Nineteenth-Century
Literature Criticism

Guide to Gale Literary Criticism Series

When you need to review criticism of literary works, these are the Gale series to use:

If the author's death date is:

You should turn to:

After Dec. 31, 1959
(or author is still living)

CONTEMPORARY LITERARY CRITICISM

for example: Jorge Luis Borges, Anthony Burgess,
William Faulkner, Mary Gordon,
Ernest Hemingway, Iris Murdoch

1900 through 1959

TWENTIETH-CENTURY LITERARY CRITICISM

for example: Willa Cather, F. Scott Fitzgerald,
Henry James, Mark Twain, Virginia Woolf

1800 through 1899

NINETEENTH-CENTURY LITERATURE CRITICISM

for example: Fedor Dostoevski, George Sand,
Gerard Manley Hopkins, Emily Dickinson

1400 through 1799

LITERATURE CRITICISM FROM 1400 TO 1800
(excluding Shakespeare)

for example: Anne Bradstreet, Pierre Corneille,
Daniel Defoe, Alexander Pope,
Jonathan Swift, Phillis Wheatley

SHAKESPEAREAN CRITICISM

Shakespeare's plays and poetry

Antiquity through 1399

CLASSICAL AND MEDIEVAL LITERATURE CRITICISM

for example: Dante, Plato, Homer, Sophocles, Vergil,
the Beowulf poet

(Volume 1 forthcoming)

Gale also publishes related criticism series:

CHILDREN'S LITERATURE REVIEW

This ongoing series covers authors of all eras.
Presents criticism on authors and author/illustrators
who write for the preschool to junior-high audience.

CONTEMPORARY ISSUES CRITICISM

This two volume set presents criticism on
contemporary authors writing on current issues.
Topics covered include the social sciences,
philosophy, economics, natural science, law, and
related areas.

ISSN 0732-1864

Volume 12

Nineteenth-Century Literature Criticism

Excerpts from Criticism of the Works of Novelists, Poets, Playwrights, Short Story Writers, Philosophers, and Other Creative Writers Who Died between 1800 and 1900, from the First Published Critical Appraisals to Current Evaluations

Laurie Lanzen Harris
Cherie D. Abbey
Editors

Jelena Obradovic Kronick
Janet Mullane
Associate Editors

Gale Research Company
Book Tower
Detroit, Michigan 48226

STAFF

Laurie Lanzen Harris, Cherie D. Abbey, *Editors*

Jelena Obradovic Kronick, Janet Mullane, *Associate Editors*

Patricia Askie Mackmiller, Gail Ann Schulte, Robert Thomas Wilson, *Senior Assistant Editors*

Rachel Carlson, Mary Nelson-Pulice, *Assistant Editors*

Sheila Fitzgerald, Phyllis Carmel Mendelson, Emily B. Tennyson,
Anna C. Wallbillich, *Contributing Editors*

Lizbeth A. Purdy, *Production Supervisor*
Denise Michlewicz Broderick, *Production Coordinator*
Eric Berger, *Assistant Production Coordinator*
Kathleen M. Cook, Maureen Duffy, Sheila J. Nasea, *Editorial Assistants*

Victoria B. Cariappa, *Research Coordinator*
Daniel Kurt Gilbert, Grace E. Gillis, Maureen R. Richards,
Keith E. Schooley, Filomena Sgambati, Vincenza G. Tranchida,
Valerie J. Webster, Mary D. Wise, *Research Assistants*

Linda Marcella Pugliese, *Manuscript Coordinator*
Donna Craft, *Assistant Manuscript Coordinator*
Maureen A. Puhl, Rosetta Irene Simms, *Manuscript Assistants*

Jeanne A. Gough, *Permissions Supervisor*
Janice M. Mach, *Permissions Coordinator, Text*
Patricia A. Seefelt, *Permissions Coordinator, Illustrations*
Susan D. Battista, *Assistant Permissions Coordinator*
Margaret A. Chamberlain, Sandra C. Davis, Kathy Grell,
Josephine M. Keene, Mary M. Matuz, *Senior Permissions Assistants*
H. Diane Cooper, Colleen M. Crane, Mabel C. Schoening, *Permissions Assistants*
Margaret A. Carson, Helen Hernandez, Anita Williams, *Permissions Clerks*

Frederick G. Ruffner, *Publisher*
Dedria Bryfonski, *Editorial Director*
Christine Nasso, *Director, Literature Division*
Laurie Lanzen Harris, *Senior Editor, Literary Criticism Series*
Dennis Poupard, *Managing Editor, Literary Criticism Series*

Copyright © 1986 by Gale Research Company

Library of Congress Catalog Card Number 81-6943
ISBN 0-8103-5812-3
ISSN 0732-1864

10 9 8 7 6 5 4 3 2

Printed in the United States

Contents

Preface

The nineteenth century was a time of tremendous growth in human endeavor: in science, in social history, and particularly in literature. The era saw the development of the novel, witnessed radical changes from classicism to romanticism to realism, and contained intellectual and artistic ideas that continue to inspire authors of our own century. The importance of the writers of the nineteenth century is twofold, for they provide insight into their own time as well as into the universal nature of human experience.

The literary criticism of an era can also give us insight into the moral and intellectual atmosphere of the past, because the criteria by which a work of art is judged reflect current philosophical and social attitudes. Literary criticism takes many forms: the traditional essay, the book or play review, even the parodic poem. Criticism can also be of several types: normative, descriptive, interpretive, textual, appreciative, generic. Collectively, the range of critical response helps us to understand a work of art, an author, an era.

The Scope of the Work

The success of two of Gale's current literary series, *Contemporary Literary Criticism (CLC)* and *Twentieth-Century Literary Criticism (TCLC)*, which excerpt criticism of creative writing from the twentieth century, suggested an equivalent need among students and teachers of literature of the nineteenth century. Moreover, since the analysis of this literature spans almost two hundred years, a vast amount of critical material confronts the student.

Nineteenth-Century Literature Criticism (NCLC) presents significant passages from published criticism on authors who died between 1800 and 1900. The author list for each volume of *NCLC* is carefully compiled to represent a variety of genres and nationalities and to cover authors who are currently regarded as the most important writers of their era as well as those whose contribution to literature and literary history is significant. The truly great writers are rare, and in the intervals between them lesser but genuine artists, as well as writers who enjoyed immense popularity in their own time and in their own countries, are important to the study of nineteenth-century literature. The length of each author entry is intended to reflect the amount of attention the author has received from critics writing in English and from foreign critics in translation. Articles and books that have not been translated into English are excluded. However, since many of the major foreign studies have been translated into English and are excerpted in *NCLC*, author entries reflect the viewpoints of many nationalities. Each author entry represents a historical overview of critical reaction to the author's work: early criticism is presented to indicate initial responses and later selections represent any rise or decline in the author's literary reputation. We have also attempted to identify and include excerpts from the seminal essays on each author as well as modern perspectives. Thus, *NCLC* is designed to serve as an introduction for the student of nineteenth-century literature to the authors of that period and to the most significant commentators on these authors.

NCLC entries are intended to be definitive overviews. In order to devote more attention to each writer, approximately fifteen authors are included in each 600-page volume compared with about fifty authors in a *CLC* volume of similar size. Because of the great quantity of critical material available on many authors, and because of the resurgence of criticism generated by such events as an author's centennial or anniversary celebration, the republication of an author's works, or publication of a newly translated work or volume of letters, an author may appear more than once. Usually, a few author entries in each volume of *NCLC* are devoted to single works by major authors who have appeared previously in the series. Only those individual works that have been the subject of extensive criticism and are widely studied in literature courses are selected for this in-depth treatment. Lord Byron's *Don Juan* and Herman Melville's *Moby-Dick* are the subjects of such entries in *NCLC*, Volume 12.

The Organization of the Book

An author section consists of the following elements: author heading, biographical and critical introduction, principal works, excerpts of criticism (each preceded by explanatory notes and followed by a bibliographical citation), and an additional bibliography.

- The *author heading* consists of the author's full name, followed by birth and death dates. The unbracketed portion of the name denotes the form under which the author most commonly wrote. If an author wrote consistently under a pseudonym, the pseudonym will be listed in the author heading and the real name given in parentheses on the first line of the biographical and critical introduction. Also located at the beginning of the introduction are any name variations under which an author wrote, including transliterated forms for authors whose languages use nonroman alphabets. Uncertainty as to a birth or death date is indicated by a question mark.

- A *portrait* of the author is included when available. Many entries also feature illustrations of materials pertinent to an author's career, including manuscript pages, letters, book illustrations, and representations of important people, places, and events in an author's life.

- The *biographical and critical introduction* contains background information that elucidates the author's creative output. When applicable, biographical and critical introductions are followed by references to additional entries on the author in past volumes of *NCLC* and in other literary reference series published by Gale Research Company. These include *Dictionary of Literary Biography, Children's Literature Review,* and *Something about the Author.*

- The list of *principal works* is chronological by date of first book publication and identifies genres. In those instances where the first publication was in other than the English language, the title and date of the first English-language edition are given in brackets. Unless otherwise indicated, dramas are dated by the first performance, rather than first publication.

- *Criticism* is arranged chronologically in each author section to provide a perspective on any changes in critical evaluation over the years. In the text of each author entry, titles by the author are printed in boldface type. This allows the reader to ascertain without difficulty the works being discussed. For purposes of easier identification, the critic's name and the publication date of the essay are given at the beginning of each piece of criticism. Unsigned criticism is preceded by the title of the journal in which it appeared. For an anonymous essay later attributed to a critic, the critic's name appears in brackets at the beginning of the excerpt and in the bibliographical citation.

- Essays are prefaced with *explanatory notes* as an additional aid to students using *NCLC*. The explanatory notes provide several types of useful information, including the reputation of the critic, the importance of a work of criticism, a synopsis of the essay, the specific approach of the critic (biographical, psychoanalytic, structuralist, etc.), and the growth of critical controversy or changes in critical trends regarding an author's work. In some cases, these notes include cross-references to related criticism in the author's entry or in the additional bibliography. Dates in parentheses within the explanatory notes refer to other essays in the author entry.

- A complete *bibliographical citation* designed to facilitate the location of the original essay or book follows each piece of criticism. An asterisk (*) at the end of the citation indicates that the essay is on more than one author.

- The *additional bibliography* appearing at the end of each author entry suggests further reading on the author. In some cases it includes essays for which the editors could not obtain reprint rights. An asterisk (*) at the end of a citation indicates that the essay is on more than one author.

An appendix lists the sources from which material in the volume is reprinted. It does not, however, list every book or periodical consulted for the volume.

Cumulative Indexes

Each volume of *NCLC* includes a cumulative index listing all the authors who have appeared in *Contemporary Literary Criticism, Twentieth-Century Literary Criticism, Nineteenth-Century Literature Criticism,* and *Literature Criticism from 1400 to 1800,* along with cross-references to the Gale series *Children's Literature Review, Authors in the News, Contemporary Authors, Contemporary Authors Autobiography Series, Dictionary of Literary Biography, Something about the Author,* and *Yesterday's Authors of Books for Children.* Users will welcome this cumulated author index as a useful tool for locating an author within the various series. The index, which lists birth and death dates when available, will be particularly valuable for those authors who are identified with a certain period but whose death date causes them to be placed in another, or for those authors whose careers span two periods. For example, Fedor Dostoevski is found in *NCLC,* yet Leo Tolstoy, another major nineteenth-century Russian novelist, is found in *TCLC.*

NCLC also includes a cumulative nationality index to authors. Authors are listed alphabetically by nationality, followed by the volume numbers in which they appear.

A cumulative index to critics is another useful feature of *NCLC*. Under each critic's name are listed the authors on whom the critic has written and the volume and page where the criticism appears.

Acknowledgments

No work of this scope can be accomplished without the cooperation of many people. The editors especially wish to thank the copyright holders of the excerpts included in this volume, the permissions managers of the book and magazine publishing companies for assisting us in securing reprint rights, and the staffs of the Detroit Public Library, University of Michigan Library, and Wayne State University Library for making their resources available to us. We are also grateful to Anthony J. Bogucki for his assistance with copyright research.

Suggestions Are Welcome

The editors welcome the comments and suggestions of readers to expand the coverage and enhance the usefulness of the series.

Authors to Appear in Future Volumes

About, Edmond Francois 1828-1885
Aguilo I. Fuster, Maria 1825-1897
Ainsworth, William Harrison 1805-1882
Aksakov, Konstantin 1817-1860
Aleardi, Aleadro 1812-1878
Alecsandri, Vasile 1821-1890
Alencar, Jose 1829-1877
Alfieri, Vittorio 1749-1803
Allingham, William 1824-1889
Almquist, Carl Jonas Love 1793-1866
Alorne, Leonor de Almeida 1750-1839
Alsop, Richard 1761-1815
Altimirano, Ignacio Manuel 1834-1893
Alvarenga, Manuel Inacio da Silva
     1749-1814
Alvares de Azevedo, Manuel Antonio
     1831-1852
Anzengruber, Ludwig 1839-1889
Arany, Janos 1817-1882
Arene, Paul 1843-1893
Aribau, Bonaventura Carlos 1798-1862
Arjona de Cubas, Manuel Maria de
     1771-1820
Arnault, Antoine Vincent 1766-1834
Arneth, Alfred von 1819-1897
Arnim, Bettina von 1785-1859
Arnold, Thomas 1795-1842
Arriaza y Superviela, Juan Bautista
     1770-1837
Asbjornsen, Peter Christian 1812-1885
Ascasubi, Hilario 1807-1875
Atterbom, Per Daniel Amadeus
     1790-1855
Aubanel, Theodore 1829-1886
Auerbach, Berthold 1812-1882
Augier, Guillaume V.E. 1820-1889
Azeglio, Massimo D' 1798-1866
Azevedo, Guilherme de 1839-1882
Bakin (pseud. of Takizawa Okikani)
     1767-1848
Bakunin, Mikhail Aleksandrovich
     1814-1876
Baratynski, Jewgenij Abramovich
     1800-1844
Barnes, William 1801-1886
Batyushkov, Konstantin 1778-1855
Beattie, James 1735-1803
Beckford, William 1760-1844
Becquer, Gustavo Adolfo 1836-1870
Bentham, Jeremy 1748-1832
Beranger, Jean-Pierre de 1780-1857
Berchet, Ciovanni 1783-1851
Berzsenyi, Daniel 1776-1836
Black, William 1841-1898
Blair, Hugh 1718-1800
Blake, William 1757-1827
Blicher, Steen Steensen 1782-1848

Bocage, Manuel Maria Barbosa du
     1765-1805
Boratynsky, Yevgeny 1800-1844
Borel, Petrus 1809-1859
Boreman, Yokutiel 1825-1890
Borne, Ludwig 1786-1837
Botev, Hristo 1778-1842
Bremer, Fredrika 1801-1865
Brinckman, John 1814-1870
Bronte, Emily 1812-1848
Brown, Charles Brockden 1777-1810
Browning, Robert 1812-1889
Buchner, Georg 1813-1837
Campbell, James Edwin 1867-1895
Campbell, Thomas 1777-1844
Carlyle, Thomas 1795-1881
Castelo Branco, Camilo 1825-1890
Castro Alves, Antonio de 1847-1871
Channing, William Ellery 1780-1842
Chatterje, Bankin Chanda 1838-1894
Chivers, Thomas Holly 1807?-1858
Claudius, Matthais 1740-1815
Clough, Arthur Hugh 1819-1861
Cobbett, William 1762-1835
Colenso, John William 1814-1883
Coleridge, Hartley 1796-1849
Collett, Camilla 1813-1895
Comte, Auguste 1798-1857
Conrad, Robert T. 1810-1858
Conscience, Hendrik 1812-1883
Cooke, Philip Pendleton 1816-1850
Corbiere, Edouard 1845-1875
Crabbe, George 1754-1832
Cruz E Sousa, Joao da 1861-1898
Desbordes-Valmore, Marceline
     1786-1859
Deschamps, Emile 1791-1871
Deus, Joao de 1830-1896
Dickinson, Emily 1830-1886
Dinis, Julio 1839-1871
Dinsmoor, Robert 1757-1836
Dumas, Alexandre (pere) 1802-1870
Du Maurier, George 1834-1896
Dwight, Timothy 1752-1817
Echeverria, Esteban 1805-1851
Eminescy, Mihai 1850-1889
Engels, Friedrich 1820-1895
Espronceda, Jose 1808-1842
Ettinger, Solomon 1799-1855
Euchel, Issac 1756-1804
Ferguson, Samuel 1810-1886
Fernandez de Lizardi, Jose Joaquin
     1776-1827
Fernandez de Moratin, Leandro
     1760-1828
Fet, Afanasy 1820-1892
Feuillet, Octave 1821-1890

Fontane, Theodor 1819-1898
Forster, John 1812-1876
Freiligrath, Hermann Ferdinand
     1810-1876
Freytag, Gustav 1816-1895
Gaboriau, Emile 1835-1873
Ganivet, Angel 1865-1898
Garrett, Almeida 1799-1854
Garshin, Vsevolod Mikhaylovich
     1855-1888
Gezelle, Guido 1830-1899
Ghalib, Asadullah Khan 1797-1869
Godwin, William 1756-1836
Goldschmidt, Meir Aron 1819-1887
Goncalves Dias, Antonio 1823-1864
Griboyedov, Aleksander Sergeyevich
     1795-1829
Grigor'yev, Appolon Aleksandrovich
     1822-1864
Groth, Klaus 1819-1899
Grun, Anastasius (pseud. of Anton
     Alexander Graf von Auersperg)
     1806-1876
Guerrazzi, Francesco Domenico
     1804-1873
Gutierrez Najera, Manuel 1859-1895
Gutzkow, Karl Ferdinand 1811-1878
Ha-Kohen, Shalom 1772-1845
Halleck, Fitz-Greene 1790-1867
Harris, George Washington 1814-1869
Hayne, Paul Hamilton 1830-1886
Hazlitt, William 1778-1830
Hebbel, Christian Friedrich 1813-1863
Hebel, Johann Peter 1760-1826
Hegel, Georg Wilhelm Friedrich
     1770-1831
Heiberg, Johann Ludvig 1813-1863
Herculano, Alexandre 1810-1866
Hernandez, Jose 1834-1886
Hertz, Henrik 1798-1870
Herwegh, Georg 1817-1875
Hoffman, Charles Fenno 1806-1884
Holderlin, Friedrich 1770-1843
Holmes, Oliver Wendell 1809-1894
Hood, Thomas 1799-1845
Hooper, Johnson Jones 1815-1863
Hopkins, Gerard Manley 1844-1889
Horton, George Moses 1798-1880
Howitt, William 1792-1879
Hughes, Thomas 1822-1896
Imlay, Gilbert 1754?-1828?
Irwin, Thomas Caulfield 1823-1892
Issacs, Jorge 1837-1895
Jacobsen, Jens Peter 1847-1885
Jippensha, Ikku 1765-1831
Kant, Immanuel 1724-1804
Karr, Jean Baptiste Alphonse 1808-1890

Keble, John 1792-1866
Khomyakov, Alexey S. 1804-1860
Kierkegaard, Soren 1813-1855
Kinglake, Alexander W. 1809-1891
Kingsley, Charles 1819-1875
Kivi, Alexis 1834-1872
Klopstock, Friedrich Gottlieb 1724-1803
Koltsov, Alexey Vasilyevich 1809-1842
Kotzebue, August von 1761-1819
Kraszewski, Josef Ignacy 1812-1887
Kreutzwald, Friedrich Reinhold
    1803-1882
Krochmal, Nahman 1785-1840
Krudener, Valeria Barbara Julia de
    Wietinghoff 1766-1824
Lamartine, Alphonse 1790-1869
Lampman, Archibald 1861-1899
Landon, Letitia Elizabeth 1802-1838
Landor, Walter Savage 1775-1864
Larra y Sanchez de Castro, Mariano
    1809-1837
Lebensohn, Micah Joseph 1828-1852
Leconte de Lisle, Charles-Marie-Rene
    1818-1894
Lenau, Nikolaus 1802-1850
Leontyev, Konstantin 1831-1891
Leopardi, Giacoma 1798-1837
Leskov, Nikolai 1831-1895
Lever, Charles James 1806-1872
Levisohn, Solomon 1789-1822
Lewes, George Henry 1817-1878
Lewis, Matthew Gregory 1775-1817
Leyden, John 1775-1811
Lobensohn, Micah Gregory 1775-1810
Longstreet, Augustus Baldwin 1790-1870
Lopez de Ayola y Herrera, Adelardo
    1819-1871
Lover, Samuel 1797-1868
Luzzato, Samuel David 1800-1865
Macedo, Joaquim Manuel de 1820-1882
Macha, Karel Hynek 1810-1836
Mackenzie, Henry 1745-1831
Malmon, Solomon 1754-1800
Mangan, James Clarence 1803-1849
Manzoni, Alessandro 1785-1873
Mapu, Abraham 1808-1868
Marii, Jose 1853-1895
Markovic, Svetozar 1846-1875
Martinez de La Rosa, Francisco
    1787-1862
Mathews, Cornelius 1817-1889
McCulloch, Thomas 1776-1843
Merriman, Brian 1747-1805
Meyer, Conrad Ferdinand 1825-1898
Montgomery, James 1771-1854
Moodie, Susanna 1803-1885

Morton, Sarah Wentworth 1759-1846
Muller, Friedrich 1749-1825
Murger, Henri 1822-1861
Nekrasov, Nikolai 1821-1877
Neruda, Jan 1834-1891
Nestroy, Johann 1801-1862
Newman, John Henry 1801-1890
Niccolini, Giambattista 1782-1861
Nievo, Ippolito 1831-1861
Nodier, Charles 1780-1844
Novalis (pseud. of Friedrich von
    Hardenberg) 1772-1801
Obradovic, Dositej 1742-1811
Oehlenschlager, Adam 1779-1850
Oliphant, Margaret 1828-1897
O'Neddy, Philothee (pseud. of
    Theophile Dondey) 1811-1875
O'Shaughnessy, Arthur William
    Edgar 1844-1881
Ostrovsky, Alexander 1823-1886
Paine, Thomas 1737-1809
Peacock, Thomas Love 1785-1866
Perk, Jacques 1859-1881
Pisemsky, Alexey F. 1820-1881
Pompeia, Raul D'Avila 1863-1895
Popovic, Jovan Sterija 1806-1856
Praed, Winthrop Mackworth 1802-1839
Prati, Giovanni 1814-1884
Preseren, France 1800-1849
Pringle, Thomas 1789-1834
Procter, Adelaide Ann 1825-1864
Procter, Bryan Waller 1787-1874
Pye, Henry James 1745-1813
Quental, Antero Tarquinio de 1842-1891
Quinet, Edgar 1803-1875
Quintana, Manuel Jose 1772-1857
Radishchev, Aleksander 1749-1802
Raftery, Anthony 1784-1835
Raimund, Ferdinand 1790-1836
Reid, Mayne 1818-1883
Renan, Ernest 1823-1892
Reuter, Fritz 1810-1874
Rogers, Samuel 1763-1855
Ruckert, Friedrich 1788-1866
Runeberg, Johan 1804-1877
Rydberg, Viktor 1828-1895
Saavedra y Ramirez de Boquedano,
    Angel de 1791-1865
Sacher-Mosoch, Leopold von 1836-1895
Saltykov-Shchedrin, Mikhail 1826-1892
Satanov, Isaac 1732-1805
Schiller, Johann Friedrich 1759-1805
Schlegel, August 1767-1845
Schlegel, Karl 1772-1829
Scott, Sir Walter 1771-1832

Scribe, Augustin Eugene 1791-1861
Sedgwick, Catherine Maria 1789-1867
Senoa, August 1838-1881
Shelley, Mary W. 1797-1851
Shelley, Percy Bysshe 1792-1822
Shulman, Kalman 1819-1899
Sigourney, Lydia Howard Huntley
    1791-1856
Silva, Jose Asuncion 1865-1896
Slaveykov, Petko 1828-1895
Slowacki, Juliusz 1809-1848
Smith, Richard Penn 1799-1854
Smolenskin, Peretz 1842-1885
Stagnelius, Erik Johan 1793-1823
Staring, Antonie Christiaan
    Wynand 1767-1840
Stendhal (pseud. of Henri Beyle)
    1783-1842
Stifter, Adalbert 1805-1868
Stone, John Augustus 1801-1834
Taine, Hippolyte 1828-1893
Taunay, Alfredo d'Ecragnole 1843-1899
Taylor, Bayard 1825-1878
Tennyson, Alfred, Lord 1809-1892
Terry, Lucy (Lucy Terry Prince)
    1730-1821
Thompson, Daniel Pierce 1795-1868
Thompson, Samuel 1766-1816
Thomson, James 1834-1882
Tiedge, Christoph August 1752-1841
Timrod, Henry 1828-1867
Tommaseo, Nicolo 1802-1874
Tompa, Mihaly 1817-1888
Topelius, Zachris 1818-1898
Turgenev, Ivan 1818-1883
Tyutchev, Fedor I. 1803-1873
Uhland, Ludvig 1787-1862
Valaoritis, Aristotelis 1824-1879
Valles, Jules 1832-1885
Verde, Cesario 1855-1886
Vigny, Alfred Victor de 1797-1863
Villaverde, Cirilio 1812-1894
Vinje, Aasmund Olavsson 1818-1870
Vorosmarty, Mihaly 1800-1855
Warren, Mercy Otis 1728-1814
Weisse, Christian Felix 1726-1804
Welhaven, Johan S. 1807-1873
Werner, Zacharius 1768-1823
Wescott, Edward Noyes 1846-1898
Wessely, Nattali Herz 1725-1805
Whitman, Sarah Helen 1803-1878
Wieland, Christoph Martin 1733-1813
Woolson, Constance Fenimore
    1840-1894
Zhukovsky, Vasily 1783-1852

Fanny Burney

1752-1840

(Born Frances Burney; later Madame d'Arblay) English novelist, dramatist, letter writer, and diarist.

Burney is remembered for her contribution to the English novel of manners, most notably with *Evelina; or, A Young Lady's Entrance into the World*. *Evelina* achieved renown for its humor, simple prose, and insightful depiction of a young woman's coming of age in eighteenth-century England. While her novels have been overshadowed by the writings of Jane Austen, who brought the novel of manners to its highest form, she is considered a significant transitional figure who employed the methods of Samuel Richardson and Henry Fielding to create a new subgenre that made possible the domestic novels of Austen, Maria Edgeworth, and countless other successors.

Burney was born in London to Esther Sleepe and Charles Burney. Her mother died when Burney was ten, and she became very attached to her father, a prominent musician and England's first musicologist. Although Burney was a shy child and received little formal education, she met a number of artists and intellectuals through her father. Under their influence, she read extensively and, though her father preferred that she devote herself to more serious activities than writing, she began to experiment secretly with prose. One of her father's closest friends, Samuel ("Daddy") Crisp, played a particularly significant role in Burney's artistic development; he was her early confidant and encouraged her first writing attempts. In 1767, however, Burney destroyed all her manuscripts. She wanted desperately to please her father as well as her stepmother, who believed that a career in writing would diminish Burney's marriage prospects. The most significant of Burney's early manuscripts was the novel "The History of Caroline Evelyn." When she began to write again several years later, this novel formed the basis of the first part of *Evelina*.

Burney published *Evelina* anonymously, aided by her brother Charles, who disguised himself when submitting the manuscript. The novel met with immediate acclaim. Written in epistolary form, *Evelina* is strongly autobiographical; the heroine's experiences and emotions closely parallel the author's own coming of age. In *Evelina*, Burney created a heroine who is considered one of the most vibrant and realistic in English literature. To Burney's surprise, her success delighted her father; ironically, Dr. Burney had read and enjoyed *Evelina* without knowing its author. He introduced her to such prominent literary figures as Samuel Johnson and Edmund Burke, who warmly welcomed her into London's literary circles and encouraged her to continue writing. However, because Dr. Burney privately pronounced her next work, a drama entitled "The Witlings," a failure, it was never produced or published. Several critics now contend that her father objected to this parody of bluestocking society for its controversial subject. Burney next wrote *Cecilia; or, Memoirs of an Heiress,* in which she continued to explore the social mores of her era with wit and satire. It was also her first experiment in third-person narrative voice, which she employed in both her subsequent novels. While not as great a success as *Evelina, Cecilia* was generally well received. Critics favorably compared it with the works of Richardson, Fielding, and Laurence Sterne, but argued that it

lacked the spontaneity of *Evelina,* a flaw also detected in *Camilla; or, A Picture of Youth* and *The Wanderer; or, Female Difficulties,* her last two novels.

Despite Burney's popularity as an author, her family continued to be concerned about her unmarried status and future financial security. When she was offered a position as second keeper of the robes to Queen Charlotte in 1786, she accepted the prestigious post at her father's urging. However, Burney's estrangement from the society that inspired her novels made her miserable. She recorded her experience in journals and letters, published posthumously as the *Diary and Letters of Madame d'Arblay,* that are today considered a telling account of the rigors and restrictions of life at court. Several tragedies that she composed during this period also bear witness to Burney's increasing unhappiness and frustration. Eventually, she became ill and Dr. Burney obtained her release from royal service. She left court in 1791, receiving a pension of one hundred pounds a year. Soon after, Burney married Alexandre d'Arblay, a penniless French exile. The marriage was evidently very happy and, in 1794, she gave birth to their son, Alexander.

Burney resumed her novel-writing career in 1796 with *Camilla,* a satirical examination of the social restrictions of marriage. Though most commentators fault *Camilla* as a sensational work written purely for financial reasons, it was extremely popular.

Burney received a large advance before the novel's publication, and the work yielded sufficient funds to build the d'Arblays a new home, Camilla Cottage. Burney's days at Camilla Cottage were her happiest; there she wrote several unpublished comedies before traveling to France with her family in 1802. Though they intended to visit briefly, they were forced to stay until 1812 because of the outbreak of war between France and England. Upon their return to England, Burney wrote her last novel, *The Wanderer*. The most poorly received of her novels, the work was considered dated and awkwardly constructed. The novel's depiction, however, of a nineteenth-century woman struggling to earn her own living has prompted a variety of critical commentary, particularly from a feminist standpoint, in recent years.

In 1815, during Napoleon's Hundred Days, d'Arblay aided the forces against Napoleon while Burney fled to Brussels for the duration of the conflict; they returned to England later that year and settled in Bath. After d'Arblay's death in 1818, Burney moved back to London, where she began to revise her journals to add her experiences in exile during wartime. In addition, she edited her father's memoirs and correspondence, *Memoirs of Dr. Burney, Arranged from His Own Manuscripts, from Family Papers, and from Personal Recollections*. Though she claimed to have carefully edited sections to avoid including any slanderous material, detractors have charged that Burney chose to incorporate material that illuminates her own life rather than her father's. Commentators have also found her style pompous and verbose. Despite the harsh reception accorded her final works, Burney's last years were happy and quiet until her death at the age of eighty-eight.

Of Burney's novels, *Evelina* is consistently the most admired and is considered the best evidence of her keen social observation and ear for dialect. Since the novel's publication, critics have praised its characterization, humor, and engrossing plot. Most scholars agree, too, that in her first novel Burney created her most consummately human and believable heroine. They also concur that Burney never recaptured the fresh, spontaneous prose of *Evelina* and that her later works suffer from a labored style. Though *Cecilia* and *Camilla* appealed to eighteenth-century readers, critics today consider both dated and stilted. Ironically, *The Wanderer*, which was dismissed by contemporary commentators, has recently received the greatest share of critical attention for its feminist focus.

Burney's journals and letters have elicited almost as much positive critical response as *Evelina;* today, they are considered both engaging depictions of her era and valuable historical documents. Though her harshest critic, her contemporary John Wilson Croker, derided the *Diary* as egocentric, most commentators, including Thomas Babington Macaulay, George Saintsbury, and Lytton Strachey, have assessed the work as insightful and historically accurate. In the twentieth century, however, Gamaliel Bradford argued that the *Diary* merely depicted Burney's obsession with the superficial in society. In recent years, such literary figures as the novelist Margaret Drabble have termed Burney a perceptive correspondent and diarist and praised her description of life in the late eighteenth and early nineteenth centuries.

Today, Burney's stature has been eclipsed by that of her successors, most notably Austen. While most critics concur that Burney's talent as a novelist blossomed early and then faded, they also hail *Evelina* as a landmark work that initiated the tradition of the domestic novel and the novel of manners. It seems likely that Burney's importance in years to come will continue to derive from her spirited depiction of Evelina's maturation into womanhood.

(See also *Dictionary of Literary Biography*, Vol. 39: *British Novelists, 1660-1800*).

PRINCIPAL WORKS

Evelina; or, A Young Lady's Entrance into the World (novel) 1778
Cecilia; or, Memoirs of an Heiress (novel) 1782
Camilla; or, A Picture of Youth (novel) 1796
Edwy and Elgiva (drama) 1796
The Wanderer; or, Female Difficulties (novel) 1814
Memoirs of Dr. Burney, Arranged from His Own Manuscripts, from Family Papers, and from Personal Recollections (memoirs) 1832
Diary and Letters of Madame d'Arblay. 7 vols. (diary and letters) 1842-46
The Early Diary of Frances Burney, 1768-1778. 2 vols. (diary) 1889
The Journals and Letters of Fanny Burney (Madame D'Arblay). 12 vols. (diaries and letters) 1972-84

FRANCES D'ARBLAY [FRANCES BURNEY] (essay date 1767)

[*The following excerpt is drawn from Burney's introduction to her* Diary, *which she wrote at age fifteen and which was posthumously published by her niece. Here, she reveals her desire to dedicate her thoughts to someone; ironically, she chooses to confide in Nobody, because "from Nobody I have nothing to fear." Her description of Nobody foreshadows the character of Evelina, whom Burney also terms a "nobody."*]

To have some account of my thoughts, manners, acquaintance, and actions, when the hour arrives at which time is more nimble than memory, is the reason which induces me to keep a Journal—a Journal in which, I must confess, my *every* thought must open my whole heart.

But a thing of the kind ought to be addressed to somebody—I must imagine myself to be talking—talking to the most intimate of friends—to one in whom I should take delight in confiding, and feel remorse in concealment; but who must this friend be? To make choice of one in whom I can but *half* rely, would be to frustrate entirely the intention of my plan. The only one I could wholly, totally confide in, lives in the same house with me, and not only never *has*, but never *will*, leave me one secret to tell her. To *whom* then *must* I dedicate my wonderful, surprising, and interesting adventures?—to *whom* dare I reveal my private opinion of my nearest relations? my secret thoughts of my dearest friends? my own hopes, fears, reflections, and dislikes?—Nobody.

To Nobody, then, will I write my Journal! since to Nobody can I be wholly unreserved, to Nobody can I reveal every thought, every wish of my heart, with the most unlimited confidence, the most unremitting sincerity, to the end of my life! For what chance, what accident, can end my connections with Nobody? No secret *can* I conceal from Nobody, and to Nobody can I be ever unreserved. Disagreement cannot stop our affection—time itself has no power to end our friendship. The love, the esteem, I entertain for Nobody, Nobody's self has not power to destroy. From Nobody I have nothing to fear.

The secrets sacred to friendship Nobody will not reveal; when the affair is doubtful, Nobody will not look towards the side least favourable. (pp. 19-20)

> *Frances d'Arblay [Frances Burney], in an introduction to her* Diary & Letters of Madame d'Arblay: 1778-1840, Vol. I, *edited by Charlotte Barrett, The Macmillan Company, 1904, pp. 19-20.*

FANNY BURNEY (essay date 1778)

[*The following excerpt is drawn from Burney's preface to* Evelina, *originally published in 1778. She states that rather than writing a romantic fantasy, she has chosen to draw "characters from nature, though not from life, and to mark the manners of the time."*]

The following letters are presented to the Public—for such, by novel writers, novel readers will be called,—with a very singular mixture of timidity and confidence, resulting from the peculiar situation of the editor; who, though trembling for their success from a consciousness of their imperfections, yet fears not being involved in their disgrace, while happily wrapped up in a mantle of impenetrable obscurity.

To draw characters from nature, though not from life, and to mark the manners of the times, is the attempted plan of the following letters. For this purpose, a young female, educated in the most secluded retirement, makes, at the age of seventeen, her first appearance upon the great and busy stage of life; with a virtuous mind, a cultivated understanding, and a feeling heart, her ignorance of the forms, and inexperience in the manners of the world, occasion all the little incidents which these volumes record, and which form the natural progression of the life of a young woman of obscure birth, but conspicuous beauty, for the first six months after her *Entrance into the world*.

Perhaps, were it possible to effect the total extirpation of novels, our young ladies in general, and boarding-school damsels in particular, might profit from their annihilation; but since the distemper they have spread seems incurable, since their contagion bids defiance to the medicine of advice or reprehension, and since they are found to baffle all the mental art of physic, save what is prescribed by the slow regimen of Time, and bitter diet of Experience; surely all attempts to contribute to the number of those which may be read, if not with advantage, at least without injury, ought rather to be encouraged than contemned.

Let me, therefore, prepare for disappointment those who, in the perusal of these sheets, entertain the gentle expectation of being transported to the fantastic regions of Romance, where Fiction is coloured by all the gay tints of luxurious Imagination, where Reason is an outcast, and where the sublimity of the *Marvellous* rejects all aid from sober Probability. The heroine of these memoirs, young, artless, and inexperienced, is

No faultless Monster that the world ne'er saw;

but the offspring of Nature, and of Nature in her simplest attire.

In all the Arts, the value of copies can only be proportioned to the scarcity of originals: among sculptors and painters, a fine statue, or a beautiful picture, of some great master, may deservedly employ the imitative talents of young and inferior artists, that their appropriation to one spot may not wholly prevent the more general expansion of their excellence; but, among authors, the reverse is the case, since the noblest productions of literature are almost equally attainable with the meanest. In books, therefore, imitation cannot be shunned too sedulously; for the very perfection of a model which is frequently seen, serves but more forcibly to mark the inferiority of a copy.

To avoid what is common, without adopting what is unnatural, must limit the ambition of the vulgar herd of authors: however zealous, therefore, my veneration of the great writers . . . , however I may feel myself enlightened by the knowledge of Johnson, charmed with the eloquence of Rousseau, softened by the pathetic powers of Richardson, and exhilarated by the wit of Fielding and humour of Smollett; I yet presume not to attempt pursuing the same ground which they have tracked; whence, though they may have cleared the weeds, they have also culled the flowers; and, though they have rendered the path plain, they have left it barren.

The candour of my readers I have not the impertinence to doubt, and to their indulgence I am sensible I have no claim; I have, therefore, only to intreat, that my own words may not pronounce my condemnation; and that what I have here ventured to say in regard to imitation, may be understood as it is meant, in a general sense, and not be imputed to an opinion of my own originality, which I have not the vanity, the folly, or the blindness, to entertain.

Whatever may be the fate of these letters, the editor is satisfied they will meet with justice; and commits them to the press, though hopeless of fame, yet not regardless of censure. (pp. lxi-lxiii)

> *Fanny Burney, in a preface to her* Evelina; or, The History of a Young Lady's Entrance into the World, *G. Bell and Sons, Ltd., 1927, pp. lxi-lxiii.*

THE MONTHLY REVIEW, LONDON (essay date 1778)

[*The anonymous critic of the following excerpt praises* Evelina *for its plot, characterization, and style.*]

[*Evelina; or, A Young Lady's Entrance Into the World*] has given us so much pleasure in the perusal, that we do not hesitate to pronounce it one of the most sprightly, entertaining, and agreeable productions of this kind, which has of late fallen under our notice. A great variety of natural incidents, some of the comic stamp, render the narrative extremely interesting. The characters, which are agreeably diversified, are conceived and drawn with propriety, and supported with spirit. The whole is written with great ease and command of language. From this commendation, however, we must except the character of a son of Neptune, whose manners are rather those of a rough, uneducated country 'squire, than those of a genuine sea-captain.

> *A review of "Evelina, or a Young Lady's Entrance into the World," in* The Monthly Review, London, *Vol. LVIII, April, 1778, p. 316.*

THE CRITICAL REVIEW (essay date 1778)

[*In the following excerpt, the critic praises the moral content of* Evelina, *but faults its unevenness and excessive length.*]

[*Evelina; or, A Young Lady's Entrance into the World*] deserves no common praise, whether we consider it in a moral or literary light. It would have disgraced neither the head nor the heart of Richardson.—The father of a family, observing the knowledge of the world and the lessons of experience which it contains, will recommend it to his daughters; they will weep and (what is not so commonly the effect of novels) will laugh, and grow wiser, as they read; the experienced mother will derive pleasure and happiness from being present at its reading; even the sons of the family will forego the diversions of the town or the field to pursue the entertainment of Evelina's acquaintance, who will imperceptibly lead them, as well as their sisters, to improvement and to virtue.

If the author of this amusing and instructive novel possess any of Richardson's merits, he labours also under one of his principal faults. The gold is in some places beat out considerably too fine. The second volume deserves few of the solid praises which we with pleasure bestow on the first and the third. The Roman sibyl, after she had burnt part of her work, still persisted in demanding the same price for what remained; we should set a higher value upon this performance had the writer made it shorter—but perhaps, as Swift said of a long letter, he had not time. (pp. 202-03)

> *A review of "Evelina; or, a Young Lady's Entrance into the World," in* The Critical Review, *Vol. XLVI, September, 1778, pp. 202-04.*

SAMUEL JOHNSON   (essay date 1778)

[*A remarkably versatile and distinguished man of letters, Johnson was the major literary figure of the second half of the eighteenth century; his monumental* A Dictionary of the English Language *standardized for the first time English spelling and pronunciation, while his moralistic criticism strongly influenced contemporary tastes. Johnson was a close friend of the Burney family, and he encouraged Fanny's literary efforts. Such was his influence on Burney that a number of critics contend that she consciously imitated his writing style in her novels, not always to good effect. In the following excerpt from an article first published in 1778, Johnson expresses admiration for Burney's "intuitive" knowledge of the world as evidenced in* Evelina.]

Evelina seems a work that should result from long experience, a deep and intimate knowledge with the world: yet it has been written without either. Miss Burney is a real wonder. What she is, she is intuitively. Dr. Burney told me she had the fewest advantages of any of his daughters, from some peculiar circumstances. And such has been her timidity, that he himself had not any suspicion of her powers. . . . Modesty with her is neither pretense nor decorum; it is an ingredient of her nature; for she who could part with such a work for twenty pounds, could know so little of its worth or of her own, as to leave no possible doubt of her humility. (pp. 102-03)

> *Samuel Johnson, "On Miss Burney's 'Evelina',"* in Library of Literary Criticism of English and American Authors through the Beginning of the Twentieth Century: The Romantic Period to the Victorian Age, *Vol. III, edited by Charles Wells Moulton and Martin Tucker, revised edition, Frederick Ungar Publishing Co., 1966, pp. 102-03.*

HESTER LYNCH THRALE   (diary date 1782)

[*Thrale was a prominent literary figure in eighteenth-century London who is best known today as the editor of Samuel Johnson's correspondence. Though the relationship between she and Burney was often strained, Thrale drew Burney into her circle and introduced her to the notable figures of the day. In the following excerpt from Thrale's diary, she admires the vivid representation in* Cecilia, *but concludes that the novel will endure only as long as the society it describes.*]

[Fanny Burney's] new Novel called *Cecilia* is the Picture of Life such as the Author sees it: while therefore this Mode of Life lasts, her Book will be of value, as the Representation is astonishingly perfect: but as nothing in the Book is derived from Study, so it can have no Principle of duration—Burney's Cecilia is to Richardson's Clarissa—what a Camera Obscura in the Window of a London parlour,—is to a view of Venice by the clear Pencil of Cannaletti.

> *Hester Lynch Thrale, in a diary entry of May 19, 1782, in* Thraliana, The Diary of Mrs. Hester Lynch Thrale, 1776-1809: 1776-1784, *Vol. I, edited by Katharine C. Balderston, Oxford at the Clarendon Press, Oxford, 1942, p. 536.*

EDMUND BURKE   (letter date 1782)

[*Burke was an Irish-born English statesman, philosopher, and critic. Throughout his career in Parliament he aligned himself with such liberal causes as the abolition of the slave trade, taxation reform for the American colonies, and removal of political restrictions on Catholics in Ireland. In addition to his distinction as a political thinker, Burke wrote a pioneering work in the field of aesthetics,* A Philosophical Inquiry into the Origin of Our Ideas of the Sublime and the Beautiful, *and in 1759 founded the* Annual Register, *a yearly review of important events. The following letter to Burney reflects Burke's admiration for* Cecilia; *he adds that its only flaw rests in its excessive number of characters.*]

I should feel exceedingly to blame if I could refuse to myself the natural satisfaction, and to you the just but poor return, of my best thanks for the very great instruction and entertainment I have received from the new present you have bestowed on the public. There are few—I believe I may say fairly there are none at all—that will not find themselves better informed concerning human nature, and their stock of observation enriched by reading your *Cecilia*. They certainly will, let their experience in life and manners be what it may. The arrogance of age must submit to be taught by youth. You have crowded into a few small volumes an incredible variety of characters; most of them well planned, well supported, and well contrasted with each other. If there be any fault in this respect, it is one in which you are in no great danger of being imitated. Justly as your characters are drawn, perhaps they are too numerous. But I beg pardon; I fear it is quite in vain to preach economy to those who are come young to excessive and sudden opulence.

I might trespass on your delicacy if I should fill my letter to you with what I fill my conversation to others. I should be troublesome to you alone if I should tell you all I feel and think on the natural vein of humour, the tender pathetic, the comprehensive and noble moral, and the sagacious observation, that appear quite throughout that extraordinary performance.

In an age distinguished by producing extraordinary women, I hardly dare to tell you where my opinion would place you amongst them. I respect your modesty, that will not endure the commendations which your merit forces from everybody.

> *Edmund Burke, in a letter to F. Burney on July 29, 1782, in* Cecilia; or, Memoirs of an Heiress, *Vol. I by Frances Burney, edited by Annie Raine Ellis, G. Bell and Sons, Ltd., 1914, p. xxii.*

[SAMUEL BABCOCK]   (essay date 1782)

[*The following excerpt is drawn from a positive review of* Cecilia *in which Babcock especially praises Burney's delineation of char-*

acter. While he concedes that the novel is too long and consequently dull in parts, he considers it outstanding as a whole.]

The great and merited success of *Evelina* hath encouraged the fair Author to the present undertaking [*Cecilia; or, Memoirs of an Heiress*]—in which we are at a loss, whether to give the preference to the design or the execution: or which to admire most, the purity of the Writer's heart, or the force and extent of her understanding. We see much of the dignity and pathos of Richardson; and much of the acuteness and ingenuity of Fielding. The attention is arrested by the story; and in general, expectation is gratified by the several events of it. It is related in a style peculiarly nervous and perspicuous, and appears to have been formed on the best model of Dr. Johnson's. (p. 453)

[The principal characters] in this exquisite Novel are in general nicely discriminated, and properly supported. They are all directed to the main object, and all concur to the *denouement* of the plot.

The prodigality of the Harrels, and the pride of old Delville, though carried to the extreme, are yet within the bounds of probability. The character of Mrs. Delville is highly finished, and leaves a very strong impression on the mind. We see dignity struggling with tenderness. We see the GREAT and ARDENT so softened by the soothing affections of humanity, and the mild virtues of the heart, parental fondness, generous friendship, and impartial justice, which surmount some irrational, though deep-rooted prejudices, that we always meet her with admiration, and part from her with regret. We wished to have seen more of her in the concluding scenes, where the want of her disappointed us. The *volubility* of Miss Larolles is very well described; and the sprightly wit, and inconsiderate ease and hilarity of Lady Honoria Pemberton, always meet our idea of the character meant to be exhibited. We see them as perfectly as if we were conversing with the originals. We may say the same of some characters that figure in a lower circle, particularly of Hobson. The self-importance of a rich tradesman is represented to the life. It is a character that frequently occurs: but we never saw it so perfectly marked, or so uniformly supported. The story of the excellent Mr. Albany is pathetic; and the events of his life well account for the singularity of his behaviour, and the strangeness of his expressions.

We have thus far dealt only in praise—and it is as sincere as we ever paid to literary merit. Totally unconnected with the Author, and even unknown to her by name, the Writer of this Article is only concerned to discharge the debt of justice: he will call it *rigid* justice; for he hath no motive to be lenient. The Author of *Cecilia* asks no undue lenity: she doth not plead any privilege of her sex: she stands on firmer ground; and with a spirit superior to solicitation or fear, may meet the decision of impartial criticism. (pp. 456-57)

We will not, however, say, that her works are all perfection. We will not say that we can praise them *with so full soul*, as to declare, *that no defect in them doth quarrel with the noblest grace she hath, and sets it to the foil.*

The Novel is protracted to too great a length; and some parts of it are uninteresting. Every part should not be brilliant; but no part should be languid: and if the mind is not awakened, or kept attentive by events of importance, it should be so far amused as not to be indifferent even in the most trivial scenes. The character of Briggs, though in many respects highly entertaining, is in some so overcharged, as to be more like a caricature than a real picture. His penuriousness is carried beyond the limits of probability; and because unnatural, loses its

effect. His borrowing a chimney-sweeper's dress for the masquerade; his sending Cecilia a slate and a pencil, and quarrelling with his boy for being too lavish of the latter, are such instances of extreme and disgusting avarice, as can scarcely be realized; or if we can suppose them to exist, yet we imagine that *all* which the Author attempted to display of his character might have been effected without them, and the air of probability more uniformly preserved.—The dialogue, however, between *Briggs*, Albany, and Hobson, on charity, is admirable, and the discriminating features of their characters are marked with wonderful skill and precision.

The imposition of Harrel on the yielding temper of Cecilia, is a reflection on her understanding and prudence. This may be in some measure accounted for on two grounds, her general goodness of heart, and particular friendship for Mrs. Harrel: but we think her accompanying them to Vauxhall, after such a scene of horror and wickedness as she had been a witness to but a few hours before, is carrying Cecilia's benevolence and good-nature beyond all the bounds of good sense, and is rather inconsistent with that virtuous indignation which she is supposed to have felt for profligacy, imposition, and insensibility.

The affectation and insipidity of Captain Aresby, and the vacancy and cold indifference of Mr. Meadows, are, in our view, *dead weights* upon the story. To introduce a trifling character without fatiguing, or a disgusting one without nauseating the Reader, is one of the most difficult and delicate tasks of a novel-writer. We think this ingenious Writer not thoroughly successful in her attempts to ridicule the absurdity of quoting French phrases, in a silly officer; nor in exposing the rudeness of inattention in an affectedly absent man. They are both intolerable, and almost as intolerable in fiction as they would be in reality. (pp. 457-58)

We have now given our general sentiments of *Cecilia*. Its excellencies far, very far, outweigh its defects and imperfections; and quotations from it would justify our praise, if the limits of our Journal would permit us to be profuse in this respect. To the work itself we appeal; and fear not to rest our decision of its superior merits with the general sentiment of the wise and virtuous. (p. 458)

[Samuel Babcock], "'Cecilia,' a Novel," in The Monthly Review, *London, Vol. LXVII, December, 1782, pp. 453-58.*

THE EUROPEAN MAGAZINE, AND LONDON REVIEW (essay date 1795)

[*The following excerpt is drawn from a review of* Edwy and Elgiva, *the tragedy by Burney that ran only one night.*]

The success of [*Edwy and Elgiva*] was not equal to what might have been expected from the acknowledged reputation of the Author. The construction of the Play was entitled to applause, and the language was beautiful and poetical; The sentiments just, and in character, and the Performers, with one exception, exerted themselves in a manner very much to their credit. The Piece, however, was not approved; some Parts appeared to want curtailing, and some circumstances were introduced which created ludicrous associations. With all these drawbacks we cannot withhold our approbation of the Play in general, which we believe would afford much pleasure in the closet, and with a few curtailments and alterations might have claimed its place on the Theatre. (p. 272)

A review of "Edwy and Elgiva," in The European Magazine, and London Review, *Vol. XXVII, April, 1795, pp. 271-72.*

[MARY WOLLSTONECRAFT] (essay date 1796)

[*Wollstonecraft, an eighteenth-century English author, is best known for her* A Vindication of the Rights of Woman, *now considered the first great feminist document. In the following excerpt, Wollstonecraft considers* Camilla *inferior to Burney's earlier novels even though it demonstrates evidence of her talent.*]

The celebrity which miss Burney has so deservedly acquired by her two former novels, naturally roused the expectation of the public for the promised production of madame d'Arblay.

A mind like hers could not be supposed to stand still, and new combinations of character are continually ripening to court the fickle.

As a whole, we are in justice bound to say, that we think it inferiour to the first fruits of her talents, though we boldly assert, that *Camilla* contains parts superiour to any thing she has yet produced.

In her former works dramatical exhibitions of manners of the comic cast certainly excel the displays of passion; and the remark may with still more propriety be applied to the volumes before us.

The incidents, which are to mark out the errours of youth, are frequently only perplexities, forcibly brought forward merely to be disentangled; yet, there are many amusing, and some interesting incidents, though they have not a plot of sufficient importance to bind them together.

The illustrating sentiments are often excellent, and expressed with great delicacy, evincing the sagacity and rectitude of the author's mind, reflecting equal credit on her heart and understanding. In the style, it is true, there are some indications of haste; but it would be almost insidious to point them out, when so large a proportion is written so well. (p. 142)

[We] cannot avoid concluding that with more consideration the author of *Cecilia* could have produced a more finished performance. (p. 143)

> [*Mary Wollstonecraft*], *"Mrs. D'Arblay's 'Camilla; or, A Picture of Youth',*" *in* The Analytical Review, *Vol. XXIV, August, 1796, pp. 142-48.*

HORACE WALPOLE (letter date 1796)

[*An English author, politician, and publisher, Walpole is best known for his memoirs and voluminous correspondence, which provide revealing glimpses of life in England during the last half of the eighteenth century. In the following excerpt, Walpole disparages* Camilla *for its lack of insight.*]

I will only reply by a word or two to a question you seem to ask; how I like *Camilla*? I do not care to say how little. Alas! [Miss Burney] has reversed experience, which I have long thought reverses its own utility by coming at the wrong end of our life when we do not want it. This author . . . knew the world and penetrated characters before she had stepped over the threshold; and, now she has seen so much of it, she has little or no insight at all: perhaps she apprehended having seen too much, and kept the bags of foul air that she brought from the Cave of Tempests too closely tied. (p. 470)

Horace Walpole, in a letter to Hannah More on August 29, 1796, in his The Letters of Horace Walpole, Earl of Orford, *Vol. VIII, edited by Peter Cunningham, Henry G. Bohn, 1866, pp. 469-70.*

[WILLIAM ENFIELD AND GEORGE E. GRIFFITHS] (essay date 1796)

[*The authors of the following excerpt praise the structure, plot, and particularly the verisimilitude of* Camilla. *Several characters are singled out for praise, including Sir Hugh, Dr. Orkborne, and Mrs. Arlbery. The critics also note Burney's adept handling of dialogue.*]

[In *Camilla,* Mrs. D'Arblay], with equal judgment and modesty, pursues the track in which she has already acquired so much deserved reputation; without suffering herself to be diverted from her native bent by an affectation of excelling in different kinds of writing, and without catching the infection of that taste for the marvellous and the terrible, which, since the appearance of her former productions, has, with some writers, become the fashion of the day. We have not perused the story of *Camilla* without seeing reason to admire its general structure, nor without feeling ourselves interested in the occurrences and catastrophe. Our chief pleasure, however, has arisen from the highly animated scenes of life and manners which have passed before us, and from the accurate and lively portraits of various characters, which the writer has drawn, if not from individual originals, at least from that great general exemplar, the world. (pp. 156-57)

The reader's attention is throughout kept awake (though indeed somewhat harassed) by an object which never fails to excite sympathy, 'innocence suffering through its own misapprehensions;' and at the close, the solitary, deserted, self-reproaching, yet truly amiable Camilla,—reduced to the lowest state of distress and wretchedness, and just ready to expire,—then, suddenly restored, by the unexpected return of Edgar, to her disconsolate parents, to love, and to happiness—presents a succession of painful and delightful images, which must deeply interest the feeling heart.

Possibly, on a general review of the principal story, the reader may think it not quite natural that a young man like Edgar, entirely and tenderly devoted to a generous passion, should give himself up to the direction of his tutor; whose personal disappointments had rendered him harsh, distrustful, and severe, in his judgment of female characters. Edgar's mistakes might, perhaps, more properly have proceeded from that extreme sensibility which naturally produces suspicion and jealousy; and the whole character of Dr. Marchmont might have been spared. We think also, that Camilla's conduct is not always quite consistent with her natural good sense and the openness of her temper; and that she too frequently acts contrary to Edgar's advice, and, on some occasions, towards the close of the work, does not treat him with sufficient frankness. The adventures of Eugenia, the sister of Camilla, whose want of personal charms occasions her many painful mortifications, (to which, however, she at length rises superior,) form an interesting under-part of the story. The meeting with the beautiful idiot, as contrived by Eugenia's father, furnishes an admirable lesson on beauty; and the picture of idiotcy is a striking one: but we are not sure that it is sufficiently distinct from that of madness. The whole plot is, perhaps, drawn out to too great a length: some of the adventures, particularly at Southampton, might have been omitted with advantage; and Camilla's ramble (not to say her whole acquaintance) with Mrs. Mitten is unnatural. If, however, in the course of this long work, the reader should occasionally experience some degree of lassitude, and be disposed to think the writer tedious, he ought to recollect that *aliquande bonus dormitat Homerus*. Be it also remembered that there is another and more advantageous point of resemblance between Mrs. D'Arblay and Homer; namely, in the peculiar distinctness and propriety of her delineations of character. (pp. 157-58)

Among the rich and varied groupe of characters exhibited in this novel, the most prominent is that of Sir Hugh Tyrold, Camilla's uncle, whose peculiar humour gives occasion to many of the most pleasing incidents in the novel, and furnishes the principal entertainment of the work. This character is, we believe, quite original, and is drawn with admirable consistency and spirit. (p. 158)

The character of a pedant, wholly absorbed in study, and devoted to literary ambition, is well delineated in Dr. Orkborne. His preparation of books for a ride of four or five miles; his vexation, when his kind patron, during his absence, had placed a book-cafe in his room, and ordered the servants to arrange his books and papers on the shelves; and his absence of mind on several occasions, when politeness or other more powerful motives urged his attention; are described with characteristic humour. In some instances, his abstractedness is carried too far, particularly in the scene at Southampton, where he stands on the landing-place of the stairs at an inn, leaning on the banisters, refining a paragraph, in the midst of general confusion and uproar. The sprightly and eccentric Mrs. Arlbery makes a distinguished figure among the *dramatis personae*. Her entrance into the ball-room with her work-bag on her arm, while she displays her airs and graces, and distributes her commands among her obsequious attendant *beaux*, exhibits a lively picture of easy gaiety, and polite negligence. Her undaunted determination to set the opinion of the world at defiance gives to her character a whimsical singularity. She afterward discovers an excellent understanding, and becomes an useful friend to Camilla. This delineation, also, has considerable originality and consistency. (pp. 160-61)

The low-bred Mrs. Mitten, even if we allow her to be a necessary agent in the business of the story, appears too frequently, and stays too long. The romantic Melmond, at his first appearance, and in some subsequent scenes, is a caricature. In a few other instances, a similar fault may be observed: but it is by no means true that Mrs. D'Arblay's general delineations of character are "*broad farce.*" They are, commonly, portraits of real manners; and it may be difficult to find any novels, except those of Fielding, in which characters are more accurately drawn than in those of this very ingenious lady. We particularly admire the happy facility with which she gives to each person a language of his own, and preserves it uniformly through the work. (p. 161)

Such a command of the language of character, as appears through all Mrs. D'Arblay's novels, is an excellence which affords ample compensation for occasional negligences. (pp. 161-62)

Fictitious tales of this kind are often incumbered with trite sentiments and trivial remarks: but no complaint of this sort lies against the present performance. Observations arising from particular incidents are very thinly scattered through the volumes; and even the general conclusions from the story are, in a great measure, left to the reader's own reflections. The moral instruction of the piece is, however, important. Among other

useful lessons, it shews the folly of exposing young people to the temptations arising from prospects created by early declared testamentary arrangements; and it warns them of the mischievous consequences of heedlessly contracting debts, and of the dangers arising from the two extremes of severely watchful suspicion, and thoughtless imprudence. (pp. 162-63)

The great merit of the work, however, consists in more important characteristics; and we may principally recommend it to the world as a *warning* 'picture of youth;'—as a guide for the conduct of young females in the most important circumstances and situations of life. (p. 163)

> [*William Enfield and George E. Griffiths*], "Mrs. D'Arblay's 'Camilla'," in The Monthly Review, London, Vol. XXI, October, 1796, pp. 156-63.

THE SCOTS MAGAZINE   (essay date 1796)

[*In the following review of* Camilla, *the critic faults its excessive length and, with the exception of Camilla herself, its character depictions.*]

From the author of *Evelina* much was expected, but we are afraid *Camilla* will rather disappoint the generality of readers. There is, in our opinion, neither character nor incident, to keep up the attention through five long volumes, even with all Mrs. D'Arblay's good sense and nicety of discrimination; these indeed (whatever may be the general merit of the book) are most happily displayed in the character she has drawn of Camilla. It is at once amiable and engaging, uniting liveliness, sensibility, and understanding, with the softer graces; which last are, by the generality of novelists, deemed alone sufficient for their heroines, the former being considered altogether incompatible with the character. The author is by no means so fortunate in the other pictures she draws; particularly in that of Sir Hugh Tyrold and Doctor Orkburne, where she makes the most disagreeable, if not unnatural, combinations. We are sorry to see, in the former of these characters, so much benevolence united with the grossest weakness and want of judgment; and in the latter, learning and respectability with so many oddities.

> A review of "Camilla; or, A Picture of Youth," in The Scots Magazine, Vol. 58, October, 1796, p. 691.

THE ANTIJACOBIN REVIEW   (essay date 1814)

[*The following excerpt is taken from a negative review of* The Wanderer. *The critic assesses Burney's preface to the book and questions the logic of some of her assertions about the capacity of the novel as an art form. While conceding that* The Wanderer *contains "no small number of interesting situations and incidents," this commentator also contends that the novel is marred by its length and unrealistic characters.*]

The high reputation which Miss Burney enjoyed as a writer of novels raised our expectations of instruction from a new production of Madame D'Arblay [***The Wanderer; or, Female Difficulties***], very high indeed. We were not such strenuous Antigallicans as to expect that our fair author would experience any diminution of talents from her union with a native of France; nor did we believe that even a residence in that country would dim the lustre of her genius, contract the sphere of her knowledge, shake the solidity of her judgment, or lessen her powers of instruction and amusement. We opened, then, these volumes with avidity, promising ourselves a rich treat from their contents, for, grave critics as we are, we are not ashamed of avowing a predilection for good writing, when combined with good principles, though presented to us in the form, and under the proscribed, but still popular, name, of—*a novel*. We had not proceeded very far, indeed, before we paused; and, ere the first volume had been read, contrary to our usual custom, we laid down the book several times. With the second and third, the case became worse, and we were really obliged to make a great effort, to labour through the whole! Has a ten years' residence in France, then, really had the effect of incapacitating this lady from fixing the attention, or exciting the interests, of an English reader, as she was wont to do? We will not presume to answer this question in the affirmative, but, most assuredly, the present production of her pen falls very far short of her former works, in its powers of attraction.

Though we consider the prefatory dedication as disfigured by labour, pedantry, and egotism; though the author's vanity in recounting the praises which a Johnson, a Burke, and a Reynolds, bestowed on her early writings, forced a smile from us; yet is it laudable for its expressions of filial piety, and judicious in its observations on novel-writing.

> With regard to the very serious subject treated upon, from time to time, in this work, some, perhaps many, may ask, is a novel the vehicle for such considerations? Such discussions?
>
> Permit me to answer; whatever, in illustrating the characters, manners, or opinions, of the day, exhibits what is noxious or reprehensible, should scrupulously be accompanied by what is salubrious, or chastening. Not that poison ought to be infused, merely to display the virtues of an antidote: but that, where errour and mischief bask in the broad light of day, truth ought not to be suffered to shrink timidly into the shade.
>
> Divest, for a moment, the title of novel from its stationary standard of insignificance, and say! What is the species of writing that offers fairer opportunities for conveying useful precepts? It is, or it ought to be, a picture of supposed, but natural, or probable, human existence. It holds, therefore, in its hands, our best affections; it exercises our imaginations; it points out the path of honour; and gives to juvenile credulity knowledge of the world, without ruin, or repentance; and the lessons of experience, without its tears.

The author here argues illogically; for it by no means follows, because a novel is a picture of human existence, that it should either have a hold on our best affections, exercise our imaginations, indicate the path of honour, impart a knowledge of the world, or inculcate the lessons of experience; not one of these is the *necessary effect* of *a* picture of human life. A novel *may* contain a true representation of human life, and yet be destitute of any of the advantages which are here stated to be the legitimate, and, indeed, obvious, consequence of such a representation. We concur, with Mrs. D'Arblay, in her general opinion of the *capability* of novels to convey all the instruction which she here ascribes to them; but her error consists in drawing a conclusion not warranted by her premises, and in representing what a novel *ought to be,* as what a novel *actually is*.

And is not a novel, permit me, also, to ask, in common with every other literary work, entitled to receive its stamp as useful, mischievous, or nugatory, from its execution? not necessarily, and in its changeless state, to be branded as a mere vehicle for frivolous, or seductive, amusement? If many may turn aside from all but mere entertainment presented under this form, many, also, may, unconsciously, be allured by it into reading the severest truths, who would not even open a work of a graver denomination.

(pp. 347-48)

This is the criterion by which we have tried *The Wanderer*. To say, that it contains much able delineation of character, many sound and judicious reflections, and no small number of interesting situations and incidents, is only to allow it the merit which it, unquestionably, possesses. On the other hand, the story is spun out to an unconscionable, and most unnecessary, length; many of the dialogues (with which it abounds) are insufferably trifling and tedious; and some of the characters are gross caricatures of human nature, and so far unnatural. Among these last we class Elinor and Mrs. Ireton. Elinor is a female philosopher of the French school, who makes her own reason (or rather her own caprice) the sole guide of her conduct in life. To this supreme arbiter she subjects every obligation human and divine; the laws of modesty; and, almost, the distinctions of sex. Engaged to marry one man, she conceives a passion for his brother, which, instead of combating by the exercise of her reason, she anxiously cherishes; she even declares her passion for him; and, from evidence of his attachment to another woman, she endeavours to commit suicide in a public assembly. We seriously ask our readers whether this be "a *natural* and *probable* picture of human existence?" To us, it appears to be the very reverse of nature and probability. (p. 349)

Mrs. Ireton and her son are characters almost as much out of nature as that of Elinor. The lady is not only frivolous and affected, beyond all usual degrees of frivolity and affectation, but malicious as Satan himself; and is made to combine the airs of fashionable folly, with the manners of Billingsgate and Covent Garden. Women no doubt, are to be found, who are to the full as fanciful, and as self-complacent, as Mrs. Ireton is represented to be; but we disbelieve in the existence of any human being, bearing the female form, who adds to so much caprice, so much malevolence, and who, to foibles that create disgust, joins vices that excite abhorrence; for, what can be more vicious than the whole conduct of this fantastical character to Juliet? Young Ireton possesses all the bad qualities of his mother, aggravated by more direct and pointed practical malice: the object of introducing him appears to be the desire to exhibit a young man, entertaining a wish to marry, but so whimsical in his choice as to suffer every object to escape him. There may be such characters, but they are, we believe, rare, and certainly not very edifying. (pp. 349-50)

The heroine herself, though combining, of course, every perfection of mind, as well as of person, is frequently made to act inconsistently with her character. Though a woman of great sense, her conduct is occasionally extremely foolish; and in several of her interviews with Mrs. Maple, Mrs. Ireton, and Mrs. Howell, she suffers herself to be bullied, insulted, and threatened, in a way which would lead any one to suppose her wholly destitute of all strength of intellect, and of all sense of propriety. Her submission to the most unworthy conduct, and to the most repulsive situations, though repugnant to her feelings, and by no means justified by her circumstances, evidently grows out of the created necessity for encountering *difficulties*. But the *"female difficulties"* which are here exhibited, though properly named, since they are of *female creation,* are not such as necessarily arise out of the situation in which the heroine is placed, but are obviously introduced for the purpose of justifying the second title of the work;—and these constitute the least able, and worst-constructed, parts of the story. (p. 350)

Madame D'Arblay is much more conversant with the practice of amplification, than with the art of compression; and relies too much on her ability to pourtray natural characters with skill and effect. But for this circumstance, we incline to think her judgment would have led her to condense the materials of this work into one half of the compass which they now occupy. It might then have been read with interest, and might, possibly, not have injured her literary character. As it is, we cannot bestow on it, as a whole, that approbation which portions of the work deserve, nor can we, with truth, declare that her reputation as an author has derived any accession of strength from the publication of *The Wanderer*. (p. 353)

> A review of "The Wanderer; or, Female Difficulties," in The Antijacobin Review, Vol. XLVI, No. 191, April, 1814, pp. 347-54.

[JOHN WILSON CROKER] (essay date 1814)

> [*Croker was an influential Tory politician and a principal contributor to the conservative journal the* Quarterly Review. *Nicknamed the "slashing critic" for his vitriolic literary reviews, he was both admired and berated by his contemporaries. Croker's writings are now considered dated, yet they continue to attract the attention of some scholars and students of nineteenth-century literary history. In the following excerpt from Croker's negative review of* The Wanderer, *he harshly judges Burney's work. Croker contends that each successive novel after* Evelina *is increasingly marred by repetition and self-imitation and lacks the vitality and originality of her earlier works. For additional commentary by Croker, see the essays dated 1833 and 1842.*]

None of our female novelists (not even Miss Edgeworth) ever attained so early and so high a reputation as Miss Burney, or, as we must now call her, Madame D'Arblay. Her *Evelina,* published at the age of seventeen, was a most extraordinary instance of early talent, and excited an expectation of excellence which her *Cecilia* almost fulfilled, and which her *Camilla* did not altogether disappoint; but we regret to say, that *The Wanderer,* which might be expected to finish and crown her literary labours, is not only inferior to its sister-works, but cannot, in our judgment, claim any very decided superiority over the thousand-and-one volumes with which the Minerva Press inundates the shelves of circulating libraries, and increases, instead of diverting, the ennui of the loungers at watering places.

If we had not been assured in the title-page that this work had been produced by the same pen as *Cecilia,* we should have pronounced Madame D'Arblay to be a feeble imitator of the style and manner of Miss Burney—we should have admitted the flat fidelity of her copy, but we should have lamented the total want of vigour, vivacity, and originality; and, conceding to the fair author (as we should have been inclined to do) some discrimination of character, and some power of writing, we should have strenuously advised her to avoid, in future, the dull mediocrity of a copyist, and to try the flight of her own genius in some work, that should not recall to us in every page

the mortifying recollection of excellence which, though she had the good sense to admire it, she never would have the power to rival.

Such being the opinion which we should have felt ourselves obliged to pronounce on an imitator, it follows that we have a still more severe judgment to pass on Madame D'Arblay herself. We are afraid that she is self-convicted of being what the painters technically call a *mannerist;* that is, she has given over painting from the life, and has employed herself in copying from her own copies, till, instead of a power of natural delineation, she has acquired a certain trick and habitual style of portraiture:—but *The Wanderer* is not only the work of a mannerist, but of a mannerist who is *épuisée,* whose last manner is the worst, and who convinces us that, during the thirty years which have elapsed since the publication of *Cecilia,* she has been gradually descending from the elevation which the vigour of her youth had attained.

Shall we confess that we were not wholly unprepared to expect this 'lame and impotent conclusion'? In Madame D'Arblay's best works an accurate eye discovered the seeds of the defect which is now so obvious. (pp. 123-24)

The characters and incidents of *Evelina, Cecilia,* and (though somewhat more diversified) of *Camilla,* have too much resemblance. In each, the plot is a tissue of teasing distresses all of the same class, and in each, are repeated, almost to weariness, portraits of the same forms of fashionable frivolity and of vulgar middle life. (pp. 124-25)

[Even] in her best days, Madame D'Arblay's style had a predisposition to self-imitation and tautology. As this peculiar *manner,* however, was at least her own—as the figures, though repeated, were well drawn,—as the details, though minute, were vividly expressed, and as there existed, in each of these works, great and distinct beauties of character and composition, the subordinate defects of repetition and self-imitation were excused in *Cecilia* and tolerated in *Camilla,* amid the general splendour of these delightful pieces.

But in *The Wanderer* there is no splendour, no source of delight to dazzle criticism and beguile attention from a defect which has increased in size and deformity exactly in the same degree that the beauties have vanished. *The Wanderer* has the identical features of *Evelina*—but of *Evelina* grown old; the vivacity, the bloom, the elegance, 'the purple light of love' are vanished; the eyes are there, but they are dim; the cheek, but it is furrowed; the lips, but they are withered. And when to this description we add that Madame D'Arblay endeavours to make up for the want of originality in her characters by the most absurd mysteries, the most extravagant incidents, and the most violent events, we have completed the portrait of an old coquette who endeavours, by the wild tawdriness and laborious gaiety of her attire, to compensate for the loss of the natural charms of freshness, novelty, and youth. (pp. 125-26)

Violent as the incongruities of [the] chief plot of the drama must appear to our readers, we venture to assure them that they are tame and common-place, compared with the monstrous absurdities of the under-plot and of the inferior characters. . . .

We have now done with this novel, on which we should not have been justified in saying so much, but that we conceived ourselves in duty bound to attend the lifeless remains of our old and dear friends Evelina and Cecilia to their last abode. . . . (p. 129)

[*John Wilson Croker*], *"D'Arblay's 'Wanderer',"* in The Quarterly Review, *Vol. XI, No. XXI, April, 1814, pp. 123-30.*

[WILLIAM HAZLITT] (essay date 1815)

[*One of the most important commentators of the Romantic age, Hazlitt was an English critic and journalist. He is best known for his descriptive criticism in which he stressed that no motives beyond judgment and analysis are necessary on the part of the critic. A critic must start with a strong opinion, Hazlitt asserted, but must also keep in mind that evaluation is the starting point— not the object—of criticism. Hazlitt's often recalcitrant refusal to engage in close analysis, however, led other critics to question whether in fact he was capable of close, sustained analysis. Characterized by a tough, independent view of the world, by his political liberalism, and by the influence of Samuel Taylor Coleridge and Charles Lamb, Hazlitt is particularly admired for his wide range of reference and catholicity of interests. In the following excerpt, Hazlitt discusses Burney's novels, stating that there is little of "passion or character, or even manners" in her work and that she excels only in describing "external behavior." He claims further that her characters are all caricatures and that they are "superficial" and "uniform." Her lack of intellectual rigor and depth are attributed by Hazlitt to her sex, for he contends that women are more aware than men of "any oddity or singularity of character"; according to Hazlitt, women are incapable of acute perception.*]

Among those few persons who 'have kept the even tenor of their way,' the author of *Evelina, Cecilia,* and *Camilla,* holds a distinguished place.... [The author of *The Wanderer* is] quite of the old school, a mere common observer of manners,— and also a very woman. It is this last circumstance which forms the peculiarity of her writings, and distinguishes them from [other] masterpieces.... She is unquestionably a quick, lively, and accurate observer of persons and things; but she always looks at them with a consciousness of her sex, and in that point of view in which it is the particular business and interest of women to observe them. We thus get a kind of supplement and gloss to our original text, which we could not otherwise have obtained. There is little in her works of passion or character, or even manners, in the most extended sense of the word, as implying the sum-total of our habits and pursuits; her *forte* is in describing the absurdities and affectations of external behaviour, or *the manners of people in company.* Her characters, which are all caricatures, are no doubt distinctly marked, and perfectly kept up; but they are somewhat superficial, and exceedingly uniform. Her heroes and heroines, almost all of them, depend on the stock of a single phrase or sentiment; or at least have certain mottoes or devices by which they may always be known. They are such characters as people might be supposed to assume for a night at a masquerade. She presents not the whole length figure, nor even the face, but some prominent feature. In the present novel, for example, a lady appears regularly every ten pages, to get a lesson in music for nothing. She never appears for any other purpose; this is all you know of her; and in this the whole wit and humour of the character consists. Meadows is the same, who has always the same cue of being tired, without any other idea, &c. It has been said of Shakespeare, that you may always assign his speeches to the proper characters:—and you may infallibly do the same thing with Madame D'Arblay's; for they always say the same thing. The Branghtons are the best. Mr. Smith is an exquisite city portrait.—*Evelina* is also her best novel, because it is shortest; that is, it has all the liveliness in the sketches of character, and exquisiteness of comic dialogue and repartee, without the te-

diousness of the story, and endless affectation of the sentiments.

Women, in general, have a quicker perception of any oddity or singularity of character than men, and are more alive to every absurdity which arises from a violation of the rules of society, or a deviation from established custom. This partly arises from the restraints on their own behaviour, which turn their attention constantly on the subject, and partly from other causes. The surface of their minds, like that of their bodies, seems of a finer texture than ours; more soft, and susceptible of immediate impression. They have less muscular power,— less power of continued voluntary attention,—of reason—passion and imagination: But they are more easily impressed with whatever appeals to their senses or habitual prejudices. The intuitive perception of their minds is less disturbed by any general reasonings on causes or consequences. They learn the idiom of character and manner, as they acquire that of language, by rote merely, without troubling themselves about the principles. Their observation is not the less accurate on that account, as far as it goes; for it has been well said, that 'there is nothing so true as habit.'

There is little other power in Miss Burney's novels, than that of immediate observation: her characters, whether of refinement or vulgarity, are equally superficial and confined. The whole is a question of form, whether that form is adhered to, or violated. It is this circumstance which takes away dignity and interest from her story and sentiments, and makes the one so teasing and tedious, and the other so insipid. The difficulties in which she involves her heroines are indeed 'Female Difficulties;'—they are difficulties created out of nothing. The author appears to have no other idea of refinement than that it is the reverse of vulgarity; but the reverse of vulgarity is fastidiousness and affectation. There is a true, and a false delicacy. Because a vulgar country Miss would answer 'yes' to a proposal of marriage in the first page, Mad. d'Arblay makes it a proof of an excess of refinement, and an indispensable point of etiquette in her young ladies, to postpone the answer to the end of five volumes, without the smallest reason for their doing so, and with every reason to the contrary. The reader is led every moment to expect a denouement, and is as constantly disappointed on some trifling pretext. The whole artifice of her fable consists in coming to no conclusion. Her ladies stand so upon the order of their going, that they do not go at all. They will not abate an ace of their punctilio in any circumstances, or on any emergency. They would consider it as quite indecorous to run down stairs though the house were in flames, or to move off the pavement though a scaffolding was falling. She has formed to herself an abstract idea of perfection in common behaviour, which is quite as romantic and impracticable as any other idea of the sort: and the consequence has naturally been, that she makes her heroines commit the greatest improprieties and absurdities in order to avoid the smallest. In contradiction to a maxim in philosophy, they constantly act from the weakest motive, or rather from pure affectation.

Thus L. S.—otherwise *Ellis,* in the present novel, actually gives herself up to the power of a man who has just offered violence to her person, rather than return to the asylum of a farm-house, at which she has left some friends, because, as she is turning her steps that way, 'she hears the sounds of rustic festivity and vulgar merriment proceed from it.' That is, in order that her exquisite sensibility may not be shocked by the behaviour of a number of honest country-people making merry at a dance, this model of female delicacy exposes herself to every species of insult and outrage from a man whom she hates. In like manner, she runs from her honourable lover into the power of a ruffian and an assassin, who claims a right over her person by a forced marriage. The whole tissue of the fable is, in short, more wild and chimerical than any thing in *Don Quixote*, without having any thing of poetical truth or elevation. Madame D'Arblay has woven a web of difficulties for her heroine, something like the green silken threads in which the shepherdesses entangled the steed of Cervantes's hero, who swore, in his fine enthusiastic way, that he would sooner cut his passage to another world than disturb the least of those beautiful meshes. The Wanderer raises obstacles, lighter than 'the gossamer that idles in the wanton summer air,' into insurmountable barriers; and trifles with those that arise out of common sense, reason, and necessity. Her conduct never arises directly out of the circumstances in which she is placed, but out of some factitious and misplaced refinement on them. It is a perpetual game at cross-purposes. There being a plain and strong motive why she should pursue any course of action, is a sufficient reason for her to avoid it; and the perversity of her conduct is in proportion to its levity—as the lightness of the feather baffles the force of the impulse that is given to it, and the slightest breath of air turns it back on the hand from which it is launched. We can hardly consider this as an accurate description of the perfection of the female character!

We are sorry to be compelled to speak so disadvantageously of the work of an excellent and favourite writer; and the more so, as we perceive no decay of talent, but a perversion of it. There is the same admirable spirit in the dialogues, and particularly in the characters of Mrs Ireton, Sir Jasper Herrington, and Mr Giles Arbe, as in her former novels. But these do not fill a hundred pages of the work; and there is nothing else good in it. In the story, which here occupies the attention of the reader almost exclusively, Madame D'Arblay never excelled. (pp. 336-38)

> [*William Hazlitt*], *"Standard Novels and Romances," in* The Edinburgh Review, *Vol. XXIV, No. XLVIII, February, 1815, pp. 320-38.*

JANE AUSTEN   (essay date 1817?)

[*As a supreme prose stylist of the nineteenth century, Austen has secured a lasting place in English literature. Her novels* Pride and Prejudice, Mansfield Park, *and* Northanger Abbey, *from which the following excerpt is drawn, are considered classics. This commentary between two characters, John Thorpe and Catherine Morland, is taken from a discussion of literature within the novel; Thorpe harshly criticizes* Camilla, *terming it "the horridest nonsense you can imagine." While Austen criticizes Burney within the context of her novel, generations of critics have acknowledged Austen's artistic debt to Burney. The actual date of* Northanger Abbey's *composition is unknown; Austen died in 1817.*]

"I was thinking of that other stupid book, written by that woman they make such a fuss about; she who married the French emigrant."

"I suppose you mean *Camilla*!"

"Yes, that's the book; such unnatural stuff! An old man playing at see-saw. I took up the first volume once, and looked it over, but I soon found it would not do; indeed, I guessed what sort of stuff it must be before I saw it; as soon as I heard she had married an emigrant, I was sure I should never be able to get through it."

"I have never read it."

"You had no loss, I assure you; it is the horridest nonsense you can imagine; there is nothing in the world in it but an old man's playing at see-saw and learning Latin; upon my soul, there is not." (p. 394)

> *Jane Austen, "Northanger Abbey," in her* The Complete Novels of Jane Austen, Volume 2, *1950. Reprint by Vintage Books, 1976, pp. 367-542.*

[JOHN WILSON CROKER]   (essay date 1833)

[*In the following excerpt, Croker disparages the* Memoirs of Dr. Burney, *which he terms a complete literary failure. Croker argues that Burney suppressed a great deal of her father's manuscripts in order to present her own life story. The result, according to the critic, is convoluted and pompous. For additional commentary by Croker, see the essays dated 1814 and 1842.*]

We would willingly have declined the task of reviewing [**Memoirs of Dr. Burney**]. As a literary work we have not a word to say in its favour; and having no hope of improving the style of an author whose most popular production was published nearly sixty years ago, and feeling a great reluctance to give gratuitous pain to a person so respectable as Madame d'Arblay, we wish we could have evaded the subject altogether; but the duty which we owe our readers, our regard for the memory of Dr. Burney, and even our personal estimation of Madame d'Arblay herself, all concur in obliging us to offer some account of these volumes.

Dr. Burney had, as Madame d'Arblay sets out with informing us, not merely intended, but '*directed* that the Memoirs of his life should be published; and his family and friends'—very naturally—'expected them to pass through her hands' . . . ; but we regret to say, that Madame d'Arblay appears to have disobeyed the 'directions' and disappointed the 'expectations' which she thus professes to fulfil. Dr. Burney left behind, it seems, 'sundry manuscript volumes, containing the history of his life from his cradle almost to his grave:'—*those* were the Memoirs which the Doctor 'directed' to be published, and of which 'his family and friends expected' Madame d'Arblay to be the editor; but from these voluminous papers Madame d'Arblay has made very scanty extracts, and has become the *writer* of a work essentially her own, and not the *editor* of her father's recollections of his life. Her motives for this course of proceeding are not distinctly stated; but it is hinted that she considered what her father had thus left as unfit for the public eye. (p. 97)

Madame d'Arblay may have exercised a sound discretion in not giving to the public this mass of materials, *in extenso;* but we do very much doubt whether what she has suppressed could have been more feeble, anile, incoherent, or '*sentant plus l'apoplexie,*' than that which she has substituted for it. In fact, almost the only passages in these volumes, which exhibit common sense, good taste, or intelligible language, are the few sentences which are given in Dr. Burney's own words, and which, though occasionally somewhat inflated, appear simple and natural in the midst of the strange *galimatias* of pompous verbosity in which his daughter has enshrined them. For instance, could Dr. Burney's own recollections of Mrs. Cibber have been more absurdly expressed than Madame d'Arblay's version of them?—

> Mrs. Cibber herself he considered as a pattern of perfection in the tragic art, from her *magnetizing powers of harrowing* and winning at once every feeling of the mind, by the eloquent sensibility with which she portrayed, or, rather,

personified, Tenderness, Grief, Horror, or Distraction. . . .

Or could his exposition of the fascinations of gambling be more verbose and obscure than the following:—

> Gaming, with that poignant stimulus, self-conceit, which, where calculation tries to battle with chance, goads on, with resistless force, our designs, by our presumption, soon left wholly in the background every attempt at rivalry by any other species of recreation.
>
> (pp. 97-8)

These specimens will, we think, satisfy our readers that so far as style is concerned, Dr. Burney's original Memoir cannot have been much worse than that of his daughter; and that a judicious selection from the autograph manuscript would probably give a fuller and certainly a more intelligible account of this amiable man, than can be gathered from the over-anxious piety and too elaborate care of his affectionate, but injudicious, biographer. (p. 99)

We must here pause for a moment to complain of a defect in Madame d'Arblay's work even more serious than that of her style—the suppression of dates. We say *suppression;* because we cannot attribute to accidental negligence the silence of the biographer as to the time of her father's first coming to London—of his marriage—of his migration to Lynn—of the birth of his children, and particularly of Madame d'Arblay herself—of the death of his first wife—of his second marriage; and, in short, of all the leading events of the earlier part of his life. It can hardly be personal vanity which produces this silence; yet certainly no spinster of a doubtful age can have a greater aversion to accuracy in matters of date than is exhibited by this lady, who admits that she has been above fifty-five years an author and forty years a wife. But though we readily acquit Madame d'Arblay of being led by *personal* vanity to this studied concealment of dates, yet we shall by and by have occasion to show, that *literary* vanity may have been the motive of this omission, which, in a biographical work, is peculiarly puzzling and provoking. . . . (p. 100)

[Of Dr. Burney's] life we confess we should be glad to see some more distinct, intelligible, and orderly account than that now before us: which, besides the errors of style which are so ridiculous, and a want of arrangement which is exceedingly perplexing, has also the more serious fault of being anything rather than a history of the life and writings of *Dr. Burney.* Madame d'Arblay gives a hint that the original correspondence of Dr. Burney is destined to the flames, and it is not clear that his original memoirs are not threatened with a similar fate. We venture to entreat that this design may not be executed; the extracts from his own pen are certainly, as we have already said, the most satisfactory parts of these volumes, and without rating very highly the importance of the history of Dr. Burney to the general literature of the country, we think the public would be glad to see a good life of him; and if his own materials can afford such a narrative, so much the better. Madame d'Arblay's book has certainly not occupied *this* ground, and instead of being called **Memoirs of Dr. Burney,** might better be described as 'Scattered Recollections of Miss Fanny Burney and her Acquaintance.' Of her father she tells almost nothing that was not already to be found in the obituary of the *Gentleman's Magazine* and other biographies; and she does not even notice three or four musical works, which we learn from those au-

thorities he composed—a strange omission in the *Memoirs* of a musical professor.

This leads us to a second part of our task—namely, to give some account of what appears to us the *real* object of the work; and if we have covered half-a-dozen pages without touching on that essential subject, it is because Madame d'Arblay, with consummate art—or a confusion of ideas which has had the same effect as consummate art,—conceals from her readers, and perhaps from herself, that it is her *own Memoirs,* and *not* those of her father that she has been writing; and we confess that we have a strong suspicion, that it was *because* her father's auto-biography did not fulfil *this* object, that *it* has been suppressed—and this joint-stock history (in which, as in other joint-stock concerns, the managing partner has the larger share) has been substituted for it. Let us not be misunderstood. We do not complain that Madame d'Arblay should write her own Memoirs; on the contrary, we wish she had done so in her own *original* style, instead of perplexing the reader with all those awkward shifts and circumlocutions, by which her modesty labours to conceal that she is writing *her own* life, and making her father's memory, as it were, *carry double.* Very ludicrous indeed are the shifts by which she contrives to pin herself to his skirts, and still more so the awkward diffidence, the assumed *mauvaise honte,* with which, to avoid speaking in the first person, she designates herself by such circumlocutions as '*this memorialist;*' or '*the present editor;*' or '*the Doctor's second daughter;*' or when, after her marriage, she retired to a cottage in Surrey, '*the happy recluse;*' or, finally, by the more compound designation of '*the-then-Bookham-and-afterwards-West-Hamble-female hermit.*' . . . (pp. 106-07)

We must now revert to the suspicion which we have before expressed, that a little literary vanity has occasioned the remarkable suppression of dates in the earlier portion of these *Memoirs;* and this leads us to the extraordinary and interesting account of Madame d'Arblay's first appearance in the literary world. At the age of *seventeen,* as we have always seen and heard it stated, Miss Fanny Burney—without the knowledge of her father—without any suspicion on the part of her family and friends that she had any literary turn or capacity whatsoever—published anonymously her celebrated novel of **Evelina, or a Young Lady's Entrance into the World;** which emerged at once into popularity, raised its youthful author, as soon as she avowed it, to a brilliant reputation, and recommended her to the admiration and friendship of some of the most considerable men of the age. We extract her father's account of this remarkable circumstance:—

> The literary history of my second daughter, Fanny, now Madame d'Arblay, is singular. She was wholly unnoticed in the nursery for any talents or quickness of study; indeed, at eight years old she did not know her letters; and her brother, the tar, who in his boyhood had a natural genius for hoaxing, used to pretend to teach her to read; and gave her a book topsy-turvy, which he said she never found out! She had, however, a great deal of invention and humour in her childish sports; and used, after having seen a play in Mrs. Garrick's box, to take the actors off, and compose speeches for their characters; for she could not read them. But in company, or before strangers, she was silent, backward, and timid, even to sheepishness: and, from her shyness, had such profound gravity

and composure of features, that those of my friends who came often to my house, and entered into the different humours of the children, never called Fanny by any other name, from the time she had reached her eleventh year, than The Old Lady.

Her first work, *Evelina,* was written by stealth, in a closet up two pair of stairs, that was appropriated to the *younger children as a play-room.* No one was let into the secret but my third daughter, afterwards Mrs. Phillips; though even to her it was never read till printed, from want of private opportunity. . . . The book had been six months published before I even heard its name; which I learnt at last without her knowledge.But great, indeed, was then my surprise, to find that it was in general reading, and commended in no common manner in the several Reviews of the times. Of this she was unacquainted herself, as she was then ill, and in the country. When I knew its title, I commissioned one of her sisters to procure it for me privately. I opened the first volume with fear and trembling; not having the least idea that, without the use of the press, or any practical knowledge of the world, she could write a book worth reading. The dedication to myself, however, brought tears into my eyes; and before I had read half the first volume I was much surprised, and, I confess, delighted.

Madame d'Arblay's account, which is very prolix and desultory, agrees with that of her father, but gives a few additional particulars—one of the first of which the reader would naturally expect to be the *age* of the writer: *that,* however, is not distinctly told; but the slight allusions which are made to the subject would seem to confirm the idea of the *extreme youth* of the author. She relates that at *eight* years she did not know her letters, though at *ten* she began scribbling, almost incessantly but always secretly, little works of invention; and that when she *attained* her *fifteenth* year (that is, we presume, when she had accomplished her *fourteenth*), she took an opportunity, while her parents were absent, of burning her heap of manuscripts. (pp. 107-08)

The good Doctor tells us that he was 'surprised and delighted;' and delighted and surprised he well might be, for even after his evidence and the more minute account given by Madame d'Arblay herself, we are utterly at a loss to comprehend how a girl of *seventeen,* slow, shy, secluded—almost neglected—never having been, as it would seem, from under the parental roof, and having seen little or nothing of life (but her own little play-room), could have written such a work as *Evelina.* We are not blind to its faults—the plot is puerile enough—the denouement incredible—the latter part very tedious—there is much exaggeration in some of the minor characters—while that of the heroine herself is left almost a blank—but the elegance and grace of the style, the vivacity of many of the descriptions, the natural though rather too broad humour, the combination of the minor circumstances, the artist-like contrast of the several characters, and, above all, the accurate and distinctive knowledge of life and manners of different classes of society—from what sources did this *child, writing by stealth, in the play-room,* derive them? (p. 109)

As to the style of these *Memoirs,* there is another cause which may have contributed to give it that strange pomposity which we have had but too much occasion to notice. A novel writer is obliged to make up for the paucity of events by a superabundance of verbal details. 'A potent, pointed, piercing, yet delicious dart' . . . ; 'eyes of the finest azure beamed the brightest intelligence'—'he flew with extatic celerity to her with whom eternal bondage would be a state celestial' . . . , and such hyperboles, may do very well to fill up the space between one event and another, and to give to imaginary beings a certain air of locality and reality; but when all this comes to be applied to *real* matter-of-fact personages, it is absurd. . . . Fictitious life, of which novels are the history, is made up of words, of epithets, of amplification, of touches—the smaller the better; real history is made up of the larger facts—of what a man *did,* not what he said,—of how a lady acted, not how she looked: fictitious life is described by fancied feelings and imputed motives—which it is given to the omniscient author alone to develope—real life, of those broad interests and plain actions of which all mankind are the witnesses and the judges—and it is, we surmise, by confounding these distinctions, that a charming novelist (for such we shall always consider the authoress of *Cecilia*) has become the most ridiculous of historians.

Even when Madame d'Arblay professes to give us the conversations of Burke, or Dr. Johnson, or Garrick, it is evident that she labours and over-labours her portraits, till they resemble the original as theatrical do real characters,—as the Napoleon or Captain Cook of a melodrama do the general or the sailor. (pp. 111-12)

[We] wish that it were possible to persuade Madame d'Arblay to separate, even now, *her own* from *her father's* **Memoirs**—to give us *them* as he wrote them, or at least as much of what he wrote as she might judge proper; and to condense and simplify into a couple of interesting (and interesting they would be) volumes, *her own* story and her contemporaneous notes and *bonâ fide* recollections of that brilliant society in which she moved, from 1778 to 1794. We lay some stress on the words *bonâ fide,* not as imputing to Madame d'Arblay the slightest *intention* to deceive, but because we think that we see in almost every page abundant proof, that the habit of *novel-writing* has led her to colour and, as she may suppose, embellish her anecdotes with sonorous epithets and factitious details, which, however, we venture to assure her, not only blunt their effect, but discredit their authority. (p. 125)

> *[John Wilson Croker], in a review of "Memoirs of Dr. Burney," in* The Quarterly Review, *Vol. XLIX, No. XCVII, April, 1833, pp. 97-125.*

MARIA EDGEWORTH   (letter date 1833)

[*Edgeworth is noted chiefly for her contributions to the English novel of manners, although she is also remembered for her charming children's stories and distinguished writings on educational theory. With her vivid novels of manners, Edgeworth continued a tradition that began with Burney and reached its finest expression in Jane Austen. In the following excerpt, Edgeworth comments on the* Memoirs of Dr. Burney. *She contends that Burney is at her best when she allows people to speak "naturally," yet she is incapable of doing so when the voice is her own; then, Edgeworth argues, Burney's writing becomes affected and false.*]

Madame d'Arblay, the author of *Evelina, Cecilia,* and *Camilla* all of which I assume you know and like, has lately published memoirs of her father, in which there are many interesting anecdotes both of her father and of her own publications and the great family affection among all her family, and also several curious anecdotes and characters of some of the most illustrious in literature and in every department of the arts of her father's day—Johnson, Garrick, Reynolds, Wyndham, Erskine, Madam Piozzi, Miss Carter, Mrs. Montague, *etc.*

In this respect it is curious: when she lets people speak naturally and when she writes naturally herself, she is very entertaining, but unfortunately she who wrote so well formerly in painting characters humorous and serious has whenever she speaks of herself some false shame, some affectation of humility or timidity, or I know not what, which spoils her style. She has a strange notion that it is more humble or prettier or better taste to call herself the *Recluse of West Hamble* or *your unworthy humble servant* or *the present memorialist* than simply to use the short pronoun *I*. This false theory leads to much circumlocution, awkwardness, and an appearance of pedantry and affectation. It becomes tiresome and ridiculous; the whole style of the book is *stilted*. But she is really so good and so good natured and her work is so free from all slander, all that can in any way injure others, that she should be treated with the same lenity she shews to others. (pp. 246-47)

> *Maria Edgeworth, in a letter to Rachel Mordecai Lazarus on June 27, 1833, in* The Education of the Heart: The Correspondence of Rachel Mordecai Lazarus and Maria Edgeworth, *edited by Edgar E. MacDonald, The University of North Carolina Press, 1977, pp. 244-47.*

[JOHN WILSON CROKER]   (essay date 1842)

[In the following excerpt, Croker continues his vituperative attack on Burney evidenced in his essays dated 1814 and 1833. He discusses her Diary, *which he claims "exceeds our worst apprehensions." The* Diary, *Croker argues, is pompous, over-written, and self-aggrandizing. While admitting that her commentary on the royal family is well written, he adds that even here she offers little insight. Because of this article, Macaulay came to Burney's defense (see excerpt dated 1843); most later critics do not concur with Croker's assessment of the* Diary.]

When we reviewed, ten years ago, that strange display of egotism which Madame D'Arblay was pleased to call *Memoirs of her Father,* we expressed a wish that she would

> *condense* and *simplify* into a *couple* of interesting (and interesting they would be) volumes her *own story* and her contemporaneous notes and *bonâ fide* recollections of that brilliant society in which she moved from 1777 to 1793 [see excerpt dated 1833].
>
> (pp. 243-44)

We were not then in the secret of Madame D'Arblay's having from her earliest youth kept the diary now presented to us [the *Diary and Letters of Madame D'Arblay*]; but we *guessed,* from many passages in the *Memoirs of Dr. Burney,* that she was in possession of copious contemporary materials for her own, and we candidly forewarned her of the kind of errors into which she was likely to fall in preparing her notes for publication. Our conjectures are now too fully verified: the interest is indeed much less than we anticipated, but in all the rest—the diffuseness—the pomposity—the prolixity—the false colouring—the factitious details—and, above all, the personal affectation and vanity of the author, this book exceeds our worst apprehensions.

At first sight the *Diary* seems a minute record of all that she saw, did, or heard, and we find the pages crowded with names and teeming with matters of the greatest apparent interest—with details of the social habits and familiar conversation of the most fashionable, most intellectual, and, in every sense, most illustrious personages of the last age. No book that we ever opened, not even Boswell's *Johnson,* promised at the first glance more of all that species of entertainment and information which memoir-writing can convey, and the position and respectability of the author, with her supposed power of delineating character, all tended to heighten our expectation; but never, we regret to say, has there been a more vexatious disappointment. We have indeed brought before us not merely the minor notabilities of the day, but a great many persons whose station and talents assure them an historic celebrity—King George III., Queen Charlotte, and their family—Johnson, Burke, Sir Joshua, and their society—Mrs. Montague, Mrs. Thrale, Mrs. Delany, and their circles—in short, the whole court and literary world; and all in their easiest and most familiar moods:—their words—their looks—their manners—and even their movements about the room—pencilled, as it would seem, with the most minute and scrupulous accuracy:—but when we come a little closer, and see and hear what all these eminent and illustrious personages are saying and doing, we are not a little surprised and vexed to find them a wearisome congregation of monotonous and featureless prosers, brought together for one single object, in which they, one and all, seem occupied, as if it were the main business of human life—namely, the *glorification of Miss Fanny Burney*—her talents—her taste—her sagacity—her wit—her manners—her temper—her delicacy—even her beauty—and, above all, her *modesty!*

We really have never met anything more curious, nor, if it were not repeated *ad nauseam,* more comical, than the elaborate ingenuity with which—as the ancients used to say that *all roads led to Rome*—every topic, from whatsoever quarter it may start, is ultimately brought home to Miss Burney. There can be, of course, no autobiography without egotism; and though the best works of this class are those in which *self* is the most successfully disguised, it must always be the main ingredient. We therefore expected, and, indeed, were very willing, that Miss Burney should tell us a great deal about herself; but what we did not expect, and what wearies, and, we must candidly add, disgusts us, is to find that she sees nothing beyond the tips of her own fingers, and considers all the rest of man and womankind as mere satellites of that great luminary of the age, the *author of Evelina.* (pp. 244-45)

We insist thus early, and thus strongly, on this extravagant egotism, not merely because it is the chief feature of the book, but for the higher and more important purpose of doing justice to the eminent persons who make a very mean and very foolish figure when thus dragged at the wheels of the triumphant car of Miss Burney,—for so we must call her, while the *Diary* is written in that name. We know that ingenious and sensible people, from not adverting to her real and sole object—namely, *herself*—have been led to consider those eminent personages as responsible for all the nonsense and twaddle which she has chosen to put into their mouths. (pp. 245-46)

In truth nothing can be so vapid as that mode of reporting conversation must inevitably be, *even in the cleverest hands.* Boswell, the best and most graphic of narrators, never attempts so hopeless a task for above two or three consecutive paragraphs, but more commonly contents himself with preserving the general spirit of the discourse—catching here and there the most striking expressions, and now and then venturing to mark an emphasis or an attitude. A clever artist may *sketch* a very lively likeness of a countenance which he has only seen *en passant*, but if he were to attempt—in the absence of the object—to fill up the outline with all the little details of form and colour, he would find that his efforts only diminished the spirit and impaired the resemblance. So it is of reporting public *speeches*—and so still more of reporting *conversations*. But even if Miss Burney had had more of Boswell's happy knack, it would not have much mended the matter, for her sole and exclusive object was—not to relate what Burke, or Johnson, or anybody else should say on general subjects, but what flattering things they said about *Fanny Burney*. The result is, that we have little amusement and less faith in the details of those elaborate dialogues, which occupy, we believe, more than half her volumes—their very minuteness and elaboration sufficiently prove that they cannot be authentic; and they are, moreover, trivial and wearisome beyond all patience. How—we will not say, the author of **Evelina** and **Cecilia**, but—how any person of the most ordinary degree of taste and talents could have wasted time and paper in making such a *much ado about nothing* we cannot conceive; nor did we—till we had read this book—imagine that *real life and proper names* could by any *maladresse* of a narrator be made so insufferably flat, stale, and unprofitable. (pp. 246-47)

Strange blindness to imagine that anything like fame was to be gathered from this deplorable exhibition of mock-modesty, endeavouring to conceal, but only the more flagrantly exposing, the boldest, the most *horse-leech* egotism that literature or Bedlam has yet exhibited. (p. 251)

It was no easy task to reconcile and carry on, *pari passu*, the pretension of modesty and the cravings of vanity; but her device, if not successful, is at least ingenious—she never, in her own proper person, very directly or outrageously praises Fanny Burney—she never absolutely says '*I am the cleverest writer— I am the most amiable woman in the world*'—on the contrary, she humbles herself with all the genuine modesty of a newly-elected *Speaker*—but then, on the other hand, she thinks it her duty, as a mere historian and relater of facts, to record, in the most conscientious detail, all the panegyrics and compliments—however extravagant—which anybody and everybody might address to her. (p. 252)

[We] cannot doubt that the natural predisposition of her mind was towards artifice and manoeuvering. It was early remarked as a prominent defect in her novels that all her heroines were exhibited as the victims of trifling annoyances and imaginary difficulties, from which two words of candour and common-sense would have extricated them. The same error runs through her own memoirs. She represents herself as thrown into confusions, embarrassments, terrors, miseries, and so forth, by the most ordinary occurrences of common life. If she is spoken to, she is in a flutter of modest agitation: if not spoken to, she is still more alarmed at such ominous silence. If complimented, she is inclined to *creep under the chair*: if not attended to she retreats into indignant seclusion. She is afraid to make tea at an evening party, lest she should appear too obtrusive; and if she does not, she is in still worse agonies, lest she should be thought supercilious.

The most trifling incident—a word or a look—if it concerns her own important self, is treated with all the pomp of history; and the idlest and most trivial conversations are registered with more detail and care than if they were evidence in a court of justice on some momentous cause. (pp. 255-56)

Some readers may be disposed to think that we have given more space to the exposure of Miss Burney's vanity and absurdity than so trivial a subject deserves; but be it recollected that the work is of considerable pretension, and that if it be not *now* reduced to its proper value, it may become hereafter a kind of authority in the history of manners, and may injuriously affect the reputation of persons whose talents it depreciates, and whose conduct it misrepresents. (p. 275)

But though the larger portion of the work, as far as it has gone, is of this worthless and vexatious character, we readily admit that there are some few episodes of a better description. In the short—alas, very short!—intervals in which Miss Burney's *amour-propre* is permitted to slumber, we pick up some amusing details of the state of society sixty years ago, and some interesting anecdotes of remarkable persons. But even these passages are written so much in the style of the 'Précieuses Ridicules,' and are spun out with such incompressible prolixity, that we confess ourselves utterly unable to separate, within any reasonable space, the grains of wheat from the bushels of chaff. We shall endeavour, however, to find room for some sketches of the most interesting subject of the work, and that which is, on the whole, the best executed,—the domestic life of George III., Queen Charlotte, and the Princesses. The Princes rarely came under Miss Burney's observation. . . .

Amongst her equals or those only a little above her in society, she is captious, perverse, pompous, and, we believe, deceitful—she is always striving to be something which she is not; but with her royal master and mistress her position was so clearly defined and so incapable of flights and fancies, that she was, as it were, pinned down to the reality, and it would seem as if the simplicity and dignity of their personal character inspired Miss Burney with short gleams of corresponding sobriety, both of feeling and description. . . . (p. 276)

We fully admit that in all she says of the royal family her narration is in better taste than any other portion of her **Diary**. We only lament that, talking so much, she says so little. . . . (p. 286)

The result of all is that we are conscientiously obliged to pronounce these three volumes to be—considering their bulk and pretensions—nearly the most worthless we have ever waded through, and that we do not remember in all our experience to have laid down an unfinished work with less desire for its continuation. That it may not mend as it proceeds, we cannot—where there is such room for improvement—venture to pronounce; and there is thus much to be said for it, that it can hardly grow worse. (p. 287)

[*John Wilson Croker*], "*Madame D'Arblay's 'Diary and Letters'*," in The Quarterly Review, *Vol. LXX, No. CXXXIX, June, 1842, pp. 243-87.*

[THOMAS BABINGTON MACAULAY]   (essay date 1843)

[*An English historian, essayist, biographer, and poet, Macaulay was a prominent social and literary critic. Known for his harsh views and antitheoretical bias, he is now primarily remembered for his extremely popular* History of England from the Accession of James the Second. *He is also known as Croker's principal detractor, and the following essay, one of the best-known estimates of Burney's work, is thought to have been prompted by Croker's attacks on Burney in 1814, 1833, and 1842. While noting many flaws in Burney's writing, Macaulay's assessment is generally positive. He documents what he terms the "pernicious" change in Burney's literary style from the simple language of*

Evelina to the more mannered style of Camilla and the later works, in which he notes a "perversion" of her powers. Therefore, while the Memoirs are tiresome, the earlier Diary is interesting and well written, according to Macaulay. He also notes that because she relied on caricature rather than characterization in her novels, Burney cannot be considered one of literature's finest artists. He argues, nevertheless, that "in the rank to which she belonged, she had few equals and scarcely any superior." By legitimizing the novel of manners, Burney thus paved the way for Austen and Edgeworth.]

Having always felt a warm and sincere, though not a blind admiration for [Madame D'Arblay's] talents, we rejoiced to learn that her *Diary* was about to be made public. Our hopes, it is true, were not unmixed with fears. We could not forget the fate of the *Memoirs of Dr Burney,* which were published ten years ago. That unfortunate book contained much that was curious and interesting. Yet it was received with a cry of disgust, and was speedily consigned to oblivion. The truth is, that it deserved its doom. It was written in Madame D'Arblay's later style—the worst style that has ever been known among men. No genius, no information, could save from proscription a book so written. We, therefore, opened the *Diary* with no small anxiety, trembling lest we should light upon some of that peculiar rhetoric which deforms almost every page of the *Memoirs,* and which it is impossible to read without a sensation made up of mirth, shame, and loathing. We soon, however, discovered to our great delight that this *Diary* was kept before Madame D'Arblay became eloquent. It is, for the most part, written in her earliest and best manner; in true woman's English, clear, natural, and lively. The two works are lying side by side before us, and we never turn from the *Memoirs* to the *Diary* without a sense of relief. The difference is as great as the difference between the atmosphere of a perfumer's shop, fetid with lavender water and jasmine soap, and the air of a heath on a fine morning in May. Both works ought to be consulted by every person who wishes to be well acquainted with the history of our literature and our manners. But to read the *Diary* is a pleasure; to read the *Memoirs* will always be a task. (p. 524)

[Madame D'Arblay] was emphatically what Johnson called her, a character-monger. It was in the exhibition of human passions and whims that her strength lay; and in this department of art she had, we think, very distinguished skill.

But in order that we may, according to our duty as Kings-at-Arms, versed in the laws of literary precedence, marshal her to the exact seat to which she is entitled, we must carry our examination somewhat further. (p. 559)

Almost every one of her men and women has some one propensity developed to a morbid degree. In *Cecilia,* for example, Mr Delvile never opens his lips without some allusion to his own birth and station; or Mr Briggs, without some allusion to the hoarding of money; or Mr Hobson, without betraying the self-indulgence and self-importance of a purse-proud upstart; or Mr Simkins, without uttering some sneaking remark for the purpose of currying favour with his customers; or Mr Meadows, without expressing apathy and weariness of life; or Mr Albany, without declaiming about the vices of the rich and the misery of the poor; or Mrs Belfield, without some indelicate eulogy on her son; or Lady Margaret, without indicating jealousy of her husband. Morrice is all skipping, officious impertinence, Mr Gosport all sarcasm, Lady Honoria all lively prattle, Miss Larolles all silly prattle. If ever Madame D'Arblay aimed at more, as in the character of Monckton, we do not think that she succeeded well.

We are, therefore, forced to refuse to Madame D'Arblay a place in the highest rank of art; but we cannot deny that, in the rank to which she belonged, she had few equals, and scarcely any superior. The variety of humours which is to be found in her novels is immense; and though the talk of each person separately is monotonous, the general effect is not monotony, but a very lively and agreeable diversity. Her plots are rudely constructed and improbable, if we consider them in themselves. But they are admirably framed for the purpose of exhibiting striking groups of eccentric characters, each governed by his own peculiar whim, each talking his own peculiar jargon, and each bringing out by opposition the oddities of all the rest. We will give one example out of many which occur to us. All probability is violated in order to bring Mr Delvile, Mr Briggs, Mr Hobson, and Mr Albany into a room together. But when we have them there, we soon forget probability in the exquisitely ludicrous effect which is produced by the conflict of four old fools, each raging with a monomania of his own, each talking a dialect of his own, and each inflaming all the others anew every time he opens his mouth.

Madame D'Arblay was most successful in comedy, and indeed in comedy which bordered on farce. But we are inclined to infer from some passages, both in *Cecilia* and *Camilla,* that she might have attained equal distinction in the pathetic. We have formed this judgment, less from those ambitious scenes of distress which lie near the catastrophe of each of those novels, than from some exquisite strokes of natural tenderness which take us here and there by surprise. We would mention as examples, Mrs Hill's account of her little boy's death in *Cecilia,* and the parting of Sir Hugh Tyrold and Camilla, when the honest baronet thinks himself dying.

It is melancholy to think that the whole fame of Madame D'Arblay rests on what she did during the earlier half of her life, and that every thing which she published during the forty-three years which preceded her death, lowered her reputation. Yet we have no reason to think that at the time when her faculties ought to have been in their maturity, they were smitten with any blight. In the *Wanderer,* we catch now and then a gleam of her genius. Even in the *Memoirs* of her Father, there is no trace of dotage. They are very bad; but they are so, as it seems to us, not from a decay of power, but from a total perversion of power.

The truth is, that Madame D'Arblay's style underwent a gradual and most pernicious change,—a change which, in degree at least, we believe to be unexampled in literary history, and of which it may be useful to trace the progress.

When she wrote her letters to Mr Crisp, her early journals, and the novel of *Evelina,* her style was not indeed brilliant or energetic; but it was easy, clear, and free from all offensive faults. When she wrote *Cecilia* she aimed higher. She had then lived much in a circle of which Johnson was the centre; and she was herself one of his most submissive worshippers. It seems never to have crossed her mind that the style even of his best writings was by no means faultless, and that even had it been faultless, it might not be wise in her to imitate it. (pp. 563-64)

In *Cecilia* the change of manner began to appear. But in *Cecilia* the imitation of Johnson, though not always in the best taste, is sometimes eminently happy; and the passages which are so verbose as to be positively offensive, are few. There were people who whispered that Johnson had assisted his young friend, and that the novel owed all its finest passages to his hand. This was merely the fabrication of envy. Miss Burney's real excellences were as much beyond the reach of Johnson, as his real excellences were beyond her reach. He could no more have written the Masquerade scene, or the Vauxhall scene, than she could have written the Life of Cowley or the Review of Soame Jenyns. But we have not the smallest doubt that he revised *Cecilia,* and that he retouched the style of many passages. . . . [When] we look into *Cecilia,* we see such traces of his hand in the grave and elevated passages, as it is impossible to mistake. (pp. 564-65)

When next Madame D'Arblay appeared before the world as a writer, she was in a very different situation. She would not content herself with the simple English in which *Evelina* had been written. She had no longer the friend who, we are confident, had polished and strengthened the style of *Cecilia.* She had to write in Johnson's manner, without Johnson's aid. The consequence was, that in *Camilla* every passage which she meant to be fine is detestable; and that the book has been saved from condemnation only by the admirable spirit and force of those scenes in which she was content to be familiar. (p. 565)

It is from no unfriendly feeling to Madame D'Arblay's memory that we have expressed ourselves so strongly on the subject of her style. On the contrary, we conceive that we have really rendered a service to her reputation. That her later works were complete failures, is a fact too notorious to be dissembled; and some persons, we believe, have consequently taken up a notion that she was from the first an over-rated writer, and that she had not the powers which were necessary to maintain her on the eminence on which good-luck and fashion had placed her. We believe, on the contrary, that her early popularity was no more than the just reward of distinguished merit, and would never have undergone an eclipse, if she had only been content to go on writing in her mother-tongue. If she failed when she quitted her own province, and attempted to occupy one in which she had neither part nor lot, this reproach is common to her with a crowd of distinguished men. (pp. 568-69)

It is not only on account of the intrinsic merit of Madame d'Arblay's early works that she is entitled to honourable mention. Her appearance is an important epoch in our literary history. *Evelina* was the first tale written by a woman, and purporting to be a picture of life and manners, that lived or deserved to live. . . .

Indeed, most of the popular novels which preceded *Evelina,* were such as no lady would have written; and many of them were such as no lady could without confusion own that she had read. (p. 569)

Miss Burney did for the English novel what Jeremy Collier did for the English drama; and she did it in a better way. She first showed that a tale might be written in which both the fashionable and the vulgar life of London might be exhibited with great force, and with broad comic humour, and which yet should not contain a single line inconsistent with rigid morality, or even with virgin delicacy. She took away the reproach which lay on a most useful and delightful species of composition. She vindicated the right of her sex to an equal share in a fair and noble province of letters. . . . Several among the successors of Madame D'Arblay have equalled her; two, we think, have surpassed her. But the fact that she has been surpassed, gives her an additional claim to our respect and gratitude; for in truth we owe to her, not only *Evelina, Cecilia,* and *Camilla,* but also *Mansfield Park* and *The Absentee.* (pp. 569-70)

[*Thomas Babington Macaulay*], "Madame D'Arblay," *in* The Edinburgh Review, *Vol. LXXVI, No. CLIV, January, 1843, pp. 523-70.*

WILLIAM MAKEPEACE THACKERAY   (essay date 1846)

[*A famed Victorian author, Thackeray is best known for his satiric sketches and novels of upper- and middle-class English life. Vanity Fair: A Novel without a Hero, a panorama of early nineteenth-century English upper middle-class society, is generally regarded as Thackeray's masterpiece. He is also credited with bringing a simpler style and greater realism to English fiction. In the following excerpt, Thackeray praises the sixth volume of Burney's* Diary. *He specifically commends the sketches of the royal family, her father, and her husband. This review appeared originally on September 25, 1846, in the* Morning Chronicle.]

[The] sixth and penultimate volume of the memoirs of the indefatigable Madame d'Arblay is the pleasantest of [the *Diary and Letters of Madame d'Arblay*]. It is as amusing as any of the numerous French works of similar nature; and has the advantage, which most of the latter do not possess, of unquestioned authenticity. The letters are genuine letters. You get portraits sketched from the life of many famous personages, who, though they figured but fifty years back, belong to a society as different and remote from ours, as that of Queen Anne or the Restoration. . . . (p. 183)

Evelina saw the First Consul; his appearance of "seriousness or sadness" sank deep into her sentimental mind. She saw all his grenadiers and generals gorgeously attired, and Cambacérès Consul No. II., "dressed richly in scarlet and gold, wearing a mien of fixed gravity and importance." The ungrateful hypocrite Talleyrand she had known, but would acknowledge no longer. Madame de Stael she patronised only a very little; the sentimentality of the impetuous Corinne was rather too boisterous for the polite and tight-laced Cecilia. She knew Cromwell-Grandison Lafayette, and shared his generous hospitality. And she wept in secret with Beauveau and Mortemar, and a great deal of the best company (returned from emigration), over the martyrdom of the Bourbon family.

In England, before she went to France, she was also a favourite in the very highest and most august company. Six lovely princesses wept over her immortal novel of *Camilla,* read it hastily in their apartments at Windsor, or "comfortably" together at Weymouth. The august eyes of Queen Charlotte moistened with tears over those dingy and now forgotten pages. The King himself had a copy and read in it, and was good-natured to the hysterically loyal Fanny d'Arblay—always ready to gush with tears at the feet of her royal master—always plunging from the embraces of one soft and kind-hearted princess into the closet and arms of another. Peace to their honest big-wigged shades! There is something queer, pleasant, and affecting in the picture which Fanny d'Arblay draws of this primitive and kindly female family of George III.; of the princesses so simple, so tender, so handsome, blooming in powder and pomatum; of the old Queen herself, that just and spotless, that economical but charitable lady. The young princesses are described as having the most romantic attachment for their interesting and romantic brothers, those models of princely chivalry and Grandisonian correctness; and the old King himself appears before us, not only as a monarch whose majestic wisdom strikes Fanny d'Arblay with speechless awe, but as a good, just, and simple father and gentleman, whose qualities inspire her with rapturous and admirable volubility of praise. Considering her gift of speech, indeed, it is a wonder that Madame d'Arblay did so little, and that we had not many hundreds of volumes of novels from her, in place of the mere score which she left behind her.

More interesting sketches than even those of the above-named famous personages are the pictures of Fanny's father and husband, such as her letters and their own exhibit them. The letters of "My dearest sir," the good old doctor at Chelsea, are as pleasant as any we know—to the highest degree lively, honest, and good-humoured. Even the multitudinousness of poor Fanny's caresses does not overpower his good temper; and after her raptures and wonders, and tears and flurry, it is the greatest relief to come upon the kind hearty prose of the jovial old scholar and gentleman, who is too good-natured even to laugh at his sentimental daughter. (pp. 183-85)

The d'Arblay portrait is a very fine one. A noble gentleman, and a Liberal, holding high rank in France, he quits the country when the Constitutional King is but a puppet in the hands of the mob. Here he and Fanny Burney give each other lessons in their native language, and correct each others exercises. What follows from this mutual instruction may be imagined: that indomitable virgin Fanny Burney is conquered in a very few lessons—and Lord Orville carries off Cecilia to love and a cottage in the country, where she writes novels and has a little baby. (p. 185)

These are the main personages and incidents of this present sixth volume. They are set before one with singular liveliness and truth, and will be read, as we take it, with kindly interest.

> *William Makepeace Thackeray, " 'Diary and Letters of Madame d'Arblay, Volume Six'," in his* Contributions to the "Morning Chronicle," *edited by Gordon N. Ray, University of Illinois Press, 1955, pp. 183-86.*

MARY ELIZABETH CHRISTIE (essay date 1882)

[*Christie provides an overview of Burney's achievement. She considers the* Diary *to be the best introduction to her work and terms* Evelina *and* Cecilia *Burney's only novels of note. Christie disagrees with critics who label Burney's work superficial; rather, she contends that "reserved" is a more accurate description.*]

Miss Burney's personages, once so fashionable and so familiar, have grown strange now that a century has passed over their heads; and though underneath the disguise of their old-world costumes they are still fresh and human, this is a secret only to be discovered at the cost of more careful reading than the modern world is apt to give to novels. This being so, we are sometimes inclined to wish that Miss Burney had described her characters more broadly, and explained the circumstances of their lives in such a running commentary as would put us quickly *au fait* of the social *milieu* of a hundred years ago. But such "posting up," however convenient some of us might find it to-day, must certainly have been tiresome to contemporary readers, and could hardly have failed to lessen the intrinsic literary value of the books. Miss Burney had more talent for dramatic presentation than for narrative, and she is only at her best when she has collected a crowd of personages on her page, and set them all talking and acting at cross-purposes. Her scenes of this description would have lost incalculably by the introduction of explanatory passages that hindered the rapid play of character and blunted the point of the dialogue. And apart from these things, which are supremely good of their kind, it cannot be said that there is any element in Miss Burney's novels that is good enough to live on its own merits.

Her plots are ingeniously constructed and coherently carried out. And the solid stuff of her characters is in consistent keeping with their surface humours. All is reasonable and natural in the wise and good personages, so that we can understand them and sympathize with them at every point of their career; but there is nothing exceptionable about them. It is impossible to get up the smallest excitement on their account; and were it not that the comedy scenes are so extraordinarily vivacious that a very quiet background is absolutely necessary to their relief, it would have to be said that the serious scenes are monotonously dull. Taken by themselves they certainly are dull—so dull that most readers attempt to skip them. But this will not do at all. They are not superficial padding, like the dull chapters of so many modern novels, but the bony structure of the plot. To leave out the serious scenes is to lose all chance of understanding the lively ones, and to find nothing but mere confusion in the whole books. The reader who has not enough persistence to read *Evelina* and *Cecilia* steadily, must give them up altogether, or prepare himself for a new effort by some extraneous reading of an introductory kind.

Without a doubt, the best introduction to Miss Burney's novels is the *Diary and Letters of Madame D'Arblay.* (And here let me say that I use the phrase, "Miss Burney's novels," to denote only *Evelina* and *Cecilia,* gladly profiting by the one little grain of advantage resulting from the double designation of the author: *Camilla* and *The Wanderer* are so much less entertaining than the earlier books, that it is a satisfaction to feel oneself literally correct in ascribing them to a different name.) Though Miss Burney never made the mistake of writing an autobiography in the form of a novel, she put a great deal of herself into Evelina, and of her ideal of life into the character and position of Cecilia; and we understand her two heroines all the better for being thoroughly acquainted with herself. Then, again, though she had no adventures, either at Streatham or at Court, which were exact parallels of the scenes in her novels, there is yet enough of general likeness between the real life described in her *Diary* and the fictitious world of her fancy to familiarize us in advance with the tone, and much of the detail, of the latter. The material is, in fact, precisely the same. Whether Miss Burney is inventing or recording, it is always the same minute detail of character and circumstance that she chooses to describe. The only difference is that, when she writes to near relations and intimate friends, she gives freer rein to her feelings than when she addresses the public. And this vein of subjectivity supplies just what is wanting to make the novels generally attractive.

The novels give an impression of a singularly keen, clever, observant woman, with a sense of the ridiculous too much developed to be a very sympathetic, or even safe, friend. The *Diary* reveals an exceptionally warm heart and a disposition very strangely compounded of good sense and sensitiveness, quick impulse and persistent loyalty, strong powers of judgment coupled with an almost morbid self-distrust, and tastes so simple and domestic that, in spite of all her friends felt at the time, and critics have written since, about the years she wasted at Court, it is difficult to escape the conviction that wherever Frances Burney's lot had fallen, her quick womanly sympathies and active interest in the affairs of life would have hindered her from giving her best time and energy to literary work. . . . She wrote *Evelina* because the world amused her, and she was too shy to say in any other way how much it amused her. She wrote *Cecilia* because the world told her it was amused by her, and that she could make her fortune by going on amusing it. But even in this second book there were indications that the natural spring was pretty nearly exhausted, while a deterioration of style betrayed the fact that her mastery of the means of literary expression was not sufficient to keep her works up to the mark when the vivacity of the first spontaneous impulse should be spent.... She used her literary talent first as an outlet for her surplus wit and wisdom, and next as a means of making money; but she had not sufficient love of literature to induce her to sacrifice to it a jot of even conventional esteem. It follows that she is seen to best advantage in the book where she appears as daughter, sister, friend, servant (there is really no other word for the position she held at Court), and finally wife and mother. In the *Diary and Letters* we not only learn how largely voluntary were the restrictions she imposed upon her literary work, but how much her private life gained in charm and usefulness and happiness by the subordination of the author's part; and, learning this, we forgive her the more easily for having partially hidden the talent which, well husbanded, might have given us more *Evelina*s and *Cecilia*s. If, indeed, there be not a sort of hypocrisy about all lamentations over sins of literary omission, and, by consequence, something superfluous in forgiveness of them. Delightful as *Evelina* and *Cecilia* are to those whose taste they suit, it is doubtful whether we should get more enjoyment out of a dozen novels of the same quality than we do out of these two. And, as has been said already, at the present moment these two are more than enough for most people. (pp. 896-98)

[*Cecilia*] is distinguished from [*Evelina*] by all the differences that are natural between the work of a shy girl who doubts her powers and fears publicity even while she seeks it, and that of a woman whose right to publish has been unimpeachably established. *Cecilia* is by far the better book of the two. It has no faults of taste, such as occur here and there in *Evelina,* and it has fewer faults of redundance. It is more ably constructed, and shows a deeper grasp of character, as well as a wider knowledge of life. It has a great many more personages, and the shades of their characters are more subtly graduated and contrasted. Above all, the situation has more of serious human interest. The plot is not, as in *Evelina,* a mere maze of circumstances to be threaded by the author's ingenuity, but a natural outcome of the characters acting in the story. On the other hand, Cecilia the heroine is a much less engaging person than Evelina the heroine. She is entirely discreet, well-bred, and virtuous, and we are duly interested in her fate from the first chapter to the last. But she wants the charm of *naïve* girlhood that makes Evelina delightful and loveable. Cecilia is too wise to be very attractive, and she suffers a further disadvantage from the colder position given to her in the book. In writing her second novel, Miss Burney dropped the epistolary form she had used in her first, and presented all her characters objectively. The change gave her greater freedom for treatment of her scenes of active comedy, but it deprived her of some favourite means of displaying the serious sides of her characters; and naturally her heroine suffered most from this deprivation. The new form also told injuriously upon Miss Burney's writing; another point in which *Cecilia* is less good than *Evelina.* It obliged her to trust less to the colloquial vein in which she excelled, and to attempt more ambitious styles that were beyond her strength. The consequence was that she fell into mannerisms, and laboured pedantically to produce stilted effects. These faults were further developed in her later books, until they resulted in an insufferable jargon. But in *Cecilia,* though they must already be called blemishes, they are not bad enough to spoil the book materially. (pp. 908-09)

[The] book ends with this quaint passage:—

The upright mind of Cecilia, her purity, her virtue, and the moderation of her wishes, gave to her in the warm affection of Lady Delisle [deaths have occurred in the family and changed old titles to new] and the unremitting fondness of Mortimer, all the happiness human life seems capable of receiving; yet human it was, and as such imperfect; she knew that, at times, the whole family must murmur at her loss of fortune, and at times she murmured herself to be thus portionless, though an HEIRESS. Rationally, however, she surveyed the world at large, and finding that of the few who had any happiness, there were none without some misery, she checked the sigh of repining mortality, and, grateful for general felicity, bore partial evil with cheerfullest resignation.

''Cheerfullest resignation'' is an important note in Miss Burney's personal memoirs. It was a virtue of which she had much need, and which she practised to perfection; and if we were forced to ascribe a purpose to her books, it would perhaps be true to say, that she aimed at promoting this mood in others, by showing how much entertainment may be got out of the trivial worries over which it is common to lose temper, and by creating interest in men and women whose qualities are not intrinsically interesting. She is sometimes accused of being superficial, because she dares so little in the direction of the stronger and deeper passions and interests of human nature. But this criticism is itself superficial: the truer word for her is *reserved*. She shut the door upon the whole range of bold speculation and unconventional feeling, because she considered these things unfit for the novelist, and especially for the female novelist to treat of. But her own feelings were deep, and her own interests and sympathies were wide; and in drawing her characters, though she seldom attempts to paint much—save in conventional outline—that goes below the surface, she yet shows at all times, by the firmness and consistency of her creations, that she possessed the root of the matter in understanding, if not in creative power and courage of execution. And, indeed, there are so few who have the power to succeed in the highest regions of imaginative romance, that when an author achieves admirable results upon the lower planes, it is wiser to rejoice than to regret that the dangerous heights have not been attempted. In the case of Miss Burney, it is certain that what is lost in boldness of conception is gained in excellence of workmanship, and that the patient industry she bestowed upon constructing plots suited to the play of the talents of which she was an easy mistress, would have been ill exchanged for vain efforts to express the deeper things which overstrain all but the strongest genius before they can find adequate expression in fiction. (p. 914)

Mary Elizabeth Christie, ''Miss Burney's Novels,'' in Contemporary Review, *Vol. XLII, December, 1882, pp. 894-915.*

GEORGE SAINTSBURY   (essay date 1895)

[*Saintsbury was an English literary historian and critic of the late nineteenth and early twentieth centuries. A prolific writer, he composed several histories of English and European literature as well as numerous critical works on individual authors, styles, and periods. His studies of French literature, particularly* A History of the French Novel, *have established him as a leading authority. Saintsbury's critical qualities have been praised by René Wellek, who commended his "enormous reading, the almost universal scope of his subject matter, the zest and zeal of his exposition," and "the audacity with which he handles the most ambitious and unattempted arguments." In the following excerpt, Saintsbury surveys the whole of Burney's writings. Like most critics he admires* Evelina, *but contends that it lacks structure. According to Saintsbury, the vitality and spontaneity that characterized* Evelina *was replaced by labor and affectation in her later novels. However, he reserves praise for the* Diary, *which he considers "delightful," if uneven. In conclusion, Saintsbury considers Burney an outstanding diarist and correspondent who was most memorable as an observant student of character in an era where she had "an extraordinarily fertile field" for study.]*

[Madame D'Arblay's] whole work has never yet, I think, been surveyed. The readers and the critics of the later novels and the *Memoirs of Dr Burney* were not acquainted with the charms of the *Diary.* The devotees of the *Diary* have very naturally said little or nothing—in some cases I believe they have known little or nothing—of anything but *Evelina* and *Cecilia.* In fact, while the *Memoirs* are not a very common book, *Camilla* and *The Wanderer* are now (in any decent condition) very uncommon ones. (p. 205)

It so happens that, as a result of the order of publication, though not of the dates of writing, Miss Burney's work falls into three natural and excellent sections for criticism. There are first the novels; then the *Memoirs of Dr Burney;* and lastly, the *Diary and Letters* early and late, though here the early comes after the late by the accident of posthumous publication. The novels pursue a steady sinking down from excellent to atrocious (for I cannot agree with some that *Cecilia* exceeds *Evelina* in anything but bulk); the *Memoirs* drop to a lower depth still; and then the *Diaries* rise to perhaps a higher height than that at which the novels began. It is unfortunate, doubtless, that the best work should be in fact all contemporaneous and all early. But it is fair to say that even in the latest written passages of the *Diary and Letters,* happy touches meet us which may be looked for absolutely in vain in the much earlier *Wanderer* and *Memoirs of Dr Burney.* (p. 206)

Evelina delectable; *Cecilia* admirable; *Camilla* estimable; *The Wanderer* impossible; *The Memoirs of Dr Burney* inconceivable; the *Diary and Letters,* whether original or "early," unequal, but at their best seldom equalled;—this might serve in the snip-snap and flashy way for a short criticism of Madame D'Arblay's work. But that work is not either in its merits or its defects to be polished off so unceremoniously. (p. 212)

Miss Burney is a satirist to some extent or she could not be so amusing as she is: but it is very small and very good-natured satire. If we compare her with her famous sisters or rather nieces in the next generation we shall find nothing in her of the inexorable justice which has been called cruelty in Miss Austen, of the severity, which sometimes comes near to savagery, of Miss Ferrier. She is even more lenient to her puppets than Miss Edgeworth herself, though she may seem to this generation too tolerant of some things in that rougher society both as she represents them in fiction, and as she records them in her actual experience.

There is avowedly very little art in [*Evelina*], and its characters, like its composition, remind us of the so-called humour-comedy of the time between Jonson and Wycherley, the principles of which had frequently been adopted by novel writers, even such great ones as Smollett. Sporadic eccentricities, accumulated more or less anyhow, form a catalogue which does as a matter of fact carry the reader from beginning to end of the story, but which exhibits hardly the slightest trace of regular plan. The

"anagnorisis" of Evelina at the end is one of the very weakest of such things (which are rather apt to be weak), and the only excuse for Mr Villars and Mrs Selwyn in not having long before softened that "reed painted like iron," Sir John Belmont, is to be found in the fact that Mr Villars throughout his letters shows himself chiefly a fool, and that Mrs Selwyn is represented as chiefly a shrew. Evelina herself pants with propriety, and blushes becomingly: and Lord Orville is not more of a stick than most of his kind. But the outrageous practical jokes of Captain Mirvan on the hapless old harridan Duval and her more hapless because more respectable French friend are overdone, and have no sort of connection with the story, while Sir Clement Willoughby's wildness is shockingly tame. Yet all these faults are far more than atoned for by the youthful zest and freshness of the general picture, by the liveliness with which the incidents, desultory as they are, pick up and succeed each other, and above all, by the incomparable sketches of the Branghtons and Mr Smith. In Poland Street, where the Burneys had lived before moving to Queen's Square, and then to Sir Isaac Newton's house just south of Leicester Square, they seem to have associated with a rather lower class of neighbours than later, and Frances used her models royally. It cannot be said that she is not at home with the upper classes: she not only knew but could draw gentlemen and ladies. Her keen as well as kind Daddy Crisp was perfectly right in ejaculating in reference to some epistolary "conversation-piece" of hers: "If specimens of this kind had been preserved of the different *Tons* that have succeeded each other for twenty centuries last past, how interesting they would have been." But Fanny was more than a mere *Ton*-painter, her best characters are more than gentlemen and ladies: they are immortals, as perhaps no others of hers are, with the doubtful exception of Sir Sedley Clarendel, the chief spot of brightness in the respectable blank of *Camilla.*

With all my sense of its defects, I never read *Evelina* (and I have read it two or three times at least during the last decade or so, as well as often earlier) without delight. Of *Cecilia* I can only borrow the famous libel on marriage, and say that to me at least "it is good, but it is not delightful." One feels immediately the presence of a much more elaborate effort, of a much maturer art, than can be found in *Evelina.* . . . I own that, after the second volume or thereabouts, I find *Cecilia* rather difficult to read. The introduction of the girl to town has much of the liveliness of *Evelina:* it was a theme evidently congenial: and though many of the details are exaggerated, especially the cockneyisms of Mr Briggs (the Branghtons, alas! are already far away), though the machinations and melodrama of the Harrels might be toned down with great advantage both to probability and pleasure, the whole is well grouped and well machined. Cecilia, moreover, has the advantage of her elder sister in character and sense. But after the point named the interest seems to me to die away and to be revived chiefly by Lady Honoria who, though she owes a good deal to Anna Howe and Charlotte Grandison, has the advantage over them of being a lady in fact as well as in name. All the Delviles are naught; Mr Monckton and Mr Albany, bad and good lay figures; while Miss Larolles, popular as she was with her own generation, does not possess very vital signs now. In other words, Miss Burney wrote *Evelina* because she had a mind to do so: she wrote *Cecilia* because she made up her mind to do so.

The signs of the collar are to me so evident in this book that I am wholly unable to accept the view of those who think that, had she been left unmolested by kings and queens, we should have had more *Evelina*s or even more *Cecilia*s from her. In the first place there are in the *Diary* certain distinct avowals, which I see no reason for assigning to mere bashfulness or mock humility, that she felt herself written out. There is at least one almost explicit hint from the experienced and affectionate Crisp that he thought she might be. And most important of all, there are the books themselves—those which come before and those which follow. Let us pay a little attention to these latter before coming to the general question.

I can see no reason, apart from a freezing of the genial current, why *Camilla* should not have been at least as good a book as *Cecilia*. . . . That *Camilla* is not a great novel I am afraid cannot be denied. It is one of its glories that Miss Austen was among the original subscribers, and the extreme Burneians have tried to extract a testimonial from this great pupil. This will not do. Camilla is indeed joined with *Cecilia* and *Belinda* in *Northanger Abbey* to receive one of those generous exaltings of contemporary work in its own craft in which young genius, as opposed to young cubbishness, often indulges. . . . The fact is that, as I must repeat, *Camilla* is *not* a great novel. (pp. 215-21)

The fact is that the whole thing, except a few separate traits, is in the vague. The author has indeed still got a plot, as she had in *Cecilia,* which is more than she had in *Evelina.* She has got some good studies for the filling in: but she does not in the least know what to do with them, and she has no grasp of life as a whole. She is constantly "off the rails;" indeed it is exceedingly rare that she is on them.

In *The Wanderer* it is not too much to say that she never gets on them at all. The opening scene of this unluckiest of books, a book which was expected, hailed, welcomed by everybody, from veterans to novices, and which sank as soon as it appeared, has a faint touch of the personal experience which was always necessary to Fanny, and which she sometimes utilised so well, in the flight of the heroine by boat from France. Madame D'Arblay had just had something very like that experience. But the rest is all stark nought. The fatal long-lost or misknown daughter business invited her once more, as in *Evelina;* and she could no more, as in *Evelina,* redeem it with humours and with the fresh insight of an unjaded eye. The progress of "the Wanderer," *alias* "the penetrated Juliet" from her sufferings in the boat, and from the vulgar persecutions of Mrs Ireton till the time when, united with Mr Harleigh, she is "embraced and owned by her honoured benefactress, the Marchioness," is a kind of nightmare of dulness. The hardened reviewer, "famoused for fight" with thousands of novels, but just saves his credit as he struggles through this fearful book, where nobody is alive, and where the adventures of the gibbering ghosts who figure in it are gibbered in a language such as hardly our own day—a nurse of monsters in style—has seen. The victims of Charlottophobia say that Miss Burney's sojourn at Court among half-Germans, and her subsequent sojourn in France, account for the frightful lingo which defaces *The Wanderer* and *The Memoirs of Dr Burney.* They forget again that only a weak plant could be stifled by such atmospheres. . . . [Whatever] the cause, the effect is not disputable, and it may be said, without remorse and without caricature, that nothing but the matter of *The Wanderer* could deserve such a style, and that the style of *The Wanderer* is, on the whole, almost too bad for the matter.

With the *Memoirs* things are, if possible, worse still in point of form, and the matter, though very much better, is almost hopelessly disfigured. Unfortunately the documents on which it is founded were mainly destroyed. Mrs Ellis, Madame D'Arblay's most faithful and most generous defender, laments the fatal misuse of these materials. They were, we know, abundant, superabundant; and Dr Burney had had opportunities such as few men have had. The actual book is a tedious rhapsody, exceedingly hard to read with any intelligent comprehension of dates and surroundings, barren in matter while full of the very worst art. . . . To quote much from that unhappy book would be unworthy of "decent gentility and education" (as Mark Pattison has it), for in more than language it *is* the "dotage," the clear dotage of a woman of delightful talent, and in some ways of true genius. It cannot be defended; to criticise it seriously were idle; and to laugh at it inhuman and base.

And so we come to the *Diary,* no part of which was issued during its author's lifetime, though it formed the basis of much of the *Memoirs of Dr Burney,* and therefore exhibits, in a way even more curious than melancholy, the fashion in which it is possible for a painter to paint his own good work into bad. This *Diary,* even yet, is understood not to be published completely, and probably never will be; but enough is extant to make it one of the bulkiest things of the kind. (pp. 222-26)

Delightful as the *Diary* is, its extreme voluminousness, and the singular inequality which here as elsewhere shows itself in the author's work, have brought upon it some rather harsh judgments, such as that it is "tiresome." I do not myself find it tiresome anywhere—even in the interminable conversations with "Mr Turbulent" and "Mr Fairly," even in the bewildering multitude of small details in the *Early Diary* which Mrs Ellis, with a patience and skill which no editor could surpass, has devoted herself to explaining, adjusting and unravelling; hardly even, though I confess that the "hardly" sometimes needs to be accentuated, in the sketches of the later years when little happened, when Madame D'Arblay either was excluded from inspiriting society or left no account of that which she did see, and when the curse of jargon, though never so evident in the *Diary* as in the published books, had laid its grasp upon her. It will not, indeed, do to expect too much or the wrong sort of things; we must not look for perpetual epigram or for frequent good stories; we must carry about with us continually the remembrance that we are in the century of Richardson and of Horace Walpole, and that Miss Burney, with all her gifts, had not those of either, while she had the voluminousness of both. (pp. 226-27)

The fact, as it seems to me, is, that Fanny Burney is in English literature our capital example of a kind of writer commoner in the old conditions of English life abroad than at home, and commoner in all countries among women than among men. In this class a talent of observation and presentation, real and charming to no small degree, is forced at a certain time, and by favourable circumstances, into not premature but perfect bloom. Its best members always remain happy and favourable subjects in point of receptivity; but they have, as a rule, no absolute root or spring of creative genius; and they do not assist the native want by any thorough study of good models. Many critics of Fanny Burney have expressed an amiable but not wholly intelligent surprise, at the very small amount that she seems to have read—brought up among unguarded books as she was—and at the somewhat limited intelligence which her critical remarks show. The fact is that she was the very reverse of bookish, and the innocent raptures over certain love letters (the work of that clever bookmaker, William Combe) in which she and her Mr Fairly indulged at Cheltenham, the comparison which in an Early Diary she makes between the *Vicar* of *Wakefield,* and some stuff of which I should have to go to the book even to remember the name, show what power of literary discrimination she had. Nor was her really creative instinct strong—*Evelina* is a chaos, though a delightful one, as far as plot or construction goes; if *Cecilia* is better we know that, putting Johnson out of question and admitting his denial of having seen the book before it was in print to the fullest, it was subjected to severe criticism and radical alteration at Crisp's hand, and was talked about between other members of the Burneian circle.

Then, it may be asked, what had she? She had much. She had an eye for character—external character, no doubt, chiefly, but still an eye for character—such as nobody else born within many years of her had. And she had, moreover, from almost her earliest youth till almost past her fortieth year, the most extraordinarily fertile field, the most extraordinarily stimulating atmosphere, of character study. The eighteenth century is admittedly the special century of the word "Society;" and Fanny Burney was in the very hotbed of the English eighteenth century. (pp. 231-33)

To her who gave us the Branghtons, Mr Smith, the first volume if not the two first volumes of *Cecilia,* Sir Sedley Clarendel even, let there be praise not in the lowest by any means. To her who gave us the quaint mixed presentation of Dr Burney's visitors, the picture of a Johnson always amiable and sometimes apologetic, the sketches of the sojourn of a young "lioness" in the most various menageries, always with credit to herself and with the result of something like immortality to the other beasts—let there be praise perhaps higher still. Historians may add that Miss Burney has given us almost our only English picture of an English Court, drawn completely from the inside, without any ill nature such as that which invalidates the truth, if it heightens the zest, of books like Hervey's, with distinct literary talent, and with total freedom from "purpose." As a diarist Miss Burney is with Pepys and Evelyn, as a letter-writer with Walpole and Chesterfield. And unlike all these, except Horace, she is a novelist as well, while I must confess that though I like the kind of *The Castle of Otranto* better than the kind of *Evelina,* I must put *Evelina* a good deal higher in its kind than *The Castle of Otranto.* (pp. 235-36)

George Saintsbury, ''Madame D'Arblay,'' in his Es-says in English Literature: 1780-1860, second series, J. M. Dent & Co., 1895, pp. 203-36.

W. D. HOWELLS (essay date 1901)

[*Howells was the chief progenitor of American realism and an influential American literary critic during the late nineteenth and early twentieth centuries. Although he wrote nearly three dozen novels, few of them are read today. Despite his eclipse, however, he stands as one of the major literary figures of his era; having successfully weaned American literature from the sentimental romanticism of its infancy, he earned the popular sobriquet ''the Dean of American Letters.'' In the following excerpt, Howells discusses* Evelina *as the first novel in which the life of a young girl has been fully and accurately depicted. In the character of Evelina, Howells discerns a real and charming person, though he concedes that her behavior and thoughts are extremely dated.*]

Camilla and *The Wanderer* are conscious, academic poses of a talent once so spontaneous. It was a talent once so spontaneous, so vivid, so unaffected, that when Fanny Burney first had before her the task of depicting the nature and behavior of "A Young Lady on her Entrance in the World," she looked in her glass for her model, and wrought with the naïveté of the true artist, especially the true artist who is also young.

It is not to be supposed that she purposely drew herself in Evelina Anville. That is not the way of good art, though the end, the effect is self-portraiture. It is essential to the charm of a fictitious character that he or she who makes it in his or her image should not be aware of doing so; and no doubt Miss Burney kept well within her illusions. If she had perfectly known what she was doing, there would have been touches of self-defence, of self-flattery in Evelina which would have spoiled our pleasure in her; but probably there were people who knew who Evelina was at the time, if Miss Burney did not, and had not to wait nearly fifty years for the *Diary and Letters of Mme. D'Arblay* to let them into the open secret. (p. 14)

Before *The Vicar of Wakefield* there had been no English fiction in which the loveliness of family life had made itself felt; before *Evelina* the heart of girlhood had never been so fully opened in literature. There had been girls and girls, but none in whom the traits and actions of the girls familiar to their fathers, brothers and lovers were so fully recognized; and the contemporaneity instantly felt in Evelina has lasted to this day. The changes since her entrance into the world have been so tremendous that we might almost as well be living in another planet, for all that is left of the world she so trembled at and rejoiced in. But whoever opens the book of her adventures, finds himself in that vanished society with her, because she is herself so living that she makes everything about her alive.

She is of course imagined upon terms of the romantic singularity which we no longer require in letting a nice girl have our hearts. Her father is of a species so very hard-hearted as to be extinct now, even in the theatre. (pp. 14-15)

It is with a fine courage that Miss Burney shows her heroine in her silliness as well as her sense, but she can do this without that suspicion of satirizing her sex which would attach to a writer of the other sex. In fact, one great charm of the story is that it is not satire at all. It is mostly light comedy; it is sometimes low comedy; it is at other times serious melodrama; but the lesson from it is never barbed, and the author's attitude towards her characters has never that sarcastic knowingness which has been the most odious vice of English novelists. (p. 20)

In few of the novels before *Evelina* could the reader help being privy to some such high-handed outrage. All over England heroines were carried off in chairs and chariots to lonely country houses, there to be kept at the mercy of their captors till the exigencies of the plot forced their release. It must have been a startling innovation that Evelina should be let off so easily as she was, but even this was not so strange as that in an age of epistolary fiction she should be allowed to portray in herself that character of a bewitching goose that she really was, and that her author should effect this without apparent knowingness, or any manner of wink to the reader. Evelina is a masterpiece, and she could not be spared from the group of great and real heroines. The means of realizing her are now as quaint and obsolete almost as the manners of the outdated world to which she was born. Nobody writes novels in letters any more; just as people no longer call each other *Sir* and *Madam,* and are *favored* and *obliged* and *commanded* upon every slight occasion; just as young ladies no longer cry out, when strongly moved, "Good God, sir," in writing to their reverend guardians; or receive prodigious compliments; or make set speeches, or have verses to them posted in public places; or go to amusements where they are likely to be confused with dubious characters. Evelina is forced to see and to suffer things now scarcely credible, and it is her business in the long letters she writes her foster-father to depict scenes of vulgarity among her city cousins which make the reader shudder and creep. She depicts other scenes among people of fashion which are not less vulgar, and are far crueller, like that where two gentlemen of rank have two poor old women run a race upon a wager and push the hapless creatures on to the contest with cheers and curses. A whole world of extinct characters and customs centres around her; but she outlives them all in the inextinguishable ingenuousness of a girlish mind which nothing pollutes, and in the purity of a nature to which everything coarse and unkind is alien. She is tempted at times to laugh at things that other people think funny, but she seems a little finer even than her inventor in all this, and it appears less Evelina than Miss Burney who expects you to enjoy the savage comedy of Captain Mervin's insulting pranks at the expense of Madame Duval. In fine, Evelina, though a goose, is perhaps the sweetest and dearest goose in all fiction. We laugh at her (we must not forget that it is she herself who lets us laugh at her), but we love her, and we rejoice in the happiness which she finds so supernally satisfying, as she passes out of the story, panting with rapturous expectation of bliss in keeping of Lord Orville. (pp. 21-3)

W. D. Howells, "Frances Burney's 'Evelina'," in his Heroines of Fiction, *Vol. I, Harper & Brothers Publishers, 1901, pp. 13-23.*

LYTTON STRACHEY (essay date 1904)

[*Strachey was an early twentieth-century English biographer, critic, essayist, and short story writer. He is best known for his biographies* Eminent Victorians, Queen Victoria, *and* Elizabeth and Essex: A Tragic History. *Critics agree that these iconoclastic reexaminations of historical figures revolutionized the course of modern biographical writing. Strachey's literary criticism is also considered incisive. In the following excerpt, he argues that since Burney's novels appeared at a time when "the English novel experienced a remarkable eclipse," her works received more positive attention than they actually deserved. According to Strachey, Burney succeeded in creating a convincing character in Evelina, but he terms the rest of her novels failures. Only the* Diary, *according to Strachey, reflects her "mirror of the world." This essay appeared originally in the* Independent Review II *in February, 1904.*]

There can be no doubt that, during the last quarter of the eighteenth century, the English novel experienced a remarkable eclipse. From the publication of *The Vicar of Wakefield,* in 1766, to the composition of *Pride and Prejudice,* in 1796, for the whole of that period of thirty years, no novel of the first class was produced at all; and few indeed of the novels which were actually written attained the level even of Miss Burney's second-class work. English prose, it is true, had never flourished more gloriously; but it reserved its magnificent outpourings for History, for Philosophy, for Oratory, for Essays, for Memoirs, for Letters, for everything, in fact, except the particular sort of prose romance which is concerned with the portrayal of human nature. Why this was the case, why, between the great constellation of Richardson, Fielding, and Sterne, and the great constellation of Jane Austen and Walter Scott, there should intervene a vast tract of literature illumined only by stars of the third magnitude—this is a mystery perhaps beyond solution, though it would be partly accounted for, if it were true that the direct study of human nature was, for some unknown reason, not interesting to the English of that generation. At any rate, whether they were (to use Johnson's phrase)

'character-mongers' or no in actual life, it seems clear that at least in literary criticism they were not. (p. 122)

It was precisely this quality of literary acumen which her contemporaries brought to bear on the novels of Fanny Burney. 'You have,' Burke wrote to her, 'crowded into a few small volumes an incredible variety of characters; most of them well planned, well supported, and well contrasted with each other' [see excerpt dated 1782]; and it is obvious that by 'characters' Burke meant just what he should not have meant—descriptions, that is to say, of persons who might exist. The truth is, that if we had been told that Delvile *père* was ten feet high, and that Mr. Morrice was made of cardboard, we should have had very little reason for astonishment; such peculiarities of form would have been remarkable, no doubt, but not more remarkable than those of their minds, which Burke was so ready to accept as eminently natural. In fact, Miss Burney's characters, to use Macaulay's phrase, are in reality nothing but 'humours' [see excerpt dated 1843], and not characters at all; and immediately this is recognised, immediately 'humours' is substituted for 'characters' in Burke's appreciation, what he says becomes perfectly just. They are indeed, these humours, 'well planned, well supported, and well contrasted with each other'; Miss Burney displays great cleverness and admirable care in her arrangement of them; and this Burke, as well as Macaulay, thoroughly understood. But such, both for Burke and for his distinguished circle, was the limit of understanding; outside that limit the God of Convention reigned triumphant. Conventional feelings, conventional phrases, conventional situations, conventional oddities, conventional loves,—these were the necessary ingredients of their perfect novel; and all these Miss Burney was able, with supreme correctness, to supply. In the culminating scene of *Cecilia,* where the conflicting passions of affection and family pride at last meet face to face, the dialogue is as wonderfully finished and as superbly orthodox as the dialogue of a second-rate French tragedy; one cannot help seeing Cecilia and Mortimer and Mrs. Delvile, in perruques and togas, delivering their harangues with appropriate gestures from the front of a Louis Quinze stage, with Corinthian columns in the background. Johnson's favourite, the mad philanthropical Albany, does indeed actually burst sometimes into downright blank verse.

> Poor subterfuge of callous cruelty!

he suddenly exclaims,

> You cheat yourselves to shun the fraud of others!
> And yet how better do you use the wealth
> So guarded?
> What nobler purpose can it answer to you,
> Than even a chance to snatch some wretch from sinking?
> Think less how *much* ye save, and more for *what;*

'And then consider how thy full coffers may hereafter make reparation for the empty catalogue of thy virtues.'

'Anan!' cries Mr. Briggs, in reply to these noble sentiments; and that—whatever it may mean—is perhaps the best rejoinder.

But it is to be feared that Miss Burney's friends did worse than misjudge her merits; it seems clear that they encouraged her faults, and turned away her energies from where her true strength lay. For, in her first work, she had succeeded in depicting one character which, though neither elaborate nor profound, was really convincing—Evelina herself. The refined, over-modest girl, around whose perplexities and sufferings and joys the troupe of usual humours dance and tumble, is delicately brought out by a sympathetic hand. Here at last is something that is more than cleverness—a little spark of genius; and it shows itself most clearly in a few little scenes and conversations, of which the following specimen may be taken as a fair example. Lord Orville, who is in love with Evelina, discovers her in the garden at an early hour, talking intimately to Mr. Macartney. Everything points (wrongly, of course) to an assignation. Evelina, who is in love with Lord Orville, returns with him to the house.

> Determined as I was to act honourably by Mr. Macartney, I yet most anxiously wished to be restored to the good opinion of Lord Orville; but his silence, and the thoughtfulness of his air, discouraged me from speaking.
>
> My situation soon grew disagreeable and embarrassing; and I resolved to return to my chamber till breakfast was ready. To remain longer, I feared, might seem *asking* for his inquiries; and I was sure it would ill become me to be more eager to speak than he was to hear.
>
> Just as I reached the door, turning to me hastily, he said, "Are you going, Miss Anville?"
>
> "I am, my lord," answered I; yet I stopped.
>
> "Perhaps to return to—but I beg your pardon!" He spoke with a degree of agitation that made me readily comprehend he meant to *the garden;* and I instantly said: "To my own room, my lord." And again I would have gone; but, convinced by my answer that I understood him, I believe he was sorry for the insinuation; he approached me with a very serious air, though at the same time he forced a smile, and said: "I know not what evil genius pursues me this morning, but I seem destined to do or say something I ought not; I am so much ashamed of myself, that I can scarce solicit your forgiveness."

That is a small picture, perhaps, of a small affair; it describes hardly more than a turn to and from a door; but it possesses qualities of beauty, of restraint, of quick imagination, of charming feeling, of real atmosphere, that make it approach, in its tiny way, close to perfection. But this quiet sort of miniature analysis Miss Burney repeated in none of her later books. Cecilia is a burlesque Evelina, a wax figure whose refinement has become a settled affectation, whose modesty is an obsession, who blushes every time her lover's name is mentioned, who is scandalised when he proposes, and is too maidenly to be married. Henceforward Miss Burney had no time for the subtleties of art; at all hazards she must be creating 'well supported' characters, and putting them into 'well planned' situations; and, her work thus cut out for her, she carried it through with credit. But it is impossible not to think that perhaps, if she had written in a more discriminating age, she would have developed her own peculiar vein as it deserved, instead of working others of inferior ore with implements too heavy for her strength. Fortunately for us indeed, she was left to herself in one domain; for her *Diary* flourished beyond the reach of criticism, deep-rooted in her own most private nature, and fed with truth. . . . It is here that Madame D'Arblay appears at full length; it is here that she shows us her mirror of the world, gives us the relish of real persons, real intimacies, real conversations. Who would not be willing to abolish for ever

the whole elaborate waste of *Cecilia,* for the sake of those few pages in the *Diary,* where, looking down upon the crowded benches of Westminster Hall, we can see distinct before us the pale face of Hastings, and watch the Managers in their box and the Duchesses in their gallery, while we listen alternately to the tedious droning of the lawyers, to the whispered flatteries of Mr. Windham, and the stupendous oratory of Burke? (pp. 123-26)

> *Lytton Strachey, "The Wrong Turning," in his* Literary Essays, *Harcourt Brace and Company, 1949, pp. 120-26.*

PAUL ELMER MORE (essay date 1906)

[*More was an American critic who, along with Irving Babbitt, formulated the doctrines of New Humanism in early twentieth-century American thought. The New Humanists were strict moralists who adhered to traditional conservative values in reaction to an age of scientific and artistic self-expression. In regard to literature, they believed that the aesthetic qualities of a work of art should be subordinate to its moral and ethical purpose. More was particularly opposed to Naturalism, which he believed accentuated the animal nature of humans, and to any literature, such as Romanticism, that broke with established classical tradition. His importance as a critic derives from the rigid coherence of his ideology, which polarized American critics into hostile opponents (Van Wyck Brooks, Edmund Wilson, H. L. Mencken) or devoted supporters (Norman Foerster, Stuart Sherman, and, to a lesser degree, T. S. Eliot). He is especially esteemed for the philosophical and literary erudition of his multi-volumed* Shelburne Essays. *In the following excerpt from that work, More praises Burney's* Diary *as a unique collection of portraits that aptly capture the era in which they were created. More adds, however, that all her writings lack personal emotion.*]

[In her *Diary,* Fanny Burney] was a true prophet in looking forward to the days when time should be more nimble than memory, for in old age she read over the record with great care, blotting out what might give offence if printed, adding here and there explanatory comments, and leaving a mass of correspondence for her executors to weave into the narrative. Her Nobody develops first into a chosen circle of listeners, and then into a public as gigantic as Polyphemus himself. There are thus three distinct elements in the *Diary* whose intermingling may add not a little to its irregular charm. Yet it is a pity, on the whole, that the thought of this final audience ever entered her brain, for it led to a circumspection and to erasures which have probably rendered the limitations of her mind unnecessarily obvious.

But of these it will be sufficient to speak later on. Just now I should like, if possible, to convey to the reader something of the exhilaration which I have myself brought from this renewed acquaintance with so full and spritely a book. I understand, of course, the difficulty of that task. To those who do not already know the *Diary* what notion can be given in a brief essay of that overflowing story of sixty-two years, and to those who have read it how dry and inadequate any summary will seem! Yet, with the latter class, at least, there is a ground of assurance. It is good to recall in solitude the speech and acts of a dear friend; it is good also to sit with one who has known him, and to talk over his generous ways. In that interchange of memories the striking events of his life come out more prominently, and his clever words tickle the ears again as if newly spoken; we pass from one point to another of his character as if, in journeying over a fair country, we were carried by some seven-league boots from hilltop to hilltop, with no care for the humbler valleys where the prospect is concealed. Such a dialogue, indeed, I should wish these essays to be—a dialogue in which the reader plays an equal part with the writer in cherishing the memory of the great moments and persons of our literature.

And it is on one of these eminences of her career that we meet with the subject of this essay at the opening of the present *Diary.* "This year," it begins, "was ushered in by a grand and most important event! At the latter end of January the literary world was favoured with the first publication of the ingenious, learned, and most profound Fanny Burney! I doubt not but this memorable affair will, in future times, mark the period whence chronologers will date the zenith of the polite arts in this island! This admirable authoress has named her most elaborate performance, *Evelina: or, a Young Lady's Entrance into the World.*" (pp. 38-40)

In some ways the first chapters of the *Diary,* in which the subject of *Evelina* predominates, are the most entertaining of all. The author's transitions from modesty to innocent vanity, her freshness and vivacity, make the record read like the scenes of a fine comedy. Though the book was dedicated to her father, he was one of the last to discover its authorship, and from his lips the knowledge passed to "Daddy" Crisp, her mentor and friend of Chessington, than whom no more tantalising figure exists in English letters. . . . (pp. 42-3)

And then comes the visit to Streatham, the residence of Mr. Thrale, the brewer, and his wife, where Dr. Johnson made himself so thoroughly at home that nearly a century later the ink spots might be seen which he had dabbled over the floor and walls of his two rooms. The burly, melancholy, tender-hearted dictator forms, so to speak, the chorus of all these early chapters. No wonder that his approbation almost crazed Fanny with agreeable surprise, so she says, and gave her such a flight of spirits that she danced a jig to Mr. Crisp, without any preparation, music, or explanation—to that good man's no small amazement and diversion. (pp. 43-4)

The journey of the court to Oxford is filled with interesting details, and the experience of the maids of honour at Nuneham, Lord Harcourt's place near by, their wandering through empty halls and questionable chambers, can only be paralleled by the story of Wilhelm Meister's troupe at the castle of the duke. More absorbing still, not without an undertone of genuine awe, is the recital of the King's illness. She touches lightly on the raving of her royal master, and on the brutal treatment he underwent, as was the custom in those days with the insane. It was her duty each morning to transmit the pages' report of the night to the afflicted Queen, and once to report those horrors was enough. (p. 52)

It is but fair to add that the limitations of Miss Burney's own mind throw the narrowness of the court into undue prominence. Of the political activities which centred around George III. and which were the only real life of the court, as, indeed, they were of England at that time, she has not a word to say. There is just a glimpse of the intrigues to set the Prince of Wales as regent over the poor mad King, but not even a hint of the larger movements that were converting England from a kingdom to an empire, and changing its government from an oligarchy to a democracy. Those last years of the eighteenth century were big with importance from that side, and sometimes the blindness of Miss Burney to all but the small personalities of the palace is more than annoying. Even at the trial of Warren Hastings, which she heard from the most advantageous posi-

tion, she displays the same obtuseness of mind. Her account of that scene as a piece of large pictorial writing is extraordinary, but her sympathy and her understanding are confined solely to the persons involved. No suspicion seems to have entered her mind that this gorgeous drama represents a change in the conduct of an empire; she is merely incensed against Burke because he is in opposition to her beloved master; her judgment does not extend beyond pity for an accused friend. Yet in a way she occasionally exhibits unusual shrewdness. Her comments to Mr. Windham on the failure of Burke's eloquence is a notable piece of literary criticism—the only criticism in the whole *Diary,* I believe, which is not a mere repetition of the faded platitudes of the day. (pp. 54-5)

The marriage with M. D'Arblay was not long deferred, and for a while we have a pretty idyl of domestic life in a little cottage built on the proceeds from a third novel, and supported by Fanny's scanty pension. From this there is an abrupt transition to the intrigues of Napoleon's court, the excitement of the Restoration, the confusion of the Hundred Days, the suspense at Brussels during the battle of Waterloo, from which Thackeray drew his famous scene in *Vanity Fair,* and the second Restoration. The interest never flags in these chapters, and it would not be easy to find elsewhere a more vivid description of the perturbations and blind currents of fear that lay hold of the individual during these great national catastrophes. One feels the general paralysis of lesser life, while somewhere in the background dark and stupendous powers are wrestling for the mastery.

In England, again, the interest gradually wanes to the close of the writer's life. Yet there are passages of this later record which display, perhaps, more literary skill of the conscious sort than any of the earlier parts. The adventure at Ilfracombe, for example, is told with an art at once realistic and imaginative, and the tale of her husband's death has over it a quiet and ineffable pathos. Macaulay has written harshly of the petrified style adopted by Mme. D'Arblay in her declining years [see excerpt dated 1843]. The censure is deserved, no doubt; and yet for sheer beauty of words she never wrote anything comparable to this expression of her feelings when she heard that the long-delayed end had fallen: "How I bore this is still marvellous to me! I had always believed such a sentence would at once have killed me. But his sight—the sight of his stillness, kept me from distraction! Sacred he appeared, *and his stillness I thought should be mine, and be inviolable.*" (pp. 57-8)

A "little character-monger" Johnson had called her in her youth, and no phrase can better describe the trait which lends interest to this long *Diary.* Nowhere else in English will you find anything just like this series of portraits, in which the eccentricities and mannerisms of the age are caught up with so unerring a fidelity and so gentle a malice. In this respect, the two of her novels which still live, *Evelina* and *Cecilia,* are properly mere excursions in the more realistic transcript of life. Occasionally, to be sure, there is a passage of capital narration, but it is always of a purely personal sort. What we miss in the *Diary* and the novels alike is any note of passion and any immediate reflection on life, and only this limitation prevents her work from ranking with the great French autobiographies, with which a comparison most naturally occurs. Fanny was a prude, we are told, and she was also, I fear, something of a snob, but the fault did not lie entirely in her own character. Not a little of it must be charged to the state of English society. The fact is, she was a victim of that peculiarly British worship of the social order which from the days of Hobbes had been slowly permeating the national consciousness. That worship was not incompatible with sound statesmanship, or with profound political philosophy as in the case of Burke; it did not lessen the manly independence of a Johnson, and it could serve to whet the barbed arrows of a Walpole. But on a yielding, feminine character such as Miss Burney's its influence was almost omnipotent, so that her prudishness and her snobbery became not so much individual as national; and they are, one must admit, none the less easy to stomach for that reason. There was an actual dead line for her mind. Custom lay like a crust between what was proper and what was unspeakable. Above were the family, the State, the Church, the social order; below were gathered all the ruinous emotions of the untamed heart, not the immoral or indecent things, merely, for these, as a matter of fact, might be harmless among gentlemen, but the passionate, rebellious things that create their own law. Richardson had been able to show the working of that seething underworld without shocking society, but only by throwing the burden of responsibility on poor Clarissa's shoulders as the result of filial disobedience. With our Fanny that crust never for a moment really breaks, and her satire skates over the surface of life with unfaltering dexterity.

If this were all, we might call her modest rather than prudish; but into that same forbidden limbo is relegated every immediate and penetrating reflection; it is as if the reverend Constitution of the land had been builded on the law, Thou shalt not think the thing that has not been thought. English literature as a body has, alas! served that law only too well, and we turn elsewhither for quick and logical thought; but in this long diary the lack is unusually apparent. I cannot recall in all the eight volumes of this record kept for seventy-three years a single sentence that shows any immediate reaction of the writer's mind on the troublesome problems of existence. She seems to have passed through the world without experience and without questioning; and at the end we still think of her as the girl, very English and very innocent, scribbling her satire in the protection of the great Sir Isaac's observatory. Perhaps we cover up her defects by remembering that Newton himself, despite his mightiness in science, was but a child when he came to reflect on human life; and certainly there are few more entertaining books and few names fairer and dearer to us than hers. (pp. 58-61)

> *Paul Elmer More, "Fanny Burney," in his* Shelburne Essays, fourth series, *G. P. Putnam's Sons, 1906, pp. 35-61.*

GAMALIEL BRADFORD   (essay date 1914)

[*Bradford considers the* Diary *artificial and contrived because, he argues, Burney was always concerned with appearances. Unlike many other critics, Bradford contends that she was too "amiable" and intellectually timid to be an astute observer of society and character.*]

[Frances Burney] wrote a diary or diary-like letters almost from the cradle to the grave. For reasons which will appear later we do not know so much about her intimate self as might be expected from such minuteness of record; but her external life, the places she dwelt in, the people she saw, the things she did, are brought before us with a full detail which is rare in the biography of women and even of men.

She was as little of a Bohemian in soul as any one who ever lived. Yet her career had something of the nomadic, kaleidoscopic character which we are apt to call Bohemian. She met all sorts of people and portrayed all sorts, from the top of

society to the bottom. And through this infinite diversity of spiritual contact she carried an eager eye, an untiring pen, and a singularly amiable disposition. (p. 108)

"Poor Fanny's face tells what she thinks, whether she will or no," said Dr. Burney. Her face might. Her diary does not. To be sure, she herself asserts repeatedly that she writes nothing but the truth. "How truly does this Journal contain my real, undisguised thoughts; . . . its truth and simplicity are its sole recommendation." No doubt she believed so. No doubt she aimed to be absolutely veracious. No doubt she avoids false statements and perversion of fact. Her diary may be true, but it is not genuine. It is literary, artificial, in every line of it. She sees herself exactly as a man—or woman—sees himself in a mirror: the very nature of the observation involves unconscious and instinctive posing. (pp. 111-12)

It was impossible for the woman to look at herself in any but a literary point of view.

Take, for instance, the address to *Nobody,* with which the diary opens [see excerpt dated 1767]. It sets the note at once. There is not the slightest suggestion of a sincere, direct effort to record the experiences of a soul; merely an airy, literary coquetting with somebody, everybody, under the Nobody mask.

A single breath of fresh air is enough to blast the artificiality of the whole thing. Turn from a page of the diary to any letter of Mrs. Piozzi [Hester Lynch Thrale]—some of them are given in the diary itself. A coarse woman, a passionate woman, a jealous woman—but, oh, so genuine in every word. Her loud veracity sweeps through Fanny's dainty nothings like a salt-sea breeze. And do not misunderstand the distinction. Fanny could not have told a lie to save her life. Mrs. Piozzi probably tossed them about like cherries or bonbons. But Mrs. Piozzi, laughing or lying, was always herself, without thinking about herself. Fanny was always thinking—unconsciously, if one may say so—of how she would appear to somebody else. (p. 112)

[Our] diarist helps us less than she ought. Yet even she cannot write two thousand pages, nominally about herself, without telling something. The very fact of such literary self-consciousness is of deep human interest. It is to be noted, also, that she does not conceal herself from any instinct of reserve. She is willing to drop pose and tell all, if she could; but she cannot. Such thoughtless self-confession as Pepys's would have been impossible to her. I do not think that once, in all her volumes, does she show herself in an unfavorable light.

But we can detect what she does not show. We can read much, much that she did not mean us to read. And lights are thrown on her by others as well as by herself.

To begin with, how did she bear glory? For a girl of twenty-five to be thrown into such a blaze of it was something of an ordeal. She herself disclaims any excessive ambition. She could almost wish the triumph might "happen to some other person who had more ambition, whose hopes were sanguine, who could less have borne to be buried in the oblivion which I even sought." She records all the fine things that are said of her, the surmises of eager curiosity, the ardent outbursts of family affection, the really tumultuous enthusiasm of ripened critical judgment. But she is rather awed than inflated by it; at least, so she says. (pp. 112-13)

With [the] various opportunities of human contact and with [her] natural shrewdness, Madame D'Arblay's diary should have been a mine of varied and powerful observation of life.

It is not. She presents us with a vast collection of figures, vividly contrasted and distinguished in external details and little personal peculiarities; but rarely, if ever, does she get down to essentials, to a real grip on the deeper springs and motives of character. This is in large part due to the eternal literary prepossession which I have already pointed out. You feel that the painter is much more interested in making an effective picture than a genuine likeness. But Miss Burney's deficiencies as a psychologist go deeper than this technical artificiality and are bound up with one of the greatest charms of her personal temperament. For an exact observer of character she is altogether too amiable. I do not at all assert that a good student of men must hate them. Far from it.

> There is a soul of goodness in things evil,
> Would we observingly distil it out

is an excellent warning for the psychologist. But Miss Burney is really too full of the milk of human kindness. It oozes from every pore. (p. 117)

It is thus that her really vast gallery of portraiture is cruelly disappointing. Turn from her to Saint-Simon or Lord Hervey, turn even to the milder Greville or Madame de Rémusat, and you will feel the difference. George the Third was not Louis the Fourteenth, nor Queen Charlotte, Queen Caroline. But George and his wife were hardly the beatific spirits that appear in this diary. Miss Burney cannot say enough about her dear queen, her good queen, her saintly queen. Mrs. Thrale remarks: "The Queen's approaching death gives no concern but to the tradesmen, who want to sell their pinks and yellows, I suppose." And this is refreshing after so much distillation of soul perfumery.

In short, though she was far from a fool, Miss Burney's views of humanity do more credit to her heart than to her head. If the paradox is permissible, she was exceedingly intelligent, but not very richly endowed with intelligence—that is, she was quick to perceive and reason in detail, but she had no turn for abstract thinking. . . . Timid intellectually—not morally—Miss Burney certainly was. Such learning as she had she carefully disguised, and in this, no doubt, she had as fellows other eighteenth-century women much bigger than she. But when she gets hold of an attractive book she waits to read it in company. "Anything highly beautiful I have almost an aversion of reading alone." Here I think we have a mark of social instincts altogether outbalancing the intellectual. (p. 118)

And as her intelligence was perhaps not Herculean, so I question whether her emotional life, just and tender and true as it unquestionably was, had anything volcanic in it. She had certainly admirable control of her feelings; but in these cases we are never quite sure whether the force controlling is strong or the force controlled weak. Her love for her husband was rapturous—in words. Words were her stock in trade. It was also, no doubt, capable of supreme sacrifice; for her conscience was high and pure. Still, that "drooping air and timid intelligence" haunt me. She seems to approach all life, from God to her baby, with a delicious spiritual awe; so different from Miss Austen, who walks right up and lifts the veil of awe from everything. Miss Burney, indeed, stands as much in awe of herself as of everything else; and hence it is that, writing thousands of words about herself, she tells us comparatively little.

One thing is certain, she was a writer from her childhood to her death. Her own experiences and all others were "copy," first and foremost. "I thought the lines worth preserving; so flew out of the room to write this." She was always flying out

of life to preserve it—in syrup. The minute detail with which she writes down—or invents—all the conversations of her first love affair is extraordinary enough. Still, as she had no feeling in the matter herself, it was less wonderful that she could describe—not analyze—the young man's. But she did love her father. She did love her husband. That she could go from their death-beds and write down last words and dying wishes, all the hopes and fears of those supreme moments, with cool, artistic finish and posterity in her eye, is a fine instance of the scribbling mania.

It is, therefore, as an authoress that we must chiefly think of her. It is as the fêted, flattered, worshiped creatress of *Evelina* that her girlish figure gets its finest piquancy. . . . (p. 119)

> Gamaliel Bradford, "Madame D'Arblay," in The North American Review, Vol. CXCIX, No. 698, January, 1914, pp. 108-19.

REGINALD BRIMLEY JOHNSON (essay date 1918)

[*Johnson assesses* Evelina *and* Cecilia *and discusses the influence of Samuel Richardson on Burney's novels. According to Johnson, Richardson initiated the analysis of women in English literature, but Burney was the first to provide psychological insight into the female mind. The critic stresses that although she lacked technical finesse and the ability to draw subtle characterizations, Burney pointed the way toward the perfection of the domestic novel.*]

[If] *Evelina* was modelled on the work of Richardson, and the fathers of fiction, who had so recently passed away, it nevertheless inaugurated a new departure—the expression of a feminine outlook on life. It was, frankly and obviously, written by a woman for women, though it captivated men of the highest intellect.

We need not suppose that Johnson's pet "character-monger" set out with any intention of accomplishing this reform; but the woman's view is so obvious on every page that we can scarcely credit the general assumption of "experienced" *masculine* authorship, which was certainly prevalent during the few weeks it remained anonymous. (p. 12)

It is obvious that we can only realise the precise nature of what she accomplished for fiction by comparing her work with Richardson's, since Fielding, Smollett, and Sterne wove all their stories about a "hero," and even Goldsmith drew women through the spectacles of a naïvely "superior" and obviously masculine vicar. Richardson, on the other hand, was admittedly an expert in the analysis of the feminine. We must recognise a lack of virility in touch and outlook. The prim exactitude of his cautious realism, however startling in comparison with anything before *Pamela*, has much affinity with what our ancestors might have expected from their womenkind. Yet his women are quite obviously studies, not self-revelations. . . . For all his extraordinary insight Richardson can only see woman from the outside. Our *consciousness* of his skill proves it is conscious. His world still centres round the hero: the rustic fine gentleman, the courtly libertine, or the immaculate male.

Fanny Burney reverses the whole process. To begin with external evidence: it is Evelina who tells the tale, and every person or incident is regarded from her point of view. The resultant difference goes to the heart of the matter. The reader does not here feel that he is studying a new type of female: he is making a new friend. Evelina and Cecilia speak for themselves throughout. There is no sense of effort or study; not because Fanny Burney is a greater artist or has greater power to conceal her art, but because, for the accomplishment of her task, she has simply to be herself. It is here, in fact, that we find the peculiar charm, and the supreme achievement, of the women who founded the school. By never attempting professional study of life outside their own experience, they were enabled to produce a series of feminine "Confessions"; which remain almost unique as human documents. We must recognise that it was Richardson who had made this permissible. He broke away, for ever, from the extravagant impossibilities and unrealities of Romance. He copied life, and life moreover in its prosaic aspect—the work-a-day, unpicturesque experience of the middle-class. But still he lingered among its crises. (pp. 13-16)

It was reserved for Fanny Burney, and still more Jane Austen, to "make a story" out of the trivialities of our everyday existence; to reveal humanity at a tea-party or an afternoon call. This is, of course, but carrying on his reform one step further. The women, besides introducing the new element of their own especial point of view, made the new realism strictly *domestic;* and learned to depend, even less than he, upon the exceptional, more obviously dramatic, or less normal, incidents of actual life. If Richardson invented the ideal of fidelity to human nature, Miss Burney selected its everyday habits and costume for imitation. Evelina's account of "shopping" in London would not fit into Richardson's scheme; while the many incidents and characters, introduced merely for comic effect, lie outside his province.

Miss Burney's ideal for heroines, indeed, must seem singularly old-fashioned to-day; nor do we delight in *Evelina* for those passages to which its author devoted her most serious ambitions. She does not excel in minute, or sustained, characterisation; nor have we ever entirely confirmed the appreciation which declares that her work was "inspired by one consistent vein of passion, never relaxed." The passion of Evelina—by which, however, the critic does *not* mean her love for Orville—has always seemed to us melodramatic and artificial. We have little, or no, patience with those refined tremors and heart-burnings which completely prostrate the young lady at the mere possibility of seeing her long-lost father. It is not in human nature to feel so deeply about anyone we have never seen, of whom we know nothing but evil.

No blame attaches to Miss Burney as an artist in this respect, however, because she was intent upon the revelation of *sensibility,* that most elusive of female graces on which our grandmothers were wont to pride themselves. Any definition of this quality, suited to our comprehension to-day, would seem beyond the subtleties of emotional analysis; but we may observe, as some indication of its meaning, that no *man* was ever supposed, or expected, to possess it. Sensibility, in fact, was the acknowledged privilege of *ladies*—as distinguished at once from gentlemen or women; particularly becoming in youth; and indicating the well-bred, the elegant, and the fastidious. . . . Evelina is scarcely more natural about her transports at discovering a brother, or in the final *satisfaction* of her filial instincts, than in her alarm about "how He would receive her," already mentioned.

We are not justified, on the other hand, in supposing that a heroine should only exhibit sensibility on some real emotional catastrophe. There was a tendency . . . in "elegant females" to be utterly abashed and penetrated with remorse, covered with shame, trembling with alarm, and on the verge of hysterics—from joy or grief—upon most trivial provocation. A tone, a look, even a movement, if unexpected or mysterious, was generally sufficient to upset the nice adjustment of their

mental equilibrium. "Have I done wrong? Am I misunderstood? Is it possible he *really* loves me?" The dear creatures passed through life on the edge of a precipice: on the borderland between content, despair, and the seventh heaven.

The wonder of it all comes from admitting that Miss Burney actually reconciles us to such absurdities. Except in the passionate scenes, Evelina's sensibility is one of her chief charms. In some mysterious and subtle fashion, it really indicates the superiority of her mind and her essential refinement. She will be prattling away, with all the naïveté of genuine innocence, about her delight in the condescending perfections of the "noble Orville," and then—at *one* word of warning from her beloved guardian—the whole world assumes other aspects, no man may be trusted, and she would fly at once to peace, and forgetfulness, in the country. We smile, inevitably, at the "complete *ingénue*"; but the quick response to her old friend's loving anxiety, the transparent candour of a purity which, if instinctive, is not dependent on ignorance, combine to form a really "engaging" personality.

It may be that we have here discovered the secret of sensibility—a perception of the fine shades, and instant responsiveness to them. (pp. 17-21)

It is impossible, I think, to put Cecilia herself on a level with Evelina; though I personally have always felt that the more crowded canvas of the *book* so entitled, and its greater variety of incident, reveal more mature power. But it is less spontaneous and, in a certain sense, less original. To begin with, Cecilia is always conscious of her superiority. Like her sister heroine, a country "miss," and suddenly tossed into Society without any proper guidance, she yet assumes the centre of the stage without effort, and queens it over the most experienced, by virtue of beauty and wealth. It may be doubted if she has much "sensibility" for everyday matters: whereas the lavish expenditure of emotional fireworks over the haughty Delviles, and the melodramatic sufferings they entail, are most intolerably protracted, and entirely destroy our interest in the conclusion of the narrative. The occasional scene, or episode, we complained of in *Evelina,* is here extended to long chapters, or books, of equally strained passion on a more complex issue. Fortunately they all come at the end, and need not disturb our enjoyment of the main story; though, indeed, the whole plot depends far more on melodramatic effect. Mr. Harrell's abominable recklessness, and his sensational suicide, the criminal passion of Mr. Monckton, and the story of Henrietta Belfield, carry us into depths beyond the reach of *Evelina,* where Miss Burney herself does not walk with perfect safety. And, in our judgment, such experiences diminish the charm of her heroine.

Yet in the main Cecilia possesses, and exhibits those primarily feminine qualities which now made their first appearance in English fiction, being beyond man's power to delineate. She, too, is that "Womanly Woman" whom Mr. Bernard Shaw has so eloquently denounced. She has the magnetic power of personal attraction; the charm of mystery; the strength of weakness; the irresistible appeal with which Nature has endowed her for its own purposes: so seldom present in the man-made heroine, certainly not revealed to Samuel Richardson and his great contemporaries.

For the illustration of our main theme, we have so far dwelt upon the revelation of womanhood achieved by Miss Burney. It is time to consider, in more detail, her application of the new "realism," her method of "drawing from life," now first recognised as the proper function of the novelist. It is here that her unique education, or experience, has full play. Instead of depending, like Richardson, upon the finished analysis of a few characters, centred about one emotional situation, or of securing variety of interests and character-types, *à la* Fielding, by use of the "wild-oats" convention, she works up the astonishing "contrasts" in life, which she had herself been privileged to witness, and achieves comedy by the abnormal mixture of Society. Thus she is able to find drama in domesticity. Her most original effects are produced in the drawing-room or the assembly, at a ball or a theatre, in the "long walks" of Vauxhall or Ranelagh: wherever, and whenever, mankind is seen only at surface-value, enjoying the pleasures and perils of everyday existence. (pp. 24-7)

Of what must seem, to our thinking, the extraordinary licence permitted to persons accounted gentlemen, Miss Burney avails herself to the utmost; and Evelina is scarcely less often embarrassed or distressed by Willoughby's violence and the insolence of Lord Merton, than by the stupid vulgarity of the Branghtons and "Beau" Smith. We have primarily the sharp contrast between Society and Commerce—each with its own standards of comfort, pleasure, and decorum; and secondarily, a great variety of individual character (and ideal) within both groups. The "contrasts" of Cecilia are, in the main, more specifically individual, lacking the one general sharp class division, and may be more accurately divided into one group of Society "types," another of Passions exemplified in persons obsessed by a single idea. (p. 28)

It is primarily, indeed, a most diverting picture of manners; and if, as we have endeavoured to show, Miss Burney advanced on Richardson by the revelation of womanhood in her heroines, the realism of her minor persons must be applauded rather for its variety in outward seeming than for its subtlety of characterisation. (pp. 29-30)

Of any particular construction Miss Burney was entirely guiltless; in this respect, of course, lagging far behind Fielding. She has no style, beyond a most attractive spontaneity; writing in "true *woman's* English, clear, natural, and lively" [see excerpt by Macaulay dated 1843]. Under the watchful eye of Dr. Johnson, indeed, she made some attempt at the rounded period, the "elegant" antithesis, in *Cecilia:* but, regretting the obvious effort, we turn here again, with renewed delight, to the flowing simplicity of her dramatic dialogue.

There is no occasion, at this time of day, to dwell upon her sparkling wit, though we may note in passing its obviously feminine inspiration—as opposed to the more scholarly subtleties of Fielding—and its patent superiority to, for example, the kitten-sprightliness of Richardson's "Lady G." We cannot claim that Miss Burney made any particular *advance* in this matter; but, here again, her work stands out as the first permanent expression—at least in English—of that shrewd vivacity and quickness of observation with which so many a woman, who might have founded a salon, has been wont to enliven the conversation of the home and to promote the gaiety of social gatherings. We must recognise, on the other hand, that, if commonly more refined than her generation, Miss Burney has yielded to its prejudice against foreigners in some coarseness towards Madame Duval; as we marvel at her father's approval of this detail—while actually deploring the vigour of her contempt for Lovel, the fop!

Finally, for all technicalities of her art, Miss Burney remains an amateur in authorship, who, by a lucky combination of genius and experience, was destined to utter the first word for

women in the most popular form of literature; and to point the way to her most illustrious successors for the perfection of the domestic novel. (pp. 30-1)

Reginald Brimley Johnson, "The First Woman Novelist," in his The Women Novelists, *1918. Reprint by Books for Libraries Press, 1967; distributed by Arno Press, Inc., pp. 7-34.*

ERNEST A. BAKER   (essay date 1934)

[*Baker contends that Burney's literary significance rests on her ability to vividly describe everyday life and to avoid the sentimentalism of her day, replacing it with natural comedy. Baker expresses admiration for her earliest novels and for her style, which he labels warm and sympathetic. However, he faults* Cecilia *for its excessive number of grotesque characters and terms* Camilla *"a rambling, dull, and amateurish production." Further, Baker notes that the formula that had been effective in* Evelina *becomes forced and repetitive in Burney's later works.*]

Fanny Burney provides an interlude of natural comedy in the long monotone of solemn and pretentious sentimentalism. She was not entirely immune from the chief foible of her time. But she was aware of that foible, she laughed at its aberrations in others, and she usually succeeded in checking it in herself. Fanny Burney, at any rate, was never an affected person. Effusions of tears occur in her pages such as other periods would have thought unseemly. She was a warm-hearted, sympathetic creature, of normal sensibilities; and, if she dwelt more tenderly upon a pathetic scene than is the wont in less demonstrative times, it was simply because this was the habitual tone of her society. In comparison with her fellow-novelists she was an anti-sentimentalist. If she is compared with such men and women of her own world as Walpole, Mrs Delany, or Mrs Montagu, the attitude in this respect is much the same in her novels and their letters. All were still under the sway of the didactic spirit, prone to moralize, apt to drop into a sentimental mood. Sane as they were, it did not take much to melt them. In the days of Fanny's youth, everybody was expected to go into tears at any affecting news, at a signal act of magnanimity or show of fine character. What Fanny quietly thought of it may be read between the lines in many a passage in her diaries. There is the great traveller Mr Bruce, for instance, "the Abyssinian giant." When he hears about the young lady at her first concert, who "sighed and groaned, and groaned and sighed, and at last she said, 'Well, I can't help it!' and burst into tears. 'There's a woman,' cried Mr Bruce, with some emotion, 'who could never make a man unhappy! Her soul must be all harmony!'"

There were, of course, all this time sets of people who had no patience with the absurdities of the sentimental school. Fanny Burney was a natural girl who did not rush to either extreme. She was anti-sentimentalist to the same extent as Dr Johnson, but not more consistently so than Goldsmith. (pp. 154-55)

Fanny Burney's importance in the history of the novel is not . . . that she broke with sentimentalism, nor is it that she extended in any way the scope of fiction; it is, rather, that she came so near to what may be called a direct transcript of life. The impressions of a sharp-eyed observer went straight into literature with a minimum of the simplifying, ordering, or interpreting process implied in such realism, for instance, as Fielding's. At her best, she seems to reproduce what she sees. There is only, as it were, a narrow and vanishing margin between literature and life. Scores of pages in her diaries may be put side by side with pages from her novels to illustrate this. Contrary to what has been repeatedly alleged, she was an omnivorous novel-reader. But she learned less from others than she knew by instinct of how to reproduce the movement and sparkle of social commerce and the singularities of individuals. Her indiscriminate reading—and she was not a good critic—was responsible for the conventions and artificialities that marred her simple truthfulness. She was best when story and all the regulation framework of fiction was lost to sight in the vividness of a scene apparently written down exactly as she saw and heard it. It was an innate faculty that she was gifted with, and her very first novel published shows that gift fully developed. But she had had to develop it; she had gone through her course of training, although this first novel came out when she was only twenty-six. (p. 156)

Evelina, or a young lady's entrance into the world . . . is a novel in letters; but, although Fanny Burney would not have liked the comparison, the letters are used more as in Smollett's *Humphry Clinker,* to bring out the humour of different points of view, than for disclosing thoughts and feelings in the most agitating crises. Her aim was modest: "I have only presumed to trace the accidents and adventures to which a 'young woman' is liable. I have not pretended to show the world what it actually *is,* but what it *appears* to a girl of seventeen:—and so far as that, surely any girl who is *past* seventeen may safely do." But she was not content to do simply this: it was incumbent upon her, at least she thought so, to arrange the accidents and adventures in the conventional order now required of a novel. There must be a plot, and of course a chequered love affair; and she fulfils these obligations by putting her young woman under a cloud, providing all the due episodes of tragic tension, and ending with an act of recognition that dissipates the cloud, and brings satisfaction to all that deserve it. Fanny Burney had long ago noted in her diary what was her own idea of a good novel. "I cannot be much pleased without an appearance of truth; or at least of possibility—I wish the story to be natural though the sentiments are refined; and the characters to be probable though their behaviour is excelling." Her first approximates to this better than her later novels; yet the conventional secret marriage and the conventional problem, whether the wicked baronet who is Evelina's father will recognize his daughter and restore her rights, detract from the proper interest of the book, which is in the jostling together of a crowd of oddly-matched characters. (pp. 160-61)

Vulgarity was not a new thing in novel or play; but no one had made it the principal theme as Fanny Burney did in the central chapters of *Evelina.* The squabbling of the Branghton sisters, the pinchbeck gentility of the City beau, Mr Smith, the uncouth attentions of the one and the ill-bred sneers of the others, their conceited airs and their prostration when confronted by a real baronet: it is all first-class comedy. (p. 162)

Sir Clement Willoughby, too, although not quite free from exaggeration, is drawn with consummate skill and goes through his difficult part with magnificent address. Madame Duval would have been better but for some uncertainty on the part of her creator, who seems to have meant her chiefly as a butt for ridicule, a vulgar and uneducated Frenchwoman, which, of course, she was not. But as often happens with low-comedy figures, Madame Duval proved too much for the author's intentions, and shows herself not a bad sort of woman at all. She turns the tables on the formidable Sir Clement in one scene, to the general applause. Nor was Fanny successful with her salt-water captain; a young lady of her propriety could not be, as she conceived him, like one of Smollett's brutal seamen.

"I can only give you a faint idea of his language," she says, "and, besides, he makes use of a thousand sea-terms, which are to me quite unintelligible." Hence she was handicapped in the one talent, for lifelike speech, that served her with the most intractable of her other oddities. No wonder that Captain Mirvan was regarded as a libel on his profession. The horseplay perpetrated on the unlucky Madame Duval is, for reasons not dissimilar, another blot on the story. Then there is the unfortunate episode in which Fanny slips into the rôle of the contemporary novelist of sensibility. The melancholy and suicidal Mr Macartney, the desperate man of sentiment, is as bad as Mackenzie's Harley at his worst, who was to be a spectacle to the world three years later. But Fanny's attitude in this and other scenes of artificial pathos, in *Cecilia,* for instance, ought to be compared with such a passage in her diary as that of the misanthropic young lady. . . . She was delineating all sorts of life, now sympathetically and now with satire, and when she touched upon sentimentalism it was always with some respect.

Fanny Burney's second novel was a more ambitious and a more elaborate production; the subject again is a young lady's entry upon life, and again the comic delineation of character is adapted to the expectations of readers at the circulating library by means of an absorbing love affair and the problematical issues of a plot. But the plot is both more complicated and more far-fetched: it is at once an intricate scheme for the display of a large and diversified crowd of characters, and a means of providing an ample allowance of excitement, suspense, and surprise. Novelists had yet to learn how characters can be left to show themselves off spontaneously, without such an artificial framework as can have very little interest for thoughtful readers. The nature of the plot is hinted in the title: *Cecilia, or Memoirs of an Heiress.* . . . (pp. 163-64)

[The] Harrel underplot and the rest of the subordinate complications are ingeniously attached to the main business; it is a piece of clever melodrama, but mechanical, not truly motived. Fanny Burney does not understand the fundamentals of character; her concern is with the differences and oddities of human nature, not with that which is universal. Hence, apart from a few scenes of concentrated comedy, her novels are inferior to the diaries in the very characteristics which are her strength.

It was, however, the Delvile affair and the harrowing struggle between the claims of family and those of love that riveted the attention of most of her contemporary readers; and next to this the Harrel episode, which was regarded as a tragic and powerful illustration of the nemesis waiting upon folly and vice. (p. 165)

Fanny said herself that the scene between the mother and son, in which Mrs Delvile is so frenzied with "grief and horror" that she suddenly cries "My brain is on fire" and breaks a blood-vessel, was the very scene for which she wrote the whole book, "and so entirely does my plan hang upon it, that I must abide by its reception in the world, or put the whole behind the fire." . . . The history of the unfortunate carpenter and his family, reduced to poverty because Mr Harrel had neglected to pay his bills, and the death of the little boy, would have done honour to the contemporary *comédie larmoyante.*

Yet the excellence of *Cecilia* lies elsewhere. Its true merit is in the many scenes, too many unfortunately, in which the character-monger makes her fops and eccentrics exhibit their mannerisms and idiosyncrasies. Goldsmith had glanced at the "paltry affectation, strained allusions, and disgusting finery," which are too frequently "the badges of ignorance, or of stupidity,'' and made his Chinese visitor seize his hat and leave the room because he aimed ''at appearing rather a reasonable creature, than an outlandish idiot.'' But by Fanny Burney's time these extravagants had become a social plague, and admirable sport for the satirist. Of course, they figure in the diary. Fanny does not repine at being placed on a sofa next ''the thin quaker-like woman'' Mrs Aubrey, when it enables her to evade Miss Weston, ''for the extreme delicacy of Miss Weston makes it prodigiously fatiguing to converse with her, as it is no little difficulty to keep pace with her refinement, in order to avoid shocking her by too obvious an inferiority in daintihood and *ton*.'' But she makes a select muster of such exquisites and grotesques in *Cecilia;* our only complaint is, not that there are so many, but that she makes them perform the same antics too often; the same situation is so often repeated that she exhausts the possibilities of her creations, and all but exhausts the reader's enjoyment of them. (pp. 166-67)

There are so many of them that they have to be drawn up in ear-marked groups, each representing some folly that will soon be driven out by a new affectation. ''The present race of Insensibilists'' are still on speaking terms with the followers of Miss Larolles, head of the Voluble tribe, and the Supercilious, led by Miss Leeson. But they are threatened by the sect of the Jargonists, and are hard put to it to maintain their pre-eminence. Mr Meadows, ''since he commenced Insensibilist, has never once dared to be pleased, nor ventured for a moment to look in good humour!'' (pp. 167-68)

Between the dates of *Cecilia* and of her third novel, *Camilla, or a picture of youth* . . . , Fanny Burney had gone through experiences that changed her history. For several trying years she served Queen Charlotte as second mistress of the robes, and in 1793 she married General d'Arblay. Her diary went on steadily, limpid and lively as ever, in contrast to her novels, which in ease and vivacity show a gradual declension from the first of all. She was a great admirer of *Rasselas,* and of its author, who gave her advice, and has rashly been suspected of actually lending a hand in parts of her writings. A stiffness and formality in the dialogue, and more of it in the narrative prose, point, even in *Cecilia,* to the influence of the admired Johnson; in *Camilla* the trail of second-rate Johnsonian English is over everything. And yet in the unstudied entries in her diary she could mingle dialogue and story with masterly ease. (pp. 169-70)

Never after *Evelina* did Fanny Burney succeed in her fiction in creating [an] illusion of having transferred reality, unimproved and untampered with, to the printed page; very far from it in *Camilla,* in perusing which the reader marvels how the vivacious diarist could be guilty of such a rambling, dull, and amateurish performance. It is the general history of a set of young people at the marriageable age, and in particular of the way one couple, contrary to their elders' designs, fall in love with each other, and in spite of misunderstandings and other vicissitudes reach the happy goal. There is hardly anything else in it, except the common accidents, the petty troubles. In *Evelina*, the author could make the trivialities of life interesting, by quietly revealing what usually passes unnoticed. Here she labours the insignificant and relates at great length and in conscientious detail what merits no attention, until the reader is bored to death. And in place of the freshness and impromptu liveliness of *Evelina* and the diary, she writes with a forced vivacity vacant of charm, and at times with a formality and Johnsonian pedantry that benumb.

To obtain the hand of an object he so highly admired, though but lately his sole wish, appeared now an uncertain blessing, a suspicious good, since the possession of her heart was no longer to be considered her inseparable appendage. His very security of the approbation of Mr and Mrs Tyrold became a source of inquietude; and, secret from them, from her, and from all, he determined to guard his views, till he could find some opportunity of investigating her own unbiased sentiments.

When love stories are written in that jargon, a lingo more repellent than even Captain Aresby's, only the infatuated or those in duty bound will read them once, and nobody twice. Towards the end sundry tragic incidents are contrived and set forth in the wildest emotional language: the prize scene in *Cecilia* is a piece of quiet narrative in comparison. Fanny Burney was always given to repeating situations and exhibitions of character. Here the same scene occurs again and again, with only minor variations. There is less of the melodrama of the Harrel chapters in *Cecilia;* but such as there is in *Camilla* she expands, dwelling on trifles, making endless fuss about nothing. Some of the characters are pleasant enough, if they would not keep on displaying their familiar traits: the good-hearted, optimistic, foolish old baronet, Sir Hugh Tyrold, whose well-intended but misguided impulses lead to so much trouble; the learned, absent-minded tutor, Dr Orkborne, always ruminating on his great work, never alive to what goes on around him or to his responsibilities for his pupils; the self-satisfied bumpkin Dubster, such a nuisance to the young ladies who cannot shake off his attentions; and the coxcomb, Sir Sedley Clarendel, who talks like Mr Meadows. . . . (pp. 171-72)

What secrets of the novelist's art she revealed to Jane Austen it would be venturesome to particularize; but that she stands somewhere between the broad realism of Fielding and the finer portraiture of her successor, and between his rich comedy and her demure irony, is manifest. Naturally, her contemporaries learned from her a good deal, of simpler modes of telling a domestic story, and of other interests than crude sentimentalism. (p. 173)

Ernest A. Baker, ''Fanny Burney,'' in his The History of the English Novel: The Novel of Sentiment and the Gothic Romance, *Vol. 5, H. F. & G. Witherby, 1934, pp. 154-74.*

DAVID CECIL (essay date 1949)

[*Cecil, an important English literary critic who has written extensively on eighteenth- and nineteenth-century authors, is highly acclaimed for his work on the Victorian era. Cecil does not follow any school of criticism; his literary method has been described as appreciative and impressionistic. His essays are characterized by their lucid style, profound understanding, and conscientious scholarship. Cecil defines the goal of his criticism in the preface to his* Early Victorian Novelists. *In order to encourage a love for literature, he endeavors to ''discriminate and, as far as it is in my power, to illuminate the aesthetic aspects of* [these] *novels which can still make them a living delight to readers.'' In the following excerpt, Cecil discusses Burney's importance in literary history as the first author to combine the stylistic methods of Samuel Richardson and Henry Fielding; from Fielding she acquired ''a satirical panorama of society'' in a ''feminine key,'' and from Richardson she gained psychological insight and analysis. Cecil also praises Burney's talents as a storyteller, especially her ability to recreate eighteenth-century society. However, Cecil*] *notes that Burney lacked the intelligence and artistic power to "make her different talents pull together, fuse them in a harmonious whole."*]

Fanny Burney had a typically English talent; she was a bright, light, humorous observer of the outward scene, not a psychological analyst; and, like Fielding, what attracted her about the novel form was the opportunity it provided for giving an entertaining picture of the world about her. In their main lines her novels are of the Fielding type, satirical panoramas of society centering upon an agreeable hero and heroine, and held together rather loosely by a symmetrical plot, culminating in their happy marriage. Perhaps the shortest way to sum up her place in the history of English Letters is to say that she was the first writer to translate the Fielding-type of novel into the feminine key.

This meant altering it considerably. Fielding was an intensely masculine character: Fanny Burney was equally intensely feminine, using the word, it must be owned, not wholly in its best sense. She was an English lady of a recognisable type, lively, civilised, and, within certain limits, extremely observant, but petty, fussy, a slave to convention and far too easily shocked. *Evelina*, we recall, is so horrified at the coarseness of *Love for Love* that she is quite unable to get any pleasure out of its brilliance. This is not at all like Fielding: and such a difference of outlook imposed a very different perspective on her creator's panorama of English society. Inevitably it is much narrower. Fielding is free to move his heroes all over the place: now they are talking to squires, now to gamekeepers, now they are flirting with ladies of title in London boudoirs, now drinking at the tavern with the postboy, now at a ball, now at a gaming-house, now following the hunt, now in Newgate jail. Their sisters—Miss Burney's heroines—were shut off from all these phases of life except those to be observed at the squire's house, the boudoir, and the ball. Even there the scope of her observation was limited by convention. She heard only such parts of the conversation as were thought suitable for a young lady's ears. In compensation, however, she had time to examine in great detail what she was permitted to see—Fielding's young men never observed the texture of social intercourse so minutely—and, under the microscope of her undeviating attention, one aspect of the social scene stood out as it had never stood out to him. . . . By nature, women are observers of those minutiae of manners in which the subtler social distinctions reveal themselves. Fanny Burney seized her opportunity with avidity. In her hands, for the first time in the English novel, social distinctions are the dominant subject of the story. She is the first novelist—though very far from being the last—to make a thorough study of snobbery.

Further, although her plots are constructed within the same convention as Fielding's, their emphasis is different. The Fielding type of plot turns on love and marriage; but Fielding was not particularly interested in the feelings of his hero and heroine for each other. . . . Fielding, like most very masculine men, has no objective interest in observing the process of courtship. Fanny Burney had; and she gives up a great deal of her space to tracing it.

It is in her treatment of this aspect of her theme that she reveals the influence of Richardson. Though she did not see life as a whole dramatically, one drama did interest her: the central drama of any young lady's life—the drama of getting married. Confronted with this spectacle she becomes for the time being a psychologist. How does a young lady feel on first meeting a marriageable young man? How does she discover her growing sentiments towards him? What steps does she take to check or to cherish them? How far by observing his behaviour, governed as it is outwardly by the rules of formal good manners, is she able to interpret the fluctuation of his feelings towards her? In Fanny Burney's novels, for the first time, the process of an ordinary, legitimate, everyday courtship becomes the central theme of an English novel. (pp. 78-81)

However, Miss Burney is no mere imitator of Richardson. A woman herself, she could enter into a girl's feelings much more realistically than he could. And anyway Richardson's mind tended always to pierce beneath a particular drama, to explore the fundamental moral situation that it illustrates. Besides, with him, analysis of character occupies most of the book. With Fanny Burney the courtship which is the subject of analysis is merely the central theme of the action; and the action is, as we have seen, secondary to her picture of society as a whole.

Fanny Burney's range, then, the area of experience in which her creative talent shows itself, is that concerned with respectable society and respectable courtship. Her three chief books all follow the same plan. An inexperienced young girl—Evelina or Cecilia or Camilla—is cast into the social world. We see it through her clear innocent eyes in all its variety. Soon—for Fanny Burney's heroines are usually both lovely and financially eligible—a cloud of suitors surrounds her. By the end of the book she has chosen a husband. In the meantime she has visited London, the country—usually a spa—has moved in good society and bad. By the end, in addition to getting married, she has managed to acquire a knowledge of the world.

It is an excellent subject for a novelist, and in many ways Fanny Burney was well equipped to do it justice. She had a vigorous, varied, vivacious talent that could control and vitalise a great deal of diverse material. Further, she was a natural story-teller: she gets the plot going at once, and sustains it by an unflagging talent for inventing incidents. Even though these are sometimes unconvincing, they do not bore the reader. Always they are related with spirit. And anyway no single one goes on too long. After the long-windedness of many eighteenth-century novels Fanny Burney's comes as a welcome relief. Moreover—it was her outstanding talent—she was extremely observant of the surface of existence. Fanny Burney can bring to life not only her central figures but the whole world they live in. To open *Cecilia* or *Evelina* is to be transported straight into eighteenth-century London, crowded, shrill, diverse, bustling, with its curious blend of elegance and crudeness, of ceremoniousness and brutality. Now we are with the middle classes, gossiping with a merchant in the room behind his shop, or out for an evening's pleasure with a flashy city beau at the shilling ball at Hampstead; now we are moving in the beau monde at a masquerade, or at Ranelagh rubbing shoulders with languid fops and rattle-pated ladies; now crowding up the stairs to the Italian Opera, now at a fashionable concert overhearing the conversation of two frivolous debutantes. . . . (pp. 81-3)

In each place Fanny Burney picks out infallibly the particular detail of scene or speech that brings it alive and stirring before our mental eye. And she relates what she sees with just that touch of slight caricature, that stroke of Hogarthian style, which gives it aesthetic life and quality.

Nor is her observation confined to the general scene. She had a lively gift for drawing individual character. It shows itself in two ways. Her most typical successes are in that tradition of realistic humorous portraiture which she learnt from Fielding and Smollett, and which they in their turn had inherited from the comic drama—"character parts", to use a stage phrase, made up of one or two strongly marked idiosyncrasies, drawn in a convention of slight caricature, and revealing themselves directly in dialogue: Evelina's vulgar cousins, the Branghtons, and their friend Mr. Smith; the fashionables who aroused the contempt of Cecilia, Miss Larolles, Miss Leeson, the absurd Mr. Meadows who thought it dowdy to appear to enjoy anything. Captain Aresby with his conversation all scattered over with French phrases, the miserly Mr. Briggs. Fanny Burney does not present them with subtlety. The Branghtons are always vulgar, Meadows is always bored, Miss Larolles is always chattering like a magpie. All the same, they are not mere conventional types. Their creator had an extremely sharp ear for dialogue, for the particular accent of silliness or pomposity which distinguishes one fool from another. She may represent these figures only in one aspect, but that aspect is drawn straight from life; and life still throbs in it. (pp. 83-4)

Fanny Burney was a woman of the world, though this world was a little narrow. The average second-class female novelist in the nineteenth century, nervously aware of more elements in life than she can get into focus, retains a youthful uncertainty, a jejune vagueness of vision.

Fanny Burney had one more weapon in her armoury, extremely useful for the presentation of the "courtship" element in her stories; an instinctive delicate perception of the processes of feeling in a young girl's heart. Sensitively she can perceive the significance of the small gesture, the almost imperceptible movement indicating the hidden trend of emotion. (pp. 88-9)

Power of story-telling, of character-drawing, ability to trace the process of feeling—with these gifts why should Fanny Burney not have done better than she did? No doubt it is primarily due to a weakness in the essential quality of her talent. The lack of subtlety in her character-drawing, the impression of thinness she makes as compared with the greatest authors, are symptoms of a fundamental lack of mental distinction. Vivacious though her scene may be, it lacks that peculiar individuality of vision which stamps the work of the great creative novelists. So, we feel, might any clever eighteenth-century lady have described the world, had she possessed a turn for writing. Fanny Burney must inevitably have been a minor novelist, for she had not been endowed with a major talent. This, however, is no reason why she should not have been consistently good at her own level; but she is not even that. Even at her best—even in *Cecilia* and *Evelina*—her work is marred by serious faults. For one thing, she could not make her different talents pull together, fuse them in a harmonious whole. This weakness appears conspicuously in her treatment of character. She had, as we have seen, a talent for analysis and a talent for comic presentation: but she never applies both to the same figures. Her comedy characters—the Branghtons and the Larolles—though vividly dramatised, are shallowly conceived. They talk vivaciously and convincingly, but we are never allowed to penetrate beneath that talk to discover the combination of qualities which went to produce their comic exterior. What they are like we see vividly, but not why they were like that. Mrs. Delvile, on the other hand, is diagnosed but not dramatised. A serious type, unsuitable for presentation in a comic convention, she required a far more subtle talent to make her personality vivid on the stage than was needed for the Branghtons. Fanny Burney did not possess such a talent. Her observation was not intelligent enough to enable her to vitalise a

deep complex nature whose demeanour was uncoloured by any obvious idiosyncrasies. The consequence is that, though we understand Mrs. Delvile, we never "see" her.

Fanny Burney's books also suffer from the fact that she does not stay within the limitations of her talent. She could have been pretty certain of success if she had only sought to show her reader what a young lady could see: her view of the social scene, her vision of her own heart and its emotions. But she refused to be bound down in this way; in the Madame Duval and Captain Mirvan episodes in *Evelina* she attempts the brutal masculine farce of Smollett: in the Macartney episodes she has a try at tragic drama involving suicide and despair. Fanny Burney, in fact, frequently commits the novelist's greatest sin; she goes outside her true creative range. It was not altogether her fault. The Fielding formula for novel-writing was not a fully matured instrument; it had not solved the problem of reconciling form with fact. (pp. 90-2)

Where Fielding failed Fanny Burney was not likely to succeed. Her plots are clumsy as well as improbable. To what extraordinary lengths and improbabilities is she forced to go to prevent Cecilia marrying Delvile before the end of the last volume! Moreover, the fact that she imposed a stagey plot on a realistic picture of life involved her in all sorts of material outside her range; and unluckily she was not so powerful and creative an artist as to be able to sweep the reader away so irresistibly that he overlooks her lapses. Indeed, she is hardly an artist at all in the fullest sense of the word. The novel to her was not the expression of an imaginative conception, but merely a means of recording her observations of the world, which she organised into an artificial unity by using any convention of story-writing she found to her hand. Only if she had lived in an age that had presented her ready-made with a thoroughly sound model for a plot, could she have achieved consistently good work. As it was, she was a victim of any influence that crossed her path. *Evelina,* her first book, reveals her at her best and her worst. There is a peculiar charm exhaling from this first fresh sparkling gush of her talent. The Branghton scenes show her comedy at its brightest; Evelina's relation to Orville reveals Fanny Burney's perception at its most sensitive. Both these strains in her story are conceived well within her range.

Alas, this cannot be said of its other elements. The story of the courtship and the picture of the social scene are incongruously combined first of all with an unsuccessful essay in Smollettian farce—the Captain Mirvan-Madame Duval scenes—and secondly with a melodramatic romance in the manner of the novelist of sensibility, featuring a brother saved at the last moment from suicide by the intervention of a hitherto unknown sister, and a father plunged into repentant tears at the sight of his long-lost and also tearful daughter. By the time she wrote *Cecilia,* Fanny Burney had learnt to prune her books of the wildest of these extravagances. There is no more Smollettian farce, and not so much sentimental melodrama. The plot is conceived in a quieter tone. But in its quiet way it is extremely improbable, turning as it does on the idea that two devoted lovers are prevented from marrying because the young man would have to change his surname to something less aristocratic if he did marry. Moreover, plot and character are not so integrated that one seems directly the result of the other. Here Fanny Burney shows conspicuously her inferiority to Jane Austen: she imposes her plot on a picture of life; the action does not arise inevitably from the situation. The Monckton intrigue, for instance, is nothing but a piece of machinery invented to keep the story going.

Furthermore, her prejudiced, enthusiastic, feminine spirit had only escaped from one influence to fall under another. . . . All the same, *Cecilia* is the most sustainedly successful of her books; though it lacks the dewy freshness of *Evelina,* it maintains a steadier level and reveals a deeper insight into character. *Camilla* and *The Wanderer* written some years after show a decline in every respect. The moralism is more aggressive than ever, and the language more stilted; even the comedy is by comparison fatigued and laboured. (pp. 92-5)

No—Fanny Burney was not an artist, she was not even an efficient craftsman; she approached her work without understanding the capacities either of her own talent or of the form which she had chosen. Responsive and undiscriminating, she lay open to any literary influence that came her way; with the consequence that the harmony of her work, even at its best, is jarred by the introduction of incongruous elements.

Yet she deserves an honourable place in the history of English literature. In her first two books, at any rate, the flame of her creative talent still burns bright enough to keep the whole alive and delightful: and her influence on the course of the novel is yet more important than her achievement. She was the first writer to detect how it might be possible to combine the methods of Richardson and Fielding. *Cecilia,* in particular, is both a novel of analysis and a comic picture of social life. Fanny Burney had not a strong enough talent herself to fuse the two with complete success. . . . [However, from] the next century onwards novels were written largely by women and, still more largely, for women. Women have remained passionately interested both in the drama of respectable courtship and the varieties of the social scene. In consequence, a huge proportion of the novels published in the nineteenth century took as their subject a picture of a society seen through the clear, unsophisticated eyes of a young girl freshly launched into it, and grouped round the story of her courtship. Such stories indeed are written still. They are all Fanny Burney's children. (pp. 95-6)

> David Cecil, "Fanny Burney," *in his* Poets and Story-Tellers: A Book of Critical Essays, *Constable & Company, Ltd., 1949, pp. 77-96.*

MIRIAM J. BENKOVITZ   (essay date 1957)

[*Benkovitz provides an analysis of Burney's drama,* Edwy and Elgiva. *Arguing that the work "is a failure in style," Benkovitz faults Burney's penchant for "contrived pathos and over elaboration in language." For additional commentary by Benkovitz, see the essay dated 1959.*]

Edwy and Elgiva is the story of the tragic conflict between Eadwig, the youthful tenth-century king of the West Saxons, and the monks of England with the struggle focused ostensibly on Eadwig's marriage to Aelgifu, daughter of his foster mother. Madame d'Arblay's version of these remote and shadowy events strongly reflects David Hume's in his *History of England.* Her phraseology often suggests familiarity with other authors: Swift, Shakespeare, Rousseau, the sermon writers whose works were always available for the edification of Queen Charlotte's court; but Hume is the single most important influence. Madame d'Arblay follows him in the account of Edwy's marriage, in her characterization of Dunstan, and in attributing to Dunstan as leader of the opposition a place of prominence that may have belonged to Oda, Archbishop of Canterbury. Furthermore the incidents incorporated into the play generally follow those related by Hume and in the same sequence except as in the case of Elgiva's excommunication, where Miss Burney changed the order of incidents for greater dramatic motivation.

The piece takes the form of an emasculated heroic play done, on the whole, in a severely neo-classic manner. *Edwy and Elgiva* does not observe the unities of time and place; but it scrupulously maintains a five act structure with liaison of scenes, it endorses the ancient rule that no more than three speaking characters be on the stage at once, and it has unity of action. Love, in the best heroic tradition, is the preoccupation of both hero and heroine. The mere sight of Edwy seems to compensate for the agony that Elgiva suffers, agony that ranges from excommunication to the apprehension of violent death. Edwy's passion for her is constantly at white heat and apparently always has been, for he reminds her,

> Have I not loved Thee from my earliest dawn?
> My Reason & my Love, like two fair twins
> Grew in thy sight, & fasten'd on thy charms.

So obsessed is he with his love that he ignores his duties as king; even at the celebration of his own coronation, he forsakes his nobles to go to Elgiva. For her, Edwy sacrifices his kingdom, his followers, and eventually his life. Indeed, he dies pointing to her corpse and speaking her name. Certainly the proportions of these emotions were heroic enough to satisfy both Dryden and Chesterfield in their demand for tragedy "rais'd above the Life." (pp. vii-viii)

[The] story she chose was innately dramatic in several of its events. The best known occurred during the coronation in 956 when the young king, having deserted his nobles for Elgiva, was found by Dunstan in her company and forced back to the banquet hall. Another has to do with Elgiva's capture, her torture, and forced removal as an exile to Ireland. Still another involves her unexpected return after torture and disfigurement, with her beauty still glowing, only to be caught up by a tragic death. And there were others: Dunstan's frequent visitors from outer space, the rebellion against Edwy, and the defection of his brother Edgar. Furthermore the choice of heroic drama as the form of her play made Madame d'Arblay's task less exacting, for it reduced the necessity of revealing the essential qualities of human nature through continuous dramatic action. The high born people of her play need not exhibit a tragic flaw in character and a subsequent alteration in action to compensate. If Edwy's love nullified every other ideal, if it led to his rejection of life, he still had no flaws. There were none. There were instead villains in the persons of Dunstan and his followers to provide reasons, external reasons, for the acute pain of Edwy and Elgiva.

But the dramatic form that made Madame d'Arblay's task easier also provided a snare. In the grandiloquence of the heroic she lost the striking quality of her story's events. She had shown in *Evelina* and occasionally in *Cecilia* that she could write sharp, well paced, and characteristic dialogue. In *Edwy and Elgiva,* however, she had an unparalleled opportunity for eloquence. This she took at the expense of valid emotion. The result is artificial pathos. Even the death scene occurs in an atmosphere of self-conscious elegance where the spectacle has more stress than the significance of death. In other words, verbal quality is not organic to the play. That is not saying merely that she wrote poor poetry. She did, of course, in whatever sensibility it is evaluated. Her verses have no poetic patterns, no metaphorical multiplicity. They have no rhythms so metrical or so innate in their language as to belong especially to poetry. That statement about verbal quality as an element of a dramatic organism does say something else: even though heroic drama in its insistence on a fictional environment ''rais'd above the life'' may permit an exaggerated diction or syntactical design, these surely must be equivalent to the quality of some experience however distended beyond every day reality it may be. In the case of *Edwy and Elgiva,* experience, instead of being explored or recreated, is exploited. Feeling degenerates into mere rhetoric, and the quality of feeling is obscured by the language and its arrangement. Thus the failure of *Edwy and Elgiva* is a failure in style.

Nevertheless, the play has an importance of its own in a consideration of Madame d'Arblay's work. She had produced one good novel and one almost good novel. She was constantly busy with a journal and letters that would place her in the front rank of journalists and letter writers in the time of Boswell and Walpole. If this play is a failure, it is also a typical part of her work, for it exhibits a definite tendency toward contrived pathos and over elaboration in language. This tendency developed into so prominent a characteristic in Madame d'Arblay's last works, such as *The Wanderer* and the *Memoirs* of her father, that they are nearly impossible to read. *Edwy and Elgiva* possibly marks the very point of decline in the career of a woman of real literary achievement. (pp. xii-xiv)

> *Miriam J. Benkovitz, in an introduction to* Edwy and Elgiva *by Madame d'Arblay, edited by Miriam J. Benkovitz, Shoe String Press, 1957, pp. vii-xiv.*

MIRIAM BENKOVITZ (essay date 1959)

[*Benkovitz contends that Burney intentionally omitted or distorted much of the material on her father in the* Memoirs of Dr. Burney, *creating a superficial and uneven portrait. The critic questions Burney's motivation and states that her purpose was solely to praise and elevate Dr. Burney; however, in so doing, she neglected all the complexity of character that makes biography compelling. For additional commentary by Benkovitz, see the essay dated 1957.*]

[When] Mme d'Arblay prepared the misnamed *Memoirs of Dr. Burney* she chose to pervert or to eliminate nearly all the material her father had recorded as autobiography.

Even a superficial reading of the *Memoirs* shows that the book is not one of Fanny's more successful writings. Too much has already been said, and in too many quarters, about the constantly increasing ostentation of her language and its bizarre arrangement. That Mme d'Arblay was guilty of pompous, obese language in the *Memoirs* is unquestionable. Furthermore, the book fails to focus on Dr. Burney. That was not due to the author's incompetence. On the contrary, it was a part of her design, for Mme d'Arblay stated in the 'Preface' that she felt privileged as a biographer to enrich her 'plain recital of facts' by adding anecdotes remembered since childhood. She said that while nothing was included that did not belong to Dr. Burney's 'history', the incidents were not 'always rigidly confined to his presence' if letters or diaries or her memory could supply characteristic accounts of notable people. What is more, her accuracy in the use of these materials may be doubtful; J. W. Croker, when he reviewed the *Memoirs* in *The Quarterly Review* for April 1833, thought so [see excerpt above]. (pp. 257-58)

Fanny's notion of fact where Dr. Burney was concerned had all the gloss and lustre that her real devotion to her father, as well as the sentimental ideal of what her devotion ought to be, could give it. The lines which she placed on the title-page of

the *Memoirs,* lines first written with some variation for *Evelina* in 1777, suggest her limited perspective:

> O could my feeble powers thy virtues trace,
> By filial love each fear would be suppress'd;
> The blush of incapacity I'd chace,
> And stand—Recorder of thy worth!—confess'd.

Her material, then, was evaluated wholly by one criterion. As long as it praised or elevated Dr. Burney it was fact.

Unfortunately such an attitude in biography is limiting. It does not admit the insignificant, the contradictory, the whole mysterious complexity of human character. And in the *Memoirs* it ignores the excitement and the continuity of zest and energy that sustained Burney in his shabby existence on the outskirts of the English musical and theatrical world until he could satisfy his own vision of the adventure of life inseparable from the adventures of the intellect. It ignores on the one hand his urbanity, his capacity as a showman which he brought even to his own musical evenings at the house in St. Martin's Street, and it ignores on the other hand his stiff morality and his lack of wisdom where his children, and especially his daughters, were concerned. It disregards his provincial caution in matters of money. And it slights his iridescent interests, his ardent enthusiasm for a confusion of books and papers and people. It neglects the restless vigour that kept him alert and talkative at the end of a long day when, usually at eleven, the Burney family with any guests invited to remain sat down to supper, an excuse, as Fanny said, 'for chatting over baked apples'. Instead Mme d'Arblay's concept of biography produced a smooth, impenetrable façade without the dimensions of human intricacy. And whatever her own opinion, she succeeded only in making her father seem a pedant, a prig, and a snob.

This she did in the first place, so far as she made use of her father's recollections and so far as the few extant scraps allow that use to be judged, through distorting incidents recorded by her father. Here are two crucial examples. The fragment of Burney's account begins in the middle of a sentence:

> . . . I liked were Prior's, [which] I borrowed, and not being rich enough to purchase, I transcribed. And from a borrowed Shakespear, I made extracts of such passages as I was most delighted [with] long before the beauties of Shakespeare were published.
>
> In the height of summer I robbed my sleep of a few hours in order to meet some other boys at a Bowling-green: and used to tie a string to one of my great toes, [which] I put out at the window of my room, by [which] I was waked as soon as it was light, by an apprentice at next door.

In the *Memoirs* this became:

> . . . the ardour of young Burney for improvement was such as to absorb his whole being; and his fear lest a moment of daylight should be profitless, led him to bespeak a labouring boy, who rose with the sun, to awaken him regularly with its dawn. Yet, as he durst not pursue his education at the expense of the repose of his family, he hit upon the ingenious device of tying one end of a ball of packthread round his great toe, and then letting the ball drop, with the other end just within the boy's

reach, from an aperture in the old fashioned casement of his bed-chamber window.

This was no contrivance to dally with his diligence; he could not choose but rise.

(pp. 260-61)

Mme d'Arblay's further attempt to misrepresent her father, and more specifically to conceal the social order to which he belonged all his life, is apparent in her omission from the *Memoirs* of numerous incidents in her father's record. The record of his early life set Burney in a social level and in the profession of musician; the interests of the professional musician permeated almost everything he wrote. He gave an account of the great fire in Cornhill in which 'at least 200 houses were destroyed', but not without adding that among them was 'The Swan Tavern where the famous concert had been held, under the direction of Stanley, the celebrated blind Organist'. Even the confusion that resulted in 'all London and a considerable part of the nation' when the rebellion of 1745 broke out, Burney described hastily, squeezing it between his narrative of musical and theatrical affairs. But his daughter transformed him from a professional to a fashionable dilettante by all but ignoring the musical and theatrical connexions that he had from earliest boyhood. (p. 262)

Mme d'Arblay omitted completely boyhood reminiscences so dear to Dr. Burney that, in one way or another, he referred to them in most of the things he wrote as well as in his autobiography; that is, the theatrical and musical life of Chester. Nowhere in the *Memoirs* did Mme d'Arblay even mention Whiteman, first violin player of Chester; Harry Alcock, who was the next 'first fiddle'; or the state composer and master of Dublin's band, Matthew Dubourg, whom young Burney heard play in Chester. (p. 263)

Furthermore Mme d'Arblay made short work of Dr. Burney's theatrical connexions during his first stay in London. Beyond the statement that 'the young musician had the advantage of setting to music a part of the mask of Alfred' and that this brought him into a friendship with the poet James Thomson, she said nothing about Burney's participation during 1745 in the alteration of *The Masque of Alfred* from a spectacle of two acts 'to a regular tragedy of five acts, with incidental songs, duets and chorus'. (pp. 263-64)

Indeed, so blatant are Mme d'Arblay's omissions and distortions in the *Memoirs* that a comparison with Burney's holograph autobiography brings up at once the question of intention.

Closely related is the quality of style in the *Memoirs,* the extravagant piling of grandiloquence on bombast which far outdistances 'elegant variation'. It is tempting to regard this style as symptomatic of Mme d'Arblay's intention to misrepresent Dr. Burney's character. This question might be examined in the light of all she wrote or, if that is too sweeping, in relation to everything except the journals and letters after 1782, the year *Cecilia* appeared. In any event the conclusion can at best be no more than surmise.

Nor can there be any certainty why Mme d'Arblay presented her father exactly as she did. As a 'memorialist' she is a failure, and her *Memoirs* are reprehensible. Yet an awareness of her achievement as novelist and journalist elicits an apology. In 1828, when she began the *Memoirs*, Mme d'Arblay was seventy-six years old. She had outlived nearly every member of her immediate family. The society to which she belonged had scattered decades earlier, and the world in which she felt at

ease had disappeared. Being a Burney no longer mattered as it once had in fashionable and intellectual London. Perhaps her father's papers with their wealth of memories seduced her into an attempt to recapture the lost splendour of the years with Mrs. Thrale and Dr. Johnson, David Garrick, Sir Joshua Reynolds, and Edmund Burke; even to renew the unhappy years at the court of George III and the hazardous ones in France, by 1828 softened by nostalgia and time. (p. 268)

> *Miriam Benkovitz, "Dr. Burney's Memoirs," in* The Review of English Studies, *n.s Vol. X, No. 39, August, 1959, pp. 257-68.*

HARRISON R. STEEVES (essay date 1965)

[*Steeves provides a detailed discussion of* Evelina, *which he terms "the first novel to examine seriously, through a woman's eyes, the effects of the usages of the time upon the position and the life of a woman." Further, Steeves notes the literary influence of Tobias Smollett in* Evelina *in Burney's comic technique, which he deems ineffective and superfluous. However, Steeves concedes that despite the faulty attempt to imitate Smollett's humor,* Evelina *is a successful epistolary novel. Burney's later works, Steeves argues, fail because their humor is both inappropriate and dated.*]

[*Evelina* has] a lasting importance in the history of English fiction as the first novel to examine seriously, through a woman's eyes, the effects of the usages of the time upon the position and the life of a woman. We say the "first" novel to accomplish this, for while Mrs. Behn, Mrs. Manley, and Mrs. Heywood had written fiction more or less in the interest of their sex, no one would think of calling their fictions serious examinations of the social environment. Yet the significance of *Evelina* as a "first" we can note and dismiss. The story impressed the readers of its time as an engaging portrait of an intelligent young lady capable of appraising and recording a new and exacting social experience. It is still a thoroughly readable novel for much the same reasons.

It is not surprising that *Evelina* has seemed to appeal to women rather than men. For a large part of our interest in fiction depends upon our recognition of faithfulness to life in the particular terms on which we know it. There are aspects of the feminine that a gifted woman writer can not only realize but represent with a surer hand than a mere male. (p. 204)

The bare theme of *Evelina* is simple and romantic—a youngish man, wealthy and well-placed, in love with a charming but at first awkward girl. Awkwardness is, in fact, very much a part of her charm, and it is drawn for us with a delicate humor as well as deep understanding of teen-age self-consciousness. (p. 205)

Many readers have felt that *Evelina* is a concoction, not an artistic composition; that is, that too many incongruous elements have been taken into its plot. But upon this point it is unsafe to try to lay down laws. The central plot is the budding and growth of the affection of Evelina and Orville, which ripens into a somewhat conventional romance. Below the surface of the story is the mystery of Evelina's paternity, relevant because the question of her legitimacy must have a good deal to do with her chances of a brilliant marriage. The denouement is Orville's supplanting of his rivals, acknowledgment of Evelina by her noble father (who *had* married her mother!), and, naturally, the marriage of the lovers. This is a unified and in most respects what might be called a standard plot.

There are two substantial subplots. The first is introduced solely for "comic relief." In it, a Captain Mirvin, a rough naval officer, and son-in-law of the gentlewoman who brings Evelina to London, carries on a running warfare of meaningless quarrels with Madame Duval, Evelina's grandmother, a grossly vulgar one-time English barmaid, long separated from Evelina by her residence in France. It is Madame Duval's intrigues, her impudence, and her utter social impossibility, that account for the fact that after his wife's death Evelina's father has disowned her entire family, and therefore Evelina. Madame Duval's relations on the other side of the family—the Branghtons—are a rather diverting study in social pretensions, and because of their connection with Evelina, although they are not related, they supply a low-comedy accompaniment to Evelina's interest and activity in the life and amusements of the upper classes.

The second subplot introduces halfway through the story an impoverished Scotch poet, Macartney, and toward the very end of the story the girl he is in love with, Miss Belmont. Their link with the action is that Evelina's friendly interest in Macartney's unhappy situation introduces complication into the maturing understanding between Orville and herself. In addition, both Macartney and Miss Belmont are connected incidentally, but not indispensably, with the solving of the problem of Evelina's parentage and position.

If a subplot is to be justified, it should have a recognizable and more or less continuous connection with the central story. The first subplot in *Evelina,* the episodes introducing Madame Duval and Captain Mirvin, is enlivened by the lowest sort of lampooning humor and practical jesting. Without being highbrow, we can safely regard such comic relief as tedious and effete, although many serious novelists and dramatists have condescended to employ it. Comedy, in itself, is another matter, but today most of us would prefer the comedy that gives flavor to a predominantly serious work, to the comedy that takes over intermittently the entire flow of action and introduces a separate set of characters for the purpose. But however it is handled, the important question is whether it is good comedy.

Candor obliges us to say that Fanny Burney's is not. Her comic interludes are obviously modeled upon Smollett, whose "humor" she thought "exhilarating." But Smollett's comedy is rough and masculine; Miss Burney's is rough and feminine. There is a difference.

Since these comic scenes are not particularly successful, they are superfluous; and since they are pinned carelessly to the central theme through the mere fact that Evelina's grandmother is the victim of them, their usefulness for plot is extremely slight. Captain Mirvin himself, introduced only to make life miserable for Madame Duval, is no more than a parasite upon the action. The goings and comings of the Branghtons, however, are more organic; and although Miss Burney's depiction of their smugness and bad manners is often schoolteacherish rather than amusing, they have a redeeming use. For the Branghtons' affected imitation of the ways of high life presents a strong contrast to Evelina's naturalness and modesty. Furthermore, their ideas of public entertainment, including the theaters, the opera, and the amusement gardens, give us some of the best close-up knowledge we have as to the way Londoners of the time actually diverted themselves.

The second subplot—the Macartney-Belmont story—is better integrated with the main story than the Duval-Mirvin-Branghton episodes. For Miss Belmont is the innocent subject of an imposture which has foisted her upon Evelina's father as his legitimate daughter, in Evelina's place. That complication is acceptable, since it accounts for her father's rejection of Evelina's proper claims. Macartney, however, Miss Belmont's admirer and suitor, has no useful part in the story beyond furnishing a means of stalling the latter part of the action (call it "creating suspense," if you prefer) in order to roughen the road to the marital bliss of Evelina and Orville. The fact that Macartney turns out to be the natural son of Evelina's father, and therefore her half-brother, is only another instance of the fact that plot can be stretched and padded by the use of easy coincidence. On the whole, all that can be said for this second subplot is that it fattens the story without adding materially to its interest. *Evelina,* then, is not a unified or sharply focused story, not even by the standards prevailing before Miss Burney wrote. And its lack of unity is especially unsatisfactory because the attached episodes are not in themselves very interesting.

Characterization in *Evelina* is sound when it is serious; crudely disappointing when Miss Burney is tempted to copy Smollett (which she does, in spite of her dictum that "imitation cannot be shunned too sedulously"). After all, Smollett's vulgar characters have redeeming humanity. Captain Mirvin is only a pestiferous clown. Even the serious characters, however, are conceived with only limited originality, and, except for Evelina herself, who is in temper and training Miss Burney's *alter ego,* they are not profoundly studied. One character, however, is not cut from the familiar eighteenth-century pattern. This is Mrs. Selwyn, a society warhorse, strong-minded and strong-willed, who chaperones Evelina to Bristol, and does her capable best to restore sweet concord to the two lovers. (pp. 211-14)

Strong-minded women were only grudgingly appreciated in Evelina's day; so it is not surprising that she prefers the soft virtues to the rational. But Mrs. Selwyn *is* a creation, tough with dandified males, but aware of character and desert, and amusing in the hearty promulgation of her likes and dislikes. I am not sure that there is a single woman character in the fiction of the period who comes as close as she does to the high bearing and salutary irony of Jane Austen's women. (p. 215)

I have stressed these critical shortcomings in critical fairness. *Evelina* is an altogether readable novel in spite of them. In any summary view of Miss Burney's performance we must balance against the errors and omissions that arise from her inexperience, as well as from the still tentative art of the novel, certain achievements that were important in themselves and that add something to the artistic tradition.

In the first place, as an epistolary novel, *Evelina* is relatively free from much of the awkwardness of narrative through the medium of letters. Writers of fiction in this period gave up slowly a form which seemed to lend itself advantageously to the most mediocre, but the disadvantages of which seemed to overbalance its advantages. Miss Burney, however, used it conscientiously and convincingly. Evelina's letters, contrasted with Pamela's, sound like letters, not dissertations. The correspondence is limited to a well-integrated group of interesting characters; it does not exceed our idea of what letters can actually accomplish; and it conveys happily the spirit of the incidents it depicts, and not merely their details.

For readers of later days, Miss Burney's outlook upon the social spectacle of the time is both intelligent and entertaining, though like all her contemporaries, she tends to think in social absolutes. Bourgeois society she observes only in terms of its aspirations or its shortcomings; people are either polite or common. Evelina herself belongs to the first group; Madame Duval and the Branghtons to the second. On the whole, the novel shows acceptance rather than doubt of the urban caste system. And in the course of the heroine's social education we see not only maturing sagacity and *politesse* but a slow and partly unconscious indoctrination in the snootiness that seemed at that time all but inseparable from aristocratic status. The Branghtons are tried by somewhat different standards from those which Evelina brought with her from the country. She discovers, and reiterates, that nice people do not live up two flights of stairs. She assimilates distinctions; Ranelagh has more tone than Vauxhall (something not quite so clear in other novelists); the really best people go to the opera to listen—not to parade and talk; she learns the right streets, and at length can pick out the right people. . . . (pp. 217-18)

Miss Burney's pictures of good society are informing because she knows good society. There is far more effective instruction in manners in *Evelina* than in Richardson's novels, which were written for the explicit purpose. She can also interpret manners; she knows sincerity from pretense; manners can be really good only when they are an ornament to character.

Undeniably, in *Evelina* Miss Burney's youth and her sex worked powerfully in her favor. Her novel owes its freshness and piquancy to her still romantic and hopeful years, its special percipience to the fact that she was instinctively faithful to her sex, and unwilling to portray it equivocally or cynically. If she deals unkindly with a Madame Duval or a Miss Branghton, it is because she feels that they are not only unladylike but unwomanly.

Whether or not we can find pleasure in *Evelina* will depend upon whether we can override natural prejudices against "dated" situations and dialogue. For Miss Burney's art is conventional and uninventive. Could it have been greatly different, since she was not only the child of her age, but the somewhat pampered pupil of upper middle-class intellectuals when the woman intellectual was occupied largely with herself, while her male contemporaries were busy with intrigue, or perhaps with politics?

Miss Burney's three later novels show a steady progress in complacent failure. She is a literary Bourbon, learning nothing and forgetting nothing. And she is unaware that her audience is moving away from her as surely and rapidly as time itself.

Cecilia . . . was published when Miss Burney was thirty. *Evelina* had been begun, at least, in her early youth. *Cecilia* is, therefore, not surprisingly, a maturer work in almost every respect; also in all-round merit the best novel of her writing. It embodies a good theme; it is developed rationally upon a substantial plot; its characters are credible. Here, indeed, Miss Burney's understanding of that unpredictable and unaccountable thing we know as character is penetrating and deep. Cecilia herself would be a meritorious creation for a novelist of a much later date. Her view of herself as a woman and her attitude toward marriage are no longer adolescent—although in fact she is just reaching years of discretion.

These are positive merits. The negative merits of *Cecilia* are, first, that it is for its time fairly free from conventional sentiment, and second, that to an important extent the thought and action of its characters are not confined by the environmental determinism of Fielding and Smollett. That is largely because Miss Burney is an intelligent woman choosing to create and develop intelligent women characters. This latter attainment has large importance in the subsequent history of the novel;

for it is one of the many respects in which Jane Austen learned from the partial and tentative success of her predecessor. Further, the principal characters in *Cecilia* are clearly conceived and vividly projected. In these determinants of quality, Miss Burney has more than carried on the success of *Evelina;* she has shown added maturity and more skilful command of her medium. What is wrong, then, with *Cecilia*?

It is precisely what is wrong with *Evelina:* a fatuous insistence upon long and tiresome comic interludes. In *Cecilia,* however, the comic characters are not the vulgarians that we met in *Evelina;* they are a sort of chorus of men and women of the *haut monde* who are the purveyors of fashionable chitchat and scandal. As background characters in their proper place, and with no greater part in the story than is called for by their choral function, they are not uninteresting. But as a constant space-consuming interruption to an otherwise well-managed narrative, they are intrusive and at length obnoxious.

There is an error here (as in *Evelina*) not only in taste but in judgment. For these characters are meant to ridicule the vacuous ostentation of people of fashion. Not satirically, however, but with false and condescending humor; false because it lacks the grace of feminine humor, in which Miss Burney had some proficiency, and condescending because it is written down to the level of an audience that she realized and understood only imperfectly. That it is not only an aesthetic error but an error in judgment is clear in the fact that these people and their talk annoy and bore the very likeable Cecilia herself (as Duval *et al* did Evelina). How then could Miss Burney expect them to entertain the reader? (pp. 218-19)

Evelina is a good novel weakened by humorous irrelevancy. *Cecilia* is a nearly first-rate novel, *spoiled* by the same defect and unredeemed by the entertaining freshness of *Evelina*.

In her third novel, *Camilla* . . . , we find added evidence that maturity seemed to contribute almost nothing to Miss Burney's literary experience. Its principal is a kind of retake of Evelina, but without Evelina's common sense and feminine resourcefulness. She is also, Miss Burney herself tells us in the conclusion, excessively sentimental. The novel as a whole, however, does not seem over-sentimental except in that it is one of the most lachrymose of the period; and by this time tears seem to have become a literary property rather than a touchstone of feeling.

The theme of the story is a common one: an exalted romantic attachment repeatedly interrupted by temporizing and almost deliberate misunderstanding. But there is more interest here than is generally found in the typical situation; for both the young lovers are made to suffer through the solemn cautions and safe advice of, in the girl's case, a devoted mother, and in the young man's case, a generally sensible tutor who has outlived two unfortunate marital ventures. Suspense, however, depends less upon anything integral for plot than upon the fact that at the moment when a word might clarify an ambiguous situation, a door is likely to open and someone appear with a summons to dinner.

The novel is further weakened by the author's ignorance of, or indifference to, some of the most obvious desiderata of realism. The story abounds in coincidence—even to the hero's at last discovering by the sheerest accident the heroine, ill almost to the point of death, in a mean wayside inn. And what is to be thought of a novel that allows significant knowledge to depend, not once but on four separate occasions, upon the accidental reading of a mislaid confidential letter? The plot itself is only moderately satisfactory, hinging as it does upon some improbable financial distresses which accumulate into a deluge before the plot is resolved by marriage to a young man with plenty of what is needed.

But the fatal defect in *Camilla* is neither structural faults nor sentimental prepossessions. Nor—and this must be mentioned too—dialogue carried on in the most stilted Johnsonese. It is the very fault that we have seen in the two earlier novels— interruption of an interesting continuity by disappointing comedy, unattached to anything essential to the plot.

It would be wrong, however, to dismiss *Camilla* as a novel without redeeming merits, even though its merits are those rather of discreet avoidance than of intelligent invention. In the first place, Miss Burney sees that sentimentalism has had its day. *Evelina* is perfumed with sentimentality; the young Cecilia (like Richardson's Signorina Clementina della Porretta) goes temporarily mad through sentimental distress over the seeming loss of her lover; but Camilla, still the victim of her "sensibility," is given us as an example of emotional extravagance, no longer lovely, but shameful and harmful. That is a gain for the novel.

Further, the "machinery" of sentimental fiction has undergone changes for the better in *Camilla.* Fainting, either spontaneous or tactical, is going out of vogue. There are few lapses from the perpendicular in *Camilla,* I should guess no more than a half a dozen, which, considering the literary temper of the times, is a conservative allowance for a novel of almost half a million words. And formal love-making no longer calls for exalted speech-making. Only one of the galaxy of male lovers in *Camilla* goes through the conventional rigmarole of despair and threatened death—and he is a hypocritical fortune-hunter who implements his passionate appeal with a pistol, and whom someone before the end of the story has the good judgment to shoot.

We are scarcely under obligation to deal largely with Fanny Burney's—or at this point we had better say Madame d'Arblay's—last novel, *The Wanderer.* . . . It appeared after Jane Austen's star had risen; and its reminiscent, even antiquated, social perspective places it under great disadvantage in comparison with Miss Austen's bright modernity. *The Wanderer* was written, Miss Burney tells us, over a period of more than ten years, during most of which she had lived with her husband in Paris, through the aftermath of the French Revolution and part of the Napoleonic wars. But the social history of this bitter and sustained international turmoil scarcely enters into the movement of the story, except as a dim background for the heroine, who has escaped from France in disguise as a half-clothed beggar, to undergo in England a life of slow social torture while she waits for restoration of friends and fortune.

It is far from a consistently interesting novel, but it has interesting points. In social environment, *dramatis personae,* complication, and long stretches of group-characterization for comic (and sometimes social-satiric) effect, it shows family resemblance to its three predecessors. Yet one cannot help feeling that its author has almost pitifully lost touch with living reality. There are the same gallants, the same human cats, the same giddy society girls, the same embarrassments for the heroine, the same noble and incredibly disinterested lover, and the same liberal use of helpful coincidence; but all these are taken over from the stock in trade of fiction at the time *Evelina* was written. (pp. 220-21)

The Wanderer has moved up somewhat with the spirit of the age. Miss Burney had already touched the humanitarian note in *Cecilia's* determination to spend her fortune in aid for the oppressed lower classes, and in *Camilla* there is a brief but revealing glance at the miseries of the English prison system. In *The Wanderer* she becomes a participant in the feminist movement, still in its infancy. Two characters in the novel carry the burden of demonstrating the oppressions that attached to woman's position. The first is the heroine, successively known as L.S., Incognita, Miss Ellis, and Juliet, whose sufferings are traceable mainly to the simple fact that she was born a woman, and therefore subject to all the taboos, disqualifications, and special discomforts and inconveniences of the woman's lot. The other "advanced woman" is a prematurely conceived feminist rebel, a tough-minded female who is not willing to accept her soft feminine destiny, but who carries her independence to the extreme of going all but mad because she cannot, in view of his unwillingness, take entire bodily possession of the subject of her desperate passion—who is, it may be guessed, the lover of the heroine. This new motive shows some contact with what was going on in the world, but it is argued (for it *is* argument) confusedly; it is mixed up with vague generalizations about the ill effects of the French Revolution; and its powerful voice is the half-crazed Elinor, whose character is liberated not only from the stultifying conventions, but from common sense.

In her attitude toward the extremes of sensibility Mme. d'Arblay carries on the mission she assumed in *Camilla*—to show the darker side of emotional thinking and acting, although there are still in profusion the tears of sensibility. Here there is again an advance in maturity, but it is merely responsive to the changed attitude of a later generation.

But it is not fair to expect too much of the good Fanny Burney. The best examples before her of unquestionable *excellence* in the English novel were the novels of Fielding, and Fielding's virtues are entirely masculine. Her outlook and her gifts were a woman's, and in opening up a woman's world (no doubt in the main for women readers) she had to find her own way, confining herself to that world as a woman was then permitted to know it—even though it was her own—under the disadvantages of limited contacts and the continuing overweening and unarguable assumptions of male superiority.

We are told by the literary taxonomists that Miss Burney's novels are "novels of manners." That is by way of saying that she is a close and intelligent observer of characters in a specific social setting. There, undoubtedly, lies her proficiency—in the depiction of *both* characters and social environment. Burney's women, however, are always more human than her men. While the world acknowledges a place for a "man's woman," we find less enthusiasm for a "woman's man." And whether or not it is true that Jane Austen and George Eliot shared the same ineptitude in the characterization of their men, it would be hard to deny that Miss Burney's women are drawn with a sure hand; her men are not. But her novels are always *about* women; men are appendages. All her novels but her last take their titles from her heroines' names, and the "Wanderer" is itself an appellation that Miss Burney applies to her principal. (pp. 222-23)

Miss Burney's heroes are pure-minded and prematurely wise young men who from their earliest appearance are destined to be not only the husbands, but the mentors and spiritual confidants of her heroines throughout a long and unfailingly happy life together. But on the fringes of her action she almost invariably presents her young men as anything from juvenile comics and mischief-makers to deep and devious villains. It may be suspected that this ambiguous attitude betrays a somewhat imperfect acquaintance with young men as they are, or with the society of the time in which they moved. More probably, it may reflect shyness and emotional immaturity. It is worth pondering that Miss Burney married at the age of forty-three, although her heroines are always married off, or at least firmly engaged, in their teens.

If we could extract from these novels their labored and sometimes gross humor, their wearisome interactions of casual scenes in the social panorama, and the author's unhappy propensity to turn high moments into rhetorical melodrama, we should have left a well-managed narrative with satiric incisiveness that sometimes is comparable to Jane Austen's. But a novel can be, after all, little or nothing but what it was meant to be; and the defect of Miss Burney's work is that after the writing of *Evelina* she was never too sure of her intentions. As an artist, she understood her talents only imperfectly; she took herself too seriously—that is painfully evident in the fatuous introduction to *The Wanderer;* she no doubt over-valued mere labor; and perhaps she over-priced her really substantial prestige as a woman of the upper intellectual and social world.

Yet there is *Evelina*—not pure gold, but certainly not to be forgotten. (pp. 224-25)

> Harrison R. Steeves, "'A Young Lady's Entrance into the World': Frances Burney," in his Before Jane Austen: The Shaping of the English Novel in the Eighteenth Century, Holt, Rinehart and Winston, 1965, pp. 204-25.

ROSE MARIE CUTTING (essay date 1975)

[*In the following feminist assessment, Cutting offers a defense of Burney's last and most disparaged novel,* The Wanderer. *The critic contends that despite the novel's artistic weaknesses—poor plot, weak characterization, and ineffective dialogue—it is historically significant as an early portrait of a woman's struggle for self-sufficiency. Cutting probes the plight of women in Western culture and notes that particularly in* The Wanderer, *women torment each other; according to Cutting, the novel "effectively dramatizes the historic poverty of women."*]

The *Wanderer* has many weaknesses: an improbable plot; faulty characterization; monotonous repetition; pompous, even bombastic diction; a convoluted syntax intended to be elegant but thwarting comprehension and enjoyment. Nevertheless, these sins do not destroy the importance of the book. As its subtitle indicates, the theme of the novel is "female difficulties." In a general sense, all of Fanny Burney's novels depict the "female difficulties" of the heroine. But her last novel departs from the rest because it examines problems of a more elementary nature. In fact, the *Wanderer* analyzes the mental, economic and social dependence of women, and predicts their struggle toward independence. To those who will heed her message, Fanny Burney's dramatization of everywoman in a cruel world provides some startling glimpses into the hell reserved for women in Western culture. (p. 47)

[The] *Wanderer* presents one of the earliest women in fiction to demand a measure of self-sufficiency. Elinor Joddrell preaches the liberal ideas of the French Revolution: the customs, traditions and institutions that police man's behavior are "arbitrary" or man-made rather than "natural"; when a man rec-

ognizes his constraints as self-inflicted, he can take an active stand against them and thus effect his own liberation.

Elinor proudly and continually proclaims her own liberation. Unlike most women who willingly submit to their subservient state, she possesses an "independent spirit," a "liberated mind," a "free soul." She declares her intention of casting off "the trammels of unmeaning custom," of "acting" and "thinking" for herself.

Viewing herself as "the champion of her sex," Elinor hopes to teach a new freedom to the women of England, "tame animals of custom . . . who always act by rule," cowards who let the fear that they might "offend or alarm the men" prevent them from demanding the independence that is their right. By submitting to the limitations imposed upon them, women become their own worst enemies. Hence Elinor preaches liberation through mental revolution. Women must first ask themselves some elementary questions: Do they truly want to accept a cultural role in which all actions and even all thoughts are "prescribed by rule" and "limited to what has been done before"? Do they really believe that the "narrow . . . sphere" conventionally allotted to them is all they deserve or all they want?

"Nature" guarantees the "rights of women," according to Elinor, and no one can truly refute them or deny the natural "equality" of the sexes. The existing inequities result from man-made restrictions; as Elinor tells the "Wanderer" (Juliet Granville), men "render us insufficient" and "then speak of us as if we were so born." Elinor harangues at some length on the specific ways in which the growth of women is stunted. The laws and institutions of society are set up to restrict the behavior of women and keep them in an inferior position. Men "dare not" allow women the same education or the same "opportunities for distinction" that they grant to themselves. Men unfairly judge women by a standard they would never apply to their own sex, disparaging the mental capacity of women because of the relative weakness of their bodies. . . . (pp. 47-8)

The *Wanderer* was far ahead of its time in posing the following question: Does society provide sufficient resources and opportunities so that women can support themselves? Juliet's struggle for economic independence forms the major part of the novel. Her identity as the daughter of an English aristocrat is not established until the end of the novel. Moreover, forced into an illegal marriage with a brutal officer of the French Revolution, Juliet conceals her true name to prevent this man from finding her and, therefore, cannot receive help from friends or relatives. (Her pseudonym, "Ellis," lacks the romantic and aristocratic connotations of "Juliet Granville": moreover, it suggests the feminine pronoun in French and hence is appropriate for a woman, stripped of the protection of family and social position, who is reduced to the condition of "everywoman.") Although Juliet is pursued by a mysterious stranger, the *Wanderer* is not a gothic romance, providing only thrills and terror. Juliet differs from Anne Radcliffe's heroines (and indeed from the heroines of Fanny Burney's previous novels) by engaging in the practical business of earning a living.

At the end of the novel, of course, Juliet comes into her inheritance and marries the hero. Fanny Burney certainly did not preach the gospel of salvation through a job to women. Yet Juliet's fight for "self-dependence" lasts through five volumes, and the "motto" of her story is clearly formulated: human beings "whether *female* or male, [must] learn to suffice to themselves.'' The *Wanderer* thus anticipates the demands of modern feminists with regard to a key issue. For Fanny Burney shows that the ability to earn a living wage is as vital for women as for men.

Juliet holds a series of jobs selected to cover the occupations open to women in her society—including women of the upper and lower classes, women of talent and education and women with a minimum of ability and training. She soon learns ''her helplessness to resist any species of indignity, while accepting an unearned asylum'' and hence works determinedly towards self-sufficiency. (pp. 50-1)

Predictably, a career in the arts does not pay off in providing Juliet with a reliable means of support, and so she willingly subjects herself to a different form of social humiliation. Seeking out occupations normally filled only by women of the lower classes, she works as a seamstress (first, independently, then for a milliner, and next in the shop of a mantua maker) and also serves as a shopkeeper. Such occupations naturally do not resolve Juliet's difficulties. As a seamstress, Juliet has to turn out goods with the regularity of a machine, and yet must constantly worry about the possibility that new orders will not come in or that customers will not pay their bills for completed work. (p. 52)

Juliet's efforts at supporting herself constitute a ''vanity of female wishes.'' Hence she studies women's occupations with an interest that reflects her creator's concern over the ''dearth of useful resources [which] was a principal cause in adversity of Female Difficulties.'' (pp. 52-3)

Most women in Fanny Burney's society—whether from the country, village or city—passed their lives as servants or as wives, or filled both of these roles. Juliet never sinks into a cook or a housemaid, and her marriage to Harleigh comes as the appropriate conclusion to the novel. Nevertheless, Fanny Burney does not slight the most common feminine occupations, for she devotes an entire volume to Juliet's experiences as a hired companion—a job that combines the domestic and personal services usually rendered by servants and by wives.

Mrs. Ireton often provides ''insulting'' descriptions of the behavior she expects from the woman she refers to as her ''humble companion.'' She demands a companion ''who would never think of taking such a liberty as to give her own opinion; but who would do, as she ought, with respect and submission.'' To ''do as she ought,'' of course, means to exist for the purpose of supplying services to Mrs. Ireton. Juliet loses her right to exist as a separate individual; all of her time belongs to her employer; her own needs and wishes are illegitimate. (p. 53)

A position as a ''humble companion'' does not bring economic security—let alone economic independence. Like most women throughout history, Juliet is not allowed to earn anything she can call her own. She remains totally dependent upon the fickle will of her employer, who takes a malicious joy in reminding Juliet that the room in which she sleeps, the clothes she wears, even the food she eats all actually belong to her employer. Moreover, although Juliet works hard to provide a fair exchange of labor for her support and inwardly believes that her services are truly ''useful,'' she is openly scorned as a ''toadeater'' and a ''parasite'' by Mrs. Ireton's relatives and other servants.

Juliet's quest for self-sufficiency ironically leads her into an occupation calculated to keep her in a state of dependency and even of physical and moral slavery. Thus her plight functions

as an appropriate metaphor for the fate of most women throughout history. Whether they lived as servants or as wives, true freedom was impossible for women. And, like Juliet, they seldom received respect or a just economic recompense for the vital domestic services they performed. . . .

Mrs. Ireton's name is a key to her disposition. Well skilled in ''the art of ingeniously tormenting,'' she delights in insulting and humiliating Juliet, keeping up a constant string of verbal attacks when the two are alone. For instance, she maliciously compliments Juliet on her skill in applying the ''red and white'' and sarcastically asks for instructions in Juliet's ''favorite art of face-daubing.'' (p. 54)

On first glance, of course, Juliet's sufferings seem atypical. Hopefully, most women were lucky enough to escape a mistress or a husband as cruel as Mrs. Ireton. But, as with so much that seems strained in the novel, the savagery that Juliet encounters is a good key to the position of women in Western culture. In fact, such savagery also pervades Fanny Burney's other novels. (pp. 54-5)

The people who persecute Juliet change and the torments vary, but she meets so much cruelty throughout the novel that her experiences take on the repetitious, irrational and extreme quality of a nightmare. As in a nightmare, she is trapped, cannot find a way out, and cannot make any progress, for each new situation brings more abuse and does not result in the independence she struggles to achieve. Realistically, of course, Juliet cannot solve her problems. She has no means of supporting herself and hence cannot win the autonomy that would free her from the danger of maltreatment.

Juliet's relationship with Mrs. Ireton is a case in point. More than once, she is driven to defying her irascible mistress and even quitting her job. But she reluctantly accepts Mrs. Ireton's ''protection'' when the latter wants her back again. All other means of support have failed for Juliet; she is penniless and frightened of the rakes who are pursuing her. The helplessness of women because of their historic poverty and limited opportunities for economic independence is forcibly depicted in Juliet's sufferings.

Women are the chief victims and the chief oppressors in Fanny Burney's cruel world. Like so many who suffer from tyranny, they vent their frustrations on anyone weaker than they are—and the weak are usually women. In addition to the heroine, there are a few ''good'' women in the *Wanderer,* blandly conventional and impossibly virtuous characters. But the ''three furies''—female ogres who relentlessly persecute the heroine—are powerfully drawn. Mrs. Ireton naturally belongs to this group, as does Elinor Joddrel's aunt, Mrs. Maple. Juliet also lives for a time with the latter, who proves herself as consistently brutal as Mrs. Ireton. If Juliet walks into a room without being summoned, Mrs. Maple humiliates her by protesting against such effrontery. When Juliet must pick up a letter at the post office, Mrs. Maple tells her to walk the eight miles (in the middle of December) rather than expect the use of the coach. To her sorrow, Juliet discovers that Mrs. Howell, who completes the unholy trinity, fully equals the other ''furies'' in vindictiveness. This genteel lady is so mortified by having mistaken an unknown ''wanderer'' for a woman of consequence that she twice tries to have Juliet put into jail.

Most of the men whom Juliet meets hardly treat her more humanely than the women. Harleigh, of couse, is consistently courteous and respectful. Otherwise, the relationship between men and women is a virtual state of war. Even men with generally admirable characters—such as the young nobleman who is later revealed as Juliet's half-brother—believe their manhood demands that they carry on the war by attempting to seduce Juliet. And Juliet is continually harried by rakes who devote their lives to preying on unprotected women. (pp. 55-6)

But the sex war is only one aspect—and the least original one—of the cruel world in Fanny Burney's novels. Unlike the male novelists who preceded her, Fanny Burney focuses on the means by which society warped women. The women Juliet meets are moral cowards or they are as sadistic and brutal as the "three furies."

The reason for Mrs. Ireton's discontent is explored at length. She is a classic example of a woman with nothing to live for; her desperate efforts to find satisfaction result in elaborate methods of "killing time." (p. 57)

Mrs. Ireton's sadism (her desire to direct the spite that inevitably results from her own sense of futility against anyone weak enough to become her victim) provides a perfect example of Erich Fromm's contention that destructiveness—whether directed against the self or against others—results from "unlived life."

Most women treat Juliet harshly out of fear rather than malice. As might be expected, Elinor Joddrell is the best spokeswoman for the pressures that turned women into frightened conformists and hypocrites. (pp. 57-8)

The *Wanderer* is a powerful study in paranoia. The reader shares Juliet's agony as she becomes acutely aware of the suspicion directed against her, a suspicion which was likely to be turned against any woman but was intensified by Juliet's anomalous position. Wherever she goes and whatever she does, Juliet is surrounded by spies. Most of the women and many of the men in the novel seem to be leagued against her, eagerly waiting for violations of decorum or of morality. Whenever a rake has maneuvered her into a situation that looks compromising, whenever Harleigh or a friendly male seek an innocent interview with her, she is observed by a scandalmonger determined to believe her guilty.

In a "misery of helplessness," Juliet laments over the fact that women are unfairly judged by appearances and constantly exposed to calumny. And Juliet learns the sad result of this constant suspicion when she is branded a moral leper, an outcast from all respectable society, because she is suspected of being an adventuress. Henceforth women who value their reputations can have nothing to do with her, and men believe they have a license to seduce her. It is no wonder that women become moral cowards rather than suffer such a punishment for overstepping the proscriptions imposed upon them.

The corruption starts at an early age. Elinor Joddrell's fourteen-year-old sister befriends Juliet when the latter lives with Mrs. Maple and gives Selina music lessons. Although she is good-natured and free of malice, Selina lacks the courage to publicly acknowledge her feelings towards a woman who is living as a dependent in her aunt's house. Repeatedly, when other people are present, Selina wounds her friend by turning away from Juliet as though she had never seen her before.

Even before Juliet becomes a pariah, her uncertain social status makes it difficult for women to treat her with any degree of humanity. Like Selina, other women seldom are courageous enough to admit they know Juliet. For instance, when Juliet goes to play her harp at a social gathering, no woman dares to acknowledge her presence. (pp. 58-9)

After the suspicious circumstances of her arrival in England become known, Juliet is ostracized so completely that she does indeed become an "invisible woman." Even when she attends church, no other woman has the fortitude to acknowledge an acquaintance with her. One Sunday, Juliet stands in the vestibule of the church, looking helplessly out at the torrent of rain that has trapped her there. The women who previously had befriended her, including Selina, Juliet's former pupils, and their mothers, walk past as though she does not exist. (p. 59)

Quite justifiably, Juliet once complains to Elinor about the "severe DIFFICULTIES OF A FEMALE, who without fortune or protection, had her way to make in the world." Elinor replies by scornfully telling Juliet to rebel against society as she had done:

> Debility and folly! Put aside your prejudices
> and forget that you are a dawdling woman, to
> remember that you are an active human being,
> and your FEMALE DIFFICULTIES will van-
> ish into the vapour of which they are formed.
> Misery has taught me to conquer mine! and I
> am now as ready to defy the world, as the world
> can be ready to hold me up to ridicule.

Elinor, of course, ignores the fact that few women would be willing to become social outcasts, no matter how much they might inwardly rebel. Instead, they were so intimidated by the necessity of presenting a decorous appearance to a hostile world, that they almost inevitably succumbed to moral cowardice.

Moreover, Juliet's specific complaint—that women had no means of earning a living when they needed to—was a realistic problem that no amount of self-assertion could overcome. Elinor's independence was possible only because of her private fortune. Women had to inherit money or be rescued from poverty and misery by men willing to marry them. Juliet, who struggled so valiantly at so many different occupations, knew from experience "the difficulty of obtaining employment, the irregularity of pay, the dread of want," and hence had valid reason for asking: "what is freedom but a name, for those who have not an hour at command from the subjection of fearful penury and distress?" The *Wanderer* effectively dramatizes the historic poverty of women, and the dependency which results from this poverty. Since women have not yet freed themselves from the economic, social, and mental bondage that constitute the history of their sex, Fanny Burney's last novel still has much to say to the modern reader about "female difficulties." (pp. 59-60)

Rose Marie Cutting, "A Wreath for Fanny Burney's Last Novel," in Illinois Quarterly, *Vol. 37, No. 3, Spring, 1975, pp. 45-64.*

MARGARET DRABBLE (essay date 1976)

[*Drabble is a noted modern English novelist. In the following excerpt, she favorably appraises Burney's journals as the work of "an ordinary woman, with an extraordinary gift."*]

How hard it is to make up one's mind about Miss Burney. Not because she is, as a character, elusive: on the contrary, she reveals all, she leaps to life in her letters, she chatters away over the centuries as though confident that we would be (as we on the whole are) interested in her son's colds, her social engagements, her impressions of foreigners both famous and obscure. It is easy enough to imagine her; the problem lies, as with an old but often irritating friend, in deciding what one really feels about her. She is so pretty, so trivial, so timid, so ambiguous about fame and society, so bourgeois, so lacking in moral independence, even, occasionally, so vulgar; and yet, just as one has decided that she represents all that was to be most deadening for Victorian womanhood, she will reveal herself as courageous, strong, daring. And, of course, she is always entertaining, when she tries to be so. She is an inspired gossip, an acute observer of the smallest details of dress and manners. Her account of the French social kiss is as amusing today as it was when she wrote it, in 1802, and could well be studied by those who, like her, have to contend with the difference between bourgeois and aristocratic manners, between the English and the French. The mouths of the two meeting persons, she tells us, ''should advance merely to retreat, and that then each party should present the right cheek, for the sole purpose of drawing it hastily away, that each may present the left, which, with the same rapidity, approaches only to retire.'' Her account of her initiation into this practice, and of her occasional mistakes, is the stuff of social comedy and social history.

Not all the letters in [*The Journals and Letters of Fanny Burney*] are equally interesting. . . . Fanny Burney did not object to writing different accounts of the same incident to different friends, so we have to listen several times to the poor woman's anxiety over the dilemma presented by the attentions of the notorious Mme de Stael. We also have to pay a great deal of thought to her son Alex's worms. Volume five opens in 1801, with Fanny married and a mother, and her husband M. d'Arblay about to set off for France to sort out his inheritance: Volume six ends ten years later, with Fanny's return to England, after an unexpectedly prolonged absence, spent largely in Paris itself. So, inevitably, the chief interest of these volumes lies in their portrait of post-revolutionary France, of Napoleon, of the lives of former aristocrats and landowners. The letters dealing with the delayed departures of both the d'Arblays are less than gripping, but as soon as Fanny sets sail to follow her husband the story comes to life.

She is an excellent narrator, and does not waste good material: the horrors of sea sickness, the fatigue of travelling with small children, the alarms of customs officials, the surprise at finding the French at Calais are neither swarthy gipsies nor bloody monsters, as she admits she had anticipated—all this is recounted to her father in vivid detail. And she continues to write home, during her ten years' stay, describing old friends rediscovered, new friends, ceremonies, parties, dresses, illnesses. Her chief interest is not politics, but people, and their public behaviour. Although married to a Frenchman, and acquainted in England with many French emigrés, she starts off with the common English belief that French women are likely to wear too little clothing, and to behave in an immoral manner. We see her relief as she builds up a little circle of thoroughly respectable proper friends, of sound morals.

And yet there is something in her that hankers after the dashing, the improper. She appreciates the wit of French conversation, so much more entertaining and intelligent than most that she had to endure during her five years' imprisonment at court in England: she writes with admiration of Caroline Murat's ''Cleopatra style'' beauty and her ''very pleasure-loving eyes'', and she evidently finds it painful to obey propriety and break off her connection with Mme de Stael, of whose charm, vivacity and good humour she had written so warmly on their first meeting in England. . . .

It is such a waste, to see Fanny Burney draw back from some of the aspects of life that fascinated her, and to note her continuing obsequious letters to Miss Planta and the English royal family. If Fanny had not spent five gruelling years at court holding gloves and emptying snuff boxes, if England had got rid of its monarchy in a revolution, if Fanny had been ten years younger when she went to Paris . . . but there she was, a woman in her forties, with a small and delicate boy, born late, a woman who enjoyed her little suburban house in Passy, who was more interested in the curious French habit of living up lots of flights of stairs, in the curious French passion for over-showy military uniforms, than she was in the rights of women. She was what she was. It is idle, perhaps, to speculate on the influence she might have had, had her life been slightly different.

Morally timid she was, but a reader of these volumes must end with a deep admiration for her physical courage. Her two voyages, to Calais in 1802, and home from Dunkirk in 1812, were undertaken alone, without her husband's support, in a dangerous political climate, and bad weather, and she coped with them admirably. But the most striking passage she ever wrote is the description of the mastectomy that she endured in 1811, without anaesthetics, fully conscious, her face covered with a cambric handkerchief. She had suffered for some years from a painful lump in the breast, and finally the distinguished army surgeon, Dr Larrey, told her he would have to operate. Her account of his behaviour towards her, her emotions as the ordeal approached, her faintness at the sight of the ''immense quantity of bandages, compresses, spunges, lint,'' and finally of her actual sensations during the surgery, is enough to make one thank God that one was born in the twentieth century. If she could have felt it proper to use this material in fiction, what a novel she might have written. As it is, her gift for noting the telling detail of tone, expression, for remembering dialogue, makes this description as vivid as a piece of film.

There is no prudery or squeamishness here, but a bravery and common sense all the more striking for its historical context. Fanny Burney certainly knew how to rise to an emergency. . . . Finally, one cannot help but like the woman, even though she is suburban in spirit, even though she refers to her husband, Mrs. Elton style, as her *caro sposo*, even though she often, like a true female gossip, praises a friend's character at the expense of her face (who would like to be called highly accomplished, highly gifted, and very ugly?) One likes her because she is so interesting, and so ordinary at the same time.

An ordinary woman, with an extraordinary gift.

> *Margaret Drabble, ''Travels of a Housewife,'' in*
> The Spectator, *Vol. 236, No. 7704, February 21,*
> *1976, p. 20.*

PATRICIA MEYER SPACKS   (essay date 1976)

[*An American essayist, biographer, and educator, Spacks has written extensively on eighteenth-century poetry. In the following excerpt, Spacks offers a feminist interpretation in which she analyzes the autobiographical nature of Burney's novels and delineates the pattern of personal experiences reflected in the structural composition of her works. According to Spacks, Burney's journals and letters reveal her psychological perception and understanding of women. This insight, Spacks contends, is evident in Burney's heroines, particularly in their search for self-discovery. Spacks finds* The Wanderer *remarkable from a historical viewpoint, if not an artistic one. She proposes that Burney's novels offer a truer self-portrait than her diaries because the fictional form allowed her greater freedom in expressing her own thwarted de-*

sires. Finally, Spacks stresses that Burney's novels are important for revealing "the dynamics of fear in a woman's experience."]

As novelist and as writer about herself, Fanny Burney takes a position in every respect opposed to Laurence Sterne. Committed to propriety as he to its opposite, apparently unaware of the formal possibilities or implications of her conventional plots, feeling that the most important question about novels concerned their moral influence, she reminds the reader that Tristram Shandy's conviction of the impossibilities of art does not represent the only conceivable viewpoint. The moral and psychological organization of her fiction and her diaries insists on the order of life itself. Keeping an intermittent record of herself for more than seventy years, she reveals not the chaos of experience but the reiteration of pattern. The rational structure of her prose helps her to assert the significant structure of her life.

A woman's vision? It seems important to say so. *Tristram Shandy* is organized to reveal the pervasiveness of male fear, demonstrating in form and in substance how the terror of impotence spreads through every endeavor. The entire mass of Fanny Burney's writing forms itself as centrally in relation to female fear—not of the absence of power but of failure of goodness and consequent loss of love. Tristram's fears reduce his life to disorder; Miss Burney's (and her heroines') have ordering force, defending against chaotic possibility.

Unique in her century in having left to posterity both a group of novels and the rich private record of voluminous letters and diaries, Miss Burney also provides through her published work a basis for investigating the relationship between avowedly autobiographical and purportedly fictional accounts of experience. . . . Both demonstrate the shaping of experience by a special sensibility, the artistry of pattern almost as manifest in letters and journals as in fiction. The pattern of Fanny Burney's life as she perceives and interprets it resembles the structures that shape her fictions, both converting psychological defense into literary tactics. (pp. 158-59)

[The diary demonstrates] the literary and personal virtues with which their author has always been credited: her sharp ear for speech rhythms, her eye for social detail, her sensitivity to manners as an index of moral quality, her devotion to her family, and her extreme propriety. The interpretative structure that forms her account of her life's happenings depends upon strategies of concealment. The idea of virtue provided Fanny Burney—as it has many women—a first line of defense. Goodness has always been a source of female force, a guard against enemies without and within. Miss Burney, hiding behind her impeccable morality, protects her inner life. (p. 159)

Reading the mass of the journals, one gradually realizes the energy of the decorous woman's verbal self-presentation, structured by her determination to be perceived as good, and her fear of negative judgment. The action of Fanny Burney's vast collections of journals and letters, like that of most women's writing in her century, derives from her attempt to defend—not to discover, define, or assert—the self. Both her choices and her ways of describing them testify to her productive and self-protective solution to unescapable problems of women's existence. That solution provides psychic space for her imaginative life, thus making her literary career possible, and also shapes the operations of her imagination. (pp. 160-61)

To define the strengths and weaknesses of Fanny Burney's fictional achievement . . . may lead at least to speculation about the reasons for her superiority to her female contemporaries.

Her strengths are more far-reaching than has been generally recognized. *Evelina* has been praised as though it consisted only of a collection of skillful character sketches. . . . It has been admired ever since its own time for the accuracy of its social detail and conversation. But it also manifests a high level of psychological insight closely related to the self-knowledge that emerges from even the youthful diaries. Fanny Burney may write better fiction than other women of her era partly because she has come to terms more fully than they with the realities of the female condition. (p. 176)

Self-discovery of a woman in hiding constitutes the subject of the novels, as of the journals. Fanny Burney's heroines hide specifically because they are women, driven to concealments in order to maintain their goodness. They do not, except in brief moments, openly resent their fates. Yet the tension suggested by a formulation that asserts the simultaneity of discovery and hiding pervades Miss Burney's fiction. She constructs elaborate happenings to articulate conflict, locate happiness, and apportion blame. Her transformations of life in fiction, while insisting on the essential order of experience, also hint their author's awareness of the psychic costs of such affirmation. Anxiety dominates the Burney novels, despite their happy endings. However minute its pretexts—and often they seem trivial indeed—its weight is real, deeply experienced by the central characters and, to a surprising extent, shared even by readers who can readily dismiss its nominal causes. In fact, the causes lie deep; the heroines suffer profound conflicts.

Evelina, of the four heroines, has the fewest and most trivial real problems. Like Cecilia and Juliet in *The Wanderer* she is in effect an orphan (her father, though alive, has refused to acknowledge her), but she has a benevolent guardian and devoted friends. (pp. 176-77)

The difficulties the novel nominally concerns itself with, according to its writer's direct assertion, derive mainly from Evelina's social inexperience. Nothing happens except "little incidents," but virtue, feeling, and understanding finally receive their just reward, the heroine's "conspicuous beauty" providing the means to this appropriate end. More obviously than stories such as Jane Barker's tale of a merman and his paramour, this tale represents a familiar female fantasy: a potent vision of virtue recognized and rewarded despite its incidental errors—specifically, in this instance, Fanny Burney's own kind of virtue. But the novel has a level of realism lacking in many other fictions by female writers. It concerns itself with a young woman's entrance into a genuinely imagined social world, dominated, like Fanny Burney's own, by forms and manners, and very real in its pressures, cruelties, and arbitrary benignities. (p. 177)

Direct comments in the novel about the world emphasize its danger, its superficiality and hypocrisy, and its sinister power. The world threatens individual identity. Mr. Villars, living in retirement, fears its effects on Evelina. He also recognizes the world's inescapable power. Only the frivolous wholeheartedly accept worldly values, but no one escapes them. The choices for women consist mainly of options to refuse or to accept rather than possibilities to act. Evelina acts meaningfully and independently once, when—in an improbable and overwritten scene—she snatches the pistols from a suicidal young man. She then faints. . . . Evelina makes quite explicit her desire (which she shares with her creator) to find a lover or husband to fill the same role as father or guardian. She assumes the utter propriety of remaining as much as possible a child: ignorant, innocent, fearful, and irresponsible.

Proving her sagacity, her lover values her for precisely these qualities. Like Evelina's guardian, whom in many respects he resembles, he believes the world is opposed to rationality and values the woman who knows nothing of it. Shortly before he proposes, he summarizes Evelina's character for a group of his fashionable friends, explaining the occasional "strange" elements in her behavior as effects "of inexperience, timidity, and a retiring education," praising her as "informed, sensible, and intelligent," and glorifying "her modest worth, and fearful excellence"... . Fearfulness has become an index of goodness. (pp. 178-79)

But *Evelina* also contains one minor woman character who does not refrain: the redoubtable Mrs. Selwyn. "She is extremely clever; her understanding, indeed, may be called *masculine;* but, unfortunately, her manners deserve the same epithet; for, in studying to acquire the knowledge of the other sex, she has lost all the softness of her own"... . No one likes Mrs. Selwyn, and since a woman's fate in the world depends largely on the degree to which she is liked, this fact alone presumably urges negative judgment of a female who feels entitled on the basis of her strong mind to act aggressively in company. She alone, for instance, feels free to remark devastatingly (and accurately) on masculine idiocy in the presence of its perpetrators... . The novelist thus suggests that she is aware, although she has not yet fully acknowledged it, that Evelina's choices, proper as they are, do not exhaust the tempting possibilities for intelligent women.

Evelina chooses dependency and fear, a choice no less significant for being thrust upon her. It amounts to the declaration of the identity that achieves her social and economic security. The identity she cares about most is given her from without by husband and father. The problem in achieving her woman's identity differs from its male equivalent, from Tom Jones's search for his identity, for example. Her education in society teaches her not to relinquish but to use her innocence and her fears. (pp. 179-80)

But the dominant dream of female withdrawal that preserves individual integrity, protects private feeling, and attracts the perfect lover suggests more clearly than any utterance in her diary the young author's longings and hopes. *Evelina,* like the letters and journals, concentrates on a woman's attempt to preserve and defend herself with the few obvious resources at her disposal. The success of that attempt reaffirms Fanny Burney's personal decisions. (p. 180)

As autobiography, in other words, this novel reveals more than the diaries. Allowing Miss Burney to articulate repressed aspects of her personality, it reminds us of the degree to which her constant professions of fear and her insistent withdrawals represent not true timidity but a socially acceptable device of self-protection. The writing and publishing of novels—a public act—also involves self-protection; no one holds the author personally responsible for Captain Mirvan's sadism or Mrs. Selwyn's ferocious commentary. Through imagining such sadism and such commentary, she permits herself the impermissible. She both declares the high value of her own mode of dealing with the world and compensates for the restrictions of her propriety.

After *Evelina* came *Cecilia,* insistently moral, carefully controlled, much too long, and containing some disturbing implications. The power of wealth gives its heroine initial security; her experience teaches her insecurity. Altogether a more sinister fable than *Evelina,* despite its insistent morality, *Cecilia*

acknowledges more openly the high psychic cost of female compliance. The permeating sense of anxiety here derives largely from the increasingly explicit recognition of the difficulties and inherent limitations of women's social position. Cecilia has wealth, intelligence, beauty, adequate social status, and the nominal freedom to do whatever she wants. In fact, as she discovers, she possesses all the concomitants, but no real freedom and no power. She must use her energies for self-suppression. . . . Never does she question—any more than Evelina questions—the necessity to be good. Like Evelina, she is rewarded by marriage. But the diminishment she undergoes in order to achieve it and the torments she endures along the way suggest a dark view of women's fate.

The heroine of *Camilla* suffers yet greater diminishment. Like Evelina, Camilla is inexperienced, powerless, and poor; like Evelina, she learns that she must preserve inexperience, use powerlessness, and emphasize her dependency. Unlike Evelina, she perceives some alternatives to this procedure before discovering their impossibility.

Because of her lack of knowledge of the world, Camilla cannot deal with sophisticated values. Her fiancé Edgar feels that she should not try: she should stay out of the world rather than endeavor to confront it. Knowledge for a woman, from his point of view, constitutes a moral equivalent of rape. Men encourage women to remain ignorant, foolish, and cowardly. . . . The lessons Camilla learns elaborate the implications of Cecilia's learning and Evelina's. She discovers that apparent sources of power disintegrate in a woman's grasp, that her fears offer more dependable guides than her ambitions, and that only through dependency can she find female success. The world she inhabits contains more multitudinous causes for terror even than Cecilia's: prison, illness, death, betrayal, and poverty. The anxiety, which in *Evelina* issued most often in the heroine's repeated experience of confusion, now has far more serious correlatives.

The balance struck in *Evelina* between acceptance of female self-concealment as a useful strategy and resentment against the world that makes hiding necessary for women becomes with each successive novel more precarious. Yet Fanny Burney's personal life was increasingly happy; her letters state explicitly that marriage brought her unprecedented contentment. *Camilla,* composed in the joyful period after the birth of her son, expresses a jaundiced view of the world. (pp. 180-82)

None of these first three novels directly protests women's lot, although each more vividly than its predecessor implies the author's awareness that women's fears acknowledge the intolerable dilemmas of their social position. Yet the ideal marriages that conclude the stories suggest that by willing acceptance of fear and restriction women can achieve happiness. Unhappy marriages also exist in these novels, but their moral causes are carefully specified. The heroines have only to avoid the weaknesses that produce them. Fanny Burney glorifies a fugitive and cloistered virtue as uniquely appropriate for women. Still, the strong women of whom she and her heroines disapprove and the trains of disaster that pursue young women aspiring to even mild independence, hint at some resentment of the social necessities apparently so fully accepted.

In 1792 Mary Wollstonecraft published *A Vindication of the Rights of Women.* Some time before 1800, Fanny Burney began writing her last novel, **The Wanderer: or, Female Difficulties,** published in 1814. There is no evidence that she read Mary

Wollstonecraft. Yet *The Wanderer* articulates female protest in terms vividly analogous to the social critic's, although nominally only to refute such protest. Mary Wollstonecraft's attack on the existing system of female education and on the assumptions that governed women's conduct focuses on issues already implicit in Fanny Burney's first three novels. (pp. 182-83)

Concerned with possibilities of social action, Mary Wollstonecraft interests herself in the question of collective female identity: how women can understand themselves as women. Fanny Burney, as a novelist, involves herself rather in the development of individuals, but *The Wanderer* implies some relation between collective and individual possibility through the striking character of Elinor Joddrell, a young and attractive woman of good family who under the influence of revolutionary ideas from France has developed a rather remarkable vision of her own resources and rights. She claims "the Right of woman, if endowed with senses, to make use of them," moving to eloquent questions about larger privileges. "Must even her heart be circumscribed by boundaries as narrow as her sphere of action in life? Must she be taught to subdue all its native emotions? To hide them as sin, and to deny them as shame? . . . Must every thing that she does be prescribed by rule? . . . Must nothing that is spontaneous, generous, intuitive, spring from her soul to her lips?" (pp. 183-84)

These questions, which describe with only slight exaggeration the emotional program followed by Fanny Burney herself, justify Elinor from her own point of view in boldly declaring her love for a man who has indicated no romantic interest in her, claiming her individual right to violate social expectation, and enlarging for herself alone the narrow boundaries of permitted emotional expression. The novel's action makes a fool of her. The man she loves does not reciprocate her feelings. She threatens and attempts suicide repeatedly in increasingly melodramatic fashion but never quite achieves it. She strikes grand attitudes and makes grand speeches, finally to disappear from the scene and reform in quiet obscurity. Juliet, the novel's heroine, concurs in her lover's judgment that Elinor needs to be brought to her senses. (p. 184)

[More] systematically than *Cecilia* or *Camilla*, *The Wanderer* expresses conscious resentment of the female condition. The "female difficulties" alluded to in the subtitle impede the heroine's attempt to achieve economic and personal independence. Juliet, like Cecilia, is an orphan; like Evelina she suffers from her parents' secret marriage and the resultant mystery about her birth and status; like all the Burney heroines, she falls in love early but faces countless external obstacles to love's fulfillment. Unlike any of her predecessors, though, she must depend on her own resources for emotional and economic survival. An exile from France, where she has been educated, penniless as a result of an accident, forbidden to reveal her origins, background, or even her name, she must make her own way in England. She herself understands her problem, in its particular ramifications, as peculiar to her sex and as illustrating the limitations of social definitions of the female state. (pp. 184-85)

The most interesting aspect of *The Wanderer* is the degree to which Juliet has internalized the social expectations that nullify her continuing struggle. She wins limited social recognition by demonstrating her mastery of the ladylike accomplishments of harp-playing and singing, and her competence in "the useful and appropriate female accomplishment of needle-work". . . . Forced against her will to appear in private theatricals, she thus acquires a further opportunity to display the range of her

talents and skills. Perhaps more significantly, the play enables her to demonstrate "those fears of self-deficiency . . . which . . . often, in sensitive minds, rob them of the powers of exertion". . . . In its first scene, she shows herself a totally incompetent actress because of her fears; later she rouses herself to triumph. . . . Impossible not to think of Miss Burney with her consistent social display of her fears, but one may be surprised, in the particular novelistic context, to find fear glorified as an index of sensitivity. Juliet brings herself to give harp lessons in order to earn a living, but when her ambiguous status and background make her lose pupils, she is unwilling to use her talents in a public musical performance—partly because Harleigh hints that to participate in such an undertaking might obviate the possibility of honorable marriage. Although financial necessity drives the heroine to determine upon performance at last, on the actual occasion she faints before she has to play. She then takes a job as companion to an irascible and tyrannical older woman, effectively dramatizing her social condition of dependency.

Increasingly Juliet finds herself relying—always limited, of course, by considerations of propriety—on financial, emotional, and physical help from men. Money embarrasses her, as it did her creator. She needs it nonetheless, and she needs the self-esteem of winning it by her own efforts, but almost equally she needs the quite opposed self-esteem derived from never even appearing to do wrong. (pp. 185-86)

Elinor points out how inconsistently men—hence, the world—judge women. They declare women unable to act as meaningfully as men because of their natural limitations, although men have in fact barred women from action by controlling their education. On the other hand, while estimating woman below themselves, they also elevate her above, requiring "from her, in defiance of their examples!—in defiance of their lures!—angelical perfection". . . . Juliet, who attempts—largely unsuccessfully—to defy the prohibition of meaningful action, entirely accepts this other impossible standard with its goal of "angelical perfection." For her virtue rather than her action, she wins reward: the man of her choice. (p. 186)

On the novel's final pages, the author summarizes Juliet as "a female Robinson Crusoe, . . . reduced either to sink, through inanition, to nonentity, or to be rescued from famine and death by such resources as she could find, independently, in herself". . . . But only in brief intervals has her survival depended on herself. Elinor seems right about the limited possibilities for women in existent social conditions, although wrong in her hope of enlarging them. . . . Juliet, too, is recovering from her dream of independence. Fanny Burney's imagining of a female Robinson Crusoe is an imagining of despair. For Juliet as a heroine must struggle not only with the obstacles supplied by a hostile physical and social environment but with those created by her own standard of femininity; no psychic or religious conversion can rescue her. Femininity wins; all else is only a dream. Juliet and Elinor in different ways illustrate a female fantasy of self-realization and self-definition through action rather than avoidance. Testing that fantasy, Juliet discovers its frailty. The fear of doing wrong finally controls her, teaching her her helplessness. (p. 187)

[*The Wanderer*'s] elaborate plot, didactically disposed characters, and old-fashioned rhetoric compose a moralistic artifice rather than a realized fiction; it seems an imitation of theory, not of life. Yet its relation to life as Fanny Burney knew it lies deeper than one might suppose. . . . To use goodness as a stance toward the world (the tactic adopted by the character

Juliet as well as by her creator) embodies some claim of strength: Juliet achieves moral superiority if not economic success. But it is an underdog's device, understood explicitly as such by the character who employs it. Goodness amounts to Juliet's only viable resource; her obsessive fear of wrongdoing implies her terror of losing her single weapon for battling the world. And her resentment of being so handicapped in life's struggle expresses itself in her repeated recognition that women know nothing and can do nothing to help themselves. They must allow themselves to be helped and must invite infantilization; they must avoid so much that finally they virtually avoid life itself. Given the detailed realizations along the way of what the female plight means, the happy ending of *The Wanderer* and the novel's artifices of plot and character seem to comprise a bitter mockery, so inadequate are artifices of plot to solve the problems here richly exposed. Fanny Burney was unable to integrate her deep perceptions of the female condition into a believable fiction—perhaps her habits of fear and avoidance made her fear and avoid the implications of her insight. But *The Wanderer* too contains its autobiographical revelations. Less careful than the journals, the novel reveals that the longing for freedom, confessed in moments of despair at the restrictions of Court life, extended farther than Fanny Burney directly acknowledged, vividly reflecting her awareness that fear of wrongdoing as a principle of action itself exemplifies the severe restrictiveness of female possibility. (p. 188)

[The] later novels, creaky of plot and increasingly impenetrable in rhetoric, seriously explore the possibilities for women to assert individual identities. More clearly than Fanny Burney's letters and diaries, the novels betray her anger at the female condition, although she also acknowledges the possibility of happiness within that condition. Imagining female defiance, she imagines also its futility in those heroines dominated, like herself, by fears of doing wrong. The atmosphere of anxiety she vividly evokes suggests what conflicts attend a woman's search for identity. The Burney female characters face endless struggle between what they want to have (independence, specific husbands, friends, pleasure, work) and what they want to be (angelically perfect): between the impulses to action and to avoidance. However important or negligible the specific images of this conflict, it stands behind the action and the characterization of all the novels.

The record of the journals, extending chronologically far beyond the writer's marriage, makes it clear that her commitment to D'Arblay, fulfilling as it was, did not mark the happy ending to her experience as it did for all her fictional heroines. Marriage resolved or simplified conflicts, granting Fanny Burney permission to act (through writing) while yet remaining conspicuously good; it thus provided energy. It also generated new dramas: classic Oedipal struggles, symbolic dilemmas about where and how to live, and conflicts of interest between Fanny's old family and her new—dramas that the journals expose more freely than they had revealed the problems of the author's youth, although in fact the problems remain in many respects essentially the same. The plot of the diaries thus necessarily differs from that of the novels, which never explore post-marital experience.

Yet the fictional inventions uncover the inner realities of the writer's mature as well as her youthful life. Indeed, comparison of Fanny Burney's personal record with her novels suggests the possibility that fiction may more vividly than autobiography delineate the shape of an author's private drama. The external events of Miss Burney's life, as reported in her diaries, supply small excitements, minor clashes, and tiny resolutions. The events of her novels increasingly emphasize important happenings—in *The Wanderer,* political as well as personal happening. Her heroines must cope with grotesque misunderstandings, malicious enemies, and bitter strokes of fate. They suffer more than they can comprehend—more perhaps even than their author comprehends. They express both their creator's wishes and her conviction that such wishes must be punished: the real essence of the inner drama that is more palely reflected in the relatively trivial events she chooses to record in diary and letters.

Fiction is fantasy. Both the strength and the weakness of Fanny Burney's novels derives from this fact. The books betray their author's longing for more grandiose experience than her powerful sense of decorum would allow her even to know she wanted. All except *Cecilia,* that fable of the poor little rich girl, rely on the deeply satisfying fairytale structure in which the hero (in these cases the heroine) with no apparent assets survives a series of demanding tests, winning by the power of goodness, triumphing over those seemingly more advantaged, and finally achieving the royal marriage that symbolizes lasting good fortune. But Fanny Burney betrays conflicting fantasies, which lessen her fiction's energy: on the one hand the dream of self-assertion and success in the face of all obstacles, on the other the fearful fantasy of nemesis for female admission of hostility and female attempts at self-determination. However she heightens happenings to melodramatic impossibility, ignoring logic and straining rhetoric to insist on the importance of her tale, her stories work against themselves. In her direct accounts of herself, with her sense of morality firmly in control, the conflict between the impulse to freedom and the commitment to propriety—its resolution in action always predictable and its emotional dynamics often compelling—shapes a persuasive narrative. But the world of fiction holds forth the possibilities of greater freedom, possibilities that Fanny Burney could not adequately handle, although they enabled her to reveal herself.

Fiction is form, and form is fiction. The forms that tempted Miss Burney, in life and in literature, were moral structures that assured her that virtue found its reward. Around her she could see evidence to the contrary, particularly in female fates. (pp. 188-90)

Fiction is public communication. Fanny Burney's consciousness of this fact expresses itself, characteristically, most often in statements of what she has left out of her novels in order to avoid contaminating young minds. Thus, she boasts that *Camilla* contains no politics because "they were not a *feminine* subject for discussion" and "it would be a better office to general Readers to carry them wide of all politics, to their domestic fire sides." As usual, she is avoiding wrong. But public communication has a positive as well as a negative aspect. In the youthful diaries, writing for "nobody," Fanny expressed a deprecating sense of self; all her letters and diaries insist upon her modesty. The more impersonal expression of fiction enabled her to enlarge her self-image by splitting herself into infinitely virtuous heroines and ingeniously aggressive minor characters, by dramatizing her sense of virtue through those heroines who suffer endlessly in their efforts toward the right, and by expressing ideas that she could not allow herself to endorse through such figures as Mrs. Selwyn and Elinor Joddrell. Only in rare moments of the private record—as when she complains that Mrs. Thrale showers her with too many gifts—does Fanny Burney betray her hostility. The open record of fiction provided greater protection: she could simultaneously convey both anger and her disapproval of anger. (p. 191)

Fiction, finally, may constitute autobiography. Through Fanny Burney's novels, through their flaws and their positive achievements, she conveys her private self more emphatically, more explicitly, than she does in the diaries. Not needing to exercise reductive moral control over every character, she can use her fantasies to communicate her feelings and her conflicts, the interior drama that her decorous life largely concealed. She quotes Mme. de Genlis: "The life of every Woman is a Romance!" The remark, implying an interpretation of actual experience in terms of literary categories, suggests a useful way to read the diaries and letters—perceiving the extent to which, even in her personal record, it is Fanny Burney's fictions that reveal herself. Writing novels, she allows herself to convey the impermissible sides of her nature and to enlarge the permissible. Writing journals, she confines herself largely to the surfaces of her life; yet she uncovers the depths by the unchanging form of her self-interpretation, by her wistful, persistent fantasy of flawless virtue, and by her insistence on shaping her account of all that happens to her in terms of the struggle for virtue. She tells the story of an uneventful life as a romance rich in drama.

Fanny Burney's novels and her journals alike reveal the dynamics of fear in a woman's experience. They also reveal some ways in which the imagination deals with emotion, demonstrating how useful are the disguises of fiction in clarifying the truths of personality and how much the forms and perceptions of fiction become necessary material for the autobiographer. (pp. 191-92)

> *Patricia Meyer Spacks, "Dynamics of Fear: Fanny Burney," in her* Imagining a Self: Autobiography and Novel in Eighteenth-Century England, *Cambridge, Mass.: Harvard University Press, 1976, pp. 158-92.*

LILLIAN D. BLOOM AND EDWARD A. BLOOM (essay date 1979)

[*Bloom and Bloom discuss the structure of Burney's novels, which they consider to be similar to fairy tales but with strongly moral overtones. The critics also examine the noticeable decline in the quality of Burney's later novels and explore their autobiographical elements. The Blooms analyze how each novel reflects Burney's changing attitudes and perception; the early works depict her "need to be pulled by an inner tension," while her final novels do not indicate the same sort of personal inspiration. According to the critics, both* Camilla *and* The Wanderer *are evidence of Burney's fading imagination and creative impetus.*]

[Fanny Burney] wrote what seems to be almost a contradiction in terms but which is in actuality a traditional genre. She wrote in the mode of a naturalistic fairy tale whose theme, like that of the Cinderella story in modern dress, concerned "Trial, Recognition and Judgement" in the course of which the humble shall be raised. The plot moved in near-linear progression from episode to episode through to its successful resolution. Upon this plot she superimposed a number of characters marked by one attribute, utilized a series of real, if vaguely described, periods of time and locale: we travel from Berry Hill, Dorsetshire, or Bury, Suffolk, or Etherington, Hampshire, to London with stopovers at fashionable watering spas and resorts like Clifton, Tunbridge Wells, Southampton, and Brighton. Within the narrative architecture is a set of values that motivates or fails to motivate her fictional people, from the middle class

to the gentry and nobility—the values of common sense and circumspection, of financial solvency and honesty.

Despite a simply arranged plot, her fiction is structured upon levels, both dramatic and moral, and with no clear-cut divisions among them. Providing cohesion was the fairy tale which appealed paradoxically to her conscious desire to write realistic literature, "lyrical images of unchanging human predicaments and strong unchanging hopes and fears, loves and hatreds." And while the events in such narratives are usually extraordinary, "they are always presented as ordinary," something that could happen to anyone. The tradition of the fairy tale bolstered a tremulous optimism, a need to project herself as an idealized heroine whose virtue could conquer social worlds. Ultimately, the energy that infuses both *Evelina* and *Cecilia* arises from the author's turmoil, whether unconscious or not, and the feeling first of release and then of joyous wholeness as the work of art emerges. The charm of these two novels is that they have the knack of universal speech, directing themselves to our recollections of childhood. We suffer with each young heroine and her myriad trials on a journey of recognition; we triumph with her as she overcomes at great cost perplexities and struggles. . . . Fanny Burney's first two novels unfold as psychodramas. They excite both the reader and inventor with their detailing of dangers faced by the heroines. And heroines they are, for as characters their weaknesses are outmatched by a moral vitality which bests the "monsters" in their path and eventually bestows upon them the reality of a safe place at a superficially glittering but primary level of consciousness.

Evelina and *Cecilia* can do so much because like other works in the mode of the fairy tale they involved the teller in a primary process of "fantasy, recovery, escape and consolation." To weave her first tale, Fanny Burney, the unpretty Miss Nobody—almost morbidly reclusive and twenty-six years old—could fantasize herself as "the most amiable, the most perfect of women," aged seventeen, sought after by eligible young men, and won by the most eligible. The molding of *Evelina,* with its power of arresting strangeness, offered her a temporary escape and recovery from a feeling of inadequacy. It consoled with a vision of a "sudden joyous turn"—the end of loneliness—that lay within her grasp. The novel, in short, suffused her and itself with the reward of achievement, which readers found contagious. Whether or not they knew the history of Fanny Burney, they empathized with Evelina and therefore with her creator.

With attributes Fanny Burney wished for herself, Evelina is a fairy tale heroine facing the trials of initiation. She is young, extravagantly lovely, sensitive, and innocent. As Lady Howard explains the ingenue's appeal: "Her face and person answer my most refined ideas of complete beauty: and this . . . is yet so striking, it is not possible to pass it unnoticed. . . . Her character seems truly ingenuous and simple; and, at the same time that nature has blessed her with an excellent understanding, and great quickness of parts, she has a certain air of inexperience and innocency that is extremely interesting." Just as Fanny Burney is secure in her corner, so Evelina is safe at Berry Hill. But neither has any alternative, at least figuratively, but to go out into the world and contend with its snares and enticements. The novelist knew intuitively what her heroine had to learn, that the journey is in fact a moral encounter. (pp. 222-24)

If the novelist and heroine share purity and fortitude, it is Evelina who is imaginatively dramatized in tests not merely of place but of people, all of whom represent pressures of one kind or another. There are the importunate fops and snobs like Mr. Lovel, would-be seducers and "enthusiasts" like Sir Clement Willoughby, a crude grandmother, vulgar relations like the shopkeeper Branghtons, a "Court-Calendar Bigot" Mrs. Beaumont, and the waspish duenna Mrs. Selwyn, each sketched in unsubtle lines to suggest a type. Indeed, the heroine and her creator become virtually one when each searches for an all-attentive father who can establish the identity so necessary for self-knowledge. Evelina gasps at the horror of parental rejection but her words highlight Fanny Burney's reaction to a parent who would turn from a loving daughter to a second marriage. (p. 225)

Harassed by people who "cannot learn who she is," she is very much like Miss Nobody until she is claimed by a parent. Autobiography in part stimulates fiction when Evelina, bewildered by "her ignorance of the forms and inexperience in the manners of the world," meets each social crisis with alarm moderated by courage. With each encounter and escape, she approaches ever-nearer the competence "to see it such as it really is." Typical of any number of naturalistic fairy tales, Fanny Burney's first novel emanates from the inventive self. While it points the way to a tranquil future, it concentrates on the process of change survived by the heroine rather than on the actual joy to be realized. Evelina learns the lessons of prudence, lessons acquired the hard way during the six months of perpetual trial and self-recognition.

Whatever the biographical elements in this first novel, it is after all a fiction in which (true to its mode) all loose threads are finally tied together. . . . Ethically, the marriage [of Evelina and Lord Orville] symbolizes the finish of all ordeals and all punishments for acts of imprudence; it symbolizes an elevated moral wholeness "and, at the same time, that separation anxiety is forever transcended when the ideal partner has been found with whom the most satisfying personal relationship is established."

Despite similarity of themes and structures, *Evelina* and *Cecilia* differ from each other with the shifting of Fanny Burney's impressions of life and change of situation. *Cecilia* irradiates less élan than its predecessor, the heroine from Bury never doubting the presence of threatening forces, never asking why but simply conceding the inevitability of menace. Even as her creator had burst forth from her locked world only to find herself enmeshed in a variety of social demands, so Cecilia sensed that confusions daily multiply, their net thrown about the innocent and guilty alike. About to come of age and without any guardian on whom to rely for moral tuition, she was more readily convinced than the younger Evelina "that a struggle against severe difficulties in life is unavoidable, is an intrinsic part of human existence—but that if one does not shy away, but steadfastly meets unexpected and often unjust hardships, one masters all obstacles and at the end one emerges victorious." The triumph is sustained, but the victor is battered.

Cecilia moves forward from *Evelina* because the Fanny Burney of 1782 had matured in more than chronological time. In the four and a half years that separated the two works, the novelist proved that a first literary success could be duplicated by one still more praiseworthy. In adjusting to the ways of a highly stratified society, she virtually forced her earlier alter ego Miss Nobody into quiescence. (pp. 225-26)

Cecilia and Fanny Burney share several worldly characteristics and, indeed, suspicions of them. Both were cynical of the London round for each "came too late into the school of fashion to be a ductile pupil." Nonetheless, their attitudes toward parties swivelled with the mood of the moment. If author and protagonist were attracted to an orderly serenity as an ideal, too much tranquillity drugged them into lassitude. They grew weary of spending their time alone and they "sighed for the comfort of society, and the relief of communication." Yet sighs did not diminish Cecilia's commitment to spurn those affairs where "every thing is languid and insipid," where one passes "the present moment in apparent gaiety and thoughtlessness." Similarly, on 23 December 1782, Fanny Burney wrote in her *Diary:* "I begin to grow most heartily sick of this continual round of visiting, and these eternal new acquaintances. I am now arranging matters in my mind for a better plan; and I mean, henceforward, never to go out more than three days in the week; . . . I really have at present no pleasure in any party, from the trouble and tiresomeness of being engaged to so many." Her second work of fiction matched the changes in self and in new perceptions of the world. The novel, despite its emulation of a fairy tale plot or because of it, mirrored the reality of its author's soul. . . .

That there are autobiographical details written into *Cecilia* is undeniable. Yet it remains an artistic effort in which phantasmagoric intentions impelled the creative act. Tonally darker than the first novel, it takes on a decisive somberness that is alleviated only with the "good" catastrophe. The trials that Cecilia must undergo are socially more tense and serious than those met by Evelina. Ironically the new heroine appears so untouched by what is sordid about her that she is likened to fairy tale royalty, as a guileless underling exclaims: "O, if I could chuse who I would be, I should sooner say Miss [Cecilia] Beverley than any princess in the world!" . . . As irony piles on irony, her position in society—her affluence and grace—intensifies the severity of her tests and subsequent suffering. Not only do individuals—stock, polarized characters though they may be—confine her quest for rational freedom but so does the world with vapidity, hypocrisy, boredom, and the persistence of unwanted suitors whose declarations amounted to "determined persecution." (p. 227)

In *Cecilia* Fanny Burney tried a new motif, one borrowed from a fairy tale tradition and yet one to which she could relate inwardly. She wrote the novel quickly, whipped on by paternal goading and her own ambitions. As she wavered between day dream and artistic reality, the jolt was sometimes so intense that she collapsed, certain that she was dangerously ill. Dedicated to the completion of the fiction, she nevertheless—as her *Diary* indicates—felt on occasion a driving urge to thrust it aside, to flee from demands that cut her off from normal associations. In a peculiar combination of desire and invention, she built upon the flight motif, used it in this novel and in the two to come. Cecilia therefore when most isolated—driven from her home and repudiated by her father-in-law—seeks relief in a "defensive process." She runs through the streets of London in search of young Delvile, who symbolized the end of her loneliness and the assuagement of anxiety. But as Fanny Burney guessed and her protagonist was to act out, flight merely inhibits; it throttles the impulse "to see it such as it is" and to recognize who one is. Cecilia races as if over sword blades, her emotional endurance lessening with each moment. She has tormented the self with such ferocity that release comes only with a vast fatigue, a fatigue so near to madness that it lies beyond speech and thought. Fanny Burney, who sensed that everyone has a breaking-point, achieved a vicarious escape this time through her heroine's silent agony.

Because the novelist saw life as future-oriented, Cecilia recovers, is united with her husband "upon principles rational, and feelings pleasant". . . . Nonetheless a change is rung upon the usual happy conclusion. In a new awareness that compromise often accompanies maturity, Fanny Burney sees to it that "the hero and heroine are neither plunged in the depths of misery, nor exalted to UNhuman happiness". . . . Specifically Cecilia surrenders her inheritance so that the Delvile name may be retained and the marriage consummated. The ending merely reaffirms that the accent throughout the work is on the protagonist's broadening adaptability to pressures both from within and without. Capable of being socially flexible, she will not, however, capitulate in matters of moral integrity. At such times when she had to dig in, she reveals a forthrightness of judgment to which the effervescent Evelina could not rise. (p. 228)

If we generalize from *Evelina* and *Cecilia*, Fanny Burney needed to be pulled by an inner tension, torn between a fairy tale world she envisioned for herself and the frustrations or uncertainties with which she lived. Her fiction, then, gave shape to fantasies of a beautiful, ever-young damsel struggling against adversity to glorious success, fantasies that made her life tolerable, even when she was petted by the exacting Streatham coterie. Her early fiction also satisfied a deeply rooted necessity to attract her father's attention and favor so that he could refer to her as "my daughter the young novelist." Ultimately, her first two novels had to assimilate the shadow known as Miss Nobody, a shadow so evanescent that it often disappeared only to return and tantalize.

None of these drives were present when she worked on *Camilla*. The paradox is that she was far too happy to write a successful novel, far too self-assured about herself as a wife and mother—hence as an artist. (p. 231)

Camilla is her paean to life, full of energy and vitality. But for all its verve and inventiveness, it remains an externalized novel, visibly and schematically contrived, a solecistic jumble of Gallic constructions and verbiage, an attenuated version of the two novels that preceded it.

Fanny Burney deliberately wrote a large book, knowing that she would print it by subscription and that under such circumstances size determined price. Everything and everybody that appeared in the earlier novels reappeared—multiplied in number. If Evelina and Cecilia were projections of an idealized self, Camilla Tyrold was simply a literary composite of the two previous protagonists. As such, she was more ingenuous than Evelina and more tried than Cecilia. Like the latter, she ends her journey in flight and madness. But where the one collapsed in silence, Camilla raved: she gave way "to despair; to screams rather than lamentations, to cries rather than tears. Her reason felt the shock as forcibly as her heart; the one seemed tottering on its seat, the other bursting its abode. Words of alarming incoherency proclaimed the danger menacing her intellects, while agonies nearly convulsive distorted her features, and writhed her form." Quite obviously, if we use this description as the tonal clue to the whole, then the near-tragedy of *Cecilia* had evaporated into the melodrama of *Camilla*.

But one protagonist was insufficient for this sprawling new novel that had a subplot and hence a secondary heroine—Eugenia, another daughter in the Tyrold family. A typical fairy tale figure, she serves as the sacrificial victim, "free from guile." She has been scarred by small-pox and crippled by a fall from a see-saw. Her pock-marked face, her hump-backed diminutive stature are counterpointed by an intellectual and spiritual beauty, a sensibility that can rise to rapture. Hers is a two-fold test: she must see herself as others see her and, even in the course of tearing through an English countryside, she must honor the vows of a forced marriage with Alphonso Bellamy, who proves his villainy by the way he gnashes his teeth. The two plots join in the near-destruction of a once cohesive family and in the misery of the two heroines. They learn little from the struggles they endure, their naiveté no match for rampant misfortunes. Each, however, is rescued by a *deus ex machina* finish which makes the happily-ever-after marriage possible even for the hapless Eugenia and certainly for Camilla.

Fanny Burney wanted more for her plot and sub-plot than merely the trial and journey motifs of the fairy tale. Eager to capture a maximum audience in 1796, she sought to cater to as many popular tests as possible. She had learned as early as *Cecilia* that "a crying volume" earned more money "in 6 months than a heavy merry thing"; she therefore permitted few emotional restraints in *Camilla*. The novel had its comic scenes and situations—some of the best she had ever devised—but they were subsumed by an overriding sentimentality. (pp. 231-32)

The novel had still another popular craving to satisfy, a "Udolphoish" terror. In imitation of the financially successful Mrs. Radcliffe, Fanny Burney sketched several gothic scenes, which attempted to achieve the verbal macabre: a lengthy description of a bier, its corpse unknown, carried through thick woods, Camilla alone with the dead man, and Camilla hysterically seeing spectral "Forms" at her bedside. In this huge novel genre warred with genre, almost every incident spawned its counterpart, and innumerable characters were variations on a few moral traits—levity, calculating selfishness, heroic propriety, innocence, scholarly dedication, generosity. (p. 232)

The monetary exigency that spurred on the composition of *Camilla* also forced *The Wanderer, or Female Difficulties.* . . . Where *Camilla* in its form and episodes burst forth torrentially, *The Wanderer* had a slow and arduous birth.

Never before had she spent so much time on the writing of a novel. Questions naturally arise. Was she uninterested in its destiny despite financial pressures? Did she find the imaginative process slowed down or emotionally enervating? To such questions the answers are a probable yes. During much of *The Wanderer*'s composition, she had to adjust to the pleasant distractions of new French friends and traditions. (p. 233)

The Wanderer was a palpable agony for her to write. But her ten years in France were for the most part without conflict. Her anxieties, if they still existed, were quieted by an intimate family group. Her fiction, however, suffered. Without the goad of inner turmoil, she could instil no conflict in that portion of the novel sketched while she spent her "time either by her own small—but precious fire-side; . . . perfectly a stranger to all personal disturbance." Early in the narrative, we meet the heroine, more visibly a fairy tale creature than her predecessors. As she starts her journey into the world, she undergoes a rebirth or a virtually magic transformation, not unlike that of Cinderella: " 'twas but an hour or two since, that you were the blackest, dirtiest, raggedest wretch I ever beheld," said Mrs. Ireton, "and now—you are turned into an amazing beauty!" As the Incognita or Wanderer "without even a name," she suggests to some that she must "be a princess in disguise." Humiliated by "wicked" stepmothers in the guise of employers—Mrs. Maple, Mrs. Ireton, Mrs. Howell—she captivates the hero: "Charming, charming creature! he cried, what can have cast thee into this forlorn condition? and by what means—

and by whom—art thou to be rescued.'' The answers are long in coming. After the characters and basic situation are introduced, the novel for almost three volumes is afflicted by stasis.

With Fanny Burney's homecoming in 1812 the psychological problems with which she had to cope were the catalyst for the violent movement that marks the last two volumes of the novel. In this case, however, tension, while forcing inventiveness, did not allow her to escape self by accepting the destiny of a fiction with a design of its own. Specifically, her inner conflicts were so tied up with day-to-day survival—even with the hardships of living on £7.10s. a quarter—that they made for literary artifice rather than organic creativity. In the fourth volume the Incognita, now named Juliet, races so rapidly through the New Forest that she is easily lost in a welter of huts, hovels, and farmhouses. In the last volume new complexities momentarily spring up as the protagonist is hounded by persecutors and self-imposed obligations, which she terms her ''situation'' and ''fate.'' But all anguish begins to level off when documents are found to establish what we already know: that ''this so long concealed and mysterious, but most lovely incognita, is the daughter of the late Lord Granville and the granddaughter of the late Earl of Melbury!'' As the fifth volume ends, all fairy tale motifs conjoin to show Juliet welcomed by her aristocratic family, the inevitably right marriage to the hero, her friends rewarded in and enemies exiled from the happy land. (pp. 233-34)

The Wanderer was published in March 1814. The reviews appeared almost immediately—harsh and even hostile, but she seemed indifferent to them or at least prepared to rationalize their severity. By the autumn of that same year, when most of the reviews had been printed, she continued to be detached. Her personal life was so tumbled about that she could not pay more than passing attention to her literary reputation. Her father had died in the previous April; her son's performance at Cambridge was unpredictable; her husband's new military duties in Restoration France disappointed her. . . .

We can only guess whether she read the reviews. We do know that she never doubted the right of readers to be critical or to switch loyalties as the situation warranted. ''I think,'' she wrote to her brother, ''the public has its full right to criticize—& never had the folly and vanity to set my heart upon escaping its late severity, while reminiscence keeps alive its early indulgence''. . . . For all her capacity to reminisce, no one was more bewildered than Fanny Burney by her literary decline. Had she suspected it, she would never have bet £1,500 on *The Wanderer*. But bewilderment did not preclude an acceptance of the fact. Now sixty-two, she found the Muses too ''skittish'' to capture. As she had once described them, ''one, with Bowls & Daggers pursues—another with a Mask escapes—However, I wind round & round their Recesses, where of old I found them—or where, rather they found *me*,'' they never met again. And probably she did not wish to flush them out. With the death of her father in 1814 and of her husband four years later, her power to fantasize had no centers from which to move outward. The day-dreams closed in on themselves, eluding for the last twenty-six years of her life the creative zest that once consciously ordered her successful fiction. (p. 235)

Lillian D. Bloom and Edward A. Bloom, ''Fanny Burney's Novels: The Retreat from Wonder,'' in Novel: A Forum on Fiction, Vol. 12, No. 3, Spring, 1979, pp. 215-35.

JANET TODD (essay date 1980)

[*Todd discusses Burney's depiction of female friendship in* Cecilia *and* The Wanderer. *According to Todd, these two novels reflect the darker side of the bond between women.*]

The search for the correct female friend forms part of the . . . complicated plots of Fanny Burney, the main painter of sentimental female friendship in England and France in the late eighteenth century. Although less perfect than *Evelina,* her first, triumphant novel, her later works more engagingly depict female relationships, and both *Cecilia* and *The Wanderer* deeply probe the dangers and rewards of female ties. If in the main Burney paints with dark colors, the sombreness conveys regret for a lightness she rejects from both fear and principle. Haywood and Lennox find friendship an asylum in a predatory world; Mme de Grafigny wishes it were so but cannot discover it. Burney seems close to Richardson in seeing it not only rare but dangerously tempting.

In *Cecilia,* the heroine's path is strewn with uncomfortable women. She inherits some from childhood and has no strength to repudiate the legacy; others she takes to meet her psychic needs. Lonely and rich, she wants mother-figures to guide her (feeling betrayed when they prove flexible), and daughters to call forth her benevolence. Like Wollstonecraft's Mary, similarly rich and isolated, she seems unable to find and like an equal.

In Mrs. Delvile, the parent of her lover, Cecilia discovers a kind of mother. Initially the older woman repels with her haughtiness, but later she is won by Cecilia's exemplary resignation to her will. Certainly Cecilia's position is unconventional: she will inherit a fortune on marriage only if her husband agrees to take her name, so playing the woman. It is a humiliating condition no man of metal seems ready to meet, and Mrs. Delvile is heartily opposed to her son's marrying so ignominiously. Finally she comes to accept a clandestine marriage, but it is to Cecilia as penniless orphan not mastering heiress. For her condescension, she sinks in Cecilia's esteem, and her raptures over her new daughter-in-law fail to impress: ''Your mother, in her tenderness forgot her dignity,'' Cecilia remarks icily to her lover. Little mitigated by Mrs. Delvile's approval, the antisocial, secret marriage still horrifies, and Cecilia repeats its shocking facts, as fascinated and appalled as the Sadian heroine exulting over her intricate incest.

In the young daughterlike Henrietta, Cecilia tries to unite friendship and benevolence, as Wollstonecraft's Mary and Austen's Emma also try. Henrietta interests through her youthful need, her melancholy state, her loveliness and ''the uncommon artlessness of her conversation,'' all of which excite in Cecilia ''a desire to serve, and an inclination to love her.'' But the friendship is a disturbed one. Cecilia soon discovers that her friend and she crave the same man, and their joint infatuation disperses for a while their dream of living together. They cannot unite, muses Cecilia, unless they are both rejected. The man determines their relationship and rules their affection.

A striking example of this male ordering of friendship occurs when, after a long absence, Cecilia and Henrietta reencounter each other in front of a male visitor. At once they dissolve into the raptures of sentimental friendship, but are interrupted by the man commenting rudely: ''The young ladies . . . have a mighty way of saluting one another till such time as they get husbands: and then I'll warrant you they can meet without any salutation at all.'' The quick put-down, so reminiscent of Lovelace's insistent belittling of female friendship, chills Cecilia, and she immediately checks "the tenderness of her fervent young friend."

Toward the end of the novel after the two women have lived for a time together, Cecilia is abruptly isolated and plunged downward. Burney is adept at such dramatic reductions, which deprive her characters of all props of money, caste, and gallantry. Impoverished and alone, Cecilia is finally driven insane—headed, it seems, for the exemplary, eulogistic death of Clarissa. But women novelists are less prone to kill their heroines, and, when the mandatory delirium is past, Cecilia is en route for the happy ending. Awakening from her healing sleep, she first encounters Henrietta, who has rushed to her bedside and answered her friend's madness with her own frenzied love. Lost friendship appears to lead both women to insanity; psychic health requires a reunion.

Although decently happy, the ending of *Cecilia* is marred by the heroine's earlier suffering. No wedded bliss can compensate for such degradation. The bliss is further diminished when Henrietta is ejected, packed off with an old lover of Cecilia's. While rich and powerful, the heroine could entertain and support her friend, but seemed unfit for her male lover; shorn of money and weakened into dependence, she is a proper wife, and the symbol of her earlier independent power must be dismissed. As Clarissa well knew, when women grasp a legacy, they somehow dissolve it. Severely qualified as the rhapsody of marriage is, then, it is no accident that the novel's last word should be "resignation."

Many of the motifs of female friendship recur in Fanny Burney's final, little appreciated novel, *The Wanderer; or, Female Difficulties,* which presents her most ambiguous and complex portrait of female relationships. Like Cecilia, the heroine of this work is degraded to the depths of society, severed from friends and relatives, and deprived of all signs of domestic worth. Like Cecilia again, she treads a bitter path through defective women who fail her at every turn and, worse, humiliate her with a nastiness not seen in fiction since the whores baited the saintly Clarissa. But at the end her suffering is rewarded and she receives the sentimental prize denied Cecilia—a sister-friend.

The story of *The Wanderer* is Burney's most improbable; it concerns Juliet, a young woman whose name we learn only in the third volume and whose circumstances are divulged even later; indeed her tale is so complex it is little wonder she refuses to tell it. Reduced initially to the denuded state of Cecilia toward the end of her novel, Juliet must prove over and over again the difficulties of females. Her sorry lot is darkened by disjunction of character and circumstance: socially anomalous as a lone woman, she must strive for self-respect and independence. "Is it only under the domestic roof,—that roof to me denied!—that woman can know safety, respect, and honour?" she cries at one point, and the answer is for her certainly yes; teaching a little music, sewing a fine seam, and companioning the old and irascible do not ward off destitution, and, more public, less feminine efforts appall. In this difficult context, then, Juliet must discover the limits and strengths of female association.

The heroine enters two contrasting relationships, both extreme in their way. One is with the extraordinary Elinor, a woman deeply impressed and impeded by French and feminist sentiments; the other unites her with the gentle Aurora, a young girl who remains always sweetly amiable and feminine. Juliet is bandied about between these extremes, confounded by the

one, comforted by the other, but she never wavers in her allegiance. She may sometimes benefit the wild Elinor, but her heart is always Aurora's and it is for her she sheds the most copious and delicious tears.

Elinor is mocked from the start as "the champion of her sex," a fierce Wollstonecraft who insists like the older sister in *Lasselia* on forcing her love on a man. She is most feminist when most demented, hysterically asserting "rights . . . which all your sex, with all its arbitrary assumption of superiority, can never disprove, for they are the Rights of human nature; to which the two sexes equally and unalienably belong." To prevent our accepting such assertion, it is given a bizarre context. Elinor is threatening murder and suicide, wielding not the feminine penknife but a real pistol; yet like her predecessors she is easily disarmed and all her exotic suicide attempts fail. Violence—both verbal and physical—should be masculine.

Nonetheless, Elinor impresses in spite of coercion from her context. Indeed the novel's horrifying picture of female degradation in Juliet strengthens Elinor's rhetoric (even as Elinor's grotesqueries underscore Juliet's stress on feminine propriety). . . . (pp. 312-16)

In a world where femininity is virtue and the heroine seeks only to embrace it, the feminist Elinor is ridiculous, mocked by her exaggerated actions, her uncontrollable passions, and her desperate shiftings from principle to love. As the book proceeds, she disintegrates, appearing only in quixotic episodes. Maddened by rejection, for example, she "rent open her wound, and tore her hair; calling, screaming for death, with agonizing wrath." She seeks death as she had sought a man, parodying the passive exemplary ending Clarissa achieved and Cecilia almost suffered, but her impotent frenzy suggests only the author's sadism. Elinor is denied active love and active death.

Juliet's second friend contradicts Elinor in all her postures. Lady Aurora enters first to sustain the fainting heroine, and her other actions are as discreetly supportive. The two women join in a sentimental, tearful friendship, blessed and sanctioned by the hero and reversing the feminist alliance fitfully imagined by Elinor. . . . (p. 317)

In *The Wanderer,* friendship reaches new heights in sisterly love. Yet in its success it reveals its flaws. If the novel supports the display of friendship, it seems to vitiate its substance. Elinor though given room to show her force, is rejected, and Aurora herself is more a rapturous shade of Juliet than an equal. Women in both *Cecilia* and *The Wanderer* may console each other and compensate for loss, but they can rarely spur to action. Both heroines ultimately act alone, if they act at all, and come to grief in solitude. The most promising tie of Juliet with Elinor is rejected in ridicule, although their union might have released the androgynous power Wollstonecraft described. Certainly Juliet could have used such a union as psychic model when she sought her own feminine strength. As it is, Elinor is cast out and the feminine left to grow effeminate. (p. 318)

[Sentimental friendship in the novel] provides a relationship into which two women can enter with passion and propriety, and it supplies a code of behavior that eases them toward each other. Yet, when it approaches fulfillment as it does in *The Wanderer,* its limitation appears. Seemingly the last bastion of the female self against the reductive claims of patriarchy, it yet fearfully retrenches when it might subvert, rendering the woman more accepting, not more desperate. In the structure of the novel, too, sentimental friendship defuses. The heroine avoids working out her difficult tie with the man who will define her, but instead flees him or simply accepts him on the final page. Left with an impotent friendship, the two women may become not androgynous but schizophrenic, while the model of the female alliance remains the duplication of sisters. (p. 319)

> Janet Todd, ''The Literary Context,'' in her *Women's Friendship in Literature, Columbia University Press, 1980, pp. 305-58.**

ADDITIONAL BIBLIOGRAPHY

Adelstein, Michael E. *Fanny Burney.* Twayne's English Authors Series, edited by Sylvia E. Bowman, no. 67. New York: Twayne Publishers, 1968, 169 p.
> An examination of Burney's life and work.

Agress, Lynne. ''Wives and Servants: Proper Conduct for One's Proper Place.'' In her *The Feminine Irony: Women on Women in Early-Nineteenth-Century English Literature,* pp. 114-45. Rutherford, N.J.: Fairleigh Dickinson University Press, 1978.*
> A discussion of Burney's work that especially focuses on *Evelina.* The critic contends that the novel's message is that a young woman must marry well in order to lead a happy life.

Backscheider, Paula R. ''Woman's Influence.'' *Studies in the Novel* XI, No. I (Spring 1979): 3-22.*
> An analysis of the means by which Evelina learned to influence the men around her.

Bloom, Edward A. Introduction to *Evelina; or, The History of a Young Lady's Entrance into the World,* by Fanny Burney, edited by Edward A. Bloom, pp. vii-xxxi. London: Oxford University Press, 1968.
> Traces the thematic and structural development of *Evelina.* According to Bloom, the novel's most effective aspects are comedy, characterization, and the dual narrative provided by Evelina and Villars's letters.

Bradbrook, Frank W. ''The Feminist Tradition.'' In his *Jane Austen and Her Predecessors,* pp. 90-119. Cambridge: Cambridge at the University Press, 1966.*
> Acknowledges Austen's literary debt to Burney.

Dobson, Austin. *Fanny Burney (Madame D'Arblay).* English Men of Letters. London: Macmillan & Co., 1904, 216 p.
> An important biography. Dobson's work was considered the standard study of Burney until the publication of Joyce Hemlow's *The History of Fanny Burney* (see annotation below). Though Dobson's observations are now dated, they are still considered insightful.

Doody, Margaret Anne. ''Deserts, Ruins and Troubled Waters: Female Dreams in Fiction and the Development of the Gothic Novel.'' *Genre* X, No. 4 (Winter 1977): 529-72.*
> Discusses the significance of female dreams and madness in a number of eighteenth-century novels. Doody devotes several pages to *Cecilia* and *Camilla.*

Edwards, Averyl. *Fanny Burney: 1752-1840, A Biography.* London: Staples Press, 1948, 170 p.
> A brief biography.

Gosse, Edmund. ''The Age of Wordsworth: 1780-1815.'' In his *English Literature, an Illustrated Record: From the Age of Johnson to the Age of Tennyson,* Vol. IV, rev. edition, pp. 1-106. New York: Macmillan Co., 1923.*
> An illustrated biographical entry.

Grau, Joseph A. *Fanny Burney: An Annotated Bibliography.* New York: Garland Publishing, 1981, 210 p.
> A detailed primary and secondary bibliography.

Hahn, Emily. *A Degree of Prudery: A Biography of Fanny Burney.* Garden City, N.Y.: Doubleday & Co., 1950, 179 p.
> A biographical study widely regarded as condescending in approach.

Hale, Will Taliaferro. ''Madame D'Arblay's Place in the Development of the English Novel.'' *Indiana University Studies* III, No. 28 (January 1916): 5-35.
> A discussion of the increasing artificiality of Burney's style that Hale believes culminated in *Camilla* and *The Wanderer.* According to Hale, both novels are unreadable, and he blames the influence of Johnson and Burney's father.

Hemlow, Joyce. ''Fanny Burney: Playwright.'' *University of Toronto Quarterly* XIX, No. 2 (January 1950): 170-89.
> Discusses Burney's dramatic writings and their role in her literary career.

———. ''Fanny Burney and the Courtesy Books.'' *PMLA* LXV, No. 5 (September 1950): 732-61.
> Demonstrates the influence on Burney's novels of contemporary works discussing the conduct of young ladies.

———. *The History of Fanny Burney.* Oxford: Oxford at the Clarendon Press, 1958, 528 p.
> The definitive biography by the foremost Burney scholar.

Hill, Constance. *Fanny Burney at the Court of Queen Charlotte.* London: John Lane, The Bodley Head, 1912, 364 p.
> A biography covering the years 1786 to 1791.

[Hunt, J. H. Leigh.] ''Men and Books.'' *The New Monthly Magazine* XXXVII, No. CXLV (January 1833): 48-59.*
> A discussion of the *Memoirs of Dr. Burney.* Hunt contends that Johnson's influence on Burney ''spoilt her style.''

Jeaffreson, J. Cordy. ''Frances D'Arblay.'' In his *Novels and Novelists from Elizabeth to Victoria,* Vol. I, pp. 312-39. London: Hurst and Blackett, 1858.
> A lengthy biographical sketch with a few derogatory comments about Burney's novels.

MacCarthy, B. G. ''The Domestic Novel—The Novel of Manners.'' In her *The Female Pen: The Later Women Novelists, 1744-1818,* Vol. 2, pp. 87-128. Cork: Cork University Press, 1947.
> Documents Burney's literary decline following the publication of *Evelina.*

Masefield, Muriel. *The Story of Fanny Burney: Being an Introduction to the ''Diary and Letters of Madame d'Arblay.''* New York: Haskell House Publishers, 1974, 160 p.
> An account of Burney's life and times.

Saintsbury, George. ''The New Paradise of the Novel.'' In his *The Peace of the Augustans: A Survey of Eighteenth Century Literature as a Place of Rest and Refreshment,* pp. 105-76. London: G. Bell and Sons, 1916.*
> A general overview of Burney's works, with special attention paid to *The Wanderer.* Saintsbury terms Burney's last novel ''a clumsy and immensely long ado about nothing.''

Staves, Susan. ''Evelina; or, Female Difficulties.'' *Modern Philology* 73, No. 4, Part 1 (May 1976): 368-81.
> Contends that the focus of *Evelina* is the heroine's powerful anxiety. Staves believes the book's psychological implications render it a far more serious work than it is often considered to be.

Stevenson, Lionel. ''Terror and Edification (1775-1800).'' In his *The English Novel: A Panorama,* pp. 148-76. Boston: Houghton Mifflin Co., Riverside Press, 1960.*
> A historical overview detailing the circumstances under which Burney composed her novels.

Tourtellot, Arthur Bernon. *Be Loved No More: The Life and Environment of Fanny Burney.* Boston: Houghton Mifflin Co., 1938, 381 p.
> A biographical and historical study based largely on Burney's diary.

Voss-Clesly, Patricia. *Tendencies of Character Depiction in the Domestic Novels of Burney, Edgeworth, and Austen: A Consideration of Subjective and Objective World.* 3 vols. Salzburg Studies in English Literature: Romantic Reassessment, edited by James Hogg, no. 95. Salzburg: Universität Salzburg, 1979.

>A comparative analysis of selected works. Voss-Clesly states that her intention is "to demonstrate the perfection of technique in character depiction in the domestic novels of Burney, Edgeworth, and Austen."

Wagenknecht, Edward. "The Romance of the Tea-Table: Fanny Burney, the First 'Lady Novelist'." In his *Cavalcade of the English Novel,* revised edition, pp. 134-38. New York: Henry Holt and Co., 1954.

>An assessment of *Evelina* and *Cecilia.* While Wagenknecht considers *Cecilia* to be the more successful from a technical standpoint, he also admires the freshness of *Evelina* and asserts that Burney's greatest strength is her ability to accurately recreate the life of London society.

White, Eugene. *Fanny Burney, Novelist; A Study in Technique: "Evelina," "Cecilia," "Camilla," "The Wanderer."* Hamden, Conn.: Shoe String Press, 1960, 93 p.

>A study of Burney's novels focusing on plot, characterization, style, and narrative technique.

Woolf, Virginia. "Fanny Burney's Half-Sister." In her *Collected Essays,* Vol. III, pp. 147-57. London: The Hogarth Press, 1967.

>A sketch of the life of Maria Allen Rishton, who Woolf suggests was the model for Evelina.

George Gordon (Noel) Byron, Lord Byron

1788-1824

English poet, dramatist, and satirist.

The following entry presents criticism of Byron's poem *Don Juan* (1819-24). For a complete discussion of Byron's career, see *NCLC*, Vol. 2.

Don Juan is considered Byron's foremost achievement and one of English literature's greatest long poems. Variously described as a satire, epic satire, mock epic, and novel in verse, the unfinished work eludes critical categorization despite the consensus that it contains some of the finest satire in the English language. Writing in an animated and virtually unclassifiable style, Byron utilized a variety of narrative perspectives to comment on a wide range of human concerns—from the nature of the universe to the common physical sensations of everyday existence. The poet's ironic observations and brutally candid portrayal of human strengths and weaknesses earned the widespread condemnation of his contemporaries, who subjected *Don Juan* and its author to an unforgiving and almost relentless campaign of personal slander and critical abuse. Today, however, critics regard Byron's complex, profoundly skeptical, and ruthlessly realistic work as a remarkable anticipation of both the mood and the thematic preoccupations of modern literature. *Don Juan* is now firmly established as one of the most important (if least characteristic) works of the Romantic era.

Public perception of Byron's character and private life greatly influenced the contemporary reception of *Don Juan*. Much of Byron's art was autobiographical, and he was often inspired to write in reaction to contemporary opinions of his life and poetry. Therefore, a grasp of the major events of his adult life is considered essential to an understanding of *Don Juan*, the work that most clearly reflects both his mature personality and his attitudes toward the age in which he lived. A critical history of the poem must take into account the series of events that transformed Byron in the space of only four years from a minor poet into England's most famous expatriate.

The unique relationship between Byron and his audience that later played an important part in the reception of *Don Juan* began with the publication of the first two cantos of his poem *Childe Harold's Pilgrimage: A Romaunt*. When *Childe Harold* appeared in the spring of 1812, Byron became England's most celebrated author virtually overnight, gaining access to the country's highest social and literary circles. His remark, ''I awoke one morning and found myself famous,'' reflects the suddenness with which the poet and his melancholy autobiographical hero were transformed into objects of universal interest. The close association in the public mind between Byron and his protagonists, first established with *Childe Harold*, continued throughout his career and profoundly affected his later life and the critical reception of his subsequent works.

For several years following his initial rise to fame with *Childe Harold,* Byron enjoyed unprecedented popularity. The publication in 1813-14 of the first three of his ''Eastern Tales,'' with their vaguely autobiographical heroes and exotic settings, furthered his hold upon the popular imagination and reinforced the idea that Byron created his protagonists in his own image. According to one contemporary account, the poet ''was really

the only topic of almost every conversation—the men jealous of him, the women of each other.'' Byron played the part of Regency dandy with aplomb, leading an active social life and carrying on a series of affairs with married women, notably Lady Caroline Lamb and Lady Jane Oxford. In 1814, however, the poet became engaged to Annabella Milbanke, a wealthy heiress whose naïveté and reputation for moral virtue sharply contrasted with Byron's wealth of worldly experience. Married in early 1815, Byron and his wife were together scarcely a year before she left him in January, 1816. The reasons for their separation have been the subject of extensive research, and while no conclusive proof has ever been brought forth, biographers suggest that Byron may have had an incestuous relationship with his half-sister, Augusta Leigh, prior to the marriage, and that his wife may have learned of it. Whatever its actual cause, Byron's estrangement from his wife and the sensational rumors concerning his conduct destroyed his place in the public esteem. The object of universal scorn and opprobrium, he was attacked in the press and snubbed by the society that had so recently lionized him. After deciding to go abroad, Byron signed a deed of separation from his wife on April 21, 1816. Four days later he left England forever.

Byron never forgot the sudden turn of public opinion in England against him. His meteoric rise to fame and equally abrupt exile hardened him against a society whose rigid notions of decorum and respectability he had always regarded with suspicion. He left the country alienated and bitter, convinced that he was "more sinned against than sinning." Byron's belief that he was the victim of British "cant"—of a social system that valued appearances more than reality—later surfaced in the unadorned realism and attack on human hypocrisy that figure prominently in *Don Juan*.

Following his departure from Britain, Byron spent the summer of 1816 in Geneva, Switzerland, and that autumn settled in Northern Italy, where he valued both the climate and the relatively tolerant social code. He continued to write and soon became known for his dissipated mode of life and numerous casual liaisons with Italian women. In September, 1817, Byron read a recently published poem by his friend and fellow English satirist, John Hookham Frere. Known as "Whistlecraft," Frere's work was a mock heroic Arthurian romance written in the style and ottava rima stanza form of the fifteenth-century Italian poet Luigi Pulci. The possibilities for satire, comedy, verbal wordplay, and thematic digression suggested by Frere's imitation of Pulci delighted Byron, and in October he incorporated these elements into *Beppo: A Venetian Story*, a light satire on Venetian morality and customs. Often seen by critics as a rehearsal of the stanzaic form and narrative style of *Don Juan*, *Beppo* was a critical and popular success when it appeared in February of 1818. The work's reception pleased Byron and prompted him to investigate the rich tradition of Italian burlesque poetry written in ottava rima, including the works of Pulci, Francesco Berni, and Giambattista Casti. Under the influence of these Italian models, he began working on *Don Juan* in July, 1818.

The flexible style and structure Byron borrowed from the Italian burlesque tradition allowed him a freedom of expression not found in his earlier works. Critics point out that in *Beppo* his art was for the first time not merely a product of the dark and melancholy aspects of his character, but instead reflected the full range of his personality. The ottava rima form and burlesque manner gave him a means of expressing the mischievous, playfully cynical, and comic sides of his genius. In *Don Juan*, however, he combined the stylistic elements and mode of narration he had borrowed from the Italian poets with a wide range of other literary influences, including the epics of Virgil and Homer, the works of such satirists as François Marie Voltaire, Miguel de Cervantes, Alexander Pope, and Jonathan Swift, and the picaresque novels of Tobias Smollett, Henry Fielding, and Laurence Sterne. Byron also incorporated a broad selection of nonfiction materials, including passages from historical works, directly into his text. This eclectic combination of literary and factual materials resulted in a work satiric in tone, epic in scope, and harshly realistic in its portrayal of human behavior and events. The poem's rambling design and the possibilities for thematic digression inherent in its burlesque style permitted Byron to discourse on numerous topics, including his complex dissatisfaction with the nature of life and his contempt for the "cant and hypocrisy" of the society that had first encouraged his vices and then driven him into exile. With the intention to satirize, shock, and reform, he lashed out in *Don Juan* at everything he considered unjust in society and the world.

Don Juan follows the adventures of a youthful protagonist who bears little resemblance to the heartless libertine of popular European legend. A passive character, Byron's Don Juan reacts to rather than manipulates the world around him. Brave, resourceful, but essentially without motivation or direction, Juan is the victim of society. By casting society in the role of villain—as the corrupting influence on an innocent incarnation of the most notorious profligate in European literature—Byron reversed the Don Juan legend to suggest that society, not the individual, bears the responsibility for evil in the world. Juan's story, however, represents only a part of *Don Juan*. The hero's series of adventures as overprotected teenager, castaway, lover, slave, soldier, kept man, and ornament in English society also enables Byron to deliberate on an almost limitless array of social, political, poetical, and metaphysical topics. Byron's use of a narrator with a distinct personality, as well as the presence of the poet's own voice in the work, allows him simultaneously to tell Juan's story and to comment on it from various perspectives, a technique that contributes to the ironic qualification of nearly every level of meaning in the poem. *Don Juan* is therefore not merely a poem about a youthful adventurer, but rather a vast collection of alternately tender and satirical speculations on the human condition, with particular emphasis on the nature of perception.

Byron recorded his thoughts on numerous aspects of *Don Juan*, from the genesis of the poem up through the various stages of its publication, in letters to his friends and advisers in London. Often facetious, deliberately outrageous, and exaggerated in tone, the letters capture Byron's reactions to the literary recommendations of his friends and to the poem's critical reception. When his publisher John Murray and the group of advisers Byron called the "Synod" received the first installments of *Don Juan* from Italy, they were horrified that he planned to publish it. In their view, Byron's attack on the Poet Laureate Robert Southey in the Dedication, his satire of Lady Byron in the character of Donna Inez, and the irreverent attitudes toward sex and religion throughout the poem made publication impossible. The poet persevered, however, fighting during the early months of 1819 to save *Don Juan* from alterations or omissions. After reluctantly agreeing to delete the slanderous Dedication and several controversial stanzas, Byron decided to publish the poem anonymously. The first two cantos, with neither Byron's nor Murray's name on the title page, appeared in July, 1819—to unprecedented critical hostility.

Byron had anticipated the outcry against *Don Juan*, but even he was surprised by its vehemence. Though reviewers had questioned the moral tendencies of his previous works, he had enjoyed a relatively benevolent relationship with the press prior to his separation from Lady Byron. Yet with his departure for the continent and the widespread reports of his dissipation and sexual excesses in Italy, many journals turned against him. Thus when *Don Juan* was published, Byron was damned both for the contents of the poem and for his past and present improprieties. Although Byron often derided published appraisals of his poetry, he never ceased to be aware of and interested in public opinion. His intense concern with his press underscores the importance of his relationship with his critics. The early reception of *Don Juan* is particularly significant in this respect because Byron responded in the poem to commentary on its previously published parts.

Setting the harsh tone for much of the criticism of the poem published during Byron's lifetime, the influential Scottish journal, *Blackwood's Edinburgh Magazine*, struck the first heavy blow against *Don Juan* in its August number for 1819. The anonymous critic consistently praised the artistic power of the work, yet sharply censured its moral implications and subject matter. The *Blackwood's* article exemplifies most contemporary reviews in that it deals as much with Byron's life as with *Don Juan*. Critics seized upon the autobiographical aspects of the poem, particularly the satiric portrait of Lady Byron, and used them to attack Byron personally. *Blackwood's* called the poet a "cool unconcerned fiend," and similar epithets were bestowed upon him by numerous other periodicals. He was urged to reform his life and return to England. Yet despite the character assassination and indignant outrage expressed in the early reviews, critics consistently acknowledged that Byron would be without peer as a poet but for his moral failings. Applauded for his intellect but savaged for his ethics, the poet was subjected to (in his own words) "hyperbolical" praise for the power of his verse and "diabolical" abuse for what the *Literary Chronicle* referred to as his "indecent allusions, double entendres," and "mockery of religion." Literary historians have attributed the clamor against *Don Juan* to various causes, including conservative bias against Byron's liberal politics, personal animosity by those he satirized, and genuine offense at the moral stance of the poem. The political dimensions of the work's reception can be seen in a review of the first two cantos by the poet Leigh Hunt. Among the few contemporary critics to praise *Don Juan* wholeheartedly, Hunt defended both its morality and realism in the pages of his liberal journal, the *Examiner*. Hunt's defense is also a broad attack on conservative values and politics, and his position demonstrates the extraliterary issues that profoundly affected the poem's initial reception.

Byron composed and published the remaining cantos of *Don Juan* over the next five years: Cantos III-V appeared in August, 1821; Cantos VI-XIV were published in three volumes in July, August, and December, 1823; and Cantos XV and XVI followed in March, 1824. With a few notable exceptions, the poem remained the object of violent critical hostility. Among the prominent critics to speak out against it was Francis Jeffrey, who in a sober 1822 article in the powerful *Edinburgh Review* broke the journal's silence on *Don Juan* to lament the moral tendencies of all Byron's works. Hunt persisted in his outspoken defiance of the "cant and hypocrisy" of the major journals, and the critic John Gibson Lockhart published an anonymous pamphlet defending the poem in 1821, but their voices were scarcely heard above the general chorus of condemnation. Though the poet was discouraged at first by the uproar, Byron's belief that *Don Juan* constituted his best work, as well as the occasional support of such men as Lockhart and Percy Bysshe Shelley, convinced him to carry on with the poem—which, despite its vilification by the critics, sold extremely well following the relatively poor sales of the first two cantos. Regardless of the poem's popularity, however, Murray refused to handle it after the publication of the fifth canto, and Leigh Hunt's brother John published the remaining installments. Byron's association with Hunt, who was regarded as a lower-class radical by the conservative journals, further alienated the critics, who accused Byron of lowering himself by consorting with the "Cockneys." Only the criticism of his mistress, Countess Teresa Guiccioli, persuaded him to actually stop writing *Don Juan;* though at her request he broke it off in July, 1821, he resumed the poem the following spring.

Byron continued to work on *Don Juan* until his departure from Italy for Greece in July, 1823. The Greek War of Independence from Turkey had captured his interest from its inception in 1821, and he decided to aid the struggle for freedom. In Greece, however, he found dissension among rival factions of the insurgents and indecisiveness on the part of their leaders. Disillusioned, but steadfast in his purpose, Byron was engaged in plans to assist the Greek cause when he became gravely ill in the spring of 1824 while staying at Missolonghi, Greece. He died on April 19, less than a month after the publication of the last completed cantos of *Don Juan*.

In the immense outpouring of grief throughout England and Europe following Byron's death, fascination with his life and character overshadowed critical consideration of his works. The social and literary phenomenon of "Byronism" that for the next twenty-five years exerted a powerful influence on European culture resulted primarily from the cult of his personality and the "Byronic Heroes" of his early verse tales and derived little from the satiric poet who had written *Don Juan*. Thus, while critics and biographers produced a large body of material on Byron in the decade following his death, they generally ignored or dismissed *Don Juan*. Notable exceptions were Sir Walter Scott, who lauded the all-encompassing subject matter of the poem, and John Ruskin, who defended its morality (see *NCLC*, Vol. 2). Their views represented those of a minority, and as early Victorian critics began to react against the popular obsession with Byron as a personality, *Don Juan* was lost in the general decline of his reputation as a poet. The poem subsequently received little critical attention of importance until 1866, when Algernon Charles Swinburne published one of the first important descriptions of its style (see *NCLC*, Vol. 2). Extolling the vitality and strength of Byron's verse, the critic also asserted that *Don Juan* could be best appreciated only when taken as a whole. Swinburne's opinion, while not profoundly influential at the time, anticipated the attempts of twentieth century critics to treat the poem as a structurally and thematically unified work.

Throughout the nineteenth century, the question of *Don Juan's* alleged immorality occupied a prominent place in criticism of the poem. On the European continent, Byron's enormous popularity and influence did not decline as dramatically as in England. Free from the societal constraints that compelled most Victorians to decry the morality of *Don Juan,* such continental critics as Hippolyte Taine and Georg Brandes were able to write candid and thorough appraisals of the poem. Thus, Taine explored the satirical strengths of *Don Juan,* praising Byron's attack on English hypocrisy; and Brandes admired the realism and honesty of the work, describing it as the "one great poem of the nineteenth century which can be compared with Goethe's *Faust*." The accolades of Taine and Brandes notwithstanding, during the remainder of the nineteenth century *Don Juan* continued to elicit more casual critical asides and belletristic debate than scholarly study. However, the gradual revival of Byron's reputation as a poet toward the end of the Victorian era, and the landmark publication in 1898-1901 of the Coleridge-Prothero edition of his works, paved the way for serious critical consideration of *Don Juan* in the twentieth century.

The period from 1900 to the centenary of Byron's death in 1924 yielded an increasing amount of appreciative commentary on the poet, most of it of a broad and biographical nature. This renewal of interest was stimulated in part by the Coleridge-Prothero edition. Although it did not lead directly to a rise in the reputation of *Don Juan*, this work nevertheless provided critics with a scholarly and complete text (including fourteen previously unpublished stanzas of the uncompleted seventeenth canto) that later served as the source material for criticism of the poem in the 1930s and 1940s. Despite such pioneering works as Claude M. Fuess's *Lord Byron as a Satirist in Verse*, the majority of critics and biographers in the early twentieth century continued to discuss *Don Juan* only in general and often defensive terms—the issue of the poem's morality remained a problem for many writers. In the 1930s, influential studies by T. S. Eliot (see *NCLC,* Vol. 2), William J. Calvert, and Ronald Bottrall confirmed the value of substantive critical analysis of various facets of *Don Juan,* including its language and range of literary influences. The publication in 1945 of full-length books on *Don Juan* by Elizabeth French Boyd and Paul Graham Trueblood initiated the modern proliferation of critical interest in the poem. Both the serious approach and quantity of essays on the poem during this period helped to establish it as Byron's most important work.

Since 1945, scholars have focused on the structure, style, literary background, and philosophy of *Don Juan.* The appearance in 1957 of both Leslie Marchand's definitive biography of Byron and the variorum edition of the poem edited by Truman Guy Steffan and Willis W. Pratt provided critics with a wealth of primary source material and information about the work's composition, textual history, and place in Byron's oeuvre. These seminal works served as an impetus for the explosion of increasingly detailed and sophisticated writing on the poem in the 1960s. Because of Byron's declared contempt for poetic systems of any kind and the unique nature of the work itself—its autobiographical elements, constantly shifting perspective, and tendency to self-mockery—most critics responded with a flexible, eclectic, and comprehensive approach. This trend is exemplified by the successful attempts of writers to find meaningful structure in the poem's deliberately meandering and seemingly disconnected narrative. While many earlier commentators viewed *Don Juan* as chaotic and improvisatory, critics during the last forty years have argued that the poem derives thematic unity and narrative purpose from a series of recurring and contrasting motifs and metaphors. The themes of nature versus civilization, appearance versus reality, and the Christian doctrine of the Fall outlined by, respectively, Boyd, Ernest J. Lovell, Jr., and George M. Ridenour are among those that lend unity and coherence to the poem, according to critics. Scholars have also explored how the structural principles of the classical epic contribute to the design of *Don Juan* and how Byron both utilized and reacted against epic conventions. In discussing the style of *Don Juan,* critics have dealt with such topics as Byron's use of multiple narrative perspectives and the influence of classical, Italian, and eighteenth-century English literature on the imagery, versification, and language of the poem. M. K. Joseph demonstrated how the different narrative personas in *Don Juan* promote its complex levels of meaning and rich variety. Lovell, Ridenour, and Jerome J. McGann also published influential essays on the stylistic elements of the poem, exploring its irony, rhetoric, and gradations of tone. In three prominent studies of the literary background of *Don Juan,* A. B. England, András Horn, and Peter Vassallo outlined the diverse array of literary traditions revealed in the structure, style, and philosophy of the poem, emphasizing both its complex heritage and its uniqueness.

While as late as 1959 Northrup Frye could state that "we have not yet shaken off our nineteenth-century inhibitions about Byron" (see *NCLC,* Vol. 2), critical squeamishness about the moral influence of *Don Juan* evolved in the 1950s and 1960s into a concern with what many commentators saw as the poem's fundamentally pessimistic philosophy and destructive view of life. Brian Wilkie argued that both philosophically and structurally *Don Juan* represents a nihilistic "epic of negation," a position upheld by Robert C. Gleckner, who found the poem both "grim" and "despairing." Alvin B. Kernan's contrasting vision of the poem as primarily comic has not found wide acceptance, although the majority of critics today perceive the poem as largely positive in purpose and effect. This view was summarized by M. H. Abrams, who maintained that the targets of Byron's satire uniformly deserve his violent attacks. In answer to the charge that *Don Juan* is unremittingly harsh and negative, Abrams asserted that "the satire constantly, though silently, assumes as moral positives the qualities of courage, loyalty, generosity, and above all, total candor; it merely implies that these virtues are excessively rare, and that the modern world is not constituted to reward, to encourage, or even to recognize them." Abrams's conception of the poem has been affirmed by numerous critics, who have found *Don Juan* as applicable to Western society in the second half of the twentieth century as it was in Byron's day. In praising the poem, recent critics have singled out not only Byron's tremendous energy, virtuosic language, and brilliant satire, but also his dynamic championing of human freedom. Today *Don Juan* is accorded the status Paul Elmer More claimed for it at the turn of the century when he pronounced the poem "the epic of modern life."

LORD BYRON (letter date 1818)

[*Byron's first recorded reference to* Don Juan *(by name) is contained in the following passage from a letter to his close friend and fellow poet Thomas Moore. Despite his often-quoted and seemingly innocuous assertion that the poem was "meant to be a little quietly facetious upon every thing," Byron frankly admits that* Don Juan *will probably meet with a hostile reception.*]

I have finished the First Canto (a long one, of about 180 octaves) of a poem in the style and manner of *Beppo,* encouraged by the good success of the same. It is called *Don Juan,* and is meant to be a little quietly facetious upon every thing. But I doubt whether it is not—at least, as far as it has yet gone—too free for these very modest days. However, I shall try the experiment, anonymously, and if it don't take, it will be discontinued. It is dedicated to S[outhey] in good, simple, savage verse, upon the [Laureate's] politics, and the way he got them. But the bore of copying it out is intolerable; and if I had an amanuensis he would be of no use, as my writing is so difficult to decipher.

My poem's Epic, and is meant to be
  Divided in twelve books, each book containing,
With love and war, a heavy gale at sea—
  A list of ships, and captains, and kings reigning—
New characters, &c. &c.

The above are two [sic] stanzas, which I send you as a brick of my Babel, and by which you can judge of the texture of the structure. (pp. 67-8)

> *Lord Byron, in a letter to Thomas Moore on September 19, 1818, in his* "The Flesh Is Frail": Byron's Letters and Journals, 1818-1819, Vol. 6, *edited by Leslie A. Marchand, Cambridge, Mass.: The Belknap Press, 1976, pp. 66-9.*

LORD BYRON (letter date 1818)

[*In the following excerpt, Byron asks his friend John Cam Hobhouse to negotiate with Murray or another bookseller to publish* Don Juan *and explains the principal reason for his attack on Southey in the Dedication to the poem. The last portion of the excerpt is one of a series of passages in Byron's letters in which he defends the controversial aspects of* Don Juan *by pointing to similar "freedoms" in the works of well-known and highly respected authors of the past.*]

I request you to read—& having read—and if possible approved to obtain the largest or (if large be undeserved—) the fairest price from [Murray] or any one else.—There are firstly—the first Canto of **Don Juan**—(in the style of **Beppo**—and Pulci—forgive me for putting Pulci second it is a slip—"Ego et Rex meus")—containing two *hundred* Octaves—and a dedication in verse of a dozen to Bob Southey—bitter as necessary—I mean the dedication; I will tell you why.—The Son of a Bitch on his return from Switzerland two years ago—said that Shelley and I "had formed a League of Incest and practiced our precepts with &c."—he lied like a rascal—for they *were not Sisters—one* being Godwin's daughter by Mary Wollstonecraft—and the other the daughter of the present Mrs. G[odwin] by a *former* husband.—The Attack contains no allusion to the cause—but—some good verses—and all political & poetical.—He lied in another sense—for there was no promiscuous intercourse—my commerce being limited to the carnal knowledge of the Miss C[lairmont]—I had nothing to do with the offspring of Mary Wollstonecraft—which Mary was a former Love of Southey's—which might have taught him to respect the fame of her daughter. . . . As [*Don Juan*] is as free as La Fontaine—& bitter in politics—too—the damned Cant and Toryism of the day may make Murray pause—in that case you will take any Bookseller who bids best;—when I say *free*—I mean that freedom—which Ariosto Boiardo and Voltaire—Pulci—Berni—all the best Italian & French—as well as Pope & Prior amongst the English permitted themselves;—but no improper words nor phrases—merely some situations—which are taken from life. (pp. 76-7)

> *Lord Byron, in a letter to John Cam Hobhouse on November 11, 1818, in his "The Flesh Is Frail": Byron's Letters and Journals, 1818-1819, Vol. 6, edited by Leslie A. Marchand, Cambridge, Mass.: Belknap Press, 1976, pp. 76-8.*

LORD BYRON (essay date 1818)

[*Byron wrote the following unfinished preface to Cantos I and II of* Don Juan *in late 1818, but it was never printed during his lifetime. In his remarks, Byron belittles Wordsworth's concept of the relation between imagination and poetry by parodying the latter's introductory note to "The Thorn" and ridiculing the poem itself. Critics agree that Byron's assault upon Wordsworth demonstrates the gulf in artistic ideals and poetic method that separated the two men; as McGann has asserted, the preface is an "attack upon the Romantic exaltation of the imagination as a divine poetic faculty" (see excerpt dated 1976). Many also contend that Byron's comments reflect his desire to discredit what he felt was an inferior school of poetry; his vilification of Southey in the final part of the preface is considered an attempt to suggest that the strengths of* Don Juan *will derive from the reality of his experience rather than from imaginary situations.*]

In a note or preface (I forget which) by Mr W. Wordsworth to a poem—the Subject of which as far as it is intelligible is the remorse of an unnatural mother for the destruction of a natural child—the courteous Reader is desired to extend his usual courtesy so far as to suppose that the narrative is narrated by "the Captain of a Merchantman or small trading vessel lately retired upon a small annuity to some inland town—&c. &c." I quote from memory but conceive the above to be the sense—as far there [*sic*] is Sense of the note or preface to the aforesaid poem—as far as it is a poem.—The poem—or pro-

duction—to which I allude is that which begins with—"There is a thorn—it is so old"—and then the Poet informs all who are willing to be informed—that it [*sic*] age was such as to leave great difficulty in the conception of it's ever having been young at all—which is as much as to say either that it was Coeval with the Creator of all things, or that it had been *born old*, and was thus appropriately by antithesis devoted to the Commemoration of a child that died young.—The pond near it is described according to mensuration

> I measured it from side to side
> Tis three feet long, & two feet wide

Let me be excused from being particular in the detail of Such things as this is the Sort of writing which has superseded and degraded Pope in the eyes of the discerning British Public and this Man is the kind of Poet who in the same manner that Joanna Southcote found many thousand people to take her Dropsy for God Almighty re-impregnated, has found some hundreds of persons to misbelieve in his insanities, and hold his art as a kind of poetical Emanuel Swedenborg—or Richard Brothers—or Parson Tozer—half Enthusiast and half Imposter.—This rustic Gongora and vulgar Marini of his Country's taste has long abandoned a mind capable of better things to the production of such trash as may support the reveries which he would reduce into a System of prosaic raving that is to supersede all that has hitherto by the best & wisest of our fathers has [*sic*] been deemed poetry;—and for his success—and what mountebank will not find the proselytes? (From Count Cagliostro to Madame Krudner) he may partly thank his absurdity—& partly his having lent his more downright and unmeasured prose to the aid of a political party which acknowledges it's real weakness—though fenced with the whole armour of artificial Power and defended by all the ingenuity of purchased Talent, in liberally rewarding with praise & pay even the meanest of its advocates.—Amongst these last in self-degradation, this Thraso of poetry—has long been a Gnatho in Politics—and may be met in print at some booksellers and several trunkmakers, and in person at dinner at Lord Lonsdale's. The Reader who has acquiesced in Mr W. Wordsworth's supposition that his "Misery oh Misery" is dated by the "Captain of a small &c." is requested to suppose by a like exertion of Imagination that the following epic Narrative is told by a Spanish Gentleman in a village in the Sierra Morena on the road between Monasterio & Seville—sitting at the door of a Posada with the Curate of the hamlet on his right hand a Segar in his mouth—a Jug of Malaga or perhaps, "right Sherris" before him on a small table containing the relics of an Olla Podrida—the time Sunset;—at some distance a groupe of black eyed peasantry are dancing to the sound of the flute of a Portuguese Servant belonging to two foreign travellers who have an hour ago dismounted from their horses to spend the night on their way to the Capital of Andalusia—of these one is attending to the story—and the other having sauntered further is watching the beautiful movements of a tall peasant Girl whose whole Soul is in her eyes & her heart in the dance of which she is the Magnet to ten thousand feelings that vibrate with her Own. Not far off a knot of French prisoners are contending with each other at the grated lattice of their temporary confinement—for a view of the twilight festival—the two foremost are a couple of hussars, one of whom has a bandage on his forehead yet stained with the blood of a Sabre cut received in the recent skirmish which deprived him of his lawless freedom;—his eyes sparkle in unison and his fingers beat time against the bars of his prison to the sound of the Fandango which is fleeting before him.—Our friend the Storyteller—at some distance with a small elderly audience is supposed to tell his story without being much moved by the musical hilarity at the other end of the village Green.—The Reader is further requested to suppose him (to account for his knowledge of English) either an Englishman settled in Spain—or a Spaniard who had travelled in England—perhaps one of the Liberals who have subsequently been so liberally rewarded by Ferdinand of grateful memory—for his restoration.—Having supposed as much of this as the utter impossibility of such a supposition will admit—the reader is requested to extend his supposed power of supposing so far as to conceive that the dedication to Mr Southey—&several stanzas of the poem itself are interpolated by the English Editor. He may also imagine various causes for the tenor of the dedication. It may be presumed to be the production of a present Whig who after being bred a transubstantial Tory—apostatized in an unguarded moment—&incensed at having got nothing by the exchange has in utter envy of the better success of the Author of Walter Tyler—vented his renegado rancour on that immaculate person for whose future immortality & present purity we have the best authority in his own repeated assurances, or it may be supposed the work of a rival poet ob-scured, if not by the present ready popularity of Mr Southey—yet by the Postobits he has granted upon Posterity & usurious self-applause in which he has anticipated with some profusion perhaps the opinion of future ages who are always more enlightened than Contemporaries—more especially in the eyes of those whose figure in their own times has been disproportioned to their deserts. What Mr Southey's deserts are—no one knows better than Mr Southey—all his latter writings have displayed the writhing of a weakly human creature conscious of owing it's worldly elevation to it's own debasement—(like a man who has made a fortune by the Slave-trade, or the retired keeper of a Gaming house or Brothel) and struggling convulsively to deceive others without the power of lying to himself.—But to resume—the dedication may be further supposed to be produced by some one who may have a cause of aversion from the said Southey—for some personal reason—perhaps a gross calumny invented or circulated by this Pantisocratic apostle of Apostacy—who is sometimes as unguarded in his assertions—as atrocious in his conjectures and feeds the cravings of his wretched Vanity disappointed in it's nobler hopes—& reduced to prey upon such Snatches of fame as his contributions to the *Quarterly Review*—and the consequent praise with which a powerful Journal repays it's assistants can afford him—by the abuse of whosoever may be more consistent—or more successful than himself;—and the provincial gang of scribblers gathered round him. (pp. 3-7)

> *Lord Byron, "Preface to Cantos I and II," in his* Don Juan, a Variorum Edition: Cantos I-V, Vol. II, *edited by Truman Guy Steffan and Willis W. Pratt, University of Texas Press, 1957, pp. 3-7.*

LORD BYRON   (letter date 1819)

[*In the following excerpt, Byron reacts to the editorial suggestions of his friends and advisers in London, who repeatedly asked him to alter or omit portions of the poem. Though he agrees to remove from the Dedication several stanzas attacking Viscount Castlereagh and an obscene pun on Southey's first name, he protests against any piecemeal tampering with his text, declaring "in no case will I submit to have the poem mutilated."*]

With regard to the Poeshie—I will have no "cutting & slashing" as Perry calls it—you may omit the stanzas on Castle-

reagh—indeed it is better—& the two "*Bobs*" at the end of the 3d. stanza of the dedication—which will leave "high" & "adry" good rhymes without any "*double* (or Single) Entendre''—but no more—I appeal—not "to Philip fasting" but to Alexander drunk—I appeal to Murray at his ledger—to the people—in short, **Don Juan** shall be an entire horse or none.—If the objection be to the indecency, the Age which applauds the "Bath Guide" & Little's poems—& reads Fielding & Smollett still—may bear with that;—if to the poetry—I will take my chance.—I will not give way to all the Cant of Christendom—I have been cloyed with applause & sickened with abuse;—at present—I care for little but the Copyright,—I have imbibed a great love for money—let me have it—if Murray loses this time—he won't the next—he will be cautious—and I shall learn the decline of his customers by his epistolary indications.———But in no case will I submit to have the poem mutilated.—There is another Canto written—but not copied—in two hundred & odd Stanzas,—if this succeeds—as to the prudery of the present day—what is it? are we more moral than when Prior wrote—is there anything in **Don Juan** so strong as in Ariosto—or Voltaire—or Chaucer? (p. 91)

> *Lord Byron, in a letter to John Cam Hobhouse and Douglas Kinnaird on January 19, 1819, in his "The Flesh Is Frail": Byron's Letters and Journals, 1818-1819, Vol. 6, edited by Leslie A. Marchand, Cambridge, Mass.: Belknap Press, 1976, pp. 91-2.*

LORD BYRON   (letter date 1819)

[*In the following excerpt from a letter to Murray, Byron insists that the possibility* Don Juan *might offend his audience should not keep the poem from being published. The quality of the poetry, Byron maintains, will decide its fate both for his era and for posterity.*]

If the poem has poetry—it would stand—if not—fall—the rest is "leather & prunella,"—and has never yet affected any human production "pro or con."—Dullness is the only annihilator in such cases.—As to the Cant of the day—I despise it—as I have ever done all it's other finical fashions,—which become you as paint became the Antient Britons.—If you admit this prudery—you must omit half Ariosto—La Fontaine—Shakespeare—Beaumont—Fletcher—Massinger—Ford—all the Charles second writers—in short, *Something* of most who have written before Pope—and are worth reading—and much of Pope himself.... (p. 95)

> *Lord Byron, in a letter to John Murray on January 25, 1819, in his "The Flesh Is Frail": Byron's Letters and Journals, 1818-1819, Vol. 6, edited by Leslie A. Marchand, Cambridge, Mass.: Belknap Press, 1976, pp. 94-5.*

LORD BYRON   (letter date 1819)

[*The following excerpt from a letter to Murray exemplifies Byron's dissatisfaction with what he felt was the hypocritical double standard of his "cursed puritanical committee," which consistently praised the poetry of* Don Juan *while condemning its morality. The final sentence of the excerpt is perhaps the most famous of his claims that the moral message of the poem was there for those who wished to find it.*]

I have written to you several letters—some with additions—& some upon the subject of the poem itself which my cursed puritanical committee have protested against publishing—but we will circumvent them on that point in the end. I have not yet begun to copy out the second Canto—which is finished;—from natural laziness—and the discouragement of the milk & water they have thrown upon the first.—I say all this to them as to you—that is for *you* to say to *them*—for I will have nothing underhand.—If they had told me the poetry was bad—I would have acquiesced—but they say the contrary—& then talk to me about morality—the first time I ever heard the word from any body who was not a rascal that used it for a purpose.—I maintain that it is the most moral of poems—but if people won't discover the moral that is their fault not mine. (pp. 98-9)

> *Lord Byron, in a letter to John Murray on February 1, 1819, in his ''The Flesh Is Frail'': Byron's Letters and Journals, 1818-1819, Vol. 6, edited by Leslie A. Marchand, Cambridge, Mass.: Belknap Press, 1976, pp. 98-9.*

LORD BYRON   (letter date 1819)

[*In the following excerpt from a letter to Murray, Byron continues to protest against any alterations in the poem, insisting ''You sha'n't make* Canticles *of my Cantos.'' He also scoffs at Murray and his friends' suggestion that he write a serious work in the epic style.*]

The Second Canto of *Don Juan* was sent on Saturday last by post in 4 packets—two of 4—& two of three sheets each—containing in all two hundred & seventeen stanzas octave measure.—But I will permit no curtailments except those mentioned about Castlereagh & the two ''Bobs'' in the introduction.—You sha'n't make *Canticles* of my Cantos. The poem will please if it is lively—if it is stupid it will fail—but I will have none of your damned cutting & slashing.—If you please you may publish *anonymously*[;] it will perhaps be better;—but I will battle my way against them all—like a Porcupine.—So you and Mr. Foscolo &c. want me to undertake what you call a ''great work'' an Epic poem I suppose or some such pyramid.—I'll try no such thing—I hate tasks—and then ''seven or eight years!'' God send us all well this day three months—let alone years!—if one's years can't be better employed than in sweating poesy—a man had better be a ditcher.—And works too!—is *Childe Harold* nothing? you have so many ''*divine*'' poems, is it nothing to have written a *Human* one? without any of your worn out machinery.—Why—man—I could have spun the thought of the four cantos of that poem into twenty—had I wanted to book-make—& it's passion into as many modern tragedies—since you want *length* you shall have enough of *Juan* for I'll make 50 cantos. (p. 105)

> *Lord Byron, in a letter to John Murray on April 6, 1819, in his ''The Flesh Is Frail'': Byron's Letters and Journals, 1818-1819, Vol. 6, edited by Leslie A. Marchand, Cambridge, Mass.: Belknap Press, 1976, pp. 105-06.*

LORD BYRON   (poem date 1819)

[*In the following stanzas from Canto I of* Don Juan, *Byron outlines his plans for the poem in a series of half-facetious comments on the relation between his poetic methods and the literary conventions of the Classical epic. In differentiating his work from that of his ''epic brethren gone before,'' Byron asserts that his ''story's actually true,'' establishing early on his consistent claim that the details of the poem were taken from life. His discussion of the ''factual'' source materials for the poem is followed by a parody of the Ten Commandments that was regarded as blasphemous by many of his contemporaries. In his ''poetical commandments'' Byron attacks the Lake Poets, offering John Dryden,*

Alexander Pope, and John Milton in their place as literary models and commenting satirically on the other major poets of his day. Byron turns from parody to a series of remarks on the morality of the poem in which he insists that the moral is there for those who wish to find it. This assertion gives way to speculation about the probable reception of his work, and Byron playfully accuses the editor of the British Review *of having taken a bribe to review the poem favorably (for the reaction of editor William Roberts see excerpt dated 1819). In the last two stanzas of the canto, Byron offers his hope that the poem will succeed. He concludes by sarcastically quoting a passage from Southey's* Epilogue to the Lay of the Laureate. *Cantos I and II of* Don Juan *were first published on July 15, 1819.*]

[*Canto I, stanzas 6-7*]

> Most epic poets plunge in ''medias res,''
>   (Horace makes this the heroic turnpike road)
> And then your hero tells, whene'er you please,
>   What went before—by way of episode,
> While seated after dinner at his ease,
>   Beside his mistress in some soft abode,
> Palace, or garden, paradise, or cavern,
> Which serves the happy couple for a tavern.
>
> That is the usual method, but not mine—
>   My way is to begin with the beginning;
> The regularity of my design
>   Forbids all wandering as the worst of sinning,
> And therefore I shall open with a line
>   (Although it cost me half an hour in spinning)
> Narrating somewhat of Don Juan's father,
> And also of his mother, if you'd rather.
>
>   (pp. 24-5)

• • • • •

[*Canto I, stanzas 200-11*]

> My poem's epic, and is meant to be
>   Divided in twelve books; each book containing,
> With love, and war, a heavy gale at sea,
>   A list of ships, and captains, and kings reigning,
> New characters; the episodes are three:
>   A panorama view of hell's in training,
> After the style of Virgil and of Homer,
>   So that my name of Epic's no misnomer.
>
> All these things will be specified in time,
>   With strict regard to Aristotle's rules,
> The *vade mecum* of the true sublime,
>   Which makes so many poets, and some fools;
> Prose poets like blank-verse, I'm fond of rhyme,
>   Good workmen never quarrel with their tools;
> I've got new mythological machinery,
> And very handsome supernatural scenery.
>
> There's only one slight difference between
>   Me and my epic brethren gone before,
> And here the advantage is my own, I ween;
>   (Not that I have not several merits more,
> But this will more peculiarly be seen)
>   They so embellish, that 'tis quite a bore
> Their labyrinth of fables to thread through,
> Whereas this story's actually true.
>
> If any person doubt it, I appeal
>   To history, tradition, and to facts,
> To newspapers, whose truth all know and feel,
>   To plays in five, and operas in three acts;
> All these confirm my statement a good deal,

But that which more completely faith exacts
Is, that myself, and several now in Seville,
Saw Juan's last elopement with the devil.

If ever I should condescend to prose,
   I'll write poetical commandments, which
Shall supersede beyond all doubt all those
   That went before; in these I shall enrich
My text with many things that no one knows,
   And carry precept to the highest pitch:
I'll call the work "Longinus o'er a Bottle,
Or, Every Poet his *own* Aristotle."

Thou shalt believe in Milton, Dryden, Pope;
   Thou shalt not set up Wordsworth, Coleridge,
      Southey;
Because the first is crazed beyond all hope,
   The second drunk, the third so quaint and mouthey:
With Crabbe it may be difficult to cope,
   And Campbell's Hippocrene is somewhat drouthy:
Thou shalt not steal from Samuel Rogers, nor
Commit—flirtation with the muse of Moore.

Thou shalt not covet Mr. Sotheby's Muse,
   His Pegasus, nor any thing that's his;
Thou shalt not bear false witness like "the Blues,"
   (There's one, at least, is very fond of this);
Thou shalt not write, in short, but what I choose:
   This is true criticism, and you may kiss—
Exactly as you please, or not, the rod,
But if you don't, I'll lay it on, by G—d!

If any person should presume to assert
   This story is not moral, first, I pray,
That they will not cry out before they're hurt,
   Then that they'll read it o'er again, and say,
(But, doubtless, nobody will be so pert)
   That this is not a moral tale, though gay;
Besides, in canto twelfth, I mean to show
The very place where wicked people go.

If, after all, there should be some so blind
   To their own good this warning to despise,
Led by some tortuosity of mind,
   Not to believe my verse and their own eyes,
And cry that they "the moral cannot find,"
   I tell him, if a clergyman, he lies;
Should captains the remark or critics make,
They also lie too—under a mistake.

The public approbation I expect,
   And beg they'll take my word about the moral,
Which I with their amusement will connect,
   (So children cutting teeth receive a coral);
Meantime, they'll doubtless please to recollect
   My epical pretensions to the laurel:
For fear some prudish readers should grow skittish,
I've bribed my grandmother's review—the British.

I sent it in a letter to the editor,
   Who thank'd me duly by return of post—
I'm for a handsome article his creditor;
   Yet if my gentle Muse he please to roast,
And break a promise after having made it her,
   Denying the receipt of what it cost,
And smear his page with gall instead of honey,
All I can say is—that he had the money.

I think that with this holy new alliance
   I may ensure the public, and defy
All other magazines of art or science,
   Daily, or monthly, or three monthly; I
Have not essay'd to multiply their clients,
   Because they tell me 'twere in vain to try,
And that the Edinburgh Review and Quarterly
Treat a dissenting author very martyrly.

"Non ego hoc ferrem calida juventâ
   Consule Planco," Horace said, and so
Say I; by which quotation there is meant a
   Hint that some six or seven good years ago
(Long ere I dreamt of dating from the Brenta)
   I was most ready to return a blow,
And would not brook at all this sort of thing
In my hot youth—when George the Third was King.
                                    (pp. 135-43)

· · · · ·

[*Canto I, stanzas 221-22*]

   But for the present, gentle reader! and
      Still gentler purchaser! the bard—that's I—
   Must, with permission, shake you by the hand,
      And so your humble servant, and good bye!
   We meet again, if we should understand
      Each other; and if not, I shall not try
   Your patience further than by this short sample—
   'Twere well if others follow'd my example.

   "Go, little book, from this my solitude!
      I cast thee on the waters, go thy ways!
   And if, as I believe, thy vein be good,
      The world will find thee after many days."
   When Southey's read, and Wordsworth understood,
      I can't help putting in my claim to praise—
   The four first rhymes are Southey's every line:
   For God's sake, reader! take them not for mine.
                                    (pp. 147, 149)

> *Lord Byron, in his* Don Juan, a Variorum Edition:
> Cantos I-V, Vol. II, *edited by Truman Guy Steffan*
> *and Willis W. Pratt, University of Texas Press, 1957,*
> *503 p.*

BLACKWOOD'S EDINBURGH MAGAZINE   (essay date 1819)

[Blackwood's Edinburgh Magazine *was founded in 1817 by William Blackwood as a Tory rival to the Whig-supported* Edinburgh Review. *Edited by Blackwood himself, the magazine became one of the most powerful literary organs of the period. Notable for the violence and personal tone of its criticism, Blackwood's (or "Maga," the nickname by which it was widely known) featured the pseudonymous writing of such men as John Gibson Lockhart and John Wilson, who both quickly established themselves among the prominent critics of the day. Blackwood's was the first of the major periodicals to discuss* Don Juan, *and the overwhelmingly negative review excerpted below set the tone for much of the criticism of the poem during Byron's lifetime. The anonymous critic (thought to be either Wilson or Lockhart) consistently praises the artistic power of the work, yet harshly condemns its moral implications and subject matter. Reserved for particular censure are Byron's satirical portrait of Lady Byron as Donna Inez, which the critic terms "brutally, fiendishly, inexpiably mean," and the shipwreck scene, described as "the best and the worst part of the whole." The latter judgment exemplifies the separation between aesthetic and moral considerations common to early notices of the poem. Byron was bothered by the review (see excerpt from his letter of December 10, 1819) and wrote* Some Observations upon an Article in Blackwood's Magazine *(see excerpt dated 1820) in reply.*]

It has not been without much reflection and overcoming many reluctancies, that we have at last resolved to say a few words . . . to our readers concerning this very extraordinary poem. The nature and causes of our difficulties will be easily understood by those of them who have read any part of **Don Juan**—but we despair of standing justified as to the conclusion at which we have arrived, in the opinion of any but those who have read and understood the whole of a work, in the composition of which there is unquestionably a more thorough and intense infusion of genius and vice—power and profligacy—than in any poem which had ever before been written in the English, or indeed in any other modern language. Had the wickedness been less inextricably mingled with the beauty and the grace, and the strength of a most inimitable and incomprehensible nature, our task would have been easy: But SILENCE would be a very poor and a very useless chastisement to be inflicted by us, or by any one, on a production, whose corruptions have been so effectually embalmed—which, in spite of all that critics can do or refrain from doing, nothing can possibly prevent from taking a high place in the literature of our country, and remaining to all ages a perpetual monument of the exalted intellect, and the depraved heart, of one of the most remarkable men to whom that country has had the honour and the disgrace of giving birth.

That Lord Byron has never written any thing more decisively and triumphantly expressive of the greatness of his genius, will be allowed by all who have read this poem. That (laying all its manifold and grievous offences for a moment out of our view) it is by far the most admirable specimen of the mixture of ease, strength, gayety, and seriousness extant in the whole body of English poetry, is a proposition to which, we are almost as well persuaded, very few of them will refuse their assent. With sorrow and humiliation do we speak it—the poet has devoted his powers to the worst of purposes and passions; and it increases his guilt and our sorrow, that he has devoted them entire. What the immediate effect of the poem may be on contemporary literature, we cannot pretend to guess—too happy could we hope that its lessons of boldness and vigour in language, and versification, and conception, might be attended to, as they deserve to be—without any stain being suffered to fall on the purity of those who minister to the general shape and culture of the public mind, from the mischievous insults against all good principle and all good feeling, which have been unworthily embodied in so many elements of fascination.

The moral strain of the whole poem is pitched in the lowest key—and if the genius of the author lifts him now and then out of his pollution, it seems as if he regretted the elevation, and made all haste to descend again. To particularize the offences committed in its pages would be worse than vain—because the great genius of the man seems to have been throughout exerted to its utmost strength, in devising every possible method of pouring scorn upon every element of good or noble nature in the hearts of his readers. Love—honour—patriotism—religion, are mentioned only to be scoffed at and derided, as if their sole resting-place were, or ought to be, in the bosoms of fools. It appears, in short, as if this miserable man, having exhausted every species of sensual gratification—having drained the cup of sin even to its bitterest dregs, were resolved to shew us that he is no longer a human being, even in his frailties;—but a cool unconcerned fiend, laughing with a detestable glee over the whole of the better and worse ele-

ments of which human life is composed—treating well nigh with equal derision the most pure of virtues, and the most odious of vices—dead alike to the beauty of the one, and the deformity of the other—a mere heartless despiser of that frail but noble humanity, whose type was never exhibited in a shape of more deplorable degradation than in his own contemptuously distinct delineation of himself. To confess in secret to his Maker, and weep ever in secret agonies the wildest and most phantastic transgressions of heart and mind, is the part of a conscious sinner, in whom sin has not become the sole principle of life and action—of a soul for which there is yet hope. But to lay bare to the eye of man and of *woman* all the hidden convulsions of a wicked spirit—thoughts too abominable, we would hope, to have been imagined by any but him that has expressed them—and to do all this without one symptom of pain, contrition, remorse, or hesitation, with a calm careless ferociousness of contented and satisfied depravity—this was an insult which no wicked man of genius had ever before dared to put upon his Creator or his Species. This highest of all possible exhibitions of self-abandonment has been set forth in mirth and gladness, by one whose name was once pronounced with pride and veneration by every English voice. This atrocious consummation was reserved for Byron.

It has long been sufficiently manifest, that this man is devoid of religion. At times, indeed, the power and presence of the Deity, as speaking in the sterner workings of the elements, seems to force some momentary consciousness of their existence into his labouring breast;—a spirit in which there breathes so much of the divine, cannot always resist the majesty of its Maker. But of true religion terror is a small part—and of all religion, that founded on mere terror, is the least worthy of such a man as Byron. We may look in vain through all his works for the slightest evidence that his soul had ever listened to the *gentle voice* of the oracles. His understanding has been subdued into conviction by some passing cloud; but his heart has never been touched. He has never written one line that savours of the spirit of meekness. His faith is but for a moment—"he believes and trembles," and relapses again into his gloom of unbelief—a gloom in which he is at least as devoid of HOPE and CHARITY as he is of FAITH.—The same proud hardness of heart which makes the author of **Don Juan** a despiser of the Faith for which his fathers bled, has rendered him a scorner of the better part of woman; and therefore it is that his love poetry is a continual insult to the beauty that inspires it. The earthy part of the passion is all that has found a resting place within his breast—His idol is all of clay—and he dashes her to pieces almost in the moment of his worship. Impiously railing against his God—madly and meanly disloyal to his Sovereign and his country,—and brutally outraging all the best feelings of female honour, affection, and confidence—How small a part of chivalry is that which remains to the descendant of the Byrons—a gloomy vizor, and a deadly weapon!

Of these offences, however, or of such as these, Lord Byron had been guilty abundantly before, and for such he has before been rebuked in our own, and in other more authoritative pages. There are other and newer sins with which the author of **Don Juan** has stained himself—sins of a class, if possible, even more despicable than any he had before committed; and in regard to which it is matter of regret to us, that as yet our periodical critics have not appeared to express themselves with any seemly measure of manly and candid indignation.

Those who are acquainted, (as who is not?) with the main incidents in the private life of Lord Byron;—and who have not seen this production, (and we are aware, that very few of our Northern readers have seen it)—will scarcely believe, that the odious malignity of this man's bosom should have carried him so far, as to make him commence a filthy and impious poem, with an elaborate satire on the character and manners of his wife—from whom, even by his own confession, he has been separated only in consequence of his own cruel and heartless misconduct. It is in vain for Lord Byron to attempt in any way to justify his own behaviour in that affair; and, now that he has so openly and audaciously invited inquiry and reproach, we do not see any good reason why he should not be plainly told so by the general voice of his countrymen. It would not be an easy matter to persuade any Man who has any knowledge of the nature of Woman, that a female such as Lord Byron has himself described his wife to be, would rashly, or hastily, or lightly separate herself, from the love which she had once been inspired for such a man as he is, or was. Had he not heaped insult upon insult, and scorn upon scorn—had he not forced the iron of his contempt into her very soul—there is no woman of delicacy and virtue, as he *admitted* Lady Byron to be, who would not have hoped all things and suffered all things from one, her love of whom must have been inwoven with so many exalting elements of delicious pride, and more delicious humility. To offend the love of such a woman was wrong—but it might be forgiven; to desert her was unmanly—but he might have returned and wiped for ever from her eyes the tears of her desertion;—but to injure, and to desert, and then to turn back and wound her widowed privacy with unhallowed strains of cold-blooded mockery—was brutally, fiendishly, inexpiably mean. For impurities there might be some possibility of pardon, were they supposed to spring only from the reckless buoyancy of young blood and fiery passions,—for impiety there might at least be pity, were it visible that the misery of the impious soul were as great as its darkness;—but for offences such as this, which cannot proceed either from the madness of sudden impulse, or the bewildered agonies of self-perplexing and self-despairing doubt—but which speak the wilful and determined spite of an unrepenting, unsoftened, smiling, sarcastic, joyous sinner—for such diabolical, such slavish vice, there can be neither pity nor pardon. Our knowledge that it is committed by one of the most powerful intellects our island ever has produced, lends intensity a thousand fold to the bitterness of our indignation. Every high thought that was ever kindled in our breasts by the muse of Byron—every pure and lofty feeling that ever responded from within us to the sweep of his majestic inspirations—every remembered moment of admiration and enthusiasm is up in arms against him. We look back with a mixture of wrath and scorn to the delight with which we suffered ourselves to be filled by one who, all the while he was furnishing us with delight, must, we cannot doubt it, have been mocking us with a cruel mockery—less cruel only, because less peculiar, than that with which he has now turned him from the lurking-place of his selfish and polluted exile, to pour the pitiful chalice of his contumely on the surrendered devotion of a virgin-bosom, and the holy hopes of the mother of his child. The consciousness of the insulting deceit which has been practiced upon us, mingles with the nobler pain arising from the contemplation of perverted and degraded genius—to make us wish that no such being as Byron ever had existed. It is indeed a sad and an humiliating thing to know, that in the same year there proceeded from the same pen two productions, in all things so different, as the Fourth Canto of **Childe Harold** and this loathsome **Don Juan**.

Lady Byron, however, has one consolation still remaining, and yet we fear she will think it but a poor one. She shares the scornful satire of her husband, not only with all that is good, and pure, and high, in human nature,—its principles and its feelings; but with every individual also, in whose character the predominance of these blessed elements has been sufficient to excite the envy, or exacerbate the despair of this guilty man. We shall not needlessly widen the wound by detailing its cruelty; we have mentioned one, and, all will admit, the worst instance of the private malignity which has been embodied in so many passages of **Don Juan;** and we are quite sure, the lofty-minded and virtuous men whom Lord Byron has debased himself by insulting, will close the volume which contains their own injuries, with no feelings save those of pity for Him that has inflicted them, and for Her who partakes so largely in the same injuries; and whose hard destiny has deprived her for ever of that proud and pure privilege, which enables themselves to despise them. As to the rest of the world, we know not that Lord Byron could have invented any more certain means of bringing down contempt inexpiable on his own head, than by turning the weapons of his spleen against men whose virtues few indeed can equal, but still fewer are so lost and unworthy as not to love and admire. (pp. 512-15)

[The] best and the worst part of the whole is without doubt the description of the shipwreck. As a piece of terrible painting, it is as much superior as can be to every description of the kind—not even excepting that in the Aeneid—that ever was created. In comparison with the fearful and intense reality of its horrors, every thing that any former poet had thrown together to depict the agonies of that awful scene, appears chill and tame.

> Then rose from sea to sky the wild farewell,
> Then shrieked the timid—and stood still the brave—
> Then some leaped overboard with dreadful yell,
> As eager to anticipate their grave:
> And the sea yawned around her like a hell,
> And down she sucked with her the whirling wave—
> Like one who grapples with his enemy,
> And strives to strangle him before he die.
>
> And first one universal shriek there rushed,
> Louder than the loud ocean, like a crash
> Of echoing thunder. And then all was hushed
> Save the wild wind, and the remorseless dash
> Of billows; but at intervals there gushed,
> Accompanied with a convulsive splash,
> A solitary shriek, the bubbling cry
> Of some strong swimmer in his agony.

But even here the demon of his depravity does not desert him. We dare not stain our pages with quoting any specimens of the disgusting merriment with which he has interspersed his picture of human suffering. He paints it well, only to shew that he scorns it more effectually; and of all the fearful sounds which ring in the ears of the dying, the most horrible is the demoniacal laugh with which this unpitying brother exults over the contemplation of their despair. Will our readers believe that the most innocent of all his odious sarcasms is contained in these two lines?

> They grieved for those that perished in the cutter,
> And also for the biscuit, casks, and butter.

(p. 518)

"Remarks on 'Don Juan'," in Blackwood's Edinburgh Magazine, *Vol. V, No. XXIX, August, 1819, pp. 512-18.*

[WILLIAM ROBERTS] (essay date 1819)

[*Roberts was editor of the highly conservative* British Review *from 1811 to 1822, during which time he exercised a tight control over all contributions and wrote a large number of the reviews himself. Under his guidance the* Review *was a staunch supporter of the moral and political values of the evangelical wing of the Church of England. All of the journal's articles on Byron were written by Roberts, and over the years he was consistently critical of the moral qualities of the poet's works. When in the first canto of* Don Juan *(see excerpt dated 1819) Byron jocularly accused Roberts of having accepted a bribe to review the poem favorably, the critic took the charge seriously, responding with a solemn and censorious article from which the following excerpt is drawn. After refusing to quote from the poem because of its alleged indecency, Roberts denies ever having taken a bribe and insists that the anonymous work cannot be by Byron, who he states would never have made such an accusation. Byron penned a lengthy satirical reply under the pseudonym "Wortley Clutterbuck" (see excerpt dated 1819).*]

Of a poem so flagitious that no bookseller has been willing to take upon himself the publication, though most of them disgrace themselves by selling it, what can the critic say? His praise or censure ought to found itself on examples produced from the work itself. For praise, as far as regards the poetry, many passages might be exhibited; for condemnation, as far as regards the morality, all: but none for either purpose can be produced, without insult to the ear of decency, and vexation to the heart that feels for domestic or national happiness. This poem is sold in the shops as the work of Lord Byron; but the name of neither author nor bookseller is on the title page: we are, therefore, at liberty to suppose it not to be Lord Byron's composition. . . . (pp. 266-67)

[The] strongest argument against the supposition of its being the performance of Lord Byron is this, that it can hardly be possible for an English nobleman, even in his mirth, to send forth to the public the direct and palpable falsehood contained in the 209th and 210th stanzas of the first canto of this work. No misdemeanor, not even that of sending into the world obscene and blasphemous poetry, the product of "studious lewdness," and "laboured impiety," appears to us in so detestable a light as the acceptance of a present by an editor of a review as the condition of praising an author; and yet the miserable man (for miserable he is, as having a soul of which he cannot get rid), who has given birth to this pestilent poem, has not scrupled to lay this to the charge of "The British Review;" and that not by insinuation, but has actually stated himself to have sent money in a letter to the Editor of this journal, who acknowledged the receipt of the same by a letter in return, with thanks. No peer of the British realm can surely be capable of so calumnious a falsehood, refuted, we trust, by the very character and spirit of the journal so defamed. We are compelled, therefore, to conclude, that this poem cannot be Lord Byron's production; and we, of course, expect that Lord Byron will, with all gentlemanly haste, disclaim a work imputed to him, containing a calumny so wholly the product of malignant invention.

Lord Byron could not have been the author of this assertion concerning us (an assertion implicating himself as well as us—for to have tendered such a bribe would have been at least as mean as to have received it); not only because he is a British peer, but because he has too much discernment not to see how little like the truth such a statement must appear concerning a "Review" which has so long maintained, in the cause of public and private virtue, its consistency and purity, independently

of all party and of all power. He knows in what a spirit of frankness and right feeling we have criticised his works, how ready we have been to do justice to their great poetical merit, and how firm and steady we have been in the reprobation of their mischievous tendency.

If Lord Byron had sent us money, and we had been so entirely devoid of honesty, feeling, and decency, as to have accepted it, his Lordship would have had sense enough to see, that to publish the fact would have been at once to release us from the iniquitous contract.

If somebody personating the Editor of the "British Review" has received money from Lord Byron, or from any other person, by way of bribe to praise his compositions, the fraud might be traced by the production of the letter which the author states himself to have received in return. Surely then, if the author of this poem has any such letter, he will produce it for this purpose. But lest it should be said that we have not in positive terms denied the charge, we do utterly deny that there is one word of truth, or the semblance of truth, as far as regards this "Review" or its Editor, in the assertions made in the stanzas above refered to. We really feel a sense of degradation as the idea of this odious imputation passes through our minds.

We have heard, that the author of the poem under consideration designed what he has said in the 35th stanza as a sketch of his own character:

> Yet Jóse was an honourable man,
> That I must say, who knew him very well.

If then he is this honourable man, we shall not call in vain for an act of justice at his hands, in declaring that he did not mean his word to be taken when, for the sake of a jest (our readers will judge how far such a mode of jesting is defensible) he stated, with the particularity which belongs to fact, the forgery of a groundless fiction. (pp. 267-68)

[*William Roberts*], "'Don Juan': A Poem," in *The British Review, Vol. XIV, No. XXVII, August, 1819, pp. 266-68.*

WORTLEY CLUTTERBUCK [PSEUDONYM OF LORD BYRON]
(letter date 1819)

[*The following excerpt is drawn from the satirical letter Byron composed in August 1819 in response to Roberts's remarks in the* British Review *(see excerpt dated 1819). Writing in a mock-serious tone of high sarcasm, Byron ridicules the language and substance of the article and insults both Roberts and the* British Review. *Byron's remarks illustrate his attitude toward what he felt was the "cant and hypocrisy" inherent in most contemporary criticism of the poem, and according to Douglas K. Morris in Alvin Sullivan's* British Literary Magazines, 1789-1836, *the poet's attack caused Roberts to become a "literary laughingstock" and give up editorship of the* Review.]

My Dear Roberts,

As a believer in the Church of England—to say nothing of the State—I have been an occasional reader, and great admirer of, though not a subscriber to, your "Review," which is rather expensive. But I do not know that any part of its contents ever gave me much surprise till the eleventh article of your twenty-seventh number made its appearance. You have there most vigorously refuted a calumnious accusation of bribery and corruption, the credence of which in the public mind might not only have damaged your reputation as a barrister and an editor, but, what would have been still worse, have injured the circulation of your journal; which, I regret to hear, is not so extensive as the "purity (as you well observe) of its," &c. &c. and the present taste for propriety, would induce us to expect. The charge itself is of a solemn nature, and, although in verse, is couched in terms of such circumstantial gravity, as to induce a belief little short of that generally accorded to the thirty-nine articles, to which you so frankly subscribed on taking your degrees. It is a charge the most revolting to the heart of man, from its frequent occurrence; to the mind of a lawyer, from its occasional truth; and to the soul of an editor, from its moral impossibility. You are charged then in the last line of one octave stanza, and the whole eight lines of the next, viz. 209th and 210th of the first canto of that "pestilent poem," *Don Juan,* with receiving, and still more foolishly acknowledging the receipt of, certain monies, to eulogize the unknown author, who by this account must be known to you, if to nobody else. An impeachment of this nature, so seriously made, there is but one way of refuting; and it is my firm persuasion, that whether you did or did not (and *I* believe that you did not) receive the said monies, of which I wish that he had specified the sum, you are quite right in denying all knowledge of the transaction. If charges of this nefarious description are to go forth, sanctioned by all the solemnity of circumstance, and guaranteed by the veracity of verse (as Counsellor Phillips would say) what is to become of readers hitherto implicitly confident in the not less veracious prose of our critical journals? what is to become of the reviews? And, if the reviews fail, what is to become of the editors? It is common cause, and you have done well to sound the alarm. I myself, in my humble sphere, will be one of your echoes. In the words of the tragedian Liston, "I love a row," and you seem justly determined to make one.

It is barely possible, certainly improbable, that the writer might have been in jest; but this only aggravates his crime. A joke, the proverb says, "breaks no bones;" but it may break a bookseller, or it may be the cause of bones being broken. The jest is but a bad one at the best for the author, and might have been a still worse one for you, if your copious contradiction did not certify to all whom it may concern your own indignant innocence, and the immaculate purity of the "British Review." I do not doubt your word, my dear Roberts, yet I cannot help wishing that in a case of such vital importance, it had assumed the more substantial shape of an affidavit sworn before the Lord Mayor.

I am sure, my dear Roberts, that you will take these observations of mine in good part; they are written in a spirit of friendship not less pure than your own editorial integrity. I have always admired you; and not knowing any shape which friendship and admiration can assume more agreeable and useful than that of good advice, I shall continue my lucubrations, mixed with here and there a monitory hint as to what I conceive to be the line you should pursue, in case you should ever again be assailed with bribes, or accused of taking them. By the way, you don't say much about the poem, except that it is "flagitious." This is a pity—you should have cut it up; because, to say the truth, in not doing so, you somewhat assist any notions which the malignant might entertain on the score of the anonymous asseveration which has made you so angry.

You say, no bookseller "was willing to take upon himself the publication, though most of them disgrace themselves by selling it." Now, my dear friend, though we all know that those fellows will do any thing for money, methinks the disgrace is more with the purchasers; and some such, doubtless, there are, for there can be no very extensive selling (as you will perceive by that of the "British Review") without buying. You then add, "what can the critic say?" I am sure I don't know; at present he says very little, and that not much to the purpose. Then comes, "for praise, as far as regards the *poetry, many* passages might be exhibited; for condemnation, as far as regards the morality, all." Now, my dear good Roberts, I feel for you and for your reputation; my heart bleeds for both; and I do ask you, whether or not such language does not come positively under the description of "the puff collusive," for which see Sheridan's farce of "The Critic" (by the way, a little more facetious than your own farce under the same title) towards the close of scene second, act the first.

The poem is, it seems, sold as the work of Lord Byron; but you feel yourself "at liberty to suppose it not Lord B.'s composition." Why did you ever suppose that it was? I approve of your indignation—I applaud it—I feel as angry as you can; but perhaps your virtuous wrath carries you a little too far, when you say that "no misdemeanour, not even that of sending into the world obscene and blasphemous poetry, the product of studious lewdness and laboured impiety, appears to you in so detestable a light as the acceptance of a present by the editor of a review, as the condition of praising an author." The devil it doesn't!—Think a little. This is being critical overmuch. In point of Gentile benevolence or Christian charity, it were surely less criminal to praise for a bribe, than to abuse a fellow creature for nothing; and as to the assertion of the comparative innocence of blasphemy and obscenity, confronted with an editor's "acceptance of a present," I shall merely observe, that as an editor you say very well, but as a Christian barrister, I would not recommend you to transplant this sentence into a brief.

And yet you say, "the miserable man (for miserable he is, as having a soul of which he cannot get rid")—But here I must pause again, and inquire what is the meaning of this parenthesis. We have heard of people of "little soul," or of "no soul at all," but never till now of "the misery of having a soul of which we cannot get rid;" a misery under which you are possibly no great sufferer, having got rid apparently of some of the intellectual part of your own when you penned this pretty piece of eloquence.

But to continue. You call upon Lord Byron, always supposing him *not* the author, to disclaim "with all gentlemanly haste," &c. &c. I am told that Lord B. is in a foreign country, some thousand miles off it may be; so that it will be difficult for him to hurry to your wishes. In the mean time, perhaps you yourself have set an example of more haste than gentility; but "the more haste the worse speed."

Let us now look at the charge itself, my dear Roberts, which appears to me to be in some degree not quite explicitly worded:

I bribed my *Grandmother's* Review, the British.

(pp. 41-5)

Some thought the allusion was to the "British Critic;" others, that by the expression, "my Grandmother's Review," it was intimated that "my grandmother" was not the reader of the review, but actually the writer; thereby insinuating, my dear Roberts, that you were an old woman; because, as people often say, "Jeffrey's Review," "Gifford's Review," in lieu of "Edinburgh" and "Quarterly;" so "my Grandmother's Review" and Roberts's might be also synonymous. Now, whatever colour this insinuation might derive from the circumstance of your wearing a gown, as well as from your time of life, your general style, and various passages of your writings,—I will take upon myself to exculpate you from all suspicion of the kind, and assert, without calling Mrs. Roberts in testimony, that if ever you should be chosen Pope, you will pass through all the previous ceremonies with as much credit as any pontiff since the parturition of Joan. It is very unfair to judge of sex from writings, particularly from those of the ''British Review.'' We are all liable to be deceived; and it is an indisputable fact, that many of the best articles in your journal, which were attributed to a veteran female, were actually written by you yourself; and yet to this day there are people who could never find out the difference. But let us return to the more immediate question.

I agree with you that it is impossible Lord Byron should be the author, not only because, as a British peer, and a British poet, it would be impracticable for him to have recourse to such facetious fiction, but for some other reasons which you have omitted to state. In the first place, his lordship has no grandmother. Now the author—and we may believe him in this—doth expressly state that the ''British'' is his ''Grandmother's Review;'' and if, as I think I have distinctly proved, this was not a mere figurative allusion to your supposed intellectual age and sex, my dear friend, it follows, whether you be she or no, that there is such an elderly lady still extant. And I can the more readily credit this, having a sexagenary aunt of my own, who perused you constantly, till unfortunately falling asleep over the leading article of your last number, her spectacles fell off and were broken against the fender, after a faithful service of fifteen years, and she has never been able to fit her eyes since; so that I have been forced to read you aloud to her; and this is in fact the way in which I became acquainted with the subject of my present letter, and thus determined to become your public correspondent. (pp. 45-7)

Shall I give you what I think a prudent opinion? I don't mean to insinuate, God forbid! but if, by any accident, there should have been such a correspondence between you and the unknown author, whoever he may be, send him back his money: I dare say he will be very glad to have it again: it can't be much, considering the value of the article and the circulation of the journal; and you are too modest to rate your praise beyond its real worth.—Don't be angry,—I know you won't,—at this appraisement of your powers of eulogy; for on the other hand, my dear friend, depend upon it your abuse is worth, not its own weight,—that's a feather,—but *your* weight in gold. So don't spare it: if he has bargained for *that,* give it handsomely, and depend upon your doing him a friendly office.

But I only speak in case of possibility; for, as I said before, I cannot believe in the first instance, that you would receive a bribe to praise any person whatever; and still less can I believe that your praise could ever produce such an offer. You are a good creature, my dear Roberts, and a clever fellow; else I could almost suspect that you had fallen into the very trap set for you in verse by this anonymous wag, who will certainly be but too happy to see you saving him the trouble of making you ridiculous. The fact is that the solemnity of your eleventh article does make you look a little more absurd than you ever yet looked, in all probability, and at the same time does no good; for if any body believed before in the octave stanzas, they will believe still, and you will find it not less difficult to prove your negative, than the learned Partridge found it to demonstrate his not being dead, to the satisfaction of the readers of almanacs.

What the motives of this writer may have been for (as you magnificently translate his quizzing you) ''stating, with the particularity which belongs to fact, the forgery of a groundless fiction,'' (do pray, my dear R., talk a little less ''in King Cambyses' vein'') I cannot pretend to say; perhaps to laugh at you, but that is no reason for your benevolently making all the world laugh also. I approve of your being angry; I tell you I am angry too; but you should not have shown it so outrageously. Your solemn ''*if* somebody personating the Editor of the,'' &c. &c. ''has received from Lord B. or from any other person,'' reminds me of Charley Incledon's usual exordium when people came into the tavern to hear him sing without paying their share of the reckoning—''If a maun, or *any* maun, or *any other* maun,'' &c. &c.; you have both the same redundant eloquence. But why should you think any body would personate you? Nobody would dream of such a prank who ever read your compositions, and perhaps not many who have heard your conversation. But I have been inoculated with a little of your prolixity. The fact is, my dear Roberts, that somebody has tried to make a fool of you, and what he did not succeed in doing, you have done for him and for yourself. (pp. 47-9)

Wortley Clutterbuck [pseudonym of Lord Byron], ''Letter to the Editor of 'My Grandmother's Review','' in The Liberal, *Vol. 1, No. 1, October, 1822, pp. 41-50.*

LORD BYRON   (letter date 1819)

[*The following excerpt from a letter to Murray contains many of Byron's most famous remarks on* Don Juan, *including his extended defense of the poem's rapid juxtaposition of levity and seriousness, a discussion of his lack of concrete plans for continuing the work, and the often-quoted statement ''do you suppose I could have any intention but to giggle and make giggle?''*]

You are right—Gifford is right—Crabbe is right—Hobhouse is right—you are all right—and I am all wrong—but do pray let me have that pleasure.—Cut me up root and branch—quarter me in the ''Quarterly''—send round my ''disjecti membra poetae'' like those of the Levite's Concubine—make—if you will—a spectacle to men and angels—but don't ask me to alter for I can't—I am obstinate and lazy—and there's the truth.—But nevertheless—I will answer your friend [Francis Cohen] who objects to the quick succession of fun and gravity—as if in that case the gravity did not (in intention at least) heighten the fun.—His metaphor is that ''we are never scorched and drenched at the same time!''—Blessings on his experience!—Ask him these questions about ''scorching and drenching.''—Did he never play at Cricket or walk a mile in hot weather?—did he never spill a dish of tea over his testicles in handing the cup to his charmer to the great shame of his nankeen breeches?—did he never swim in the sea at Noonday with the Sun in his eyes and on his head—which all the foam of ocean could not cool? did he never draw his foot out of a tub of too hot water damning his eyes & his valet's? did he never inject for a Gonorrhea?—or make water through an ulcerated Urethra?—was he ever in a Turkish bath—that marble paradise of sherbet and sodomy?—was he ever in a cauldron of boiling oil like St. John?—or in the sulphureous waves of hell? (where he ought to be for his ''scorching and drenching at the same time'') did he never tumble into a river or lake fishing—and sit in his wet cloathes in the boat—or on the bank afterwards ''scorched and drenched'' like a true sportsman?———''Oh for breath to utter''———but make him my compliments—he is a clever fellow for all that—a very clever fellow.———You ask me for the plan of **Donny Johnny**—I *have* no plan—I *had* no plan—but I had or have materials—though if like Tony Lumpkin—I am ''to be snubbed so when I am in spirits'' the poem will be naught—and the poet turn serious again.—If it don't take I will leave it off where it is with all due respect to the Public—but if continued it must be in my own way—you might as well make Hamlet (or Diggory) ''act mad'' in a strait waistcoat—as trammel my buffoonery—if I am to be a buffoon—their gestures and my thoughts would only be pitiably absurd—and ludicrously constrained.—Why Man the Soul of such writing is it's licence?—at least the *liberty* of that *licence* if one likes—*not* that one should abuse it—it is like trial by Jury and Peerage—and the Habeas Corpus—a very fine thing—but chiefly in the *reversion*—because no one wishes to be tried for the mere pleasure of proving his possession of the privilege.———But a truce with these reflections;—you are too earnest and eager about a work never intended to be serious;—do you suppose that I could have any intention but to giggle and make giggle?—a playful satire with as little poetry as could be helped—was what I meant—and as to the indecency—do pray read in Boswell—what *Johnson* the sullen moralist—says of *Prior* and Paulo Purgante. . . . (pp. 206-08)

Lord Byron, in a letter to John Murray on August 12, 1819, in his ''The Flesh Is Frail'': Byron's Letters and Journals, 1818-1819, Vol. 6, *edited by Leslie A. Marchand, Cambridge, Mass.: Belknap Press, 1976, pp. 206-10.*

LORD BYRON   (letter date 1819)

[*Writing to a friend in a self-consciously rakish idiom, Byron asserts that whatever its indelicacies,* Don Juan *is a great poem because it reflects the reality of worldly experience.*]

As to **Don Juan**—confess—confess—you dog—and be candid—that it is the sublime of *that there* sort of writing—it may be bawdy—but is it not good English?—it may be profligate—but is it not *life*, is it not *the thing*?—Could any man have written it—who has not lived in the world?—and tooled in a post-chaise? in a hackney coach? in a Gondola? against a wall? in a court carriage? in a vis a vis?—on a table?—and under it?—I have written about a hundred stanzas of a third Canto—but it is damned modest—the outcry has frightened me.—I had such projects for the Don—but the *Cant* is so much stronger than *Cunt*—now a days,—that the benefit of experience in a man who had well weighed the worth of both monosyllables—must be lost to despairing posterity.—After all what stuff this outcry is—Lalla Rookh and Little—are more dangerous than my burlesque poem can be. . . . (p. 232)

Lord Byron, in a letter to Douglas Kinnaird on October 26, 1819, in his ''The Flesh Is Frail'': Byron's Letters and Journals, 1818-1819, Vol. 6, *edited by Leslie A. Marchand, Cambridge, Mass.: Belknap Press, 1976, pp. 231-33.*

LORD BYRON   (letter date 1819)

[*Despite his professed indifference to public and critical opinion of* Don Juan, *Byron was keenly interested both in the reaction of his audience to the poem and in the views of those critics he respected. The excerpt below reveals his ongoing concern with various aspects of the poem's success and reputation, including imitations of the work by other authors, the number of copies sold, and the notion expressed by many reviewers that it was unfit for women to read.*]

Murray sent me a letter yesterday—the impostors have published—*two* new *third* Cantos of **Don Juan**—the devil take the impudence of some blackguard bookseller or other there-*for*. . . .—[He] told me the sale had not been great—1200 out of 1500 quarto I believe (which is nothing after selling 13000 of the **Corsair** in one day) but that the ''best Judges &c.'' had said it was very fine and clever and particularly good English & poetry and all those consolatory things which are not however worth a single copy to a bookseller—and as to the author—of course I am in a damned passion at the bad taste of the times—and swear there is nothing like posterity—who of course must know more of the matter than their Grandfathers.—There has been an eleventh commandment to the women not to read it—and what is still more extraordinary they seem not to have broken it.———But that can be of little import to them poor things—for the reading or non-reading a book—will never keep down a single petticoat;—but it is of import to Murray—who will be in scandal for his aiding as publisher.———He is bold howsomedever—wanting two more cantos against the winter—I think that he had better not—for by the larkins!—it will only make a new row for him. (p. 237)

Lord Byron, in a letter to Richard Belgrave Hoppner on October 29, 1819, in his ''The Flesh Is Frail'': Byron's Letters and Journals, 1818-1819, Vol. 6, *edited by Leslie A. Marchand, Cambridge, Mass.: Belknap Press, 1976, pp. 236-38.*

[LEIGH HUNT]   (essay date 1819)

[*An English poet and essayist, Hunt is remembered as a literary critic who encouraged and influenced several Romantic poets, especially John Keats and Percy Bysshe Shelley. In his criticism, Hunt articulated the principles of Romanticism, emphasizing imaginative freedom and the expression of a personal emotional or spiritual state. Although his critical works were overshadowed by those of such prominent Romantic critics as his friends Samuel Taylor Coleridge, William Hazlitt, and Charles Lamb, Hunt's essays are considered both insightful and generous to the fledgling writers he supported. Critics have described Hunt's relations with Byron as complex and difficult. The magazine they founded together in 1822, entitled the* Liberal, *failed after only a few issues, and their personal interaction was strained by temperamental and class differences. Hunt, however, was one of the few early critics of* Don Juan *to praise the poem without also faulting its morality. In the following excerpt from his review of the first two cantos, he condemns the widespread charge that Byron had eulogized vice and corruption. Arguing for the importance of realism in art, Hunt asserts that the truthful portrayal of vice in* Don Juan *is less dangerous and more instructive than the exaggeration of its horrors by the* ''prudish and very suspicious moralists'' *who had labeled the poem immoral.*]

Some persons consider [**Don Juan**] the finest work of Lord Byron,—or at least that in which he displays most power. It is at all events the most extraordinary that he has yet published. His other poems, with the exception of that amusing satire—**Beppo,** are written for the most part with one sustained serious feeling throughout,—either of pathos, or grandeur, or passion, or all united. But **Don Juan** contains specimens of all the author's modes of writing, which are mingled together and push one another about in a strange way. The ground-work (if we may so speak of a stile) is the satirical and humourous; but you are sometimes surprised and moved by a touching piece of human nature, and again startled and pained by the sudden transition from loveliness or grandeur to ridicule or the mock-heroic. The delicious and deep descriptions of love, and youth, and hope, came upon us like the ''young beams'' of the sun breaking through the morning dew, and the terrific pictures of the misery of man and his most appalling sensations, like awful flashes of lightning;—but when the author reverses this change, he trifles too much with our feelings, and occasionally goes on, turning to ridicule or hopelessness all the fine ideas he has excited, with a recklessness that becomes extremely unpleasant and mortifying. What, for instance, can be more beautiful and at the same time true to nature than where,—just after a very anti-pathetic description of the confusion of *Julia* at her husband's sudden appearance, and her contrivances and lovers' falsehoods to elude his search for the beloved youth, he says (speaking of their alarm at the expected return of the old gentleman)—,

> Julia did not speak,
> But pressed her bloodless lip to Juan's cheek.
>
> He turn'd his lip to hers, and with his hand
>   Call'd back the tangles of her wandering hair;
> Even then their love they could not all command,
>   And half forgot their danger and despair.

What more calculated to "harrow up one's soul" than the following stanzas, which come in the very midst of some careless jests on the abstract ludicrousness of the wretched shifts of starving sailors in a becalmed boat, surrounded by a boundless prospect of the ocean? The Italics are our own.

> The seventh day, and no wind—the burning sun
>   Blister'd and scorch'd; and, stagnant on the sea,
> They lay like carcases! and hope was none,
>   Save in the breeze which came not: *savagely*
> *They glared upon each other*—all was done,
>   Water, and wine, and food,—and you might see
> The *longings of the cannibal arise,*
> *(Although they spoke not)* in their *wolfish* eyes.
>
> At length one whispered his companion, who
>   Whispered another, and thus it went round,
> And then into a *hoarser murmur* grew,
>   An ominous and wild and desperate sound;
> And when his comrade's thought each sufferer knew,
>   'Twas but his own, suppress'd till now, he found:
> And *out they spoke* of lots for flesh and blood,
> And who should die to be his fellow's food.

Then, immediately following this awful passage, comes an affected delicacy at the tearing up of *Julia's* letter to *Juan* to make the lots ("materials which must shock the muse"), and a *sang froid* account of the division of the body: shortly after follow some terrific lines relating the dreadful consequences of this gorging of human flesh; and a little farther on there is a laughable description of *Juan's* dislike to feed on "poor Pedrillo," and his preference for "chewing a piece of bamboo; and some lead," the stanza ending with the irresistible fact, that

> At length they caught two boobies and a noddy,
> And then they left off eating the dead body.

It is not difficult to account for this heterogeneous mixture,— for the bard has furnished us with the key to his own mind. His early hopes were blighted, and his disappointment vents itself in satirizing absurdities which rouse his indignation; and indeed a good deal of bitterness may be found at the bottom of much of this satire. But his genius is not naturally satirical; he breaks out therefore into those frequent veins of passion and true feeling of which we have just given specimens, and goes on with them till his memory is no longer able to bear

the images conjured up by his fine genius; and it is to get rid of such painful and "thick-coming" recollections, that he dashes away and relieves himself by getting into another train of ideas, however incongruous or violently contrasted with the former. This solution will, we think, be borne out by the following affecting description of the poet's feelings. Observe in particular the remarkable parenthesis after the first line, whose pregnant meaning seems to have compelled him to take refuge in a lighter and more humourous idea:—

> But now at thirty years my hair is grey—
>   (I wonder what it will be like at forty?
> I thought of a peruke the other day)—
>   My heart is not much greener; and, in short, I
> Have squandered my whole summer while 'twas May,
>   And feel no more the spirit to retort; I
> Have spent my life, both interest and principal,
> And deem not, what I deem'd, my soul invincible.
>
> No more—no more—Oh! never more on me
>   The freshness of the heart can fall like dew,
> Which out of all the lovely things we see
>   Extracts emotions beautiful and new,
> Hived in our bosoms like the bag o' the bee:
>   Think'st thou the honey with those objects grew?
> Alas! 'twas not in them, but in thy power
> To double even the sweetness of a flower.
>
> No more—no more—Oh! never more, my heart,
>   Canst thou be my sole world—my universe!
> Once all in all, but now a thing apart
>   Thou canst not be my blessing or my curse.

Here is some evidence that the poet is not without the milk of human kindness, and to our minds there is much more in the rest of the volume. His bent is not, as we have said, satirical, nor is he naturally disposed to be ill-natured with respect to the faults and vices of his fellow-creatures. There is an evident struggle throughout these two cantos in the feelings of the writer, and it is very fine to see him, as he gets on, growing more interested in his fiction, and pouring out at the conclusion in a much less interrupted strain of rich and deep beauty. (pp. 700-01)

Don Juan is accused of being an "immoral" work, which we cannot at all discover. We suppose that this charge more particularly alludes to the first canto. Let us see then on what foundation it rests. The son of a Spanish patrician, educated in the most prudish manner by a licentious, yet affectedly virtuous mother, falls in love with the young wife of an old man. She returns his affection, and their passion being favoured by opportunity, she gives way to her natural feelings, and is unfaithful to her marriage vows, the example (observe) being set her by this very husband's intrigues with *Juan's* mother. Now Lord Byron speaks lightly of the effect of any scruples of conscience upon her, and of her infidelity; and this, it is said, has tendency to corrupt the minds of "us youth," and to make us *think* lightly of breaking the matrimonial contract. But if to do this be immoral, we can only say that Nature is immoral. Lord Byron does no more than relate the consequences of certain absurdities. If he speaks slightingly of the ties between a girl and a husband old enough for her father, it is because the ties themselves *are* slight. He does not ridicule the bonds of marriage generally, or where they are formed as they should be: he merely shows the folly and wickedness of setting forms and opinions against nature. If stupid and selfish parents will make up matches between persons whom difference of age or disposition disqualifies for mutual affection, they must take the consequences:—but we do not think it fair that a poet should be exclaimed against as a promoter of nuptial infidelity because he tells them what those consequences are. In this particular case, too, the author does not omit some painful consequences to those who have sinned according to "nature's law." *Julia,* the victim of selfishness and "damned custom," is shut up in a convent, where no consolation remains to her but the remembrance of her entire and hapless love; but even that was perhaps pleasanter to her than living in the constant irksomeness of feigning an affection she could not feel.

There are a set of prudish and very suspicious moralists who endeavour to make vice appear to inexperienced eyes much more hateful than it really is. They would correct Nature;—and they always over-reach themselves. Nature has made vice to a certain degree pleasurable, though its painful consequences outweigh its present gratification. Now the said prudes, in their lectures and sermons and moral discourses (for they are chiefly priests) are constantly declaiming on the *deformity* of vice, and its almost total want of attraction. The consequence is, that when they are found to have deceived (as they always are) and immoral indulgence is discovered to be not without its charms,—the minds of young persons are apt to confound their true with their false maxims, and to think the threats of future pain and repentance mere fables invented to deter them from their rightful enjoyments. Which then, we would ask, are the immoral writings,—those which, by misrepresenting the laws of nature, lead to false views of morality and consequent licentiousness?—or those, which ridicule and point out the effects of absurd contradictions of human feelings and passions, and help to bring about a reformation of such practises.

Of the story in the second canto it is unnecessary to say much, for these remarks will apply to both. We suppose there has been some sermonizing on the description of the delight arising from the "illicit intercourse" of *Juan* and *Haidee.* People who talk in this way can perceive no distinctions. It certainly is not to be inculcated, that every handsome young man and woman will find their account in giving way to all their impulses, because the very violent breaking through the habits and forms of society would create a great deal of unhappiness, both to the individuals, and to others. But what is there to blame in a beautiful and affectionate girl who gives way to a passion for a young shipwrecked human creature, bound to her by gratitude as well as love? She exacts no promises, says the bard, because she fears no inconstancy. Her father had exposed her to the first temptation that comes across her, because he had not provided against it by allowing her to know more of mankind. And does she not receive, as well as bestow, more real pleasure (for that is the question) in the enjoyment of a first and deep passion, than in becoming the wife of some brother in iniquity to whom her pirating father would have trucked her for lucre?

The fact is, at the bottom of all these questions, that many things are made vicious, which are not so by nature; and many things made virtuous, which are only so by calling and agreement: and it is on the horns of this self-created dilemma, that society is continually writhing and getting desperate. (pp. 701-02)

[Leigh Hunt], in a review of "Don Juan, Cantos 1st and 2d," in The Examiner, *No. 618, October 31, 1819, pp. 700-02.*

M. N. [PSEUDONYM OF WILLIAM MAGINN]   (poem date 1819)

[In addition to the over sixty reviews of Don Juan *published in the British press during Byron's lifetime, there also appeared numerous pamphlets, poems, continuations, and other forms of "Byroniana" inspired by the work. The following poem is considered one of the best examples of such extra-critical material. Maginn was an Irish essayist, short story writer, poet, critic, and editor who became one of the most prominent journalists in England during the first half of the nineteenth century. One of the principal early contributors to* Blackwood's, *he is credited by many scholars with inventing the* Noctes Ambrosianae, *the popular series of imaginary conversations published in* Blackwood's *between 1822 and 1835. His articles range from burlesques in verse to literary criticism and contain a rich blend of farcical humor, classical allusions, and political commentary. In the following poem, entitled "'Don Juan' Unread," a parody of Wordsworth's "Yarrow Unvisited," Maginn states that although the excesses of Byron's earlier works were tolerable, "Don Giovanni" takes matters too far and should be left alone. The critic makes disparaging references to the political and social circles Byron had frequented in England as well as puns and jests associating the poet with other liberal writers of the day, including the "Cockneys" Hunt, Keats, and Hazlitt. Though scarcely complimentary, "'Don Juan' Unread" represents a softening of the harsh stance* Blackwood's *had taken towards the poem in its August number (see excerpt dated 1819).]*

Of Corinth Castle we had read
    The amazing Siege unravelled,
Had swallowed *Lara* and the *Giaour,*
    And with *Childe Harold* travelled;
And so we followed cloven-foot
    As faithfully as any,
Until he cried, "Come, turn aside
    And read of Don Giovanni."

Let Whiggish folk, *frae* Holland House,
    Who have been lying, prating,
Read *Don Giovanni,* 'tis their own,
    A child of their creating!
On jests profane they love to feed,
    And there they are—and many;
But we, who link not with the crew,
    Regard not *Don Giovanni.*

There's Godwin's daughter, Shelley's
        wife,
    A writing fearful stories;
There's Hazlitt, who, with Hunt and Keats
    Brays forth in Cockney chorus;
There's pleasant Thomas Moore, a lad
    Who sings of Rose and Fanny;
Why throw away these wits so gay
    To take up *Don Giovanni.*

"What's *Juan* but a shameless tale,
    That bursts all rules asunder?
There are a thousand such elsewhere
    As worthy of your wonder."
Strange words they seem'd of slight and
        scorn;
    His Lordship look'd not *canny;*
And took a pinch of snuff, to think
    I flouted *Don Giovanni.*

O! rich, said I, are *Juan's* rhymes,
    And warm its verse is flowing!
Fair crops of blasphemy it bears,
    But we will leave them growing,
In Pindar's strain, in prose of Paine,
    And many another Zanny,
As gross we read, so where's the need,
    To wade through *Don Giovanni.*

Let Colburn's town-bred cattle snuff
   The filths of Lady Morgan,
Let Maturin to amorous themes
   Attune his barrel organ!
We will not read them, will not hear
   The parson or the granny;
And, I dare say, as bad as they
   Or worse, is *Don Giovanni.*

Be *Juan* then unseen, unknown!
   It must, or we may rue it;
We may have virtue of our own;
   Ah! why should we undo it?
The treasured faith of days long past,
   We still shall prize o'er any;
And we shall grieve to hear the gibes
   Of scoffing *Don Giovanni.*

When Whigs with freezing rule shall come,
   And piety seem folly;
When Cam and Isis curbed by Brougham,
   Shall wander melancholy;
When Cobbett, Wooler, Watson, Hunt,
   And all the swinish many,
Shall rough-shod ride o'er church and state,
   Then hey! for *Don Giovanni.*

                           (pp. 194-95)

> *M. N. [pseudonym of William Maginn], "Don Juan Unread," in* Blackwood's Edinburgh Magazine, *Vol. VI, No. XXXII, November, 1819, pp. 194-95.*

LORD BYRON   (letter date 1819)

[*In the excerpt below, Byron expresses his dissatisfaction with the August 1819 review of* Don Juan *in Blackwood's (see excerpt above). Byron's irritation over the review eventually prompted him to write a rebuttal of its criticisms in* Some Observations upon an Article in Blackwood's Magazine *(see excerpt dated 1820).*]

I have finished the third Canto of *D[on] J[uan]*—but the things I have read & heard discourage all further publication—at least for the present. . . . I perceive Mr. Blackwood Magazine and one or two others of your missives—have been hyperbolical in their praise—and diabolical in their abuse.——I like & admire Wilson—and *he* should not have indulged himself in such outrageous license—it is overdone and defeats itself—what would he say to the grossness without passion—and the misanthropy without feeling of Gulliver's travels?—when he talks of Lady Byron's business—he talks of what he knows nothing about—and you may tell him that no one can more desire a public investigation of that affair than I do. . . .—These fellows first abused me for being gloomy—and now they are wroth but I am or attempted to be facetious. . . . Your Blackwood accuses me of treating women harshly—it may be so—but I have been their martyr.—My whole life has been sacrificed *to* them & *by* them. (pp. 256-57)

> *Lord Byron, in a letter to John Murray on December 10, 1819, in his "The Flesh Is Frail": Byron's Letters and Journals, 1818-1819, Vol. 6, edited by Leslie A. Marchand, Cambridge, Mass.: Belknap Press, 1976, pp. 256-58.*

WILLIAM WORDSWORTH   (letter date 1820?)

[*One of the major English poets of the nineteenth century, Wordsworth was central to English Romanticism. His incorporation of the elements of colloquial speech into his poetry in such collections as* Lyrical Ballads *revolutionized the language of English verse. Important also as a critic, Wordsworth expressed in his theoretical writings his belief that neither the diction nor the content of poetry should be stylized or elaborate and that the value of a poet was to feel and express the bond between human beings and nature. Relations between Byron and Wordsworth were characterized by mutual antagonism. Byron disliked Wordsworth's poetic innovations and frequently satirized and insulted the poet and his works. Wordsworth is the subject of ridicule throughout* Don Juan, *and in his letters Byron often referred to the poet as "Wordswords" and "Turdsworth." For his part, Wordsworth considered Byron irresponsible and believed that the natural settings in Canto IV of* Childe Harold *had been plagiarized from his works. In the following excerpt from a letter presumed to be to Henry Crabb Robinson, Wordsworth asks Robinson to encourage the editor of the* Quarterly Review *to condemn* Don Juan, *which Wordsworth felt could corrupt the English character. For the* Quarterly's *first comments on* Don Juan, *see the excerpt dated 1822. Though the precise date of Wordsworth's letter is unknown, Sir Charles Frith has tentatively assigned it to January 1820.*]

You will probably see Gifford, the Editor of the *Quarterly Review;* tell him from me, if you think proper, that every true-born Englishman will regard the pretensions of the *Review* to the character of a faithful defender of the institutions of the country, as *hollow,* while it leaves that infamous publication ***Don Juan*** unbranded; I do not mean by a formal Critique, for it is not worth it; it would also tend to keep it in memory; but by some decisive words of reprobation, both as to the damnable tendency of such works, and as to [the] despicable quality of the powers requisite for their production. What avails it to hunt down Shelley, whom few read, and leave Byron untouched?

I am persuaded that ***Don Juan*** will do more harm to the English character, than anything of our time; not so much as a *Book;*—But thousands who would be afraid to have it in that shape, will batten upon choice bits of it, in the shape of Extracts. (p. 850)

> *William Wordsworth, in an extract from a letter to Henry Crabb Robinson in January, 1820? in* The Correspondence of Henry Crabb Robinson with the Wordsworth Circle (1808-1866): 1844-1866, Vol. II, *edited by Edith J. Morley, Oxford at the Clarendon Press, Oxford, 1927, pp. 850-51.*

ROBERT SOUTHEY   (letter date 1820)

[*Though his works attract little attention today, Southey was a significant member of the Lake School of poetry. His writings received serious critical assessment from his contemporaries, and in 1831 he was appointed Poet Laureate. While interest in his social theories has increased since his death, his reputation as a creative writer—especially as a poet—has declined. The history of his quarrel with Byron is long and involved (for Byron's explanation of his attack on Southey in the Dedication to* Don Juan *see excerpt from his letter of November 11, 1818), but their mutual dislike was essentially a product of the vast political, personal, and religious differences that separated them. Byron considered Southey a traitor to the liberal cause and an inferior poet who had sacrificed his integrity to become Poet Laureate. Southey reveals his attitude toward Byron in the following excerpt from a letter to Walter Savage Landor. Here, Southey disparages Byron's use of the Italian ottava rima stanza and calls* Don Juan *"a foul blot on the literature of his country." Though the Dedication to* Don Juan *had been suppressed, Southey was aware of its contents, and in 1821 he publicly attacked Byron in the preface to his* A Vision of Judgment. *Referring to his adversary as the leader of the ''Satanic School'' of poetry, he initiated a series of bitterly hostile exchanges culminating in Byron's satirical masterpiece* The Vision of Judgment, *a parody of Southey's poem which eclipsed its model.*]

A fashion of poetry has been imported which has had a great run, and is in a fair way of being worn out. It is of Italian growth,——an adaptation of the manner of Pulci, Berni, and Ariosto in his sportive mood. Frere began it. What he produced was too good in itself and too inoffensive to become popular; for it attacked nothing and nobody; and it had the fault of his Italian models, that the transition from what is serious to what is burlesque was capricious. Lord Byron immediately followed; first with his *Beppo,* which implied the profligacy of the writer, and, lastly, with his *Don Juan,* which is a foul blot on the literature of his country, an act of high treason on English poetry. The manner has had a host of imitators. The use of Hudibrastic rhymes (the only thing in which it differs from the Italian) makes it very easy. (p. 21)

> *Robert Southey, in a letter to Walter Savage Landor on February 20, 1820, in his* The Life and Correspondence of Robert Southey, Vol. V, *edited by Rev. Charles Cuthbert Southey, Longman, Brown, Green and Longmans, 1850, pp. 20-2.*

LORD BYRON   (essay date 1820)

[*The following excerpt is drawn from an essay Byron wrote in reaction to the ''Remarks on 'Don Juan' '' in* Blackwood's *(see excerpt dated August 1819). He protests against ''being everlastingly taken, or mistaken for my own protagonist.'' Byron accuses* Blackwood's *of ignoring* Don Juan *in order to attack him personally, insisting that even if his personal life were the business of the press, he has suffered enough for his sins by being separated from his wife and exiled from England. In a portion of the essay not excerpted below, Byron critiques the poetry and poets of his day, explaining the reasons for his attacks on the Lake Poets and comparing their works unfavorably with those of Pope, Dryden, and Milton. Dated by Byron March 15, 1820, this essay was never published during his lifetime.*]

'The life of a writer' has been said, by Pope, I believe, to be *'a warfare upon earth.'* As far as my own experience has gone, I have nothing to say against the proposition; and, like the rest, having once plunged into this state of hostility, must, however reluctantly, carry it on. An article has appeared in a periodical work, entitled 'Remarks on *Don Juan,*' which has been so full of this spirit, on the part of the writer, as to require some observations on mine.

In the first place, I am not aware by what right the writer assumes this work, which is anonymous, to be my production. He will answer, that there is internal evidence; that is to say, that there are passages which appear to be written in my name, or in my manner. But might not this have been done on purpose by another? He will say, why not then deny it? To this I could answer, that of all the things attributed to me within the last five years,—Pilgrimages to Jerusalem, Deaths upon Pale Horses, Odes to the Land of the Gaul, Adieus to England, Songs to Madame La Valette, Odes to St. Helena, Vampires, and what not,—of which, God knows, I never composed nor read a syllable beyond their titles in advertisements,—I never thought it worth while to disavow any, except *one* which came linked with an account of my 'residence in the isle of Mitylene,' where I never resided, and appeared to be carrying the amusement

of those persons, who think my name can be of any use to them, a little too far.

I should hardly, therefore, if I did not take the trouble to disavow these things published in my name, and yet not mine, go out of my way to deny an anonymous work; which might appear an act of supererogation. With regard to *Don Juan,* I neither deny nor admit it to be mine—every body may form their own opinion; but, if there be any who now, or in the progress of that poem, if it is to be continued, feel, or should feel themselves so aggrieved as to require a more explicit answer, privately and personally, they shall have it.

I have never shrunk from the responsibility of what I have written, and have more than once incurred obloquy by neglecting to disavow what was attributed to my pen without foundation.

The greater part, however, of the 'Remarks on *Don Juan*' contain but little on the work itself, which receives an extraordinary portion of praise as a composition. With the exception of some quotations, and a few incidental remarks, the rest of the article is neither more nor less than a personal attack upon the imputed author. It is not the first in the same publication: for I recollect to have read, some time ago, similar remarks upon *Beppo* (said to have been written by a celebrated northern preacher); in which the conclusion drawn was, that 'Childe Harold, Byron, and the Count in *Beppo,* were one and the same person;' thereby making me turn out to be, as Mrs. Malaprop says, *'like Cerberus, three gentlemen at once.'* That article was signed 'Presbyter Anglicanus;' which, I presume, being interpreted, means Scotch Presbyterian. I must here observe, and it is at once ludicrous and vexatious to be compelled so frequently to repeat the same thing,—that my case, as an author, is peculiarly hard, in being everlastingly taken, or mistaken for my own protagonist. It is unjust and particular. I never heard that my friend Moore was set down for a fire-worshipper on account of his Guebre; that Scott was identified with Roderick Dhu, or with Balfour of Burley; or that, notwithstanding all the magicians in *Thalaba,* any body has ever taken Mr. Southey for a conjuror. . . . (pp. 474-75)

In the course of this article, amidst some extraordinary observations, there occur the following words:—'It appears, in short, as if this miserable man, having exhausted *every species* of sensual gratification,—having drained the cup of sin even to its bitterest dregs, were resolved to show us that he is no longer a human being even in his frailties,—but a cool, unconcerned fiend, laughing with a detestable glee over the whole of the better and worse elements of which human life is composed.' In another place there appears, 'the lurking-place of his selfish and polluted exile.'—'By my troth, these be bitter words!'— With regard to the first sentence, I shall content myself with observing, that it appears to have been composed for Sardanapalus, Tiberius, the Regent Duke of Orleans, or Louis XV.; and that I have copied it with as much indifference as I would a passage from Suetonius, or from any of the private memoirs of the regency, conceiving it to be amply refuted by the terms in which it is expressed, and to be utterly inapplicable to any private individual. On the words, 'lurking-place,' and 'selfish and polluted exile,' I have something more to say.—How far the capital city of a government, which survived the vicissitudes of thirteen hundred years, and might still have existed but for the treachery of Buonaparte, and the iniquity of his imitators,—a city which was the emporium of Europe when London and Edinburgh were dens of barbarians,—may be termed a 'lurking-place,' I leave to those who have seen or heard of

Venice to decide. How far my exile may have been 'polluted,' it is not for me to say, because the word is a wide one, and, with some of its branches, may chance to overshadow the actions of most men; but that it has been 'selfish' I deny. If, to the extent of my means and my power, and my information of their calamities, to have assisted many miserable beings, reduced by the decay of the place of their birth, and their consequent loss of substance—if to have never rejected an application which appeared founded on truth—if to have expended in this manner sums far out of proportion to my fortune, there and elsewhere, be selfish, then have I been selfish. To have done such things I do not deem much; but it is hard indeed to be compelled to recapitulate them in my own defence, by such accusations as that before me, like a panel before a jury calling testimonies to his character, or a soldier recording his services to obtain his discharge. (pp. 475-76)

The writer continues:—'Those who are acquainted, *as who is not?* with the *main* incidents of the private life of Lord B.,' etc. Assuredly, whoever may be acquainted with these 'main incidents,' the writer of the 'Remarks on *Don Juan*' is not, or he would use a very different language. That which I believe he alludes to as a 'main incident,' happened to be a very subordinate one, and the natural and almost inevitable consequence of events and circumstances long prior to the period at which it occurred. It is the last drop which makes the cup run over, and mine was already full.—But, to return to this man's charge: he accuses Lord B. of 'an elaborate satire on the character and manners of his wife.' From what part of *Don Juan* the writer has inferred this he himself best knows. As far as I recollect of the female characters in that production, there is but one who is depicted in ridiculous colours, or that could be interpreted as a satire upon any body. But here my poetical sins are again visited upon me, supposing that the poem be mine. If I depict a corsair, a misanthrope, a libertine, a chief of insurgents, or an infidel, he is set down to the author; and if, in a poem by no means ascertained to be my production, there appears a disagreeable, casuistical, and by no means respectable female pedant, it is set down for my wife. Is there any resemblance? If there be, it is in those who make it. I can see none. In my writings I have rarely described any character under a fictitious name: those of whom I have spoken have had their own—in many cases a stronger satire in itself than any which could be appended to it. But of real circumstances I have availed myself plentifully, both in the serious and the ludicrous—they are to poetry what landscapes are to the painter; but my *figures* are not portraits. It may even have happened, that I have seized on some events that have occurred under my own observation, or in my own family, as I would paint a view from my grounds, did it harmonise with my picture; but I never would introduce the likenesses of its living members, unless their features could be made as favourable to themselves as to the effect; which, in the above instance, would be extremely difficult.

My learned brother proceeds to observe, that 'it is in vain for Lord B. to attempt in any way to justify his own behaviour in that affair; and now that he has so *openly* and *audaciously* invited enquiry and reproach, we do not see any good reason why he should not be plainly told so by the voice of his countrymen.' How far the 'openness' of an anonymous poem, and the 'audacity' of an imaginary character, which the writer supposes to be meant for Lady B., may be deemed to merit this formidable denunciation from their 'most sweet voices,' I neither know nor care; but when he tells me that I cannot 'in any way *justify* my own behaviour in that affair,' I acquiesce,

because no man can '*justify*' himself until he knows of what he is accused; and I have never had—and, God knows, my whole desire has ever been to obtain it—any specific charge, in a tangible shape, submitted to me by the adversary, nor by others, unless the atrocities of public rumour and the mysterious silence of the lady's legal advisers may be deemed such. But is not the writer content with what has been already said and done? Has not 'the general voice of his countrymen' long ago pronounced upon the subject—sentence without trial, and condemnation without a charge? Have I not been exiled by ostracism, except that the shells which proscribed me were anonymous? Is the writer ignorant of the public opinion and the public conduct upon that occasion? If he is, I am not: the public will forget both, long before I shall cease to remember either. (pp. 477-78)

I will now return to the writer of the article which has drawn forth these remarks, whom I honestly take to be John Wilson, a man of great powers and acquirements, well known to the public as the author of the *City of the Plague, Isle of Palms,* and other productions. I take the liberty of naming him, by the same species of courtesy which has induced him to designate me as the author of *Don Juan.* Upon the score of the Lake Poets, he may perhaps recall to mind that I merely express an opinion long ago entertained and specified in a letter to Mr. James Hogg, which he the said James Hogg, somewhat contrary to the law of pens, showed to Mr. John Wilson, in the year 1814, as he himself informed me in his answer, telling me by way of apology, that 'he'd be damned if he could help it;' and I am not conscious of any thing like 'envy' or 'exacerbation' at this moment which induces me to think better or worse of Southey, Wordsworth, and Coleridge as poets than I do now, although I do know one or two things more which have added to my contempt for them as individuals. And, in return for Mr. Wilson's invective, I shall content myself with asking one question; Did he never compose, recite, or sing any parody or parodies upon the Psalms (of what nature this deponent saith not,) in certain jovial meetings of the youth of Edinburgh? It is not that I think any great harm if he did; because it seems to me that all depends upon the intention of such a parody. If it be meant to throw ridicule on the sacred original, it is a sin; if it be intended to burlesque the profane subject, or to inculcate a moral truth, it is none. If it were, the *unbelievers' Creed,* the many political parodies of various parts of the Scriptures and liturgy, particularly a celebrated one of the Lord's Prayer, and the beautiful moral parable in favour of toleration by Franklin, which has often been taken for a real extract from Genesis, would all be sins of a damning nature. But I wish to know, if Mr. Wilson ever has done this, and *if* he *has, why he* should be so very angry with similar portions of *Don Juan*?—Did no 'parody profane' appear in any of the earlier numbers of *Blackwood's Magazine*?

I will now conclude this long answer to a short article, repenting of having said so much in my own defence, and so little on the 'crying, left-hand fallings off and national defections' of the poetry of the present day. Having said this, I can hardly be expected to defend *Don Juan,* or any other '*living*' poetry, and shall not make the attempt. And although I do not think that Mr. John Wilson has in this instance treated me with candour or consideration, I trust that the tone I have used in speaking of him personally will prove that I bear him as little malice as I really believe at the *bottom of his heart* he bears towards me; but the duties of an editor, like those of a taxgatherer, are paramount and peremptory. I have done. (pp. 494-95)

Lord Byron, ''Reply to Blackwood's 'Edinburgh Magazine' [*Some Observations upon an Article in 'Blackwood's Magazine'*], in his The Works of Lord Byron: Letters and Journals, Vol. IV, *edited by Rowland E. Prothero, revised edition, Charles Scribner's Sons, 1900, pp. 474-95.*

P. B. SHELLEY   (letter date 1820)

[*Regarded as a major English poet, Shelley was a leading figure in the English Romantic movement. His* Defence of Poetry, *in which he investigated poetry's relation to the history of civilization, was an important contribution to nineteenth-century aesthetics. Influenced by the French philosopher Jean-Jacques Rousseau and the German poet and pre-Romanticist Johann Gottfried von Herder, Shelley viewed both poetry and human society as a continuing evolution of ideas. Byron and Shelley first met in 1816 in Switzerland following the former's final departure from England, and they remained friends until Shelley's death in 1822. In the following excerpt from a letter to Byron, Shelley praises Cantos I-II of* Don Juan, *citing the power, beauty, and truth of the writing and expressing only mild apprehension about the poem's ''bitter mockery'' of human nature. While Chew (see Additional Bibliography) has suggested that in ''studying Shelley's opinions of Byron one must bear in mind (his) facile, generous, and ill-considered enthusiasms,'' Shelley was nevertheless the only major English Romantic poet to speak favorably about* Don Juan *during Byron's lifetime.*]

I have read your **Don Juan** in print, and I observe that the *murrain* has killed some of the finest of the flock, i.e., that your bookseller has omitted certain passages. The personal ones, however, though I thought them wonderfully strong, I do not regret. What a strange and terrible storm is that at sea, and the two fathers, how true, yet how strong a contrast! Dante hardly exceeds it. With what flashes of divine beauty have you not illuminated the familiarity of your subject towards the end! The love letter, and the account of its being written, is altogether a masterpiece of portraiture; of human nature laid with the eternal colours of the feelings of humanity. Where did you learn all these secrets? I should like to go to school there. I cannot say I equally approve of the service to which this letter was appropriated; or that I altogether think the bitter mockery of our common nature, of which this is one of the expressions, quite worthy of your genius. The power and the beauty and the wit, indeed, redeem all this—chiefly because they belie and refute it. Perhaps it is foolish to wish that there had been nothing to redeem. (p. 198)

P. B. Shelley, in a letter to Lord Byron on May 26, 1820, in his The Letters of Percy Bysshe Shelley: Shelley in Italy, Vol. II, *edited by Frederick L. Jones, Oxford at the Clarendon Press, 1964, pp. 197-99.*

JOHN KEATS (AS REPORTED BY JOSEPH SEVERN) (conversation date 1820)

[*Keats is considered a key figure in the English Romantic movement and one of the major poets in the English language. Critics note that though his creative career spanned only four years, he achieved remarkable intellectual and artistic development. His poems, notably those contained in the collection* Lamia, Isabella, The Eve of St. Agnes, and Other Poems, *are valued not only for their sensuous imagery, simplicity, and passionate tone, but also for the insight they provide into aesthetic and human concerns, particularly the conflict between art and life. The philosophical and artistic differences between Keats and Byron kept them from admiring or even understanding one another's work. Keats once remarked in a letter that Byron ''describes what he sees—I de-*

scribe what I imagine,'' a difference of approach reflected in the following excerpt in which Keats condemns the shipwreck scene from Don Juan. *Keats's comments, introduced and reported from memory by his friend Joseph Severn, were made in October 1820 while on board a ship sailing from England to Italy.*]

When we had passed the bay of Biscay, where we . . . had been in danger & great fright from a storm of three days— Keats took up Ld Byrons **Don Juan** accidentally as one of the books he had brought from England & singular enough he opened on the description of the Storm, which is evidently taken from the Medusa frigate & which the taste of Byron tryes to make a jest of—Keats threw down the book & exclaimed,

> this gives me the most horrid idea of human nature, that a man like Byron should have exhausted all the pleasures of the world so compleatly that there was nothing left for him but to laugh & gloat over the most solemn & heart rending since [scenes] of human misery this storm of his is one of the most diabolical attempts ever made upon our sympathies, and I have no doubt it will fascenate thousands into extreem obduracy of heart—the tendency of Byrons poetry is based on a paltry originality, that of being new by making solemn things gay & gay things solemn. . . .

John Keats, as reported by Joseph Severn, in his comments of October, 1820, in The Keats Circle: Letters and Papers, 1816-1878, Vol. 2, *edited by Hyder Edward Rollins, Cambridge, Mass.: Harvard University Press, 1948, p. 134.*

LORD BYRON   (letter date 1821)

[*Byron made various pronouncements about his plans for carrying on the plot of* Don Juan (*see also the excerpt from his conversation with Thomas Medwin dated 1822*), *but the following comments from a letter to Murray (written after completing the fifth canto) are his most complete and important statement about how he intended to continue the unfinished poem.*]

The 5th. is so far from being the last of *D. J.* that it is hardly the beginning.—I meant to take him the tour of Europe—with a proper mixture of siege—battle—and adventure—and to make him finish as *Anacharsis Cloots*—in the French revolution.— To how many cantos this may extend—I know not—nor whether (even if I live) I shall complete it—but this was my notion.— I meant to have made him a Cavalier Servente in Italy and a cause for a divorce in England—and a Sentimental ''Wertherfaced man'' in Germany—so as to show the different ridicules of the society in each of those countries——and to have displayed him gradually gaté and blasé as he grew older—as is natural.—But I had not quite fixed whether to make him end in Hell—or in an unhappy marriage,—not knowing which would be the severest.—The Spanish tradition says Hell—but it is probably only an Allegory of the other state.——You are now in possession of my notions on the subject. (p. 78)

Lord Byron, in a letter to John Murray on February 16, 1821, in his ''Born for Opposition'': Byron's Letters and Journals, 1821, Vol. 8, *edited by Leslie A. Marchand, Cambridge, Mass.: Belknap Press, 1978, pp. 77-9.*

JOHN BULL [PSEUDONYM OF JOHN GIBSON LOCKHART] (essay date 1821)

[*Although Lockhart wrote several novels, his fame rests primarily on his biography of Sir Walter Scott and his critical contributions to* Blackwood's *and the* Quarterly Review. *From 1817 to 1825 he was one of* Blackwood's *principal contributors; his trenchant wit contributed to the magazine's early success and earned him the nickname of "The Scorpion." Later, as editor of the* Quarterly, *he was a less acerbic critic. Today he is regarded as a versatile, if somewhat severe, critic whose opinions of his contemporaries, though lacking depth, are generally considered accurate when not distorted by political animosities. It was Lockhart who produced what is considered the first genuinely engaging criticism of* Don Juan *when in 1821 he published the anonymous pamphlet from which the excerpt below is drawn. Free from the editorial constraints and formality that characterize nearly all of the early reviews of the poem published in periodicals, the pamphlet is written in a familiar and humorous style. Although Lockhart qualifies his praise for* Don Juan, *his tone in general is laudatory and candid. The critic finds the poem more sincere than Byron's previous publications and calls it "by far the most spirited, the most straightforward, the most interesting, and the most poetical" of his works. Lockhart also suggests that a disparity exists between critics' public opinions and their more sincere private views of* Don Juan: *"every body thinks as I do of it, although they have not the heart to say so." Ultimately, Lockhart predicts that the poem will endure as a masterpiece when the works of Byron's contemporaries have been forgotten. Byron read the pamphlet with pleasure (see excerpt from his letter dated June 29, 1821) and asked Murray to find out who had written it.*]

You are a great poet, but even with your poetry you mix too much of that at present very saleable article against which I am now bestirring myself. The whole of your misanthropy, for example, is humbug. You do not hate men, "no, nor woman neither," but you thought it would be a fine, interesting thing for a handsome young Lord to depict himself as a dark-souled, melancholy, morbid being, and you have done so, it must be admitted, with exceeding cleverness. In spite of all your pranks, (**Beppo**, &c. **Don Juan** included,) every boarding-school in the empire still contains many devout believers in the amazing misery of the black-haired, high-browed, blue-eyed, bare-throated, Lord Byron. How melancholy you look in the prints! Oh! yes, this is the true cast of face. Now, tell me, Mrs. Goddard, now tell me, Miss Price, now tell me, dear Harriet Smith, and dear, dear Mrs. Elton, do tell me, is not this just the very look, that one would have fancied for Childe Harold? Oh! what eyes and eyebrows!—Oh! what a chin!—well, after all, who knows what may have happened. One can never know the truth of such stories. Perhaps her *Ladyship* was in the wrong after all.—I am sure if I had married such a man, I would have borne with all his little eccentricities—a man so evidently unhappy.—Poor Lord Byron! who can say how much he may have been to be pitied? I am sure I would; I bear with all Mr. E.'s eccentricities, and I am sure any woman of real sense would have done so to Lord Byron's: poor Lord Byron!—well, say what they will, I shall always pity him;—do you remember these dear lines of his—

> It is that settled ceaseless gloom,
> The fabled Hebrew wanderer bore,
> That will not look beyond the tomb,
> But cannot hope for rest before.

—Oh! beautiful! and how beautifully you repeat them! You always repeat Lord Byron's fine passages so beautifully. What think you of that other we were talking of on Saturday evening at Miss Bates's?

> ——Nay, smile not at my sullen brow,
> Alas! I cannot smile again.

I forget the rest;—but nobody has such a memory as Mrs. E. Don't you think Captain Brown has a look of Lord Byron?

How you laugh in your sleeve when you imagine to yourself (which you have done any one half-hour these seven years) such beautiful scenes as these:—they are the triumphs of humbug: but you are not a Bowles: you ought to be (as you might well afford to be) ashamed of them. You ought to put a stop to them, if you are able; and the only plan I can point out is, that of making a vow and sticking to it, as I have done, and ever, I hope, shall do, of never writing a line more except upon the anti-humbug principle. You say you admire Pope, and I believe you: well, in this respect, I should really be at a loss to suggest a better model; do you also, my Lord, "stoop to truth, and (de)moralize your song." Stick to **Don Juan**: it is the only sincere thing you have ever written; and it will live many years after all your humbug Harolds have ceased to be, in your own words,

> A school-*girl's* tale—the wonder of an hour.

Perhaps you will stare at this last piece of my advice: but, nevertheless, upon my honour, it is as sincere as possible. I consider **Don Juan** as out of all sight the best of your works; it is by far the most spirited, the most straightforward, the most interesting, and the most poetical; and every body thinks as I do of it, although they have not the heart to say so. Old Gifford's brow relaxed as he gloated over it; Mr. Croker chuckled; Dr. Whitaker smirked; Mr. Milman sighed; Mr. Coleridge (I mean not the madman, but the madman's idiot nephew) took it to his bed with him. The whole band of the "Quarterly" were delighted; each man in his own *penetralia*, (I except, indeed, Mr. Southey, who read the beginning very placidly, but threw the Don behind the fire when he came to the cut at himself, in the parody on the ten commandments); but who should dare to say a word about such a thing in the "Quarterly"? Poor Mr. Shelley cannot publish a wicked poem which nobody ever read, or was likely to read, but the whole band were up in arms against him: one throwing in his face his having set fire to a rotten tree when he was a boy at Eton; and another, turning over the leaves of his own travelling memorandum book to discover the very date at which Mr. Shelley wrote himself ["atheist"], in a Swiss album; and the whole of these precious materials handed forthwith to———I know whom. But not so with the noble Don. Every body poring over the wicked, smiling face of Don Juan,—pirated duo-decimo competing it all over the island with furtive quarto; but the devil a word of warning in the high-spirited, most ethical, most impartial "Quarterly Review." No; never a word—because—because—the wicked book contained one line ending with

> —My grand-dad's narrative.

—and its publisher was—no it was not—Mr. John Murray.

Firstly. They would not speak of it at all, because it would never have done to speak of it without abusing you; and that was the *"vetitum nefas,"* through which it is only real sons of the "Japeti genus" (like me) that dare run. Secondly, They could not speak of it without praising it, and that would have been doing something against themselves—it would have amounted to little less than coming in as accessories to the crime of *lese majesté* against the liege Lord of the "Quarterly" Reviewers, and of all other reviewers who print their Reviews—Humbug.—But even this is nothing to the story that is told (God knows with what truth!) of Blackwood—I mean the *man* Blackwood, not the *thing* Blackwood,—the bibliopole, not the magazine. This worthy bibliopole, it is said, actually refused to have *Don Juan* seen in his shop; *"procul, procul, esto profane,"* was the language of the indignant Master William Blackwood to the intrusive Don Juan. Now, had Lord Byron, (forgive the supposition,) had Lord Byron sent *Don Juan,* with five hundred thousand million times more of the devil about him than he really has exhibited, to that well-known character Christopher North, Esq. with a request to have the Don inserted in his Magazine,—lives there that being with wit enough to keep him from putrefying, who doubts the great KIT would have smiled a sweet smile, and desired the right honourable guest to ascend into the most honourable place of his upper chamber of immortality? This is clear enough; and then came the redoubted Magazine itself,—(why, by the way, have you delayed so long publishing that letter upon it which many have seen, and of which all have heard?)—what could it do? could it refuse to row in the wake of the admiral? could the clay rebel against the potter? No, no; a set of obsequious moralists meet in a tavern, and after being thoroughly maddened with tobacco smoke and whiskey punch, they cry out—"Well, then, so be it; have at *Don Juan.*" Upon a table all round in a roar of blasphemy, and by men hot from ——'s, and breathing nothing but pollution, furious paragraph after furious paragraph is written against a book of which the whole knot would have been happy to club their brains to write one stanza,—a book which they had all got by heart ere they set about reviewing it, and which thousands will get by heart after all the reviews they ever wrote shall have sunk into the "melodious wave" of the same Lake, where now slumber gently side by side, the fallen and fettered angel of the "Isle of Palms" . . . , and the thrice rueful ghost of the late "much and justly regretted" Dr. Peter Morris.

From the pure "Quarterly," and its disowned, if not discarded, Cloaca, the leap is not "Wilsonian" to the "Edinburgh." *Don Juan* was not reviewed there neither; but Little's poems were; "aye, there's the rub." It was very right to rebuke Tom Moore for his filth; but what was his filth to the filth of *Don Juan?* Why, not much more than his poetry was (and is) to the poetry of *Don Juan.* This, indeed, was straining at the shrimp, and swallowing the lobster; and what was the reason for it? Your Lordship knows very well it is to be found in a certain wicked page of a certain wicked little book of yours called *English Bards and Scotch Reviewers* . . . , the suppression of which, by the way, is another egregious piece of humbug on the part of your Lordship. Had you never written that little book, (I wish you would write a better on the same subject—now that you are a man)—Mr. Francis Jeffrey, that grave doctor of morality, would have flourished his thong and laid on with all his might, and Don Juan would have scratched his back, for he would have thought a flea had skipped within his linens. The thong was not flourished, the healing stripe was withheld, and the Don slumbered undisturbed. (pp. 80-8)

Enough, however, for the present, of these gentlemen: for their hour is not yet come, and I meant no more than to give them a jog in passing. (p. 88)

I will not insult *Don Juan* by saying that his style is *not* like that of Signior Penseroso di Cornuaglia; in truth, I think the great charm of its style is, that it is not much like the style of any other poem in the world. It is utter humbug to say, that it is borrowed from the style of the Italian weavers of merry *rima ottava;* their merriment is nothing, because they have nothing but their merriment; yours is every thing, because it is delightfully intermingled with and contrasted by all manner of serious things—murder and lust included. It is also mere *humbug* to

accuse you of having plagiarized it from Mr. Frere's pretty and graceful little Whistlecrafts. The measure to be sure is the same, but then the measure is as old as the hills. But the spirit of the two poets is as different as can be. Mr. Frere writes elegantly, playfully, very like a gentleman, and a scholar, and a respectable man, and his poems never sold, nor ever will sell. Your *Don Juan* again, is written strongly, lasciviously, fiercely, laughingly—every body sees in a moment, that nobody could have written it but a man of the first order both in genius and in dissipation;—a real master of all his tools—a profligate, pernicious, irresistible, charming Devil—and, accordingly, the *Don* sells, and will sell to the end of time, whether our good friend Mr. John Murray honours it with him *imprimatur* or doth not so honour it. I will mention a book, however, from which I do think you have taken a great many hints—nay, a great many pretty full sketches for your Juan. It is one which (with a few more) one never sees mentioned in reviews, because it is a book written on the anti-humbug principle. It is—you know it excellently well—it is no other than FAUBLAS, a book which contains as much good fun as *Gil Blas,* or *Moliere*—as much good luscious description as the *Heloise;* as much fancy and imagination as all the Comedies in the English language put together—and less humbug than any one given romance that has been written since Don Quixote—a book which is to be found on the tables of Roués, and in the desks of divines and under the pillows of spinsters—a book, in a word, which is read universally—I wish I could add,—in the original. Your fine Spanish lady, with her black hair lying on the pillow, and the curly-headed little Juan couched under the coverlid,—she is taken—every inch of her—from the *Marquise de B——;* your Greek girl (sweet creature!) is *La petite Contesse,* but she is the better, because of her wanting even the semblance of being married. You have also taken some warm touches from Peregrine Proteus, and if you read Peregrine over again you will find there is still more well worth the taking.

But all this has nothing to do with the charming *style* of *Don Juan,* which is entirely and inimitably your own—the sweet, fiery, rapid, easy—beautifully easy, anti-humbug style of *Don Juan.* Ten stanzas of it are worth all your *Manfred* . . .—and yet your *Manfred* is a noble poem too in its way; and Meinherr von Goëthe has exhibited no more palpable symptom of dotage than in his attempt to persuade his *"lesende publicum"* that you stole it from his *Faustus* . . . ; for it is, as I have said, a noble and an original poem, and not in the least like either *Don Juan* or *Faust,* and quite inferior to both of them. I had really no idea what a very clever fellow you were till I read *Don Juan.* In my humble opinion, there is very little in the literature of the present day that will really stand the test of half a century, except the *Scotch* novels of Sir Walter Scott and *Don Juan. They* will do so because they are written with perfect facility and nature—because their materials are all drawn from nature—in other words, because they are neither made up of cant, like Wordsworth and Shelley, nor of humbug like *Childe Harold* . . . and the *City of the Plague* . . . , nor of Brunswick Mum, like the *Rime of the Ancient Mariner* . . . , nor of milk and water like Mr. Barry Cornwall. (pp. 90-3)

> *John Bull [pseudonym of John Gibson Lockhart], "Letter to the Right Hon. Lord Byron," in John Bull's "Letter to Lord Byron" by Alan Lang Strout, University of Oklahoma Press, 1947, pp. 63-110.*

LORD BYRON (letter date 1821)

[In the following excerpt from a letter to Murray, Byron confesses that the humorous spirit and straightforward honesty of Lockhart's

pamphlet (see excerpt dated 1821) had pleased him, though Lockhart was not among the men he suspected of having written it.]

I have just read "John Bull's letter"—it is diabolically *well* written—& full of fun and ferocity.—I must forgive the dog whoever he is.—I suspect three people—one is *Hobhouse*—the other—Mr. Peacock (a very clever fellow) and lastly Israeli—there are parts very like Israeli—& he has a present grudge with Bowles & Southey &c. There is something too of the author of the Sketch-book in the Style. Find him out. (p. 145)

> Lord Byron, in a letter to John Murray on June 29, 1821, in his "Born for Opposition": Byron's Letters and Journals, 1821. Vol. 8, *edited by Leslie A. Marchand, Cambridge, Mass.: Belknap Press, 1978, pp. 144-45.*

THE MONTHLY MAGAZINE (letter date 1821)

[The Monthly Magazine was founded in 1796 by Richard Philips. A liberal periodical, the Monthly *is described by Kenneth Curry in* British Literary Magazines, 1789-1836 *as "antiministerial" in politics, "Dissenting and Unitarian" in religion, and "sympathetic to young writers such as Coleridge, Southey, and Lamb." The anonymous critic of the following excerpt was one of a number of reviewers who discovered that Byron had incorporated passages from a work by Sir G. Dalzell called* Shipwrecks and Disasters at Sea *in the shipwreck scene from Canto II of* Don Juan. *While the critic insists that Byron ought to have acknowledged his use of Dalzell's material, he or she also asserts that the interest of the shipwreck scene is not "at all decreased, but, on the contrary, increased, by learning that the horrors of such a scene were actually experienced by some of our fellow creatures." Quotations from both works showing Byron's extensive borrowings followed this review. The poet responded privately to the charge of plagiarism by admitting his debt to Dalzell (see excerpt from his letter of August 23, 1821).]*

Lord Byron has been so long, and so deservedly esteemed as the greatest poet of the present age, that it is with a feeling of the utmost deference, I presume to offer for insertion in your valuable and widely circulated Magazine, the following extracts from the Second Canto of his ***Don Juan,*** with corresponding passages from a work entitled "Shipwrecks and Disasters at Sea," in 3 vols.

To attempt a criticism upon the writings of his Lordship, were it even possible, would require a much abler pen, and a far maturer judgment than I possess; and not without timidity do I venture to ask if, in the following stanzas which I have selected, plagiarism the most glaring, is not sufficiently evident? Accident furnished me with the narratives from which Lord Byron appears to have derived most of the incidents in that part of his ***Don Juan,*** in which is so admirably described a storm and shipwreck. Most readers of taste have doubtless heard or perused that portion of the poem, and whilst their feelings have been harrowed by his appalling and heart-rending recital, few, perhaps, were aware that his Lordship was indebted for the most prominent features therein exhibited, to the work above-mentioned. The interest excited by the well-imagined sufferings of the hapless crew of the vessel in which Juan embarked, will not, I am sure, be at all diminished, but, on the contrary, increased, by learning that the horrors of such a scene were actually experienced by some of our fellow-creatures.

Possessed, as is his Lordship, of an imagination, fertile beyond most, it is impossible for a moment to suppose that he could

have occasion to borrow from the writings of any one; and doubtless his motive in thus illustrating his narrative with incidents which are well authenticated to have occurred, was to render his descriptions the more natural. But from what cause is it that there are no notes subjoined, acknowledging the sources from which he derived them?

I trust the freedom with which the charge of plagiarism is here advanced against so renowned a poet, will be justified by the importance of keeping even renown within the pale of honesty.

> C.E.S., in a letter to the editor of "The Monthly Magazine," in The Monthly Magazine, *London, Vol. LII, No. 357, August 1, 1821, p. 19.*

LORD BYRON (poem date 1821)

[In the following introductory stanzas to Canto IV of Don Juan, *Byron muses on how his approach to poetry has been shaped by the effects of time and experience on his emotions and perception of life. He comments also on the charges of immorality that had been brought against the first two cantos of the poem, maintaining that his critics condemned him for "Not what they saw, but what they wish'd to see." Cantos III-V of* Don Juan *were first published on August 8, 1821.]*

[*Canto IV, stanzas 1-7*]

Nothing so difficult as a beginning
    In poesy, unless perhaps the end;
For oftentimes when Pegasus seems winning
    The race, he sprains a wing, and down we tend,
Like Lucifer when hurl'd from heaven for sinning;
    Our sin the same, and hard as his to mend,
Being pride, which leads the mind to soar too far,
Till our own weakness shows us what we are.

But Time, which brings all beings to their level,
    And sharp Adversity, will teach at last
Man,—and, as we would hope,—perhaps the devil,
    That neither of their intellects are vast:
While youth's hot wishes in our red veins revel,
    We know not this—the blood flows on too fast;
But as the torrent widens towards the ocean,
We ponder deeply on each past emotion.

As boy, I thought myself a clever fellow,
    And wish'd that others held the same opinion;
They took it up when my days grew more mellow,
    And other minds acknowledged my dominion:
Now my sere fancy "falls into the yellow
    Leaf," and imagination droops her pinion,
And the sad truth which hovers o'er my desk
Turns what was once romantic to burlesque.

And if I laugh at any mortal thing,
    'Tis that I may not weep; and if I weep,
'Tis that our nature cannot always bring
    Itself to apathy, for we must steep
Our hearts first in the depths of Lethe's spring,
    Ere what we least wish to behold will sleep:
Thetis baptized her mortal son in Styx;
A mortal mother would on Lethe fix.

Some have accused me of a strange design
    Against the creed and morals of the land,
And trace it in this poem every line:

I don't pretend that I quite understand
My own meaning when I would be *very* fine;
    But the fact is that I have nothing plann'd,
Unless it were to be a moment merry,
A novel word in my vocabulary.

To the kind reader of our sober clime
    This way of writing will appear exotic;
Pulci was sire of the half-serious rhyme,
    Who sang when chivalry was more Quixotic,
And revell'd in the fancies of the time,
    True knights, chaste dames, huge giants, kings
        despotic;
But all these, save the last, being obsolete,
I chose a modern subject as more meet.

How I have treated it, I do not know;
    Perhaps no better than they have treated me
Who have imputed such designs as show
    Not what they saw, but what they wish'd to see;
But if it gives them pleasure, be it so,
    This is a liberal age, and thoughts are free:
Meantime Apollo plucks me by the ear,
And tells me to resume my story here.

                                        (pp. 344-47)

Lord Byron, in his Don Juan, a Variorum Edition:
Cantos I-V, Vol. II, *edited by Truman Guy Steffan
and Willis W. Pratt, University of Texas Press, 1957,
503 p.*

*A portrait of Annabella Milbanke, the future Lady Byron,
in 1812.*

LORD BYRON   (letter date 1821)

[*In the following excerpt from a letter to Murray, Byron responds
to the* Monthly Magazine's *charge (see excerpt dated 1821) that
he had plagiarized Sir G. Dalzell's* Shipwrecks and Disasters at
Sea *in Canto II of* Don Juan.]

With regard to the charges about the "Shipwreck"—I think
that I told both you and Mr. Hobhouse years ago—that [there]
was not a *single circumstance* of it—*not* taken from *fact*—not
indeed from any *single* shipwreck—but all from *actual* facts
of different wrecks.—Almost all ***Don Juan*** is *real* life—either
my own—or from people I knew.——By the way much of the
description of the *furniture* in Canto 3d. is taken from *Tully's
Tripoli*—(pray *note this*)—and the rest from my own observation.——Remember I never meant to conceal this at all—
& have only not stated it because *D Juan* had no preface nor
name to it.—If you think it worth while to make this statement—do so—in your own way.—*I laugh at such charges*—
convinced that no writer ever borrowed less——or made his
materials more his own. (p. 186)

*Lord Byron, in a letter to John Murray on August
23, 1821, in his* "Born for Opposition": Byron's
Letters and Journals, 1821, Vol. 8, *edited by Leslie
A. Marchand, Cambridge, Mass.: Belknap Press,
1978, pp. 186-87.*

LORD BYRON   (letter date 1821)

[*Here, Byron reveals his frustration with the difficulties inherent
in publishing a poem in England while residing in Italy. He accuses Murray of being careless with the typesetting of* Don Juan
*and of taking advantage of his absence from England to omit and
alter controversial portions of the poem.*]

I have received the ***Juan***s—which are printed so *carelessly*
especially the 5th. Canto—as to be disgraceful to me—& not
creditable to you.—It really must be *gone over again* with the
Manuscript—the errors are so gross—words added—changed—
so as to make cacophony & nonsense.——You have been
careless of this poem because some of your Synod don't approve of it—but I tell you—it will be long before you see any
thing half so good as poetry or writing.——Upon what principle have you omitted the *note* on Bacon & Voltaire? and one
of the concluding stanzas sent as an addition? because it ended
I suppose—with—

    And do not link two virtuous souls for life
    Into that *moral Centaur* man & wife?

Now I must say once for all—that I will not permit any human
being to take such liberties with my writings—because I am
absent.—I desire the omissions to be replaced (except the stanza
on Semiramis) particularly the stanza upon the Turkish marriages—and I request that the whole be carefully *gone over*
with the M.S.S.—I never saw such stuff as is printed—Gul-
leyaz—instead of Gul*beyaz* &c. Are you aware that Gul*beyaz*
is a real name—and the other nonsense?—I copied the *Cantos*
out carefully—so that there is *no* excuse—as the Printer reads
or at least *prints* the M.S.S. of the plays without error.——
If you have no feeling for your own reputation pray have some
little for mine.——I have read over the poem carefully—and
I tell you *it is poetry.*—Your little envious knot of parson-
poets may say what they please—time will show that I am not
in this instance mistaken.——

Desire my friend Hobhouse to correct the press especially of
the last Canto from the Manuscript—as it is—it is enough to

drive one out of one's senses—to see the infernal torture of words from the original.—For instance the line

And pair their rhymes as Venus yokes her doves

is printed—

and *praise* their rhymes &c.—

also "precarious" for "precocious"—and this line stanza 133.—

And this strong extreme effect—to tire no longer.

Now do turn to the Manuscript—& see—if I ever made such a *line*—it is *not verse.*———No wonder the poem should fail—(which however *it wont* you will see) with such things allowed to creep about it.———Replace what is omitted—& correct what is so shamefully misprinted,—and let the poem have fair play—and I fear nothing. (pp. 192-93)

> *Lord Byron, in a letter to John Murray on August 31, 1821, in his "Born for Opposition": Byron's Letters and Journals, 1821, Vol. 8, edited by Leslie A. Marchand, Cambridge, Mass.: Belknap Press, 1978, pp. 192-93.*

P. B. SHELLEY   (letter date 1821)

[*Shelley's assessment of Cantos III-V of* Don Juan *is even more complimentary to Byron than his comment on the earlier cantos (see excerpt dated 1820). In his letter, Shelley praises the conception, originality, events, and language of the poem, declaring "nothing has ever been written like it in English."*]

Many thanks for [Cantos III-V of] *Don Juan*—It is a poem totally of its own species, & my wonder and delight at the grace of the composition no less than the free & grand vigour of the conception of it perpetually increase.—The few passages which any one might desire to be cancelled in the 1st & 2d Cantos are here reduced almost to nothing. This poem carries with it at once the stamp of originality and a defiance of imitation. Nothing has ever been written like it in English—nor if I may venture to prophesy, will there be; without carrying upon it the mark of a secondary and borrowed light.—You unveil & present in its true deformity what is worst in human nature, & this is what the witlings of the age murmur at, conscious of their want of power to endure the scrutiny of such a light.—We are damned to the knowledge of good & evil, and it is . . . well for us to know what we should avoid no less than what we should seek.—The character of Lambro—his return—the merriment of his daughters guests made as it were in celebration of his funeral—the meeting with the lovers—and the death of Haidée,—are circumstances combined & developed in a manner that I seek elsewhere in vain. The fifth canto, which some of your pet Zoili in Albemarle St. said was *dull*, gathers instead of loses, splendour & energy—the language in which the whole is clothed—a sort of [chameleon] under the changing sky of the spirit that kindles it—is such as these lisping days could not have expected,—and are, believe me, in spite of the approbation which you wrest from them—little pleased to hear. One can hardly judge from recitation and it was not until I read it in print that I have been able to do it justice.—This sort of writing only on a great plan & perhaps in a more compact form is what I wished you to do when I made my vows for an epic.—But I am content—You are building up a drama, such as England has not yet seen, and the task is sufficiently noble & worthy of you. (pp. 357-58)

> *P. B. Shelley, in a letter to Lord Byron on October 21, 1821, in his* The Letters of Percy Bysshe Shelley:

> Shelley in Italy, Vol. II, *edited by Frederick L. Jones, Oxford at the Clarendon Press, 1964, pp. 357-59.*

JOHANN WOLFGANG von GOETHE   (essay date 1821)

[*A preeminent figure in German literature, Goethe was a shaping force in the major literary movements of the late eighteenth and early nineteenth centuries. He is best known for his verse drama* Faust *and his early novel* Die Leiden des jungen Werthers. *Goethe held a high opinion of* Don Juan, *one reflected in the following excerpt from his* Ueber Kunst und Alterthum, *first published in 1821. In his remarks, written to accompany a translation of the first five stanzas of the poem, Goethe praises Byron's daring approach to subject matter and language and defends the morality of the work.*]

Don Juan is a work of infinite genius, misanthropical with the bitterest inhumanity, yet sympathetic with the deepest intensity of tender feeling. And since we now know the author and esteem him, and do not wish him to be otherwise than he is, we enjoy thankfully what he dares with overgreat independence, indeed insolence, to bring before us. The technical treatment of the verse is quite in accord with the singular, reckless, unsparing content. The poet spares his language as little as he does his men, and as we examine it more closely we discover indeed that English poetry has a cultivated comic language which we Germans wholly lack. (pp. 205-06)

In translating *Don Juan* there are many useful things to be learned from the Englishman. There is only one joke which we cannot imitate from him,—one that gets its effect by a singular and dubious accent in words which look quite differently on paper. The English linguist may judge how far the poet in this case has wantonly exceeded the proper limits. (p. 206)

Possibly we may be reproached for spreading in translation such writings as these through Germany, thus making an honest, peaceful, decorous nation acquainted with the most immoral works that the art of poetry ever produced. But according to our way of thinking, these attempts at translation should not be intended for the press, but may serve as excellent practice for talented brains. Our poets may then discreetly apply and cultivate what they acquire in this way, for the pleasure and delight of their countrymen. No particular injury to morality is to be feared from the publication of such poems, since poets and authors would have to cast aside all restraint to be more corrupting than the papers of the present day. (p. 207)

> *Johann Wolfgang von Goethe, "Byron's 'Don Juan',"* in his *Goethe's Literary Essays, edited by J. E. Spingarn, Harcourt Brace Jovanovich, 1921, pp. 205-07.*

LORD BYRON (CONVERSATION WITH THOMAS MEDWIN) (conversation date 1822)

[*Medwin was a cousin of Shelley's who had almost daily contact with Byron for approximately four months during the latter part of 1821 and the beginning of 1822. Shortly thereafter, he published a record of their conversations. Byron's friends almost immediately denounced the work as factually inaccurate, and it is considered by modern scholars to be one of the least reliable of the contemporary accounts of the poet. Despite its questionable accuracy, however, critics value Medwin's book both for capturing something of Byron's manner in conversation and for its occasional record of opinions not revealed elsewhere. In the excerpt below, Byron discusses the concept of* Don Juan *as an epic and his projected plans for the poem. Modern discussions of the work's epic qualities often cite his comment, "If you must have an epic, there's* Don Juan *for you." For additional remarks by Byron on his plans for the poem, see also the excerpt from his letter of February 16, 1821.]*

People are always advising me, [said Byron] to write an epic. You tell me that I shall leave no great poem behind me;—that is, I suppose you mean by great, a heavy poem, or a weighty poem; I believe they are synonymous. You say that **Childe Harold** is unequal; that the last two Cantos are far superior to the two first. I know it is a thing without form or substance,— a *voyage pittoresque*. But who reads Milton? My opinion as to the inequality of my poems is this,—that one is not better or worse than another. And as to epics,—have you not got enough of Southey's? There's 'Joan d'Arc,' 'The Curse of Kehama,' and God knows how many more curses, down to 'The Last of the Goths!' If you must have an epic, there's **Don Juan** for you. I call that an epic: it is an epic as much in the spirit of our day as the 'Iliad' was in Homer's. Love, religion, and politics form the argument, and are as much the cause of quarrels now as they were then. There is no want of Parises and Menelauses, and of *Crim.-cons.* into the bargain. In the very first Canto you have a Helen. Then, I shall make my hero a perfect Achilles for fighting,—a man who can snuff a candle three successive times with a pistol-ball: and, depend upon it, my moral will be a good one; not even Dr. Johnson should be able to find a flaw in it!

Some one has possessed the Guiccioli with a notion that my **Don Juan** and the Don Giovanni of the Opera are the same person; and to please her I have discontinued his history and adventures; but if I should resume them, I will tell you how I mean him to go on. I left him in the seraglio there. I shall make one of the favourites, a Sultana, (no less a personage,) fall in love with him, and carry him off from Constantinople. Such elopements are not uncommon, nor unnatural either, though it would shock the ladies to say they are ever to blame. Well, they make good their escape to Russia; where, if Juan's passion cools, and I don't know what to do with the lady, I shall make her die of the plague. There are accounts enough of the plague to be met with, from Boccaccio to De Foe;—but I have seen it myself, and that is worth all their descriptions. As our hero can't do without a mistress, he shall next become man-mistress to Catherine the Great. Queens have had strange fancies for more ignoble people before and since. I shall, therefore, make him cut out the ancestor of the young Russian, and shall send him, when he is *hors de combat*, to England as her ambassador. In his suite he shall have a girl whom he shall have rescued during one of his northern campaigns, who shall be in love with him, and he not with her.

You see I am true to Nature in making the advances come from the females. I shall next draw a town and country life at home, which will give me room for life, manners, scenery, &c. I will make him neither a dandy in town nor a fox-hunter in the country. He shall get into all sorts of scrapes, and at length end his career in France. Poor Juan shall be guillotined in the French Revolution! What do you think of my plot? It shall have twenty-four books too, the legitimate number. Episodes it has, and will have, out of number; and my spirits, good or bad, must serve for the machinery. If that be not an epic, if it be not strictly according to Aristotle, I don't know what an epic poem means. (pp. 163-66)

> *Lord Byron, in a conversation with Thomas Medwin in 1822, in* Journal of the Conversations of Lord Byron *by Thomas Medwin, Henry Colburn, 1824, pp. 163-66.*

[FRANCIS JEFFREY] (essay date 1822)

[Jeffrey was a founder and editor (1803-1829) of the Edinburgh Review, *one of the most influential magazines in early nineteenth-century England. A liberal Whig and politician, Jeffrey often allowed his political beliefs to color his critical opinions. His literary criticism, perhaps the most characteristic example of "impressionistic" critical thought during the first half of the nineteenth century, stressed a personal approach to literature. Though he became famous for his harsh criticism of the Lake Poets, Jeffrey was an exponent of moderate Romanticism and praised the work of Keats, Byron, and Scott. Like the* Quarterly Review *(see excerpt dated 1822), the* Edinburgh *initially refused to comment on* Don Juan, *and Jeffrey first expressed his opinion of the poem in a review, excerpted below, of Byron's* Cain, Sardanapalus, *and* The Two Foscari. *Considered one of the most thoughtful pieces of criticism written on* Don Juan *during Byron's lifetime, Jeffrey's remarks deal not only with the poem itself, but also with the effects of the poem on Byron's reputation in England. In contrast to the majority of contemporary critics, Jeffrey provides a sober and frank discussion of the reasons for the widespread outcry against Byron and the poem. The critic charges that despite their beauty and power,* Don Juan *and Byron's works in general "have a tendency to destroy all belief in the reality of virtue." He concludes by comparing Byron's works unfavorably with those of Scott. Byron admired Jeffrey and respected his opinions (see* Don Juan, Canto X, *stanzas xi-xix), but whether he read these remarks and reacted to them is not known.]*

We have a word or two to say on the griefs of Lord Byron. . . . He complains bitterly of the detraction by which he has been assailed—and intimates that his works have been received by the public with far less cordiality and favour than he was entitled to expect. We are constrained to say that this appears to us a very extraordinary mistake. In the whole course of our experience, we cannot recollect a single author who has had so little reason to complain of his reception—to whose genius the public has been so early and so constantly just—to whose faults they have been so long and so signally indulgent. From the very first, he must have been aware that he offended the principles and shocked the prejudices of the majority, by his sentiments, as much as he delighted them by his talents. Yet there never was an author so universally and warmly applauded, so gently admonished—so kindly entreated to look more heedfully to his opinions. He took the praise, as usual, and rejected the advice. As he grew in fame and authority, he aggravated all his offences—clung more fondly to all he had been reproached with—and only took leave of Childe Harold to ally himself to Don Juan! That he has since been talked of, in public and in private, with less unmingled admiration—that his name is now mentioned as often for censure as for praise—and that the exultation with which his countrymen once hailed the greatest of our living poets, is now alloyed by the recollection of the tendency of his writings—is matter of notoriety to all the world; but matter of surprise, we should imagine, to nobody but Lord B. himself.

He would fain persuade himself, indeed, that this decline of his popularity—or rather this stain upon its lustre—for he is still popular beyond all other example—and it is only because he is so that we feel any interest in this discussion;—he wishes to believe, that he is indebted for the censures that have reached him, not to any actual demerits of his own, but to the jealousy of those he has supplanted, the envy of those he has outshone, or the party rancour of those against whose corruptions he has testified;—while, at other times, he seems inclined to insinuate, that it is chiefly because he is a *Gentleman* and a *Nobleman* that plebeian censors have conspired to bear him down! We scarcely think, however, that these theories will pass with Lord

B. himself—we are sure they will pass with no other person. They are so manifestly inconsistent as mutually to destroy each other—and so weak, as to be quite insufficient to account for the fact, even if they could be effectually combined for that purpose. *The party* that Lord B. has offended, bears no malice to Lords and Gentlemen. Against its rancour, on the contrary, these qualities have undoubtedly been his best protection; and had it not been for them, he may be assured that he would, long ere now, have been shown up in the pages of the *Quarterly,* with the same candour and liberality that has there been exercised towards his friend Lady Morgan. That the base and the bigotted—those whom he has darkened by his glory, spited by his talent, or mortified by his neglect—have taken advantage of the prevailing disaffection, to vent their puny malice in silly nicknames and vulgar scurrility, is natural and true. But Lord B. may depend upon it, that the dissatisfaction is not confined to them,—and, indeed, that they would never have had the courage to assail one so immeasurably their superior, if he had not at once made himself vulnerable by his errors, and alienated his natural defenders by his obstinate adherence to them. *We* are not bigots, nor rival poets. We have not been detractors from Lord Byron's fame, nor the friends of his detractors; and *we* tell him—far more in sorrow than in anger—that we verily believe the great body of the English nation—the religious, the moral, and the candid part of it—consider the tendency of his writings to be immoral and pernicious—and look upon his perseverance in that strain of composition with regret and reprehension. We ourselves are not easily startled, either by levity of temper, or boldness, or even rashness of remark; we are, moreover, most sincere admirers of Lord Byron's genius—and have always felt a pride and an interest in his fame. But we cannot dissent from the censure to which we have alluded; and shall endeavour to explain, in as few and as temperate words as possible, the grounds upon which we rest our concurrence.

He has no priestlike cant or priestlike reviling to apprehend from us. We do not charge him with being either a disciple or an apostle of Satan; nor do we describe his poetry as a mere compound of blasphemy and obscenity. On the contrary, we are inclined to believe that he wishes well to the happiness of mankind—and are glad to testify, that his poems abound with sentiments of great dignity and tenderness, as well as passages of infinite sublimity and beauty. But their general tendency we believe to be in the highest degree pernicious; and we even think that it is chiefly by means of the fine and lofty sentiments they contain, that they acquire their most fatal power of corruption. This may sound at first, perhaps, like a paradox; but we are mistaken if we shall not make it intelligible enough in the end.

We think there are indecencies and indelicacies, seductive descriptions and profligate representations, which are extremely reprehensible; and also audacious speculations, and erroneous and uncharitable assertions, equally indefensible. But if these had stood alone, and if the whole body of his works had been made up of gaudy ribaldry and flashy scepticism, the mischief, we think, would have been much less than it is. He is not more obscene, perhaps, than Dryden or Prior, and other classical and pardoned writers; nor is there any passage in the history even of Don Juan, so degrading as Tom Jones's affair with Lady Bellaston. It is no doubt a wretched apology for the indecencies of a man of genius, that equal indecencies have been forgiven to his predecessors: But the precedent of lenity might have been followed; and we might have passed both the levity and the voluptuousness—the dangerous warmth of his romantic situations, and the scandal of his cold-blooded dis-

sipation. It might not have been so easy to get over his dogmatic scepticism—his hard-hearted maxims of misanthropy—his cold-blooded and eager expositions of the non-existence of virtue and honour. Even this, however, might have been comparatively harmless, if it had not been accompanied by that which may look, at first sight, as a palliation—the frequent presentment of the most touching pictures of tenderness, generosity, and faith.

The charge we bring against Lord B. in short is, that his writings have a tendency to destroy all belief in the reality of virtue—and to make all enthusiasm and constancy of affection ridiculous; and that this is effected, not merely by direct maxims and examples, of an imposing or seducing kind, but by the constant exhibition of the most profligate heartlessness in the persons of those who had been transiently represented as actuated by the purest and most exalted emotions—and in the lessons of that very teacher who had been, but a moment before, so beautifully pathetic in the expression of the loftiest conceptions. When a rash and gay voluptuary descants, somewhat too freely, on the intoxications of love and wine, we ascribe his excesses to the effervescence of youthful spirits, and do not consider him as seriously impeaching either the value or the reality of the severer virtues; and in the same way, when the satirist deals out his sarcasms against the sincerity of human professions, and unmasks the secret infirmities of our bosoms, we consider this as aimed at hypocrisy, and not at mankind: or, at all events, and in either case, we consider the Sensualist and the Misanthrope as wandering, each in his own delusion—and pity those who have never known the charms of a tender or generous affection. The true antidote to such seductive or revolting views of human nature, is to turn to the scenes of its nobleness and attraction; and to reconcile ourselves again to our kind, by listening to the accents of pure affection and incorruptible honour. But if those accents have flowed, in all their sweetness, from the very lips that instantly open again to mock and blaspheme them, the antidote is mingled with the poison, and the draught is the more deadly for the mixture! (pp. 446-49)

This is the charge which we bring against Lord Byron. We say that, under some strange misapprehension as to the truth, and the duty of proclaiming it, he has exerted all the powers of his powerful mind to convince his readers, both directly and indirectly, that all ennobling pursuits, and disinterested virtues, are mere deceits or illusions—hollow and despicable mockeries for the most part, and, at best, but laborious follies. Love, patriotism, valour, devotion, constancy, ambition—all are to be laughed at, disbelieved in, and despised!—and nothing is really good, so far as we can gather, but a succession of dangers to stir the blood, and of banquets and intrigues to sooth it again! If this doctrine stood alone, with its examples, it would revolt, we believe, more than it would seduce:—but the author of it has the unlucky gift of personating all those sweet and lofty illusions, and that with such grace and force and truth to nature, that it is impossible not to suppose, for the time, that he is among the most devoted of their votaries—till he casts off the character with a jerk—and, the moment after he has moved and exalted us to the very height of our conception, resumes his mockery at all things serious or sublime—and lets us down at once on some coarse joke, hard-hearted sarcasm, or fierce and relentless personality—as if on purpose to show

Whoe'er was edified, himself was not—

or to demonstrate practically as it were, and by example, how possible it is to have all fine and noble feelings, or their appearance, for a moment, and yet retain no particle of respect for them—or of belief in their intrinsic worth or permanent reality. Thus, we have an indelicate but very clever scene of the young Juan's concealment in the bed of an amorous matron, and of the torrent of 'rattling and audacious eloquence' with which she repels the too just suspicions of her jealous lord. All this is merely comic, and a little coarse:—But then the poet chuses to make this shameless and abandoned woman address to her young gallant, an epistle breathing the very spirit of warm, devoted, pure and unalterable love—thus profaning the holiest language of the heart, and indirectly associating it with the most hateful and degrading sensuality. In like manner, the sublime and terrific description of the Shipwreck is strangely and disgustingly broken by traits of low humour and buffoonery;—and we pass immediately from the moans of an agonizing father fainting over his famished son, to facetious stories of Juan's begging a paw of his father's dog—and refusing a slice of his tutor!—as if it were a fine thing to be hard-hearted—and pity and compassion were fit only to be laughed at. In the same spirit, the glorious Ode on the aspirations of Greece after Liberty, is instantly followed up by a strain of dull and cold-blooded ribaldry;—and we are hurried on from the distraction and death of Haidee to merry scenes of intrigue and masquerading in the seraglio. Thus all good feelings are excited only to accustom us to their speedy and complete extinction; and we are brought back, from their transient and theatrical exhibition, to the staple and substantial doctrine of the work—the non-existence of constancy in women or honour in men, and the folly of expecting to meet with any such virtues, or of cultivating them, for an undeserving world;—and all this mixed up with so much wit and cleverness, and knowledge of human nature, as to make it irresistibly pleasant and plausible—while there is not only no antidote supplied, but everything that might have operated in that way has been anticipated, and presented already in as strong and engaging a form as possible—but under such associations as to rob it of all efficacy, or even turn it into an auxiliary of the poison.

This is our sincere opinion of much of Lord B.'s most splendid poetry—a little exaggerated perhaps in the expression, from a desire to make our exposition clear and impressive—but, in substance, we think merited and correct. We have already said, and we deliberately repeat, that we have no notion that Lord B. had any mischievous intention in these publications—and readily acquit him of any wish to corrupt the morals, or impair the happiness of his readers. Such a wish, indeed, is in itself altogether inconceivable; but it is our duty, nevertheless, to say, that much of what he has published appears to us to have this tendency—and that we are acquainted with no writings so well calculated to extinguish in young minds all generous enthusiasm and gentle affection—all respect for themselves, and all love for their kind—to make them practise and profess hardly what it teaches them to suspect in others—and actually to persuade them that it is wise and manly and knowing, to laugh, not only at self-denial and restraint, but at all aspiring ambition, and all warm and constant affection. (pp. 449-51)

It seems to be Lord Byron's way . . . never to excite a kind or a noble sentiment, without making haste to obliterate it by a torrent of unfeeling mockery or relentless abuse, and taking pains to show how well those passing fantasies may be reconciled to a system of resolute misanthropy, or so managed as even to enhance its merits, or confirm its truth. With what different sensations, accordingly, do we read the works of [Scott and Byron]!—With the one, we seem to share a gay and gorgeous banquet—with the other, a wild and dangerous in-

toxication. Let Lord Byron bethink him of this contrast—and its causes and effects. Though he scorns the precepts, and defies the censure of ordinary men, he may yet be moved by *the example* of his only superior!—In the mean time, we have endeavoured to point out the canker that stains the splendid flowers of his poetry—or, rather, the serpent that lurks beneath them. If it will not listen to the voice of the charmer, that brilliant garden, gay and glorious as it is, must be deserted, and its existence deplored, as a snare to the unwary. (pp. 451-52)

[Francis Jeffrey], "Lord Byron's Tragedies," in The Edinburgh Review, Vol. XXXVI, No. LXXII, February, 1822, pp. 413-52.

[REGINALD HEBER]   (essay date 1822)

[*Heber was the author of several well-known hymns, and in 1822 he became the bishop of Calcutta. In the following excerpt from a review of Byron's dramas in the powerful conservative journal the* Quarterly Review, *Heber explains why the periodical had refused to critique* Don Juan *and harshly condemns the moral tendencies of Byron's works. The fact that neither the* Quarterly *nor the* Edinburgh Review *(see excerpt by Francis Jeffrey dated 1822) had reviewed* Don Juan *when it was first published became something of a literary scandal in England, where both periodicals held a powerful influence. The reasons why both journals initially refrained from reviewing the poem are complex, but it is assumed that the* Edinburgh's *longtime support for Byron and the fact that his publisher Murray was also the publisher of the* Quarterly *prevented them from attacking him. Heber's explanation of censure by silence may also be taken into account. Byron read the critic's remarks and attributed their severity to political pressure on Heber to take a hard line against* Don Juan *(see excerpt from his letter of December 25, 1822).*]

Several years have passed away since we undertook the review of any of Lord Byron's Poetry. Not that we have been inattentive observers of that genius whose fertility is, perhaps, not the least extraordinary of its characteristics, of whose earlier fruits we were among the first and warmest eulogists, and whose later productions———though hardly answering the expectation which he once excited—would have been, of themselves, sufficient to establish the renown of many scores of ordinary writers. Far less have we been able to witness, without deep regret and disappointment, the systematic and increasing prostitution of those splendid talents to the expression of feelings, and the promulgation of opinions, which, as Christians, as Englishmen, and even as men, we were constrained to regard with abhorrence. But it was from this very conflict of admiration and regret;—this recollection of former merits and sense of present degradation;—this reverence for talent and scorn of sophistry, that we remained silent. The little effect which our advice had, on former occasions, produced, still further tended to confirm us in our silence,—a silence of which the meaning could hardly, as we conceived, be misunderstood, and which we wished Lord Byron himself to regard as an appeal, of not the least impressive kind,—to his better sense and taste and feelings. We trusted that he would himself, ere long, discover that wickedness was not strength, nor impiety courage, nor licentiousness warmheartedness, nor an aversion to his own country philosophy; and that riper years, and a longer experience, and a deeper knowledge of his own heart, and a more familiar acquaintance with that affliction to which all are heirs, and those religious principles by which affliction is turned into a blessing, would render him not only almost but altogether such a poet as virgins might read, and Christians praise, and Englishmen take pride in.

With these feelings we have altogether abstained from noticing those strange, though often beautiful productions, which, since the appearance of the Third part of his **Childe Harold,** have flowed on, wave after wave, redundant as that ocean which Lord Byron loves to describe, but with few exceptions, little less monotonous,—and stained, in succession, with deeper and yet deeper tokens of those pollutions, which, even in the full tide of genius, announce that its ebb is near. We knew not any severity of criticism which could reach the faults or purify the taste of **Don Juan,** and we trusted that its author would himself, ere long, discover, that if he continued to write such works as these, he would lose the power of producing any thing better, and that his pride, at least, if not his principle, would recall him from the island of Acrasia. (pp. 476-77)

> [Reginald Heber], *"Lord Byron's Dramas," in* The Quarterly Review, *Vol. XXVII, No. LIV, July, 1822, pp. 476-524.*

LORD BYRON   (letter date 1822)

[*Here, Byron describes to Moore the contents and purpose of Cantos VII-VIII of* Don Juan. *For additional comments by Byron on this part of the poem, see his preface to Cantos VI-VIII dated 1823.*]

I have written three more cantos of **Don Juan,** and am hovering on the brink of another (the ninth). . . . [These] cantos contain a full detail (like the storm in Canto Second) of the siege and assault of Ismael, with much of sarcasm on those butchers in large business, your mercenary soldiery, it is a good opportunity of gracing the poem with * * *. With these things and these fellows, it is necessary, in the present clash of philosophy and tyranny, to throw away the scabbard. I know it is against fearful odds; but the battle must be fought; and it will be eventually for the good of mankind, whatever it may be for the individual who risks himself. (p. 191)

> *Lord Byron, in a letter to Thomas Moore on August 8, 1822, in his "In the Wind's Eye": Byron's Letters and Journals, 1821-1822, Vol. 9, edited by Leslie A. Marchand, Cambridge, Mass.: The Belknap Press, 1979, pp. 190-91.*

LORD BYRON   (letter date 1822)

[*In this excerpt from a letter to Murray, Byron reacts to Heber's comments on* Don Juan *in the* Quarterly Review *(see excerpt dated 1822). Byron defends his satiric intent and protests that the licentious parts of the poem are relatively harmless compared with the works of such authors as Henry Fielding, Ariosto, and Tobias Smollett.*]

[What] the Writer says of D[on] J[uan] is harsh—but it is inevitable—He must follow—or at least not directly oppose the opinion of a prevailing & yet not very firmly seated party— a review may and will direct or "turn away" the Currents of opinion—but it must not directly oppose them.—**Don Juan** will be known by and bye for what it is intended a *satire* on *abuses* of the present *states* of Society—and not an eulogy of vice;—it may be now and then voluptuous—I can't help that— Ariosto is worse—Smollett (see Lord Strutwell in vol 2d. of R[oderick] R[andom]) ten times worse—and Fielding no better.——No Girl will ever be seduced by reading D[on] J[uan]— no—no—she will go to Little's poems—& Rousseau's ro-

mans—for that—or even to the immaculate De Stael——they will encourage her—& not the Don—who laughs at that— and—and—most other things. (p. 68)

> *Lord Byron, in a letter to John Murray on December 25, 1822, in his "A Heart for Every Fate": Byron's Letters and Journals, 1822-1823, Vol. 10, edited by Leslie A. Marchand, Cambridge, Mass.: Belknap Press, 1980, pp. 67-70.*

LORD BYRON   (letter date 1823)

[*In the following extract from a letter to Bryan Waller Procter, Byron discusses the English Cantos of* Don Juan *as a reflection of his own experience of high society in England, describing also his purpose in the poem as a whole.*]

As to what **D**[on] **J**[uan] may do in England—you will see. If you had had the experience which I have had of the *grande monde* in that and other countries, you would be aware that there is no society so intrinsically (though hypocritically) *intrigante* and profligate as English high life.

I speak what I do know—from what I have *seen* and *felt personally* in my youth—from what I have undergone and been made to undergo—and from what I know of the whole scene in general, by my own experience, and that of others; and my acquaintance was somewhat extensive. I speak of seven years ago and more; it may be bettered now. . . .

They mistake the object of **Don Juan,** which is nothing but a satire on affectations of all kinds, mixed with some relief of serious feeling and description. At least this is the object, and it will not be easy to bully me from "the farce of my humour." (p. 116)

> *Lord Byron, in a letter to Bryan Waller Procter on March 5, 1823, in his "A Heart for Every Fate": Byron's Letters and Journals, 1822-1823, Vol. 10, edited by Leslie A. Marchand, Cambridge, Mass.: The Belknap Press, 1980, pp. 115-17.*

LORD BYRON   (essay date 1823)

[*In his preface to Cantos VI-VIII of* Don Juan, *originally published July 15, 1823, Byron explains his attack on Robert Stewart, viscount Castlereagh, the marquis of Londonderry, who had served as foreign secretary of England from 1812 to 1822. To Byron and many of his Whig friends in England, Castlereagh symbolized conservative ignorance and repressive tyranny. Castlereagh had recently committed suicide, but as the following remarks indicate, Byron felt that the foreign secretary left a legacy of oppression which his death could not absolve. In the poet's mind, men like Castlereagh were responsible for the carnage and brutality depicted in the portrayal of the Siege of Ismail (Cantos VII-VIII). In the second part of the preface, Byron expresses his contempt for what he considers the false and hypocritical accusations of his critics. Contesting the charges of blasphemy that had been brought against portions of* Don Juan, *he concludes by attacking the "*Cant *which is the crying sin of this double-dealing and false-speaking time."*]

The details of the Siege of Ismail in two of the following Cantos (i.e. the 7th and 8th) are taken from a French work entitled "Histoire de la Nouvelle Russie." Some of the incidents attributed to Don Juan really occurred, particularly the circumstance of his saving the infant, which was the actual case of the late Duc de Richelieu, then a young volunteer in the Russian service, and afterwards the founder and benefactor of Odessa, where his name and memory can never cease to be regarded with reverence. In the course of these cantos, a stanza or two will be found relative to the late Marquis of Londonderry, but written some time before his decease. Had that person's Oligarchy died with him, they would have been suppressed; as it is, I am aware of nothing in the manner of his death or of his life to prevent the free expression of the opinions of all whom his whole existence was consumed in endeavouring to enslave. That he was an amiable man in *private* life, may or may not be true; but with this the Public have nothing to do; and as to lamenting his death, it will be time enough when Ireland has ceased to mourn for his birth. As a Minister, I, for one of millions, looked upon him as the most despotic in intention and the weakest in intellect that ever tyrannized over a country. It is the first time indeed since the Normans, that England has been insulted by a *Minister* (at least) who could not speak English, and that Parliament permitted itself to be dictated to in the language of Mrs. Malaprop.

Of the manner of his death little need be said, except that if a poor radical, such as Waddington or Watson, had cut his throat, he would have been buried in a cross-road, with the usual appurtenances of the stake and mallet. But the Minister was an elegant Lunatic—a sentimental Suicide—he merely cut the "carotid artery" (blessings on their learning) and lo! the Pageant, and the Abbey! and "the Syllables of Dolour yelled forth" by the Newspapers—and the harangue of the Coroner in an eulogy over the bleeding body of the deceased—(an Anthony worthy of such a Caesar)—and the nauseous and atrocious cant of a degraded Crew of Conspirators against all that is sincere or honourable. In his death he was necessarily one of two things by the *law*—a felon or a madman—and in either case no great subject for panegyric. In his life he was—what all the world knows, and half of it will feel for years to come, unless his death prove a "moral lesson" to the surviving Sejani of Europe. It may at least serve as some consolation to the Nations, that their Oppressors are not happy, and in some instances judge so justly of their own actions as to anticipate the sentence of mankind.—Let us hear no more of this man; and let Ireland remove the Ashes of her Grattan from the Sanctuary of Westminster. Shall the Patriot of Humanity repose by the Werther of Politics!!!

With regard to the objections which have been made on another score to the already published Cantos of this poem, I shall content myself with two quotations from Voltaire:—

> La pudeur s'est enfuite des coeurs, et s'est refugiée sur les livres.

> Plus les moeurs sont depravés, plus les expressions deviennent mesurées; on croit regagner en langage ce qu'on a perdu en vertu.

This is the real fact, as applicable to the degraded and hypocritical mass which leavens the present English generation, and is the only answer they deserve. The hackneyed and lavished title of Blasphemer—which, with radical, liberal, jacobin, reformer, &c. are the changes which the hirelings are daily ringing in the ears of those who will listen—should be welcome to all who recollect on *whom* it was originally bestowed. Socrates and Jesus Christ were put to death publicly as *Blasphemers*, and so have been and may be many who dare to oppose the most notorious abuses of the name of God and the mind of man. But Persecution is not refutation, nor even triumph: the "wretched Infidel," as he is called, is probably happier in his prison than the proudest of his Assailants. With his opinions

I have nothing to do—they may be right or wrong—but he has suffered for them, and that very Suffering for conscience-sake will make more proselytes to Deism than the example of heterodox Prelates to Christianity, suicide Statesmen to oppression, or over-pensioned Homicides to the impious Alliance which insults the world with the name of "Holy"! I have no wish to trample on the dishonoured or the dead; but it would be well if the adherents to the Classes from whence those persons sprung should abate a little of the *Cant* which is the crying sin of this double-dealing and false-speaking time of selfish Spoilers, and—but enough for the present. (pp. 3-5)

> *Lord Byron, "Preface to Cantos VI-VIII," in his Don Juan, a Variorum Edition: Cantos VI-XVII, Vol. III, edited by Truman Guy Steffan and Willis W. Pratt, University of Texas Press, 1957, pp. 3-5.*

LORD BYRON   (poem date 1823)

[*In the following introductory stanzas to Canto VII of* Don Juan, *Byron discusses the philosophy, methods, and purpose of the poem—as well as the hostile reception accorded the previous cantos. Cantos VI-VIII of* Don Juan *were first published on July 15, 1823.*]

[*Canto VII, stanzas 1-7*]

Oh Love! O Glory! what are ye? who fly
   Around us ever, rarely to alight;
There's not a meteor in the Polar sky
   Of such transcendant and more fleeting flight.
Chill, and chained to cold earth, we lift on high
   Our eyes in search of either lovely light;
A thousand and a thousand colours they
Assume, then leave us on our freezing way.

And such as they are, such my present tale is,
   A non-descript and ever varying rhyme,
A versified Aurora Borealis,
   Which flashes o'er a waste and icy clime.
When we know what all are, we must bewail us,
   But, ne'er the less, I hope it is no crime
To laugh at *all* things—for I wish to know
What after *all*, are *all* things—but a *Show?*

They accuse me—*Me*—the present writer of
   The present poem—of—I know not what,—
A tendency to under-rate and scoff
   At human power and virtue, and all that;
And this they say in language rather rough.
   Good God! I wonder what they would be at!
I say no more than has been said in Dante's
Verse, and by Solomon and by Cervantes;

By Swift, by Machiavel, by Rochefoucault,
   By Fenelon, by Luther, and by Plato;
By Tillotson, and Wesley, and Rousseau,
   Who knew this life was not worth a potato.
'Tis not their fault, nor mine, if this be so—
   For my part, I pretend not to be Cato,
Nor even Diogenes—We live and die,
But which is best, you know no more than I.

Socrates said, our only knowledge was
   "To know that nothing could be known"; a pleasant
Science enough, which levels to an ass
   Each Man of Wisdom, future, past, or present.
Newton (that Proverb of the Mind) alas!
   Declared, with all his grand discoveries recent,

That he himself felt only "like a youth
Picking up shells by the great Ocean—Truth."

Ecclesiastes said, that all is Vanity—
   Most modern preachers say the same, or show it
By their examples of true Christianity;
   In short, all know, or very soon may know it;
And in this scene of all-confessed inanity,
   By saint, by sage, by preacher, and by poet,
Must I restrain me, through the fear of strife,
From holding up the Nothingness of life?

Dogs, or Men! (for I flatter you in saying
   That ye are dogs—your betters far) ye may
Read, or read not, what I am now essaying
   To show ye what ye are in every way.
As little as the Moon stops for the baying
   Of Wolves, will the bright Muse withdraw one ray
From out her skies—then howl your idle wrath!
While she still silvers o'er your gloomy path.

(pp. 66-70)

> *Lord Byron, in his* Don Juan, a Variorum Edition:
> Cantos VI-XVII, Vol. III, *edited by Truman Guy
> Steffan and Willis W. Pratt, University of Texas Press,
> 1957, 569 p.*

JAMES KENNEDY AND LORD BYRON   (conversation date 1823)

*[Kennedy was a Scottish army doctor who, in a series of meetings
with Byron beginning in August, 1823, tried to convert the poet
to orthodox Christianity. Despite speculation that Byron may have
been making sport of Kennedy and leading the young man on for
his own amusement, most critics now assume that Byron was
sincere. Kennedy's record of their interviews is also regarded as
genuine and reliable. In the following excerpt from Kennedy's
account of one of their conversations, the two men discuss Byron's
portrayal of vice in* Don Juan *and his purpose in depicting high
society as predominantly corrupt and immoral.]*

"Even in [*Don Juan*]," said Lord B., "I have been equally
misunderstood. I take a vicious and unprincipled character, and
lead him through those ranks of society, whose high external
accomplishments cover and cloke internal and secret vices, and
I paint the natural effects of such characters; and certainly they
are not so highly coloured as we find them in real life."

"This may be true; but the question is, what are your motives
and object for painting nothing but scenes of vice and folly?"
"To remove the cloak, which the manners and maxims of
society," said his lordship, "throw over their secret sins, and
shew them to the world as they really are. You have not,"
added he, "been so much in high and noble life as I have been;
but if you had fully entered into it, and seen what was going
on, you would have felt convinced that it was time to unmask
the specious hypocrisy, and shew it in its native colours."

"My situation," I replied, "did not naturally lead me into
society, yet, I believe, before the publication of your book,
that the world, especially the lower and middling classes of
society, never entertained the opinion, that the highest classes
exhibited models of piety and virtue; nay, from circumstances,
we are naturally disposed to believe them worse than they really
are."

"It is impossible you can believe the higher classes of society
worse than they are in England, France, and Italy, for no
language can sufficiently paint them." "But still, my lord,
granting this, how is your book calculated to improve them,

and by what right, and under what title, do you come forward
in this undertaking?" "By the right," he replied, "which every
one has who abhors vice united with hypocrisy." (pp. 92-3)

> *James Kennedy and Lord Byron, in a conversation
> in 1823, in* Conversations on Religion, with Lord
> Byron and Others *by James Kennedy, 1830. Reprint
> by Carey & Lea, 1833, pp. 92-3.*

THOMAS MOORE   (essay date 1830)

*[Considered a minor Romantic poet, Moore is best known for his
exotic epic poem* Lalla Rookh *and was second only to Byron as
the most popular poet during the English Romantic era. Today,
however, his works are regarded as maudlin and lacking in depth.
A close friend of Byron, Moore was entrusted by the poet with
his memoirs, which Byron's friends and advisors later destroyed
despite Moore's objections. His biography of Byron, from which
the following excerpt is drawn, is regarded as remarkably balanced and reliable given the author's proximity to his subject.
Moore comments upon what he sees as the unique combination
of genius and profligacy in* Don Juan, *speculating also upon the
circumstances and personality that gave rise to it. The Life, Letters, and Journals of Lord Byron* was first published in 1830.]*

[Never] did pages more faithfully, and, in many respects, la-
mentably, reflect every variety of feeling, and whim, and passion, that, like the rack of autumn, swept across the author's
mind in writing them. Nothing less, indeed, than that singular
combination of attributes, which existed and were in full activity in his mind at this moment, could have suggested, or
been capable of the execution of, such a work. The cool
shrewdness of age, with the vivacity and glowing temperament
of youth,—the wit of a Voltaire, with the sensibility of a
Rousseau,—the minute, practical knowledge of the man of
society, with the abstract and self-contemplative spirit of the
poet,—a susceptibility of all that is grandest and most affecting
in human virtue, with a deep, withering experience of all that
is most fatal to it,—the two extremes, in short, of man's mixed
and inconsistent nature,—now rankly smelling of earth, now
breathing of heaven,—such was the strange assemblage of contrary elements, all meeting together in the same mind, and all
brought to bear, in turn, upon the same task, from which alone
could have sprung this extraordinary poem,—the most powerful and, in many respects, painful display of the versatility
of genius that has ever been left for succeeding ages to wonder
at and deplore.

> *Thomas Moore, in an extract from* The Life, Letters
> and Journals of Lord Byron *by Lord Byron, edited
> by Thomas Moore, John Murray, 1932, p. 386.*

H. A. TAINE   (essay date 1863-64)

*[Taine was a French philosopher, critic, and historian who stud-
ied the influence of environment and heredity on the development
of human character. In his well-known work,* Histoire de la littérature anglaise, *from which the following excerpt is drawn, Taine
analyzes literature through a study of race and milieu. In his
critique of* Don Juan, *Taine praises Byron's satirical attack on
British hypocrisy. The critic mocks many of the stock charges of
immorality that had been made against the poem, at the same
time decrying what he sees as Byron's excessive cynicism and
misanthropy. Taine contends that the sheer power and satirical
abandon that* Don Juan *displays are, in the final analysis, disturbing in their lack of restraint. "There is," he asserts, "a
derangement of heart and mind in the style of* Don Juan," *one
that exhausted Byron and caused the last cantos of the poem to
"drag." Taine's* Histoire *was first published in 1863-64.]*

[Byron] went in search of a hero, and did not find one, which, in this age of heroes, is 'an uncommon want.' For lack of a better he chose 'our ancient friend Don Juan,'—a scandalous choice: what an outcry the English moralists will make! But, to cap the horror, this Don Juan is not wicked, selfish, odious, like his fellows; he does not seduce, he is no corrupter. When the occasion rises, he lets himself drift; he has a heart and senses, and, under a beautiful sun, all this feels itself drawn out: at sixteen a youth cannot help himself, nor at twenty, nor perhaps at thirty. Lay it to the charge of human nature, my dear moralists; it is not I who made it as it is. If you will grumble, address yourselves higher: here we are painters, not makers of human puppets, and we do not answer for the structure of our dancing-dolls. Look, then, at our Juan as he goes along; he goes about in many places, and in all he is young; we will not strike him with thunder, therefore; that fashion is past: the green devils and their capers only come on the stage in the last act of Mozart. And, moreover, Juan is so amiable! After all, what has he done that others don't do? If he has been a lover of Catherine II., he only followed the lead of the diplomatic corps and the whole Russian army. Let him sow his wild oats; the good grain will spring up in its time. Once in England, he will behave himself decently. I confess that he may even there, when provoked, go a gleaning in the conjugal gardens of the aristocracy; but in the end he will settle, go and pronounce moral speeches in Parliament, become a member of the Society for the Suppression of Vice. If you wish absolutely to have him punished, we will make him end in hell, or in an unhappy marriage, not knowing which would be the severest. The Spanish tradition says hell; but it probably is only an allegory of the other state.

At all events, married or damned, the good folk at the end of the piece will have the pleasure of knowing that he is burning all alive.

Is it not a singular apology? Would it not aggravate the fault? Wait; you know not yet the whole venom of the book: together with Juan there are Donna Julia, Haidee, Gulbeyaz, Dudu, and the rest. It is here the diabolical poet digs in his sharpest claw, and he takes care to dig it into our foibles. What will the clergymen and white-chokered reviewers say? For, in short, there is no preventing it: we must read, in spite of ourselves. Twice or three times following we meet here with *happiness;* and when I say happiness, I mean profound and complete happiness—not mere voluptuousness, not obscene gaiety: we are miles away from the pretty rascalities of Dorat, and the unbridled licence of Rochester. Beauty is here, southern beauty, sparkling and harmonious, spread over everything, over the luminous sky, the calm scenery, corporal nudity, freshness of heart. Is there a thing it does not deify? All sentiments are exalted under his hands. What was gross becomes noble; even in the nocturnal adventure in the seraglio, which seems worthy of Faublas, poetry embellishes licentiousness. The girls are lying in the large silent apartment, like precious flowers brought from all climates into a conservatory:

> One with her flush'd cheek laid on her white arm,
> And raven ringlets gather'd in dark crowd
> Above her brow, lay dreaming soft and warm; . . .
> One with her auburn tresses lightly bound,
> And fair brows gently drooping, as the fruit
> Nods from the tree, was slumbering with soft breath,
> And lips apart, which show'd the pearls beneath. . . .
> A fourth as marble, statue-like and still,
> Lay in a breathless, hush'd, and stony sleep;
> White, cold, and pure . . . a carved lady on a
>   monument.

However, 'the fading lamps waned dim and blue;' Dudu is asleep, the innocent girl; and if she has cast a glance on her glass,

> 'Twas like the fawn, which, in the lake display'd,
> Beholds her own shy, shadowy image pass,
> When first she starts, and then returns to peep,
> Admiring this new native of the deep.

What will become now of Puritan prudery? Can the proprieties prevent beauty from being beautiful? Will you condemn a Titian for its nudity? What gives a value to human life, and a nobility to human nature, if not the power of attaining delicious and sublime emotions? You have just had one—one worthy of a painter; is it not worth that of an alderman? Will you refuse to acknowledge the divine because it appears in art and enjoyment, and not only in conscience and action? There is a world beside yours, and a civilisation beside yours; your rules are narrow, and your pedantry pedantic; the human plant can be otherwise developed than in your compartments and under your snows, and the fruits it will then bear will not be less precious. You must confess it, since you relish them when they are offered you. Who has read the love of Haidee, and has had any other thought than to envy and pity her? She is a wild child who has picked up Juan—another child cast ashore senseless by the waves. She has preserved him, nursed him like a mother, and now she loves him: who can blame her for loving him? Who, in presence of the splendid nature which smiles on and protects them, can imagine for them anything else than the all-powerful feeling which unites them. . . . O admirable moralists, you stand before these two flowers like patented gardeners, holding in your hands the model of bloom sanctioned by your society of horticulture, proving that the model has not been followed, and deciding that the two weeds must be cast into the fire, which you keep burning to consume irregular growths. Well judged: you know your art.

Beyond British cant, there is universal hypocrisy; beyond English pedantry, Byron wars against human roguery. Here is the general aim of the poem, and to this his character and genius tended. His great and gloomy dreams of juvenile imagination have vanished; experience has come; he knows man now; and what is man, once known? Does the sublime abound in him? Do you think that the great sentiments—those of Childe Harold, for instance—are the ordinary course of his life? The truth is, that he employs most of his time in sleeping, dining, yawning, working like a horse, amusing himself like an ape. According to Byron, he is an animal; except for a few minutes, his nerves, his blood, his instincts lead him. Routine works over it all, necessity whips him on, the animal advances. As the animal is proud, and moreover imaginative, it pretends to be marching for its own pleasure, that there is no whip, that at all events this whip rarely touches its flanks, that at least his stoic back can make as if it did not feel it. It is harnessed in imagination with the most splendid trappings, and thus struts on with measured steps, fancying that it carries relics and treads on carpets and flowers, whilst in reality it tramples in the mud, and carries with it the stains and stinks of every dunghill. What a pastime to touch its mangy back, to set before its eyes the sacks full of flour which load it, and the goad which makes it go! What a pretty farce! It is the eternal farce; and not a sentiment thereof but provides him with an act: love in the first place. Certainly Donna Julia is very lovable, and Byron loves her; but she comes out of his hands, as rumpled as any other. She has virtue, of course; and better, she desires to have it. She plies herself, in connection with Don Juan, with the finest arguments; a fine thing are arguments, and how proper they are to check passion! Nothing can be more solid than a firm purpose, propped up by logic, resting on the fear of the world, the thought of God, the recollection of duty; nothing can prevail against it, except a *tête-à-tête* in June, on a moonlight evening. At last the deed is done, and the poor timid lady is surprised by her outraged husband; in what a situation! There anent read the book. Of course she will be speechless, ashamed and full of tears, and the moral reader duly reckons on her remorse. My dear reader, you have not reckoned on impulse and nerves. To-morrow she will feel shame; the business is now to overwhelm the husband, to deafen him, to confound him, to save Juan, to save herself, to fight. The war having begun, it is waged with all kinds of weapons, firstly with audacity and insults. The single idea, the present need, absorbs all others: it is in this that woman is a woman. This Julia cries lustily. It is a regular storm: hard words and recriminations, mockery and defiance, fainting and tears. In a quarter of an hour she has gained twenty years' experience. You did not know, nor she either, what an actress can emerge, all on a sudden, unforeseen, out of a simple woman. Do you know what can emerge from yourself? You think yourself rational, human; I admit it for to-day; you have dined, and you are at ease in a pleasant room. Your machine does its duty without disorder, because the wheels are oiled and well regulated; but place it in a shipwreck, a battle, let the failing or the plethora of blood for an instant derange the chief pieces, and we shall see you howling or drivelling like a madman or an idiot. Civilisation, education, reason, health, cloak us in their smooth and polished cases; let us tear them away one by one, or all together, and we laugh to see the brute, who is lying at the bottom. Here is our friend Juan reading Julia's last letter, and swearing in a transport never to forget the beautiful eyes which he caused to weep so much. Was ever feeling more tender or sincere? But unfortunately Juan is at sea, and sickness sets in. . . . Many other things cause the death of Love:

'Tis melancholy, and a fearful sign
Of human frailty, folly, also crime,
That love and marriage rarely can combine,
Although they both are born in the same clime;
Marriage from love, like vinegar from wine—
A sad, sour, sober beverage. . . .
An honest gentleman, at his return,
May not have the good fortune of Ulysses; . . .
The odds are that he finds a handsome urn
To his memory—and two or three young misses
Born to some friend, who holds his wife and riches,—
And that *his* Argus bites him by—the breeches.

These are the words of a sceptic, even of a cynic. Sceptic and cynic, it is in this he ends. Sceptic through misanthropy, cynic through bravado, a sad and combative humour always impels him; southern voluptuousness has not conquered him; he is only an epicurean through contradiction and for a moment:

Let us have wine and women, mirth and laughter,
Sermons and soda-water the day after.
Man, being reasonable, must get drunk;
The best of life is but intoxication.

You see clearly that he is always the same, in excess and unhappy, bent on destroying himself. His ***Don Juan,*** also, is a debauchery; in it he diverts himself outrageously at the expense of all respectable things, as a bull in a china shop. He is always violent, and often ferocious; black imagination brings into his stories horrors leisurely enjoyed,—despair and famine of shipwrecked men, and the emaciation of the raging skeletons

feeding on each other. He laughs at it horribly, like Swift; more, he plays the buffoon over it, like Voltaire. . . . With his specimens in hand, Byron follows with a surgeon's exactness all the stages of death, satiation, rage, madness, howling, exhaustion, stupor; he wishes to touch and exhibit the naked and ascertained truth, the last grotesque and hideous element of humanity. Look again at the assault on Ismail,—the grape-shot and the bayonet, the street massacres, the corpses used as fascines, and the thirty-eight thousand slaughtered Turks. There is blood enough to satiate a tiger, and this blood flows amidst an accompaniment of jests; it is in order to rail at war, and the butcheries dignified with the name of exploits. In this pitiless and universal demolition of all human vanities, what subsists? What do we know except that life is 'a scene of all-confess'd inanity,' and that men are,

Dogs, or men!—for I flatter you in saying
That ye are dogs—your betters far—ye may
Read, or read not, what I am now essaying
To show ye what ye are in every way?

What does he find in science but deficiencies, and in religion but mummeries? Does he so much as preserve poetry? Of the divine mantle, the last garment which a poet respects, he makes a rag to stamp upon, to wring, to make holes in, out of sheer wantonness. At the most touching moment of Haidée's love, he vents a buffoonery. He concludes an ode with caricatures. He is Faust in the first verse, and Mephistopheles in the second. He employs, in the midst of tenderness or of murder, pennyprint witticisms, trivialities, gossip, with a pamphleteer's vilification and a buffoon's whimsicalities. He lays bare the poetic method, asks himself where he has got to, counts the stanzas already done, jokes the Muse, Pegasus, and the whole epic stud, as though he wouldn't give twopence for them. Again, what remains? Himself, he alone, standing amidst all this ruin. It is he who speaks here; his characters are but screens; half the time even he pushes them aside, to occupy the stage. He lavishes upon us his opinions, recollections, angers, tastes; his poem is a conversation, a confidence, with the ups and downs, the rudeness and freedom of a conversation and a confidence, almost like the olographic journal, in which, by night, at his writing-table, he opened his heart and discharged his feelings. Never was seen in such a clear glass the birth of a lively thought, the tumult of a great genius, the inner life of a genuine poet, always impassioned, inexhaustibly fertile and creative, in whom suddenly, successively, finished and adorned, bloomed all human emotions and ideas,—sad, gay, lofty, low, hustling one another, mutually impeded like swarms of insects who go humming and feeding on flowers and in the mud. He may say what he will; willingly or unwillingly we listen to him; let him leap from sublime to burlesque, we leap then with him. He has so much wit, so fresh a wit, so sudden, so biting, such a prodigality of knowledge, ideas, images picked up from the four corners of the horizon, in heaps and masses, that we are captivated, transported beyond limits; we cannot dream of resisting. Too vigorous, and hence unbridled,—that is the word which ever recurs when we speak of Byron; too vigorous against others and himself, and so unbridled, that after spending his life in braving the world, and his poetry in depicting revolt, he can only find the fulfilment of his talent and the satisfaction of his heart, in a poem in arms against all human and poetic conventions. To live so, a man must be great, but he must also become deranged. There is a derangement of heart and mind in the style of ***Don Juan,*** as in Swift. When a man jests amidst his tears, it is because he has a poisoned imagination. This kind of laughter is a spasm, and you see in one man a hardening of the heart, or madness; in another, excitement or disgust. Byron was exhausted, at least the poet was exhausted in him. The last cantos of **Don Juan** drag: the gaiety became forced, the escapades became digressions; the reader began to be bored. A new kind of poetry, which he had attempted, had given way in his hands: in the drama he only attained to powerful declamation, his characters had no life; when he forsook poetry, poetry forsook him; he went to Greece in search of action, and only found death. (pp. 302-09)

> *H. A. Taine, "Lord Byron," in his* History of English Literature, *Vol. II, translated by H. van Laun, 1871. Reprint by Henry Holt and Company, 1885, pp. 271-312.*

GEORGE BRANDES (essay date 1875)

[*Brandes, a Danish literary critic and biographer, was the principal leader of "Det moderne gennbruch" ("the modern breaking-through"), the intellectual movement that helped to bring an end to Scandanavian cultural isolation. He believed that literature reflects the spirit and problems of its time and that it must be understood within its social and aesthetic context. Brandes's major critical work,* Hovedstrømninger i det 19de aarhundredes litteratur, *first published in 1875 and excerpted below, won him admiration for his ability to view literary movements within the broader context of all of European literautre. Here, Brandes describes Don Juan as the "one poem of the nineteenth century which can be compared with Goethe's* Faust." *The critic contrasts the detailed realism and ruthless honesty of Byron's approach with Goethe's more intellectually profound but less tangible treatment of his subject. Brandes argues that as an epic of modern life, "the strong, practical, historical spirit of Don Juan carries, as it were, more weight with it than the philosophical spirit which inspires Faust." The quotation from the Book of Daniel that concludes this essay also appears in Canto VIII of Don Juan.*]

[**Don Juan**], which, with its savage dedication to Southey, had to be published, not only anonymously, but actually without any publisher's name on the title-page, and which, as Byron said, had more difficulty in making its way into an English drawing-room than a camel in passing through the eye of a needle, is the one poem of the nineteenth century which can be compared with Goethe's *Faust;* for it, and not the comparatively insignificant **Manfred**, is Byron's poem of universal humanity. Its defiant motto is the famous speech in *Twelfth Night:* "Dost thou think, because thou art virtuous, there shall be no more cakes and ale?—Yes, by Saint Anne, and ginger shall be hot i' the mouth, too!'"—a motto which promises nothing but offence and satiric pleasantry. Nevertheless it was with justifiable and prophetic pride that Byron said to Medwin: "If you must have an epic, there's **Don Juan** for you; it is an epic as much in the spirit of our day as the *Iliad* was in that of Homer" [see excerpt dated 1822]. It was Byron who produced what Chateaubriand imagined he had produced in *Les Martyrs,* namely, the modern epic poem—which it was not possible to construct, as Chateaubriand had attempted to do, on a Christian-Romantic basis, or as Scott had thought it might be done, on the foundation of national history and manners. Byron succeeded because he took as his foundation nothing less than the most advanced civilisation of the century.

Juan is no Romantic hero; neither his mind nor his character raises him much above the average; but he is a favourite of fortune, an exceptionally handsome, proud, bold, lucky man, who is led more by his destiny than by intention or plan—the proper hero for a poem which is to embrace the whole of human life. It would never have done for him to have any special

province; for, from the very beginning, there was no limit set to the scope and reach of the work.

The poem rises and falls like a ship borne upon sunlit and storm-tossed billows; it passes from one extreme to another. (pp. 342-43)

Not only does it contain, in extraordinary variety, representations of the strange contradictions in human life, but each of these contradictions is followed out to its extremest development. In each case the sounding-lead of the poet's imagination has been let down to the bottom, both in the psychological and in the external, tangible situation. Goethe's antique temperament inclined him, wherever it was possible, to moderation; even in *Faust*, where, in terrible earnest, he lifts the veil from human life, he lifts it with a careful hand. But the result of this moderation is often a deficiency in the highest potency of life. In Goethe's works the geniuses of life and death are seldom allowed unlimited space in which to spread their giant wings. Byron has never the desire to tranquillise his reader, never thinks of sparing him. He himself is not calm until he has said everything there is to say; he is a mortal enemy of the idealism which beautifies by selecting this, rejecting that; his art consists in pointing to reality and nature, and crying to the reader: Know these!

Take any one of his characters—take Julia, for instance. She is twenty-three; she is charming; almost without being aware of it, she is a little in love with Juan; she is contented with her husband of fifty, but also, almost unconsciously, has a faint wish that he could be divided into two of five-and-twenty. After a hard struggle to remain virtuous she gives way; but for a time there is nothing base or comical in the relations of the lovers. Then Byron shows her to us in a difficult position; the pair are surprised by the husband; and all at once we discover a new stratum of her nature—she lies, she deceives, she acts a part with astounding facility. She was not, then, good and amiable, as she at first appeared to be? We were mistaken? Not at all. Byron shows us yet another deeper-lying stratum of her soul, in the famous farewell letter she writes to Juan, an effusion of sincere womanly feeling, one of the gems of the poem. Mental agony does not incapacitate for devotion; love does not preclude deceit; nor deceit extreme delicacy and beauty of feeling at given moments. And the letter—what becomes of it? Juan reads it, sighing and weeping, on board ship; in the middle of its affecting comparison of the manner in which men love with that in which women love, he is interrupted—by sea-sickness. Poor letter, poor Julia, poor Juan, poor humanity!—for is not this human life? Once again, poor letter! After the shipwreck, when the crew of the boat have devoured their last ration and have long gazed hungrily at each other's famished figures, they agree to determine by lot which one of them shall be killed and eaten by the others. Search is made for paper, but not a scrap is to be found in the boat except Julia's poetical and loving letter; it is snatched from Juan and cut into squares, which are numbered. One of these numbered squares brings death to Pedrillo. Is there, then, really a sphere in the firmament of heaven where idealistic love and cannibal instincts are to be found side by side, nay, meet upon one square inch of paper? Byron answers that he knows one—the Earth.

From the shipwreck scene we are transported straight to Haidée. Compared with her, all the Greek maidens of Byron's earlier poems are immature attempts. Nowhere in the whole range of modern poetry had the love of a child of nature been so beautifully described. Goethe's best girl figures, Gretchen and Clärchen, charming as they are, are little *bourgeoises; we* feel that their creator was a Frankfort citizen, to whom nature revealed herself in his position as a member of the middle class, and culture displayed itself at a small German court. In Byron's most beautiful female characters there is nothing bourgeois—no middle-class manners and customs have modified their free naturalness. We feel, when we read of Juan and Haidée, that Byron is a descendant of Rousseau; but we also feel that his high and independent social position, in combination with the character of the fortunes that had befallen him, had given him a much more emancipated view of human nature than Rousseau ever attained to. (pp. 344-46)

What reader (especially if he comes straight from the erotic hypocrisy of the literature of the French reactionary period) but feels carried away by this strong current of warm youthful passion, by the poet's ardent enthusiasm for natural beauty, and by his profound scorn for the prudishness of conventional morality! Is there, then, a world, a world of law in which 2 and 2 make 4, an animal world in which all the lowest and most disgusting instincts may come to the surface at any moment, and yet in which such revelations of beauty in human life—revelations lasting for a moment, or a day, or a month, or a year, or an eternity of years—occur? Yes, answers Byron, there is such a world, and it is the world in which we all live. And now, away from these scenes to the slave market, to the seraglio, to the battlefield, to systematic murder and rape and the bayoneting of little children!

The poem is made up of such contrasts and contradictions. But it is not a sensuous, playfully satiric epic of the nature of Ariosto's; it is a passionate work, instinct with political purpose, full of wrath, scorn, threats, and appeals, with from time to time a loud, long blast on the revolutionary war trumpet. Byron does not merely describe horrors; he interprets them. After quoting "the butcher" Suwarrow's rhymed despatch to Catherine announcing the capture of Ismail, he adds:

> He wrote this Polar melody, and set it,
>   Duly accompanied by shrieks and groans,
> Which few will sing, I trust, but none forget it—
>   For I will teach, if possible, the stones
> To rise against earth's tyrants. Never let it
>   Be said that we still truckle unto thrones;—
> But ye, our children's children! think how we
> Show'd *what things were* before the world was free!

If, considering both from this point of view, we compare *Don Juan* with *Faust*, the great poem of the beginning of the century, we feel that the strong, practical, historical spirit of *Don Juan* carries, as it were, more weight with it than the philosophical spirit which inspires *Faust*. And if we place it for a moment in imagination beside its Russian offspring, Pushkin's *Jevgeni Onjoegin,* and its Danish offspring, Paludan-Müller's *Adam Homo,* the fresh sea breeze of nature and fact in the English poem seems to us all the stronger in contrast with the polish and the political feebleness of the Russian, and the narrow morality of the clever Danish poem. In *Don Juan* we have nature and fact; in *Faust,* nature and profound reflection. *Don Juan* gives us in full, broad detail the human life which *Faust* condenses into a personification; and the whole work is the production of an indignation which has written where it can be read by the mighty of all ages its *"Mene, Mene, Tekel, Upharsin."* (pp. 347-48)

George Brandes, "Culmination of Naturalism," in his Main Currents in Nineteenth Century Literature:

Naturalism in England, Vol. IV, *translated by Mary Morison, William Heinemann, 1905, pp. 342-57.*

ERNEST HARTLEY COLERIDGE   (essay date 1903)

[Coleridge served as poetry editor of the 1898-1904 edition of Byron's complete works and also edited several collections of the writings of his grandfather, Samuel Taylor Coleridge. In the following excerpt, the critic suggests that Byron's conception of Juan's character may have been influenced by S. T. Coleridge. The critic also maintains that Byron's occasional violations of taste and morality in Don Juan *are not significantly offensive in the context of the poem as a whole, where they contribute to the poet's realistic portrait of the "great things of the world."]*

Great works, in which the poet speaks *ex animo,* and the man lays bare the very pulse of the machine, are not conceived or composed unconsciously and at haphazard. Byron did not "whistle" *Don Juan* "for want of thought." He had found a thing to say, and he meant to make the world listen. He had read with angry disapproval, but he had read, Coleridge's *Critique on* [Maturin's] *Bertram . . . ,* and, it may be, had caught an inspiration from one brilliant sentence which depicts the Don Juan of the legend somewhat after the likeness of Childe Harold, if not of Lord Byron: "Rank, fortune, wit, talent, acquired knowledge, and liberal accomplishments, with beauty of person, vigorous health, . . . all these advantages, elevated by the habits and sympathies of noble birth and natural character, are . . . combined in Don Juan, so as to give him the means of carrying into all its practical consequences the doctrine of a godless nature. . . . Obedience to nature is the only virtue." Again, "It is not the wickedness of Don Juan . . . which constitutes the character an abstraction, . . . but the rapid succession of the correspondent acts and incidents, his intellectual superiority, and the splendid accumulation of his gifts and desirable qualities as coexistent with entire wickedness in one and the same person." Here was at once a suggestion and a challenge.

Would it not be possible to conceive and to depict an ideal character, gifted, gracious, and delightful, who should "carry into all its practical consequences" the doctrine of a mundane, if not godless doctrine, and, at the same time, retain the charities and virtues of uncelestial but not devilish manhood? In defiance of monition and in spite of resolution, the primrose path is trodden by all sorts and conditions of men, sinners no doubt, but not necessarily abstractions of sin, and to assert the contrary makes for cant and not for righteousness. The form and substance of [*Don Juan*] were due to the compulsion of Genius and the determination of Art, but the argument is a vindication of the natural man. It is Byron's "criticism of life." *Don Juan* was *taboo* from the first. The earlier issues of the first five cantos were doubly anonymous. Neither author nor publisher subscribed their names on the title-page. The book was a monster, and, as its maker had foreseen, "all the world" shuddered. Immoral, in the sense that it advocates immoral tenets, or prefers evil to good, it is not, but it is unquestionably a dangerous book, which (to quote Kingsley's words used in another connection) "the young and innocent will do well to leave altogether unread." It is dangerous because it ignores resistance and presumes submission to passion; it is dangerous because, as Byron admitted, it is "now and then voluptuous;" and it is dangerous, in a lesser degree, because, here and there, the purport of the quips and allusions is gross and offensive. No one can take up the book without being struck and arrested by these violations of modesty and decorum; but no one can master its contents and become possessed of it as a whole without perceiving that the mirror is held up to nature, that it reflects spots and blemishes which, on a survey of the vast and various orb, dwindle into *natural* and so comparative insignificance. Byron was under no delusion as to the grossness of *Don Juan.* His plea or pretence, that he was sheltered by the superior grossness of Ariosto and La Fontaine, of Prior and of Fielding, is *nihil ad rem,* if it is not insincere. When Murray (May 3, 1819) charges him with "approximations to indelicacy," he laughs himself away at the euphemism, but when Hobhouse and "the Zoili of Albemarle Street" talked to him "about morality," he flames out, "I maintain that it is the most moral of poems" [see excerpt from his letter of February 1, 1819]. He looked upon his great work as a whole, and he knew that the "*raison d'être* of his song" was not only to celebrate, but, by the white light of truth, to represent and exhibit the great things of the world—Love and War, and Death by sea and land, and Man, half-angel, half-demon—the comedy of his fortunes, and the tragedy of his passions and his fate. (pp. xvii-xix)

> Ernest Hartley Coleridge, "Introduction to 'Don Juan'," in The Works of Lord Byron: Poetry, Vol. VI by Lord Byron, edited by Ernest Hartley Coleridge, revised edition, Charles Scribner's Sons, 1903, pp. xv-xx.

J. F. A. PYRE (essay date 1907)

[*Pyre argues that Byron "discovered himself" in* Don Juan *because he transcended the limitations in subject matter, style, and technical ability that had characterized his earlier works. Admitting that the poem is often "shocking," the critic nevertheless considers it the most effective expression of Byron's "immense talent."*]

It was in *Don Juan* that [Byron] found himself. . . . The grand, gloomy, and self-torturing misanthrope who dominates all Byron's early romances, as well as *Childe Harold, Manfred,* and *Cain,* illustrates only one phase of an exceedingly complicated and variable temperament. When Byron discovered himself in *Don Juan,* his mind had matured, his way of life had become more wholesome, his technical ability had reached its height; what was of particular importance, he had learned to write more slowly and with greater patience; his daily stint was two octaves of *Don Juan.* The scheme of the poem was such as to allow him to deploy all his powers. Flesh and blood narrative, description which *is* the thing, satire in all keys, sentiment, trenchant reflection, are woven together with a mastery and ease which continually astonish, and never tire, though they sometimes shock. He is, by turns, comical and savage, pathetic and terrible, romantic and burlesque, earnest and reckless, intellectual and voluptuous; he laughs and weeps, prays and blasphemes, sings, shouts, threatens, cajoles, caresses, stabs right and left. Half a dozen stanzas as cleverly keyed and turned as the . . . satire of the blue-stockings would be sufficient to make the fame and determine the bent of a minor poet, such as Praed; and this represents only one of a thousand moods. And yet, *Don Juan* is not a series of passages; the narrative swims forward without effort; our eyes are continually on the hero; our heart aches with the meaning of it all. It is a shallow view of this poem which regards it as a mere string of studied disenchantments, lewdnesses, cynicisms, and blasphemies. It is the panorama of life as Byron saw it, "with all its imperfections on its head," a mixture of good and evil, which he was bound to render frankly as it appeared to him, and as he

lived and judged it,—not well perhaps, but passionately, fearlessly, and as a citizen of the world. Byron's recent editor [Paul Elmer More] is not wrong in calling *Don Juan* the "epic of modern life."

Byron's view of life was, after all, essentially moral. He was deeply and sincerely interested in the moral aspect of things; only, he laid the stress elsewhere than on the conventional morality of his day. That conventional morality—often a mere matter of appearances—he stigmatized as cant; he hated that cant, not comically, at bottom, but earnestly, savagely; and he assailed it with furious blows, shocked without mercy or caution. There is no doubting his sincerity when he cries out in his letters, "It is the most moral of poems;" his contempt is as genuine as it is bitter, when he says to the British nation,—

> You're not a moral people and you know it,
> Without the need of too sincere a poet.

But he was less interested in private, domestic morality than in public, political morality. Nothing could more clearly present this contrast than his terrible arraignment of George III, in *The Vision of Judgment.* And herein, he took a large, a continental view,—not an insular, British view. Perhaps he was wrong, but he was sincere. Further, his treatment of this theme is essentially poetical. He creates a myth, a political myth. His assaults on individuals are not, for the most part, the result of personal rancor, though this sometimes added to the zest of his attack. He erected a mythus of political devildom, and its heroes were Castlereagh and Wellington and George III, and, most of all, Southey, the recalcitrant laureate, the idealization, in his mind, of pusillanimous time-serving, of scribbling, prosperous British cant.

There is no doubt that *Don Juan* is often shocking; perhaps the sum total of its impression is that of a terrible disorder of enormous and varied powers, often ill-directed. There is no mistaking the inferiority of Byron's force to that of Shelley, in attractiveness, in sweetness, radiance, and charm; but there is, likewise, no mistaking Byron's superiority in massiveness, in variety, and in effectiveness. Shelley, who understood Byron thoroughly, was not deceived on that point [see excerpts dated 1820 and 1821]; he well knew which was the mightier spirit. Shelley, too, not being one of the canters, readily saw that in *Don Juan* the immense talent of his great contemporary had first found the means of freely rendering itself effective. (pp. 550-51)

> J. F. A. Pyre, "Byron in Our Day," in The Atlantic Monthly, Vol. 99, No. 4, April, 1907, pp. 542-52.

CLAUDE M. FUESS (essay date 1912)

[*Fuess's* Lord Byron as a Satirist in Verse *is considered the first important twentieth-century study to discuss* Don Juan *at length. The critic describes the poem as primarily satirical, rather than narrative or epic. Fuess explores not only the political, social, and personal targets of Byron's derision, but also the nature of his satire, which the critic describes as destructive, skeptical, and founded on doubt. In his conclusion, Fuess maintains that the poem is first and foremost a product of Byron's unique personality. "Don Juan is Byron," he argues, "and in this fact lies the explanation of its strength and weakness."*]

[Whatever] may have actuated Byron in beginning *Don Juan* and however uncertain he may have been at first about its ultimate purpose, it soon grew to be primarily satirical. He himself perceived this in describing it to [Moore] in 1818 as "meant to be a little quietly facetious upon everything" and in characterizing it in 1822 as "a *Satire* on *abuses* of the present states of society" [see excerpts dated September 19, 1818, and December 25, 1822]. Despite the intermingling of other elements, the poem is exactly what Byron called it—an "Epic Satire." His remark "I was born for opposition" indicates how much at variance with his age he felt himself to be; and his inclination to pick flaws in existing institutions and to indulge in destructive criticism of his time had become so strong that any poem which expressed fully his attitude towards life was bound to be satirical. Just as the cosmopolitan outlook of the poem is due partly to Byron's long-continued residence in a foreign country, so its varied moods, its diverse methods, and its wide range of subject matter are to be attributed, to a large extent, to the fact that the composition of *Don Juan* extended over several years during a period when he was growing intellectually and responding eagerly to new ideas. The work is a fair representation of Byron's theories and beliefs during the period of his maturity, when he was developing into an enlightened advocate of progressive and liberal doctrines. It is an attack on political inertia and retrogression, on social conventionality, on cant and sham and intolerance. The intermittent, erratic, and somewhat imitative radicalism of a few of his earlier poems has changed into a persistent hostility to all the reactionary conservation of the time. *Don Juan* is satiric, then, in that it is a protest against all that hampers individual freedom and retards national independence.

The pervasive satiric spirit of *Don Juan* has varied manifestations. In a few passages there are examples of rancor and spite, of direct personal denunciation and furious invective, that recall the satire of *English Bards*. The attacks on Castlereagh and Southey, on Brougham and Lady Byron are in deadly earnest, with hardly a touch of mockery. At the same time Byron relies mainly on the more playful and less savage method which he had learned from the Italians and used in *Beppo.* He himself expressed this alteration in mood by saying,

> Methinks the older that one grows,
> Inclines us more to laugh than scold.

It is noticeable, too, that in *Don Juan* petulant fury is much less conspicuous than philosophic satire. Byron is assailing institutions and theories as well as men and women. To some extent the poem is a medium for satisfying a quarrel or a prejudice; but to a far greater degree it is a summary of testimony hostile to the reactionary early nineteenth century. The poet still prefers, in many cases, to make specific persons responsible for intolerable systems; but he is gradually forsaking petty aims and rising to a far nobler position as a critic of his age.

The satire in *Don Juan* is still more remarkable when we consider the field which it surveys. Byron is no longer dealing with local topics, but with subjects of momentous interest to all humanity. He is assailing, not a small coterie of editors or an immodest dance, but a bigoted and absolute government, a hypocritical society, and a false idealism, wherever they exist. More than this, he so succeeds in uniting his satire, through the force of his personality, with the eternal elements of realism and romance, that the combination, complex and intricate though it is, seems to represent an undivided purpose.

Perhaps the loftiest note in Byron's protest is struck in dealing with the political situation of his day. Despite his noble birth and his aristocratic tastes, he had become, partly through temperamental inclination, partly through association with Moore

and Hunt, a fairly consistent republican, though he took care to make it clear, as Nichol points out, that he was "for the people, not of them." (pp. 165-68)

Such doctrine was, of course, not new in Byron's poetry. He had already spoken eloquently and mournfully of the loss of Greek independence; he had prophesied the downfall of monarchs and the triumph of democracy; and he had inserted in *Childe Harold* that vigorous apostrophe to liberty:

> Yet, Freedom, yet thy banner, torn but flying,
> Streams like the thunder-storm *against* the wind.

In *Don Juan,* however, Byron is less rhetorical and more direct. In expressing his

> Plain sworn downright detestation
> Of every despotism in every nation,

he does not hesitate to condemn all absolute monarchs; moreover he displays a sincere faith in the ultimate success of popular government:

> I think I hear a little bird, who sings
> The people by and by will be the stronger.

Such lines as these show a maturity and an earnestness that mark the evolution of Byron's satiric spirit from the hasty petulance of *English Bards* to the humanitarian breadth of his thoughtful manhood. Like "Young Azim" in Moore's *Veiled Prophet of Khorassan*, he is eager to march and command under the banner on which is emblazoned "Freedom to the World."

It is characteristic of Byron's later satire that he applied his theory of liberty to the current problems of British politics by assailing the obnoxious domestic measures instituted by the Tory ministry of Lord Liverpool, by condemning the English foreign policy of acquiescence in the legitimist doctrines of Metternich and the continental powers, and by attacking the characters of the ministers whom he considered responsible for England's position at home and abroad. The England of *Don Juan* was the country which Shelley so graphically pictured in his *Sonnet: England in 1819:*—

> An old, mad, blind, despised, and dying king, . . .
> Rulers who neither see, nor feel, nor know,
> But leech-like to their fainting country cling,
> Till they drop, blind in blood, without a blow, . . .
> A people starved and stabbed in the untilled field.

It was a nation exhausted by war, burdened with debt, and seething with discontent. . . . For these conditions Byron blamed Castlereagh, the Foreign Secretary.

Byron had never met Castlereagh and had never suffered a personal injury from him; his rage, therefore, was directed solely at the statesman, not at the man. The Secretary had long been detestable to Irish Whigs like Moore and English radicals like Shelley; it remained for Byron to track him through life with venomous hatred and to pursue him beyond the grave with scathing epigrams. For anything comparable aimed at a man in high position we must go back to Marvell's satires on Charles II and the Duke of York or to the contemporary satire in 1762 on Lord Bute. Byron's Castlereagh has no virtues; the portrait, like Gifford's sketch of Peter Pindar, is all in dark colors. The satire is vehement and personal, without malice and without pity.

Byron also attacked Wellington, but in manner ironic and scornful, as a leader who had lost all claim to the gratitude of the people by allying himself with their oppressors. For George, who as Regent and King, had done nothing to redeem himself with his subjects, Byron had little but contempt. In satirizing these men, however, Byron was perhaps less effective than Moore, over whose imitations of Castlereagh's orations and "best-wigged Prince in Christendom," people smiled when Byron's tirades seemed too vicious.

Through the method commonly called dramatic, or indirect, Byron assailed English politicians in his portrayal of Lord Henry Amundeville, the statesman who is "always a patriot—and sometimes a placeman," and who is representative of the unemotional, just, yet altogether selfish British minister. The type is drawn with considerable skill and with much less rancor than would have been possible with Byron ten years before. Indeed the satire resembles Dryden's in that it admits of a wide application and is not limited to the individual described. (pp. 168-71)

Byron's iconoclastic tendencies showed themselves also in his attack on English society, in which he aimed to expose the selfishness, stupidity, and affectation of the small class that represented the aristocratic circle of the nation. In dealing with this subject he knew of what he was speaking, for he had been a member and a close observer of "that Microcosm on stilts yclept the Great World." His picture of this upper class is humorous and ironic, but seldom vehement. In a series of vivid and often brilliant character sketches he delineates the personages that Juan, Ambassador of Russia, meets in London, touching cleverly on their defects and vices, and unveiling the sensuality, jealousy, and deceit which their outward decorum covers. (p. 172)

He describes their life as dull and uninteresting, a gay masquerade which palls when all its delights have been tried. Its prudery conceals scandal, treachery, and lust; its great vices are hypocrisy and cant—"cant political, cant religious, cant moral." Indeed the satire of *Don Juan,* from Canto XI to the point where the poem is broken off, is an attack on pretence and sham, and a vindication of the free and natural man. Byron's motive may have been, in part, the desire for revenge on the circle which had cast him out; but certainly he was disgusted with the narrowness and conventionality of his London life, and his newly acquired jesting manner found in it a suitable object for satire. (p. 173)

It is not at all surprising that a large portion of *Don Juan* should be devoted to two subjects in which Byron had always been deeply interested—woman and love. Nor is it at all remarkable, in view of his singularly complex and variable nature, that the poem should contain not only the exquisite idyll of Haidée but also line after line of cynical satire on her sex. Though Byron's opinion of women was usually not complimentary, sentiment, and even sentimentality of a certain sort, had a powerful attraction for him. . . . At the same time the conventional assertions of woman's inconstancy and treachery so common in his earlier work recur frequently in *Don Juan.*

Love, according to Byron's philosophy, can exist only when it is free and untrammelled. The poet's too numerous amours and the general laxity of Italian morals had joined in exciting in him a prejudice against English puritanism; while his own unfortunate marital experience had convinced him that "Love and Marriage rarely can combine." The remembrance of his married life and his observation in the land of his adoption were both instrumental in forming his conclusion:

> There's doubtless something in domestic doings,
> Which forms, in fact, true love's antithesis.
>
> (pp. 174-75)

Nothing in the first two cantos of *Don Juan* was more offensive to Hobhouse and the "Utican Senate" to which Murray submitted them than the poorly disguised portrayal of Lady Byron in the character of Donna Inez. Though Byron explicitly disavowed all intention of satirising his wife directly, no one familiar with the facts could possibly have doubted that this lady "whose favorite science was the mathematical," who opened her husband's trunks and letters, and tried to prove her loving lord mad, and who acted under all circumstances like "Morality's prim personification" was intended to represent the former Miss Milbanke and present Lady Byron.

Doubtless there is something artificial and affected in much of Byron's cynical comment on women and love; but if we are inclined to distrust this man of many amours who delights in flaunting his past before the eyes of his shocked compatriots, we must remember that there is probably no conscious insincerity in his words. Byron frequently deludes not only his readers but himself, and his satire on women, when it is not a kind of bravado, is merely part of his worldly philosophy.

The philosophical conceptions on which *Don Juan* rests are, in their general trend, not uncommonly satirical; that is, they are destructive rather than constructive, skeptical rather than idealistic, founded on doubt rather than on faith. It is the object of the poem to overturn tottering institutions, to upset traditions, and to unveil illusions. Byron's attitude is that so often taken by a thorough man of the world who has tasted pleasure to the point of satiety, and who has arrived at early middle age with his enthusiasms weakened and his faith sunk in pessimism. This accounts for much of the realism in the poem. Sometimes the poet, in the effort to portray things as they are, merely transcribes the prose narratives of others into verse, just as Shakspere borrowed passages from North's *Plutarch* for *Julius Caesar.* More often he undertakes to detect and reveal the incongruity between actuality and pretence, and to expose weakness and folly under its mask of sham. (pp. 175-77)

Byron's materialistic and skeptical habit of mind is often put into phraseology that recalls the "Que sais-je?" of Montaigne. Rhetorical disquisitions on the vanity of human knowledge and of worldly achievement had appeared in *Childe Harold;* in *Don Juan* the poet dismisses the great problems of existence with a jest:

> What is soul, or mind, their birth and growth,
> Is more than I know—the deuce take them both.
>
> (p. 178)

Byron, then, refused to accept any of the creeds and idealisms of his day. His own position, however, was marked by doubt and vacillation, and he took no positive attitude towards any of the great problems of existence. Experience led him to nothing but uncertainty and indecision, with the result that he became content to destroy, since he was unable to construct. (p. 179)

Byron's satire [in *Don Juan*], in assuming a wider scope and a greater breadth of view [than in his earlier works], in growing out of the insular into the cosmopolitan, has also blended itself with romance and realism, with the lyric, the descriptive, and the epic types of poetry until it has created a new literary form and method suitable only to a great genius. His satiric spirit, in assailing not only individuals, but also institutions, systems, and theories of life, in concerning itself less with literary grudges and personal quarrels than with momentous questions of society, in progressing steadily from the specific to the universal, has undergone a striking evolution. The tone of his satire has become less formal and dignified, and more colloquial, while a more frequent use of irony, burlesque, and verbal wit makes the poem easier and more varied. Byron joins mockery with invective, raillery with contempt, so that **Don Juan,** in retaining certain qualities of the old Popean satire, seems to have tempered and qualified the acrimony of **English Bards**. The inevitable result of this development was to make **Don Juan** a reflection of Byron's personality such as no other of his works had been. **Don Juan** is Byron; and in this fact lies the explanation of its strength and weakness. (pp. 186-87)

> *Claude M. Fuess, in his* Lord Byron as a Satirist in Verse, *1912. Reprint by Russell & Russell, Inc., 1964, 228 p.*

VIRGINIA WOOLF   (diary date 1918)

[*A British novelist, essayist, and short story writer, Woolf is one of the most prominent literary figures of the twentieth century. Like her contemporary James Joyce, with whom she is often compared, Woolf is remembered as one of the most innovative of the stream of consciousness novelists. She was concerned primarily with depicting the life of the mind, and she revolted against traditional narrative techniques and developed her own highly individualized style. Woolf's works, noted for their subjective explorations of characters' inner lives and their delicate poetic quality, have had a lasting effect on the art of the novel. Woolf was a discerning and influential essayist as well as a novelist. Her critical writings, termed ''creative, appreciative, and subjective'' by Barbara Currier Bell and Carol Ohmann, cover almost the entire range of literature and contain some of her finest prose. In the following excerpt from her diary, Woolf muses on the readability, casual fluent style, and all-encompassing subject matter of Byron's poem.*]

In the absence of human interest, which makes us peaceful & content, one may as well go on with Byron. Having indicated that I am ready, after a century, to fall in love with him, I suppose my judgment of **Don Juan** may be partial. It is the most readable poem of its length ever written, I suppose;·a quality which it owes in part to the springy random haphazard galloping nature of its method. This method is a discovery by itself. Its what one has looked for in vain—a[n] elastic shape which will hold whatever you choose to put into it. Thus he could write out his mood as it came to him; he could say whatever came into his head. He wasn't committed to be poetical; & thus escaped his evil genius of the false romantic & imaginative. When he is serious he is sincere; & he can impinge upon any subject he likes. He writes 16 canto's without once flogging his flanks. He had, evidently, the able witty mind of what my father Sir Leslie would have called a thoroughly masculine nature. I maintain that these illicit kind of books are far more interesting than the proper books which respect illusions devoutly all the time. Still, it doesn't seem an easy example to follow; & indeed like all free & easy things, only the skilled & mature really bring them off successfully. But Byron was full of ideas—a quality that gives his verse a toughness, & drives me to little excursions over the surrounding landscape or room in the middle of my reading. And tonight I shall have the pleasure of finishing him—though why, considering that I've enjoyed almost every stanza, this should be a pleasure I really dont know. But so it always is, whether the books a good book or a bad book. (pp. 180-81)

> *Virginia Woolf, in a diary entry of August 8, 1918, in her* The Diary of Virginia Woolf: 1915-1919, *Vol. I, edited by Anne Olivier Bell, The Hogarth Press, 1977, pp. 180-81.*

JOHN DRINKWATER   (essay date 1925)

[*Drinkwater was a minor English poet, biographer, and dramatist. His biography of Byron, from which the following excerpt is drawn, is still considered a valuable study of the poet. In his remarks on* Don Juan, *Drinkwater dismisses the notion that the work is offensive and declares it ''the greatest comic poem in our language.''*]

The objections first made against [**Don Juan**] are not in themselves wholly unreasonable. In parts it is lewd, it is bitter, it is savage, it is shocking; that is to say, it would be these things if it were not as a whole, and in its own idiom, ''surpassingly beautiful.'' But this beauty lifts it utterly above all offence. Byron's plea that the poem was an exposure and not a celebration of vice was at best a concession to the cant morality of some of his friends who ought 'to have known better. To claim that **Don Juan** edifies us by its precepts is the folly of pretence indeed. We care nothing for its example. But that anyone could be hurt by reading it, Hobhouse, for example, must have known in his heart to be as inconceivable as we know it. It seems almost indelicate to acknowledge the complaints. The poem is not perfect. As a single work it sometimes seems too long, with weak periods, as Byron confessed; but this impression might have been removed had it been longer, that is, if the design had been completed. To judge a poem of over twelve thousand lines one has to test the impression formed from page to page by the architectural effect made by the whole when we have finished reading, and the architectural effect of **Don Juan** necessarily remains uncertain. But, with these reservations, we can but add a modest word to the general eulogy that has recognised the greatest comic poem in our language. For that, all things considered, **Don Juan** is. On such a scale, with such indomitable energy, with so passionate a fertility of invention, and with resources of metre and diction so inexhaustible, the comic spirit in English verse has never approached this performance. It is the inspiration of **Don Juan** more than anything else that makes us conscious of the sublime impertinence of the Trelawnys and the Lady Blessingtons who thought to show off their wits against Byron's. Even the good friends, the Hobhouses, the Murrays, and the Moores, recede into diminutive distances as we are intoxicated by passage after passage of this transfiguring humour. Byron might well be tired for the moment of the circumstance of poetry—tired, that is, of sending packets to London; but the impetus of his genius, far from abating, was gathering force when he went to die at Missolonghi. (pp. 361-62)

> *John Drinkwater, in his* The Pilgrim of Eternity: Byron—A Conflict, *Hodder and Stoughton Limited, 1925, 416 p.*

WILLIAM J. CALVERT   (essay date 1935)

[*Calvert's* Lord Byron: Romantic Paradox *was one of the first studies of the poet to explore the contrast between the Classical and Romantic aspects of his personality and work. In his comments on* Don Juan, *Calvert traces the range of Classical, Italian, and eighteenth-century English influences on the poem. Beginning with the premise that* Don Juan *is ''the greatest of informal epics,'' the critic engages in an extended discussion of Byron's ''real preface'' to the poem in which the poet makes a series of half-facetious remarks on the relation between his methods and the literary conventions of the Classical epic (see excerpt from Canto I of* Don Juan *dated 1819). Calvert believes that in* Don Juan, *Byron first reconciled the conflict between the conservative and revolutionary facets of his character and art, ''not revolting against the past, but adapting the past to the present.''*]

Don Juan is the greatest of informal epics. There is no attempt at sustaining a grand style; and when the author does lapse into it, he hastens to cover it over with puerilities or whimsicalities, as a man might do in conversation. On just this side *Don Juan*, like *Beppo*, is the glorification of chitchat, what a whimsical man would write to a woman with whom he is alternately sarcastic, in love, angry, and tenderly playful. The style, possessing a directness and power of passionate utterance, and a complexity, nay inconsistency of thoughts, depends, for its effectiveness, upon the carelessness, the slovenliness of ordinary speech. If for the instant it rises above itself, it does so but for a time. "A nondescript and ever varying rhyme," it has the inconsequence and the wit, the glow, and the lucidity that are to be found in the correspondence. Byron, for the first time in poetry, as formerly in his letters and his conversation, had the right to utter whatever came into his head, without thought of consequences, to

> rattle on exactly as I'd talk
> With anybody in a ride or walk.

He might speak seriously, or with tongue in cheek, but at any moment he could fall back upon the plea of humor, when taken to task for an assertion. The result of the method—or mood, for it is the most unmethodical of methods—which would have been fatal in the hands of a lesser man, is a "wonderful fertility of thought and expression," that moved even Croker to enthusiasm. "The 'Protean' style of *Don Juan*, instead of checking (as the fetters of rhythm generally do) his natural ability, not only gives him wider limits to range in, but even generates a more roving disposition. I dare swear . . . that his digressions and repetitions generate one another, and that the happy jingle of some of his comical rhymes has led him on to episodes of which he never originally thought."

The digressions, however, are but part of the business. Byron had never been thoroughly at home when pursuing a rigid scheme, and his bent had been always to break away from the fetters of design. For long his muse had "admired digression," particularly at genial moments. In the plan of the whole, digressions are the humor of it. "He digresses because he has much to say; because his poem is a criticism of life" [according to Chew (see Additional Bibliography)]. But he also digresses to relieve a situation, to show that things are not so serious as they seem, or that there are other things worth talking about, or that the real subject of the poem is Byron and what Byron thinks, not the miscellaneous adventures of Juan. In bulk the digressions have "an analogy with the general system of his character, and the wit and poetry which surround . . . hide the darkness of the thing itself." They do not intrude upon the narrative. They are but a stage, or an ever recurring background, against which Juan's travels pass in strong relief.

Into the cauldron go many things, wit, poetry, passion, imagination, philosophy, epigram, irony, idealism, sarcasm, sentiment. The style is indeed "Protean." Sometimes the elements are fused one with another; but usually they contrast strikingly. The gravity serves to heighten the fun, and light sentiment to deepen the succeeding impression of gloom. Nothing is forbidden in this frolic of the fancy. Remarks on the technique of writing intrude into the text, as they had in Cervantes, Pulci, Casti, and occasionally Ariosto. The author admits us behind the scenes as he writes, and points out to us how the show is manipulated. There are comments on the form,

> Also, our Hero's lot, howe'er unpleasant
> (Because this Canto has become too long)
> Must be postponed discreetly for the present.

And there are good-natured admissions of the straits to which an author is carried by "the wicked necessity of rhyming":

> (The rhyme obliges me to this; sometimes
> Monarchs are less imperative than rhymes) . . .
>
> The 'tu's' too much—but let it stand—the verse
> Requires it.

Yet there is a unity of tone, gained, if not by uniformity, by a consistent return to the note of humor. When the author grows too metaphysical, quite forgets "this poem's merely quizzical, and deviates into matters rather dry," he brings himself back to earth with a single stroke of his pen, and resumes his gaiety. Even those recollections of his former work which occur again and again are transformed either in their expression or by the turn of the final couplet. The following passage, for instance, though distinctly reminiscent of the *Prophecy of Dante*, and *The Lament of Tasso*, is nevertheless neither, but unmistakably *Don Juan*:

> Men who partake all passions as they pass
>   Acquire the deep and bitter power to give
> Their images again as in a glass,
>   And in such colors that they seem to live;
> You may do right forbidding them to show 'em
> But spoil (I think) a very pretty poem.

The ottava rima allowed and encouraged this final humorous sally, by its couplet at the end of each stanza. But it is important for more than its flexibility in the hands of its user. It carried with it memories of great Italian literature that had gone before. Authority, for the first time, Byron does not seem to have worried about. But the stimulation of example worked strongly upon him. He always showed the tendency to adopt a style suggested by the works of another. In *English Bards*, it had been the style of Gifford and Churchill, rather than of Pope; in *Childe Harold*, that of the Spenserian stanza, in many hands; and in the early tragedies, Shakespeare's. It may be said that he was inspired rather than that he copied. But he was open to the stimulus of diction or of a lilt, which carried him as decidedly as the flow of his thought. Whatever came into his head from a contrasting style, if it worked its way into the composition, was felt to be foreign matter, and set off by quotation marks. In the case of *Don Juan*, the background is that of the Italian romance and burlesque epic. *Whistlecraft*, though it may have suggested to Byron a similar effort to translate the manner of the Italians into English, was not the inspiration of his poem; the answer to the contrary is that the two are essentially unlike. Neither is Pulci, nor Berni, nor Casti, nor the three of them, enough to explain the "tradition" of *Don Juan*. There are echoes of *Jerusalem Delivered*, and of *Orlando Furioso*, both great epics removed by a nobility of treatment from burlesque, as definite as echoes of closer models. Even Spenser, from his connection with Ariosto in critical parlance, is sometimes mirrored, though grotesquely, in the style.

This is not to say that Byron slavishly copied, or even imitated. Good evidence may be adduced to show that he did not. But in writing *Don Juan* he had the earlier epics constantly in mind. He had the advantage of observing and testing the methods of others before trying them himself. He fell heir to suggestions in technique that are lacking to the pioneer in a form of art. He shaped and stamped the whole with his personality; but without the example of a long tradition, he could hardly have produced *Don Juan*.

All this has been made clear by Mr. Fuess, in *Lord Byron as a Satirist in Verse* [see excerpt dated 1912], and by Mr. Waller, in his preface to Frere's *The Monks and the Giants*. What they have not considered necessary to point out is another and modifying influence—the Rules, or the background of the neoclassic tradition. Our epic, as I have been at pains to assert, is an essentially humorous composition. It laughs at all things, or attempts to. And for that reason it is impossible, as in a more responsible work, to say, "Lo here!" and "Lo there!" and let quotation end the argument. It is necessary, for understanding, to enter into the spirit of raillery, and this the present study, as a serious investigation, cannot pretend to do. Byron's irony, at its best, like Swift's, succeeds in meaning and not meaning exactly what it says, at one and the same moment. It seems to remark that the present is a very serious matter, but that it must not be taken seriously. It at once ridicules its subject and ridicules its own ridicule, until the reader is at a loss to determine what the author believes. The latter remains aloof from the question, turns it over and over in his hand, looks at it, and says something quizzical about it. It is not always safe to say that he is sarcastic. He is having intellectual fun. His mind is fermenting.

Of such a nature is Byron's real preface to **Don Juan,** placed by him near the end of the first canto. It can only be recognized for what it is, a humorous discussion of the standards of literary composition, as they had been accepted in the age of Pope. It is not, because it is humorous, necessarily sarcastic, any more than the preface of Martinus Scriblerus to the *Dunciad* is an attack on neoclassic canons. It merely shows, as did that other preface, that the canons are in the author's mind and that his sense of humor is working on them. The announcement of purposes cannot be taken literally, because we know that they were not, and were not likely to be, followed.

These thirteen stanzas, which I have been pleased to call a preface, are even more of a burlesque than the notice of Scri-

Byron in 1813. The poet considered this portrait true to life.

blerus. They are a hodge-podge of neoclassical ethics and reminiscences, thrown together into an unbelievable though plausible statement of good intentions. The poem, it is asserted, is an epic. Therefore there are to be twelve books, and three episodes. Each book is to contain, "with love and war, a heavy gale at sea, a list of ships, and captains, and kings reigning"— a catalogue of ships, in the manner of the *Iliad*. There will be a panoramic view of Hell, after the style of Virgil and Homer, new mythological machinery, and "very handsome supernatural scenery." All is to be written "with strict regard to Aristotle's rules," except that there will be less embellishment, a greater care for the truth—"This story's actually true." There is to be a moral, which nevertheless may be hard for some people to find. If in time the author should descend to prose, he will write new poetical commandments, to supersede all those just now accepted, with others much severer, to be entitled "Longinus o'er a Bottle, or Every Poet his *own* Aristotle." Now he says nothing; but if he were to speak, he would command reverence for Milton, Dryden, Pope, and Crabbe, and scorn of the Lake School:

> Thou shalt not write, in short, but what I choose;
>   This is true criticism, and you may kiss—
> Exactly as you please, or not—the rod;
> But if you don't, I'll lay it on, by G-d.

The passage might very well be judged alone, in the spirit of the whole poem. Here is Byron disporting himself with what in other moods he reverences. He is committing sacrilege against poetry and religion by burlesquing both the Rules and the Ten Commandments. But it is all in fun. He means no harm to either the Ten Commandments or the Rules, though they have their funny side, and one may point it out, in such a poem as this. Incidentally, he has arrived at a truth, that his standards are his own because they are his, and when he preaches them he is imposing himself upon others. But that is no admission that he does not believe in them, and will not uphold them stoutly.

The passage might very well be judged alone, but it is better to check it up with other portions of the satire. The occasional references to Horace and Pope are not reverential, but neither are they carping. Homer is referred to humorously as a model, when Byron is obviously not in an Homeric vein. There is a recollection that even Homer nods, and a serious echo of Homer in the description of the army at night. Aristotle is dealt with as irreverently, but more respectfully. For while the appeal to "the opinion of the critic . . . from Aristotle *passim*" is ironical, another passage,

> As I have a high sense
> Of Aristotle and the Rules, 't is fit
> To beg his pardon when I err a bit,

is not clearly so. There is, indeed, a constant resort to "the ancient epic laws," with a tendency to quote them and then disobey them, or to bring them in wherever they are most incongruous. *In medias res* is cited, only as "the usual method, but not mine—my way is to begin with the beginning." Aristotle's principle of the beginning, middle, and end, is echoed in "the riddle of epic Love's beginning—end—and middle" and in an extended precept consciously quite as obvious as Aristotle's analysis:

> Firstly, begin with the beginning—(though
>   That clause is hard); and secondly, proceed;
> Thirdly, commence not with the end.

Byron, in his own way, was declaring his independence as conclusively as any of his contemporaries were doing. But there is a difference in the point of view. He is, in the last analysis, not revolting against the past, but adapting the past to the present, though less rigidly than he has done in his tragedies. As the poem proceeds, citations and comments prove that the great critics and established writers of the past are in his thoughts, if he does not obey their injunctions to the letter. He has precept and standard in mind; but here he must to a great extent adapt precept to his own situation. Aristotle had laid down no rule for the burlesque epic. As it had been claimed in the age before, that his pronouncements in the *Poetics* would have been modified by a perusal of the *Aeneid,* so much the more would they have been affected by the newer and far different epics. After all, the laws of poetic composition had been distilled from the usages of great writers. Every additional great writer was like past great ones, but he differed from them insofar as his purposes and the nature of his task demanded. It was no disloyalty to one's predecessors to work out one's own practices. If Byron was in need of a "lofty wing plumed by Longinus or the Stagyrite," he after all sang "Knights and Dames . . . such as the times may furnish." There is no advantage in taking Aristotle too literally. *Don Juan* "shall have twenty-four books, the legitimate number. Episodes it has, and will have, out of number; and my spirits, good or bad, must serve for the machinery. If that be not an epic, if it be not strictly according to Aristotle, I don't know what an epic means." Of course that is not strictly according to Aristotle, any more than Byron was sure of writing only twenty-four cantos; but it was what Aristotle might have approved of, if he had faced Byron's problem in Byron's time. *Don Juan* is an epic, but a modern epic, that cannot be judged completely in terms of an inherited critical jargon. "If you must have an epic, there's *Don Juan* for you; it is an epic as much in the spirit of our day as the *Iliad* was in Homer's. Love, religion, and politics form the argument. . . . There is no want of Parises and Menelauses, and of *Crim-cons* into the bargain. In the very first canto you have a Helen. Then, I shall make my hero a perfect Achilles for fighting . . . and, depend upon it, my moral will be a good one; not even Dr. Johnson should be able to find a flaw in it." The proposition is advanced jocularly, as was fitting in any serious discussion of *Don Juan.* And in just the proper manner, the truth is neatly summed up.

Byron's chief concern, in his adherence to the classics, was one of form. There is some talk about morality, and a mention of coloring

> With Nature manners which are artificial,
> And rend'ring general that which is especial.

In the incongruity of the application of the Rules to modern circumstances lies much of the fun. But Byron was not really concerned with the spirit of Aristotle. His classical spirit is more subconscious than conscious, a disinclination to let himself go completely, a reaction from excess, or the correction of a momentary extravagance; it is derived from his immediate forbears, Pope and Johnson, rather than from the dictates of Aristotle. When he quoted or paraphrased the critics, it was the more obvious precepts that impressed him. As in the dramas his chief concern had been the Unities, so here it was matters of where to begin and how to continue, not, for instance, the doctrine of imitation. One of the most classical of all maxims is, perhaps, that "men should know why they write, and for what end"; and it is in complete and conscious command of his powers that much of his classical quality consisted. To

speak approximately, Byron knew what he was going to do and went deliberately about doing it. (pp. 189-98)

William J. Calvert, in his Byron: Romantic Paradox, *1935. Reprint by Russell & Russell, Inc., 1962, 235 p.*

RONALD BOTTRALL (essay date 1939)

[*Bottrall asserts that Byron's mastery of the rhythms and vocabulary of colloquial speech is one of the major strengths of* Don Juan. *According to the critic, the "amazing variety of tone and the tremendous rhythmic energy of* Don Juan *come from Byron's complete understanding of the spoken language." Bottrall concludes that Byron's familiarity with the idiom of everyday conversation contributed to the greatness of* Don Juan *and "vivified and renewed the English poetic tradition." This essay was originally published in the* Criterion *in January 1939.*]

A great deal of English poetry from 1780 to 1870 and most of it from 1870 to 1900 was written on the assumption that if only an experience is felt sincerely enough and intensely enough it will find its own words, which will be the best words, and its own form, which will be the best form. The presence of the 'daimon' of inspiration is enough. This accounts for much of the slovenliness and 'inattention' of Shelley, Browning and Swinburne. All three of them were technically competent, and at least one, in a narrow way, a great technician, but they really saw the problems of the subject, the material and the form as *one* problem; once mastered by the conviction of 'genuine' inspiration they treated the formal problem as an unavoidable but inessential corollary. In the worst work of Coleridge, Shelley and Browning indeed a mere outline of a poem is given; the reader has to do the formal work for himself. With Swinburne the problem is somewhat different; technique (by which he meant a double sestina rather than a villanelle) is an end in itself. Byron's greatness in the ottava rima poems is that he evolved a form perfectly adapted to his subject and his material, and so was able to use the whole range of the language with a virility and momentum such as is found nowhere else in nineteenth century poetry. The amazing variety of tone and the tremendous rhythmic energy of *Don Juan* come from Byron's complete understanding of the spoken language. In his controversy with Bowles [over the value of Pope's work] Byron continually emphasizes the importance of execution, and he came to hate 'flowers of poetry' and to despise 'the mart For what is sometimes called poetic diction.' He went back to Pope to learn precision of statement and the problems of relating technique to material, and to Dryden to learn how the complete resources of the language might be enlisted.

T. S. Eliot in a very interesting essay [see *NCLC,* Vol. 2] cites the following stanza as an example of Byron's colloquial power:

> He from the world had cut off a great man,
> Who in his time had made heroic bustle.
> Who in a row like Tom could lead the van,
> Booze in the ken, or at the spellken hustle?
> Who queer a flat? Who (spite of Bow-street's ban)
> On the high toby-spice so flash the muzzle?
> Who on a lark with black-eyed Sal (his blowing)
> So prime—so swell—so nutty—and so knowing?

It is brilliant, but it is a *tour de force.* Byron is doing far more cleverly the sort of thing that Harrison Ainsworth was doing in 'Nix my doll pals, fake away' or Henley in 'Villon's straight tip to all cross coves' with its famous refrain 'Booze and the blowens cop the lot.' Byron in exile was showing that he still remembered the thieves' cant which he heard when he was a dandy and used to spar with Gentleman Jackson and Molineaux. When Eliot compares this stanza to Burns he is being most misleading. Burns was using a vernacular which was his native speech, Byron was faking a brilliant *pastiche*. What Byron has in common with Burns is not his use of a vivid vernacular or his homely turn of phrase, but his method of familiar, ironical address, his generous regard for the common people and his large humanity.

The language of Byron was aristocratic, and though it had a great tradition behind it, this language is charged with a lower poetic potentiality than the Scots of Burns. There is thus far less explosive force in Byron's phrasing than in that of Burns, but there is an equally powerful use of the rhythms of colloquial speech. In *Don Juan* Byron is writing as he spoke to his friends and equals, and at the same time writing great verse.

> Where's Brummell? Dished. Where's Long Pole
>   Wellesley? Diddled.
> Where's Whitbread? Romilly? Where's George the
>   Third?
> Where is his will? (That's not so soon unriddled).
> And where is 'Fum' the Fourth, our 'royal bird'?
> Gone down, it seems, to Scotland, to be fiddled
> Unto by Sawney's violin, we have heard:
> 'Caw me, caw thee'—for six months hath been
>   hatching
> This scene of royal itch and loyal scratching.
>
> Where is Lord This? And where my Lady That?
> The Honourable Mistresses and Misses?
> Some laid aside like an old Opera hat,
> Married, unmarried and remarried; (this is
> An evolution oft performed of late).
> Where are the Dublin shouts and London hisses?
> Where are the Grenvilles? Turned as usual. Where
> My friends the Whigs? Exactly where they were.

The huddled speed of question and answer, parenthesis, court gossip, innuendo, thrust and repartee, is breath-taking. Every phrase keeps, however, the normal word-order, and the rhythms of everyday speech run with and into the intricate stanza, giving an extraordinary effect of energy harnessed and then liberated at the highest pressure. Here Byron displays the whole rhythmic potentiality of colloquial English.

A remark of Goethe, 'So bald er reflectirt ist er ein Kind,' has often been brought against Byron since Arnold quoted it [see *NCLC,* Vol. 2]. Goethe, in fact, did not intend it to be taken as a general criticism, he was speaking of Byron's irritability in the face of hostile criticism; but Arnold's wider application of the remark is in part justified. The 'thought' that we find in *Childe Harold,* the 'metaphysics' of *Cain,* are those of an undergraduate, if not of a child; but Byron could forge out *poetic* thought.

> Don Juan saw that Microcosm on stilts,
> Yclept the Great World; for it is the least,
> Although the highest: but as swords have hilts
> By which their power of mischief is increased,
> When Man in battle or in quarrel tilts,
> Thus the low world, north, south, or west, or east,
> Must still obey the high—which is their handle,
> Their Moon, their Sun, their gas, their farthing candle.

We have only to compare this with the tangled metaphors [of] . . . *Childe Harold* to note a fundamental difference. Here the metaphors are not loosely impressionistic, they are used

structurally to build up a fine piece of poetic logic. Through such eighteenth century poems as Pope's *Elegy to the Memory of an Unfortunate Lady,* this stanza may even be brought into relation with Metaphysical poetry.

T. S. Eliot speaks of Byron's 'imperceptiveness to the word' and his 'schoolboy command of language.' This, I confess, I cannot understand. Byron was certainly, in his way, at least as perceptive to the word as Swinburne was in his. It is true that his interest was rather in the fundamental rhythmic movement of speech than in the word, but that was, at the time, to the good. Augustan theories of diction were too much obsessed by the word, and a Wordsworthian theory of poetics, carried to its logical end, could only debilitate and desiccate the language. Byron by bringing to his verse the colloquial force of his prose vivified and renewed the English poetic tradition. (pp. 220-23)

> Ronald Bottrall, ''Byron and the Colloquial Tradition in English Poetry,'' in English Romantic Poets: Modern Essays in Criticism, *edited by M. H. Abrams, Oxford University Press, 1960, pp. 210-27.**

ELIZABETH FRENCH BOYD (essay date 1945)

[*Boyd and Paul Graham Trueblood (see Additional Bibliography) were the first critics to publish full-scale studies of* Don Juan. *The serious critical attention they lavished on the work helped pave the way for the proliferation of* Don Juan *studies in the next two decades. Boyd's* Don Juan: A Critical Study *is still admired today for its interpretive acumen and scholarly insight. In the following excerpt, the critic examines the intellectual content of* Don Juan. *Arguing that ''Nature vs. Civilization'' forms the work's greatest theme, Boyd here analyzes Byron's treatment of ''Love, Tempest and Travel, War, and Society.'' As she probes Byron's views on each of these subjects, Boyd also traces the literary influences and biographical events that helped shape them.*]

Although the style of *Don Juan* is personal and subjective, the themes are universal and are handled objectively—playfully, on the surface, as Byron freely confesses, but with an underlying seriousness. The grand theme, implicit in the story and the satire, is Nature vs. Civilization, or as Byron might have defined it, if anyone had pinned him down with a question, Truth and Feigning, or Reality and Appearance. In Byron's mind, it runs through everything, from natural and political history to metaphysics. Byron's preoccupation with it is typically romantic.

To clothe the major argument, he uses a multitude of themes, departments of human experience and thought, some of which he takes the trouble to name from time to time in the course of the poem. The lists differ in details, but the best summary appears at the end of Canto VIII—''Love—Tempest—Travel—War.'' In Canto XIV, after many preliminary hints in Cantos X-XIII, he adds:

> A bird's eye view, too, of that wild, Society;
>   A slight glance thrown on men of every station.

He remarked to Medwin [see excerpt dated 1822] that *Don Juan* is about Love, War, and Religion, the classic subjects of the epic. We might append to the list, also, the topics for digression—what Byron calls his ''lucubrations''—on metaphysics, freedom, education, literary criticism, his personal confessions, and a host of lesser subjects.

But omitting all these, tempting as they are, for the purpose of brief but comprehensive discussion I propose to analyze only what Byron has to say on Love, Tempest and Travel, War, and Society. (p. 58)

At the outset, we must note that the principal substance of Byron's thought is conveyed in his story. It is easy in reading *Don Juan* to be too much diverted by the digressions and to regard the story as comparatively trivial, a thread of interest barely strong enough to hold the poem together and keep the reader's curiosity alive from canto to canto. Byron writes as if he were himself very little concerned with it and was being forced only by convention to return to it and keep it spinning.

We might easily be deceived by this negligent attitude and assign it to feebleness and inertia in storytelling, forgetting that a large part of Byron's poetic apprenticeship consisted of concentrated galloping narratives. But there is an important difference in the *Don Juan* narrative from the short tales like the *Corsair* or *Mazeppa*. In the tales, the emphasis is upon action and passion, but in *Don Juan* Byron was attempting to *add* to a straight story of adventure the novelistic virtues of elaborate psychological realism and intellectual theme. Instead of the romantic world of oriental or Gothic coloring, *Don Juan* treats of the real world, and all its values are true to life. This made a different and a much greater tax on Byron's powers of invention, imagination, and expression. We must remember the unsuccessful attempts he had persistently made to write novels, and his recent experience in composing dramas.

Whether *Don Juan* is a successful novel or not, it must be judged as a novel, on its merits as a story, if we care to understand what Byron has to say through it. To be sure, the first person digressions re-enforce and explain the story, but even without the digressions the story would stand firm. Byron's ideas are implicit in the characters and the action.

This is a new departure in Byron's practice in writing narrative poetry. His definitions of poetry—that it is a mirror of life, the passions in action—were made in refutation of the practice of psychological novelists, especially Madame de Staël, who "reason upon the emotions." Now he is borrowing their technical weapons to refute their prevailing views. We are reminded of Goethe's judgment, that Byron "as soon as he thinks, is a child." But Goethe put this judgment in so forcible a metaphor merely to stress the greatest power of Byron—the power to give expression in words to the electric thrill of passionate emotion. Goethe meant that Byron was not a clear and original thinker; he did not mean to call him brainless and unreflecting. Granted that Byron is muddled, inconclusive, and derivative in his ideas, nevertheless it is important to recognize the intellectual content of *Don Juan,* if only to understand and feel more intensely its passion.

As Byron turned over "all the adventures that he had undergone, seen, heard of, or imagined, with his reflections on life and manners," the epic theme of love naturally occupied a very large position in his thoughts. For all his too well known amours, strange to say, Byron has been accused of exhibiting very little knowledge of the female heart because he made the women in his verse tales stereotyped romantic dolls. As a matter of fact, he was a very accurate reader of feminine character, aided, perhaps, as Moore suggests, by the feminine traits of his own mind. He had made a prolonged and deep study of women and the passion between the sexes, not only in his own experience but from books. He had much to say upon love—first love, pure natural love, impure selfish love, the hypocrisies of fashionable love, love in marriage, and marriage without love—and upon the effect of love in the lives of women and the careers of men.

In his reading on this subject, Byron had acquired a wide knowledge of quasi-philosophical and psychological thought about love and the nature of man. On the one hand, he had read practically everything in self-observation and analysis from Montaigne to Rousseau, and the criticisms and endorsements of these philosophers in the comments of people like Grimm and Diderot. On the other hand, he knew the mass of fiction portraying and analyzing the progress of love, especially books like Marmontel's *Contes Moraux,* which tend to reduce romantic imaginations and substitute worldly wisdom on matters of love and marriage. He knew and condemned Mme. de Staël's highly elaborate psychologizing on the tender passions. He was among the first to admire Constant's *Adolphe* as profoundly true and realistic in characterization, though he thought it highly improbable in plot. Wieland's *Agathon,* we know from Moore, was supplying him with its realistic information on the progress of passion as he embarked on Canto III of *Don Juan.*

Byron could not fail to agree with Grimm, who said, in justifying Montaigne and Bayle for what has been called "the licentiousness of their bold reasonings on human nature":

> They thought they might permit themselves to
> enter into rather minute details upon the subject
> of a passion which has so much influence on
> the whole economy of our existence; which
> formed, and which constantly modifies society,
> and is in fact, the most active and the most
> powerful principle by which it is moved.

Byron was for pushing the inquiry further, to find out new truths about this mainspring of human life. Commenting at the end of Canto XIV on the growing relationship between Adeline and Juan, he writes:

> . . . for Truth is always strange—
> Stranger than fiction; if it could be told,
> How much would novels gain by the exchange!
> How differently the World would men behold!
> How oft would Vice and Virtue places change!
> The new world would be nothing to the old,
> If some Columbus of the moral seas
> Would show mankind their Souls' antipodes.

Not less truth is needed, but more; and Byron believed that faithful adherence to clearly observed facts is the way to acquire it. With this conviction of the importance of love and of faithfulness to reality in describing it, Byron chose the famous legend of Don Juan and set about retelling it in the light of truth. Love is the most important theme in the poem, viewed from the standpoint of the general theme, Nature vs. Civilization.

To begin with Byron's conclusions, we may gather from some one hundred stanzas scattered through *Don Juan* the essence of his thought on love. It is complete and satisfactory, artistically coherent with the actions and characters of the poem, but it is not theoretically consistent, and it is filled with romantic paradox and wonder and awe at the unplumbed mystery, Man. To the first mention of love in Canto I, the digression on the sweetness of first love, Byron instantly appends the corollary of wonder at Man, the inscrutable creation.

In the story of Don Juan, Byron rejects the simple diabolism of the Spanish legend. Fundamentally, he says, the nature of man is good, and love is one of his most beautiful and sublime instincts. If Don Juan becomes a libertine monster, a man worthy of Hell, the fault lies in society, which has wrecked his primal nobility and twisted his good impulses to evil ends. This is Byron's Rousseauism.

But almost in the same breath, he repudiates this view as too narrow and incomplete. Love is now the God of Evil . . . ; not Evil in itself, but the gateway of all evil. Part of the evil occasioned by love is to be laid to society, it is true; but the individual cannot be exempted, for the transient purity of love gives place only too soon to selfish passions, extravagances and errors which bring upon the individual his own proper punishment:

> The Heart is like the sky, a part of Heaven,
>   But changes night and day, too, like the sky;
> Now o'er it clouds and thunder must be driven,
>   And Darkness and Destruction as on high:
> But when it hath been scorched, and pierced, and riven,
>   Its storms expire in water-drops; the eye
> Pours forth at last the Heart's blood turned to tears,
> Which makes the English climate of our years.
>
> The liver is the lazaret of bile,
>   But very rarely executes its function,
> For the first passion stays there such a while,
>   That all the rest creep in and form a junction,
> Like knots of vipers on a dunghill's soil—
>   Rage, fear, hate, jealousy, revenge, compunction—
> So that all mischiefs spring up from this entrail,
> Like Earthquakes from the hidden fire called
>   'central.' . . .

With this rather unsatisfactory piece of poetical anatomy (Hobhouse objected to it as grotesque), Byron tries to express his understanding of the dual nature of man, wherein the physical and spiritual, the evil and the good are inextricably mixed. From the perversion of a pure instinct to an unbounded passion come all the woes we bring on our own heads:

> The Nightingale that sings with the deep thorn,
>   Which fable places in her breast of wail,
> Is lighter far of heart and voice than those
> Whose headlong passions form their proper woes.
>
> And that's the moral of this composition,
>   If people would but see its real drift. . . .

Evil is inherent in the nature of man; he does not have to learn it from society, though society frequently succeeds in first evoking it. The heart and the liver are both parts of man's nature, and evil and pure instincts spring side by side. Thus Byron attempts to reconcile Rousseauism with the older views of human nature in the philosophies of Aristotle and Calvin.

Closely allied with Byron's wonder at human nature in general, but on a lower and slightly patronizing plane, is his philosophizing on the nature of women. He recommends to "young beginners" in the science of psychology a "quiet cruising o'er the ocean, Woman." Here he also makes a distinction between women in a state of nature, like Haidée, and women whose bondage to society damages more or less their natural goodness and calls out in them their worse natures.

It has been suggested that Byron shared Pope's rather cynical view in his *Moral Essay on the Characters of Women*, that women are mere pretty animals who possess but two ruling passions: the love of pleasure and the love of sway. But though Byron did not like to see a woman eat, he was not so con-

temptuous as that. In *Don Juan,* he assigns as a woman's ruling passion the need to love and to be loved:

> Man's love is of man's life a thing apart,
>   'T is a woman's whole existence; Man may range
> The Court, Camp, Church, the Vessel, and the Mart;
>   Sword, Gown, Gain, Glory offer, in exchange
> Pride, Fame, Ambition, to fill up his heart,
>   And few there are whom these cannot estrange;
> Men have all these resources, We but one—
> To love again, and be again undone. . . .

So Julia, from the convent where she has been shut up, writes her farewell letter to Juan as he is setting forth on his adventures. This truism, by the way, first met Byron's attention in Mme. de Staël's *Corinne*. It stands as a text for the fates of all the heroines of *Don Juan,* from gentle Julia and innocent Haidée, to the great whore Catherine II, who was at least "three parts woman."

Pity for the sad lot of women is a keynote in many passages. Women, Byron thinks, can really love but once, and that love is invariably betrayed:

> . . . for Man, to man so oft unjust,
>   Is always so to Women: one sole bond
> Awaits them—treachery is all their trust;
>   Taught to conceal, their bursting hearts despond
> Over their idol, till some wealthier lust
>   Buys them in marriage—and what rests beyond?
> A thankless husband—next, a faithless lover—
> Then dressing, nursing, praying—and all's over. . . .
>
> Poor Thing of Usages! coerced, compelled,
>   Victim when wrong, and martyr oft when right,
> Condemned to child-bed, as men for their sins
> Have shaving, too, entailed upon their chins,—
>
> A daily plague, which in the aggregate
>   May average on the whole with parturition,—
> But as to women—who can penetrate
>   The real sufferings of their she condition?
> Man's very sympathy with their estate
>   Has much of selfishness, and more suspicion,
> Their love, their virtue, beauty, education,
> But form good housekeepers—to breed a nation. . . .

This, and much more, from Byron, who called himself the "martyr to and by women," is sympathy indeed. Thus he enlarged on the Elvira theme of the legend. His sympathy for women leads him to condone, while wondering at, their conscious arts and wiles, handed down traditionally from maid to maid, to fit them first for the marriage market and then for the managing of a husband. It excuses their casuistry in love, their reckless impulsiveness, and their tigress-like fury when they are betrayed.

The simplicity of this Byronic view of women, however true to nature and to the condition of women in Byron's day, belies somewhat the subtlety and the effect of infinite variety in the portraits of individual women in *Don Juan*. Byron's observation and dramatic characterization in this particular are more comprehensive than his philosophizing. These women, fundamentally mere lovers and objects of love, like the earlier Byronic heroines, are now endowed with complete personalities, and exhibited at every age and at every stage of their careers. In the earlier tales, the predominant importance of the Byronic hero relegated the heroines to the background, where they show only in silhouette. In *Don Juan* they are set forth "in the round." Byron recognized their loyalty and capacity for friendship. He understood the spiritual craving in love experienced by the good and sensitive woman. Lady Adeline, for example, found something lacking in her noble husband, Lord Henry:

> A something all-sufficient for the *heart*
> Is that for which the sex are always seeking:
> But how to fill up that same vacant part?
> There lies the rub—and this they are but weak in.
> Frail mariners afloat without a chart,
> They run before the wind through high seas
> breaking;
> And when they have made the shore through every
> shock,
> 'T is odd—or odds—it may turn out a rock. . . .

On the whole, he admitted the potential humanity of women, but thought it criminally stifled by the prevailing conditions of society.

Byron's view of marriage is uncompromisingly unfavorable; some of the bitterest verses of *Don Juan* are reserved to condemn this, to him, uncomfortable and artificial state of being. Love is an institution of nature, but marriage of society, and the two are rarely compatible. This romantic view, hallowed by the ages, was no conventional pose with Byron. His own experience of unhappy marriage and of cicisbeism in Italy confirmed what he read from Pope's *Eloisa* to Rousseau's *Nouvelle Héloise*. Especially in England, he says, where marriages depend upon money, no matter what hypocritical society may declare to the contrary, matrimony is the opposite of love. He takes up Scott's phrase and proves that Love is not the ruler of Camp, Court, and Grove, but that Money is. . . . In a bitter syllogism, he shows that heaven cannot be love, because heaven sanctions only matrimony, and everybody knows that, first, matrimony and love are incompatible, and second, all unmarried love is sin and therefore unheavenly.

Especially he condemns the hypocrisy of society and individuals toward love. He begins in Canto I attacking the hypocrisy of parents and husbands toward love and marriage, and in the last cantos he is still spurring to the charge. All hypocrisy in love is wicked and one of the prime evil effects occasioned by love, especially the hypocrisy of "Platonics" and other forms of self-deception. As a literary critic, he condemned the hypocrisy of romantic amatory writing. He thought the duty of the poet is to speak out plainly and with full responsibility, and he tried in the various and successive love episodes of *Don Juan* to exemplify his conception of the truth about love. (pp. 58-65)

None of Juan's love episodes is for Byron strictly autobiographical, but the whole story contains his explanation of the havoc wrought in his life by love affairs and the ruin of his reputation. This, Byron says, is how the human being is evolved whom the world ignorantly dubs a Don Juan. Hypocrisy, violence, and vicious self-indulgence in individuals combine with an unnatural civilization to ruin the pristine beauty and purity of the human heart.

The general theme of *Don Juan*, Nature vs. Civilization, is illustrated not only in the love episodes and their effect upon the hero, but in Juan's travels. . . . Byron deliberately enlarged the scope of the legend and broadened his hero's career by taking him on a tour of Europe and giving him the conventional picaresque novel adventures. *Don Juan* is a story of travel as well as a story of love, and travel ranks in importance only second to love as the source of change in Juan's character. Just as Byron enlarged upon the Elvira theme of persecuted innocent womankind, so, in the inclusion of shipwreck and travel, he expanded according to his own gifts and interests the hints in the original Don Juan legend. What exactly had Byron to say in his use of the themes of tempest and travel?

The story of Don Juan in Tirso de Molina's *El Burlador de Sevilla* begins with a seduction in Italy from which Don Juan escapes to Spain. His ship is wrecked on a rock off Tarragona, and only he and his valet escape by swimming. A poor fishergirl succours Don Juan, and he repays her hospitality by seducing her. The convention of shipwreck and near-drowning persisted in all the subsequent versions of the story, except Da Ponte's and Goldoni's, as if to illustrate the proverb that the villain cannot drown but is reserved for a more appropriate death.

But the tempest and the sea journey mean more for Byron than a mere following of the Don Juan legend, or indeed of epic and picaresque novel conventions. It is appropriate to the general theme that a violent convulsion of physical nature should follow, in this series of romantic-realistic contrasts, the tempest in the teapot of civilized Seville. (p. 70)

The ocean stood for escape and liberation to Byron. Those who remember the wonderful effect of climax and release produced by the famous lines to the ocean at the end of *Childe Harold* will recall that it is achieved by a sudden shift of viewpoint. The Pilgrim of Eternity does not stand on the seashore of ruined empires and look at the unchanging ocean; instead, he contemplates the shores of Africa and Europe from the middle of the Mediterranean. It is a view landward from the sea, and at once the ocean becomes the impassive, unchanging floor of the world, while the solid lands around turn into "the graves of Empires" that "heave but like some passing waves," as Byron restated it at the end of Canto XV in *Don Juan*.

The untamed sea, symbol for Byron of escape, oblivion, and eternal nature, provided in his own experience the sheer space and loneliness that were enough to sponge out old life and refresh him for the new. But for Don Juan, who experiences the sea at its most impersonally cruel and tedious, the wreck and the sufferings in the longboat and the final exhausting efforts of swimming were meant to intensify the naturally purifying effect of a sea voyage. . . . [They] make credible his Garden-of-Eden innocence and his integrity in the Haidée episode. Natural love and passionate violence are appropriately introduced by a rude commotion in physical nature and a stark tale of human struggle for survival against natural forces.

Sticking to reality, however, Byron could not give his hero a sea voyage, much less a wreck, every time he wanted to ring down the curtain on one of his shattering experiences and prepare him and the reader for the next. True, Don Juan has another short voyage from Lambro's island in the Cyclades to Constantinople. But the mere sight of Ilion in the distance, though it affords Byron and the reader a breathing space to muse on mutability, could not refresh the wounded forlorn Juan.

Byron here introduces other conventions of picaresque fiction; first, the troupe of wandering actors. Byron claims that the story of the Italian opera company sold into slavery by their impresario is a fact, the truth of which he learned in Venice in 1817. The topics, however, of "Raucocanti's eloquent recital" he may have derived from Goldoni's amusing comedy *L'Impresario della Smyrna*,—the whims of the prima donna, the bellowing basso, the dancers, the cracked voices, the catarrhs, and the jealousies. But this dim diversion and object lesson in optimism, and even the passing of time and healing of his wounds were hardly sufficient to restore Juan to a semblance of hope and health. What syncope, time, travel, and new scenes were not wholly able to accomplish, philosophy completed, in the shape of the sturdy Englishman, Johnson. Candide also found solace in a philosophical fellow traveler, when his spirits were at their lowest ebb. Johnson, taking up where Raucocanti's cheerful optimism left off, flatters and shames Juan by precept and example into a courageous frame of mind:

> By setting things in their right point of view,
>   Knowledge, at least, is gained; for instance, now,
> We know what slavery is, and our disasters
>   May teach us better to behave when masters.

Travel serves not only to pass the time and change the scene, so that the hero may grow up and the whole view of European society be unrolled before his eyes; but travel and the firsthand experience it brings are meant to be as powerful educators of Juan as any of his affairs of the heart.

Steeped in the English aristocratic tradition of the grand tour, Byron wrote to his mother in 1808:

> . . . when I return [from the tour of the East] I may possibly become a politician. A few years' knowledge of other countries than our own will not incapacitate me for that part. If we see no nation but our own, we do not give mankind a fair chance;—it is from *experience,* not books, we ought to judge of them. There is nothing like inspection, and trusting to our own senses.

This humanistic conviction remained with him all his life. He learned to hold a cosmic view not only from Cuvier but from a glimpse of the stars through Herschell's telescope, and he acquired a continental outlook not only from books but from experience. Though he read travel books eagerly, he knew how and why to distrust them. He plumed himself, if not on the extent, at least on the duration and the thoroughness of his travels. It might be shown that travel was the source, or at least the re-enforcement, of his political views and activities. In literature, he scorned the stay-at-homes like Hunt and Keats and Wordsworth and Southey—what could they know of the world? Making the most poetic capital of his travels, he dealt with the best-known publisher of travel literature.

If one contrasts the travelogue qualities of *Childe Harold* and *Don Juan,* the different uses made of travel in each poem strikingly illustrate the growth of this conviction in Byron's mind and his intention concerning travel in *Don Juan. Childe Harold* is a sight-seeing tour, a negative forth-faring to seek escape. The monuments of the past, whether the handiwork of man or of nature, are its objects, as the ruin of empires is its embracing theme. Modern civilization and contemporary life enter the picture only as foils, or to point the moral lessons of antiquity. In *Don Juan,* however, we travel in the world of 1789-91. Sight-seeing occupies a minimum of either Juan's or the reader's attention. If Juan does not feel like looking at Cape Sigeum, usually the reader is not allowed to look at it either. If Juan stops at Canterbury to inspect the Cathedral and its relics, it is to point up a contrast between his dreams of old English heroism and the actuality of the highway robbery about to occur to him; or to give a chance for sarcasm on un-Christian Christians, through the irony of Leila's remarks on the Cathedral. These are the only bits of sight-seeing *per se* recorded at

any length in *Don Juan;* for the rest, Juan is hurried in a "kibitka," or the Empress's imperial coach, or the English stage-coach, through scenes suggested with only enough detail to provide that sense of elapsing time and space necessary for the story.

The important objects of travel in *Don Juan* are modern societies and modern people and their effect on the unfolding consciousness of the hero. *Don Juan* is not a travelogue, but a *Wanderjahr.* The reader sees the world, now through the eyes of Byron, and now through those of Juan, but the different angles of vision are trained on the present, on the modern, actual world. *Childe Harold* is a passive contemplative travelogue; *Don Juan* is the travels of a man of action.

To the educative influences of contact with rude nature and personal experience of distance and physical hardship, Byron adds firsthand acquaintance with a wide variety of peoples, places, and manners. But he makes another use of travel, as the technical device for conveying satire. He uses the technique of travel and the eyes of a voyager from another civilization to give the utmost point to the satire on his own. Juan, assisted by Byron's asides, is the favorite eighteenth century traveling philosopher from China all over again, only in the dress of a modern Spaniard-cosmopolite. The natural man, whether he is a Spaniard, or a Chinese, or a Scythian (as in the *Voyage of Anacharsis*), views society through unaccustomed eyes and thus sees it truly. Travel in *Don Juan* serves a double purpose. It fosters and chastizes the hero, educating him as no mother or book learning in Seville could do; and it educates the reader, by juxtaposing view after view of the modern real world.

Juan's itinerary is dictated partly by the legend and by Byron's own experience, but also by the purposes of satire and the use of the travel theme to illustrate Nature vs. Civilization. The story necessarily starts in Spain, in keeping with the legend, and the Spanish civilization is even more pointedly ripe for satire than the English. It goes to England inevitably, since English society and English responsibility in continental politics are principal butts of the satire. But what is the significance of Greece and of Russia? Greece, enslaved under Turkey, and Russia, tyrannical and treacherous, the remote corners of Europe, provide contrasts to the homelands of both Juan and Byron, and give unparalleled opportunities for reflection on the themes of nature and civilization, war, tyranny, and freedom. (pp. 71-4)

The Greek War of Independence really began as far back as 1770 in preliminary skirmishes between the Greek highlanders and the Turks. It flared up again, simultaneously with the French Revolution, during the Russian-Turkish war of 1787-91. Major Lambro Katsones, the original of Byron's Lambro, joined with Captain Andrutsos, a famous klepht, in campaigns by land and by sea with the Turks during 1790-92. The conflicts between the Greeks and the Turks on the one hand and the Russians and Turks on the other were therefore an historical ingredient of the world that Juan entered when he was washed up on Lambro's island.

We begin to hear rumblings from the great world of political warfare from the moment Lambro appears on the scene—a pirate from choice, but also as a patriotic rebel against the Turks. At Constantinople, the soldier of fortune Johnson is being sold into slavery as a prisoner of war; he had been captured in the battle of Widdin between the Russians and the Turks. The Sultan is preoccupied by "his daily council" on the war against Catherine, and the Russian victories, which had recently increased. When Juan and Johnson escape, they therefore naturally head for the Russian encampment on the banks of the Danube. Juan is following out the text that Man may supplement, or substitute for, Love by seeking Glory in the Camp and the Court. In the introduction of the theme of war, Byron's epic satire departs widely from the simple unity of the Don Juan legend, but it is still concerned with the central moral problems of the legend, honor and the ends for which men live.

Nowhere else in ***Don Juan*** did Byron deal a stronger blow for progressive and liberal thought than in Cantos VII-VIII, condemning wars of conquest. With all the Napoleonic world, he had been meditating furiously on war and conquest through the whole span of his adult life. This was the period when the ideas of isolated philosophers, poets, and groups, who for centuries past had inveighed against war, began, under the stress of current events, to spread to the multitudes and to take shape in political and social organizations for world peace, and the outlawing of war. (pp. 76-7)

In May 1816, [Byron] visited Waterloo, one year after its soil likewise had run red with blood. The famous passage in ***Childe Harold,*** Canto III, was the result, with its introductory stanzas on the futility of a war which has eclipsed the glory of Napoleon in vain, for it has brought no freedom from oppression. The conclusion of this passage, while celebrating those gallant men who fought and fell there in what they thought to be the cause of liberty, denies that their brief glory and the lasting fame of Waterloo equally compensate for the destruction caused by their loss:

> Their children's lips shall echo them, and say—
> 　　'Here, where the sword united nations drew,
> Our countrymen were warring on that day!'
> And this is much—and all—which will not pass away.

To the futility of wars of conquest that accomplish no good but only destruction, Byron added the folly of setting any store by military glory. Applying his Aristotelian ethics to Napoleon's career, he moralizes on the Napoleonic wars, begun with such fair promise for the freedom of Europe, and evolving, through Napoleon's unbridled lust for war, into the worst type of conquest:

> 　　　. . . There is a fire
> And motion of the Soul which will not dwell
> 　　In its own narrow being, but aspire
> Beyond the fitting medium of desire. . . .
>
> This makes the madmen who have made men mad
> 　　By their contagion. . . .

Not only at Waterloo, and in the eager following of the post-mortems and the myths of Napoleon's career (fed to Byron by such people as Stendhal and Hobhouse), but also in the preparations for Italian rebellion, Byron continued to meditate upon war. "Revolutions," he recognized, "are not made with rose-water." Though he had not yet experienced battle himself, he had been near enough to it in imagination. By the time he wrote ***Don Juan,*** Cantos VII-VIII, his ideas had settled into a creed.

All wars, he thought, are terrible, hells upon earth, but wars in support of freedom are justifiable, even praiseworthy. He had indeed perceived that "Revolution alone can save the earth from Hell's pollution." War, however, embodies every human crime conceivable, but the worst is that it breeds a colossal hypocrisy, a blindness of ignorance and party prejudice. War hypocrisy induces hero worship for a general, a "butcher in large business," who has enriched himself by war, while it forgets the miseries and murders of untold anonymous millions. It allows a poet, who should know better, to call "Carnage God's daughter." "War cuts up not only branch, but root." It destroys in one hour, at the command of one mad leader, what nature can scarcely rebuild in thirty years. The pursuit of the hollow glory of individual fame, alive only in the throat of quickly forgetful mobs, is the worst folly and hypocrisy of all. This is the will-o'-the-wisp that keeps up the spirit of militarism and glorifies martial prowess.

History, Byron thought, ought to be written to divest war of its charm. The public should be let in on the facts behind the headlines in their morning papers, behind the long casualty lists, where names as often as not are misspelled:

> History can only take things in the gross;
> 　　But could we know them in detail, perchance
> In balancing the profit and the loss,
> 　　War's merit it by no means might enhance,
> To waste so much gold for a little dross,
> 　　As hath been done, mere conquest to advance.
> The drying-up a single tear has more
> Of honest fame, than shedding seas of gore.
>
> And why?—because it brings self-approbation. . . .

From the public standpoint, war is wasteful; and from the private, war does not give the individual the meed of honor and glory he is seeking. The momentary fame of military glory is "nothing but a child of Murder's rattles."

Byron uses his theme of war in civilized Europe to illustrate again his general theme of nature and civilization. One extraordinary digression occurs in Canto VIII at the height of the battle, when Ismail had been entered but not taken,—the stanzas on Daniel Boone, 61-67:

> 'God made the country, and man made the town,'
> So Cowper says—and I begin to be
> 　　Of his opinion, when I see cast down
> Rome—Babylon—Tyre—Carthage—Nineveh—
> 　　All walls men know, and many never known;
> And pondering on the present and the past,
> To deem the woods shall be our home at last:—. . .

Byron, who was an admirer of Americans and American freedom, had received a caller in Ravenna, "a young American, named Coolidge," early in 1821. Coolidge and Byron talked about civilization and savagery and the pursuit of happiness. "The greatest (said Byron) of all living puzzles is, to know for what purpose so strange a being as man was created." He pumped Coolidge for tales of the American wilderness, and among other narratives, the young man related "that of Daniel Boon, the backwoodsman of Kentucky, which made a strong impression upon him." Boone, then, was chosen as the good modern hero, the natural man, to counterbalance bloody Suvaroff (*videlicet* Wellington, and other military heroes of civilization):

> [Boone] left behind a name
> For which men vainly decimate the throng,
> 　　Not only famous, but of that *good* fame,
> Without which Glory's but a tavern song—
> 　　Simple, serene, the *antipodes* of Shame,
> Which Hate nor Envy e'er could tinge with wrong;
> 　　An active hermit, even in age the child
> Of Nature—or the Man of Ross run wild. . . .

> So much for Nature:—by way of variety,
>   Now back to thy great joys, Civilization!
> And the sweet consequence of large society,
>   War—pestilence—the despot's desolation,
> The kingly scourge, the lust of notoriety,
>   The millions slain by soldiers for their ration,
> The scenes like Catherine's boudoir at threescore,
> With Ismail's storm to soften it the more.

But this pessimism, even cynicism, is not Byron's final comment. He did not utterly despair of civilization, for he was at pains to lash its follies and crimes in this protracted satire, and the reforming satirist must always hope in his heart that his words will take effect. Moreover, Byron foresaw, though ironically only in a distant millennium removed by geological ages from the present, that happy period when wars, cutthroat conquerors, and tyrants will be as strange relics of an earlier civilization as the bones of mammoths seem to us.

"Conquest and its consequences," as Byron points out, are "what make Epic poesy so rare and rich." As in the love theme he refuted the popular notion of a Satanic Don Juan, and as in the travel theme he rejected the descriptions and rhapsodies of the travel books, so in the theme of war his epic satire dealt with war only to condemn it.

In the broad sense, all of Byron's *Don Juan* deals with society, the modern European world both east and west. But the last six cantos are especially concerned with the state of society in England, and the field of thought embraces both society at large and the *haut monde* of London's West End. The latter ranked foremost in Byron's thought, for he considered the "grand, *grand monde*" as a kind of tail that wags the dog. But he never lost sight of the nation as a whole, and its position in European society, while concentrating on the manners and characters of the "four thousand." The keynote is sounded in Canto X, with Juan's first sight of the white cliffs of Dover, a lament for Britain, no better than a slave gaoler of other slave nations, when it *"might have been"* the noblest in history. At the conclusion of the canto, pausing with Juan to contemplate the view of London,

>   a wilderness of steeples peeping
>   On tiptoe through their sea-coal canopy,

Byron deplores the mistaken activity of Mrs. Fry. Why should Mrs. Fry waste her time preaching in Newgate? She ought to go to work on hardened and imperial sin in the houses of the great:

> Tell them, though it may be, perhaps, too late—
>   On Life's worn confine, jaded, bloated, sated—
> To set up vain pretence of being *great*,
>   'T is not so to be *good*. . . .

In general, Byron condemns English society for its materialism, its selfish irresponsibility, its frigidity, and its unnaturalness. He deals in Canto XII with the power of money, as it is specifically exercised in "the marriage mart." He ridicules abstract theorists, like Malthus, who set up new philosophical codes for an already artificial society, living by unnatural conventions. In Canto XIII, he deals with the ennui of the members of Society, where the acme of polish is represented by Horace's *nil admirari*, and a country house party is made up of "two mighty tribes, the *Bores* and *Bored*." Hunting, matchmaking, intrigues, and French cookery (the last word in artificiality), form the outer trimmings of Lord Henry's real reason for being in the country, political fence mending in the interests of main-

taining the grand principles, Place and Patronage. Even the native ghost is treated by all except Juan as a subject of no importance, or an occasion for pastime and jest.

Seeming, not being, cant, hypocrisy, and heartlessness are the qualities Byron most deplores in English society. He reveals them, with exquisite lightness of touch, in action in the shifting tides of fashion, fads, and conventional pleasures. For success in this society, Juan must cling to the precepts, *"carpe diem"* and "be not what you seem but what you see."

The questions how far Byron's view of English society is true and trustworthy, and how valid his criticism of it may be, are illuminated interestingly by the Countess of Blessington. Her *Conversations with Lord Byron*, which should certainly be read in conjunction with **Don Juan**, Cantos XI-XVI, took place, however, after he had completed Canto XV. Her point of view can have had no substantial effect on the poem. But it is interesting that Byron's talks with her and his reading of the Count D'Orsay's Journal (destroyed without ever being published) seem to have stimulated him into hurrying the poem through the press. On the day that he warned D'Orsay through the Earl of Blessington that there were remarkable coincidences between the Journal and **Don Juan,** Byron wrote off to Hunt for proofs of the remaining cantos urgently needed for correction. The corrections, however, as they are noted by E. H. Coleridge, took the form only of the usual improvements in diction and phrasing and the addition of two or three stanzas. Perhaps the quality of the Blessingtons' conversation saved Byron from a few errors of taste and rapport which he might have made, had he not had that timely contact with people who were more recently acquainted with the high society he was describing. The Countess, and even Trelawney and other visitors, noticed how old-fashioned Byron's manners and speech had become during his exile from England. He impressed Trelawney as not having realized that the Regency Buck had become passé. Lady Blessington declares that Byron's knowledge and understanding of English society were very imperfect. "Byron sees not, that much of what he calls the usages of cant and hypocrisy are the fences that protect propriety. . . ." Ultra-feminine as her comment doubtless is, nevertheless it is the answer of the latest fashion, the Victorian, to Byron's indictment of society.

Some cancellations, therefore, have to be made by the careful reader of Byron's cantos; something must be subtracted both for his imperfect and perhaps self-deceiving view, and for the change in manners from the eighteenth to the nineteenth century that he never understood, though he felt it keenly. A strong and ample residue of permanent good sense remains, however, and the best proof of that is the use that later Victorian satirists of society made of his poem—Bulwer Lytton, Disraeli, Thackeray, Meredith, and Trollope, to name only the most prominent.

No complete verdict can be passed on Byron's picture of English society, since it is an unfinished fragment. But that it is quintessential, a mine for future writers on the subject, and the most diverting and sparkling passage of **Don Juan,** no reader can deny. The story of Don Juan and his love affairs, expanded to include the whole of Europe, tempest and travel, war and peace, is at last brought home to the responsible apex of European society, its most privileged class, the British aristocracy. (pp. 78-82)

Elizabeth French Boyd, in her Byron's "Don Juan":
A Critical Study, *Rutgers University Press, 1945,
193 p.*

C. M. BOWRA (lecture date 1948-49)

[*Bowra, an English critic and literary historian, is considered among the foremost classical scholars of the first half of the twentieth century. He is known for his objective approach to literature, which reflects his refusal to adhere to any fixed literary tradition. In his remarks on* Don Juan, *Bowra contrasts the satirical realism of the poem with the more conventionally Romantic attitudes toward reality and the imagination expressed both in Byron's earlier works and in those of his great contemporaries. The critic argues that in* Don Juan *Byron cast off the false Romantic persona he had created in such works as* Childe Harold *and spoke candidly for the first time about his perceptions of society, life, and himself. According to Bowra, Byron did not entirely reject a Romantic outlook, but the complexity and changeability of his character forced him to question and accept only with qualification many of the assumptions his contemporaries took for granted. The critic maintains that* Don Juan's *frequent lapses into farce during moments of high seriousness reflect the tension in Byron's mind between "Romantic longings" and his fundamentally skeptical view of the universe. It is this tension, Bowra insists, that gives the poem its enormously varied perspective and rich complexity of tone. The critic's comments are drawn from a series of lectures he delivered in 1948-49.*]

Don Juan is Byron's masterpiece because into it he put the whole of his real self and nothing of the false self which he had manufactured for his earlier poems. And just because it is true to experience, the technique is entirely adequate and cannot be blamed for carelessness. In it Byron speaks not in a slack version of the grand manner, but with the rich ebullience of his conversation and his incomparable letters. He uses the whole living language as he himself knew it and spoke it. It is wonderfully natural and unaffected, and the tone of the words responds with perfect ease to Byron's wayward moods. If he derived his form from Pulci's *Morgante Maggiore,* he showed excellent judgement in doing so. For Pulci has something of Byron's careless gaiety and of his ability to temper seriousness with mockery. The *ottava rima* with its easy progress is well adapted to story-telling, and the clinching couplet in each stanza gives excellent opportunities for epigram such as were denied by the Spenserian stanzas of **Childe Harold.** The easy flowing stanzas suit Byron's different effects, and though they lack polished art, they are a perfect vehicle for what he has to say. They are so flexible that in them Byron's carelessness does not matter and indeed becomes a virtue, since it is part of his conversational manner. All kinds of elements pass easily into this style. It is equally suited to lyrical description and scurrilous satire, to sustained narrative and personal outbursts, to stately declamation and slapdash slang. The brilliantly ingenious rhymes keep it fresh and lively, and the sprightly, uninhibited movement of the stanzas is in perfect accord with the darts and flashes of Byron's mind.

In **Don Juan** Byron speaks as freely and as candidly about himself as Wordsworth does in *The Prelude.* Of course, **Don Juan** is cast in the form of objective narrative and deals with imaginary incidents, but what holds it together and provides its amazing vitality is Byron's personality, and the contrast with Wordsworth's self-portrait shows how far apart the two men were. Their differences of taste and of temperament are matched by their differences of outlook on the nature of poetry. When Wordsworth conceived the idea of *The Prelude,* he was entirely absorbed in his Romantic creed and believed that his was a dedicated task which must be fulfilled through communion with nature. In his earlier work Byron had assumed some of the airs appropriate to such a creed without feeling its mystical appeal. But when he wrote **Don Juan,** he wished to

do something different. He decided that he must tell the truth in the hope of making men better. He was not surprised that **Don Juan** shocked a large number of people, but he held that he himself was not to blame. . . . His purpose was to expose the hypocrisy and the corruption of the high society which he knew so well, and in his hero to depict

> a vicious and unprincipled character, and lead
> him through those ranks of society, whose high
> external accomplishments cover and cloak internal and secret vices.

Byron knew his subject from the inside, and, though his moral earnestness may sound impertinent to those who think that they are better men than he, there is no doubt of his sincerity. He wished to expose a disgraceful sham by telling the full truth about it.

In other words, Byron turned from his own kind of Romantic escape to satirical realism. At the outset nothing could be more alien to the serious Romantic spirit, the essence of which was to concentrate on some mysterious corner of existence and to extract the utmost possible from it. In writing **Don Juan,** Byron was no doubt moved by more than one reason. In the first place, he seems to have seen that his early art was not worthy of his real capacity, and he wished to replace it by something which satisfied the artist in him. In the second place, he was outraged by the behaviour of English society, which had first petted and idolized him and then turned malignantly on him. He felt that such behaviour deserved punishment, and he knew how to inflict it. In the third place, he was compounded of so many elements that he had, sooner or later, to find a poetry which should contain them all. His earlier work reflected something in himself, especially his discontent and his longing for some dramatic splendour of circumstance and character. But in him the dreamer and the solitary were countered by the wit and the man of the world, and these could not be kept permanently out of his work. His creative spirit moved not on a single, straight line like that of Wordsworth or Shelley, but by devious and circuitous paths. But when he wrote **Don Juan,** he had found his direction. He wished to tell the truth as he saw it with all the paradoxes and contradictions of his nature. The result is an extremely personal document in which the whole of Byron is contained. The exaggerations and the fantasy of the story only serve to bring into prominence and set in a clear perspective his individual views of existence and his conflicting feelings about it.

Byron differs from the authentic Romantics not merely in his low estimate of the imagination but in the peculiar quality and power of his wit. Indeed, his wit rises largely from his loss of belief in the imagination. Once he ceased to believe in the reality or the relevance of his wilder inventions, he turned on himself and laughed. All these fine ideas, he seems to say, are rather ridiculous: we have only to look at them in practice to see what they mean and how unlike the reality is to the dream. . . . Even his emotions were at war with one another, and he would pass by sudden leaps from love to hatred and from admiration to contempt. He was a true child of his age in the uncertainty of his temperament and its wayward responses to experience. But since he was extremely intelligent and observant, he did not deceive himself into thinking that all his responses were right. He marked their inconsistencies and treated them with ironical disdain as part of our human imperfection. At the outset **Don Juan** is a criticism of the Romantic outlook because it says that human beings may have beautiful dreams but fail to live up to them.

In embarking on this realistic and satirical task, Byron was careful not to exaggerate on certain matters which concerned him. He saw that though he had largely outlived his wilder notions or seen their limitations in actual life, they still counted for something and could not altogether be rejected. His aim was to put them in a true setting, to show both their strength and their weakness, to assess them at their right worth. So his poem moves, as it were, on two lines. On the one hand he gives an abundance of delightful poetry to some subjects which the Romantics would approve and which still appealed to him. On the other hand he stresses with wit and irony the defects and contradictions and pretences which belong to these subjects. His acid temper works on his material and destroys anything false or pretentious in it, with the result that his Romantic longings are countered by a searching irony and are not allowed to claim too much for themselves. If the special successes of Wordsworth and Shelley were possible because humour never raised its head in the sacred places of their imagination, Byron's success comes from the opposite cause, that through humour he gave a new dimension and a greater truth to his creations. His poetry comes closer to the common man because it is more mixed and more complex than was allowed by his great contemporaries in their austere devotion to ideal worlds.

Byron's dual approach to his subject is reflected in a mannerism which is extremely common in *Don Juan.* He will begin to discourse seriously of a subject and speak nobly and finely about it, only to end with some calculated anticlimax, which makes us think that after all he does not care very much about what he has said. We almost feel that he has tricked us by making us respond to a serious topic, only to say that there is nothing in it. But this is not a correct analysis of what Byron does. When he treats of love or nature or liberty in this way, it is not because he has seen through them or wishes us to think that he has. The moods of admiration and of mockery exist concurrently in him and are merged in his outlook. As a poet he feels the one strongly and writes about it with all his powers, but as a man of the world he sees that other men may ridicule him, and he forestalls them by getting in the first laugh. His mockery is partly protective, partly the expression of a sincere conviction that few things in life are what they appear to be and that most things, however noble in some aspects, are ridiculous in others. Byron makes no attempt to harmonize the two points of view, but is content that life should be like this. Nor can we say that he is wrong. Laughter is entitled to have its way where it will, and nothing is ultimately the less serious because in some moods and in some times we make fun of it.

Byron differed from his Romantic contemporaries in the complex character of his response to experience. In his earlier poetry he had tried to look at things from almost a single point of view, but in *Don Juan* he abandoned this and exploited the whole range of his feelings. Whereas the other Romantics tended to follow a single principle in their approach to life, Byron followed his own wayward, changing moods. Just as the Romantics were in their own way perfectly true to themselves, so was Byron in his, but his nature was more complicated than theirs and could not be confined to a single channel. If he lacks their simplicity and the special power which comes with it, he makes up for this by the range of his tastes and the wonderful variety of his responses. Of course, the result is that he misses the peculiar intensity of the great Romantics, but he makes much of many themes which are beyond their reach, and gives in *Don Juan* a panorama of contemporary life which is much richer than anything they could have produced. Those who saw in *Don Juan* the epic of the age were not entirely wrong. It

touches many facets of actual life and gives an appropriate poetry to each. Byron had an omnivorous taste for experience and tried most things that came his way. The result is that his great poem provides a vivid and searching commentary on the contemporary scene.

Though Byron abandoned the Romantic view of the imagination and practised a new realistic art, he did not altogether abandon some themes and ideas which meant much to the Romantics. He seems rather to have applied his critical mind to their favourite topics and to have kept only what he thought to be real and true. If he had no sense of a transcendental order behind reality, he did not forsake all the subjects in which his contemporaries looked for it. Rather, he felt that matters like nature and love were sufficient in themselves to inspire poetry, and that he need not look beyond them for something else. (pp. 153-59)

Byron's position with regard to the other Romantics can be seen in his attitude towards nature. He loved it beyond question, and was perhaps happiest when he was alone with it. But his conception of nature lacked the mystery which Wordsworth, Coleridge, and Keats found in it. Or rather, he found a different mystery, more immediate and more homely, which absorbed his being and engaged his powers without opening doors into some unknown world. In his own way perhaps he had a religion of nature, and we need not disbelieve him when he says:

> My altars are the mountains and the Ocean,
> Earth—air—stars,—all that springs from the great
>   Whole,
> Who hath produced, and will receive the Soul. . . .

But though Byron might hold such a belief, it was not what inspired his poetry of nature. His genius was set to work not by a sense of immanent divinity but simply by what he saw and by the appeal which it had for him. (pp. 159-60)

A second Romantic subject to which Byron gave great attention is love. In this he was far more adventurous than Wordsworth and more experienced than Keats. If he had an equal in the importance which he attached to love, it was Shelley, but Shelley's view of it was quite different. For Shelley love is a union of souls, foreordained in some celestial scheme of predestination, and guided by the powers which move the universe. Byron saw nothing in such speculations. (pp. 165-66)

Though Byron felt the claims of ideal love and longed for it, he believed that it is inevitably frustrated by society and spoiled by the corrupt instincts of men. He shows how life blunts a man's finer feelings and obliterates even his memories of the purest love. He tempers his Romantic ideal with realistic considerations, but the result is that the ideal remains as alluring as before.

In his treatment of nature and of love, Byron shows what he gained from the common outlook of his age and what affinities he had with his Romantic contemporaries. But deeper perhaps than his interest in these two subjects was something else which lay at the centre of his being and determined much that was best in him. Byron was representative of his generation in his belief in individual liberty and his hatred of tyranny and constraint, whether exercised by individuals or by societies. (pp. 169-70)

In Byron the ideals of 1789 were still a living force. He saw that the free fulfilment of the human self would be possible only when the powerful obstacles of thrones and courts were removed, and that the cruelest of tyrannies is that which seeks to enslave the mind.

In the great appeals for liberty which ring through *Don Juan,* and in the attacks which Byron makes on its enemies, we can see the fundamental purpose of the poem. Byron set out to tell the truth, but his views were determined by a powerful and positive belief in the worth of individual man. He resembled Blake in his condemnation of senseless cruelty and of the hypocrisy which it breeds for its support. He was appalled by the habits of high society which claimed to do one thing and did another, and hid its vices under good manners and high-sounding principles. It evoked his sharpest irony:

> Oh for a *forty-parson power* to chant
> Thy praise, Hypocrisy! Oh for a hymn
> Loud as the virtues thou dost loudly vaunt,
> Not practise! Oh for trump of Cherubim! . . .

He hoped that by telling the truth he would awake the world to the evils which blighted its happiness, and expose its respected social system as a corrupt and corrupting sham. On the positive side, what he liked was the free play of the affections as he depicted it in his ideal love-scenes and in the care-free happiness of his Greek island. Much more than any other poet of the time, he had a keen appreciation of the natural man and thought his ordinary pleasures right and worthy of protection. He might not agree with the moral code of his age and his country, but he had his own values. Above all, he thought that truthfulness is a paramount duty, and that only through it can mankind be liberated from many ugly and degrading bonds.

Though *Don Juan* stands almost alone among poems of the Romantic age, it belongs to it and is in its own way a true product of it. Though Byron rejected the Romantic belief in the imagination, he was true to the Romantic outlook in his devotion to an ideal of man which may have been no more than a dream, but none the less kept his devotion despite the ordeal of facts and his own corroding scepticism. He knew how difficult this ideal was to realize and what powerful obstacles it met in the corruption of society and the contradictions of human nature. He made many discoveries, seldom creditable, about himself and other men, and that is why at times he seems cynical and disillusioned. Disillusioned perhaps he was, in the sense that he had few hopes that all his dreams would come true; but cynical he was not, at least about the matters which lay nearest to his heart. It was not their worth which he questioned, but the possibility of translating them into fact. Of course, he rejected any suggestion that he treated his task seriously, and no one could accuse him of being solemn. But serious he is, not merely when he speaks directly about his convictions, but when he presents them with irony and mockery. He made a bold attempt to put the whole of himself into *Don Juan,* and the result is something quite outside the range of his great contemporaries. The alternations of his moods are matched by the extraordinary range of his subjects. There seems to be almost no topic on which he has not got something interesting or witty or penetrating to say. The story is only half the poem; the other half is a racy commentary on life and manners. *Don Juan* is the record of a remarkable personality, a poet and a man of action, a dreamer and a wit, a great lover and a great hater, a man with many airs of the eighteenth century and yet wholly of the nineteenth, a Whig noble and a revolutionary democrat. The paradoxes of his nature are fully reflected in *Don Juan,* which is itself both a romantic epic and a realistic satire, and it owes the wide range

and abundant wealth of its poetry to the fact that Byron had in himself many Romantic longings, but tested them by truth and reality and remained faithful only to those which meant so much to him that he could not live without them. (pp. 171-73)

C. M. Bowra, "'Don Juan'," in his The Romantic Imagination, *1949. Reprint by Oxford University Press, 1961, pp. 149-73.*

ERNEST J. LOVELL, JR. (essay date 1957)

[*In his influential analysis of the structure of* Don Juan, *Lovell argues that the unifying principle of the poem is thematic and derives from Byron's recurring motif of the ironic contrast between appearance and reality. According to the critic, the irony resulting from Byron's continuous juxtaposition of actuality and illusion binds together all of the work's seemingly disparate and disconnected elements. In order to demonstrate the importance of this theme to the poem as a whole, Lovell traces the ironic contrasts and multiple self-deceptions that play a part in each of Juan's adventures. The critic also attempts to show the complexity and variety of tone inherent in Byron's approach to irony, which Lovell insists is never merely one-dimensional or repetitive. In contrast to earlier commentators, Lovell asserts that Byron's use of irony is a mature, profoundly considered, and sincere reflection of his philosophical beliefs. For an alternative viewpoint on the poem's unifying principle, see excerpt by Ridenour dated 1960.*]

The prerequisite to any consideration of the art of *Don Juan* is an analysis of its unity, denied or overlooked often enough to make its explication at this time a task of prime critical importance. Unity denied, the poem is reduced at once to a picaresque series of loosely jointed fragments, however brilliant. It must be clearly demonstrated, therefore, that there is a controlling, unifying principle at work throughout and, more particularly, that each main narrative episode, without exception, is somehow integral to a larger structure.

That unifying principle, I suggest, is the principle of thematic unity—here, the basically ironic theme of appearance versus reality—the difference between what things seem to be (or are said or thought to be) and what they actually are. Thematic unity established, it can then be seen readily that the most significant structure is a complex and carefully considered organization of ironically qualified attitudes and that manner and matter, consequently, are flawlessly fused; for irony is here integral to both theme and mode. It is inherent in the theme, hence it functions also as a necessary principle of narrative structure; and it is, at the same time, the primary device for manipulating manner or mode, to achieve a variety of richly mixed, fully orchestrated tonal qualities, which are themselves reconciled by and subordinated to the dominant theme. In terms of substance, this means that the diverse materials and the clash of emotions gathered together in the poem are harmonized finally by Byron's insight into the difference between life's appearance and its actuality, into the highly mixed motives which ordinarily control men and women, and into their genius for self-deception and rationalization.

A summary, then, of the consistently organic relation between episode and theme is the essential prelude to any purely stylistic discussion of *Don Juan.* Such a summary of the narrative or dramatic expression of theme will make clear, in the course of it, that Byron's irony is neither shallow, cynical, insincere, incidental, nor typically romantic, whether the latter type be understood as self-irony, self-pitying disillusion, or the willful destruction of the dramatic illusion. It is, instead, ordinarily the precise, necessary, fully orchestrated, and artistically functional expression of his own hard-won point of view, almost never a mere attitude adopted for its own sake, the tone of it almost never that of the simple irony of a reversed meaning.

At the risk of grossly oversimplifying the rich complexity of a great poem, then, one may begin by recalling the original hypocrisy of Juan's education, incomplete and thus false to the actual facts of life. Indeed, the entire poem may be read as a richly humorous investigation of the results stemming from a canting, maternal education which attempted to deny the very physical foundations of life. Because Juan has been so ill-educated, he is correspondingly ill-equipped to deal wth Julia, understanding neither his own emotional state nor hers, until too late, and so is sent ironically on his travels, "to mend his former morals," while Inez, undaunted, takes to teaching Sunday school. Before this, however, in a passage of far-reaching irony, Juan, transformed temporarily into a nympholeptic nature poet, has engaged in obscure Wordsworthian communings with nature, ludicrously deceiving himself and overspiritualizing the natural world. This self-delusion neatly balances and underlines that of Julia, who, overspiritualizing her passion, engages in the deliberately engendered hypocrisy of Platonic love. Here, as well as elsewhere, the appearance-versus-reality theme focuses on the moral danger of denying the physical basis of life and love, although Byron does not overlook the ideal end of either. The tone of all this comic but quite meaningful irony is deepened, finally, by the criminal hypocrisy of Inez in using her own son, unknown to him, to break up Julia's marriage. Indeed, one form taken by the philosophic irony underlying the first canto suggests that cant and hypocrisy may endanger the very continuity of civilized tradition. But the crowning stroke, after the irony of Julia's tirade while her husband searches her bedroom, is that she who has so viciously deceived herself with so much talk about spiritual love should be sent to live in a convent, where presumably she may contemplate the spiritual forever.

Byron points again at the wrongheadedness of such ill-founded love, hypocritically denying its own physical basis, when he allows Juan to become seasick in the midst of protesting his eternal devotion to Julia while rereading her pathetic letter. One may profitably compare Auden's dramatization of the tension between an asserted life-long fidelity in love and the mutabilities of physical experience, in "As I Walked Out One Evening." But if life and love must be viewed "really as they are," so also must death. When the ship's company would resort self-deceptively to prayers and "spirits" for identical reasons, to enable them to face the reality of drowning, Juan keeps them from the "spirit room," symbolically, at pistol point, while Byron without preaching attacks an easy crisis religion. The sentimental illusion of Julia's spiritual love, however, is dissipated for good with the appropriate final disposition of her famous letter. Its disposition is quite equal to that accorded Damian's note to May, in *The Merchant's Tale*, and it has much the same function—to strip the tinsel savagely and finally from false sentiment and reveal it for what it is. It is also at once grimly, ironically appropriate that the loser in the drawing of lots should be Juan's tutor, representative of that hypocritical race, instruments of Inez, who are responsible finally for Juan's being where he is. The chief satire of the shipwreck episode, however, is not directed against either the sentimental falsification of the great traditions or of the experience of love, but against the overspiritualization of nature, against "this cant about nature" preached gravely by those

who, concerned too exclusively with the "beauties of nature," would overlook its destructive aspects.

Byron's use of ironic qualification within a lyric context, to achieve the illusion of increased comprehensiveness and complexity, is especially noteworthy in his treatment of Haidée's romantic paradise, which could no more exist on half-truths than Milton's Garden of Innocence. It is also a significant paradox that Juan and Haidée, lacking a common language, communicate nevertheless more precisely than if they shared the same tongue. But the tone of the Haidée episode is much more nearly similar to that of *Romeo and Juliet*, qualified and enriched as it is by such discordant elements as those supplied by the witty Mercutio and the bawdy Nurse, than it is to that of *Paradise Lost*. Byron has qualified the lyricism of the episode explicitly with the character of Zoe, who cooked eggs and "made a most superior mess of broth" while Haidée's world turned back its clock to paradise.... Zoe, a graduate of "Nature's good old college," the perfect complement to the innocence of Haidée, pure "child of Nature," is thus an important ally in enabling Byron to avoid overspiritualizing the romantic love of Juan and Haidée and abstracting one element of the experience to imply that it is the whole.

> I'll tell you who they were, this female pair,
>   Lest they should seem princesses in disguise;
> Besides, I hate all mystery, and that air
>   Of clap-trap, which your recent poets prize;
> And so, in short, the girls they really were
>   They shall appear before your curious eyes,
> Mistress and maid; the first was only daughter
> Of an old man, who lived upon the water.

Space allowing, one might pursue here the full thematic and tonal implications of such ambiguities as those resulting from Byron's skillful fusion of tragedy, comedy, and satire in the character of Lambro (which permits, among other far-reaching effects, a subtle divorce of the Rousseauistic union of virtue and taste). Or one could explore Lambro's resemblance to the old Byronic hero as well as to Byron himself . . . and hence his implied kinship to Juan. The boy or child imagery descriptive of Juan and the mother imagery descriptive of Haidée . . . add another element of richness to the characterization. And the ironic frame, audaciously suspended and unnoticed over eighty-five stanzas . . . , which results from Lambro's unknown presence, encloses with telling effect the famous lyric on the isles of Greece (ironically enframed a second time by the Southeyan poet who sings it), the equally famous Ave Maria stanzas, and the stanzas to Hesperus. Here Byron achieves an effect quite as complex as that resulting in *The Waste Land* from Eliot's use of the same lines from Sappho, for more directly satiric purposes. Although it is impossible to discuss here these subtle, significant variations of tone and theme, or the consequent added dimensions, it may be said that nowhere else, perhaps, as in the third canto has Byron so skillfully manipulated the knife-edge dividing comedy and tragedy, or suggested more fully, within a successfully maintained romantic frame and setting, the ambiguities and rich complexities of actual existence.

Having successfully established and developed the central theme of appearance versus reality, Byron presumably felt free to permit himself a farcical variation on it: Juan disguised as a woman in a Turkish harem. But the harem episode also lays bare the romanticized Turkish travel book, the Oriental tale, and, perhaps, the romantic submissiveness of Byron's own early Oriental heroines. For Juan is literally a "slave to the passions.'' Who but Byron could have taken the old cliché, read it literally, and so have turned its seamy side inside out—to reveal the ridiculous nature and self-defeating characteristics of purely sensual love, allowing us, notwithstanding—by means of the magnificently mixed tone—to pity its symbol as a woman! But Gulbeyaz, the enslaved specialist in love who should have known better, also represents the final self-deception of one who thinks that love, the free gift of self-surrender, may be bought and commanded. And to the extent that love, Juan's chief interest and most serious occupation, is equated in the poem with all of life, Byron is saying, without heroics, that life itself is impossible without freedom, however attractive a loving or benevolent despot may seem to be, or whatever luxuries may seem to surround the "escape from freedom."

Byron prepared for his ironic demolition of modern war, "Glory's dream unriddled," in his portrait of the Sultan, disguised as lord of all he surveys except his latest favorite wife and the Empress Catherine, whose boudoir he so well might have graced, as Byron points out, to the furtherance of both "their own true interests." The two courts of the opposing rulers, each so seriously concerned with "love," form of course an ironic frame for the bloody siege of Ismael, the narrative vehicle of Byron's attack on the false heroics of war. Although the irony is too pervasive to describe, it may be recalled that the immediate theme is not an unqualified pacifism but the hypocrisy and cant of war ("the crying sin of this double-dealing and false-speaking time"), with especial attention to the unsavory paradox of a Christian war of conquest and the attendant Christian mercies of the invading Russians, shortly to become members of the Holy Alliance. But Byron's satire does not depend on a simple reversal of the hypocrisy of war; his tone is carefully qualified, as it ordinarily is, with the result that the satire is never thin or one-dimensional. Successfully avoiding the easy resolution of a comment on the general meaninglessness of war, he can thus frankly recognize its excitement, the intense loyalties and the heroism it evokes, and the paradoxical acts of generosity it calls forth.

Juan at the court of Catherine completes the ironic frame of the war cantos and allows Byron to play his own variation on the old theme of "to the brave the fair"—the sickening lust of the gentle sex to possess a uniform and see "Love turn'd a lieutenant of artillery"—only to show that such generous reward of the returning hero will debilitate him and that such a surrender of arms (to other arms) may well bring him nearer death, even, than his wars did. Meanwhile the relations between Catherine and Juan are without hypocrisy, and are known to all. Juan even has an official title. Gross as Catherine's appetites are, they are not so reprehensible as the hypocrisy of Inez's letter . . . , which serves the further purpose of recalling, without naming, Julia's hypocrisy of Platonic love and Byron's insistence on the necessity of recognizing the physical basis of love. The Catherine episode qualifies the latter insight by making the obvious point that the merely physical, lacking spiritual warmth, will sicken even the greatest lover and force him to more temperate climates.

As Juan moves on across the Continent, Byron ironically deflates the tradition of the picturesque tour . . . , chiefly by rhyming a roll call of famous cities and a list of natural resources. When Juan reaches England, where hypocrisy and cant can achieve a dazzling multiplicity of aspects, Byron's satiric exposition of the difference between appearance and reality rises, without shrillness, to its greatest heights. He reveals pretense to be the pervading rottenness of an entire culture—

beginning with the irony of the attempted highway robbery, shortly after Juan arrives in the land of freedom, law, and order, and closing with the magnificent final irony of the Duchess of Fitz-Fulke disguised as the ghost of the Black Friar, emblematic of a land where the sensual comes draped in the robes of the spiritual, while a country girl in a red cape is brought before the lord of the manor charged with immorality. It is a land where the wealthy, to escape the press of the city, crowd together in the country. Assembled in all their boredom and frivolity at Norman Abbey, weighty with the great traditions of the past, they may well remind us of Eliot's similarly ironic juxtaposition of richly traditional setting and spiritual poverty in *The Waste Land*. In Juan's England, even the food masquerades in foreign dress, fit nourishment for a hypocritical people. Things in *Don Juan*, then, are never what they seem, not even the title character, the "natural" man at home in every "artificial" society, the exile and wanderer never haunted by a sense of quest. He finds equilibrium in the "changeable" sex and his moments of eternity in the symbol of the physical here and now. He is the world's most famous lover, yet he never seduces a woman. Although he treads a rake's progress, he does so without becoming cynical or worldly minded. He is a man famous in love and war, yet a child in search of a mother (who will also be mistress and goddess), and he finds her, repeatedly, in woman after woman!

An effort, however inadequate, has already been made to indicate that the functional irony of *Don Juan* is seldom the simple irony of a reversed meaning. To abstract the meaning of the narrative in an attempt to suggest the pervasive unity of the main theme and establish the organic relation of each of the chief episodes to it, may suggest that some oversimplification has taken place. As a corrective, therefore, it may be well to say again that Byron repeatedly used irony as a qualifying device within the larger frame of his satire, and so saved it regularly from oversimplification, thinness, and monotony of tone. The point, which deserves to be emphasized, may be illustrated by a brief analysis of the richly mixed tone characteristic of Byron's feminine portraits. It is significant that *Don Juan* combines and reconciles within itself the extremes of the love poem and of the satire, mingling and fusing attitudes of almost pure approval and almost complete disapproval—at once a great hymn to love and a satire on women, and frequently concerned with the comedy of love. Thus the satire may merge so successfully with comedy or at other times with tragedy that it is often hardly recognizable as "serious" satire: seldom or never is it narrowly satiric or expressive of unqualified disapproval. The tone, in other words, is almost never "pure."

Consider Julia, for example. Is she a hypocritical self-deceiver viciously leading herself and Juan on with the cant of Platonic love, or is she a woman betrayed originally into marriage with an old man, led deliberately into a trap by Inez, and sentenced finally by society to a convent, to pay for a single indiscretion? Is she a tragically pathetic figure or a comically shrew-tongued termagant? Byron, it seems, can have it several ways at once, as he does also (though in different wise and reconciling other extremes) with Haidée, the island goddess who is also Juan's mistress, mother, and nurse, attended by the earthy figure of Zoe. There is also the richly ambiguous Lambro, at once an affectionately comic parody of the Byronic hero and the unwitting agent of tragedy, who sheds his own ambiguous light over the entire episode. Byron, of course, was quite aware of the romantic character of the Haidée episode, and so repeatedly qualified and enriched its tone with heterogeneous materials, creating an atmosphere of lyrical tenderness, but at the same time intellectually awake to the physical actualities. In the final tragedy he asserts the validity of the romantic vision, but he is aware too (as the violent shift in tone at IV, 74, indicates) that life must go on, as dangerous, as ludicrous, or as humiliating as ever, despite tragedy or the death of romance. Thus Byron was able to explore fully the experience of ideal, romantic love without ever forcing his romanticism. Although he bases the dream squarely on a physical foundation, supporting and guarding the lyrical motif with numerous discordant elements, his is not in any sense the self-contradictory attitude of romantic irony. The romance is not canceled out but intensified.

Byron's treatment of Gulbeyaz offers an instructive contrast to that of Haidée and illustrates how skillfully he can qualify and develop a tone which is basically comic. The Sultana, who loses the game of love by reason of the very device which made it possible for her to win, Juan's disguise, is the woman comically scorned by Juan in petticoats. But she is at the same time genuinely pathetic in her frustrated tears, which turn, note, metaphysically and murderously, into a tempest that nearly drowns Juan finally, sewed up in a sack. (Byron develops a tear-tempest figure over several stanzas, V, 135-37.)

In the portrait of Adeline, however, neither predominantly romantic as Haidée nor comic as Gulbeyaz, but present for purposes of pure satire, Byron uses ironic qualification with perhaps even greater skill. Here his chief concern was social satire, focusing on English hypocrisy, and Adeline, clearly, was to be one of its chief exponents. We see her entertaining her country guests in a bid for their votes, then ridiculing them when they have left. We see her indeed as acquiescent hostess to all the hypocrisy and pretense assembled at Norman Abbey; and we see her inevitably deceiving herself, with the subtle deceit of an ill-understood friendship for Juan. But in ironic qualification of all this deception, she has most of the solid virtues and all the charm of the polished society which she reflects and symbolizes at its best. And, paradoxically, it is this very quality of polished smoothness which gives rise, simultaneously, to Byron's satire and to his sympathetic approval. The coldly polished manners of these frozen Englishmen, with their philosophy of *nil admirari*, reduce them to a comically bored, colorless sameness; but it is the same quality of self-discipline which accounts for the achievements and virtues of Adeline, making her a perfectly gracious hostess, a musician, and a poetess, able to admire Pope without being a bluestocking. Despite the effort required and the vacancy in her heart, she can love her lord, nevertheless, "conjugal, but cold." And although she is falling in love with Juan, she refuses to admit it even to herself. But such restraint and self-discipline, Byron knew, is won at the price of bottling up and suppressing the emotions beneath a layer of ice, thus doubly distilling them and ironically intensifying their explosive qualities, enabling them the more effectively to break down the cold and icy walls of polished restraint. . . . Even Adeline's hypocrisy with her country guests arises out of a kind of sincerity, her *mobilité*. Thus recognizing the complex origins of hypocritical social conduct at the very time that he is attacking hypocrisy, achieving a triumph of mixed tone, Byron can acknowledge the attractiveness of Adeline, one of his most subtle projections of the appearance-versus-reality theme. He elevates her to something like a symbol of one aspect of the English character, and allows her, "the fair most fatal Juan ever met," his richly endowed and highly ambiguous "Dian of the Ephesians" . . . , to merge finally, with his other goddesses of love, into the complex and all-embracing figure of "Alma Venus Genetrix." . . . (pp. 131-40)

Don Juan does therefore show a significant thematic unity. Its most significant structure is a considered organization of attitudes expressed by means of a rich variety of ironically qualified tones, and each of the chief narrative episodes bears an organic relation, clear but subtly varied, to the larger theme. (p. 140)

> *Ernest J. Lovell, Jr., "Irony and Image in Byron's 'Don Juan'," in* The Major English Romantic Poets: A Symposium in Reappraisal, *Clarence D. Thorpe, Carlos Baker, Bennett Weaver, eds., Southern Illinois University Press, 1957, pp. 129-48.*

GEORGE M. RIDENOUR (essay date 1960)

[*Ridenour's* The Style of "Don Juan" *is considered one of the most important studies of the poem. According to Oscar Santucho, "besides being an astonishingly good critical treatment of* Don Juan *. . . , Ridenour's book is also remarkably seminal in its suggestions of methodology, issues, and main lines of study that will be followed during the sixties." In the excerpt below, Ridenour argues that the unity and coherence of* Don Juan *result from Byron's recurring use of the Christian doctrine of the Fall as a metaphor. According to the critic, the outwardly chaotic and conflicting ingredients of the poem are linked together by a regular series of images representing the moral and artistic descent of humankind from a state of grace. In his outline of Byron's portrayal of both art and nature in terms of the metaphor of the Fall, Ridenour explores what he views as the poem's paradoxical vision of existence.*]

One of the principal obstacles to an appreciation of ***Don Juan*** on the part of many serious readers of poetry in our day has been what seems to them the irresponsible nature of Byron's satire. They feel that, clever as the poem undoubtedly is in parts, taken as a whole it is immature, exhibitionistic, lacking in integrity. This has caused distress on both moral and aesthetic grounds. But though it is not prudery to refuse assent to the implications of the poet's vision, it would be unjust to deny due praise to the style of that vision—its special grace and swagger. Certain obvious faults in the manner of the poem may be frankly conceded. Byron is sometimes careless, and there are times when he is obviously showing off. Sometimes, though rarely in ***Don Juan***, he is guilty of bad taste.

But it is not these things, I suspect, that constitute the real problem. It has more to do with the uncertainty of the satirist's point of view as compared, say, with Horace or Pope. Satirists are normally conservatives and are proceeding at least ostensibly on the basis of a generally accepted (or in any case familiar) system of norms, principles, and attitudes. That this is not true of Byron in the way in which it is true of Horace or Pope (though the consistency of both is liable to some criticism) is clear enough. Byron is notoriously a rebel, and rebels have not enjoyed high critical esteem lately.

But Byron is not a consistent rebel. There is, for example, his apparently snobbish insistence on Juan's birth and breeding. And his views on women would hardly commend themselves to emancipated spirits. But then what were Byron's views on women (or aristocrats)? They seem to undergo such remarkable shifts in the course of sixteen cantos that it is not easy to say. The apparent lack of structure in terms of which these shifting points of view can be assimilated is, I gather, the basic problem of ***Don Juan*** for the modern reader. It is not so much "What does he stand for?" (that is not always self-evident in the most traditional of satires), as "How do his various professions fit together?" In short, is *Don Juan* a chaos or a unity?

The question is natural and not unanswerable. The answer, however, cannot be in terms of a system. . . . Byron had a temperamental aversion to system. He is not to be categorized either intellectually or poetically. But this is not to say that his vision is incoherent. It is, in fact, elaborately coherent. And it is with what seem to me the dominant modes of this coherence that I shall be largely concerned.

In the first place, Byron, rebel that he is, is perfectly willing to make use of traditional concepts for his own ends. Some elements of the Christian myth especially commended themselves to him both as man and as poet. Whether it was the result of the Calvinistic influences of Byron's Scottish childhood, whether it was personal experience, aesthetic, the product of his own experience, or any combination of these factors, Byron seems throughout his life to have had peculiar sympathy with the concept of natural depravity. Lovell has asserted that "Byron held consistently to a belief in the existence of sin and the humanistic ideal of virtue as self-discipline. The fall of man—however he resented the injustice of its consequences—is the all-shadowing fact for him." Whatever one may think of this as a biographical generalization, it is clearly true of the imagination of the poet of *Don Juan*—with the reservation that in the poem the Christian doctrine of the Fall is a *metaphor* which Byron uses to express his own personal vision. In *Childe Harold* . . . he developed an original reading of the Prometheus myth for similar purposes.

The myth of the Fall, then, is an important means of organizing the apparently contradictory elements of *Don Juan*. In the context of Byron's reading of the myth, Helene Richter's and William J. Calvert's interpretation of Byron in terms of a classic-romantic paradox [see excerpt dated 1935] and Antonio Porta's very similar Rousseau-Voltaire split are seen as elements in a vision not readily to be categorized under any of these headings.

Byron introduces Canto IV with a stanza on the perils of poetry:

> Nothing so difficult as a beginning
>   In poesy, unless perhaps the end;
> For oftentimes when Pegasus seems winning
>   The race, he sprains a wing, and down we tend,
> Like Lucifer when hurled from Heaven for sinning;
>   Our sin the same, and hard as his to mend,
> Being Pride, which leads the mind to soar too far,
> Till our own weakness shows us what we are. . . .
>   (pp. 19-22)

What one immediately notices is the connection between this stanza and the imagery of flight we have met with in the Dedication. One thinks particularly of Blackbird Southey "overstraining" himself and "tumbling downwards like the flying fish," or even more, perhaps, of the ominous reference to the Tower of Babel. Here again a fall results from the attempt at a flight beyond one's proper powers. And, indeed, the motif is recurrent throughout the poem. At the beginning of Canto XI, for example, Byron describes the "spirit," some of whose metaphysical flights he had been discussing, as a liquor (a "draught," "Heaven's brandy") which is a bit too heady for the "brain." . . . Metaphysical speculation is a kind of drunkenness, and the image is one of genial diminution. Then, with a characteristically Byronic modulation of the image of "indisposition," he adds:

> For ever and anon comes Indigestion
>   (Not the most "dainty Ariel"), and perplexes
> Our soarings with another kind of question. . . .

Man's loftiest flights are subject to the unpredictable activities of the digestive system. (The further modulation of the image in stanzas 5 and 6, by which physical ills, just now seen as hazards to spiritual flight, become incentives to religious orthodoxy, strikes me as adroit.) The passage is only one of many emphasizing man's physical nature and the folly of forgetting it or trying to pretend that it is other than it is.

But both the stanza on poets and the lines on metaphysics differ in at least one important way from those passages in the Dedication which also make use of the image of flight. In the Dedication, while the satire is not merely personal, it does take the form of an attack on a real individual or group. This is a common device of satire, and one which Byron continues to use throughout the poem. But in *Don Juan* the satiric implications of the image are characteristically generalized. It is "we" who fall, and it is "*our* soarings" that are perplexed. Byron is making a comment on human beings in general, on human nature. And if the comment is not remarkably optimistic, neither is it broodingly grim.

The point is of particular importance with regard to the first passage ("Nothing so difficult, etc."). For what Byron is speaking of here is not merely a quality of bad poets; it is something that he sees as characteristic of *all* poets, including himself. A poet, to earn the name, *must* sometimes soar. How seriously he takes this may be seen from one of his most extended (and savage) attacks on Wordsworth. As usual, in order to appreciate properly a particular passage of *Don Juan*, it is necessary to see how it fits its context. The passage in question, stanzas 98-100 of Canto III, stands as the climax of a variation on one of the most important themes of the poem, the social significance of language (cf. the Dedication). The section has been initiated with the song of the island laureate, "The Isles of Greece." Here poetry is fulfilling its proper function (as it does not, we are told, in the case of Laureate Southey), serving the real interests of society rather than merely flattering its rulers. For

> . . . words are things, and a small drop of ink,
>   Falling like dew, upon a thought, produces
> That which makes thousands, perhaps millions,
>   think. . . .

Furthermore, in order to fulfill its social function poetry must be socially accessible. Hence the relevance of the attacks on Wordsworth's obscurity:

> He there [in the *Excursion*] builds up a formidable dyke
>   Between his own and others' intellect. . . .

These, then, are the most important considerations lying behind the stanzas on Wordsworth with which the section concludes:

> We learn from Horace, "Homer sometimes sleeps;"
>   We feel without him,—Wordsworth sometimes
>   wakes,—
> To show with what complacency he creeps
>   With his dear "*Waggoners*," around his lakes.
> He wishes for "a boat" to sail the deeps—
>   Of Ocean?—No, of air; and then he makes
> Another outcry for "a little boat,"
> And drivels seas to set it well afloat.
>
> If he must fain sweep o'er the ethereal plain,
>   And Pegasus runs restive in his "Waggon,"
> Could he not beg the loan of Charles's Wain?

Or pray Medea for a single dragon?
Or if, too classic for his vulgar brain,
He feared his neck to venture such a nag on,
And he must needs mount nearer to the moon,
Could not the blockhead ask for a balloon?

"Pedlars," and "Boats," and "Waggons!" Oh! ye
    shades
Of Pope and Dryden, are we come to this?
That trash of such sort not alone evades
    Contempt, but from the bathos' vast abyss
Floats scumlike uppermost, and these Jack Cades
    Of sense and song above your graves may hiss—
The "little boatman" and his *Peter Bell*
Can sneer at him who drew "Achitophel!" . . .

(pp. 22-4)

The first complaint made about Wordsworth is that he not only does not soar, he creeps. And he creeps around lakes, permitting Byron to emphasize his alleged provinciality and limitation by repeating the lake-ocean contrast of the Dedication. But this lake-ocean contrast is present only by implication in the explicit ocean-air contrast. While any flight is necessarily through the air, Byron is here taking advantage of its associations of triviality and bluff in order to discredit the flight of a poet whose characteristic motion is that of creeping around lakes. Byron's playing with the common Scriblerian notion of the proximity of the high and the low is brought out even more clearly by the highly Swiftian comments on the scum floating to the top "from the bathos' vast abyss."

But the satirist is also offended at the vehicle chosen for the poet's flight—"a little boat." There is something essentially improper, apparently, in a poet's soaring off in a boat, especially a little one. Perhaps he feels the symbol too private (cf. the final contrast between the fanciful *Peter Bell* and the public, socially relevant "Achitophel"), or, perhaps merely childish. It is not, at any rate, a proper bardic conveyance. Real poets ride the winged horse Pegasus (a persistent image in *Don Juan*, and an important one). Wordsworth's choice of a little boat, the satirist suggests, is a tacit admission of poetic inadequacy. Pegasus is far too spirited a steed for him: "He feared his neck to venture such a nag on."

In contrast to the creeping and floating of Wordsworth, the satirist bends and soars. The first refers to the natural gesture of the truthful muse, who is scrupulous in following her sources:

A brave Tartar Khan—
Or "Sultan," as the author (to whose nod
In prose I bend my humble verse) doth call
This chieftain—somehow would not yield at all. . . .

And this is no means the only time that we shall be reminded of the famous couplet from the "Epistle to Dr. Arbuthnot":

That not in Fancy's Maze he wander'd long,
But stoop'd to Truth, and moraliz'd his song. . . .

(pp. 24-6)

In contrast both with the creeping and floating Wordsworth and the bending of the satiric muse is the soaring poet of the beginning of Canto X:

In the wind's eye I have sailed, and sail; but for
    The stars, I own my telescope is dim;
But at the least I have shunned the common shore,
    And leaving land far out of sight, would skim
The Ocean of Eternity: the roar

Of breakers has not daunted my slight, trim,
    But *still* sea-worthy skiff; and she may float
Where ships have foundered, as doth many a boat. . . .

One notices first of all the elements common to this stanza and the section on Wordsworth. Here again there is flight described in terms of floating in a boat. But what were there images of contempt are here images expressive of a disarming modesty (an old rhetorical shift particularly valuable to the satirist, whose pose inevitably implies pretensions of personal merit). To be sure, he presents himself as an explorer of the Ocean (cf. the ocean-lake contrast) of Eternity, but then he owns that he has no very clear view of the stars, and that his "slight, trim, / But *still* sea-worthy skiff" merely "skims" the ocean, floating on its surface. It is important to notice that while he makes no very extravagant claims as to his discoveries on the "Ocean of Eternity," he does claim some credit for having undertaken the voyage. He even asserts that it is of social (or generally human) utility, a point to which we shall return.

We are now perhaps in a position to profit from another look at the passage from which we set out:

Nothing so difficult as a beginning
    In poesy, unless perhaps the end;
For oftentimes when Pegasus seems winning
    The race, he sprains a wing, and down we tend,
Like Lucifer, when hurled from Heaven for sinning;
    Our sin the same, and hard as his to mend,
Being Pride, which leads the mind to soar too far,
Till our own weakness shows us what we are. . . .

The passage is, as I shall try to show, a particularly clear statement of one version of the poem's central paradox. For the moment it is enough to see how Byron is complicating the traditional images of flight and fall. It is not merely that the satirist's attacks on particular kinds of poetry and particular literary figures are elements in a more general criticism of a particular state of society (as the island Laureate puts it: "The heroic lay is tuneless now— / The heroic bosom beats no more!"). But Byron has associated the poetic "flight" with diabolic pride, and he means it. Whatever may have been his own personal convictions regarding the myth of the war in heaven, it serves the poet as an indispensable metaphor for some concepts and attitudes which seem to have been very important to him and which are of central importance for a proper understanding of his greatest poem. The movement of the thought is roughly as follows: to be a poet is a fine and valuable thing; poets, to be worthy the name, must essay the grand manner (soar); but soaring is a manifestation of the prime sin. It is this kind of paradox that Byron's reading of the myth of the Fall is designed to sustain and justify.

Byron most commonly, however, plays with the notion of fall in terms of the Fall of Man:

We have
Souls to save, since Eve's slip and Adam's fall,
    Which tumbled all mankind into the grave,
Besides fish, beasts, and birds. . . .

We have here at the very least an admission of man's radical imperfection, presented in terms of the Christian myth. Eve slipped, Adam fell, and mankind became subject to death. And—this is very important—not mankind alone. "Fish, beasts, and birds" shared the curse of death placed on our First Parents. Nature, too, fell. We live in a fallen world.

This fact may help explain Byron's notoriously ambiguous attitude toward the arts of civilization. They are at one time emblems of man's degeneration from an original paradisal state; at another they embody high human values. We are told, for example, that Haidée

> . . . was one
> Fit for the model of a statuary
>   (A race of mere imposters, when all's done—
> I've seen much finer women, ripe and real,
> Than all the nonsense of their stone ideal). . . .

And of the Sultana we learn that she was "so beautiful that Art could little mend her." . . . Here, of course, there is the implication that whatever might be true of Gulbeyaz, there are women whom art might conceivably improve. But then we are told, with reference to Juan's dress uniform at the court of Catherine the Great, that "Nature's self turns paler, / Seeing how Art can make her work more grand." . . . The statements, taken in themselves, are clearly contradictory. But again this is not indecision or confusion. Not only do both points of view have their validity, but Byron supplies us with a consistent metaphor in terms of which the fact may be contemplated. That basis is again the Christian myth of the Fall.

Four stanzas preceding the last passage quoted, Byron writes of the new Fall of Man that will occur when, according to Cuvier, the earth will next undergo one of its periodic convulsions and a new world is formed (Byron seems to think temptation integral to creation, and fall the inevitable consequence of temptation). He speaks with some compassion of

> . . . these young people, just thrust out
> From some fresh Paradise, and set to plough,
> And dig, and sweat, and turn themselves about,
>   And plant, and reap, and spin, and grind, and sow,
> Till all the arts at length are brought about,
>   Especially of War and taxing. . . .

The development of the arts of civilization, of which the art of poetry is exemplary, is clearly a consequence of the Fall, part of the taint of Original Sin.

I have thus far been stressing the negative side of the paradox. It is time now to imitate the poet himself and shift the emphasis to the positive pole. This change in emphasis may conveniently be considered with regard to the four beautifully modulated octaves with which Byron opens Canto X. He is here making explicit the mythic presuppositions in terms of which he is proceeding:

> When Newton saw an apple fall, he found
>   In that slight startle from his contemplation—
> 'Tis *said* (for I'll not answer above ground
>   For any sage's creed or calculation)—
> A mode of proving that the Earth turned round
>   In a most natural whirl, called "gravitation;"
> And this is the sole mortal who could grapple,
> Since Adam—with a fall—or with an apple.
>
> Man fell with apples, and with apples rose,
>   If this be true; for we must deem the mode
> In which Sir Isaac Newton could disclose
>   Through the then unpaved stars the turnpike road,
> A thing to counterbalance human woes:
>   For ever since immortal man hath glowed
> With all kinds of mechanics, and full soon
> Steam-engines will conduct him to the moon. . . .
>
> (pp. 26-30)

The concluding couplet of the first octave suggests that ever since the Fall of Adam man has suffered from a lack, a something wanting or a something wrong, with which Newton was the first successfully to contend. The reference is, of course, to the traditional notion of aberrations entering into a perfect creation with the Fall of Man, the crown of creation. Man, who in his paradisal state had ruled all things, now becomes subject to the vicissitudes of a fallen natural order. Byron sees a symbol of this state of subjection in natural man's helplessness before the law of gravity. The idea of fall, then, which we have already examined in connection with the Scriblerian concept of bathos, is here given much greater range by being associated with the force which in the physics of Byron's day was regarded as the governing principle of the natural order. As Byron sees it, since the Fall men naturally fall (morally and physically). The imaginative concept is very close to Simone Weil's notion of sin: "When . . . a man turns away from God, he simply gives himself up to the law of gravity."

The second octave is most explicit: "Man fell with apples, and with apples rose." In a celebrated passage of his journal Baudelaire observes that true civilization "does not consist in gas or steam or turn-tables. It consists in the diminution of the traces of Original Sin." But while Byron would probably not argue with this definiton of civilization, his own views are rather more catholic. In his eyes gas and steam and turn-tables are legitimate and even important means for "the diminution of the traces of Original Sin." They are civilization's way of contending with and rising above a fallen nature. Scientific advance of the kind represented by Newton is "A thing to counterbalance human woes." And while there is mild irony in the picture of immortal man glowing over his gadgets and his steam engine to the moon, Byron's awareness of absurdity is clearly a complicating rather than a negating element.

Yet Byron is not merely (or even principally) interested in scientific advance. The art he is most concerned with is, as we have seen, the art of poetry:

> And wherefore this exordium?—Why, just now,
>   In taking up this paltry sheet of paper,
> My bosom underwent a glorious glow,
>   And my internal spirit cut a caper:
> And though so much inferior, as I know,
>   To those who, by the dint of glass and vapour,
> Discover stars, and sail in the wind's eye,
> I wish to do as much by Poesy.
>
> In the wind's eye I have sailed, and sail; but for
>   The stars, I own my telescope is dim;
> But at the least I have shunned the common shore,
>   And leaving land far out of sight, would skim
> The Ocean of Eternity: the roar
>   Of breakers has not daunted my slight, trim,
> But *still* sea-worthy skiff; and she may float
> Where ships have foundered, as doth many a boat. . . .
>
> (pp. 30-2)

We have met this last stanza before. Here the poet, who has been discussing scientific investigation, applies the image of exploration to his own pursuit. If Newton was an explorer, so too in his modest way is he. This is a corollary to what he has said about the necessity of poetic "flight," the social utility of poetry, and the importance of a poet's rising above provinciality. The poet, who has been speaking of how science helps repair the faults in nature that arose as a result of the Fall, announces that it is his aim "to do the same by Poesy."

Poetry too, then, is being seen as not merely emotional relief (though it is that) or relief from ennui (though it is that too), but ''A thing to counterbalance human woes,'' an agent of civilization in its struggle for ''the diminution of the traces of Original Sin.''

The point is made only slightly less explicitly in the first two stanzas of Canto VII:

> O Love! O Glory! what are ye who fly
>   Around us ever, rarely to alight?
> There's not a meteor in the polar sky
>   Of such transcendent and more fleeting flight.
> Chill, and chained to cold earth, we lift on high
>   Our eyes in search of either lovely light;
> A thousand and a thousand colours they
> Assume, then leave us on our freezing way.
>
> And such as they are, such my present tale is,
>   A nondescript and ever-varying rhyme,
> A versified Aurora Borealis,
>   Which flashes o'er a waste and icy clime.
> When we know what all are, we must bewail us,
>   But ne'ertheless I hope it is no crime
> To laugh at *all* things—for I wish to know
> *What*, after *all*, are *all* things—but a *show?* . . .
>
>   (pp. 32-3)

The claims here are rather more modest, but the principle is the same. Byron's ''wasteland'' symbol is that of a frozen world. Since Byron sometimes believed in Cuvier's theory of periodic destruction and recreation of the earth, and since on at least one occasion he conceived the annihilation of life on our world as the result of freezing (in the fragment ''Darkness''), he may be thinking of a kind of progressive chill leading to final annihilation. At any rate the ''icy clime'' is not a cultural wasteland. It is presented rather as a state natural to man, an inevitable symbol of a fallen world. Man is ''chained to cold earth'' (like Prometheus on ''icy Caucasus'') and is able to alleviate his sufferings only by his own efforts—by love and glory and, as we learn in the second stanza, by poetry. This very poem is presented as an attempt to give color, form, warmth to a world naturally colorless, indefinite, and chill.

The poem, like the meteor, exercises a double function. First of all, it sheds light (''flashes o'er a waste and icy clime''), the light that reveals the rather grim truth about the state of man on earth (''when we know what all are, we must bewail us''). But the poem, even while revealing the melancholy state of man, helps him to come to terms with it. The act of exposing the sad reality exposes the absurdity of the pretense that it is otherwise, while providing through art a means of dealing with it without the hypocrisy and self-deception integral to Love and Glory:

> Dogs, or men!—for I flatter you in saying
>   That ye are dogs—your betters far—ye may
> Read, or read not, what I am now essaying
>   To show ye what ye are in every way.
> As little as the moon stops for the baying
>   Of wolves, will the bright Muse withdraw one ray
> From out her skies—then howl your idle wrath!
> While she still silvers o'er your gloomy path. . . .

This I take to be the true rationale behind the alleged ''cynicism'' of *Don Juan*. It is thus a prime expression of the positive pole of the paradox whose negative aspects we have already examined.

The argument thus far, then, would run something as follows. Byron, in developing the world of *Don Juan,* makes use of the Christian concepts of· sin, fall, and the fallen state. He is writing a poem in terms of such a world. The poem is presumably going to be of help with regard to man's fallen condition. But at the same time, like all products of civilization, the act of writing poetry holds in itself the danger of fall. It inevitably implies, for example, participation in the original sin of pride and revolt. Or, to reverse the emphasis (as Byron does), there is ''evil'' in art, but there is also a good which can help at least to overcome the evil. And this paradox is based on a still profounder one, a vision of the radically paradoxical nature of ''the way things are''—that is, of nature itself. For, as we have seen, in the world of *Don Juan* nature is fallen and stands in need of redemption. And at the same time, nature is valuable both in itself and as a norm against which a corrupt civilization may be exposed. For the Christian, nature is fallen and must be redeemed. But though fallen, nature is God's creation and must of necessity retain the imprint of the Creator (hence the possibility of ''natural theology''). (pp. 34-5)

[As I observed in the preface,] ''The underlying principle of Byron's universe seems to be that its elements are in their different ways both means of grace and occasions of sin.'' Now the religious image is misleading if one understands it in too moral a sense. The point is not that a thing is good if used properly and bad if used improperly. It simply *is* both good and bad. But it is *good* and *bad*. I make use of theological terminology because Byron does, and he does so because it is expressively necessary for him. The universe, as Byron sees it, is not merely inconveniently arranged, or not arranged at all and so humanly neutral. There is, from man's viewpoint at least, something profoundly wrong about it and about his place in it. But at the same time there is generous provision of means and opportunities of dealing with this wrongness and making it humanly right. But these means and opportunities have a way of being closely allied with the primary causes and manifestations of the wrongness. All this is not what *Don Juan* is about. It is about coming to terms with such a world. But something very like this is what *Don Juan* presupposes. (p. 49)

> *George M. Ridenour, in his* The Style of ''Don Juan,'' *1960. Reprint by Archon Books, Hamden, CT, 1969, 168 p.*

M. K. JOSEPH (essay date 1964)

[*Joseph explores the implications of the various narrative personas in* Don Juan. *The critic maintains that the variety of narrative perspectives allows Byron to simultaneously tell the story of his protagonist and comment on the events from several points of view. Joseph identifies three separate levels of narration, including the* ''narrative centered on Juan,'' *the* ''narrator, who is a partly fictitious persona,'' *and* ''Byron himself.'' *The interaction between each of these levels, Joseph asserts, gives the poem its richness and complexity. He also examines the relation and significance of the different levels of narration in various episodes of the poem, demonstrating how their combined effect transcends their individual limitations to form an intricate dialogue of contrasting views on the human condition.*]

In *Beppo,* Byron had already identified and practised the device of comic digression. In *Don Juan,* he exploits it to the full and one of the features of the poem that may strike us at first as merely comic or even whimsical is the whole technique of commenting on the writing as it goes, digressing about digressions, apologising or explaining, and generally teasing the reader by involving him in the fiction, and then withdrawing from it with the reminder that it *is* only fiction after all.

> . . . But to my subject—let me see—what was it?
>   Kind reader! pass
>   This long parenthesis: I could not shut
> It sooner for the soul of me, and class
>   My faults even with your own! which meaneth, Put
> A kind construction upon them and me:
> But *that* you won't—then don't—I am not less free.
>
> 'Tis time we should return to plain narration,
>   And thus my narrative proceeds. . . .
>
>   However, 'tis no time to chat
> On general topics: poems must confine
>   Themselves to Unity, like this of mine.
>
>   . . . I'm ''at my old lunes''—digression, and forget
>   The Lady Adeline Amundeville. . . .

This is a method already implicit in the comic epic, and Fielding's introductory chapters in *Tom Jones* had already mastered it in prose, claiming the right to comment as he pleased on life and literature—

> Reader, I think proper, before we proceed any further together, to acquaint thee, that I intend to digress, through this whole history, as often as I see occasion; of which I am myself a better judge than any pitiful critic whatever.

And Sterne, who also equated writing with ''conversation'', provided Byron with an example of digression used even more pervasively and informally, as a major part of the structure of the book—

> . . . in all my digressions . . . there is a masterstroke of digressive skill, the merit of which has all along, I fear, been overlooked by my reader . . . and it is this: That tho' my digressions are all fair, as you observe,—and that I fly off from what I am about, as far, and as often too, as any writer in *Great Britain;* yet I constantly take care to order affairs so that my main business not stand still in my absence.
>
>   .   .   .   .
>
> Digressions, incontestably, are the sunshine; they are the life, the soul of reading!—take them out of this book, for instance,—you might as well take the book along with them;—one cold eternal winter would reign in every page of it; restore them to the writer;—he steps forth like a bridegroom,—bids All-hail; brings in variety, and forbids the appetite to fail.

Don Juan was, in fact, described by some as ''a *Tristram Shandy* in rhyme''; but Hazlitt, in noting this, perceptively added that ''it is rather a poem written about itself''.

It is, in fact, characteristic of much great art to be ''about itself'' in this way. It bounds and impersonalises itself by insisting on its own nature, not by trying to sustain an illusion; or perhaps we should say that the illusion is so persistent that it survives even when the sleight-of-hand is revealed. All art is about life: all art is about art. These statements are equally and simultaneously true. *One* of the main things that art does is to reflect on itself—as in Hamlet's speech to the players, or

A portrait of Byron in Venice in 1818.

the defence of the religious epic in *Paradise Lost,* or the chinese-box structure of *Les Faux-Monnayeurs,* or the sections on language in the *Four Quartets,* or (in this case) the digressions in *Don Juan*.

The most perfect examples are to be found in certain types of painting, in which the picture becomes, as it were, its own *event*. The grandest and most moving of these is perhaps *Las Meniñas* of Velasquez, in which the painter's studio is itself the scene and subject, the recorder is himself part of what he records. The princess, the dwarfs, the attendants are arrested in a moment whose transient nature is emphasised by the fact that Velasquez himself is shown recording it. It moves us because it is both transient and permanent, remote and present. Such is, in a very pure form, the method by which art reinforces itself by insisting on what it is; and such art must be painted (literally or figuratively) from a mirror.

In *Don Juan,* then, we are conscious of two or possibly three levels—there is the picaresque narrative centred on Juan; there is the narrator, who is a partly fictitious *persona;* and, as a possible third level, there is Byron himself. By distinguishing them in this way, we can keep the actual personality of Byron from obtruding into a critical estimate of the poem. It is a strong and complex personality, and is subject to quite conflicting interpretations; it can be taken as that of a vain and timid poseur (as in Fairchild or Erdman) or of a kind of secular messiah (as in Wilson Knight). The treatment of the personality in the poetry, which has been taken by John Wain as ''a short cut to arriving at a sense of his own tangible existence'', is for Paul West [see *NCLC,* Vol. 2] part of an attempt to repudiate, and even to repudiate his repudiation—''he was lonely early on; and, late, he feared even to cherish the principle of elimination itself—for fear of being typed once again''. It is W. W. Robson, in his excellent lecture, who effectively reconciles and disposes of both by pointing out that, characteristically, Byron achieves the feat of simultaneously playing a role and being aware of it—

The Byronic predicament may not be simply or wholly what it purports to be; but to give both its illusion of itself, and its reality, is a remarkable achievement.

And this process of simultaneous self-dramatisation and self-detachment finds its realisation in the dissociation of hero and narrator in **Don Juan**. In the half-serious forecasts he made concerning the continuation of the poem—the "Werther-faced man", cavalier servente, Anacharsis Clootz, and so on—it is notable that Byron forecasts the use of a method which he does not exploit in the poem as it stands. Juan acquires experience, and takes on (physically at least) the character of his surroundings; but, whatever Byron may have intended, he is not an *intellectual* chameleon, like Wieland's *Agathon:* "He appeared to be alternately a devout enthusiast, a Platonist, a Republican, a Hero, a Stoic, a Voluptuary; yet he was neither of all these, though at different times he passed through these several changes, and received a shade from each of them." Juan encounters a wide variety of attitudes to life, but does not impersonate them. He experiences love in multitudinous aspects, natural disaster, slavery, war, the court, the aristocracy, while remaining fundamentally a rather pleasant and well-behaved young man, exceptional only in his power to arouse the desires of woman, and only just beginning to be shadowed by experience, "*blasé* and *gâté*".

The essential method of the poem is, again, something different from that of the *bildungsroman*. It consists, not only in a rapid presentation of a whole panorama of human experience, but in a technique of simultaneously presenting and commenting on this experience. The experience is conveyed to the reader as emotional reality: in the same moment, it is distanced from him by the continual interposition of the commentary. We are with Juan in Julia's bedroom, in the sinking ship, in the harem, on the battlefield, at Catherine's court and at the house-party; at the same time, all these are but speaking pictures, held up for our laughter, sympathy and judgement by the half-masked figure of the commentator. And (as will be argued later) what is true in the broad plan is true also in detail; various characteristic devices that Byron uses in the handling of language and imagery serve to reinforce this effect of simultaneously presenting experience and fixing it as the fiction that it is.

When Medwin attempted to identify Byron with Don Juan, as well as with Harold, Byron "laughed at the remark"—the laughter of polite non-agreement. Byron had already striven to dissociate himself from Harold; he achieves complete dissociation from his hero in **Don Juan** by the device of the narrator. "He repudiates even the *persona* of **Don Juan**", writes Paul West. Of course—and this is because he wishes to insist that it *is* a *persona;* because he avoids the romantic confusion of mask and face, of art and life. His true *persona* is that of the showman-narrator.

The general method had already been consciously exploited in *Beppo*, and Byron is well aware that he is using it as a distinctive part of **Don Juan,** claiming the same liberty as Sterne and Fielding—

> But let me to my story: I must own,
> If I have any fault, it is digression;
> Leaving my people to proceed alone,
> While I soliloquize beyond expression;
> But these are my addresses from the throne,
> Which put off business to the ensuing session:

> Forgetting each omission is a loss to
> The world, not quite so great as Ariosto.

And so he speaks of himself as "now and then narrating, now pondering", as the mood takes him; he cries "I won't reflect" yet admits that "thought . . . sticks to me through the abyss of this odd labyrinth"; he even denies that the poem is intended as a narrative at all—

> This narrative is not meant for narration,
> But a mere airy and fantastic basis,
> To build up common things with common places.

More seriously, he claims for poetry its traditional role as a moral medium, and makes this the special function of his digressions—

> O, pardon me digression—or at least
> Peruse! 'Tis always with a moral end
> That I dissert, like Grace before a feast:
> For like an aged aunt, or tiresome friend,
> A rigid guardian, or a zealous priest,
> My Muse by exhortation means to mend
> All people, at all times and in most places;
> Which puts my Pegasus to these grave paces.

The actual amount of digression varies surprisingly in different parts of the poem. . . . The average of the whole poem is about one-third; but in the earlier cantos (I-VIII—up to Ismail) he seems to have aimed at something more like a quarter. Sometimes it goes well below this, in particularly active cantos, such as II (the shipwreck) and V (the seraglio); only once does it rise well above it, in Canto III (Juan and Haidée), where it amounts to almost forty per cent. But when Juan reaches St Petersburg, the percentage increases immediately, shooting up to nearly sixty per cent; Canto XII, with its elaborated comments on women and the marriage market, carries over seventy per cent on a slender thread of narrative—the highest in the whole poem. None of the later cantos go below about forty per cent, except for XIII (about thirty per cent) and the last, XVI, which drops suddenly below twenty per cent again; but in these two, much of the material centred on Juan is concerned to broaden the social picture—Norman Abbey, the house-party, meals, Lord Henry as magistrate—rather than to advance the actual story.

Of course, it is not always easy to separate the narrative proper from commentary which arises out of and may remain fairly closely entwined with it; nor is it always a simple matter to separate commentary from "digression" properly so-called—passages in which Byron temporarily takes leave of the story to make some personal aside or general statement, for which there is no immediate basis in the story.

An extreme case is such as one finds in the stanza on "the name of 'Mary'" near the beginning of Canto V. Byron is describing the view of Constantinople, and recalls Lady Mary Wortley Montagu's description of it. By a kind of free association, this sets off a brief reflection on the name, obviously recalling the early attachment to Mary Chaworth. It has no immediate relation to the story, though there may be a tenuous link to the mention of Petrarchan love three stanzas earlier; and Byron immediately checks it and returns to the story, and from the pathetic to the realistic mode.

At other times, the effect is more deliberately farcical. For example, there is the passage in which Byron is describing the stormy coast of Haidée's island. The image of creaming champagne, used to describe "the small ripple spilt upon the beach", sets him off into a digression in praise of wine, and the sparkling passage in which he prescribes hock and soda-water as a hangover-cure. After this he returns, with deliberate nonchalance, to the scenery—

> The coast—I think it was the coast that I
> Was just describing—Yes, it *was* the coast . . .

In these and many other cases, the substance of the digression can be related *thematically* to the poem as a whole; but its *dramatic* function in the immediate context is to keep alive our sense of the narrator, interposing him between ourselves and the story.

But there are many longer and less simple cases. Take, for example, the evening passage at the end of Canto III. This (following immediately upon a digression on digressions and an attack on Wordsworth) takes its point of departure from the actual situation of the lovers, Juan and Haidée, together in the twilight. But it shifts away from this to the evening angelus, the Ave Maria, Byron's religion, the pinewoods at Ravenna and Boccaccio's phantom huntsman, all leading into a generalised evening hymn, itself partly a translation from Dante. The last line of this—"Ah! surely nothing dies but something mourns!" leads on to the detached stanza about the flowers on Nero's tomb. A lengthy process of association, governed by the general notion of twilight, has led completely away from the lovers in the Cyclades, to the poet's actual present, the human affections, and the storied past. Having thus "pondered" at length, Byron abruptly changes the tone and returns to the poem—

> But I'm digressing; what on earth has Nero
>   Or any such like sovereign buffoons,
> To do with the transactions of my hero,
>   More than such madmen's fellow man—the moon's?

And he proceeds to cut the canto in half and tie up the loose ends.

Here the linkages are mainly personal and emotional. In other cases again, the commentator consciously leaves the story in order to elaborate a kind of intellectual structure around it. An extended and formally defined example occurs in the middle of the Julian adventure. Byron begins by inviting the reader to allow for the lapse of time between June and November. He then launches out into the six anaphoristic stanzas, built up on an elaborate system of structural repetition and variation and using an extremely wide range of reference, in praise of "first and passionate love", which make a complete lyric in themselves. The climax of this uses the images of the fall and of Prometheus, and these allow for a striking modulation of tone in the following stanzas, which describe the imperfect and Promethean nature of modern man, with copious illustrations from this

> patent age of new inventions
> For killing bodies, and for saving souls . . .

The effect of the whole passage is to lay out broadly several basic themes of the poem—the panoramic variety of human experience, the quality of passion, fallen man, the mixed nature of civilisation. And although the general manner is assured and genial, there is also a sombre undertone of mortality:

> Few mortals know what end they would be at,
>   But whether glory, power, or love, or treasure,
> The path is through perplexing ways, and when
> The goal is gain'd, we die, you know—and then—

Byron as narrator, mediating between the poem and the reader, allows himself the widest possible range of movement. . . . In the full analysis, both digression and comment play their part in the full and complex development of the poem. In the end, nothing is irrelevant. If we take, for example, Canto IX as one of the most "digressive" cantos (nearly sixty per cent), we find that its only real *incident* is Juan's arrival at court and his meeting with the impressionable Empress. Yet around this Byron weaves a full commentary on wars just and unjust, and on tyranny; he states his political credo; he links together his two main epic themes, of love and war; he describes the varied and paradoxical nature of love, and woman's ambiguous role as destroyer and replenisher; and he sets the whole thing in a Cuvieresque framework of worlds destroyed and reborn, of recurrent Falls and Deluges.

Leave out the narrative element, and **Don Juan** becomes an indefinitely extensible medium for personal apologia and topical commentary, not unlike the *Cantos* of one of Byron's modern counterparts, Ezra Pound. But the narrative is a considerable asset in itself: it is the sustaining element which makes the whole poem possible, the picture from which the garrulous narrator takes off and to which he returns. The narrative supplies a relatively fixed element in the poem, the commentary an indefinitely variable one; and the richness of the poem is due to the interplay between them. And whereas in the earlier poetry, and particularly in **Childe Harold,** Byron's almost inveterate habit of accretion tended to blur and change the contours of the poem, in a *poème à tiroir* like **Don Juan** it becomes an essential part of the total effect.

As a final instance, let us return to Canto III, which is an interesting example of the full range of the poem: it contains something of nearly all its effects, and the overlapping and related layers of meaning can be clearly seen.

On the first layer, that of epic narrative, there is little action beyond the Odyssean homecoming of Lambro; but there is the splendid and vigorous account of feasting, décor and costume, culminating in the dazzling description of Haidée herself in all the pride of youthful beauty, love and power. On a slightly different level, within the picture but pointing outside it, are the characters of Lambro and the poet. What they have in common is the theme of Greek freedom and decadence—Lambro the embittered patriot turned pirate, the poet a turncoat moved to a moment of patriotic honesty. Lambro is historical—as, in a perennial sense, is the poet; but further, Lambro as "sea-attorney", merchant and fond father is an incisive satire on law, trade and family and on the idea of the "great man"; and the poet is, specifically, a kind of Levantine Southey.

As a third layer, there are, running through the story of Lambro's return and arising out of it, a series of reflections on love and marriage, on woman's inconstancy and the mingled pains and pleasures of family life.

At a fourth and further remove is the satire on the Lakers and the declaration of literary allegiance to Pope and Dryden. At a fifth, the concluding "evening voluntary" provides the setting for a personal declaration of religion. On another level again, there is Byron the man, actually riding at twilight through the Ravenna pinewoods, recalling "Boccaccio's lore and Dryden's lay". And as seventh, and all-embracing level, there is Byron the poet arranging, controlling, digressing and conscious of digression, and finally cutting the canto in two with a reference to Aristotle.

Between these layers, lights and reflections shift continually to and fro, too many to be named. The Byron who rides through the Ravenna woods is also, in a different way, the Byron who brooded over Marathon. The reflections on marriage and the family hearth which enlarge Lambro's story are also an expression of Byron's own nostalgia for his household gods. The stanza on Nero and the jaunty dismissal reflect back on the cruel but tender Lambro. And the Byron who burlesques Southey in the form of the poet is also the Byron who digresses directly to attack the Lakers, and who himself, as poet, is consciously manipulating all the complex levels of the poem.

In an unpublished preface to **Don Juan,** Byron appears to be sketching in rather fully the person of the narrator and the setting in which the story is supposed to be told—a passage drawn directly from his memories of Andalusia in 1809:

> The Reader . . . is requested to suppose . . . that the following epic Narrative is told by a Spanish Gentleman in a village in the Sierra Morena on the road between Monasterio & Seville—sitting at the door of a Posada with the Curate of the hamlet on his right hand a Segar in his mouth—a Jug of Malaga or perhaps, "right Sherris" before him on a small table containing the relics of an Olla Podrida—the time Sunset;—at some distance a groupe of black eyed peasantry are dancing to the sound of the flute of a Portuguese Servant belonging to two foreign travellers . . . [see excerpt dated 1818].

—and so on. It would be pleasant to find that this was the actual narrator of the poem; but Byron is, in fact, mainly concerned here with parodying Wordsworth's prose introduction to "The Thorn". And although he begins the poem with what appears to be a completely fictitious narrator, an old family friend, bachelor and man of the world, he soon allows this figure to fade out, and by the end of Canto I, the narrator, bidding farewell to his youth and accepting middle-age, is clearly Byron himself. Or rather, to make a necessary distinction, the narrator is Byron as he allows himself to appear in the poem, and can be treated (if we wish) as a kind of fiction.

All the digressive passages are, of course, in some degree personal—they imply attitudes which help to build up, stroke by stroke, the *persona* of the narrator. To these he adds more specific personal characteristics, such as his liking for late hours and "morning slumber"; although there is also a contrary process by which personal traits are sometimes effaced from the poem. In various passages scattered throughout the poem, he recalls familiar items from his own life and experience, as for example in the reference to his grandfather, "Foul-Weather Jack" ("my grand-dad's Narrative''); to his youthful dealings with Jewish moneylenders; to **English Bards,** Jeffrey and Scotland; or to his life as social and literary "lion". Later, in more forgiving terms, he recalls his marriage—

> I'll not gainsay the generous public's voice,
> That the young lady made a monstrous choice.

—and remembers with gratitude those women friends (like Lady Holland, Lady Jersey and Miss Mercer Elphinstone) who had remained loyal to him in the disaster of 1816.

The nature and placing of personal references is not by any means uniform, but varies quite markedly in the course of the poem; and in examining this, it will be useful to make a distinction between "Juan's present" (the time during which the story occurs, about 1789-91), "narrator's present" (the actual period of writing, 1818-23) and "narrator's past" (various times, but particularly 1809-11, the period of his early travels and the first **Childe Harold**). Both kinds of personal reference are particularly common in the early cantos into which (Steffan suggests) material from the suppressed Memoirs has "spilled over''. Already, at the end of Canto I, we have Byron in 1818, humorously accepting middle-age—

> But now at thirty years my hair is gray—
>   (I wonder what it will be like at forty?
> I thought of a peruke the other day)
>   My heart is not much greener; and, in short, I
> Have squander'd my whole summer while 'twas May,
>   And feel no more the spirit to retort; I
> Have spent my life, both interest and principal,
> And deem not, what I deem'd, my soul invincible.

—regretting the lost "freshness of the heart", and bidding farewell to love and ambition. Later, there is a glimpse of Byron at a Venetian masquerade, and soon the scene shifts to Ravenna—the haunted "evergreen forest" of *la Pineta di Classe,* scene of his daily rides, Gaston de Foix's column, Dante's tomb, the "enormous rooms" and "long galleries" of the Palazzo Guiccioli, while, in a vivid afterthought, he adds an account of the commandant slain on his doorstep.

At the same time, he is freely recalling the events of his Mediterranean journey in 1809-11, and these arise naturally enough in cantos which return to the same earlier scene. Thus he throws in a personal recollection of Cadiz and its stormy bay; makes his usual boast of having swum the Hellespont; significantly recalls his visit to the site of Troy, that "vast, untill'd and mountain-skirted plain'', where he had "stood upon Achilles' tomb''; and similarly describes the seas rolling up the Bosphorus, as viewed from the "Giant's Grave". Much later, there is a stray reference to the jackals at Ephesus, but direct references to the early **Childe Harold** period are confined largely to the first five cantos, which are also framed, in terms of "narrator's present", by Byron's life at Venice and Ravenna.

After the resumption of the poem in Canto VI, the narrator-pattern changes. There is in fact a marked lack of direct autobiographical references of this type in Cantos VI-IX, where both narrative element and commentary are particularly rich; and they tend to disappear again in the later cantos, from XII on, although these exploit personal experience in a different way, and are full of personal comment. But direct personal and contemporary references tend to cluster again in Cantos X-XI, around Juan's return to England. This becomes almost a vicarious return for Byron himself: at the same time, the fact of his continued exile serves to remind him of all that has happened since 1816, in the new, post-Napoleonic world.

Time has passed: it is now the autumn of 1822, and Byron is approaching thirty-five

> . . . getting nigh grim Dante's "obscure wood,"
>   That horrid equinox, that hateful section
> Of human years, that half-way house, that rude
>   Hut, whence wise travellers drive with
>   circumspection
> Life's sad post-horses o'er the dreary frontier
>   Of age, and looking back to youth, give *one* tear;—

and as Juan first sights the white cliffs of England, Byron recalls his own seven-year exile—"seven years (the usual term of transportation)''.

Three years before, in the Wellington stanzas (originally intended for Canto III but transferred to Canto IX), he had given vent to his feeling about one of the dominant figures of the years after Waterloo. Now, in Canto XI, as he introduces and builds up his picture of the English scene, particulars and events of the recent past accumulate, and serve to mark out the "narrator's present" very clearly, as a particular time with a history of its own. The narrator becomes himself the defeated and exiled "grand Napoleon of the realms of rhyme", and in the *Ubi sunt* stanzas he accumulates a mass of topical references to the world which has dissolved and vanished during the years of his exile—the deaths of "Napoleon the Grand" and of the suicide Castlereagh, of George III himself, and his son's "unhappy Queen" Caroline and her loved daughter, of convivial Sheridan and his old enemy Romilly and many others, all dead—

> Statesmen, chiefs, orators, queens, patriots, kings,
> And dandies, all are gone on the wind's wings.

And now George IV, the "royal bird", has gone down to Scotland for the "royal itch and loyal scratching" of 1822, while the Congress of Allied Sovereigns meets at Verona, "doing all that's mean".

Recurrently, throughout the poem, we are reminded of the narrator as a person who lives in a particular time and place, with a contemporary history, all a generation later than the "present" in which Juan himself lives. The reader is kept aware of this, as part of the framework in which the story is shown to him (even, at this distance of time, adding a new "framework" of his own: the world of 1960, framing the world of 1820, framing the world of 1790 . . .). At least once, a specific and datable event from the narrator's life is built into the poem, in Byron's account of the murdered commandant at Ravenna, and the effect of this is complex. It provides the occasion for one of Byron's major meditations on human mortality, and shows how his "ponderings" shift from real life into the poem. It harmonises generally with the episodes of slave-market, seraglio, battlefield and imperial-court, recalling earlier despotisms and inhumanities in the troubled world of 1820. But it is also valuable for its very gratuitousness, as if to emphasise that the narrator is *here,* a real person living quite apart from the poem, while all the time, on the other level, Juan is *there,* on the way towards romantic adventures in the seraglio.

Elsewhere, the relation between the two worlds of the poem is more direct. The obvious case is the Wellington stanzas, which Byron consciously moves up into their appropriate place at the beginning of Canto IX, immediately after the siege of Ismail. He explained this to Moore [see excerpt dated August 8, 1822], when asking him to return the only extant copy of the stanzas:

> The reason I want the stanzas again which I sent you is, that as these cantos contain a full detail (like the storm in Canto Second) of the siege and assault of Ismael, with much of sarcasm on those butchers in large business, your mercenary soldiery, it is a good opportunity of gracing the poem with * * *. With these things and these fellows, it is necessary, in the present clash of philosophy and tyranny, to throw away the scabbard.

The juxtaposition of events in the "narrator's present" and in "Juan's present" brings together Ismail and Waterloo, Suvarov and Wellington, the age of Catherine the Great and the age of

the Holy Alliance, and the effect is mutual: not only does the present comment on the past, but the past illuminates the present; and both develop one of his leading themes, the horror of war and its legitimacy only in self-defence—

> War's a brain-spattering, windpipe-slitting art,
> Unless her cause by Right be sanctified.

Finally, there is one major point at which Byron directly compares his two time scales, and contrasts the present with the past. This occurs when Juan, in London in 1791, sees Parliament in session, with an idealised version of George III on his constitutional throne, and his son, the Prince of Wales, still "first gentleman of Europe" and darling of the Whigs—

> There too he saw (whate'er he may be now)
>   A Prince, the prince of princes, at the time
> With fascination in his very bow,
>   And full of promise, as the spring of prime.
> Though royalty was written on his brow,
>   He had *then* the grace too, rare in every clime,
> Of being, without alloy of fop or beau,
>   A finished gentleman from top to toe.

This is the "great George" who "now weighs twenty stone", and who ironically serves as a living link between the two time-levels of the poem, a reminder that time not only kills, but, even worse, corrupts. Such might be the fate even of Juan himself.

Is it true to speak, as Ridenour does, of the poem's "narrowing the gap between speaker and protagonist"? Perhaps—if the poem had continued to the length and along the lines adumbrated by Byron himself. But in the poem as we have it, Juan has matured in the ways of the world without ceasing to be himself: "he has changed in manner but not in nature", says Steffan, "and that manner is not a spurious veneer or even a glossy varnish but a penetrating finish that has brought out the natural grain, to which he himself has applied a natural social polish".

The narrator is already bidding farewell to youth, love and ambition soon after the poem opens; he ages with it, moving into the shadows of Dante's "obscure wood". Juan has not yet lost "the freshness of the heart", though perhaps he is beginning to be in danger of it. The poem as it stands remains a kind of inverted Portrait of Dorian Grey: it is Juan, the figure in the picture-frame, who remains unlined, angelic, poised and experienced in the end, but with a kind of innocence; it is the narrator and commentator who ages. Between them there remains the perpetual pathetic-ironic contrast between the ardours and innocence of youth, the humorous disappointment and sadness of middle-age; and the like-unlike relation of narrator and hero runs like a giant simile through the whole poem. "Memories are a form of simile", writes Graham Greene: "when we say something is 'like' we are remembering."

Byron's long-distance flirtation with the Faust legend finds its resolution at last in the plan to treat the *other* great legend, and remake it in such a way that the theme of damnation through excess and daring appears in a form more congruent to himself and to his age. For this is to be a Don Juan *de nos jours,* firmly set in the historical period of a generation earlier, of Europe on the eve of the French Revolution. It is beside the point to complain, or affect surprise, as so many have done, that this Don Juan seems to have so little in common with the myth. This is Don Juan *circa* 1790: he is as much like the Don Juan of Tirso, Molière and Mozart as Shaw's Jack Tanner; and if Byron had followed out one of his plans, he might have claimed that the embrace of the guillotine was an appropriate modern equivalent for the handclasp of the walking statue.

This in itself is the first major step towards lending fresh interest to the twice-told tale. The second consists in casting the story in the form of comic epic, blending the tradition of Fielding and Sterne with that of the Pulcian and Bernesque poem. The third, and Byron's master device, consists in adding the superstructure of the showman-narrator. For here is the narrator of 1820, the "broken Dandy", raconteur and moralist, describing the world of 1790 in order to satirise his own world, portraying a corrupt society on the brink of war and revolution in order to satirise what appears to him a society again on the brink of revolution and war. This also answers those, like Johnson [see Additional Bibliography], who attempt to limit the real range of Don Juan; and reinforces the argument of those, like Wilson Knight, who believe that the rage of the public against *Don Juan* was the rage of the conservative against someone who implicitly threatened them with the same kind of castigation that had befallen European society a generation earlier. The poem might, at least, be taken to proclaim that the age of revolutions was not yet over—a disquieting thought in the age of the Holy Alliance.

Once we begin to see *Don Juan* in this way, a partial parallel may help to clarify the matter. What Byron is using, in a less rigorously developed form, is an anticipation of the structure of Thomas Mann's *Doctor Faustus*. Mann's work is, of course, carried through to completion with forethought and exactitude. Yet its method is fundamentally the same: in retelling the other great myth in modern form, Mann uses his narrator, Zeitblom, in such a way as to draw the parallel between the diabolic collapse of the great German genius, Adrian Leverkühn, the modern Faust, in 1930, and the collapse of German civilisation in the last years of the war.

The comparison serves to define more closely the basic method of *Don Juan*. And as Escarpit points out, the effect is to substitute a "psychological time" for a "fictional time" in the narrative—or rather, to superimpose one upon the other. Present and past comment one upon the other, and the result is a view of human experience richer and more complex than would have been possible in simple narrative. Carried all the way, such a technique might lead to a pure relativism such as that of Durrell's *Alexandria Quartet*, which has suggestions of a modern Don Juanism—the highly personal and imaginative view of society from a standpoint outside England (even when it includes the English scene), the interpolated reflections, the calculated longueurs, the turning and re-turning of human experience till it reaches a state of relativism more extreme than anything in Byron. For Byron stops short at the point where it is still possible to assert a traditional morality and a common human feeling, even, at times, by describing the effects of their absence. The "distancing" effect created by the major strategy of the narration, and also by the prevailing tactics of multiple simile, *objet trouvé*, verbal *collage*, linguistic impurity, and so on, enables the narrator to preserve a moral normality while at the same time expressing his mocking and ironic despair of a world that he sees as morally abnormal. (pp. 194-209)

> *M. K. Joseph, in his* Byron the Poet, *Victor Gollancz Ltd., 1964, 352 p.*

ALVIN B. KERNAN (essay date 1965)

[*Kernan contends that the view of life expressed in* Don Juan *is primarily comic. He focuses on how various aspects of the poem, including plot, characterization, and scope, reflect the values and methods traditionally ascribed to the comic genre. The critic maintains that the poem as it stands suggests an optimistic appraisal of life that reflects Byron's delight in the vitality, variety, and beauty of the world. A conception of the poem as pessimistic, argues Kernan, places too much emphasis on the mood of the first few cantos and fails to take into account the last completed portion of the work.*]

Byron deliberately chose to narrate the youthful adventures of his hero before he arrived at the cynicism and hardened depravity which qualify his zest for life in the older legend and the versions of Tirso de Molina, Molière, and Mozart. Byron's Juan is the pure embodiment of all those virtues which comedy shows as the key to successful life. These virtues are in origin natural, innate in man, though they are refined and improved upon in some varieties of comedy—principally Shakespeare's—by the order, still natural in origin, of society. Juan is the very essence of the natural, as the Romantics understood that term. He is lively and vital,

> A little curly-headed, good-for-nothing,
>   And mischief-making monkey from his birth. . . .

As a youth he is tall, slim, lithe, and handsome—the human form of the beautiful and well-proportioned world of comedy. He possesses all the natural virtues—courage, quick wit, passionate feelings, uprightness, frankness, warmth—and all the natural appetites for love, food, and pleasure. These instincts are not destructive in him but lead to beneficent actions, to enjoyment, pity, love, concern for others.

Juan's heart is sound enough, and he does have sense enough to come in out of the rain, but by academic standards his mind is somewhat deficient. This is perfectly proper in the world of comedy where, since truth is obvious and value apparent, the analytic intellect can lead only to confusion and loss. Occasionally, Juan does attempt deep thought, but his nature always saves him, as in this effort to probe the cosmos and construct a metaphysic:

> He thought about himself, and the whole earth,
>   Of man the wonderful, and of the stars,
> And how the deuce they ever could have birth;
>   And then he thought of earthquakes, and of wars,
> How many miles the moon might have in girth,
>   Of air-balloons, and of the many bars
> To perfect knowledge of the boundless skies;—
> And then he thought of Donna Julia's eyes. . . .

Juan's instincts are too clear and direct to allow him to lose himself in useless theoretical speculation and to forget the real and meaningful, a woman's beautiful eyes. The healthy limitations of his mind are realized by his speech, or more precisely, his failure to speak very often. His usual silence is emphasized by the loquaciousness of those around him, particularly the garrulous narrator who can never stop talking. Without question Juan is at his best when he neither tries to think or speak, for thinking always involves him in ludicrous tangles, and his few speeches are either commonplace or hopelessly romantic.

Nor does Juan learn very much from his experiences. By the end of the poem he has become a suave young diplomat, more courteous and formal than he was as a boy, but no more profound and still oblivious of those sad realities of life with which the narrator, who has traveled Juan's path before him, is forced to live. It is not only that Juan lacks the ability to organize and schematize life, but chiefly that he lacks that mental function which is the source of so much of the narrator's suffering: memory. Where the narrator cannot forget his loves, his youth, and his images of men who are now only dust and names, Juan's regrets for yesterday last only one intense moment and then are gone as yesterday ceases to be. He suffers horribly when first separated from Donna Julia and vows,

> Sooner shall Earth resolve itself to sea,
> Than I resign thine image, oh, my fair! . . .

But the image fades quickly enough as he becomes sea-sick, struggles for survival in an open boat, and then finds another love. . . . Juan is a comic hero of the romantic variety, a Ferdinand rather than a Falstaff, but his virtues still enable him to live that life of immediacy which can always be described in somewhat cruder terms by a more earthy comic approach to life. When Juan and an Englishman named Acres are chained together in a Turkish slave market, Juan announces in his inflated style: not for the

> present doom
> I mourn, but for the past;—I loved a maid. . . .

To which Acres replies that he understands, for he too cried when his first wife died, and again when the second ran away, but that he had run away from the third.

While Juan continues to take himself quite seriously, never quite seeing the wonderfully efficient way he manages to stay alive and happy in a constantly changing world, he is constantly being undercut by a comic sense of life more basic and honest than his own. The narrator and characters like Acres know that, since all things pass, there is no point in worrying or of taking yourself and your passions too seriously. At the same time, of course, Juan's delicacy and refinement in taking his pleasures call into question the lower comic values, and in this way the tone is complicated even within the comic portions of the poem. But whatever form the comic values may take—pure love or pure pleasure—the comic way of life remains a natural, unthinking instinct for what is good and a freedom in moving with the full stream of life.

For this way of life to be workable, it is necessary that the comic hero live in a world friendly to him and suitable to his virtues. The stream of life to which he commits himself cannot carry him to disaster but must cast him in the way of pleasure and joy. Viewed from one angle, Juan does live in a beneficent world. He often lands in temporary trouble, but bad luck is only momentary and usually turns out to be good luck in disguise. (pp. 187-91)

[If] lack of introspection, a poor memory, and a mind which has very limited analytical powers are to be valuable assets, they must be located in a world which is not only good enough to be trusted but of such a nature that any attempt to understand its operations through reason be futile and ludicrous. The relativism characteristic of *Don Juan* creates just such a world. Variety, plenitude, and mutability combine to make ridiculous all received philosophies and religions, to destroy any belief in history and progress, and to make laughable any attempts to speculate on and systematize the workings of the universe. And why worry about it, says comedy. Everything may change, but nothing can be done about it; and the world as immediately sensed is full of joy and pleasure. Women's eyes flash beauty, wine excites wonderfully, the pulse beats, torrents crash down mountainsides, and the whole spectacle of nature is a satisfying display of the richness, power, and springing vitality of the world. The over-all somberness of *Don Juan* often obscures

this romantic and comic joy in life, man, and nature; but it is regularly present, and it validates both Juan's trust in the life known to his senses and feelings and his thoughtless commitment of himself to whatever chances the world offers.

But though the comic world is essentially good, it always allows for forces which attempt to pervert this good. The way of the world is inevitable, however, and these anti-life forces have no real chance of success. Foolishness, not evil, constitutes the opposition in comedy. Since in *Don Juan* the comic way is to give oneself to life and move with it through change, foolishness is necessarily any attempt to stay life, to deny its pleasures, and to cramp it into any rigid, permanent form, a philosophical system or a marriage bed. The poem is filled with characters who attempt to do just this. Donna Inez and her efforts to educate Juan by means of sermons and homilies which try to stifle his natural impulses and curb his passions; the stiff, placid, aristocratic ladies and gentlemen who gather at Norman Abbey, scarcely able to breathe within their stays and their rigid sense of propriety; the Turkish sultan who buys, locks away, and guards elaborately the numerous but unused beauties of his harem. The narrator, in his digressions, provides a host of parallels: the art of the Lake poets, which imposes ludicrous boundaries on human nature; Coleridge's metaphysics, which pretends to enfold the mysteries of the universe; Plato's philosophy of the ideal, which insists that the physical is unreal and that the passions can be controlled; the ridiculous attempts of tyranny through the ages to enslave men and contain their drive toward political freedom; the laughable pretensions of polite society to order and bottle up man's natural appetites. But restraint and enfolding are also treated as inescapable realities of life which take such forms as physical ageing which stiffens and binds the once-free body, the tendency of the mind to remember what once was and therefore to suffer in the painful grasp of memory, the inevitable movement of time toward decay and death, that ultimate form of containment and stillness which contains all other forms of enslavement.

The attempts to impose bonds on life and the hero's successful escapes from each of the snares constitute the comic plot of *Don Juan*. Juan's pedantic tutors try to eradicate his passions, and Donna Julia's careful parents try to lock her into a marriage with a wealthy old man; but when the two young people meet, their love flares and destroys all barriers to pleasure. Caught in her bedroom, muffled under the bedclothes, his exit barred by an enraged husband, Juan, naked, nearly murders the old man and his servants to break free. Finding the garden gate, the last barrier to freedom, locked, Juan opens it and then relocks it from the outside, leaving the prisoners of society inside. Becalmed on the sea in an open boat, most of the survivors of a shipwreck turn cannibals and perish as a result, but Juan plunges into the sea and, aided by the current, swims to an island where he finds Haidée and the full enjoyment of natural love. But even on this Edenic island, restraints exist, and Haidée's papa, to give him his comic epithet, returns suddenly, has Juan bound, and ships him off to a Turkish slave market. From here on Juan's life is a continued series of escapes from a variety of bonds, political, physical, social, and amorous which the world attempts to impose upon him. (pp. 191-94)

Juan rambles over all Europe, going from love to shipwreck to prison to war to court and back to love again. As he moves through his spacious world, time takes no toll of him. He grows less impulsive, but at the end of the poem he is still young and passionate and ready for further adventures. In himself, like a figure of myth rather than a mere man, he contains the timeless energy and appetite of the human race. Byron suggests in several places that he plans to reduce Juan to marriage, disillusionment, and old age, but he can never bring himself to do it. Juan's ultimate escape from the poet's plans may be a result of the accident of Byron's death, but the adventure on which the poem ends is a climactic comic image of all the tests Juan has earlier endured, and once again his vitality and felt sense of life triumph. The scene is Norman Abbey, the country house of the Amundeville family, where Juan has gone as the member of a house party. Here, all is restraint and confinement. The water of the artificial lake is still, the skies overcast and gray, the landscape autumnal and dreary, the castle—a "Gothic Babel"—heavy and earthbound because its many dissimilar parts and styles lack any soaring quality and life-giving unity. The upper-class English men and women of the party are equally lifeless. Their clothes and manners are stiff and smooth, their vitality smothered in a fashionable ennui, their moral spots varnished over, and their only interests dinner and sleep. Beauty here is completely self-possessed, and Byron describes the great beauties of the party as locked in ice or buried deep within the polished surfaces of a gem. Whenever life does burst forth in this society it is destroyed by gossip and ostracism—as Byron had once been destroyed—or is brutally restrained. Two poachers are caught in huge steel traps and then imprisoned; a young unmarried girl with child, a "poacher upon Nature's manor," is made to wear a scarlet coat and hauled for sentencing before a Justice of the Peace.

This concentration of confinement and tyranny is further focused in the ghost of a Monk who has haunted the castle since Henry VIII dissolved the monastery and gave the lands to the Amundevilles. Juan and the ghostly Monk are worthy antagonists, and their combat raises to the mythic level the comic struggle which has heretofore been presented realistically. On one side we have the ultimate comic hero whose blazing vitality cannot weaken or be entrapped; on the other side the ultimate comic antagonist, the very spirit of the anti-vital. The ghostly form of the Monk makes him completely bodiless, and his monkishness is the absolute form of asceticism and a strict, religious ordering of life. His ceaseless search for revenge on those who have robbed him is the final extension of that perversion of life to a sterile emptiness which overtakes those characters in *Don Juan* who cramp their natural instincts too severely. (pp. 197-98)

After several appearances, the "sable Friar in his solemn hood" comes to fetch Juan from his bed. The door creaks on his entrance and seems to say, "Lasciate ogni speranza, voi, ch'entrate!" and the words over the entrance to Dante's Hell sum up all the many forms of damnation in *Don Juan*. Though terrified of this "darkening darkness," Juan moves to fight once more, and as he advances, the Monk retreats until pressed against a courtyard wall. Juan's hand reaches forward and presses a "hard but glowing bust." The sable frock and dreary cowl fall away to reveal,

> In full, voluptuous, but *not o'er*grown bulk,
> The phantom of her frolic Grace—Fitz-Fulke!

These are the last lines of the poem, though Byron may have written a few stanzas more, and while they have a realistic explanation—the Duchess of Fitz-Fulke is a rather forward beauty who has been eyeing Juan for some time and has taken advantage of the story of the ghost to get to his chamber unobserved—they are at the same time a climactic image of the comic triumph of life over death. The illusion of a pale, bloodless world moving toward sterility and death is transformed by

courage, vitality, and good chance into a living, breathing, and satisfying immediacy.

Unfortunately, the majority of readers do not go past the Haidée episode or Juan's Turkish captivity, and for that reason overestimate the pessimistic qualities of the poem. But *Don Juan* as Byron left it ends on an affirmation of the goodness of life, and the entire poem is thus framed by a comic view of experience. (pp. 198-99)

Alvin B. Kernan, "'Don Juan'," in his The Plot of Satire, *Yale University Press, 1965, pp. 171-222.*

BRIAN WILKIE (essay date 1965)

[*In the following excerpt from his full-scale study of the epic tradition in Romantic poetry, Wilkie explores the concept of* Don Juan *as "epic of negation." According to the critic, the characterization, plot, and ultimate purpose of the poem represent a reaction against the heroic values and literary conventions of the traditional epic. Wilkie examines at length Byron's ironic and satirical treatment of various epic conventions, including especially the contrast between Juan's adventures and those of the stock epic hero. Byron's rejection of the traditional notion of heroism, according to Wilkie, forms part of the poem's fundamental skepticism about the nature of life itself.* Don Juan's *negative inspiration, contends the critic, in combination with its lack of concrete form and inconclusiveness, suggest that the universe has no real order or purpose. "It is," he asserts, "one of the very few poems which truly assert and exemplify philosophic nihilism."*]

Of the major English Romantic poems none reminds us of its debt to epic tradition so often or insistently as Byron's *Don Juan*. At the same time the poem is obviously unheroic, though not simply mock-epic. This is only one of the countless puzzles and contradictions which criticism of the poem must deal with. If criticism's task is to elucidate the central meaning of a work and the principles of order that give it coherence, then surely *Don Juan* is one of the most recalcitrant of subjects for the critic. Almost any interpretation of its "meaning" must ignore a good deal of conflicting or anomalous evidence. It is sometimes said that *Don Juan,* while lacking formal unity, has a thematic unity which arises from Byron's repeated harping on the same strings: the baseness and hypocrisy of marriage, the meanness of despotism, and so forth. This critical point is useful, but even on many of his pet themes Byron is far from consistent. His attack on marriage hardly wavers at all, but his commitment to, say, popular rule is not nearly so firm; he surmises, for example, that if monarchs were in fact overthrown he would probably become an ultra-Royalist. . . . Nothing is so easy as to catch Byron in the act of contradicting himself—except that "catch" is the wrong word, since Byron admits his inconsistency and even makes a virtue of it.

> Also observe, that like the great Lord Coke,
> (See Littleton) whene'er I have expressed
> Opinions two, which at first sight may look
> Twin opposites, the second is the best.
> Perhaps I have a third too in a nook,
> Or none at all—which seems a sorry jest;
> But if a writer should be quite consistent,
> How could he possibly show things existent? . . .

Don Juan is sometimes treated as a great poem *manqué,* a brilliant achievement which might have been far better if Byron had devoted himself to it with more serious single-mindedness, if he had labored more zealously to order his heterogeneous material in the way that great poems do. But such regrets ignore what Byron insistently implies or states, both in *Don Juan* itself and in his comments on it, namely that the poem is calculatedly formless, aesthetically and in its ideas. It is one of the very few poems which truly assert and exemplify philosophic nihilism. (pp. 188-89)

[In] *Don Juan* Byron wanted to create a poem that was deliberately and in every sense inconclusive, since he wanted to show life itself as ultimately without meaning, despite its enthralling variety and the high flavor its particular episodes could have. For the last two or three hundred years this view of life has been common among thinking men, and for such men in our own day it is probably the most common of all. But one does not usually write a long narrative poem to assert such a philosophy. Byron did so because, it would seem, he felt the pressure of what he considered specious orthodoxies and systems all around him—some of them old, many of them new. Therefore the fact of life's insignificance was something that urgently needed to be asserted in his day. Byron's comments on *Don Juan* stress again and again its relevance to the age; in his own way Byron was trying to be doctrinal to a nation. But his doctrine was to be the denial of particular doctrines and of the very notion of doctrine, even that last infirmity of the noble skeptic, defiant fist-shaking curses at the gods who are not there. (There is plenty of this in Byron's other late poems, of course, a fact that renders even more significant the generally tolerant skepticism of *Don Juan;* the rule dramatizes the exception.) And what more striking vehicle could Byron have used to assert the emptiness of man's enterprise than the epic, a form in which the statement that after all there is no final Truth, or that if there is one we have no way of knowing it, has the kind of jarring effect it would have if one heard the statement from a pulpit? (pp. 211-12)

[One] of Byron's basic strategies for emptying *Don Juan* of meaning is to play against one another different attitudes toward epic. Just as important, though, are his ironic adaptations of more specific traditional epic devices. Most of these are directed against epic values themselves, and not simply against Byron's own age, though of course at times and for particular satiric effects Byron does choose to compare modern life unfavorably with the past in the way I have outlined earlier. But although he sometimes feels the satirist's impulse to correct contemporary abuses, that purpose is, I believe, subordinate to the basic philosophic message of the poem.

For the most part, Byron's twisting of epic conventions involves the hero and his function. The central fact about Don Juan is that he has no mission. Except in Canto I, where Byron wants to show him as a green adolescent, the Don is not an absurd figure at all; he shows himself capable of noble and generous-minded behavior, as in his exhortation to the sailors to die like men rather than like brutes, his defiance of Gulbeyaz, and his rescue of Leila. Nor, if we except his amours, is he usually passive in any ordinary sense; he responds with instant action to the holdup by Tom and is instrumental in turning the tide of battle at Ismail. His passivity, so-called, strikes us only when we think of him as an epic protagonist, and even then not because he is not active enough but because his actions do not form a meaningful sequence leading him toward definitive achievement. The disjointedness of his "progress" is nowhere better illustrated than in Byron's mystifying and cavalier silence about how the harem episode turns out—this after he has created more narrative suspense than in any other part of the poem. As a man of action, an adventurer, Don Juan is not so

totally unlike Byron's swashbuckling protagonists as he has been said to be; as an epic protagonist, however, his aimlessness is dearly felt.

Nor, on the whole, is the Don's lack of a mission a satiric comment on the impossibility of modern heroism, as is the portrait of Lambro . . . or (more facetiously or indirectly) those of Tom the highwayman and Lord Henry Amundeville. . . . Don Juan's most impressive derring-do is evident in the siege of Ismail, where more than anywhere else in the poem Byron draws a serious equation between modern and ancient heroism. Moreover, one of the most striking facts about Juan is his ability to live in the world while somehow remaining unaffected by it. Byron shows him as having been a little spoiled and over-sophisticated by his tenure as Catherine's favorite, but not very significantly. . . . Nowhere, in fact, are Juan's polite distance from the group and superiority to the fiats of modern convention and fashion more strongly emphasized than in the English cantos, where for satiric purposes he might most easily have been shown as corrupted or limited by the triviality of the world he is part of. Juan's failure to have a mission is, rather, part of Byron's attempt to depict realistically the actual conditions of all heroism, the fact that although a hero may be admirable and do some impressive things, his deeds cannot lead to any meaningful result. And this, of course, is just the opposite of what epic usually tries to demonstrate.

"You have so many *'divine'* poems," Byron wrote to Murray, "is it nothing to have written a *Human* one? without any of your worn-out machinery" [see excerpt from his letter of April 6, 1819]. And part of his aggressive jesting about his epic plan for *Don Juan* was the statement that "my spirits, good or bad, must serve for the machinery." That there is a pun here on *spirits* is borne out by the poem itself, where Byron sometimes claims to be writing while half-drunk or suffering from a hangover (perhaps we are meant to compare the nocturnal visitations of Milton's Muse) and also plays at introducing ghosts as machinery:

> And now, that we may furnish with some matter all
> Tastes, we are going to try the supernatural. . . .

But—to mention the most obvious meaning last—by "spirits" Byron also means his whim and disposition. He would seem to have introduced "machinery" into his epic in the only form he could accept—random, calculatedly digressive speculations, notably on metaphysical and religious subjects. For it is precisely through "machinery" that the epic poets have most imaginatively stressed the meaningful, destined role that their heroes play. Byron's hero is under tutelage to no fore-seeing gods; his progress—or lack of progress—is determined by the merest whim of his creator, Byron himself, who repeatedly appears *ex machina* to explain the cosmic meaning—that is, lack of meaning—of his poem and of his hero's actions. If we regard the author's almost never-failing comments on his own digressiveness and tendency to metaphysical speculation as in themselves a joke, we must admit that it becomes frayed by the time Byron has repeated it five or six times. The joke is richer, I believe, if we see his digressiveness and highhanded manipulation of his action as analogous to the oscillation of epic narrative between the hero and his guiding destiny, between earth and heaven. This idea might also explain Byron's occasional references to his poem as "fiction," which seem to contradict flagrantly his more typical insistence that he is being factual or truthful. But it is important to Byron that he have it both ways, for he is trying to say, in effect, that if we are honest, if we respect truth and fact, we must see epic heroism as a poet's pipe-dream; truth is fact, and that heroism is a fiction is *a* fact. (pp. 212-14)

For choosing a legendary epic hero Byron had good precedents in epic and its theory. Don Juan is, specifically, a legendary lover, and this fact too is intended to have epic reverberations. When Juan and Johnson are parting from the women before plunging into gruesome, nightmarish battle, Byron observes that Juan never left women "Unless compelled by fate, or wave, or wind, / Or near relations." . . . In the background, I believe, is the memory of Aeneas's abandonment of Dido so that he may fight and found an empire and perhaps of Hector's farewell to Andromache. In the context, which is Byron's savage attack on war and the ideal of martial glory through explicit parallels with epic tradition, the further implication is obvious: Byron is endorsing love as the alternative to war and thus reversing the antifeminism which is implied in one form or another by almost every traditional epic. (pp. 214-15)

Byron continues throughout the poem to suggest the same point—that love is a higher calling than war and other types of conventional prowess—and to evoke ironically the cliché of woman as an obstacle to heroism. Haidée is doubtless a Nausicaa, but she is also a Dido, giving herself unreservedly to her shipwrecked lover and dying for it. The "nuptials" stanzas . . . , the mention of the Stygian river . . . , the fatalistic tone ("deeds eternity can not annul" . . .)—all these make the parallel fairly convincing. An ironic reflection on conventional heroism follows once again, however; almost immediately after the consummation of the "nuptials" Byron writes a stanza celebrating "worthies Time will never see again," including Caesar, Pompey, and Belisarius, all of whom were "heroes, conquerors, and cuckolds." . . . Sex, in short, is a reality, a fact, which Juan and Haidée have confronted in their private, human way; the same force, in a degraded form, returns upon conventional heroes to remind them—and Byron's readers—of facts of life which are ignored at one's peril. To cap the irony (though the effect is also to alter and embitter the irony, to direct it at life rather than at heroism), Fate intervenes—not to set the hero back on the high path of heroism but to despatch him over the heroic Mediterranean waves to a slave market. That Byron thought out the parallel as schematically as I have described it is admittedly doubtful, but that he wrote in this spirit seems fairly certain. (pp. 215-16)

Byron's contemporaries often accused him of degrading human nature [see excerpt from *Don Juan* dated 1823]:

They accuse me—*Me*—the present writer of
The present poem—of—I know not what,—
A tendency to under-rate and scoff
At human power and virtue, and all that;
And this they say in language rather rough. . . .

In the lines following these Byron defends himself by citing the examples of Dante, Solomon, Cervantes, Swift, and a number of other writers of the past, but (here, at least) he does not deny the charge. The current trend in criticism is to regard these contemporary objections, with which Keats, for one, agreed, as shortsightedness which mistook satire for scurrility. But Byron's critics were not so blind as we sometimes assume they were. It is true that Shelley, whom one would expect to be sensitive on such a point, defended Canto V as containing nothing which "the most rigid asserter of the dignity of human nature could desire to be cancelled," but that he should make this defense at all is significant, and, besides, Canto V would have appealed to Shelley because of its idealistic speeches about love and its defiant attitude toward tyranny. But in many crucial ways *Don Juan* does subvert the idea that man is noble, especially through attacks on heroism's clay feet, both today and in the past.

What his contemporaries really did fail to appreciate was Byron's reluctance to destroy such illusions. His defense against the public outcry was that truth must be served first. His Muse, he maintains,

mostly sings of human things and acts—
And that's one cause she meets with contradiction;
For too much truth, at first sight, ne'er attracts;
And were her object only what's call'd glory,
With more ease too she'd tell a different story. . . .

These last lines were no empty boast, as Byron's early exotic tales could testify. Byron believed that the heroic ideal had never been more than a dream. But, although the dream was based on false values, it nevertheless could be bracing and invigorating. He could not or would not abandon any of these conflicting views, and he states his dilemma poignantly in the "Aurora Borealis" stanzas. Man's highest ideals are love and glory, which "fly / Around us ever, rarely to alight."

Chill, and chained to cold earth, we lift on high
Our eyes in search of either lovely light;
A thousand and a thousand colours they
Assume, then leave us on our freezing way.

Such, too, is his own "non-descript and ever varying rhyme . . . Which flashes o'er a waste and icy clime."

When we know what all are, we must bewail us,
But, ne'er the less, I hope it is no crime
To laugh at *all* things—for I wish to know
What after *all*, are *all* things—but a *Show*? . . .

Byron's italics, which he always uses skillfully and accurately, are often important to his mood and meaning; here the italicizing in "*all* things" suggests that Byron intends the phrase to mean, not the total of discrete things and experiences, but rather the "allness" of things, the sum of things considered as having or not having coherent meaning. So defined, "*all* things" are simply appearance, a show, a spectacle, like the Aurora Borealis. True love and glory, which if they existed might give meaning to life, are so foreign to its actual conditions as to be pure illusion. The overtones of Byron's statement are, in different ways, Dante's pity, when he first leaves Hell, for the "northern widowed clime" which does not know the stars he now can see, and Milton's gloomy apprehension that his epic enterprise may be defeated by cold climate and an age too late.

But for Byron the "cold and icy clime" is not so much his own age as the human lot in general, earthbound but prone to find beauty in its illusory visions. Byron too finds these illusions beautiful, even beneficent. And therefore he sometimes feels that his campaign for honesty is misguided; though glory and high ideals be will-o'-the-wisps, to expose them as sham is to destroy the illusions without which nations and individuals cannot flourish. *Don Quixote* is the saddest of all tales; its "hero's right, / And still pursues the right," but

Cervantes smiled Spain's Chivalry away;
A single laugh demolished the right arm
Of his own country;—seldom since that day
Has Spain had heroes. . . .

This reluctance by Byron to smash even false idols helps account for certain especially insistent paradoxes in the poem.

The English cantos, for example, have often irritated, bored, or puzzled critics. The treatment of England seems anticlimactic. Byron has skillfully whetted our appetites for this section; throughout the first ten cantos England is often the subject even when she does not furnish the setting or the actors. The sharpness of Byron's frequently interpolated attacks on England makes us expect savage satire in the English cantos themselves, but on the whole this is not what we get. We get delicate social satire at most, and often not even that; Byron sometimes seems to have turned into a novelist, with the novelist's minute and relatively neutral interest in the workings of a social group.

Much of this is true, but it is important to recognize that Byron is still writing an epic. *Don Juan,* despite its inclusive European setting, is very much a national epic poem; that is, it comes close to being one in the negative sense applicable to *Joan of Arc*—through its vilification of the poet's own country. Hence (ironically in more than one way) Byron's dedication of the poem to the official spokesman for English values, the epic renegade Southey, and hence his bitterness toward the other false poetic prophets of his country, his obsession with the dirt of English politics, his rhetorical celebration of England as a nation which has traded its sometime greatness for universal abhorrence and the status of "first of slaves" . . .—all of which is an inversion of the usual epic rhetoric. But Byron cannot use an inverted epic tradition in the service of a positive cause; he does not have one. Since by Canto X he has thoroughly deflated ancient as well as modern heroism, the false values of men in general as well as English illusions, he cannot consistently adopt the attitude of moral superiority he has implicitly promised to assume and which the satirist and the Southey of *Joan* do assume. He cannot compare the English unfavorably with an idealized alternative group.

But neither does Byron simply become a novelist; at the same time that he is probing the minutest details of English life, often tolerantly or with bemused fascination, he never allows society to become the unquestioned framework of his action; he maintains his epic vista by keeping us aware of the totality of time and of the place of Englishmen in their heroic tradition, such as it is. He conjures up the Black Prince, Thomas à Becket, Cressy, and the Druids; he reminds us of British achievements in the cause of liberty; he traces the history of Norman Abbey and of its personages. References to epic tradition are very many: the bluestockings ask Juan if he saw Ilion, matchmaking ladies are implicitly compared to the Virgilian gods ("'Tantaene!' Such the virtues of high station"), there are the Cervantes stanzas calling *Don Quixote* a "real Epic," there is a subtle comparison of the Menelaus-Paris-Helen triangle to Lord Henry-Adeline-Juan, a parallel is drawn between the feast at Norman Abbey and the battles and feasts in Homer.

The result of all this is an ambivalent treatment of the English. To the extent that he has undermined the whole notion of heroism Byron can be tolerant toward the English; to the extent that they make pretensions to the loftiest heroism or significance and to the extent that Byron himself feels the need to believe in a heroic ideal, he shows the English to be seriously inadequate. But neither of these judgments is that of the vitriolic satirist; even Byron's criticisms of the English in the later cantos are sad rather than angry or stridently contemptuous in tone. Byron is no Swift, even when he is criticizing; while he

denounces he often seems to be asking, candidly and without rhetorical self-righteousness, how anything can really be expected of so frail a being as man.

Byron's criticism of the English returns again and again to the same point: that they lack individuality. . . . One thinks of Byron's loathing of Suwarrow because he tends to think of men and of things "in the gross, / Being much too gross to see them in detail" . . . and the leveling of the same charge at History:

> History can only take things in the gross; . . .
> The drying up a single tear has more
> Of honest fame, than shedding seas of gore. . . .

The reason, Byron explains, is that such an act of individual kindness "brings self-approbation," and by contrast we think of the oblivion which, he is constantly telling us, awaits the hero who looks for that generalized, immortal good will called Glory.

This concern with the individual as superior to and more real than the mass is only one aspect of Byron's championing of "fact" as opposed to wider, more generalized vision and doctrine, which he associates not only with philosophy but also with poetry. "But still we Moderns equal you in blood," he apostrophizes Homer,

> If not in poetry, at least in fact,
>   And fact is truth, the grand desideratum!
> Of which, howe'er the Muse describes each act,
>   There should be ne'ertheless a slight substratum. . . .

Elsewhere he declares:

> But then the fact's a fact—and 'tis the part
>   Of a true poet to escape from fiction
> Whene'er he can; for there is little art
>   In leaving verse more free from the restriction
> Of truth than prose. . . .

His own Muse "gathers a repertory of facts." . . .

Byron uses the word *fact* in a curiously ambivalent way. It sometimes means "truth" as distinguished from lies or fiction or sham. To use the word so is to use it in the satirist's, or corrective, sense. But it can also have a more philosophical sense; here *fact* refers to the isolated, unrationalized phenomenon, frequently in opposition to the "ideal." When Byron writes, "fact is truth, the grand desideratum," he is not so much stating that the two words are semantically equivalent as hazarding a definition of the nature of things, which are what they are without reason or connection with one another, without a unifying "Idea." This is where the emotional conflict in Byron becomes apparent. In *Don Juan* Byron repeatedly sneers at philosophical idealism, especially in its Platonic form, though also in others—Berkeley's for example. . . . Yet almost as often Byron states or implies that the world is a tawdry place compared with what one can imagine its being. His view, of course, is that such imagining is simply dreaming; there is virtually no serious attempt to say that what exists as thought must have an analogue outside the individual mind or that whatever is thought is *ipso facto* real. But Byron cannot help feeling a deep sense of loss because reality is so much less than dream. From the satirist's viewpoint *fact* is a word to be used with angry gusto; from the viewpoint of the epic poet-prophet *fact* suggests the dreariness of the human lot. Yet, Byron seems to be saying, fact is all we have and we must live with it.

It is this stubborn insistence that in spite of the temptation to dream we are dupes if we go beyond isolated phenomena to a systematic belief in a "Truth" behind the phenomena that makes *Don Juan* a sad and frightening poem; clearly, fact is all that Byron will admit, but it is not always enough for him. In this respect he is similar to many twentieth-century existentialists. But he differs from many, perhaps most, of them in that he feels sadness rather than anger at man's lonely meaninglessness and in his avoidance of the position that by egoistic fiat one can create a valid kind of reality. He refuses, that is, to turn his kind of skepticism into what is popularly called a "philosophy." I am still referring to *Don Juan,* be it understood; in other poems Byron is capable of taking both of these existentialist positions.

Perhaps, after all, *Don Juan* does imply a certain kind of heroic ideal. It is not the heroism of the scientist, for whom "fact" is of utterly no consequence except as it contributes to system and generality; the kind of heroism Byron implies is much more consistent with technology, which deals with limited facts and situations and leaves ultimate questions alone. The two passages in praise of Newton . . . emphasize respectively Newton's modest denial of having discovered ultimate truth and his usefulness to progress in mechanics; it is Wordsworth rather than Byron who admires the Newton of "strange seas of thought." On the other hand, we cannot attribute heroism to the mean sensual man whose respect for facts arises from mere unreflectiveness. The heroism implied by *Don Juan* is that of the man who can think and think and think and be a skeptic. It consists in tolerant, unembittered unbelief accepted in spite of a serious need for a sense of meaning and direction in life.

In a way it is surprising that Keats should have denounced Byron so severely, for Byron is very close to preaching—and in *Don Juan* exemplifying—the Negative Capability that Keats had once urged. The Keats who had once endorsed that attitude later became, as we have seen, a diligent seeker for answers. But even if, with his Shakespeare and thrush, he had never fretted after knowledge, his uncertainty would have been different from the uncertainty Byron acknowledges. Keats advocated Negative Capability in a spirit of optimism; he assumed that one could gain positive knowledge by not interposing labels and formulas between oneself and the object. He also assumed, though, that there is an order in the world and especially in life which, independent of the formulas of thought, will make itself apparent to a person who is patient and alertly perceptive. Byron's negative capability is more negative and also, in a way, more heroic. Without a flag to fight under, without goal or obvious reward, it skirmishes endlessly against protean falsehood—and without even the adrenal stimulus of the will to disbelieve.

But although *we* may call this heroism, Byron does not; he endorses no heroic ideal as such, this one or any other. And this fact brings me to some final comments pertinent to him. . . . (pp. 217-24)

[When] they were working in the tradition of epic the Romantics generally expressed heroic values that were not relativistic. Byron is obviously an exception; in *Don Juan* we find precisely that typically modern distrust of objective values to whose influence the decline of epic and epic heroism, along with a host of other vanished certainties, is so often attributed. It is true that when critics or historians, especially those antipathetic to the Romantics, bring the charge of relativism against them, the complainants usually have in mind what they would consider a vague and specious spirituality in the Romantic creeds and are not adverting to Byron's considered, hardnosed Pyrrhonism. Often, indeed, critics make a reservation in Byron's favor as for a man who appreciated better and cherished more dearly than his contemporaries the threatened heroic standards of earlier ages. Nevertheless, it must be admitted that Byron helps corroborate the actual substance of the charge.

Surely there is an irony here. Byron appears, in different poems and in different parts of *Don Juan,* both as the Romantic poet who broke most violently with the moral values of the past and as the last exponent of larger-than-life, "traditional" heroism; the poet of titanic defiance of God and man is the same poet who created the most unheroic of epic heroes. Is this irony simply one more to be added to the long list of unresolved paradoxes concerning Byron? Perhaps, but I think there is a plausible solution. It has to do with the paradox of progressivism and conservatism in epic. . . . [Although] Byron does not really believe in heroism, past or present, he defines this nonexistent thing to himself in a curiously rigid way. Both when he is denying the possibility of heroism and when he is portraying a titanically powerful figure capable of shaking earth's foundations and the firmament, Byron regards heroism as something alien to the familiar norms of human experience, as something either contemptibly fake or superhuman. Heroism is for him one specific *style* of action rather than the *substance* of a code of values. But in the great literary epics there are different styles of action and, which is more important, such styles are by-products of heroism, not values themselves identifiable with heroism. Both Aeneas and Turnus can defy, boast, fight, and kill, but for Virgil Aeneas is a true hero and Turnus at best a hero *manqué*. Byron, in short, makes in some ways the same erroneous estimate of traditional heroism as do many writers on epic today; he identifies heroism too exclusively with certain of its manifestations in some particular age or ages. (The matter is complicated, of course, by the fact that such misunderstanding is functional to his deliberate, undermining skepticism in *Don Juan*.) It is interesting to notice how consistently Byron associates heroism with such terms as "fame" and "glory," which two values he systematically contrasts with the familiar realities of human experience and with such aspects of individual inner life as "self-approbation." . . . (pp. 224-25)

Byron, then, exemplifies the paradox of the epic in a negative way. The definitive epic poets and those Romantic poets who tried to place themselves in the tradition believed in the possibilities of their own ages because they also believed that greatness had existed in the past and could therefore provide a foundation on which to build newer and grander structures. One can also state this the other way around: their belief in progress committed them to an appreciation of the values of the past; even Keats, who in *Hyperion* was not much interested in any doctrine of historical continuity, implicitly salutes the past by calling up earlier statements paralleling his own statement of an essentially timeless truth. But Byron plays past and present against each other, denying that there has been greatness in the past, yet also evoking an illusory idea of earlier greatness as a judgment on his own uninspired age. Heroism, according to this view, cannot evolve; neither can the epic; nothing can come of nothing. (p. 226)

Brian Wilkie, "Byron and the Epic of Negation," in his Romantic Poets and Epic Tradition, *The University of Wisconsin Press, 1965, pp. 188-226.*

ROBERT F. GLECKNER (essay date 1967)

[*Expanding on Ridenour's conception of* Don Juan *as a series of variations on the theme of the Fall (see excerpt dated 1960),*

Gleckner contends that the structure of the poem derives from an ongoing cycle of contrasts between Byron's emotional and rational responses to the world. The critic asserts that the poem is based not on Byron's portrayal of various versions of the Fall, but on his alternately hopeful and despairing reactions to a world already irrevocably fallen. Like Wilkie (see excerpt dated 1965), Gleckner sees Don Juan *as primarily nihilistic in its perspective on the human condition. Byron, he argues, was struggling to come to grips with his own refusal to view the horrors of life with anything but the most uncompromising honesty and realism. The result, according to Gleckner, is the voice of a man trying to retain his sanity "amid the wreck of all paradises and all worlds."*]

It requires some temerity for anyone, after the fine work of Steffan and Ridenour to write again on *Don Juan.* Yet Byron's development as a poet must be seen whole, continuous, and perhaps surprisingly consistent, encompassing all of his poetry. If . . . his prophetic voice, which grows in power and conviction through the poems of 1816 and after, modulates itself into the colloquial chatter and banter of the Pulci-Berni mode, we should not be put off. Essentially the voice is still the same; its message has not changed: the various voices heard in *Hours of Idleness*, the tales, *Childe Harold,* and the plays have now, in effect, become one voice, remarkably supple and resilient and telling. As such, it concentrates all the voices of man into the presentation of a vision of the world, a "vision" in a truer sense than that implied in the only poem he wrote with the word in its title, *The Vision of Judgment.* Whereas there Byron adapts a conventional mode to destroy the efficacy of Southey's idea of vision (and that of others), in *Don Juan* the prophecies of Dante and Tasso are transformed into what is perhaps the only kind of coherent view available to Byron in his time—a fragmented, chaotic, digressive panorama of the world's waste and the unending self-destruction and corruption of man. If one must call it anti-romantic, or negatively romantic, as Morse Peckham might say, in so doing we are only recognizing the inevitability of the form and voice of the poem in Byron's age.

I must confess at the outset that I find the poem a grim one—funny, even hilarious at times, irreverent, coarse, moral and immoral at once, but through it all, despairing. It is a poem of endless cycles or, as Ridenour has put it, endless repetitions of the Fall, which form the skeletal framework for the myriad variations Byron plays upon the nature of the fallen. Furthermore, it is a poem written (or narrated) from the point of view of the fallen, and this central fact determines both the form and style of the entire work. It is not written from above, or chanted mysteriously from within the temple of prophecy, or thundered divinely from the mount; the gaze of the poet is level with life, the accents of his voice the very accents of all men. "Byron is caught," as Ridenour says,

> and he knows he is caught and he must manage to live in terms of this awareness. This is what he is engaged in coming to terms with, and *Don Juan* is the final expression of the *quality* of this acquiescence. It is clearly a frightening vision, and Byron does not try to minimize the terror. In *Don Juan* at any rate, he wastes little time in feeling sorry for himself or us. If he has no real answers, the firmness with which he poses the question is not contemptible, and the poise with which he manages, for the most part, to keep his fragmentary world from breaking up is really astonishing. For it is ultimately up to him. It is his attitude alone that can give it what coherence it is susceptible of.

Though Ridenour is certainly correct here, I should prefer a somewhat different emphasis. "Caught" in the chaos he envisions, Byron's problem, as I see it, is less to live with his awareness than to remain sane in the face of it. For it is clearly an insane world:

> Shut up the World at large, let Bedlam out;
>   And you will be perhaps surprised to find
> All things pursue exactly the same route,
>   As now with those of *soi-disant* sound mind. . . .

His sanity is maintained by the very act of creating as coherent a vision of incoherence as is possible, not so much in the quality of his acquiescence as in the quality of his triumph over his own fallen nature and over the horror of his vision. At the same time, as we have seen, the very means to the maintenance of sanity—creation—also gluts the despair out of which that creation comes—an interaction between poet and poem that Steffan sees but interprets quite differently. The precarious balance of laughter and despair in *Don Juan* is a testament to this quest for sanity. As Maurois says, the poem is the mask for "a strong and bitter philosophy beneath light-hearted gaiety and whimsical rhymes"; or, as Louise Swanton Belloc put it more tellingly and accurately a century earlier, the work of *Don Juan* is flowers crowned with thorns. Victor Hugo was quite right in protesting the identification of Voltaire and Byron: "Erreur! il y a une étrange différence entre le rire de Byron et le rire de Voltaire: Voltaire n'avait pas souffert."

I should say, then, but for a quite different reason from that which prompted the popular outcry against *Don Juan* in Byron's time and immediately thereafter, that the poem is not moral, despite all of Byron's protestations to the contrary. Fundamentally, it has to do not with morality or immorality but with nothingness, with a world devoid of value and humanity, a world in which even the "good" (in *any* sense) quickly destroys itself in its very effort to be what it is. It was not, as William Blackwood thought, Byron's "grossness or blackguardism," his "vile, heartless, and cold-blooded" attitude, that degraded "every sacred and tender feeling of the human heart"; it was simply that those sacred and tender feelings were no longer a property of man—except in those fleeting and paradoxical moments when he found them again only to die in the act of rediscovery. (pp. 329-32)

Don Juan must also be seen as an immensely compassionate poem. . . . Byron's poet *does* have a heart. If it can no longer be his sole world, his universe, in a sense the world and universe, shivered into a chaos of feeling elements that brokenly live on, like those of his own heart, have, through the medium of his own experience, loss, and suffering, become *his* heart. As such, the poet's heart is both blessing and curse—blessing in that it represents the essence of his humanity, bruised and beaten yet puissant and warmly breathing, curse in that it leads him to that fundamental sympathy which is the cause of its brokenness and his own despair. The illusion of a world separate, untaintable, and invulnerable, set apart from the slow stain of mundane affairs, is gone forever except in dreams, but in its place is not a heart insensible but a heart whose capacity has been enlarged beyond that of the private, parochial dream. It is this heart that speaks to us in the Haidée episode, which I take to be the fulcrum as well as the symbolic core of the entire poem; it is this heart that envisioned a Haidée, a Dudù, an Aurora Raby, a Leila, that weeps over the carnage of Ismail, that responds to the sparks of humanity, however few, in the characters of Gulbeyaz, Lambro, Baba, and even Suwarrow. But as that heart naturally and inevitably goes out to the essentially human, so it must be constantly restrained for sanity's sake by the laughter of the sophisticate, the sneer of the world-ling, the reasoned pessimism of the philosopher, the jokes of the buffoon, and the realism of the prophet-poet. The response of each mask in its own way claims for itself the honesty and clear-sightedness of vision, for in none of them is found the deceit and hypocrisy with which man masks his heart in the world, "Corroding in the cavern of the heart" all feeling,

> Making the countenance a masque of rest
> And turning Human Nature to an art. . . .
>
> (pp. 336-37)

The structure of the poem, then, whatever coherence it commands through the metaphor of the Fall or patterns of experience or overlapping themes, is built solidly on the thesis and antithesis of the poet's emotional and rational responses to the world. He is constantly being torn by his heart's involvement and restored by his cooler, dispassionate judgment; and both of these dynamic movements cohere in the consistent vision of the universe as a vast sea of desolation and ruin. Again and again the prophet-poet molds the evidence of his eyes into an image of the earth as it is, only to withdraw from it in horror to the safety of his own mind and one of his cerebral masks. (pp. 337-38)

What Steffan sees as the manner triumphing over the matter of the poem on occasion, as wit crackling merely "for the sake of isolated jest," as Byron becoming at times intoxicated with his own brilliance and humor, are not always signs of the poet's loss of his sure grasp of the materials, technique, and structure of the poem. It may be the result of Byron's often expressed determination that the poem, whatever else it might be, should not be dull. I take these sallies, however, not merely as an antidote to dullness or, as Steffan suggests, a natural outcome of the "itch for variety and paradox" symptomatic of Byron's "vigorous and boisterous mind." I see them as the result of his mind's constant and fearful attempt to wean him from the sorrows of the heart; from the overflow of compassion that could throw him from the brink of precarious sanity into the abyss of unutterable despair; from the perils of his clear vision of nightmarish darkness to the more comfortable facetiousness of manners within which lurked, ironically, his basic softness and warmth and humanity.

The theme of love in **Don Juan** is also related to the metaphor of Eden and the Fall, as Ridenour has noted. Of love, he writes, "the most powerful force undermining the paradisal relationship is the very force that made it a paradise in the first place . . . love recreates for the individual son of Adam the paradisal state lost by the first Adam. . . ." Although I agree with this idea, once again I would give it a different emphasis. As Ridenour sees it, love for Byron is "the most potent enemy to innocence (as embodied in young love)," and it is also Adam's "experience of such love" which led to the Fall. Perhaps. It is more important that for Byron true love does indeed re-create paradise, indeed *is* paradise regained, but, as the tales and *Childe Harold* have told us, that re-creation is only momentary or illusory: . . . in the very act of being most human and warm man is betrayed by circumstances or the world (or perhaps even by God) in such a way that his essential humanness is sacrificed or lost the moment it is gained. Once that lesson is learned, man in his new and bitter wisdom thenceforth steels his heart against further loss, sorrow, and despair by "manning" himself through an exercise of will and mind—and in so doing he denies the very humanity whose "loss" was so severe a blow. (pp. 339-40)

But man, as I have said, and as Byron has so often indicated in his earlier poems, learns from his loss and from the world. Steeling his heart, he becomes more a man and less a human, and thus can survive or even triumph over the world on its own terms. Juan in the court of Catherine the Great, fresh from the slaughter of Ismail, is the symbol of this transformation: in full and gaudy uniform, the obvious hero: "He / Seems Love turned a Lieutenant of Artillery!" . . . A variant upon this theme is Lambro, the fisher of men; in a searing parody of Christ, he fishes for wandering merchant vessels only to confiscate their cargoes and sell the crews into slavery or slaughter them in battle. . . . To clinch his point Byron also describes the more civilized piracy, slavery, and slaughter of love amid society in exactly the same phrase, "Fishers for men." . . .

Such gentlemanly and polite conflict is but the superficial mask for what men truly are once their hearts have been steeled and their bodies and minds manned to do battle. For that truth we must look to the archetypal war and waste which for Byron characterize life when it was not "This paradise of Pleasure and *Ennui*" . . . , "that Microcosm on stilts, / Yclept the Great World." . . . The Siege of Ismail is his terrifyingly coherent vision of the shattered, violent, bestial world that is left after the death of the heart and the loss of Eden. (pp. 343-44)

[War] and bloody cruelty, "Hell's pollution" . . . , Byron sees not merely for what it is but as an emblem of civilization:

> Now back to thy great joys, Civilisation!
> And the sweet consequence of large society,
>   War—pestilence—the despot's desolation,
> The kingly scourge, the lust of notoriety,
>   The millions slain by soldiers for their ration,
> The scenes like Catherine's boudoir at threescore,
> With Ismail's storm to soften it the more. . . .

Amid the heat of battle and the overpowering bloodlust, even "War forgot his own destructive art / In more destroying Nature" . . . , the nature of man whose heart has been buried or destroyed in his cerebrating manhood:

> All that the mind would shrink from of excesses—
>   All that the body perpetrates of bad;
> All that we read—hear—dream, of man's distresses—
>   All that the Devil would do if run stark mad;
> All that defies the worst which pen expresses,—
>   All by which Hell is peopled, or as sad
> As Hell—mere mortals who their power abuse—
> Was here (as heretofore and since) let loose. . . .

It is **The Siege of Corinth** all over again, or the nightmarish wasteland ride of **Mazeppa,** or the damp horror of **The Prisoner of Chillon,** or the visions on the field of Waterloo of **Childe Harold,** or the mad conflagration of **Sardanapalus,** or any of the numberless insane slaughters in Byron's poetry—all perpetrated by the human mind bereft of the heart's softness and love. It is visions such as these that call forth from Byron unrestrained imprecations against the God or gods who permit the carnage. **Cain** and **Heaven and Earth** are but the intellectualized versions of, for example, this passage in the shipwreck scene in Canto II:

> 'T was twilight, and the sunless day went down
>   Over the waste of waters; like a veil,
> Which, if withdrawn, would but disclose the frown
>   Of one whose hate is masked but to assail.
> Thus to their hopeless eyes the night was shown,

And grimly darkled o'er the faces pale,
And the dim desolate deep: twelve days had Fear
Been their familiar, and now Death was here. . . .

Thus man is both destroyer and destroyed, victim and victimizer, and the gods (or God) made in man's image but conspire to sink him in the vast deep of desolation. "The sparrow's fall / Is special providence," he writes in another place, echoing *Hamlet:*

> though how it gave
> Offence we know not; probably it perched
> Upon the tree which Eve so fondly searched. . . .

In another canto, quoting Wordsworth out of context in a passing attack upon his favorite target among the Romantic poets, Byron turns the passage upon itself to give us a version of the new Trinity overseeing the battle of Ismail:

> "Carnage" (so Wordsworth tells you) "is God's
> daughter:"
> If *he* speak truth, she is Christ's sister, and
> Just now behaved as in the Holy Land. . . .

Byron's prophecy, then, is clearly not based on cause and effect—if you go on so, the result will be so—but rather it is what he refers to facetiously in Canto XV as the prophecy of *is* and *was* . . . ; of "a plain man" . . . who "Without, or with, offence to friends or foes" will "sketch" the "world exactly as it goes" . . . ; who makes "addresses from the throne" . . . in the guise of merriment because his fundamental humanity "cannot always bring / Itself to apathy" . . . ; who denounces "all amorous writing" in a poem dedicated to love and the death of the heart . . . ; who feigns stoicism only to reveal his hurt more fully; who hates not but knows that he is hated . . . ; who knows that he is unheard yet declaims all the louder for his loneliness; who weeps while knowing that his tears are but the ocean poured into a sieve . . . ; and whose voice crying in the wilderness, feeding its own despair, is the only hope discernible amid the wreck of all paradises and all worlds. (pp. 345-47)

> *Robert F. Gleckner, in his* Byron and the Ruins of
> Paradise, *The Johns Hopkins University Press, 1967,*
> *365 p.*

A. B. ENGLAND (essay date 1975)

[*In contrast to previous critics, England argues that the style of* Don Juan *was more significantly influenced by the poetry of Jonathan Swift than that of Alexander Pope. Conceding Byron's admiration for Pope and the latter's tangible influence on* Don Juan, *the critic nevertheless asserts that the rhetoric of the poem shows a greater affinity with Swift's "burlesque style" than with Pope's more precisely structured approach to poetic diction. England compares several passages from* Don Juan *with excerpts from Swift's works in order to demonstrate shared stylistic traits. The critic also maintains that the chaotic vision of the universe expressed in* Don Juan *has more in common philosophically with Swift's works than those of Pope. Parts of the critic's remarks originally appeared in his longer study,* Byron's "Don Juan" and Eighteenth-Century Literature: A Study of Some Rhetorical Continuities and Discontinuities.]

In this essay I want to discuss some of the relationships between Byron's poetic style in *Don Juan* and the English poetry of the early eighteenth century. There has been no extended treatment of the subject since Ronald Bottrall's essay written more than thirty years ago [see excerpt dated 1939], in which he tried to

counteract F. R. Leavis's argument that the relationship between Byron's poetry and that of Pope is not really very close. Although it has become commonplace to mention Byron's intense admiration of Augustan poetry and especially of Pope, nearly all of the comparisons that one encounters are briefly made and undeveloped, usually because the author is concentrating on something else. In making some further comparisons now, I shall be concerned not with matters of direct influence (though evidence of that certainly appears in some of the passages I shall discuss), but with continuities such as those to which T. S. Eliot refers in 'Tradition and the Individual Talent' when he writes that the most 'individual' parts of a poet's work 'may be those in which the dead poets, his ancestors, assert their immortality most vigorously. To define such continuities is obviously a means of clarifying the place which *Don Juan* occupies in the English literary tradition. And in attempting to do this, I shall introduce a rather different kind of emphasis from that which has so far been prevalent. For it seems to me that the almost exclusive emphasis on Pope has been misplaced, and that the most important connections are with a kind of poetry quite different from his. (pp. 94-5)

While it is important, I think, to recognise the occasions on which the poem's rhetoric is related to Pope's, it also needs to be said that the impulse towards order which those occasions represent appears in a poem which is most of the time imitative of a reality that lacks the coherence in which Pope believed. Therefore, if the style of *Don Juan* is more than sporadically connected with any part of Augustan poetry, that part is not the one represented by Pope. There was, however, a kind of poetry being written in the early eighteenth century which in its style and in the concept of reality implied by that style was radically different from Pope's. And the major practitioner of it was Swift.

Swift's poetry is of course extremely varied, but both he and Pope felt that it tended to possess certain predominant characteristics. And they both referred to these characteristics through the use of the word 'burlesque'. Swift at one point imagines himself being requested to 'suspend a While, / That same paultry *Burlesque* Stile,' and Pope's list of 'authorities for poetical language' recommended Butler and Swift 'for the burlesque style.' Byron also uses the same word to describe his own poetry in *Don Juan* when he says that 'the sad truth which hovers o'er my desk / Turns what was once romantic to burlesque'. . . . Nowadays, of course, the meaning of the word is very generalised, but when Pope and Swift refer to the 'burlesque style' it is clear that they have in mind a fairly definite set of rhetorical expectations. These expectations are based largely on the style of Butler's *Hudibras*, which was widely imitated in the early eighteenth century, and which Swift's poetic manner often resembles. It has been pointed out that burlesque poetry began as an attempt to achieve comic effects by describing the figures and actions of classical epic in a colloquial and vulgar style. And the comedy in *Hudibras* is achieved largely through the juxtaposition of words that possess fairly elevated connotations with words that ordinarily belong to a more commonplace context. The burlesque style thus achieves some of its major effects by exploiting contrasts between radically different kinds of words. But the intention of the burlesque poet, when he juxtaposes kinds and levels, is in no way—as it is in Pope's satires—to criticise failures of discrimination. On the contrary, when the burlesque poet juxtaposes, say, the heroic and the commonplace, his intention is to amuse us by persuading us to entertain the idea of a possible connection between the two. Thus, while the burlesque style is essentially based on the concept of a hierarchical structure, it tends to undermine rather than to affirm that structure. (pp. 100-01)

I would suggest that in the following stanza from *Don Juan* Byron shows an affinity of both style and temperament with [Swift's burlesques] . . . :

> Her favourite science was the mathematical,
> Her noblest virtue was her magnanimity,
> Her wit (she sometimes tried at wit) was Attic all,
> Her serious sayings darkened to sublimity;
> In short, in all things she was fairly what I call
> A prodigy—her morning dress was dimity,
> Her evening silk, or, in the summer, muslin,
> And other stuffs, with which I won't stay puzzling. . . .

If we look at the sequence, 'mathematical', 'Attic all', 'what I call', we witness a progressive diminution of the power which the first rhyme-word ordinarily has to communicate meaning. For the fragmentation of that word's sound-structure is pushed to such an extreme that the reader is made retrospectively to sense 'mathematical' more strongly as a physical object than as an embodiment of meaning. The rhymes not only damage the word's integrity, they reduce it to the status of a cipher whose meaning is of no account. Such is the kind of thing that tends to happen in this stanza to words denoting those pursuits and talents of which Donna Inez is so proud. It happens in the sequence, 'magnanimity', 'sublimity', 'dimity', where the juxtaposition of the imposingly abstract and the prosaically physical does not imply that any hierarchical distinction needs to be made between them. On the contrary, Byron is throughout the stanza making the point that the 'magnanimity' and the 'sublimity' of Donna Inez are as superficial as the articles of clothing made out of 'dimity', so that the apparently gratuitous details about what she wears in fact follow naturally upon the description of her moral, intellectual and emotional characteristics. Moreover, it is not only Donna Inez's personality which is diminished by this stanza. For when words like 'magnanimity' and 'sublimity' are made to participate in such absurd verbal patterns as this, the dignity and the serious values which are normally attached to them tend to be obscured or even momentarily obliterated. The words appear to be introduced because of their capacity to serve the ends of Byron's verbal farce, and they consequently suffer a reduction—just as in . . . [passages] by Swift, words suggestive of intellectual activity suffer a reduction for the same reason.

The manner in which Swift juxtaposes contrasting items in his poetry constantly tends to undermine hierarchies, and to enforce the concept of an absurd reality in which levels tend to merge rather than to separate. At one point in 'On Poetry: A Rapsody' he suggests that if a satirist does not fully identify the individuals he attacks it will be difficult, merely from a description of their characteristics and activities, to be sure who is referred to:

> A publick, or a private *Robber;*
> A *Statesman,* or a South-Sea *Jobber.*
> A *Prelate* who no God Believes;
> A [Parliament], or Den of Thieves.
> A Pick-purse at the Bar, or Bench;
> A Duchess, or a Suburb-Wench. . . .

Only a name distinguishes the morally coalescing levels, and if the juxtapositions are incongruous in appearance they are not in fact. Rather than enabling the reader to make clear, confirmatory distinctions, Swift's rhetoric implies that it is hard to separate one level clearly from another, that accepted lines of demarcation are in reality blurred. And the use of juxtaposition here is very much like that which appears time after time in *Don Juan*. A clear example occurs in the first of the following three lines:

> The statesman—hero—harlot—lawyer—ward
> Off each attack, when people are in quest
> Of their designs, by saying they *meant well.* . . .

Byron's point is that all of these apparently disparate kinds of person tend both to do harm and to claim that their good intentions excuse that harm. When he places these items next to one another within the line, therefore, his intention is to suggest that the distinctions between them are not really so clear as they are ordinarily assumed to be. His use of juxtaposition is like Swift's in that it stresses an unrecognised homogeneity beneath the surface differences. A similar effect is given when he writes of the starving Juan:

> He fell upon whate'er was offered, like
> A priest, a shark, an alderman, or pike. . . .

The second line of this couplet vividly illustrates the difference between the two kinds of juxtaposition that I have been discussing. When Pope places 'Friendship' and 'ten Pound', or bibles and billets-doux close to each other within the poetic line, he is seeking to confirm traditional hierarchic distinctions rather than to imply a real absence of differentiation. The confused surface of his line, in which disparate items are brought unharmoniously together, may imitate the disorder of the satirised object's mind. But there exists for Pope a reality which possesses the order of a hierarchical structure and in which spiritual and materialistic values are clearly separate. His juxtapositions reach beyond the chaotic surfaces he describes to suggest that there is clarity, distinction, coherence in the nature of things. The structure of Byron's line, however, holds 'priest', 'shark', 'alderman' and 'pike' in close conjunction, and he wishes us to see them as being so conjoined in reality; the apparently distinct levels coalesce in fact, not just in the mind of a satirised object who cannot perceive the way things truly are. The juxtapositions do not reach beyond the confused world that they describe towards a coherent ethical structure against the reality of which that world is judged. Rather, the line seems to mimic a reality which is much more deeply disordered than that which Pope perceives, and Byron's juxtapositions offer no reassuring access to a fundamental coherence in the nature of things. They mimic the only reality that the poet knows; they do not ironically define failures to perceive a real hierarchy behind the confusion of immediate particulars. (pp. 102-05)

In a fairly recent attempt to define the burlesque style, Francis Bar has suggested that one of its major tendencies is to enumerate miscellaneous specifics without organising them into coherent patterns. The device originated as part of the burlesque poet's attempt to create all kinds of discontinuity and incoherence in opposition to the high degree of formal order associated with epic poetry. And a similar kind of stylistic tendency appears in Swift's poetry, often when he is not consciously concerned with being anti-epic. A typical example occurs in 'A Description of a City Shower', where Swift is in fact parodying Virgil's description of a storm in the first book of the *Georgics,* and where the connection with the burlesque tradition is particularly strong:

> To Shops in Crouds the daggled Females fly,
> Pretend to cheapen Goods, but nothing buy.
> The Templer spruce, while ev'ry Spout's a-broach,

Stays till 'tis fair, yet seems to call a Coach.
The tuck'd-up Sempstress walks with hasty Strides,
While Streams run down her oil'd Umbrella's Sides.
Here various Kinds by various Fortunes led,
Commence Acquaintance underneath a Shed.
Triumphant Tories, and desponding Whigs,
Forget their Fewds, and join to save their Wigs. . . .

Here, Swift enumerates the various items in such a way as to avoid any ethical or thematic classification of them. There is, of course, a kind of relationship between the various individuals in that they all have a common purpose. But this is a superficial, fortuitous connection, and the passage is carefully organised to give the impression that the speaker is observing quite randomly, noting items without selecting or ordering them. Because of this it seems inappropriate to define the succession of items in the way it is defined by the following statement; 'the city's corruption is betokened . . . in the behaviour of the citizens caught in the downpour. Hypocrisy, or falseseeming, is the essence of their natures. Tories and Whigs, in the face of the threatening deluge, discard their ostensibly principled differences and reveal their true common purposes. Such ethical classification of the poem's various details has the effect of attributing to them a much greater degree of generic life than they actually have. It simply cannot be assumed that a series of particulars in Swift's poetry is likely to possess the kind of morally significant coherence that such series do in Pope's. In this instance Swift is intent on preserving the sheer miscellaneousness of the juxtaposed items, and they are not allowed to participate in any significant patterns of generic contrast or similarity. His picture shows no evidence of coherent composition, and its specific elements seem likely to spill over the edges of any frame that might irrelevantly be imposed on them.

In the second canto of *Don Juan,* when he describes the multitudinous chaos wrought by the storm at sea, Byron also accumulates particulars without forming them into coherently thematic patterns:

Some went to prayers again, and made a vow
Of candles to their saints—but there were none
To pay them with: and some look'd o'er the bow:
Some hoisted out the boats; and there was one
That begged Pedrillo for an absolution,
Who told him to be damned—in his confusion.

Some lashed them in their hammocks; some put on
Their best clothes, as if going to a fair;
Some cursed the day on which they saw the Sun,
And gnashed their teeth, and howling, tore their
hair. . . .

The items in this passage are carefully selected so as to give the impression that no process of selection has gone on, and they are arranged in a sequence which gives the impression that they have not been arranged at all. Only in the first two lines of the second stanza, with their juxtaposition of the private and the public, do we find items achieving a degree of relationship with each other through the principle of generic contrast. Elsewhere, they appear to stand next to one another only because they do so in that actuality which Byron's rhetorical pattern imitates, and which he purports to register by a process of random notation. Especially in the movement from those who 'went to prayers' to those who 'looked o'er the bow' there is a studied discontinuity, a lack of significant progression. And the reference to the second of these two groups of people is ostentatiously gratuitous; by simply looking 'o'er the bow'

they take on no generic or otherwise significant life, and Byron creates the illusion that he points them out only because they are there. Byron's rhetorical structure, therefore, is designed so as to appear to be inclusive of individual items which not only enforce no theme, but do not even belong to any ordered world of kinds. And the movement between these disconnected particulars is as imitatively discontinuous as that in 'A Description of a City Shower'.

In passages like this, it is made to appear that an unstructured external reality finds its way, unorganised and untransformed, into the fabric of Byron's poetry. No evident design within the rhetoric opposes itself to or resists the chaotic multiplicity that is being presented. And this stylistic tendency becomes especially noticeable when the subject matter which is being treated is of a dull or repetitive nature. (pp. 107-10)

Don Juan is, of course, an extremely varied poem, and it is not dominated by any one style. But the kind of rhetoric I have described in comparing Byron with Swift appears much more frequently than that which [is often emphasized] in comparing Byron with Pope, and it is more central to the poem in that it is closely related to the kind of world-view which *Don Juan* as a whole tends to enforce. I have tried to describe some aspects of what I take to be a genuine stylistic continuity, and one which connects both Swift and Byron with the tradition of English burlesque poetry. (pp. 110-11)

> *A. B. England, "The Style of 'Don Juan' and Augustan Poetry," in* Byron: A Symposium, *edited by John D. Jump, Macmillan, 1975, pp. 94-112.*

JEROME J. McGANN (essay date 1976)

[*In the following excerpt, McGann discusses Byron's conception in* Don Juan *of the relation between imagination and poetry, emphasizing how it differed from that of other great English Romantic poets. The critic argues that in contrast to such contemporaries as Wordsworth and Keats, Byron saw the imagination primarily as an analytic rather than a creative faculty—one to help clarify reality rather than embellish poetry. McGann's remarks are based in part on his analysis of Byron's attitudes as reflected in the unpublished preface to the poem (see excerpt dated 1818).*]

When Wordsworth attacked the "poetical diction" which his age had inherited, and when Coleridge said that objects as objects are fixed and dead, both spoke from a similar perspective. Behind them lay the territory entered first, and initially mapped, by Locke. A pile of stones, a pair of shoes, a table: unless these things are lit up with the life of the perceiver, they have no meaning. They are mere objects, fixed and dead. Outward forms do not win us to life; the fountains are within, in the individual imagination, whence all meaning comes. So too for Wordsworth: once "poetical diction" represented the outpouring of a vital expression, but long usage had deadened these forms, which now use poets. Poetical language is mere convention which the poets follow, and to which they subject their vision.

No one can fail to see the force, and real importance, of such ideas. At the same time, we have increasingly come to accept this particular Romantic position uncritically, and without realizing its serious limitations. These limitations ultimately fall to the awareness that such a view constricts the functional world in which living operations are carried out. Life is "within," meaning is personal, the individual is the source and end and test of what is real and true. Yet surely nothing could be less true than these ideas, unless it were the opposite set of ideas, that the individual had no impact upon the meaning of his own experience, or, for that matter, on the experience of others. (p. 156)

[The] whole point of *Don Juan* was to attack the "Romantic" position especially. The power of the attack is based upon Byron's sense that "tuism" . . . was as crucial a factor in human affairs, public and private, as was "universal Egotism." . . . Human meaning in the world cannot simply be seen from the perspective of the individual, as if his life gave life to reality, as if the person alone were the jar in Tennessee about which "the whole creation moved." For Byron, the person existed in context, and the interaction of the two developed the reality we call the human world.

One example will have to suffice. Let us recall, for a moment, the object fixed and dead—all those "its" out there which seem merely to sit still. For a Romantic of the Imagination, a table, a pair of shoes, a particular locution: these "things" need our life to live, they need to be reinvested with new life by the individual. But in what sense is this so? A fixed and dead table we pass every day, unimaginatively, may be having a very imaginative time of it. It may not be in *our* lively world, but it is in *the* world, and we may be merely unaware of the various contexts other than our own in which that table is having a continuous importance and life. Nor does the table, or the contexts in which it moves and has its being, need any one of us particularly. It is at least as much our loss, as much as it may be the table's or the table's world's loss, if we fail to find any of our life in terms of it. The table and its world will go on living without us. (pp. 156-57)

A pair of shoes is not simply a pair of shoes. If they are not ours, they are—or have been, or will be, or might be, or might have been—someone else's. In any case, they have a human meaning, though our own limited perspective may close us from that meaning. *Don Juan* is constantly trying to remind Byron's contemporaries, and us, that the meaning of events passes beyond human perception because the contexts of events are always larger than our own awareness. Insisting upon the primacy of the Imagination, we become less imaginative, more self-absorbed, Lake-locked.

We do not have to depend solely upon our imaginations. The world is more benevolent than that, or perhaps more chastening; and "outward forms" (like simple manners in a Jane Austen novel) can come in aid of imagination even as feeling can come in aid of feeling. Outward forms can teach the fixed imagination a few things too, from a life that is not the imagination's own. Don Alfonso, in *Don Juan*, gets an infuriating lesson in this truth when a mere "pair of shoes" is part of a message which he had already "imagined," but which, without the shoes, he could not decode.

> A pair of shoes!—what then? not much, if they
>   Are such as fit with ladies' feet, but these
> (No one can tell how much I grieve to say)
>   Were masculine; to see them, and to seize,
> Was but a moment's act.—Ah! well-a-day!
>   My teeth begin to chatter, my veins freeze!
> Alfonso first examined well their fashion,
> And then flew out into another passion. . . .

The "meaning" of the pair of shoes, though already imagined by Don Alfonso, is not created by his imagination. The shoes, in context, have their own meaning which Alfonso does not give, but in which he is deeply implicated. (It would be a

complex problem, for example, to explain fully how the shoes got where they are.) The meaning of the shoes is constituted in a reality larger than Don Alfonso, larger than Don Juan (whose shoes they are), larger than the room in which all the characters are now placed. Don Alfonso imagined himself a cuckold, but reality made him one. Moreover, he is a fool by imagination, and in reality. Don Alfonso wants to triumph over his imagined disgrace by imagining what he knows (to borrow a phrase from Shelley). Things are not so easily arranged, however, for life has more contexts than one may at any point imagine. The scene of Don Alfonso's imagination is also being imagined from other perspectives: by Donna Julia, by her maid, by Juan. None of these imaginations ultimately wins out, however, for Byron has yet another imagination of the scene, which is the surprising imagination of "Circumstance, that unspiritual god" (*Childe Harold* . . .). Byron arranges the scene, first, to show how different perspectives and contexts overlap in what appears to be "one" place (it is in fact many places); and second, to analyze critically the (for example, Blakean) idea that a particularly strong imagination or context necessarily triumphs over others in the affairs of life by reason of its strength. But the actual event is never so neat, for strength itself is a fact and idea whose meaning is determined by relative contexts. Even when we seem to be gaining control of a situation, for example, multiple contexts are arranging events differently. Every victory which brought Napoleon closer to Moscow, which he finally took, was only another defeat in his accumulating catastrophe.

Byron controls the bedroom scene, but only in poetry, and only to show that life is the measure of imagination, not vice versa. That scene, like all of *Don Juan*, puts poetry in its place: it represents, and if necessary reveals, the world, which is its standard. Imagination is part of the human world, not its defining idea. The human world exists as history, tradition, and facts before it ever can begin to exist as will or idea. We find ourselves somewhere particularly, in a world we never made—which may be reason for many different sorts of reactions. But however we respond to it, we cannot live in any world, even a purely inward world, unless we live in a larger world. Struggling with that larger world is one of the terms of life that are given to us, determined for us, in advance. Romantic rebellion, egoism, imagination are, we should be pleased to say, very conventional ways of behaving. If men are the masters of things, as in some sense they are, they have much more to thank (or curse) for this state of affairs than themselves, much more even than their particular human history. Biology is not in fact man's creation, but only his idea. The responsibility for being human is not something men invented in their self-conscious minds alone. The "sciences of the artificial," including imagination, are merely the ways men have developed for dealing functionally with the contexts in which they find themselves. For Byron, this often meant the construction of imaginative systems which exposed the fact, and importance, of context itself. (pp. 157-59)

Unlike Coleridge, Byron was far from being a profound theorist of poetry; nor was he a great intellectual polemicist for the new poetical ideas of his day, as Blake, Wordsworth, and Shelley were. He was not even, like Keats, a subtle critic and anatomist of his own ideas about being a writer. When we read his *Reply to Blackwood's* . . . [see excerpt dated 1820] and his epistolary "answers" to Bowles we find a very traditional set of ideas about poetry. (pp. 159-60)

The contrast with Keats is glaring. "I am certain of nothing but of the holiness of the Heart's affections and the truth of

Imagination—What the imagination seizes as Beauty must be truth—whether it existed before or not." Such an exaltation of the imagination was, for Byron, absurd. Merely to be able to imagine something . . . was no guarantee of the truth of imagination. Though he admitted that "it must be" so, Keats said that he had "never yet been able to perceive how any thing can be known for truth by consequitive reasoning." Therefore, in his pursuit of truth through poetry Keats swore allegiance to the imagination and depreciated the "rational" poetry of Pope. But Byron kept faith with the Enlightenment: "We are sneeringly told that [Pope] is the 'Poet of Reason,' as if this was a reason for his being no poet." And again: "He who can reconcile poetry with truth and wisdom, is the only true '*poet*' in its real sense."

For Keats, however, Imagination *was* Truth—that is what his phrase "the truth of Imagination" means. But for Byron "the truth of Imagination" was the truth, or truths, which could be brought to light with the aid of the devices of poetry, including the aid of imagination. The subject (truth) of poetry was not the poetic process itself—truth as imagination, in the Romantic formulation—but the human world of men and women in their complex relations with themselves, each other, and their environments, both natural and cultural.

The consequence of Byron's position is an idea about imagination (and poetic invention) which may now strike us, the late inheritors of Romantic ideas about poetry, as extremely novel. We tend, because of our immediate literary tradition, to equate imagination with creativity. Indeed, the idea that the imagination is "creative" is so entrenched in our thinking that we no longer examine what it means. For Byron, the imagination was creative only in a specific sense, that is, it was the source of the poet's *inventio*. Byron's old-fashioned poetics led him to regard invention as one of the poet's tools (others he specifically mentions are thought, design, characterization, description, eloquence, versification). Consequently, invention or creativity was a means to an end. The ultimate purpose of the imagination was not to create, as High Romanticism suggested, self-generated and self-justifying worlds and orders. Rather, it was to present fictive conditions in terms of which the human world would be more clearly revealed and, being revealed, would be more susceptible to human judgment. In the end, Byron's "imagination" is not creative (in the Romantic sense), it is analytic and critical (in the philosophic sense). *Don Juan* is Byron's textual evidence for his position.

In the prose "Preface" to his epic Byron initiated his attack upon the Romantic exaltation of imagination as a divine poetic faculty [see excerpt dated 1818]. The texts he has most immediately in mind are Wordsworth's "Preface to Poems, 1815" and Coleridge's *Biographia Literaria*, especially chapters 13-14. Byron's strategy in his Preface is ironic and indirect. He opens with a reference to Wordsworth's brief prose preface to "The Thorn," in which the "Reader is desired to extend his usual courtesy so far as to suppose that the narrative is narrated by 'the Captain of a Merchantman or small trading vessel lately retired upon a small annuity to some inland town—&c. &c.' I quote from memory but conceive the above to be the sense— as far [as] there is Sense of the note or preface to the aforesaid poem—as far as it is a poem." The word "suppose," here and in the remainder of the Preface, is used to locate the poetical power praised so highly by Wordsworth and Coleridge, "exertion of Imagination" (as Byron later says in his Preface).

Byron goes on to quote from "The Thorn" and to denounce such poetry in broad invective. The point of his attack does not become clear, however, until the second part of the Preface, where he ironically asks:

> The Reader who has acquiesced in Mr. Wordsworth's supposition . . . is requested to suppose by a like exertion of Imagination that the following epic Narrative is told by a Spanish Gentleman in a village in the Sierra Morena on the road between Monasterio and Seville—sitting at the door of a Posada with the Curate of the hamlet on his right hand a Segar in his mouth— a Jug of Malaga or perhaps, "right Sherris" before him on a small table containing the relics of an Olla Podrida.

Byron's supposition continues at great length and the detail of his imagined setting is rich and complex. When he finishes his description he again turns directly to the reader: "Having supposed as much of this as the utter impossibility of such a supposition will admit—the reader is requested to extend his supposed power of supposing so far as to conceive." This remark introduces the final section of the Preface, but it also works back across the first two parts by elucidating the meaning of "supposing" and imagination in poets and readers.

First, Byron is ridiculing Wordsworth, the exalter of imagination, for his lack of imagination. His implied argument is that if Wordsworth really had a powerful imagination—as powerful as Pope's, for example—he would not have had to preface "The Thorn" with a prose statement explaining (however thinly) the context of the poem's story. The argument works by assuming, for the moment, Wordsworth's own notions about imagination and poetry. Wordsworth's poem ought to have made all the matters detailed in his preface clear in the poetry itself, if they were in fact relevant to the poetry. But the fact is, Byron implies, that Wordsworth's poetry is as dull and

Byron's Italian mistress, Countess Teresa Guiccioli.

''unimaginative'' as his prose. The wit of the argument is particularly complex because Byron is also alluding to Wordsworth's remarks on verse and prose, and their relation to poetry, in the ''preface'' to *Lyrical Ballads.*

In the second place, Byron's own prose ''supposition,'' which is highly detailed, is meant to illustrate what imagination in a writer actually entails. His excellent point is that a good writer does not ask of his reader ''a like exertion of Imagination'' in supposing what a particular poem is about, but performs that office himself. The reader is not supposed to suppose but to enjoy and judge on the basis of the poet's supposings. ''Poets do need imagination,'' Byron is saying, ''and here is one (modest) writer's ability to imagine something for his readers.'' The example is meant to contrast with Wordsworth's feeble imaginations, on the one hand, and to make the point that the reader should not be required to perform the poet's function. Indeed, as Byron says, it is an ''utter impossibility'' for the reader to ''suppose'' or imagine what the poet must invent.

The last part of the Preface recapitulates the critique set out in the previous sections and introduces a wholly new perspective on imagining, invention, and supposing. The reader ''may . . . imagine various causes for the tenor'' of the dedicatory stanzas to *Don Juan.* Further: ''the dedication may be . . . supposed to be produced by some one who may have a cause of aversion from the said Southey—for some particular reason.'' The Preface, in short, concludes with a series of requests that the reader ''imagine'' the actual truth lying behind the fictions of *Don Juan.* As in his supposition about the ''Spanish Gentleman in a village in the Sierra Morena,'' Byron goes on to provide in great detail the ''imagined'' circumstances with which much of *Don Juan,* and in particular the ''Dedication,'' is concerned. The truth of Imagination in *Don Juan* is thus made to be not poetical imagining but actual fact—realities of time, place, circumstance.

Byron's Preface implies that poets should use imagination to reveal the truth about something outside poetry altogether. Poetic imaginings are not ''true,'' they are one of the poet's most useful means for getting at and clarifying what is true. In *Don Juan* itself the point is handled repeatedly—for example, when Byron speculates: what ''if our quarrels should rip up old stories''? He answers the question at the end of the stanza: ''science profits by this resurrection— / Dead scandals form good subjects for dissection.'' . . . The poet's imaginings—dead or live scandals, or even purely invented histories—form the basis for increasing our understanding of the real and the human world, as Byron's scientific metaphor emphasizes. We study, analyze, and make judgments about reality by ''dissecting,'' as it were, the poet's fictive representations. (pp. 160-63)

[Imagination] in *Don Juan* is not a creative but an analytic instrument. *Don Juan*'s inventions serve an intellectual (and, ultimately, moral) purpose. Nor is Byron's poem, like *The Eve of St. Agnes,* its own reason for being. *Don Juan* does not imagine itself, as Keats's poem does, it imagines the world. It is ''created'' to clarify the world of men, rather than the world of poetic processes. Of course, all poetry except the purely aesthetic (if any such exists) must and does do this; but *Don Juan* was specifically written to warn its age, and succeeding ages, against the solipsistic dangers latent in the new theories of poetry (''the reveries . . . of prosaic raving''). *Don Juan* was an attempt to restore poetry to its proper place and functions, both for its own good and for the benefit of the world it was meant to serve. (p. 165)

Jerome J. McGann, in his ''Don Juan'' in Context, The University of Chicago Press, 1976, 184 p.

FREDERICK L. BEATY (essay date 1985)

[*In the following excerpt from his full-length study of Byron's satires, Beaty explores the concept of* Don Juan *as ''epic satire.'' The critic examines Byron's familiarity with various aspects of the satiric tradition, noting how the poet used the framework of the Classical epic to create the unique satiric form of* Don Juan. *In his discussion, Beaty focuses on Byron's imitation of Roman satire, or* satura, *in Canto V of the poem and studies the ''satiric spirit'' which permeates the whole. The critic contends that despite the multitude of influences and styles it displays,* Don Juan *is primarily a collection of different forms of satire bound together by Byron's anti-heroic approach to the conventions of the epic.*]

The form of *Don Juan* is so indeterminate as virtually to defy categorization. Since the classical epic, Roman satire, Italian epic romance, mock-heroic poetry, the picaresque novel, Restoration comedy, the realistic novel, the novel of manners, the pantomime, Gothic romance, the ballad, the lyric, and neoclassical satire have all left their imprint on the poem, it is not surprising that the receptacle containing such varied ingredients should be amorphous. Critics who have felt uneasy about calling *Don Juan* a ''hold-all'' have resorted to designating it as a metrical novel, a mock-epic, an epic carnival, an epic of negation, epic satire, or merely satire. While excellent cases can be made for all these labels, none is utterly satisfactory for the poem as a whole. One of the few delineations with which no critics would cavil is James R. Thompson's description of *Don Juan* as ''a kind of generic explosion produced by the nineteenth-century pressure to redefine form in highly personal terms.''

What is undeniable, in any case, is that the form, or formlessness, accurately reflects Byron's view of life and man's disordered, incongruous, and unpredictable world. His concept of artistic form, as McGann has maintained, is not concerned with internal unity but, in the Horatian tradition, with rhetoric and function. Form, either in the classical sense of a preconceived mold or in the Romantic sense of a product of organic development, has little meaning for *Don Juan.* So long as a poetical work was ''simple and entire,'' as Byron translated the Horatian dictum in *Hints from Horace,* and also was organized in such a way as to express most effectively what the poet had to say, form could take care of itself. Byron's repeated assertions that the cantos of *Don Juan,* whether organized around topics or episodic narrative, could go on almost indefinitely suggest a looseness of structure and an open-endedness that challenge conventional notions of form. The shapelessness of *Don Juan,* however, was not a serious problem with regard to satire. Since its Roman inception, satire has been thought of as a hodgepodge (*farrago*), a medley, or a miscellaneous collection. It has tended to be so unstructured that, as Northrop Frye affirmed, ''a kind of parody of form seems to run all through its tradition.'' Acquaintance with the tradition, which included many varieties of satire and different levels of style appropriate to them, had taught Byron that there was actually no prescribed form.

He was sufficiently skilled as a classicist to appreciate what the Romans called formal satire. In Latin *satura* designated only a particular literary genre—a seemingly unordered poem mixing unfavorable criticism with moral observations. In English, however, the term *satire* could be applied to any artistic composition in which the author's intention was to arouse contempt for his subject. More loosely, it might refer to isolated passages in compositions that were not predominantly derogatory, to the temper characterizing such works, or even to the techniques employed to degrade. It is revealing that in letters and conversations Byron most frequently referred to *Don Juan* as a satire. It is also significant that early reviewers saw the poem primarily as satire—on everything, including the epic. And whatever the generic modulations of the poem, its substance is undeniably permeated by the satiric spirit, even in instances when that spirit, as both Ernest J. Lovell and Alvin B. Kernan [see excerpts dated 1957 and 1965] have observed, is so thoroughly blended with either comedy or tragedy that it can hardly be identified as "serious" satire. Since there was no satiric form adequate to a large composition, a more comprehensive genre, such as the epic, was needed as a carrier—one in which a variety of intentions, including the satiric, could function. Within this matrix Byron was able to incorporate not only many kinds of satire but in one instance, the Constantinople episode, an illustration of *satura*.

His conscious adaptation of both the form and substance of Roman satire in Canto V suggests that he wished that portion to be seen in the light of a continuing tradition. This imitation was his way of announcing his genre and establishing his pedigree. His two introductory stanzas beginning that canto advertise his intention of forsaking "amorous writing" in favor of an edifying variety that attaches morals to every error and attacks all the passions. Properly interpreted, the narrator's role becomes that of the Roman satirist with Stoic inclinations. Moreover, the dialogue in which Johnson explains his Stoic philosophy to Juan . . . is an authentic replica of the dialogue form in which both Horace and Persius treated Stoic doctrines. Horace actually invented the satiric dialogue and used it with subtle irony to involve prolocutor and adversary in a dramatic skit. Persius, though strongly inclined toward dramatic conversations even when the presence of his opponent in a debate had to be imagined, used the Horatian innovation as framework for only two whole satires, while Juvenal was even less disposed toward dialogue form. It was Pope, in his *Imitations of Horace,* who proved to be most skillful of all in pitting speakers against one another in an evolving discussion. Pope's example probably inspired Byron to attempt a similar feat. (pp. 138-40)

Byron's skill in combining various ingredients drawn from Roman satire into a traditional satiric form deserves special attention. Though the subject of Johnson's discourse derives primarily from Persius, the general tone of the dialogue more closely resembles the Horatian mixture of genial humor and wry cynicism than the earnest didacticism of Persius. Yet it was Byron's originality in readapting classical materials that earned him a place as a contributor to the tradition. His conversion of metaphorical enslavement into physical reality and his use of Constantinople's slave market as a microcosm of mercantile society, where everyone offers himself to the highest bidder, ingeniously and vastly enriched the possibilities for a thematic conflict between freedom and slavery in that episode. Even Stoic philosophy is so modernized as to be assimilable into Robert Walpole's truism on human venality ("all have prices, / . . . according to their vices" . . .) and to be assailable ultimately as a philosophy of insensibility ("To feel for none is the true social art / Of the world's stoics—men without a heart" . . .). And the dialogue between Johnson and Juan is more than an unresolved debate on Stoicism. As a dramatic mode of dialectic, it stimulates each speaker to a revelation of his own perspective, as well as to a deeper perception of the limitations inherent in his own outlook. Through his naive

questioning of Johnson's cynical approach, Juan serves as friendly adversary or *provocateur* in evoking the differences between sentimental youth and disillusioned age. One of Byron's finest achievements in this *sermo* is the unexpected combination of a crescendo suggesting a modified Stoicism as the key to survival and an ironic coda questioning its validity as a guide to life.

Possibly because Byron saw a number of parallels between Constantinople, which he called "Rome transplanted" (V. 86. 8), and Rome under the early caesars, he drew many other suggestions for his fifth canto from Roman satire and thereby emphasized further his connection with that still vital tradition. The narrator's frequent references to the role of capricious fortune in that section are reminiscent of Juvenal and, to a lesser degree, Horace rather than of Moslem belief. It is likely that Byron had mentally assimilated the extensive commentary Madan wrote for Juvenal's tenth satire on the significance of Fortuna in pagan Rome. Certainly Byron was indebted to the substance of two Juvenalian satires (VI and X) for the encounter involving Juan and the lustful sultana Gulbeyaz. For ideas, phraseology, and analogies he also drew on Madan's notes about the nymphomaniac empress Messalina and her determination to force the handsome Gaius Silius to become her husband. Much of the broad sexual jesting in the fifth canto echoes that of Juvenal. Castration, for example, in addition to being an accepted Turkish practice, may have been suggested by hints in Juvenal's tenth that Madan had explicated. While circumcision remained a notable difference between Christian and Moslem in Byron's day, as his earlier letters observed, he would also have recalled the recurrent jests in Horace, Persius, and Juvenal about Jewish circumcision. Juan's transvestism, as well as its sexual overtones, had precedents in Juvenal and in Madan's notes to Satires II and X. But throughout that episode it is not so much the imitation of the model that deserves study as the ingenious transformation of Juvenalian materials in the alembic of Byron's imagination. Byron's achievement, in altering even the "tragic satire" of Juvenal into half-serious comedy dealing with feminine lust, masculine chastity, marital fidelity, and tyranny over all that should be free, shows how completely he could absorb the ingredients of Roman satire into his own creation.

While the imitation of *satura* is evident only in Canto V, the overall randomness of *Don Juan* suggests satiric content. It is primarily through the satiric spirit, especially as it is assimilated into epic form, that Byron's satire functions. Despite the poem's open defiance of epic conventions, the narrator repeatedly claims that *Don Juan* is an epic and that its contents (love, war, shipwreck, and even a "view of hell") qualify it for that designation. There is good reason, furthermore, to believe that Byron took those claims seriously, that he intended something more than another comic epic in the Italian tradition. It would be easy, especially in the early cantos, to assert that *Don Juan* is a mock-epic since that subgenre not only incorporates satire in its burlesque of epic conventions but also uses the ideals of previous epics to illustrate, by allusion, the contrast between earlier greatness and contemporary pettiness. But as Brian Wilkie has shown [see excerpt dated 1965], *Don Juan* is not just a mock-epic. Byron was determined that, unlike his "epic brethren gone before," he would write a *true* epic depicting man and his world realistically. On the assumption that *Don Juan* in scope and purpose deserved to be compared to Homer's *Iliad,* Byron told Thomas Medwin in late 1821 or early 1822 that his poem was "an epic as much in the spirit of our day as the Iliad was in Homer's" [see excerpt dated 1822]. Evidently he thought it mirrored the religious, political, and social attitudes of his own era as comprehensively and accurately as Homer's epic had reflected his age. Byron's invocation of Homer's aid before the siege of Ismail . . . , his use of language less formal and stylized than Virgil's or Milton's, and his rejection of a providential or teleological design for background of the protagonist's ''heroism'' indicate that Byron in some ways felt a closer affinity with Homer than with the later epic poets. But fundamental changes in the inherited tradition were necessary to produce a modern epic depicting the ideals—or lack of them—in contemporary society, and satire was essential in sharpening its negative features.

When in 1823 Byron called *Don Juan* an ''Epic Satire'' . . . , he acknowledged its hybrid nature. His poetic commentary on *Don Quixote* . . . suggests the relationship that Byron apparently saw between satire and epic. Even though Cervantes may have assumed that in our corrupt world only a fool or a madman could champion chivalric values, he was not, in Byron's judgment, ridiculing the noble idealism for which Quixote fights. Cervantes' ''hero'' is ''right'' in

> Redressing injury, revenging wrong,
>   To aid the damsel and destroy the caitiff;
> Opposing singly the united strong,
>   From foreign yoke to free the helpless native. . . .

Yet we smile at the spectacle the deluded knight makes of himself, and, reflecting on the folly of defending virtue, we realize the melancholy plight in which Cervantes has involved us. Thus what Cervantes may have begun as satire on the absurdities of knight-errantry resulted in a ''real Epic unto all who have thought.'' . . . By demolishing the traditional concept of heroism, he destroyed the old form of epic romance. In its place he provided a genuine, realistic epic, the only kind viable in a skeptical, disillusioned age.

This reading of *Don Quixote* has implications for Byron's interpretation of epic satire in *Don Juan*. Like Cervantes, Byron strove through satire to banish a false vision of life. In the course of achieving that goal he produced, like Cervantes, a literary form that radically readapted epic traditions, the epic hero, and the very idea of heroism—a form that could integrate other literary genres into itself and accommodate satire as part of its realistic approach. The union of such an epic and satire was more compatible than might have at first appeared, for the traditions of the two genres already met on common ground. Love, war, shipwreck, banquets, and glimpses of Hades, essential ingredients in the epic, were also standard fare in Roman *satura* and neoclassical adaptations. In *Don Juan* epic of a negative thrust could easily exist in symbiotic relationship with satire. The epic element, impelled by narrative, was identifiable with the onward momentum of life; the satiric, conversely, with whatever threatened man's progress. True heroism and idealism, however rare, were not to be scorned, though their goals were usually unattainable and their adherents often appeared foolish to a cynical world. This ironic situation, as Byron saw it, represented the dilemma of modern man, and ''Epic Satire'' was his way of embodying it.

Quite likely the term *epic satire* also had another association for Byron. Although he may have thought of *Don Juan* in its earliest stages as primarily in the *genus tenue* and the casual Horatian mode, as the poem developed more grandiose proportions he acquired a loftier sense of its mission—one comparable to the Juvenalian concept of satire in the *genus grande*. Particularly from careful study of Juvenal's Satires I, VI, X,

and XV, Byron learned that true-to-life satire might be as edifying as tragedy or epic. Even though Juvenal respected the great epics of the past, he had the utmost contempt for poetasters of his day who strained beyond their abilities to attempt the highest genres. Traditional epic and tragedy, with their artificial conventions, impracticable ideals, and hackneyed mythological subjects, seemed no longer viable to Juvenal because they were irrelevant to contemporary life. What was needed, in view of the corruption permeating every stratum of Roman society, was a literature of truth rather than of literary invention—in short, one that depicted reality as Juvenal saw it. If satire was to supersede the outworn genres in the old poetic hierarchy and assume their instructive functions, the satirist was obliged to aspire to a *genus grande* that would approximate, even while radically readapting, epic form. In practice Juvenal substantiated those assumptions through elevated rhetoric, an impassioned style, and a heroic determination to amend society through exposure of wrong-doing. . . . Juvenal's frequent imitation of epic, whether with serious intent or, when style was inappropriate to subject matter, for humorous effect, further showed that he strove for a nobler goal than that ordinarily associated with the satires of Horace and Persius. It may well be that Juvenal's works, to which Byron repeatedly returned over the years, deepened his concept of satire so that it evolved beyond a youthful lashing out at whatever displeased him into a sophisticated view of life encompassing all things human. (pp. 142-46)

Frederick L. Beaty, in his Byron the Satirist, *Northern Illinois University Press, 1985, 236 p.*

ADDITIONAL BIBLIOGRAPHY

Abrams, M. H. Headnote to *Don Juan*, by Lord Byron. In *The Norton Anthology of English Literature*, Vol. 2, 3d ed., edited by M. H. Abrams, pp. 395-97. New York: W. W. Norton & Co., 1974.
    A brief biographical and critical introduction to excerpts from the poem.

Bewley, Marius. ''The Colloquial Mode of Byron.'' *Scrutiny* XVI, No. 1 (March 1949): 8-23.
    A response to Bottrall's ''Byron and the Colloquial Tradition in English Poetry'' (see excerpt dated 1939). Bewley argues that the style of Byron's mature satires has more in common with the verse of the seventeenth-century Caroline poets than with that of the English Augustan poets.

Blackstone, Bernard. ''*Don Juan*.'' In his *Byron: A Survey*, pp. 287-349. London: Longman, 1975.
    Explores the psychosexual and metaphysical dimensions of the poem and its relation to Byron's works as a whole. Blackstone structures his remarks around a series of quotations from William Blake's *For the Sexes: The Gates of Paradise* and T. S. Eliot's ''Burnt Norton.''

Bloom, Harold. ''The Digressive Balance: *Don Juan*.'' In his *The Visionary Company: A Reading of English Romantic Poetry*, pp. 272-88. Garden City: Doubleday & Co., Anchor Books, 1963.
    An exegesis of *Don Juan* from Bloom's influential study of the English Romantic poets.

Bostetter, Edward E. ''Byron.'' In his *The Romantic Ventriloquists: Wordsworth, Coleridge, Keats, Shelley, Byron*, pp. 241-301. Seattle: University of Washington Press, 1963.
    Contains two sections devoted to *Don Juan*. In the first, ''The Humbler Promontory,'' Bostetter focuses on Byron's characterization in the English cantos. In the second, ''Hock and Soda

Water,'' the critic explores Byron's growth as a conscious and confident artist in the later portions of the poem.

———, ed. *Twentieth Century Interpretations of Don Juan: A Collection of Critical Essays.* Englewood Cliffs, N.J.: Prentice-Hall, 1969, 119 p.

A collection of seminal essays and other commentary on *Don Juan.* Topics discussed include the poem's structure, themes, and style.

Brownstein, Rachel Mayer. ''Byron's *Don Juan:* Some Reasons for the Rhymes.'' *Modern Language Quarterly* XXVIII, No. 2 (June 1967): 177-91.

Argues that Byron's use of ''brilliant, outrageous rhymes'' in *Don Juan* contributes to the iconoclastic nature of the poem.

Chew, Samuel C. *Byron in England: His Fame and After-Fame.* London: John Murray, 1924, 415 p.

A thorough and highly respected study of Byron's reputation in England from 1808 through the first decade of the twentieth century. Chew chronicles the changing critical fortunes of *Don Juan* and devotes chapters to the poem's early reception and continuation by other authors.

Clancy, Charles J. *Review of ''Don Juan'' Criticism: 1900-1973.* Salzburg Studies in English Literature: Romantic Reassessment, edited by James Hogg, vol. 40. Salzburg: Universität Salzburg, 1974, 93 p.

A survey of important commentary on *Don Juan* in the twentieth century. Clancy summarizes and evaluates twenty-two major studies and provides a selected bibliography.

———. *Lava, Hock and Soda-Water: Byron's ''Don Juan.''* Salzburg Studies in English Literature: Romantic Reassessment, edited by James Hogg, vol. 41. Salzburg: Universität Salzburg, 1974, 273 p.

An extended study of *Don Juan* based on the thesis that it ''begins and ends a comic epic.'' Clancy explores Byron's use of epic conventions and comic devices in each episode of the poem in order to demonstrate that the work is primarily comic and positive in effect rather than satirical or negative.

———. ''Aurora Raby in *Don Juan:* A Byronic Heroine.'' *Keats-Shelley Journal* XXVIII (1979): 28-34.

Examines the character of Aurora Raby in *Don Juan.* Clancy argues that she represents the female counterpart of the ''Byronic hero.''

Cooke, M. G. ''A Sad Jar of Atoms?: Antidromic Order in 'Don Juan'.'' In his *The Blind Man Traces the Circle: On the Patterns and Philosophy of Byron's Poetry,* pp. 128-74. Princeton: Princeton University Press, 1969.

Examines the influence of Restoration comedy as an ordering principle in *Don Juan.* Cooke contends that the poem's literary background is only of minor importance to its structure and philosophy. Byron, the critic argues, rejected the organizational and philosophic possibilities in each of his literary influences because they failed to address the epistemological concerns that led him to create a ''gospel of uncertainty.''

England, A. B. *Byron's ''Don Juan'' and Eighteenth-Century Literature: A Study of Some Rhetorical Continuities and Discontinuities.* London: Associated University Presses, 1975. 197 p.

A study of the influence of eighteenth-century English literature on *Don Juan.* England concludes that although Byron borrowed from his predecessors, there exists no direct line of continuity between the poem and eighteenth-century literature.

Hagelman, Charles W., Jr., and Barnes, Robert J., eds. *A Concordance to Byron's ''Don Juan.''* Ithaca, N.Y.: Cornell University Press, 1967. 981 p.

A concordance to the Variorum edition of the poem.

Hirsch, E. D., Jr. ''Byron and the Terrestrial Paradise.'' In *From Sensibility to Romanticism: Essays Presented to Frederick A. Pottle,* edited by Frederick W. Hilles and Harold Bloom, pp. 467-86. New York: Oxford University Press, 1965.

Argues that the ''recurrent visions'' of paradise on earth in *Don Juan* testify to ''Byron's persistent faith in the possibilities of

life.'' Hirsch sees the poem as ultimately positive in its outlook on human existence.

Horn, András. *Byron's ''Don Juan'' and the Eighteenth-Century English Novel.* Swiss Studies in English, edited by O. Funke, vol. 51. Bern: Francke Verlag, 1962, 75 p.

A study of the influence of Fielding, Sterne, and Smollett on *Don Juan.*

Johnson, Edward Dudley Hume. ''*Don Juan* in England.'' *ELH* 11, No. 2 (June 1944): 135-53.

Asserts that much of the contemporary outcry against the morality of *Don Juan* was in fact sincere and not merely ''cant and hypocrisy'' as Byron charged and later critics have tended to believe. Johnson argues that in the years after Byron left the country, the growing influence and popularity of orthodox religion in England contributed to public condemnation of the poem.

Kroeber, Karl. ''Byron: The Adventurous Narrative.'' In his *Romantic Narrative Art,* pp. 135-67. Madison: University of Wisconsin Press, 1960.

Focuses on *Don Juan* as a novel in verse. Unlike earlier commentators, Kroeber asserts that the ''novelistic qualities'' of the poem show a greater affinity with the developing nineteenth-century novel than with eighteenth-century fiction.

Lauber, John. ''*Don Juan* as Anti-Epic.'' *Studies in English Literature, 1500-1900* VIII, No. 4 (Autumn 1968): 607-19.

Explores the thesis that in *Don Juan* Byron set out to ''destroy the epic form by a comprehensive attack on the whole tradition of epic poetry—its style, its structure, and its values.''

Manning, Peter J. *Byron and His Fictions.* Detroit: Wayne State University Press, 1978, 296 p.

A psychoanalytic study of Byron's works containing four chapters on *Don Juan.* Manning explores such subjects as how the poem functioned as a catharsis for Byron and what Juan's relationships with women reveal about the poet's own experience with and attitudes toward the opposite sex.

Marchand, Leslie A. *Byron's Poetry: A Critical Introduction.* Cambridge: Harvard University Press, 1968, 261 p.

A highly regarded general introduction to Byron's poetry. Marchand focuses on *Don Juan* as a reflection of Byron's personality.

———. ''Narrator and Narration in *Don Juan.''* *Keats-Shelley Journal* XXV (1976): 26-42.

Contends that Byron's personality as narrator forms the only real structure in *Don Juan* and that attempts to find a systematic plan in the poem distort its meaning.

Martin, Philip. ''*Don Juan.''* In his *Byron: A Poet before His Public,* pp. 173-219. Cambridge: Cambridge University Press, 1982.

Investigates the relationship between Byron and his audience and how his refusal to accede to their demands in *Don Juan* allowed him to transcend the limitations of his other works.

Reiman, Donald H., ed. *The Romantics Reviewed: Contemporary Reviews of British Romantic Writers: Byron and Regency Society Poets,* 5 vols. New York: Garland Publishing, 1972.

Reprints over sixty contemporary reviews of *Don Juan.*

———. ''*Don Juan* in Epic Context.'' *Studies in Romanticism* 16, No. 14 (Fall 1977): 587-94.

Explores the concept of *Don Juan* as epic. Reiman discusses Byron's use of epic conventions and how the poem represents an epic of modern life.

Ridenour, George M. ''The Mode of Byron's *Don Juan.''* *PMLA* LXXIX, No. 4, Pt. 1 (September 1964): 442-46.

A study of narrative viewpoint and irony in the poem.

Ruddick, W. ''Don Juan in Search of Freedom: Byron's Emergence as a Satirist.'' In *Byron: A Symposium,* edited by John D. Jump, pp. 113-37. London: Macmillan, 1975.

Examines the reasons why, in Ruddick's view, Byron was able to express the full range of his personality and intellect only in *Don Juan* and his other late satires.

Rutherford, Andrew. *Byron: A Critical Study*. Stanford: Stanford University Press, 1961, 253 p.

An influential study of Byron's works containing five chapters on *Don Juan*. Rutherford discusses such topics as Byron's conception of the relationship between the poet and society and *Don Juan*'s composition, realism, and portrayal of politics.

————. *Byron: The Critical Heritage*. The Critical Heritage Series, edited by B. C. Southam. New York: Barnes & Noble, 1970, 513 p.

A collection of excerpted reviews, letters, and commentary on Byron and his works from 1808 to 1909, including numerous pieces on *Don Juan*.

Santucho, Oscar José, and Goode, Clement Tyson, Jr. *George Gordon, Lord Byron: A Comprehensive Bibliography of Secondary Materials in English, 1807-1974, with a Critical Review of Research*. Scarecrow Author Bibliographies, No. 30. Metuchen, N.J.: Scarecrow Press, 1977, 641 p.

A detailed bibliography of secondary materials on Byron and his works.

Sheraw, C. Darrell. "*Don Juan*: Byron as Un-Augustan Satirist." *Satire Newsletter* X, No. 2 (Spring 1973): 25-33.

Disputes the idea that *Don Juan* belongs within the Augustan tradition of English poetry. Sheraw argues that the poem's satire is distinctly modern rather than Augustan in approach.

Stavrou, C. N. "Religion in Byron's *Don Juan*." *Studies in English Literature* III (Autumn 1963): 567-94.

A study of Byron's attitudes toward religion in *Don Juan*.

Steffan, Truman Guy, and Pratt, Willis W., eds. *Byron's "Don Juan": A Variorum Edition*, 4 vols. 2nd ed. Austin: University of Texas Press, 1971.

The definitive text of the poem. Volume I contains an extended discussion by Steffan of *Don Juan*'s composition and history, as well as his critical commentary. Volumes II-III present the text of the poem itself, and Volume IV consists of notes on the text by Pratt.

Trueblood, Paul Graham. *The Flowering of Byron's Genius: Studies in Byron's "Don Juan."* Palo Alto, Calif.: Stanford University Press, 1945, 183 p.

Contains chapters on *Don Juan*'s development, contemporary reviews, and satiric importance.

————. *Lord Byron*. Twayne's English Author Series, edited by Sylvia E. Bowman, no. 78. New York: Twayne Publishers, 1969, 177 p.

Contains a biographical and critical discussion of *Don Juan*'s genesis, composition, style, structure, and themes.

Vassallo, Peter. *Byron: The Italian Literary Influence*. London: Macmillan, 1984, 192 p.

Explores the influence of Italian literature on Byron's works, especially *Beppo* and *Don Juan*.

Weinstein, Leo. "The Romantic Don Juan." In his *The Metamorphoses of Don Juan*, pp. 78-94. New York: AMS Press, 1967.*

Discusses Byron's use of the Don Juan legend.

Isabella Valancy Crawford

1850-1887

(Also wrote under pseudonym of Dennis Scott) Irish-born Canadian poet, short story writer, novelist, and fairy tale writer.

Crawford is considered one of the most outstanding Canadian poets of the nineteenth century. Blending imaginative and realistic styles, she depicted in her poetry the culture, scenery, and character types of the Canadian frontier. Although Crawford received little recognition in her own time, many modern critics commend her vivid nature imagery and energetic prose and verse styles; in addition, they claim that her poetry constitutes a substantial contribution to the development of Canadian literature.

Scholars disagree on certain details of Crawford's biography, but the general facts of her life are clear. She was born in Dublin, Ireland, in 1850. Her father, a physician, having difficulty supporting the family, decided to emigrate, and the family set out for North America sometime between 1850 and 1856. They lived briefly in Wisconsin before settling in Peterborough, Ontario, where her father resumed his medical practice with little financial success. The family's life on the Canadian frontier proved to be hard, tedious, and devoid of cultural amenities. Crawford, however, received an excellent education at home and read widely in the classics and in Italian and French literature. Her particular favorites included the poetry of Dante Alighieri, Henry Wadsworth Longfellow, and Alfred, Lord Tennyson. As a child, Crawford composed stories and poems, many of which were influenced by the rugged beauty of the Ontario landscape. Encouraged by friends and hoping to contribute to the family's income, she entered and won a short story competition in 1873. Although the sponsoring company soon declared bankruptcy and Crawford received only a small portion of the prize, this event marked the beginning of her literary career. After her father's death in 1875 the family's financial difficulties became more acute, and Crawford began selling her work to magazines and newspapers in Canada and the United States. Most of her work, including the 1886 novel, *The Little Bacchante; or, Some Black Sheep,* appeared in the Canadian journals *Toronto Globe* and in the *Evening Telegram* between 1879 and 1887. Yet she could barely make a living and in 1880 moved with her mother to Toronto, the center of the Canadian publishing industry. Crawford found no full-time employment as a writer, and in 1884 she published, at her own expense, a volume of her poetry, *Old Spookses' Pass, Malcolm's Katie, and Other Poems.* She managed to sell only about fifty copies of the book. Undaunted, Crawford resumed writing poetry and prose for local newspapers and was at work on a serial novel when she died suddenly of heart failure in 1887.

Old Spookses' Pass, Malcolm's Katie, and Other Poems, the only volume of Crawford's work to be published in her lifetime, forms the basis for her poetic reputation. "Old Spookses' Pass," influenced by Tennyson, realistically portrays the life and adventures of cattle ranchers in the Rocky Mountains. Written in the idiom of the American cowboy, the poem is characterized by dramatic action and a brisk narrative pace. Crawford modeled "Malcolm's Katie" on Tennyson's pastoral romances; skillfully interweaving plot, characterization, and imagery, she

conveys in the poem the atmosphere of farm life on the Canadian frontier. In addition to the two title poems, the collection includes many short lyrics, songs about native Indians, and patriotic pieces written in a variety of styles and enhanced by Crawford's use of Norse, classical, and oriental motifs. During the 1870s, Crawford wrote a series of lyrics, first published in *The Collected Poems of Isabella Valancy Crawford,* which detail a philosophical debate between an optimist and a disillusioned artist. These pieces were compiled by scholars as a single, narrative poem and published in 1977 as *Hugh and Ion.*

Although critics have focused most of their attention on Crawford's poetry, since the publication during the 1970s of several of her prose works, including *Selected Stories of Isabella Valancy Crawford* and *The Halton Boys,* they have begun to examine her prose writings as well. She wrote in several different prose genres, including the novel, short story, and fairy tale. These works share such characteristics as a popular, sentimental style, broad subject matter, and unusual description. Scholars have praised Crawford's characterizations and settings in *The Halton Boys* and *Fairy Tales of Isabella Valancy Crawford,* but they have also faulted her tendency toward didacticism throughout her prose works.

Although her poems have been frequently anthologized, Crawford's works have only recently been analyzed for their significance to Canadian literary history. Early reviews of *Old Spookses' Pass, Malcolm's Katie, and Other Poems* were generally complimentary, particularly in England, but her reputation as an important Canadian poet did not become established until the 1905 publication of *The Collected Poems*. Her reputation was further enhanced by the publication in 1959 of James Reaney's extensive discussion of Crawford's development of symbolism, which caused a resurgence of critical interest in her poetry. Many critics now laud the diversity of Crawford's poetic oeuvre, her original treatment of nature, and her stylistic experimentation. They particularly emphasize her imagery and myth-making imagination and maintain that her poetry successfully combines realistic detail with intricate symbolism and nationalistic sentiment. Additionally, Crawford's innovative use of native landscape and Indian lore is viewed by many critics as her most valuable contribution to Canadian literature.

Today, Crawford is remembered primarily for her colorful portrayal of Canadian frontier life, for her bold use of imagery, and for her role in helping to shape a Canadian national literature. According to Northrop Frye, she possessed "the most remarkable mythopoeic imagination in Canadian poetry."

PRINCIPAL WORKS

Old Spookses' Pass, Malcolm's Katie, and Other Poems
  (poetry) 1884
The Little Bacchante; or, Some Black Sheep   (novel)
  1886; published in newspaper *Toronto Globe*
The Collected Poems of Isabella Valancy Crawford
  (poetry) 1905
Selected Stories of Isabella Valancy Crawford   (short
  stories) 1975
Fairy Tales of Isabella Valancy Crawford   (fairy tales)
  1977
Hugh and Ion   (poetry) 1977
The Halton Boys   (novel) 1979

*This novel was written between 1876 and 1879.

THE SPECTATOR   (essay date 1884)

[*In the following excerpt from an early review of Crawford's* Old Spookses' Pass, Malcolm's Katie, and Other Poems, *the critic hails the work as one "full of promise."*]

[*Old Spookses' Pass, Malcolm's Katie, and Other Poems*] is a volume that comes from a country as yet unfertile of literature. If the harvest is as good as the first-fruits, it will be well, for Miss Crawford writes with a power of expression quite unusual among aspirants to poetic fame. The first poem is written in the dialect which we commonly associate with the Western States, and tells in a vigorous fashion (though not without a curious, and we should think, inappropriate sprinkling of ornate literary English), the story of a stampede of cattle in a pass of the Rocky Mountains. "Malcolm's Katie" is a love-story, spoiled in a way by an immoderate use of rhetoric (witness "Alfred's" speech . . . , such a tirade as surely never was delivered over a camping-fire in the woods), but still powerful. Miss Crawford's blank verse is indeed of no ordinary kind. . . . The passage descriptive of forest scenery in Part II, of the same poem

is also noteworthy. . . . [On] the whole, this volume seems full of promise. (p. 1381)

> *A review of "Old Spookses' Pass, Malcolm's Katie, and Other Poems," in* The Spectator, *Vol. 57, No. 2938, October 18, 1884, pp. 1381-82.*

THE SATURDAY REVIEW, LONDON   (essay date 1885)

[*The following excerpt is from a largely positive review of* Old Spookses' Pass, Malcolm's Katie, and Other Poems.]

More humour, vivacity, and range of power are to be found in Miss Crawford's poems than in most recent American verse. "Old Spense" is an excellent example of racy untrained humour; so also are "**The Deacon and his Daughter**," and "**Farmer Stebbin's Opinions**," though these and others are a little too suggestive in style of the *Biglow Papers*. "**Old Spookses' Pass**" is a graphic and exciting recital of a stampede of a herd of cattle in a terrible thunderstorm by night, in which the narrator tells, in his stirring and vigorous vernacular, how his herd was saved from destruction by the mysterious apparition who, with lasso and whip, turned the leader of the maddened beasts just as they were making for a precipice. The remaining poems are of a more conventional cast, and a love story, called "**Malcolm's Katie**," and the longest poem in the collection, is marred by much extravagant incident. (p. 693)

> *A review of "Old Spookses' Pass; and Other Poems," in* The Saturday Review, London, *Vol. 59, No. 1543, May 23, 1885, pp. 692-93.*

THE ILLUSTRATED LONDON NEWS   (essay date 1886)

[*In the following excerpt, drawn from an early review of* Old Spookses' Pass, Malcolm's Katie, and Other Poems, *the critic points out Crawford's errors in versification and grammar, but contends that she is a true poet nevertheless.*]

A very unpretentious-looking little volume is *Old Spookses' Pass, Malcolm's Katie, and Other Poems:* by Isabella Valency Crawford . . . ; and at the first glance, even after the first few stanzas, one is not disposed to think that to send it so many miles, so many thousand miles indeed, for the opinion of English readers, was a happy thought either for them or for the writer. But a different conclusion is soon drawn: the first piece, notwithstanding the unpoetical, slangy diction in which (after a questionable modern fashion) it is written, shows a depth of feeling and a power of description indicative of the real poetic faculty, and the second piece causes us to feel grateful to the author for giving us the opportunity of reading what is truly a beautiful, charming little poem, abounding in noble sentiments, picturesque narration, glowing language, and pathetic touches, combined with simple, impressive dignity. If this little volume be a fair specimen of our Canadian brethren's minor muse, their higher and more ambitious efforts must be very noteworthy indeed. The most striking blemishes in this extremely promising collection are faulty versification, and grammatical or orthographical errors; but the former can be easily remedied by care and study, and the latter are no doubt due, in many instances, to mistakes of the press. Indeed, the writer expressly states that there are at least a hundred and fifty such mistakes, which have been allowed to go uncorrected from consideration of expense. These matters, the versification and the errors that may be ascribed partly to the hurry of composition in two senses, are of comparatively little importance: that which is inborn, which cannot be acquired by any training or any amount of attention and application, which belongs to those only whose birth has been watched by Melpomene with gentle smile, is the one thing needful; and that is exhibited in no small degree. That the pieces are unequal it can scarcely be necessary to state; this is always the case, and it should be sufficient for the writer's and the reader's satisfaction to know that the best are very good indeed. Such, at least, is the opinion of one who has derived much pleasure from them, and felt much admiration for them. The question whether poetry may not be considered to lose in height what it gains in breadth, to be degraded to some extent, by the adoption of that slangy phraseology which has been mentioned, and which, though it adds to the reality, detracts from the grace and delicacy of a poem, there is here neither space nor inclination to discuss.

A review of "Old Spookses' Pass, Malcolm's Katie, and Other Poems," in The Illustrated London News, *Vol. LXXXVIII, No. 2450, April 3, 1886, p. 360.*

HECTOR W. CHARLESWORTH (essay date 1893)

[*In the excerpt below, Charlesworth praises the "dramatic forcefulness" of Crawford's poetry.*]

[Late] years have seen the birth of a school of [Canadian] woman poets whose works show a breadth and virility unapproached by the womansingers of the rest of the continent. One of them, whose soul burned with passionate delight in the vigor and beauty and freedom of Canada and Canadian things, has already passed away. This was the late Isabelle Valancey Crawford [*sic*], a poet whose fame among us came after her death; in [*Old Spookses' Pass, Malcolm's Katie, and Other Poems*] are found passages so rich in color and warmth and beauty as to make the pale analytic verses of the magazine blue-stocking seem weak and colorless indeed. . . . The gentlemen poets— many apologies for the phrase, sirs—in whom Canada is rich, have none of her dramatic forcefulness. She loved grandeur of the titanic description, and her passion for Nature in her richest colors was intense. She sings of

> A cusp'd dark wood caught in its black embrace
> The valleys and the hill, and from its wilds
> Spik'd with dark cedars, cried the whip-poor-
> will.
>
> A crane, belated, sailed across the moon;
> On the bright, small, close-link'd lakes green
> islets lay;
> Dusk knots of tangl'd vines, or maple boughs,
> Or tuft'd cedars, toss'd upon the waves.

Or, turning elsewhere at random, one finds something about

> Torn caves of mist, wall'd with a sudden gold,
> Reseal'd as swift as seen—broad, shaggy
> fronts,
> Fire-ey'd and tossing on impatient horns
> The wave impalpable—

Miss Crawford's lines do not sound like a woman's at all. Her imagery is always grand and never grandiloquent; her lines burn pictures into the brain that cannot be forgotten, and in reading them one cannot help feeling that she wrote with a consciousness that her word-painting was for all time. (pp. 189-90)

Hector W. Charlesworth, "The Canadian Girl: An Appreciative Medley," in The Canadian Magazine

of Politics, Science, Art and Literature, *Vol. I, No. 3, May, 1893, pp. 186-93.**

E. J. HATHAWAY (essay date 1895)

[*In the following excerpt, Hathaway commends Crawford's varied style, narrative skill, and talent for description.*]

[*Old Spookses' Pass, Malcolm's Katie, and Other Poems*] contains one of the most delightfully varied collections of poems ever issued by a Canadian writer. . . . The spirit of Canadian freedom pulses throughout the pages, and though her themes are not always local, they everywhere bear the impress of a sturdy independence. The first piece in the book, "**Old Spookses' Pass,**" is a remarkable picture of western life; a little drawn out, it may be, but stirring and powerful throughout. . . . Many of her scenes and characters are drawn from Canadian pioneer life, and expressed in the dialect of the frontiersman or the recognized speech of the rural inhabitant. "**Old Spookses' Pass,**" a ranchman's midnight experience with a stampeding herd, is a vigorous descriptive poem and full of action. A vivid picture is given of the night in which the stampede takes place. The dark sky overhead; the thick oppressive night air, in which one feels intuitively that something fearful is to happen; the deep breathing of the mustang and an occasional quiver of his flanks; the great white moon throwing its river of brightness over the mighty herd.

> Tearin' along the indigo sky,
> Wus a drove of clouds, snarl'd an' black;
> Scuddin' along to'ards the risin' moon,
> Like the sweep of a darn'd hungry pack
> Of preairie wolves to'ard a bufferler,
> The heft of the herd, left out of sight;
> I dror'd my breath right hard, fur I know'd
> We wus in fur a 'tarnal run thet night.

In a moment

> The herd wus up!—not one at a time,
> *Thet* ain't the style in a midnight run,—
> They wus up an' off like es all thair minds
> Wus rolled in the hide of only one.

The narrative is carried through the somewhat lengthy poem with the same vigorous swing. There is masculine strength in it; and it seems almost incredible that so vivid an experience could be described by one who had no part in it.

"**Old Spense**" is another descriptive poem of great merit. It is inclined to be wordy, perhaps, and is a little artificial, but the writer has hit off some capital pictures of human life. (p. 570)

Her descriptive poems are redolent of exquisite beauty. Everything that was beautiful on the earth seemed to appeal to her for adoration. The great forces of nature had no terrors for her—rather did they fill her soul with nobler thoughts. . . .

If there is one element in Miss Crawford's writings more distinctly visible than another it is that of power—virility it would be called if applied to a man. Her work throughout is characterized by bold, vigorous treatment, purity of thought and felicity of expression.

> Roses, Senors, roses!
> Love is subtly hid
> In the fragrant roses,

Blown in gay Madrid.
Roses, Senors, roses!
Look, look, look and see
Love hanging on the roses,
Like a golden bee!
Ha! Ha! shake the roses—
Hold a palm below;
Shake him from the roses,
Catch the vagrant so!

There is something peculiarly attractive about these lines. They even seem fragrant themselves with the perfume from that sunny land. The writer has caught the spirit of the scene, and in fancy we see the great circus with its tiers of gaily-dressed people watching eagerly to see the "bold bull bleed," and in our own ears there rings the sweet refrain of the flower girls song.

Roses by the dozen!
Roses by the score!
Pelt the victor with them—
Bull or Toreador.

(p. 571)

E. J. Hathaway, "Isabella Valancy Crawford," in
The Canadian Magazine of Politics, Science, Art and
Literature, *Vol. V, No. 6, October, 1895, pp. 569-72.*

LAWRENCE J. BURPEE (essay date 1901)

[*In the excerpt below, Burpee extols Crawford's versatility and originality and compares her with such writers as Ben Jonson and James Russell Lowell. Deeming "Malcolm's Katie" her "strongest and most ambitious work," Burpee briefly discusses Crawford's handling of narrative and imagery in that and several other poems.*]

In reviewing the course of Canadian literature, or at any rate the English portion of it, a fact that at once strikes the attention is the high place attained by women, in verse as well as in fiction. Having in view its youth and sparse population, Canada has given birth to a larger proportion of genuine women of letters than perhaps any other country, ancient or modern. In fiction, which could hardly be said to exist in Canada prior to a year or two ago, women now divide the honors almost equally with men. Close on a score of Canadian women could be mentioned who are at present building up a solid reputation as writers of good fiction. In poetry the women of the Dominion have been equally active and successful. Among them, through her works, though now no longer in the flesh, is one who should rank as one of the sweetest and most genuine singers of her time,—Isabella Valancy Crawford. I say "should rank" advisedly; for her work has never yet received the recognition it deserved, and least of all in her native country. "A prophet," etc.

Miss Crawford only published one small book of verse, but that is instinct throughout with the very spirit of poetry. It is impossible to help being impressed with the sincerity and high lyrical quality of her work, as well as its striking originality and versatility. The wonder grows when it is remembered that this was the first effort of a young and practically untrained intellect. (pp. 575-76)

Although her prose was of some merit, it was not the medium best suited to the peculiarly lyrical cast of her genius. In verse alone could she adequately express herself, and in verse she embodied the best fruits of her heart and mind.

Old Spookses' Pass is made up of a number of poems covering a surprisingly wide range of thought, and showing Miss Crawford's remarkable command over many of the most difficult forms of verse. Here we find, besides purely lyrical pieces, narrative, descriptive, dialect, and many other forms.

The poem into which she put her strongest and most ambitious work, and which, on the whole, may be taken as her most sustained effort, is "**Malcolm's Katie.**" (p. 577)

[In portions] of the poem there is a perfect riot of imagery. Metaphors and onomatopoeia abound, and the poet reveals a talent for the choice of pregnant words. Here is introduced a love-song which can only be compared in sweetness and the delicacy of its form and thought to Ben Jonson's immortal lyric:—

O, Love builds on the azure sea,
   And Love builds on the golden sand,
And Love builds on the rose-wing'd cloud,
   And sometimes Love builds on the land.

O, if Love build on sparkling sea,
   And if Love build on golden strand,
And if Love build on rosy cloud,
   To Love these are the solid land.

O, Love will build his lily walls,
   And Love his pearly roof will rear,—
On cloud or sand, or mist or sea,
   Love's solid land is everywhere.

(p. 578)

Isabella Crawford's remarkable versatility is illustrated when we go from the above narrative poem to the ballad of "**Old Spookses' Pass.**" This is the most important of a number of poems in the book written in that form of narrative dialogue which Lowell, John Hay, Bret Harte, and others have made so familiar. (p. 580)

The narrative is vigorous, spirited, precise, and strikingly true to nature,—indeed, extraordinarily so, coming from the pen of a young writer, and a woman who had never travelled west of Ontario. (p. 581)

Interspersed through the narrative are passages of shrewd, homely soliloquy, showing much keeness of perception and knowledge of human nature. . . .

The dramatic vigor of the poet's style, already seen in "**Malcolm's Katie,**" is further revealed in "**The Helot,**" here combined with passion, intensity, and brilliant color. The Spartan, restrained, cold-blooded, and unsympathetic, teaches his child a lesson in self-control—the supreme virtue of his race—by forcing his slave to drink himself into a state of absolute brutality. He plies the Helot with fiery wine, until, maddened with its fumes, enraged by the contemptuous scorn of the Spartan, and smarting under the consciousness of the wrongs of his race, the slave rises in his physical might, and strikes the cold Spartan in his one vulnerable spot,—the life of his only child. (p. 582)

Here is a richness and mature dignity that give promise of the very highest type of verse,—a promise unhappily only partly fulfilled, owing to the early death of the poet. She already possessed a grasp of lyrical form and language rarely surpassed in modern verse. (p. 583)

Constantly in this book one comes across striking lines, pregnant with thought and enriched with brilliant imagery and color:—

> Viewless the cord which draws from far
> To the round sun some mighty star;
> Viewless the strong-knit soul-chords are!

> Thought white as daisies snow'd upon the lawn.

> In space's ocean Suns were spray.

> Long sway'd the grasses like a rowing wave
> Above an undertow.

> . . . ancient billows, that have torn the roots
> Of cliffs, and bitten at the golden lips
> Of firm, sleek beaches, till they conquer'd all,
> And sow'd the reeling earth with salted waves.

These passages are taken almost at random from poems which space will not permit me to deal with otherwise. I give them to illustrate the almost uniform high quality of the poet's verse. (p. 585)

It would be possible to add many additional selections to those given, showing the exceptionally wide and catholic range of Miss Crawford's thought, and its maturity, as well as her originality, precision, sincerity, and the high lyrical quality of her verse. It is not too much to say that these gifts, so seldom found together in the same writer, justly entitle her, especially if we credit her with the promise of even better work held out by that which she did perform, to a high place, not alone among those who were her contemporaries, but among the intellectual leaders of the century. Had she lived for another ten or fifteen years, she would have outgrown the slight faults which occasionally appear in her work, nearly always faults of inexperience; and there is every reason to believe that she would have produced even finer and more polished, though hardly truer, verse than she did in her short lifetime. The world lost in her a genuine poet, one of those rare singers who, like Chatterton, are taken away before they have more than begun their life's work. (p. 586)

Lawrence J. Burpee, "Isabella Valancy Crawford: A Canadian Poet," in Poet Lore, *Vol. XIII, No. 4, Winter, 1901, pp. 575-86.*

ETHELWYN WETHERALD (essay date 1905)

[*In this excerpt from her introduction to* The Collected Poems, *which prompted the twentieth-century rediscovery of Crawford, Wetherald, a Canadian poet herself, praises Crawford as "purely a genius." She singles out freshness of perspective, lively imagery, and universal themes as the main characteristics of Crawford's style.*]

[Crawford] is purely a genius, not a craftswoman, and a genius who has patience enough to be an artist. She has in abundant measure that power of youth which persists in poets of every age—that capacity of seeing things for the first time, and with the rose and pearl of dawn upon them—and, as a part of this endowment, the poet's essential lightheartedness and good sense. Perhaps the most satisfying allurement in her poetry is its directness. It is as if she spoke to us face to face, and we gain the instant impression of a vigorous and striking personality, arresting our attention and "crying into us with a mighty directness and distinctness, in words that could not be more forcibly ordered," the athletic imagery that crowded her brain.

In "**Old Spookses' Pass**" her grasp on character and situation is passionately firm and strong. The verses are built up of cowboy language, through which her wit plays lambently, and the sense of her vividly wild, free spirit, showing in every line, brings the conviction that she must have been an eye-witness of the scene so glowingly thrown before us. (pp. 17-18)

This is large, forcible verse, direct and simple and vividly picturesque. Everything Miss Crawford has written is alive with her own personality, but in "**Old Spookses' Pass**" virility and sincerity are the clearest notes. In it, as in all her work, one is made to feel that behind the rich colouring, and what one is occasionally tempted to call the dashing and splendid verbal display, there are enduring forces of character.

The extent to which our poet's environment concerns us is that in which it is bodied forth in her writings. With her life and literature were one. When we read of

> The hollow hearts of brakes,
> Yet warm from sides of does and stags,

or gaze with her at

> The slaughtered deer,
> His eyes like dead stars cold and drear.
>
> • • • • •
>
> And the sharp splendour of his branches,

or hear the strong north wind,

> That rushed with war-cry down the steep ravines,
> And wrestled with the giants of the wood;

or feel the atmosphere of a certain day,

> All set about with roses and with fire,—
> One of three days of heat which frequent slip,
> Like triple rubies, in between the sweet,
> Mild emerald days of summer;

or follow the motion of the shadow-grey swift that, from the airy eave,

> Smites the blue pond, and speeds her glancing wing
> Close to the daffodils;

or enter into the lives of her fellow-adventurers in the New World, braced by poverty and "happy in new honeymoons of hope," we recognize the inmates and furnishings of her forest surroundings. It is true her imagination travelled far,—but not into regions of super-refinement. She knows the faith of the cowboy and the loyal heart of the backwoodsman, and her sense of humour is entertained by the rugged eccentricities of Old Spense and Farmer Stebbins. Her Muse, like Max's soul, shows a virile front, full-muscled and large-statured. (pp. 19-20)

Of the poems which have hitherto not appeared in book form, there are in some an Oriental prodigality of colours and images which almost affright the everyday imagination. Such is "**The Inspiration of Song,**" which at first glance appears to be an inspired medley of starry distances, fine-flamed diamonds, immortal roses, banks of violets, the heavy wings of slow centuries, rarest gems of every hue, flowering walls and "a tawny lion with a mane that tossed in golden tempests round his awful eyes." But the fundamental design beneath this wealth of decoration is strong and sufficient. Miss Crawford ornaments with a lavish hand, but she demands immense structures to work upon. (pp. 22-3)

The attentive reader of our Isabella will find that she voices the universal heart, not only in its deepest pangs, but in its highest happiness—the happiness of assured love. The poem, **"Love's Forget-me-not,"** is that rare combination of absolute simplicity with complete freedom from the least taint of the commonplace which is the final achievement of poetic souls. (p. 26)

"Malcolm's Katie," Miss Crawford's longest poem, is peculiarly rich in descriptive passages. Here we find in profusion the qualities and powers she has taught us to expect in her work—strong and coherent thought, imagery unhackneyed and unstrained, with a diction as concise, ringing and effective as the blows of its hero's axe. (p. 27)

But it is the splendour of Miss Crawford's descriptions—the report she gives of visual feasts—that most profoundly holds her reader. Canadian poets have been accused of "treating Nature as if she had been born and brought up in Canada," so authentically does the dew of first-hand observation lie upon their lines. Our Isabella, in the grace of her country-nurtured girlhood, found a pulse and living colour in every natural object. Among the timbered hills of "hiding fern and hanging fir" she passed her days making pictures that differ from those of most word-painters in that they are at once vivid and intelligible. Always she has stuff of thought to express, and if the stream of her utterance is at times a little impeded, like that of a leaf-choked brook in October, it is because of an excess of riches. It is this that ensures her against shallowness—that bane of the poet who writes because he chooses and not because he must. Strong, ardent, self-sufficing, finding in her hard life a challenge to which her spirit heroically responded, and in her solitary environment the right and true atmosphere of her bright-winged muse, Isabella Valancy Crawford is a brilliant and fadeless figure in the annals of Canadian literary history. (pp. 28-9)

> *Ethelwyn Wetherald, in an introduction to* The Collected Poems of Isabella Valancy Crawford *by Isabella Valancy Crawford, edited by J. W. Garvin, William Briggs, 1905, pp. 15-29.*

KATHERINE HALE (essay date 1923)

> [*A prominent Crawford critic, Hale offers a balanced assessment of her career. Characterizing her work as "the poetry of youth," Hale analyzes Crawford's style and praises her "brilliant, pure, sophisticated, and yet spontaneous" poetic voice. Hale acknowledges some immaturity and lack of humor in her work, but maintains that Crawford's handling of imagery and verse make her a first-rate poet.*]

[Open *The Collected Poems of Isabella Valancy Crawford*] and you find the eternal poet, no longer thwarted by life but rich amazingly, overflowing with thought and full of ecstasy—an authentic voice of wide range and a timbre that probably came out of long inheritance; brilliant, pure, sophisticated and yet spontaneous.

In any analysis of the art of Isabella Valancy Crawford it must be remembered that hers is the poetry of youth, written in days of struggle and literary obscurity that seem, in their comparative nearness, incredibly remote. She was caught in the smoothest decades of Victorianism. The giants existed, and fought among themselves in a sort of holy war, but there was no rush of young insurgents clamouring to break new lances. She was far from the centres of art where *camaraderie* naturally exists. Alone she must work out her methods, the rhythms of

world poetry moving far away in distant lordly strides. But she possessed in herself the neccessary elements: tingling life, imagination rather than fancy, a sensuous love of beauty, invention, which always means a large knowledge of the world's facts, and, as she was no specialist, the transmutation of more than one gift adding its subtle power. (pp. 96-7)

[She] rather reminds one at times of Walt Whitman's democrat, who felt himself "taller than the redwoods of California" and "strong enough to handle hell." She is essentially dramatic, even in her treatment of nature. Her oak is "a dark loud lion of a tree." (pp. 97-8)

Her wood flowers are "gay enamelled children of the swamp," and who but she could write of "a morn so like a dove with jewelled eyes"?

Like all creators this poet garnered from the past but lived vividly in the present. How she would have moulded the sensitive mercurial stuff of our day is problematic; what register of new perceptions it might have awakened it is perhaps idle to conjecture. Her constructive faculty was very great. Immaturity is evident in a certain lack of perspective, for, in spite of several dialect poems obviously intended to please an unsophisticated public, she had not lived long enough to acquire the gift of humour. With it, she would have been full-armed. Her work is, of course, the truest biography. It would seem that she had been grounded in Dante and had put on Tennyson, though, as in the case of most disciples, she outdoes her master in mannerisms. But while the early work abounds in imitative methods in its essence, it is not for a moment derivative. Indeed, its spontaneity is infectious. The clear-flowing lines seem to spring out of some glad, secret fountain of being. And there is great verbal colour. (pp. 98-9)

In her way she is an experimenter in form. You feel her touching the rich embroidery to design new patterns. Sometimes she uses an irregular rhyme, but seldom an irregular rhythm. In the poem **"March"** the amphibrach foot is used effectively without rhyme, and it is not an old-fashioned mind that could write such a line—a hundred others might be quoted—as "her laugh—a zigzag butterfly of silver sound." But she has her old-world moods when the reader gets the impression of a weaver of mediaeval tapestries. The forms and images are quaint—hundreds of years old. She writes of minstrels and wine-bowls, of steeds and lances and groves and hermits and golden-tressed maidens, old castles, black moats and trembling doves. She loves the adjective "ruddy," and quite overdoes it, and perpetually she uses the symbol of the rose. But no matter how ornate a poem may appear at a first reading, soon comes the piercing thought that makes short work of mere "poetic" words, the golden line that carries one away by sheer magic. A picture-maker always, more than that a dramatist, she understands the value of suspense and withdrawal, as well as a short, dry attack. The poetry of to-day is sharper than it was in her day; it makes use of clearer contrast. In many ways she was a forerunner.

The inclination to classical themes may have been a means of escape from a colourless environment. It was also a natural outcome of early training and reading. Such poems as **"The Helot," "Caesar's Wife," "Curtius"** and **"Vashti the Queen"** are examples of this phase. They are written in blank verse, and in this form Miss Crawford excels, making of it a magnificent and rarely flexible instrument.

But there is an inherent oriental quality that, with the exception of Marjorie Pickthall, no Canadian possesses in anything like the same degree. (pp. 99-101)

The home of Robert Strickland in Lakefield, Ontario, where the Crawfords lived from 1863 to 1869.

A sense of conscience is not always included among the singing leaves of a poet's wreath, but this poet possessed it. In "**The King's Garments**" occurs the famous lines:

> For Law immutable hath one decree,
> 'No deed of good, no deed of ill can die;
> All must ascend unto my loom and be
> Woven for man in lasting tapestry,
> Each soul his own.'

But I like better the careless dismissal, as of an account closed, with which she wills away the flesh in a poem called "**His Clay**":

> The flesh that I wore chanced ever to be
> Less of my friend than my enemy.
>
> So bury it deeply—strong foe, weak friend—
> And bury it cheaply—and there its end.

Of love of country this poet wrote in her own strange bright language. There was a day when lines like these met the casual gaze of readers of a Toronto newspaper:

> If destiny is writ on night's dusk scroll,
> Then youngest stars are dropping from the hand
> Of the Creator, sowing on the sky
> My name in seeds of light. Ages will watch
> Those seeds expand to suns, such as the tree
> Bears on its boughs, which grow in Paradise.

No poet long maintains this plan of rapture. Shakespeare and Dante sustained it in repeated measures. Keats and Shelley in brief lyric songs, every real poet in certain magic lines. It is the last thought of the writer to compare the magic lines of this Canadian poet with those of any other, much less with the masters of English song. One can only stress the obvious fact that she did leave rare and beautiful snatches of poetry, marked by her own original imprint, which always bore a certain splendour rather akin to the clear colours of the Ontario landscape that she knew and loved. (pp. 102-03)

[Crawford's poetry shows] the remarkable versatility of the poet. Her sea songs are few and rarely quoted, hence "**Good-Bye's the Word**," which is as fresh as though written yesterday. "**Between the Wind and the Rain**," "**The Butterfly**" (the original title of "**The Mother's Soul**"), "**The Camp of Souls**" and "**Laughter**," to mention only a few of the lyrics, take us worlds away one from the other, in concept and mood. (pp. 103-04)

Lines from "**Malcolm's Katie**" cannot be omitted in any summary of the poet's output. Here one gets a vivid imagination at work on a foundation of actual experience. The life of the woods is the drama, with a somewhat insipid love-story used as a connecting link.

In "**Gisli the Chieftain**," an old Norse Saga is converted into a narrative poem that for sheer dramatic imagery would have made the writer notable, had no other work been published. The pictures are superb—unforgettable. (pp. 104-05)

There is an ancient myth that poets thrive in poverty and neglect and that the tongues and pens of hostile critics are so much fuel to their flame. Witter Bynner, the American poet, has recently said "One had to be a poet indeed a quarter of a century ago to endure the attacking obloquy." Judging from the criticisms of the day, however, women, with the possible exception of Mrs. Browning, who had been bold enough to write "The Cry of the Children," a protest against juvenile labour in the factories and mines in England, were not even dignified by "attacking obloquy." They were merely "poetesses." Isabella Valancy Crawford was never a "poetess," and perhaps her work refutes the theory that to have great artists there must be great audiences. One of the robust race whom no circumstance, however untoward, can altogether quell, she goes singing on in lines that may, or may not, be better known to-morrow than they are to-day. (p. 107)

> *Katherine Hale, in her* Isabella Valancy Crawford, *The Ryerson Press, 1923, 125 p.*

JOHN W. GARVIN (essay date 1927)

[*Garvin's edition of* The Collected Poems *(1905) was instrumental in the revival of critical interest in Crawford. In the excerpt below, he evaluates her importance and predicts that her poetry will be more fully appreciated in the course of time.*]

A genius is always original and distinctive. Apart from that kind of personality, a great poet is invariably impersonal in his or her verse. This is markedly true in the poetic output of Miss Crawford. None of the trials and disappointments in her life find expression there. She is courageous and optimistic to a degree. She sings with a radiant outpouring of her spirit, because she must sing. Her exquisite nature poems are invariably personification. Read "**The City Tree**," "**Said the Daisy**," "**Said the West Wind**," "**Said the Canoe**," etc. Yet human joys and tragedies had their strong appeal too, for she wrote numerous poems permeated by intense human interest. She might have written, I think, poetical dramas of a high order of merit. Her blank [verse] is rarely equalled, and she had constructive imagination and the gift of objective characterization. (p. 132)

The world has known few great women poets. Between Sappho and Elizabeth Barrett Browning, whom can we name? Between the latter and 1887, who equalled Isabella Valancy Crawford, and who has surpassed her since? She wrote the first Western poem of surpassing merit, "**Old Spookses' Pass**." "**The Helot**" is of such power and quality that it makes all other poems with a similar theme sink into insignificance. But I need not enumerate further. The more Canada develops in nationhood, the more Miss Crawford's poetry will be loved and her memory revered. (p. 133)

John W. Garvin "Who's Who in Canadian Literature: Isabella Valancy Crawford," in The Canadian Bookman, *Vol. IX, No. 5, May, 1927, pp. 131-33.*

V. B. RHODENIZER (essay date 1930)

[*Rhodenizer briefly comments on Crawford's style, deeming her "Canada's greatest female poet."*]

[Crawford's] outstanding literary merits are formal excellence, verbal music, philosophical insight, emotional intensity and range, and dramatic imagination almost universal in scope. The last two in particular give to her poetry variety, from the most delicate lyric play of Celtic fancy to the elemental grandeur of primitive epic. Her narrative poems, whether in blank verse or in rhymed stanza, whether in dialect or in literary language, describe settings with a Keats-like vividness, and at times present dramatic situations, both serious and comic, with Shakespearean effectiveness. Her lyrics include Shelley-like interpretations of the spirit of personified natural objects, and Browning-like dramatic lyrics presenting great emotional moments in the lives of persons of many social ranks, countries, and periods. Notwithstanding her broad sympathy, she was essentially Canadian in spirit. She has an unrivalled position as Canada's greatest female poet. (pp. 167-68)

V. B. Rhodenizer, "Early Poets," in his A Handbook of Canadian Literature, *Graphic Publishers Limited, 1930, pp. 160-69.**

E. K. BROWN (essay date 1944)

[*Though he acknowledges that a good deal of her work was "careless and unsatisfactory," Brown praises Crawford's imaginative style and realistic depiction of Canadian life.*]

Isabella Valancy Crawford is the only Canadian woman poet of real importance in the last century; and her **"Malcolm's Katie,"** a long narrative of backwoods life in primitive Ontario, is the best image a poet has given us of Canadian living in the years following Confederation. Malcolm Graem is a stern, silent, Scottish Canadian farmer, who has made his fields from the wilderness and every time he surveys them feels a rugged pride in property and accomplishment. His daughter Katie has the grace and the softer virtues that belong to a time of consolidation rather than back-breaking pioneer effort; but her love goes out to Max, a lumberman, who is a representative of a Canada more primitive than Katie's father's, a Canada where adventure is a deeper satisfaction than achievement, though achievement is not scorned. Clearly, in her way of presenting these personages, as in her style, Miss Crawford follows Tennyson, the Tennyson of the modern idylls; but in the style there is a density, at times a confused richness, which express a nature more nervous and ardent than Tennyson's.

Nowhere does her style appear to better advantage than in the description of nature, in such passages as these:

> At morn the sharp breath of the night arose
> From the wide prairies, in deep-struggling seas,
> In rolling breakers, bursting to the sky;
> In tumbling surfs, all yellow'd faintly thro'
> With the low sun; in mad conflicting crests,
> Voic'd with low thunder from the hairy throats
> Of the mist-buried herds. . . .

and

> In this shrill Moon the scouts of winter ran
> From the ice-belted north, and whistling shafts
> Struck maple and struck sumach, and a blaze
> Ran swift from leaf to leaf, from bough to bough;
> Till round the teeming forest flashed a belt of flame,
> And inward lick'd its tongues of red and gold
> To the deep tranced inmost heart of all.

Both these passages come from the opening of the second part of **"Malcolm's Katie,"** in which with more impressive result than anywhere else in her poetry Miss Crawford sought to convey the teeming vitality of nature. The density and confused richness in her manner, sometimes a fatal flaw, are here wholly appropriate: they do aid her in making the reader feel that nature is enormously and even terrifyingly alive. Not until Duncan Campbell Scott wrote his major nature poems was any other Canadian poet to rival Miss Crawford's adequacy in handling wild nature.

One of the most powerful forms in which Miss Crawford rendered nature was the combination of the dense and rich style with dialect which recalls the *Biglow Papers.* **"Old Spookses' Pass"** is written in this dialect, and there is much more than quaintness, there is a rare force of surprise and insight when the luxuriant and original imagery is set in humble dialect:

> An' the summer lightnin', quick an' red,
> Twistin' an' turnin' amid the stars,
>   Silent as snakes at play in the grass,
> An' plungin' their fangs in the bare old skulls
>   Uv' the mountains frownin' above the Pass;
> An' all so still that the leetle crick,
>   Twinklin' an' crinklin' from stone tew stone
> Grows louder an' louder . . .

The passages that have been quoted suggest another of her powers, the power of fantastic imagination: indeed it is only because her imagination is wildly fantastic that those passages were written, that nature in her poetry is such a wild and exciting thing. In very trifling pieces this imagination appears to arrest the attention, in such comparisons as that of a girl's mobile eyes with "a woodbird's restless wing," a light laugh with "a zigzag butterfly," the flash of a jewel with the "silent song of sun and fire." The multitude of such images makes it unsafe to neglect even her most careless and unsatisfactory poems—and very much of her work is careless and unsatisfactory.

Often her poetry is unsatisfactory simply because it is carelessly conventional. She is very likely in her more relaxed passages to use a diction like Cameron's, in which fields are "gemmed" with flowers, a canoe has "polished sides" like a queen's, a mother's hair is "the holy silver of her noble head." There is a great deal of this sort of language in her poetry, and even in the middle of some of her intensely wrought passages it comes to mar the fine effect. In the second part of **"Malcolm's Katie,"** where she is at her very best, she can speak of a tree as

> The mossy king of all the woody tribes

or of superb health as denoted by

> The rose of Plenty in the cheeks.

This carelessness, the sign of flagging energy and dubious taste, is perhaps, all in all, not so grievous a disappointment as some of the tricks played Miss Crawford by what is so often her strength—that very fantastic imagination some of whose flights have been recorded. Of these tricks I shall give but one example, a passage which has by some been highly admired:

> For love, once set within a lover's breast,
> Has its own sun, its own peculiar sky,
> *All one great daffodil,* on which do lie
> The sun, the moon, the stars all seen at once.

The utter lawless wildness of such a comparison is the penalty paid for the fantastic successes; and there is a great deal of such wildness, most of it far less acceptable than the lines quoted.

Some time ago it was said that in **"Malcolm's Katie"** Miss Crawford had given us the one poetic account of real Canadian living in the years following Confederation. She was able to do so because, despite her fantastic vein, she lived in the real Upper Canadian world of her time. She tells, for instance, of how into the edges of settlement came the business men:

> . . . smooth-coated men, with eager eyes,
> And talk'd of streamers on the cliff-bound lakes,
> And iron tracks across the prairie lands,
>
> And mills to crush the quartz of wealthy hills,
> And mills to saw the great wide-armed trees,
> And mills to grind the singing stream of grain. . . .

And over against this picture of the coming of a business civilization—how much there is in that one epithet, "smooth-coated"—in her best-known lyric, **"The Song of the Axe,"** she celebrates the pioneer glory. She frames the song admirably, placing just before it the line:

> While the Great Worker brooded o'er His work

and after it this claim of Max's:

> My axe and I—we do immortal tasks—
> We build up nations—this my axe and I.

In the framework and in the tone of the song itself Miss Crawford comes nearer to Whitman than any of her contemporaries. The song itself is moving:

> Bite deep and wide, O Axe, the tree,
> What doth thy bold voice promise me?
>
> I promise thee all joyous things,
> That furnish forth the lives of kings!
>
> For ev'ry silver ringing blow
> Cities and palaces shall grow!
>
> Bite deep and wide, O Axe, the tree,
> Tell wider prophecies to me.
>
> When rust hath gnawed me deep and red,
> A nation strong shall lift his head!
>
> His crown the very Heav'ns shall smite,
> Æons shall build him in his might.
>
> Bite deep and wide, O Axe, the tree;
> Bright Seer, help on thy prophecy!

The old clothes are still there, but the new spirit is strong enough to shine through them, and to animate. . . . Miss Crawford's vision was not strictly national . . . ; but it was often fixed . . . on the real significance of the life immediately around her. (pp. 42-6)

> E. K. Brown, "The Development of Poetry in Canada," in his On Canadian Poetry, *revised edition,*

1944. Reprint by The Tecumseh Press, 1977, pp. 28-87.*

DESMOND PACEY (essay date 1952)

[*In this brief excerpt from an essay originally published in 1952, Pacey criticizes Crawford's melodramatic style.*]

Miss Crawford's poems are vigorous and energetic, and to the description of a storm or a stampede of cattle she can give compelling speed and force. She sees similitudes everywhere, and image is piled upon image until we are almost breathless from the pressure:

> The late, last thunders of the summer crash'd,
> Where shriek'd great eagles, lords of naked cliffs.
> The pulseless forest, lock'd and interlock'd
> So closely bough with bough and leaf with leaf,
> So serfed by its own wealth, that while from high
> The moons of summer kissed its green-glossed locks,
> And round its knees the merry West Wind danc'd;
> And round its rings, compacted emerald,
> The South Wind crept on moccasins of flame. . . .

This, surely, gives the sense of the confused intensity of a Canadian forest. But even here the confusion is more apparent than the intensity, and when Miss Crawford turns from nature to man her essentially melodramatic imagination becomes painfully obvious. The two title poems of [*Old Spookses' Pass, Malcolm's Katie, and Other Poems*], for example, are melodramatic extravaganzas in which the good lines are almost lost in the wild confusion of the whole. **"Old Spookses' Pass"**, the account of a cattle stampede on the prairies, has some fine descriptive passages, but it also has much trite moralizing, stale sentiment and strained pathos. **"Malcolm's Katie"**, praised even by the judicious E. K. Brown as "the best image a poet has given us of Canadian living in the years following Confederation" [see excerpt dated 1944], conducts a group of pasteboard characters through a wildly improbable sequence of events. Violent deaths and fortuitous rescues occur on almost every page, and the dialogue is stilted and unnatural. Even the descriptive passages are frequently strained, as in this account of an autumn night:

> The land had put his ruddy gauntlet on,
> Of harvest gold, to dash in Famine's face;
> And like a vintage wain deep dryed with juice
> The great moon faltered up the ripe, blue sky,
> Drawn by silver stars—like oxen white
> And horned with rays of light.

Such boldness of fancy is admittedly superior to a timid conventionalism such as Mair or Goldsmith gave us, but it is surely extreme to call such writing good poetry. The term for this type of art, obviously, is rococo: it is tastelessly and clumsily florid. No amount of regret for the harsh circumstances among which Miss Crawford's life was lived and her poetry was written should blind us to this fact. (pp. 69-70)

> Desmond Pacey, "The Confederation Era (1867-1897)," in his Creative Writing in Canada: A Short History of English-Canadian Literature, *second edition, The Ryerson Press, 1961, pp. 35-88.**

R. E. RASHLEY (essay date 1958)

[*In this negative assessment of "Malcolm's Katie," Rashley faults Crawford's "external" depiction of nature and "pseudo-Indian imagery.'' He maintains that the poem does not succeed as a stylistic experiment, although he does acknowledge that Crawford began to explore ''the attitudes created by pioneering'' in such poems as ''Malcolm's Katie.'']*

Isabella Valancy Crawford writes against a background of civilization already accomplished in the older parts of Canada. Her **''Malcolm's Katie,''** which at first glance might seem to be a poem of the pioneer type, on reading turns out to be a popular romance in a pioneer setting. There is just a suggestion of the pioneer type of survey in the description of the growth of the settlement, but it is too rapid to give much colour to the poem:

> So shanties grew
> Other than his amid the blackened stumps;
>
> . . . . .
>
> There the lean weaver ground anew his axe,
> Nor backward looked upon the vanished loom,
> But forward to the ploughing of his fields,
>
> . . . . .
>
> The pallid clerk looked on his blistered palms
> And sighed and smiled, but girded up his loins
> And found new vigour as he felt new hope.
> The lab'rer with trained muscles, grim and grave,
> Looked at the ground, and wondered in his soul
> What joyous anguish stirred his darkened heart,
>
> . . . . .
>
> Then came smooth-coated men with eager eyes
> And talked of steamers on the cliff-bound lakes;
> And iron tracks across the prairie lands;
> And mills to crush the quartz of wealthy hills;
> And mills to saw the great wide-armed trees;
> And mills to grind the singing stream of grain:

The story attempts to give some of the experience of pioneering along with some of the vitality and force of nature against which the pioneer was pitted. Nature is external, as with the pioneer poets, but it is now conceived as a powerful force in itself. The effort to give this force expression leads to a blind alley of experiment in style. The pseudo-Indian imagery is no more real to us than the poetry using it is real to the Indian; it is, in fact, a failure to make the world of nature available as spiritual substance. There is a great difference between Crawford's Indian summer:

> She will linger, kissing all the branches;
> She will linger, touching all the places,
> Bare and naked, with her golden fingers,
> Saying, ''Sleep and dream of me, my children;
> Dream of me, the mystic Indian Summer,''—

and Campbell's:

> Along the line of smoky hills
> The crimson forest stands
> And all the day the blue-jay calls
> Throughout the autumn lands.

The difference is not simply that one is more familiar with the style of Campbell's poem, but that his style is the one which best expresses experience of people with the season. **''Malcolm's Katie''** is an extension of the range of pioneer sensibilities but it has none of the nativeness of the sixties poets. This would seem to be true of the remainder of Crawford's work. The attitude toward Toronto in the poem of that name

is precisely the attitude of the pioneer group, pride in accomplishment. It is a poetic version of the preamble to the first edition of the *Anglo-American Magazine*'s series of articles on Canada, ''It is meet that we should rejoice over the triumph of civilization, the onward progress of our race, the extension of our language, institutions, tastes, manners, customs and feelings.'' **''Canada to England''** expresses the dual loyalty of the pioneers, and the cry ''Man hath dominion'' is the cry of the pioneer trumphant in a man-centered world. The environment is conquered and man has, out of his own capacities, produced something of value. There is an extension of the sensibilities of the pioneer group in the concept of nature and the attempt to find imagery for the experience of the pioneer with nature. Perhaps in **''Malcolm's Katie''** and poems like **''His Clay''** there is an effort to present one realization of the attitudes created by pioneering, the intellectual and emotional stuff that escapes Goldsmith and the earlier writers. (pp. 54-6)

R. E. Rashley, ''Extensions of Pioneer Poetry,'' in his *Poetry in Canada: The First Three Steps, The Ryerson Press,* 1958, pp. 53-8.*

JAMES REANEY   (lecture date 1959)

[In the following excerpt, drawn from one of the most seminal commentaries on Crawford, Reaney discusses her development and use of an "individual Bible" of symbols. In addition, he analyzes the relationship between imagery, symbol, and theme in Crawford's poetry and asserts that "Malcolm's Katie" is the only completed poem that includes her entire "alphabet of symbols." Reaney asserts that Crawford's primary importance as a poet lies in her ability "to translate [Canada's] still mysterious melancholy dominion into the releasing potentially apocalyptic dominion of poetry." His comments were originally delivered as a lecture in a series entitled "Our Living Tradition."]

The first impression that the reader has about Crawford's poetry is her tendency to see landscape as humanized. She is continually creating a mythology. Just as the Greeks made the world about them a world of half-human satyrs and nymphs, river gods and rainbow goddesses, so in Crawford ''the frost bit sharp like a silent cur,'' the Night steals like a ''dark giant,'' the snow is a ''white squaw.'' Indian—North American Indian—poetry and mythology seem to have helped her here and she is one of the few Canadian poets to do much with what would seem an obvious way to come upon real knowledge of what symbolic grammar best fits our environment. One first discovers then that Crawford sees the Canadian landscape as half-human—as potentially under human imaginative control. (p. 275)

To show you Crawford's mythopoeic imagination as neatly as possible I should like to speed up her poems a bit until they coalesce into a pattern or an epic diagram I find there. Every poet who gets beyond the scrappy lyric stage into something more organized generally has the Bible behind him for assistance in laying out larger narrative patterns and in spelling out the alphabet and paradigms of a symbolic language that can handle bigger subjects than the private images of one's life can. By bigger subjects I mean creation, flood, exodus, annunciation, incarnation, crucifixion, harrowing of Hell, Pentecost, the Bridegroom and the Bride, and Apocalypse. However each poet has his own Bible, his *own* ordered imagination of what the whole of reality is like. It is important that he have his own since that is the only way vision is ever attractive and convincing; we feel that this particular person (poet) saw every eccentric and individual corner of his life as having some sort of contact with Eternity. We are thus taught by the individuality of a poet's handling of the universal language to trust in a similar effect on our individuality. Crawford's poems produce the following individual Bible and as I say I am doing with her what you do with the Mutascope pictures at the fall fair: put your one cent in and turn very slowly; the Indian's tomahawk will never dispose of the cowboy's scalp, but turn faster and instead of individual images one gets an individual narrative.

In the beginning there was a huge daffodil which contained all reality, was all reality—its centre was everywhere and its circumference nowhere. It was both inside out and outside in at the same time. What upheld this huge daffodil? It was caused, like the reality that existed before God created the angels, by a Trinity of the "one beloved, the lover and sweet love." In the world of the daffodil there was neither day nor night—the stars, moon, the sun shone all at once, not spelling each other off as they do in our fallen world or drowning each other out either. Crawford suggests that this daffodil apocalypse is possible whenever two human beings love each other.

But for some unaccountable reason the daffodil shattered—broke apart, divided. Perhaps, as the theosophist Jacob Boehme puts it, the unity of God wanted to show forth its wonders. One of those wonders is pain and another is evil and another is good; sometimes when one has experienced all three of these one wishes that God would stop showing forth his wonders and tuck Himself back into daffodil unity again. At any rate Crawford's daffodil breaks up, breaks up into tree and lake, eagle and dove, eagle and swan, the queen of heaven looking at herself in a glassy lake, wind and ship, cloud and caged skylark, whip and stampeding herd, good brother and evil brother, paddle and lily bed, smouldering darkness and prickly starlight, aristocratic Spartan and beaten Helot, Isabella Valancy Crawford and King Street, Toronto.

This division can produce the greatest agonies, the most fearful dread, even a disastrous swing into an abyss—in **"Old Spookses' Pass"** it is referred to as a gulch—which might as well be called the black daffodil world, a world of complete opposition to all return of the golden daffodil unity with which we began our Crawford Bible. This black daffodil might in turn be called complete nothingness and seems to be a sort of necessary condition of return to the first daffodil. Both the strictly moral and the atheistic live here, but horrible as they are they serve a purpose.

In between the black daffodil and the glorious one we have the divided pairs already mentioned. The evil brother is sometimes clever enough to see that he is as much a child of the daffodil as his good brother and that they are really working at the same reconstruction of Eternity. Only if the good brother is extremely stupid will the evil brother become a completely black daffodil abyss type, but then of course he becomes so extremely horrible that the tension of dread arouses the good brother's intelligence and he rights a lopsided dangerous situation. The stampeding herd of cattle rocket on straight towards nothingness; eventually a mysterious whip descends from the darkness which turns their flowing shapelessness into a revolving circle that mills about and mills about until it stands still.

Out of this still dark circle flares up the great daffodil vision again. This vision does not return from a fleeing away from evil and chaos; in several of her poems Crawford is quite insistent that the daffodil springs from stepping back into the

chaos and disorder and stilling it with the imagination within oneself. In connection with the good brother aspect of things she twice mentions gyres, and so I assume that just as evil may be seen as a line that spins itself up into a circle so the world of good is also a revolving spiralling shape of some sort whose narrow part gives you a vision of Eternity but not the actuality of it. This can only come from descending back towards the black spinning chaos of stampeding cattle again. So the daffodil at the beginning breaks up into a spinning black whirlpool and a spinning white whirlpool. Obviously this is speeding up Crawford considerably and I've had to squeeze to get some things the right shape particularly when she didn't give me very much to go on. I am particularly glad that she mentions gyres, a concept that eases the organization of any visionary system since it explains how things can get from one state to another, also go through a bewildering number of diverse experiences and yet still remain attached to the single undivided point of Eternity on which the gyre spins. One may ask, "Did she know she was doing this?" Probably not. It is potentially there; it would be there if enough pressure had been put on her by an informed and interested reading public.

When one first reads Crawford's collected poems the two things that stay in one's mind at almost a sub-verbal level are a yellow shape that's the justly praised passage about love having "its own sun, its own peculiar sky / All one great daffodil" and a whirling dark shape ("Round spun the herd in a great black

A manuscript page from "A Hereditary Prince," an early version of The Halton Boys.

wheel'') from **"Old Spookses' Pass."** They loom so importantly in one's mind that they catch hold of the rest of her poetry in an organizing way that cannot simply be wish-fulfillment or system-fulfillment fantasy on my part.

Then too she herself shows signs of using her images grammatically rather than intuitively; the daffodil appears again in the **"Roman Rose-Seller"**:

> . . . Love's of a colour—be it that
> Which ladders Heaven and lives amongst the Gods;
> Or like the Daffodil blows all about the earth.

She is not just the sweet singer who delves about among her free associations and her private experience and her intuitions to produce, usually, a different flower for love each time. Like the great symbolic linguists she is interested in finding one symbol for love, a symbol peculiarly hers, and using it again and again so that the reader sees in each fresh use of the recurring symbol not only what it means but what it carries with it from the last passage he saw it in. It is in this way that canons of poetry are formed, that a reader gets the chance to feel he can understand a whole complicated series of lyrics in one final look. . . . [The] recurring daffodils give Crawford's work a feeling of order, give this reader the feeling that she was developing an organized symbolic language. If the recurring daffodils seem too scanty, just try to count up the water lily images: they endlessly recur and are always associated with the moment of love that can produce the possession of Eternity. Then too there is the recurring image of opposites—wind and ship, Spartan and Helot already mentioned. Apparently therefore she was a poet who was battling her way out of the nineteenth-century literary dilemma. I refer to the fact that most people—readers and critics—seemed then to think that the only way to write poetry was to sit down and hope something hatched out of one's private intuition hen house. Crawford I see as refusing to sit; she goes about and organizes.

After my Mutascope run-through of Crawford which produced . . . the daffodil, white circle, black circle, and back-to-daffodil progression I feel I should go back and fill it in a bit with references to actual poems for fear you might think I have made this all up myself. (pp. 275-79)

The daffodil comes from **"Malcolm's Katie"** and represents the hero's feeling that no matter what complications the fallen world provides—the toil of clearing the forest, the disappearance of sun and stars in the clouds of smoke from burning logs—in his heart he has a world beyond such complications, the daffodil world of his love.

When the daffodil splits up we get in a very interesting poem called **"Gisli, the Chieftain,"** a poem that takes some extremely daring imaginative leaps, a dialogue between good and evil, two brothers out of the same father who is a mysterious God:

> Said the voice of Evil to the ear of Good,
> Clasp thou my strong right hand,
> Nor shall our clasp be known or understood
> By any in the land.

Evil goes on to say that he works for his own destruction, that his toil is bleak, that he suffers, and that it is only ignorant man who calls him ''Evil''; actually he is just another son of God, or son of the Daffodil, with peculiarly difficult work assigned to him. This is an extremely sophisticated view of good and evil and reflects the fine mental equipment and training Crawford started out with. Most Canadian poets have either

to break through a shell of nonsense about Hell being an absolutely permanently separate state from Heaven or else are brought up to regard these extremely interesting and useful symbols as not having any spiritual use at all. Her cowboy in **"Old Spookses' Pass"** refuses to believe in the conventional devil whom God somehow allows to throw logs across the railway tracks of individual lives. The engines that fall off are then in Presbyterian fashion thrown into the scrapheap of Hell. But Crawford's cowboy sees both good and evil as parts of God; there is evil and guilt in the world, summed up in the symbol of the black stampede of cattle to the abyss, but the evil brings one to God not away from Him; it calls forth the organization of mercy and love which turns the dark rushing line into a circle that is the basis for paradise. After the stampede has been stopped the cowboy feels a faith and an innocence that had not been present in his heart for years. The guilt and evil within him has finally forced a total reorganization of his soul in the direction of Eternity. Crawford usually refuses to take a moral attitude; her attitude is always that of imaginative exuberance that would rather tell a story than condemn. In **"Farmer Stebbins' Opinions"** the old farmer is impatient of ''moral twitters'' and prefers to listen to God, to the God who talks in the images and symbols of a natural world, a world Crawford always sees as a humanized one, already part of the human mind:

> I talk tew them in simple style
> In words uv just three letters,
> Spelled out in lily-blow an' reed,
> In soft winds on them blowin'.

This impatience with morality and intellect (and I think she is also impatient with just the aesthetic attitude too since her best poems always have a muscular symbolic organization that keeps the reader from sinking into a beautiful mood) springs, of course, from a feeling that imagination sees reality so much better, frees man so much more efficiently. From imagination's point of view, sorrow and evil prevent the soul from collapsing ''like a mist'' into a ''chaos'' of ''soft, gilded dreams, / As mists fade in the gazing of the sun'' (**"Malcolm's Katie,"** VI). Evil is a basis for unity, not something to be fled from and rejected.

Various exciting poems show other ways of looking at the world of opposites represented above by the two brothers. The wind invites a ship out into the ocean for a suicide pact (**"Said the Wind"**); a caged skylark cries to a cloud who eventually swoops it away (**"Said the Skylark"**); a Spartan exhibits a drunken Helot to his little boy as a dreadful moral example—the Helot kills the little boy in an action that shows the dreadful snapping back of balance between good and evil that has to occur whenever very moral people start tampering with this balance (**"The Helot"**). In **"The Inspiration of Song"** a figure very similar to the Shekinah figure of cabalism, or the veiled Anima Mundi figure who stands at the end of Spenser's epic, lives in a tower above a glassy lake. This sounds to me like Spenser's version in the *Hymnes* of the Holy Ghost, a female figure apparently the wife of God of whom the whole created world is reflection, i.e., ''made at her behest.'' Wherever Crawford got this extremely interesting figure, she stands for the human imagination and what she drops down to the passing imaginers living in the fallen divided world is flowers—images, symbols—not tracts nor moods nor pebbly truths.

Death is the doorway for many: a black arrow, two arrows, and a white butterfly introduce, respectively, an Indian warrior, a Viking warrior, and a child, into a world where opposites have disappeared:

> Never upon them the white frosts lie,
>   Nor glow their green boughs with the ''paint of
> death'';
> Manitou smiles in the crystal sky,
>   Close breathing above them His life-strong breath;
> And He speaks no more in fierce thunder sound,
> So near is His happy hunting ground.
>
>   (**''Camp of Souls''**)

Nevertheless in the midst of life itself the door stands open:

> And love is a cord woven out of life,
> And dyed in the red of the living heart
> And time is the hunter's rusty knife
> That cannot cut the red strands apart.
>
>   (**''Camp of Souls''**)

Perhaps the two best poems in which the return is discussed are **''The Lily Bed''** and **''Between the Wind and the Rain.''** In the former take one large lake covered with waterlilies in blossom and reflecting the forest about it; someone in a canoe sticks a scented red-cedar paddle into the lily-bed and appears to remain entangled there for the whole day. This image which Solomon might have borrowed for his canticles is simply allowed to expand for what seems dozens of couplets; not only is the paddle identified with the lily bed but the image of the forest finally becomes unified with the reflecting lake:

> The wood, a proud and crested brave;
> Bead-bright, a maiden, stood the wave
>
>   •   •   •   •   •
>
> Till now he stood, in triumph's rest,
> His image painted in her breast.

One is left with more than a mood by this poem for the whole point of it seems to be that this has been a moment out of the daffodil world. In **''Between the Wind and the Rain''** the situation is this: one of the lovers—apparently the woman—cannot abide the coming storm although it is obvious that everything in the landscape or rather gardenscape about them is beginning to intensify beautifully at the very prophecy of the coming rain:

> . . . and the round chestnut stirs
> Vastly but softly at thy prophecies.
> The vines grow dusky with a deeper green.

The woman wants to be like the eagle that flies above the storm. (''Beats on a sunlight that is never marred'') and to ''circle star-ward, narrowing my gyres / To some great planet of eternal peace.'' But this is not the way of Love into Eternity; it is more like the second best way back—that of the arrows of Death already mentioned. The way one wants Eternity is to have it right in the centre of the Time/Space ambush redeeming thereby as much of Time and Space as possible. So the man says that the eagle does not avoid the storm but comes back into it with what he now knows about the ''planet of eternal peace.'' The storm, by the way, is the same image as the whirling black circle we have already discussed in connection with **''Old Spookses' Pass''**:

> And there he rends the dove, and joys in all
> The fierce delights of his tempestuous home.

Then comes a very beautiful passage in which both lovers watch the approach of the storm. The daffodil moment is closing in

and yet it is a moment of terror as well as delight when the two opposing states collide:

> O Prophet Wind, close, close the storm and rain!
> Long swayed the grasses like a rolling wave
> Above an *undertow;* the mastiff cried;
> Low swept the poplars, *groaning* in their hearts;
> And iron-footed stood the gnarled oaks,
>
>   •   •   •   •   •
>
> *Lashed* from the pond, the wary Cygnets sought
> The carven steps that plunged into the pool;
> The peacocks *screamed* and dragged forgotten plumes;
> On the sheer turf all shadows subtly died
> In *one large shadow* sweeping o'er the land;
> Bright windows in the ivy blushed *no more;*
> The ripe, red walls grew *pale,* the tall vane *dim.*
> Like a *swift offering to an angry god,*
> O'erweighted vines shook plum and apricot
> From trembling trellis, and the rose trees poured
> A red *libation* of sweet, ripened leaves
> On the trim walks; to the high dove-cote set
> *A stream of silver wings and violet breasts,*
> The *hawk-like storm* down swooping on their track.

I should like to call attention to the words I have italicized in this passage—how they suggest the approach of the terrible evil brother, the dark shadow, how the whole passage shows a very orderly closed garden world suddenly joining with some mysterious bubbling black force. The hawk-dove conclusion is a way Crawford has put this particular union of opposites in other poems.

Just in the split second before the rain descends, the moment of dread collapses and the daffodil world springs up:

>   ''Where'er thou art,'' I said,
>   ''Is all the calm I know. Wert thou enthroned
>   In maelstrom or on pivot of the winds,
>   Thou holdest in thy hand my palm of peace.''

The most exciting and tremendous flowering of the daffodil comes by grasping the pivot of the winds, by holding extreme opposites in one's being at one time for as long as one possibly can.

The story of **''Malcolm's Katie''** on the surface sounds wildly implausible and even ludicrous. Since Crawford is attempting a myth about the whole business of being a Canadian she has no time to fret about making her poem vulgarly believable in its low mimetic areas. Just tell yourself the story of ''The Eve of St. Agnes'' where the interest lies not in a plausible story but in soaking the reader's head in various rich sensual moods and your merriment will soon force you to realize that it's not a plausible story Keats is interested in. Similarly with the first chapters of Genesis or the Apocalypse of St. John. Since **''Malcolm's Katie''** is the only poem Crawford completed which includes all the alphabet of symbols I have been discussing as lying behind her other poems I thought I would take it out for separate discussion. (pp. 279-85)

What Crawford was doing [in the poem] is what thousands or maybe hundreds of Canadian ladies have been attempting in droves for at least a century—the Canadian pioneer novel. **''Malcolm's Katie''** has much the same plot as Grace Campbell's *Thorn-Apple Tree* but whereas *Thorn-Apple Tree* is completely plausible, there is nothing very imaginative about it except the illustrations. . . . In Crawford's story what one holds one's breath at is the tremendously exciting way in which she grasps what happens to a soul in a pioneer setting. She may not have managed to make the low mimetic level of her story very plausible—only a Dante or Shakespeare can give you that effortless feeling of reality on all levels of their work; but in the way the story is told on a second level using natural forces as symbols that combine the human and the superhuman, this is remarkably successful:

> The pulseless forest, locked and interlocked
> So closely bough with bough and leaf with leaf,
> So serfed by its own wealth, that while from high
> The moons of summer kissed its green-glossed locks,
> And round its knees the merry West Wind danced,
> And round its ring, compacted emerald,
> The South Wind crept on moccasins of flame,
> And the red fingers of th' impatient Sun
> Plucked at its outmost fringes, its dim veins
> Beat with no life, its deep and dusky heart
> In a deep trance of shadow felt no throb
> To such soft wooing answer.

This is the dark brother, the brooding monster of Nature out of which Canadian civilization has just begun to emerge. Max faces it with an axe which shapes it into a useful garden and farm monster not the brooding selfish darkness that wells up in the magnificent phrase "serfed with its own wealth." On the other side of the monster dragon forest, as in all dragon-killing legends, stands Katie—the heroine. Conquer the dragon forest and you conquer the wrath of Katie's father, another brooding darkness in the narrative. Symbolically the tree that falls on Malcolm is a completely plausible tree. The villain Alfred, who represents a particularly chaotic and nothinged aspect of the "dark brother" forest, has at that moment made a most brutal attack on Max's grasp of Eternity. Max has just said very confidently that he is in love and "thus do I / Possess the world and feel eternity." It is either now or never for the monster and he crunches down upon him. Alfred, the villain, is given a very striking speech about Time that corresponds to the flowing linear aspect of the stampeding herd in **"Old Spookses' Pass."** He sees Time as just one long terrifying stampede to Nothingness Gulch:

> The ceaseless sweep of her tremendous wings
> Still beat them down and swept their dust abroad.
> Her iron finger wrote on mountainsides
> Her deeds and prowess, and her own soft plume
> Wore down the hills. Again drew darkly on
> A night of deep forgetfulness; once more
> Time seemed to pause upon forgotten graves;
> Once more a young dawn stole into her eyes;
> Again her broad wings stirred, and fresh, clear airs
> Blew the great clouds apart; again she said,
> "This is my birth—my deeds and handiwork
> Shall be immortal!"

A series of stampedes, actually. But eventually even Alfred can go only so far into nothingness. The world of love turns him into a whirling dark circle upon which the daffodil world can be built, upon which Max and Katie are brought together again. The story shows the lily-bed and daffodil aspect of things returning after the now familiar break-up into opposites of one sort or another—Max separated from Katie, Max against the forest, Max against Alfred; with the successful conquest of forest and Alfred, the lovers inhabit a new world with its own sun and its own peculiar sky.

This structure which I have described as present in both Crawford's whole work and in more concentrated form in her best narrative poem is a memorable achievement on her part and worth attention on our part since it involves the Canadian situation so deeply. I really don't know what else there is to say except that in this poet those interested in developing their imaginations in Canada may find some indication of just how to go about developing that imagination in Canada. She was one of the first to translate our still mysterious melancholy dominion into the releasing potentially apocalyptic dominion of poetry. This translation must go on if we are to have a civilization in Canada. I give you the primer this long-dead woman stumbled on—so simple really: a daffodil filled with the moon, the stars and the sun; two brothers, a long rushing line, and a black circle that revolves ever more slowly and more slowly. (pp. 285-88)

> *James Reaney, "Isabella Valancy Crawford," in* Our Living Tradition, *second and third series, edited by Robert L. McDougall, University of Toronto Press, 1959, pp. 268-88.*

JOHN B. OWER   (essay date 1967)

[*In the following excerpt from his detailed critical study of "The Canoe," Ower analyzes Crawford's imagery in order to illustrate his contention that the poem is "a study in the psychology of the primitive mind." He also comments on Crawford's portrayal of love, death, and sexuality.*]

A convenient starting point for an analysis of **"The Canoe"** is the fact that the poem constitutes, both in the viewpoint of its narrator, the canoe, and in her account of her "masters twain", a study in the psychology of the primitive mind. Particularly notable is Crawford's remarkable awareness of the animating and myth-making proclivities of primitive man. That is, as is evident in some of the most striking similes and metaphors in **"The Canoe"**, the poet is familiar with the tendency of the primitive to see everything in terms of life, and of human life in particular:

> Thin, golden nerves of sly light curl'd
> Round the dun camp, and rose faint zones,
> Half way round each grim bole knit,
> Like a shy child that would bedeck
> With its soft clasp a Brave's red neck;
>
> Sinuous, red as copper snakes,
> Sharp-headed serpents, made of light,
> Glided and hid themselves in night.

Another significant aspect of Crawford's treatment of the primitive mentality is her romantic sense of its primal and direct character. In **"The Canoe"**, . . . the poet evidently finds in the behaviour of the "savage" Indian a sort of psychological apocalypse of the basic forces of human nature. This is particularly evident in Crawford's lyric in the love-song of the two braves, with its frank expression of impulses and emotions which at first appear scarcely less elemental than those of the hounds who dream of "the dead stag stout and lusty":

> My masters twain sang song that wove
> (As they burnish'd hunting blade and rifle)
> A golden thread with a cobweb trifle—
> Loud of the chase, and low of love.
>
> O Love, art thou a silver fish?
> Shy of the line and shy of gaffing,

Which we do follow, fierce, yet laughing,
Casting at thee the light-winged wish.

Even if **"The Canoe"** were simply a poetic study in the psychology of uncivilized man, it would still do considerable credit to Crawford's powers of insight and imagination. However, as Reaney has shown, Crawford is not merely a clever poetical dilettante, but an artist with a vision of sufficient dimensions to come to grips with the great questions of human existence [see excerpt dated 1959]. It is therefore reasonable to assume that her remarkable re-creation of the primitive mind in **"The Canoe"** is not simply an anthropological study, but possesses a wider frame of human reference. One obvious possibility follows from the supposition that Crawford sees in the primitive the direct expression of man's primal psychic impulses. This is that she is using the mentality of the Indian in essentially the same way as Wordsworth employs that of the peasant: to exemplify or explore in the workings of a simple and uninhibited mind certain basic principles of man's psychic activity which are normally buried, suppressed or modified in the case of the civilized person. In terms of modern psychology, Crawford might be dealing in **"The Canoe"** with those forces which in the European normally belong to the realm of the subconscious, but which nonetheless exert a pervasive influence upon his life. It would then of course be possible that the external world as it is seen through the myth-making and animating focus of the primitive mind becomes a symbolic projection of the psychological realities with which the poet is dealing.

An analysis of **"The Canoe"** along the lines just proposed may begin with the love-song of the two braves. This lyric occupies a central position in Crawford's poem, and we may divine that it is intended to stand out as a kind of climax or core, to which the preceding and following lines function essentially as a prologue and epilogue. It is accordingly significant for our line of argument that the song is concerned with a paradox involving one of the fundamental impulses of man's psychic life. The paradox, which under normal circumstances would exist only in the subconscious of civilized man, is that human love in its sexual aspect is also violence, and is destructive as well as creative, death-dealing as well as life-giving:

> O Love, art thou a silver fish?
> Shy of the line and shy of gaffing,
> Which we do follow, fierce, yet laughing,
> Casting at thee the light-wing'd wish,
>
> • • • • •
>
> O Love! art thou a silver deer,
> Swift thy starr'd feet as wing of swallow,
> While we with rushing arrows follow;
> And at last shall we draw near,
> And over thy velvet neck cast thongs—
> Woven of roses, of stars, of songs?

The darker aspect of sexuality is expressed in the song of the braves in terms of the pursuits of fishing and hunting. These images of force and slaughter are of course offset in the song by what Reaney would term the "golden daffodil" images of laughter, song, lily, rose, gold, silver and gems. However, the manner in which the song is introduced ironically undercuts the positive implications of these images:

> My masters twain sang songs that wove
> (As they burnish'd hunting blade and rifle)
> A golden thread with a cobweb trifle—
> Loud of the chase, and low of love.

Similarly, the predominance of "golden daffodil" symbols in the second stanza of the lyric is implicitly offset by the imagery of violence and death in the line immediately following. In the primitive or sub-conscious context of **"The Canoe"**, the creative and life-giving aspects of sexuality are thus paradoxically accompanied, and even overshadowed, by a dark lust for destruction and death. In terms of the symbolic scheme outlined by Reaney, **"The Canoe"** is thus a "black daffodil" poem, in which the chase of love is still essentially the dark line of the rush to annihilation. It is only near the conclusion of Crawford's poem that we receive symbolic hints that this black line is becoming the "black circle" in which evil is ordered and redeemed.

The dark vision of sexuality in the love-song of the braves is reinforced by the imagery in the passages which precede and follow it. Thus, the almost domestic tenderness of the "erotic" treatment of the canoe with which Crawford's poems open is ironically undercut by the grim references to the hunting and fishing activities of the braves, which involve numerous images of shooting, stabbing, binding and hanging. We should particularly notice in the lines preceding the love-song the description of a deer, which has been shot, bound and hung from boughs:

> My masters twain the Slaughter'd deer
> Hung on fork'd boughs—with thongs of leather.
> Bound were his stiff, slim feet together—
> His eyes like dead stars cold and drear. . .

The psychological paradox just outlined, with its emphasis on the dark aspects of human sexuality, is also reflected in the animating and myth-making images of **"The Canoe"**, of which there are several striking examples in the lines preceding the love-song of the braves. It will be noted that the relevant similes and metaphors are all images of light. The source of this light is in each case the campfire of the two braves, whose designation as a "camp-soul" indicates that it serves as a symbol of the source and centre of primitive consciousness in the psychic activity of the "savage" mind. In the images under consideration, either the light of this "camp-soul" or what is revealed by it carries sinister implications of malignity. Thus, the extended simile concerning the "faint zones" of light cast by the campfire on the trunks of pine trees . . . expresses the frightened paralysis of human innocence and love in the face of the dark powers of cruelty and violence that reside in man. A similar sense is conveyed by the image in which the firelight becomes a human figure who lays an "anxious" hand on the foam-flecked shoulder of a hanging deer, and peers into his dead eyes. In this strange metaphor, we evidently have a recognition of the consequences of a lust for violence and slaughter in which there is a child-like mixture of fascination and fear. The two images just mentioned thus depict an essentially naïve consciousness suddenly becoming aware of the innate capacities for evil in the human soul. However, in neither of them is the firelight itself seen as something sinister, as it is when it becomes "Thin, golden nerves of sly light", or "Sharp-headed" snakes slithering into the darkness. In both of these latter images there is a suggestion, not of the naïveté which we find elsewhere in **"The Canoe"**, but of the subtlety of the serpent who tempted Eve.

Seen with regard to the traditional value of light as a symbol of goodness, love and life, the above images with their sinister implications apparently involve an ironic reflection of the psychological paradox which Crawford is treating elsewhere in **"The Canoe"**. In connection with "primitive" sexuality, and perhaps the whole of man's fundamental psychic life, creativity is overshadowed by destructiveness, and love by bloodlust and violence. On a symbolic level, the light of the "camp-soul" which represents the psychic life of the primitive is thus really akin to darkness. This paradox of a light which embodies blackness is suggested symbolically by the redness of the firelight in three of the above images. This colour has of course appropriate associations with blood and burning, together with its connotations of violence, lust and death. This "demonic crimson" is in turn probably intended to be contrasted with the silver fish and the silver deer of love which we find in the song of the two braves.

The symbolic pattern which runs through the myth-making and animating imagery of the "prologue" to the love-song is of course carried on into the "epilogue" in the radical simile in which "slaughter'd" fish, reddened by the light of the camp-fire, are compared with scimitars stained with the blood of "new-dead" wars. However, in the final myth-making image of **"The Canoe"**, there is a reversal of the symbolic values of the images just discussed.

> The darkness built its wigwam walls
> Close round the camp, . . .

This metaphor is of course an image of darkness rather than of light, but the darkness in this case is evidently that of the "black circle," in which the line of evil and destruction has become the whirl from which the golden daffodil will ultimately re-emerge. This positive connotation is implicit in the reference to the weaving of a wigwam wall, which is not only an image of an upward gyration, but also one of creation rather than of destruction. Thus, in symbolic opposition to a light which is really darkness, we have in the last myth-making image in **"The Canoe"** a darkness from which light and order are beginning to be born, just as they are in the first stages of the Creation in Genesis. The nascence of light from blackness, and of cosmos from chaos, is likewise suggested in the last two lines of the poem by the white shapes, albeit still "thin-woven and uncertain", which press at the "curtain" of shadows. In psychological terms, we presumably see in the closing images of **"The Canoe"** a representation of the first stages of a transformation of the dark side of man's nature into "sweetness and light". (pp. 54-9)

[For] Crawford the psychological paradox explored in **"The Canoe"** is really a microcosmic reflection of a metaphysical situation, and . . . she therefore sees a definite analogy between the constitution of man's psyche and that of the cosmos which he inhabits. . . .

Whatever its basis, such an "analogical" vision would have important implications with regard to the symbolic value of Crawford's poetry. The perception of a radical correspondence between the internal and external worlds would make it possible for her to write a "double-barrelled" poetry, in which metaphysical and psychological questions were treated in one and the same set of symbolic images. The action of a poem like **"The Canoe"** could in this case take place within the human mind, and yet at the same time extend to embrace the whole of the cosmos. Crawford's poetry would thus involve a double apocalypse, in which the depths of man's mind and those of the universe surrounding him were simultaneously revealed. (p. 59)

If **"The Canoe"** really does function symbolically on two levels, what would be the significance of its dual revelation in terms of the frame of reference provided by Crawford's overall vision of man and the universe? How could the double apocalypse of the poem fit into the Biblical pattern of Creation, Fall, Redemption and Apocalypse which Reaney sees as the backbone of Crawford's poetic system? To put a further question which is closely related to the first two, what message could **"The Canoe"** be meant to convey to the civilized European who is the poet's intended audience? On the psychological level, we have already indicated that the primitive outlook of **"The Canoe"** is intended to illustrate a sinister paradox in the fundamentals of human psychology, which would in turn be of basic importance for civilized man, even if in his case it were suppressed or buried below the level of his normal consciousness. In terms of the Biblical schema which Reaney sees as providing the "bigger subjects" of poetry, this inseparable union of creativity and destructiveness, good and evil, in man's basic mental activities may be seen as the psychological aspect of his fallen state, with its frightening ramifications of his life. For Crawford, this fallen condition is presumably shared by the savage and the civilized man alike. In the case of the European at least, its negative side may be repressed or sublimated through the censorship of morality, but this control is at best imperfect, and for Crawford it will never bring humanity back to heaven. The good and evil, creation and destruction, which are so intimately linked in the depth of the human psyche are in fact complementary aspects of the "golden daffodil" unity which is man's spiritual goal, and both are necessary for its attainment. What is needed is not for man to attempt to suppress the evil side of his fallen nature, but rather to organize and transform it by means of his powers of creativity and love. In order for him to do so, it is necessary for him to plunge into its darkness, as Dante descends into the Inferno on his way to God. Only by so doing will man's nature finally be redeemed, and return to its unfallen unity. The Indian braves of **"The Canoe"** may be seen as pointing out this dark journey which must be taken by all men, including the European, in order to achieve redemption. The emphasis in **"The Canoe"** falls upon the negative aspect of this process although, as we have seen, there is a symbolic suggestion at the end of the poem of the ordering and transmuting of the evil in man.

The significance of **"The Canoe"** on a metaphysical level can be best approached by a consideration of the wilderness landscape of the poem as it is seen by the primitive mind. . . . Crawford sees the task of the European in the New World as being the redemption of the dark wood by converting it into a garden once again. However, in order to "save" the wilderness, he must first plunge into it like the Indian braves of **"The Canoe"**, and temporarily experience the terrors of its darkness. This preliminary step in the process of redeeming nature is of course analogous to the psychological plunge into his own fallen soul which is an essential part of man's return to the golden daffodil. In fact, Crawford undoubtedly sees the two processes as being inseparably related in actual practise. The settling of a country like Canada would involve for her a simultaneous redemption of both the outer and inner worlds. In **"The Canoe"**, Crawford emphasizes the essential element of evil and terror which is involved in this re-creative process, with only suggestions towards the end of the poem of the rebirth of light and order from darkness and chaos. (pp. 60-1)

John B. Ower, "Isabella Valancy Crawford: 'The Canoe'," in Canadian Literature, *No. 34, Autumn, 1967, pp. 54-62.*

A manuscript page from The Halton Boys.

FRANK BESSAI (essay date 1970)

[*Bessai explores Crawford's development of myth, imagery, and theme in "The Dark Stag," "The Lily Bed," "The Canoe," "Malcolm's Katie," and "The City Tree." He also discusses her style, especially in "The Lily Bed" and "The Canoe," in relation to Victorian poetic conventions, noting that Crawford achieves her most striking effects in a "peculiarly subconscious way."*]

In attempting a summary of the qualities exhibited by **"The Dark Stag,"** what comes to mind first is its melodrama, sustained by a taut, almost headlong succession of concrete and violent metaphors. That Crawford finds it necessary to provide us with occasional hints that she is writing a poem about the coming of an autumn dawn in the Canadian wilderness, may indicate that her method of doing so is unnecessarily ornate, over-wrought, and subject to overinvention. From the standpoint of tradition, she seems to have reshaped materials from Greek myth; but while the results may be as Rashley has it, pseudo-Indian [see excerpt dated 1958], they do not seem to be pseudo-mythological. She has given us *her* myth of a Canadian dawn; and in this personal, romantic sense, one surely does not require it to be culturally authentic. The poem has an overtly narrative structure which contains her basic metaphorical conception (with its mythological undertones) of the night as a stag accompanied by his love, the "snow-white doe," who is the "pale, pale Moon." In their frantic flight from the hunter Sun and his dog-like winds, the pair "beat the stars

down as they go" but soon the moon falls victim and the stag's tears "fall in rain" as the hunter pursues relentlessly, aiming his shafts of light at his victim. Finally the stag "sinks in space—red glow the skies, / the brown earth crimsons as he dies." The Indianization of the action may subsume the fateful story of Memnon, son of Aurora, and, as with the Ethiopian king, here too all nature participates in the rites of death. Crawford brings in the birds of the air and the marsh, the fierce pike of the northern lake, the red glare of autumn sumach, although perhaps significantly only the "shy loon" mourns; the rest of nature either participates in the destruction, as do the hound-like winds, or provides an environment of violence such as the "silver-warriors," who are "the strong, fierce muskallunge." In the lines which follow, the natural scene takes on the metaphor of an Indian conclave, perhaps a war assembly where "red torches of the sumach glare, / Fall's council-fires are lit." Her myth of the Canadian dawn is a story of combat and struggle; two lovers are violently severed, although not before they themselves "beat the stars down"; the noble stag himself "stamps the lilied clouds" before he is destroyed by his even fiercer foe. It is not enough to say that Crawford frequently views natural events in terms of violent struggle which is, of course, the total impression the poem makes . . . , but even here she mythologizes, howbeit incidentally, on her favourite theme of Love. Its innately destructive aspect is hinted at briefly, but the emphasis is on the violence in its severance. This is an aspect of the love theme she dwells on more fully in **"Malcolm's Katie."**

Thematically **"The Lily Bed"** moves in the opposite direction, both in terms of the love motif, which here is a coming together, and on the natural level, which depicts through gentle, loving motion a sense of peace and beauty, conveyed in imagery of union. In fact, the unique aspect of the poem is that these two levels are inseparable, a remark which suggests the greater complexity of this poem to the **"Dark Stag."** As in the latter, this poem begins with a narrative decoy, which serves at the same time as a refrain, subtly varied to underline three stages of a congress presented to us in terms of a sexual idyll. Once again, as in **"The Dark Stag,"** there is a comprehensive natural landscape, represented by the fish, the dragon fly, and the oriole, that bears witness to the central action. The narrative cluster that evokes the stillness of the scene, depicted as a sachem seated in a sunlit harvest lodge, though somewhat overfreighted with adjunctory metaphors, is nevertheless an appropriate way to direct us to the anthropomorphic centre of the poem, wherein the pine forest and the lily-surfaced lake are presented respectively as an Indian brave and a maiden who are lovers. The cedar paddle and the canoe made of bark have already served early in the poem to introduce us to the theme of embracing lovers. Their amorous intertwining is subtly indicated later by the unexpected substitution of a personal pronoun:

> His lips, soft blossoms in the shade,
> That kissed her silver lips—hers cool
> As lilies on *his* inmost pool.

Here the lilies on *his* rather than her pool underscore the complete merging of the forest and the lake, the two complementary segments of the landscape which the poem is about.

In the next couplet, we find Crawford explicating, perhaps a trifle overtly, the precise relationships of her metaphorical construct, to tell us, in effect, that she is writing a poem about the day-long reflection of the forest on the lake's surface:

> Till now he stood, in triumph's rest,
> His image painted on her breast.

But the poetical conception of this union as a sexual act of conquest is included in the lines, in terms primitive enough, in the allusion to the brave's painted image, to further the central theme. That is to say, the poem does not pause at this point for any parsing of what has already been said. While the description of the lake isle as a bead from the wampum belt of Manitou may, like the sachem's lodge of stillness, be a gratuitous ornamentation, the poem returns immediately thereafter to its metaphorical centre: the Indian canoe among the water lilies, whose amorous motion, no matter what all else it suggests, never loses the sharply defined rocking of a real canoe on quiet water. The poet's final structural problem, to find a way to introduce the notion of passing time without relinquishing the metaphorical complex of lake and canoe, suffers again from overinvention, in that we get a causative sequence not unlike that in the children's story of the old lady trying to get her pig over a stile. But after the rather shrill and gaudy congeries of the Evening Star (also equipped with a lodge) grasping the mane of a sunset cloud to make it neigh evening winds, there is a strong and sure return to the pines and lilies, wherein the wind-puff metaphorically serves to climax their love-act and bring the poem to an end with the approach of twilight.

One element of the poem's conception may be questioned. The means by which Crawford has chosen to anthropomorphize the forest as Indian brave in bark canoe, wherein only the cedar paddle and the bark of the canoe provide logical links with the forest, may be regarded as tenuous even though it is a way of introducing the primary image of motion. That she is aware of this as a possible flaw emerges in her attempt to strengthen the brave's forest connection by the line ''Of loud strong pines his tongue was made.'' But we should observe that the next line of the couplet delineates him in a way that denies the appropriateness of a stronger identification with the forest, as being prejudicial to the mystical oneness of the wilderness which is the poem's theme. In this respect, the tenuous association of brave and forest seems strongly justified, and we should admit that, aside from those incidental lapses which critics in general tend to find in her work, ''The Lily Bed'' is a well-made poem. We are bound to observe also, that the poem's most astonishing quality lies in what I have already called a narrative decoy: although the poem is dramatic, it only appears to conform to the linear rudiments of a story told. Instead, Crawford gives us a concatenation of metaphors that are capable of being assimilated as a lyric tableau: the poem is in one piece, and not in a succession of pieces. In this we must note that she has, seemingly without help, begun to transcend the poetics of the Victorians, to invent for herself a modern idiom. This idiom can be more comprehensively explored when we turn to ''The Canoe,'' her most successful poem.

The poem's title, which is ''Said the Canoe'' in the 1905 Garvin edition, forces us from the beginning to accept a purposeful metaphysical oddity: the *persona* of this poem is a talking canoe, that describes, in a strangely lyrical way, the evening camp of two Indian hunters who are its masters. Once more, as in ''The Lily Bed,'' we have the rudiments of narrative: the stanzas move through the consecutive steps of making camp. First the canoe describes how it is beached, in metaphors that suggest a woman being put to bed by two lovers. The lyrical strain, always implicit in the metaphorical freight of the poem, breaks easily into the braves' love words to their canoe, suggesting an emotional dimension which will be expanded later in the love song they sing around the campfire.

The lighting of the campfire brings into the poem the opportunity for a complex interplay of metaphorical devices, which has so far only been hinted at in the furry skins that cover the lover-canoe. The flickering glow of firelight is described in images that range from the ambivalence of ''Thin nerves of sly light curled'' through a comprehensive spectrum of emotional values. The centre is the powerfully unifying simile of the flames seen as the wavering hands of a child that fears to clasp the red neck of a warrior brave: by this means, the ''love-as-life'' theme already established is extended and subtly modified. But the metaphors that continue the description of the firelight deepen the sinister ''love-as-death'' tone, while at the same time integrating and organizing the lyrical structure. Thus, while the line about the ''hollow hearts of brakes / Yet warm from sides of does and stags'' is easily related to the initial image of the snugly bedded canoe and emerges naturally from the description of the firelight curling around, metaphorically embracing, the surrounding trees, the line's primary function is to link the plumed hunter through the sharp-headed snakes of his arrows with this slaughtered quarry in the next verse.

The hanging up of the slaughtered deer by the canoe's hunter masters continues to employ the firelight ambivalently: first, from its sinister, ash producing, death related side, to provide the eerie glow against which the deer's eyes reflect like dead stars, and the hard lineaments of its corpse with its stiff bound feet and clotted foam on the side and flanks, can be illuminated. But the imagery of life and love, already presented in terms of the firelight as child caressing brave, now briefly returns to alleviate the stark impression of death, and the firelight is seen once more as a life-fostering force, a red and anxious palm caressing the deer's splendid antlers.

The song which the hunters sing, as they polish their knives and rifles, is paradoxically introduced by the reporting canoe as weaving ''a golden thread with a cobweb trifle,'' to suggest the delicately apprehensible connections that unify and give value to the primitive and subconscious sensibility. The brave's song, which is the heart of the poem, contains two motifs, hunting and love presented as inseparable segments of experience. The hunting song, which is also a love song, suggests the true extent of Crawford's metaphysic. Love for her is a universal and ambivalent power that inhabits equally the forces of creation and destruction, of life and death, and permits them to merge in the guise of art. Love and the chase are explicitly linked by the hunters' song: they pursue the deer and the fish as creatures whose loveliness in life they admire, in order to kill them and make them over ritually into bejewelled trophies, flower-decked artifacts of death. In this process, the firelight, functioning as the ambivalent symbol of the human sensibility, assists in the actual scene before us, making the deer's eyes shine like dead stars, exposing the sculptured outlines of the deer's trussed body as *nature morte*, illuminating the strung fish as ruddy swords. By means of the sword image presented in a stanza that frames the hunters' love song with the corpses of their quarry, Crawford has managed a remarkable feat of metaphorical compression, wherein the fish as trophies embody also the instruments of death. What happens here is more or less in accordance with Reaney's approach, for the entire contents of the poem—the hunters, the fire, the deer and the fish, love and the chase—are here all comprehended in the single icon of the sword [see excerpt dated 1959].

Besides turning the poem towards the quiet close, the next two stanzas have the minor function, according to Crawford's habitual practice, of enlarging her scheme with surrounding nature as the life-fostering element as comprised in the image of the pine boughs that are piled, as earlier for their canoe, to provide a resting place for the hunters. The same boughs gratuitously cushion the sleeping hounds, who dream of death and the chase; and the reversion to an animal sensibility progresses to the weird image of the bat flitting over the campfire's subsiding flames. To read the final stanza, with Ower, as involving "the nascence of light from the blackness, and of cosmos from chaos" is to place too negative an interpretation on the poem's contents [see except dated 1967]. While the hunters no doubt represent the means to explore the primitive sensibility, they function as metaphors for a timeless ordering, a ritual-producing element in the human psyche, for which no regeneration is demanded or necessary. Accordingly, the "pressed shapes, thin, woven and uncertain / As white locks of tall waterfalls' should be interpereted not as cosmos intruding on chaos, but rather the reverse. It is the savage and unimaginable heart of the wild that intrudes, with the dying fire, on the hunter's camp.

Finally, we may return to the conceit of the talking canoe to observe that it provides, as artifact, the overriding symbol of man's ordering use of, and involvement with, nature. The personification of the canoe as "slender lady of the tides" suggests the primitive beginnings of poverty as myth; its bedding, covered with blanket of fur, a ritual that involves the forces of love equally present in the hunt. To have the canoe speak the poem is an ultimate means to contain metaphorically the idea of man's ordering impact on the wilderness.

"**The Canoe**" may be taken as the finest example of Crawford's departure from traditional poetry. . . . When she writes poems like "**The Canoe**," she is writing, we are bound to say, out of profound, naive, and original genius. It is only fair to add that much of her poetry is easily placed in the tradition, even the minor tradition, of her time, where she does not exceed by much the gentle capacities of a Jean Ingelow or a Mrs. Hemans.

When we turn to her major narrative poem, "**Malcolm's Katie**," such salient aspects of the Victorian tradition are at once apparent, particularly in the sentimental and melodramatic surface aspects of the story itself. (pp. 408-14)

The basic lineaments of this romance may well be absurd; no critic has ever claimed otherwise. But if we approach even so seemingly ridiculous a plot armed with some knowledge of Crawford's mythic propensities, as revealed for instance in "**The Canoe**," we discover at once the underlying structure of a metaphysical scheme containing the familiar ingredients of love and struggle and death. Moreover, these abstractions assume a panoramic form against the broad background of a narrative poem that contains aspects of a Canadian myth. Perhaps the best place to begin such an analysis is in the scene where Alfred confronts Max in the forest to persuade him that Katie is unfaithful. There is a long exchange between the two of them, in which each reveals his mythic essence.

In lyrical exuberance, Max, the conquerer of the wilderness, exults in the might of his axe:

> Bite deep and wide, O Axe, the tree!
> What doth thy bold voice promise me?
> I promise thee all joyous things,
> That furnish forth the lives of kings;
> In every silver ringing blow
> Cities and palaces shall grow.

And turning to Alfred,

> See, friend, he cried, to one that looked and smiled,
> My Axe and I, we do immortal tasks,
> We build up nations, this my axe and I.

"Oh," Alfred replies, with a cold, short smile, "Nations are not immortal!" and in a long speech on time and the crumbling of empires, he concludes, "Naught is immortal save immortal—Death!" But Max smiles a superior smile as he rejoins,

> O preach such gospel, friend,
> To all but lovers who most truly love;
> For *them,* their gold-wrought scripture glibly reads,
> All else is mortal but immortal—Love!

Alfred cries, "Fools, fools," "most immortal fools!"

On the simplest level, Max stands for the life-affirming myth of progress which must inform a healthy pioneer society, set in opposition to Alfred as the life-denying world-historical principle of decadence and decay. Thus, also, Alfred himself has no wish to be a builder, but is content to inherit the work of others. Malcolm may be described as representing the pioneering movement of progress run down to a point halfway between the positions of Max and Alfred. He has been a pioneer, he is now content to hold—and in a bourgeois way to value—what he has. Into this larger historical tension Crawford inserts the more specifically human and personal principle of love. It is, of course, created in Katie. On the mystical mythological level, Katie represents *das Ewig Weibliche*—the universal power of love incarnate that flows in all directions and invests all positions. Its sinister aspect, or link with death— what we might call the *Liebestod* theme— is revealed in all the principal characters. First, in Katie, when her love for Max leads her into the perilous excess of dancing on the logjam; second, in Max, when he is almost killed by the tree his love-and-progress axe chops down; finally, and most spectacularly, in Alfred, when he jumps with Katie into the millrace. The point of this episode, which can hardly be sought in the area of psychological realism, is that Alfred, as the professed principle of anti-love and anti-progress, or, to put it another way, as the angel of Death, has himself been defeated by the superior power of love. But Alfred's final desire to assimilate love in death is defeated by the providential arrival of love-and-progress. Again, on the level of realism, Max's spectacular arrival is an absurd coincidence. What we have, therefore, in the scheme of the poem, is the triumph of love as a life-force set in the context of a myth of progress that is finally able, in the naming of the child, to overcome and transcend all obstacles. Crawford's poem, in its basic lineaments, thus invests the pioneering drive, ordinarily conceived of as a heroic or masculine stereotype, with an energy which is primarily feminine; she writes what might be termed a feminine epic.

The large plot-framing sections of "**Malcolm's Katie**," in which the seasons are Indianized, are commonly regarded as gratuitous ornamentation, providing evidence that Crawford is not a narrative poet. That her lyrical gifts and her penchant for anthropomorphizing nature constantly interfere with the flow of the narrative is indeed true. But it is not true that these sections are merely gratuitous. Rather, they provide a means, in the personifying of the seasons, to deepen and extend the historical, social, and specifically human aspects of her story in all its dimensions of love, progress and death. (pp. 414-16)

That "**Malcolm's Katie**" is nevertheless a failure is due in no small part to the expectations which we ordinarily bring to narrative poetry of the nineteenth century. We expect a story with a measure of psychological credibility, the clear lines of which the presence of a mythical substratum should not obscure. Crawford is not equal to this task. But in the narrative tradition of Canadian poetry, **"Malcolm's Katie"** should be accorded an honourable place.

Finally, **"The City Tree,"** although in every respect a traditional achievement, may be mentioned because even it demonstrates the peculiarly subconscious way in which Crawford achieves her strongest effects. The *persona* of the poem is literally the city tree itself, standing "within the stormy, arid town," expressing with nostalgia all the elements in nature that are missing from its existence:

> When to and fro my branches wave and sway,
> Answ'ring the feeble wind that faintly calls,
> They kiss no kindred boughs, but touch alway
> The stones of climbing walls.

There are consolations for the tree in the broad shade it provides for city men "as they lie / Pillowed on horny hand." Even more, from the tree's point of view, the shy eyes of children are a happy substitute for the absent violets. They look up "To where my emerald branches call and wave / As to the mystic skies." This poem, in its wistful recognition of the poet's own role of isolated artist scarcely known in her own lifetime, might be called the spiritual autobiography of Isabella Valancy Crawford. Metaphorically the poem tells the story of the still young writer transplanted in her last years because of family tragedy and poverty from the wilderness world which was her chief inspiration. It is the story of natural genius and unflinching courage, of the power of a lonely and loving spirit. (pp. 417-18)

> *Frank Bessai, "The Ambivalence of Love in the Poetry of Isabella Valancy Crawford," in* Queen's Quarterly, *Vol. LXXVII, No. 3, Autumn, 1970, pp. 404-18.*

DOROTHY LIVESAY   (essay date 1973)

[*The following excerpt is from Livesay's essay on a then-unpublished manuscript of* Hugh and Ion, *which she refers to as* The Hunters Twain. *She maintains that the poem "confirms [Crawford's] virtuosity" and that it demonstrates her concern for social and moral problems in nineteenth-century Canada.*]

[The reader is entitled to ask: how does the publication of Crawford's **The Hunters Twain**] fundamentally change the critics' view of Isabella Valancy Crawford?

In my opinion it adds to her stature and confirms her virtuosity. It illustrates that she saw herself as a narrative-philosophical poet whose role it was to define the epic aspects of immigration, settlement and pioneer life in Ontario. Further, more than any other Canadian poet of her period, Crawford is shown to be deeply aware of the social, class and moral clashes that arise in a free-enterprise society. Although perhaps she is best known and loved for her lyrics in praise of love, she was no mere lyricist. She possessed a political conscience.

This unpublished manuscript is valuable in another, literary sense. It gives a clue as to Crawford's creative method, "the poet at work". She wrote at white heat impelled by passion. The result is often wordy and even chaotic, showing little regard for syntax, spelling, punctuation or the dangers of repetition. There is clear evidence that she did spend time on revision, but it is difficult to see the rationale behind her revisions. . . . At times she uses inversion of subject and predicate

with great force (as was true in **"The Helot"** and in **"Malcolm's Katie"**) but she relies on this rhetorical device too often. What emerges however, from this method of composition (and it is also true of **"Malcolm's Katie,"** which I take to be earlier than *The Hunters Twain*) is that Crawford worked on a generous scale with a broad canvas in view; and out of this wide documentation of detail and theme she allowed her imagination to lift her free into pure lyric song. She responds to the wilderness with love, not fear; and she believes that love will win, if only man will work *with* nature and not against her. In this sense Crawford is the most modern of the Confederation Poets and the most relevant for us here and now in the Seventies. (p. 97)

> *Dorothy Livesay, "The Hunters Twain," in* Canadian Literature, *No. 55, Winter, 1973, pp. 75-98.*

PENNY PETRONE   (essay date 1974)

[*In this excerpt from her introduction to the* Selected Stories *of Isabella Valancy Crawford, Petrone surveys characterization, settings, dialogue, imagery, and structure. Although she finds the quality of Crawford's stories uneven, she praises her realism and technical expertise and concludes that "Extradited" is Crawford's best story. Petrone's introduction was written in 1974.*]

For the most part [Crawford's settings in her stories] are either so vague and generalized that they do not convey any sense of real locality, as in **"La Tricoteuse,"** or they are so overloaded with description that the reader is overwhelmed, as in **"Tudor Tramp."** But occasionally Crawford's settings are convincing and effective. For example, in **"Extradited,"** by presenting brief glimpses of the clearing at the right moment, with a control that is unusual for her, Crawford captures the stark grimmness of the backwoods farm. Although the circle described in her romances of high society was completely alien to her own life, Crawford in **"A Five-O'Clock Tea,"** with a few carefully selected details to create a plausible drawing-room setting, skilfully projects the luxury and elegance of the *haute-monde*.

Frequently Crawford uses dialogue and dialect to sustain the realism of her settings. The trivial conversation of *bon-vivant* colonels drinking tea from little Chinese teacups helps to suggest the superficial "social whirl" which is the setting of **"A Five-O'Clock Tea."** The idioms and rhythms of Irish brogue and the illiterate speech of current general usage achieve homespun simplicity and regional colour in **"Extradited."** Part of Crawford's claim to documentary accuracy may be based pon this ability to catch the peculiarity of language—the rhetorical rhythms and vernacular phrases of the country speech of her day.

Although Crawford's characterizations are usually stereotyped, her heroines are often portrayed with spunk, with physical and moral strength, emotional and intellectual independence. Self-reliance distinguishes Crawford's two female protagonists in **"Extradited"** and in **"In the Breast of a Maple."** Although Marie de Meury's characterization lacks subtlety, her attitude towards men and marriage at a time when any marriage was considered better than none is an independent one. Bessie O'Dwyer's stubbornness in resisting her husband's wishes for the sake of her son's financial security is symbolic of attempts by frontier mothers to make life less harsh for their children.

Crawford's skill as a comic writer is evident in several selections. In **"The Grasshopper Papers"** her views on the subjects of cremation and the habits of grasshoppers are humorous. Her waspish commentary on unmusical girls in "A Five-O'Clock Tea" is a bit of social comedy:

> Musical girls, generally with gold eye-glasses on chill, aesthetic noses, play grim classical preparations, which have as cheerful an effect on the gay crowd as the perfect, irreproachable skeleton of a bygone beauty might have, or articulate, with cultivation and no voices to speak of, arias which would almost sap the life of a true child of song to render as the *maestro* intended.

In "The Halton Boys," Sim's visit with the billy-goat to Lyon's bedroom is only one of several amusing episodes involving this young pickpocket who is converted to a respectable member of the Halton farm community. "In the Breast of a Maple" demonstrates Crawford's skill with elements of burlesque—comic pantomime, caricature, and coarse wit.

In her prose, as in her poetry, Crawford's power lies in her use of imagery. The same sensual images which distinguish her poetry are found in her prose. In "Tudor Tramp":

> Lake Ontario rounded higher against the sky full bosomed yet from the early floods—every leaf was plump with juices the barks of trees moist with sap.

"In the Breast of a Maple" reveals the same eroticism:

> Mademoiselle de Meury's knee moved under her clinging woollen skirt, showing itself boldly like that joint in the statue of the Venus de Milo.

At times Crawford's images attain the force of symbol. Throughout "In the Breast of a Maple," Dalmas is caricatured with small animal images which, from their cumulative effect, achieve the power of symbol.

Crawford's lyrical abilities and use of irony often contribute significantly to the effectiveness of her stories. A poet's eye and ear transform the bleak backwoods barn of "Extradited" into an Oriental temple:

> The rude doors stood open, a vigorous purple haze, shot with heavy bars of crimson light, filled the interior: a Whip-Poor Will chanted from a distant tree, like a muezzin from a minaret.

In the same story irony heightens the emotional impact of the conflict between Bessie and Sam and produces the tension which underlies the tale.

The selections [in the *Selected Stories of Isabella Valancy Crawford*] reveal Crawford's difficulty with form: structure and style. Ponderous authorial interpolations and convoluted descriptive passages weaken the narrative structure of "Tudor Tramp." And yet "In the Breast of a Maple," "A Five-O'Clock Tea," and "Extradited" reveal an awareness of form. The burlesque-like mood permeating "In the Breast of a Maple" gives it a unifyingly comical effect. "A Five-O'Clock Tea" achieves fusion of matter and form: the events take place in an upper class drawing room within a few hours. Given the situation, the imaginative reader can suspend disbelief long enough to project himself into a world that seems perfectly plausible. In "Extradited" Crawford reveals her technical artistry as a writer

of short stories because she has here attempted to integrate characterization, situation, mood and idea into an organic whole.

And although Crawford's language is extravagantly romantic, there are times when her languge is direct and plain and she achieves an epigrammatic restraint, as in the following pithy expressions of homespun wisdom spoken by her old peasants in "La Tricoteuse": "caterpillars deform the comeliest vines," "wives are not good bridles in mouths of wild asses." We must remember too, that in her Canadian fiction Crawford was struggling for a new language to describe the Canadian wilderness. How to describe the wild grandeur of the new environment has been the Canadian writer's dilemma. In "Tudor Tramp" and to a lesser degree in "In the Breast of a Maple" and "Extradited," Crawford comes to imaginative grips with the seasons and the landscape with a highly imaginative representation which one usually associates with poetry. And when her romantic imagination conjures up a busy world of Indian spirits living in the Canadian skies, as in her exploration of "Indian Summer" in "The Grasshopper Papers," her myth-making skills and individuality, as in the best of her poetry, are graphically revealed.

The dominant expression left by the selections of this volume is of its uneven quality. And yet their variety of themes and narrative styles seems to suggest that Crawford was experimenting with various kinds of prose in order to perfect her artistry.

Her three pieces "A Five-O'Clock Tea," "In the Breast of a Maple," and "Extradited," produced in the last few years of her life, show that Crawford viewed the short story as an art form at a time when serious criticism of it was barely underway. The last two stories, moreover, demonstrate her concern for realism at a time when Canadian subject matter was still strongly romantic. We must remember, too, she died at the age when George Eliot produced her first novel. Although it is impossible to trace her development as a prose writer, since no dates of composition or possible publication of the bulk of her work exists, there is reason to believe that Crawford would have improved if she had lived longer.

Crawford's writings represent early English-Canadian prose activity. Her fictional portrayals of Canadian life give us glimpses into the literary past of our country. Her story "Extradited" merits attention for two additional reasons: the theme has a wider application than to the events of the story, because the problem that Bessie faces is one which men have faced since the beginning of time. It reveals Crawford's vision of life: the necessity of sorrow in life and the importance of the power of love. Because of its literary competence, its historical realism and the psychological truth which is at its base, therefore, "Extradited" commands a legitimate place in the annals of the literature of Canada. (pp. 12-16)

> *Penny Petrone, in an introduction to* Selected Stories of Isabella Valancy Crawford, *by Isabella Valancy Crawford, edited by Penny Petrone, University of Ottawa Press, 1975, pp. 9-16.*

ROY DANIELLS (essay date 1976)

[*Daniells briefly discusses Crawford's style, subject matter, and themes in the context of Canadian, Romantic, and Victorian literature. He lauds her originality and her "fusion of inner and outer worlds as if by accident."*]

Another page from Crawford's manuscript of The Halton Boys, *with her pseudonym.*

[Crawford's poem **"Said the Canoe"**] succinctly and clearly embodies the elements of Crawford's originality as a poet. The Canadian landscape, the landscape of a pioneer country, is grasped objectively; yet it is at once and completely infused with intensely subjective realizations of love and struggle and death. . . .

This capacity for an intense projection into her poems of her feelings about love and struggle and death separates her from the other post-Confederation poets; she is in the line of Emily Brontë rather than Wordsworth or Tennyson. It also differentiates her poems from the general run in her generation, in that they tend to invite two readings—a straightforward and an esoteric—with very different results. **"Malcolm's Katie,"** her longest and best known piece, is on the face of it a preposterously romantic love story on a Tennysonian model in which a wildly creaking plot finally delivers true love safe and triumphant. To add that there are some nice pictures of the struggles and satisfactions of clearing the land and building homes in the wilderness is not to add much. What makes this poem also "ancestral, important, haunting" is its ability to pull the raw landscape into an interior world of living passion and fulfilment. Katie's lover, Max, achieves this movement of absorption in a superb passage, central to the poem. It follows an objective description of felling and burning trees.

> And Max cared little for the blotted sun,
> And nothing for the startled, outshone stars;
> For love, once set within a lover's breast,
> Has its own sun, its own peculiar sky,
> All one great daffodil, on which do lie
> The sun, the moon, the stars, all seen at once
> And never setting, but all shining straight

> Into the faces of the trinity—
> The one beloved, the lover, and sweet love.

As we should expect, these images are counterpointed by others, of utter insensibility and the threat of death by water.

> O you shall slumber soundly, tho' the white,
> Wild waters pluck the crocus of your hair,
> And scaly spies stare with round, lightless eyes
> At your small face laid on my stony breast!
>
> > (p. 424)

Crawford achieves her fusion of inner and outer worlds as if by accident. **"Old Spookses' Pass"** begins as a shapeless tale of cattle-driving by an illiterate cowboy with a turn for moralizing, but before the poem ends we have experienced the authentic shudder of a haunted mountain defile, of a stampede in darkness and the crash of thunder. The landscape imposes its inner presence unmistakably, though the poem seems to have few formal merits. Elsewhere—notably in such pieces as **"The Mother's Soul"** and **"Said the Skylark"**—we find standard Victorian diction, versification, and sentiment emitting an unexpected intensity and sincerity of emotion and the occasion is always the same, an escape of the soul into a natural universe filled with love. The child's soul springs into the arms of its dead mother under the kind light of moon and stars. Or to the caged bird comes the cloud from the open sky,

> And murmuring to him said:
> "O Love, I come! O Love, I come to cheer thee!
> Love, to be near thee!"

It has been often remarked that Crawford is unusual among Canadian poets by her strong mythopoeic feeling for nature. Yet the passages where this faculty is most apparent may be read simply as her habitual infusion of external landscape with her passionate apprehension of love, of struggle, of death. Thus the dark Stag of Night is hunted by the Sun:

> His antlers fall; once more he spurns
> > The hoarse hounds of the day;
> His blood upon the crisp blue burns,
> > Reddens the mounting spray;
> His branches smite the wave—with cries
> > The loud winds pause and flag—
> He sinks in space—red glow the skies,
> The brown earth crimsons as he dies,
> > The strong and dusky stag.

Comparisons between Crawford and the great Victorians and parallels between her and other post-Confederation poets can be multiplied. She has the same range of subjects as, say, Longfellow, the spectrum that runs from an immediate sensuous knowledge of woods and fields to a scholarly and poetic feeling for Rome and Greece. Her poems bring us medieval lovers, and helot of Sparta, Margaton by the stream, classical shepherds, Vikings of the sagas, Indians of legend and real life, biblical figures, and poor exiles from Erin. Patriotism, faith and hope and charity, the round of the seasons, farewells and welcomes: the standard items of Victorian sensibility are present, down to dialect stories of simple countryfolk.

Ideal love is her dominant theme and best expressed obliquely, as we have seen, through some description of nature. Her overt love poems . . . lack proper psychic distance, are too immediate, too revealing.

> A golden heart graved with my name alone . . .
> "A golden prophet of eternal truth,"

I said, and kissed the roses of her palms,
And then the shy, bright roses of her lips;
And all the jealous jewels shone forgot
In necklace and tiara as I clasped
The gold heart and its shamrocks round her neck.
My fair, pure soul! My noble Irish love!

Her true and characteristic inner intensity is better revealed in such a poem as **"The Lily Bed"**:

His cedar paddle, scented, red,
He thrust down through the lily bed;

Cloaked in a golden pause he lay
Locked in the arms of the placid bay. . . .

All lily-locked, all lily-locked,
His light bark in the blossoms rocked.

Their cool lips round the sharp prow sang,
Their soft clasp to the frail sides sprang. . . .

There are many passages, especially in **"Malcolm's Katie,"** where the dogged, hopeful spirit of pioneer settlers is expressed and this has some interest of an historical and sociological kind. But the conquest of our terrain in which she played her real part was the assimilation of Canadian landscape into the realm of the imagination, or, conversely, the infusion of passionate love, love strong enough to overcome death, into the substance of the simple Canadian scene. This is her triumph, her spiritual victory, her legacy to our uncertain age. (pp. 424-26)

> Roy Daniells, "Crawford, Carman, and D. C. Scott," in Literary History of Canada: Canadian Literature in English, Vol. I, edited by Carl F. Klinck, second edition, University of Toronto Press, 1976, pp. 422-37.*

FRANCES FRAZER   (essay date 1978)

[In this excerpt from her assessment of Crawford's fairy tales, Frazer maintains that the tales are inferior to the poetry.]

[Crawford's fairy tales] might better have been left in peace and obscurity. They are unlikely to interest anyone except the most devoted Crawford enthusiasts, and even these are unlikely to find in them much sustenance for ther enthusiasm. In her poetry, Crawford had several "best" styles. She could write lushly passionate but reassuringly precise descriptions of nature; quirky, provocative expressions of complex thoughts and emotional states; carefully inoffensive but exuberantly comic pioneer dialect poems (**"Old Spookses' Pass,"** **"Old Suspense,"** **"The Deacon and His Daughter"**). She sometimes approached Blakeian mysticism, as in the brotherly invitation of Evil to Good that concludes **"Gisli, the Chieftain."** She could be effectively laconic:

. . . the flesh that I wore chanced to be
Less of my friend than my enemy.

So bury it deeply,—strong foe, weak
    friend—
And bury it cheaply,—and there its end!

(**"His Clay"**)

But in these principally flat and ornately verbose stories, little of her intelligence, her verbal flair, or her humour is apparent.

Of the six, **"The Waterlily"** is the most satisfying as a story. (p. 74)

Next I would rank **"The Vain Owl and the Elf,"** not for its plot but for a walk-on character, Swift the squirrel, a more obliging than ardent suitor of his cousin Jettie. His character is amusingly revealed as Jettie begs help from an elf to escape her engagement to a pompous owl. Swift is broken-hearted, she says.

"Oh, certainly," replied Swift, turning his head quite over his shoulder, in order to observe the elegant markings of the fur on his back.

Swift is likely to kill himself, she says.

"Most decidedly, adorable Jettie!" remarked Swift politely.

Moved more by his own love of mischief than belief in Swift's suicidal passion, the elf distracts the poor, unlovely owl into lifelong barn servitude by playing on his vanity.

Vanity is also the moral pivot of the two least storylike tales in the book. **"The Rose and the Rainbow"** is a fable on the theme of Rupert Brooke's "Heaven," involving a number of self-ful envisioners of celestial delights. The rose defines the moral, a Hans Christian Anderson favourite: "in this world everyone sees with his own heart and wishes, and is all the world to himself." And vanity is explicitly condemned in the poem appended to **"The Rival Roses,"** though it is hard to see how the catastrophe of the frail tale was invoked by it, unless one believes in a fanatically puritanical Providence. (pp. 74-5)

The two remaining tales are thin, wish-fulfilling fantasies—one about a romance between a bewitched butterfly prince and a queen of violets, the other of a shipwrecked child tended by fairies who sound . . . scarcely big enough to splint her eyelash, should she break one.

Of course there is a qualitative difference between weak stories by an able writer and weak stories by an inept one. These are a cut above the ones ordinarily displayed on supermarket shelves. (p. 75)

> Frances Frazer, "Crawford's Fairies," in Canadian Literature, No. 78, Autumn, 1978, pp. 74-6.

FRANK M. TIERNEY   (essay date 1981)

[In this excerpt from his evaluation of The Halton Boys, Tierney discusses Crawford's blending of aristocratic and democratic themes and of English and American juvenile fiction styles. He also praises Crawford's inventive characterization and settings as well as her unobtrusive incorporation of the didactic elements in the novel.]

The Fairy Tales and **The Halton Boys** both reveal surprising and pleasurable streams in Crawford's creative impulse. **The Halton Boys** in particular reveals her adjustment from a tendency toward material and psychological realism to a romantic, youthful realism, fit for the taste of her young audience and the requirements of the genre. The book presents an unusual blend of aristocratic and democratic elements in characterization and plot. . . . (p. 15)

Crawford's venture into juvenile prose fiction was consistent with the pattern followed by major writers of adult literature, most of whom wrote stories for young people at some time during their careers, or had their books taken over by children. (p. 16)

Crawford's story was written for the same audience as that of . . . [other] women writers and expresses, therefore, much of the same tone and mores. But the sympathetic modern reader who is prepared to understand and accept the limitations imposed by the period and the genre will be pleasantly surprised by her use of this traditional framework, and her innovative creation of unusual characters and fresh settings.

The reader will not be surprised to find such well-worked machinery of the time as a boarding school, the students' favorite store and meeting place, the feuds between Juniors and Seniors, and the class system operational within this framework; but there is a sudden delightful move away from these traditional elements to such scenes as a circus, a pig-pen, and a murky river bank, and to a hero—the eleven-year-old Simfletcher—who is independent of all elements of the traditional mode. The reader is suddenly confronted with the real thoughts and sensations of childhood, of wisdom without the loss of innocence, and is given a judicious, humorous blending of the expected and the unexpected, the familiar and the unfamiliar. The late nineteenth century North American young readers could more readily identify with Simfletcher's personality, quick wit, lively imagination, and exploits than with such familiar figures of virtue, as Larry Halton or "Old Gentle" (Professor Harkleboy). There is in this book a real awakening of the imagination that gives it life beyond the audience and time for which it was written.

This story, therefore, is an unusual blend of the English and American juvenile fiction of the later nineteenth century. The English story written at that time addressed itself largely to boys and contained strong class consciousness; the American story for juveniles had very little class consciousness and eliminated more of the differences between stories for boys and stories for girls. *The Halton Boys* is a cross between the English and the American with the latter dominating the settings, plot, tone, and characterization.

Feeling for the North American way of life evolves through the rural scenes. The barnyards, the small town, the circus, and the folksy characters form the bulk of the plot, the excitement and the dramatic impact on the story. (pp. 16-17)

Yet the first two chapters of *The Halton Boys* have an English thrust in setting and tone. Perhaps this would lead some readers to assume that it would convey didactically the values of Rugby, as found for example in Thomas Hughes' *Tom Brown's School Days.* . . . Crawford was experienced with both American and English literary characters and characterization; many characters in *The Halton Boys* . . . have a touch of the colouring found in Charles Dickens' work. The personality of Larry Halton and of some background characters at the outset and even in the final paragraphs produce this same British flavor; but the heart of the work does not. The principle of equality found throughout most American fiction of this type emerges repeatedly, though implied rather than expressed, through the wisdom and leadership of the "lower class" characters, and the emotional unevenness and intellectual limitations of some of the principal characters who represent aristocratic values. The blend works. It reveals an interesting side of Crawford's creative impact: her contribution to the transition in juvenile fiction of the period from the aristocratic structure to the democratic framework that dominates modern stories.

Crawford's story does not suggest a conscious plea for the American way of life or a rejection of the English; the two systems blend into a single unique framework, in which both serve their functions well and both emerge as attractive. The most striking difference between Crawford's story and the tra-

ditional framework is in some of the characterization and the subtle suppression of class power. In fact, the aristocratic structure remains but is ignored and transcended by Simfletcher. This principle of equality is in harmony with the feelings of most of the youth of North America at that time.

Another element of equality emphasized in juvenile literature written in America in that period was the slowly elevating position accorded to women in society and the increased opportunities offered to them for education. Crawford is inclined to describe their plight but prudently, considering the genre and the audience, suppresses the temptation and protects the artistic integrity of her work.·. . . The effusive display of feeling, another aspect of the age that is abundant in this story, will require some adjustment for modern readers, especially to the character Larry Halton. Larry is quickly moved to strong emotional responses of love, of sorrow, of regret, in a manner that is demonstrative beyond the comprehension of most young readers today, who are experienced largely in realism. But sensibility was a popular element in characterization during Queen Victoria's reign; tears flowed from men and women without hesitation and with ease; so when Larry, and his brother Lyon too, toward the end of the book, manifest this romantic trait with occasional self-indulgence, this would capture the sentimental young reader, and perhaps many adult readers of the time as well. The display of an acute sensibility is not now fashionable, but the modern reader may be sympathetic because Crawford's incidents and endings always follow naturally and the pathos is genuine.

Today's reader may also think the thematic preoccupation with character-building is overworked. This too was a central pillar of nineteenth century writing for the young audience. . . . The principal, Mr. Beaufield, Larry Halton's guardian Mr. Standish, the narrator, and Larry himself all accept and proclaim through the work the essential need for the highest moral character and leadership, and project its importance into their future lives at the end of the story. But Crawford has welded this theme unobtrusively and artistically into the work. It is an ingredient common to this type of literature in Crawford's time that she has handled with artistic success. Crawford knew how to capture and retain the interest of young readers, whose general criteria for a good story have always been adventure, variety of exciting incidents, the presence of a central character with lofty ideals, and a circle of interesting supporting characters and challenging foils; all presented with suspense, humor, and realistic language and dialogue. Crawford succeeds in creating this fusion in *The Halton Boys* in eight short chapters. (pp. 18-20)

Crawford has taken a simple and traditional plot and surrounded, integrated, and developed it with innovation, colorful settings, interesting subplots, fascinating and dynamic characters, to create a story that is additional evidence of her talent.

Crawford's story is outside of the prevailing trend of young people's fiction of the time. It is akin to the small, growing stream of stories for boys that focus on the common boy as hero, the best examples of which were written about the same time as *The Halton Boys: Tom Sawyer* . . . and *Huckleberry Finn.* . . . But *The Halton Boys* is not only a distinctive variation on the usual didactic story of the time; it is also a story that implies a contrast of the traditional with the new, the aristocratic with the democratic.

Larry, the stereotyped aristocratic ideal, does not measure up to heroic standards in emotional stability, intellectual astuteness, decision making, or action when he is outside of his sheltered environment. His heroic image largely dissolves as he is faced with challenges outside of his experience. He tends, under these circumstances, to self pity, and to stasis. It is the young orphan Simfletcher, poor, uneducated, culturally deprived, and socially destitute, who, through spontaneous, creative, decisive action, solves one problem after another, from hiding the identity of Lyon, to ultimately saving his life and uniting the brothers. Sim is cool and constant. He is the democratic child of America from the mould of the Huckleberry Finns and Tom Sawyers, expressing, however, a unique witty personality.

This story, therefore, is satisfying reading, calling into play the imaginations of boys, teenagers, and adults alike. It is a humorous novel which also stimulates appreciation for language. There is ample colorful dialect and a pleasing variety of narrative language to harmonize with the rhythms, structures and tones of the speakers and situations, as well as to comment objectively. *The Halton Boys* presents a pleasing spectrum of moral, social, and cultural levels of character portrayal, and a hero in Simfletcher who is outside the traditional nineteenth century heroic framework. (p. 25)

> Frank M. Tierney, *"Isabella Valancy Crawford's 'The Halton Boys',"* in Canadian Children's Literature: A Journal of Criticism and Review, *No. 22, 1981, pp. 15-26.*

An illustration for Crawford's short story "A Five-O'Clock Tea."

DOROTHY FARMILOE (essay date 1983)

[*In this excerpt from her full-length critical biography of Crawford, Farmiloe discusses her significance and reputation.*]

If the poet is the sum total of everything he touches and everything that touches him, as Yeats implied in "Mohini Chatterjee," then it is no wonder there are so many diverse strains in Crawford's work. Beginning with the Paisley years, she wove the experiences of her own life into universal themes. She was the first Canadian poet to take images from the Native way of life, with which she was acquainted, and to consciously form them into symbols. Stemming from a sincere admiration for the Native culture which in turn was based on respect for the earth, her early imagery became the *leitmotif* of her most fully realized poetry. Worked out independently of other naturalists of the time like Thoreau, Crawford's "gospel of the woods and plains" was based ond the Ojibway survival skills she had observed as a child. Eventually her love of the wilderness and its sustaining, life-giving properties evolved into a philosophy that advocated living in harmony with the environment instead of exploiting it. In this, as in so many other ways, she was years ahead of her time.

She was an anomaly among contemporary women writers. No other Victorian spinster—with the exception, perhaps, of Emily Dickinson who was not writing for publication—has dared to write so erotically. Crawford was the first Canadian writer of either sex to transform landscape into sexual geography, the first to use what we now call Freudian terms to communicate physical love-making. When Pauline Johnson writes of the song her paddle sings, the paddle remains just that—a paddle. Under Crawford's pen it becomes a vivid erotic symbol.

Her prose is less erotic and less socially committed than her poetry, although in places in her fiction she breaks through social conventions to stand revealed as one of the most openminded observers of the nineteenth-century scene. In at least one novel she strikes out at racial prejudice. At a time when racism was rampant in Ontario and the Separate Schools Act gave legal sanction to segregated schools for "Coloured People," she was writing sympathetically in a style surging with psychological undercurrents about a love affair between a white mistress and her black servant. Crawford's handling of this explosive situation in **"Pillows of Stone"** outshines in every way Lillian Hellman's *Toys in the Attic* which came some eighty years later. (pp. 72-3)

One of her recurring themes is that of suffering, reconciliation and redemption through love. Critics have argued that *Hugh and Ion* with its conflict revolving around hope versus despair would have reconciled the contraries to move in this direction. It is hard to agree with such an assessment when the major thrust of *Hugh and Ion* as it stands is otherwise. There is little to counter the Falcon Lady's "away with love," nothing to effectively dispute Ion's bleak vision of the future when he stands on a cliff to prophesy "the birth of ruins and the horrid flames of bursting worlds." Hugh's argument for a resolution based on Christian love is unconvincing in the face of Ion's pervasive despair. Crawford's most cynical poems—**"War," "The Pessimist,"** and *Hugh and Ion* among them—are renditious of hard realism based on the oppression she saw around her. Although she speaks out against oppression, she sees no justice for the sufferers. Her long narrative poem **"The Helot"** condemns aggression and tyranny (by implication), but when the slave rebels against the master, the uprising results in his death and the death of an innocent child. She brought the theme to a grim finality in **"The Pessimist"**:

> Build slightly, builders! From enslaved nations
>   Burst the blind lin'd human tides,
> And on their necks, thro' night of desolations,
>   Again old chaos rides.

Given the destruction and suffering wrought by the wars of aggression in the twentieth century, the nightmare prophesy contained in **"The Pessimist"** has been fulfilled to a frightening degree. (p. 74)

Working on her own, she integrated her various themes into an artistic vision that encompassed not only the present as she saw it but the future as well. Her prophesies are one of her most noteworthy and least understood achievements.

Crawford's literary reputation has been diminished because of her excesses. Her habit of piling on at least one adjective and sometimes three or four in front of every noun does not sit well with our sense of streamlined modernity. Far from being a "plethora of heady empty words," however, her exuberance had meaning and purpose. The Victorians liked decoration—they liked their china heavily flowered, their lettering scrolled and curlicued, their furniture ornately carved. In time we may come to appreciate Crawford's flowery descriptions to the same degree that we now appreciate other Victorian embellishments for what they are: the embodiment of a peculiar age. In relation to the other arts, Crawford's poetry, particularly her descriptive nature poetry, is possibly the finest example of what could be called, for want of an existing literary term, Florid Victorian. We have to remember that was what sold.

Crawford wrote to earn her living. What her genius might have produced if she had not had to cater to the market-place to the extent she did is hard to say. As things were, and regardless of her own preferences, she was forced to churn out the kind of reading matter that was popular at the time—patriotic ditties and mawkishly sentimental verses that found a ready market in the newspapers of the day. The **Collected Poems,** actually a volume of selected pieces, contains too many of these bread-and-butter efforts. Like other writers who turned out a body of inferior works in addition to the masterpieces they are remembered for—Emily Dickinson is but one example—Crawford inadvertently bequeathed a collection of mediocre works to posterity. What is needed at this time is a discerning editor who can put together a new *Selected Poems* so that her genius can emerge in full brilliance. (p. 75)

Posterity has not yet accorded her her rightful place on the literary ladder; but even as things stand now, the best of her poetry and prose is enough to assure her an enduring place among the masters of nineteenth-century literature. (p. 76)

> *Dorothy Farmiloe, in her* Isabella Valancy Crawford: The Life and the Legends, *The Tecumseh Press, 1983, 90 p.*

ADDITIONAL BIBLIOGRAPHY

Brooks, Marshall. " 'Malcolm's Katie': The Interior View." *Canadian Literature,* No. 76 (Spring 1978): 134-35.
Discusses Crawford's treatment of nature in "Malcolm's Katie." Brooks suggests that Crawford also explores her own state of mind in the poem.

Frye, Northrop. *The Bush Garden: Essays on the Canadian Imagination.* Toronto: Anansi, 1971, 256 p.*
Includes references to Crawford's themes and imagery. In particular, Frye praises Crawford's imaginative powers.

Hughes, Kenneth J. "Democratic Vision of 'Malcolm's Katie'." *CV II* I, No. 2 (Fall 1975): 38-46.
A study of Crawford's sociological and political ideas in "Malcolm's Katie." Arguing that her views are "clearly idealist" in the poem, Hughes discusses Crawford's treatment of workers and landowners and concludes that she came to believe that "the politics of egalitarian love is the answer to the politics of hierarchical power."

Hughes, Kenneth J., and Sproxton, Birk. " 'Malcolm's Katie': Images and Songs." *Canadian Literature,* No. 65 (Summer 1975): 55-64.
An analysis of Crawford's imagery in "Malcolm's Katie" in relation to the poem's themes. Hughes and Sproxton focus on ring, garden, and sun/moon images as those most central to the poem's meaning. In addition, they comment on the dramatic and thematic function of various songs in "Malcolm's Katie."

Jones, D. G. *Butterfly on Rock: A Study of Themes and Images in Canadian Literature.* Toronto: University of Toronto Press, 1970, 197 p.*
A survey of Canadian poetry in relation to Canadian culture. Jones briefly discusses Crawford's portrayal of nature and praises her manner of integrating its destructive and benevolent aspects.

Kyte, E. C., ed. "Isabella Valancy Crawford." In his *A Catalogue of Canadian Manuscripts Collected by Lorne Pierce and Presented to Queen's University,* pp. 100-04. Toronto: Ryerson Press, 1946.
Describes the Crawford manuscripts, many of which have never been published, located in the Pierce collection at Queen's University, Kingston, Ontario.

Livesay, Dorothy. "Tennyson's Daughter or Wilderness Child?: The Factual and the Literary Background of Isabella Valancy Crawford." *Journal of Canadian Fiction* II, No. 3 (Summer 1973): 161-67.
An overview of Crawford's life and career. Livesay also briefly analyzes *Hugh and Ion,* which she refers to as *The Hunters Twain.* She contends that Crawford was influenced by Tennyson's style, but that she adapted it to suit her perception of the Canadian frontier.

Martin, Mary F. "The Short Life of Isabella Valancy Crawford." *The Dalhousie Review* 52, No. 3 (Autumn 1972): 390-400.
An account of Crawford's life. Though brief, Martin's essay initiated a revival of critical interest in Crawford in the 1970s.

Mathews, Robin. " 'Malcolm's Katie': Love, Wealth, and Nation Building." *Studies in Canadian Literature* 2, No. 2 (Summer 1977): 49-60.
Explores the implicit social and economic values expressed in "Malcolm's Katie" and their relation to Crawford's vision of Canada's future.

Ross, Catherine Sheldrick. "Isabella Valancy Crawford: Solar Mythologist." *English Studies in Canada* IV, No. 3 (Fall 1978): 305-16.
Analyzes Crawford's frequent use of sunlight and darkness imagery. According to Ross, Crawford's "monomyth of the sun's ceaseless struggle with darkness" was also her symbol for human struggle.

———. "I.V. Crawford's Prose Fiction." *Canadian Literature,* No. 81 (Summer 1979): 47-58.
Discusses themes, style, and symbolism in Crawford's prose fiction. Ross posits that Crawford's prose attests to her stature as "a mythopoeic writer" and contributes to our understanding of her narrative style in the longer poems.

Stich, K. P. "The Rising Village, the Emigrant and 'Malcolm's Katie': The Vanity of Progress." *Canadian Poetry,* No. 7 (Fall-Winter 1980): 48-55.*
Suggests that Crawford's vision of Canadian nationalism was influenced by her concern about growing commercialization and industrialization and is, therefore, often disillusioned or satirical.

Suo, Lynne. "Annotated Bibliography on Isabella Valancy Crawford." *Essays on Canadian Writing,* No. 11 (Summer 1978): 289-314.
> A comprehensive annotated listing of works by and about Crawford. Suo also includes information about early reviews in Canadian, British, and United States journals.

Tierney, Frank M. Introduction to *The Halton Boys* by Isabella Valancy Crawford, pp. xv-xli. Ottawa: Borealis Press, 1979.
> A study of the two extant manuscripts of *The Halton Boys.* Tierney discusses Crawford's emendations to the manuscripts as indications of her emerging style.

――――. ed. *The Crawford Symposium.* Re-Appraisals: Canadian Writers, edited by Lorraine McMullen. Ottawa: University of Ottawa Press, 1979, 158 p.
> A transcript of the Crawford Symposium held at the University of Ottawa in 1977. Included are essays by such critics as Dorothy Livesay, Penny Petrone, Margo Dunn, and Kenneth Hughes, as well as a checklist of writings by and about Crawford.

West, David S. " 'Malcolm's Katie': Alfred as Nihilist Not Rapist." *Studies in Canadian Literature* 3, No. 1 (Winter 1978): 137-41.
> A reply to Mathews's article on "Malcolm's Katie." West contends that the rape images in the poem are figurative and pertain to Alfred's nihilistic philosophy and his desire for death.

Yeoman, Ann. "Towards a Native Mythology: The Poetry of Isabella Valancy Crawford." *Canadian Literature,* No. 52 (Spring 1972): 39-47.
> Studies Crawford's handling of such symbols as the lily-bed, circle, fire, and stampede. Yeoman concludes that Crawford's importance to Canadian literature lies in the fact that "she understood [the] need for a unifying and identifying language of symbols as necessary to the development of a native culture and literature."

Henry Kendall

1839-1882

(Born Thomas Henry Kendall. Also wrote as The Meddler, The Mopoke, N.A.P., A Literary Hack, and Henry Clarence Kendall) Australian poet and journalist.

Kendall is considered the most important Australian poet of the nineteenth century. Primarily noted for his contribution to the development of his country's literature, Kendall extols the beauty of Australia in many of his poems. Critics have generally praised his nature imagery, particularly his detailed descriptions of the Australian landscape and coastland, as well as his lyric ability.

Kendall's brief but arduous life has been chronicled by many of his critics; indeed, some have attributed the melancholy tone that pervades much of his poetry to the personal difficulties that plagued him throughout his life. Born near Ulladulla, a village in the province of New South Wales, Australia, Kendall moved in 1844 with his family to Sydney, where his father secured a position as a civil servant. The family's brief financial stability was shattered, however, when Kendall's father was convicted of forgery. After a two-year prison term, he held various jobs, and the family moved frequently as he sought permanent work. Following his death in 1852, the family was separated.

In 1855, Kendall began work as a cabin boy on his uncle's whaling vessel. He returned to Sydney in 1857, and, by working at various jobs, was soon able to reunite his family. At this time, Kendall began contributing verse to several Australian newspapers, including the Sydney *Empire*, edited by the successful writer Joseph Sheridan Moore. The publication of Kendall's first collection, *Poems and Songs*, proved to be an important breakthrough in his career. Because of its success, he became acquainted with other Australian literary figures, including James Lionel Michael. A prominent attorney and a poet himself, Michael hired Kendall as his clerk and encouraged him to submit poetry to the English journal the *Athenaeum*, which published three of his poems to favorable reviews in 1862.

In 1863, Kendall was appointed to a clerkship at the Surveyor General's Office. Despite his popularity as a poet, he continued to struggle to support his family. His financial difficulties increased when he married Charlotte Rutter in 1868. One year later, Kendall fled to Melbourne with his wife and infant daughter in an attempt to escape his creditors. Yet he was unable to support his family by journalism alone, and his second collection of poetry, *Leaves from Australian Forests*, was a financial failure. The year 1870 brought even greater tragedy: Kendall was tried for forgery, his daughter died of malnutrition, and his wife left him to return to her family in Sydney. In 1871, Kendall was committed to an asylum, where he was treated for depression, opium addiction, and alcoholism. Although he was released that same year, he was readmitted in 1873. Kendall's friends had arranged a newspaper editorship for him upon his subsequent release, but he refused it. Setting out for Sydney on foot, he became ill and was taken in by a family in Gosford, who supported and employed him during his recuperation.

During his stay in Gosford, Kendall worked as a bookkeeper and wrote satirical verse and political essays for Sydney newspapers. In 1876, he moved to Camden Haven, where he and his wife reconciled their differences. With renewed vigor, he submitted a poem to the International Exhibition in Sydney that won a prize and subsequently became immensely popular. Kendall's final and most successful collection, *Songs from the Mountains*, appeared in 1880 and firmly established him as Australia's leading poet. The following year, Kendall accepted a post as inspector of forests, but the strain of constant travel, coupled with his frail health, led to his death from tuberculosis in 1882.

Kendall's greatest achievement was in the lyric mode, which, with its highly subjective and emotive character, was particularly suited to his personal and melancholic poetic voice. However, many critics have argued that his poetry is uneven in quality, contending that while his finest poems show a sure handling of imagery and language, others are weak and repetitive in form and theme. Because much of his poetry demonstrates the influence of the English poets Algernon Charles Swinburne and Alfred, Lord Tennyson, some critics suggest that Kendall's work suffers from the obvious marks of imitation. In his first collection, *Poems and Songs*, Kendall celebrates the beauty of the southeastern Australian coast, a particular focus for many of his poems. Scholars agree that despite flaws, the work does show promise, containing melodious verse and powerful nature imagery; yet his handling of both subject and meter is considered awkward and forced. In *Leaves from Australian Forests,* Kendall demonstrates greater metrical skill and a broader range of subject. Here, he depicts life in the Australian bush and describes the clash between the aboriginal and European cultures. In the opinion of many critics, *Songs from the Mountains* does not evince any appreciable progress. Several commentators have noted in particular Kendall's continuing inability to describe human feeling, for while his response to nature in this volume is strong and direct, his statements on the human condition remain vague and abstract.

Most critics agree that Kendall's powerful nature imagery and lyricism constitute his lasting contribution to Australian poetry. However, he has been the subject of diverse critical commentary, and modern scholars have reached little consensus regarding certain aspects of his work. For example, there is virtually no agreement concerning which of his poems are his best. Kendall is known to most readers through a handful of poems that have been published for generations in anthologies of Australian writings. Yet some commentators argue that his best work is found in the lesser-known poems, which they feel truly reveal his depth and range. Another topic of dissension is the autobiographical nature of his writings. While some critics regard his work, particularly his more melancholy poetry, as a direct manifestation of his personal difficulties, others claim that this aspect reflects a conscious artistry. And while some call him the quintessential Australian poet, others find in his work a universal appeal that transcends the limits of a particular time or place.

Although he holds a minor place in the history of world literature, Kendall remains an important figure in Australian literary history. He brought a personal and evocative vision to an emerging national literature, and it is as the lyrical voice of the Australian landscape that he is remembered today.

*PRINCIPAL WORKS

Poems and Songs   (poetry)   1862
Leaves from Australian Forests   (poetry)   1869
Cantata: Written Expressly for the Opening of the Sydney
    International Exhibition   (poetry)   1879
Songs from the Mountains   (poetry)   1880
Poems of Henry Kendall   (poetry)   1886
The Poetical Works of Henry Kendall   (poetry)   1966

*Much of Kendall's verse was originally published in Australian newspapers.

HENRY KENDALL   (letter date 1862)

[*Kendall wrote the following letter to the editors of the London* Athenaeum *upon sending three of his early poems to that publication. Although Kendall admits that his education is meager and his social background humble, he asks the editors to judge his work on the basis of its literary merit, rather than its "immaturity."*]

The inclosed papers will have travelled 16,000 miles when you receive them, and on that account I hope you will read them. I am an Australian and a self-educated one; hence there may be technical errors in what I send. Their immaturity must be

passed over for the reason that I have not reached my twentieth year. In a maze of 'crude imitations' perhaps if there is anything holding out a promise of future excellence tell me of it. Don't turn from me, as others have done, because I am a native of a country yet unrepresented in literature, but read what is sent before you condemn. Rejecting the magnificent patronage of our would-be literary magnates, I appeal to a greater authority for kinder treatment. If there is hope, give me some encouragement by noticing me in your journal; if there is none, I shall be satisfied with *your* decision. I cannot send any of my later writings, because they are too long, and too Australian to be cared for by Englishmen. *They,* at least, are my own. But even in these, which were written while I was in my eighteenth year, I have striven to be original. And a very good opportunity I have had, being not in a position to afford to buy books, and living out of the reach of them, in the backwoods of the Colony. (pp. 551-52)

> *Henry Kendall, in a letter to the editor of "The Athenaeum" on July 19, 1862, in* A Century of Australian Song, *edited by Douglas B. W. Sladen, W. Scott, 1888, pp. 551-52.*

THE ATHENAEUM   (essay date 1862)

[*In the following excerpt from the 1862* Athenaeum *review of Kendall's verse, the critic suggests that Kendall shows promise as a poet and, most importantly, that he possesses a natural talent.*]

We have sent out poets to Australia . . . and Australia cannot as yet be said to have paid us back in poetic coin. Not that there is failure of musical issue on that continent. Indeed, much verse is in circulation among the gold-finders and the backwoodsmen. From Hobart Town to Moreton Bay every newspaper has its poets, who set events to music, like the Grecian singers and the Northern skalds. Of the rhymes of these poets, not a trifle finds its way to [the offices of the *Athenaeum* on] Wellington Street, Strand. By nearly every mail comes an appeal from the neglect which genius finds in the Colonies to the more liberal and impartial literary courts of the mother-country, justified by parcels of manuscript verse and newspaper cuttings, which the hopeful writer expects us to read with patience and indulgence. Who could refuse? The poor fellow—often a clever fellow—lives 16,000 miles away. He has no friends on this northern side of the globe. You do not know him. He has never seen you—perhaps never will see you. He has no other claim on your kindness than his poverty of resource. Often his appeal against the injustice of Colonial editors has very slight foundation: his verses halt, his cases differ, his illustrations fail. But we read with hope. . . . By the last mail from Sydney came to us the usual parcel from an unknown hand. The note which accompanies the verses sent for our inspection is dated Sydney, and signed Henry Kendall. (pp. 550-51)

[We] think better of Mr. Kendall's verse than of the usual receipts from Australia. Mr. Kendall has much to learn; but he has received from Nature some of that strong poetic faculty and power which no amount of learning can bestow. The spirit of nearly all the writings under our hand is dark and sorrowful, but of their energy and vigour there can be little doubt. (p. 552)

Most readers who examine the structure of these pieces ["**The River and the Hill**," "**Kiama**," and "**Fainting By the Way**"] will agree with us that a man who can execute such work at the age of twenty may hope, in his riper years and experience, to be heard of again in the world of letters. (p. 560)

"The 'Athenaeum' Review of Kendall's Manuscript Poems," in A Century of Australian Song, *edited by Douglas B. W. Sladen, W. Scott, 1888, pp. 550-60.*

G. B. BARTON (essay date 1866)

[*Although Barton calls Kendall's* Poems and Songs *"a work of genius," he notes that the book's greatest distinction lies "in the promise it affords of future excellence." He particularly praises Kendall's genius for description, lyrical gift, and originality.*]

Considering the circumstances under which [*Poems and Songs*] was produced—the author's youth, his privations, his want of sufficient education—it is entitled to the very highest praise. Its merit is so great as to justify us in pronouncing it a work of genius. . . . If his fame be compelled to rest upon the productions he has already published, then there is certainly little chance of that fame being a very extensive one. The value of his book lies principally in the promise it affords of future excellence. It may be that Mr. Kendall is incapable of higher efforts, and that he has already exhausted the powers bestowed upon him. In that case, we can look for nothing but repetitions of what he has already written—repetitions marked rather by mannerism than by thought. That remains to be seen. But, on the other hand, it is equally possible that Mr. Kendall is capable of infinitely higher things; and if so, it will be no small credit to this colony that it should, at so early a period of its history, have produced a man of great poetic genius.

One striking merit in Mr. Kendall's poetry is, that its colouring is strictly local, and that he has endeavoured to give voice to the majestic scenery of his native land. Whatever opinion may be formed of his poetry, it cannot be denied that it is distinctly Australian poetry. This is a hopeful sign; inasmuch as it speaks of a mind naturally original, and averse to imitation. He has not commenced the practice of his Art by studying Tennyson, but by studying the wild and splendid scenery that surrounded him at his birth. His capacity in descriptive poetry is very great; in fact, it appears to be the distinctive mark of his genius. He has an artist's eye for a landscape, and if his shading is rather too dark, his outlines are none the less true. No local writer has reproduced the scenes familiar to us with so much effect. And again, he has sought inspiration in the characters and events of this country—endeavouring to paint the wild society of the interior as well as its peculiar scenery. He has chanted the savage melodies of the aboriginals—painted the sufferings of the explorers—and given a poetic interest even to the life of stockmen. These are facts which mark him out as an Australian poet, and an original poet: for there is no writer in this field whom he could imitate. This portion at least of his writings may be pronounced perfect. (pp. 192-94)

There is a degree of originality and power about [several of Mr. Kendall's] productions which is not often met with. No author can be pointed out as the obvious model on which they were framed. The writer's style, as regards both thought and expression, is peculiarly a style of his own. If, for instance, we compare the various descriptive poets in the language, we shall not find one whose mode of treatment bears much resemblance to Mr. Kendall's. This may arise from the difference between English and Australian scenery; but if we take in the American poets also, we shall yet fail to find one who has painted scenery in similar colours. It is this originality of style which no doubt gives rise to the charge of obscurity so often

brought against Mr. Kendall's poems. He uses language of his own. To some extent, this amounts to mannerism: but, on the whole, he deserves commendation for his taste and judgment in selecting words. So far as thought is concerned, he does occasionally become obscure—that is he fails to bring out his meaning distinctly, and leaves upon the reader's mind only some vague impression of solemnity. This, however, does not occur so frequently as to justify the charge. As Coleridge says, "A poem is not necessarily obscure because it does not aim to be popular. It is enough if a work be perspicuous to those for whom it is written, and 'fit audience find, though few.'" There are not many readers of a cultivated class who can experience much difficulty in comprehending Mr. Kendall's writings, if they choose.

Judging from what he has already written, his genius lies wholly in a lyrical direction. He has manifested power in no other form of poetry: but in so young a writer, it is impossible to decide the limits of his power. The lyrics he has written are by far the finest that have yet been written in Australia. They are distinguished by perfect harmony of versification, as well as by force of conception; and altogether they form a nearer approach to what we conceive to be genius, as opposed to talent, than any other poetry we have yet produced. Should he live to realise the anticipations that have been formed of him, his name will reflect a lasting honour on his native country. (pp. 205-06)

G. B. Barton, "Henry Kendall," in The Poets and Prose Writers of New South Wales, *edited by G. B. Barton, Gibbs, Shallard, & Co., 1866, pp. 192-206.*

EVELYN (essay date 1869)

[*The following excerpt is drawn from a letter to the editor of* The Australasian, *a Melbourne publication. The writer challenges the views presented in an article in the* Colonial Monthly Magazine, *in which the anonymous critic stated that Kendall's early work was his finest. This reader contends instead that Kendall's more mature productions reveal his considerable artistic development.*]

Since the publication of *Poems and Songs* in 1862 Mr. Kendall has progressed, and like a luxuriant vine has gained a wider scope and finer culture. The faculty which originally seemed solely lyrical has visibly expanded, and we have now from him blank verse imitations; descriptive narratives, abounding in dramatic force; and clear, faithful transcripts of historic incidents. With all this he has preserved his uniqueness. His singular command of terse Saxon adjectives, his rushing alliteration, the musical blendings of his iambic lines, the distinctness with which he photographs an impression upon the mind by a single aptly, selected word, are still as solely Kendall's as on the day when he wrote the **"Swarthy Wastelands, Wild and Woodless;"** the song of the **"Cattle Hunters,"** or the alloquy to Sheridan Moore. He has grown to have a purer taste, he has tapped founts of deeper beauty of expression, but he is still as original, as singular, and as Australian as the shadowy fern in a grove of English oaks.

This improvement is most marked in the delicious delicacy of suggestiveness of such poems as **"Illa Creek," "Mountain Moss,"** or **"Moss on a Wall,"** (the latter of which is descriptive of a grass-grown spot in the heart of this busy city of Melbourne,) and in the fuller, more matured thought of the **"Death in the Bush,"** published in the recently issued *Australian Annual,* which is even surpassed in my opinion by many of his later poems which at present have not passed beyond the manuscript stage. What, for instance, can be more finished than the lines:—

> A little patch of dark-green moss,
> Most surely grown of gentle ways;
> (With all its deep delicious floss)
> In slumbrous suns of summer days.

Or, again—

> A gracious growth of tender moss,
> Whose nights are soft, whose days are sweet.

Placing these side by side with some of the outpourings of his muse which have appeared in your journal, there is, it seems to me, sufficient to assure us that we have in Australia a poet who has passed somewhat beyond the undeveloped or rudimentary stage assigned him by the reviewer of the *Colonial Monthly*. . . .

"But," says the reviewer, "the spirit of Kendall is sanguine, and deeply joyous." Is this so? Literary men and the intellectualists in our community must be the judges. For my part, after following Mr. Kendall's career for years (no easy task, for many of his best writings never find a publisher in this colony), it has seemed to me his one predominant characteristic is pensiveness; not that which springs from a sickly sentimentalism or a morbidly excited imagination, but the sombreness of tone which most fitly harmonises with Australian scenery, the appreciation of the melancholy beauty and stillness of forest life; the deep-pervading sense of the Divine infinity which is expressed in the works of nature; the love for and inborn sympathy with solitude; the unaffected mournful interest in human beings; the solemn pathos which lies in their everyday life; and the mysteries and doubt which overhang religious speculation. These thoughts trouble him, the nature which always hints and whispers solemn tales perplexes him; the religious doubts which will arise puzzle him; but his philosophy rises above it, teaching a purer, higher lesson, in the words—

> A man is manifest when he wisely knows,
> How vain it is to halt, and pule and pine,
> Whilst under every mystery haply flows
> The finest issue of a love divine.

But this love for nature, the desire to seek solace apart from man, is not merely a negative dislike, it appears to be a positive antipathy. Associated by his daily avocation with the populous city of Sydney, he yet yearns to be away from it. He longs for the freshness of the country with the anxiety of a child. In **"Moss on a Wall,"** he writes:—

> From faithless lips and fickle lights,
> The tired pilgrim sets his face,
> And thinketh here of sounds and sights,
> In many a lonely forest place.

And in **"Dungog,"** a poem as yet unpublished, he is still more explicit:—

> I've seen the deep wild Dungog fells,
> And hate the heart of towns.

But in this appreciation of scenic beauty, this weariness at the cramped artificial life of a commercial town—this eagerness to be away from it and commune with the beloved objects which seem to have such a music for him, I can trace none of the joyous childlike disposition, the buoyancy, the exhilaration in the face of danger, ascribed to him. For this reason, then, I raise the pen to ask the public of these colonies not to take

on trust what the reviewer of the *Colonial Monthly* has written, or what I have ventured to remark in these pages, but to read Mr. Kendall's writings, and shape their judgment by kind perusal. Let us not regard him as an immature, uncultivated rhymester, who may attain excellence hereafter, but as a poet who has already shown true strength, who, whether it be good or ill, has attained a distinctive style, who has given expression to the national voice of Australia, who seeks to give his adopted country a place amongst the song-cages of the world—a poet as yet, perhaps, not fully developed, but one with a marvellous command of language and rythm and imagery, and a thorough artist—a man whose name will be green in the eyes of posterity as that of one of the first teachers of beauty in this strangely new land.

> Evelyn, "Mr. Kendall's Poetry," in The Australasian, Vol. VI, No. 146, January 16, 1869, p. 72.

S. S. T[OPP] (essay date 1876)

[*In the following excerpt, the critic notes the unevenness of Kendall's poetry in* Leaves *from Australian Forests. He claims that far too much of the volume reveals Kendall's penchant for imitation, but remarks that when his subject is his native Australia, Kendall's verse shows his mastery of meter and his descriptive power.*]

[Mr. Kendall's] muse has unfortunately, so far, not been a prolific one. The best of his poems are to be found in a small volume, entitled *Leaves from Australian Forests*. This volume, together with a few fugitive pieces scattered through the columns of various colonial periodicals, make up the sum total of his contributions to the literature of his native country. Mr. Kendall's forte is undoubtedly lyrical poetry; indeed he seldom attempts any other kind. His few narrative poems in blank verse, such as **"A Death in the Bush"** and **"The Glen of Arramatta,"** are by no means among his happiest efforts. Not that these poems are destitute of merit, as both of them, the latter more especially, contain several fine passages; but, on the whole, they lack interest, and do not afford scope for Mr. Kendall's peculiar merits. The turn of the verse, and indeed of some of the expressions, remind us strongly of Tennyson's shorter pieces in blank verse; for instance, **"Dora"** and **"Aylmer's Field."** His great fault indeed seems to be a tendency to imitate previous poets. He reminds us, in some respects, of the mocking-bird of America, which can imitate exactly the note of every other songster. Unlike the mocking-bird, however, he possesses a natural note of his own, of which, unfortunately, he gives us too little. This imitative tendency is admitted by the poet himself in one of his sonnets, where he asks the reader of his poems to accept them kindly—

> Even though there be
> Some notes that unto other lyres belong:
> Stray echoes from the elder sons of song;
> And think how from its neighbouring, native sea
> The pensive shell doth borrow melody.

We think that this apology, although gracefully worded, will scarcely save the poet from the reader's condemnation, when he finds that in a volume of about 150 pages more than a third of the poems are imitations more or less close of other poets. Mr. Kendall's imitations, indeed, sometimes approach so nearly to the originals, as to be termed by the harsher name of plagiarisms. . . . [Perhaps] the most unfortunate of all his imitations, and indeed the worst thing he ever wrote, is **"After the Hunt,"** which reads like a miserable burlesque of "The Bells"—

> Underneath the windy mountain walls
>   Forth we rode an eager band,
> By the surges and the verges and the gorges,
>   Till the night was on the land—
>   On the hazy mazy land!
> Far away the bounding prey
>   Leapt across the ruts and logs,
> But we galloped, galloped, galloped on,
>   Till we heard the yapping of the dogs!
> The yapping and the yelting of the dogs.

It is almost incredible that a poet, with so exquisite an ear for the music of poetry as this poet possesses, should have deliberately printed in his collected poems such trash as this, which has the additional demerit of being vague and almost meaningless. Mr. Kendall is indeed a veritable chameleon of poetry, and reflects the colours of any poet he may have been recently studying. Another defect in his poetry, and a serious one, is the absence of all human interest, which characterises most of his poems. He is as a rule too purely descriptive. He writes beautifully about the sky, the flowers, the mountains, the birds, the winds, and the rivers, but he dissociates these things from human beings altogether, and seems to look at them as something apart and far off from the concerns of humanity. He does not even show how they affect his own mental moods. **"The Hut by the Black Swamp"** is a notable example of this. Here in a poem of seventy or eighty lines he describes a deserted hut in the bush. The treatment of the subject reminds one somewhat of Hood's "Haunted House." He tells us with great affluence of language and pomp of style that the moss never grows on the hut, the birds do not sing over it, the wild dog howls past it, the nettle entwines it, the adder makes his lair in it, and so on. Why? Because at some time or other a murder was committed there; but as to who committed the murder, who was the victim, what the circumstances were under which it was committed, or even how the poet himself is affected by the contemplation of it, we are left entirely in the dark. . . . It is to be regretted that Mr. Kendall should have given us so few poems upon essentially colonial subjects. The title of his volume is *Leaves from Australian Forests.* The reader will doubtless be somewhat puzzled to discover the connection between "Australian Forests" and such poems as **"Daphne," "To Damascus," "A Spanish Love Song," "The Voyage of Telegonus,"** &c. Anyone who, after perusing these, turns to Mr. Kendall's poems on purely Australian subjects such as **"Ghost Glen," "Illa Creek," "At Euroma," "On a Cattle Track," "Coogee,"** and **"Sutherland's Grave,"** will perceive an essential difference between the two classes. The latter poems are almost perfect; as original as they are inimitable. The former, though well written and musical, are comparatively commonplace, such as many second and third-rate poets in England could have written. Why should a colonial-born poet go out of his way to sing the well-worn story of "Daphne," and such other old world themes. But enough of censure. Let us now turn to the more pleasing duty of pointing out Mr. Kendall's merits. As a descriptive poet he stands easily first among colonial writers, while as a master of metre he will bear comparison with the best among English poets. His perfect command of all the technicalities of poetry—rhyme, alliteration, assonance—is something wonderful. Take the following:—

> May catch the sense like subtle forest spells.

> Nor comes the bird whose speech is song,
>   Whose songs are silvery syllables.

> Ah! in his life, had he mother or wife,
>   To wait for his step on the floor?
> Did beauty wax dim while watching for him
>   Who passed through the threshold no more?
> Doth it trouble his head? He is one with the dead;
>   He lies by the alien streams,
> And sweeter than sleep is death that is deep,
>   And unvexed by the lordship of dreams.

> His should be a grave by mountains, in a cool and thick mossed lea,
> With the lone creek falling past it, falling ever to the sea.
> His should be a grave by waters, by a bright and broad lagoon,
> Making steadfast splendours hallowed of the quiet shining moon.

Lines like these are perfect, and linger in the memory like strains of music, quite apart from the meaning they convey. It must be admitted, however, that Mr. Kendall seldom sacrifices the sense of a passage to its poetic form, as many great masters of metre do. He abounds also in those curiously felicitous expressions which are more than anything else characteristic of a genuine poet—passages in which not a word could be altered without spoiling the picture. . . . A characteristic which must strike every reader of Mr. Kendall is his extreme melancholy. He fully exemplifies Shelley's line, "Our sweetest songs are those which tell of saddest thought." His best poems are full of a pensive sadness which would seem to be inspired by a contemplation of the Australian bush. Its vastness, its thick undergrowth, its monstrous trees, its desolation, its silence, all produce a depressing effect, which every one who has travelled through it must have observed, and are certainly not calculated to inspire one with light and cheerful musings. This vein of sadness is not peculiar to Mr. Kendall, but is apparent in Harpur, Gordon, and indeed all our poets who have passed much of their time in the bush. There is plenty of sweetness, but little "light" in Mr. Kendall's song. On the whole, however, he must be pronounced to be a true poet, though with a somewhat narrow scope. His best poem is undoubtedly **"Ghost Glen."** We regret that we have not space to extract it, for although it has been frequently quoted, it is well worthy of repetition. Had Mr. Kendall always written like this, praise and blame would have been alike thrown away upon him. As it is, we can only wish that he may live to give us many more poems of equal excellence. (pp. 205-11)

> *S. S. T[opp], "Australian Poetry," in* The Melbourne Review, *Vol. I, April, 1876, pp. 202-30.**

DOUGLAS B. W. SLADEN (essay date 1887)

[In the following excerpt, Sladen favorably compares Kendall's verse to that of his contemporaries, particularly the Australian poet Adam Lindsay Gordon. According to Sladen, Kendall has no equal as a "forest-poet" and "has written the most beautiful and the most terrible scenes we have of existence in the depths of the Bush." Taking issue with Barton's assessment of Kendall (see excerpt dated 1866), Sladen contends that he should be valued most for his forest poetry.]

Kendall is, in our opinion, unquestionably a poet of a higher order than Gordon, if being "of a higher order" may be taken to mean approaching more nearly to the level of the masters of song. It is our honest opinion that since Shelley and Keats died no one has so nearly approached them. He touched the lyre with something of the lyric musicality which made Shelley the father of the dactylic modern measures. He had somewhat of the marvellous Shelleian gift of detecting the Protean spirit of Nature in its myriad changes of form; and, like poor Keats, he could steal the loveliness of a southern summer and coin phrases whose "beauty is a joy for ever." (p. 8)

Kendall is essentially a Bush poet—an Australian Bush poet—not as Gordon was, but (excluding from our consideration the white intruder into the primeval forests) more essentially than Gordon was. For he was a much closer and more reverent observer of animal and vegetable life. He was the friend of nature—with man he was less intimate. In depicting the robust, muscular, dare-devil bushman—stockman or trooper—Kendall cannot be compared with Gordon, who only had to reflect his own life, as the great Italian painters painted their own portraits from mirrors. Gordon wrote, as he lived, like a man who would "put his horse" at anything or "square up" to anybody. But as a Bush-landscape-painter Kendall has no equal in Australia.

In his admirable "Poets and Prosewriters of New South Wales," . . . Mr. G. B. Barton, reviewing Kendall's first book . . . , made some remarks which have received a substantial endorsement from the Poet's later writings. (pp. 12-13)

Mr. Barton's remarks have in the main been borne out, but he claims too much. Kendall could paint loneliness admirably well. No one has drawn finer pictures of that aspect of Bush life which is peace or dreariness according as one pines for solitude or pines for society. He has written the most beautiful and the most terrible scenes we have of existence in the depths of the Bush—of the utter forsakenness of the explorer's fate. But for poems of what Mr. Barton calls the "wild society of the interior," we should not go to Kendall. He could put himself on the standpoint of the lonely bushman, as we have said, admirably well; but he had little sympathy with the roistering side of the bushman's nature. His own nature was too delicate, too poetic, too beautiful. This side of Bush life was reserved for men of rougher fibre, more robust and dashing in their genius. In Gordon the man overshadowed the poet, in Kendall the poet the man. . . . Kendall wrote like a poet who had been to the races; Gordon like a poet who had raced. But we have no wish to decry Kendall because he could not rival Gordon in bushman's ballads and never wrote an Australian Hiawatha like George Gordon McCrae. He could unmistakably throw himself into the feelings of a dying explorer. Take, for instance, his description of the death of the two explorers immortalized in Melbourne—Burke and Wills—published when the poet was only twenty, which brings out the main idea much more forcibly than two far more beautiful pieces, **"At Euroma"** and **"Leichhardt,"** in which the beauty of the poems rather cloaks the action. (pp. 14-15)

So far we have not been quite in accord with Mr. Barton. We know now, though he did not then, that while he was writing in New South Wales to laud Kendall as the first Station-life poet, poems that have now a world-wide celebrity were being written on the same subject in Victoria, and no one would claim that Kendall had competed with Longfellow by producing an aboriginal poem to compare with Hiawatha. Nor do we think that in his poems on exploration he throws up the stern realities like Gordon . . . or P. J. Holdsworth and others. In his poem on Leichhardt especially it will be seen that his poetical soul loved to dwell more on the so-called poetical aspects than on the grim practical ones. For few poets have had such

a delicate, tender, poetical soul as this native-born New South Welshman—who might justly be called the Australian Shelley. Indeed, as we pointed out above, in his brilliant appreciation of colour, his swift recognition of that Proteus, the spirit of Nature in all her changes of form, in the delicate music of his verse, his marvellous ease, his felicity and fecundity of expression, and his courageous assertion of opinions which men are generally unwilling to proclaim, he had much to make him remind us of the immortal author of "Queen Mab."

Kendall was as bold in bringing into prominence his adherence to Romanism in a secular, or at best an undenominational, community, as Shelley was in letting his peculiar views be known in a community which persecuted the unorthodox. But though he had so much in common with Shelley, the influence of Swinburne is much more apparent in this Australian poet's writings, than the influence of Swinburne's master. But the genius of the man is shown most, perhaps, by his handling of the language and the metres which the polished rapier-thrusting buffoonery of Mr. Gilbert's opera-libretti has overwhelmed with ridicule, except when they are handled by true poets. Kendall can write long poems with the antepenultimate rhyme, put an utterly bald expression like "two-and-thirty years ago" into a position of emphasis and solemnity, and yet not fall from the sublime. Some of his most serious "In Memoriam" poems would be quite comic, if one did not feel the restraining power of the man's genius. He could solemnify. There is such a true breath of religiousness about his poems, though they never preach, that scoffs are disarmed; and his genius is further demonstrated by the fact that he has written one of the two or three prize poems that are worth reading after the event with which they are connected has passed. His poem for the opening of the Sydney Exhibition is magnificent—we should say, perhaps, the finest prize poem written in the English language. The rest of Mr. Barton's claims we most cordially endorse, for, as a Bush landscape painter, Kendall has never had an equal, especially in the gloomier tints.

What a power of word-painting he had may be seen from his poems, **"The Hut by the Black Swamp,"** **"Cooranbean,"** and **"The Curse of Mother Flood,"** especially the first of them, because it shows in contrast the quiet beauty of his landscape painting and the intenseness of his lurid compositions. **"Cooranbean"** is, to our mind, the weirdest and most blood-curdling, at the same time as it is the most beautiful and powerful of Kendall's lurid pieces. In fierceness of curses it is surpassed by **"The Curse of Mother Flood"**; but that poem always strikes us as less natural and more of a rhetorical exercise.

But Kendall is seen at his very best, not in these lurid colours, but in the delicate tints of light and shadow, the lovely contrasts of moss and stream, the languorous shade, the sleepy perfumed air, the luxuriance and the untroddenness of his native forests. In fact, he is essentially a forest-poet: his genius did not exult upon the mountain-top, it luxuriated in the dells, as the reader will see while he himself luxuriates in those delicious pieces of the mountain-forest—**"Bell-Birds,"** **"Mooni,"** and **"Orara"**—the last-named a mint of beautiful thoughts and expressions. (pp. 16-18)

[With] that cultivated class of intellect that delights to be made the confidante of Nature, as Gilbert White, Richard Jefferies, and John Burroughes, have made it, and revels in all that is genuinely redolent of a forest-life that is fresh to it, we venture to prophesy that Kendall will become a supreme favourite as soon as he is recognized. He was a child of the Australian forest, and continued such all his life. No one who did not love the forest as a mother could have written his Shelleian **"September in Australia"**; and the little poem entitled **"The Warrigal"** (**"Wild Dog"**) will prove that he observed animal life as faithfully as still life and landscape. And we venture to think that there is nothing more Landseer-like in the whole range of Australian poetry than this brilliant lyric. We ourselves give the palm among Kendall's poems to **"After Many Years."** It is as pathetic as a masterpiece of Tom Hood—something to be remembered with "Fair Inez" and "The House where I was Born" for music and tenderness. (p. 18)

> *Douglas B. W. Sladen, in an introduction to* A Century of Australian Song, *edited by Douglas B. W. Sladen, White and Allen, 1887, pp. 2-34.**

OLIPHANT SMEATON (essay date 1895)

[*Smeaton compares Kendall's works to those of his contemporaries, notably Gordon, Alfred Domett, and James Brunton Stephens. Ranking Kendall as one of Australia's foremost poets, Smeaton cites "Araluen," "Hy-Brasil," and "Mooni" as his finest productions.*]

[The popularity of Kendal (sic)] is still on the increase. During his lifetime his fame was somewhat overshadowed by that of Gordon, whose poetry was more in accord with the spirit of the time. But with the more general diffusion of culture throughout the great continent, his works are daily becoming more popular—not that Gordon is valued the less, but that Kendal is prized the more. Essentially an idyllic poet, he is one to whom Australasians, weary of the turmoil and "the briars of this work-a-day world," may turn for pictures of peaceful Arcadian beauty, even as long ago the critical and thought-weary Alexandrians rejoiced in the idyllic landscapes of the Greek pastoral poets, Theocritus, Bion, and Moschus.

Kendal's vocabulary, though not so surprisingly full as that of Domett and Stephens, claims its chief merit in its choiceness. Invariably, it is absolutely the best word possible under the circumstances of the case which he selects; while, as regards the other two, their excessive ornament begets diffuseness. By a chasteness of taste and a severe beauty more Greek than Anglo-Saxon, of vocabulary, idiom, and poetic imagery, Kendal's work is characterised. To Swinburne's *Atalanta in Calydon,* much of it bears a close resemblance in pervading atmosphere, and from these general attributes arise the fact that the more cultured section of the Australasian community are his most fervent admirers. His sources of figurative comparison are both numerous and characterised by aptness and propriety. (pp. 496-97)

Kendal's imagery, flashing, clear-cut, and pellucid, a picture often in a word, if less broadly effective than that of Stephens, is more invariably true. As a metrist, Kendal cannot compare with Domett, Stephens, or Gordon. He is more tenderly sweet than any, but not so varied. The measures he essayed, some of them of great beauty, as, for instance, **"Euroclydon,"** he moulded to his will with the ready ease of a master. As compared with the others, however, his range was narrow. But within that range he is as mellifluous as Stephens, and the dainty grace of many of his sonnets, modelled on those of Rossetti, such as **"A Mountain Spring," "By a River,"** and **"Rest,"** are only inferior to those of his master. . . .

Kendal is essentially an idyllic poet, and it is to be regretted he confined his work to merely fugitive pieces. Feeling, perhaps, he had not the strength of pinion for a longer flight . . . ,

he wisely kept within his range. Lyrics of an exquisite and dainty grace, meriting praise the highest, he has written; as, for example, **"Outre-Mer," "Brothers from Far-Away Lands," "The Song of the Cattle Hunters,"** and his splendid **"Hymn of Praise."** . . . (p. 497)

Kendal is a master both of passion and pathos. Some of his love-poems, as the sonnets **"To Laura," "Merope," "Mary Rivers,"** &c., are charged with the very soul and spirit of love-sick longing, yet chastened and purified by a sense of the intrinsic dignity of human nature. . . . There is [a] . . . passionate *abandon* to the sweet sway of love, with nevertheless a subtle sense of self-respect throughout it all. Kendal's verse also is weighted with a burden of pathos often too deep for tears. In common with Miss Jennings Carmichael, his emotional power lies in the natural and unfeigned character of the pathos he expresses. The circumstances are not framed to suit the preconceived emotion, but the latter arises naturally out of the circumstances. No one could read without being deeply moved his delicately pathetic **"Araluen,"** written upon the death of his own daughter, **"Hy-Brasil," "After Many Years," "The Street,"** that terribly tragic retrospect of his own life, and finally, **"Mooni,"** wherein is represented the high-water mark of Kendal's genius. (p. 498)

Kendal's claim to the chief place among Australasian singers is based upon his wonderful "many-sidedness," on the remarkable manner wherein all the qualities essential to the composition of a really great singer are combined in him. His genius is more eclectic, more composite, than that of any of his great Antipodean compeers. In harmony between sense and sound, and in intellectual strength—qualities the most important whereby to appraise the value of a poet's work—Kendal takes a place amongst the foremost of his fellows. In **"Hy-Brasil"**—that marvel of rich word-painting and rhythmic music as estimated by Antipodean standards of excellence—he never betrays a single weak line, while in all his poems the sign manual of intellectual strength is more or less present. In some, indeed, it borders upon the purely didactic, that being during the brief period when the spell of Robert Browning had fallen over him. Intellectual subtilty in him never tends to obscurity.

Kendal's specialty being idyllic poetry, he is less vividly epical in presentation than Gordon, less dramatically so than Stephens. This is borne home to the mind when one reads Kendal's racing poem, **"How the Melbourne Cup was Won,"** after Gordon's "How we Beat the Favourite," or his **"Ghost Glen,"** or **"The Hut by the Black Swamp"** after Stephens's "Midnight Axe." His faculty of humour was less broadly effective than theirs, but is more delicately playful. It was more subtly seasoned with the true Attic salt of wit, if less pitilessly sardonic. Stephens and Gordon expose shams with the steely, blue rapier-blade of sarcastic invective; Kendal genially laughs them out of fashion, even as "Cervantes smiled Spain's chivalry away." As the most compositely eclectic genius Australasia has yet produced, Kendal's place every year is becoming more widely admitted, and it will be long, I fear, before the dainty grace and rounded sweetness of his verse will be surpassed. (pp. 498-99)

> *Oliphant Smeaton, "A Gallery of Australasian Singers," in* The Westminster Review, *Vol. CXLIV, No. 5, November, 1895, pp. 477-503.**

A. G. STEPHENS (essay date 1919)

[*A journalist, editor, and publisher, Stephens was one of the most prominent Australian literary critics of the late nineteenth and early twentieth centuries. In the following excerpt from a review first published in a 1919 issue of the* Bookfellow, *Stephens characterizes Kendall as the quintessential Australian poet. In addition, he lauds the melodiousness of his verse and acknowledges the influence of such poets as Tennyson, Swinburne, Edgar Allan Poe, and Christina Rossetti. For additional commentary by Stephens, see the excerpt dated 1928.]*

There has been no writer more generically Australian than Kendall; the Spirit of the Bush hovers over his poetry. Australia contains all landscapes; all climates; only a part of the southeast coast was known to Kendall, but he had drawn that part into his blood. As a nervous, delicate boy, all eyes and ears, at Ulladulla—as a nervous, solitary man at Coorumbene, labouring to imprison his dreams in verse—he lived in a close communion with Nature: he is poet of Nature and himself—not a poet of Humanity.

Past river and mountain, flower and moss, past the words that try to portray his feeling, Nature in Australia pervades his work like a brooding atmosphere of feeling. His selected poems as published, with prize odes, obituary pieces, and rhyming efforts to win the popular ear—do not display fully this obsession of Nature remarkable in his early work. It is the permanent background of Kendall's poetry, from which here and there he was able to draw Australian colours visible in words.

> The soft white feet of afternoon
>   Are on the shining meads,
> The breeze is as a pleasant tune
>   Among the happy reeds.
> The air is full of mellow sounds,
>   The wet hill heads are bright,
> And down the fall of fragrant grounds
>   The deep ways flame with light. . . .
>   (p. 147)

Kendall's model in blank verse must have been Milton, but he writes in a softer strain. In long rhymed lines he was sometimes successful, but his short lyric measures have a higher musical quality. The value of his work remains chiefly personal and Australian; he has but a small place in the rank of English poets. In the Australian literary rank he will stand always among the first. Innocence, sensitive feeling, sympathy with Nature, sing sweetly and sadly in his melodies.

An unlettered youth, with genius in place of schooling, it was inevitable that Kendall should imitate and sometimes echo the English poets that he loved. Perhaps the influence of Poe is strongest in his early verse; Tennyson, Christina Rossetti, and Swinburne appear later. Occasionally he seized a complete phrase—as in Coogee's 'gaps and fractures fringed with light' from Patmore's description of the retreating clouds of a thunderstorm. His persistent use of refrain he learned perhaps from Poe; the trick of excessive alliteration that spoils some of his work he caught from Swinburne.

Past these debts, he has his own strong sense of rhythm and sweet, instinctive melody. Wind blows and water runs through his poetry; still more than he saw the vision of the Bush he heard its singing voice. And his instrument of interpretation? Considering Kendall's poetry in its range from wild cries and clamour to the softest, sweetest music, we may say and believe that Kendall was an Irish harp in Australia. (p. 148)

A. G. Stephens, "Henry Kendall," in Twentieth Century Australian Literary Criticism, *edited by Clement Semmler, Oxford University Press, Melbourne, 1967, pp. 147-48.*

A. G. STEPHENS   (essay date 1928)

[In this discussion of Kendall's literary career, Stephens assesses the differences between his early and late works. According to Stephens, the early poetry demonstrates the author's natural and spontaneous poetic energy, while much of the later poetry is artificial, written from memory rather than feeling. Thus, Stephens argues that Kendall's "rare power of seeing and feeling and singing was not supported by an equal power of knowledge or an equal power of thought. For that reason, . . . Kendall remains in the scale of literature a sweet poet, with a particular Australian value: not a sublime poet with universal value." For additional commentary by Stephens, see the excerpt dated 1919.]

Poems and Songs abounds with natural truth, keen vision, and warm feeling: expressed in passages of melodious beauty. Kendall learned to write more thoughtfully: his later work shows wider knowledge of literature. But it loses fresh and ardent poetical energy: it loses much of that feeling of pure and exalted communion with Nature which is Kendall's peculiar quality in Poetry.

Here are some lines from **"The Muse of Australia"** which Kendall placed first in *Poems and Songs:*—

> Where the pines with the eagles are nestled in rifts
>   And the torrent leaps down to the surges,
> I have followed Her, clambering over the clifts,
>   By the chasms and moon-haunted verges:
> I know She is fair as the angels are fair;
> For, have I not caught a faint glimpse of Her there?
> —A glimpse of her face, and her glittering hair,
>   And a hand with the harp of Australia!
>
> I never can reach you, to hear the sweet voice
>   So full with the music of fountains:
> Oh, when will you meet with that soul of your choice
>   Who will lead you down here from the mountains?
> A lyre-bird lit on a shimmering space!
> It dazzled mine eyes; and I turned from the place,
> And wept in the dark for a glorious face
>   And a hand with the harp of Australia!

Here is a passage from a poem written about seventeen years afterwards:—

> What though a sky of new strange beauty shines
> Where no white dryad sings within the pines,
> Here is a land whose large imperial grace
> Must tempt thee, Goddess! in thy holy place:
> Here are the dells of peace and plenilune,
> The hills of morning and the slopes of noon:
> Here are the waters dear to days of blue
> And dark-green hollows of the noontide dew:
> Here lies the harp, by fragrant wood-winds fanned,
> That waits the coming of thy quickening hand:
> And shall Australia, framed and set in sea
> August with glory, wait in vain for thee?

You feel that a difference between these poems is the difference between the torrent and the lake: between Poetry springing rapturously from its source of feeling, and Poetry sleeping calmly among the hills of Memory. One poem is natural: the other is artificial. That is the characteristic difference between Kendall's poetry in youth and his poetry in age. In the beginning he wrote because he was impelled by an inspiring force: in the end he often compelled himself to write. (p. 9)

[Kendall's second book of poems, *Leaves from Australian Forests,*] represents the maturity of his talent: before the downfall of his health and reputation. Less original, less impetuous than the lad who wrote *Poems and Songs,* Kendall at this period wrote in studied imitation of the style of praised English poets. The work is often good; but we miss the salt-sea tang, the wild-wood savour, the bright blood of the boy.

"September in Australia" (1869) is an example. Two stanzas:—

> September, the maid with the swift, silver feet!
>   She glides and she graces
> The valleys of coolness, the slopes of the heat,
>   With her blossomy traces:
> Sweet month! with a mouth that is made of a rose,
>   She lightens and lingers
> In spots where the harp of the Evening glows
>   Attuned by her fingers.
>
> O, season of changes—of shadow and shine—
>   September the splendid!
> My song hath no music to mingle with thine,
>   And its burden is ended:
> But thou, being born of the winds and the sun,
>   By mountain, by river,
> Mayst lighten, and listen, and loiter, and run
>   With thy voices for ever.

That poem has beauty: yet, if you compare its spirit with the spirit of **"Morning in the Bush"** or **"Evening in the Bush"** (1862) you will see that Kendall is farther from essential truth. His vision is less clear, his description is less exact: he writes around his subject rather than out of his subject. (p. 12)

Nevertheless the ripe fruit of Kendall's middle poetical period has its own excellence. For example:—

> Sometimes we feel so spent for want of rest
> We have no thought beyond. I know, to-day,
> When tired of bitter lips, and dull delay
> With faithless words, I cast mine eyes upon
> The shadows of a distant mountain-crest,
> And said: That hill must hide within its breast
> Some secret glen, secluded from the sun . . .
> O, mother Nature! would that I could run
> Into thy arms, and, like a wearied guest
> Half blind with lamps and sick of feasting, lay
> An aching head on thee . . . Then, down the streams
> The moon might swim, and I should feel her grace
> While soft winds blew the sorrows from my face,
> So quiet in the fellowship of dreams.

With feeling, and with expression, that sonnet takes a high place in English poetry. Read it aloud; and observe how naturally the thought makes a harmonious shape of words: curving from the first statement, the need of rest, through the images of mountain, glen, and streams to the final picture of rest secure. Linger upon the beauty of the last four lines: where the words fall into place like the notes of a musical instrument touched tenderly.

Here is another passage of Kendall at his height:

> Sing, son of Sorrow! is there any gain
> For breaking of the loins, for melting eyes,
> And knees as weak as water?—any peace,
> Or hope, for casual breath and labouring lips:

> For clapping of the palms, and sharper sighs
> Than frost?—or any light to come for those
> Who stand and mumble in the alien streets
> With heads as grey as Winter,—any balm
> For pleading women—and the love that knows
> Or nothing left to love?

That also is classic poetry; since it expresses perfectly human sympathy with sorrow. Those lines help to prove how rightly we esteem poetry: because, with the touch of apt words in harmony, the poet sharpens the keen edge of the fact, and in our minds makes life itself more living.

In the lofty sky of Poetry, these poems rise higher than Kendall's beautiful descriptions of Australian scenery; because they are not limited by a particular landscape: they appeal to all readers of English. The human value of literature is measured by its effect upon the greatest number of minds during the longest time. Our own national poetry is better for us than the national poetry of other peoples; yet the human spirit of literature shines beyond nations and periods. In a literary view the best Australian poetry is that which embraces the feelings and thoughts of mankind everywhere through the ages. Transcending the national, it becomes universal. (pp. 12-13)

Kendall lacked the steadfast strength of a great writer: he could not build his dreams into a palace of poetry: he wandered and wondered and sang. His true poetry is like one of the Australian streams that he loved: not a grand river, yet beautiful to sense and spirit: murmuring with soft sound through a wilderness of shady delight.

Kendall excels also in portraying simple affection. He sings of love and hope as well as of failure and disaster; yet the doom of sorrow overshadowed him: his keynote of temperament is sad. . . .

Kendall wrote descriptive and critical essays in prose. These show interesting material well expressed: without remarkable originality or force. Kendall's mind was of ordinary capacity, with an extraordinary kind of capacity. His rare power of seeing and feeling and singing was not supported by an equal power of knowledge or an equal power of thought. For that reason, and for the reason that only a little of his persistent labour achieved the height of his talent, Kendall remains in the scale of literature a sweet poet, with a particular Australian value: not a sublime poet with universal value.

Kendall wrote many satirical verses: humorously critical: cleverly displaying keen observation and bright wit; but usually without dignity and weight. (p. 13)

[In his closing years] Kendall had overstrained body and mind: he had fallen too far: he was a broken man. He wrote verses that were sometimes well turned and polished, but usually lacking his former energy. He had lost heart and hope; yet his poetical impulse persisted. He won a prize offered for an ode to commemorate the International Exhibition at Sydney; and he gathered the material of a third book, *Songs from the Mountains,* published at Sydney in 1880. Here Kendall's fire falls often to a glow of gorgeous language. He attempts—sad bard!—to win popularity. There are many eloquent lines: as in the address **"To a Mountain"**:—

> . . . Round thy lordly capes the sea
> Rolls on with a superb indifference
> For ever. In thy deep, green, gracious glens
> The silver fountains sing for ever. Far

Above dim ghosts of waters in the caves,
The royal robe of morning on thy head
Abides for ever. Evermore the wind
Is thy august companion; and thy peers
Are cloud, and thunder, and the face sublime
Of blue mid-heaven. On thy awful brow
Is Deity; and in that voice of thine
There is the great, imperial utterance
Of God, for ever: and thy feet are set
Where, evermore, through all the days and years,
There rolls the grand hymn of the deathless wave.

That is a passage which does not sound quite truly in poetry: it is skillfully made rather than naturally sung. The splendid words seem like the padding of a slight emotion; strengthened by the impressive refrain of ''for ever'' and ''evermore.'' Observe that the closing lines repeat the idea of the lines at the beginning.

Sweeter poetically are Kendall's verses of personal sorrow, his melodious moan for the dream of youth vanished, the hope of glory fled. He writes in **"Orara"**:—

The soft white feet of afternoon
Are on the shining meads:
The breeze is as a pleasant tune
Amongst the happy reeds.

and continues:

The world is round me with its heat,
And toil, and cares that tire:
I cannot, with my feeble feet,
Climb after my desire.
But, on the lap of lands unseen,
Within a secret zone,
There shine diviner gold and green
Than man has ever known:
The glory of a larger sky
On slopes of hills sublime
That speak with God and Morning, high
Above the ways of Time.

Such stanzas of defeat do not soar high in the sky of Poetry. When Kendall writes of his failure to write, remember that Poetry achieves its end and does not fail. Kendall's gloomy and self-pitying strain is sickly, not healthy. Yet we, who know and admire his effort and his work, can appreciate the tender sentiment of his last vision, and can sympathise with his sorrow. (p. 14)

A. G. Stephens, "Henry Kendall," in Australian Writers, *Vol. I, 1928, pp. 2-16.*

ARCHIE JAMES COOMBES   (essay date 1938)

[*The following excerpt is from a survey of Kendall's works that treats his style, structure, and themes. Coombes's remarks are largely negative. He claims that Kendall's poetry is monotonous and notes no appreciable evolution in style or subject although he does acknowledge Kendall's success in depicting scenes from nature.*]

The poems presented in his first volume, *Poems and Songs,* . . . were all written before Kendall had completed his twenty-first year, and it is only to be expected that certain immaturities should be evident. These, however, are counterbalanced by other qualities of definite promise which entitle the book to

rank as the best collection of lyrics till then issued in Australia. As a poet's first volume it must be considered satisfactory.

Poems and Songs provides ample evidence of Kendall's careful observation of the facts of nature, for he relies upon his skill in that direction for the major portion of his work. Scenic description was a thing of ease to him, so much so that the exuberance of youth led him to overcrowd his scenes. He grips detail with power, and displays occasional touches of delicacy and deftness of phrasing.

His rhythms are smooth and free, at times light and graceful, but more characteristically a monotony prevails in the movement of his verses. The musical quality of many of his lines marks a certain delicacy of his ear for tonal effects. Echoes there are of older poets, as might be expected in youthful verse, but Kendall's native gift for melody is also freely exercised.

Immaturity is more apparent in the thought and feeling of these poems than in their structural mechanism. The poet exhibits a tenderness of sensibility, but the range of experience through which it moves is very limited, and to atone for this limitation, youth leaves him no remedy but the shadows of experience and the fictions of feeling that imagination is able to create. His thought is coloured by melancholy, and is marked by a predilection for dismal groping. His feeling, though sensitive, is flabby. He is never an exhilarant. The yearning of inexperience, instead of finding an outlet in healthy activity of mind, either seeks the drugged solace of sentimentalism, or nerves itself upon the strong waters of horror. At this stage of his development, therefore, his feelings were a false guide, and he realized that happiness eluded him.

Leaves from Australian Forests . . . is a mature production, marked by a finer metrical skill and grace on the one hand, and by a deepening of his dismal tendencies on the other. The volume contains some of Kendall's most popular poems, such as **"September in Australia," "Bell Birds," "Araluen," "Illa Creek," "Moss on a Wall," "Arakoon,"** and **"Mountain Moss."**

"September in Australia," and **"Bell Birds,"** perhaps the best known of his poems, are fine examples of skill in mingling graceful movement with chiming melody, an art in which Kendall has no equal among Australian poets. His manipulation of repetition and change in vowel and consonant effects is full of subtle pleasure to the ear, through which the sense of beauty is stirred even where the substance of the verses may be thin.

"Araluen," "Illa Creek," "Moss on a Wall," and **"Mountain Moss,"** illustrate the poet's tenderness and accuracy of observation when alone with nature in her sweet seclusion. His verses flow with the liquid grace of the streams he loves, and bear within them the purity and freshness of the quiet woodland dells. In such poems as these we see Kendall at his best.

The majority of the pieces in this volume are descriptive, but in many of them the description is intended as the setting for some story or reflection upon life. In such cases the poet proves his possession of graphic power, but with a fatal kink for gloom. Too many of his subjects are essentially ugly, and the art he employs to render them vivid fails to redeem in them the effects of ugliness. Occasionally, however, where the sentiment is not over-wrought, there is a genuine power in his pathos. **"A Death in the Bush"** is a good example of such work. In this poem, as also in **"The Glen of Arawatta"** he echoes the voice of Charles Harpur, whom he does not excel.

Songs from the Mountains . . . is the most easily read of his three publications, although there is no appreciable advance upon his former volume, either in subject or treatment. There are similar descriptions, and similar reflections, and the record of emotional experience is much the same. Variety is added to this last work by the inclusion of a series of efforts at satire and humour; but beyond a certain fidelity of description there is only the smallest literary value in these pieces. At best Kendall is a thin laugher.

The best things in this volume again are those in which he describes the streams and the woodlands, or reflects with affection or sadness upon past happiness associated with them. **"Orara," "Narrara Creek," "Mooni," "Names Upon a Stone,"** and **"After Many Years,"** rank with those poems on similar subjects in his previous volume as being the most characteristic work he produced.

"Hy-Brazil," a religious fantasy, is a successful piece in the poet's favourite fifteen-syllabled metre. **"To a Mountain,"** the dedicatory poem introducing the volume, is perhaps the best example of the poet in a thinking mood; and the verses on **"The Sydney International Exhibition"** are eloquent and harmonious and prove his happy facility in phrase and imagery.

The volume also includes a variety of ugly themes, which are rendered gripping and vivid; but their stark realism repels rather than attracts. Few readers find pleasure in having their feelings desolated; and rightly so. Error of taste in choice of a subject is as grave a defect in an artist as error of treatment in subjects chosen. Kendall's taste was defective.

Kendall produced a great deal of verse for the newspapers and periodicals of his day which did not reappear in book form during his lifetime. More recent researches have brought to light many of these pieces which are now to be found in various complete editions of his works. In these poems he breaks no new ground, but they serve to illustrate more fully the several powers already displayed in his published volumes.

To read Kendall in the mass is to impose on oneself a wearying task. An immense deal of what he wrote is but the husk and chaff of literature which exerts upon the reader the cumulative effect of metrical garrulity without the compensating pleasures one associates with poetry. Though his best pieces excel in melody and grace of movement, very many of his poems pursue a course of unrelieved monotony, and it will be found that of such poems the chief offenders are those written in lines of excessive length. The ear, held in expectancy of rhyme or rest over intervals of fifteen, sixteen, and seventeen syllables for page after page, ultimately revolts against the weight and continuity of the burden laid upon it; and, whilst an undue load is thus laid upon the ear, the reader's power of visualizing the sequence of objects diminishes, with the result that though the sound and movement go on and on interminably, the sense subsides and fades in defeat, and the reader's interest is alienated.

Weariness is also assured for the reader in the monotony of subject and treatment which prevails. Landscape pictures, some of them photographic in reality, abound, greatly in excess of the pleasures literary scenery affords. One grows oppressed by rock and ridge and plain and sea, whose solitude is diversified with little more than what weather conditions furnish. Barren and desolate scenes intrude with a severity that is almost ironical of the beauty of life; and macabre effects, moving the sense of the terrible and horrible, disturb, but neither temper nor purify the emotions. The poet establishes his intensity,

achieves realistic dismalness, but annihilates tragic beauty, and the reader grows impatient of excessive suffering.

Then, too, although possessing a genius for words, Kendall possessed no genius for life, either actively as a participator, or imaginatively as a spectator, and, therefore, in the absence of the buoyancy and versatility that is bred of action, and knows triumph and revolt as well as suffering, the personal factor in his verse presents a monotony of tears and defeat, of submission and the weariness of wailing. It has been argued that Kendall the poet should not be condemned for the failures of Kendall the man, and in a sense the argument holds good. But it must also never be forgotten that in lyric poetry personality is an element of prime importance. It is the crystal through which experience shines, and upon its excellence depends the very soul of the poetic product. Burns failed in life perhaps as woefully as Kendall, but the soul of Burns sang free from the shackles of circumstance. The same cannot be said of Kendall. In contact with life his personality founders, and the reader in time grows weary of foundering in his company.

Furthermore, Kendall's personality, even apart from its insatiable craving for pity, is essentially insipid. There is no positive passion in any of his work, and consequently his poems strike out surprisingly little heat and surprisingly little colour in the reader's mind. One is left with a minimum of refreshment, and something of the feeling of having been fed with a species of beauty from which the vital and fertilizing element has been withheld. One's interest languishes in a monotony of unfulfilled expectation.

Hence the average reader, desiring to derive pleasure from his acquaintance with Kendall, is more likely to be rewarded by reading him in judicious selections than by attempting him in the mass.

Temperamentally unfitted to be an exponent of Australian sentiment, and lacking the substance to qualify him as a representative of Australian thought, Kendall is more truly a poet and more truly Australian in portraying the shadowed beauty of the coastal brushes, with their quiet streams, and moss-grown rocks, and dells of fern and foliage. In such surroundings remote from the pageant of daily life, the spirit of place descends upon him, kindling his genius. The genuine Kendall shines in the result, for his heart had its home in the wild-wood. . . . His ambition had been to write

> The perfect verses to the tune
> Of woodland music set;

and despite his own too modest disclaimer he approached more nearly to the realization of his ideal than he knew. **"Orara"** and **"Dungog"** are two of a happy group of poems which serve to illustrate this fact. He shows a subtle accuracy in his perceptions of nature. He sees his scene faithfully and reflects in his verse its movement and light and shade; he hears his scene intuitively and translates to his lines its delicacies of tonal change; and above all he feels his scene with tenderness and informs his utterance with a poise and atmosphere whose simplicity and grace are identical with nature's own. The reactions of such scenes upon him move trains of gentle reflection and chastened emotion that are justly mingled with the substance of his song. Within such limits his adequacy as a poet is beyond denial. (pp. 26-33)

Archie James Coombes, "Henry Kendall," in his Some Australian Poets, *1938. Reprint by Books for Libraries Press, 1970; distributed by Arno Press, Inc., pp. 23-33.*

P[ATRICK] I[GNATIUS] O'LEARY   (essay date 1954)

[O'Leary contends that Kendall's poetry was molded by external rather than internal forces. Even though Kendall wrote from memory, according to this critic, his subjects had a "material" rather than a personal basis. O'Leary also notes that melancholy informs most of Kendall's poetry, but underscores the power in that melancholy, for Kendall was able to reflect the natural beauty of life around him as well as the unattained hopes of the past.]

Almost every force that moulded the lineaments of Kendall's poetry is an external one. Often—indeed, it is his most characteristic note—he sings of things, events, places, drawn from out of that storehouse of hoarded recollection and vague shapes of the bygone which is memory. But these all have a material basis. Mostly they associate with remembered scenes and impressions of the country he knew and loved so well in his opening years, and until his early twenties. Over all of them plays his fancy—there is little that is imaginative in Kendall's poetry—now a gleam and now a gloom—the "rain and the sunbeams shine mingled together." It is this "shadowy brightness," to use a phrase of Yeats's, that makes up no small part of that melancholy which is in so much of his poetry.

We may strain the effect of maternal influences upon Kendall too far, perhaps, but it cannot, I think, be questioned that to them must be ascribed this aspect of his poetry—this and a certain astonishing felicity of phrase, which, should, assuredly, have stayed Arnold in his search for specimens of that which he claimed was genuinely Celtic. And, with these, Kendall's love of natural beauty in any manifestation.

The final verses of "Orara," from the original manuscript.

I say natural beauty in any manifestation. But most of the described beauty which we meet in Kendall's poetry is a loveliness extracted from his beloved places by the Clarence, and in those parts of Australia unvisited by the raids of drought, Lawson's "red marauder." Kendall was no poet of the spanning plains, of the dusty, dry and haggard spaces where summer is dominant and pitiless. What he sings of were not slimy and all but dried up waterholes, but "waters unkissed by the summer." He sings of those places where he says:

> October, the maiden of bright yellow tresses,
> Loiters for love in these cool wildernesses;
> Loiters knee-deep in the grasses to listen,
> Where dripping rocks gleam and the leafy pools glisten.

Though the stimulus to poetry in Kendall may appear to be immediately external in source, the brooding and shaping spirit so coloured with the gray cast of regret is his own gentle, wavering, indecisive nature. It is this that places on his recorded impressions that unmistakable something which is Kendall's own—and no one else's. We may say what we will of his poetry; that it lacks strength, robustness, passion, intensity. But there it is—a lovely thing, even though it possesses more of backward-glancing pensiveness and melancholy than of—

> Songs interwoven of lights and of laughters,
> Borrowed from bell-birds in far forest rafters.

How lovely his poetry is at its best! Let us, then, judge it by that best, forgetting the debts to Shelley, Tennyson and Swinburne—very real debts as they are—those

> . . . notes that unto other lyres belong
> Stray echoes from the elder sons of song.

Forgetting these and his descents into poor verse, how fine, how beautiful Kendall is at his best! What poet would disdain the very line I have just quoted: "Stray echoes from the elder sons of song"? (pp. 24-6)

There was in Kendall a melancholy that may be almost called predestinate, if I do not do injustice to a very express word. He gives the sense of his going forth to battle, and always falling. He did not grapple with the realities of to-day. He sat and brooded over the unattained hopes of yesterday. He commiserated with himself and exhibits a self-piteousness which is pathetic. Kendall was defective in sustained strength, in intellectual and creative stamina. He was the muser who conceived a palace of art, of beauty, and magnificence that he could not fashion into form. He dreamed and longed and designed. But his dreams and designs were frailties, but beautiful frailties like gossamers, dew-gemmed and sunlit.

Kendall's is a cry of achievement withheld, of frustration. It is constantly ringing in his loveliest lines. He purposed and failed to make

> . . . a cunning harmony
> Of words and music caught from glen and height,
> And lucid colours born of woodland light,
> And shining places where the sea-streams lie;
> But this was when the heat of youth glowed white;
> And since I've put the faded purpose by.

And again he tells

> The world is round me with its heat,
> The toil, and cares that tire:
> I cannot, with my feeble feet
> Climb after my desire.

That note recurs again and again in his poetry.

Kendall I hold to be still our most melodious poet. In lyric faculty, in gift of pure song, in delicate apprehension of certain aspects of natural beauty, he excels all other Australian poets. He describes himself as

> Longing for power and the sweetness to fashion
> Lyrics with beats like the heart-beats of passion.

He did not lack "the sweetness." It was the "power" he wanted. (pp. 26-7)

> P[atrick] I[gnatius] O'Leary, "Henry Clarence Kendall," in his *Bard in Bondage, edited by Joseph O'Dwyer, The Hawthorn Press, 1954, pp. 22-7.*

T. INGLIS MOORE (essay date 1956)

[*Assessing Kendall's place in the history of Australian literature, Moore maintains that the poet was the first native craftsman to render the beauty of the Australian environment in verse. He argues that although Kendall is a genuine poet, anthologies of Australian literature fail to reflect the scope and variety of his work. In addition, Moore notes that many collections of Kendall's poetry contain a disproportionate number of his inferior verses and therefore fail to fully convey his talents as a romantic, classicist, and realist. This essay was written in 1956.*]

[Historically,] Kendall is important as the first poet to assimilate the Australian environment and express it with any fullness: earlier poets, such as Tompson, Wentworth, and Woolls, had only given fitful glimpses. Even Harpur, despite the keenness of his eye, had painted only a few local scenes, and these objectively, without the warmth of Kendall's passionate love of the bush. Kendall enlarged, with richer details, the variety of scene and mood introduced by Harpur. Indeed, he brought a significant development to the concept of the Australian landscape. The first concept of the early settlers was of a romantically picturesque and exotic land. This merged into one of a country marked by "gloomy monotony" or "weird melancholy", to use the phrases of Wentworth and Marcus Clarke. Harpur expressed this somberness, associated with the tragedies of pioneer settlers, in his forceful poem "The Creek of the Four Graves". Kendall expanded it in the poems grouped together . . . in the section entitled **"Death in the Bush".** His own temperament responded to its tragic and melancholy tones. A number of lyrics also describe the harshness of the dry inland plains. He added, however, three new elements to the concept of the Australian landscape. First, he celebrated his joy in the beauty of the coastal forests, mountains, and streams—a loveliness of radiant sunlight and singing waters. In the second place, he wrote of the country not as a nostalgic exile but as a patriot hymning his homeland. Finally, he introduced that sacerdotal feeling for the bush, with qualities of religious awe and adoration, coupled with a reaching out for a universal significance, which has since become a distinctive trend in Australian nature poetry. "I recognise in Poetry", he once wrote, "a revelation of Divinity beyond all revelations: a religion past all religions." In **"To a Mountain"** he identifies this poetic revelation of divinity with nature, in kinship with Wordsworth and Emerson. Thus Kendall created a new Australia of the mind—a country made beautiful, beloved, and sacred.

In the historical development of Australian poetry Kendall was significant, not only for this original and seminal contribution to the assimilation of the environment, but also as the best craftsman of verse that had yet appeared, the first poet to win recognition overseas, and a pioneer in various themes and forms. He was one of the first, along with Harpur, to treat the aboriginal as a serious subject, to celebrate the explorers, and to handle historical incidents. He wrote narratives as well as lyrics. He pioneered songs of bush life—of cattle-hunters, possum-hunters, and wild kangaroos—anticipating Gordon, and was a forerunner of the bush balladists in his colloquial ballads of bullock-drivers and shingle-splitters.

Kendall's true claim to consideration, however, rests on his achievement as a genuine poet. This has been blurred by the two forms in which he has been generally represented: the few poems published in anthologies of Australian poetry fail to indicate his scope and variety, whilst the collected editions of his poems, such as those edited by Sutherland and Stevens contain so many poor verses that they swamp the finer lyrics. Kendall's ear and taste were both defective, so that he can only be judged fairly by means of a selection confined to his best work. (pp. xvi-xvii)

[There] were three Kendalls: the romantic, the classical, and the realist poet. The traditional legend of Kendall as purely a melancholy romantic, all gentleness and pathos with no robustness or humour, gives only half the truth. True, he was largely a poet of this character. He believed that "the Poetry of Retrospection" was the best poetry: "There is at all times a mellowed beauty associated with the sunsets of yesterday which we do not find in the noon of to-day, and cannot anticipate for the morn of to-morrow". This was perhaps a rationalization of the melancholy lying in his temperament or evoked by his sufferings, since he constantly recurs to regret for the past or the wistfulness of frustration. Here he is in contrast to Mary Gilmore, another poet strongly retrospective, who looks to the past for a sturdy tradition that will build the future. Not only are Kendall's personal lyrics plaintive, but his tales of the bush past and his aboriginal verses are invariably sombre. He was an incorrigible addict to elegies. In his elegiac melancholy he is entirely romantic, just as he is in many of his nature lyrics, with their constant personal note.

From his romantic sadness Kendall extracts a grave sweetness, a melodic charm. His true talent, however, is not that of the romantic lyrist expressing his own emotions, like Burns and Shelley. Although his feeling is sincere, he lacks the poetic power to communicate it fully. Perhaps he himself gave the key to this defect when, writing of the poetic temperament, he said, "I have enough of that acute sensibility to work myself into a constant flutter of excitement". His sensibilities lay too close to the surface, and fluttered too easily, so that his emotional expression often became facile and superficial. It is a major failing that he rarely achieves a true intensity of passion—a failing of which he himself was conscious. His poems of the affections are often sentimental, often trite, and even insipid. His lapses of taste led frequently to bathos. His anger emerges in abuse, over-violent; his self-pity grows lachrymose. Grasping at tragedy, he could reach only half-way to pathos. Only a few of the poems of personal sentiment attain an even standard, such as the **"The Voice in the Wild Oak"**, **"After Many Years"**, **"Names Upon a Stone"**, and **"Outre Mer"**. Here the warm, sincere feelings are expressed simply and effectively.

Contrary to tradition, the truth about Kendall is that he wrote better when using a classical objectivity than when he is singing most subjectively as a romantic poet. In his poems on classical themes or those on biblical subjects in a neo-classical mode he can achieve the classic virtues: simplicity, clarity, detachment, and the force of economy. Thus **"The Voyage of Telegonus"** and **"King Saul at Gilboa"**, like such tales of the bush as **"The Glen of Arrawatta"** and **"A Death in the Bush"**, have true narrative, descriptive, and dramatic power. In such poems Kendall is stronger because he has passed beyond the enervating pathos of his personal tragedy to an impersonal vigour. It is significant that one of the worst of his elegies is **"Araluen"**, the lament for his baby daughter, when his feelings were most deeply stirred, whilst his best elegy is the one on a nameless aboriginal in **"The Last of His Tribe"**. **"Beyond Kerguelen"** shows strikingly the strength Kendall could achieve when, forgetting himself in objective description, he allowed his imagination free play.

Undoubtedly the best poems are those, such as **"Orara"**, **"Mooni"**, and **"Araluen"** (the river), where his religious passion for beauty in nature inspired him with rapture, exalted his imagination, and heightened his poetic power to describe the natural scene. In such lyrics the pattern is repeated of the poet rising to fine description, then declining into the diminuendo of the wistful, plaintive ego. His poetic salvation came when he lost his self in a wider outside world, either of nature or literature, since Kendall the poet was a far stronger character than Kendall the man.

This truth is further borne out by the realistic satires, topical verses, bush songs, and ballads. Once again Kendall exercises a native strength and liveliness when diverted from himself and his woes. The satires, although frequently heavy-handed to crudeness, carry some lusty punches. The descriptions of cattle-hunters and shingle-splitters, taken from life, are vivid and vigorous. Ballads such as **"Bill the Bullock-Driver"**, **"Jim the Splitter"**, and **"Billy Vickers"** were pioneering efforts. Naturally they did not compass the colloquial assurance of Paterson's balladry. Yet they have a similar realistic treatment, gift for characterization, and touch of ironic humour. Despite a few "literary" lapses and touches of priggishness, on the whole they come freshly, smacking of the soil. It was unfortunate that Kendall and his critics tended, in the fashion of the day, to dismiss his bush realism as not conforming to the romantic tradition of poetry then current, just as the nationalists discounted the classical pieces as un-Australian. Yet the robustness of both classical and realistic verses suggests that if Kendall had not met an early death he might well have turned from his introspective melancholy to develop this promising vein of extrovert sturdiness.

Kendall's originality has been doubted, and he has been denounced for an "unpardonable" imitative tendency. Here his imitations must be distinguished from his borrowings. Some poems are frankly imitative of the style of English writers (e.g., he published **"Ogyges"** with the note: "After the manner of Tennyson's 'Tithonus' and Horne's 'Orion'"), but in this he followed a long-established poetic practice, and the result must be judged on its own poetic merits. Thus **"The Voyage of Telegonus"** is Tennysonian, whilst **"To a Mountain"** is Wordsworthian; yet both are good poems. In the first the imagination shown is Kendall's own, whilst the feeling of the second is highly personal, felt on the pulse of experience. **"Campaspe"** has merits as an exercise "after the manner" of Swinburne. His borrowings from the poets in whom he was saturated, on the other hand, are unconscious, except where he takes lines from Gordon with an open avowal. So, too, he freely admits that his work contains "Stray echoes from the elder notes of song", not as purposive filchings but as unwitting

"plunder of perfumes". Such echoes can be detected in lines or phrases caught from Horne, Wordsworth, Patmore, and Christina Rossetti, for example. Elsewhere we find language, rhythms, and rhymes reminiscent of Poe, Longfellow, Keats, Shelley, Tennyson, and Swinburne.

Here it must be noted that, despite the influence of Swinburne in some later poems, in historical fact Kendall was Swinburnian before he had ever read Swinburne—indeed, before Swinburne had published anything but an early drama. Kendall's *Poems and Songs* appeared in 1862, whereas Swinburne's *Atalanta in Calydon* did not appear till 1865, the *Poems and Ballads* till 1866. The use of alliteration, long lines and anapestic rhythms which we regard as Swinburnian had already been employed by Kendall in his first book, in which we find the characteristic elements he developed later as his own distinctive style. As H. M. Green pointed out, "he has a marked poetic personality and a music that is quite individual, in spite of the echoes" [see Additional Bibliography]. If Kendall—like many another poet—unconsciously made minor levies, he was no mere imitator. He forged his own idiom. His emotion is always his own. His local scenes were experienced.

On the other hand, his style, if his own, like Touchstone's Audrey, was also at times, like her, "a poor thing". His language was apt but conventional, wanting that freshness and element of surprise that delight one in Neilson and McCrae. Often he succumbed to the obvious alliteration and the showy, but shallow, phrase, as when he writes:

> And, softer than slumber, and sweeter than singing,
> The notes of the bell-birds are running and ringing.

Actually the notes of the bell-bird come, not "softer than slumber", but as sharp, metallic tinkles; they also come *staccato*, not *sostenuto*: ringing, but not running. Kendall had a fatal facility with words, so that he often grew garrulous and diffuse. The original energy is dissipated in a welter of words. An equal fluency with rhythms betrayed him into metrical regularity, creating monotony. Too often his verse flows on like a stream, without variation of cadence or subtlety in the melody. His blank verse, although mellifluous or dignified, usually has not the pith and sinew of Harpur's. He never mastered the sonnet form. In the types of verse, moreover, his talent was limited. His racing rhymes miss the easiness of Gordon or Paterson. His lighter verses often show a heavy hand or fall into doggerel. His satires, with some exceptions, tend to much railing with little wit. In content his poetry as a whole has little body of ideas. The intellectual element is either conventional or tenuous, although he had the ideas of the poetic imagination.

By absolute standards these defects reduce Kendall to a minor poet. In Australian poetry his place at present would probably be somewhere near the bottom rung of the best dozen poets, along with Victor Daley. True, he is superior to both Harpur and Gordon, and to such later lyrists as Quinn and Wilmot. His work is slight, however, beside that of such philosophical and intellectual poets as Brennan and O'Dowd, Baylebridge and FitzGerald. Technically he is limited compared with such craftsmen as Slessor and Douglas Stewart. In the pure lyric, where comparison is fittest, his poetry is surpassed by the artistry of McCrae, the sudden magic of Neilson, the compressed power of Mary Gilmore at her best, and the disciplined intensity of Judith Wright.

On the other hand, Kendall is a true poet who should hold an honourable place in our poetry, a born singer, a graphic painter of landscape, and a versatile craftsman.

He still remains one of the sweetest of our singers, with a natural rhythmic flow and a melody always graceful, often memorable. In spite of the weaknesses already mentioned, he had considerable metrical skill, writing effectively in many forms. Thus he can pass from the stirring, swinging dactyls of "**Beyond Kerguelen**" to the grave quietness of the blank verse in "**Ogyges**", from the crisp ring of the couplets in "**King Saul at Gilboa**" to the mourning cadences of "**The Last of His Tribe**". Skilful craftsmanship achieves the contrast between the dignified movement of the rhetoric in "**The Sydney International Exhibition**", the rollicking run of "**The Song of Ninian Melville**", the epigrammatic curtness of "**Billy Vickers**", stinging like the flick of a stock-whip, and the graceful ripple of "**September in Australia**" or "**Bell-Birds**". He is usually most effective in his lyrics of short lines, where the garrulity unloosed in longer measures is curbed to an economy that still compasses a melodious grace, as in "**Orara**" and "**Araluen**". Yet "**Beyond Kerguelen**", as Oscar Wilde declared, "has a marvellous music about it".

As a descriptive poet he caught, like Roberts, Streeton, and Gruner in painting, the light and shade of the Australian scene. It was significant that he began his first volume with a symbolical image of sunlight: "A lyre-bird lit on a shimmering space". His work abounds in phrasing of pictorial force, as in the pictures of Kerguelen as "this leper of lands in the cold"; of the Araluen River as:

> Daughter of grey hills of wet,
> Born by mossed and yellow wells—

of "Summer's large, luxurious eyes"; of Leichhardt perishing

> On the tracts of thirst and furnace—on the dumb, blind
>   burning plain,
> Where the red earth gapes for moisture, and the wan
>   leaves hiss for rain.

There are memorable pictures of the bush-fire's legacy:

> Black ghosts of trees, and sapless trunks that stood
> Harsh hollow channels of the fiery noise
> Which ran from bole to bole a year before,
> And grew with ruin,

or the sunlight after rain by the Orara:

> The air is full of mellow sounds;
>   The wet hill-heads are bright;
> And, down the fall of fragrant grounds,
>   The deep ways flame with light.

In the finest lyrics Kendall rises to a felicity where the imaginative vision matches the music of the song. (pp. xviii-xxiii)

> *T. Inglis Moore, in an introduction to* Selected Poems
> of Henry Kendall *by Henry Kendall, Angus and Robertson, 1957, pp. vii-xxiii.*

THOMAS THORNTON REED (essay date 1960)

[*Reed is considered the foremost authority on Kendall. In addition to compiling and editing Kendall's complete works, Reed has written a biography of the poet. In the following excerpt from his critical study of Kendall, Reed discusses his use of varied poetic forms. He calls Kendall's work the "poetry of remembrance" because of its highly personal nature and notes the poetic strength in its quietude and peace. Reed maintains that despite the uneven quality of Kendall's work, he remains a "true poet."*]

To those who know only the best of his poetry—the poems which are included in anthologies and selections—Kendall must appear as the singer of sweet and melancholy songs of the beautiful eastern coastlands of the Australian continent, a shy, diffident, and introspective dreamer whose narrow range of music is filled with regretful memories and the consciousness of failure. If, however, one reads his poetical writings as a whole one realises that, although his greatest poems deal with the fertile forests of New South Wales, with wistful longings, opportunities lost or denied, and dreams unfulfilled, there remains a considerable body of verse which deals with other themes and which is often written in happier and livelier moods. In his collected poems are to be found songs of the bush and the sea, tales in verse with Australian, Biblical, and Classical settings, poems of love and passion, popular ballads, and stinging satires. It is true that these fall short of his best work and that the time must come, if it has not already arrived, when his lesser poems will be read only by the student and the enthusiast; yet they have their importance for all who would know of the development of our Australian literature because Kendall was a pioneer in many fields of verse.

Long before Gordon and others had written the bush ballads and galloping rhymes, which have been taken by many as typically Australian poetry, Kendall was experimenting with this type of verse. As early as October 1860 he had written "**The Curlew Song**", and in June 1861 "**Wild Kangaroo**", which he followed in November of the same year with "**The Song of the Cattle Hunters**". (pp. 9-10)

If these songs and others like them—e.g. "**The Opossum Hunters**" . . . , "**On a Cattle Track**" . . . , "**After the Hunt**" . . . and a later poem, "**Song of the Shingle Splitters**" . . .—are compared with the rough bush songs which preceded them and the more popular ones which were to follow from other hands, it will be seen that Kendall falls between two stools. His bush songs fail to reach the height of poetry on the one hand, while on the other they are too poetical to achieve the easy familiarity which marks the true bush ballad. (p. 11)

Nor could he quite attain the sophistication of later poets who carried on the tradition begun by the early unknown singers. Poems such as Gordon's "The Sick Stockrider", or Paterson's "The Man from Snowy River" could never have been written by Kendall. His love of description led him to overlay his ballads, as he overlaid his narrative blank verse, with an ornateness which changes them into something which is neither ballad nor lyric. "**The Opossum Hunters**" is an outstanding example of this trait. . . .

"**Song of the Shingle Splitters**" is the best that Kendall achieved in his peculiar style. . . . (p. 12)

But it was nearly twenty years after his first ballad had been written that the "**Song of the Shingle Splitters**" was composed at Brisbane Water.

The lack of versatility, the ingrained habit of irrelevant description, and the clinging to the formal trappings of verse, which prevented his compassing the careless conversational ease of the best ballads, prevented him from excelling in his poems of the race course. Despite the fact that he was a good horseman and, in his later years, when these verses were written, well acquainted with the turf from his association with the Fagans, who owned and raced horses, his racing poems are filled with conventional and stilted expressions and smell of the study lamp. Their rhythm is perfect but their metaphors and similes sound forced when the poems are compared with

Gordon's "How we Beat the Favourite", or Ogilvie's "How we Won the Ribbon".

On the other hand Kendall's character sketches of bushmen in *Songs from the Mountains* (for example, **"Bill the Bullock Driver"** and **"Jim the Splitter"**) are in their way masterpieces. The metres are simple, the expressions used are natural, and Kendall is completely at his ease. . . . Bill the Bullock Driver, Jim the Splitter, and Jack Hayes are men whom Kendall knew and appreciated for their definite characteristics. Forgetting his "singing robes", he draws them as he knows them, and, unlike the lay figures which too often appeared in his earlier poems, we have men of flesh and blood. (pp. 13-14)

In infancy, childhood, youth, and early manhood Kendall had the opportunity of observing the aborigines of Australia, if not in their purely native state at least uncivilised and retaining many of their customs and much of their independence. At Ulladulla, Wollongong, and Grafton he was in touch with the remnants of native tribes which were fast being dispossessed of their hunting grounds and whose numbers were rapidly dwindling. Between the years 1860 and 1870 he composed several poems about them (e.g. **"Kooroora"**, **"Urara"**, **"Ulmarra"**, **"Uloola"**, **"Aboriginal Death Song"**, and **"The Last of His Tribe"**). The first three of these he included in *Poems and Songs* . . . , and the last in *Leaves from Australian Forests*. . . . In these poems he shows a sympathy with and an understanding of the aborigines. He depicts their savagery, but credits them with being men of like passions with himself. The best of these poems, which is also one of his outstanding lyrical achievements, is **"The Last of His Tribe"**. . . . It was given its present title when it was included in *Leaves from Australian Forests* in 1869. With a deep sincerity and a simplicity of style it expresses, in an appropriate metre, the sadness of a dying race. . . . (pp. 14-15)

His later poems about the aborigines (such as **"Black Lizzie"**, **"Black Kate"**, and **"Peter the Piccaninny"**) are entirely different in character. They deal not with the unspoiled natives but with those de-tribalised and de-graded "blacks" who, living in contact with a civilisation greatly more advanced than their own, had become debased both by their condition of dependence and by the vices they had acquired from the white man. Though he pitied them he could not respect them as he had done their untamed brethren, and his verses deal with them as subjects for playful laughter but do not do so quite as happily as the similar verses of J. Brunton Stephens. In his early poems he had seen them as romantic subjects—in his later verses he gazes upon them with disillusioned eyes.

Kendall produced neither a long narrative poem, nor a group of shorter narrative poems linked by a common theme, though it is probable that he would have done so had the circumstances of his life allowed him sufficient leisure and freedom from anxiety for the work. Short lyrical outbursts may spring forth in the midst of a hurried and distracted life, but composition needing sustained effort and continuous inspiration seldom survives anxiety, interruption, pressing daily work, and intemperate habits. (pp. 15-16)

Kendall wrote only four narrative poems with Australian settings—**"On the Paroo"**, **"A Death in the Bush"**, **"The Glen of Arrawatta"**, and **"Our Jack"**. In these he follows in the steps of Charles Harpur but does not surpass him. Though Harpur is rougher and less musical than Kendall, Harpur is more successful in his "Creek of the Four Graves" than is Kendall in his most ambitious narrative poem, **"Orara"**. . . .

Kendall's treatment allows description to overlay the narrative which, because of its paucity of incident and failure to bring the characters to life, sinks under the verbiage in which it is enveloped. There are rare passages of beauty and isolated lines and phrases which arrest the mind, but the blank verse, though workmanlike, is pedestrian. Kendall lacked the simplicity and verve, needed by the skilled storyteller, and failed to compensate for these failings with a sustained beauty of musical expression which alone could have saved his narrative poetry from the insipidity which pervades it.

Kendall's Biblical narrative poetry is dull. It lacks a deep apprehension of religious truths as well as sharing in the defects of his Australian narrative verse. Though he thought highly enough of **"Achan"** to include it in *Poems and Songs,* and of **"To Damascus"** and **"King Saul at Gilboa"** to include them in *Leaves from Australian Forests,* he did not include **"Elijah"**, **"Manasseh"**, or **"Rizpah"**, which were written in Melbourne between June and December 1870, in *Songs from the Mountains*. If one considers these narrative poems and also his other religious verse (e.g. **"Gehazi"**, **"An Easter Hymn"**, and **"Hymn of Praise"**), one is forced to admit that they appear rather poetical exercises than the outbursts of deep religious fervour, informed with an understanding of the doctrines and truths which underlie the stories and themes involved. Ardent devotion is no guarantee of great religious poetry, it is true, but neither can great religious poetry spring from a loosely held faith. We cannot transmit to others what we have not ourselves. It is not to be understood from this judgment that Kendall's sincerity is to be questioned. He was a man of strong religious convictions and of high moral principles. The contention put forward may best be illustrated by reference to a specific poem, **"An Easter Hymn"**, which by the expressions used in it implies beliefs concerning the Blessed Virgin Mary which Kendall did not hold and which could only have been employed by him in a purely "poetical" sense. The testimony of his son, given to the present writer, and the evidence of his letters support this statement. The fact does not need elaboration and is merely referred to in accounting for his failure as a religious poet. He was well read in the Bible and his poems contain many biblical references which must be lost upon some modern readers but which would have been understood and appreciated by his contemporaries.

Kendall included five poems on Classical themes in *Leaves from Australian Forests* and two in *Songs from the Mountains*. These poems were praised by his contemporaries but have lost favour with succeeding generations. The two written in blank verse—**"The Voyage of Telegonus"** and **"Ogyges"**—are obviously, and admittedly, attempts in the style of Tennyson, and, falling short of his high standard, suffer by comparison. The lyrics—**"Daphne"**, **"Syrinx"**, **"Merope"**, and **"Galatea"**—are pleasant and reveal a sincere affection for the ancient myths but, apart from that, have no claim to the approval or delight of a generation whose education is unlikely to include, in the ordinary course, some Latin and a little Greek and to whom poems on classical themes appear artificial and unjustifiable unless of superlative beauty or deep universal human interest. As with the Bible, so with the Classics, it is only a minority to-day who can read poems containing allusions to these great literatures without frequent recourse to dictionaries and encyclopaedias. If the day ever comes again when every educated man and woman has a working knowledge of the characters of ancient classical mythology and history and of the great men and women of the Scriptures Kendall's poems involving this knowledge may become popular—but not till then. Men may approve their beauty and extol their sentiments, but they will not read them for pleasure.

Though Kendall included only four memorial poems in his volumes of verse he wrote many others during his life and published them in newspapers and periodicals. Some were written to commemorate prominent men of the day with whom Kendall was not personally acquainted, while others, more interesting and intimate, were written in memory of fellow men of letters whom he knew and admired.

Though none of these poems can be ranked amongst his best poetry they are all of great interest because they reveal Kendall's judgment on certain of his contemporaries. (pp. 17-19)

Kendall's ceremonial odes and cantata librettos, though lofty and dignified in strain and revealing capable craftsmanship, are of the head rather than of the heart. They pleased his contemporaries, who delighted in such exercises, and they brought him public recognition and financial benefits—they were deliberately written for those ends—but they are not the work by which he will be remembered as a poet. (p. 21)

Kendall tried his hand at the sonnet, and there remain twenty-eight examples of his work in this beautiful but exacting poetical form. Unfortunately he does not appear to have understood the rigid requirements of the rhyme sequences nor the function of octave and sestet. His sonnets do not follow the Petrarchan, Shakespearean, Spenserian, or Miltonic forms, but are composed of fourteen decasyllabic iambic lines rhymed just as Kendall felt like rhyming them. Many fine expressions and isolated lines of great beauty are to be found in these poems, but there are none, except the two dedicatory sonnets in *Leaves from Australian Forests,* which rise above the handicap Kendall set himself when he disregarded the rules which govern the sonnet.

In his early years Kendall produced a number of conventional love poems (**"Etheline"**, **"Aileen"**, **"Bellambi's Maid"**, **"Clari"** and others), and thought well enough of them to include them in his first book of poems in 1862. Not one of them is distinguished by anything other than the smoothness of its music and the correctness of its sentiments. They do not appear to have sprung from real emotional experience and they undoubtedly touch no chord of emotion in those who read them. As the years passed, however, and his experience deepened he wrote with truer insight and deeper passion. This stronger and fuller tone is found in his second volume of verse, *Leaves from Australian Forests* . . . , and, though to modern ears poems such as **"A Spanish Love Song"**, and **"Campaspe"** seem almost staid in their expressions and sentiments, to our Victorian ancestors they appeared outspoken and frank. (pp. 23-4)

In *Leaves from Australian Forests* are six poems which deal with Kendall's disappointed love for Rose Bennett, the most famous of which is **"Rose Lorraine"**. . . . [This is] the most beautiful love lyric ever written by an Australian. (p. 24)

Throughout his poetical career Kendall delighted to sing of the natural beauties of his native land, confining himself principally to the part he knew intimately and which is the most beautiful portion of the continent—the south-eastern coastline. With the heart to love and the eye to admire scenic loveliness he combined an intimate and firsthand knowledge of the flora and fauna of New South Wales. His pictures, at their best, are vivid, clear, and simple. . . . (p. 29)

It is not often that he paints the sterner aspects of Australian scenery with its "stark desolations and a waste of plain". He

prefers to tell of its "affluence, Which makes the heart of Nature glad", of "noonday dew in cool green grasses", "rainy hill-heads", and

> Folded woods that hide the grace
> Of moss and torrents strong.

But when he does touch upon the sterner side of Australian bush life his pictures are arresting. . . . Poems and passages from poems, in which the great desert tracts of the continent of Australia are described, form a dark background to the gracious greenness of which Kendall most frequently sang. It is well that he wrote of those places because these things are true of by far the greater part of Australia. The cool, moist dells, the bubbling streams, and the sheltered, shady gullies are the exception not the rule.

As a nature poet Kendall is content to be a singer through whose voice the beauties which delight the eye may be transmuted into song. He had no philosophy, gained from the contemplation of or from communion with Nature, which he sought to teach. His outlook was conventionally Christian without trace of incipient animism or pantheism. One may discover passages which would lend themselves, taken in isolation, to theories of Nature worship . . . but they are misleading because they are connected with his theories of poetical inspiration and not with philosophical or religious belief.

Kendall had definite ideas about the nature of poetry and the function of the poet which may be discovered in his poems, his letters, and his prose articles. For him the true poet was the sleepless artist, who drew his inspiration from nature . . . and he acknowledged clearly the sources from which his inspiration was drawn. . . . (pp. 31-3)

Without true inspiration the poet was for Kendall only an "accomplished mechanic". In his very earliest days of writing he said, "I think there is a fearful gap between thought and language. Perhaps there is no rarer endowment of the poet than a gift of exact expression—the power of subjugating language to thought; so that he can conscientiously feel that the whole truth which was in him has been laid before the world in all its unclouded simplicity." Like Wordsworth he sought to express experiences and emotions which were strongly felt, recollecting them in tranquillity and turning them into song. "I like," he said in a letter to Brereton, "the Poetry of Retrospection. When the personal element is prominent, it is always the happiest kind of verse. There is at all times a mellowed beauty associated with the sunsets of yesterday, which we do not find in the noon of to-day, and cannot anticipate for the morn of to-morrow. To-day is too real for us; to-morrow is too mythical for us. But yesterday is for ever like an eloquent background in a noble picture. And therefore, I think, we see clearest and sing sweetest when our thoughts are with the sobered lights and shadows of the days and nights of the past." This considered statement made when he was nearly twenty-six years of age reveals why his poetry is what it is—the poetry of remembrance. That it is wistful remembrance is due to the circumstances of his life. (pp. 34-5)

Though Kendall was forced by circumstances to live in cities for the greater part of his adult life, his heart was always in the bush. His longing to be there is expressed in a number of his poems. . . . (p. 37)

This love of the peace, solitude, and beauty of the bush was one of the reasons why, when he was appointed Inspector of Forests, he left Camden Haven not for Sydney, where he would have been near his headquarters and at the centre from which all his journeys would be taken, but for the little town of Cundle on the Manning River. He loved too the native names of his native land and wove them into his verses—Kiama, Bellambi, Narran, Barwan (Barwon), Arakoon, Paroo, Woolli, Dandenong, Warra (Warrah), Benar, Woollombi, Mooni, Narrara (Narara), Gerringong, Corrimal, Araluen, and Jamberoo; and though he may at times use expressions and terms taken from England and which Australia has not adopted (e.g. dell, lea, glade, runnel, and wold), his descriptions are of a land he knew and loved—the trees are Australian trees, the rivers are Australian rivers, and the bright sunshine and the summer heat belong to a country very different from that whose poets fired his imagination and poured music into his soul.

Yielding himself to the deep and all-pervading love of the Australian bush he pours forth unpremeditated songs in which are blended, without reserve, the innermost experiences of his soul. The ''serene surprises of the sun'', ''the water-moons splendid'', ''the lyre-bird lit on a shimmering space'', the ''fern-matted streams'', and the ''unfooted dells, And secret hollows dear to noontide dew'' all become the vehicles of his own emotional life. Through them he reveals the quiet reflection of his mind, the tender contemplative emotions of his heart, and the past weaknesses of his will. The most beautiful aspects of the natural scenery of Australia are enshrined in songs whose sweetest notes flow from the sadness and the sorrow of human life. Because of this Kendall's strength as a poet is to be sought and found in quietness and peace. This simple serenity marks his earliest work. . . . It also marks his latest. . . . (pp. 37-8)

When all the dross has been noted in Kendall's collected poetical works—and in this critical estimate the temptation to forget his failures has been rigidly avoided—there remains a valuable residue of pure gold. Despite the inequality of his workmanship, his frequently conventional diction, his curious lapses of taste, and his occasional sentimentality, Kendall is nevertheless a true poet. (p. 39)

Above all things Kendall is sincere—he speaks unrestrainedly from his heart and is at no pains to cloak and hide his real character. Had he been more reticent, more defiant, and unrepentant he might have written the robust and objective verses which some have wished that he had written. These would, however, have been false—the projection of an imaginary self into songs whose setting was a real and deep love of Australia. Kendall, the true Kendall, was a shy, diffident man, whose prevailing characteristic was a gentle melancholy, and who unashamedly mingled his personality with all that he wrote. He does not shrink from singing of ''faculties forfeited—hopes beyond reaching''. . . . (pp. 41-2)

There can be no doubt that for all the shyness and diffidence in his character he restrained neither the form nor the content of his verses. Had he revised his poems more severely it is possible that he would have left many thoughts unexpressed but in so doing he would have failed to reveal himself as completely as he did. That revelation is so intimately bound up with the beauty of his work that one can hardly wish that he had been a sterner critic of his poems. But such thoughts and such judgments, since they can avail us nothing, are best set aside in regretful silence. Kendall's gift to his native land is his imperishable poetry in which he himself is for ever revealed—with all his faults and failings. (p. 42)

Thomas Thornton Reed, in his Henry Kendall: A Critical Appreciation, *Rigby Limited, 1960, 66 p.*

A. C. W. MITCHELL   (essay date 1969)

[*In the following excerpt, Mitchell charts the development of Kendall's poetic vision. Outlining what he considers a system of images that reveals a coherent poetic philosophy, Mitchell specifically addresses the importance of forests and water in Kendall's poetry and relates those images to his themes.*]

This essay will be concerned with an examination of Kendall's poetry for a system of images that amount to a loose poetic philosophy, an attitude of mind that is formulated emotionally rather than logically, but in any case consistently. Although one should not attach too much importance to the phrase 'Kendall had brains' (he is a poet, after all, not a philosopher), there is nevertheless a coherence of imagery and themes throughout his poetry. That is one distinguishing feature about Kendall: he is consistent. His poetry all fits together.

To begin with the obvious, Kendall is always writing about forests. The point does not need elaborating, for most of his poems have as their setting a forest. But the forest is little more than a setting. Kendall is instead concerned with what the forest conceals, whether it is a creek or wind or blossom or some other thing. Indeed, it is the fact of concealment itself that intrigues him, and not so much what is concealed. The function of the forest in his nature poems (which include most of his love poems) is primarily to conceal, and consequently to dissipate light and heat. The focus of his attention is on something removed, on the unseen and unknown. (The connection with his poems of lament for absent loved ones is self-evident.) But the forests are always there: they *locate* the emotional statement.

In the forests is a creek, a river, a pool, and because of the forest it is seen only in a diffused light. Sometimes there are clearings into which the sunlight penetrates more clearly, but in any case there is not enough heat and light to negate the coolness of the forest. Half-light, coolness, shade, these are clearly significant details, and often they are implied by the presence of moss—**"Deniehy's Grave," "Bell Birds", "Moss on a Wall"**. The absence of moss in **"The Hut by the Black Swamp"** suggests that for Kendall moss represents more than serenity and undisturbed nature, that it is a sign of grace, just as its pointed absence indicates both depravity and the scorching heat of direct blazing sunlight. Accompanying the refreshing coolness of the dells, glens and gullies are the breezes, the 'woodwinds' which, amplified, become gales and storms, just as the cool light can become the withering heat that causes drought and desert—the harsh realities. One of the reasons why **"Christmas Creek"** and **"Leichhardt"** fail as poems is that the realities are brought into too close juxtaposition to the ideal. The artifice is excessively apparent without the forests as a buffer. Kendall's common practice is to widen the divorce between the two by establishing his creeks within a context of poetic dream, the impulse to creativity; and since the creek is more often remembered than immediate, it is removed from the hostile present. This is not an evasion of the poet's responsibility to face the reality of the present; it is instead a means of safeguarding the mystery of that which is most vital to Kendall, the ideal. He takes it as almost axiomatic that the present is hostile to the poetic sensibility.

In brief, this amounts to a polarity of the real and the ideal, in which Kendall associates the ideal with the creative impulse and with Nature, and the real with the sordid actuality of city life and the hot plains that deny the sentiments he attaches to Nature. Thus the 'ballads', which self-consciously draw attention to their departure from the poetical (**"No poet is Bill"**,

"**Jim is poetical rarely**"), either have very little relation to Kendall's favourite landscapes and define a social environment instead, or use the contrast to stress the insensitivity of their subjects. . . . Admittedly this amounts to little more than the conventional opposition between nature and society—the city is all din and noise and strife, the forests are quiet and blessed and sacrosanct. But there is a difference, and it is Kendall's variation from the conventional that invites the reader's critical interest. Kendall does not really know very much about his creeks—they come from somewhere up in the mountains and they go down to the sea, itself a massive and ambivalent symbol. Judith Wright has identified the mountain as an important symbol for Kendall [see excerpt dated 1965], but she protests too much, I think, in interpreting it as a father-figure. Donovan Clarke rightly contends that the sea is an important image, but he does not relate it to Kendall's real themes [see excerpt dated 1957-58]. What is needed is a larger scheme which embraces both sea and mountain as well as the rest of Kendall's imagistic and thematic preoccupations.

The creek is the vital connection; and as was suggested above, in some way it connotes the ideal, the poetic vision. The point is that these creeks have been seen. That is, for Kendall the ideal exists, it is actual. Now it will be recalled that in "**Orara**" he speculates about the upper brook—the creek must come from somewhere, from lands untrodden and unknown. A new world is guaranteed, where is to be found

> that light for which I look
> In vain through all the world.

The little scenes of beauty he has seen, and remembered, and celebrated in his poems are fragments of the larger vision which, it is important to note, is conceived in terms of light. The creek is the overflow into the real world of some hidden natural reservoir. In other words, Kendall's pattern of images represents a transcendentalist scheme, where up in the cool mountains is the rarer air, the finer tone, the higher transcendental experience, and down on the plains are the soulless cities and commonplace reality, exposure to dust and the burning sun. It is not a profoundly thought out system—Kendall was no Kant or Emerson, although he may very well have read them in J. L. Michael's library, for example. And in any case his system of thought is in the first place conceived in poetic terms, in images. Most certainly it is articulated in images.

Sometimes he translates his thought into a specifically religious frame of reference. There is a fairly strong religious vein in Kendall, and Inglis Moore quotes him: 'I recognize in Poetry a revelation of Divinity beyond all revelations, a religion past all religions'. Moore is ambiguous in arguing that Kendall reaches out for a universal significance, but it is true enough that Kendall reaches out after something undefined. That is where the larger body of Kendall's work meets with his religious poetry, where the indefinite or undefined is contemplated with religious feeling. And one might add that the process of 'indefinition' is functional. . . . To take two such unlikely examples as "**Song of the Shingle Splitters**" and "**Bill the Bullock Driver**", one finds that they express an attitude, which might as well be called religious, towards the celebration of that ideal which Kendall intuitively knew to be located in nature—not in landscape but in nature—but which continually eluded him. The poems don't really posit the presence of God in the bush; besides, it was customary then to think of the bush as especially God-forsaken. The difference between Kendall and Bill the Bullock Driver is that Kendall is aware of the sacred nature of the hills where the ideal, focused for the moment in the idea

of God, may be revered, adored, celebrated, or what you will. Bill, on the other hand, is blissfully oblivious to the living glory about him. Similarly, when Kendall writes 'God in the woodland dwells', he is more interested in what this says about the woodland than what it says of God's whereabouts. And the context of the poem bears this out—the birds singing 'sweet hymns by the waterfalls' informs us of the attitude of the listener rather than about who is being praised in the hymns and why.

Kendall's poetic frame of reference clarifies itself progressively throughout his career. Clearly, selected poems show this much more convincingly than others. I have chosen to remark on certain of Kendall's better known poems for the sake of convenience, although the miscellaneous poems that Reed has collected together confirm the points that are made here. Three poems from Kendall's first volume, "**The Song of the Cattle Hunters**", "**The Barcoo**", and "**The Muse of Australia**", while not particularly remarkable in themselves, serve to introduce Kendall's imagistic scheme.

The first line of "**The Song of the Cattle Hunters**" is typical of him: 'While the morning light beams on the fern-matted streams'. Morning light is not strong light, which is anathema to Kendall, yet it has to penetrate the ferns in order to beam on the streams. The word 'beam' is in fact too strong for the sense, and it is justified only by the demand for an internal rhyme. This establishes a principle which looms large in Kendall's poetic practice: he is perfectly happy to compromise the sense, provided that the sound remains melodious. It is pertinent that he habitually referred to his poems as 'songs', whereas Adam Lindsay Gordon, for example, insisted on calling his poems 'rhymes'—the distinction underlines the very different preconceptions these two had about poetry, and indicates at least some of the reasons for their widely dissimilar achievements.

Streams hidden amongst the ferns are seen only in glimpses, in the morning light; but having announced the poetic setting, Kendall apparently abandons these details as he is carried away by the rhythm. Yet there is also the scale of value mentioned before—the cattle hunters gallop down from the ridges and gullies to the yardrails on the plain. Up in the ridges and gullies is where the echoes and caves and fern-matted streams are, whereas down on the lowlands and plains the echoes die away, even if the lowlands are filled with 'sound'. Kendall is fond of such indefinite words as sound, song, cry, note, noise, voice, tone and tune. All these are deliberately chosen because they are imprecise. What kind of a sound is 'sound'? The only means we have of defining the indefinite here is by the sound pattern. In the lines

> Like a wintry shore that the waters ride o'er,
> All the lowlands are filling with sound,

the full vowel sounds indicate a kind or roaring like the thunder of waves in the first stanza.

In "**The Barcoo**" the action is reversed: 'we', the squatters, leave the plains that are dotted with sheep and cattle, and depart for the unknown, or at least unfamiliar. In "**The Song of the Cattle Hunters**", the riders descended from the upper levels of the unknown to the unmysterious, domestic and familiar plains. Leaving the 'blind courses / And sources of rivers that all of us know', the squatters

> speed for a Land where the strange Forests sleep
> And the hidden creeks bubble and brattle!

The sleeping forests are related to Kendall's poetic dream, but that does not emerge until later. The immediate point is the juxtaposition of the strange forests and the lively hidden streams. The adjective 'blind' applied to what is known, is cryptic. The river courses are blind because they lead nowhere, figuratively and metaphorically. The metaphor is more interesting—the known is limited precisely because it is known; hence one seeks the unknown, the indefinite. That is why the streams are so often hidden from the full light of day. Exposed, they become dried up; or known, they become unmysterious, blind. The paradox can be presented in these terms: Kendall is vitally aware of the unknown, the intuited. Bill the Bullock Driver, we saw, was unaware of 'the mighty magnificent temples of God / In the hearts of the dominant hills'. Kendall uses the adjective 'blind' there too. Bill is blind to the hills because he sees too easily. That is, he does not *see* them, he merely perceives.

The second stanza of **"The Barcoo"** announces the symbolic quest, the searching for waters. Most often the quest remains a speculation in the mind, a meditation that pursues the stream up through forests and mountains to its source. Much less frequently it faces the possibility of confronting 'beds of hot gravel / And clay-crusted reaches where moisture hath been'.

The third of these early poems, **"The Muse of Australia"**, locates that elusive and hard-pressed damsel in the mountains. There is a variation on the hidden stream motif: the poet has caught a faint glimpse of the Muse. That momentary vision is submerged, however, and it is sound that becomes dominant:

> I never can reach you, to hear the sweet voice
> So full with the music of fountains!

His complaint is that she has not heeded his solicitations, or those of any other poet for that matter. No one has yet led her down from the heights; the word 'here' is important—'Who will lead you down here from the mountains?' His present plane is not up in the regions that the muse inhabits. Of course this is purely conventional, imitating the Greek muses on the heights of Olympus; these are Australian mountains inhabited by a local muse, and he as a poet has not been permitted to ascend the scale of ideality. His vision is limited to the prosaic 'down here'—and yet he has caught a faint glimpse of her.

Then comes a surprising shift in tone, and it is in this that Kendall shows his true colours as a poet. We don't really accept this fiction of muses roaming about the mountains, pursued by imploring would-be poets. Kendall suddenly switches from thin conventional posturing to the intensely real:

> A lyre-bird lit on a shimmering space;
> It dazzled mine eyes, and I turned from the place,
> And wept in the dark. . . .

Unfortunately this is followed by more in the previous vein, which effectively ruins the poem and the impact of those unprecedented and surprisingly intense lines. Given the situation, the search for the Muse, it does not take much to depersonalise the young lady, however appealing: she stands revealed as a somewhat clumsy personification of the ideal. On other occasions the ideal is a utopia, or euphoria, or the headwaters of a creek, and so on. The poem then says that the ideal, the transcendental, has eluded the poet, as it always must. The lyre-bird, however, is a sign, a promise. One notices that it appears in 'a shimmering space', and dazzles the eyes. The point is stressed because Kendall frequently makes a statement through some detail of the intensity of light. Here the shim-

mering space reflects too much light. It is perhaps a warning not to approach too close to the sphere of the ideal. One can see too much, after all; it is not good for us, given the human condition, to be exposed to too much light, to too intense a vision. The poet turns away from the place where he has seen the bird, because the incident registers for him a moment of intense experience, a momentary confrontation with something from the realm of the ideal. The intensity is, in typical romantic fashion, both delightful and painful to him. That ambiguity is contained in the verb 'dazzled'. He has to turn away, not as a denial but as an admission of his human inability to entertain or confront any manifestation of the transcendental. He acknowledges as much when he weeps in the dark.

One of the earlier poems of the second volume, **"The Last of His Tribe"** . . . , displays the same frame of reference but is more interesting in the way it demonstrates Kendall's use of the poetic dream. An aborigine is turned into a hunter again as he relives the past in his mind, in a context of wind and rain and thunder. The hunting is remembered, not actual, just as Kendall's streams are remembered rather than actual. The moaning of a creek replies to the aborigine's own mournfulness, and establishes some identification between his life and the natural order, so that the echo he hears from the hills *is*, for him, a corroboree song. The 'streamy' nature of association leads him further and further into the recollected past, until finally he is confronted by the woman that gleams like a Dream. She is in fact part of his dream, a dream which has become so vivid to him that the figure being dreamed has become actual. Once again it is the gleaming that, like dazzling and shimmering, emphasizes the intensity of this moment. It is worth remarking on the opposition between thought and dream here. Kendall, like many of the mid-nineteenth-century poets, and not just those in Australia, used the device of the poetic dream fairly often, in a sense with which perhaps we no longer sympathize, at least not readily. The dream is one of the poet's mental processes; it does have some relation to thought. It is associated with the visionary, and seems to be a means of apprehending or intuiting the transcendental. Since the transcendental is essentially the undefined, the vagueness and 'indefinition' of dreaming is particularly appropriate in this process of apprehension. So here the aborigine has proceeded beyond the stage of cogitation, of smouldering thought, when one is aware of distinctions in time for example, of the separation of the past from the present. He has proceeded beyond thought to dream, which is a no less viable order of contemplation. The dream does not focus precisely on remembered actions but depends on the strength of the emotions aroused by those recollections for its immediacy; and when the emotion is overpowering, the dream becomes so intense that it merges into present reality. So the woman steps out of the dream to beckon him to his ancestors, and she is seen in terms of that strange mysterious light which bathes all Kendall's heightened perceptions. That is to say, the last stanza transcends the level of perception of the preceding stanza, which conveys only a speculative vision. The poem moves towards the spiritual, whether the spirit-woman is one of the aboriginal creator beings or whether one prefers to think of her in specifically Christian terms as of an angelic order of being. The real point lies in the Dream. The poem resolves itself into a contemplation of ideal being, of the higher life made viable through the dream process, and presented within a context of stream, wind, forest and echoes. (pp. 102-09)

[*Leaves from Australian Forests*] begins with a dedication followed by two prefatory sonnets. The second of these is a modest confession of some over-enthusiastic imitation of other poets, **"Stray echoes from the elder sons of Song"**. The first sonnet is much more interesting because it combines allusions to a number of the themes and images that comprize Kendall's poetic frame of reference; and the statement is such as to confirm that this is no unconscious pattern that is being elucidated. It is an important poem, for it reveals Kendall's understanding of his own aims and attitudes and achievements as a poet; it is as important as another contemporary statement, Gordon's dedicatory poem in *Bush Ballads and Galloping Rhymes*. Indeed, it is not impossible that Gordon's 'A Dedication' is in part a reply to Kendall.

Kendall does not see himself as a wild romantic—he is no Byron or Shelley or Poe, all of them very much in vogue at the time. Rather, his poetry is, or is in intention, 'a cunning harmony of words and music'. Harmony rather than passion: we arrive at that conclusion ourselves anyway, but Kendall too was quite aware of his preference. In practice he emphasized the music more than the words, if by words one understands the literal statement. (pp. 109-10)

Kendall derives his harmony from glen and height, and 'lucid colours born of woodland light'. We have seen that the glens and heights signify the transcendental vision, that they locate the ideal; our attention is now directed to the forest light and the shining places of the sea-streams. These recall the dazzling lyre-bird and shimmering space in virtually the equivalent 'prefatory' poem of the first volume, for lucid properly means not clear but shining, bright, resplendent. All this excitement in the luminous and visionary belongs to the past, however, for this was the kind of poetry he tried to write in the ardour of his youth (heat means ardour and vitality here, and is not to be confused with that other withering heat that evaporates both the forest-streams and the lyric impulse).

The sestet of the sonnet concedes a kind of defeat: the intensity of the vision has faded, his poetic statement is halting and faulty. And yet he still claims certain true accents that catch the 'sense'—that is, they capture our sensibility in the sporadic moments when he manages to convey something of his own response to the unfooted dells and secret hollows. And he indicates the intensity of his experience by confusing not the senses but the natural scene; here, for example, he focuses on an apparent paradox in the noontide dew. Dew, more commonly associated with morning or evening, is referred instead to the height of day. Secret forest hollows, here and elsewhere in his poetry, are valued precisely because they permit and preserve the rarer state of being.

Inevitably in a study of Kendall, one comes round to remarking on **"Bell Birds"**. Such remarks are generally directed towards the poem's verbal facility and its sound pattern; but to leave these aside for the moment, it is enough to argue that from the present point of view the details are all consistent with it. The echoes in the first line are of course the echoes of the birds' song, yet here as elsewhere what prompts the echo is not so important as the echo itself. In the remote forest glens, the natural conditions are amenable to echoes, and conversely echoes are a sign, a guarantee, of the sanctity of that particular locality. Echoes, birdsong, forest breezes, and sounds of creeks and waterfalls all comprize for Kendall the audible manifestation of the ideal—the truly, because naturally, harmonious.

The stream *lives* in the mountain, and through the various trees struggles the 'light that is love to the flowers'. Kendall is unusually explicit here about his interpretation of the filtered light that preoccupies him. It represents love because it is a benediction, a blessing. Open sunlight is too strong, is destructive, whereas this softer light caresses rather than distresses. It is more the heat that is filtered out than the light.

There has been some critical exception taken to the couplet

> And softer than slumber, and sweeter than singing
> The notes of the bell-birds are running and ringing.

Inglis Moore, for example, complained that the notes of the bird are not soft, but sharp metallic tinkles, and that they come ringing but not running [see excerpt dated 1956]. The original energy of the poem, he says, is dissipated in a welter of words. That is true, but it misses the point, which is that the blurring of detail is deliberate. Kendall was not Gould, nor was he merely describing the landscape. He didn't want to be precise, to be definite, for to define is to limit and to fragment experience where he was attempting to construct a sense of completeness, of organic wholeness with which to identify himself, if not of the transcendental interfusion of things. It has already been seen how the dream acts as a medium between the real and the ideal, and that is why the echoing birdsong is softer than slumber. Similarly, singing implies the whole orchestra of natural sound, and that explains how the bell-birds can be 'sweeter than singing', because this is an intimation of the rarer order of things. In just this poem alone, it is to be noted how often Kendall indicates the desired interfusion: rain and sunbeams are mingled together, colours are grouped, the 'watermoons' scatter and blend, his memories of childhood are mixed with the sights and sounds of the forest, songs are interwoven, and of course there is the famous—or infamous—'sing in September their songs of the Maytime'. The effect of this interfusion is to suggest a new dimension, a private sanctuary out of time, remote from the tyranny of the city and its alleys, and safe from the oppression of sun and heat ('When fiery December sets foot in the forest'). We penetrate beyond the temporal and mutable to a timeless and changeless existence. It is both real and unreal—unreal, because we can't really know it, except from such fragmentary evidence as the bell-birds, the creeks, the echoes and the dazzling lyre-bird, and yet real precisely because we have that evidence. The bell-birds exist only as voices and songs, they are not seen. (pp. 110-12)

[In *Songs from the Mountains*,] Kendall's statement of his poetic themes becomes much more precise. Although his poems begin to decline from the nervous vitality of his middle period, this is compensated by increased assurance and control in technique. By the time Kendall had mastered his medium and discovered his subject, his talent was on the wane. Still, the controlling vision remained with him. It would be excessively wearisome to reiterate the same set of poetic coordinates in relation to the poems of this volume; it is sufficient to draw attention to a couple of poems in which Kendall is explicit about his themes. (p. 112)

["**Mooni**"] opposes his remorse and sense of offence to that 'power in forest places' he had celebrated in happier moments. The unusually direct religious statement can be accounted for by his excessive conviction of shame; our present interest, however, is in his lament for lost innocence, his nostalgia for the days when he was

> the shining sharer
> Of that larger life, and rarer
> Beauty. . . .

Once again the luminous quality is expressed in an unusual context. He is the *shining* sharer, and the detail is repeated a few stanzas later when he recalls the metamorphosis that sometimes used to take place in him:

> When the large supreme occasion
> Brought the life of inspiration,
> Like a god's transfiguration
> Was the shining change in me.

All this took place in the hallowed precincts of Mooni Creek, where still the noonday dew gleams in the cool green grass, and the River Spirit dreams. His poignant regret is that he no longer has access to this secret, private inner world; by his recent lapse, he has exiled himself to 'the burning Outer world— its sneers and spurning'.

Most of the preceding comments are applicable to **"Orara"**. It is not the only poem that attempts to include within itself Kendall's complete vision, for **"After Many Years"** to name just one tries to achieve this; in a sense all of the poems do. **"Orara"** more successfully than any of them expounds Kendall's intuitive apprehension of the transcendental. When he writes of the radiant brook unknown to him beyond its upper turn, one pauses at the quality of that radiance. The next stanza repeats the emphasis, for he hears the 'singing silver life'. It is possible to restrict the meaning of this, for if 'silver life' is a metaphor for the creek that 'lives' like the one in **"Bell Birds"**, then Kendall has stated no more than that he listens to the sound of the creek. But there is more, if only by suggestion. The metaphor carries its own vitality; it insists on a new order of experience. The creek promises an untrodden land, it has a hidden source that is denied to him. Yet he can accept that loss because the light that he has been seeking exists within his 'dream'. It is a shining, 'diviner green and gold', the rarer beauty that is partly manifested in the filtered light of the creeks and the forests. It is, then, no absolute loss, provided that he maintains belief in his poetic vision. Indeed, it would not do to confront the transcendental, to test his radiant Dream, for its validity depends upon 'that nameless grace, The charm of the Unknown'. One appreciates how Kendall throughout his career had been working towards this point, through the allusive and indefinite, the blurred outlines and the deliberately imprecise nouns and adjectives. It is a limited transcendentalism, however, a philosophy of aspiration and vision adequate to support his poetry. It is a personal 'myth' constructed to account for the mystery of his controlling vision, and expressed most commonly in terms of light. In this poem Kendall at last discovered his subject and reconciled himself to the impossibility of achieving any but the most limited identification with the ideal, and if not for the first time here, then this is his most effective exposition of his new acceptance. He renounces vain striving and within the terms of his pattern of thought accepts his limitations, content that

> My spirit fancies it can hear
> The song I cannot sing.

The dedicatory poem of the third volume repeats this conclusion (**"After Many Years"** appeared in print before **"To a Mountain"**): while acknowledging the transfigured life and the light ineffable, it also confesses Kendall's growing inability to articulate his Dream.

Towards the end of his life Kendall wrote:

> I have led a hard life full of sorrow and toil;
> hence the work I have done in the domain of

literature is only a poor adumbration of what I might have accomplished in happier circumstances.

He was grovelling in his own despondency, but at the same time it reminds us that his whole attitude is in the conditional tense. Everything is in terms of what might be, or what might have been. It is debatable whether this indicates pessimism or persistent hopefulness—a gloomy optimism. His is a philosophy of the unattained and unattainable ideal. He is not to be under-rated, just as he is not to be accepted at his own appraisal. After much effort he discovered what Brennan was later to say so much more simply: 'We use poetry to express not the perfect beauty, but our want of it, our aspiration towards it', and in tracing the process of this discovery we follow Kendall's development from a colonial acceptance of the tritely poetical towards a more sincere, because more painfully evolved, awareness of what poetry is. (pp. 112-14)

> *A. C. W. Mitchell, "The Radiant Dream: Notes on Henry Kendall," in* Australian Literary Studies, *Vol. 4, No. 1, May, 1969, pp. 99-114.*

KENNETH SLESSOR (essay date 1970)

[*Unlike many critics, including Green (see Additional Bibliography), Slessor contends that Kendall's work does not genuinely reflect the sorrows of his life. Indeed, he considers Kendall's "principal failure as a poet . . . [to be] his inability to derive any deeper poetic significance from experience than a superficial statement of sad facts."*]

With the exception of a very few pieces—four or five at the most—that come uncomfortably close at times to lachrymose self-pity or even to the pangs of post-alcoholic repentance, Kendall's work does not seem to have been darkened by the successive calamities of his life. Indeed, it often keeps up a kind of Christmas cracker chirpiness that would make the world seem all anapaests and "elfin bells" and "blue-eyed days".

In verses such as the "Dedication" of his *Poems,* the lines to his daughter Araluen or the piece called **"Persia"**, there is a sense of guilty self-reproach mingled with allusions to his "suffering" and "bitterness". (p. 81)

But the "suffering" and "bitterness" are not analysed in the writing that comes out of them. They cause no spiritual or philosophic change; they do nothing to the poet or his poetry. There is no hardening of the will, no summoning up of either courage or detachment, only a damp kind of remorse and self-flagellation. Instead, Kendall is off into abstractions that have nothing to do with human realities, into "dells of dewy myrtle" and "the glory of a larger sky On slopes of hills sublime". The verses called **"On a Street"** are said by H. M. Green to be "a terrible piece of half-concealed autobiography". Kendall, on the other hand, said that the verses refer to "poor W—— ——of Melbourne". If Green is correct and Kendall is really writing about a personal experience, **"On a Street"** must be assumed to touch the very bottom of hopeless self-abasement. Yet Kendall can come to no conclusion about his moral prostration, he can offer no cure for his own disease, all he can produce is a final rather hurried reference to Jesus Christ's mercy and promptly, as if a wand were waved, the sun comes out, the "woods" are bright with gold and green, and we are back with the dingles and dells and elfin bells again. (p. 82)

[**"On a Street"**] illustrates Kendall's principal failure as a poet—that is, his inability to derive any deeper poetic significance from experience than a superficial statement of sad facts. It would be possible to demonstrate this failure in many other of Kendall's works, but I propose to deal now only with a few of his verses that have been quoted in anthologies or mentioned approvingly by critics. H. M. Green is one of those critics, and he is a critic whom I greatly respect, for he is capable of cool detachment yet at the same time of that illuminating fervency without which literary comment would become as factual and bony as arithmetic. Green has declared that, in his poem called **"Orara"**, Kendall was "able to maintain a high level almost throughout". The height of a level, of course, must be measured from a defined base, and if Green's base is taken to mean the plane of reasonably good poetry, I feel compelled to disagree with him. It *is* a high level, perhaps, if it is considered on the scale of much of Kendall's other verse, but even so this level is not maintained "almost throughout". (p. 83)

If choice by anthologies offers any guide, Kendall's best work is evidently considered to be **"September in Australia"**. These verses have been reprinted steadily in almost every general collection of Australian poetry published in the last half-century. The title, **"September in *Australia*"**, seems to me to declare at once a self-conscious attitude, as if Kendall's eyes were on those English "sons of song" for whose approval Harpur yearned, reminding them of the peculiar and perhaps rather regrettable natural fact that in this country Spring comes in September and not in May. The verses (like **"Beyond Kerguelen"**, **"Lilith"**, **"Moss on a Wall"**, **"Narrara Creek"** and several others) might be said to belong to the dwarf-Swinburne school—that is to say, Swinburne, after a considerable amount of brandy, might have had some difficulty in remembering whether or not he had written them in somebody's album during the course of the night. (p. 85)

By far the greatest quantity of Kendall's verse, however, is written, not in Swinburnian metres, but in the long, lolloping line of Tennyson's "Locksley Hall". There are pages and pages of **"Euterpe"**, **"Hy-Brasil"**, **"Araluen"**, **"Mary Rivers"**, **"Pytheas"**, **"Leichhardt"**, **"Coogee"**, **"Christmas Creek"**, **"The Fate Of The Explorers"**, **"Sutherland's Grave"**, and **"Fainting By The Way"**, all equally hard on the wind and exhausting to the patience in their sing-song protractions. Lord Tennyson himself may be considered to have overindulged in these fatally easy and temptingly capacious trochees which allow so much margin for a rhyme to be found by even the dullest-witted poet. Yet Tennyson wrote only 98 couplets in the metre, most of them technically superb. Kendall wrote more than 270, most of them laborious and artificial.

I must touch very quickly on a few other verses that have been praised or quoted. **"Bell-Birds"** has been given prominence, I suppose, because its subject is so pleasantly associated in most readers' minds with Australian scenery. But it is essentially "woodland" English in character and allusion, and it is badly written at that—mosses and sedges, banks and ledges, "brakes of the cedar and sycamore bowers"—if it were not for the "creeks", these bell-birds could sing in Berkeley Square. Moreover it contains two atrocious rhymes, "unfolden-golden" and "childhood-wildwood".

"Mooni" is more pretentious but just as defective. What can be said to excuse lines like "Winds may hiss with heat, and hurtle", or "Feels in flowerful forest arches" or "Like the affluent morning dream" or "Sin and shame have left their trace" or "When the large, supreme occasion" or "Something of the grand old season"? **"After Many Years"** is pretty and trivial and sentimental and as English Victorian as bulrushes

and pampas grass and pressed flowers, with its "woodland music", its "brood", its inevitable "rose" and its "slopes of moss".

If I believed in the psycho-analytical approach to criticism of verse, which I don't, I would probably be able to find a reason for Kendall's curious obsession with moss. If the term may be used, his lines are larded with moss. It grows everywhere, in short lines, in long lines, in anapaests, in trochees, in sonnets or in odes, and it is generally rhymed with "floss". I feel that Kendall would certainly have ended his life more happily if, towards the close of his lugubrious career, Sir Henry Parkes had seen fit to appoint him, not an Inspector of Forests, but an Inspector of Moss. (pp. 87-8)

> *Kenneth Slessor, "Kendall and Gordon," in his* Bread and Wine: Selected Prose, *Angus and Robertson, 1970, pp. 74-91.**

A. D. HOPE   (essay date 1973)

[*In the following excerpt from his introduction to a collection of Kendall's works, Hope calls for a reassessment of his poetry. According to Hope, Kendall's critical reputation and reception have been marred by three prevailing views, which he labels "false, partial, or irrelevant": 1) that Kendall is primarily a nature poet, although his works do not exclusively depict the Australian landscape, 2) that his works show the influence of other writers, and "imitation is always deplorable," and 3) that much of Kendall's verse is humorous, satirical, and polemical, which "cannot be poetry of the highest order."*]

The earliest writers of a country have an interest which does not depend on their literary merits alone. They are articulate voices from a past which has left fewer first-hand impressions than we should like to have. We can see in their work the beginning of characteristic styles and traditional attitudes of mind and, even if they were not very good writers, the fact that they were the first leads us to treat their faults with a certain indulgent regard. Henry Kendall shares this indulgence but his claim to attention rests on the fact that he was a true poet, that his best work is still very much alive and has survived on its merits, and not merely for its historical interest. (p. ix)

Kendall's poetry, like his character, needs some reassessment. Criticism has not dealt with it unfairly. There is a limit to what can be profitably said of the work of a minor poet and there is not much new that can be said about Kendall's. But some false, partial, or irrelevant views have come to be taken almost for granted and distort his real achievement as a result. There are, in the main, three of these. The first is the idea that Kendall is primarily a poet of nature and concerned with natural description. This in itself is questionable, but it has led to irrelevant argument as to whether Kendall was able to describe Australian scenery in its own terms, whether his was genuine *Australian* poetry or not, so that the only relevant question: whether it was genuine *poetry* or not, was sometimes overlooked. This concern with national character, in turn, has acquired a bare semblance of discussing a literary question, because of the assumption that Australia must eventually develop a distinct and distinctive language, literature, and culture of its own. Thus any writing that was not readily distinguishable from the main body of English letters was apt to be condemned as second-hand and therefore second-rate. If one clears the mind of this tedious cant, it is easy to see that a good poem like **"King Saul at Gilboa"** is no worse because its subject is not Australian and that a bad poem like **"September in Aus-**

tralia" is no better because its subject is. And the latter is not a bad poem because it describes the Australian landscape, or weather, in September in terms so general and in language so 'English' that it has no distinctively Australian note about it. It is a bad poem because it is full of meretricious verbal tricks, tasteless metrical jingles, vapid ideas, and embarrassing platitudes of feeling. . . . (pp. xv-xvi)

"To a Mountain," on the other hand, is equally 'general' in its language. There is nothing to show that this is an Australian mountain in the Australian bush except for the fact the poet is writing in Australia, and it is not only a good poem but one of Kendall's best. It is a beautiful and elevated invocation, in plain and moving language, Kendall's profession of faith and his central vision of the world he celebrates. . . . It is a noble and sustained music which, whatever it may owe to Wordsworth and Tennyson, is Kendall's own voice. Had he been an English poet writing in England it would have won him a recognition sometimes denied or grudgingly bestowed by critics who would like it to include a few gum trees, bungalows and woolly-butts to guarantee that it is a genuine Australian product.

Kendall saw himself as a descriptive poet. He felt his task to be that of assimilating the scenery and the aspects of nature in a new country to the poetic tradition of another and thereby transplanting and continuing the tradition. But he also felt himself, as Wordsworth did, to be the chosen instrument and voice of nature, deeply inspired and not merely deliberate in his choice of subject. . . . Those who have disputed Kendall's opinion of himself have usually overlooked the fact that both the language of poetry that Kendall and his readers accepted and the scenery they knew have changed since the nineteenth century. In fact it is because Kendall felt at home with the traditional vocabulary of poetry and did not feel it necessary to drag in many specifically Australian terms, that he is sometimes accused of writing 'like an Englishman.' The truth about Kendall's nature poems is that there are some real successes and that the same prevailing weakness spoiled many others as spoiled much of his narrative, lyric, and satirical verse. **"Beyond Kerguelen,"** for example, which so impressed critics as different as Roy Campbell and Oscar Wilde, is indeed impressive. But it is so in spite of its tedious and sometimes inept double rhymes, its obtrusive, meaningless and quite inexorable alliteration, and the number of trite and flabby epithets in its description. In fact it is a puzzle how it should still manage to convey its impression of gloomy power under all this frippery, as it undoubtedly does.

On the whole it is better to consider Kendall's best poems than to argue that his strength lay in one particular poetic mode. If other modes have not been given their due, it is because of the persistence of certain critical fallacies, which were common in the last century and, long after they have been discredited elsewhere, still appear in our estimates of Australian poets. One of these fallacies has already been touched on and there are two others which have affected the assessment of Kendall's poetry. One is the notion that imitation is always deplorable and usually a mark of inferior work, and the other is the notion that humorous, satirical, and polemical verse cannot be poetry of the highest order or cannot be poetry at all.

Much of Kendall's poetry shows clear influences of other poets in style and verse technique. He was well aware of this and

in the second of the two fine sonnets that served as preface to his *Leaves from Australian Forests* he admits it:

> So take these kindly, even though there be
>   Some notes that unto other lyres belong:
>   Stray echoes from the elder sons of Song;
> And think how from its neighbouring, native sea
> The pensive shell doth borrow melody.

Nor was it simply a matter of involuntary echoes. There is evidence that Kendall carefully studied the technique of Tennyson's verse of which his own catches many familiar mannerisms. It has been pointed out that Kendall was writing in a style which might have been taken as an imitation of Swinburne, before Swinburne. . . . [Indeed,] Kendall has learned something from Swinburne, has improved on his mentor and yet is definitely and characteristically himself. He was in addition well aware of the faults of the more obvious, the melodiously unmeaning Swinburne, and could parody them to good effect as he does in his satire on a sectarian sermon against the Roman Catholics, **"A Psalm for the Conventicle."** No one who reads this delightful and technically sophisticated skit in its entirety could imagine Kendall a slavish or unconscious imitator of Swinburne. (pp. xvi-xix)

[The] poems of Kendall's which show the influence of poets such as Tennyson and Swinburne, and which have subjects not connected with this country, have often been underrated in comparison with inferior poems of more direct local appeal. It may be said that on occasion imitation saved Kendall from errors of taste and judgement to which he was prone but on other occasions it was imitation of admired models which led him into it. He was rarely happy with running or tripping metres. If he learned a nobler music from the blank verse of Tennyson, he fell a prey to the sentimental language and metres of *Maud*. He was seduced by the vapid prettiness of Poe and the vulgar lyric tenor of Moore's Irish melodies. Swinburne confirmed his liking for excessive and crude alliteration, and Browning perhaps for clumsy and inept feminine rhymes. The trochaic eight-foot couplets of 'Locksley Hall' seem particularly to have taken his fancy and he nearly always used them inappropriately. But when all this is said there remains enough poetry of quality to keep his name alive.

Finally there is his satiric and humorous verse. A good deal of this fails outright, though it seemed to have been successful enough at the time. But in some of it Kendall shows that, like most of the poets before him, Wentworth, Robinson, Tompson, and Harpur in particular, the late eighteenth-century tradition in poetry was still alive for him. He could write heroic couplets with point and finish. Though the language at times betrays the Victorian taste, the movement of the lines is Augustan. . . . [His] is a style that owes nothing to Romantic and Victorian practice. Kendall wrote a good deal of his best poetry in heroic couplets. **"The Austral Months"** deliberately breaks up the closed couplet form but the dedication to *Leaves from Australian Forests,* **"King Saul at Gilboa," "The Sydney International Exhibition," "The Far Future," "The Gagging Bill,"** and **"The Bronze Trumpet,"** show how versatile he was with the Augustan verse form and the surprising effects he could produce with what was regarded in his day as an exhausted style. The prejudice against Augustan verse and Augustan canons of poetry and the prejudice against formal satire are both still very much alive and appreciation of Kendall's work has suffered accordingly. It is for this reason, for example, that one of his finest and best sustained poems, that on the Sydney International Exhibition, is so often dismissed either as competent rhetoric or as a dignified and capable exercise which never manages to achieve poetry.

If one comes to Kendall's poetry freed from the sorts of critical bias I have mentioned, his achievement may wear a different look from that usually set on it. (pp. xx-xxii)

The lyric mode is commonly said to be that in which Kendall was most at home. It is true that his best known and most popular poems are lyrics like **"Bell-birds," "September in Australia," "Rose Lorraine,"** and **"The Last of his Tribe."** He certainly had the touch. But it was an uncertain touch. The exuberance of lyric metres often ran away with him, he never learned to select and compress, and the emotions though sincere enough are often facile and easy emotions, sometimes to the point of the lachrymose, the pretty-pretty, the melodramatic, or the plain sentimental. As in other modes, he is best when he keeps to iambic metres; the language is then in the main plain and direct, the stanzas firmly knit, and the syntax that of ordinary speech. . . . Rhyme was something he never managed well and even his best lyrics are apt to be marred with inept devices too plainly introduced to get a rhyme:

> River, myrtle-rimmed and set
>   Deep amongst unfooted dells—
> Daughter of grey hills of wet,
>   Born by mossed and yellow wells—
> Now that soft September lays
>   Tender hands on thee and thine,
> Let me think of blue-eyed days,
>   Star-like flowers, and leaves of shine!

This use of an unidiomatic participial phrase, *hills of wet, leaves of shine,* is a particularly common and nearly always a disastrous mannerism. At once the whole poem goes soft and seems flabby and contrived. It is worse when Kendall tries anapaestic or others of the tripping, cantering, and prancing metres. He then tends to assume the voice of stage-Irish sentiment—a legacy of his early fondness for Tom Moore:

> Often I sit, looking back to a childhood,
> Mixt with the sights and the sounds of the wildwood,
> Longing for power and the sweetness to fashion,
> Lyrics with beats like the heart-beats of Passion;

It was a fatal longing; when he indulged it he produced comic or merely embarrassing parodies of passion. . . . Kendall's successful lyrics in fact are few. There is a pensive charm about **"Arakoon," "Orara," "Araluen,"** and **"Moss on a Wall"; "Rose Lorraine"** is a charming love-poem; **"The Hut by the Black Swamp"** has a dark power, and **"Outre Mer"** a haunting music. The memorial verses for Marcus Clarke, for J. L. Michael, and for Archdeacon McEncroe are beautiful. . . . The Aboriginal poems, **"The Last of his Tribe," "Kooroora," "Uloola," "Aboriginal Death Song,"** and so forth, are not successful poems though Kendall has been justly praised for his humanity and feeling for the unfortunate native tribesmen. He makes the mistake of dramatizing their situations from the outside, indeed from the literary resources of European views of the noble savage and in language that has incongruous overtones of 'Ossian,' 'Thalaba,' and 'The Lay of the Last Minstrel.' (pp. xxii-xxiv)

His most interesting poems are the four longish narratives, **"The Voyage of Telegonus," "The Glen of Arrawatta," "A Death in the Bush,"** and **"King Saul at Gilboa."** To these should be added **"Ogyges"** which is less a narrative than what Browning would have called a dramatic monologue. All re-

count a pathetic or tragic death and all show a sure understanding of the different sorts of treatment required by different kinds of narrative. Each in its way is a moving and effective poem. **"The Voyage of Telegonus"** is the least successful of the four. It is in the nature of an exercise in the manner of Tennyson, and in places the imitation is enfeebled Tennyson rather than Tennyson assimilated and mastered. Kendall really caught the magic of the Poet Laureate's music and made it his own in another poem, **"Ogyges,"** written on the model of Tennyson's 'Tithonus.' For all that, **"The Voyage of Telegonus"** manages to tell its story dramatically and with a real sense of tragic fate. (p. xxv)

"The Glen of Arrawatta" and **"A Death in the Bush"** are each essays not in tragic but in pathetic narrative. There is no contest of wills, no clash of desire and duty, no concern with fate or inevitable doom. Each is a simple tale of mishaps typical of the early settlement of the country. In the first a pioneer returning to his property is ambushed and murdered by the blacks, in the other a settler and his wife making a new life in the bush meet disaster when the husband becomes ill and dies in their lonely hut. The pathos of the situation in each case depends not so much on what happens to the victims— people are murdered and die of disease everywhere—nor on the nature of the people concerned—there is little in the way of character drawing—but on the loneliness and isolation in which they meet their fates. It is this that appeals to the imag-

Kendall toward the end of his life.

ination, and in order to do this effectively Kendall has told the actual events in plain and everyday language, without much elaboration, and by setting these events in a full description of the surroundings he has evoked the fear and pathos of the circumstances of each death with remarkable force and vividness. . . . The whole narrative technique is quite different from that of "**The Voyage of Telegonus.**" It goes back in fact to an older day—to the narrative technique of the late eighteenth century, the technique of the early Wordsworth in such poems as 'The Old Cumberland Beggar,' the world of the novel of sentiment, of 'The Shipwreck' of Falconer, 'The Deserted Village' of Goldsmith, and Crabbe's 'Tales of the Borough.' In this world Kendall was more at home than with the new styles of the great Victorian poets. When he had a theme which could be treated in the manner of the late Augustans or the earlier Romantics, his taste was surer, his touch was firmer, and his imagination moved at a higher poetic level. As a tale in verse "**A Death in the Bush**" can stand beside some of the best of Lawson's prose tales in the same vein. (pp. xxvi-xxvii)

"**King Saul at Gilboa**" is perhaps Kendall's most astonishing performance. It tells the story, freely expanded by the poet, of Saul's last battle and suicide. . . . What is astonishing about the poem is the tragic force of its language, and the tense, driving energy of its verse. In spite of a few Victorian touches of language, it is essentially eighteenth-century verse and the models are Pope's *Homer* and Dryden's *Virgil*, particularly the latter. But it is by no means mere imitation of the heroic Augustan metres. It has an accent which is Kendall's own and shows that the Augustan style was still alive and developing in Australia in the 1860s. The couplets are nearly all closed, the lines end-stopped, the language dense and terse. The balance is about the centre of the line, so that the effect is one of stiff and formal verse. Yet the connection of the syntax, the urgent movement of event on event, is so precipitous that it is hard to find a passage that can be quoted without seeming incomplete. It is a masterly performance in which the precipitous movement of the syntax reinforces the fatality and drama of the battle, while the stiffness of the verse form accentuates the impression of Saul's agony. In tragic force it would be hard to match in nineteenth-century English poetry, just as it would be hard to parallel the way in which a nineteenth-century poet is able to draw a new music from the Augustan instrument.

> And as in Autumn's fall, when woods are bare,
> Two adverse tempests meet in middle air,
> So Saul and Achish, grim with heat and hate,
> Met by the brooks and shook the scales of Fate;
> For now the struggle swayed, and, firm as rocks
> Against the storm-wind of the equinox,
> The rallied lords of Judah stood and bore
> All day the fiery tides of fourfold war.
> But he that fasted in the secret cave,
> And called up Samuel from the quiet grave,
> And stood with darkness and the mantled ghosts
> A bitter night on shrill Samarian coasts,
> Knew well the end: of how the futile sword
> Of Israel would be broken by the Lord;
> How Gath would triumph . . .

Had Kendall always written like this he might be among the masters.

It is the same with his satire. Those in contemporary style and manner are crude in abuse, and deplorable in their attempts at wit and humour, though they may have been effective at the time as political squibs and amusing caricatures of local types.

The best of them are the portraits of the back-block knowall, the bullock-driver, and the shingle-splitter. These are genuine Theophrastan 'characters,' but spoiled by a self-consciousness in the author who keeps telling his readers not to expect culture and refinement from such characters. The worst are the sectarian and political lampoons which display a vulgarity of mind surprising in the fastidious and gentle Kendall. But as soon as he tries formal satire, as he does in "**The Gagging Bill,**" and "**The Bronze Trumpet**" . . . , the discipline of the heroic couplet and his natural sympathy for the Augustan techniques carries him to another plane. These are satires which are also poetry. Wit was not one of his accomplishments but sometimes indignation could bring out the proper eloquence of satire in him:

> Is this your model ruler?—turn and shout,
> Ye boobies, while I trot your idol out!
> Here is the man who on an evil date
> Was pitchforked hither through the devil's gate—
> Who crouched for years outside the social pale
> Nor showed his hoof, nor advertised his tail—
> Whose cunning seized upon the earliest chance
> When men were fooled by blatant utterance—
> Who crept to power in his peculiar mode
> And stuck at nothing on the nasty road—
> Who ran with every wind, and gained his ends
> By buying foes and sacrificing friends!

The virtues of this succinct and lucid writing have not been appreciated because the standards of the age that taught Kendall have been out of fashion and because of the habit of thinking of Kendall as a Victorian poet. It has also been deprecated because Kendall is here attacking Henry Parkes, the man who befriended him and who continued to befriend him after the attack. But this is beside the point. This is a public poem on a public issue in which Kendall believed, and with a good deal of justice, that Parkes was doing something dangerous and disgraceful. Had "**The Gagging Bill**" been the product of an eighteenth-century poet its merits would long ago have been recognized. "**The Bronze Trumpet**" is not quite so successful. It has its moments, but on the whole it is too long, does not keep to the point enough, and lacks the incisive thrust and impact of the later poem. (pp. xxviii-xxx)

In spite of its forbidding title ["**The Sydney International Exhibition**"] is an able and effective poem. Its subject is not so much the exhibition as Australia, the new nation in the south seas just beginning to feel itself as a nation. Kendall was genuinely and unaffectedly patriotic, and like many of his contemporaries he saw something more than an official and commercial enterprise of self-advertisement in the great exhibition of 1879. . . . The poem unfortunately begins with two of Kendall's worst lines, and takes another twenty lines or so to get off the ground. But from then on it rings true and shows Kendall at his best, as plainness, dignity, enthusiasm, and imagination combine in splendid music. It is a puzzle to understand how critics could dismiss it as an exercise, a rhetorical performance. In an age which has forgotten what public poetry is like and which suffers from the delusion that rhetoric and poetry are incompatible, this might pass. But the qualities that distinguished the poetic genius of Augustan poetry have been long enough rediscovered and recognized for critics not to miss the fine lyric movement within the discipline of the couplet, the genuine voice of passion, and the noble imagination of lines . . . describing the changes which had taken place on the site of Sydney since its foundation nearly a century before. . . . Kendall in this poem touched the true eloquence of poetry. It has been his misfortune that, because for once he rose above the personal, romantic strain of Victorian poetry and achieved the eighteenth-century ideal of a common public style in a great public poem, it has been neglected as though it were no more than a piece of competent pastiche. **"The Sydney International Exhibition,"** like so much of Kendall's work, has flaws and weaknesses which would make one hesitate to describe it as a great poem. But it is a remarkable poem and one by which he may be remembered when his more personal and subjective verse is forgotten. It is unwise to predict even this, for though the faults of Kendall's verse are easy enough to see, he continues to be a poet who inspires affection and respect in spite of them. (pp. xxxi-xxxiii)

> *A. D. Hope, in an introduction to* Henry Kendall *by Henry Kendall, edited by Leonie Kramer and A. D. Hope, Sun Books, 1973, pp. ix-xxxiii.*

ADDITIONAL BIBLIOGRAPHY

Clarke, Donovan. "Henry Kendall—A Study in Imagery: Parts I and II." *The Australian Quarterly* XXIX, No. 4 (December 1957): 71-9; XXX, No. 1 (March 1958): 89-98.
    A reevaluation of Kendall's poetry based on Clarke's interpretation of the poet's use of myth. The critic traces the development of Kendall's personal mythology, focusing in particular on his recurrent use of water imagery and the water journey throughout his major works.

——. "Kendall's Views on Contemporary Writers: A Survey of His Correspondence." *Australian Literary Studies* 1, No. 3 (June 1964): 170-79.
    Surveys Kendall's letters to determine his opinions of his own works and those of his contemporaries.

Elliott, Brian. "Channels of Coolness." In his *The Landscape of Australian Poetry*, pp. 100-19. Melbourne, Australia: F. W. Cheshire, 1967.*
    Discusses Kendall's ability as a landscapist—a poet who "looked with his ears and felt with his eyes."

Goldie, Terry. "The Aboriginal Connection: A Study of Charles Mair's *Tecumseh* and Henry Kendall's 'The Glen of Arrawatta'." *World Literature Written in English* 21, No. 2 (Summer 1982): 287-97.*
    A comparison of Kendall's poem "The Glen of Arrawatta" with the verse drama *Tecumseh* by the nineteenth-century Canadian poet Charles Mair. Goldie focuses on Kendall's depiction of Australian aborigines and Mair's description of Canadian Indians.

Green, H. M. "Kendall." In his *Fourteen Minutes: Short Sketches of Australian Poets and Their Works from Harpur to the Present Day*, edited by Dorothy Green, pp. 12-18. Sydney, Australia: Angus and Robertson, 1950.
    Asserts that Kendall's work is not typically Australian in focus. According to Green, Kendall concentrates on a very narrow segment of Australian culture and landscape and therefore cannot be considered to represent the native Australian voice.

Hope, A. D. "Henry Kendall: A Dialogue with the Past." *Southerly* 32, No. 3 (September 1972): 163-73.
    Contends that unfavorable nineteenth-century interpretations of Kendall's work have influenced twentieth-century evaluations. Hope asserts that Kendall's poetry deserves more thorough critical treatment.

Hope, A. D. "Considered Opinions: Three Early Australian Poets." In his *Native Companions: Essays and Comments on Australian Literature, 1936-1966*, pp. 103-26. Sydney, Australia: Angus and Robertson, 1974.*
    Argues for a reevaluation of the poetry of Kendall and his predecessor Charles Harpur. Hope asserts that literary biases have undermined estimates of their poetry and praises Kendall's "King Saul at Gilboa" and "The Voyage of Telegonus," as well as Harpur's "The Witch of Hebron."

Mackaness, George. "A Memory of Henry Kendall." *Southerly* 24, No. 4 (December 1964): 228-31.
    Presents several previously unpublished poems by Kendall.

Perkins, Elizabeth. "Harpur's Notes and Kendall's 'Bell Birds'." *Australian Literary Studies* 5, No. 3 (May 1972): 277-84.*
    Maintains that Kendall's poem "Bell-Birds" was inspired by Harpur's notes to his "The Kangaroo Hunt."

Reed, T. T. "Kendall's Satirical Humour." *Southerly* 42, No. 4 (December 1982): 363-84.
    Discusses the *Sydney Punch* editors' unfavorable opinions of Kendall and provides background information on the poet's satirical writings.

Wilde, W. H. *Henry Kendall*. Boston: Twayne Publishers, 1976, 182 p.
    A major study of Kendall which includes a selected bibliography of the poet.

Wright, Judith. "Henry Kendall." In her *Preoccupations in Australian Poetry*, pp. 19-44. Melbourne: Oxford University Press, 1965.
    A survey of Kendall's major poems that focuses on imagery and symbolism, written by an Australian poet.

Comte de Lautréamont

1846-1870

(Pseudonym of Isidore Lucien Ducasse) French poet.

A minor French poet, Lautréamont is primarily known for his notorious work, *Les chants de Maldoror (The Lay of Maldoror)*, which, with its shocking and often repugnant imagery, was embraced and championed by the surrealists. Indeed, many members of the surrealist movement considered him their chief nineteenth-century precursor. Yet he was virtually unknown during his lifetime, and it was not until the 1920s when French- and English-language studies of his work began to appear that he developed a limited but devoted following. Since the 1970s, a resurgence of critical interest has brought Lautréamont to the attention of scholars, although he remains unknown to most readers. His obscurity stems, in part, from his small body of writings. Lautréamont wrote only two works: *Maldoror,* which forms the basis of his reputation both with the surrealists and with the majority of modern commentators, and *Poésies,* which has attracted increasing scholarly attention in recent years.

An air of mystery surrounds Lautréamont and continues to affect critical reception of his works. Until the 1970s, no portrait of the author was believed to exist, and even now very little is known about his brief life. Lautréamont was born Isidore Lucien Ducasse in 1846 in Montevideo, Uruguay, where his father was a French consular officer. In 1859, he left Uruguay to continue his studies in France. He first enrolled in the *lycée* at Tarbes and in 1863 transferred to the *lycée* at Pau. In 1867 or 1868, Lautréamont moved to Paris, ostensibly to attend L'École Polytechnique, although he never registered. He remained in Paris and is believed to have composed both *Maldoror* and *Poésies* during this period. Lautréamont died in 1870 of unknown causes.

The publishing history of Lautréamont's work reflects the continuing enigma of Lautréamont as a poet and as a man. *Maldoror* was published in two parts: the first canto appeared anonymously in 1868, and the full work was published the following year under the pseudonym by which he is known today, Comte de Lautréamont. However, because the publisher feared that violence in the work would lead to prosecution, *Maldoror* was never distributed to booksellers. Not until 1874 was the full text of *Maldoror* released to the public. The author's only other literary work, *Poésies,* appeared in 1870 with his given name on the title page. The connection between these two works remained unknown until 1890, when the editor of a volume of *Maldoror* uncovered the author's real name. The significance of his use of two different names has been an ongoing subject of controversy, and many critics have questioned what, if any, relationship exists between the author's signature and his intent.

Maldoror is Lautréamont's most celebrated work. Analyses of the text often focus on the meaning of the names the author selected for himself and for his hero, and their significance to the work. Maldoror, the hero, is alternately said to mean *aurore du mal,* dawn of evil, and *mal d'aurore,* evil from the beginning; while the pseudonym Lautréamont is said by some to represent *L'autre Amon,* the other Sun King, others believe it was taken from Eugène Sue's novel *Latréaumont,* in which

the hero, like Maldoror, is both arrogant and blasphemous. The form of *Maldoror* is also subject to interpretation: it is generally considered poetry, yet it is written in prose, and some critics have described it as a novel. Its six cantos, divided into about sixty strophes, detail the experiences of the hero, a demonic, rebellious figure who is part man and part beast and whose most frequent target is God. Deliberately challenging and insulting, Maldoror views himself as a rival monarch, equal to God, who in turn is depicted as degraded and debased. Similarly, in describing the relationship between humans and animals, Lautréamont reduces humans to the level of apes, divesting them of all sublimity. As the narrator observes, "I use my genius to depict the delights of cruelty"; indeed, murder, eroticism, sadomasochism, violence, blasphemy, and obscenity all play a part in Maldoror's life story. In the words of Georges Lemaître, *Maldoror* "constitutes a tremendous and amazing epic of Evil."

The focus of critical discussions of *Maldoror* has been largely defined by the surrealist writers, who acclaimed Lautréamont's handling of the theme of rebellion, as well as his depiction of the unconscious and his use of imagery. Critics who have interpreted the work primarily as an expression of the unconscious have concentrated on the nightmarish, hallucinatory atmosphere that lends *Maldoror* its deeply unsettling quality. Other critics have dealt more extensively with the imagery in

Maldoror. Lautréamont often juxtaposed two entirely unrelated and dissimilar elements, as in his frequent use of metaphors beginning with the phrase "beau comme," or "beautiful as"; for example, his line "beautiful as the fortuitous meeting of a sewing machine and an umbrella on a dissection table" has been frequently quoted as the paradigm of the surrealist analogical system. While some critics have hailed these constructions, including S. A. Rhodes, who praised the "irrational apprehension of a secret unity and harmony," others see in them the possibility for destroying all figurative language. In addition to its imagery, the work's several narrative stances have also been the subject of commentary. Modern scholars have noted that the shifting point of view in *Maldoror* blurs the distinction between the narrator, hero, and reader. Through this method, Lautréamont confuses the bounds of fiction in *Maldoror*, implicitly compromising his readers by involving them in the hero's grotesque activities.

Lautréamont's other work, *Poésies*, contains two sections. In the first, which is written in prose, Lautréamont outlines his aesthetics. He denounces the personal poetry of the romantic writers and terms school graduation speeches the masterpieces of the French language, thus repudiating imaginative literature in favor of works whose purpose is utility and morality. The second part includes a series of maxims or aphorisms, arranged in no apparent order, which espouse optimism, practicality, and religion. Many of the maxims are only slightly revised versions of passages by Blaise Pascal, Luc de Clapiers Vauvenargues, François de La Rochefoucauld, Jean de La Bruyère, Dante Alighieri, William Shakespeare, and others.

Poésies, like *Maldoror*, has been accorded various interpretations, and critics have debated both the nature of the work and its meaning. Some regard it as the preface to a new collection of poems that either was lost or that Lautréamont intended to write but never completed; this view is supported by his letter dated March 12, 1870, in which he refers to having composed a preface of sixty pages. Other critics contend that the work is complete as is. According to most critics, defining the relationship between the strikingly different *Poésies* and *Maldoror* is crucial to an understanding of the author, and scholars have turned to his correspondence for clues to his intent. In the aforementioned letter, Lautréamont asserted, "I have completely changed my method, to sing exclusively of *hope, expectation,* CALM, *happiness,* DUTY"; and in a letter dated February 21, 1870 describing a work in progress, Lautréamont claimed, "I take up the most beautiful poetry of Lamartine, Victor Hugo, Alfred de Musset, Byron and Baudelaire, and correct it in the direction of hope; I outline how it ought to have been done." Such comments have led some readers to view *Poésies* as a thorough repudiation of the views expressed in *Maldoror*. In addition, they regard the author's rejection of his pseudonym and publication of *Poésies* under his own name as further proof of his philosophical reversal. Yet many consider this view simplistic and note that the work's ironic tone undermines its pious content. Recent critics have denied that the two works are contradictory, arguing instead that *Poésies* complements rather than repudiates the earlier text. In this view, *Poésies* is seen as an attempt to undermine traditional literary forms. According to Paul Knight, the author employs three techniques: challenging his own views as expressed in *Maldoror;* reworking passages from earlier writers; and incorporating conflicting ideas within the text. Knight summarized the opinion of many modern critics in describing *Poésies* as "a continual process of contradiction, negation, replacement and correction."

Critical response to Lautréamont during his lifetime was negligible. Essentially unknown at his death, only with the 1890 edition of *Maldoror* did his works begin to receive limited attention. He was rescued from obscurity by the surrealists, who revered him and adopted him as one of their exemplars. Beginning in the 1920s with the writings of the surrealists, French-language studies on Lautréamont were published by many important authors—including Léon Bloy, Rémy de Gourmont, Valéry Larbaud, André Breton, Tristan Tzara, Phillipe Soupault, André Malraux, André Gide, Léon Pierre Quint, Gaston Bachelard, Maurice Blanchot, Antonin Artaud, and Albert Camus—yet few of their comments have been translated into English. Studies in English also began to appear in the 1920s, and their number increased gradually until the 1970s, when his works began to receive a greater share of scholarly attention. Still, few English-language critics have accorded Lautréamont the degree of respect and attention granted by French writers. Today, the author of both *Maldoror* and *Poésies* is recognized primarily for his influence on surrealism.

PRINCIPAL WORKS

Les chants de Maldoror: Chant premier   (poetry)   1868
Les chants de Maldoror: Chants I, II, III, IV, V, VI
   (poetry)   1869
   [*The Lay of Maldoror*, 1924]
Poésies I, II   (poetry)   1870
   [*Lautréamont's Preface to His Unwritten Volume of
    Poems* published in *New Directions 9*, 1946]
Oeuvres complètes   (poetry and letters)   1927
Poésies and Complete Miscellanea   (poetry and letters)
   1978

COMTE DE LAUTRÉAMONT   (essay date 1868)

[*The following excerpt is from strophes 1-4 of the first canto of* Maldoror, *which was originally published in 1868. Lautréamont begins by discouraging those who lack "rigorous logic" from reading his work, and he introduces his protagonist, Maldoror. Lautréamont also describes his purpose in writing: "I use my genius to depict the delights of cruelty: delights which are not transitory or artificial; but which began with man and will end with him." Many critics have cited the importance of this initial direct address in involving the reader in the text.*]

May it please heaven that the reader, emboldened and having for the time being become as fierce as what he is reading, should, without being led astray, find his rugged and treacherous way across the desolate swamps of these sombre and poison-filled pages; for, unless he brings to his reading a rigorous logic and a tautness of mind equal at least to his wariness, the deadly emanations of this book will dissolve his soul as water does sugar. It is not right that everyone should read the pages which follow; only a few will be able to savour this bitter fruit with impunity. Consequently, shrinking soul, turn on your heels and go back before penetrating further into such uncharted, perilous wastelands. Listen well to what I say: turn on your heels and go back, not forward, like the eyes of a son respectfully averted from the august contemplation of his mother's face; or rather like a formation of very meditative cranes, stretching out of sight, whose sensitive bodies flee the chill of winter, when, their wings fully extended, they fly powerfully through silence to a precise point on the horizon, from which suddenly a strange strong wind blows, precursor of the storm. The oldest crane, flying on alone ahead of the others, shakes his head like a reasonable person on seeing this, making at the same time a clack with his beak, and he is troubled (as I, too, would be, if I were he); all the time his scrawny and featherless neck, which has seen three generations of cranes, is moving in irritated undulations which foretoken the quickly-gathering storm. Having calmly looked in all directions with his experienced eyes, the crane prudently (ahead of all the others, for he has the privilege of showing his tail-feathers to his less intelligent fellows) gyrates to change the direction of the geometric figure (perhaps it is a triangle, but one cannot see the third side which these curious birds of passage form in space) either to port or to starboard, like a skilled captain; uttering as he does so his vigilant cry, like that of a melancholy sentry, to repulse the common enemy. Then, manoeuvring with wings which seem no bigger than a starling's, because he is no fool, he takes another philosophic and surer line of flight.

* * * * *

Reader, perhaps it is hatred you wish me to invoke at the outset of this work! What makes you think that you will not sniff—drenched in numberless pleasures, for as long as you wish, with your proud nostrils, wide and thin, as you turn over on your belly like a shark, in the beautiful black air, as if you understood the importance of this act and the equal importance of your legitimate appetite, slowly and majestically—its red emanations. I assure you, they will delight the two shapeless holes of your hideous muzzle, if you endeavour beforehand to inhale, in three thousand consecutive breaths, the accursed conscience of the Eternal One! Your nostrils, which will dilate immeasurably in unspeakable contentment, in motionless ecstasy, will ask nothing better of space, for they will be full of fragrance as if of perfumes and incense; for they will be glutted with complete happiness, like the angels who dwell in the peace and magnificence of pleasant Heaven.

* * * * *

I will state in a few lines that Maldoror was good during the first years of his life, when he lived happily. That is that. Then he noticed that he had been born evil: an extraordinary fatality! As far as he could, he hid his real character for a large number of years; but in the end, because of the concentration this required, which did not come naturally to him, the blood used to rush to his head every day; until, no longer able to bear such a life, he flung himself resolutely into a career of evil-doing . . . a sweet atmosphere! Who would have thought so! Whenever he kissed a little pink-faced child, he felt like tearing open its cheeks with a razor, and he would have done so very often, had not Justice, with its long train of punishments, prevented him. He was no liar, admitted the truth and said that he was cruel. Human beings, did you hear that? He dares to say it again with this trembling pen. So it is a power stronger than will . . . Curse! Could a stone escape from the laws of gravity? Impossible. Impossible, for evil to form an alliance with good. That is what I was saying in the above lines.

* * * * *

There are those whose purpose in writing is, by means of the noble qualities of heart which their imagination invents or which they themselves may have, to seek the plaudits of other human beings. For my part, I use my genius to depict the delights of cruelty: delights which are not transitory or artificial; but which began with man and will end with him. Cannot genius be allied with cruelty in the secret resolutions of Providence? Or can one, being cruel, not have genius? The proof will be seen in my words. You have only to listen to me, if you wish . . . Excuse me, for a moment it seemed as if my hair was standing on end; but it is nothing, for I had no trouble in putting them back in place again with my hand. He who sings does not claim that his cavatinas are utterly unknown; on the contrary, he commends himself because his hero's haughty and wicked thoughts are in all men. (pp. 29-32)

> *Comte de Lautréamont, in his* Maldoror and Poems, *translated by Paul Knight, Penguin Books, 1978, 287 p.*

EPISTEMON [PSEUDONYM OF ALFRED SIRCOS]   (essay date 1868)

[*The following essay, which was originally published in the French journal* La jeunesse, *September 1-15, 1868, was the only contemporary critical review of the first edition of* Maldoror. *Sircos notes the poem's power, originality, and affinity to the works of Musset, Byron, and Goethe.*]

The first effect produced by reading [*Les chants de Maldoror*] is of astonishment: the hyperbolic bombast of the style, the savage strangeness, the desperate vigour of conception, the contrast of this impassioned language with the dullest lucubrations of our time, at first cast the mind into a deep amazement.

Alfred de Musset mentions somewhere what he calls "the Sickness of the Century": it is uncertainty about the future, contempt for the past, or incredulity and despair. Maldoror is stricken with this malady; sceptical, he grows wicked, and turns all the powers of his genius towards cruelty. Cousin to *Childe Harold* and *Faust,* he knows men and despises them. Envy eats him up, and his heart, always empty, incessantly excites itself with gloomy thoughts without ever being able to attain that vague and ideal objective he seeks and guesses at.

We will not carry the criticism of this book any further. It should be read, to feel the powerful inspiration animating it, the dark despair diffused within these lugubrious pages. Despite its faults, which are numerous, the incorrectness of style, the disorder of the scenes, we think this work will not be mistaken for other current publications: its uncommon originality assures us of that. (pp. 145-46)

> Epistemon [*pseudonym of Alfred Sircos*], "*Contemporary Reactions to Lautréamont: The First Review,*" *in* Poésies *and Complete Miscellanea by Isidore Ducasse, edited and translated by Alexis Lykiard, Allison & Busby, 1978, pp. 145-46.*

COMTE DE LAUTRÉAMONT   (letter dates 1869-70)

[*The following excerpt contains letters from Lautréamont to different recipients. The first letter is written to Verboeckhoven, the Belgian associate of the publisher Lacroix, to whom Lautréamont had sent* Maldoror *when Lacroix refused to distribute it. This letter includes a famous passage in which Lautréamont compares his work with that of other nineteenth-century writers. In the second letter, also to Verboeckhoven, Lautréamont announces that he has "disowned" his past and now espouses only hope. The third letter is written to Darasse (alternately spelled Durasse), a banker whose list of clients included Lautréamont's father. In this letter also, the poet apparently rejects his earlier work. Lautréamont's reference in the last two letters to a work in progress, a preface of sixty pages, is often assumed to be the* Poésies, *and*] *many critics cite these letters when discussing the meaning of that work.*]

[*To Monsieur Verboeckhoven, October 23, 1869*]

I have sung of evil as did Misckiéwickz, Byron, Milton, Southey, A. de Musset, Baudelaire, etc. Naturally I have somewhat exaggerated the diapason so as to do something new in the way of this sublime literature which sings of despair only to oppress the reader and make him desire the good as remedy. It is always therefore, the good one sings, in short, only by a method more philosophical and less naïve than that of the old school, of which Victor Hugo and a few others are the sole surviving representatives. Sell, I am not preventing your doing so: what must I do for that? State your terms. What I should like is that the service of criticism be made in the style of the principal *lundistes* [those who followed the French critic Sainte-Beuve]. They alone shall judge in the 1st and last resort the beginning of a publication which will only, of course, see its end much later, when I'll have seen mine. Thus the moral at the end is not yet drawn. However there is already an immense suffering on every page. Is that then evil? Of course not. I would be grateful to you, since if the critics speak well of it, I could in subsequent editions delete some passages that are too powerful. So what I desire above all is to be judged by the critics, and once known, it'll be plain sailing. (pp. 121-23)

* * * * *

[*To Monsieur Verboekhoven, February 21, 1870*]

Has Lacroix given up the edition, or what has he done with it? Or have you refused it? He has told me nothing about it. I have not seen him since then.—You know, I have disowned my past. I now sing only of hope; but for that one must first attack the doubt of this century (melancholias, sadnesses, sorrows, despairs, lugubrious whinnies, artificial mischiefs, puerile pride, comical maledictions etc., etc.). In a work I will deliver to Lacroix during the 1st days of March, I take up the most beautiful poetry of Lamartine, Victor Hugo, Alfred de Musset, Byron and Baudelaire, and correct it in the direction of hope; I outline how it ought to have been done. I am correcting at the same time 6 of the worst bits of my confounded old book. (p. 127)

* * * * *

[*To Monsieur Darasse, March 12, 1870*]

I have had a book of poetry published by M. Lacroix. . . . But once it was printed he refused to let it appear, because life was painted there in colours that were too bitter, and he feared the Attorney General. It was something in the genre of Byron's Manfred and Mickiewicz's Konrad, but far more terrible, however. Publication cost 1200 francs, of which I had already found 400. But the whole thing went down the drain. That made me open my eyes. I told myself that since the poetry of doubt (of today's volumes not 150 pages will remain) has reached such a point of gloomy despair and theoretical nastiness, therefore it's because it is radically false; and the reason is that *it discusses principles, and one must not discuss them:* it's more than unjust. The poetic moans of this century are only hideous sophisms. To sing of boredom, suffering, miseries, melancholias, death, darkness, the sombre, etc., is wanting at all costs to look only at the puerile reverse of things. Lamartine, Hugo, Musset have voluntarily metamorphosed into sissies. These are the Great-Soft-Heads of our epoch. Always snivelling! That is why I have completely changed method, to sing exclusively of *hope, expectation,* CALM, *happiness,*

DUTY. And thus I rejoin with the Corneilles and Racines the chain of good sense and composure brusquely interrupted since the poseurs Voltaire and Jean-Jacques Rousseau. My book will not be finished for 4 or 5 months. But in the meanwhile I would like to send my father the preface, consisting of 60 pages; published by Al. Lemerre. He will thus see I am working and will send me the full sum for printing the book later. (pp. 127-29)

> *Comte de Lautréamont, in extracts from three of his letters: to Monsieur Verboekhoven on October 23, 1869 and February 21, 1870 and Monsieur Darasse on March 12, 1870, in* Poésies and Complete Miscellanea *by Isidore Ducasse, edited and translated by Alexis Lykiard, Allison & Busby, 1978, pp. 121-29.*

BULLETIN du BIBLIOPHILE et du BIBLIOTHÉCAIRE   (essay date 1870)

[*In this extract from the French journal* Bulletin du bibliophile et du bibliothécaire *of May, 1870, the anonymous critic predicts that* Maldoror *"will doubtless remain unknown in France."*]

[*Les chants de Maldoror*] was published, we are informed, in a small edition and then suppressed by the author, who has disguised his real name under a pseudonym. It will find a place among the bibliographical curiosities, no preface, a series of visions and reflections in bizarre style, a sort of Apocalypse whose meaning it would be futile to guess. Is it some sort of wager? The writer seems very serious and nothing is more lugubrious than the scenes he presents to his readers' eyes. We mention this strange work because it will doubtless remain unknown in France. (pp. 146-47)

> *"Contemporary Reactions to Lautréamont: Extract from 'Bulletin du bibliophile et du bibliothécaire', Issue of May, 1870," in* Poésies and Complete Miscellanea *by Isidore Ducasse, edited and translated by Alexis Lykiard, Allison & Busby, 1978, pp. 146-47.*

RÉMY DE GOURMONT   (essay date 1891)

[*Gourmont, a French poet, novelist, critic, and essayist, was one of the founders of the influential* Mercure de France, *a journal that championed the symbolist movement in France during the late nineteenth century. Gourmont is considered one of the most perceptive and sensitive of the symbolist critics, and his work is noted for its detached and objective tone. He was an individual of broad interests and encyclopedic knowledge, as is evidenced in his essays on such diverse topics as aesthetics, biology, and religion. Gourmont is also remembered as the critic who championed the works of Friedrich Nietzsche, Stéphane Mallarmé, J. K. Huysmans, and Jean Marie Villiers de l'Isle Adam in France. In the following excerpt, Gourmont praises the novelty, originality, abundance, and arrangement of imagery and metaphor in* Maldoror. *In addition, like many later critics he discusses Lautréamont's sanity. Gourmont questions whether Lautréamont was in fact mad, or was instead "a superior ironist, a man forced by a precious scorn for mankind to feign a madness whose incoherence is wiser and more beautiful than the average reason." This essay was originally published in 1891.*]

He was a young man of savage and unexpected originality, a diseased genius and, quite frankly, a mad genius. Imbeciles grow insane and in their insanity the imbecility remains stagnant or agitated; in the madness of a man of genius some genius often remains: the form and not the quality of the intelligence has been affected; the fruit has been bruised in the fall, but has preserved all its perfume and all the savor of its pulp, hardly too ripe.

Such was the adventure of the amazing stranger, self-adorned with this romantic pseudonym: Comte de Lautréamont. (p. 141)

The *Chants de Maldoror* is a long poem in prose whose six first chants only were written. It is probable that Lautréamont, though living, would not have continued them. We feel, in proportion as we finish the reading of the volume, that consciousness is going, going—and when it returns to him, several months before his death, he composes the *Poésies,* where, among very curious passages, is revealed the state of mind of a dying man who repeats, while disfiguring them in fever, his most distant memories, that is to say, for this infant, the teachings of his professors!

A motive the more why these chants surprise. It was a magnificent, almost inexplicable stroke of genius. Unique this book will remain, and henceforth it remains added to the list of works which, to the exclusion of all classicism, forms the scanty library and the sole literature admissible to those minds, oddly amiss, that are denied the joys, less rare, of common things and conventional morality.

The worth of the *Chants de Maldoror* is not in pure imagination: fierce, demoniac, disordered or exasperated with arrogance in crazy visions, it terrifies rather than charms; then, even in unconsciousness, there are influences that can be determined. "O Nights of Young," the author exclaims in his verses, "what sleep you have cost me!" And here and there he is swayed by the romantic extravagances of such English fictionists as were still read in his time, Anne Radcliffe and Maturin (whom Balzac esteemed), Byron, also by the medical reports on eroticism, and finally by the bible. He certainly had read widely, and the only author he never quotes, Flaubert, must never have been far from his reach.

This worth I would like to make known, consists, I believe, in the novelty and originality of the images and metaphors, by their abundance, the sequence logically arranged like a poem, as in the magnificent description of a shipwreck, where all the verses (although no typographic artifice betokens them) end thus: "The ship in distress fires cannon shots of alarm; but it founders slowly . . . majestically." So, too, the litanies of the Ancient Ocean: "Ancient Ocean, your waters are bitter. I greet you, Ancient Ocean. Ancient Ocean, O great celibate, when you course the solemn solitudes of your phlegmatic realms . . . I greet you, Ancient Ocean." (pp. 142-44)

Alienists, had they studied this book, would have classified the author among those aspiring to pass for persecuted persons: in the world he only sees himself and God—and God thwarts him. But we might also inquire whether Lautréamont is not a superior ironist, a man forced by a precious scorn for mankind to feign a madness whose incoherence is wiser and more beautiful than the average reason. There is the madness of pride; there is the delirium of mediocrity. How many balanced and honest pages, of good and clear literature, would I not give for this, for [the] words and phrases under which he seems to have wished to inter reason herself! (p. 148)

Maldoror (or Lautréamont) seems to have judged himself in making himself apostrophised thus by his enigmatic Toad: "Your spirit is so diseased that it perceives nothing; and you deem it natural each time there issues from your mouth words that are senseless, though full of an infernal grandeur." (p. 150)

Rémy de Gourmont, "Lautréamont," in his The Book of Masks, *translated by Jack Lewis, 1921. Reprint by Books for Libraries Press, Inc., 1967, distributed by Arno Press, Inc., pp. 141-50.*

TRISTAN TZARA   (essay date 1922)

[*Tzara was a Rumanian-born poet who wrote in French. He was one of the founders of dadaism, a nihilistic literary movement that existed during and just after World War I. As a protest against the insanity of war, the dadaists attempted to pervert the tenets of art and philosophy. These writers argued for the importance of instinctive expression and experimented with the "disintegration" of language, attempting to destroy the relationship between ideas and language. In the late 1920s and 1930s, Tzara collaborated with the surrealists, who adopted and gave further expression to many of the ideas of the dadaists. Tzara's comments on Lautréamont originally appeared in March, 1922, in the French journal* Littérature.]

Mal d'or or gold of dolour

Mal d'or or gold has destroyed the door of death.

His madness was not sublime—which is why it still lives on. Who dares to combat a reality because it is served up as a form of reproach?

TO SEE: necessity of a cerebral trigger.

Those people whose uncertainties show themselves in pretensions and whose pride rises in the form of cerebral saliva, those people for whom swamps and excrement have determined the rules of philosophical pity, will see, one of these days, this immeasurable malediction destroy their filthy, feeble muscles. The Comte de Lautréamont has gone beyond the tangential point which separates creation and madness. For him, creation is already mediocrity. On the other hand it is unpronounceable solemnity. The frontiers of wisdom are unexplored. Ecstasy devours them with neither hierarchy nor cruelty.

The dolour that freezes the brains, pulverises the crystal of its blood, and leads the chaos of the sheathing of the hulls of old boats, of the lining of old coats, down a strange channel of pathetic regrets. Whether imaginary or exaggerated, dolour drinks silence, and accompanies the high-pitched force that is constantly trying to dissolve itself in the magic, universal delirium tremens.

The liberty of his faculties, which are bound by nothing, which he turns in all directions and especially towards himself, the strength to humble himself, to demolish, to cling to every blemish, with a sincerity far too intimate to interest us, are the highest human attitude because, transformed, as actions, they ought to culminate in the annihilation of that strange mixture of bones, flour and vegetation: humanity. The mind of this negative man, who was ever ready to be killed by the merry-go-round of the wind and to be trampled on by a hail of meteors, goes beyond the sickly hysteria of Jesus and other tireless windmills installed in the sumptuous apartments of history.

Don't love if you want to die in peace.

Mal'dor or gold of dolour

Mal d'or or gold has destroyed the door of death
by his brilliance and the music of the zephyr's frogs. (pp. 97-8)

Tristan Tzara, "Note on the Comte de Lautréamont, or the Cry," in his Seven Dada Manifestos and Lampisteries, *translated by Barbara Wright, John Calder, 1977, pp. 97-8.*

WILL BRAY   (essay date 1922)

[*This excerpt marks the beginning of English-language criticism of Lautréamont. Bray assesses Lautréamont's importance in the early twentieth century. He specifically notes the effect of the developing field of psychology, with its investigations into the unconscious, on perceptions of Lautréamont's writings.*]

The age has been far more reluctant to concede the genius of Isidore Ducasse ("Comte de Lautréamont" . . .), than is the case, perhaps, of any other of the extraordinary personalities of the past century. His writings, speciously damned as the maunderings of a madman, were regarded up to very recently as having little interest, save for the alienist. . . .

In France, however, the younger generation, which otherwise might well have been stifled by the sterile traditions of the preceding art-period, has taken Ducasse to its heart, and is producing a literature of great fertility, freedom, invention, aggressiveness. It is postulated that the post-war period is, or is to become, a very pregnant one, an age of unrivalled physical attainments and of the desperation born thereof. To the period which has just set in, the personality of Ducasse, like that of Rimbaud, exercises a dominant attraction. These two were the vaticinal spokesmen for a state of mind whose brutality and beauty none could have foretold.

The nineteenth century, again—it always serves as a point of departure—was enmeshed in a vicious cycle of quiddities and casuistries from which the spirit emerged into either an unhealthy Christianity or a hybrid Epicureanism. Ducasse, like Rimbaud, was neither pagan nor Christian. We are extricated from these dreaded categories as we are from the fruitless *post hoc ergo propter hoc.*

The *Songs of Maldoror* form a legend on an heroic scale of the naked human passions working out their destinies. Since we have come to know more familiarly the cavernous recesses of the mind and the momentous play of the unconscious in the diurnal existence, the presumption of a Ducasse becomes pardonable. The contained, complex social nature of man drops off like an outworn robe. There is escape at last from the buttonmoulder who menaced *Peer Gynt.* The standard associations of thought are forsworn; the motivation verges from the most frightful niceties of observation to gestures of gigantic scope, while the human rôle in the drama of nature becomes that of Prometheus. Man is a beast again; his laughter, his weeping, his howling, are as insistent and clamorous as those of the other beasts in the jungle.

With the nullification of human reason, the mind abandons itself to a sort of destructive sincerity, whereby all may be denied or posited, and nothing is impossible. The gift of song in man becomes atavistic again, chanting against pain, hunger and danger. In *Maldoror* the incantations assume the rhythm of the baying of hounds, the long swell of sea-waves, or the furious velocity of a life that is consumed like a flame across the sky.

Will Bray, "Exordium to Ducasse," in *Broom, Vol. 3, No. 1, August, 1922, p. 3.*

S. A. RHODES   (essay date 1931)

[*Rhodes compares Maldoror with Rimbaud's Illuminations, noting elements of kinship between the two writers. Both Lautréamont and Rimbaud described unreal worlds with flashes of keen poetic insight, according to Rhodes, and both were rebels who eventually denounced their earlier works. While praising the simple and accessible language that drew the surrealists to Lautréamont, Rhodes contends that Maldoror lacks the "magic art" that characterizes Rimbaud's works.*]

The most that [a] worshipful disciple and admiring critic could do would be scant justice . . . to requite Lautréamont for the oblivion into which he had unjustly fallen until resurrected by the love of his surrealist followers. He had hoped to see "promptly, some day or other, the consequences of his theories accepted by some literary school or other. . . ." But he had to wait much longer than Rimbaud to find his Verlaine. And yet no poet is more like Rimbaud, within certain reservations, than he.

In *Les Chants de Maldoror* we awake in a world of utter irreality, the same as in *Illuminations.* But whereas we behold in the latter a free spirit lost to human sight, Maldoror makes intermittent descents upon the earth, like an eagle swooping down upon its prey. He is a resistless typhoon let loose upon all things, human and divine, spreading, like a scourge, fear, hatred, and death, hovering on the brink of madness and ecstasy, planting his black standard in the eddying currents of dissolving life, until his spirit writhes and whirls as in some irrepressible, satanic doomsday. Nevertheless, Maldoror's acerbated nihilism is consequential, almost Euclidean in its severe formalism. It draws its *raison d'être* from an anterior positivism (his father gave a series of lectures on Comte's philosophy to the *élite* of Montevideo society), and from a contemporaneous, voluptuous mysticism of his irascible, thwarted spirit. Both are expressions of an irrational idealism and faith in a real paradise, which, however, becomes a "paradise lost," that Maldoror pretends to rediscover. Therein lies his only madness. He is an optimist *à rebours.* With lucid eyes, he sallies forth to challenge God and men, good and evil, to tear it all asunder, and thus to "atteindre à l'infini par les moyens les plus insensés." Maldoror, at once rival and judge of God, becomes a fiercer antagonist than Milton's Lucifer. His war-cries are the apotheosis of satanism and sadism; it is nihilism gnawing its own entrails; revolt lifting its hydra head and spitting fire and venom at its own heart. He boasts of reverting the current of Christian religion, and seeks to pit his pride, revolt, triumphant invective against humility, resignation, and martyrdom. He abhors not only man-made God, but also God-made man. He divests himself of all vestiges of conscience, and thus breaks loose from God's bondage—consciousness of good and evil, human solidarity, regret, remorse. He becomes a free spirit, alike unto and equal to God. With this reservation, however, that in order to be, he needs God. That is why his conflict ends in an impasse. Rimbaud, sky adventurer, sought to dethrone the Biblical deities in order to enthrone what he considered a more absolute and universal principle. Lautréamont seeks to destroy the throne along with the monarch. He does not propose to replace one anthropomorphic concept with another perhaps as absurd. Failing in that, his struggle must end, as it actually does, in a draw. Unlike Rimbaud, he does not feel the need of inventing a new prosody. Rimbaud was a prophet. Lautréamont is a pure rebel. Under his whip the French language becomes snarling, biting, scorching. But it is still a human language, exalted to the pitch of madness. It stays entirely within the precincts of simple symbolic interpretation. And so his hallucinated rebellion remains lucid and rationally expressed. He is simplicity personified compared to Rimbaud.

Therein may lie the reason why the surrealists turn instinctively to Lautréamont rather than to Rimbaud. The latter's hermetical idiom screens the inner labor of his artistic alchemy. No expression was incantatory enough for him; no prosody sufficiently magic. He often worked over and chiselled his verse and prose, as the numerous variants he has left behind testify. Lautréamont on the other hand must have written with a frenzy quasi-mystic, with that "écriture automatique" which is something quite different from what Rimbaud's "alchimie du verbe" calls for. A year was all he needed to compose his six cantos. His verbal imagination is not as rich or colorful as that of the author of *Illuminations*. He is more accessible, despite the ambiguous but refreshing quality of much that he wrote, as in his striking and yet simple simile: "beau . . . comme la rencontre fortuite sur une table de dissection d'une machine à coudre et d'un parapluie!" There is no apparent kinship between a sewing machine and an umbrella on a dissecting table. The gist of the expression lies in an irrational apprehension of a secret unity and harmony. The older image was a simple photographic transposition of a visible aspect of reality. The poet's idea or emotion was transfixed on the poetic negative as a vivid, rational image. The analogy was easy to grasp because the image was pictorial. The symbolist expressed his idea or emotion through impressionistic rather than photographic images. Nerval, Lautréamont, Rimbaud, do away with the camera and the impression. Instead of showing reality through analytical, imitative *clichés,* they illumine it as with flashes of lightning.

Such flashes are not as common in Lautréamont as in Rimbaud. In fact **Les Chants de Maldoror** are told with the Biblical directness of the *Book of Job,* or Milton's *Paradise Lost,* although, of course, they do not measure up to these poems. Maldoror recalls rather Byron's Cain or Manfred. This suggests that Lautréamont's is only a second-hand originality. It does not detract from his luster, for originality in art as in literature is purely formal. He himself admits indebtedness to Young, Blake, Mickiewicz, Baudelaire. In his attempt to equal them, his muse forces the note a little. But for sheer power, passion, and thunderous rhetoric, **Les Chants de Maldoror** merits comparison with another nineteenth century prose-poem, with Nietzsche's *Also sprach Zarathustra.* Maldoror is like Zarathustra in certain traits, and unlike him in others. Both are of the same stature, portentous and satanic, spreading anarchy with the fire of their flaming tongues, destroying a civilization from the roots up. But Maldoror is more desperate. He is another Lucifer, whereas Zarathustra is less fierce and more human.

To return to the subject of the kinship between Lautréamont and Rimbaud, the remarkable coincidence that presided at the effulgence, almost the same year, of two poets, both adolescents, of similar verve, poetic frenzy, and spiritual import, witnessed also the almost identical recantation by each of what they had erstwhile adored and created. Just as Rimbaud burnt immediately after publication as much of the edition of *Une Saison en Enfer* as he could lay his hands on, and then turned his back to poetry forever, so Lautréamont (with less consistency perhaps, for unlike Rimbaud he does not seem to have planned abandoning the literary career, although M. Pierre-Quint supposes he might have had he lived) turned with invective and scorn, in the preface to *Poésies,* upon the monument of apostasy he had erected in **Les Chants de Maldoror.** In a letter of February 21, 1870 [see excerpt above], he declares: "You know, I have abjured my past. I sing hope only now. . . ." Maldoror becomes "ce cas pathologique d'un égoïsme formidable." Rousseau, Musset, Balzac, Baudelaire, are put down as "des écrivains funestes," and Byron, Manfred, Werther, all his former idols, become a "série bruyante des diables en carton." He calls back "les vertus offensées et leurs impér-

issables redressements," casts anathema upon all literature, except baccalaureate and commencement addresses, "les chefs-d'oeuvre de la langue française," and whatever can edify a girl of fourteen (Nineteenth Century model). All this sounds paradoxical, illogical, like human reason digging its own grave. He died the year of the preface. So that his last words, as in the case of Rimbaud, would imply a complete renunciation of art. This seems to be the only sense in which the surrealists understand the recantation. They foresee the passing of literature as such, of the written word as a creation of the idle fancy, of poetasters as clowns juggling verses in the face of the eternal tragedy which is life. For them, either the "will to power," in art as in life, or the "will to death." A more literal interpretation of Lautréamont's renunciation they refuse to accept. (pp. 286-89)

[Despite] the surrealists' gallant efforts to reinterpret and reintegrate Lautréamont's genius, I doubt if he will ever rise to the pinnacle of fame that his spiritual brothers, Rimbaud, Laforgue, know. Because Lautréamont lacks that magic art that turns Rimbaud's most shrieking outbursts of madness into immortal poetry. Lautréamont is a religious (or anti-religious, it is all the same), delirious dreamer, primarily. He is a fanatic, Quixotic rebel who uses the medium of poetry to give vent to his dynamic passions, as Lucifer might handle God's thunder. He is a poet because he makes use of poetic symbols; because his prophetic, or satanic frenzy lifts him to the heights of poetry. (p. 290)

> *S. A. Rhodes, "Lautréamont 'Redivivus'," in The Romanic Review, Vol. XXII, No. 4 (October-December, 1931), pp. 285-90.*

EDMUND WILSON (essay date 1931)

[*Wilson is generally considered twentieth-century America's foremost man of letters. A prolific reviewer, creative writer, and social and literary critic endowed with formidable intellectual powers, he exercised his greatest literary influence as the author of* Axel's Castle (*excerpted below*), *a seminal study of literary symbolism, and as the author of widely read reviews and essays in which he introduced the best works of modern literature to the reading public. In the following excerpt from his discussion of dadaism as an outgrowth of the symbolist movement, Wilson briefly reviews Lautréamont's life and works, describing him as* "the patron saint of Dadaism." *The report mentioned by Wilson that Lautréamont was assassinated by the secret police of Napoleon III, though widely believed at the beginning of this century, has been discredited by recent scholars.*]

[The writer] of the first Symbolist generation whom the Dadaists seem most to have admired was a man named Isidore Ducasse, the author of the **Chants de Maldoror,** who signed himself "Comte de Lautréamont." Ducasse was a Frenchman born in Uruguay, who came to Paris in 1867 when he was twenty-one and, full of the literature of the Romantics from Byron to Baudelaire, composed an immature but not unpromising book in which the expression of what had become by that time the conventional attitudes of Romanticism was given a slightly new accent and handled in a slightly new way. **Les Chants de Maldoror** is full of the familiar ferocities and blasphemies, the familiar sombre confessions of uncommon and magnificent sins, carried, however, to unprecedented lengths by a young writer who evidently felt that his predecessors had set him a high standard to surpass; but the images of his nightmares and tirades have that peculiar phantasmagoric quality which was to be characteristic of Symbolism. Very little is known about Ducasse, but he has been identified with considerable plausibility with a man of the same surname, a particularly violent social-revolutionary orator who attracted a certain amount of notice at the popular meetings authorized by Napoleon III on the eve of the Franco-Prussian War. Ducasse was found dead in his room one morning, three years after he had come to Paris, and there are reasons for believing that he was murdered by Napoleon's secret police. At any rate, a legendary Ducasse, thin, catlike, small and dry, with a shrill grating voice and a "tête de décapité," half-buffoon but with a demon's energy, hushing crowds with his bloodthirsty speeches and dashing down at top speed during his solitary nights a book of sadistic and scandalous visions, became the patron saint of Dadaism. (pp. 254-55)

> Edmund Wilson, "Gertrude Stein," in his Axel's Castle: A Study in the Imaginative Literature of 1870-1930, *Charles Scribner's Sons, 1931, pp. 237-56.**

ALBERT THIBAUDET (essay date 1936)

[*Thibaudet was an early twentieth-century French literary critic and follower of the French philosopher Henri Bergson. His work is considered versatile, well informed, and original, and critics cite his unfinished* Histoire de la littérature française de 1789 à nos jours, *first published in 1936 and excerpted below, as his major critical treatise. In this work, Thibaudet classified authors by the generations of 1789, 1820, 1850, 1885, and 1914-18, rather than by literary movements. Thibaudet groups Lautréamont with Verlaine, Mallarmé, Rimbaud, and Corbière, labeling them "the dissidents of 1870."*]

Verlaine was the faun, Mallarmé the mystic, Rimbaud the child, Corbière the mystic. Among all these dissidents there certainly had to be an authentic dissenter from reason, a madman, his madness presented by genius. This was the case with Lautréamont. Although he never wrote a line of verse, Lautréamont brought an unaccustomed parcel of poetry into literature with *Les Chants de Maldoror:* a frenzied monologue in six songs, an oratorical surge, a proclamation of ferments of violence and violator, of sensual and sexual, of redskin and antediluvian in a creature of letters cast up from an austral world on to some unexpected shore of France. A pre-Columbian idol and a sea serpent, Maldoror has given French literature what England has asked in vain of Loch Ness: its monster. With him as with the four others, a limit of literary creation was reached—hyperbole! (p. 426)

> Albert Thibaudet, "The Dissidents," in his French Literature from 1795 to Our Era, *translated by Charles Lam Markmann, Funk & Wagnalls, 1968, pp. 421-27.**

PAUL ÉLUARD (essay date 1936)

[*Éluard, along with Breton, founded the surrealist movement in France. Though he formally abandoned the movement in 1938, Éluard never ceased utilizing the methods he developed as a surrealist. Today, he is particularly acclaimed for his skilled use of imagery in accordance with surrealist methods, as well as the strength of his lyrics, the economy of his language, and the vivid texture of his poetry. Here, Éluard offers a brief tribute to the works of Lautréamont and Sade, highlighting their violence and power.*]

There is no portrait of the Marquis de Sade in existence. It is significant that there is none of Lautréamont either. The faces of these two fantastic and revolutionary writers, the most desperately audacious that ever were, are lost in the night of the ages.

They both fought fiercely against all artifices, whether vulgar or subtle, against all traps laid for us by that false and importunate reality which degrades man. To the formula: '*You are what you are,*' they have added: '*You can be something else.*'

By their violence Sade and Lautréamont strip solitude of all its adornments. In solitude each being, each object, each convention, each image also, premeditates a return to its own non-becoming reality, to have no longer a secret to reveal, to lie hatching peacefully and uselessly in the atmosphere it creates.

Sade and Lautréamont, who were solitary to the last degree, have revenged themselves by mastering the miserable world imposed upon them. In their hands they held earth, fire and water, the arid enjoyment of privation, and also weapons; and anger was in their eyes. They demolish, they impose, they outrage, they ravish. The doors of love and hate are open to let in violence. Inhuman, it will arouse man, really arouse him, and will not withhold from him, a mere accident on earth, the possibility of an end. Man will emerge from his hiding-places and, faced with the vain array of charms and disenchantments, he will be drunk with the power of his ecstasy.

He will then no longer be a stranger either to himself or to others. (pp. 179-80)

> Paul Éluard, "Poetic Evidence," in Surrealism, *edited by Herbert Read, 1936. Reprint by Faber and Faber Limited, 1971, pp. 169-84.**

GEORGES HUGNET (essay date 1936)

[*In this excerpt from his essay on the antecedents of the surrealist movement, Hugnet stresses Lautréamont's willingness to confront moral and philosophical issues and his experimental approach to language.*]

Here I am concerned merely to enumerate in the immediate past, from the time of Gérard de Nerval and Charles Baudelaire, whose flashes of Surrealism gleam on the romantic current, those who have heard the surrealist call even although they have not always responded, those who have striven for the liberation of the spirit, those who by means of technical discoveries, by virtue of a new sensibility and strange imagery, have sought the freedom of the imagination. Two names at once suggest themselves: Lautréamont and Arthur Rimbaud. How right Lautréamont was when he wrote in 1869: 'A l'heure que j'écris, des nouveaux frissons parcourent l'atmosphère intellectuelle: il ne s'agit que d'avoir le courage de les regarder en face.' It is a fact that after the supernaturalism of Nerval, the poetic lycanthropy of Borel, and certain arresting images of Baudelaire, an acceleration set in with Lautréamont. Indeed, it is evident that the writer of this sentence could look squarely at what others had merely given a passing glance. He brought into question the rôle of spirituality, of morality, all human laws, the purpose of literature. Facing that from which others had hypocritically turned aside, uttering his great tempestuous cry, he threw into the night of humanity a dazzling light which fell on shame and agony and on the most poignant despair. In his powerful romantic language, with its wild apostrophes, full of the most astounding images, he tried to deliver man from his illusory obsessions; throwing all notions of good and evil into the scales, he marked on the dial the hollowness of human justice. Lautréamont's contribution is thus more intellectual and moral than formal. I wish I could insist more on the *disquieting* aspect of Lautréamont, for everyone avoids speaking about it. He terrifies, stupefies, strikes dumb. Lautréamont is, par excellence, the Surrealist. His importance is considerable and not to be compared with anyone else's. His new conception of the poet, his feeling for a kind of beauty which can only be inadequately described as *experimental,* his monstrous lucidity, make of him a colossus before which one can only bow down. That is why, with this man for whom any approximation is vain, who is unapproachable in his wonderful solitude, I have thought it best, from among so many cruel and haughty pages, to emphasise what in his work is most personal: his similes. By the estrangement and disorientation of propositions—an essentially surrealist method of resolving apparent oppositions—he pointed the way to André Breton's 'beauté convulsive.' (pp. 188-90)

> *Georges Hugnet, "1870 to 1936," in* Surrealism, *edited by Herbert Read, 1936. Reprint by Faber and Faber Limited, 1971, pp. 185-251.**

ANDRÉ BRETON   (essay date 1938)

[*Although Breton was a French poet, novelist, and critic, he is principally recognized today as a founder of the surrealist movement. The author of several* Manifestes du surréalisme, *he developed many of the movement's theories, including the belief in "écriture automatique," or automatic writing. Breton was profoundly interested in psychological theory and the world of dreams, and he sought in both his creative and theoretical writings to liberate art from its dependence on rational thought by tapping directly into the unconscious—which contributed to the striking imagery characteristic of surrealist writings. Breton's fascination with the unconscious also led him to the poetry of Lautréamont, whom he revered. Despite changes in surrealist aesthetics, Breton consistently championed Lautréamont's works as the inspiration for the movement. Here, Breton explains, in part, his admiration for the poet. His comments were originally published as an introduction to the 1938 edition of Lautréamont's* Oeuvres complètes *and were reissued in Breton's* Anthology of Black Humour.]

One must recover the colours used by Lewis in *The Monk* to paint the apparition of the infernal spirit behind the features of an admirable young man, naked to his crimson wings, his limbs caught in an orbit of diamonds under an antique breath of roses, a star on his forehead and his gaze imprinted with a savage melancholy. . . . [One must] recover these colours to situate, in the extraliterary atmosphere (and that is to say the least), the dazzling figure of black light, the comte de Lautréamont. In the eyes of certain poets of today, *Les Chants de Maldoror* and *Poésies* sparkle with an incomparable brilliance. They are the expression of a total revelation that seems to exceed human possibilities. This is the whole of modern life, sublimated in a single blow in what is specifically its own. His backdrops revolve on the swinging doors of the ancient suns that illuminate the sapphire floor, the lamp with the silver beak, winged and smiling, advancing over the Seine, the green membranes of space and the shops on the rue Vivienne, prey to the crystalline rays from the centre of the earth. An absolutely virgin eye alerts itself to the scientific perfection of the world, disregarding the consciously utilitarian character of that perfection, situating it, with all the rest, in the light of the apocalypse. *Definitive apocalypse*: in this work the great instinctive pulsebeats are lost and exalted upon contact with the asbestos cage enclosing a white-hot heart. For centuries to come, everything thought and explored most audaciously will find here, for-

mulated in advance, its magic law. The word, no longer style, suffers with Lautréamont a fundamental crisis, marking a *recommencement.* Thus are drawn the limits within which words can enter into rapport with words, and things with things. A principle of perpetual mutation overtakes objects and things alike, tending towards their total deliverance which involves that of man. In this regard the language of Lautréamont is at once a dissolvant and a germinative plasma without equivalent.

The accusations of madness, of proof by absurdity, of an infernal machine, which have been voiced and even repeated about such a work, demonstrate very well that criticism has never approached it without sooner or later acknowledging its own failure. This is because, brought down to a human scale, this work, which is the very setting for all mental interferences, inflicts a tropical climate on the sensibility. Léon-Pierre Quint, in his very lucid work, *Le Comte de Lautréamont et Dieu,* extracts some of the most imperious qualities of this message that can be received only with gloves of fire:

1. 'Evil' for Lautréamont (as for Hegel) being the form under which the motive force of historical development presents itself, it is important to fortify it in its *raison d'être,* which cannot be done better than by establishing it on prohibited desires, inherent in such primitive sexual activity as is manifested in particular by sadism.

2. Poetic inspiration, according to Lautréamont, comes as the product of a rupture between common sense and the imagination, a rupture most often consummated in favour of the latter and obtained by the voluntary, vertiginous acceleration of the verbal flow. (Lautréamont speaks of the 'extremely rapid development' of his sentences. As we know, the systematisation of this kind of expression inaugurated surrealism.)

3. Maldororian revolt cannot be revolt forever if it must indefinitely spare one form of thought at the expense of another; thus in *Poésies* it necessarily assumes its own dialectical position.

The flagrant contrast offered by these two works from a moral point of view makes any other explanation unnecessary. Yet, as one searches deeper for that element capable of effecting their unity, their identity, from a psychological point of view, one discovers that it rests principally on humour—the various operations which are, here, the resignation of logical thought, of moral thought, and subsequently of the two new methods of thought defined by opposition to these latter, but which do not recognise any other common factor: playing against the evidence, appealing to the mob of the boldest comparisons, torpedoing solemnity, reconsidering wrong side out, transposed, those celebrated 'thoughts' or maxims, etc. All that analysis reveals in this regard of the procedures in play yields with interest to the infallible representation that Lautréamont leads us to make of humour as he envisages it—humour developing with him its supreme power and completely subjecting us to its law. (pp. 193-95)

> *André Breton, "'Anthology of Black Humour': Isidore Ducasse, Comte de Lautréamont," translated by Stephen Schwartz, in his* What is Surrealism? Selected Writings, *edited by Franklin Rosemont, Pluto Press, 1978, pp. 193-95.*

HENRY MILLER   (essay date 1944)

[*An American novelist, essayist, and critic, Miller was one of the most controversial authors of the twentieth century. The ribaldry and eroticism of such works as* Tropic of Cancer *and* Tropic of Capricorn *made him one of the most censored major writers of all time. Many of Miller's best-known works are autobiographical and describe the author's quest for truth and freedom as well as his rejection of the social, political, and moral strictures of modern civilization. According to Kenneth Rexroth, Miller wrote for those "to whom the values, the achievements, and the classics of the dominant civilization are meaningless and absurd." Miller's essay on Lautréamont, written in response to the New Directions edition of* Maldoror, *was originally published in the Autumn, 1944, issue of* Accent. *Here, he ruminates on the importance of Lautréamont and particularly on the theme of God in* Maldoror. *Miller underscores the power and intensity of the poem, declaring that "the style, the effect, the intent, everything about this black bible is monstrous."*]

"Everything was working towards its destiny: the trees, the plants, the sharks. All—except the Creator!" Thus sings Lautréamont in the third canto [of *Maldoror*] where the Omnipotent is made to assume the role of He Who Gets Slapped. But that was all long ago, as Isidore himself says, only to add quickly: "but I think he knows where I am now." (I wonder.) And then, in one of the most revelatory passages of the entire work, he continues: "He avoids my place and we both live like two neighboring monarchs who are aware of one another's respective powers, cannot overcome one another, and are weary of the useless battles of the past."

Like two neighboring monarchs! Or, The Ego and his Own . . .

Maldoror deals almost exclusively with God the Omnipotent One. God in man, man in God, and the Devil take the hindmost. But always God. This is important to stress, because should it become overnight a best seller (due to those by-products so hungrily sought after by Anglo-Saxons, viz., lust, cruelty, vice, hate, vindictiveness, rage, violence, despair, ennui, rape, etc.), God may be forgotten and only the ferocious little Isidore Ducasse, alias the Comte de Lautréamont, remembered. God had a hand in the creation of this book, as he did in the creation of *A Season in Hell, Flowers of Evil* and other so-called disturbing works, which are disturbing only because we are loath to recognize the shadow as well as the majesty of the Almighty. It is most important to emphasize this because, unless the miracle happens or Chance be defeated, some obscure and innocent printer will, like Etienne Dolet, take the rap and go to the gibbet.

Almost seventy-five years after the appearance of this infamous work (which, incidentally, failed to establish a precedent for the *Hundred and Twenty Days*) an eminent American lawyer, elated over the decision rendered by Judge Woolsey (James Joyce vs. America), raves publicly in a Foreword to a cheap edition of *Ulysses,* about the body-blow then (1933—year of forgotten miracles) delivered the censors. "The necessity," says he, "for hypocrisy and circumlocution in literature has been eliminated. Writers need no longer seek refuge in euphemisms. They may now desribe basic human functions without fear of the law." This is precisely what the young Isidore did. He asked no quarter and he gave none. His predecessor was Jonathan Swift and his chief executor was the Marquis de Sade who spent most of his life in jail. Isidore escaped with a whole skin by dying young. In time he came to be for André Breton and his group what Rimbaud was for Claudel and the unknown galaxy to follow.

Baudelaire was a rain of frogs, Rimbaud a nova (which still blazes), and Lautréamont a black messenger heralding the death of illusion and the nightmare of impotence to follow. Had there been only these three sinister luminaries in the whole of the

nineteenth century that century would have claim to being one of the most illustrious in all literature. But there were others— Blake, Nietzsche, Whitman, Kierkegaard, Dostoievski, to cite just a few. In the middle of this amazing century a border line was crossed, and there will be no returning. Almost every European nation, and even America, contributed to this putsch: it was the century of great gangsters in every walk of life, in every realm, including the celestial.

The three great bandits were Baudelaire, Rimbaud and Lautréamont. And now they have become sanctified. Now we see that they were angels in disguise. Seventy-five years behind time, like a derailed train which finds it own way, even through Pontine marshes, cemeteries and the crooked deals of financiers, Lautréamont arrives in America. (pp. 624-26)

"I go on existing, like basalt! In the middle as in the beginning of life, angels resemble themselves: how long it has been since I ceased to resemble myself!" Thus he laments in the fourth canto, which opens: "It is a man or a stone or a tree about to begin the fourth canto." *It is.* It is like nothing ever before invented, not even the Fourth Eclogue of Vergil. But so indeed are the other cantos. They do not even resemble one another: they are angel-lamps. Sometimes they "bellow like vast flocks of buffaloes from the pampas." Or they spout sperm, like the sperm whale. Or they impersonate themselves, like "The Hair" which the Creator left behind in the brothel, to his great embarrassment. To get the true flavor of them one has to visualize this young Montevidean (who "probably died of some respectable bourgeois disease induced by his unhealthy and Bohemian habits of life") pounding the piano as he composed them. They are French only in the language chosen. There is something Aztec, something Patagonian, in all of them. Something too of Tierra del Fuego, which lies buried like a dislocated toe in the chill waters that wrap it round. And perhaps too something of Easter Island. Not perhaps—*certainly,* most certainly.

What I wonder is not how the Anglo-Saxon will take this book, but how the Oriental will. Tamerlane could not have inspired in his own people the feelings he awakened in the peoples he slaughtered. Similarly, Ramakrishna has become for the Westerner a sort of "monster" of ecstasy. Lautréamont, following his own example exclusively, took the European gong (which had been sounding its own death knell for centuries) and literally kicked the gong around. This does not make him in the least like Cab Calloway, nor Minnie the Moocher. It makes him more and more like Lautréamont, which (to us) is insufferable.

It might be called a new Bible, written from a new Sinai, expressly for "the boa of absent morality and the monstrous snail of idiocy." The mysterious brothers are implicated, as well as the neighboring monarchs—*and the angel-lamp.* Nor can we ignore his first cruel love, the shark, with all her fins. Marvelous. Marvelous throughout, and not like the ink spots— just here and there. Pluto rising, God and man sealed in one death. Enter now the janissaries of Satan and his camelot the machine. Enter the weird birds and beasts from North America. Enter Broken Blossom and Broken Brow, followed in strict sequence by that movie which we are still making, called "The Slaughter of the Innocents." (pp. 626-27)

Suddenly, as if a volcano had erupted under the floor of a boudoir, just when France is about to receive her first mortal blow, comes a burst of passion black as pitch. Passion, I say, and not luke-warm piss from a printer's soiled bladder. All personal feuds have passion, even if the feud is only with the Creator. Isidore had one feud, one passion. He was alone. But *alone*, mind you, and that in a world where even to take a walk, as one French genius put it laconically, costs money. There was no sadder world than the world of the nineteenth century—for those who had wings. What does one do in such periods? One takes wing. One flees. One sails aloft with the albatross. But whither? *That* we are just beginning to discover. *Wing it first*, that's the moral of the nineteenth century. And leave the world of snails and boas to sink like a diseased cork.

It is the habit of critics to deal with style and such things. There is no style here to talk about. It was out of style even before it was written. Understand, please, that we are dealing with a Bedouin in a button factory. We have, if you insist, the ode, the litany, the apostrophe, the invective, the jeremiad, the bromide, the round dance, the refrain, the revolver shot, the death and the resurrection, the apocrypha, the curse and the maul, together with the vocabulary of a diamond cutter pickled in Malmsey—all in full glory like a six-masted schooner. There is also the foam on the beer, even the louse, if you are itchy. You will learn nothing from analyzing these ingredients and scaffoldings. Someone crucified himself: that's all that matters. And he had an evil name, worse than it sounds. (But it always rings like a tocsin, no matter what the language!) You will also find tenderness in these cantos, and abysmal humility. And if you have never travelled to the nadir, then here is the opportunity.

When Isidore took himself to Paris the whole world was rolling down hill. A veritable toboggan slide, but taking place in the Unconscious, as we imagine. A right jolly *dégringolade* it was. So jolly that some, like Wordsworth, Tennyson and other infatuates, were sticking their toes through Heaven's bangled tambourine. Then began a series of the most unethical assassinations, now taking on the proportions of a pogrom. (We're still at the threshold . . . livelier things are in store, don't fret.) When the split could no longer be concealed a fusion took place, a piece of expert welding, and dream and reality—like two boxers in the arena—shook hands. The man who had sawed the two realms apart folded up like a jack-knife. It was as if he had sawed the Virgin Mary in two on a busy street, fired a revolver to summon the police, waited calmly for the next bus, and then at some unpredicted *carrefour* transferred to a vehicle more to his liking. Ordinarily, were such a man apprehended, he would be put in a strait-jacket. Not Isidore. He lives beyond apprehension. He writes those advertisements in the sky which when read backwards always spell Maldoror. A golden roar of pure spite, malice, vituperation. In it is the roar of gold—pure gold, not gleet-gold. And in it too is pure evil, not the counterfeit of spinsters and clericals. (How little genuine evil is in the world! And how much gold! And what do all these black crucifixes mean?)

"NOW WE ARE IN THE MIDST OF REALITY, INSOFAR AS THE TARANTULA IS CONCERNED."

The style, the effect, the intent, everything about this black bible is monstrous. So is the image of Kali. So is mathematics, if only you would think about it. So are the good deeds of little men. So are the legends of heroes. And so finally and inevitably is the Creator, seen from here below. Otherwise would it not be too simple, like a beautiful dream, say, that had turned sour? And why not monsters now and then, in a world packed with fools and angels? (pp. 627-29)

Henry Miller, "Let Us Be Content with Three Little New-Born Elephants," in "Accent" Anthology: Se-

lections from "Accent," a Quarterly of New Literature, 1940-1945, *edited by Kerker Quinn and Charles Shattuck, Harcourt Brace Jovanovich, 1946, pp. 624-29.*

GEORGES LEMAÎTRE   (essay date 1947)

[*In this excerpt from his discussion of the forerunners of surrealism, Lemaître characterizes Lautréamont as a* révolté, *or one whose goal is destruction. According to Lemaître, the poet uses sarcasm and irony to create an evil, nightmarish world in which Maldoror rejects God and attacks all human values. Lemaître also briefly examines the subliminal sources of Lautréamont's imagery.*]

Lautréamont appears to belong to the type of extreme or absolute *révolté*. While with Baudelaire and Rimbaud revolt was but a transitory stage, a means of clearing the way to a higher sphere of self-realization, with Lautréamont it seems to have been a real end in itself. His attacks are not confined to the domain of human morals, human society, or human reason; they are directed against even God Himself. God, as the first source of all things, is held responsible for the appalling atrocity that constitutes life on this earth. The spectacle of the gaping, raw wound which life inflicts on the unfortunate animated beings who inhabit the globe is held to be the just punishment of its original Cause and Creator. "J'ai reçu la vie comme une blessure. . . . Je veux que le Créateur en contemple, à chaque heure de son éternité, la crevasse béante. C'est le châtiment que je lui inflige." . . . Maldoror stands forth like a modern Prometheus, challenging and insulting the Supreme Deity, deliberately turning his own existence into a continuous, withering blasphemy.

First, he sets himself to disintegrate the world of God's creation by virulent and caustic sarcasm. All kinds of forms and shapes, principles and ideas, are made to appear impossibly preposterous. Maldoror systematically jumbles and confuses all normal connections and values; grave problems are treated as mere bubbles; trifles are investigated with methodical thoroughness. A feeling of utter absurdity slowly pervades a universe turned topsy-turvy. The concentrated acid of the author's irony dissolves all the aspects of the world that we know into an inconsistent and odious nightmare.

But the most corrosive of all the means of destruction at his disposal is undoubtedly the existence of Evil itself. **Les Chants de Maldoror** constitutes a tremendous and amazing epic of evil. Evil is here presented, without indictment, explanation, or excuse, simply as a stupendous fact dominating the whole creation. Malefic influences are shown creeping irresistibly everywhere; and Evil, developing and expanding monstrously, finally dwarfs everything else into insignificance, all but eclipsing the very spirit of God Himself.

The feeling of guilt, intoxicating as a powerful drug, causes Maldoror to experience a curious surge of exaltation, temporarily giving to an otherwise desperate and miserable existence a zest of lurid and violent intensity. Scenes of cruelty and lust, sadistic murders, torture of living bodies, profanation of corpses, are all evoked with a wealth of gory detail that creates a haunting impression of inescapable horror. The gripping fascination exerted by horror upon certain inferior but very deep-seated strata of common human nature is here brought to a climax, and the morbid appeal possessed by certain of Lautréamont's pictures goes far to disclose the unavowed and perhaps unsuspected elements lurking at the bottom of man's subconscious mind.

Lautréamont himself obviously did not draw these pictures with any cold-blooded consideration of their import and possible effects. He seems to have obeyed an impulse from within which bade him pour out a flood of images, without restraint or discrimination, from the innermost recesses of his soul. The continuous, though uneven flow of his sentences, in which the most unusual associations come together in overpowering abundance, precludes the idea that this is a deliberate combination of heterogeneous fragments artificially pieced together. It is nothing more nor less than the current of secret, turbid subconscious thought which is allowed to come to the surface and escape through the free, uncontrolled outlet of spontaneous verbal procreation. Every metaphor brings forth an image which in turn begets a comparison; so the poet watches—without trying to interfere with—the amazing procession of strange things coming from the depths of his own being, realizing that this automatic development can reveal a new world, truly momentous and fundamental, which dialectical intelligence would certainly fail to approach.

The new world brought to light by the vision of Maldoror is not without an internal logic of its own, but it is marked by a prodigious efflorescence of weird forms with their roots spreading down into the uncertain substratum of subliminal dreams. We catch glimpses of ambiguous creatures, half-human, half-plant, suggesting a monstrous submarine flora stranded after the ebb of some preternatural tide; again, swarming legions of polymorphic beings are shown crawling on the face of some bald, arid immensity. . . . All that phantasmagoria, imbued with the elemental forces of fabulous epochs, evokes the primal mysteries which must have haunted the dreams of men from the very dawn of time. Even now it arouses in us dormant memories, the remnants of an almost vanished consciousness of potential cosmic forces whose display is for ever endowed with an enthralling, awe-inspiring grandeur.

Alternating with the recurrent themes of inevitable malediction and universal suffering are the shrill notes of demented, passionate frenzy, the chaotic torment of mutual destruction, or the anguished appeals of a lone victim pursued in the dark, shrieking with fear. But above it all sounds the voice of fierce, exasperated human pride, constantly struck down, yet indestructible, always rising again, always ready to rebel and fight; then, joining in a tremendous chorus of demoniac fury, taking up the original motif of desperate revolt against God. (pp. 37-40)

> Georges Lemaître, "The Forerunners," in his From Cubism to Surrealism in French Literature, *revised edition, 1947. Reprint by Greenwood Press, Publishers, 1978, pp. 19-49.*

OSCAR A. HAAC (essay date 1950)

[*Haac focuses on* Poésies, *examining both the work itself and its significance in Lautréamont's oeuvre. In portions of the essay not excerpted below, Haac surveys critical reaction to* Poésies *and outlines the conflicting interpretations of its relationship to* Maldoror. *In the following remarks, Haac contends that the extant portion of* Poésies *consists of two parts, an introduction and the text. Basing his opinion on internal evidence, Haac claims that there are two basic links between* Maldoror *and* Poésies: *they share similarities in structure and spirit. Haac concludes, therefore, that* Poésies *does not represent a recantation or contradiction of Lautréamont's earlier beliefs; instead, Haac views the*

An imaginary portrait of Lautréamont at nineteen, by Salvador Dali. Copyright Librairie José Corti. Used with permission.

work as a continuation of the violent mockery of God and humankind first presented in Maldoror.]

The essential continuity linking *Maldoror* to *Poésies* is twofold. First it is structural. The initial section of each of the six songs of *Maldoror* contains comment on literary method or on the author's relationship to the reader. This pattern is also true in *Poésies*. Of the two sections we have, the first only is an introduction discussing the validity of other authors and general aims. The second section, contrary to accepted opinion, is a part of the principal text. We gather from it that the poems are dramatic developments of sweeping generalizations; they are distorted maxims. As Ducasse states, "a maxim, to be well formed, must not be corrected. It must be developed!"

The other parallel between *Maldoror* and *Poésies* is one of fundamental spirit, or rather of violence. As *Maldoror* had done, *Poésies* claims universal authority and wants to encompass all of human experience, thereby satisfying the author's drive for originality and revolt. Both works give free reign to his imagination, a medium for powerful visions and a road to success. They re-evaluate morals while providing material in which his unusual verbal power can manifest itself.

The difference is merely one of presentation. *Maldoror* painted fuller scenes, yet "not to make the reader better understand but to develop my thought!'' On the other hand, in *Poésies,* Ducasse is proud that not even Racine had been able to condense his poetry into maxims. The starting point has changed from the episode to the formula, from physical violence to absolute principles. However the spirit remains.

In *Maldoror,* . . . Ducasse mocked the hypocritical public, not himself. He wanted to make sure that every last dullard saw himself parodied. In the sixth song, the chronological link to *Poésies,* this becomes most clear. Ducasse shocks the reader by protesting against inkwell and pen, by showing that the virtuous police cannot find Maldoror by commenting in his profound style which will seem ''naïve'' and by claiming that he forgot the beginning of a sentence. Oratorical questions are inserted where the stupid reader will expect them. Mervyn is lost because of his bourgeois virtues; Lautréamont admits that he aims to stupify the reader, or better, to hypnotize him. Poor reader, he will pity Mervyn like the Rhinoceros. Let him be shot then as was this symbolic quadruped, since he will not comprehend the beauty of Mervyn hung on the Vendôme column, circling it, with his blond hair shining like the tail of a comet. The author explains that this is a scene no novelist ever dreamed of, and adds that, as a poet, he is concerned only with facts beyond the normal course of nature. Surely these passages foreshadow no restraint!

Shall we assume that *Poésies* was altogether different? By examining first the introduction (section 1), then the text (section 2), let us see whether the maxims take the shape of laws within a logical philosophy, or whether they are designed, like *Maldoror* to exasperate the reader. In the introduction, Ducasse sets out methodically to contradict every accepted notion of literary fame and of traditional criticism, while asking who is ill in his mind here, the author or the reader. He then proposes as examples of literary glory three grotesque models: Villemain, prize orations and ''appreciation'' of Voltaire. The polished Villemain is said to be more valuable than Eugène Sue. This cannot be sincere because Ducasse kept his pen-name derived from Sue's novel *Latréamont* and realized Sue's popularity. Sue is set below Villemain simply because this will shock the public. For the same reason Ducasse glorifies the speeches accompanying the distribution of prizes in the schools, admittedly dull, and despised by the author who always hated school restrictions and professors. He adds to these absurd ideals ''an appreciation of Voltaire . . . preferable to his works'' and dares the reader to understand: ''Creusez le mot appréciation!''

It has been said that Ducasse, in his supposed transformation, attached himself strongly to the classical writers. A close look at the text proves this argument to be a fallacy. He was either unfamiliar with classical drama, or purposely offending common sense, when he refused the literary description of passion, unless it were subordinated to high morality as in Corneille, and when he said that Racine could very well have written the *Discourse on Method* of Descartes. These backhanded compliments just do not apply. Médée, Attila and the treacherous Cléopâtre of *Rodogune* are hardly symbols of virtuous passion, nor is Phèdre's love for her stepson a tribute to reason. If Lautréamont exclaims that Racine represents a poetic perfection which has not been surpassed ''by a single millimeter,'' it is not to worship Racine whom he later attacks, but to throw down the gauntlet before all contemporary poets, telling them that they have accomplished nothing. All recent literary figures are condemned in a series of parallel developments which become increasingly grotesque. From Sénancourt to the roman-

tics, Hugo, Musset, and Lamartine, from Balzac to Baudelaire and Flaubert, the accepted authors are mocked as tear jerkers, infantile jesters, or with epithets such as ''Byron, the jungle hippopotamus.'' Ducasse mentions the classic only the better to disparage his contemporaries, and to appear most original himself.

Final proof that he is bent on misguiding the reader is furnished by the obvious contradictions in the poems themselves (section 2). These contradictions are so significant because the author proclaims: ''The lack of contradiction is the mark of certainty!'' For instance, Racine is set up as a hero of logic, then rejected since he failed to condense his tragedies into maxims or to write for the masses. The first of these objections is a negation of dramatic art, the second is meaningless as applied to the time of Racine or to Lautréamont's own works, which are anything but popular literature. There are other examples. Ducasse presents as the ideal author the moralist who is also a good writer and calls him preferable to the poet. Soon thereafter poets are set above philosophers. On another occasion he states: ''I do not accept evil!'' Soon he reverses himself by saying that not pleasures, but only boredom and complete acceptance of evil fate can overcome misfortune. This nihilistic argument concludes with the outcry: ''Ill fortune is not in us . . . but in Elohim,'' but Elohim is God, the principle identified with the good by the unsuspecting reader!

Still Ducasse fears that he will be misunderstood, and rightly so, judging by past critics. He asks: ''Must I write in verse to separate myself from the multitude?'' This means: does it not suffice that I compose my poems in prose, that I pervert every principle, that I consistently violate my own dictum that the lack of contradiction is the mark of certitude? Indeed, certainty is not in *Poésies* if lack of contradiction be a prerequisite. Yet it was certainty which the transformists wanted to find here.

We conclude that we actually possess a group of Lautréamont's poems in the second section of *Poésies,* that they are distorted maxims claiming universal authority and that their meaning is clear, though both surrealists and their enemies often failed to see it, and distorted their appraisal by symbolic interpretations of the author's death. Ducasse merely shifted his approach after *Maldoror,* but he still mocks all morals in the poems, and public opinion in his introduction to them. His motto: ''I replace evil by good'' is but a challenge disguised as a pronouncement of human wisdom. In *Poésies* Satan Maldoror speaks again, Maldoror who once asked in surprise: How can it be that I am so wicked and yet but the son of men? Ducasse planned once more to shock the christian reader and represent to him extreme vice and evil. Dante and Milton were models to be outdone in their portrayals of hell, spirits to be stripped of their symmetrical and rational thinking, so that the unlimited will to pervert could be pictured. (pp. 371-75)

> *Oscar A. Haac, ''Lautréamont's Conversion: The Structure and Meaning of 'Poésies','' in* Modern Language Notes, *Vol. LXV, No. 6, June, 1950, pp. 369-75.*

WALLACE FOWLIE (essay date 1950)

> [*Fowlie is one of the most respected and versatile scholars of French literature. His works include translations of major dramatists and poets of France as well as critical studies of the major figures and movements of modern French letters. The following excerpt is drawn from his treatise on surrealism both as a literary movement and as a description of a profound psychological state.*

Fowlie examines several of the major figures of surrealism as well as the nineteenth-century writers who most profoundly influenced them, including Lautréamont. Using Lautréamont as a symbol, Fowlie attempts to describe the temperament of the modern artist. He begins by arguing that the temperament of romantic artists and their modern successors was one of individualism, which derived from the artists' experience of solitude. According to Fowlie, Lautréamont bridged the gap between the romantic intuition and the surrealist dogma that solitude was essential to the creative process. Fowlie argues that because Lautréamont's work was created entirely from personal experience, Maldoror does not reflect external reality. Instead, Lautréamont's solitude enabled him to journey into himself to discover and depict universal experiences and archetypal emotions. This quality, according to Fowlie, assured Lautréamont's importance to the surrealists. For further criticism by Fowlie, see excerpt dated 1967 and Additional Bibliography.]

The experience of solitude probably explains more about modern literature and art than any other single experience. And I am thinking of the solitude of such different geniuses as Vigny in his ivory tower, Hugo on his islands, Rimbaud in his voyages and escapes, Claudel in his religious meditations, Joyce in his exile from Dublin. In his solitude, which is his inheritance, the modern artist has had to learn that the universe which he is going to write or paint is in himself. He has learned that this universe which he carries about in himself is singularly personal and unique as well as universal. To find in oneself what is original and at the same time what can be translated into universal terms and transmitted, became the anxiety and the occupation of the modern artist. The romantics held this belief partially and intuitively. The surrealists made it into a creed and a method. Surrealism was actually founded on the doctrine that the artist does not belong to any one period and that he must discover solely in himself his universe.

The man who did more than any other to bridge the gap between the romantic perception, only faintly illuminated, and the surrealist dogmatism was Isidore Ducasse, who called himself Comte de Lautréamont. (pp. 29-30)

The surrealists have venerated the obscurity and the solitude of Lautréamont's life. The absence of any photographic resemblance of him has incited them to create imaginary portraits based upon the literary testament which he left. *Les Chants de Maldoror* come from a single mind, from the sensibility of one man who lived in almost total solitude in the midst of modern European civilization and who, like Rimbaud (who was writing his first poems when Lautréamont died), traversed in the space of just a few years, approximately 1865-1870, a whole century of human experience. A few readings which are traceable in his work, in addition to the particular kind of solitude he lived, were sufficient to call forth from him a series of images and of themes, whose intensity and meaning go very far in explaining much of modern art. His temperament, formed by a modern genus of solitude, created a series of images, which are those of the modern artist, and which seemingly can be explained best in terms of this mysterious temperament.

· · · · ·

It is important to remember that for the surrealists, Lautréamont was much more significant than a mere literary figure could ever be. He is their ancestor not so much by virtue of having created a new literary atmosphere or a new literary work, as by virtue of having created a domain inclusive of literature and art but far more extensive. For the surrealists the language of Lautréamont seems to have a dissolving power. What he literally committed to the page is striking and bold and almost unthinkable at times, but what is important is the degree of life and vision, and particularly of futurity in life and vision, which can be evoked from the work. Its language and its image may therefore dissolve into a reality greater than they, a reality which is not translatable into language. (pp. 31-2)

At the beginning of Lautréamont's work, in the first canto of *Maldoror,* we learn that the experience which is going to be related is the career of evil. On page 3, Lautréamont says that Maldoror, after living for a few years, made the discovery that he had been born wicked, and "il se jeta résolument dans la carrière du mal" [see excerpt dated 1868]. This phrase, "the career of evil," is a violent announcement for a work of art. It prepares us at the outset for a sombre revelation and informs us that the work is to be read as a book of negation. The subject matter is to be the disaster and catastrophe of human experience. The narrative of *Maldoror* is therefore not to be what we often find in literary works—a sublimation or an embellishment of life. It is to be the reverse of all that—the going backwards of man (since evil is the negation of the good), the plunge into human existence at a point which will often appear, as we read *Les Chants de Maldoror,* pre-historical, a point in time before human existence began. The large number of animals, and particularly of sea animals (sharks, whales, crabs, frogs, octopuses) and birds of all kinds, which inhabit the pages of *Maldoror,* accentuate this important theme of the reversal of chronology, this turning back of man in order to track down the origin of his dilemma and anguish and evil.

Throughout the six cantos, Lautréamont maintains, as one of his primary themes, the relationship of man with the physical universe, with what often appears to be the prehistoric physical universe. The hero Maldoror, who is in many respects the outstanding surrealist hero, is conceived of as a man still very close to his memory of animals, still very close to the time when he himself participated in an animal existence. He is the hero closely and fervently animalistic, and hence sadistic; the being who moves and acts in accordance with cruelty. He finds himself midway between two beings: between the purely physical being, such as a shark, and the purely spiritual being whom he calls God. Maldoror finds himself equally distributed between matter and spirit, and therefore equally drawn toward animals and toward God. But since the cantos are to narrate his career of evil, he describes his sadistic impulses more exclusively than his spiritually motivated impulses. The initial phrase, "the career of evil," implies that Maldoror feels closer allegiance to the physical than to the spiritual, that he is going to attempt to live solely by sadistic evil. Yet, the career of evil never completely obliterates the career of the spirit, and Maldoror states, also in the first canto, his need for the infinite: *Moi, comme les chiens, j'éprouve le besoin de l'infini.* But such a need as this is followed by the need to feel himself the son of a shark or of a tiger.

I suppose that never has a literary hero felt so perfectly ambivalent as Maldoror. This evenly partitioned ambivalence, unique perhaps in Lautréamont, has its antecedents throughout the history of man, in the age-long struggle between good and evil, God and Lucifer, the spiritual and the material, the unicorn and the lion. The duality of man is inescapably reflected in art. (pp. 33-5)

The duality of man and the duality of all art are . . . exemplified in the very particular duality of the artist whose temperament or temperamental ambiguities are projected in highly dramatic fashion in Lautréamont. The permanent drama of man is the struggle between good and evil. This is treated directly and vehemently in *Les Chants de Maldoror.* But it is prefigured in the permanent drama of every artist. This drama is the struggle to attain some harmony between the two needs of the artist: first, the need to be a man of the world, that is, a man who somehow understands the world and the reasons for the customs of the world; and second, the need to be the specialist, chained to his palette or his marble or his language.

The conflict in every artist is the need to understand the world and the need to live apart from it. But he has to understand the world not in the usual moral and political way, but in a manner which I have already described as prehistorical. The great artist—and this I take to be the surrealist lesson of Lautréamont—has to be able to return to those shadowy worlds existing before birth and after death. The great artist has to remember everything: not merely the wars and revolutions of his time, but of time before time, of the war in heaven, of apocalyptic wars and infernal punishments.

Most men are simply curious about history and politics. But in the artist, this curiosity grows into a monstrous kind of passion, into a force which is fatal and irresistible. It makes of him a singular being capable of all metamorphoses. This is, to a large extent, the subject matter of *Les Chants de Maldoror.* On one level, Maldoror is able to metamorphose himself into an animal, in much the same way as a character of Kafka changes into a cockroach. But on the other level, his tortuous pride and his memory make him desirous of equaling God. Again in the first canto, we come upon this sentence: *il voudrait égaler Dieu.* This surrealist metamorphosis of Maldoror, which moves in two directions, one toward the physical and the other toward the spiritual, is really the annihilation of time, by which the hero is able to descend into the mysterious past when man was one with God. He has never recovered from the haunting memory of some distant and buried crime which turned him against God.

To use the word consecrated and especially defined in French literature by Charles Baudelaire, the modern artist has become the "dandy." *Le dandy* is the being dramatized and allegorized by Lautréamont in his character Maldoror. The dandy, according to Baudelaire, has critical intelligence and a finely developed sensitivity and character, but he is constantly aspiring to a coldness of feeling, a hardness of character, an insensibility, an inscrutability. This is a tight-fitting mask which he must forge every day in order not to betray himself when in the world. The dandy learns how to feign hostility and indifference until they become naturally instinctive in him. His fear is the same as Maldoror's fear—that to appear sincere in his worldly relationships would be equivalent to appearing ridiculous. (pp. 35-7)

[The case of Maldoror] is an instance and a deep study of the Baudelairian dandy and hence of the modern artist—the man who has to see the world, who has to live in its center, and who all the time has to remain hidden from the world. Such an ambiguous rôle, which I think can be traced to the early Renaissance when Christendom began its secularization, allows us quite justifiably to consider the modern artist the secularized priest, the one who, forced by his vocation to live apart from the world, is nevertheless the profoundest conscience of the world, the most accurate recorder and interpreter of the world's problems.

· · · · ·

In this light, the experience of solitude for the modern artist is religious. It is the experience of a sacrament. Both prepa-

ration and absolution, it effects a complete change in the human being. The solitude of Lautréamont, who was known personally by so few people, whose itinerary, only eighty years ago, through such a modern city as Paris, is not traceable, and the solitude of his hero Maldoror who contemplates one scene after another in the world, only to lay waste to it when he himself participates in it, have the same secret force of a destiny. Solitude seems to be the destined climate and need and fulfillment of the modern artist. Baudelaire, in his personal journal, *Mon coeur mis à nu,* acknowledges this same thought: *sentiment de destinée éternellement solitaire.*

The center of this inescapable solitude is the scene of Lautréamont's revolt against God, made all the more dramatic and bare because of the solitude. *Les Chants de Maldoror* illustrate what Baudelaire analyzed as the modern type of beauty, namely a commingling of mystery and tragedy. *Mystère* and *malheur* were the words Baudelaire used, and he referred to Milton's Satan as a leading type of virile beauty. This Baudelairian definition of the beautiful might easily be applied to the art of other periods, to the *Oedipus* of Sophocles and the *Phèdre* of Racine, for example, but Lautréamont, writing in the wake of Baudelaire's doctrine, made a shocking and violent use of it, and the surrealists held steadfastly to this particular illustration of the theory.

The celebrated scene between Maldoror and a female shark which takes place almost at the end of the second canto, would serve to depict the Baudelairian and surrealist type of beauty, as well as to indicate the main traits of Maldoror's revolt against God, and hence the dandy's indifference about life.

The scene is prefaced by an important passage dealing precisely with the theme of solitude, of predestined solitude which may well explain the excessive action of sadism and bestiality. Maldoror says that he had searched everywhere for a kindred spirit, for a soul which resembled his, but he had found no one. By day a young man had approached him, offering his friendship, but Maldoror had turned him aside. By night he had spoken to a beautiful woman but had been unable to accept her love. This is the setting of a parable. The first act of the drama now begins. Maldoror, seated on a rock by the shore, watches a storm rise up and hurl a large ship against a reef. The drowning men try to prolong their lives because they fail to recognize the fish of the sea as their ancestors. Fetishistically, Maldoror prods his cheek with a sharp piece of iron in order to increase the suffering of the victims from the boat. This is the first strong note of sadistic pleasure which Maldoror is deriving from the shipwreck scene. He takes his gun and finishes off those few who are on the point of escaping, especially a boy who, stronger than the rest, swims to only 200 meters off the shore. But Maldoror says that he was tired of always killing, that his pleasure had diminished, that he was not really so cruel as later he was accused of being. We half see in such a statement that cruelty is a willed regimen, an experimentation. Yet Maldoror makes no effort to excuse himself: he acknowledges that, when he commits a crime, he knows what he is doing.

A second act, more terrifying than the first, begins when the ship finally sinks into the sea and the many survivors are left floundering about on the surface. A school of sharks adds a new horror to the scene and the water becomes crimson with blood. At that moment a huge female shark, famished, arrives and destroys all but three of the male sharks. Maldoror kills one of these with his gun, and then dives into the ocean to attack with his bare hands and a knife one of the sharks while the female slays the one remaining monster. Alone, then, in the water with the female shark, Maldoror unites with her in a ferocious embrace. This, of course, is the culmination of the drama, which is in itself a kind of metamorphosis. Maldoror recapitulates the introductory theme, when he says that the shark resembles him, that he is no longer alone and that he has experienced his first love.

Such a scene as this, I might say, in the violence of its beauty and its horror, has not been exceeded in the writings and the paintings of the surrealists. For a scene of comparable power and awesomeness, one would perhaps have to go to Dante's *Inferno,* to the circle, for example, where thieves are punished by having their bodies united with the bodies of snakes. This shark scene of the second canto is exemplary of two fundamental literary qualities mentioned by Baudelaire in his work, *Fusées,* two qualities rigorously adhered to by the surrealists— supernaturalism and irony. The attraction of the shark is at least mysterious if not supernatural, and Maldoror's first discovery of love in his mating with the sea monster is strongly ironic, according to any ordinary measurement of human standards.

The act of love is here portrayed in a scene which reveals its most primitive aspect of torture—as the act of prayer might easily be portrayed in its most primitive aspect of magic. But for our specific purpose, which is an understanding of the meaning of surrealism, this scene, so strongly primitive in its ferocity and incredibility, so reminiscent of our dream world where we cohabit with monsters, might help us to establish the myth of the artist, as specifically enacted by Maldoror. Again we return to Baudelaire, for textual confirmation in his journal, *Mon coeur mis à nu,* where he writes that only three types of men are respectable, as judged by the temperament of the artist. These are the priest, the warrior and the poet. All other men exercise what Baudelaire scornfully calls professions; that is, I suppose, perfectly measurable and conventionalized lives. With each of these three types, Baudelaire associates a verb, that is, a strong action. For the priest, it is "to know," for the warrior, "to kill," for the poet, "to create." These combined roles in the artist—of priest, warrior, poet; or of knower, killer, creator—form the myth of the artist, and are, curiously enough, quite evident in Maldoror's scene with the female shark. First he presides over it as a priest might preside over a complicated ritual: he predicts and knows it and seems even to control it. And then, like the warrior, he participates in actual destructiveness and slaughter. Finally, like the poet, he creates a new form of himself in his union with the monster.

The entire passage shows the combined contradictions of feeling which every artist experiences before the spectacle of life: the feelings of horror and ecstasy. The ecstasy of the priest, who knows transcendently, and the horror of the warrior, who kills in obedience to a deeply imbedded primitive instinct, have to be combined in the creation of the poet which is the formalized metaphor of horror and ecstasy. The orderly evolution of the three verbs, *to know, to kill, to create* is at once the expression of a temperament and the process of a myth. It is in close accord with the aesthetic doctrine which defines the beautiful in terms of mystery and tragedy. (pp. 37-41)

Every human life is more characterized by mystery and secretiveness than by comprehensiveness and lucidity. For the surrealists the secret of Lautréamont's life was the sign of the inaccessible character of his work. The difficulty or obscurity of artistic form always comes from the mysteriousness or inaccessibility of the content. The content of *Les Chants de Maldoror,* as is evident from the shark episode is perhaps the most

incomprehensible of all possible themes, because it is the insubordination of man to God. This theme of man's revolt against God is in almost all of the greatest literary works: in Aeschylus, in the story of Moses, in Dante's *Inferno,* where it is the only subject, in Milton, Goethe, Baudelaire. Maldoror's pride is that of the damned, whose beauty is horror and whose memory is ecstasy.

* * * * *

The newness of Maldoror and his specifically surrealistic character is his exaggeration of revolt, its absolute quality, and the humanized and degraded portraiture he gives of God. Maldoror appears not only in a state of revolt against God, but as a rivaling and neighboring monarch to God. In his need to equal God, he utters extreme blasphemy and at the same time he creates metaphorically in his writing an important aspect of art usually called the "grotesque." The long passage which terminates the third canto is a brothel scene in which Maldoror listens to the speech of a gigantic hair fallen from God's head. The blasphemy consists of thinking of God as having committed sin and crime. The divine misdemeanors had awakened from their sleep of centuries in the catacombs under the brothel, which significantly was once a convent, the nuns who, like those of us living in the modern world, are overcome with a strange *malaise* and anxiety. So, God Himself receives the stigmata and has to strive to rehabilitate Himself in the world of men. God talks about His shame as being endless as eternity: *ma honte est immense comme l'éternité.* In such scenes in which God is degraded, Maldoror reveals himself as an integral anarchist, as the destroyer not only of human but also of divine values.

If the writer Lautréamont was in revolt against what was currently accepted in his day as "literature," namely the well-rounded inflated sentence of romantic style, his character Maldoror was in revolt against conventionalized feelings and respected taboos. The surest and cruelest way to overcome dramatized feelings and pompous and stubbornly stated affiliations is to make fun of them. *Les Chants de Maldoror,* even in such serious scenes as those of the female shark and the hair from God's head, contain an aspect of the modern type of humor and the comic which is so important in the work of Picasso, Joyce, and Proust. I am confident that Lautréamont and the surrealists were scornful of the traditional type of comedy, as exemplified in Aristophanes and Molière. They were as strongly opposed to the exaggerated verbal logic of romanticism, of a Chateaubriand, for example, whom Lautréamont called the "melancholy Mohican," as they were opposed to the intellectual logic and rule of good common sense, which have always been extolled and exemplified by the culture of France. Lautréamont and the surrealists, in their rôle of ardently minded revolutionaries, would have been mortified in using any of the traditional forms of comedy and tragedy. Blasphemy, which is a combination of the serious and the comic, is their mode. When art is somewhat dominated by the grotesque (which is always allied with blasphemy) the spirit of modern man is more at ease in considering the serious, the tragic, the religious. I am thinking here not only of Lautréamont and the surrealists, of Picasso, Proust, and Joyce, but also, to a lesser degree, of course, of *The New Yorker,* Mickey Mouse, Charles Chaplin, Fernandel.

Maldoror, in his many experiences of violence and revolt, is trying to destroy the voice of his conscience, to forget the lessons of tradition and convention. He turns against the family, as the prodigal son did, and initiates a fervent line of modern prodigal sons, of whom the most illustrious are Rimbaud and Gide. In him, love and hate are perfectly fused, as they must inevitably be in any real experience of blasphemy. Both the writer and his creature, both Lautréamont and Maldoror, are the same adolescent who makes of his revolt, so equally composed of love and hate, a search for the absolute. This is a mark of adolescents: they are the most fervent seekers of the absolute. As they grow older, only the few among them who become by vocation poets, philosophers, and saints remain seekers of the absolute.

So, the adolescent revolutionist turns against his family, against the books of his schoolmasters, and against his society. But after knowing during their adolescence the passion of revolution, most revolutionists become lovers. Lautréamont, as far as his book is concerned, did not become lover. His book deals only with the principle of destruction, and not with the principle which follows destruction, when the revolutionist becomes lover, namely the principle of possession. Lautréamont, then, represents the first stage of an evolution. He is the pure example of revolutionist. (pp. 42-4)

> *Wallace Fowlie, "Lautréamont: The Temperament," in his* Age of Surrealism, *1950. Reprint by Indiana University Press, 1960, pp. 28-44.*

ALBERT CAMUS   (essay date 1951)

[*An Algerian-born French novelist, essayist, dramatist, and short story writer, Camus was one of the most important literary figures of the twentieth-century. Throughout his varied writings, Camus consistently, often passionately, explored his major theme: the belief that people can be happy in a world without meaning. He defended the dignity and decency of the individual and asserted that through purposeful action one can overcome the apparent nihilism of the world. His notion of an "absurd" universe is premised on the tension between life in an irrational universe and the human desire for rationality. Although this world view has led Camus to be linked with the Existentialists, he himself rejected this classification. In his* L'homme revolté, *first published in 1951 and excerpted below, Camus examines the nature and history of rebellion, emphasizing individual revolt. Camus discusses Lautréamont's contradictory attitude toward revolt and discerns therein a desire for annihilation. Maldoror represents total revolt against God and the physical universe and the destruction of all boundaries, which results in the refusal to recognize rational consciousness. Yet in* Poésies, *Lautréamont appeared to repudiate his earlier view, embracing banality and conformity. Thus, Camus claims that "the* Songs [Maldoror], *which exalted absolute negation, are followed by a theory of absolute assent* [in Poésies], *and uncompromising rebellion is succeeded by complete conformity—all this with total lucidity." According to Camus, in* Poésies *Lautréamont succumbed to the nihilistic temptation for conformity and thus presaged "the taste for intellectual servitude which flourishes in the contemporary world."*]

Lautréamont demonstrates that the rebel dissimulates the desire to accept appearance behind the desire for banality. In either case, whether he abases or vaunts himself, the rebel wants to be other than he is, even when he is prepared to be recognized for what he really is. The blasphemies and the conformity of Lautréamont illustrate this unfortunate contradiction, which is resolved in his case in the desire to be nothing at all. Far from being a recantation, as is generally supposed, the same passion for annihilation explains Maldoror's invocation of the primeval night and the laborious banalities of the *Poésies.*

Lautréamont makes us understand that rebellion is adolescent. Our most effective terrorists, whether they are armed with bombs or with poetry, hardly escape from infancy. The *Songs of Maldoror* are the works of a highly talented schoolboy; their pathos lies precisely in the contradictions of a child's mind ranged against creation and against itself. Like the Rimbaud of the *Illuminations,* beating against the confines of the world, the poet chooses the apocalypse and destruction rather than accept the impossible principles that make him what he is in a world such as it is.

"I offer myself to defend mankind," says Lautréamont, without wishing to be ingenuous. Is Maldoror, then, the angel of pity? In a certain sense he is, in that he pities himself. Why? That remains to be seen. But pity deceived, outraged, inadmissible, and unadmitted will lead him to strange extremities. Maldoror, in his own words, received life like a wound and forbade suicide to heal the scar (*sic*). Like Rimbaud he is the one who suffers and who rebelled; each, being strangely reluctant to say that he is rebelling against what he is, gives the rebel's eternal alibi: love of mankind. (pp. 82-3)

From the romantics to Lautréamont, there is . . . no real progress, except in style. Lautréamont resuscitates, once again, with a few improvements, the figure of the God of Abraham and the image of the Luciferian rebel. He places God "on a throne built of excrement, human and golden," on which sits, "with imbecile pride, his body covered with a shroud made of unwashed sheets, he who styles himself the Creator." "The horrible Eternal One with the features of a viper," "the crafty bandit" who can be seen "stoking the fires in which young and old perish," rolls drunkenly in the gutter, or seeks base pleasures in the brothel. God is not dead, he has fallen. Face to face with the fallen deity, Maldoror appears as a conventional cavalier in a black cloak. He is the Accursed. "Eyes must not witness the hideous aspect which the Supreme Being, with a smile of intense hatred, has granted me." He has forsworn everything—"father, mother, Providence, love, ideals—so as to think no longer of anything else but himself." Racked with pride, this hero has all the illusions of the metaphysical dandy: "A face that is more than human, sad with the sadness of the universe, beautiful as an act of suicide." Like the romantic rebel, Maldoror, despairing of divine justice, will take the side of evil. To cause suffering and, in causing it, to suffer, that is his lot. The *Songs* are veritable litanies of evil.

At this point mankind is no longer even defended. On the contrary, "to attack that wild beast, man, with every possible weapon, and to attack the creator . . ." that is the intention announced by the *Songs.* Overwhelmed at the thought of having God as an enemy, intoxicated with the solitude experienced by great criminals ("I alone against humanity"), Maldoror goes to war against creation and its author. The *Songs* exalt "the sanctity of crime," announce an increasing series of "glorious crimes," and stanza 20 of Song II even inaugurates a veritable pedagogy of crime and violence.

Such a burning ardor is, at this period, merely conventional. It costs nothing. Lautréamont's real originality lies elsewhere. [In a footnote, Camus adds: It accounts for the difference between *Songs I,* published separately, which is Byronic in a rather banal way, and the other *Songs,* which resound with a monstrous rhetoric.] The romantics maintained with the greatest care the fatal opposition between human solitude and divine indifference—the literary expressions of this solitude being the isolated castle and the dandy. But Lautréamont's work deals with a more profound drama. It is quite apparent that he found this solitude insupportable and that, ranged against creation, he wished to destroy its limits. Far from wanting to fortify the reign of humanity with crenelated towers, he wishes to merge it with all other reigns. He brought back creation to the shores of the primeval seas where morality, as well as every other problem, loses all meaning—including the problem, which he considers so terrifying, of the immortality of the soul. He had no desire to create a spectacular image of the rebel, or of the dandy, opposed to creation, but to mingle mankind and the world together in the same general destruction. He attacked the very frontier that separates mankind from the universe. Total freedom, the freedom of crime in particular, supposes the destruction of human frontiers. It is not enough to condemn oneself and all mankind to execration. The reign of mankind must still be brought back to the level of the reign of the instinct. We find in Lautréamont this refusal to recognize rational consciousness, this return to the elementary which is one of the marks of a civilization in revolt against itself. It is no longer a question of recognizing appearances, by making a determined and conscious effort, but of no longer existing at all on the conscious level.

All the creatures that appear in the *Songs* are amphibious, because Maldoror rejects the earth and its limitations. The flora is composed of algae and seaweed. Maldoror's castle is built on the waters. His native land is the timeless sea. The sea—a double symbol—is simultaneously the place of annihilation and of reconciliation. It quenches, in its own way, the thirst of souls condemned to scorn themselves and others, and the thirst for oblivion. Thus the *Songs* replace the *Metamorphoses*, and the timeless smile is replaced by the laughter of a mouth slashed with a razor, by the image of a gnashing, frantic, travesty of humor. This bestiary cannot contain all the meanings that have been given to it, but undoubtedly it discloses a desire for annihilation which has its origins in the very darkest places of rebellion. The "stultify yourselves" of Pascal takes on a literal sense with Lautréamont. Apparently he could not bear the cold and implacable clarity one must endure in order to live. "My subjectivity and one creator—that is too much for one brain." And so he chose to reduce life, and his work, to the flash of a cuttlefish's fin in the midst of its cloud of ink. The beautiful passage where Maldoror couples with a female shark on the high seas "in a long, chaste, and frightful copulation"—above all, the significant passage in which Maldoror, transformed into an octopus, attacks the Creator—are clear expressions of an escape beyond the frontiers of existence and of a convulsive attack on the laws of nature.

Those who see themselves banished from the harmonious fatherland where justice and passion finally strike an even balance still prefer, to solitude, the barren kingdoms where words have no more meaning, and where force and the instincts of blind creatures reign. This challenge is, at the same time, a mortification. The battle with the angel, in *Song II,* ends in the defeat and putrefaction of the angel. Heaven and earth are then brought back and intermingled in the liquid chasms of primordial life. Thus the man-shark of the *Songs* "only acquired the new change in the extremities of his arms and legs as an expiatory punishment for some unknown crime." There is, in fact, a crime, or the illusion of a crime (is it homosexuality?) in Maldoror's virtually unknown life. No reader of the *Songs* can avoid the idea that this book is in need of a *Stavrogin's Confession.*

But there is no confession and we find in the *Poésies* a redoubling of that mysterious desire for expiation. The spirit appropriate to certain forms of rebellion which consists . . . in reestablishing reason at the end of the irrational adventure, of

rediscovering order by means of disorder and of voluntarily loading oneself down with chains still heavier than those from which release was sought, is described in this book with such a desire for simplification and with such cynicism that this change of attitude must definitely have a meaning. The *Songs,* which exalted absolute negation, are followed by a theory of absolute assent, and uncompromising rebellion is succeeded by complete conformity—all this with total lucidity. The *Poésies,* in fact, give us the best explanation of the *Songs.* "Despair, fed by the prejudices of hallucination, imperturbably leads literature to the mass abrogation of laws both social and divine, and to theoretical and practical wickedness." The *Poésies* also denounce "the culpability of a writer who rolls on the slopes of the void and pours scorn on himself with cries of joy." But they prescribe no other remedy for this evil than metaphysical conformity: "Since the poetry of doubt arrives, in this way, at such a point of theoretical wickedness and mournful despair, it is poetry that is radically false; for the simple reason that it discusses principles, and principles should not be discussed" (letter to Darassé [see excerpt dated 1869-70]). In short, his reasoning recapitulates the morality of a choirboy or of an infantry manual. But conformity can be passionate, and thereby out of the ordinary. When the victory of the malevolent eagle over the dragon hope has been proclaimed, Maldoror can still obstinately repeat that the burden of his song is nothing but hope, and can write: "With my voice and with the solemnity of the days of my glory, I recall you, O blessed Hope, to my deserted dwelling"—he must still try to convince. To console humanity, to treat it as a brother, to return to Confucius, Buddha, Socrates, Jesus Christ, "moralists who wandered through villages, dying of hunger" (which is of doubtful historical accuracy), are still the projects of despair. Thus virtue and an ordered life have a nostalgic appeal in the midst of vice. For Lautréamont refuses to pray, and Christ for him is only a moralist. What he proposes, or rather what he proposes to himself, is agnosticism and the fulfillment of duty. Such a sound program, unhappily, supposes surrender, the calm of evening, a heart untouched by bitterness, and untroubled contemplation. Lautréamont rebels when he suddenly writes: "I know no other grace but that of being born." But one can sense his clenched teeth when he adds: "An impartial mind finds that enough." But no mind is impartial when confronted with life and death. With Lautréamont, the rebel flees to the desert. But this desert of conformity is as dreary as Rimbaud's Harrar. The taste for the absolute and the frenzy of annihilation sterilize him again. Just as Maldoror wanted total rebellion, Lautréamont, for the same reasons, demands absolute banality. The exclamation of awareness which he tried to drown in the primeval seas, to confuse with the howl of the beast, which at another moment he tried to smother in the adoration of mathematics, he now wants to stifle by applying a dismal conformity. The rebel now tries to turn a deaf ear to the call that urges him toward the being who lies at the heart of his rebellion. The important thing is to exist no longer—either by refusing to be anything at all or by accepting to be no matter what. In either case it is a purely artificial convention. Banality, too, is an attitude.

Conformity is one of the nihilistic temptations of rebellion which dominate a large part of our intellectual history. It demonstrates how the rebel who takes to action is tempted to succumb, if he forgets his origins, to the most absolute conformity. And so it explains the twentieth century. Lautréamont, who is usually hailed as the bard of pure rebellion, on the contrary proclaims the advent of the taste for intellectual servitude which flourishes in the contemporary world. The *Poésies* are only a preface to a "future work" of which we can only surmise the contents and which was to have been the ideal end-result of literary rebellion. But this book is being written today, despite Lautréamont, in millions of copies, by bureaucratic order. Of course, genius cannot be separated from banality. But it is not a question of the banality of others—the banality that we vainly try to capture and which itself captures the creative writer, where necessary, with the help of the censors. For the creative writer it is a question of his own form of banality, which must be completely created. Every genius is at once extraordinary and banal. He is nothing if he is only one or the other. We must remember this when thinking of rebellion. It has its dandies and its menials, but it does not recognize its legitimate sons. (pp. 83-8)

> Albert Camus, "The Poets' Rebellion," in his The Rebel: An Essay on Man in Revolt, *translated by Anthony Bower, revised edition, 1956. Reprint by Vintage Books, 1960, pp. 81-100.**

THOMAS GREENE (essay date 1954)

[*Asserting that Lautréamont's work is as closely related to the earlier romantics as it is to the later surrealists, Greene characterizes Maldoror as a romantic hero.*]

[Lautréamont's] relationship to the Romantic movement has tended to be blurred in France by the emphasis on his relationship to Surrealism, and yet *Maldoror* points backward as well as forward. Many passages seem at first reading uninspired reworkings of hackneyed Romantic material. But even in these passages the tone betrays itself with a pomposity or absurdity that turns the Romantic ardor into bathos. At this stage one concludes that the whole book is an enormous piece of Romantic irony. But this conclusion is not really accurate either. The truth might be better stated by saying that *Maldoror* assumes the full responsibility for attitudes which many romantics only play at; it pushes Romantic ideas and Romantic poses to their extremes. Sometimes it pushes them into absurdity, sometimes into ugliness, sometimes into a kind of splendor. It pushes Romantic irony to *its* extreme, to the point that the seriousness of a situation is always jeopardized without being destroyed. Ultimately the question of a given passage's seriousness is unanswerable.

In this sense *Maldoror* is rather a book about Romantic literature than a book about "life," and as such it is an extremely illuminating study. It may be that you could understand Byron better by reading *Maldoror,* where his name is never mentioned, than by reading any number of critical or biographical analyses. On a conscious level Lautréamont may have read Byron superficially and imperceptively, but as a writer he produced a searching anatomy of Byron's role and his poetry.

Perhaps because of this integrity, this fidelity to the responsibilities of Romanticism, Lautréamont succeeded in realizing the destructive impulse which had driven and misdriven his literary predecessors as it was to drive his disciples. In all the literature of revolt few books succeed in destroying so well as *Maldoror.* If it were only superficially shocking, cheaply sensational, it could be easily dismissed. It is certainly these things among others. But as a whole it is a profoundly unsettling book. From its symphonic opening sentence which warns off the innocent or casual reader [see excerpt dated 1868], it follows the strategy of outrage: the outrage of morality, which is Lautréamont's peculiar comedy; the outrage of nature, which is his peculiar violence; the outrage of language, which is his

peculiar rhetoric. A blend of comedy, violence and rhetoric produces that bitter savor which only a few, wrote Lautréamont, can taste without danger.

. . . . .

Les Chants de Maldoror dramatize the existence of a hero who is nominally committed to evil and whose record of assault and murder provides the narrative pretext for most of its episodes. In the phantasmagorical universe of which he is the center, Maldoror is hostile to virtually everything: in his Machiavellian ravages of the innocent few and the brutalized many among his fellow men he is only a little less implacable than in his feud with an extraordinarily disagreeable and anthropomorphic God. Some of the most sensational episodes which describe the forms of Maldoror's sadism are repellent and disgusting; they contain passages which one does not willingly reread. But Maldoror's sadism, and even the sadism of these extreme episodes, is at least partly redeemed by a psychological denseness about him, a queer paradoxical ambivalence which qualifies even the most brutal and forthright of his acts.

The first paradox in Maldoror's psychology is his moral consciousness. All the events of his universe are charged with profound ethical significance for him, and he seems to respond almost entirely to ethical motives—to disgust for the brutality of God and man on the one hand, to remorse for his own brutality on the other. His sexual aggressions often seem motivated less by physical impulse than by a fanatic will of almost Puritanical sternness and earnestness. It is a kind of moral indignation, a perverted Calvinism, which turns Maldoror away from God and man and drives him to seek the sin which is absolutely unprovoked and hideous, the sin which is the perfect crime.

In his awareness of innocence, in his protest against authority and in the solitude of his individualism, Maldoror embodies most of the tenets of Romantic morality. The influence of the Satan of Milton, whom we know Lautréamont to have read, and probably of Mary Shelley's monster in *Frankenstein,* which he would seem to have read from internal evidence, played roles in the conception of Maldoror, but by far his most direct ancestor was the Byronic hero as typified by Lara, Cain, Manfred and the Corsair. Lautréamont mentions each of these characters at various points in the *Poésies,* and in *Maldoror* he borrowed feelings and attitudes they all embody—the nervous fatigue, the sense of isolation, the thirst for the superhuman with its concomitant frustration. (pp. 529-31)

The urge "by good or ill to separate himself" from those who share his mortal state underlies most of Maldoror's behavior. The very fact of his humanity is in doubt throughout the book; sometimes he would seem to belong to the class of sinister, demonic, invulnerable personages who people Romantic literature from Maturin's Melmoth through Polidor's Vampire and Hugo's Han d'Islande to Sue's Wandering Jew. Maldoror himself is not always sure of his own condition. This uncertainty heightens his Byronic urge to be different from human beings.

From the ambivalence of this uncertainty Lautréamont derives some of his most grotesque comedy, comedy which characteristically concludes with the chastening recognition that Maldoror is indeed human. See for instance Maldoror's long address to the sea—perhaps the most polished and controlled single episode of the book—in which his impulse toward the super- or sub-human is confronted with this recognition of his human condition. The episode consists of a declamation divided into ten sections, each of which is concluded with the refrain *"Je te salue, vieil océan!"* The whole is prefaced by an injunction to the reader who, being human, will probably prove too weak and too excitable to enjoy it anyway.

> *Je me propose, sans être ému, de déclamer à grande voix la strophe sérieuse et froide que vous allez entendre. Vous, faites attention à ce qu'elle ne manquera pas de laisser, comme une flétrissure, dans vos imaginations troublées.... Il n'y a pas longtemps que j'ai revu la mer et foulé le pont des vaisseaux, et mes souvenirs sont vivaces comme si je l'avais quittée la veille. Soyez néanmoins, si vous le pouvez, aussi calmes que moi, dans cette lecture que je me repens déjà de vous offrir, et ne rougissez pas à la pensée de ce qu'est le coeur humain.*

> [I propose to proclaim in a loud voice and without emotion the cold and grave chant that you are about to hear. Consider carefully what it contains and guard yourself against the painful impression it cannot fail to leave like a blight upon your troubled imaginings.... Not long ago I saw the sea once again and trod upon the bridges of ships; my memories of it are as lively as if it had all happened yesterday. If you are able, however, be as calm as I am as you read what is to follow (for already I regret offering it to you) and do not blush for the human heart.]

Beneath the cold formality of a passage like this one lies a faint reminiscence of French classical tragedy. But basically the passage evokes the classical declamation only to parody it, and there is a buffoonishness about Maldoror's pose which qualifies, but never destroys, the significance of what follows. In particular the pose of disdainful condescension to the human—and therefore inferior—reader, announces the sardonic comedy which is to underly the whole episode. The implication of Maldoror's non-humanity is continued in each of the following apostrophes to the sea, which is always compared favorably with the derisory and feeble race of man. These progressively extended and rhetorical apostrophes culminate in the climactic question to which they have been tending: *"Réponds-moi, océan, veux-tu être mon frère?"* As though in answer, the sea surges up in a magnificent series of waves, before which Maldoror, in a burst of terror and awe, prostrates himself, thus losing ironically his vaunted frigidity.

> *Oh! quand tu t'avances, la crête haute et terrible, entouré de tes replis tortueux comme d'une cour, magnétiseur et farouche, roulant tes ondes les unes sur les autres, avec la conscience de ce que tu es, pendant que tu pousses, des profondeurs de ta poitrine, comme accablé d'un remords intense que je ne puis pas découvrir, ce sourd mugissement perpétuel que les hommes redoutent tant, même quand ils te contemplent, en sûreté, tremblants sur le rivage, alors, je vois qu'il ne m'appartient pas, le droit insigne de me dire ton égal.*

> [Oh, when you advance, your crest high and terrible, surrounded by your tortuous coils as by a royal court, magnetic and wild, rolling your waves one upon the other, full of the con-

sciousness of what you are; and when you give utterance from the depths of your bosom as if you were suffering the pangs of some intense remorse which I have been unable to discover, to that perpetual heavy roar so greatly feared by men even when, trembling on the shore, they contemplate you in safety: then I perceive that I do not possess that signal right to name myself your equal.]

The recognition of his inferiority to the sea, and the resulting implication of his human condition, produces a spasm of rage in Maldoror which yields in its turn to resignation, resignation to a life in human society even though that life must be ridiculous. *"Faisons un grand effort, et accomplissons, avec le sentiment du devoir, notre destinée sur cette terre. Je te salue, vieil océan!"* This, the conclusion of the episode, reveals a sudden humility which renders the preceding comedy more warm and more significant.

If Maldoror is repeatedly faced with the fact of his own humanity, he is also faced with his difference from most of his fellow men. The divergent sensibility which sets off the Romantic hero from an unfeeling society is parodied by the cumbersome inflexibility of Maldoror's mental processes. At moments he is actually pedantic and toward the end of the book he lapses into stretches of unreadable double talk which mimic the hyper-precision of scientific jargon. He is, moreover, incapable of laughter. *"Moi, je ne sais pas rire. Je n'ai jamais pu rire, quoique plusieurs fois j'aie essayé de la faire. C'est très difficile, d'apprendre à rire."* Once, in a grotesque attempt to imitate his fellows, Maldoror widens the corners of his mouth with his penknife to force it into a laugh. For an instant he believes that he has succeeded, but presently, through the falling blood, he recognizes that he has failed. This terrible and brilliant image dramatizes in its insane way the spiritual isolation of the Romantic hero and all his clumsy maladjustment with a power which few Romantic poets equaled. Maldoror's illogicality, which is really an excess of misplaced logic, translates the apparent illogicality of his hyper-conscious moral sensibility.

Thus the comedy of **Maldoror** dwells on the conflict between the pro-human and anti-human motives of the Romantic hero-saint. Ultimately of course the hero fails to be a saint, as he has to fail; the pressures upon him are too confusing, his own behavior too ambiguous, to permit him the purity either of the perfect martyrdom or the perfect crime. But his conflict leads him to repeated essays, and the elements which I have called comic are interwoven with elements of sickening violence. It is as though Maldoror had taken upon himself to dramatize an epigram which his creator could not possibly have read, this remark from the *Journaux Intimes* of Baudelaire: *"Quand j'aurai inspiré le dégoût et l'horreur universels, j'aurai conquis la solitude."* (pp. 531-34)

> *Thomas Greene, "The Relevance of Lautréamont,"* in Partisan Review, *Vol. XXI, No. 5, September-October, 1954, pp. 528-39.*

GASTON BACHELARD (essay date 1956)

[Bachelard was an influential French philosopher and critic. Although he began his career as a philosopher of science, he concluded it as an expert in phenomenology, as his interest gradually turned from rational, scientific thought to the creative imagination. Many of Bachelard's writings focus on poetic imagery and

its relation to the creative process, and their approach is characterized by an emphasis on psychoanalytic theory. Unlike Sigmund Freud, who regarded dreams as manifestations of an individual's motivations, Bachelard, like Carl Jung, considered dreaming to be a revelation of the collective unconscious. Bachelard thus looked to dreaming, or rêverie, *for certain primitive archetypes—especially the traditional elements of earth, air, fire, and water—and studied representations of each in poetic imagery. Today, Bachelard's importance rests on his efforts to establish relationships between science, psychology, and poetry, and on his insight into the links between imagery and the unconscious. Bachelard also wrote a lengthy study entitled* Lautréamont, *first published in 1939 and revised in 1956, that is largely untranslated. This work, a portion of which is excerpted below, is considered a major psychoanalytic study of Lautréamont. Bachelard describes* Maldoror *as a phenomenology of aggression, citing in particular the work's "complex of animal life." Lautréamont includes a variety of animals, according to the critic, to represent the full range of human vices. In the original text, the comments below were preceded by an introductory chapter in which Bachelard described the results of his statistical study of Lautréamont's use of animal imagery.*]

Struck by this enormous biological production, this extraordinary confidence in animal movement, I undertook a systematic study of Lautréamont's bestiary. I attempted in particular to single out the most significant animals, the animal functions which Lautréamont most clearly sought. A quick statistical survey of the 185 animals of Ducasse's bestiary gives prominence to the dog, the horse, the crab, the spider, and the toad. But I soon discovered that a more or less formal statistical study would shed very little light on the Lautréamont problem, and that it might even present it in the wrong terms. Indeed, if we limit ourselves to noting animal forms and keeping an exact account of their appearances, we neglect the essential part of the *Ducasse complex;* we forget the dynamic vitality of this production. In order to be psychologically exact, I felt obliged to reconstitute the dynamic value, the *algebraic weight* which gives the measure of the different animals' vital actions. Reliving the **Chants de Maldoror** was the only way to go about it. It was not enough to *observe* their life. I therefore strove honestly to experience the intensity of Ducasse's action. And only after adding a dynamic coefficient did I recast my statistics. . . .

For example, in the **Chants de Maldoror,** the dog and the horse are not sufficiently dynamic to be kept in the first rank. They are external means. Maldoror spurs on a charger, arouses a dog's anger, but he does not penetrate into the heart of animal movement. Nothing in the **Chants de Maldoror,** for instance, allows us to relive the profound experience of the centaur, that creature so misunderstood by the mythologists of the past—who always saw syntheses of images where syntheses of acts should be seen. Thus, in the **Chants de Maldoror** the horse does not rear up; he transports. The dog hardly exceeds the function of aggressiveness imposed upon him by his bourgeois owner. This is a sort of delegated aggression. It lacks the straightforwardness characteristic of Ducasse's kind of violence. Another proof that the dog and the horse are but external images, seen images, is that they do not metamorphose; their forms do not swell as do those of so many other creatures of the bestiary; the dog's muzzle does not multiply and activate the triple violence of a Cerberus. Neither horse nor dog bears any mark of the teratological power which characterizes Ducasse's imagination. There is nothing in them that is still constantly growing. They represent no monstrous impulsion. Finally, as one can see, animals such as the dog or the horse, in the **Chants de Maldoror,** do not in any way designate a

dynamic complex. They do not belong to the cruel escutcheon of the Comte de Lautréamont.

I tried to determine, in addition, if the well-known statement, *"As for me, I use my genius to depict the delights of cruelty"* [see excerpt dated 1868], might not provide the dominant key to his works. But once again I had to admit that ordinary cruelty, represented by the tiger and the wolf, was lacking in dynamism. The image of the tiger, with its classic cruelty, would rather block the development of the complex. In any case, it seems to me that it is these blocked images which catch the mind of certain readers. As astute a critic as René Lalou, for example, remains outside of *lautréamontisme.* In his opinion, the beautiful sentence which praises the delights of cruelty is soon *"diluted in trite expressions."* One will not receive this impression of dilution if, instead of starting with massive and ready-made cruelty, summed up in a traditional animal, one restores to cruelty its multiplicity, and disperses it over all the functions of inventive aggression.

The animal favored by Lautréamont's dynamic imagination is the crab, in particular the "tourteau." The crab would rather lose its claw than loosen its hold. Its body has less bulk than its pincers. If we were to imitate Lautréamont's teratological exaggeration, we might express the motto of the crab as follows: *one must live to pinch, and not pinch to live.*

Since only biological movement is significant in the type of imagination which I am describing, sudden substitutions become possible: the crab is a louse, the louse is a crab. *"O venerable louse . . . Beacon of Maldoror, where do you guide his steps?"* Then, fiery pages follow one after another. In the middle of the second *chant,* there appear those passages, devoted to the louse, which have been taken as tasteless ventures, created in a frenzy of unwholesome and puerile originality, and which indeed are completely incomprehensible in terms of a theory of static imagination—the imagination of completed forms. But a reader willing to accept *animalizing* phenomenology will read in a different spirit; he will recognize the action of a special force, the thrust of a characteristic life. Certainly, animality is at its peak in its virulence: it pushes, grows, dominates. The blood-loving louse *"would be capable, through an occult power, of becoming as big as an elephant, of crushing men like blades of wheat."* Therefore, it must be kept *"in high esteem, above all animals of Creation"*:

> If you find a louse in your path, go your way. . . .
>
> You can pet an elephant, not a louse.
>
> O louse, with your wrinkled eyeball, as long as the rivers shed their sloping waters into the abysses of the sea, . . . as long as the mute void has no horizon . . . , thy reign will be assured over the universe and thy dynasty will stretch links of its chain from century to century. I salute thee, rising sun, celestial liberator, thou, invisible enemy of man. . . .

These passages have often been cited as if they were a parody written by a schoolboy. This interpretation disregards the breadth of an original language, its dehumanized sonority brought to the level of an outcry. Psychologically, it is a refusal to experience that strange myth of metamorphoses, which remains cold and formal in certain ancient authors like Ovid, and which takes on a sudden new life in more recent authors who return unconsciously to primal impulsions.

In spite of the lessons of natural history or the wisdom of common sense, we must associate Ducasse's eagle and vulture with the louse and the crab. The talon and the beak, which are adapted to each other in animal nature by a vital synergy, must take on, in an imagination given over entirely to the dynamics of animal movement, an imaginative synergy with the claw. The eagle's beak, in Lautréamont's bestiary, is nothing but a claw: the eagle does not devour, it tears. Maldoror asks himself: *"Is it my sick mind's delirium, a secret instinct independent of my reasoning, like that of the eagle tearing up its prey, which forced me to commit this crime?"* Cruelty can have all sorts of reasons—except need or hunger.

The eagle, like the louse, like the crab, like all the vigorously imagined animals of the bestiary, can change dimensions. If combat is necessary, *"it will click its curved beak for joy,"* it will become *"enormous."* Then, *"the eagle is terrible, it makes huge bounds which shake the earth."* As we can see, this is still the same squandering of force—but always a specific force—which grows proportionately with the obstacle, which must always overcome resistance and produce victoriously the weapons of its crime, the animal organs of its offense. . . .

These phantasms are not whimsical contrivances; they are, originally, desires for specific actions. They are produced by a motive imagination of great sureness, of astounding inflexibility. (pp. 38-41)

LES

CHANTS DE MALDOROR

CHANT PREMIER

PAR ***

Prix : 30 centimes

PARIS
IMPRIMERIE BALITOUT, QUESTROY ET Cⁱᵉ
7, RUE BAILLIF ET RUE DE VALOIS, 18
—
AOUT 1868

The unsigned title page of the first edition of Maldoror.

Gaston Bachelard, "The Dynamic Imagination of Lautréamont," in his On Poetic Imagination and Reverie: Selections from the Works of Gaston Bachelard, *translated by Colette Gaudin, The Bobbs-Merrill Company, Inc., 1971, pp. 38-41.*

WALLACE FOWLIE   (essay date 1967)

[*Fowlie's comments on Lautréamont are drawn from his book-length study on violence in French literature during the past one hundred years. In portions of his essay on Lautréamont not excerpted below, Fowlie examines each of the episodes of* Maldoror *and provides a stanza-by-stanza explication of its symbolism, with special attention to the theme of violence. In the following excerpt, he summarizes the work's importance to early twentieth-century writers, highlighting Lautréamont's view of the artist's role in society. In addition, Fowlie interprets the symbolism in* Maldoror *as Lautréamont's exploration of the subconscious. For further criticism by Fowlie, see excerpt dated 1950 and Additional Bibliography.*]

Les Chants de Maldoror appears today a work of imitation, with countless literary echoes and allusions, composed in an almost declamatory style. The title *chants* (cantos) announces the genre of the epic, of the poetic narratives with scenes of violence and war. This is adhered to, to some extent. But an aspect of romanticism is also present throughout the work: a predilection for verbal eloquence, for blasphemy, for imprecation, for the turbulent atmosphere of the Gothic tale.

Although the first edition of *Les Chants* appeared in 1869, it was destined to exert no influence on the nineteenth century. But it became, in the twentieth century, with the writings of Rimbaud, composed at the same time, a work that has counted considerably in the literary consciousness of the modern period. . . . In their revelation of the subconscious, Lautréamont and Rimbaud indicated certain directions that modern poetry was to follow. . . . (p. 20)

Rimbaud's legacy has been exploited far more than Lautréamont's, not only because of the greater originality and power of his writing, but because of his life story, because of his human adventure and personality. Rimbaud's power of invention, his power to expand what he invented, and his ultimate demolition of literature, gave to his work and his example an extraordinary uniqueness. He established a relationship with forms of anxiety which reappear virulent and provocative in the twentieth century. These anxieties, in a histrionic and highly stylized manifestation, are the subject matter of *Les Chants de Maldoror.* The macabre is deliberately cultivated in the themes of lycanthropy, vampirism, murder, bestiality. The hero's name Maldoror would seem to be *aurore du mal,* "dawn of evil." We are at the beginning of time, because each human being, in his subconscious, relives the history of man. The fears of primitive man are orchestrated by Lautréamont in his stanzas; all the instinctive impulses of sexuality and egoism are celebrated as if they were necessary rites of purification. Monsters of the sea, animals of prey, insects, and vermin are everywhere on these pages. Pictorially they appear as they would in the imagination of a child, but they symbolize the basic drives of man in his destructiveness. They are used by Lautréamont in asking philosophy's great questions. Who is man? Why is he evil? The first syllable of the hero's name: *mal,* announces this preoccupation with the problem of evil. Lautréamont remains close to the tradition of Baudelaire in the analysis he offers of the perverse pleasure taken in perpetrating acts of evil. These acts would not be called evil if Baudelaire and Lautréamont did not believe in the existence of God. (p. 21)

To attach an absolute value to *Les Chants de Maldoror,* or to any book, for that matter, would be futile. Literary value is imponderable. But it would be difficult to exaggerate the moral and the aesthetic use that the book had for a generation of French writers and artists, those who worked approximately in the second quarter of the twentieth century. In addition to the themes specifically announced and elaborated in *Maldoror,* the book is also about the reasons for literary creation, about the madness itself of writing. The term of madness, in its medical sense, was used by early critics of Lautréamont, by Léon Bloy, for example, to explain the behavior and the writings of this young man, but today such an explanation would appear too facile and erroneous.

Lautréamont unquestionably had the conviction that the artist must be different from other men, must live in some other way than in accordance with the fixed standards of the bourgeoisie. His writings represent an attack on the traditional poses of romanticism, on the languorous and sentimental attitudes of the poets, on the moonlit scenes of peacefulness and medita- tions. He followed and exalted the more vigorous romanticism of a Berlioz, in his resounding periods and inflated style, and of a Delacroix, in the rich colors of his scenes. He was the youthful writer, who, with Rimbaud, felt he had been cheated and tricked by destiny. He refused, during the brief span of his writer's career, to compromise with society or with any of the forces that habitually promise success to the aspiring artist. In this regard, Rimbaud and Lautréamont closely resembled one another.

But the meditations of Lautréamont on humanity culminated in a greater sense of disgust and hate. . . . (p. 22)

In his systematic visions, in his tone of scorn and sarcasm for what is human, Lautréamont revived and prolonged the ro- manticism of despair and revolt, a resonant lyricism more rem- iniscent of Byron than of anything French. *Les Chants de Mal- doror* is the work of an unhappy and even desperate adolescent. In the beauty of his writings, he derived some degree of sat- isfaction by demolishing the world, by upsetting the moral values of the world. In his experience of solitude, Lautréamont saw only himself and his Creator. All the scenes he depicted have to do with the epic struggle, the oldest struggle of man- kind, between man himself and God.

What meaning can be given to this work? The exterior literal meaning of the various episodes is not sufficient. The narrative, with its multiple literary echoes, is in reality a study of man's fundamental complexes. (p. 23)

Everything is presented as enigmatic in the long series of ep- isodes which compose *Les Chants de Maldoror:* dreams, myths, symbols, realistic effects. The son's hostility toward his father (or man's effort to liberate himself from his Creator) is the most apparent theme of the work. There are several examples of the traumatic experience of a child being brutally separated from his family: in the second canto, the child running after the omnibus; in the fourth canto, the child taking refuge in the ocean and being transformed into an amphibian; and the story of Mervyn in the sixth canto. (pp. 33-4)

Literature is primarily a movement of discovery, of self-dis- covery. In its extreme examples—*Les Chants de Maldoror* is one of these—the discovery of the individual is almost equiv- alent to the beginning of madness. To know oneself is dan-

gerous, and this danger is emphasized throughout the cantos. The symbolic presentation of the writing, where it is impossible to fix on one meaning alone, where several interpretations occur to the reader, is a way of disguising the danger. The immediate literal interpretation is the shock of melodrama that holds the attention of the reader only momentarily. Then the plethora of possible meanings form a kind of net in which the reader is caught. He flounders about trying to find his way out, trying to widen one of the meshes that will permit him to escape. The libidinous tendencies and the death wishes of the subconscious are so numerous and so urgent that the reading of such a work as *Les Chants de Maldoror* provides an almost too exact representation of them. It is difficult to bear the power of the subconscious when it is cast into recognizable forms of violence. Lautréamont is telling us that the individual first recognizes himself as such in his relationship with his father, both his human father and his supernatural Creator. But as soon as this recognition takes place, a combat ensues. A combat for survival, which will challenge all the powers of a man. The long genital life of an adolescent, as he grows and develops, will constantly recapitulate this combat. Mervyn's story is both his renouncing of his father and his search for a father.

Infrequently Lautréamont alludes to the strong words of "min- otaur" and "labyrinth," striking symbols for his conception of the life of an individual. Life is not static. It is constantly moving, both progressing and retrogressing. In his subcon- scious, man creates his own labyrinth, and then in his conscious life he tries to explore it. Each man therefore plays the two roles of Minotaur, of monster for whom the labyrinth is de- signed, and Theseus, who heroically tries to encounter the Minotaur and slay him. *Les Chants de Maldoror* is the meeting between Theseus-Lautréamont and the Minotaur-Maldoror. The cantos are the labyrinth. They are the literary expression of man seen in his labyrinthine ways.

As a writer, Lautréamont is totally conscious in his labors of reconstructing the labyrinth, classically logical in the ordering of his sentences and in their transitions. But behind these formal aspects, he is searching for the obscure forces of a psyche, searching in his movements toward the future and toward the past for the meaning of the drives and the emotions in a man's life. The danger of such an exploration is that of losing one's way, of complete alienation from conscious life. But in the labyrinth of *Les Chants,* in each phase of the search, the hero finds his way, even if it is momentarily, as in the popular horror story, of the *série noire* type: Fantômas, James Bond, Fu Manchu. Whenever Lautréamont speaks directly to the reader about his work, he emphasizes his logic and his prudence in the way in which he reveals the unusual and the fantastic. In order to approximate the great reason for life, he procedes reasonably.

It is indeed reasonable to look upon sleep and nightmares as experiences that reveal the subconscious. Sleep, madness, and death are states where the deepest ego comes to life. A con- scious effort to see clearly into oneself is quite different from the vision provided by the subconscious. Lautréamont is both analyst and psychoanalyst: analyst in the lucidity of his form, and psychoanalyst in the obscuring of his meaning.

The writer is always to some degree the recreator of myths. In the figure of Maldoror, whose name could easily mean the dawn, the light of evil, one can see the recreation of the Chris- tian myth of Lucifer, of the fallen archangel whose name means light. And in the name Ducasse chose for himself, Lautréa- mont, some critics believe they can see L'autre Amon, or

Amon-Râ, the Egyptian sun god, the other sun. The defiance of Maldoror is of such proportions, the violence of his actions and his thoughts is so extreme, that he becomes the personification of evil, an epic figure in the very greatness of that which he opposes.

The psychoanalysis of a character reveals what Maldoror reveals in a literary form: the close relationship existing between the subconscious and the symbol. The labyrinth and the desert can easily symbolize the subconscious; the one composed of too many conflicting paths, and the other, pathless. From Greece and from Egypt come the two myths of the minotaur and the sphinx, two figures who complement one another: the minotaur with the animal head and the human male body, the sphinx with the female head and the animal's body.

Maldoror encounters the minotaur in the numerous episodes of bestiality, and the sphinx in his efforts to explain the enigmas of existence. The supernatural powers he manifests, the swiftness of his movements, his ubiquity make him appear as an archangel hesitating between good and evil, fearful of God and wanting to be God. (pp. 34-6)

> Wallace Fowlie, "Lautréamont's Epic," in his Climate of Violence: The French Literary Tradition from Baudelaire to the Present, *The Macmillan Company,* 1967, pp. 20-36.

ANNA BALAKIAN (essay date 1970)

[*Balakian is a critic of French literature who has written extensively on writers of the symbolist, surrealist, and dadaist movements. Here, she identifies the imagery and themes of Lautréamont's work that attracted the surrealists. She asserts that an important influence on his work that he shared with twentieth-century writers was Darwin's theory of evolution. Balakian maintains that evolutionary theory precipitated a spiritual crisis in Lautréamont by shattering his illusion of human perfectibility: Lautréamont felt that evolution's stress on the relationship between humans and animals degrades humans to the level of beasts. In addition, Lautréamont regarded the struggle for survival as proof that destruction is a law of nature. Thus, Lautréamont derived Maldoror's theme from his "recognition of the brutal origin and the biological universality of evil," and he based its imagery on analogies between humans and beasts. For further criticism by Balakian, see Additional Bibliography.*]

Lautréamont's imagery, its hallucinatory force, the subconscious train of thought which it reveals, its occasional basis in the absurd create a point of contact with the surrealists. But these obvious characteristics have been rather easily explained away by critics all the way from Remy de Gourmont to as recent a researcher as Jean-Pierre Soulier . . . as manifestations of neurosis and eventual psychosis. Clinical explanations minimize however the very qualities that have endeared Ducasse to the surrealists and enflamed their imagination. It is this conscious moral and spiritual perspective more than literary manifestations of an unbalanced mind that indicated a major departure from his contemporaries and brought him closer in line with twentieth-century aesthetic and philosophic thought.

The surrealists preferred to see in the *Chants de Maldoror* either new figurations of the old Greek myths of man's tormented passage through the enigma of life, or an acute metaphysical rebellion in a world losing its anthropocentric focus. Surrealists Marcel Jean and Arpad Mezei . . . were inclined to explain Lautréamont as a tortured victim of his own inherited traits, "Theseus and Minotaur all at once," and thus identified the author with his diabolical character, Maldoror. On the other hand, Breton and Léon Pierre-Quint have seen Ducasse as a very lucid, proud rebel, who can objectivize his plight in *the other,* Maldoror, and create the catharsis of the protest of the damned. In his magnificent book on Lautréamont . . . , which is at the same time a profound study of the very nature of revolt, Léon Pierre-Quint calls *Les Chants* "the great contemporary work of revolt," and "the overwhelming expression of supreme revolt." It is indeed in the light of a conscious and direct protest that Lautréamont's work is most poignant and most relevant to the development of the surrealist climate. The isolation of the young man in Paris and his severance from family ties were more likely to have produced benign melancholia than subversive attack on man and God.

There was a greater factor to cause disturbance in the sensitive adolescent's development than geographical or affective disorientation. The historical dates provide more decisive data sometimes than sundry personal letters. He came of age in the era of the advent of Darwinism. Lautréamont's work is closely involved with the spiritual upheaval caused by the theory of evolution in the second half of the nineteenth century. This scientific event proved as disturbing to that epoch as non-Euclidian geometry and the explorations of un-human space have been to a later era.

The theory of evolution was welcomed in France by biologists; the philosophers saw in it a dislocation in moral values. The notion of the soul seemed to be put in jeopardy. This moral shock and its inevitable effect upon religious orientation supplied the major impetus for Lautréamont's writings, for his venom, his rejections, his diffidence, and eventually served as a provocation for his wry, dark humor in facing up to the universe and its Creator. (pp. 52-4)

Darwinism and the positivist atmosphere in which it flowered affected the work of Lautréamont in the same way that the theory of the Great Chain of Being influenced the Romanticists. From plant to animal, from animal to man, from man to the angel, from the angel to God had been the graded path to perfection as visualized by pantheist writers such as Victor Hugo. In his metaphysical poem, *Dieu,* Hugo made animal, man, and the angel plod on their way toward the discovery of the infinite, each according to his relative spiritual capacity. Although a general relationship was sensed by the Romanticists between the other species and man, the proportion between nothingness and perfection was considered entirely different for the inferior forms of life as compared with that in man, and therefore man's belief in his superiority was not shaken. But with Darwinism the scale of gradual perfectibility was disturbed, for each species was considered perfect in its own fashion. But if we then move from the biological concept of perfection to its philosophical implications, man's aspiration toward the absolute is blocked by the very reshuffle of the biological role which promises him only the dark mystery of disappearing as easily and irrevocably from the face of the earth as a fly or a butterfly. Finding himself a descendant of the ape and a brother to the leech, man can no longer believe himself created in the image of God.

Lautréamont did not come to this notion serenely. Endowed with a propensity for mysticism, he should have lived in a world which accepted miracles and spiritual revelations equal to the scope of his vast imagination. It was a bitter disappointment for him to discover the extent of man's limitations. Maldoror, the half-man, half-beast hero of his work, wanders day and night without rest or respite, troubled by horrible nightmares and by phantoms that hover about his bed and trouble his sleep. He is tormented by his dual combat with God and with man. Lautréamont and his shadowy protagonist, who serves to exteriorize occasionally his own anguish, are indignant at being chained to "the hardened crust of a planet," and of being "imprisoned within the walls of their intelligence." Yet, Lautréamont cannot quench his passion for the infinite. And if it is true that he shares the destiny of the animal, then his own unanswered but unabated longing for the infinite must exist in the lowliest creatures. Indeed, the dogs that bark must be thirsty for the infinite, "like you, like me, like all the rest of humans. I, even as the dogs, feel the need for the infinite. I cannot, I cannot satisfy this need. I am the son of man and of woman, so I have heard. I am surprised . . . I thought I was more." He is angry with God for not having made him *more*. He chides Him for having committed such a blunder: "The Creator should not have engendered such a vermin." He is equally angry with man for having been fool enough to harbor the illusion of his dignity for so long. When he refers to man as "this sublime ape" there is disdain, sarcasm, and regret in the use of the terminology.

A less virile and vigilant young man in the throes of such a spiritual crisis might have sought release from his tension by escape, either in terms of physical or intellectual evasion. The examples of such culminations to revolt are numerous in literature. The originality of Lautréamont, and the very thing which endeared him to a future generation of artists, is his refusal to be diverted from his intellectual dilemma. Art did not mean to him a form of consolation or a palliative, but on the contrary a confrontation of the problem, a search, perhaps a revelation however painful it might be.

Les Chants de Maldoror attests to Lautréamont's facing up to the tremendous rearrangement of a world in which man is to be considered a material organism and therefore conditioned by the same nonmoral impulses as the beasts. This is not really an attitude of revolt, for revolt implies refusal to accept. Young Isidore accepts a totally earthbound condition: "The stone would long to escape from the laws of gravity. Impossible!" But he accepts it with repugnance as he sets out to portray man through the eyes of his disillusionment: "Let my war against man be eternal since each recognizes in another his own degradation." No longer are vestiges of the sublime qualities of man to be seen in the animal, as the Romanticists had believed; but on the contrary the undesirable or ugly aspects of animals are mirrored in human beings. Lautréamont begins with a hideously unflattering picture of the *dear reader,* calling him a monster, referring to his mouth as a snout and comparing his movements to those of a shark. Human eyes are like a sea hog's, circular like a night bird's. When man stretches his neck it looks like a snail's; his legs remind Lautréamont of a toad's hind limbs. Man's facial expressions are those of a duck or a goat, his baldness that of a tortoise shell, his nakedness that of the worm. The cries of a dog, a child, a cat, a woman have a definite kinship in his picture of the universe.

The analogies between man and beast form the core of his imagery in *Les Chants de Maldoror*. The similarity is by no means limited to physical attributes. Human movements and attitudes are often drawn into very complicated mental associations with animal behavior: "Just like the stercoraceous, birds that are restless as if always famished, enjoy the polar seas, and venture only accidentally into more temperate zones, like them I was uneasy and dragged my legs forward very slowly." Here is his concept of a human state of mind: "The mind is dried up by a condensed and continually strained re-

flection, it howls like frogs in a swamp, when a band of ravenous flamingos or famished herons fall upon the weeds of its shores." He compares the style of a writer to "an owl serious unto eternity." By accepting a close link between man and other living organisms in his metaphors, he destroys old aesthetic values; beauty becomes for him something entirely unorthodox: "He seemed beautiful like the two long tentacle-shaped filaments of an insect," or "The beetle, beautiful as the trembling of the hands of an alcoholic." It is farfetched analogies such as these which André Breton has called the surrealism of Lautréamont. The following image has become famous because of the number of times it has been cited as the perfect surrealist image: "The vulture of the lambs, beautiful as the law of arrestment of the development of the chest in adults whose tendency to growth is not in relation to the quantity of molecules that their organism assimilates, vanished into the high reaches of the atmosphere." Even death has a beauty likened to a characteristic of the animal: "Each one has the common sense to confess without difficulty that he does not perceive at first a relation, no matter how remote, which I point out between the beauty of the flight of a royal kite, and that of the face of a child, rising sweetly above an open casket, like a water lily piercing the surface of the waters."

If man's physical characteristics are akin to those of the animal, his social behavior can also be seen to derive from that of the lower forms of life. Man's social incompatibility, for instance, becomes as natural a phenomenon as that of various species of fish that practice their own brand of isolationism in ocean habitats. . . . (pp. 57-61)

The theory of evolution accorded Lautréamont a means of reexamining moral issues. In [the French translation of Darwin's *Origin of the Species*] . . . , the universal and inevitable destructiveness in all nature was eloquently brought out: "a law of inevitable destruction decimates, either the young or the old, at each successive generation, or only at periodic intervals." In line with this basic struggle for survival described by Darwin, the translator's introduction pointed out that if destruction is a basic law of nature, then the fundamental rule of morality would be the efforts of each species for self-preservation. The recognition of the brutal origin and the biological universality of evil is a basic theme of *Les Chants de Maldoror*. Lautréamont accepts man's sinful inclinations as the same type of manifestation as the eagle's instinct to tear up his prey. The judges of man's cruelty to man are no other than the eagle, the crow, the pelican, the wild duck, the toad, the tiger, the whale, the shark, or the seal, for he has surpassed the cruelty of all of these.

If man is physically and spiritually no more than a sublime ape, then the angel cannot be very far from this same stage; he appears to Maldoror in the guise of a crab and laughs like a lamb. As the concept of gradual perfection is minimized, even God is divested of his sublimity.

Once the physical and moral characteristics of human beings have been reduced to the level of those of the animals, there remains only one reason for man's greater unhappiness as compared with the attitude of other living organisms on earth: it is the illusion he has of his superiority. In his own moment of disillusionment, therefore, Lautréamont seeks to reduce human pride and thereby find peace through a fraternization with the animal world and finally through actual metamorphosis. He discourses with the greatest of ease with animals (among whom are some of the principal characters of his work): the snake, the beetle, the toad. He seeks a bond with the most despicable of animals: the vampire is his friend, the scorpions his companions; he makes love to the female shark, is consoled by the serene and majestic toad. I do not agree with Bachelard that Lautréamont's obsession with animals is a manifestation of "the phenomenology of aggression." If hostile, violent acts are perpetrated, as he says, to forestall his own vulnerabilty to suffering, the evidence seems to show that Maldoror suffers as much as the animals with which he associates. Lautréamont is making an attempt to revise the anthropocentric notion of the universe, and the process is wrought with pain and stoical humiliation. The pantheists had also felt a certain affinity with all created beings, but the bond had been considered hierarchic, and man's love of God's other creatures placed on a somewhat patriarchal plane. In Lautreamont's vision of the universe, however, the fraternization of man with beast, Maldoror's actual intercourse with animals, are based on a sordid form of democracy and a powerful atavism whereby man seeks justification for his instincts and attitudes by putting them on a par with those of the lowest forms of animal life.

Maldoror achieves complete identification with the other species. With joy he lives as a shark, or a hog, or a pretty cricket: "The metamorphosis never appeared to my eyes as anything but the high and magnanimous reverberation of perfect happiness for which I had been waiting a long time." He envisions with equanimity two brothers changed into a single spider. Going one step further, he contemplates the possibility of new species: he sees himself as a hybrid, half-bird, half-man, or he imagines with scientific precision a man with the appendages of a duck in close communion with water life: "I saw swimming in the sea, with large duck's feet in place of the extremities of the legs and arms, bearing a dorsal fin proportionally as fine and as long as a dolphin's, a human being, with vigorous muscles, and which numerous schools of fish (I saw, in this procession, among other inhabitants of the waters, the torpedo, the anarnak of Greenland, and the horrible scropene) followed with the very ostensible marks of the greatest admiration . . . The porpoise, who have not, in my opinion, stolen the reputation of good swimmers, could hardly follow from afar this amphibian of a new species." In still another instance, his disgust for mankind makes him assume partially the shape of a swan and live at peace with the fish. "Providence, as you can see, has given me in part the organism of a swan. I live in peace with the fish, and they procure the food which I need."

It is significant to note the difference between these metamorphoses and the *Metamorphosis* of Kafka. Gregor Samsa, transformed into a tremendous insect, feels nothing but contempt and fear in his new condition. He senses an eternal barrier between himself and humanity. His metamorphosis symbolizes his exclusion from the rest of society, his tremendous loneliness that nothing can cure. On the contrary, Lautréamont feels no disgust; to him the tentacles of an insect are beautiful. It is, rather, the return to his former shape that he considers a misfortune. His metamorphosis is not the terrible thing it is in Kafka's story, but an affront to that human hypocrisy he cannot tolerate. Basically, then, he is not such a pessimist as Kafka for he finds relief from his dissatisfaction with humanity—unwholesome though the manner may be—through his identification with other forms of life.

Nonetheless Lautréamont's attempts to take man down from his self-appointed pedestal and to integrate him with a more closely knit animal kingdom produce a tragic note throughout his writings. Although on the one hand he concedes a dreary sort of materialism that endows man with as little immortality

as a butterfly, his innate mysticism produces undertones of a protest against a totally materialistic concept of life as pungent as his determined intent to undermine the traditional faith in human superiority.

The mood fluctuates between insolence and derision on the one hand, and on the other, the despair of Adam chased from paradise. Although he was obsessed by the seeing of the animal in man, he did not achieve a total portrayal of man as a beast. Even in comparing Maldoror's crime to that of the eagle he unconsciously pointed to the great difference by adding: "yet as much as my victim, I suffered." For all his self-imposed materialism he could not rid himself of the notion of immortality. The very evil he saw in man and in beast he explained by their common rage against the inability to fathom the absolute. Although he humiliated God before his creatures he could not deny His omnipresence. And although man and beast are pictured as being equally ephemeral yet there exists for all a paradise, described in eloquent terms by brother toad who will share it with Maldoror.

What dazzled the surrealists and intensified their admiration for Lautréamont was his ability to confront the human condition squarely in all its abject and tragic facets yet to discover at the same time a weapon for self-preservation in his battle with God. It was what Breton called in his *Anthologie de l'Humour Noir* a "humor that reached its supreme power and that brings us physically and totally under its law." Léon Pierre-Quint had earlier seen in this two-edged instrument of attack and self-protection the basic metal of the modern comic, which has something sacred about it and is at the antipodes of the old: it is aimed at the irremediable plight of man although humor allows Lautréamont a moment of exemption from the target of his derision. Léon Pierre-Quint says that Lautréamont put an infernal machine at each junction of his thought process: "When Lautréamont responds with humor to Maldoror's cries of fury as he stands in judgment over Jehovah and as an executioner over men, he has truly attained the revolt of the mind, and it is superior to the integral nihilism of the destroyers of society."

Lautréamont died too young to have reached any philosophical conclusions. The ultimate picture which **Les Chants de Maldoror** leaves is twofold. True, on the one hand there is the image of man on a plane little (if at all) above that of the beast; but at the same time Lautréamont's tableau of the animal world is endowed, through his longing for fraternity, with the human qualities he would deny: wisdom, kindness, sympathy, at times even a certain "douceur." As a result his apostrophes to the lowliest creatures, touched as they are with an undercurrent of pathos and compassion, transform many a passage of the work from a derision of mankind to a mockery of those who would deny man any powers beyond those of animals. "I thought I was more than that!" is the chant that soars above the absurd fraternizations. The bold manner in which Lautréamont came to grips with "the great problem of life," whether he transferred his concern to his alter ego, the brother of the leech, or took it upon himself directly, gave his work a universal and timeless character, and set the tragic but unresigned and sometimes sardonic tone, characteristic not of his age but of a future one. (pp. 61-6)

*Anna Balakian, "Lautréamont's Battle with God,"
in her* Surrealism: The Road to the Absolute, *revised
edition, Dutton, 1970, pp. 50-66.*

PAUL ZWEIG (essay date 1972)

[*Zweig's full-length study of Lautréamont is divided into several
parts. He begins by outlining the literary traditions upon which*

Maldoror is based, acclaiming the continuing relevance of its vision. Zweig then provides a lengthy discussion of Lautréamont as a new type of Narcissus—a defiant, violent revolutionary with a profound need to understand the depths of his own personality. The final portion of the work contains extracts from Lautréamont's writings. In the following excerpt, Zweig discusses Lautréamont's relationship to nineteenth-century literature. He argues that Maldoror, like the Gothic novel and the roman noir, differs from realistic works by celebrating the supremacy of the individual in revolt against society. The creation of such works, according to Zweig, requires psychic freedom, and he examines passages from Maldoror to determine whether such freedom drove Lautréamont insane.]

Les Chants de Maldoror is undoubtedly the masterpiece of nineteenth-century satanism. The poem's savagery and dark humor have rarely been equaled in literature. Lautréamont's hero, Maldoror, is a terrifying yet strangely comic figure, as when he transforms himself into a giant squid fastening his suckers in the Creator's armpit, or leaps headfirst into the ocean to copulate with his "living portrait," a female shark. Rarely has poetry expressed such a mood of demonic revolt.

The originality of **Maldoror** does not lie only in its subject matter, of course. Since the *petit romantisme* of Petrus Borel and Aloysius Bertrand in the 1830s, a current of somber hallucinatory poetry had taken over the foreground of French literature, in Gérard de Nerval's hermetic sonnets and his dream epic, *Aurélia;* in Baudelaire's *Fleurs du Mal,* and Charles Nodier's tales; also in the vast wave of popular literature represented by the *roman noir.* (p. 5)

Novelists like Thackeray or Jane Austen, or Balzac himself (in most of *The Human Comedy*), describe and celebrate the pattern of "realities" which compose a life. They present us with unique characters playing out their lives in equally unique social circumstances. In the *roman noir,* on the other hand, it is not the pattern which is celebrated, not the "realistic," highly articulated history, but the energies which disrupt the history. The hero of the *roman noir,* and of the Gothic novel before it, is perverse and essentially mysterious; he is a character whose allegiance to himself is so compelling that he refuses to be imprisoned by the limits of circumstance and society, by the prison of the ordinary to which novels are committed. Such heroes are "evil" because they come from elsewhere, like falling stars, or like devils. They are criminals (Rocombole and Vautrin), or condemned exiles (Melmoth); they are solitary characters whose consolations lie not in companionship and society, but in the demonstration of their own compelling vitality. They are also victims, men of *ressentiment,* and therefore every impulse of their character is an act of revenge upon the society to which they cannot belong and refuse to belong.

In this sense, the *roman noir* and the Gothic novel are antinovels. And the rebellious mood of the late French Romantics grows out of this tradition of avenging energies. There is a somber Rousseauism in Nerval, Baudelaire, Lautréamont and Rimbaud. "Man was born free but everywhere he is in chains" [Rousseau]. To undo the chains, these men chose to undo the pattern of society in their own psyches. This is the impetus of Rimbaud's drug experiments, his "reasoned unreasoning of the senses," of Nerval's fascination with the archaic freedom of dream images. And this is the commitment Isidore Ducasse expresses in a letter to his publisher a year before his death: "I have celebrated evil, as Mickiewitz, Byron, Milton, Southey, Alfred de Musset, Baudelaire, etc., did before me. Naturally I exaggerated the tone a little, to create something new in the mode of that sublime literature . . ." [see excerpt dated 1869-70].

Ducasse's declaration of intention echoes the disingenuousness of his immediate ancestor, Baudelaire, who wrote of his *Fleurs du Mal,* "Since famous poets have long since staked out the more flowery realms of poetic subject matter, I thought it would be interesting . . . to extract beauty out of evil." The innocuous "literary" tone of Lautréamont's letter points to an ambivalence in **Maldoror** which one finds equally in the whole tradition he identifies himself with. On the one hand, in writing his poem he embraced a cultural form, a convention for which his rhetorical gifts were uniquely fitted. What he is doing is "literary." Like Baudelaire, and his other avowed masters, he has chosen among subject matters. But the genre he has chosen mines a dangerous territory of inward sentiments, it draws upon images, energies, and emotions which are blind and unsocializable. That is why they attract him. They express an impregnable "freedom" which the poet experiences in his own psyche: freedom from morality and authority; freedom from society; eventually, in **Maldoror,** freedom from the confinement of the human form itself. To fulfil his "literary" commitment, and dramatize the animus of revolt and *ressentiment* which the genre demands, the poet must walk a tightrope into the archaic revolts of his psyche, closer than one perhaps should ever be to the permanent insanity which lies beneath the outer walls of personality. At the end of his Second Canto, Lautréamont exclaims:

> No . . . don't let that haggard pack of diggers and shovels come deeper through the land mines of this impious song! The crocodile won't change a word of the vomit pouring from the inside his skull. Too bad if some furtive shadow, excited by the worthy goal of avenging humanity, which has been unjustly attacked by me, should slide open the door of my room, brushing along the wall like a seagull's wing, to plunge a knife through the ribs of the scavenger of celestial wrecks! The clay might as well dissolve its atoms this way as any other. . . .

Apparently Lautréamont understood the danger of his poem, and was fascinated by it. The starkness and the strange immediacy of the language here characterize **Maldoror.** The entire poem seems to take place at an intersection between literature and madness. The language is warped into uniqueness by the associative pressures of the primitive mind (the unconscious), and yet controlled, magnificently, by the rhetorical form of which the poet never loses sight. The result makes the poem seem self-generating and monolithic. One experiences **Maldoror** as a unique vision of cruelty and revolt, a poem whose rhythm is so compelling that it must be "authentic," a true if terrifying cry from the depths.

This undoubtedly explains the reverence for Lautréamont expressed by André Breton, and the French surrealists, who insisted that **Maldoror** must never be allowed to enter literary history, inserted between "this fellow and that fellow"; that Lautréamont had, at all costs, to be rescued from "literature." It also explains the feeling of scandal created when large passages in **Maldoror** were found to have been cribbed word for word from naturalist encyclopedias, and others were shown to echo, in a style just short of plagiarism, a whole panoply of popular writers from Michelet and Victor Hugo, to Goethe, Byron, Baudelaire, Sue, Shakespeare and others, too. In fact, on the evidence, few works of literature in the nineteenth century (which was so compelled by the romantic values of "authenticity" and "sincerity") were as resolutely literary as Lautréamont's late Gothic epic.

Ultimately, the fascination *Maldoror* continues to exert on readers probably will be defined by this enigma of a poem which breathes a uniqueness that is all but hallucinatory, while clinging at every moment to all its cultural and literary origins. In the end, one cannot decide whether Isidore Ducasse was a master of rhetorical effects, and a very great master at that, or a man driven mad by writing, whose poem must be read as a history of his madness.

What is one to make, for example, of passages like the following:

> The brother of the leech walked slowly in the forest. Several times he stops, opening his mouth to speak. But each time his throat contorts, refusing to release the aborted effort. At last he cries out: O Man, when you see a dead dog on its back, wedged into a lock so that it can't float away, don't act like everyone else and pick the worms out of its swollen stomach with your hands, contemplate them wonderingly, open a knife, and then cut up a number of them, saying to yourself, you too will be just like that dog. What mystery are you searching for? Not me, or the four webbed claws of the sea-bear of the Boreal ocean, have been able to discover the problem of life. Beware, night approaches, and you've been here since morning. What will your family and your little sister say when they see you coming home so late? Wash your hands, take the road that goes to where you sleep. . . . What's that creature down there, on the horizon, who dares to approach me fearlessly, with oblique, tormented leaps? What majesty, mixed with serene sweetness! Its gaze is deep, although it is tender. Its enormous eyelids flap in the breeze, and seem to be alive. It is unknown to me. When I look into its monstrous eyes my body trembles for the first time since I sucked the dry tits of what they call a mother. A halo of blinding light surrounds him. When he has spoken, everything in nature becomes quiet, and shudders. Since you want to come to me, as if drawn by a magnet, I won't stop you. How beautiful he is! It hurts me to say it. You must be strong, because your face is more than human, sad as the universe, beautiful as suicide. I abhor you with all my might, and would rather see a snake wound around my neck from the beginning of time, than your eyes. . . . What! It's you, toad! . . . fat toad! . . . unfortunate toad. . . . Pardon! . . . Pardon! . . . What are you doing on this earth of the damned? But what have you done to your viscous and fetid warts, to seem so lovely?
>
> (pp. 6-10)

In a moment of madness, I could take you by the arms and twist them like a wash that you wring dry, or break them with a snap, like two dry branches, and then use force to make you eat them. Taking your head in my hands, sweetly and caressingly, I could press my avid fingers into the lobes of your innocent brain, with a smile on my lips, extracting a usable fat to wash my eyes, which hurt with life's eternal insomnia. Sewing your eyelids together with a needle, I could shut out the spectacle of the universe, making it impossible for you to find your way; I wouldn't be the one to guide you. Lifting up your virgin body with an arm of steel, I could seize you by the legs and roll you around me like a slingshot, concentrating my forces on the last circumference, as I heave you against a wall. Each drop of blood will stain a human breast, and frighten men, placing them before an example of my evil deeds! . . . Don't worry, I'll order half a dozen of my servants to guard the venerated remains of your body, and keep them from the hunger of wild dogs. The body is probably stuck to the wall like a ripe pear, and hasn't fallen to earth; but dogs can make high leaps, if you don't watch out. . . .

The language is taut and controlled. The images never seem stereotyped or compulsive. On the contrary, the aura of dreamlike surprise in the first passage, the sadistic violence in the second, are positively sharpened by a fine line of humor which creates the impression of artistic control in the midst of frenzy. Or is the impression we get rather one of psychotic detachment, resulting from the emotional disassociation of the illness, as the psychiatrist Jean-Pierre Soulier argues in his study *Lautréamont: Génie ou Maladie Mentale?*

The debate concerning Lautréamont's sanity is an old one. Léon Bloy, who came across an old copy of *Maldoror* in the 1880s, was the first to make the judgment that "this is a madman speaking, the most deplorable, most painful of madmen." Since then, virtually every critic from Remy de Gourmont to Maurice Blanchot has felt obliged to reinterpret the evidence and decide for or against, sane or not sane. The arguments have all had a single deficiency. Virtually nothing is known of Isidore Ducasse, aside from the barest outlines of his life, a few letters, and a sample of his handwriting. The only evidence is *Maldoror,* and there a problem arises. The partisans of sanity and genius point to the exquisite artistic control which virtually never lapses in the poem, and decide that such a coherence is proof that the author was sane. But they are answered quite professionally that a whole category of mental illness, which used to be called *folie raisonante* or *délire d'interpretation* ("reasoning madness," "delirium of interpretation") and is now called schizophrenia or paranoia, can manifest itself precisely in such a sustained, gloriously flawless system of language, that loss of control need have nothing to do with psychosis until a very advanced stage. In such cases the control in psychosis is strangely misapplied, creating a world of coherent but exaggeratedly idiosyncratic, and even archaic images. (pp. 10-11)

Isidore Ducasse may or may not have written his epic under the pressure of encroaching psychosis; but *Maldoror* is, by its own frequent admission, a book of the mad, whose half-humorous intention is to liberate the reader into madness.

Throughout the poem Lautréamont toys with the suggestion of his own insanity, accusing the All-Powerful of having placed his "soul between the boundaries of madness, and those furious thoughts which kill more slowly. . . ." . . . At one point he describes a striking scene in which Maldoror is haunted by a spectre, as in the spookiest of Gothic novels:

> what shadow casts the image of its shriveled silhouette upon my wall with such incredible

power. . . . A flock of hungry birds hover near your face; they love meat that doesn't belong to them, and defend the usefulness of pursuit, beautiful as skeletons plucking leaves of the panoccos in Arkansas. . . . But maybe you don't have a face; your shadow walks on the wall in a feverish shake of human vertebrae, like the deformed symbol of a ghostly dance. . . .

The episode builds in a crescendo of grotesque imagery, until at last Maldoror is forced to recognize the phantom which has been haunting him:

> There's only one thing left to do: break this mirror into pieces with the help of a stone. . . . It's not the first time the nightmare of the momentary loss of memory has set up residence in my imagination, when, by inflexible optic laws, I have been confronted with the ignorance of my own image. . . .

Such hints of mental disassociation become more frequent and more elaborate in the poem as Lautréamont develops the conception of his liberating insanity, which is like an expedition into some exotic domain where all identities, all forms have become unstable. "It is a man, or a stone, or a tree that will begin the Fourth Canto. . . . In the middle as at the beginning of life angels stay the same; how long is it since I stopped resembling myself?" (p. 13)

Then at last, after the reader has been cajoled, dazzled, chilled, and yet compelled too, by the satanic transformation which *Maldoror* has enacted before his eyes, Lautréamont turns to him in a passage of double talk, mingled with startling argument:

> My friend, isn't it true that, to a certain extent, my poem has won you over? Then what keeps you from going the rest of the way? The limit between your taste and mine is invisible; you'll never really understand it; proof that the limit itself doesn't exist. In which case, consider this (I only touch on the question here): it may not be impossible that you've signed a treaty of alliance with obstination, agreeable daughter of the mule, copious spring of intolerance. If I didn't know that you weren't stupid, I wouldn't complain about this. There is no need for you to get stuck in the membraned carapace of an axiom you think is unshakeable. Other axioms are unshakeable too, and they advance parallel to yours. If you have a strong preference for caramel (that admirable farce of nature), no one will think it's a crime; but someone whose intelligence is more active and capable of greater things, may prefer arsenic and pepper, and have good reasons to do so, without meaning to impose their peaceful domination over those who tremble with fear before a shrew-mouse, or the talking expression of the surfaces of a cube. . . .

The effect of the passage is comic, and yet convincing in its way. Only by loosening his grip on the forms of his own sanity, can the reader demonstrate true broadness of mind. Otherwise he will remain locked in the axioms of reason as in a prison, and will never understand the enjoyment he has hypocritically taken in the "mind-blowing" episodes of *Maldoror*. Besides, the reader had better be careful, because at that very moment

"new thrills are appearing in the intellectual atmosphere," and what better way could there be to meet them than to plunge, cathartically, into the bath of *Maldoror*'s insane vision.

Isidore Ducasse would have been surprised by the accuracy of his prophecy. A year or two later Rimbaud appeared on the literary scene, occupying precisely the place Isidore Ducasse had designated for him. Maldoror turns out to have been a kind of John the Baptist. But Ducasse was dead by the time the new literature erupted. (pp. 13-14)

Lautréamont rarely leaves his reader with the comfort of an abstract formulation. He concludes the above "therapeutic" exhortations with a course of practical advice that seals the argument once and for all. Rarely have the tools of discourse been used for such manipulative and ultimately grotesque ends:

> Believe me, in all things habit is necessary; and since the instinctive disgust which you felt when you first began reading, has notably diminished, in inverse proportion to the pages you've turned, like a large boil which has been lanced, there is hope, although your head is still sick, that your cure will quickly reach its final period. In my opinion, it's obvious that you're in full convalescence; although your face is thin, alas! But . . . have courage! You have an unusual mind, I love you, and haven't given up hope of your complete deliverance, as long as you take a few medicinal ingredients, which I'm sure will hasten the final disappearance of all your symptoms. For an astringent and tonic nourishment, first of all, you will tear off your mother's arms (if she's still alive), cut them into small pieces and eat them, in a single day, without betraying the trace of an emotion on your face. If your mother is too old, take another surgical specimen, a younger and fresher one, whose flesh is more easily scraped, and whose tarsal bone, when she walks, finds good support to balance forward: your sister, for example. . . . The most lenitive mixture I advise is a basin full of pitted blenoragic pus in which has been dissolved beforehand a pilous cyst of the ovary, a follicular chancre, an inflamed foreskin peeled back from the glans by a paraphymosis, and three red slugs. If you follow my prescription, my poetry will receive you with open arms, like a louse severing the root of a hair with its kisses.

The violence of *Maldoror* is committed to a kind of ironic pedagogy. The poem's satanic vision, we are told mockingly, is indeed therapeutic. It is meant to cure the reader of what Mathurin (one of Lautréamont's favorite writers), called "the curse of sanity." (pp. 14-15)

> *Paul Zweig, in his* Lautréamont: The Violent Narcissus, *Kennikat Press, 1972, 122 p.*

ALEX DE JONGE (essay date 1973)

[In the following excerpt, de Jonge discusses Maldoror *as a subversive text, focusing on its ability to alter the reader's perceptions of the world. According to de Jonge, Lautréamont "wants us to understand that we are prisoners confined for ever in the nightmare of our culture." To free us, the poet attempts to shock the reader with obscenity and blasphemy. Because Lautréamont chal-*

lenges our basic assumptions about society, de Jonge claims,
official culture cannot afford to acknowledge him; thus, his works
remain obscure, and he is dismissed either as a mere adolescent,
or as a madman.]

Lautréamont begins his principal work *Les Chants de Maldoror* with a warning; unless the reader proceeds with real caution Lautréamont's poetry will poison his brain [see excerpt dated 1868]. This may appear a hysterical and exaggerated threat, but it is nothing of the sort, the author is perfectly right. Read in one way the work will make the reader aware of appetites and desires that he never knew he had; he may not like what he finds, or he may like it too much. Reading in another way he will discover that Lautréamont delicately picks at the threads that hold his world-view together until, gently and undramatically, its fabric falls apart at the seams. But however he may choose to interpret or judge *Les Chants de Maldoror,* he may be certain of one thing; it is a work that does not leave the reader as it found him.

Lautréamont forces his readers to stop taking their world for granted. He shatters the complacent acceptance of the reality proposed by their cultural traditions, and makes them see that reality for what it is: an unreal nightmare all the more hair-raising because the sleeper believes that he is awake.

The desire to bring his readers to full consciousness, make them see who and where they are, underlies every word that Lautréamont wrote. Above all he wants us to understand that we are prisoners confined for ever in the nightmare of our culture. He is traumatically disturbed by the knowledge that we can only see the world as our culture would have us see it; that our view of reality is strictly the limited view that you enjoy from a cell window.

In order to make us acknowledge this truth emotionally as well as intellectually, Lautréamont sets out to disturb us. Coolly, deliberately, he breaks every kind of taboo. His blasphemies are so extreme that they continue to disturb in an age of irreligion; his sadistic eroticism has lost none of its edge in a world no longer shocked by death camps and hard porn.

Lautréamont is not, however, content simply to shock his readers. He also asks them questions, questions such as 'What is literature?' 'What is meaning?' 'What is man?' And, finally, 'What is God?' Although he supplies no answers he makes us realise that the questions need to be asked, because the obvious answer answers nothing. Thus Lautréamont seeks to heighten awareness in his readers, to teach them to think and feel for themselves.

His instrument of education is language. With an extraordinary blend of surrealism and logic he uses language as a model to build patterns that clarify and articulate the issues at stake. The models are not designed to provide answers, but to *explicate* the questions, taking that word in its etymological sense of *explicare*—to unfold.

It is this process of unfolding that makes Lautréamont important. He is not just another minor poet, a rich and untapped vein of scholarship material, to be written about because he is there. If we read him with both eyes open, we shall see that his poetry unfolds before us the essential elements of our culture-pattern—post-Renaissance capitalist Europeans with a Christian ancestry.

The most important lesson that his models teach is that man is at the mercy of his culture-pattern. Culture creates for each one of us a 'grid'; a set of categories of similarity and difference that forms the entire series of values and beliefs through which we interpret our world. It is a great deal harder to change the grid than it is to be changed by it, because it constitutes the base-elements of a cultural language. It is an enormous mistake to assume that language is something we manipulate; usually it is language that manipulates us. . . . [Each] individual is at the mercy of his language. He may feel that it leaves him free to do as he pleases, but that sense of freedom is an illusion. He is always restricted by the range of choices that language offers him. He can only criticise it in terms of its own making. It creates for him a prison from which there can be no escape. . . . [Language] creates what might be termed a one-dimensional situation; one in which it is impossible to make an act of effective judgment, because the very situation renders us quite unable to conceive of any genuine alternative. The individual is not free to give his own answer, because no answer he gives can be his own.

Lautréamont is obsessed with the fact that our answers are not our own, but simply the products of our culture, of our particular place in space and time. What we think of as being our truth is nothing of the sort; it is imposed upon us by circumstance, making us at the very least the prisoners of our culture.

Lautréamont cannot secure our release. As von Humboldt implied, you cannot escape from this prison, you can only change cells. What he can do is make us realise that we are 'inside', show us the walls, the bars on the window, and perhaps, something beyond. This is the next best thing to escape; once we know where we are, and realise that all action and judgment is shaped by our situation, we experience a strange liberation. The better we know our prison, the larger our cell seems to become. Not even Lautréamont can arrange a break-out, but he can make prison-life more bearable.

It is to this end that Lautréamont blasts his readers with blasphemy and obscenity. He tries to break down their prejudices, the inhibitions founded on good taste and taboo that culture builds into them as a defence against any truth that might threaten it. He goes on to try to make them understand the actual nature of their predicament. It is precisely because his work considers these fundamental questions, questions that pose an essential threat to the culture-pattern in that they seek to expose its limitations, that the immediate response of the culture in question is to reject Lautréamont as unreadable.

There are certain fundamentally subversive works that official culture cannot afford to acknowledge. They offer too great a threat, because they infringe the area of silence surrounding society's basic taboos. We all know the proposition 'Tell me what you read and I'll tell you who you are'. Much more revealing is the proposition 'Tell me what you censor and I'll tell you who you are'. Some of the most significant facts about a society are to be found in its cultural dustbins, among the objects that it rejects because they do not conform to its patterns.

Official culture subscribes to the Berkeleyan thesis, whereby an author exists only in so far as the public is aware of him. It has endeavoured to make Lautréamont vanish by pretending he is not really there. He does not loom large in the official canon of nineteenth-century European poetry. It was significantly left to the surrealists of the 1920s to recognise him as a writer of the utmost importance. Their admiration for him was boundless—no wonder. Surrealism represents one of the most radical rejections of official culture that we know. The surrealists considered that their civilisation had most perfectly expressed itself in such masterpieces as the Battle of the Somme. They found it more difficult to admire its lesser creations. For them *Les Chants de Maldoror* expressed a refusal to accept the rationalistic commonsense world-view that formed the basis of that civilisation. They felt it was a work that the establishment could not afford to face; a work to be taken very seriously indeed.

Not so official criticism. Because the author challenges basic assumptions and declines to accept cultural conventions as the truth, his writing is quite unlike anything else in the cultural tradition. It cannot be matched against a predecessor, it lacks 'formative influences'. Because it demands a totally new way of reading, official criticism dismisses it as impossible to read.

But even if Lautréamont were easy to read, he would still be rejected out of hand. The work is easier to explain away than to accept. So great is the violence it inflicts that it inspires immediate resentment. It is simpler to dismiss it. (pp. 1-4)

Official criticism finds it convenient to treat *Les Chants de Maldoror* as a curiosity, an exhibit in the literary freak-show. This enables it to dismiss its hair-raising obscenity as schoolboy extravagance. The patronising treatment of the author as a foul-mouthed innocent enables the critic to dodge the violent eroticism of his work. He does not have to take account of scenes in which innocent children are raped to death with the aid of a pen-knife and a bulldog, in which God is caught in an informal moment resting in a whore's crib. Such scenes are mere adolescent indiscretions, they do not matter, are not really there. This kind of dismissal has been used to take care of writers such as Céline, not *really* anti-Semitic, and William Burroughs, not a real writer, since he enjoys the support of a fortune built on the sale of office machinery. The alternative—to accept the works as meaning what they say—would be unthinkable.

But Lautréamont is precisely concerned with the unthinkable. Hence the deliberate flouting of taboo, the persistent intention to name the unnameable that emerges in such passages as this:

> It is time to apply a brake to my inspiration
> and to pause for a moment on my way, as you
> do when you look at a woman's vagina.

What is to be done with an author, a nineteenth-century author at that, who uses *that word*? The answer is obvious. He must be hidden. You either pretend he does not exist, or you put him away. You do not, on any account, read him.

It is no coincidence that a great predecessor of Lautréamont's, one of the most prolific novelists of the eighteenth century, has been subjected to just such a conspiracy of silence and sequestration. The Marquis de Sade spent most of his adult life behind bars, and his writing has been kept in the quarantine of the pornographers' lists ever since. It would be unthinkable to treat de Sade as literature; to read him with both hands. This is why the case against him is always made out on literary grounds. We are informed that his works are formless, repetitive, boring, that they are not even erotic. He is both a bad writer and a bad pornographer. Official criticism labels him unreadable, so no one tries.

Just as de Sade has been dismissed as a repetitive lunatic, so there have been attempts to explain Lautréamont by suggesting that he was mad. Known to be the work of a madman, the writing is no longer a threat. It ceases to have meaning and becomes a curiosity: a text with a clinical or documentary value. (pp. 5-6)

A much more convincing dismissal of Lautréamont is furnished by the 'near-miss' approach, whereby *Les Chants de Maldoror* just fails. Albert Camus has described it as the work of 'a schoolboy who was nearly a genius' [see excerpt dated 1951]. This constitutes the most generous and damning of rejection slips. 'Very well done. This was extremely interesting. Do carry on and send us anything you do when you're grown up.' It is a little odd to find Camus writing like this about a work that anticipates his own interest in the cultural outsider by more than half a century.

This brief review of the critical reaction to Lautréamont tells us more about the critics than it does about the object of their criticism. Reading Lautréamont and reflecting about what he has to say will often lead one into areas of speculation that may have little to do with French poetry in the last century, but that have a great deal to do with the way we live and think now. Since he writes about the relationship between the individual and his culture, he can perform the invaluable service of helping us to discover who and where we are. (p. 6)

[Before] entering the world of Maldoror the reader should beware. At its strongest Lautréamont's strange blend of bombast, blasphemy and obscenity is very disturbing. It will be recalled that the author began his work with a warning. With its invocation, its absurdly complicated style and its bizarre imagery, it is an excellent introduction to Lautréamont's nightmare:

> Please heaven that the reader, rendered for a
> moment bold and savage at what he reads, find
> his rough and wild path, without getting lost,
> across the desolate marshes of these sombre
> poison-ridden pages; for unless his reading be
> supported by a rigorous logic and a mental
> alertness at least the equal of his sense of mis-
> trust, the deadly vapours of this book will sat-
> urate his soul as water saturates sugar.

The reader has been warned. (p. 7)

Alex de Jonge, in his Nightmare Culture: Lautréamont and "Les Chants de Maldoror," *St. Martin's Press, 1973, 189 p.*

LEO BERSANI (essay date 1976)

[*In the following excerpt, Bersani examines the metamorphosis of identity in* Maldoror. *He begins by commenting on the work's sadomasochistic quality, which, despite its violence, is often insubstantial and reveals a literary self-consciousness. Bersani then examines narration in the work, trying to determine the identity of its various speakers. Arguing that the shifting narrative stance symbolizes metamorphosis, Bersani also discusses how Lautréamont uses language to both create and destroy identity. Because every aspect of the work contributes to the crumbling of fixed identities, Bersani describes* Maldoror *as "one of literature's most daring enterprises of decentralization."*]

[In] spite of its consistently "respectable" diction, *Maldoror* is a steady stream of blasphemy and obscenity. Thematically, the book is unoriginal and boringly adolescent. It is a long diatribe against the evil nature of God and of man, at the same time that it documents the evil of its own hero, Maldoror. Lautréamont doesn't even bother to make the moral point of view consistent. At times, man is the virtuous victim of a malevolent God; at other times, he more than deserves whatever punishments he may have to suffer. Occasionally, Maldoror is the moral martyr who defends man against the persecutions of an unjust Creator. But he is also (and more often) the persecutor of his fellow men (if we can call Maldoror a man), and the book is full of Maldoror's spectacularly sadistic attacks on others—preferably on adolescent boys. *Les Chants de Maldoror* could be taken as the model for a very special literary genre: the sadomasochistic comic book.

Almost at the very beginning of the first canto, the narrator announces that he uses his genius "to depict the delights of cruelty!" [see excerpt dated 1868]. It's true that the reader's potential terror is forestalled by the manner in which Lautréamont both ridicules his own most terrifying inventions and smothers them in a kind of pasty dull prose. Nonetheless, the inventions themselves are remarkably wild and gruesome. Here is the narrator's description of his first view of God:

> . . . I slowly raised my mournful eyes, ringed with great bluish circles, towards the inverted bowl of the firmament, and dared to try and penetrate, young as I was, the mysteries of heaven. Not finding what I was seeking I raised my [terrified lids] higher . . . higher yet . . . until at last I perceived a throne built of human excrement and gold upon which was enthroned with idiot pride and robed in a shroud made from unlaundered hospital sheets, that one who calls himself the Creator!
>
> In his hand he held the decaying trunk of a [dead] man and he lifted it successively from his eyes to his nose and from his nose to his mouth, where one may guess what he did with it. His feet were bathed in a vast morass of boiling blood to the surface of which there suddenly arose like tapeworms in the contents of a chamber-pot, two or three cautious heads which disappeared instantly with the speed of arrows; for an accurate kick on the nose was the well-known reward for such a revolt against the law, caused by a need to breathe the air, for men are not, after all, fish!
>
> Amphibians [at the very most], they swam between two waters in that unclean juice! And when the Creator had nothing left in his hands he would seize another swimmer by the neck with the two first claws of his foot as in a pincers and raise him up out of that ruddy slime (delicious sauce!)
>
> (pp. 191-92)

But the cruelty of Maldoror is somehow insubstantial. Lautréamont is always adding the corny comment which takes the bite out of his indignation. For example, soon after the long passage I quoted in the previous paragraph, the narrator refers to God's lower jaw (as He chews up men) moving "his beard full of brains," and adds: "O reader, doesn't this last detail make your mouth water?" It is as if he were doing a tongue-in-cheek imitation of a straight horror story. At times he seems intent on outdoing the most extravagant Gothic inventions or the most impassioned romantic monologues, and at other times he deliberately—and rather grandly—dismisses his own success by longwinded, flat comments. Lautréamont is like a student showing he can excel in a certain type of written exercise—and showing at the same time that he doesn't even care about the effects that exercise is supposed to produce. The ultimate in showing off includes a suggestion of indifference to showing off.

An imaginary drawing of Lautréamont by Valloton.

"I have sung of evil," Lautréamont wrote in a letter, "as did Mickiewicz, Byron, Milton, Southey, A. de Musset, Baudelaire, etc." [see excerpt dated 1869-70]. To fill in the "etc." with other appropriate names would make for an impressive anthology of literary sources. Other critics have emphasized Lautréamont's bookishness; his work invites us to a feast of literary source-hunting. What I referred to a moment ago as a certain insubstantiality in *Maldoror*'s violence derives mainly from the way in which that violence is continuously being exposed as an act of literary virtuosity. *Les Chants de Maldoror* seems to be about nothing more than Lautréamont's ability to write *Les Chants de Maldoror*. But it is this very extremity of literary self-consciousness in Maldoror which gives to the book its ontological originality. It is as if Lautréamont were so immersed in literature that he could begin to conceive of identities being constrained by nothing outside of literature. He makes the easy but radical step from a *nom de plume* to an *identité de plume,* and the result is a revolutionary decentralization of self, and an extraordinary psychic mobility.

The biographical Isidore Ducasse is almost lost, both to literary history and to the works which attribute their authorship to a fictive Comte de Lautréamont. But then where is this unreal Lautréamont in his own book? The narrative "I" sometimes reports on Maldoror as if the latter were clearly distinct from the former. At times, the narrator is omniscient and insightful; at other times, he seems to be a stupefied and not particularly well-informed spectator of Maldoror's activities. But there are also moments when, without indicating that he is quoting Maldoror, the narrator speaks with Maldoror's voice, and Lautréamont, his narrator, and his hero are fused into one. Thus the identity presumably "behind" *Les Chants de Maldoror*— that of Isidore Ducasse—gets lost in its derivations. And the indeterminate voice we hear—does it belong to Ducasse? to Lautréamont? to an omniscient narrator outside of the story? to a narrator participating in the story, even if only as a spectator? or, finally, to Maldoror?—also shifts indeterminately along various attitudes. Its moral personality is sometimes sadistic, sometimes humane; it belongs to "someone" ready to defend men, and then to torture them, someone who both sings "the delights of cruelty" and sheds tears over men's cruelty to one another.

The sliding of identities in *Maldoror* isn't limited to various names or various moral attitudes. Lautréamont responds to the suggestions for self-transformation in literary comparisons. Early in Canto One, he (who?) writes that he would have liked to be the "son of a female shark," and then he describes his physical appearance: "No one yet has seen the green furrows in my forehead, nor the protruding bones of my emaciated face, resembling the bones of some great fish, or the rocks which cover the seashore, or the rugged Alpine mountains which I climbed often when my hair was of a different color." What is to prevent him from becoming that which he resembles? He confesses to having lived "a half-century in the form of a shark among the submarine currents that extend along the African coast," and in one of his happiest dreams he lives in a pig's body. The capacity for metamorphoses is shared by everyone in the book. In the Mervyn short story which constitutes Canto Six, Maldoror becomes a black swan. God is a rhinoceros, and one of his archangels "had taken on the form of a hermit crab large as a vicuna." Elsseneur and Reginald are changed into a giant spider so that they may punish Maldoror for trying to kill them by sucking the blood from his neck every night for twenty years.

What makes these metamorphoses so powerful in *Maldoror* is precisely what might seem to condemn them to triviality: their purely literary derivation. They have their source in an imagination unconstrained by any sense of responsibility to the real. And the invisible Ducasse finds his peculiar liberty of self-effacement and self-transformation both frightening and exhilarating. What the isolated and bookish author of *Les Chants de Maldoror* seems to discover is that, alone with words, one experiences the extent to which language doesn't merely describe identity but actually produces moral and perhaps even physical identity. We can of course choose to be literal-minded and insist that no amount of self-comparisons will suffice to change us into sharks. But in trying to account for the originality of *Maldoror,* I think that we have to allow for a kind of dissolution or at least elasticity of being induced by an immersion in literature. (pp. 192-94)

With Lautréamont, we see for the first time the *destructuring* possibilities of language. There is a kind of verbal terrorism which murders sense without even disrupting legitimate verbal orders and sequences. The attack against structure in *Maldoror* is carried out in the most rigorously structured way; each sentence, each stanza, each canto, and the succession of cantos are prodigies of controlled composition. What disintegrates the composed work and the composed self in *Maldoror* is a kind of exacerbated receptiveness to the very procedure of thought which generally helps us to compose a self or a literary work: that is, to comparisons. Instead of making reality intelligible by establishing relations among distinct units of experience, comparison in Lautréamont dislocates reality by violating two

conditions never stated in any specific comparison, but which guarantee the epistemological usefulness of all comparisons. First of all, Lautréamont refuses to acknowledge that there has to be any recognizable similarity of nature between the two terms of a comparison, and secondly he doesn't hesitate to convert an analogy into an identity. Lautréamont's most original comparisons are not an extension of our sense of affinities; they do not make us suddenly see, in a flash of recognition which is generally thought of as part of the poetic shock, unsuspected relations among "distant" elements of reality. Here are two examples of the much-praised "beau comme" construction which appears most frequently in Cantos Five and Six:

> Although he [the pelican being described by the narrator] possessed no human countenance, he appeared to me as beautiful as the two long tentaculiform filaments of an insect; or rather as a sudden interment; or again as the law of the restoration of mutilated organs; and especially as an eminently putrescible liquid!

> [Mervyn] is as handsome as the retractability of the claws of birds of prey; or again, as the uncertainty of the muscular movements of wounds in the soft parts of the posterior cervical region; or rather as the perpetual rat trap, reset each time by the trapped animal, that can catch rodents indefinitely and works even when hidden beneath straw; and especially as the fortuitous encounter upon a dissecting table of a sewing machine and an umbrella!

These comparisons have no educational, no cognitive function. What they do is simply to move us away from their supposed points of departure. There is no resemblance between Mervyn's beauty and a "perpetual rat trap" or the meeting on a dissecting table of a sewing machine and an umbrella. Proust writes that "truth" in literature begins only when the writer establishes the relationship between two different objects or when, "comparing qualities shared by two sensations, he makes the essential nature common to both sensations stand out clearly by joining them in a metaphor, in order to remove them from the contingencies of time. . . ." Nothing could be more alien to the poetics of *Maldoror*. Lautréamont's comparisons are strategies for leaps of being. The word "like" does not draw disparate aspects of our experience into a single structure; instead of being a technique of enclosure (as it is in part for Proust), metaphor in *Maldoror* is an invitation to metamorphosis. The second term of a comparison doesn't illuminate the first term; rather, it proposes that we forget it, that we almost literally jump away from it.

Les Chants de Maldoror is one of literature's most daring enterprises of decentralization. It is a major document among modern efforts to break away from what Jacques Derrida has been brilliantly anatomizing as the Western cultural habit of referring all experience to centers, or beginnings, or origins of truth and being. With Lautréamont, such points of departure are authentically negligible. And every aspect of his work contributes to the dispersion or the crumbling of fixed identities. By a happy misfortune of literary history, Isidore Ducasse is as fictive a personality for us as the invented Lautréamont who takes credit for the adventures of an imaginary Maldoror, adventures told by a narrator elusively floating among various physical and moral identities. And where exactly can we locate Ducasse-Lautréamont's imagination? *Maldoror* (and this is even truer of the *Poésies*) is the work of a plagiarizing genius; or, to turn the formula around, it testifies to the genius of plagiarism, to the appeal of wandering among styles and episodes all of which could simply be designated as *other*. They belong to or come from neither Ducasse nor his presumed sources. *Maldoror* is at once so like and so unlike those sources that it transcends its own limitations and forces us to renounce the critical compulsion to make attributions.

Lautréamont's work is ''about'' the capacity of being to glide from one form to another. From the stylistic level of the narrator's comparisons to the ''characters''' fabulous transformations, we are somewhat tauntingly put through a circus of metamorphoses. There is also Lautréamont's unrelenting ironic self-consciousness. Always willing to destroy his effects, to deflate the pose of anguish with a trivial detail or a corny joke, to allow the melodramatic and the prosaic to cancel each other out, to make such monstrously long and boring sentences that we can't even be sure he wants to be read, Lautréamont manages to disappear from a statement at the very moment he makes it. He is the master of irony—if we take irony to be something more radical than a discrepancy between apparent significance and real significance. Irony is the style of a mind in constant metamorphosis. In Lautréamont, as Maurice Blanchot has written in *Lautréamont et Sade*, the ironic statement hides no definite meaning but merely designates the author's absence from his statements. The narrator's ''person'' in *Maldoror*—whoever or whatever that may be—is never where he is speaking; he is, bizarrely, perhaps nothing more than a somewhere else. (pp. 195-97)

> *Leo Bersani, ''Desire and Metamorphosis,'' in his* A Future for Astyanax: Character and Desire in Literature, *Little, Brown and Company, 1976, pp. 189-229.**

ROBIN LYDENBERG   (essay date 1977)

[*In the following study of* Maldoror, *Lydenberg analyzes the ways in which Lautréamont blurs the distinctions between the narrator, the reader, and the text. She identifies in the narrative of* Maldoror *the progressive stages leading up to a major shift in the status of the reader: the fictionalized reader, who identifies with the personages in the text; the compromised reader, who confuses the bounds of fiction and becomes a participant; the educated reader, who learns to become the ideal reader—the double of the narrator; and the immobilized reader, who is hypnotized by Lautréamont's intimidating and convoluted style. Lydenberg argues that by redefining the role and identity of the reader, ''Ducasse is perhaps the first author to deal explicitly with the phenomenology of reading.''*]

Much of contemporary criticism has turned from analyses of the novel's relation to reality or society to analyses of the more immediate relationship between the literary work and its reader. The recent revival of critical interest in the works of Isidore Ducasse may be attributed in part to this 19th-century writer's systematic exploration of the nature of the reading process. In his article ''Une lecture compromettante,'' Roger Borderie presents Ducasse's *Les Chants de Maldoror* ... as a unique representation of the phenomenology of reading, as an exercise in supreme compromise. Never before, he claims, have the reader and what he reads been so completely joined; never before has a book been written so exclusively to be read.

While Borderie acknowledges that a concentration on the reader's activity is a latent characteristic of all literary discourse, he fails to credit an entire tradition of narratives preceding *Les Chants* in which the narrator/reader relationship is the major content of the fiction. A concern with the activity of the reader *as* reader is certainly a central focus in a novel like Laurence Sterne's *Tristram Shandy,* and Sterne himself recognizes his debt to a tradition of novels about the writing and reading of fiction, particularly to the works of Rabelais and Cervantes. In order to assess properly the uniqueness of *Les Chants,* it is necessary to understand Ducasse's assimilation and transformation of the techniques or reader involvement already developed by his predecessors.

In *La Révolution du langage poétique,* Julia Kristeva also presents Ducasse's work as a radical literary breakthrough, but her study clarifies in some detail the ways in which *Les Chants* both continue and deviate from conventional discourse. Linguistic traditionalism is defined by a structural opposition of the narrative ''je'' (*narrateur*) with a ''tu'' (*narrataire*) who is the receiver of the discourse, the other, the reader. Any play or interplay of the ''figurants du texte''—''je'' ''tu'' and ''il''—is camouflaged in the conventional narrative, logically justified by plot structures and a traditional use of fictional personae.... As innovative and self-conscious as their works may be, Ducasse's predecessors in the classical narrative never fully abandon the logical security of individual identity. It is precisely in the uncertainty of all identity in *Les Chants* that Ducasse's reader finds himself most exposed and endangered.

When the dividing line which differentiates *narrateur* and *narrataire* is blurred, the reader loses the security of his distance from the narrative. Confused and manipulated by arbitrary shifts in the discourse, he finds himself gradually assimilated into the text and implicated in its production. The process of *Les Chants* is a redefinition of the function and identity of the reader.

Ducasse elaborates theoretical guidelines for this new science of reading in *Poésies I* and *Poésies II,* a series of aphorisms published one year after *Les Chants.* Ducasse demonstrates his theories by reproducing in this later work his own activity as a reader. In what he calls reading ''appréciation,'' Ducasse substitutes his own formulations within the most well known quotations from Pascal, Vauvenargues and others, often completely reversing their original meaning. His continual metamorphoses of these classical texts replace the conventional passive receptivity of the reader with a more aggressive and creative involvement in the making of a text. Reproducing the same confusion he imposes on his own reader in *Les Chants,* Ducasse will repeatedly ''serre de près la phrase d'un auteur'' until it becomes his own, *narrateur* and *narrataire* converging in the corrected text. In this new poetry authorial identity becomes communal (''La poésie doit être faite par tous. Non par un.'') and all meaning is thrown into a flux of continual correction and reversal. Thus both content and identity are obscured and undermined, leaving only the ''fil indestructible de la poésie impersonnelle''—Ducasse's rigorous and convoluted rhetoric.

Each reader's assumptions about the relationship between narrator and reader and the responsibilities of the narrative to meaning and structure are laid bare and contradicted in *Les Chants* and *Poésies.* Beyond the conventional activity of creating or inventing an audience, the narrator of *Les Chants* practices what he calls the cretinising of each individual reader and the tradition embodied in that reader's expectations. *Les Chants* cannot be dismissed as the wild flailings of adolescent anarchy, for Ducasse's radicalism is carefully and dialectically structured. Rather than simply denying or circumventing the narrative tradition which precedes him, Ducasse attempts to encompass the movement of literary history itself, assimilating the very conventions he seeks to overthrow by absorbing and manipulating his audience. Ducasse achieves this gradual assimilation by a series of rhetorical devices which progress from fictional analogies for the reader's situation to his direct involvement and even imprisonment in the discourse. Through the contradictions, the illogicalities, the verbal accumulations and convoluted digressions which characterize his style, Ducasse transforms the conventions of an artificial rhetoric into a rhetoric come alive as the immediate and disturbing experience of the reader. I propose to trace in the narrative of *Les Chants* the progressive stages leading up to a major shift in the status of the reader in literary discourse which has ushered us into an age of modern revolutionary poetics.

The reader fictionalized.

Let us begin by examining the vestiges in *Les Chants* of one of the more conservative devices of the self-conscious fictional narrative: the use of consistent and identifiable ''personnages'' whose experiences within the fiction suggest analogies with the reader's situation in the discourse. The danger of confusing literature with life, of misunderstanding the relationship between fiction and reality, are pointedly dramatized in the novel from Cervantes' Don Quixote to that character's more tragic descendant Emma Bovary. While the classical novel may indirectly warn the reader not to expect reality to conform to fiction, Ducasse is more concerned with asserting his autonomy as an author warning his readers to abandon any expectation that *Les Chants* will conform to the conventions of reality.

After five *chants* of poetic chaos Ducasse introduces (although in his own stylistically unorthodox manner) a highly conventional novelistic framework supported by an elaborate network of ''bourgeois'' clichés. It is within the security of this familiar genre of the family novella that Ducasse indirectly asserts some of his most violent threats against the reader. The hero of this little drama is one Mervyn, an ingenuous adolescent whom we first encounter dutifully returning home from his fencing lesson. The narrator is irritated by Mervyn's expectation that he will, in fact, reach home safely; and omnisciently aware of the dangerous Maldoror lurking nearby, he concludes somewhat sadly, somewhat maliciously, ''Que ne fuyait-il donc? C'était si facile . . . cependant, il lui est impossible de deviner la réalité. Il n'est pas prophète.'' . . . It is Mervyn's expectation of happiness and normalcy which must be punished, and as we shall see Maldoror carries out that punishment rigorously.

The history of Mervyn and Maldoror demonstrates most clearly the danger of retaining any expectations of the written word. Maldoror first approaches his prey in writing, and it is Mervyn's romantic and naive reading of Maldoror's letter which eventually causes his demise. Always hoping for the best, Mervyn accepts on faith the vow of mutual confidence and trust which Maldoror offers him. In what Lautréamont hails as a ''scène unique qu'aucun romancier ne retrouvera,'' Mervyn is made to suffer for this expectation of sincerity. A meeting is arranged between the two, but instead of the brotherly embrace Mervyn awaits anxiously, the young man is quite unceremoniously stuffed in a sack and smashed against the parapet of the Pont du Carrousel. The reader has been forewarned by analogy against any similar misinterpretation of the respectful formality and concern which often characterize Lautréamont's direct addresses to *his* audience. The reader's relationship to *Les Chants* is thus hopelessly paradoxical. Confronted with an arbitrary and unpredictable fictional world, the

reader is totally dependent on the guidance of the narrator, but he is also repeatedly advised to distrust the poses and promises of that persona.

The perverse self-contradictions of the narrator of *Les Chants* are further complicated by Ducasse's stance in *Poésies,* where he adopts a highly conventional moral voice in total opposition to the amorality of the reckless comte de Lautréamont. The narrator of *Poésies* anticipates and discourages any critical objections to this polar reversal by asserting forcefully, ''Je ne permets à personne, pas même à Elohim, de douter de ma sincérité.'' . . . This aphorism should not be read as a claim to sincerity—for in this ''poésie impersonnelle'' sincerity is only one pose among many—but as Ducasse's exercizing of the absolute authorial will which establishes the narrative voice above question, like all other first principles and absolute truths, ''à ne pas discuter.''

The narrator of the conventional self-conscious novel often mobilizes his resistance to the interference of readers and critics, asserting an absolute control over fictional events and the order of their revelation. Sterne's Tristram, for example, declares he would tear out the next page of his book if he thought the reader could guess its contents. Like his predecessors, the narrator of *Les Chants* will not tolerate any assumption on the reader's part which would question his arbitrary autonomy. Lautréamont's tyrannical domination, however, extends beyond the aesthetics of storytelling to annex the territory of logic itself. Mervyn may be denied his expectations of the future, but the reader of *Les Chants* is even denied any certainty as to the apparent reality of the present of the discourse. The original version of the final stanza of Chant I, ''Ce premier chant finit ici,'' reads more tauntingly in a later variant, ''S'il est quelquefois logique de s'en rapporter à l'apparence des phénomènes, ce premier chant finit ici.'' The confusion and uncertainty which dominate the fictional world of *Les Chants* are reproduced here not by analogy but in the immediate experience of the reader, in his perception of the material structure of the written text.

While the reader may gradually learn to protect himself against the unexpected and the illogical by abandoning all assumptions in his reading of *Les Chants,* he is still forced to witness acts of violence perpetrated against more naïve and innocent victims in the course of the fiction. In Chant II, stanza 4, the narrator relates the story of a helpless child chasing after an omnibus in the hopes that it may carry him to safety. The passengers are all indifferent to the fate of the child and even annoyed at his continual cries. There is only one spectator who reacts indignantly to this injustice: ''L'adolescent se lève, dans un mouvement d'indignation, et veut se retirer, pour ne pas participer, même involontairement, à une mauvaise action. Je lui fais un signe, et il se remet à mon côté.'' . . . Maldoror's coercion of the adolescent, who is not allowed to disassociate himself from the inhumanity of his fellow men, mirrors Ducasse's insidious corruption of an audience committed to the ingestion of his terrible fictions.

While the reader may learn from such fictional analogies to distance himself from the fiction, he cannot so easily escape his function within the discourse as the consciousness through which the narrative is realized. As Ducasse insists in *Poésies,* the reader always ''makes'' what he reads.

In addition to peopling his fictional world with characters who are essentially writers and readers, Ducasse also practices the convention of addressing his readers directly in several fic-

tionalized incarnations: the intimidated adolescent, the sceptical philosopher or the courageous but imprudent explorer of
the text. (pp. 211-16)

The reader compromised.

Against the opposition *narrateur/narrataire* which establishes
the reader's distance from the text, Ducasse practices in *Les
Chants* an intermittent and unpredictable confusion of the ''je''
and ''tu'' of the discourse, creating a free and unlimited fictional space in which fixed identity and function may be temporarily dissolved. Once again asserting his arbitrary autonomy
within the narrative, Ducasse challenges the laws of a consistent grammar which would assume the identification and differentiation of ''personnages.'' The effect of this confusion of
pronouns is that the reader may become, beyond analogy and
artificial rhetoric, an actual participant in the fiction.

One clear example of this technique of assimilation appears
early in *Les Chants* in the torture scene in Chant I, stanza 6.
The stanza begins with an impersonal structure using ''on''
and the extratemporal verb form: ''On doit laisser pousser ses
ongles pendant quinze jours. Oh! comme il est doux d'arracher
brutalement de son lit un enfant [. . .] de faire semblant de
passer suavement la main sur son front [. . .] d'enfoncer les
ongles longs dans sa poitrine molle.'' . . . The narrative continues with a similarly hypothetical and impersonal description
of the drinking of the child's blood and tears, but the impersonal
''on'' is replaced by a communal persona rendered specific
and individual as the object of the narrator's direct address:
''Homme, n'as-tu jamais goûté de ton sang, quand par hasard
tu t'es coupé le doigt?'' Having initiated the reader's involvement on these as yet inoffensive grounds, the narrator increases
his assumptions by implying that he shares with the reader a
certain predilection for the taste of blood. Assumption becomes
intimacy as the narrative presumes to conjure the reader's memories and ''réflexions lugubres'': ''ne te souviens-tu pas d'avoir
un jour [. . .] porté la main, creusée au fond sur la figure
maladive mouillée par ce qui tombait des yeux; laquelle main
ensuite se dirigeait fatalement vers la bouche, quit puisait à
longs traits, dans cette coupe, tremblante comme les dents de
l'élève qui regarde obliquement celui qui est né pour l'op-
presser, les larmes?'' . . . Surely not every reader will recognize
himself in this romantic misanthrope, but in his deciphering
of the text the details of these actions are embedded in the
reader's memory and become part of his past (poetic) experience.

From the first innocent admission that he may have on occasion
tasted his own blood and tears, the reader soon finds himself
portrayed in somewhat more compromising circumstances. The
narrator accomplishes this transition through the parenthetical
analogy, ''comme les dents de l'élève,'' which associates the
reader's hypothetical private preoccupations with the sado-ma-
sochistic scene about to be described in the fiction. From this
analogy the narrator's reasoning follows logically:

> Donc, puisque ton sang et tes larmes ne te dé-
> goûtent pas, nourris-toi, nourris-toi avec con-
> fiance des larmes et du sang de l'adolescent.
> Bande-lui les yeux, pendant que tu déchieras
> ses chairs palpitantes; et, après avoir entendu
> de longues heures ses cris sublimes, semblables
> aux râles perçants que poussent dans une ba-
> taille les gosiers des blessés agonisants, alors,
> t'ayant écarté comme une avalanche, tu te pré-
> cipiteras de la chambre voisine, et tu feras sem-

blant d'arriver à son secours [. . .]. Comme le
cœur déborde de pouvoir consoler l'innocent à
qui l'on a fait du mal: ''Adolescent [. . .] par-
donne-moi.'' . . .

(pp. 216-18)

The narrative has progressed from an impersonal third person
to a series of hypothetical actions addressed to an abstract and
rhetorical ''tu'' and finally to an imperative address which
seems to button-hole the actual reader and designate to him
very specific words which, in his reading, he does in fact
pronounce. There is an imperceptible shift of the discourse into
an immediate present tense in which the adolescent is consoled
and begged for forgiveness in the voice of the reader. Because
this shift takes place in a subtle grammatical slippage within
the discourse rather than in an overt characterization of some
particular reader/''personnage'' the reader has not foreseen the
necessity of disassociating himself from the ''tu'' of the text.
Thus at this very early point in *Les Chants* Ducasse has implicated his audience in one of Maldoror's most terrible deeds,
as each reader discovers himself mouthing the hypocritical
words of the evil torturer.

The territorial overlapping in *Les Chants* of the arena of the
fictional adventures and the interaction of narrator and reader
in the discourse have a disorienting effect on the reader's conception of his place in textual structure. Just as the critic who
continues to read the chronicles of Gargantua and Pantagruel
after the narrator has dismissed all ''grabeleurs de correction''
becomes by definition part of Rabelais' accepting audience,
any reader who fails to turn back at the warning on the first
page of *Les Chants* has established his complicity throughout
the rest of the text. ''Il n'est pas bon,'' we are told, ''que tout
le monde lise les pages qui vont suivre; quelques-uns seuls
savoureront ce fruit amer sans danger. Par conséquent, âme
timide, avant de pénétrer plus loin dans de pareilles landes
inexplorées, dirige tes talons en arrière et non en avant. Écoute
bien ce que je te dis: dirige tes talons en arrière et non en
avant.'' . . . Merely by proceeding in the text the reader has
sanctioned any ''fruit amer'' Ducasse may offer in the course
of *Les Chants,* and from the outset the reader shares with the
narrator the complicity of all fallen men. While the reader may
still disassociate himself from the specific ''personnages'' of
Rabelais' drinking companions or hypocritical censors, from
the pompous Sir or Madam of *Tristram Shandy,* Ducasse's text
is far more threatening because it addresses us all ultimately
in our most basic function as readers, continually calling into
question our understanding of the limits and responsibilities of
that function.

The reader educated.

Despite the complicity generated between narrator and reader
by Ducasse's confusion of the ''figurants du texte,'' no reader
could experience in *Les Chants* a communion with the author.
It is precisely this sentimental conceit of the discourse as a
meeting of souls, as an intimate interaction between ''je'' and
''tu'' which Ducasse has set out to undermine. The theory of
an impersonal poetry which Ducasse develops in *Poésies* frequently defines itself in opposition to the abuses of a romanticism which indulges itself in the display of sentimentality.
Ducasse's directives against such behavior are severe: ''Si vous
êtes malheureux, il ne faut pas le dire au lecteur. Gardez cela
pour vous.'' . . . Ducasse is particularly impatient with the
passive role the sentimental poet adopts with his readers: ''Il
existe une convention peu tacite entre l'auteur et le lecteur,
par laquelle le premier s'intitule malade, et accepte le second

comme garde-malade. C'est le poète qui console l'humanité! Les rôles sont intervertis arbitrairement.'' . . . In *Les Chants* Ducasse attempts to correct this error, and by reversing in his turn the roles of author and reader once again he returns his discourse to one of the earliest novelistic metaphors: literature as a cure. (pp. 218-19)

Ducasse sees his contemporaries (''nos époques phtisiques''), infected by the morbid self-indulgence of their ailing authors, as particularly in need of the curative powers of a literature which establishes the author as doctor, the reader as patient and the text as beneficial medication. He appropriates and applies this convention in *Les Chants* to his own radical purposes, and his offers to cure the reader are as ambiguously hostile as his aggressive gestures of friendship. Ducasse's text, in fact, operates as a cure only in that the reader is gradually less repulsed by what he encounters there.

In the voice of a patient but conservative school master, Lautréamont insists on the necessity of practice and discipline to conquer our instinctive repulsion to his words. He is hopeful that the reader's continual ''application à la lecture'' will increase his tolerance for *Les Chants,* carrying him from convalescence to complete deliverance. The numbing of the reader's sensibilities caused by his reading of the text must be followed up by a regimen which also demands complicitous actions. Again we find that the narrative shifts from hypothesis and analogy into imperative and concrete action. With no change in the tone of his bedside manner, the narrator prescribes the following ''substances médicamenteuses'': ''Comme nourriture astringente et tonique, tu arracheras d'abord les bras de ta mère (si elle existe encore), tu les dépèceras en petits morceaux, et tu les mangeras ensuite, en un seul jour, sans qu'aucun trait de ta figure ne trahisse ton émotion. Si ta mère était trop vieille, choisis un autre sujet chirurgical, plus jeune et plus frais . . . ta soeur, par exemple.'' . . . The dutiful patient will be rewarded with the open embrace of the text, likened to the vampire-kiss of the louse at the hair root. There is no sentimental elective affinity in the treatment offered by the narrator of *Les Chants,* for his cure threatens to be more of an infection. While we hardly feel constrained to obey Lautréamont's detailed instructions for our future conduct, the insinuating device of the reader's hypothetical crime draws the audience more deeply into the text than all of Rabelais' rhetoric of conviviality.

Although Ducasse's version of the curative powers of literature operates only negatively and destructively, one might argue that his motive is the same as that of the classical author: to remake the audience in the image of the narrator. The success and even the survival of the reader of *Les Chants* depends on his ability to become as ferocious as the text and as vigilant as its narrator. Like the speaker who introduces Baudelaire's *Les Fleurs du Mal,* Lautréamont ultimately addresses himself to an ideal reader—a double or brother. Because of his hyperbolic nature, this search often leads Lautréamont to posit impossible prerequisites for his audience: ''Celui qui, pendant un jour, a poursuivi l'autruche à travers le désert, sans pouvoir l'atteindre, n'a pas eu le temps de prendre de la nourriture et de fermer les yeux. Si c'est lui qui me lit, il est capable de deviner, à la rigueur, quel sommeil s'appesantit sur moi.'' . . . These descriptions of a hypothetical ideal reader often grow into extended metaphorical fictions within what begins as a digression from the fictional content of the narrative. Thus Lautréamont's simple assertion that he is tired spins into the following convoluted elaboration:

Mais, quand la tempête a poussé verticalement un vaisseau, avec la paume de sa main, jusqu'au fond de la mer; si, sur le radeau, il ne reste plus de tout l'équipage qu'un seul homme, rompu par les fatigues et les privations de toute espèce; si la lame le ballotte, comme une épave, pendant des heures plus prolongées que la vie d'homme; et, si, une frégate, qui sillonne plus tard ces parages de désolation d'une carène fendue, aperçoit le malheureux qui promène sur l'océan sa carcasse décharnée, et lui porte un secours qui a failli être tardif, je crois que ce naufragé devinera mieux encore à quel degré fut porté l'assoupissement de mes sens. . . .

For those of us who have not lived through such an experience Ducasse conveniently provides an identical storm in Chant II, stanza 13.

An experience accessible only in the fiction itself becomes the necessary training for a proper reading of the narrative. The world of *Les Chants* once again begins to feel uncomfortably claustrophobic. Reality and fiction no longer present a dual structure, for fiction has replaced reality by establishing itself as the primary existential experience. Lautréamont equates the reader's witnessing of his fictional storm with an understanding of life: ''Celui qui n'a pas vu un vaisseau sombrer au milieu de l'ouragan, de l'intermittence des éclairs et de l'obscurité la plus profonde, pendant que ceux qu'il contient sont accablés de ce désespoir que vous savez, celui-là ne connaît pas les accidents de la vie.'' . . . Only the imaginative reader who has successfully absorbed the shipwreck scene already described in this stanza has the proper knowledge of ''les accidents de la vie'' demanded by the narrative.

This particular scene, however, does not portray the vicissitudes of life but the arbitrary control of the narrator/hero who explicitly states his intention to destroy all the passengers on the ship. The ''accidents de la vie'' must be understood in the literary context of the author's autonomy. What the reader actually witnesses is the destruction of fictional content as embodied in the ship and its passengers. After a slow and detailed account of the drownings and wreckage, the scene is finally literally consumed by sharks, leaving only the narrator and the triumphant survivor of the shipwreck feast, ''la femelle du requin,'' sinking to the bottom of the sea in a hideous embrace.

The shipwreck episode begins, in fact, with the narrator's fruitless search for a ''semblable,'' for ''quelqu'un qui eût les mêmes idées que moi,'' and here ends with the recognition of the shark as his very image. This shark may be Ducasse's ideal reader who devours the text and survives, who braves the poisonous cure, traverses the ''marécages désolés'' and emerges not only as part of the fiction but in the image of its maker.

No reader will ever achieve this ideal assimilation into the fiction of *Les Chants* or the image of its narrator, for Ducasse's discourse depends on the continuing process of confrontation, confusion and correction which is the reader's education and the life of the text. Ducasse introduces *Poésies I* with the following declaration: ''Je remplace la mélancolie par le courage, le doute par la certitude, le désespoir par l'espoir, la méchanceté par le bien, les plaintes par le devoir, le scepticisme par la foi, les sophismes par la froideur du calme et l'orgueil par la modestie.'' . . . In this arbitrary reversal of the pose he cultivated in *Les Chants,* Ducasse discredits the entire system of moral dualism within which his earlier work was misinterpreted. In its denunciation of the dark romanticism of *Les Chants, Poésies* continue the education of the reader, warning him that any conventional assumptions about the sincerity or consistency of a writer's work may be met with such hostile contradiction. Ironically, critical assessments which respond to *Poésies* as Ducasse's renunciation of his previous work, as a chronological development of his personal morality, merely corroborate the necessity of an infinite ducassian pedagogy.

If the reader could become the ideal *narrataire,* the impossible double of the narrator, the perpetual struggle within the discourse of *Les Chants* would be reduced to the sterility of a shallow mirror reflection. The terror and temptation of Ducasse's narrator to be his own reader, to merge completely with the "other" who stands outside the text, is a dilemma he shares with many radical poets. The total autonomy of the narrator who would become his own reader, however, threatens to produce a frightening isolation. As technician the narrator would play the master ventriloquist, framing and manipulating the audience's responses; but his powers can only be realized within the dialogue of the discourse, against the continued resistance of some "other" who is the reader.

The reader immobilized.

Despite repeated warnings to the reader not to trust the narrator's apparent intentions to educate his audience, to illuminate for them the mysteries of heaven and earth, *Les Chants* have been hailed by critics as a guide to the complexities of the reading process. If the reader looks to this narrative for direction, however, he must be prepared to adjust to a circuitous methodology, for Ducasse's only pedagogical aim is to provide the reader with a lesson in endless contradiction. Ducasse promises, for example, to set down in his poetic aphorisms the laws and the source of a new poetic science. . . . He punctuates those promises with tyrannical demands for his reader's blind faith in the laws and sources which must remain unspoken and unexamined.

The ultimate aim of the new poetry, Ducasse also insists in *Poésies,* must be a practical and not a mystical truth. Thus the reader's education in *Les Chants* and *Poésies* consists of direct experience in the assertive and manipulative powers of language. The reader learns to match the aggressiveness of Ducasse's philosophical pronouncements or extravagant fictions with an equivalent resistance. Ducasse's works overcome the contradiction of their content in the common battle of wills which is generated by Ducasse's hostile and assimilative brand of discourse.

In the pedagogy of the more conventional narratives of Rabelais and Sterne the reader is instructed in the proper approach to the text, but he is expected to apply these novelistic lessons to his extraliterary life. Ducasse's instruction leads us only from *Les Chants* to *Poésies,* and from *Poésies* to an infinite network of other texts, past and future, conventional and apocryphal. The fierce rhetoric of *Les Chants* threatens to imprison the reader permanently within his function in the literary discourse, leaving him no private space, cutting off his extraliterary afterlife. The infinite pedagogy of *Les Chants* and *Poésies* threatens the complete assimilation of the reader and his immobilization under the hypnotic spell of Ducasse's style. (pp. 219-24)

[In an] attempt to fix his audience in its function, Lautréamont assigns to the reader an obedient posture: silent, hands humbly folded over his breast and eyes lowered—an attitude which mimics the posture of reading. "O vous," he continues, "qui que vous soyez, quand vous serez à côté de moi, que les cordes de votre glotte ne laissent échapper aucune intonation [. . .] n'essayez nullement de me faire connaître votre âme à l'aide du langage." . . . As fierce as the narrator's impositions of silence and servility on the reader may be, such directives remain pure rhetorical bravado which the actual reader may still resist by terminating or interrupting his reading. Behind the artificial conventions of such direct addresses to the reader, however, Ducasse is operating a far more devious and powerful weapon which will assure the helpless immobility of his audience: the hypnotic power of his intimidating and convoluted style.

While earlier novels treated the problem of the reader's involvement in a fiction as a general numbing of his consciousness which endangers his ability to distinguish literature from reality, Ducasse is perhaps the first author to deal explicitly with the phenomenology of reading. The narrator of *Les Chants* describes the immobility and estrangement caused by the reading process in which the reader is taken by surprise, uncertain of where he is being led. Ducasse has made every effort to take advantage of the "remarquable stupéfaction" to which readers of fiction are particularly susceptible. The stupefaction that results from reading *Les Chants* is not the conventional magnetism of an ideal or adventurous fictional world which replaces the reader's banal reality, but rather the stupefaction of confusion. The real hypnotic and assimilative power of Ducasse's work lies in his use of language, for the audience's concentration is riveted to the text in an effort to follow the mere syntactic progress of a sentence.

Ducasse's syntax mirrors his narrative style: both are infinitely digressive. The stylistic arabesques of his digressions leave content further behind with each parenthetical elaboration. One of the first laws of the poetic science of manipulation which Ducasse practices is revealed in *Poésies I:* "Il faut que la critique attaque la forme, jamais le fond de vos idées, de vos phrases. Arrangez vous." . . . Ducasse has arranged his defense against conventional critics by obscuring the meaning of his own phrases through the reversals and contradictions within and between *Les Chants* and *Poésies.* The logical and metaphorical spirals of Ducasse's digressions and "corrections" continually disorient the reader who loses his way, as he has lost his independent identity, in the stylistic maze of the discourse.

The following digression, for example, prepares the return to Lautréamont's interrupted description of a hanging with this single sentence:

> Pour clore ce petit incident, qui s'est lui-même dépouillé de sa gangue par une légèreté aussi irrémédiablement déplorable que fatalement pleine d'intérêt (ce que chacun n'aura pas manqué de vérifier, à la condition qu'il ait ausculté ses souvenirs les plus récents), il est bon, si l'on possède des facultés en équilibre parfait, ou mieux, si la balance de l'idiotisme ne l'importe pas de beaucoup sur le plateau dans lequel reposent les nobles et magnifiques attributs de la raison, c'est-à-dire, afin d'être plus clair (car, jusqu'ici je n'ai été que concis, ce que même plusieurs n'admettront pas, à cause de mes longueurs, qui ne sont qu'imaginaires, puisqu'elles remplissent leur but, de traquer, avec le scalpel de l'analyse, les fugitives apparitions de la vérité, jusqu'en leurs derniers retranche-

ments), si l'intelligence prédomine suffisamment sur les défauts sous le poids desquels l'ont étouffée en partie l'habitude, la nature, et l'éducation, il est bon, répété-je pour la deuxième et la dernière fois, car, à force de répéter, on finirait, le plus souvent ce n'est pas faux, par ne plus s'entendre, de revenir la queue basse (si, même, il est vrai que j'aie une queue) au sujet dramatique cimenté dans cette strophe. . . .

(pp. 224-26)

In traditional rhetoric this single sentence merely constitutes an extended digression. In Ducasse's living rhetoric, however, we may discern his aggressive attempt to intimidate and manipulate the reader, who must follow the narrative's tortuous path if he is ever to find his way back to the fictional content.

This single digression resumes and demonstrates the process of Ducasse's education and assimilation of the reader. Insinuating his way through the digression to unearth what he calls the fugitive apparitions of truth, Lautréamont is also attempting to unearth the reader, to raise him, despite the weight of defects ingrained in him by habit, nature and education, to the higher level of the "nobles et magnifiques attributs de la raison," to the contemplation of those absolute and indiscussible laws of poetic science. For Ducasse the truth is only to be found in these digressive flights which realize the ideal poetry he describes in *Poésies*. Leaving behind the "accidents" and "phénomènes" of the fiction, the dialogue of *narrateur* and *narrataire* proceeds unencumbered by content, liberated from the limits of time, space and identity.

The laws of gravity, however, defeat the narrator's digression, bringing him back down to earth to the content "cimenté dans cette strophe." The reader—whom the narrator has threatened by turns to absorb, to destroy, to carry away with him into the thinner air of pure reason—returns with some relief to more solid ground. While Lautréamont seems to extend his control by dictating his own epitaph to be delivered by the humbled reader, "Il faut lui rendre justice. Il m'a beaucoup crétinisé," he is also acknowledging that the reader *will* outlive him.

Lautréamont's impossible program of destruction, his struggle against the "Grand Objet Extérieur," his attempts to violate convention, to confound content, and to absorb and annihilate his readers, leave behind material traces: the text of *Les Chants de Maldoror*. Instead of the culminating execution with which both reader and text have been threatened from the beginning of the narrative, the final gesture of *Les Chants* points to survival, to the perpetuation of the struggle between *narrateur* and *narrataire*.

The narrative ends where it began, with an invitation to the reader. The infinite pedagogy of Ducasse's prose will practice on the inexhaustible generations of students he summons to try their will and intellect against the hypnotic power of *Les Chants.* As he suggests in *Poésies,* the corrective activity of reading merely develops the latent content of a text, and so in the end as in the beginning the reader serves the discourse, realizing and revitalizing its exploration of the immediate experience of reading. (pp. 226-27)

Robin Lydenberg, "Surviving Lautréamont: The Reader in 'Les Chants de Maldoror'," in L'Esprit Créateur, Vol. XVII, No. 3, Fall, 1977, pp. 211-27.

PAUL KNIGHT (essay date 1978)

[*In this excerpt, Knight analyzes* Poésies. *He disputes the critical interpretation that this work represents a refutation of the views expressed in* Maldoror. *Instead, because of the polysemous nature of Lautréamont's thought, Knight describes* Poésies *as "a continual process of contradiction, negation, replacement and correction." For further criticism by Knight, see Additional Bibliography.*]

Whereas *Maldoror* has come to be accepted, or at least tolerated as a brilliant aberration, the *Poems* have met with resistance and rejection, frequently from professed admirers of *Maldoror.* What is to be made of what Camus [see excerpt dated 1951] called the 'laborious banalities' of the *Poems*? Is Ducasse, at the same time as discarding his nom de plume, repudiating *Maldoror*?

These questions suggest that we are presented with a choice between *Maldoror* and the *Poems,* between Lautréamont and Ducasse, that one or the other of these texts must be the statement of the author's 'real' intentions, his 'real' philosophy. But in fact the need for such a choice is illusory. The *Poems* do not repudiate *Maldoror,* they complement and correct the earlier text. They ensure that the process of radical interrogation which begins in *Maldoror* does not end when that book is closed. The danger is that, however strong the impression left by *Maldoror,* its memory will, like that of all other books and events, be effaced, relegated to a compartment of consciousness where it will crumble and decay, perhaps less rapidly than other books we have read but just as inevitably. The *Poems* prevent this, reminding us that *Maldoror* is more than a gesture of defiance, revolt, blasphemy—it is, essentially, a process of infiltration of literary forms, of undermining from within a text, of ironic self-awareness. The *Poems* take up this process in another form. *Maldoror* is itself subjected to that process, just as a whole set of literary assumptions and concepts are called in question in *Maldoror.* With the *Poems,* Lautréamont/Ducasse breaks out of the static and linear categories of beginning and end; this process, made explicit in the *Poems,* will only come to an end with the death of the author, or if he gives up writing altogether (though even then it can be taken up by others, it is not the prerogative of an individual writer alone): 'The phenomenon passes. I seek the laws.' *Maldoror* is, in every sense of the word, a phenomenon, a stage in the process. But this process aims far beyond the 'fabrication' of a single text: 'The science I am establishing is a science distinct from poetry. I am not writing the latter. I am trying to discover its source.'

By the author's own admission, the *Poems* are not poems. They are maxims, conclusions reached after a syllogistic process in which terms have been omitted, assertions which claim the status of self-evident truth: 'The maxim does not need to be proved. One point in an argument requires another. The maxim is a law which contains a number of arguments. The closer the argument comes to the maxim, the more perfect it becomes. Once it has become a maxim, it rejects the evidence of a transformation.' The adoption of the maxim form in vogue in the seventeenth and eighteenth centuries in France seems to underline the author's advocacy of classical values, his contempt for an age of uncertainty, experimentation, revolt. Ducasse diagnoses the disease of contemporary literature, exhaustively listing its symptoms:

Upheavals, anxieties, deprivation, death, exceptions in the physical and moral order, the spirit of negation, brutishness, hallucinations wilfully induced, torture, destruction, sudden reversals of fortune, tears, insatiability, servitude, wildly burrowing imaginations, novels, the unexpected, the forbidden, the mysterious, vulture-like chemical peculiarities which watch over the carrion of some dead illusion, precocious and abortive experiments, bug-like obscurities, the terrible monomania of pride, the inoculation of profound stupors, funeral orations, jealousies, betrayals, tyrannies, impieties, irritations, acrimonies, aggressive outbursts, dementia, spleen, reasoned terrors, strange anxieties which the reader would prefer to be spared, grimaces, neuroses, the bloody screw-plates by which logic is forced to retreat, exaggerations, lack of sincerity, catch-words, platitudes, the sombre, the lugubrious, creations worse than murders, passions, the clan of assize-court novelists, tragedies, odes, melodramas, extremes perpetually present, reason howled down with impunity, odours of milk-sops, mawkishness, frogs, octopi, sharks, the simoun of the deserts, all that is somnambulous, shady, nocturnal, somniferous, noctambulous, viscous . . . it is time to react against these repulsive charnel houses which I blush to name, to react against everything which is supremely shocking and oppressive.

It will immediately strike every reader that all the vices so vehemently condemned here are to be found in plenty in *Maldoror.* It is passages such as this which have led some readers of *Maldoror* to interpret the *Poems* either as a rejection of that text or as a proof of its author's 'insincerity.'

The more we read *Maldoror* and the *Poems,* the more inappropriate and incommensurate this accusation of insincerity seems—it is difficult to see how the criterion of sincerity can usefully be applied to Lautréamont's work and in particular to the *Poems,* which is a continual process of contradiction, negation, replacement and correction. If, however, we insist on applying this criterion, Ducasse tells us that: 'I allow no one, not even Elohim, to doubt my sincerity.'

This process of correction takes three main forms in the *Poems:* the revision of *Maldoror;* the rewriting of passages from Descartes, Pascal, La Rochefoucauld, Vauvenargues and others; and then there is internal contradiction: what is asserted at one point is denied at another, and vice-versa; mutually contradictory propositions are presented with the same dogmatic self-assurance (so that the maxim, would-be vehicle of irrefutable truths, is also called in question, its claims to self-evidence revealed as spurious).

The murderous hostility to mankind which runs through *Maldoror* gives way, in the *Poems,* to what appears a more positive judgement. In *Maldoror,* Lautréamont had written: 'I have seen men surpassing the hardness of rock, the rigidity of cast steel, the insolence of youth, the senseless rage of criminals, the falseness of the hypocrite . . . I have seen them wearing out moralists who have attempted to discover their heart, . . . bringing upon themselves implacable anger from on high . . . prostituting women and children, thus dishonouring the parts of the body consecrated to modesty; . . . show me a man who is good . . . But at the same time increase my strength tenfold; for at the sight of such a monster, I may die of astonishment: men have died of less.' The revised version in the *Poems* reads: 'I have seen men wearing out the moralists who attempted to discover their heart, and bringing upon themselves blessings from above. They showed respect to childhood and to age, to

all that breathes . . . , they paid homage to woman and consecrated to modesty the parts of the body which we refrain from naming. The firmament, whose beauty I acknowledge, the earth, image of my heart, were invoked by me, in order to represent myself as a man who did not believe himself good. The sight of this monster, had it ever proved to be real, would not have killed me with shock: it takes more than that to kill a man. All this needs no comment.' It is naïve to see in this second passage a 'development' from a pessimistic to an optimistic view of human nature. Ducasse explicitly warns against such an interpretation: 'If these sophisms were corrected by their corresponding truths, only the corrections would be true; while the work which had been thus revised would no longer have the right to be called false. The rest would be outside the realm of the true, tainted with falsehood, and would thus necessarily be considered null and void.' Here we are beyond the critique of literary forms and structures. The limitations of a mode of thinking which reduces the complexity of things to sterile antitheses are exposed. Those who are imprisoned in this thought-structure—who are not, at least momentarily, liberated from it by the reading of *Maldoror* and the *Poems*—will misinterpret both these texts, seeing in them the same kind of antitheses as between good and evil, true and false: 'Good is the victory over evil, the negation of evil. If one writes of the good, evil is eliminated by this fitting act. I do not write of what must not be done. I write of what must be done. The former does not include the latter. The latter includes the former.' For Ducasse, what must be done includes what must not be done. Good includes or contains evil: the two are not seen as diametrically opposite. A pseudo-logic is at work here, using pseudo-syllogisms; the conclusions reached in this process do not follow from the propositions on which they are allegedly based. The most dogmatic and self-assured statements are the least tenable. It is as if Ducasse is intentionally building a house in which the foundations inevitably give way when the roof is put on: 'Several certainties have been contradicted. Several falsehoods remain uncontradicted. Contradiction is the sign of falsehood. Non-contradiction is the sign of certainty.'

The *Poems* frequently contradict assertions from *Maldoror.* Whereas in the latter the novel was acclaimed as the 'best,' the 'definitive formula,' in the *Poems* it is condemned because 'the moral conclusion is lacking.' An apparently clear case of outright contradiction—or is it? Is it the overdue contradiction of a falsehood which has been uncontradicted up to now, or was the original proposition from *Maldoror,* despite the irony behind it, one of the several certainties which have been contradicted?

Pascal had written: 'In writing down my thoughts, they sometimes escape me; but that reminds me of my weakness, which at every moment I forget; and this teaches me as much as the thoughts I have forgotten, for I tend only to know my own insignificance.' For Pascal, the experience of writing is humbling, a blow to intellectual pride, because he cannot grasp his thoughts. It is a confrontation with his own insignificance, another reason for abandoning himself to God's inscrutable will. The same experience has the opposite effect on Ducasse, who rewrites Pascal's text as follows: 'When I write down my thoughts they do not escape me. This action reminds me of my strength which at every moment I forget. I learn as I link my thoughts together. But I am only moving towards the realization of one thing: the contradiction between my mind and nothingness.' Nothing could illustrate more clearly the absolute contradiction between Ducasse's thinking and Pascal's. Ducasse justifies this form of revision, replacement, in these terms:

'Plagiarism is necessary. It is implied in the idea of progress. It clasps an author's sentence tight, uses his expressions, eliminates a false idea, replaces it with the right idea.' For Ducasse, the adoption of Pascal's style is an essential part of the refutation of his ideas. In the *Poems,* the process is not always one of simple refutation. An idea may also be taken as a starting-point and then extended, explored in several possible permutations (in accordance with Ducasse's dictum that 'to be well-wrought, a maxim does not need to be corrected. It needs to be developed'). Vauvenargues—earlier acknowledged as the source of a 'quotation'—had written: 'One cannot judge life by a falser rule than death.' Ducasse writes: 'One can only judge the beauty of life by the beauty of death.' 'As long as my friends are alive, I will not speak of death.' 'One can only judge the beauty of death by the beauty of life.' Vauvenargues' maxim is neither affirmed nor rejected, but, typically, developed in several directions and at the same time deprived of its aura of certainty, finality. In the *Poems* there is nothing final, nothing exempt from correction, development, replacement. It is futile to try to pin Lautréamont/Ducasse down to a standpoint, a 'philosophy,' however complex, because there is no standing still; the process goes on, and in it every statement is 'valid' only in its place, is sure to be developed, revised, effaced later: 'I do not need to bother about what I will do later. What I am doing now I had to do. I do not need to discover the things I will discover later. In the new science, everything comes in its place—that is its excellence.'

The *Poems* were Ducasse's last work (he died a few months after they were published). But because his work is essentially a process, and because this process is not, and cannot be, the possession of any individual, it goes on: 'Poetry must be made by all. Not by one.' . . . So many-sided is the work that there are many possibilities suggested by the work which have still to be exploited. *Maldoror* and the *Poems* have lost none of their impetus, their disquieting novelty. They remain a 'permanent publication.' (pp. 246-52)

> *Paul Knight, "Introduction to 'Poems',"* in Maldoror and Poems *by Comte de Lautréamont, translated by Paul Knight, Penguin Books, 1978, pp. 246-52.*

KATHY J. PHILLIPS   (essay date 1980)

[*Phillips discusses the final canto of* Maldoror, *which contains the story of Mervyn and which Lautréamont himself considered the most important part of the work. She analyzes several antithetical relationships, describing how the concept of "loosing and capturing, scattering and gathering" recurs in the work's imagery, theme, and structure.*]

The climactic scene of Maldoror swinging Mervyn around his head in Canto VI draws together motifs from the rest of the work and serves as a model for the operation of the book, demonstrating how it incorporates—and copes with—violence. Maldoror and Mervyn together form a visual image that suggests, in a remarkably condensed way, Lautréamont's two basic approaches to writing, the narrative and the poetic, at the same time that it sums up his two basic attitudes toward people, love and hate. Both poetry and narration become strategies of desire. Because this last scene illuminates both theme and structure, the sixth canto (despite its parody of narrative techniques: the gothic novel, epic epithets and battles) justifies Lautréamont's tongue-in-cheek claim that it is the most important part of the work, to which everything else is "frontispice . . . l'explication préalable de ma poétique future. . . ."

Maldoror climbs to the top of the Vendôme column, tosses a cable for Aghone to attach to Mervyn, then runs around the balustrade to lift Mervyn from the ground like a kite, until Mervyn is circling in the same plane as Maldoror's outstretched arm. At the high point of tension, Maldoror lets go of the rope. In a surreal apotheosis, Mervyn's body flies to the Panthéon dome, where his skeleton, ludicrously clutching straw flowers called "immortelles," remains glued, on display.

The bizarre and gory scene, described with incongruous mathematical precision and detachment, suggests first Lautréamont's general view of the reader-writer-work relation. Exercising complete control over his characters, the author projects the ordered pattern of a literary work. The book is related to him (as the two bodies), but it is not self-expression (Lautréamont emphasizes this point in *Poésies*). Like the ellipse that Mervyn's body describes, the book follows laws of its own throughout its elaboration, until at the last moment it stops changing, adopting the final "immortal" shape (already dead) which anyone may approach and see.

The ellipse described by Mervyn repeats an image that has been important throughout the book. The slingshot, and an implicit counterpart, the lasso, use the same overhead swinging motion, but for opposite effects, either to loose or to capture. The dual image also expresses Maldoror's two most basic, and paradoxical, impulses, striking and embracing. But these two actions designed to put him in contact with another person are still "mediated" in the image. Lassoing is an embrace at a distance; slingshooting is a hit at a distance.

For Lautréamont, literature itself is the mediator. Writing is a tactic to strike or seduce; but no one gets hurt. No one is really affected. The narrator invites the reader to embrace him, but the page is, after all, an encumbrance. . . . However, Lautréamont imagines the miraculous reaction at a distance finally taking place, literally at the other end of the narrative thread. Since the image of loosing and capturing, scattering and gathering, has structural as well as thematic implications, we will be suggesting how Lautréamont expects literature to be such a tactic.

Thematically, the scene is clear only in the context of a whole series of similar scenes. Maldoror lures Mervyn to a rendezvous, then thrusts him into a sack, which he swings around in preparation for the Vendôme column scene. . . . Maldoror relates how he swung Falmer against a tree, perhaps so that Falmer's hair would tear loose in his hand. . . . Aghone's carpenter-father swings a jointing-plane to hold off the family as he crushes the children's pet canary in its cage. . . . (pp. 58-9)

The paradigms, including a central tree or column, the tearing or losing of hair, and slinging something away, have many implications: phallic control, fear of castration, protection against attackers. Maldoror letting go of the rope tied to Mervyn seems to represent a sexual release for him, showing how Maldoror can be both pushing others away or attacking them outright at the same time that he is imagining an embrace. The rope suggests, then, not only a slingshot to kill, but also the "garland of living camellias," or of seraphic lovers linked in an "ellipse."

> Amour affamé . . . créant, à la longue, une pyramide de séraphins . . . les entrelacera dans une ellipse qu'il fera tourbillonner autour de lui . . . le voyageur . . . verra . . . un être humain, emporté vers la cave de l'enfer par une guirlande de camélias vivants! . . .

A facsimile of Lautréamont's letter to Monsieur Verboeckhoven dated October 23, 1869.

Lautréamont constantly hides the impulse to embrace—literally, always in ellipsis—in a frustrated figure of annihilation,
and elaborates the carefully controlled ''pyramid'' of an art
work to commemorate the loss. (p. 60)

Writing paradigmatically, with the narration coiling back over
characters and events, is a way of expressing one half of Maldoror's motivation, the desire for unity. Disparate elements
are brought together in the common mold of the paradigm, as
Maldoror would like to see all the lovers united in the band of
living camellias. Lautréamont packs into the image of the
''fronde'' both a reminder of the literary technique of circling
back, and the memory of ribbons to tress his own private
community.

Though the sixth canto shows the narrator tightening the poetic
structure, gathering together and reducing motifs—columns,
swinging—to a common denominator, the canto also multiplies
versions and ravels out the account. While paradigmatic writing
corresponds to the ''gathering'' aspect of the image of the
ellipse, a number of different methods of narrative motion
constitute the ''scattering'' aspect. By spinning out stories,
distancing himself from the action, creating new speakers in
a box effect, and even delaying narration with tangential stories
and irrelevant asides, the author creates a counterpart to the
unity and stasis of paradigmatic writing.

Two examples of multiple speakers will show how a ''scattering'' technique is still related to creating a community. In
the story of God in the bordello . . . , the narrator makes a
refrain of the information that he has pressed himself closer to
the grating to see and hear. He overhears the speech by the
hair, lamenting its position as unwilling overseer to God's
crimes. Maldoror then overhears God's account to the hair of
how He in turn overheard Satan. A boxed series of narrators
emerges: Maldoror, hair, God and Satan. As he leaves, Maldoror replaces a sign (which he has ignored) warning the traveller that he may not return, with a new sign swearing silence.
Since Maldoror has just recounted the whole incident to the
reader, he obviously ignores this sign too. All this talk of
eavesdroppers reminds us that we are unseen witnesses at the
last remove from the action. A ''listen, then speak'' pattern
which is emerging might suggest that, more than violent action,
the book teaches articulation, and particularly the voicing of
indignation: after all, Maldoror only gains his voice at all after
witnessing God's crimes. . . . (pp. 61-2)

Another example of how the narrator multiplies speakers occurs
in the scene of the chastising spider. Putting his own first person
account in quotation marks, Maldoror admits that he gave the
spider permission to set out. The same account of the spider
setting out then starts over again, outside quotation marks,
with the confident assurance, ''Nous ne sommes plus dans la
narration . . . nous sommes maintenant arrivés dans le réel.'' . . .
Of course, that the lines recur reminds us all the more that this
is precisely narration. Giving birth to two ''adolescents,'' the
spider describes Maldoror's misdeeds against Réginald and
Elsseneur. One adolescent is Réginald, while the ''mother''
spider appears to be Elsseneur—although we may at first have
identified him with the other adolescent; the possible narrators
are thus further confused and multiplied. The two youths, having repeated Maldoror's characteristic hostile reaction to rejection, by going to war, now break out of the pattern after
hearing their own story and vow friendship. The multiplication
of speakers is counterbalanced by the youths' incarnation for
a time in the single spider with a single voice. The basic relation
of the two technical impulses is affirmed: the reduction to a
single paradigm, and the syntagmatic proliferation of detail.
The two techniques in conjunction actually make up Réginald
and Elsseneur and Maldoror's ''cure.''

Thus the ''little novel of thirty pages'' coalesces paradigms as
Lautréamont expects to gather in people; it spins out narrators
and stories and even interruptions, as Lautréamont pushes away
others. The two human impulses, love and hate, and the two
techniques, poetic (paradigmatic) and narrative, are richly condensed in the last image-event, the lasso-slingslot, which is
the culmination of the book at the same time that it sends the
reader back to the work as a whole, a literal strategy of embracing and rejecting. (p. 62)

*Kathy J. Phillips, ''The Hit at a Distance: Lautréa-
mont's Sixth Canto,'' in* Romance Notes, *Vol. XXI,
No. 1, Fall, 1980, pp. 58-62.*

ADDITIONAL BIBLIOGRAPHY

Abel, Lionel. ''A Dialogue: A, B, C on Lautréamont.'' *View* Series
IV, No. 4 (December 1944): 117, 151-54.
    A tribute to Lautréamont written in the form of two fictional
conversations.

Balakian, Anna. "A Spiritual Crisis." In her *Literary Origins of Surrealism: A New Mysticism in French Poetry*, pp. 62-97. New York: New York University Press, 1966.*
    Contends that nineteenth-century scientific progress brought on a wide-spread spiritual crisis that had a destructive effect on Lautréamont's writings.

Edson, Laurie. "*Les chants de Maldoror* and the Dynamics of Reading." *Nineteenth-Century French Studies* 12, Nos. 1 & 2 (Fall-Winter 1983-84): 198-206.
    Interprets *Maldoror* as a commentary on the cognitive process.

L'Esprit créateur XVIII, No. 4 (Winter 1978): 1-65.
    Contains five essays (one in French) on Lautréamont.

Fowlie, Wallace. "Third Cycle." In his *The Clown's Grail: A Study of Love in Its Literary Expression*, pp. 58-79. London: Dennis Dobson, 1948.*
    Studies the representations of love in *Maldoror*. Fowlie postulates that there are three cycles of love—philosophical, divine, and human—that correspond to the three ages of civilization, and he assigns Lautréamont to the final group.

———. *Lautréamont*. Twayne's World Authors Series, no. 284. New York: Twayne Publishers, 1973, 135 p.
    A biographical and critical introduction to Lautréamont. In addition to describing the author's life and works, Fowlie briefly outlines critical reaction to Lautréamont and his relationship to the decadent movement of the late nineteenth century.

Gasché, Rodolphe. "Onslaught on Filiation: Lautréamont and the Greeks." *Genre* XI, No. 4 (Winter 1978): 479-504.
    A deconstructionist examination of Lautréamont's rendering of the classical Greek myths in *Maldoror*.

Grubbs, Henry A., Jr. "The Problem of Lautréamont." *The Romanic Review* XXV, No. 2 (April-June 1934): 140-50.
    A description of *Maldoror* with a review of its early critical reception.

———. "The Division into Strophes of the *Chants de Maldoror*." *Modern Language Notes* LXVIII, No. 3 (March 1953): 154-57.
    Disparages the editorial work in most early editions of *Maldoror*.

Knight, Paul. "Introduction to *Maldoror*." In *"Maldoror" and "Poems,"* by Comte de Lautréamont, translated by Paul Knight, pp. 7-26. Harmondsworth, Middlesex, England: Penguin Books, 1978.
    Focuses on the relationship between the author, the reader, and the text to examine how Lautréamont comments in *Maldoror* on the act of writing fiction.

Lykiard, Alexis. "Preface without Memoirs." In *"Poésies" and Complete Miscellanea*, by Isidore Ducasse, edited and translated by Alexis Lykiard, pp. 7-22. London: Allison & Busby, 1978.
    An introduction to Lautréamont's *Poésies* that examines the significance of names, the importance of his letters, his critical reception, and the meaning of the work.

Moffett, Oren E. "Lautréamont in Uruguay." *The French Review* XLVIII, No. 4 (March 1975): 703-10.
    An inquiry into the author's early life in Uruguay.

Nadeau, Maurice. "The 'Stimulators' of Surrealism." In his *The History of Surrealism*, translated by Richard Howard, pp. 69-76. New York: Macmillan Co., 1965.*

From a major history of surrealism, first published in 1945, that discusses Lautréamont's importance to the movement.

Nesselroth, Peter W. *Lautréamont's Imagery: A Stylistic Approach.* Geneva: Librairie Droz, 1969, 130 p.
    A detailed study of Lautréamont's use of imagery in *Maldoror*.

———. "Lautréamont's Plagiarisms; or, The Poetization of Prose Texts." In *Pre-Text, Text, Context: Essays on Nineteenth-Century French Literature,* edited by Robert L. Mitchell, pp. 185-95. Columbus: Ohio State University Press, 1980.
    Examines Lautréamont's "borrowed descriptions," particularly his reliance on *L'encyclopédie d'histoire naturelle du Dr Chenu*. Nesselroth argues that Lautréamont created an original work by transforming such documents.

O'Brien, Justin. "A Rapprochement: M. André Gide and Lautréamont." *The Romanic Review* XXVIII, No. 1 (February 1937): 54-8.*
    Documents Lautréamont's influence on André Gide.

Porter, Laurence M. "Submission to the Father: From Chaos to Geometry in the *Chants de Maldoror*." In his *The Literary Dream in French Romanticism: A Psychoanalytic Interpretation*, pp. 100-22. Detroit: Wayne State University Press, 1979.
    Interprets Maldoror's relationship to God as a symbol for the father-son relationship.

Praz, Mario. "The Shadow of the 'Divine Marquis'." In his *The Romantic Agony,* translated by Angus Davidson, pp. 93-186. New York: Meridian Books, 1956.*
    A brief discussion of Lautréamont's work in which Praz links him to the traditions of sadism, victimization, the macabre, and the grotesque in eighteenth- and nineteenth-century French and English literature, specifically in tales of terror.

Riffaterre, Michael. "Generating Lautréamont's Text." In *Textual Strategies: Perspectives in Post-Structuralist Criticism,* edited by Josué V. Harari, pp. 404-20. Ithaca: Cornell University Press, 1979.
    A semantic study of poetic language in *Maldoror*.

Sussmann, Henry. "The Anterior Tail: The Code of *Les chants de Maldoror*." *MLN* 89, No. 6 (December 1974): 957-77.
    Discusses *Maldoror* as a violent assault on ordered literary texts that presages the direction of the development of modern literature.

Woodard, Kay B. "Celui qui lit: Reader in the Text/Reader of the Text in *Les chants de Maldoror*." *French Forum* 3, No. 2 (May 1978): 159-68.
    Explores the role of the reader in *Maldoror*.

Ziegler, Robert E. "The Environment of Aggression in *Les Chants de Maldoror*." *Rocky Mountain Review of Language and Literature* 37, No. 4 (1983): 173-80.
    Examines Lautréamont's use of the imagery of aggression in *Maldoror*.

Zimmerman, Marc. "Sade *et* Lautréamont (*sans* Blanchot): Starting Points for Surrealist Practice and Praxis in the Dialectics of Cruelty and *Humour Noir*." *Boundary 2*, Vol. V, No. 2 (Winter 1977): 507-28.*
    Discusses the relationship between the writings of Lautréamont and the Marquis de Sade, focusing on their evocation of cruelty.

Herman Melville

1819-1891

American novelist, short story writer, and poet.

The following entry presents criticism of Melville's novel *Moby-Dick; or, The Whale* (1851). For a complete discussion of Melville's career, see *NCLC*, Vol. 3.

Moby-Dick is considered one of America's greatest novels and a classic of world literature. Critics generally agree that in this work, Melville parlayed the story of a sea captain's vengeful search for a legendary whale into a narrative suffused with profound speculation concerning the nature and interrelationship of the individual, society, God, and the cosmos. The novel is also highly acclaimed as a distinctively American book. By resolutely and artfully grounding his speculations in American thought, language, and experience, Melville elevated *Moby-Dick* to the status of a national epic.

Moby-Dick is replete with details concerning whales and whaling. Although Melville gleaned some of this information from such books as William Scoresby's *An Account of the Arctic Regions* and Thomas Beale's *The Natural History of the Sperm Whale,* much of his knowledge came from his own experiences as a mariner. Having briefly served on a merchant ship in 1839, Melville joined the crew of the whaling ship *Acushnet* in 1841. The ensuing voyage had a great impact on Melville's thought and works. In addition to providing the firsthand knowledge of whaling that figures so prominently in *Moby-Dick,* the trip brought him into intimate contact with South Sea island communities whose primal existence caused Melville to begin questioning the social and theological underpinnings of his Calvinist heritage. This questioning came to the fore in the philosophical allegory of his third novel, *Mardi: A Voyage Thither,* and later emerged as a major thematic concern in *Moby-Dick.*

Melville wrote his masterpiece in 1850-51 under trying financial and artistic conditions. Family obligations left him strapped for money and writing time, and he had recently felt compelled by the poor reception granted *Mardi* to compromise his artistic instincts and produce such popular works as *Redburn: His First Voyage* and *White Jacket; or, The World in a Man-of-War.* "What I feel most moved to write," he told Nathaniel Hawthorne, "that is banned,—it will not pay. Yet, altogether, write the *other* way I cannot. So the product is a final hash, and all my books are botches." Hawthorne's friendship itself, however, went some way toward assuaging Melville's despair. The writers became neighbors when Melville moved to Pittsfield, Massachusetts, in 1850, and they visited and corresponded with each other while Melville was composing *Moby-Dick.* Hawthorne's influence on the novel is the subject of ongoing debate: Lincoln Colcord has detected Hawthorne's "transcendental" influence in *Moby-Dick,* while other critics have contrasted the writers' views. Nonetheless, Melville's dedication of *Moby-Dick* to Hawthorne attests to the fact that Melville greatly admired Hawthorne's genius and felt artistically rejuvenated by their friendship.

Melville released *Moby-Dick* for publication in late 1851. One chapter of the book, "The Town-Ho's Story," appeared in the October 1, 1851, issue of *Harper's New Monthly Magazine.* Richard Bentley subsequently issued the novel under the title

The Whale in London on October 18, 1851, followed by Harper and Brothers' publication of *Moby-Dick; or, The Whale* in New York on November 13, 1851. Bentley's English edition was an expurgated version of Melville's manuscript and did not include the epilogue.

Some critics speculate that in creating *Moby-Dick,* Melville drew on well-known stories concerning a ferocious white whale named Mocha Dick and the sinking of the Nantucket whaling ship *Essex.* In the novel, the narrator, Ishmael, recounts his ill-fated voyage as a hand on board the whaling ship *Pequod.* Outfitted with an eclectic crew including South Sea islanders, North American Indians, blacks, and New England salts, the whaler leaves Nantucket on Christmas Day, bound on a commercial hunt for whales. As the trip progresses, however, Ahab, the ship's captain, exerts his will over the crew and converts the voyage into a quest to destroy his personal nemesis, a celebrated white whale known as Moby Dick. Ahab had lost a leg to the whale in a previous encounter, and his search is further fueled by his monomaniacal conviction that Moby Dick visibly personifies all earthly malignity and evil. The story concludes with a turbulent three-day struggle between the White Whale and the *Pequod*'s crew. Lowering for Moby Dick on the third day, Ahab becomes entwined in a harpoon rope and is carried to his death by the whale, who then turns on the *Pequod* and sunders it with a fierce blow. Buoyed by a floating coffin and rescued by a passing ship, Ishmael is the sole survivor of the titanic struggle.

The relative simplicity of the novel's plot belies a density of meaning that has made *Moby-Dick* one of the most intensely scrutinized works in American literature. The novel's depth was largely unrecognized by Melville's nineteenth-century reviewers, who were uneasy with the work's unusual mixture of adventure, philosophical speculation, and cetology. Interest in the book languished, as did Melville's literary reputation, as he continued to produce works that generally mystified his contemporaries. *Moby-Dick* remained a well-kept secret, prized by a small coterie of American and British admirers, until 1921, when Raymond M. Weaver galvanized Melville studies with his biography *Herman Melville: Mariner and Mystic*. Commentators soon recognized *Moby-Dick* as the flower of Melville's genius and have since examined the novel from an astounding variety of perspectives. Overall, critical investigation has revealed *Moby-Dick* to be a work that suggests a multitude of symbolic meanings, many of which are concerned with fundamental psychological, societal, religious, and philosophical issues.

Many critics have looked to the novel as a revelation of Melville's psyche. In particular, they have focused on the relationship between Ahab and Moby Dick, treating it as a symbolic projection of Melville's oedipal sexual anxieties. Newton Arvin is one of several commentators who have interpreted the relationship as an expression of the fears and desires stemming from Melville's "excessive and . . . crippling" love for his mother. Thus, he joins numerous critics in viewing Moby Dick as a threatening parent figure who symbolically castrates Ahab by mutilating his leg. Another psychological reading is offered by Henry A. Murray, who depicts the conflict between Ahab and Moby Dick as a symbolic struggle between "an insurgent Id" and an "oppressive cultural Superego." Commentators also note the strong ties binding Ishmael and Queequeg, Ahab and Fedallah, and Ahab and Pip. The friendship between Ishmael and the tattooed cannibal, Queequeg, is considered particularly important; treated by Leslie A. Fiedler (see *NCLC,* Vol 3) and other critics as one of the most celebrated homosexual bonds in American literature, it also serves as a thematic foil to Ahab's self-imposed isolation from humankind.

Ahab's isolation is considered to have profound societal implications as well. As Charles Olson observes, Ahab's aloofness contributes to a solipsism that ultimately destroys him and his "world." Many critics take this "world" to represent American society, interpreting *Moby-Dick* as a commentary on the American way of life. Richard Chase and Harry Slochower, for example, maintain that Melville probes the capitalist foundation of American society in the novel. According to Slochower, the doomed voyage of the *Pequod* constitutes an ambivalent version of the quest for commercial and physical expansion that characterized America's early development as a nation. Chase argues that Ahab and Moby Dick represent, respectively, "the American free enterpriser" and "the implicit spiritual meaning of free enterprise." In his opinion, Ahab assumes and is finally destroyed by the whale's malignity, thus underscoring the danger of the capitalist ideal. Alternatively, Olson and other critics have detected a strong democratic theme in *Moby-Dick*. The society of the *Pequod* is "what we imagine democracy to be," notes Olson, but he also suggests that the democratic ideal is vitiated by Ahab's autocratic influence over his crew. For this critic, the novel reveals the tragic insight that "the common man, however free, leans on a leader, [and] the leader, however dedicated, leans on a straw." Murray offers an additional perspective on the social themes in *Moby-Dick,* interpreting the aforementioned symbolic struggle between id and "oppressive cultural Superego" as an implicit critique of nineteenth-century American mores and the Puritan ethic of which they were a part.

Murray traces Melville's criticism of American mores to a deep-seated disaffection with Western religion in general and Calvinism in particular. In so doing, he aligns himself with a host of critics who discern a strong anti-religious tenor in *Moby-Dick*. One such critic is Lawrance Thompson, who argues that Melville expresses his personal liberation from the tyranny of God and Christian dogma in the novel with his blasphemous treatment of the whale, who symbolizes God. According to Marius Bewley, Thompson's reading is based on the apprehension that Melville considered God to be the origin of evil in the world. For his part, Bewley takes exception to this view, arguing that although Melville struggled to understand the source and nature of evil, he affirms the positive aspects of God and creation in *Moby-Dick*. In Bewley's opinion, the whale provides a vehicle for this affirmation, serving as a "symbol of a *good* God" and as a natural agent fostering Ishmael's reconciliation with creation. As exemplified by Thompson and Bewley, most critics note important connections between *Moby-Dick* and the Christian religious tradition. At the same time, a substantial number of critics have explicated Melville's use of Eastern religious concepts in the novel, while others have stressed his independence from specific religious creeds and philosophies. The latter position is taken by Tyrus Hillway, who emphatically states that "*Moby-Dick* declares allegorically . . . total independence of subservience to any established religious or philsophical explanation of man's role in the universal order. It stands, however dangerously, as a declaration of man's freedom to control his own spiritual destiny."

In the view of many critics, Melville concerns himself in *Moby-Dick* with nothing less than the nature of the universe and mankind's role in it. Just as Ahab is preoccupied with malignity and evil and seeks to break through the "pasteboard mask" that he believes obscures the true nature of reality, so have commentators focused on these same themes. Lewis Mumford characterizes the novel as a "parable on the mystery of evil and the accidental malice of the universe" (see *NCLC,* Vol. 3). In his opinion, the parable features Ahab as the "spirit of man" heroically pitting itself against the evil and cruel energies of the universe, represented by Moby Dick. William Ellery Sedgwick (see *NCLC,* Vol. 3) also depicts Ahab as the champion of humankind, elucidating his role as a courageous quester who repudiates "all traditional conclusions, all common assumptions, all codes and creeds and articles of faith" in attempting to break through the mystery of creation. Similarly, Alfred Kazin casts Ahab as a "hero of thought" who strives to reestablish humanity's preeminence in the natural order (see *NCLC,* Vol. 3). Kazin, however, maintains that Ahab fails to accomplish his mission, and Mumford (see *NCLC,* Vol. 3) and Sedgwick both note that he severs his vital link with humankind while pursuing his heroic aims. Such considerations as these have led some commentators to question Melville's endorsement of the Ahabian world view and to turn to Ishmael for an alternative perspective. Sedgwick thus emphasizes the spiritual equanimity that enables Ishmael to keep in view "the whole circle of life's possible issues" and to preserve his sense of community with humanity, while Howard C. Horsford focuses on the ways in which Ishmael functions as a foil to Ahab's symbolical ontology. In Horsford's estimation, Ishmael counters

Ahab's insistence on the symbolic nature of experience by promoting an awareness that the universe may simply be meaningless. In two different approaches, Bewley contrasts Ishmael's affirmation of nature with Ahab's hatred of it, while Robert Zoellner opines that if Ishmael can learn to love a leviathan, he can learn to love the cosmos of which he is a symbol. James William Nechas occupies the middle ground, arguing that Melville actually underscores the uncertainty of metaphysical speculation in *Moby-Dick* by establishing Ishmael in the role of an ontological hero who "refuses to accept as true and complete any single interpretation of Moby Dick, . . . [placing] such interpretive assurance outside of human knowledge."

In addition to the abundant thematic studies of *Moby-Dick,* a small but enlightening body of criticism has been written concerning the novel's technical and formal properties. On the simplest level, *Moby-Dick* purports to be a first-person account of Ishmael's adventures. Commentators have noted several irregularities in this regard, however: Melville gradually slips from the first person to the omniscient point of view in presenting the story, and the tale itself is interspersed with numerous expository passages on whales and whaling. These practices were censured by early critics, but are now generally considered consonant with the novel's overall methods and themes. Warner Berthoff, for example, has explained Ishmael's withdrawal from the tale as a natural outgrowth of his selfless immersion in his story, while the cetological and whaling digressions in the novel have been defended by numerous writers. Included among the latter are Olson and Arvin (see *NCLC,* Vol. 3), who observe that the passages help control the novel's tempo, and Mumford (see *NCLC,* Vol. 3), who suggests that as an "imaginative synthesis," "every aspect of reality" is germane to *Moby-Dick.* In addition, Van Wyck Brooks approaches the issue from the perspective of form, opining that the expository elements in *Moby-Dick* constitute the factual "ballast" required in literary epics (see *NCLC,* Vol. 3).

Brooks's allusion to the epic qualities of *Moby-Dick* broaches the issue of the book's formal properties. Although it is organized as a novel, poetry and drama figure prominently within the work's fictional framework. The poetic qualities of *Moby-Dick* have been noted by many critics, including Kazin (see *NCLC,* Vol. 3), who maintains that rather than issuing from the reportorial perspective common to fiction, the work issues from the personal perspective common to poetry. Kazin and such writers as Yvor Winters (see *NCLC,* Vol. 3) associate *Moby-Dick* with a specific type of poetry, describing the work as an epic poem written in prose. Such commentary is usually based on a corresponding recognition of the cosmic sweep and heroic themes of *Moby-Dick,* and it also frequently acknowledges the presence of epic rhythms and rhetoric in the novel. The dramatic aspects of *Moby-Dick* have undergone similar scrutiny. Melville began reading William Shakespeare's works shortly before composing the novel, recording his admiration for the "divine William," as he called him, in various writings during this period. Consequently, a number of critics have discussed Shakespeare's influence on the novel, with many commentators focusing on Melville's use of rhythmical soliloquies approximating blank verse. Olson extends this discussion to include Shakespeare's impact on *Moby-Dick*'s characters and structure, while F. O. Matthiessen emphasizes Melville's debt to the playwright in arriving at an idiom capable of expressing "the hidden life of men, which had become his compelling absorption" (see *NCLC,* Vol. 3).

The critical commentary on *Moby-Dick,* then, clearly establishes the universality of the novel's themes. At the same time,

critics regard it as distinctively American by virtue of its subject, language, and humor. Archibald MacMechan remarked on the Americanism of the book's subject and style in 1899, noting that just as whaling was "peculiarly an American industry," so was Melville's style indigenous to his country. According to MacMechan, the writer's mode in *Moby-Dick* is "large in idea, expansive; it has an Elizabethan force and freshness and swing, and is, perhaps, more rich in figures than any style but Emerson's. It has the picturesqueness of the new world, and, above all, a free-flowing humour, which is the distinct *cachet* of American literature." In the twentieth century, Olson lauded Melville for penetrating to the core of the American experience, which the critic defines as the drive to subdue nature, and Thornton Wilder used the novel to illustrate the emergence of the American language in United States literature. Richard Chase and other critics have added a significant dimension to the discussion by exploring Melville's incorporation of tall-tale exaggeration, oratorical bombast, Barnum-like showmanship, and other hallmarks of American culture, folklore, and mythology in *Moby-Dick.* In Chase's estimation, Melville combined these elements with an epic theme, namely, the disastrous implications of capitalism. In so doing, Chase maintains, Melville united a supporting American mythology with a theme of universal significance, thus creating "*the* American epic."

The epic and American properties of *Moby-Dick* continue to be discussed as part of the ongoing critical absorption with Melville's complex masterpiece. Whatever challenges these and other issues may present to critical consensus, however, commentators have consistently described *Moby-Dick* in superlatives. Despite the overriding lack of enthusiasm for the novel in the nineteenth century, in 1899 MacMechan echoed W. Clark Russell in hailing the novel as "the best sea story ever written," and in 1919 Frank Jewett Mather, Jr., characterized it as Melville's "greatest" and "most characteristic" work (see *NCLC,* Vol. 3). Latter-day critics have been even less unstinting in their praise, ranging from Mumford's recognition of the novel as both "the best tragic epic of modern times and one of the fine poetic works of all time," to Conrad Aikens's assertion that *Moby-Dick* is "the greatest book which has come out of New England, and one of the very greatest works of prose fiction ever written in any language" (see *NCLC,* Vol. 3). This is high praise indeed for a book that Melville felt would be forgotten. "What's the use elaborating what, in its very essence, is so short-lived as a modern book?" he wrote Hawthorne (see *NCLC,* Vol. 3). "Though I wrote the Gospels in this century, I should die in the gutter."

(See also *Dictionary of Literary Biography,* Vol. 3: *Antebellum Writers in New York and the South.*)

H[ERMAN] MELVILLE (letter date 1850)

[In the following excerpt, Melville briefly discusses the composition of Moby-Dick *with Richard Henry Dana, Jr.]*

About the "whaling voyage"—I am half way in the work, & am very glad that your suggestion so jumps with mine. It will be a strange sort of a book, tho', I fear; blubber is blubber you know; tho' you may get oil out of it, the poetry runs as hard as sap from a frozen maple tree;—& to cook the thing up, one must needs throw in a little fancy, which from the nature of the thing, must be ungainly as the gambols of the whales themselves. Yet I mean to give the truth of the thing, spite of this. (p. 108)

> H[erman] Melville, in a letter to Richard Henry Dana, Jr. on May 1, 1850, in his The Letters of Herman Melville, *edited by Merrell R. Davis and William H. Gilman, Yale University Press, 1960, pp. 106-08.*

H[ERMAN] MELVILLE (letter date 1851)

[*The following remarks are taken from a letter that Melville wrote to his friend and neighbor, the noted writer Hawthorne, while he was composing* Moby-Dick. *Melville's fatigue and frustration are evident as he recounts the conditions under which he is writing the book, but so is his admiration for Hawthorne. Melville addressed Hawthorne in a more euphoric vein (see excerpt dated November, 1851) upon receiving his appreciative letter concerning the novel.*]

[The] reason I have not been to Lenox is this,—in the evening I feel completely done up, as the phrase is, and incapable of the long jolting to get to your house and back. In a week or so, I go to New York, to bury myself in a third-story room, and work and slave on my *Whale* while it is driving through the press. *That* is the only way I can finish it now,—I am so pulled hither and thither by circumstances. The calm, the coolness, the silent grass-growing mood in which a man *ought* always to compose,—that, I fear, can seldom be mine. Dollars damn me; and the malicious Devil is forever grinning in upon me, holding the door ajar. My dear Sir, a presentiment is on me,—I shall at last be worn out and perish, like an old nutmeg-grater, grated to pieces by the constant attrition of the wood, that is, the nutmeg. What I feel most moved to write, that is banned,—it will not pay. Yet, altogether, write the *other* way I cannot. So the product is a final hash, and all my books are botches. I'm rather sore, perhaps, in this letter; but see my hand!—four blisters on this palm, made by hoes and hammers within the last few days. It is a rainy morning; so I am indoors, and all work suspended. I feel cheerfully disposed, and therefore I write a little bluely. . . . If ever, my dear Hawthorne, in the eternal times that are to come, you and I shall sit down in Paradise, in some little shady corner by ourselves; and if we shall by any means be able to smuggle a basket of champagne there (I won't believe in a Temperance Heaven), and if we shall then cross our celestial legs in the celestial grass that is forever tropical, and strike our glasses and our heads together, till both musically ring in concert,—then, O my dear fellow-mortal, how shall we pleasantly discourse of all the things manifold which now so distress us,—when all the earth shall be but a reminiscence, yea, its final dissolution an antiquity. (pp. 390-91)

> H[erman] Melville, in a letter to Nathaniel Hawthorne in June, 1851, in his Herman Melville: Representative Selections, *edited by Willard Thorp, American Book Company, 1938, pp. 389-93.*

JOHN BULL (essay date 1851)

[*The following excerpt is from a review of* Moby-Dick *that originally appeared in the October 25, 1851, issue of the English periodical* John Bull. *In the course of praising the book as an unlikely but successful blend of whaling and philosophy, the critic notes the anti-religious and American strains in the novel. Censuring Melville for irreverence, the reviewer goes on to laud him*

for investing his ordinarily "repulsive" subject matter "with an absorbing fascination."]

Of all the extraordinary books from the pen of Herman Melville [*The Whale*] is out and out the most extraordinary. Who would have looked for philosophy in whales, or for poetry in blubber. Yet few books which professedly deal in metaphysics, or claim the parentage of the muses, contain as much true philosophy and as much genuine poetry as the tale of the *Pequod's* whaling expedition. Hardly has the ship set sail from Nantucket than it is, with its strangely assorted crew on board, isolated from the rest of creation; wholly engulphed, as it were, in the world of whales, a world peculiar to itself, and, as the reader of these volumes will find, as brimful of matters of deepest interest as any other sublunary world. In that wonderful world the most extravagant specimens of the genus *homo*, the offspring of Herman Melville's wild and grotesque fancy, are pursuing their career of adventure and of danger with an energy not unlike that of the whale himself; their chieftain, Captain Ahab, being a perfect match in every way for his foe-whale Moby Dick.

To give anything like an outline of the narrative woven together from materials seemingly so uncouth, with a power of thought and force of diction suited to the huge dimensions of its subject, is wholly impossible. Those who seek acquaintance with "the whale" must needs embark on board the venturesome craft, and bear company to her commander with the ivory leg and the heart of steel. They must be prepared, however, to hear much on board that singularly-tenanted ship which grates upon civilized ears; some heathenish, and worse than heathenish talk is calculated to give even more serious offence. This feature of Herman Melville's new work we cannot but deeply regret. It is due to him to say that he has steered clear of much that was objectionable in some of his former tales; and it is all the greater pity, that he should have defaced his pages by occasional thrusts against revealed religion which add nothing to the interest of his story, and cannot but shock readers accustomed to a reverent treatment of whatever is associated with sacred subjects.

All that is idiomatically American in the tone of his sentiments, and in the slang which runs through his discourse, we are most willing to forgive him. These things belong to the individuality of the author and the book. The perfect Yankee, surrounded as he is, in reality no less than in Mr. Melville's fiction, with savage and demi-savage life, is a picture which, like everything that is true to nature, possesses a charm of its own, though it may not fall within the ordinary canons of beauty. The exhibition of it is both a novelty, and a study; and the artist is entitled to his meed of praise; even though his subject should in itself be of a somewhat repulsive character. And in the present case that praise is the more abundantly due, because the artist has succeeded in investing objects apparently the most unattractive with an absorbing fascination. The flashes of truth, too, which sparkle on the surface of the foaming sea of thought through which the author pulls his readers in the wake of the whale-ship,—the profound reflections uttered by the actors in the wild watery chase in their own quaint forms of thought and speech,—and the graphic representations of human nature in the startling disguises under which it appears on the deck of the *Pequod*,—all these things combine to raise *The Whale* far beyond the level of an ordinary work of fiction. It is not a mere tale of adventures, but a whole philosophy of life, that it unfolds. (pp. 9-10)

> *"Reviews of 'The Whale' and 'Moby-Dick', 1851-1852: London 'John Bull'," in "Moby-Dick"*

as Doubloon: Essays and Extracts (1851-1970), *edited by Hershel Parker and Harrison Hayford, W. W. Norton & Company, Inc., 1970, pp. 9-10.*

THE SPECTATOR   (essay date 1851)

[*This anonymous reviewer offers a predominantly negative assessment of* Moby-Dick, *criticizing the "marvellous" elements in the story as interruptions to the plot and noting inconsistencies and improbabilities in the narrative point of view.*]

This sea novel is a singular medley of naval observation, magazine article writing, satiric reflection upon the conventionalisms of civilized life, and rhapsody run mad. So far as the nautical parts are appropriate and unmixed, the portraiture is truthful and interesting. Some of the satire, especially in the early parts, is biting and reckless. The chapter-spinning is various in character; now powerful from the vigorous and fertile fancy of the author, now little more than empty though sounding phrases. The rhapsody belongs to wordmongering where ideas are the staple; where it takes the shape of narrative or dramatic fiction, it is phantasmal—an attempted description of what is impossible in nature and without probability in art; it repels the reader instead of attracting him. . . .

The "marvellous" injures the book by disjointing the narrative, as well as by its inherent want of interest, at least as managed by Mr. Melville. In the superstition of some whalers, . . . there is a *white* whale which possesses supernatural power. To capture or even to hurt it is beyond the art of man. . . . Ahab, the master of the Pequod—a mariner of long experience, stern resolve, and indomitable courage, the high hero of romance, in short, transferred to a whale-ship—has lost his leg in a contest with the white whale. Instead of daunting Ahab, the loss exasperates him; and by long brooding over it his reason becomes shaken. In this condition he undertakes the voyage; making the chase of his fishy antagonist the sole object of his thoughts, and, so far as he can without exciting overt insubordination among his officers, the object of his proceedings.

Such a groundwork is hardly natural enough for a regular-built novel, though it might form a tale, if properly managed. But Mr. Melville's mysteries provoke wonder at the author rather than terror at the creation; the soliloquies and dialogues of Ahab, in which the author attempts delineating the wild imaginings of monomania, and exhibiting some profoundly speculative views of things in general, induce weariness or skipping; while the whole scheme mars, as we have said, the nautical continuity of story—greatly assisted by various chapters of a bookmaking kind.

Perhaps the earliest chapters are the best, although they contain little adventure. Their topics are fresher to English readers than the whale-chase, and they have more direct satire. . . .

The strongest point of the book is its "characters." Ahab, indeed, is a melodramatic exaggeration, and Ishmael is little more than a mouthpiece; but the harpooners, the mates, and several of the seamen, are truthful portraitures of the sailor as modified by the whaling service. The persons ashore are equally good, though they are soon lost sight of. The two Quaker owners are the author's means for a hit at the religious hypocrisies. . . .

It is a canon with some critics that nothing should be introduced into a novel which it is physically impossible for the writer to have known: thus, he must not describe the conversation of miners in a pit if they *all* perish. Mr. Melville hardly steers clear of this rule, and he continually violates another, by beginning in the autobiographical form and changing ad libitum into the narrative. His catastrophe overrides all rule: not only is Ahab, with his boat's-crew, destroyed in his last desperate attack upon the white whale, but the Pequod herself sinks with all on board into the depths of the illimitable ocean. Such is the go-ahead method.

"Herman Melville's 'Whale'," in The Spectator, *Vol. 24, No. 1217, October 25, 1851, p. 1026.*

HERMAN [MELVILLE]   (letter date 1851)

[*Melville received an appreciative letter from Hawthorne concerning* Moby-Dick *that has since been lost. The following excerpt from Melville's response to that letter conveys his "sense of unspeakable security" and euphoria on having won the approbation and understanding of a respected peer. Melville's allusion to his own "paltry" criticism of Hawthorne's works refers to his 1850 essay, "Hawthorne and His Mosses."*]

Your letter was handed me last night on the road going to Mr. Morewood's, and I read it there. Had I been at home, I would have sat down at once and answered it. In me divine magnanimities are spontaneous and instantaneous—catch them while you can. The world goes round, and the other side comes up. So now I can't write what I felt. But I felt pantheistic then—your heart beat in my ribs and mine in yours, and both in God's. A sense of unspeakable security is in me this moment, on account of your having understood the book. I have written a wicked book, and feel spotless as the lamb. Ineffable socialities are in me. I would sit down and dine with you and all the gods in old Rome's Pantheon. It is a strange feeling—no hopefulness is in it, no despair. Content—that is it; and irresponsibility; but without licentious inclination. I speak now of my profoundest sense of being, not of an incidental feeling. (pp. 394-95)

You did not care a penny for the book. But, now and then as you read, you understood the pervading thought that impelled the book—and that you praised. Was it not so? You were archangel enough to despise the imperfect body, and embrace the soul. Once you hugged the ugly Socrates because you saw the flame in the mouth, and heard the rushing of the demon,—the familiar,—and recognized the sound; for you have heard it in your own solitudes.

My dear Hawthorne, the atmospheric skepticisms steal into me now, and make me doubtful of my sanity in writing you thus. But, believe me, I am not mad, most noble Festus! But truth is ever incoherent, and when the big hearts strike together, the concussion is a little stunning. Farewell. Don't write a word about the book. That would be robbing me of my miserly delight. I am heartily sorry I ever wrote anything about you—it was paltry. Lord, when shall we be done growing? As long as we have anything more to do, we have done nothing. So, now, let us add Moby Dick to our blessing, and step from that. Leviathan is not the biggest fish;—I have heard of Krakens. (p. 395)

Herman [Melville], in a letter to Nathaniel Hawthorne in November, 1851, in his Herman Melville: Representative Selections, *edited by Willard Thorp, American Book Company, 1938, pp. 394-96.*

[EVERT DUYCKINCK]   (essay date 1851)

[Duyckinck, a prominent nineteenth-century American editor and the co-author of the Cyclopaedia of American Literature, *befriended Melville early in his career and visited him as he was writing* Moby-Dick. *In the review excerpted below, Duyckinck discerns three major components in the novel: whale lore; Ahab's conflict with Moby Dick, which the critic interprets as an allegorical struggle against the "moral evil of the world"; and the iconoclastic moralizing of the narrator, Ishmael. Duyckinck praises the cetological portions of the novel and describes the allegorical "romance" of Ahab and his crew as an overdrawn but "noble and praiseworthy conception." He is least pleased by Ishmael's criticism of conventional creeds and opinions, which he describes as "out of place and uncomfortable." Duyckinck concludes his review by noting that it would have been a "great glory" had Melville succeeded in controlling the "strong powers" that inform the work. Other critics who discuss the role of allegory in* Moby-Dick *include Colcord (1922) and Hillway (1979). Auden (1950), Murray (1951), Thompson (1952), and Hillway (1979) continue the discussion of Melville's treatment of religion in the novel.]*

[Mr. Melville's *Moby Dick*] is a natural-historical, philosophical, romantic account of the person, habits, manners, ideas of the great sperm whale; of his haunts and of his belongings; of his associations with the world of the deep, and of the not less remarkable individuals and combinations of individuals who hunt him on the oceans. Nothing like it has ever before been written of the whale; for no man who has at once seen so much of the actual conflict, and weighed so carefully all that has been recorded on the subject, with equal powers of perception and reflection, has attempted to write at all on it—the labors of [William] Scoresby covering a different and inferior branch of the history. To the popular mind this book of Herman Melville, touching the Leviathan of the deep, is as much of a discovery in Natural History as was the revelation of America by Christopher Columbus in geography. Let any one read this book with the attention which it deserves, and then converse with the best informed of his friends and acquaintances who have not seen it, and he will notice the extent and variety of treatment; while scientific men must admit the original observation and speculation. . . .

[The book] opens, after a dedication to Nathaniel Hawthorne, with a preliminary flourish in the style of Carlyle and the "Doctor" of etymology, followed by a hundred or so of extracts of "Old Burton," passages of a quaint and pithy character from Job and King Alfred to Miriam Coffin; in lieu of the old style of Scott, Cooper, and others, of distributing such flourishes about the heads of chapters. Here they are all in a lump, like the grace over the Franklin barrel of pork, and may be taken as a kind of bitters, a whet and fillip to the imagination, exciting it to the curious, ludicrous, sublime traits and contemplations which are to follow.

It is some time after opening with Chapter I. before we get fairly afloat, but the time is very satisfactorily occupied with some very strange, romantic, and, withal, highly humorous adventures at New Bedford and Nantucket. A scene at the Spouter Inn, of the former town, a night in bed with a Pacific Islander, and a mid-ocean adventure subsequently with a Frenchman over some dead whales in the Pacific, treat the reader to a laugh worthy of Smollet. (p. 381)

• • • • •

A difficulty in the estimate of this, in common with one or two other of Mr. Melville's books, occurs from the double character under which they present themselves. In one light they are romantic fictions, in another statements of absolute fact. When to this is added that the romance is made a vehicle of opinion and satire through a more or less opaque allegorical veil, as particularly in the latter half of *Mardi,* and to some extent in this present volume, the critical difficulty is considerably thickened. It becomes quite impossible to submit such books to a distinct classification as fact, fiction, or essay. Something of a parallel may be found in Jean Paul's German tales, with an admixture of Southey's Doctor. Under these combined influences of personal observation, actual fidelity to local truthfulness in description, a taste for reading and sentiment, a fondness for fanciful analogies, near and remote, a rash daring in speculation, reckless at times of taste and propriety, again refined and eloquent, this volume of *Moby Dick* may be pronounced a most remarkable sea-dish—an intellectual chowder of romance, philosophy, natural history, fine writing, good feeling, bad sayings—but over which, in spite of all uncertainties, and in spite of the author himself, predominates his keen perceptive faculties, exhibited in vivid narration.

There are evidently two if not three books in *Moby Dick* rolled into one. Book No. I. we could describe as a thorough exhaustive account admirably given of the great Sperm Whale. The information is minute, brilliantly illustrated, as it should be—the whale himself so generously illuminating the midnight page on which his memoirs are written—has its level passages, its humorous touches, its quaint suggestion, its incident usually picturesque and occasionally sublime. All this is given in the most delightful manner in "The Whale." Book No. 2 is the romance of Captain Ahab, Queequeg, Tashtego, Pip & Co., who are more or less spiritual personages talking and acting differently from the general business run of the conversation on the decks of whalers. They are for the most part very serious people, and seem to be concerned a great deal about the problem of the universe. They are striking characters withal, of the romantic spiritual cast of the German drama; realities of some kinds at bottom, but veiled in all sorts of poetical incidents and expressions. As a bit of German melodrama, with Captain Ahab for the Faust of the quarter-deck, and Queequeg with the crew, for Walpurgis night revellers in the forecastle, it has its strong points, though here the limits as to space and treatment of the stage would improve it. Moby Dick in this view becomes a sort of fishy moralist, a leviathan metaphysician, a folio Ductor Dubitantium, in fact, in the fresh water illustration of Mrs. Malaprop, "an allegory on the banks of the Nile." After pursuing him in this melancholic company over a few hundred squares of latitude and longitude, we begin to have some faint idea of the association of whaling and lamentation, and why blubber is popularly synonymous with tears.

The intense Captain Ahab is too long drawn out; something more of *him* might, we think, be left to the reader's imagination. The value of this kind of writing can only be through the personal consciousness of the reader, what he brings to the book; and all this is sufficiently evoked by a dramatic trait or suggestion. If we had as much of Hamlet or Macbeth as Mr. Melville gives us of Ahab, we should be tired even of their sublime company. Yet Captain Ahab is a striking conception, firmly planted on the wild deck of the Pequod—a dark disturbed soul arraying itself with every ingenuity of material resources for a conflict at once natural and supernatural in his eye, with the most dangerous extant physical monster of the earth, embodying, in strongly drawn lines of mental association, the vaster moral evil of the world. The pursuit of the White Whale thus interweaves with the literal perils of the fishery—a problem of fate and destiny—to the tragic solution of which Ahab hurries on, amidst the wild stage scenery of the ocean. To this end the motley crew, the air, the sky, the sea, its inhabitants are idealized throughout. It is a noble and praiseworthy conception; and though our sympathies may not always accord with the train of thought, we would caution the reader against a light or hasty condemnation of this part of the work.

Book III., appropriating perhaps a fourth of the volume, is a vein of moralizing, half essay, half rhapsody, in which much refinement and subtlety, and no little poetical feeling, are mingled with quaint conceit and extravagant daring speculation. This is to be taken as in some sense dramatic; the narrator throughout among the personages of the Pequod being one Ishmael, whose wit may be allowed to be against everything on land, as his hand is against everything at sea. This piratical running down of creeds and opinions, the conceited indifferentism of Emerson, or the run-a-muck style of Carlyle is, we will not say dangerous in such cases, for there are various forces at work to meet more powerful onslaught, but it is out of place and uncomfortable. We do not like to see what, under any view, must be to the world the most sacred associations of life violated and defaced.

We call for fair play in this matter. Here is Ishmael, telling the story of this volume, going down on his knees with a cannibal to a piece of wood, in the second story fireplace of a New-Bedford tavern, in the spirit of amiable and transcendent charity, which may be all very well in its way; but why dislodge from heaven, with contumely, "long-pampered Gabriel, Michael and Raphael." Surely Ishmael, who is a scholar, might have spoken respectfully of the Archangel Gabriel, out of consideration, if not for the Bible (which might be asking too much of the school), at least for one John Milton, who wrote *Paradise Lost.*

Nor is it fair to inveigh against the terrors of priestcraft, which, skilful though it may be in making up its woes, at least seeks to provide a remedy for the evils of the world, and attribute the existence of conscience to "hereditary dyspepsias, nurtured by Ramadans"—and at the same time go about petrifying us with imaginary horrors, and all sorts of gloomy suggestions, all the world through. (pp. 403-04)

So much for the consistency of Ishmael—who, if it is the author's object to exhibit the painful contradictions of this self-dependent, self-torturing agency of a mind driven hither and thither as a flame in a whirlwind, is, in a degree, a successful embodiment of opinions, without securing from us, however, much admiration for the result.

With this we make an end of what we have been reluctantly compelled to object to this volume. With far greater pleasure, we acknowledge the acuteness of observation, the freshness of perception, with which the author brings home to us from the deep, "things unattempted yet in prose or rhyme," the weird influences of his ocean scenes, the salient imagination which connects them with the past and distant, the world of books and the life of experience—certain prevalent traits of manly sentiment. These are strong powers with which Mr. Melville wrestles in this book. It would be a great glory to subdue them to the highest uses of fiction. It is still a great honor, among the crowd of successful mediocrities which throng our publishers' counters, and know nothing of divine impulses, to be in the company of these nobler spirits on any terms. (p. 404)

[*Evert Duyckinck*], "Melville's 'Moby Dick; or, The Whale'," and "Melville's 'Moby Dick; or, The Whale', second notice," *in* The Literary World, *Vol.*

IX, Nos. 20 and 21, November 15 and November 22, 1851, pp. 381-83, 403-04.

THE LITERARY GAZETTE   (essay date 1851)

[*This anonymous critic disdains* Moby-Dick *as an aimless and eccentric production unworthy of Melville's talents, expressing particular dissatisfaction with the conclusion of the novel.*]

Thrice unlucky Herman Melville! Three goodly volumes has he written, with the main purpose of honouring the Cachalot, and disparaging the *Mysticete,* and his publisher has sent them into the world in brilliant covers of blue and white, with three Greenland whales stamped in gold on·their binding. How they spout! Three unmistakeable Mysticeti, sloping heads, and jaws fringed with long combs of baleen. Shade of extinguished spermaceti, how thy light has been put out by the bookbinders!

This is an odd book, professing to be a novel; wantonly eccentric; outrageously bombastic; in places charmingly and vividly descriptive. The author has read up laboriously to make a show of cetalogical learning. He has turned over the articles Whale, Porpoise, Cachalot, Spermaceti, Baleen, and their relatives, in every Encyclopaedia within his reach. . . . [He uses this research for] stuffing to fill out his skeleton story. Bad stuffing it makes, serving only to try the patience of his readers, and to tempt them to wish both him and his whales at the bottom of an unfathomable sea. . . .

What the author's original intention in spinning his preposterous yarn was, it is impossible to guess; evidently, when we compare the first and third volumes, it was never carried out. He seems to have despaired of exciting interest about a leviathan hero and a crazy whale-skipper, and when he found his manuscript sufficient for the filling up of three octavos, resolved to put a stop to whale, captain, crew, and savages by a *coup de main.* Accordingly, he sends them down to the depths of ocean all in a heap, using his milk-white spermaceti as the instrument of ruthless destruction. How the imaginary writer, who appears to have been drowned with the rest, communicated his notes [to the publisher] is not explained. The whole affair would make an admirable subject for an Easter entertainment at Astley's. (p. 841)

Mr. Herman Melville has earned a deservedly high reputation for his performances in descriptive fiction. He has gathered his own materials, and travelled along fresh and untrodden literary paths, exhibiting powers of no common order, and great originality. The more careful, therefore, should he be to maintain the fame he so rapidly acquired, and not waste his strength on such purposeless and unequal doings as these rambling volumes about spermaceti whales. (p. 842)

A review of "The Whale," *in* The Literary Gazette, *London, No. 1820, December 6, 1851, pp. 841-42.*

WILLIAM T. PORTER   (essay date 1851)

[*Porter reviews* Moby-Dick *in his capacity as the editor of the* Spirit of the Times, *America's first sporting journal. He commends the novel for its whale lore and for the originality and dramatic interest of its story. This essay was originally published in the December 6, 1851, issue of the* Spirit of the Times.]

Moby Dick, or the Whale, is all whale. Leviathan is here in full amplitude. Not one of your museum affairs, but the real, living whale, a bona-fide, warm-blooded creature, ransacking the waters from pole to pole. His enormous bulk, his terribly destructive energies, his habits, his food, are all before us. Nay, even his lighter moods are exhibited. We are permitted to see the whale as a lover, a husband, and the head of a family. So to speak, we are made guests at his fire-side; we set our mental legs beneath his mahogany, and become members of his interesting social circle. No book in the world brings together so much whale. We have his history, natural and social, living and dead. But Leviathan's natural history, though undoubtedly valuable to science, is but a part of the book. It is in the personal adventures of his captors, their toils, and, alas! not unfrequently their wounds and martyrdom, that our highest interest is excited. This mingling of human adventure with new, startling, and striking objects and pursuits, constitute one of the chief charms of Mr. Melville's books. His present work is a drama of intense interest. A whale, 'Moby Dick'—a dim, gigantic, unconquerable, but terribly destructive being, is one of the persons of the drama. We admit a disposition to be critical on this character. We had doubts as to his admissibility as an actor into dramatic action, and so it would seem had our author, but his chapter, 'The Affidavit,' disarms us; all improbability or incongruity disappears, and 'Moby Dick' becomes a living fact, simply doubtful at first, because he was so new an idea. . . . (pp. 279-80)

Moby Dick, or the Whale, is a 'many-sided' book. Mingled with much curious information respecting whales and whaling there is a fine vein of sermonizing, a good deal of keen satire, much humor, and that too of the finest order, and a story of peculiar interest. As a romance its characters are so new and unusual that we doubt not it will excite the ire of critics. It is not tame enough to pass this ordeal safely. Think of a monomaniac whaling captain, who, mutilated on a former voyage by a particular whale, well known for its peculiar bulk, shape, and color—seeks, at the risk of his life and the lives of his crew, to capture and slay this terror of the seas! It is on this idea that the romance hinges. The usual staple of novelists is entirely wanting. We have neither flinty-hearted fathers, designing villains, dark caverns, men in armor, nor anxious lovers. There is not in the book any individual, who, at a certain hour, '*might have been seen*' ascending hills or descending valleys, as is usual. The thing is entirely new, fresh, often startling, and highly dramatic, and with those even, who, oblivious of other fine matters, scattered with profusest hand, read for the sake of the story, must be exceedingly successful. . . .

[We] must conclude by strongly recommending *Moby Dick, or the Whale,* to all who can appreciate a work of exceeding power, beauty and genius. (p. 280)

> *William T. Porter, in an extract from* Melville: The Critical Heritage, *edited by Watson G. Branch, Routledge & Kegan Paul, 1974, pp. 278-80.*

SIR NATHANIEL (essay date 1853)

[*Sir Nathaniel describes* Moby-Dick *as an unevenly written work that is seriously marred by the author's "extravagant treatment of the subject." He underscores the dualistic extremes of Melville's "maniacal" prose style, posits the existence of two authorial personalities, and then briefly remarks on the characterization of Ahab, Queequeg, Starbuck, and Stubb. For additional commentary on Melville's prose style in* Moby-Dick, *see the excerpts by MacMechan (1899), Winters (1938), Wilder (1952), Nechas (1978), and Matthiessen (NCLC, Vol. 3).*]

[Mr. Melville's] three volumes entitled *The Whale* undoubtedly contain much vigorous description, much wild power, many striking details. But the effect is distressingly marred throughout by an extravagant treatment of the subject. The style is maniacal—mad as a March hare—mowing, gibbering, screaming, like an incurable Bedlamite, reckless of keeper or strait-waistcoat. Now it vaults on stilts, and performs *Bombastes Furioso* with contortions of figure, and straining strides, and swashbuckler fustian, far beyond *Pistol* in that Ancient's happiest mood. Now it is seized with spasms, acute and convulsive enough to excite bewilderment in all beholders. When he pleases, Mr. Melville can be so lucid, straightforward, hearty, and unaffected, and displays so unmistakable a shrewdness, and satirical sense of the ridiculous, that it is hard to suppose that *he* can have indited the rhodomontade to which we allude. Surely the man is a Doppelganger—a dual number incarnate (singular though he be, in and out of all conscience):—surely he is two single gentlemen rolled into one, but retaining their respective idiosyncrasies—the one sensible, sagacious, observant, graphic, and producing admirable matter—the other maundering, drivelling, subject to paroxysms, cramps, and total collapse, and penning exceeding many pages of unaccountable "bosh." So that in tackling every new chapter, one is disposed to question it beforehand, "Under which king, Bezonian?"—the sane or the insane; the constitutional and legitimate, or the absolute and usurping? Writing of Leviathan, he exclaims, "Unconsciously my chitography expands into placard capitals. Give me a condor's quill! Give me Vesuvius' crater for an inkstand! Friends, hold my arms!" Oh that his friends had obeyed that summons! They might have saved society from a huge dose of hyperbolical slang, maudlin sentimentalism, and tragi-comic bubble and squeak.

His Yankeeisms are plentiful as blackberries. "I am tormented," quoth he, "with an everlasting itch for things remote." Remote, too frequently, from good taste, good manners, and good sense. We need not pause at such expressions as "looking a sort of diabolically funny;"—"beefsteaks done rare;"—"a speechlessly quick chaotic bundling of a man into eternity;"—"bidding adieu to circumspect life, to exist only in a delirious throb." But why wax fast and furious in a thousand such paragraphs as these:—"In landlessness alone resides the highest truth, indefinite as the Almighty. . . . Take heart, take heart, O Bulkington! Bear thee grimly, demi-god! Up from the spray of thy ocean-perishing—straight up, leaps thy apotheosis!" . . . "If such a furious trope may stand, his [Capt. Ahab's] special lunacy stormed his general sanity, and carried it, and turned all its concentrated cannon upon its own mad mark . . . then it was, that his torn body and gashed soul bled into one another; and so interfusing made him mad." (pp. 307-08)

The story itself is a strange, wild, furibund thing—about Captain Ahab's vow of revenge against one Moby Dick. And who is Moby Dick? A fellow of a whale, who has made free with the captain's leg: so that the captain now stumps on ivory, and goes circumnavigating the globe in quest of the old offender, and raves by the hour in a lingo borrowed from Rabelais, Carlyle, Emerson, newspapers transcendental and transatlantic, and the magnificent proems of our Christmas pantomimes. Captain Ahab is introduced with prodigious efforts at preparation; and there is really no lack of rude power and character about his presentment—spoiled, however, by the Cambyses' vein in which he dissipates his vigour. His portrait is striking—looking "like a man cut away from the stake, when the fire has overrunningly wasted all the limbs without consuming them, or taking away one particle from their compacted aged ro-bustness''—a man with a brow gaunt and ribbed, like the black sand beach after some stormy tide has been gnawing it, without being able to drag the firm thing from its place. . . . The amiable cannibal Queequeg occasions some stirring and some humorous scenes, and is probably the most reasonable and cultivated creature of the ship's company. Starbuck and Stubb are both tiresome, in different ways. The book is rich with facts connected with the natural history of the whale, and the whole art and process of whaling; and with spirited descriptions of that process, which betray an intense straining at effect. The climax of the three days' chase after Moby Dick is highly wrought and sternly exciting—but the catastrophe, in its whirl of waters and fancies, resembles one of Turner's later nebulous transgressions in gamboge. . . .

O author of **Typee** and **Omoo,** we admire so cordially the proven capacity of your pen, that we entreat you to doff the ''non-natural sense'' of your late lucubrations—to put off your worser self—and to do your better, real self, that justice which its ''potentiality'' deserves. (p. 308)

> Sir Nathaniel, ''Herman Melville,'' in The New Monthly Magazine, n.s. Vol. XCVIII, No. CCCXCI, July, 1853, pp. 300-08.

THE CRITIC, NEW YORK   (essay date 1893)

[*This anonymous critic focuses on the ''Whitmanesque . . . intensity and realism'' of* Moby-Dick, *emphasizing the importance of Melville's vocabulary and sea experience in sustaining these effects.*]

The undreamt poesy lying in the lives of Nantucket whalers in the fifties has for once received epical treatment [in **Moby Dick**], and the result is a marvellous Odyssey of adventure in warm seas and in icy, in halcyon and in purgatorial latitudes, over such a range of sunlit or storm-smitten billows as could occur only in actual experience before the mast in search of real whales on the real deep. Hugo never travelled; and therefore his lovely poems of the sea or his ''Hans d'Islande'' are conceived from the shore—powerful but shadowy idealizations of things he had never really seen. His empty shells Melville fills full of the living breath, the roar, the music, the vibration of the living sea, Whitmanesque in its intensity and realism, the memories of one who had lived years in the troughs or on the mountain-crests of Homeric waves, and who therefore in his work simply transcribed ineffaceable impressions. . . . [Actual] knowledge is always welcome if not indispensable in depicting the mighty phenomena of great voyages, great emotions or great deeds. This Hugo did not possess, and his phantom romances are mere husks, mere *larvae* or *simulacra*, illumined by an unnatural interior light, like a jack o' lantern, as compared with the healthy, wholesome, rude but terrible realities of such books as **Moby-Dick**.

In this story Melville is as fantastically poetical as Coleridge in the ''Ancient Mariner,'' and yet, while we swim spellbound over the golden rhythms of Coleridge feeling at every stroke their beautiful improbability, everything in **Moby-Dick** might have happened. The woe-struck captain, his eerie monomania, the half-devils of the crew, the relentless pursuit of the ever-elusive vindictive white whale, the storms and calms that succeed each other like the ups and downs of a mighty hexameter, all the weird scenery of the pursuit in moonlight and in daylight, all are so wonderfully fresh in their treatment that they supersede all doubt and impress one as absolutely true to the life. Even

the recondite information about whales and sea-fisheries sprinkled plentifully over the pages does not interfere seriously with the intended effect; they are the paraphernalia of the journey. The author's extraordinary vocabulary, its wonderful coinages and vivid turnings and twistings of worn-out words, are comparable only to Chapman's translations of Homer. The language fairly shrieks under the intensity of his treatment, and the reader is under an excitement which is hardly controllable. The only wonder is that Melville is so little known and so poorly appreciated.

> A review of ''Moby-Dick; or, the White Whale,'' in The Critic, New York, Vol. XIX, No. 582, April 15, 1893, p. 232.

ARCHIBALD MacMECHAN   (essay date 1899)

[*MacMechan, who hoped to rehabilitate Melville's reputation, discusses the qualities that make* Moby-Dick ''*the best sea story ever written.'' Focusing on the novel's literary elements, MacMechan praises Melville's treatment of structure, theme, and style and analyzes the distinctive ''Americanism'' informing* Moby-Dick. *MacMechan's essay originally appeared in the October, 1899, issue of the* Queen's Quarterly. *For additional discussion of Melville's prose style in the novel, see Sir Nathaniel (1853), Winters (1938), Wilder (1952), Nechas (1978), and Matthiessen (NCLC, Vol. 3). Further discussion of the American properties of* Moby-Dick *is provided by Olson (1947), Chase (1949), Wilder (1952), Mushabac (1981), and Rourke (see Additional Bibliography).*]

The present writer made his first acquaintance with **Moby Dick** in the dim, dusty Mechanics' Institute Library . . . of an obscure Canadian village, nearly twenty years ago; and since that time he has seen only one copy of the book exposed for sale, and met only one person (and that not an American) who had read it. Though Kingsley has a good word for Melville, the only place where real appreciation of him is to be found of recent years is in one of Mr. Clark Russell's dedications. There occurs the phrase which gives this paper its title [''The Best Sea Story Ever Written'']. Whoever takes the trouble to read this unique and original book will concede that Mr. Russell knows whereof he affirms. (pp. 138-39)

When Mr. Clark Russell singles out **Moby Dick** for such high praise as he bestows upon it, we think at once of other sea-stories,—his own, Marryat's, Smollett's perhaps, and such books as Dana's *Two Years before the Mast.* But the last is a plain record of fact; in Smollett's tales, sea-life is only part of one great round of adventure; in Mr. Russell's mercantile marine, there is generally the romantic interest of the way of a man with a maid; and in Marryat's the rise of a naval officer through various ranks plus a love-story or plenty of fun, fighting and prize-money. From all these advantages Melville not only cuts himself off, but seems to heap all sorts of obstacles in his self appointed path. Great are the prejudices to be overcome; but he triumphs over all. Whalers are commonly regarded as a sort of sea-scavengers. He convinces you that their business is poetic; and that they are finest fellows afloat. He dispenses with a love-story altogether; there is hardly a flutter of a petticoat from chapter first to last. The book is not a record of fact; but of fact idealized, which supplies the frame for a terrible duel to the death between a mad whaling-captain and a miraculous white sperm whale. It is not a love-story but a story of undying hate.

In no other tale is one so completely detached from the land, even from the very suggestion of land. Though Nantucket and

New Bedford must be mentioned, only their nautical aspects are touched on; they are but the steps of the saddle-block from which the mariner vaults upon the back of his sea-horse. The strange ship "Pequod" is the theatre of all the strange adventures. For ever off soundings, she shows but as a central speck in a wide circle of blue or stormy sea; and yet a speck crammed full of human passions, the world itself in little. (pp. 139-40)

For a tale of such length, *Moby Dick* is undoubtedly well constructed. Possibly the "Town-Ho's Story," interesting as it is, somewhat checks the progress of the plot; but by the time the reader reaches this point, he is infected with the leisurely, trade-wind, whaling atmosphere, and has no desire to proceed faster than at the "Pequod's" own cruising rate. Possibly the book might be shortened by excision, but when one looks over the chapters it is hard to decide which to sacrifice. (p. 140)

One striking peculiarity of the book is its Americanism—a word which needs definition. The theme and style are peculiar to this country. Nowhere but in America could such a theme have been treated in such a style. Whaling is peculiarly an American industry; and of all whale-men, the Nantucketers were the keenest, the most daring, and the most successful. Now, though there are still whalers to be found in the New Bedford slips, . . . the industry is almost extinct. . . . Perhaps Melville went to sea for no other purpose than to construct the monument of whaling in this unique book. Not in his subject alone, but in his style is Melville distinctly American. It is large in idea, expansive; it has an Elizabethan force and freshness and swing, and is, perhaps, more rich in figures than any style but Emerson's. It has the picturesqueness of the new world, and, above all, a free-flowing humour, which is the distinct *cachet* of American literature. No one would contend that it is a perfect style; some mannerisms become tedious, like the constant moral turn, and the curiously coined adverbs placed before the verb. Occasionally there is more than a hint of bombast, as indeed might be expected; but, upon the whole, it is an extraordinary style, rich, clear, vivid, original. It shows reading and is full of thought and allusion; but its chief charm is its freedom from all scholastic rules and conventions. Melville is a Walt Whitman of prose.

Like Browning he has a dialect of his own. The poet of *The Ring and the Book* translates the different emotions and thoughts and possible words of pope, jurist, murderer, victim, into one level uniform Browningese; reduces them to a common denominator, in a way of speaking, and Melville gives us not the actual words of American whalemen, but what they would say under the imagined conditions, translated into one consistent, though various Melvillesque manner of speech. The life he deals with belongs already to the legendary past, and he has us completely at his mercy. He is completely successful in creating his "atmosphere." Granted the conditions, the men and their words, emotions and actions, are all consistent. One powerful scene takes place on the quarter-deck of the "Pequod" one evening, when, all hands mustered aft, the Captain Ahab tells of the White Whale, and offers a doubloon to the first man who "raises" him. . . .

Then follows the wild ceremony of drinking round the capstan-head from the harpoon-sockets to confirm Ahab's curse. "Death to Moby Dick. God hunt us all, if we do not hunt Moby Dick to the death!" The intermezzo of the various sailors on the forecastle which follows until the squall strikes the ship is one of the most suggestive passages in all the literature of the sea. Under the influence of Ahab's can, the men are dancing on the forecastle. The old Manx sailor says:

"I wonder whether those jolly lads bethink them of what they are dancing over. I'll dance over your grave, I will—that's the bitterest threat of your night-women, that beat head-winds round corners. O, Christ! to think of the green navies and the green-skulled crews." (pp. 141-42)

[Melville's] humour has the usual tinge of Northern melancholy, and sometimes a touch of Rabelais. The exhortations of Stubb to his boat's crew, on different occasions, or such chapters as "Queen Mab," "The Cassock," "Leg and Arm," "Stubb's Supper," are good examples of his peculiar style.

But, after all, his chief excellence is bringing to the landsman the very salt of the sea breeze, while to one who has long known the ocean, he is as one praising to the lover the chiefest beauties of the Beloved. The magic of the ship and the mystery of the sea are put into words that form pictures for the dullest eyes. The chapter, "The Spirit Spout," contains these two aquarelles of the moonlit sea and the speeding ship side by side:

> It was while gliding through these latter waters that one sérene and moonlight night, when all the waves rolled by like scrolls of silver; and by their soft, suffusing seethings all things made what seemed a silvery silence, not a solitude; on such a silent night a silvery jet was seen far in advance of the white bubbles at the bow. Lit up by the moon it looked celestial; seemed some plumed and glittering god uprising from the sea. . . .
>
> Walking the deck, with quick, side lunging strides, Ahab commanded the t'gallant sails and royals to be set, and every stunsail spread. The best man in the ship must take the helm. Then, with every mast-head manned, the piled-up craft rolled down before the wind. The strange, upheaving, lifting tendency of the taffrail breeze filling the hollows of so many sails made the buoyant, hovering deck to feel like air beneath the feet.
>
> (pp. 143-44)

It would be hard to find five consecutive sentences anywhere containing such pictures and such vivid, pregnant, bold imagery: but this book is made up of such things. . . .

A complete scientific memoir of the Sperm Whale as known to man might be quarried from this book, for Melville has described the creature from his birth to his death, and even burial in the oil casks and the ocean. He has described him living, dead and anatomized. (p. 144)

This book is at once the epic and the encyclopaedia of whaling. It is a monument to the honour of an extinct race of daring seamen; but it is a monument overgrown with the lichen of neglect. Those who will care to scrape away the moss may be few, but they will have their reward. To the class of gentleman-adventurer, to those who love both books and free life under the wide and open sky, it must always appeal. Melville takes rank with Borrow, and Jefferies, and Thoreau, and Sir Richard Burton; and his place in this brotherhood of notables is not the lowest. Those who feel the salt in their blood that draws them time and again out of the city to the wharves and the ships, almost without their knowledge or their will; those who feel the irresistible lure of the spring, away from the cramped and noisy town, up the long road to the peaceful companionship of the awaking earth and the untainted sky; all those—and they are many—will find in Melville's great book an ever fresh and constant charm. (p. 145)

> Archibald MacMechan, "'The Best Sea Story Ever Written'," in The Recognition of Herman Melville: Selected Criticism since 1846, edited by Hershel Parker, The University of Michigan Press, 1967, pp. 137-45.

JOSEPH CONRAD (letter date 1907)

[*Conrad was born and raised in Poland and later resided in England. A major novelist, he is considered an innovator of novel structure as well as one of the finest stylists of modern English literature. He made the following remarks in response to a request by the editors of Oxford University Press that he write a preface for their proposed edition of* Moby-Dick.]

I am greatly flattered by your proposal; but the writing of my own stuff is a matter of so much toil and difficulty that I am only too glad to leave other people's books alone. Years ago I looked into **Typee** and **Omoo**, but as I didn't find there what I am looking for when I open a book I did go no further. Lately I had in my hand **Moby Dick**. It struck me as a rather strained rhapsody with whaling for a subject and not a single sincere line in the 3 vols of it. (pp. 122-23)

> Joseph Conrad, in a letter to Humphrey Milford on January 15, 1907, in Moby-Dick as Doubloon: Essays and Extracts (1851-1970), edited by Hershel Parker and Harrison Hayford, W. W. Norton & Company, Inc., 1970, pp. 122-23.

H. M. TOMLINSON (essay date 1921)

[*Tomlinson speaks of the intangible "enchanted" quality that pervades* Moby-Dick, *characterizing it as both a challenge to the reader and an affirmation of the novel's artistic greatness. These comments were originally published on November 5, 1921, in the* Literary Review.]

When one enters [**Moby Dick**] one is instantly aware of an overshadowing presence. From the opening passage there is no doubt about it. Nor is it now a fitful presence. It meets us at that entrance which is quite rightly entitled "Loomings." We go at once into a world where all is familiar—streets, ships, men, sea, and sky—but where all has been enchanted. Another spirit is there, creative, dominant, which knows us, but is itself unknown. What has happened it is impossible to say. We hear Melville's voice. It is easily recognizable. His words are familiar and the rhythm of their ordering. But they are somehow changed. They have been transmuted. They shine with an unearthly light. Their music can be even terrifying, like nameless sounds heard at night in the wilderness.

These, of course, are generalities. But who has resolved poetry into its elements? We know it only from the thrill it gives, neither of joy nor of fear, but something of each, when we encounter it. **Moby Dick** is a supreme test. If it captures you, then you are unafraid of great art. You may dwell in safety with fiends or angels and rest poised with a quiet mind between the stars and the bottomless pit.

> H. M. Tomlinson, "A Supreme Test of a Reader," in Moby-Dick as Doubloon: Essays and Extracts (1851-1970), edited by Hershel Parker and Harrison Hayford, W. W. Norton & Company, Inc., 1970, p. 148.

LINCOLN COLCORD (essay date 1922)

[*Colcord comments on the shifting narrative point of view and other technical irregularities in* Moby-Dick, *attributing them to an underlying conflict within Melville "between realism and mysticism, between a natural and an artificial manner." According to Colcord, this conflict had a particularly damaging effect on Melville's handling of the novel's ending, yet it ultimately redounded in his favor, for it served as an "intensifying medium through which the work rose to superlative heights." The critic also questions the role of allegory in* Moby-Dick, *a topic also considered by Hillway (1979). For additional discussion of the narrative point of view in the novel, see Thompson (1952), Berthoff (1962), and Nechas (1978).]*

I do not remember having seen in print a discussion of the extraordinary technical development of **Moby Dick**. In terms of the craft of writing, the book is a surpassing feat of legerdemain. Briefly, **Moby Dick** is the only piece of fiction I know of, which at one and the same time is written in the first and the third persons. It opens straightforwardly as first-person narration. "Call me Ishmael"—"I thought I would sail about a little"—"I stuffed a shirt or two into my carpet bag, tucked it under my arm, and started for Cape Horn and the Pacific." So it runs, throughout the opening scenes in New Bedford and Nantucket; the characters are real persons, seen through Ishmael's eyes; they speak real speech; the scenes are delineated with subjective realism. Melville is telling a story. His (or Ishmael's) meeting with Queequeg, and their first night together in the big feather bed at the Spouter Inn, are intensely human and alive. Even Bildad and Peleg are creations of realism. The first note of fancifulness is introduced with the Ancient Mariner who accosts Ishmael and Queequeg on the pier in Nantucket. The book, however, still holds to the technical channel of first person narration; and it is through Ishmael's eyes that one sees the "Pequod" sail from Nantucket.

Then, without warning, the narrative in Chapter twenty-nine jumps from the first to the third person; begins to relate conversations which could not possibly have been overheard by Ishmael and to describe scenes which his eye could not possibly have seen; follows Ahab into his cabin and Starbuck into the recesses of his mind, and launches boldly on that sea of mystical soliloquy and fanciful unreality across which it sweeps for the remainder of the tale. As it progresses, Ishmael sinks farther and farther from sight, and the all-seeing eye of the third person comes more and more into play.

Yet, even at this stage, the technical form of first-person narration is not entirely abandoned; is kept along, as it were, like an attenuated wraith. As the "Pequod" sights ship after ship, the narrative momentarily reappears, only to be discarded once more at the first opportunity; so that, of the main body of the book, it may truly be said that it is written in both the first and the third persons. For instance, chapter ninety-one, "The 'Pequod' Meets the 'Rosebud'": "It was a week or two after the last whaling-scene recounted, and when we [not they] were slowly sailing over a sleepy, vapoury, midday sea. . . ." This is a recurrence to first person narration in the midst of pages of third-person soliloquy. But turning to Chapter CXXVIII, "The 'Pequod' Meets the 'Rachel'": "Next day, a large ship, the 'Rachel,' was descried, bearing directly down upon the 'Pequod,' all her spars thickly clustering with men"—this might be either first or third person; the context shows it to be the latter. Ishmael has been definitely forsaken, and hereafter remains in abeyance until the end of the book; when, suddenly, he re-emerges in the epilogue.

The quarrel between the persons, however, does not by any means comprise the whole technical irregularity of *Moby Dick.* There is the introduction of the form of dramatic dialogue; an innovation singularly successful, and remarkably in keeping both with the mood of the moment when it is introduced and with the general tone of mystical formlessness pervading the whole work. There is the adroit suspending of the narrative by those absorbing chapters of plain exposition, descriptive of whales and whaling; the gradual revealing of the secrets of the whale, while the final nameless secret is withheld, while fancy and terror feed and grow on suspense. There is the totally ideal development of the characterization, as Ahab and Starbuck and Stubbs and all the rest indulge themselves in the most high-flown and recondite reflections and soliloquies. Finally, there is the bizarre method of chaptering—each chapter a little sketch, each incident having its own chapter; some of the chapters only half a page in length, others a page or two; a hundred and thirty-five chapters in all, together with forewords on etymology and extracts, and an epilogue. In short, *Moby Dick* as a technical exercise is utterly fantastic and original. Melville has departed from every known form of composition; or rather, he has jumbled many forms into a new relation, choosing among them as fancy dictated. (pp. 561-62)

I am not aware that *Moby Dick* was received at the time of its publication with any degree of surprise at its technical form, whatever surprise or opposition may have been called forth by its content. Neither am I aware that Melville himself felt that he was doing an extraordinary thing in adopting a unique but natural technical form for the expression of an original creative effort. His letters to Hawthorne during the composition of *Moby Dick* betray no self-consciousness on this score. In fact, he seems to have retained a perfectly free relation with his technical medium. (p. 562)

· · · · ·

[An exhaustion in the latter part of *Moby Dick*] seems to me to become startlingly apparent at the crisis of the book, which is reached in the last chapter. Cavilous as the criticism may sound from the viewpoint of a broader appreciation, I sincerely feel that Melville failed to reap in his crisis all that he had sown throughout the body of the tale. The chase of the white whale is splendid; in the daily fight between Ahab and this sinister embodiment of evil Melville is at his best. [Everything] goes magnificently up to the very last; but the final attack of Moby Dick on the ship, and the sinking of the "Pequod" with all her company, are inadequate to the point of anticlimax.

There should have been a more generous descriptive effort at this pass; Melville could picture a scene superbly, and he should have spared no pains to do it here. He seems instead to have adopted an affectation of simplicity. He will rest on his oars now, let the momentum of the book carry it forward, allow the various lines of suspense and horror to culminate of their own accord; in fine, he will sketch the winding up of the piece, leaving the actual descriptive effort to the reader's imagination.

But in this he made a critical error; while it is a fine thing to utilize the reader's imagination, it is disastrous to tax it too far. The last pages of *Moby Dick* do not give us the ending for which we have been prepared; which, with the keenest anticipation, we have been awaiting. Having created such intense suspense, Melville was under the imperative obligation to provide for its satisfaction a flash of equally intense realism. The imagination, having too readily devoured the feast that he has set forth, and finding its hunger only increased thereby, is

suddenly let down and disappointed. In this unhappy, defrauded state, it fastens upon the first thing at hand, which is the catastrophe itself; recognizing at once the fantastic nature of that complete oblivion which so causelessly descends on the "Pequod" and her company. For, as a matter of sober fact, a ship of her size would not, in sinking, have drawn down into her vortex an agile cat, much less a crew of whalers, used to being pitched out of boats in the open sea, and surrounded with quantities of dunnage for them to ride when the decks had gone from under.

Turning to the last chapter of *Moby Dick*, one may note that it contains but a brief paragraph describing the whale's frantic attack on the vessel. No horror is created, no suspense, no feverish excitement. It is another of art's vanished opportunities. There should have been a close-packed page or two of tumultuous visualization; then, with the gigantic whale dashing head-on toward the devoted "Pequod," a pause in the narrative, to let suspense rankle, while a few paragraphs were occupied with a dissertation on the sinking of vessels—not the sinking of vessels by whales, which matter has already been examined, but the sinking of vessels; about how difficult, how unusual, it would be for a ship to carry her whole company beneath the waves; about Starbuck's knowledge of this fact; about their frantic preparations for escape—then, loosing every ounce of reserve literary power, a description of the crash, the catastrophe, the peculiar and malignant combination of circumstances, easily to be imagined, which, in spite of common experience, did actually destroy this whole ship's company. The whale should have dashed among the debris and floating men, after the ship had gone down, to complete the work of destruction. The scene should have been cast in the form of first-person narration, and Ishmael should have been near enough to see it all. (He was adrift, it will be remembered, and did not go down with the vessel; but the return to the first person is reserved for the epilogue, while the crisis of the story is told in an especially vague form of the third person.) We should have been given a final view of the white whale, triumphantly leaving the scene and resuming the interrupted course of his destiny. In short, there are dozens of strokes of realism neglected in this chapter which plainly demand to be driven home.

Melville chose to end the book on a note of trancendentalism; he himself does not seem to have visualized the scene at all. The influence of Hawthorne, one suspects, was largely responsible for this grave error. (pp. 585-86)

The influence of Hawthorne is painfully evident throughout the last two-thirds of *Moby Dick;* painfully evident, because it is so incongruous with Melville's natural manner which is that of narrative realism; he must be there in person—he makes the scene alive with amazing vitality where he stands. In the same sense, his natural power of characterization in the descriptive or analytical field; I am not aware that he has ever put into the mouth of a single character a realistic speech. Wherever, in *Moby Dick,* he gets his best effects, he gets them through the exercise of his natural manner. Certain scenes stand out vividly. Certain pages of analytical characterization are instinct with truth and greatness. The natural impulse keeps bursting through. But the bulk of the characterization is cast in a method artificial to him; he constantly tries to raise the pitch of the tale, to inflate the value of the words. Too much of the descriptive matter likewise is forced through unnatural channels, losing the air of mastery in its adaptation to the less vigorous form of the third person.

Thus the book, in its composition, represents a struggle between realism and mysticism, between a natural and an artificial manner. It begins naturally, it ends artificially. This in a measure explains the strange confusion of the technique, the extravagant use of the two separate persons. Only the most extraordinary creative power could have struck art and achievement from such an alien blend.

What, then, of the allegory?—for we are told that *Moby Dick* is a masterpiece of this form of composition. I must confess that I did not follow the allegory closely, and did not find that it was forced on my attention; and now that I look back on the book, I fail exactly to see wherein it lies. What, for instance, does Ahab represent, and what the white whale? I am not certain that Melville meant the story to be an allegory. In fact, does he not somewhere fiercely disclaim the imputation? But it is the fate of all work done in the manner of transcendentalism to land sooner or later in the rarified atmosphere of allegory, whether it means anything or not, whether or not the allegory seems to point anywhere in particular. Transcendentalism is the stuff of allegory. Melville hated allegory, and would have hated transcendentalism, had he not just then happened to come under the influence of a transcendentalist. This put him in a bad fix, and made him, whether he willed it or not, write a book which looked like allegory. Do we need a better explanation of his turning so fiercely against the imputation?

Not because of its allegorical significance, and not, indeed, because of its mysticism, considered as a thing apart, does this book of the chase of the white whale live among the immortal works of literature; but rather because of its irrepressible triumph of realism over mysticism, because of the inspired and gripping story that builds itself up out of a passionate flow of words. For my part, I like Ahab as Ahab, not as a symbol of something or other; and Ahab lives as Ahab, marvelously enough, in spite of the wild unreality of his constant meditations and ebullitions. Yes, and because of it; the overshadowing demoniac terror of the story lends reality to unreality, charm and substance to mystical formlessness. This is the mark of genius in the creator. Yet even genius may carry things too far; Ahab manages to live as Ahab, but Starbuck—well, Starbuck struts and swells a little, betrayed by an overdose of transcendentalism.

If I have seemed to wish that *Moby Dick* had been written in the form of unalloyed narrative realism, that Melville had left off altogether his dalliance with transcendentalism, I would correct the impression now. As a piece of pure realism, the book obviously would not have been the inspired achievement that it is in its present form. The creative struggle that Melville was undergoing at the time of its composition was the intensifying medium through which the work rose to superlative heights. The chapters flow easily, as though he did not realize their duality of form and temper, but felt them to be parts of a unified, continuous product; but the grievous battle taking place within him caused him to produce what actually are gigantic fragments, struck from mountains of fire and anguish, which slowly and ponderously arrange themselves into the delineation of a majestic idea.

Moby Dick is not the allegory of Ahab's struggle with destiny; it is rather the story of Melville's struggle with art and life. Without this struggle, there would have been no agonizing greatness; only another *Typee,* a splendid tale, a perfect example of literary realism. But, given the struggle, there had to be from page to page this singular conflict in style and form and matter, the confused, reflected gleams of a hidden con-

flagration; so that to wish the conflict away would be to wish away the book's divinity. (pp. 586-87)

Lincoln Colcord, "Notes on 'Moby Dick'," *in* The Freeman, *Vol. V, Nos. 128 & 129, August 23 & August 30, 1922, pp. 559-62, 585-87.*

D. H. LAWRENCE (essay date 1923)

[*Lawrence was an English novelist, poet, and essayist who is noted for his introduction of the themes of modern psychology to English fiction. In his lifetime he was a controversial figure, both for the explicit sexuality he portrayed in his works and for his unconventional personal life. Much of the criticism of Lawrence's work concerns his highly individualistic moral system, which was based on absolute freedom of expression, particularly sexual expression. Human sexuality was for Lawrence a symbol of the Life Force and is frequently pitted against modern industrial society, which he believed was dehumanizing. Lawrence commented on* Moby-Dick *in his* Studies in Classic American Literature, *a collection of essays exploring the "true American" as revealed in the works of Hawthorne, Melville, and other writers. Lawrence asserts in his preface to* Studies *that "Americans refuse everything explicit and always put up a sort of double meaning. They revel in subterfuge." Accordingly, he approaches* Moby-Dick *as a highly symbolic work evoking a mortal conflict between the "last phallic being of the white man," represented by Moby Dick, and the "parasitic mental or ideal consciousness" of the white race, represented by the crew of the* Pequod *(see NCLC, Vol. 3). In the excerpt below, Lawrence discusses the crew and comments on the significance of the destruction of the* Pequod, *the symbolic "ship of the American soul." For further commentary on the role of symbolism in the novel, see Arvin (1950), Bewley (1959), Horsford (1962), Kulkarni (1970), Hillway (1979), and Mather, Mumford, Aiken, Winters, Sedgwick, Maugham, Auden, and Priestley (NCLC, Vol. 3).*]

You are some time before you are allowed to see the captain, Ahab: the mysterious Quaker. Oh, it is a God-fearing Quaker ship.

Ahab, the captain. The captain of the soul.

> "I am the master of my fate,
> I am the captain of my soul!"

Ahab!

"Oh, captain, my captain, our fearful trip is done."

The gaunt Ahab, Quaker, mysterious person, only shows himself after some days at sea. There's a secret about him! What?

Oh, he's a portentous person. He stumps about on an ivory stump, made from sea-ivory. Moby Dick, the great white whale, tore off Ahab's leg at the knee, when Ahab was attacking him.

Quite right, too. Should have torn off both his legs, and a bit more besides.

But Ahab doesn't think so. Ahab is now a monomaniac. Moby Dick is his monomania. Moby Dick must DIE, or Ahab can't live any longer. Ahab is atheist by this.

All right.

This *Pequod,* ship of the American soul, has three mates.

1. Starbuck: Quaker, Nantucketer, a good responsible man of reason, forethought, intrepidity, what is called a dependable man. At the bottom, *afraid.*

2. Stubb: "Fearless as fire, and as mechanical." Insists on being reckless and jolly on every occasion. Must be afraid too, really.

3. Flask: Stubborn, obstinate, without imagination. To him "the wondrous whale was but a species of magnified mouse or water-rat—"

There you have them: a maniac captain and his three mates, three splendid seamen, admirable whalemen, first-class men at their job.

America!

It is rather like Mr. Wilson and his admirable, "efficient" crew, at the Peace Conference. Except that none of the Pequodders took their wives along.

A maniac captain of the soul, and three eminently practical mates.

America!

Then such a crew. Renegades, castaways, cannibals: Ishmael, Quakers.

America!

Three giant harpooners, to spear the great white whale.

1. Queequeg, the South Sea Islander, all tattooed, big and powerful.

2. Tashtego, the Red Indian of the sea-coast, where the Indian meets the sea.

3. Daggoo, the huge black negro.

There you have them, three savage races, under the American flag, the maniac captain, with their great keen harpoons, ready to spear the white whale.

And only after many days at sea does Ahab's own boat-crew appear on deck. Strange, silent, secret, black-garbed Malays, fire-worshipping Parsees. These are to man Ahab's boat, when it leaps in pursuit of that whale.

What do you think of the ship *Pequod*, the ship of the soul of an American?

Many races, many peoples, many nations, under the Stars and Stripes. Beaten with many stripes.

Seeing stars sometimes.

And in a mad ship, under a mad captain, in a mad, fanatic's hunt.

For what?

For Moby Dick, the great white whale.

But splendidly handled. Three splendid mates. The whole thing practical, eminently practical in its working. American industry! (pp. 149-50)

Hot-blooded sea-born Moby Dick. Hunted by monomaniacs of the idea.

Oh God, oh God, what next, when the *Pequod* has sunk?

She sank in the war, and we are all flotsam.

Now what next?

Who knows? *Quien sabe? Quien sabe, señor?*

Neither Spanish nor Saxon America has any answer.

The *Pequod* went down. And the *Pequod* was the ship of the white American soul. She sank, taking with her negro and Indian and Polynesian, Asiatic and Quaker and good, businesslike Yankees and Ishmael: she sank all the lot of them.

Boom! as Vachel Lindsay would say.

To use the words of Jesus, IT IS FINISHED.

Consummatum est!

But *Moby Dick* was first published in 1851. If the Great White Whale sank the ship of the Great White Soul in 1851, what's been happening ever since?

Post-mortem effects, presumably.

Because, in the first centuries, Jesus was Cetus, the Whale. And the Christians were the little fishes. Jesus, the Redeemer, was Cetus, Leviathan. And all the Christians all his little fishes. (pp. 160-61)

*D. H. Lawrence, "Herman Melville's 'Moby Dick',"
in his* Studies in Classic American Literature, *1923.
Reprint by The Viking Press, 1964, pp. 145-61.*

LEWIS MUMFORD (essay date 1929)

[*Mumford is an American sociologist, historian, philosopher, and critic whose primary interest is the relationship between the modern individual and his or her environment. In his* Herman Melville, *excerpted below and in NCLC, Vol. 3, Mumford hails Moby-Dick as a remarkably rich "parable" in which "the white whale stands for the brute energies of existence, blind, fatal, over-powering, while Ahab is the spirit of man, small and feeble, but purposeful, that pits its puniness against this might, and its purpose against the blank senselessness of power." The critic also extols the novel as "one of the first great mythologies to be created in the modern world." The latter insight is the focus of the following excerpt, in which Mumford stresses Melville's skill and perspicacity in fusing science and imagination in* Moby-Dick. *The role of myth in the novel is also addressed by Chase (1949), Zoellner (1973), and Freeman, Arvin, Camus, and Fiedler (see NCLC, Vol. 3).*]

The epic and mythic quality of *Moby-Dick* has been misunderstood because those who examined the book have thought of the epic in terms of Homer, and the myth itself in relation to some obvious hero of antiquity, or some modern folk-hero, a Washington, a Boone, raised to enormous dimensions. "The great mistake seems to be," as Melville said in his essay on Hawthorne, "that even with those Americans who look forward to the coming of a great literary genius among us, they somehow fancy he will come in the costume of Queen Elizabeth's day; be a writer of dramas founded upon old English history or the tales of Boccaccio. Whereas, great geniuses are parts of the times, they themselves are the times and possess a corresponding colouring."

Now, *Moby-Dick* was written in the best spirit of the nineteenth century, and though it escaped most of the limitations of that period, it escaped with its finest qualities intact. Heroes and gods in the old sense, as Walt Whitman plainly saw, had had their day: they fitted into a simpler scheme of life and thought, and a more credulous sort of attitude; so far from representing the ultimate triumph of the human imagination, from which the scientific mode of thought was not merely a departure but a falling off, the old myths were but the product of a juvenile fantasy. One might still use these figures . . . ; but they stood for a mode of consciousness and feeling remote from our modern experience. Science did not, as has been foolishly believed, destroy the myth-making power of man, or reduce all his inner strivings to bleak impotence. . . . What the scientific spirit has actually done has been to exercise the imagination in finer ways than the autistic wish—the wish of the infant possessed of the illusion of power and domination—was able to express. Faraday's ability to conceive the lines of force in a magnetic field was quite as great a triumph as the ability to conceive fairies dancing in a ring: and, as Mr. A. N. Whitehead has shown, the poets who sympathized with this new sort of imagination, poets like Shelley, Wordsworth, Whitman, Melville, did not feel themselves robbed of their specific powers, but rather found them enlarged and refreshed. (pp. 190-91)

Almost all the important works of the nineteenth century . . . [expressed a] new imaginative range: they respect the fact: they are replete with observation: they project an ideal realm in and through, not over, the landscape of actuality. *Notre Dame* might have been written by an historian, *War and Peace* by a sociologist, *The Idiot* might have been created by a psychiatrist and *Salammbo* might have been the work of an archaeologist. I do not say that these books were scientific by intention, or that they might be replaced by a work of science without grave loss; far from it. I merely point out that they are conceived in the same spirit; that they belong to a similar plane of consciousness. Much as Melville was enriched by the Elizabethan writers, there is that in *Moby-Dick* which separates him completely from the poets of that day—and if one wants a word to describe the element that makes the difference, one must call it briefly science.

Now, this respect for fact, as opposed to irresponsible fantasy, did not of course exist for the first time in the nineteenth century: Defoe had this habit of mind in quite as great a measure as Melville: what is important is that in the nineteenth century it was for the first time completely wedded to the imagination. It no longer means a restriction, a dried-up quality, an incompleteness; it no longer deifies the empirical and the practical at the expense of the ideal and the aesthetic: on the contrary, these qualities are now completely fused together, as an expression of life's integrated totality. The symbolism again becomes equal to the reality. . . . Had Milton sought to tell this parable of Melville's, he would probably have recast the story of Jonah and the whale, making Jonah the hero; but in doing so he could not help losing all the great imaginative parallels Melville is able to work out, through using material hitherto untouched by previous myth or history. For Ahab's hate and the pursuit of the whale is only one part of the total symbol: the physiological character of the whale, its feeding, its mating, its whole life, from whatever sources Melville drew the data, is equally a part of it. Indeed, the symbol of Moby-Dick is complete and rounded, expressive of our present relations to the universe, only through the passages that orthodox criticism, exercised on lesser works and more meagre traditions, regards as extraneous or unimportant!

Moby-Dick, then, is one of the first great mythologies to be created in the modern world, created, that is, out of the stuff of that world, its science, its exploration, its terrestrial daring, its concentration upon power and dominion over nature, and not out of ancient symbols, Prometheus, Endymion, Orestes, or mediaeval folk-legends, like Dr. Faustus. *Moby-Dick* lives imaginatively in the newly broken soil of our own life: its symbols, unlike Blake's original but mysterious figures, are

direct and explicit: if the story is bedded in facts, the facts themselves are not lost in the further interpretation. *Moby-Dick* thus brings together the two dissevered halves of the modern world and the modern self—its positive, practical, scientific, externalized self, bent on conquest and knowledge, and its imaginative, ideal half, bent on the transposition of conflict into art, and power into humanity. This resolution is achieved in *Moby-Dick* itself: it is as if a Shakespeare and a Bacon, or, to use a more local metaphor, as if an Eakins and a Ryder, had collaborated on a single work of art, with a heightening of their several powers. The best handbook on whaling is also— I say this scrupulously—the best tragic epic of modern times and one of the fine poetic works of all time.

That is an achievement; and it is also a promise. Whitman went as far in his best poems, particularly in the *Song of Myself;* and, with quite another method, Tolstoy went as far in *War and Peace,* Dostoyevsky in the *Brothers Karamazov;* Hardy, less perfectly, approximated it perhaps in *The Dynasts;* but no one went further. It is one of the great peaks of the modern vision of life. ''May God keep us,'' wrote Blake, ''from single vision and Newton's sleep.'' We now perhaps see a little more clearly what Blake's enigmatic words mean. In *Moby-Dick* Melville achieved the deep integrity of that double vision which sees with both eyes—the scientific eye of actuality, and the illumined eye of imagination and dream. (pp. 191-94)

> *Lewis Mumford, in his* Herman Melville, *Harcourt Brace Jovanovich, 1929, 377 p.*

HART CRANE (letter date 1932)

[*Crane was an early twentieth-century American poet and essayist who is best known as the author of the poem* The Bridge, *an ambitious work intended by Crane to provide a myth for American life. The poet supports Melville in this excerpt from a letter, defending the utility of the digressive elements in* Moby-Dick.]

A way, way back you asked me a question about what I thought of *Moby Dick.* It has passages, I admit, of seeming innuendo that seem to block the action. But on third or fourth reading I've found that some of those very passages are much to be valued in themselves—minor and subsidiary forms that augment the final climacteric quite a bit. No work as tremendous and tragic as *Moby Dick* can be expected to build up its ultimate tension and impact without manipulating our time sense to a great extent. Even the suspense of the usual mystery story utilizes that device. In *Moby Dick* the whale is a metaphysical image of the Universe, and every detail of his habits and anatomy has its importance in swelling his proportions to the cosmic rôle he plays. You may find other objections to the book in mind, but I've assumed the above to be among them, at least, as I among others that I know, found the same fault at first. (pp. 404-05)

> *Hart Crane, in a letter to Solomon Grunberg on March 20, 1932, in his* The Letters of Hart Crane: 1916-1932, *edited by Brom Weber, University of California Press, 1965, pp. 403-05.*

ERNEST HEMINGWAY (essay date 1935)

[*Hemingway, the author of such critically acclaimed works as* The Sun Also Rises, A Farewell to Arms, *and* The Old Man and the Sea, *was one of the most influential and best-known American novelists of the twentieth century. Critics generally regard his distinctive writing style—terse, lucid, and unornamented—as his greatest contribution to literature. Hemingway compliments Melville's writing style in the following commentary on American authors, excerpted from his* Green Hills of Africa.]

[We] have had, in America, skillful writers. Poe is a skillful writer. It is skillful, marvelously constructed, and it is dead. We have had writers of rhetoric who had the good fortune to find a little, in a chronicle of another man and from voyaging, of how things, actual things, can be, whales for instance, and this knowledge is wrapped in the rhetoric like plums in a pudding. Occasionally it is there, alone, unwrapped in pudding, and it is good. This is Melville. (p. 20)

Ernest Hemingway, in his Green Hills of Africa, *Charles Scribner's Sons, 1935, 295 p.*

WILLARD THORP   (essay date 1938)

[*Thorp sparked modern academic interest in Melville with his scholarly introduction to* Herman Melville: Representative Selections. *One of his focuses in the essay is Melville's tortured quest for answers concerning such spiritual issues as necessity and free will and the relationship between a righteous God and an evil world. In the excerpt below, Thorp traces the quest as it is expressed in* Moby-Dick *and its predecessor,* Mardi; *he ultimately suggests that Ahab is made to suffer vicariously for Melville as a misguided quester, while "Ishmael-Melville" is delivered from the onslaught of the wrathful gods. Additional discussion of Melville's treatment of theology in the novel is provided by Thompson (1952), Bewley (1959), and Aiken (see* NCLC, *Vol. 3). For further discussion of the role of ontology in* Moby-Dick, *see Bewley (1959), Horsford (1962), Zoellner (1973), Nechas (1978), Hillway (1979), and Aiken (*NCLC, *Vol. 3).*]

Melville, in the days since his homecoming, had wrestled with the chronic problems of philosophy. In *Mardi,* as he had done with his friends in conversation, he threshed over the old arguments for the proof of consciousness, the debate between necessity and free will, the problem of a sinful world and a righteous God, the question of the moral responsibility of the natural man. (pp. lxvii-lxviii)

What troubled him ceaselessly was to know whether a master key to all these teasing questions could ever be found. An urge, deep in his nature, compelled him to "grind away at the nut of the universe" though it crack his jaws. The Penultimate will not satisfy him; he must have the Ultimate. That he might be dragged asunder in the effort to reconcile heaven and earth and find the Absolute, he knew, as well as did his creature Babbalanja. In the conversion of Taji's companions to the way of life of the Serenians, Melville represents the inclination he often felt to content himself with the natural "theology in the grass and the flower," and to follow the promptings of the heart, supplemented by Christ's gospel. "Yet, alas! too often do I swing from these moorings."

When Babbalanja is granted a vision of the Mardian Paradise he dares to ask there the question, "Why create the germs that sin and suffer, but to perish?"

"That," breathed my guide, "is the last mystery which underlieth all the rest. Archangel may not fathom it; that makes of Oro the everlasting mystery he is; that to divulge, were to make equal to himself in knowledge all the souls that are; that mystery Oro guards; and none but him may know."

This evasion contents Babbalanja. Taji it did not content. He would solve the mystery or pull down heaven. Leaving his

companions behind he seizes the helm, eternity in his eye, and steers for the outer ocean. (pp. lxviii-lxix)

[What we are] concerned with here is the place of *Moby-Dick* in Melville's quest for the Ultimate. When *Mardi* ended, Taji held the prow toward the open sea. . . . The action of *Moby-Dick* begins when Ahab, whose "quenchless feud," Melville declares, "seemed mine," tells the crew that they have signed on to chase the White Whale "round perdition's flames," till he "spouts black blood and rolls fin out." The new voyage is the continuation of the first, with this great difference, that the object of the quest has been transformed. Taji still hoped to recover . . . [lost happiness]; Ahab seeks revenge against an inscrutable and apparently capricious foe. (p. lxx)

[What] chiefly torments Ahab is to know whether he is fighting against energies from the void of death which man has himself animated, or against "some unknown but still reasoning thing." Whichever guess may be the true one, what Ahab chiefly hates is the inscrutableness of his enemy who impales him first on one and then the other of these desperate answers.

The frightfulness of the whale is incarnate in his whiteness, the "colorless, all-color of atheism," of the universal charnel-house inhabited by nothingness. To pursue him is to pursue death. If we try to solve the incarnation of his whiteness, we must to the grave to learn it. Sometimes Ahab, in this mood, thinks "there's naught beyond" the mask, behind which his foe fights, but blankness. But this mood is not frequent. To whalers who encountered Moby-Dick in times past his seeming infernal aforethought of ferocity was "not wholly regarded as having been inflicted by an unintelligent agent." Their inclination to believe in his demoniac purpose became at length in Ahab an obsession of certainty. The beast, whether agent of a devil-god or the god himself, showed purposeful malice beneath his outrageous strength. All the suspected malice of the universe, all the "subtle demonisms of life and thought" crazy Ahab saw at last practically assailable in Moby-Dick.

Before his mind was overthrown by this fatal obsession Ahab was sensitive to other elements than the demonism of the world. . . . In his calmer moments, such as prevail in . . . [his] colloquy with Starbuck in "The Symphony," he looks back longingly to the world of reason and love which he has put behind him. But these moods are few and are annihilated by the remorseless commands of the emperor who rules him. He feels himself the Fates' lieutenant acting under orders. His act is immutably decreed and was rehearsed a billion years before the ocean rolled. (pp. lxxi-lxxii)

So Ahab wills to believe. His creator knows this is delusion. Once when the ship, aglow with the flame and smoke of the try-works, drove on through the night, Ishmael-Melville dozed at the helm. The tiller smote his side, and he awoke in fright, having turned himself about in his sleep. Grateful to have escaped the fatal contingency of being brought by the lee, he meditates: "Look not too long in the face of the fire, O man! Never dream with thy hand on the helm! Turn not thy back to the compass; accept the first hint of the hitching tiller; believe not the artificial fire, when its redness makes all things look ghastly." Such wisdom Ahab trampled on. He had gazed too long on the unholy fires. He willed his mind to follow the cursed fiends who beckoned him down among them. In the chapter called "The Chart" Melville represents him as starting from his hammock at night, forced by intolerable dreams. His explanation of Ahab's anguish is explicit, and we should not pass it by. The Ahab who rushed from his sleep was not, he says, the crazy Ahab who pursued the whale. It was the innocent living soul of him that for a moment, in sleep, dissociated itself from and escaped the characterizing mind, which at other times employed it for its outer vehicle or agent.

> But as the mind does not exist unless leagued with the soul, therefore it must have been that, in Ahab's case, yielding up all his thoughts and fancies to his one supreme purpose; that purpose, by its own sheer inveteracy of will, forced itself against gods and devils into a kind of self-assumed, independent being of its own. Nay, could grimly live and burn, while the common vitality to which it was conjoined, fled horror-stricken from the unbidden and unfathered birth. Therefore, the tormented spirit that glared out of bodily eyes, when what seemed Ahab rushed from his room, was for the time but a vacated thing, a formless somnambulistic being, a ray of living light, to be sure, but without an object to colour, and therefore a blankness in itself. God help thee, old man, thy thoughts have created a creature in thee; and he whose intense thinking thus makes him a Prometheus; a vulture feeds upon that heart forever; that vulture the very creature he creates.

This significant passage makes plain the symbolic meaning of the mysterious Fedallah, the Parsee whom Ahab smuggles aboard the ship and who led his chase against the whale. Though they never spoke while they kept watch together, a potent spell joined them, "as if in the Parsee Ahab saw his forethrown shadow, in Ahab the Parsee his abandoned substance." Which is to say, that Ahab brought his own fate on board with him. This vulture that feeds upon his heart he himself created.

How is *Moby-Dick* to be read as the allegory of Melville's spiritual state in 1851? To what point has he come in his quest for the Ultimate? He invites us to inquire in the passage [in the chapter entitled "Moby-Dick"] which admits his sympathy with Ahab's feud. The wall of the mystery had been shoved menacingly near. He was like a prisoner whose only escape was by thrusting through. The ultimate answer, if it could be reached, would be complex, he now realized, and its quest perhaps dangerous to the sanity. He might have to impute the evil omnipresent in the universe to its ruler. But was this evil the work of principal or of agent? He began to suspect even that the intricate subject of all his speculations might dissolve in nothing, that there was, as he wrote to Hawthorne, no secret, "like the Freemason's mighty secret, so terrible to all children," which turns out, at last, "to consist in a triangle, a mallet, and an apron,—nothing more." In this same illuminating letter he notes that as soon as man begins to objectify the invisible world, to talk of *Me*, a *God*, a *Nature*, he prepares the noose that will hang him, like Ahab who sought to fight the intangible malignities only when he found in the White Whale their tangible incarnation.

Although Ahab was mad, as Melville knew him to be, and though he tried revenge, which is no solution to man's predicament, we must not suppose that Melville, even though defiant, would now choose to follow Ahab into the gulf, as Taji had turned his prow towards the racing tide. It is not merely for the purpose of saving the narrator that Ishmael-Melville survives the White Whale's assault. However much he sympathized with Ahab's Promethean determination to stare down the inscrutableness of the universe, Melville hurled, not himself, but Ahab, his creature, at the injurious gods. Like the mountain eagle, though he had swooped into the blackest gorge, that gorge lay within the lofty mountains. [As he confided to Hawthorne (see excerpt dated November, 1851), Melville] had written a wicked book for which Ahab was made to suffer vicariously, and he felt as spotless as the lamb. (pp. lxxii-lxxv)

> *Willard Thorp, in an introduction to* Herman Melville: Representative Selections *by Herman Melville, edited by Willard Thorp, American Book Company, 1938, pp. xi-cxxix.*

YVOR WINTERS   (essay date 1938)

[*Winters was a twentieth-century American poet and critic. He was associated with the New Criticism movement and gained a reputation as one of the most stringently anti-romantic critics of his period. Maintaining that a critic must be concerned with the moral as well as the aesthetic import of a work of art, he also believed that poetry ought to provide rational comment on the human condition, with the poet "seeking to state a true moral judgment." His critical precepts, usually considered extreme, include an emphasis on order, dignity, restraint, and morality. Here, Winters first compares the language of* Moby-Dick *to the language of epic poetry, then praises Melville's linguistic "instrument" as "an invention . . . essentially as original and powerful . . . as the blank verse of Milton." Further discussion of Melville's prose style in* Moby-Dick *is provided by Sir Nathaniel (1853), MacMechan (1899), Wilder (1952), Nechas (1978), and Matthiessen (see NCLC, Vol. 3). The novel's poetic properties receive further elucidation in the criticism of Erskine, Mumford, and Kazin (see NCLC, Vol. 3). Additional portions of Winters's essay, including his commentary on the symbolism and epic nature of* Moby-Dick, *are excerpted in NCLC, Vol. 3.*]

The language in which [*Moby Dick*] is written is closer to the poetry of *Paradise Lost* or of *Hamlet* than it is to the prose of the realistic novelist. The extremes of prosaic and of poetic language, each at a high level of excellence, might be illustrated by the prose of [Edith Wharton's] *The Age of Innocence*, on the one hand, and by one of the best sonnets of Shakespeare on the other: the extreme of prose is the recounting of individual facts; the extreme of poetry is the lyrical, in the best sense; that is, the expository concentration of a motivating concept, in language such that motivating concept and motivated feeling are expressed simultaneously and in brief space. Between these extremes, but a little nearer to the sonnet than to Mrs. Wharton, is the language of the great epic or dramatic poem: in *Macbeth*, or in *Paradise Lost*, the individual passage is never self-sustaining in the same measure as the poetry of the great sonnet by either author; even the greatest passages are dependent upon the structure and upon the total theme for their greatness, and must be read in their context if they are not to seem inferior in quality to the shorter poems. This does not mean that they are an inferior kind of poetry; it means that they are a different kind of poetry. In the prose of *Moby Dick*, this difference in texture is carried a little farther, but only a very little. The prose, of *Moby Dick*, though mechanically it is prose and not verse—except for those passages where it occasionally falls fragmentarily into iambic pentameter—is by virtue of its elaborate rhythms and heightened rhetoric closer in its aesthetic result to the poetry of *Paradise Lost* than to the prose of Mrs. Wharton. The instrument, as an invention, and even when we are familiar with the great prose of the seventeenth century as its background, is essentially as original and powerful an invention as the blank verse of Milton. On the whole, we may fairly regard the work as essentially a poetic performance. (pp. 73-4)

Artist's rendition of Captain Ahab. Culver Pictures, Inc.

Yvor Winters, "Herman Melville, and the Problems of Moral Navigation," in his Maule's Curse: Seven Studies in the History of American Obscurantism, New Directions, 1938, pp. 53-89.

WILLIAM ELLERY SEDGWICK (essay date 1942)

[*In his* Herman Melville: The Tragedy of Mind, *which was completed at the time of his death in 1942 and published in 1944, Sedgwick outlines a theory of tragedy informing* Moby-Dick, Mardi, *and other works by Melville. Between the human mind and heart, says Sedgwick, there exists a "fatal conflict, of which the heart is invariably the innocent victim." This conflict is the crux of the Melvillean "tragedy of mind," in which "the great man, the fairest possible semblance of humanity, is impelled to achieve a noble and impossible ideal, and in the very effort to achieve this ideal destroys the fairest semblance of humanity." According to Sedgwick, Ahab epitomizes this tragedy. Symbolizing mankind "sentient, speculative, purposive, religious," he pits his "royal" humanity against the awesome mystery of creation, represented by Moby Dick; however, in pursuing this "noble madness," Ahab's heroic idealism is perverted by his monomaniacal hatred for the White Whale, with the result that he forfeits his humanity and his life. Sedgwick's general comments concerning* Moby-Dick *and the "tragedy of mind" are included in NCLC, Vol. 3. The following excerpt is more narrowly focused, tracing the inner conflicts of both Ahab and Ishmael as they grapple with the inscrutablility of creation. Sedgwick contrasts the corrosive effects of Ahab's monomania, which leads to misperception and isolation from his fellows, with Ishmael's "spiritual balance," which en-*]

ables him to keep in view "the whole circle of life's possible issues" and to retain his vital sense of community with humankind. Other critics who contrast Ahab's and Ishmael's view of the world include Arvin (1950), Bewley (1959), Horsford (1962), Zoellner (1973), and Kazin (see NCLC, Vol. 3).]

Ahab pursues the truth as the champion of man, leaving behind him all traditional conclusions, all common assumptions, all codes and creeds and articles of faith. Although the universe of sea and sky opens around him an appalling abyss, and although the abyss seems the visible apprehension of his mind that the truth will prove that there is no truth, still he sails on. He will at any rate have the universe show its cards, so that a man may know how it stands with him, whether or not there is anything beyond himself to which he can entrust his dearest hopes, and then bear himself accordingly. "I feel deadly faint," he says, "faint, bowed, and humped, as though I were Adam staggering beneath the piled centuries since Paradise."

Ahab is nobly mad. Yet there are ambiguities about his conduct that this madness does not explain. Something else must be taken into account. We must discriminate in this matter of his madness. He says himself, "They think me mad—Starbuck does; but I'm demoniac, I am madness maddened!" That is just it. On his last trip, as the result of his mutilation, he fell prey to a terrible monomania. In all that he suffered in forty years of seafaring that injury affected him as nothing else. It was like Job's plague of boils that of all his humiliations touched nearest the quick. For "no turbanned Turk, no hired Venetian or Malay" could have smitten Ahab with more seeming malice.

> Small reason was there, to doubt then, that ever since that almost fatal encounter, Ahab had cherished a wild vindictiveness against the Whale, all the more fell for that in his frantic morbidness he at last came to identify with him, not only all his bodily woes, but all his intellectual and spiritual exasperations. The White Whale swam before him as the monomaniac incarnation of all those malicious agencies which some deep men feel eating in them, till they are left living on with half a heart and half a lung. That intangible malignity which has been from the beginning; to whose dominion even the modern Christians ascribe one-half of the worlds; which the ancient Ophites of the East reverenced in their statue devil;—Ahab did not fall down and worship it like them; but, deliriously transferring its idea to the abhorred White Whale, he pitted himself, all mutilated against it. All that most maddens and torments; all that stirs up the lees of things; all truth with malice in it; all that cracks the sinews and cakes the brain; all the subtle demonisms of life and thought; all evil, to crazy Ahab were visibly personified, and made practically assailable in Moby Dick.

> (pp. 109-10)

Without impairing his strength of mind and purpose, Ahab's monomania has all but possessed itself of Ahab. His noble madness still has its own consciousness and ends in view. But it is horribly disfigured and perverted by his monomania which held it like a vise. "Ahab's full lunacy subsided not, but deepeningly contracted. . . . But as in his narrow-flowing monomania not one jot of Ahab's broad madness had been left behind; so in that broad madness, not one jot of his great natural intellect had perished. That before living agent, now became the living instrument. If such a furious trope may stand, his special lunacy stormed his general sanity, and carried it, and turned all its concentrated cannon upon its own mad mark.''

The White Whale is all evil to Ahab. Nevertheless it is wrong to say, as do almost all the critics of *Moby Dick,* that Melville intended him to represent evil. The White Whale has a tremendous power to do harm. But unless the word is so denatured as to be synonymous with harmful or dangerous, he cannot be called evil. If a man sees evil in him, then it is his own evil which is reflected back at him.

The chapter called ''The Doubloon'' makes Melville's meaning here perfectly clear. Ahab has had the great gold coin nailed to the main-mast, the reward for the first man who hails Moby Dick. ''The ship's navel,'' Pip calls it. One day it happens that, one after another, Ahab, the three mates and members of the crew walk up to the coin and study the design of three mountain peaks stamped on the face of it. Each interprets it according to his own nature. For instance, Ahab makes out ''three peaks as proud as Lucifer,'' while Starbuck makes out three ''heaven-abiding peaks that almost seem the Trinity.'' Pip has been watching all this and when the last man has gone by he steals up to the coin. Now Pip has gone quite mad but ''man's insanity is heaven's sense; and wandering from all mortal reason, man comes at last to that celestial thought, which, to reason, is absurd and frantic; and weal or woe, feels then uncompromised, indifferent as his God.'' Reflecting on what he has just seen, Pip speaks the wonderful indifference of heaven's sense. ''I look, you look, he looks; we look, ye look, they look.'' The words, oddly remembered from Pip's negligible schooling, sound like gibberish, yet they sum up what has just transpired. The object is indifferent, the subject is all that is needed because the subject always sees himself. This is Pip's version of the solipsism of consciousness, a theme which Melville continually broaches in *Moby Dick.* Here, for certain, is the clue to Melville's meaning with respect to the White Whale. He stands for the inscrutable mystery of creation, as he also stands for what man sees in creation of himself.

Ahab's noble madness sprang from an excess of humanity. His monomania on the contrary is identified with mutilation. Truly a monomania, wherever it looks it sees only itself. It sees its evil in the White Whale. And Ahab's hate does not rest there. Be the White Whale agent or be he principal, Ahab will wreak his hate upon him. It was hardly in his nature not to believe in a divine power above creation. There must be a creator beyond his creation. There, too, Ahab saw his own hate reflected back at him. His soul and his religious sense could not but believe in God. His monomania, intruding itself, revealed a Satanic god.

Ahab's monomania is evil. It demands the ruthless sacrifice of love and preys on his common humanity. It implicates Ahab in ''the heartless voids and immensities of the universe.'' He has leagued himself with them. Or, to show the tragic aspect, which is so close to the aspect of evil in Ahab's case, we may put it this way: when Ahab thrust his harpoon into the flanks of Moby Dick, at that awful moment which came after nearly forty years of facing the interlinked wonders and terrors of the sea, just then the universe got its barbs into him. His human front broke down at last and the inscrutable inhumanity of the universe passed into him. (pp. 110-12)

Ahab's first words show the unkindness that his hate has wrought in him. ''Down, dog, and kennel,'' he says outrageously to Stubb. In the great scene on the quarterdeck when he makes his purpose known he is in the image of his monomania. He clubs down Starbuck's reluctance, elevates over Starbuck the pagan harpooners and binds the crew with satanic rites. But presently his humanity speaks out. His anguish is profoundly human. ''This lovely light, it lights not me; all loveliness is anguish to me.'' Pointed south, the *Pequod* sails into milder weather; there ''more than once did he put forth the faint blossom of a look, which, in any other man, would have soon flowered out into a smile.'' The painful isolation to which the mysterious laws of his being have brought him is driven home by the desolation of the seas beyond Good Hope. A school of harmless little fish has been following the *Pequod.* Ahab observes that they forsake the *Pequod* to follow in the wake of a passing vessel, homeward bound. In a tone of deep and helpless sorrow Ahab murmurs, ''Swim away from me, do ye?'' His is like King Lear's anguish, ''The little dogs and all, Tray, Blanch, and Sweet-heart, see, they bark at me.'' Another ship is hailed', '''Well, now, that's cheering,''' says Ahab, ''while whole thunder clouds swept aside from his brow.'' For some time the *Pequod* has been becalmed and now it is reported that the stranger ship brings a breeze with her. ''Better and better,'' Ahab says; then, showing that the deepest fountains of his being are not sealed up, ''Would now St. Paul would come along that way, and to my breezelessness bring his breeze!'' (p. 113)

[The drama of Ahab's inner conflict unfolds in his relationship with Pip.] Between him and Pip there is a bond of madness, the same in both, although they have come by it in opposite ways; the one from strength, the other from weakness. At any rate, Ahab begins to feel sympathy with and for Pip. If suffered to grow and ramify this feeling might cast out Ahab's hateful monomania and restore him to his humanity. Ahab sees the point. He says to Pip, ''There is that in thee . . . which I feel too curing to my malady . . . and for this hunt my malady becomes my most desired health,'' and orders him to his own cabin.

''No, no, no!'' Pip pleads, ''ye have not a whole body, sir; do ye but use poor me for your one lost leg; only tread upon me, sir; I ask no more, so I remain a part of ye.'' ''Oh! spite of million villains, this makes me a bigot in the fadeless fidelity of man!—and a black! and crazy!—but methinks like-cures-like applies to him too; he grows so sane again. . . . If thou speakest thus to me much more, Ahab's purpose keels up in him. I tell thee no; it cannot be.''

The situation here is akin to that between King Lear and his fool in the storm scenes:

> My wits begin to turn,
> Come on, my boy. How dost, my boy? Art cold?
> I am cold myself . . . Come, your hovel.
> Poor fool and knave, I have one part in my heart
> That's sorry yet for thee.

His sympathy with his fool is like a cordial to keep his madness off. It takes his mind from his own exasperation, and leads him to a broader fellow feeling with his kind.

The crisis in Ahab's spiritual drama follows in the chapter called ''The Symphony'' which occurs just before the White Whale is sighted and the chase begins. For Ahab's salvation it is necessary that his sympathies, renewed by Pip, should reach out to embrace the great community of men—the common continent of men—represented in Starbuck. And for a moment this seems on the point of consummation. It is a lovely mild day; a day such as seems "the bridal of the earth and sky." The stepmother world, Melville writes, which had so long been cruel, "now threw affectionate arms round his stubborn neck, and did seem to joyously sob over him, as if over one, that however wilful and erring, she could yet find it in her heart to save and to bless." Ahab's mood relents, and Starbuck observing this draws up to him. Then Ahab's sympathies flow forth, drawing him deeper and deeper into their common humanity. "Close! stand close to me, Starbuck; let me look into a human eye; it is better than to gaze into the sea or sky; better than to gaze upon God. By the green land, by the bright hearthstone! this is the magic glass, man; I see my wife and my child in thine eye." Starbuck abundantly rejoins, "Oh, my captain! my captain! noble soul! grand old heart, after all! . . . Away with me! let us fly these deadly waters! let us home! Wife and child, too, are Starbuck's—wife and child of his brotherly, sisterly, play-fellow youth; even as thine, sir, are the wife and child of thy loving, longing, paternal old age! Away! let us away—this instant let me alter the course!" Ahab continues to mingle his sympathies with Starbuck's landward thoughts. But, of a sudden, his mind takes off in its endless speculation; the sea-instinct surges up in him, and, almost simultaneously, his maniacal hate bares its visage. "Look! see yon albicore! who put it into him to chase and fang that flying-fish? Where do murderers go, man? Who's to doom, when the judge himself is dragged to the bar?" He looks up for Starbuck's answer, but "blanched to a corpse's hue with despair, the mate had stolen away." Ahab "crossed the deck to gaze over on the other side; but started at two reflected, fixed eyes in the water there. Fedallah was motionlessly leaning over the same rail."

By separating himself from Starbuck, Ahab has cut himself off from the common continent of man. He is doomed. The whole inward truth is reflected in the outward circumstances of his death. His boats all smashed, the rest of his men, all save two, have managed to climb aboard the *Pequod*, and she, her sides stove in by the Whale, begins to sink. Ahab dies alone, cut off, as he says, "from the last fond pride of meanest shipwrecked captains." Long before he had said to Starbuck about Moby Dick, "He tasks me; he heaps me." In "The Symphony" he had said, "What is it, what nameless, inscrutable, unearthly thing is it; what cozening, hidden lord and master . . . commands me; that against all natural lovings and longings, I so keep pushing, and crowding, and jamming myself on all the time?" The whole inward truth, as I say, is reflected in the manner of his death. On the previous day, the second in the three-day battle, Fedallah had disappeared. On the third and last day his corpse reappeared lashed round and round to the Whale's back. Then Ahab, stabbing his harpoon into the Whale, at the same moment gets caught up in his own line and is dragged after him, with his last breath shouting, "Toward thee I roll, thou all-destroying but unconquering whale; to the last I grapple with thee . . . while chasing thee, though tied to thee, thou damned Whale! *Thus,* I give up the spear!"

Yet we have one more glimpse of him. "Oh, lonely death on lonely life! Oh, now I feel my topmost greatness lies in my topmost grief," he cries at the end. His nobility is reaffirmed in these words. He speaks here as the noble victim of the tragedy of mind.

He dies in the grip of his own evil, his heart racked by hate. His "most brain-battering fight" has availed him nothing. The problem of evil, the responsibility for suffering, these mysteries have eluded him in the end. "How can the prisoner reach

outside except by thrusting through the wall? To me, the White Whale is that wall shoved near to me." "The dead blind wall butts all enquiring heads at last," says Ahab another time, hopeless of getting any answer to his final questions. The most terrifying aspect of Moby Dick in the last encounter is the featureless, wall-like countenance he presents to his assailants.

Still, defeated as he is in these respects, Ahab does not acknowledge defeat. So far as he can see he retains his sovereignty. Then by sheer strength of will he transcends all the considerations which had driven him on. . . . (pp. 114-18)

In Ahab we come to feel the same tremendous act of will which is required for a tremendous act of forgiveness, although the act itself has another form than forgiveness. He accepts fate. "This whole act's immutably decreed. 'Twas rehearsed . . . a billion years before this ocean rolled." Yet this act has a more positive force than resignation. His is "a prouder, if a darker faith." He reverses himself to take his station in the eternal, impersonal order of things, which is beyond right or wrong, justice and injustice, and to which all the forces of which a man has outward knowledge are the obedient servants. If this is surrender or abdication, it is in terms of absolute equality with all the known forces of creation. (pp. 118-19)

[Ishmael's] story turns on his mortal need to maintain himself against the strong drag he feels toward Ahab. (p. 120)

Ishmael's jeopardy can be put in the picturesque language of the fishery as Melville explains it under the headings, "Fast-Fish and Loose-Fish." A fast-fish is a whale who has been stuck and who, presumably, can be brought alongside and made fast to the ship whose harpoon has caught him. A loose-fish is still fair game for anybody: he is still free for anybody to have, himself first of all. Ahab is a fast-fish. The universe has got its barb in him. His humanity is transfixed. Ishmael, on the contrary, is a loose-fish. Will he keep himself so? Or will he like Ahab impale himself on the exasperating inscrutability of things? Will he cease to stand up a "sovereign nature (in himself) amid the powers of heaven, hell and earth"? "If any of those powers choose to withhold certain secrets, let them; that does not impair my sovereignty in myself; that does not make me tributary." But that, directly and indirectly, is what did impair Ahab's sovereignty.

The chapter called "The Whiteness of the Whale" begins with Ishmael saying, "What the White Whale was to Ahab has been hinted; what, at times, he was to me, as yet remains unsaid. . . . It was the whiteness of the Whale that above all things appalled me."

Thereupon he proceeds to follow the meaning of whiteness, tracking it down through all its associations in man's mind from time out of mind—as they appear in pageantry, story and ritual. Whiteness enhances beauty. It is associated with royalty and with royal preëminence, the same in kings and which, among peoples, gives "the white man ideal mastership over every dusky tribe." Whiteness is associated with gladness, with innocence, with the holy of holies. Yet, for all these associations, there is an ambiguity about whiteness; the same ambiguity that in the connotations of the sea seem to identify death with glory, bleached bones and desecration with spirituality.

> Is it [Ishmael asks] that by its indefiniteness it
> shadows forth the voids and immensities of the
> universe, and then stabs us from behind with
> the thought of annihilation, when beholding the

white depths of the Milky Way? Or is it, that as in essence whiteness is not so much a colour as the visible absence of colour, and at the same time the concrete of all colours; is it for these reasons that there is such a dumb blankness, full of meaning, in a wide landscape of snows— a colourless, all-colour of atheism from which we shrink? And when we consider that other theory of the natural philosophers, that all other earthly hues—ever stately or lovely emblazoning—the sweet tinges of sunset skies and woods; yea, and the gilded velvets of butterflies, and the butterfly cheeks of young girls; all these are but subtle deceits, not actually inherent in substances, but only laid on from without; so that all deified Nature absolutely paints like a harlot, whose allurements cover nothing but the charnel-house within; and when we proceed further, and consider that the mystical cosmetic which produces every one of her hues, the great principle of light, forever remains white or colourless in itself, and if operating without medium upon matter, would touch all objects, even tulips and roses, with its own blank tinge— pondering all this, the palsied universe lies before us a leper; and like wilful travellers in Lapland, who refuse to wear coloured and colouring glasses upon their eyes, so the wretched infidel gazes himself blind at the monumental white shroud that wraps all the prospect around him.

Under the spell of Ahab, yet going his own way, Ishmael catches sight or, better, has a ''sensational presentiment'' of the cleavage in creation which sprang up an active principle, in Ahab. (pp. 120-22)

The horror of whiteness, is it the soul's fear of death, the fear of extinction after death? Yes, but it goes beyond that. It is more fearful because more intimate. It is the soul's fear of itself. For in its own conscious self lies the seed of its destruction. The preoccupation with truth, with ideality, with ''ideal mastership,'' with ''spiritual things,'' nay, with the Deity itself, which are of the conscious soul, these are of the light principle, which ''great principle of light, forever remains white or colourless in itself.'' In the white light of the soul's preoccupation with truth all its earthly satisfactions seem illusory— all stale, flat and unprofitable. The vital needs of its own earth born humanity are but ''coloured and colouring glasses.'' Refusing to wear these kindly glasses, the soul finds itself in a void. It sees everywhere, as was seen in the White Whale, when he faced the staggering *Pequod,* its own featurelessness, its own colorlessness.

Ishmael felt himself on the verge of the abyss which he saw outwardly in Ahab's lurid light. In that extremity he felt within himself the source of all the tormenting ambiguities of life. What is life to one side of the soul is death to the other, and death at last to both.

Strong as his attachment to Ahab is, Ishmael is open to contrary influences. He is reluctant to share a bed with Queequeg at the inn at New Bedford, but the next morning brings a change. Ishmael is glad to accept Queequeg's offer of friendship and they share a pipe over it. Then Queequeg, according to the custom in his country, makes him a gift of half his possessions in silver and tobacco. Ishmael feels himself restored. He is in

the position that Ahab is in, much later, with Pip. Ishmael, however, goes the full length of his more kindly emotions; ''I began to be sensible of strange feelings. I felt a melting in me. No more my splintered heart and maddened hand were turned against the wolfish world. This soothing savage had redeemed it.''

While Ahab's hunt for the hated White Whale gets hotter, Ishmael's land sense struggles to preserve itself. Whereas Ahab curses ''that mortal inter-indebtedness'' which makes a man dependent on his fellows, Ishmael submits to the fact that it is ''a mutual, joint-stock world, in all meridians.'' Two thirds of the way through the book comes the chapter, ''A Squeeze of the Hand.'' Ishmael describes the operation of squeezing down lumps of sperm into a delicious aromatic milk. The work is done in tubs, and since many hands are at work in each tub, they often squeeze each other by mistake. ''Squeeze! squeeze! squeeze!'' cries Ishmael, himself melting again. ''I declare to you, that for the time I lived as in a musky meadow; I forgot all about our horrible oath. . . . I felt divinely free from all ill-will, or petulance, or malice, of any sort whatsoever. . . . Would that I could keep squeezing that sperm forever! For now, since by many prolonged, repeated experiences, I have perceived that in all cases man must eventually lower, or at least shift, his conceit of attainable felicity; not placing it anywhere in the intellect or the fancy; but in the wife, the heart, the bed, the table, the saddle, the fireside, the country; now that I have perceived all this, I am ready to squeeze case eternally.''

In the next chapter but one Ishmael's drama reaches its climax. It is night and he is taking his turn at the helm. The rest of the crew are employed in boiling blubber and have gathered around two vast cauldrons under which fires have been kindled. From his place in the stern Ishmael looks on, while ''the wind howled on, and the sea leaped, and the ship groaned and dived, and yet steadfastly shot her red hell further and further into the blackness. . . .'' While he was watching it came over Ishmael that ''the rushing *Pequod,* freighted with savages, and laden with fire . . . and plunging into that blackness of darkness, seemed the material counterpart of her monomoniac commander's soul.'' Then something happens. There just fails of being a fiery welding between his soul and Ahab's. He is conscious that something is very wrong. He cannot see the compass. There is nothing in front of him but a pit of gloom, ''now and then made ghastly by flashes of redness. Uppermost was the impression, that whatever swift, rushing thing I stood on was not so much bound to any haven ahead as rushing from all havens astern. A stark, bewildered feeling, as of death, came over me. . . . My God! what is the matter with me? thought I. Lo! in my brief sleep I had turned myself about. . . . In an instant I faced back, just in time to prevent the vessel from flying up into the wind, and very probably capsizing her. How glad and how grateful the relief from this unnatural hallucination of the night, and the fatal contingency of being brought by the lee!''

''Look not too long in the face of the fire, O man!'' Fire is idiosyncratic. It has a capricious, distorting intensity. It is the light of personal feelings, that take the universal sorrow of life as personal grievance, and reason for personal rage. And ''that way madness lies.'' ''There is a wisdom that is woe; but there is a woe that is madness. And there is a Catskill eagle in some souls that can alike dive down into the blackest gorges, and soar out of them again and become invisible in the sunny spaces.''

The freedom of spirit, alike to plunge and to soar. Here we come upon the significance of Ishmael's escape in the coffin life-preserver, which is more directly rendered when Ishmael, or rather Melville, taking a suggestion from the vapour that hangs about a whale's head "as you will sometimes see it—glorified by a rainbow, as if heaven itself had put its seal upon his thoughts"—writes, "And so through all the thick mists of the dim doubts in my mind, divine intuitions now and then shoot, enkindling my fog with a heavenly ray. And for this I thank God; for all have doubts; many deny; but doubts or denials, few along with them have intuitions. Doubts of all things earthly, and intuitions of some things heavenly; this combination makes neither believer nor infidel, but makes a man who regards them both with equal eye."

Against the strong attraction he feels for Ahab, Ishmael manages to keep his spiritual balance, his spiritual and intellectual freedom. Sharing Ahab's preceptions and feeling himself drawn to Ahab's desperate conclusions, he manages to so hold himself that he keeps in view the whole circle of life's possible issues. His soul, like Bulkington's, his sleeping partner, keeps "the open independence of her sea." (pp. 122-25)

> William Ellery Sedgwick, in his Herman Melville: The Tragedy of Mind, *Cambridge, Mass.: Harvard University Press, 1944, 225 p.*

CHARLES OLSON   (essay date 1947)

[*Olson, an American poet, essayist, and critic, is considered one of the major influences on American poetry after World War II. A central figure among the Black Mountain school of poets, he presented the fundamental theory of that school in his 1950 essay "Projective Verse," a radical statement proposing a philosophy of poetics and existence substantially based on the rejection of the rationalistic, ego-centered conventions dominating Western literature and society. Most critics consider this essay to be a powerful influence upon American poetry written in the 1960s, and its significance contributed greatly to Olson's stature as a literary cult figure. Olson's first major publication was a 1947 critical-theoretical study entitled* Call Me Ishmael. *In this work, there appear many of the topics he later addressed in "Projective Verse," including the destructiveness of the ego exemplified by the character of Ahab, as well as the utilization of forceful speech and prose rhythms dependent on breath. The following excerpt is taken from chapters of* Call Me Ishmael *in which Olson expatiates on the two "strongest forces" in* Moby-Dick: *America and Shakespeare. While the critic describes Shakespeare's influence on the novel's characters, structure, and language in conventional literary terms, his discussion of the American aspects of* Moby-Dick *is distinguished by his emphasis on the American drive to subdue nature. According to Olson, this drive issues from the spaciousness and harshness of the American environment and is personified in Ahab's peremptory desire to conquer Moby Dick. Furthermore, Ahab's assumption of leadership in pursuing this end reflects Melville's perception that "(1) democracy had not rid itself of overlords; (2) the common man, however free, leans on a leader, the leader, however dedicated, leans on a straw." For further commentary on the American properties of* Moby-Dick, *see the excerpts by MacMechan (1899), Chase (1949), Wilder (1952), Mushabac (1981), and Rourke (Additional Bibliography). The dramatic aspects of the novel are also discussed by Sedgwick (see* NCLC, *Vol. 3).*]

I take SPACE to be the central fact to man born in America, from Folsom cave to now. I spell it large because it comes large here. Large, and without mercy.

It is geography at bottom, a hell of wide land from the beginning. That made the first American story . . . : exploration.

Something else than a stretch of earth—seas on both sides, no barriers to contain as restless a thing as Western man was becoming in Columbus' day. That made Melville's story (part of it).

PLUS a harshness we still perpetuate, a sun like a tomahawk, small earthquakes but big tornadoes and hurrikans, a river north and south in the middle of the land running out the blood.

The fulcrum of America is the Plains, half sea half land, a high sun as metal and obdurate as the iron horizon, and a man's job to square the circle.

Some men ride on such space, others have to fasten themselves like a tent stake to survive. As I see it Poe dug in and Melville mounted. They are the alternatives.

Americans still fancy themselves such democrats. But their triumphs are of the machine. It is the only master of space the average person ever knows, oxwheel to piston, muscle to jet. It gives trajectory.

To Melville it was not the will to be free but the will to overwhelm nature that lies at the bottom of us as individuals and a people. Ahab is no democrat. Moby-Dick, antagonist, is only king of natural force, resource.

I am interested in a Melville who decided sometime in 1850 to write a book about the whaling industry and what happened to a man in command of one of the most successful machines Americans had perfected up to that time—the whaleship.

This captain, Ahab by name, knew space. He rode it across seven seas. He was an able skipper, what the fishing people I was raised with call a highliner. Big catches: he brought back holds barrel full of the oil of the sperm, the light of American and European communities up to the middle of the 19th century.

This Ahab had gone wild. The object of his attention was something unconscionably big and white. He had become a specialist: he had all space concentrated into the form of a whale called Moby-Dick. And he assailed it as Columbus an ocean, LaSalle a continent, the Donner Party their winter Pass.

I am interested in a Melville who was long-eyed enough to understand the Pacific as part of our geography, another West, prefigured in the Plains, antithetical.

The beginning of man was salt sea, and the perpetual reverberation of that great ancient fact, constantly renewed in the unfolding of life in every human individual, is the important single fact about Meville. Pelagic.

He had the tradition in him, deep, in his brain, his words, the salt beat of his blood. He had the sea of himself in a vigorous, stricken way, as Poe the street. It enabled him to draw up from Shakespeare. It made Noah, and Moses, contemporary to him. History was ritual and repetition when Melville's imagination was at its own proper beat.

It was an older sense than the European man's, more to do with magic than culture. Magic which, in contrast to worship, is all black. For magic has one purpose: compel men or non-human forces to do one's will. Like Ahab, American, one aim: lordship over nature. (pp. 11-13)

Beginner—and interested in beginnings. Melville had a way of reaching back through time until he got history pushed back so far he turned time into space. He was like a migrant back-trailing to Asia, some Inca trying to find a lost home. . . .

Melville went back, to discover us, to come forward. He got as far as *Moby-Dick.* (p. 14)

He had a pull to the origin of things, the first day, the first man, the unknown sea, Betelgeuse, the buried continent. From passive places his imagination sprang a harpoon.

He sought prime. He had the coldness we have, but he warmed himself by first fires after Flood. It gave him the power to find the lost past of America, the unfound present, and make a myth, *Moby-Dick,* for a people of Ishmaels. . . .

Whitman we have called our greatest voice because he gave us hope. Melville is the truer man. He lived intensely his people's wrong, their guilt. But he remembered the first dream. The *White Whale* is more accurate than *Leaves of Grass.* Because it is America, all of her space, the malice, the root. (p. 15)

Melville was no naïve democrat. He recognized the persistence of the "great man" and faced, in 1850, what we have faced in the 20th century. At the time of the rise of the common man Melville wrote a tragedy out of the rise, and the fall, of uncommon Ahab. (p. 64)

A whaleship reminded Melville of two things: (1) democracy had not rid itself of overlords; (2) the common man, however free, leans on a leader, the leader, however dedicated, leans on a straw. He pitched his tragedy right there.

America, 1850 was his GIVEN:

"a poor old whale-hunter" the great man;
fate, the chase of the Sperm whale, plot (economics
   is the administration of scarce resources);
the crew the commons, the Captain over them;

              EQUALS:
tragedy.

                                (pp. 64-5)

Melville saw his creative problem clearly:

He had a prose world, a NEW.
But it was "tragedie," old.
Shakespeare gave him a bag of tricks.
    The Q.E.D.: *Moby-Dick.*

The shape of *Moby-Dick,* like the meaning of its action, has roots deep in THE PLAYS. Melville studied Shakespeare's craft. For example, *characterization.* In at least three places Melville analyzes *Hamlet.* . . . [The] most interesting passage is in *The Confidence Man.* There Melville makes a distinction between the making of "odd" and the creation of "original" characters in literature. Of the latter he allows only three: Milton's Satan, Quixote, and Hamlet. The original character is

> like a revolving Drummond light, raying away
> from itself all round it—everything is lit by it,
> everything starts up to it (mark how it is with
> Hamlet).

Melville likens the effect to "that which in Genesis attends upon the beginning of things." In the creation of Ahab Melville made the best use of that lesson he knew how.

Structure, likewise. *Moby-Dick* has a rise and fall like the movement of an Elizabethan tragedy. The first twenty-two chapters, in which Ishmael as chorus narrates the preparations for the voyage, are precedent to the action and prepare for it. Chapter XXIII is an interlude, THE LEE SHORE. . . . With the

next chapter the book's drama begins. The first act ends in the QUARTER-DECK chapter, the first precipitation of action, which brings together for the first time Ahab, the crew, and the purpose of the voyage—the chase of the White Whale. All the descriptions of the characters, all the forebodings, all the hints are brought to their first manifestation.

Another interlude follows: Ishmael expands upon MOBY-DICK and THE WHITENESS OF THE WHALE. (pp. 65-6)

[The] book then moves up to the meeting with the *Jeroboam* and her mad prophet Gabriel . . . and, after that, in a third swell, into the visit of Ahab to the *Samuel Enderby* to see her captain who had lost his arm as Ahab his leg to Moby-Dick. . . . The pitch of the action is the storm scene, THE CANDLES. From that point on Ahab comes to repose, fifth act, in his fate.

In this final movement Moby-Dick appears, for the first time. It is a mistake to think of the Whale as antagonist in the usual dramatic sense. (In democracy the antagonisms are wide.) The demonisms are dispersed, and Moby-Dick but the more assailable mass of them. (pp. 66-7)

While the book is getting under way—that is, in the first forty-eight chapters—Melville allows only four "scientific" chapters on whaling to appear. Likewise as the book sweeps to its tragic close in the last thirty chapters, Melville rules out all such exposition. The body of the book supports the bulk of the matter on the Sperm whale—"scientific or poetic." Melville carefully controls these chapters, skillfully breaking them up: the eight different vessels the *Pequod* meets as she moves across the oceans slip in and cut between the considerations of cetology. Actually and deliberately the whaling chapters brake the advance of the plot. (pp. 67-8)

Stage directions appear throughout. *Soliloquies,* too. There is a significant use of the special Elizabethan soliloquy to the skull in Ahab's mutterings to the Sperm whale's head in THE SPHINX . . . . One of the subtlest *supernatural effects,* the "low laugh from the hold" in the QUARTER-DECK scene, echoes Shakespeare's use of the Ghost below ground in *Hamlet.*

Properties are used for precise theater effect. Ahab smashes his quadrant as Richard his mirror. Of them the Doubloon is the most important. Once Ahab has nailed the coin to the mast it becomes FOCUS. The imagery, the thought, the characters, the events precedent and to come, are centered on it. It is there, midstage, Volpone, gold.

Of the soliloquies Ahab's show the presence of *Elizabethan speech* most. The cadences and acclivities of Melville's prose change. Melville characterized Ahab's language as "nervous, lofty." In the soliloquies it is jagged like that of a Shakespeare hero whose speech like his heart often cracks in the agony of fourth and fifth act.

The long ease and sea swell of Ishmael's narrative prose contrasts this short, rent language of Ahab. The opposition of cadence is part of the counterpoint of the book. It adumbrates the part the two characters play, Ishmael the passive, Ahab the active. . . . The contrast in prose repeats the theme of calm and tempest which runs through the novel. Without exception action rises out of calm, whether it is the first chase of a whale, the appearance of the Spirit Spout, the storm, or the final chase of Moby-Dick precipitously following upon THE SYMPHONY.

As the strongest literary force Shakespeare caused Melville to approach tragedy in terms of the drama. As the strongest social force America caused him to approach tragedy in terms of democracy.

It was not difficult for Melville to reconcile the two. Because of his perception of America: Ahab.

It has to do with size, and how you value it. You can approach BIG America and spread yourself like a pancake, sing her stretch as Whitman did, be puffed up as we are over PRODUCTION. It's easy. THE AMERICAN WAY. Soft. Turns out paper cups, lies flat on the brush. N.G.

Or recognize that our power is simply QUANTITY. Without considering purpose. Easy too. That is, so long as we continue to be INGENIOUS about machines, and have the resources.

Or you can take an attitude, the creative vantage. See her as OBJECT in MOTION, something to be shaped, for use. It involves a first act of physics. You can observe POTENTIAL and VELOCITY separately, have to, to measure THE THING. You get approximate results. (pp. 68-9)

Melville did his job. He calculated, and cast Ahab. BIG, first of all. ENERGY, next. PURPOSE: lordship over nature. SPEED: of the brain. DIRECTION: vengeance. COST: the people, the Crew.

Ahab is the FACT, the Crew the IDEA. The Crew is where what America stands for got into *Moby-Dick*. They're what we imagine democracy to be. They're Melville's addition to tragedy as he took it from Shakespeare. He had to do more with the people than offstage shouts in a *Julius Caesar*. This was the difference a Declaration of Independence made. (pp. 69-70)

To MAGNIFY is the mark of *Moby-Dick*. . . . It is the technical act compelled by the American fact. Cubits of tragic stature. Put it this way. Three forces operated to bring about the dimensions of *Moby-Dick:* Melville, a man of MYTH, antemosaic; an experience of SPACE, its power and price, America; and ancient magnitudes of TRAGEDY, Shakespeare. (p. 71)

In exactly what way Ahab . . . [used reason] to fight the White Whale is a central concern of Melville's in *Moby-Dick*. In his Captain there was a diminution in his heart.

> From whaling, which America had made distinctly a part of her industrial empire, he took this "poor old whale-hunter," as he called him, this man of "Nantucket grimness and shagginess." Out of such stuff he had to make his tragic hero, his original. He faced his difficulties.

He knew he was denied "the outward majestical trappings and housings" that Shakespeare had for his Antony, his Lear and his Macbeth. Melville wrote:

> Oh, Ahab! what shall be grand in thee, must needs be plucked at from the skies, and dived for in the deep, and featured in the unbodied air!

He made him "a khan of the plank, and a king of the sea, and a great lord of leviathans." For the American has the Roman feeling about the world. It is his, to dispose of. He strides it, with possession of it. His property. Has he not conquered it with his machines? He bends its resources to his will. The pax of legions? the Americanization of the world. Who else is lord?

Melville isolates Ahab in "a Grand-Lama-like exclusiveness." He is captain of the *Pequod* because of "that certain sultanism

of his brain." He is proud and morbid, willful, vengeful. He wears a "hollow crown," not Richard's. It is the Iron Crown of Lombardy which Napoleon wore. Its jagged edge, formed from a nail of the Crucifixion, galls him. He worships fire and swears to strike the sun.

OVER ALL, hate—huge and fixed upon the imperceptible. Not man but all the hidden forces that terrorize man is assailed by the American Timon. That HATE, extra-human, involves his Crew, and Moby-Dick drags them to their death as well as Ahab to his, a collapse of a hero through solipsism which brings down a world.

At the end of the book, in the heart of the White Whale's destruction, the Crew and Ahab lie down together.

> All scatt'red in the bottom of the sea.

(pp. 72-3)

Charles Olson, in his Call Me Ishmael, *Reynal & Hitchcock, 1947, 119 p.*

RICHARD CHASE   (essay date 1949)

[*Chase provides a detailed discussion of American folk elements in* Moby-Dick. *Elaborating on the commentary of Rourke (see Additional Bibliography), he links various aspects of the novel's characterization, rhetoric, and narration to tall-tale exaggeration, oratorical bombast, Barnum-like showmanship, and other hallmarks of American folk culture. Chase concludes his analysis with a discussion of Melville's ironic treatment of the American "capitalist myth" in* Moby-Dick. *For a response to Chase's commentary, see Mushabac's essay dated 1981. Other critics who discuss the American properties of* Moby-Dick *include Mac-Mechan (1899), Olson (1947), and Wilder (1952). Like Chase, Mumford (1929), Zoellner (1973), and Freeman, Arvin, Camus, and Fiedler (see* NCLC, *Vol. 3) discuss the role of myth in* Moby-Dick, *while Zoellner (1973) and Brooks, Winters, Arvin, and Kazin (see* NCLC, *Vol. 3) also comment on the epic qualities of the work.*]

In Ishmael, Melville created a literary-mythical version of the American folk hero who, in all his rudeness and native vigor, was appearing in the popular literature of the day. Sam Slick, the creation of the humorist Thomas Chandler Haliburton, was the type. Sam Slick had been a clock peddler up and down the Eastern states and into Canada. As the frontier was gradually opened up, he had aspired westward. He had been a steamboatman on the Mississippi and a fur trader for the Astors in the Northwest. Like many folk heroes—Crockett himself—he answered the restless westward urge by sailing over the Pacific, far beyond the bounds of the land. (pp. 67-8)

Sam Slick possessed a great variety of talents and went quickly and restlessly from occupation to occupation, making the changes with great aplomb. (p. 68)

[Like Ishmael,] he could dance a competent jig. He was a taleteller, a liar, a flirt, a preacher of steadfast morality, and an enemy of every kind of cant and hypocrisy. Sam Slick was a sort of poor-man's Ishmael, a proletarian cousin of the soliloquizer of *Moby-Dick,* who, though he was an intellectual and an aristocrat by birth, ran no poor second in the variety of his pursuits and attainments. For Ishmael was not only schoolmaster and whaleman: he was also a stonemason, "a great digger of ditches, canals and wells, wine-vaults, cellars, and cisterns of all sorts," a merchant seaman, a moralist, a philosopher who swayed high in the spars above the Pacific with Plato in his head, a scientist who pretended to write an original work on the natural history of whales, a traveler who had discoursed with the king of the Arsacides, and a man whose best friend was a cannibal.

The metaphors which Ishmael uses and the tall tales he tells are comic mythology. The great metaphors of the book are metamorphoses. A whale transformed by nature into an albino is further transformed by the story into a god. The heroes of the story are transformed into titans, beasts, or machines. A whaling cruise is transformed into an allegory of the destiny of the world. The central tall tale is the yarn about the fabulous White Whale and the heroes who pursue him through a strange world of fact and fancy. The epical metaphors are supported and also given relief by innumerable incidental comic similes. Very often these similes transform men into animals and back again in a brief flight of fantasy. (pp. 69-70)

American myth and story is a special amalgam of fact and fantasy. Its peculiarity resides in its surface reliance on fact, while underneath the story wanders at large in fantasy. This pretense to fact and practicality of American folk literature helps to explain why the preponderance of fantasy has often escaped notice. How easy, after all, it is for an Ahab to lead his crew off on a fantastic hunt after a nearly mythical beast. Starbuck may warn that an old man's blasphemous vengeance won't fetch as much in the Nantucket market as a hold full of whale oil. But when Ahab shouts, ''Nantucket market! Hoot!'' the sailors listen to him and not to Starbuck. And so a whole crew of practical, money-grubbing Americans delivers itself over to the magical trance of Ahab's ascendancy. Still, paradoxically, the *Pequod* goes about the business of killing ordinary whales and filling the oil casks. But within the magic world of the book, practical pursuits are less real than the fantasy of the supreme hunt after the myth.

The soliloquist of *Moby-Dick* speaks in the style required by the basic relation between fact and fantasy in American folk art. Ishmael is nearly omnipresent in the book. The reader shares experiences with him in varying degrees of immediacy; we understand some of his emotions; we hear all of his story; but he remains elusive and impersonal. He is a nearly blank mask, not a specifically comic or tragic one. As Constance Rourke points out, this has been the characteristic of American storytellers from the earliest times; for the mask has been useful to Americans. ''In a primitive world crowded with pitfalls,'' writes Miss Rourke, ''the unchanging, unaverted countenance had been a safeguard, preventing revelations of surprise, anger, or dismay. The mask had otherwise become habitual among the older Puritans as their more expressive or risible feelings were sunk beneath the surface.'' And the mask was useful for less compelling purposes: the Yankee peddler had used it to sell his victim a clock or a story or an opinion. (pp. 72-3)

[*Moby-Dick*] is a monologue told through a mask, Ishmael; the mask is an abstraction from the full richness of American folk experience—it is the consciousness of that experience. The outward voice speaks more often and more explicitly; it describes objectively and states facts; it gives us the whole science of whaling and tells the story. Combining subtly with the inner voice of fantasy, it creates the larger metaphors and the allegory and the hundreds of incidental supporting figures of speech. Sometimes the outer voice breaks off entirely, and we hear the inner voice spinning out its fantasy as if it were reflecting on what the monologuist had been saying. Thus, after the persons of the drama have been introduced and the long spiel on ''cetology,'' at once science and sales talk, has been run through, there is a sudden silence, broken, however, by the reverie of

Ishmael on the masthead. . . . [Repeatedly] the outer voice falls silent and the underlying fantasy is allowed to emerge: the discourse has the rhythmic beat of withdrawal and return. We hear the inner fantasy in the dream of Fate and Free Will described in the chapter called ''The Mat-Maker.'' After the description of how a whale is killed and stripped of blubber comes the grim fantasy of ''The Funeral,'' soliloquizing on the monstrous carcase cut adrift from the ship and floating on the sea. In ''The Sphinx'' there is a sudden imaginative plunge into the ''awful water-land'' at the earth's foundations. After more cetology, an encounter between Ahab and Starbuck, and the sickness of Queequeg, comes ''The Pacific,'' in which the fantasy opens out into the enchanted spaces of the sea, into a sense of primeval wonder, freshness, and light, dissolving all the values of time into one contemporaneous moment of serene utopian vision. (pp. 73-4)

The taleteller stands aside while the persons of the drama perform their parts, parts which are frequently written in stage-drama form. But the separateness of the objective drama is no unbridged gulf. The drama breaks through the surface, but the sources of its energy and meaning are the sources of the soliloquy. And even on the surface the dramatic action sometimes merges with the soliloquy, so that in a chapter like ''The Dying Whale'' Ahab speaks with a voice indistinguishable from that of Ishmael. The persons of the drama, furthermore, stem from the folk personality of which Ishmael is the general mask. When Melville came to write **The Confidence Man,** he called it a ''Masquerade.'' *Moby-Dick* was also a masquerade.

In the 1840's Phineas T. Barnum emerged as the master showman of his day. His long, hard training as an editor, storekeeper, and lottery promoter in Connecticut and as a traveling showman had taught him what it was that appealed to the Americans of his time. They had developed a taste for the exotic and the strange, a reverence for violence and size, a hankering for monstrosities, abortions, and morbidities. The entertainment which offered these things must be presented, not as fairy tale or myth, but as science and education. And the upshot of the entertainment must be, not a sense of wonder and excitement, but a reassurance that no wonders really existed, none more wonderful, at any rate, than grotesque or pitiable mistakes of nature. In other words, the entertainment must be a hoax, in spite of the scientific presentation and in spite of the genuine wonder and excitement which the entertainment might momentarily provide. The Barnum method was very much in keeping with the technique of the tall-tale teller of the West and the sales talk of the Yankee peddler: the deadpan presentation of facts, the air of authenticity, the apparent unawareness of anything fantastic or strange or fabulous in what one was saying. The long American tradition of practical joking found verbal expression in storytelling and sales talk, for often both listener and talker were tacitly conscious that a hoax was being perpetrated. (pp. 75-6)

[*Moby-Dick*] is a literary-scientific extravaganza with very clear affinities to Barnum's showmanship. (p. 77)

At the beginning of *Moby-Dick,* the whole extravaganza which Ishmael is about to conduct is said to be a ''performance'' stage-managed by Fate and heralded in a celestial combination headline-and-advertisement appearing in ''the grand programme of Providence.'' It was to be ''a sort of brief interlude and solo between more extensive performances'':

> *Grand Contested Election for the Presidency*
> *of the United States*

WHALING VOYAGE BY ONE ISHMAEL
BLOODY BATTLE IN AFGHANISTAN

The spectator would behold all kinds of instructive curiosities: ''Feegeeans, Tongatabooarrs, Erromangoans, Pannangians, and Brighggians.'' And he would behold the feature attraction: an albino whale with a deformed back, ''a portentous and mysterious monster,'' the most marvelous of ''all the attending marvels of a thousand Patagonian sights and sounds''—the albino whale, the most awe-inspiring monster imaginable, than which the albino man is only less awe-inspiring.

> What is it that in the Albino man so peculiarly repels and often shocks the eye, so that sometimes he is loathed by his own kith and kin! It is that whiteness which invests him, a thing expressed by the name he bears. The Albino is as well made as other men—has no substantive deformity—and yet this mere aspect of all-pervading whiteness makes him more strangely hideous than the ugliest abortion.

At its lower levels, *Moby-Dick* is pure showmanship of the peculiarly American kind, science tacitly tending toward the fabulous, normality subtly misshaping itself into monstrosity, fact covertly throwing off images of itself and creating an elusive world of fantasy. Even Audubon had amused himself by hoaxing a foreign naturalist with imaginary species of birds and fish.

An undercurrent of humorous hoaxing runs through *Moby-Dick*. The dialogue between the proprietor of the Spouter-Inn and Ishmael, for example, is the speech of the familiar comic encounter between the humorous, whittling Yankee and the greenhorn. The inflated syntax and the exaggeration of the simulated emotions are in keeping with the atmosphere of this popular situation. . . . No doubt Melville was trying faithfully to reproduce the tone and language of the humor of his time and was able to do so with a certain amount of objectivity. Still, he had a weakness himself for this sort of thing, a fact which helps to account for the awkward verbiage and clumsy emotions into which his literary style sometimes degenerates.

Presumably one of the reasons for the popularity of the practical joke in America was the danger of life in the early days. Often a practical joke artificially creates a situation which appears dangerous, horrible, or uncanny and then disperses the sensation of terror with the sudden revelation that the whole thing is a hoax. It is the exercise of what Freud called ''anxiety''—the imaginative creation of danger, a psychic exercise designed to reduce the stature of real danger or to keep the senses alert against real danger; this has always been one of the main functions of myth. The tension of anxiety is relieved by the upshot of the practical joke, just as it is by the dénouement of story and myth. It is not surprising that amid the dangers of the whale hunt the idea of the practical joke should occur very urgently to Ishmael. In the chapter called ''The Hyena,'' Melville wrote:

> There are certain queer times and occasions in this strange mixed affair we call life when a man takes the whole universe for a vast practical joke, though the wit thereof he but dimly discerns, and more than suspects that the joke is at nobody's expense but his own. However, nothing dispirits, and nothing seems worth while disputing. He bolts down all events, all creeds, and beliefs, and persuasions, all hard things

> visible and invisible. . . . And as for small difficulties and worryings, prospects of sudden disaster, peril of life and limb; all these, and death itself, seem to be only sly, good-natured hits, and jolly punches in the side bestowed by the unseen and unaccountable old joker. That odd sort of wayward mood I am speaking of comes over a man only in some time of extreme tribulation; it comes in the very midst of his earnestness, so that what just before might have seemed to him a thing most momentous, now seems but a part of the general joke. There is nothing like the perils of whaling to breed this free and easy sort of genial desperado philosophy; and with it I now regarded this whole voyage of the Pequod, and the great White Whale its object.

A white whale was, after all, an improbable and even a comic beast. . . . He was a sluggish and confused monster who, despite his speed and strength, would allow a whaleboat virtually to beach itself on his back, a creature so insensitive to danger that he would stop to copulate in the very waters where the deadly harpooners were taking aim. He was a very tun of guts and gigantic cask of oil whom men lanced, bled, butchered, and cast away to the sharks and birds, an awkward satyr whose six-foot phallus was joked upon by mere men and skinned to make cassocks for blubber-cutters. The White Whale, for a moment at least, was the greatest of all hoaxes, of whom Stubb might sing:

> Oh! jolly is the gale,
> And a joker is the whale. . . .

Yet Moby-Dick is no hoax, or rather, the emotions and ideas he excites are no hoax. . . . If there is a hoax, it is directed against those who are looking for a hoax. Like any work of art, [*Moby-Dick*] is uncompromising in its emotions and its intellectual quality. It is as resolutely against the American grain as it is resolutely with it. (pp. 78-82)

There arose in this country in the 1830's and 1840's a most violent spirit of magniloquence. Oratory was one of the accomplishments of the folk hero. ''I can outspeak any man,'' was one of Crockett's boasts. An orotund native oratory, full of bombast, humorous mythology, and rough Americanisms, emerged, as if by necessity, to express the tumultuous feelings of the people. This oratorical language, which could be heard in various forms in tall talk, in congressional addresses, in sermons and written literature, had its effect on Melville. . . . (p. 89)

The following, from Mark Twain's *Life on the Mississippi*, will demonstrate the style in its more purely egomaniac mode:

> Whoo—oop: I'm the old original, iron-jawed, brass-mounted, copper-bellied corpse-maker from the wilds of Arkansas! Look at me! I'm the man they call Sudden Death and General Desolation! Sired by a hurricane, dam'd by an earthquake, half-brother to the cholera, nearly related to the small-pox on the mother's side! Look at me!

. . . [Its] counterpart could be heard in the House of Representatives, in such speeches as the following:

> MR. SPEAKER: When I take my eyes and throw them over the vast expanse of this expansive

country: when I see how the yeast of freedom has caused it to rise in the scale of civilization and extension on every side; when I see it growing, swelling, roaring, like a spring freshet—when I see all *this,* I cannot resist the idea, Sir, that the day will come when this great nation, like a young schoolboy, will burst its straps, and become entirely too big for its boots.

Sir, we want *elbow-room*—the continent—the *whole* continent—and nothing *but* the continent! And we will have it! Then shall Uncle Sam, placing his hat upon the Canadas, rest his right arm on the Oregon and California coast, his left on the eastern sea-board, and whittle away the British power, while reposing his leg, like a freeman, upon Cape Horn! Sir, the day *will*—the day *must* come!

These words of "General Buncombe" have their counterparts in Melville's books, though Melville is never so vulgar a phraseologist as the General. The feeling of power, openness, space, and freedom is the central emotion in many of Melville's best passages, and as any reader of **Moby-Dick** will know, Melville purges the mood of exaltation of all vulgarities, of mere power worship, muscle-flexing, or intoxication with the *mystique* of force and space. About such a piece of oratory as the one quoted above, he would have been of two minds: he would have deplored the jingoism and the mindlessness of the sentiments; but at the same time he would have felt a deep sympathy with the speaker. (pp. 89-90)

[Melville's exaltation of power, space, and freedom] is at once lyric in its poignancy and epic in the large nobility of its vision. The mood is not brutal or blind or chaotic or megalomaniac. It is serene and joyful, with the serenity and joy which follow upon the sense of great power controlled and great violence purged. It is the mood expressed by Father Mapple at the end of his sermon (which is itself perhaps the high point of American oratory):

> Delight is to him—a far, far upward and inward delight—who against the proud gods and commodores of this earth, ever stands forth his own inexorable self. Delight is to him whose strong arms yet support him, when the ship of this base, treacherous world has gone down beneath him. Delight is to him who gives no quarter in the truth and kills, burns, and destroys all sin though he pluck it out from under the robes of Senators and Judges.
>
> (p. 91)

[Much of what Ahab] does and says would have been familiar to those Americans of Melville's time who had no literary learning but who instinctively felt the values of folklore. (p. 94)

There is something of the "screamer" or the "ring-tailed roarer" in Ahab. We hear the same note of blind defiance when Ahab, deliberately grasping the lightning-rod chains, shouts his challenge to the electric storm as we do in the jauntier tones of the [hero Crockett's] boast that he could tame a streak of lightning as easily as he could a stallion and that, as a cure for love-sickness, he was accustomed to swallow thunderbolts. The unreasoning rage of Ahab against Moby-Dick had its frontier counterpart in the reckless destruction of the wilderness and its creatures which often went far beyond the needs of security. "Long exile from Christendom and civilization," Melville wrote,

"inevitably restores a man to that condition in which God placed him, *i.e.*, what is called savagery. Your true whale-hunter is as much a savage as an Iroquois." The "splintered heart and maddened hand . . . turned against the wolfish world" might become as much a way of life for the frontiersman-killer as it did for Ahab, no matter how much the Starbucks of the new country might denounce the mad hunt as a work of blasphemy against God's bounteous world.

There were many legends in the West concerning strange beasts encountered in the woods: jet-black coursers, fabulous mountain lions, and white steeds (which Melville himself mentions in "The Whiteness of the Whale"). Often these mythical beasts cast a spell over the hunter. The story of the enchanted hunter is told by Constance Rourke: At sunset a Kentucky woodsman suddenly noticed that the streams were running in the wrong direction, shadows were falling the wrong way, and the woodsman's own shadow "traveled around him like the marker on a sun dial, though much faster." The spell could be relaxed only by Indian incantations and the appearance of a snow-white fawn. Such a spell descends upon the *Pequod* at the moment when Ishmael falls into a trance and nearly turns the ship around and during the episode of the magically turned compasses. The end of **Moby-Dick,** too, recalls themes from the folk tales. Ahab, pulled into the sea by Moby-Dick, shared the fate of a hero called High-Chin Bob, who roped a mountain lion and rode off into eternity with the stricken and rampaging beast. And the tale of the ship rammed by a whale was known outside the factual accounts such as Owen Chase's account of the *Essex,* which Melville had read.

But there is a profounder similarity between Ahab and the folk heroes, a similarity with crucial implications in any estimate of American art and culture. The folk hero, writes Constance Rourke, stepped with one bound "out of a darkness which seems antediluvian." He had no history, had been through no tangible process of maturation, he was disinherited by whoever had begot and borne him, and his parents had vanished. He was, in short, Ishmael in search of his paternity. Lacking a knowable natural-human genesis, he was not quite human himself or quite of this world. "He was seldom deeply involved in situations," writes Miss Rourke; "even his native background was meagerly drawn. . . . Though he talked increasingly his monologues still never brimmed over into personal revelation. He was drawn with ample color and circumstance, yet he was not wholly a person. His mask, so simply and blankly worn, had closed down without a crack or a seam to show a glimpse of the human creature underneath." It is true of Ahab, the masked old man of whose past we have only shadowy details. He has been whaling for forty years; he has lost a leg; he has, we are told, "his humanities"; there are vague references to a girl-wife whom he married in his old age. Much of the wonder of **Moby-Dick,** as Charles Olson has said, comes from its antediluvian mood [see excerpt dated 1947]. In the Asiatic countries, wrote Melville, we still see "much of the ghostly aboriginalness of earth's primal generations, when the memory of the first man was a distinct recollection, and all men, his descendants, unknowing whence he came, eyed each other as real phantoms, and asked of the sun and the moon why they were created and to what end." To have no history is to have no humanity, to be a "phantom." Whatever is "grand" in Ahab, as Melville admits, "must needs be plucked at from the skies, and dived for in the deep and featured in the unbodied air." Phantoms are undeniably "real," as Melville says. And one can produce profoundly human works of art using phantoms for characters—Starbuck is, after all, the only *homme moyen sensuel* in *Moby-Dick*. (His name indicates this; it is a common one in Nantucket; and the other characters all have biblical or barbarian or comic names.) When Starbuck is on the point of openly mutinying, he becomes the center of the story. He is a human being with human emotions, an instinctive attachment to life, and poignant regret for what he has lost. He is Man ready to destroy the Phantoms. But he fails, and the central figure is Ahab once again, the central sun of a doomed phantom world.

Melville knew instinctively as well as intellectually this deep flaw in American culture. The American personality was unconditioned, only imperfectly human. The wealth of present experience in which this personality found itself was wonderful, rich, and exciting, but finally meaningless by itself. Melville's books therefore present the symbolic figure of Ishmael, seeking for his own humanity, looking from present to past for the revelation of his paternity, hunting for the form and substance of his own being, contesting with God and Nature the right to refuse the revelation. Space, that obsessive image of the American, is psychologically the Void—the Void of personality, experience, and consciousness which have been neutralized or emasculated. There are many symbols of this Void in Melville's books: the whiteness of the whale, the rainbow turned white, the pure emptiness behind the mask. . . . The inhuman horror of space and emptiness fascinated Melville, and it is what drags his characters off center, away from full humanity toward the unmanned—the humanly voided—condition of the titan, the beast, the machine, or the child. The American failure, he showed, was the sterilizing of the human core of personality. Melville's fictional heroes, searching for the secret of their paternity and their selfhood, seek to rehumanize and reprinciple the Void. (pp. 95-8)

Melville thought that the hope of America was to be found in the spirit of the West. Yet the West is an ambiguous image. It symbolizes vigor, accomplishment, nobility, magnanimity, but it is also the home of the setting sun and the abode of the dead. In *Mardi*, Melville envisioned stars and suns, mankind and all human empires, streaming westward, toward the "beacon by which the universe is steered." In the Pacific, too, all of life streamed out toward the West. As Ahab says, watching the dying whale:

> He turns and turns him to it,—how slowly, but how steadfastly, his homage-rendering and invoking brow, with his last dying motions. He too worships fire; most faithful, broad, baronial vassal of the sun!—Oh that these too-favoring eyes should see these too-favoring sights. Look! here, far water-locked; beyond all hum of human weal or woe; in these most candid and impartial seas, where to traditions no rocks furnish tablets, where for long Chinese ages, the billows have still rolled on speechless and unspoken to, as stars that shine upon the Niger's unknown source; here, too, life dies sun-wards full of faith.

In the West, Ahab saw the secret of his own doom, saw that he was betraying the spirit of life to be found there and giving himself over to the spirit of death. "Time was," he says, "when as the sunrise nobly spurred me, so the sunset soothed. No more. This lovely light, it lights not me; all loveliness is anguish to me, since I can ne'er enjoy. Gifted with the high perception, I lack the low, enjoying power; damned, most subtly and malignantly! damned in the midst of Paradise! Good night—Good night!'' It was Melville's most bitter, suspicious fear for the American that before his career had fairly got started in his wonderful country he might suddenly turn out to be damned in Paradise. If so, the reason would be clear: the superhuman struggle toward civilization would have abstracted man from his own emotions. To be damned is to be unmanned, to become the Mask, the Idea, the Will, the Titan.

In *Moby-Dick* a great man allows himself to be unmanned by the lure of God. The White Whale is for Ahab the mask which affirms, because of its horror and beauty, that all human, natural, and divine reality is concealed behind the masks of appearance. The tremendous mass of the sperm whale, propelled with such resources of power, has no face. The whale's head is a "dead, blind wall," as Ishmael observes; an inscrutable, menacing blankness. . . . The pursuit of the White Whale forces the hunter more and more into an inhuman, unnatural world where there is no reality but the mirage of shifting, mocking masks. It is this world which above all Starbuck fears and hates, knowing that there can be no commitment to life in such a world, no leavening of the superhuman will with human emotions. To Starbuck, the White Whale, though wondrous and terrible, is, finally, a dumb brute; and that is the fact which he will not abandon. For Starbuck it is blasphemous to strike a dumb brute with Ahab's kind of insane vengeance, a blasphemy against nature and man. This basic difference between Ahab and Starbuck is far more than a simple difference in philosophy. Their instinctive disagreement about the whale is a psychological and cultural difference.

As patriots we may enjoy with Melville his excursions into American folklore. It was, for him, a healthy impulse. Like Ahab, he was gifted with the high perception; without it *Moby-Dick* would lack the over-all structure of its universal-historical allegory. Yet underneath the high perception, supporting and nourishing it, Melville knew there must be a low enjoying power. This he sought and found in the folk spirit of his country. As Constance Rourke writes, beneath the mask the variegated folk hero was "a symbol of triumph, of adaptabilility, or irrepressible life—of many qualities needed to induce confidence and self-possession among a new and unamalgamated people." In the folk spirit, as none knew better than Melville, there was much which was destructive of its own better self. But in it he sought and found the "humanities" which Ahab had in but far too small a quantity. To have "confidence" Melville knew to be vital for his countrymen, which helps to explain the bitterness of his denunciation, in *The Confidence Man,* of the various forms of false confidence discernible in the American character. Most important, he knew that the American quest must be to come into possession of the human self. It is selfhood from which his false heroes flee in their disastrous abdications.

Moby-Dick is an American epic; so far it seems to be *the* American epic. An epic is the response of a poet to the body of received and implicit myth which his culture bequeaths to him. . . . It is fortunate that Melville had the American knack of exploitation, which allowed him to find more in the folk myths of his country than one might have thought was there and which allowed him to pluck all manner of curiosities and mythical odds and ends out of the world's store. The pack of the peddler contained a weird array of wares.

But there *is* a received and implicit myth in *Moby-Dick*. The high perception makes it into the universal allegory; the low enjoying power establishes it as the folk foundation. This myth is capitalism. *Moby-Dick* remains intransigently a story of the whaling industry; a hymn to the technical skill of the heroes and the marvelous perfection of their machine and to the majesty of what they appropriate from the sea—the sheer weight, mass, wealth, power and beauty of the whale's body; a saga of the exploitation of nature and man for profit or for righteousness. . . . There is no doubt that the voyage is an industrial enterprise bossed by Ahab, the nineteenth century type of the manager of an absentee-owned plant. All the facts are there: the wage of the sailor, the occupational hazards, the deployment of personnel, in the field, the precautions to be taken and the risks to be calculated in each operation, the nature and care of the various kinds of equipment—all the intricate parts and economy of the machine which reduced the whale by a series of lovingly described processes to the useful oil in the casks. Almost every process included the possibility that a man might be killed; if so, his death was at once the murder of an industrial worker and the ritual sacrifice of a hero.

The hunt for the White Whale is anything but an abandonment of the capitalist myth. Ahab may hoot at the Nantucket market, but he never hoots at capitalism. Quite the contrary, he accepts its full disastrous implications. Ahab is the epic transmutation of the American free enterpriser, and the White Whale is the transmutation of the implicit spiritual meaning of free enterprise. The meaning is clear: the American who exploits nature soon learns to pursue a mysterious and dangerous ideal, and this pursuit transforms him into the likeness of what he pursues. Ahab was once a child and then a man. He was injured in line of duty by the enterprise of which he was a part. A suffering man, he became dedicated. "Unmanned," he became through an abortive and illusory transfiguration a titan, a savior. Into his ken swam the obsessive White Whale, and pursuing him, the titan was transformed into his likeness—into the beast, the machine, and the purity of death.

"I try all things," says Melville in *Moby-Dick*. "I achieve what I can." His plight as an epic writer was less desperate than his words might imply, for he did not have to invent the central epic theme. That was given to him by his culture; he had merely to recognize it, though that was no doubt difficult enough. What he had to do was adduce the body of supporting mythology, clothe the skeleton with flesh and the habiliments of style. For this purpose "all things" were grist for the mill—jokes, puns, dances, ceremonies, side shows, catalogues, scientific discourses, orations, meditations, confessions, sermons, tall tales, redactions of Old World mythologies, and literary conventions. Much more so than the Homeric epic, *Moby-Dick* remains the willed, self-generating, and idiosyncratic act of a partly lost and un-cultured man. But this is the typical act of the American genius. (pp. 98-102)

> *Richard Chase, in his* Herman Melville: A Critical Study, *The Macmillan Company, 1949, 305 p.*

W. H. AUDEN (essay date 1950)

[*Auden, an Anglo-American poet, essayist, playwright, critic, editor, and translator, is considered a major twentieth-century poet and an influential literary figure. His early poetry and criticism are informed by the psychological and political theories of Sigmund Freud and Karl Marx; his later work is heavily influenced by his conversion to Christianity. While some critics charge that the radical change in Auden's aesthetic philosophy is inconsistent and contradictory, Auden believed that an artist's work is by its nature evolutionary and responsive to the changing moral and ideological climate of the age. One of his best-known critical works,* The Enchafèd Flood; or, The Romantic Iconography of the Sea, *is excerpted below. Auden begins by proposing that Father Mapple's pronouncements concerning the relationship between the self and salvation serve as "moral presuppositions" for judging the behavior of the characters in the novel. He then proceeds to apply these presuppositions to the actions and attitudes of the* Pequod's *crew, concluding that the mariners are afflicted with a variety of spiritual ills ranging from Starbuck's cowardice to Ahab's "defiant despair." NCLC, Vol. 3 includes additional commentary by Auden on* Moby-Dick. *For further commentary on Melville's treatment of religion in the novel, see the excerpts by Murray (1951), Thompson (1952), and Hillway (1979).*]

[Father Mapple's sermon] is not, as has sometimes been said, a magnificent irrelevance, but an essential clue to the meaning of the whole book. The story of Jonah is the story of a voyage undertaken for the wrong reasons, of learning repentance through suffering and a final acceptance of duty. . . . [Jonah knows the Word]; he flees from the divine command out of aesthetic pride, a fear that he will not be listened to and admired, not be an aesthetic hero. He is punished for his refusal by being confronted with the really aesthetically great, the storm and the whale, compared with which the greatest emperor is a puny weakling, and then, in the whale's belly, he is deprived of even the one gift he had, his ability to hear the Word. Humbled, he does not despair but repents and trusts in the God whom he can no longer hear. God forgives him, he is cast up on the land, and sets off to fulfill his vocation.

In drawing the moral, Father Mapple says two apparently contradictory things.

1) If we obey God, we must disobey ourselves; and it is in this disobeying of ourselves, wherein the hardness of obeying God consists.

2) Delight is to him—a far, far upward and inward delight—who against the proud gods and commodores of this earth ever stands forth his own inexorable self. (pp. 116-17)

When we have finished the book, we realise why Father Mapple's sermon was put in where it was: in order that we might know the moral presuppositions by which we are to judge the speeches and actions of Ahab and the rest. (p. 119)

The four squires are representatives of the four nonwhite Pagan races.

Queequeg is	a South Sea Islander
Tashtego	a North American Indian
Dagoo	an African Negro
Fedallah	an Asiatic

(p. 121)

In Father Mapple's terms, all four are themselves; but, since they are unconscious . . . [of God or the self], they are only potentially themselves. Queequeg is not only himself but obeys God without having to disobey himself. Fedallah obeys himself and the Devil, i.e., denies the true God.

None of the three mates is an evil man. All are physically brave, loyal and free from malice. Yet all suffer from spiritual sloth, which is a form of cowardice, so that none is his complete self; all have refused to grow up. They have, as it were, started on Ishmael's voyage and then tried to draw back, but that voyage is like a sea voyage in that once the boat has left the shore, you cannot get off, you can only play the child's game of "let's pretend we are on shore." [Like Jonah, each] of them in his own way takes ship from Tarshish to flee from the presence of the Lord.

Starbuck has gone farthest and is the most fitted for the voyage so that he suffers most from his refusal to go all the way.

He has a religious reverence for life and death; he knows that the fear of the Lord is the beginning of wisdom. That is why he will have no man in his boat who is not afraid of the whale. (pp. 123-24)

He alone of the three has an inkling that Ahab's soul is in danger, and therefore looks at him not only with mingled fear and admiration but with pity and love.

He can tell Ahab the truth, as when he rebukes him for seeking ''vengeance on a dumb brute that simply smote thee from blindest instinct,'' or again ''Moby Dick seeks thee not. It is thou, thou that madly seekest him.''

He knows that in obeying Ahab he is disobeying God, yet before Ahab's passion his knowledge and righteous fear are powerless: ''I think I see his impious end, but feel that I must help him to it. 'Tis my miserable office to obey, rebelling.''

Because fear may be the right way to begin, but it is not enough to go on with. For in the fear which is reverence is mixed the fear which is cowardice, the fear that the whole truth may be too much to encounter, that too much will be asked of me, that in fact God will not add His grace to one's own powers. Thus, Starbuck remains in the childish religious state of believing in omens like the Squid. ''Almost rather had I seen Moby Dick and fought him, than to have seen thee, thou white ghost.'' He dare not look at the Doubloon too closely. ''This coin speaks wisely, mildly, truly, but still sadly to me. I will quit it, lest Truth shake me falsely.'' And looking down into the Ocean on a beautiful calm day he sees belief and reason, faith and knowledge as contradictory. He keeps to his belief but at the cost of refusing to experience. His faith is insufficient for that. (pp. 124-25)

It is characteristic of Stubb that, of the three of them, he should be the one who is always describing himself to himself to reassure himself.

> I guess he's got what some folks ashore call a conscience, it's a kind of Tic-Dolly-Row they say—worse than a tooth-ache. Well, well, I don't know what it is, but the Lord keep me from catching it. Damn me, it's worth a fellow's while to be born into the world, if only to fall asleep. Damn me, but all things are queer, come to think of 'em. But that's against my principles. Think not, is my eleventh commandment, and sleep when you can is my twelfth. . . .

> A laugh's the wisest easiest answer to all that's queer.

> I know not all that may be coming but be it what it will, I'll go to it laughing.

> It's against my religion to get mad.

> I am Stubb and Stubb has his history but here Stubb takes oaths that he has always been jolly.

For the comic always involves standing outside a situation, and so a man who makes a religion of the comic must be humorously self-regarding. (pp. 125-26)

[The comic] does not involve suffering, either directly in the subject or indirectly by sympathetic identification with those involved in the contradiction.

There is, however, a particular religious form of the comic in which suffering is involved, i.e., a man may laugh at suffering on condition that 1) it is he who suffers, 2) he knows that, ironically, this suffering is really a sign that he is in the truth, that he who suffers is really blest.

But the suffering must be real, i.e., not enjoyed. When Stubb thinks about his wife, he says:

> What's my juicy little pear at home doing now? Crying its eyes out?—Giving a party to the last arrived harpooners, I dare say, gay as a frigate's pennant, and so am I—fa, la! . . .

It looks at first as if this might be humorous resignation, but the end of the sentence gives him away. He is not suffering at the thought of his wife's infidelity, either because he no longer loves her, or because he is not really imagining a real scene, but a comic French farce in a theatre.

A man who makes a religion out of the comic is unable to face suffering. He is bound to deny it or to look the other way. When Stubb looks at the Doubloon, he abstracts from it the features which can fit into his view of life and ignores the rest.

> There's a sermon now, writ in high heaven, and the sun goes through it every year, and yet comes out of it all alive and hearty.

Stubb, however, is not soulless, i.e., he knows that suffering and mysteries which are not comic exist:

> I wonder whether the world is anchored anywhere, if she is she swings with an uncommon long cable.

He senses, where Flask does not, the demonic qualities of Fedallah; but his solution is to put him away where he can't be seen. . . . And he gives himself away in his dream about Ahab, which is a terror dream, but on waking he does not meet this fact but says: ''The best thing you can do, Flask, is to let that old man alone; never speak to him, whatever he says.''

Starbuck fears God; Stubb fears suffering. Starbuck knows what he fears; Stubb doesn't, which makes him all the more insistent in his defence. As in a characteristic moment of frankness—the frankness itself is a defensive theatre—Stubb confesses to Starbuck: ''I am not a brave man; never said I was a brave man; I am a coward; and I sing to keep up my spirits. And I tell you what it is, Mr. Starbuck, there's no way to stop my singing in this world but to cut my throat.''

When he does not or cannot sing, he turns away like a child from the frightening world to the comforting breast, i.e., to his pipe, which is never out of his mouth. The sight of the whale's blood is slightly disquieting to him so that he substitutes a pleasant image: ''Would now it were old Orleans Whiskey,'' and his last thought in the moment of death is food. ''Oh Flask, for one red cherry ere we die.''

In his relations to his neighbor, he substitutes good-fellowship for love. (pp. 126-29)

The difficulty about good-fellowship as a principle of social conduct is that one's neighbor must also be a good-fellow, i.e., not a sufferer. Thus Stubb, who prides himself on his kindness, is the one who becomes guilty of destroying an innocent boy's sanity, for he cannot understand Pip's kind of fear, which cannot be laughed off. He does not guess what the consequences of leaving Pip in the water will be, because he has never really looked at him.

The best comment on Stubb is an aphorism of Kafka's:

> You can hold back from the suffering of the world, you have free permission to do so and it is in accordance with your nature, but perhaps this very holding back is the one suffering that you could have avoided . . . .

Flask is the least sympathetic of the three. Stubb, when confronted with mystery and suffering, looks the other way; Flask denies that it exists. Stubb would never laugh at the spectacle of a wrecked boat. Flask does. In relation to others he has the child's shamelessness and lack of dignity. For instance, his conduct in a whale-boat:

> "Lay me on—lay me on! O Lord, Lord! but I shall go stark, staring mad: See! see that white water!" And so shouting, he pulled his hat from his head, and stamped up and down on it; then picking it up, flirted it far off upon the sea; and finally fell to rearing and plunging in the boat's stern like a crazed colt from the prairie.

He is also the only one whom Peleg warns against fornication.

Towards animals he is cruel like a child.

> A nice spot. Just let me prick him there once.

Towards the mysterious, however, instead of a child's reverence, he has developed the underdog's Philistinism; he trivialises everything. The whale is only a magnified water-rat; the doubloon is only a round thing made of gold worth sixteen dollars or nine hundred and sixty cigars.

His reaction to imminent death is equally characteristic. Starbuck says, "May God stand by me now"; Stubb thinks of food; Flask thinks of his mother and money: "I hope my poor mother has drawn my part-pay ere this; if not, few coppers will now come to her for the voyage." (pp. 129-30)

Pip is more significant, as his despair is dialectically related to Ahab's. Between them they represent the two opposite kinds of despair which Kierkegaard defines as:

> The despair of weakness. i.e., The despair of willing despairingly not to be oneself

and

> The despair of defiance. i.e., The despair of willing despairingly to be oneself.

Pip is a slave, i.e., the one who has no authority, aesthetic, ethical or religious. He should never have been taken on this voyage at all, and he is innocent, for he never wanted to, knowing that he lacks the qualities required:

> Have mercy on this small Black boy down here. Preserve him from all men that have no bowels to feel fear.

His proper place is in a fairy story where fairy godmothers and animals assist him against all probability to vanquish the giant (who kills himself by mistake) and marry the Princess. But it has not been so. Papageno has been made to go through the ordeal and it has destroyed him.

He is bound to Ahab because they have both suffered a catastrophe, Ahab through his own deliberate original attack on the whale, Pip through the thoughtless action of the decent fellow Stubb. But Ahab is the exception, for whom exceptional situations are made; Pip is not. Ahab, knowing that he is the exception, is outraged by a catastrophe he was not powerful enough to command; Pip is outraged by not being up to the command of the situation. Thus Ahab's madness is directed against the whale; Pip's is directed against himself. "Seek not Pip who's now been missing long. If ye find Pip, tell all the Antilles he's a runaway; a coward, a coward, a coward. Tell them he jumped from a whaleboat. I'd never beat my tambourine over Pip, and hail him general." Having lost himself, he can only exist through the self of another, and where should he find that but in Ahab, the defiant self, so that he cannot bear to be out of sight, and he only exists in obeying him.

> Here he this instant stood; I stand in his air,— but I'm alone. Now were even Pip here I could endure it, but he's missing . . . let's try the door. What? neither lock, nor bolt, nor bar; and yet there's no opening it. It must be the spell; he told me to stay here . . . Hist! above there. I hear ivory—Oh, master! master! I am indeed down-hearted when you walk over me. But here I'll stay, though this stern strikes rocks; and they bulge through; and oysters come to join me. . . .
>
> (pp. 131-33)

Ahab on his side is bound to Pip, and to no one else, not even Starbuck. As the conscious defiant despairer, he recognises that Pip is his antitype and envies Pip's humility as Pip admires his strength. "There's that in thee, poor lad, which I feel too curing for my malady. Like cures like; and for this hunt, my malady becomes my most desired health."

If each could have had the qualities of the other added to his own, when they encountered catastrophe, i.e., if Ahab had had Pip's humility as well as his own strength and vice versa, both would have been saved.

Kierkegaard defines defiant despair as follows:

> . . . with hatred for existence it wills to be itself, to be itself in terms of its misery; it does not even in defiance or defiantly will to be itself, but to be itself in spite . . . Whereas the weak despairer will not hear about what comfort eternity has for him, so neither will such a despairer hear about it, but for a different reason, namely, because this comfort would be the destruction of him as an objection against the whole of existence. It is (to describe it figuratively) as if an author were to make a slip of the pen, and that this clerical error became conscious of being such—perhaps it was no error but in a far higher sense was an essential constituent in the whole exposition—it is then as if this clerical error would revolt against the author, out of hatred for him were to forbid him to correct it, and were to say, "No, I will not be erased, I will stand as a witness against thee, that thou art a very poor writer." . . .

Of this despair, Ahab is a representation, perhaps the greatest in literature.

Before he was born there were prophecies of some extraordinary destiny, which caused his mother to name him Ahab, after the son of Omri, of whom it is written in the book of Kings that he "did evil in the sight of the Lord above all that were before him," that reared up an altar for Baal, that he made a grove, and constructed an ivory house.

He himself declares that the prophecy was that he should be dismembered. Now a prophecy is either true or false, and in either case the only thing to do is to ignore it. If it is true, then it will happen and must be accepted when it occurs, and it is defiance either to try to make it happen or to try to avoid it. If it is false, it will not happen, and if one makes it happen one is not really fulfilling a prophecy at all but doing what one has chosen to do. (pp. 133-35)

So [Ahab] encounters Moby Dick and loses a leg. (p. 135)

It is interesting to note the occasion during the voyage when he breaks his leg, jumping off the *Enderby,* whose captain has also lost an arm to Moby Dick without despairing and whose doctor ascribes Moby Dick's apparent malice to clumsiness. The example of sanity with authority is too much for Ahab, and he must again goad himself to his resolution.

So in defiance he takes his vow: "I now prophesy that I will dismember my dismemberer. Now then, be this prophet and the fulfiller one. That's more than ye, ye great gods, ever were."

The defiant man and the obedient man use the same words "It is not I but Fate," but their meaning is opposite. (p. 137)

> *W. H. Auden, "Ishmael—Don Quixote," in his* The Enchafèd Flood; or, The Romantic Iconography of the Sea, *1950. Reprint by Vintage Books, 1967, pp. 90-151.*

NEWTON ARVIN   (essay date 1950)

[*In his* Herman Melville, *Arvin discerns four "planes of significance" in* Moby-Dick: *the literal, the psychological, the moral, and the mythic. The following excerpt represents his reading of the novel as a projection of Melville's unconscious fears and desires, many of which the critic traces to the author's "excessive and . . . eventually crippling" love for his mother, Maria Melville. Ahab is thus interpreted as a victim of Oedipal bitterness and castration; Moby Dick is taken to represent a bisexual "archetypal Parent"; and Ishmael is depicted as the lone survivor of the sexual strife, saved by his capacity to love. Arvin's commentary on the moral and mythic significance of* Moby-Dick *is excerpted in NCLC, Vol. 3. For further commentary on the psychosexual aspects of* Moby-Dick, *see the excerpts by Murray (1951), Fiedler (1966), and Auden (NCLC, Vol. 3). The role of symbolism in the novel is also considered in the criticism of Lawrence (1923), Bewley (1959), Horsford (1962), Kulkarni (1970), Hillway (1979), and Mather, Lawrence, Mumford, Aiken, Winters, Sedgwick, Maugham, Auden, and Priestley (NCLC, Vol. 3). Like Arvin, Sedgwick (1942), Bewley (1959), Horsford (1962), Zoellner (1973), and Kazin (NCLC, Vol. 3) contrast Ahab's and Ishmael's view of the world.*]

[On one plane, *Moby-Dick*] is an oneiric or dreamlike projection of Melville's unconscious wishes and obscure inward contests. *On one plane* the book is this, and on that plane only; for of course *Moby Dick* is not a dream but a work of imaginative art, and this means that it is the product of a complex creative process of which a great part has been conscious, deliberate, reflective: the formless spontaneity of an actual dream, along with much else, has been transcended. It shares with a dream, however, its sources in the unconscious, its dependence on

irrational symbols, and its power to give expression to deep, instinctive, irrational fears and desires. How much of the sway it exercises over us depends on this!

When we read *Moby Dick* in this manner we are conscious of being presented at the very outset with one dominating oneiric image, the image of self-destruction; and then, as the action unrolls itself, and Ahab advances slowly to the fore-scene, we are given its counterpart and equivalent, the image of murderous destructiveness directed outward against the Other. From one point of view, what is dreamlike in the book may be said to move back and forth between these two poles, the suicidal wish, the longing for self-extinction, and its necessary antithesis, so deeply dependent upon it emotionally, the desire to inflict death upon what is, or what one imagines to be, the source of one's suffering. To undergo a kind of suicide is the motive that, along with the idea of the Whale (so closely bound up with it), impels Ishmael in the first place to go off to sea. Whenever, he says, he finds himself involuntarily pausing before coffin warehouses, and bringing up the rear of every funeral he meets, then he accounts it high time to get to sea as soon as he can: "With a philosophical flourish Cato throws himself upon his sword; I quietly take to the ship." There follows a series of hypnotic meditations on the allurements of the sea, of water generally, in which that element figures, though in a complex and iridescent way, as a symbol of death; of a return to the primal liquidity, oblivion, nonbeing. The sailing of the *Pequod* is to be for Ishmael a temporary passage out of existence.

Meanwhile, however, the death-wish has met with a check and a corrective; Thanatos has entered into a contest with Eros, and Ishmael, in his deathful loneliness encountering the savage Queequeg, has formed a solemn friendship with him, formed what he calls a marriage; the longing to love and to be loved has evoked its own oneiric symbol, and from this point forward Ishmael gradually ceases to be the man committed wholly to death. A dreamlike "displacement" occurs and the accent shifts to Ahab, another embodiment of the self, and to Ahab's will to death, which expresses itself not directly as the conscious purpose of suicide, but indirectly as the purpose to wreak destruction on Moby Dick. It is true that Ishmael succumbs with part of his being to Ahab's ferocious hate: "A wild, mystical, sympathetical feeling was in me," he says; "Ahab's quenchless feud seemed mine." But the verb is "seemed" not "was," and already there is the possibility of Ishmael's recovering the will to live. (pp. 170-71)

[Ahab] is what our wildest, most egoistic, most purely destructive malevolence could wish to be, this old Quaker skipper from Nantucket; obsessed to the point of monomania with the will to destroy the hated thing, yet free from all mere smallnesses, "a grand, ungodly, godlike man." He is our hatred ennobled, as we would wish to have it, up to heroism. Moreover, he has in fact been terribly and vitally injured by Moby Dick. The Whale, in what looks like conscious malice, has reaped Ahab's leg away with his frightful, sickle-shaped jaw, and Ahab must now rely on a dead, artificial leg made of a Sperm Whale's jawbone. A kind of castration, in short, has been not only imagined and dreaded but inflicted, and the phallic source of vital potency has been replaced by an image of impotence and lifelessness, constructed from the skeleton of the injurer himself. Not only so, but in a kind of redoubled, repetitive, dreamlike manner, we hear that this apparently impotent limb has itself turned upon Ahab, and that before the sailing of the *Pequod* he had been found one night fallen in the streets of Nantucket with his artificial leg so twisted about that it had smitten his groin like a stake and almost pierced it.

A profound sexual injury is transparently symbolized here, and Ahab's "ivory" leg is an equivocal symbol both of his own impotence and of the independent male principle directed cripplingly against him. It had been fashioned from the polished bone of a Sperm Whale's jaw, though not of course from Moby Dick's own: what, then, does Moby Dick himself, on this deep instinctive plane, shadow forth? It would be easiest to say simply the father, the father who imposes constraint upon the most powerful instincts, both egoistic and sexual; the father also who threatens even to destroy the latter by castration and may indeed, in all but the literal sense, carry out the threat. On the deepest level, this is the oneiric truth about Moby Dick, but it is Melville with whom we have to reckon throughout, and for whom we have to remember how soon, and how overbearingly, the paternal role was played by Maria Melville. On every ground we are forced to confront a profound ambiguity in Moby Dick and to end by confessing that he embodies neither the father merely nor the mother but, by a process of condensation, the *parental* principle inclusively. Of his basic maleness there can be no question, not only because we are everywhere reminded of his preternatural power and masculine strength but because, in detail, we are required to contemplate the "battering-ram" of his head, the highly prized spermaceti with which it is so richly stored, his phallus ("The Cassock"), and his tail (with its "Titanism of power"); there is even a suggested association with the phallic serpent-god of the Ophites. Yet along with all this we cannot ignore a certain bisexuality in the image, if not literally of Moby Dick, then of the Sperm Whale generally; a bisexuality that is conveyed to us partly by the glimpses we have into his "beautiful" mouth and "the great Kentucky Mammoth Cave of his stomach"—that stomach in which, as Father Mapple's sermon reminds us, Jonah was swallowed up as in a womb—but also, and chiefly, by the obstetric imagery of the chapter . . . in which Tashtego falls into the liquid depths of a Sperm Whale's severed head and is rescued or "delivered," like a baby, by Queequeg.

Moby Dick is thus the archetypal Parent; the father, yes, but the mother also, so far as she becomes a substitute for the father. And the emotions Moby Dick evokes in us are the violently contradictory emotions that prevail between parent and child. Too little, curiously, has been made of this; what dominates most accounts of the White Whale is the simple vindictive emotion that Ahab is alleged to feel toward him, and of course there can be no question of his Oedipal bitterness toward Moby Dick: his conviction that the Whale is the embodiment of "all the subtle demonisms of life and thought"; in short, "all evil." Yet hatred of this obsessive and even paranoid sort is but the deformation of a still more deep-seated love, and Ahab is as tightly bound to Moby Dick as an unhappy child to a parent too passionately loved. The emotion, however, that the Sperm Whale inspires is not restricted to Ahab's monomaniac vengefulness: from the very outset we are conscious also of Ishmael's feelings, and though at one pole these are identified with Ahab's, at the other they are by no means the same. They are, at any rate, more openly and obviously contradictory: the "grand hooded phantom," as it swims before Ishmael's fancy, may inspire a kind of fear but it inspires also an intensity of mystical longing that is something like love. It is a sort of love that lies behind that passionate preoccupation with every detail, however trifling, that characterizes the regarded object, and it is a sort of love, though an imperfectly fulfilled one, that brings Moby Dick before our imaginations

as a creature of "majestic bulk," "pervading dignity," and "appalling beauty."

In his role of archetypal parent, in fact, Moby Dick is the object of an excessive and an eventually crippling love, as Maria Melville was for her son; and the consequence is the vital injury symbolized by the loss of Ahab's leg, an injury to the capacity for heterosexual love. Both Ahab and Ishmael suffer in this way, but Ahab far the more terribly of the two. Ishmael, by somehow preserving a complexity of feeling toward the White Whale, has preserved also his capacity for selfless love even though this is directed toward his own sex and even toward a member of his own sex, Queequeg, who embodies both the grandeur and the limitations of the primitive, the prerational, the instinctive. Nevertheless it is love that Ishmael deeply feels toward Queequeg, and it is the imagination of an even more comprehensive love that comes to him as he sits before a tub of cooling spermaceti, squeezing its congregated globules back into fragrant fluid, and washing his hands and his heart, as he does so, of "our horrible oath." The capacity to imagine an all-embracing love, which proves to be Ishmael's salvation, Ahab has fatally lost. He has lost it so far that he has succeeded in hardening his heart even toward his young wife and their child, whom he has frankly deserted; what wretched vestiges of pure human feeling are left in him go out only to the small black boy Pip, and to him reluctantly. Ahab is dedicated now to mere destruction, and he ends by attaining his suicidal wish and meeting his death by water. Ishmael, thanks to his rejection of mere hatred, survives the wreck; is picked up before he drowns by "the devious-cruising *Rachel*," the vessel that is itself a symbol of bereaved motherhood. In the end, the dream embodies a will to live triumphing over the will to die. (pp. 171-74)

Newton Arvin, in his Herman Melville, *William Sloane Associates, 1950, 316 p.*

HENRY A. MURRAY (essay date 1951)

[*In his letters to Hawthorne, Melville described* Moby-Dick *as a "wicked book" (see the excerpt dated November, 1851) and suggested that he had baptized the work in the name of the devil. Taking note of these remarks, Murray affirms the "diabolic" nature of the novel in the excerpt below, explicating* Moby-Dick *as an attack on nineteenth-century American mores and the religious traditions on which they were founded. According to Murray, Melville resented the prohibitions that were imposed on him by his Calvinist heritage and enforced by American society. Moby-Dick in turn reflects this tension, being a symbolic struggle between the "horde of primitive drives, values, beliefs, and practices which the Hebraic-Christian religionists rejected and excluded, and . . . forced into the unconscious mind of Western man," represented by Ahab and his followers, excluding Starbuck, and "the Old Testament Calvinistic conception of an affrighting Deity and his strict commandments, the derivative puritan ethic of nineteenth-century America and the society that defended this ethic," represented by Moby Dick. As the critic points out, this conflict is susceptible to psychoanalytic interpretation as a struggle between "an insurgent Id" and "an oppressive cultural Superego." Murray originally presented his remarks in a September 3, 1951, address at Williams College commemorating the centennial of the publication of* Moby-Dick. *For further discussion of Melville's treatment of religion in the novel, see the excerpts by Auden (1950), Thompson (1952), and Hillway (1979). Other commentators on the psychosexual aspects of* Moby-Dick *include Arvin (1950), Fiedler (1966), and Auden (NCLC, Vol. 3).*]

I shall not cite the abundant proof for the now generally accepted proposition that in **Moby-Dick** Melville "meant" something—something, I should add, which he considered "terrifically true" but which, in the world's judgment, was so harmful "that it were all but madness for any good man, in his own proper character, to utter or even hint of." What seems decisive here is the passage in Melville's celebrated letter to Hawthorne: "A sense of unspeakable security is in me this moment, on account of your having understood the book." From this we can conclude that there *are* meanings to be understood in *Moby-Dick,* and also—may we say for our own encouragement?—that Melville's ghost will feel secure forever if modern critics can find them, and, since Hawthorne remained silent, set them forth in print. Here it might be well to remind ourselves of a crucial statement which follows the just quoted passage from Melville's letter: "I have written a wicked book." The implication is clear: all interpretations which fail to show that *Moby-Dick* is, in some sense, wicked have missed the author's avowed intention. (pp. 440-41)

[My] version of the main theme of *Moby-Dick* can be presented . . . [briefly and is] limited to two hypotheses.

The first of them is this: Captain Ahab is an embodiment of that fallen angel or demi-god who in Christendom was variously named Lucifer, Devil, Adversary, Satan. The Church Fathers would have called Captain Ahab "Antichrist" because he was not Satan himself, but a human creature possessed of all Satan's pride and energy, "summing up within himself," as Irenaeus said, "the apostasy of the devil."

That it was Melville's intention to beget Ahab in Satan's image can hardly be doubted. He told Hawthorne that his book had been boiled in hell-fire and secretly baptized not in the name of God but in the name of the Devil. He named his tragic hero after the Old Testament ruler who "did more to provoke the Lord God of Israel to anger than all the Kings of Israel that were before him." King Ahab's accuser, the prophet Elijah, is also resurrected to play his original rôle, though very briefly, in Melville's testament. We are told that Captain Ahab is an "ungodly, god-like" man who is spiritually outside Christendom. He is a well of blasphemy and defiance, of scorn and mockery for the gods—"cricket-players and pugilists" in his eyes. Rumor has it that he once spat in the holy goblet on the altar of the Catholic Church at Santa. "I never saw him kneel," says Stubb. He is associated in the text with scores of references to the Devil. He is an "anaconda of an old man." His self-assertive sadism is the linked antithesis of the masochistic submission preached by Father Mapple.

Captain Ahab-Lucifer is also related to a sun-god, like Christ, but in reverse. Instead of being light leaping out of darkness, he is "darkness leaping out of light." The *Pequod* sails on Christmas Day. *This* new year's sun will be the god of Wrath rather than the god of Love. Ahab does not emerge from his subterranean abode until his ship is "rolling through the bright Quito spring" (Easter-tide, symbolically, when the all-fertilizing sun-god is resurrected). The frenzied ceremony in which Ahab's followers are sworn to the pursuit of the White Whale—"Commend the murderous chalices!"—is suggestive of the Black Mass; the lurid operations at the try-works is a scene out of Hell.

There is some evidence that Melville was re-reading *Paradise Lost* in the summer of 1850, shortly after, let us guess, he got the idea of transforming the captain of his whale-ship into the first of all cardinal sinners who fell by pride. Anyhow, Melville's Satan is the spitting image of Milton's hero, but portrayed with deeper and subtler psychological insight, and placed where he belongs, in the heart of an enraged man.

Melville may have been persuaded by Goethe's Mephistopheles, or even by some of Hawthorne's bloodless abstracts of humanity, to add Fedallah to his cast of characters. Evidently he wanted to make certain that no reader would fail to recognize that Ahab had been possessed by, or had sold his soul to, the Devil. Personally, I think Fedallah's rôle is superfluous and I regret that Melville made room for him and his unbelievable boat-crew on the ship *Pequod.* Still, he is not wholly without interest. He represents the cool, heartless, cunning, calculating, intellectual Devil of the Medieval myth-makers, in contrast, to the stricken, passionate, indignant, and often eloquent rebel angel of *Paradise Lost,* whose rôle is played by Ahab.

The Arabic name "Fedallah" suggests "dev(il) Allah," that is, the Mohammedans' god as he appeared in the mind's eye of a Crusader. But we are told that Fedallah is a Parsee—a Persian fire-worshipper, or Zoroastrian, who lives in India. Thus, Ahab, named after the Semitic apostate who was converted to the orgiastic cult of Baal, or Bel, originally a Babylonian fertility god, has formed a compact with a Zoroastrian whose name reminds us of still another Oriental religion. In addition, Captain Ahab's whale-boat is manned by a crew of unregenerate infidels, as defined by orthodox Christianity, and each of his three harpooners, Queequeg, Tashtego, and Dagoo, is a member of a race which believed in other gods than the one god of the Hebraic-Christian Bible.

Speaking roughly, it might be said that Captain Ahab, incarnation of the Adversary and master of the ship *Pequod* (named after the aggressive Indian tribe that was exterminated by the Puritans of New England), has summoned the various religions of the East to combat the one dominant religion of the West. Or, in other terms, that he and his followers, Starbuck excepted, represent the horde of primitive drives, values, beliefs, and practises which the Hebraic-Christian religionists rejected and excluded, and by threats, punishments, and inquisitions, forced into the unconscious mind of Western man.

Stated in psychological concepts, Ahab is captain of the culturally repressed dispositions of human nature, that part of personality which psychoanalysts have termed the "Id." If this is true, his opponent, the White Whale, can be none other than the internal institution which is responsible for these repressions, namely the Freudian Superego. This then is my second hypothesis: Moby-Dick is a veritable spouting, breaching, sounding whale, a whale who, because of his whiteness, his mighty bulk and beauty, and because of one instinctive act that happened to dismember his assailant, has received the projection of Captain Ahab's Presbyterian conscience, and so may be said to embody the Old Testament Calvinistic conception of an affrighting Deity and his strict commandments, the derivative puritan ethic of nineteenth-century America, and the society that defended this ethic. Also, and most specifically, he symbolizes the zealous parents whose righteous sermonizings and corrections drove the prohibitions in so hard that a serious young man could hardly reach outside the barrier, except possibly far away among some tolerant, gracious Polynesian peoples. The emphasis should be placed on that unconscious (and hence inscrutable) wall of inhibition which imprisoned the puritan's thrusting passions. "How can the prisoner reach outside," cries Ahab, "except by thrusting through the wall? To me, the White Whale is that wall, shoved near to me . . . I see in him outrageous strength, with an inscrutable malice sinewing it." As a symbol of a sounding, breaching, white-dark, unconquerable New England conscience what could be better than a sounding, breaching, white-dark, unconquerable sperm whale?

Who is the psychoanalyst who could resist the immediate inference that the *imago* of the mother as well as the *imago* of the father is contained in the Whale? . . . [Elsewhere, Melville exhibits] keen and sympathetic insight into the cultural determinants of his mother's prohibiting dispositions. In *Pierre*, it is the "high-up, and towering and all-forbidding . . . edifice of his mother's immense pride . . . her pride of birth . . . her pride of purity," that is the "wall shoved near," the wall that stands between the hero and the realization of his heart's resolve. But instead of expending the fury of frustration upon his mother, he directs it at Fate, or, more specifically, at his mother's God and the society that shaped her. For he saw "that not his mother had made his mother; but the Infinite Haughtiness had first fashioned her; and then the haughty world had further molded her; nor had a haughty Ritual omitted to finish her."

Given this penetrating apprehension we are in a position to say that Melville's target in *Moby-Dick* was the upper middle-class culture of his time. It was *this* culture which was defended with righteous indignation by what he was apt to call "the world" or "the public," and Melville had very little respect for "the world" or "the public." The "public," or men operating as a social system, was something quite distinct from "the people." In *White Jacket* he wrote: "The public and the people! . . . let us hate the one, and cleave to the other." "The public is a monster," says Lemsford. Still earlier Melville had said: "I fight against the armed and crested lies of Mardi (the world)." "Mardi is a monster whose eyes are fixed in its head, like a whale." Many other writers have used similar imagery. Sir Thomas Browne referred to the multitude as "that numerous piece of monstrosity"; Keats spoke of "the dragon world." But closest of all was Hobbes: "By art is created that great Leviathan, called a commonwealth or state." It was in the laws of this Leviathan, Hobbes made clear, that the sources of right and wrong reside. To summarize: the giant mass of Melville's whale is the same as Melville's man-of-war world, the *Neversink*, in *White Jacket,* which in turn is an epitome of Melville's Mardi. The Whale's white forehead and hump should be reserved for the world's heavenly King.

That God is incarnate in the Whale has been perceived by . . . [every] Catholic critic of Melville's work, as well as by several Protestant critics. . . . Of course, what Ahab projects into the Whale is not the image of a loving Father, but the God of the Old Dispensation, the God who brought Jeremiah into darkness, hedged him about, and made his path crooked; the God, adopted by the fire-and-brimstone Puritans, who said: "With fury poured out I will rule over you." "The sword without and the terror within, shall destroy both the young man and the virgin." "I will also send the teeth of beasts upon them." "I will heap mischiefs upon them." "To me belongeth vengeance and recompense."

Since the society's vision of deity, and the society's morality, and the parents and ministers who implant these conceptions, are represented in a fully socialized personality by an establishment that is called the Superego—Conscience as Freud defined it—, and since Ahab has been proclaimed "Captain of the Id," the simplest psychological formula for Melville's dramatic epic is this: an insurgent Id in mortal conflict with an oppressive cultural Superego. Starbuck, the First Mate, stands for the rational realistic Ego which is overpowered by the fanatical compulsiveness of the Id and dispossessed of its normally regulating functions.

If this is approximately correct, it appears that while writing his greatest work Melville abandoned his detached position in the Ego from time to time . . . and, through the mediumship of Ahab, "burst his hot heart's shell" upon the sacrosanct Almighty and the sacrosanct sentiments of Christendom. Since in the world's judgment, 1851, nothing could be more reproachable than this, it would be unjust, if not treacherous, of us to reason *Moby-Dick* into some comforting morality play for which no boldness was required. This would be depriving Melville of the ground he gained for self-respect by having dared to abide by his own subjective truth and write a "wicked book." . . . (pp. 441-46)

In *Civilization and its Discontents* Freud, out of the ripeness of his full experience, wrote that when one finds deepseated aggression—and by this he meant aggression of the sort that Melville voiced—one can safely attribute it to the frustration of Eros. In my opinion this generalization does not hold for all men of all cultures of all times, but the probability of its being valid is extremely high in the case of an earnest, moralistic, nineteenth-century American, a Presbyterian to boot, whose anger is born of suffering, especially if this man spent an impressionable year of his life in Polynesia and returned to marry the very proper little daughter of the Chief Justice of Massachusetts, and if, in addition, he is a profoundly creative man in whose androgynic personality masculine and feminine components are integrally blended.

If it were concerned with *Moby-Dick,* the book, rather than with its author, I would call *this* my third hypothesis: Ahab-Melville's aggression was directed against the object that once harmed Eros with apparent malice and was still thwarting it with presentiments of further retaliations. The correctness of this inference is indicated by the nature of the injury—a symbolic emasculation—that excited Ahab's ire. Initially, this threatening object was, in all likelihood, the father, later, possibly, the mother. But, as Melville plainly saw, both his parents had been fashioned by the Hebraic-Christian, American Calvinist tradition, the tradition which conceived of a deity in whose eyes Eros was depravity. It was the first Biblical mythmakers who dismissed from heaven and from earth the Great Goddess of the Oriental and primitive religions, and so rejected the feminine principle as a spiritual force. Ahab, protagonist of these rejected religions, in addressing heaven's fire and lightning, what he calls "the personified impersonal," cries: "But thou are my fiery father; my sweet mother I know not. Oh, cruel! What hast thou done with her?" He calls this god a foundling, a "hermit immemorial," who does not know his own origin. Again, it was the Hebraic authors, sustained later by the Church Fathers, who propagated the legend that a woman was the cause of Adam's exile from Paradise, and that the original sin was concupiscence. Melville says that Ahab, spokesman of all exiled princes, "piled upon the whale's white hump the sum of all the general rage and hate felt by his whole race from Adam down." Remember also that it was the lure of Jezebel that drew King Ahab of Israel outside the orthodoxy of his religion and persuaded him to worship the Phoenician Astarte, goddess of love and fruitful increase. "Jezebel" was the worst tongue-lash a puritan could give a woman. She was Sex, and sex was Sin, spelled with a capital. (pp. 447-48)

In *Pierre* Melville confessed his own faith when he said that Eros is god of all, and Love "the loftiest religion of this earth." To the romantic Pierre the image of Isabel was "a silent and tyrannical call, challenging him in his deepest moral being, and summoning Truth, Love, Pity, Conscience to the stand.'' Here he seems to have had in mind the redeeming and inspiring Eros of Courtly Love, a heresy which the Medieval Church had done its utmost to stamp out. *This,* he felt convinced, was *his* ''path to God,'' although in the way of it he saw with horror the implacable conscience and worldly valuations of his revered mother.

If this line of reasoning is as close as I think it is to the known facts, then Melville, in the person of Ahab, assailed Calvinism in the Whale because it blocked the advance of a conscience beneficent to evolutionary love. And so, weighed in the scales of its creator, *Moby Dick* is not a wicked book but a *good* book, and after finishing it Melville had full reason to feel, as he confessed, ''spotless as the lamb.''

But then, seen from another point, *Moby-Dick* might be judged a wicked book, not because its hero condemns an entrenched tradition, but because he is completely committed to destruction. Although Captain Ahab manifests the basic stubborn virtues of the arch-protestant and the rugged individualist carried to their limits, *this* god-defier is no Prometheus, since all thought of benefiting humanity is foreign to him. His purpose is not to make the Pacific safe for whaling, nor, when blasting at the moral order, does he have in mind a more heartening vision for the future. The religion of Eros which might once have been the secret determinant of Ahab's undertaking is never mentioned. . . . The truth is that Ahab is motivated solely by his private need to avenge a private insult. His governing philosophy is that of nihilism, the doctrine that the existing system must be shattered. Nihilism springs up when the imagination fails to provide the redeeming solution of an unbearable dilemma, when ''the creative response,'' as Toynbee would say, is not forthcoming, and a man reacts out of a hot heart—''to the dogs with the head''—and swings to an instinct—''the same that prompts even a worm to turn under the heel.'' This is what White Jacket did when arraigned at the mast, and what Pierre did when fortune deserted him, and what Billy Budd did when confronted by his accuser. ''Nature has not implanted any power in man,'' said Melville, ''that was not meant to be exercised at times, though too often our powers have been abused. The privilege, inborn and inalienable, that every man has, of dying himself and inflicting death upon another, was not given to us without a purpose. These are the last resources of an insulted and unendurable existence.''

If we grant that Ahab is a wicked man, what does this prove? It proves that *Moby-Dick* is a *good* book, a parable in epic form, because Melville makes a great spectacle of Ahab's wickedness and shows through the course of the narrative how such wickedness will drive a man on iron rails to an appointed nemesis. Melville adhered to the classic formula for tragedies. He could feel ''spotless as the lamb,'' because he had seen to it that the huge threat to the social system, immanent in Ahab's two cardinal defects—egotistic self-inflation and unleashed wrath—was, at the end, fatefully exterminated, ''and the great shroud of the sea rolled on as it rolled five thousand years ago.'' The reader has had his catharsis, equilibrium has been restored, sanity is vindicated.

This is true, but is it the whole truth? In point of fact, while writing *Moby-Dick* did Melville maintain aesthetic distance, keeping his own feelings in abeyance? Do we not hear Ahab saying things that the later Pierre will say and that Melville said less vehemently in his own person? Does not the author show marked partiality for the ''mighty pageant creature'' of

his invention, put in *his* mouth the finest, boldest language? Also, have not many interpreters been so influenced by the abused Ahab that they saw nothing in his opponent but the source of all malicious agencies, the very Devil? As Mr. Mumford has said so eloquently, Ahab is at heart a noble being whose tragic wrong is that of battling against evil with ''power instead of love,'' and so becoming ''the image of the thing he hates.'' With this impression imbedded in our minds, how can we come out with any moral except this: evil wins. We admit that Ahab's wickedness has been cancelled. But what survives? It is the much more formidable, compacted wickedness of the group that survives, the world that is ''saturated and soaking with lies,'' and their man-of-war God, who is hardly more admirable than a primitive totem beast, some oral-aggressive, child-devouring Cronos of the sea. Is this an idea that a man of good-will can rest with?

Rest with? Certainly not. Melville's clear intention was to bring not rest, but *unrest* to intrepid minds. All gentle people were warned away from his book ''on risk of a lumbago or sciatica.'' ''A polar wind blows through it,'' he announced. He had not written to soothe, but to kindle, to make men leap from their seats, as Whitman would say, and fight for their lives. Was it the poet's function to buttress the battlements of complacency, to give comfort to the enemy? There is little doubt about the nature of the enemy in Melville's day. It was the dominant ideology, that peculiar compound of puritanism and materialism, of rationalism and commercialism, of shallow, blatant optimism and technology, which proved so crushing to creative evolutions in religion, art, and life. In such circumstances every ''true poet,'' as Blake said, ''is of the Devil's party,'' whether he knows it or not. Surveying the last hundred and fifty years, how many exceptions to this statement can we find? Melville, anyhow, knew that *he* belonged to the party, and while writing *Moby-Dick* so gloried in his membership that he baptized his work *In Nomine Diaboli.* It was precisely under these auspices that he created his solitary masterpiece, a construction of the same high order as the Constitution of the United States and the scientific treatises of Willard Gibbs, though huge and wild and unruly as the Grand Canyon. And it is for this marvel chiefly that he resides in our hearts now among the greatest in ''that small but high-hushed world'' of bestowing geniuses. (pp. 448-51)

Henry A. Murray, ''In nomine diaboli,'' in The New England Quarterly, *Vol. XXIV, No. 4, December, 1951, pp. 435-52.*

THORNTON WILDER (essay date 1952)

[*Wilder was a prominent twentieth-century American author. Contributing to the arts as a playwright, novelist, essayist, and screenwriter, he was three times the recipient of the Pulitzer Prize, winning that award for his novel* The Bridge of San Luis Rey *in 1927, and for his plays* Our Town *in 1938 and* The Skin of Our Teeth *in 1943. The following excerpt is from a 1952 revision of Wilder's first Charles Eliot Norton lecture at Harvard in 1950. Having declared ''the American characteristics of classical American literature'' as his lecture topic, he here uses* Moby-Dick *to illustrate the emergence of a new ''American language'' in nineteenth-century literature. Wilder does not focus on Melville's linguistic and rhetorical inventions per se; rather, he emphasizes their significance as expressions of a peculiarly American way of apprehending the world. For additional criticism of the American properties of the novel, see the excerpts by MacMechan (1899), Olson (1947), Chase (1949), Mushabac (1981), and Rourke (Additional Bibliography). Melville's prose style in* Moby-Dick *is also explored by Sir Nathaniel (1853), MacMechan (1899), Winters (1938), Nechas (1978), and Matthiessen (NCLC, Vol. 3).]*

I am going to examine with you one of the most famous pages in American literature—the first direct view of the White Whale in *Moby Dick*. Our study of this page will not be primarily a literary one, but an attempt to discover these American modes of seeing and feeling—characteristics born of a nation's history and geography before they are characteristics of style. (p. 9)

The Melville of *Moby Dick,* the most widely admired work in American literature, is a notably interesting example for our study. Melville was not only writing within the tradition of English literature: he was writing very bookishly and stylishly indeed. No doubt he was conscious that the vogue for his books was beginning to be greater in England than in America; *Moby Dick* was first published in London. Under the mounting emotion of composition Melville's "Americanism" erupted in spite of himself. It can be seen progressively manifesting itself. The first eleven pages of the novel are the worst kind of English English—that is to say, the English of the contemporary New York literary cliques. There are many pages in *Moby Dick* which betray the insecurity of a writer thirty-one years old who has launched upon a mighty subject; but the page from which I am about to quote is completely successful and its success has been achieved through the presence within it of elements inherent in the nation's adventure. (pp. 19-20)

[This passage] is from Chapter 133. It affords us our first direct view of the White Whale; it is probably the most delayed entrance of a star in all literature—in my edition it is on page 538.

During the reading of this page I wish you to ask yourself a number of questions: What is its *movement* and where have you heard it before? Does its rhythm and ordering of phrase recall to you the Bible of 1611? or Elizabethan drama? or Sir Thomas Browne? Or does it seem to you to sound like a prose translation or adaptation of an epic poem? Does it, indeed, seem to be trying to capture in prose the effects peculiar to poetry? But, above all, are you aware of any elements that separate it from English literature, the English spirit recounting the English experience of life?

The whale has been sighted, "A hump like a snow-hill!" and the boats of the *Pequod* have started in pursuit.

> Like noiseless nautilus shells, their light prows
> sped through the sea; but only slowly they neared
> the foe.

Melville's emotion is gaining on him. The alliterations in *n* and *s* begin to introduce an incantatory tone which will presently be confirmed by constructions employing repetition; but the approach to a state of trance does not prevent his marking the rapidity of the boats with monosyllables, and the dragging slowness—as felt by the whalers—by open vowels.

> As they neared him, the ocean grew still more smooth; seemed drawing a carpet over its waves; seemed a noon-meadow, so serenely it spread. At length the breathless hunter came so nigh his seemingly unsuspecting prey, that his entire dazzling hump was distinctly visible, sliding along the sea as if an isolated thing, and continually set in a revolving ring of finest, fleecy, greenish foam. He saw the vast, involved wrinkles of the slightly projecting head beyond. Before it, far out on the soft Turkish-rugged wa-

> ters, went the glistening white shadow from his broad, milky forehead, a musical rippling playfully accompanying the shade; and behind, the blue waters interchangeably flowed over into the moving valley of his steady wake; and on either hand bright bubbles arose and danced by his side.

Melville's emotion is under powerful control.

We are approaching a paroxysm of swooning love and shuddering horror, but so far he has mainly presented himself to us All Eyes. The emotion is present, however, in this insistence that everything is serene and in the undulation of the rhythm. Scarcely a noun is offered which is not preceded by one or two adjectives, many of which ("projecting," "soft," "white," "broad," "blue") tell us nothing new. We call this practice a mid-nineteenth-century vice and today children are punished for it. Today such a scene—picture and emotion—would be conveyed with the economy of a telegram. But style is not only the man; it involves also the thought-world of the time, including the writer's effort to alter it. This page is an exercise in flamboyant rhetoric; it is a "purple patch," unashamed. Its triumph issues from the superimposition of novel elements upon a traditional form.

The visual details which Melville has furnished, and which he is about to furnish, are the most brilliant precision, but they do not render the scene objective, nor do they mitigate our awe and terror. The impression is that his eyes are "starting out of his head." Only the greatest authors—and Dante in chief—can thus continue to *see* while they are in a state of transport. Lesser authors relapse into abstract nouns and fashion from them a sort of cloudy "sublime."

> But these were broken again by the light toes of hundreds of gay fowl softly feathering the sea, alternate with their fitful flight; and like to some flagstaff rising from the painted hull of an argosy, the tall but shattered pole of a recent lance projected from the White Whale's back; and at intervals one of the cloud of soft-toed fowls hovering, and to and fro skimming like a canopy over the fish, silently perched and rocked on this pole, the long tail feathers streaming like pennons.

> A gentle joyousness—a mighty mildness of repose in swiftness, invested the gliding whale.

At last we have an abstract noun—four of them, and how abstractly dependent upon one another! But Melville's grasp of this visible world is so sure that we can afford a plethora of them. Abstract nouns come naturally to Americans, but they must constantly find an idiosyncratic way of employing them. New-World abstractions are very different from Old-World abstractions; they are not "essences" but generalizations; or, to express it most paradoxically, an American strives to render his abstraction concrete.

> Not the white bull Jupiter swimming away with ravished Europa clinging to his graceful horns; his lovely, leering eyes sideways intent upon the maid; with smooth bewitching fleetness, rippling straight for the nuptial bower in Crete; not Jove, not that great majesty Supreme! did surpass the glorified White Whale as he so divinely swam.

What! These whalefishers are hurrying to their death and the great blasphemer to his retribution and Melville chooses this moment to linger over the behavior of some birds and to insert an elaborated Renaissance vignette?

This beautifully wrought metaphor, though not at all classical in feeling, represents a device we frequently find in Homer. The simile which arises from the presented action begins to lead an independent life of its own; it flowers into details and developments which occasionally disturb and even reverse its relation to its original correlevant. This evocation of Jupiter not only arrests our excitement; it almost cuts us off from direct vision. This would seem to be a flaw, but its justification lies in its relation to time.

There are three times transpiring on this page. There are—as in all narration—the time of the action and the time of the narrative; Ishmael at his desk recalls and re-experiences those events from the past. But the time which is passing in the mind of Ishmael the narrator is invaded by another time which can best be called the timeless. If Melville were writing an adventure story for boys, "Joe Foster, the Young Whaler," it would indeed be lamentable to deflate our excitement at this moment. But in the realm of moral issues and total experience such human tensions are out of place. Older readers know that life is crisis. (Goethe said that the *Iliad* teaches us "that it is our task here on earth to enact Hell daily.") The house burns down and no Joe Foster rushes through the flames to rescue the child from the cradle; the survivors of the wreck turn black and expire upon their raft before Joe Foster appears upon the horizon; the consequences of the lives we have fashioned advance toward us with age and death on their heels. Homer and Melville remove us to a plane of time wherein catastrophe or rescue are mere incidents in a vast pattern.

But these birds and this fragment of mythology have another character. They proceed from another form of excitement. They have about them the hushed, glassy precision of hallucination. For those who come upon them in their place in the vast book they are like the intrusions of a dream and like the irrelevances in a moment of danger. They are that moment when the matador sees the bull dashing toward him and at the same time, out of the corner of his eye, sees that a woman in the second row is wearing three red roses and that her black scarf is being fanned by the wind. The timeless is for a moment identified with the time of all those other people and things that are not caught up in our crisis—the people who pass whistling happily under our hospital window, the people who are held up at a crossing while we drive to a burial—the birds, and the nuptials of Jupiter and Europa.

Whereupon, after this far journey into the timeless, Melville brings us back abruptly to the most concrete level of his story:

> On each soft side—coincident with the parted swell, that but once leaving him, . . . then flowed so wide away—on each bright side, the whale shed off enticings. No wonder there had been some among the hunters who, namelessly transported and allured by all this serenity, had ventured to assail it; but had fatally found that quietude but the vesture of tornadoes.

This is very extravagant writing, indeed, but, as the word "namelessly" shows, Melville is returning us for a moment to the symbolic level.

We do not have to think of the Nantucket whalefishers as subject to throes of aesthetic transport. We may read:

> It is not surprising that some men have been mistaken by the apparently serene orderliness of God-in-Nature and, swept up into *hubris,* have attempted to blaspheme against it and to set themselves up as its antagonists, only to discover that . . .
>
> Yet calm, enticing calm, oh whale! thou glidest on, to all who for the first time eye thee, no matter how many in that same way thou may'st have bejuggled and destroyed before.

The climax employs the most rhetorical—that is to say, the most potentially absurd—of all devices: the invocation to an abstraction, to an insensible or absent being. It is characteristic of our time, and related to . . . the decline of our belief in authorities and essences, that few orators can be heard saying, "Oh, Commonwealth of Massachusetts, persevere!" and few poets now address the Evening or Sweet Days of Childhood.

> And thus, through the serene tranquillities of the tropical sea, among waves whose hand-clappings were suspended by exceeding rapture, Moby Dick moved on, still withholding from sight the full terrors of his submerged trunk, entirely hiding the wrenched hideousness of his jaw. But soon the fore part of him slowly rose from the water; for an instant his whole marbelized body formed a high arch, like Virginia's Natural Bridge, and warningly waving his bannered flukes in the air, the grand god revealed himself, sounded, and went out of sight. Hoveringly halting, and dipping on the wing, the white sea-fowls longingly lingered over the agitated pool that he left.

There are some literary echoes in this passage, but they are drowned out by an influence that is not of the printed page. I find but one cadence which recalls the Bible: "suspended in exceeding rapture"; and but one reminiscence of Elizabethan, though not Shakespearean, blank verse:

> Yet calm, enticing calm, oh whale! thou glidest on, to all who for the first time eye thee. . . .

Sir Thomas Browne is never far absent; he has had his part in the evocation of Europa and in him Melville "fatally found that quietude but the vesture of tornadoes." To my ear, however, the movement of this passage is primarily oratorical.

Yet the observation that this passage has the air of being written for declamation does not distinguish it as a work of the New World. De Quincey and Carlyle and Ruskin and Chateaubriand and Victor Hugo and Kierkegaard had all been writing or were about to write prose that took its tone from forensic and pulpit eloquence. (pp. 20-7)

[The following elements] indicate that it is written in America:

1. It contains a number of locutions which reveal the emergence of the American language.

2. It is directed to a classless society—to Everybody. (p. 27)

The novel element which seems to me to be of least importance was the presence of new words and idioms. There are no examples of this in the page we are studying. "Bejuggled"— which Melville had already employed in *Mardi*—is not in most dictionaries, but ''juggled'' has a long history on both sides of the Atlantic. But if there are no new words, there are some examples of novel usage.

''The whale shed off enticings.'' There is little doubt that De Quincey or even Carlyle would have written ''shed enticements.'' ''Enticings'' will be followed in the next paragraph by ''hand-clappings.'' These verbal nouns based on the present participle are relatively rare in the plural. A number, after losing their dynamic force (paintings, savings, undertakings), have entered common use, and others (understandings, risings, mumblings) are on their way to the same static condition. But we do not say laughings, shoppings, studyings, enticings, or hand-clappings. Melville in *Moby Dick* offers us intertwistings, spurnings, coincidings, imminglings, and even ''what lovely leewardings!'' I have counted thirty-one of them. (p. 28)

Much of this coinage in Melville is mere huffing and puffing. A young man of thirty-one with barely a high-school education has remarked Shakespeare's bold inventions without having acquired the tact that controlled them. I find the plural gerunds on this page, however, completely successful.

''The whale shed off enticings.'' As foreigners who are learning our language frequently inform us, we Americans are forever putting prepositions and adverbial particles to new uses. Here the ''off'' combined with the ''enticings'' gives the impression of a continuous fulguration. It is not only an expression of vivacity and energy; it reveals our national tendency to restore to the past its once-present life rather than to immobilize it, to bury it under the preterite. In narration this assumed a great importance, for Americans wish to declare that all living things are free—and were free—and the past tenses in narration tend to suggest that we, telling the story from its latter end, see them as ''determined'' and as the victims of necessity. When we come to discuss the American time-sense and its struggle to reshape the syntax of the English language, we shall see that one of its principal aims has been to give even to the past tenses the feeling of a ''continuous present,'' a door open to the future, a recovery of the we-don't-know-what-will-happen.

On this page we are shown the bull and Europa ''rippling straight for the nuptial bower in Crete.'' Water ripples; tresses ripple. Had we read in a present-day author, English or American, that ''Leander rippled straight for Sestos,'' we would have condemned it as a vulgarity. What saves this phrase from vulgarity is the *gamut of tones* that are juxtaposed in this nineteenth-century page—which brings us to our second consideration.

A novel element in our classics of a century ago is the fact that they were written for a classless society, they were written for everybody. (pp. 29-30)

Wherein do these paragraphs from *Moby Dick* reveal the fact that Melville was addressing an undifferentiated audience? They are certainly highly ''bookish''—what with that elaborated classical allusion, that stylish subjunctive, and their high percentage of words from the Latin.

First, we observe that elevation and intensity are not solely and inseparably associated with noble images. The sublime does not wear a cothurnus. There are not two doors for words in America, no tradesmen's entrance: all can go in the front door. In the very same sentence in which Melville apostrophizes divinity we are told that God has ''bejuggled'' many a man. It is a word from the skulduggeries of the country fair

and the card game at the livery stable. We remember the horror with which Racine's contemporaries greeted the mention of a dog in tragedy, the protest of the audience against Hugo's use of the humble phrase *''Quelle heure est-il?''* in *Hernani*. Generations of critics deplored the drunken porter in *Macbeth*. What better illustration of the limited gamut of tones available for European full-throated utterance than the observation that so many of the words that describe lofty moods are also words that stem from the designations of social rank, or that run concurrently with them and derive much of their force from connotations of status: ''noble'' and *''herrlich''* and *''edel''* and *''magnifico''* and *''grande''* and *''soberano''* and ''majestic'' and even ''gentle.'' The United States is a middle-class nation and has widened and broadened and deepened the concepts of the wide and the broad and the deep without diminishing the concept of the high. We notice that the angelic host of birds that glorify the White Whale have soft toes. Toes, like noses, have not hitherto entered the exalted, the dithyrambic style. This page did not have the drawing room in view.

Second, most European exercises in the sublime, in avoiding the common and humble, avoid the specific. In the tirades of Burke and Carlyle on the French Revolution, in the impassioned visions of De Quincey and Chateaubriand, the noble is associated with a high vagueness. Audiences which are composed of the selected and the cultivated and the *Gebildeten* and the *honnêtes gens* and the *cognoscenti* are not interested in life's diversity; the pressures upon them work toward the formulation of taste and convention and the Rules of the Beautiful and an ever narrowing purity (*i.e.*, economy) in the selection of detail. But the American public was one and one and one . . . to an unlimited number. Their taste could never be codified, for it was overwhelmed by an ever enlarging vision of the universe and its multifarious character. The bigger the world is, the *less* you can be content with vagueness. The catalogues of Walt Whitman . . . are filled with this kind of apprehension. He hears a runaway slave

> . . . crackling the twigs of the woodpile,

> Through the swung half-door of the kitchen I saw him limpsy and weak, . . .

> The bride unrumples her white dress, the minute-hand of the clock moves slowly,

> The opium-eater reclines with rigid head and just-opened lips. . . .

Whitman can get a million people into his poem by making sure that not *one* of his twenty is amorphous.

What European poet, reminding us that the sunlight falls on all alike, would have selected as an illustration the reminder that it falls upon the ''Squirrel in the Himmaleh''—or have drawn from the thought so chillingly abstract a conclusion as did Emily Dickinson? (''But not for Compensation—/It holds as large a Glow/To Squirrel in the Himmaleh/Precisely, as to you.'')

Since the American can find no confirmation of identity from the environment in which he lives, since he lives exposed to the awareness of vast distances and innumerable existences, since he derives from a belief in the future the courage that animates him, is he not bent on isolating and ''fixing'' a value on every existing thing in its relation to a totality, to the All, to the Everywhere, to the Always? And does that not require of him a new way of viewing and feeling and describing any existing thing? And would that not require, in turn, a modification of the language? (pp. 31-3)

Thornton Wilder, *"Toward an American Language,"* in his *American Characteristics and Other Essays,* edited by Donald Gallup, Harper & Row, Publishers, 1979, pp. 3-33.

LAWRANCE THOMPSON (essay date 1952)

[*Thompson explicates* Moby-Dick *as a theologically subversive work in which Melville expresses his personal independence from the "tyranny" of God and Christian dogma. In the critic's estimation, Melville justifies his own attitude by "glorifying" Ahab's defiance and portraying him as a "supremely tragic hero who rises to his highest grandeur . . . even in the face of that ultimate and inevitable God-bullying indignity, death." Ironic readings of many portions of the novel, including Ishmael's rapturous meditation on brotherhood in "A Squeeze of the Hand," form a major part of Thompson's analysis. For a rebuttal, see the excerpt by Bewley dated 1959. Melville's treatment of religion in* Moby-Dick *is also discussed by Auden (1950), Murray (1951), and Hillway (1979); the author's treatment of theology in the novel is also examined by Thorp (1938), Bewley (1959), and Aiken (NCLC, Vol. 3). Thompson also discusses the narrative point of view in* Moby-Dick, *as do Colcord (1922), Berthoff (1962), and Nechas (1978).*]

[Melville's ultimate goal in *Moby-Dick*] was to tell a story which would illuminate, obliquely, his personal declaration of independence not only from the tyranny of Christian dogma but also from the sovereign tyranny of God Almighty. With appropriate irony, he turned to the Bible for inspiration, particularly to the book of Job. Without any great difficulty he could identify himself with the suffering Job, and could join Job in blaming God for all the sorrows, woes, evils which distressed and perplexed him. . . . Although he could not join Job in the final tableau of abject submission and acceptance of God's inscrutable ways, he could relish the inadequacy (as it seemed to an actual whale hunter) of those terms God used to upbraid Job for upbraiding God:

> Canst thou draw out leviathan with an hook?
>
> Canst thou fill his skin with barbed irons? or his head with fish spears?
>
> None is so fierce that dare stir him up: who, then, is able to stand before me?

In Melville's day, many laymen and theologians were agreed that God's reference to leviathan, in that Forty-first chapter of Job, was a reference to a whale; that God used the image of the whale to serve as a symbol of God's own indomitable and inscrutable attributes. Having recently returned from the professional task of slaughtering whales, Melville was naturally inclined to pounce impudently on this God-given symbol and play it for all it was worth. By extension, the symbolic image of the whale permitted him to assume, wickedly, that any concern for whaling might be considered some form of God-concern, in an allegorical sense. Already well practiced in the possibilities of allegory, he was perfectly prepared to work out simultaneous concealments and revelations in terms of those rich whaling associations (physical and metaphysical) which crammed his thoughts and memories. (pp. 147-48)

The total structure [of the novel] depends on the interplay between the action, as such, and the narrative, as such; between the story of Captain Ahab's deeds and the way that story is told by Ishmael. The artistic cross-ruff between these two factors (*what* the story is; *how* the story is told) enables Melville to present his ulterior meanings by means of sustained irony. Consequently, an egregious mistake which a reader of *Moby-Dick* can make is the mistake of settling for *what* the story is, without noticing *how* the story is presented. (p. 150)

In *Moby-Dick,* it might be said that Melville projected one aspect of himself into his narrator Ishmael, and then projected another contrasting aspect of self into his hero, Captain Ahab. Ishmael is a self-acknowledged coward, fugitive, outcast, escapist. By contrast, Captain Ahab is a brave and heroic pursuer, outspoken in his hatreds. The foil value permits Melville to conceal from certain types of readers the fact that there is a close identity of viewpoints between Ishmael and Captain Ahab. Artistically, Melville again avails himself of sustained irony by pretending a contrast between the viewpoints of his hero and his narrator. (p. 151)

[Melville's] constant interweaving of several hundred Biblical names, references, allusions, quotations, creates an ambiguous and equivocal effect which is strikingly similar to the effects achieved by Montaigne and Pierre Bayle for purposes of deception and self-protection. . . . [The] reader should quickly be able to notice that Melville's uses of Biblical allusions in *Moby-Dick* are endowed with equivocal and ambiguous meanings by the larger context which controls them; that the conventional meanings of those Biblical allusions are exactly the meanings which Melville deliberately but covertly satirizes; that the inverted meanings are those which mesh and interlock with the ulterior or total meaning of *Moby-Dick.* By contrast, the overt tendentiousness of meaning, in that astonishingly elaborate parade of Biblical allusions, provides Melville with a major device for self-protective deception and sarcastic hoodwinking. To illustrate, we need go no further afield than to consider the ambiguous values implicit in the [name of the hero, Ahab]. (pp. 151-52)

What does the conventional reader make of Ahab's name? He probably remembers the Biblical account of King Ahab, in First Kings: Ahab "did evil in the sight of the Lord." In fact, "Ahab did more to provoke the Lord God of Israel to anger than all the kings of Israel that were before him." Furthermore, it was Elijah who upbraided Ahab in the Bible, even as in *Moby-Dick,* for having forsaken the commandments of the Lord. King Ahab's sin was that he "did very abominably in following idols." Obviously, then, it is not difficult to use either one of these Ahabs, for Christian purposes, as a horrible object lesson which teaches us that while virtue and obedience are rewarded, wicked defiance is neither expedient nor profitable because it brings down retribution.

But there is one other correlation, far more interesting, between these two Ahabs. Each of them is seduced to his death by a prophet, and Captain Ahab's misleading prophet is Fedallah, whose symbolic values are complex. Consider, however, the hint in First Kings as to how it happened that King Ahab was similarly victimized: "I saw the Lord sitting on his throne, and all the host of heaven standing by him, on his right hand and on his left. And the Lord said, Who shall persuade Ahab, that he may go up and fall at Ramoth-gilead? . . . And there came forth a spirit, and stood before the Lord, and said, I will persuade him. And the Lord said, Wherewith? And he said, I will go forth, and I will be a lying spirit in the mouth of all his prophets. And the Lord said, Thou shalt persuade him, and prevail also: go forth and do so."

For Melville's anti-Christian purposes, that passage lends itself nicely to a correlated series of insinuations that God is a malicious double-crosser, a deceiver, who is not above employing "a lying spirit" (inside or outside a human being) to lead a man to his death, even as God permitted Satan to serve as agent in seducing Adam and Eve to ultimate death; much as God permitted Satan to torture poor Job. In *Moby-Dick,* Captain Ahab is motivated by such dark thoughts when he follows Job in upbraiding God for his malice. It is because of the sufferings which God (as agent or principal) inflicts on Captain Ahab that Ahab swears his unspeakable oath to seek out the emblematic White Whale in defiance. Although Melville's circular pattern of attitudinizing causes him to view Captain Ahab from various angles, and with varying degrees of sympathy, as the story unfolds, Melville ultimately chooses to justify himself by glorifying Ahab's declaration of independence from man and God; to justify himself by representing Ahab as a supremely tragic hero who rises to his highest grandeur (and says so) even in the face of that ultimate and inevitable God-bullying indignity, death.

A third major aspect of total structure, in *Moby-Dick,* is the triangulation among three whale stories: Captain Ahab's, Jonah's, Job's. Again, this structural aspect is developed ironically and deceptively, because Melville chooses to inflate his mock-serious version of the fish story, in Father Mapple's sermon; by contrast, Melville chooses to represent his anti-Christian version of the Job story, by means of scattered and cumulative insinuations. Nevertheless, the careful reader comes to appreciate that the direct quotations from the book of Job and the allusions to Job pile up until they call persistent attention to the analogy between what happened to Job and what happened to Captain Ahab. The importance of that slowly enriched analogy deflates the Ahab-Jonah parallelism to the intended antithesis or inversion. To be sure, Captain Ahab's actions, which occur as a consequence of his Job-like sufferings, should also be viewed as inversions of the lollipop ending which scholars tell us the orthodox revisionists tacked on the story of Job. Instead of accepting God's inscrutability, as Job did, Captain Ahab defies it and vows to dismember his taunting Dismemberer. While Ahab goes about that obvious business, Ishmael goes about his covert business of taunting the Taunter. With mock humility, for example, Ishmael sets up the pun value of cetology-theology in the opening paragraphs of the "Cetology" chapter, and progresses until he can exclaim, sarcastically, "What am I that I should essay to hook the nose of this leviathan? The awful tauntings in Job might well appeal to me. 'Will he (the leviathan) make a covenant with thee? Behold the hope of him is vain!'" With equally taunting mockery and sarcasm, Ishmael contemplates a dying whale (possibly a symbol of an impotent and defeated and dying God), and continues his anti-Christian sneering in these rhetorical questions, "Is this the creature of whom it was once so triumphantly said— 'Canst thou fill his skin with barbed irons? or his head with fish-spears? . . .' This the creature? this he? Oh! that unfulfilments should follow the prophets. For with the strength of a thousand thighs in his tail, Leviathan had run his head under the mountains of the seas, to hide him from the Pequod's fish-spears!''

(After the reader has become familiar with Melville's fondness for all manner of punning and equivocal word-play, he may be inclined to look more generously on my suspicion that Melville chose to name the ship of Captain Ahab and of Ishmael the *Pequod* because of the punlike suggestiveness of the ship's intention to pique God.)

Now complete this Ahab-Job-Jonah triangulation by placing the devout Father Mapple's whale-story sermon against the

other two whale stories. Immediately, one may see further reason for considering the possibility that Melville intended the Jonah story to be viewed as a fish story. But we must pause here to acknowledge the heresy of such a literary interpretation, because our leading Melville authorities insist that Melville introduces the fine rhetoric of Father Mapple to serve as a yardstick for measuring the shortcomings and sins of mad old Captain Ahab. Because the bias of these authorities has afforded them pleasure in enjoying that sermon at its face value, they resent the suggestion that Melville might possibly have written that sermon for purely satirical purposes. More than that, these authorities resent the suggestion that they themselves could possibly have fallen into one of Melville's better mouse-traps. Apparently they feel that if Melville had actually planned to trap any of his readers, he should have warned them.

So far, I have briefly sketched three aspects of the total structure of *Moby-Dick:* the sustained irony in the focus of narration; the sustained irony in some of Melville's uses of Biblical allusions; the sustained irony in the triangulation of three whale stories. (pp. 152-55)

[Each of the chapters in which Melville describes the processing of the whale into usable goods] is a sarcastic answer to the taunting insistence of Job's God that Leviathan is inscrutable and untouchable. Furthermore, each is an ironic *exemplum* or parable, capped with a stated or implied "application." Many of these chapters enable Melville to increase his ridicule of the orthodox Christian dogma that the Holy Bible is the infallible Word of God. For his sinister purpose, the Forty-first Chapter of Job was almost made to order, and he took full advantage of it. For example, let us . . . [examine] the scene in which three boats from the *Pequod* overtake and capture a "huge, humped old bull," enfeebled by age and other infirmities. We have already mentioned this passage, along with the earlier passage in which Ishmael mentioned "the awful tauntings in Job." But we need the full text, as Ishmael taunts the Taunter, dismembers the Dismemberer (italics added):

> Seems it credible that by three such thin threads the great Leviathan [note the capital "L"] was suspended like the big weight to an eight day clock. Suspended? and to what? To three bits of board. Is this the creature of whom it was once so triumphantly said—'Canst thou fill his skin with barbed irons? or his head with fish-*spears*? The sword of him that layeth at him cannot hold, the spear, the dart, nor the habergeon; he esteemeth iron as straw; the arrow cannot make him flee; darts are counted as stubble; he laugheth at the shaking of a *spear*!' This the creature? this he? Oh! that unfulfilments should follow the prophets. For with the strength of a thousand thighs in his tail, Leviathan had run his head under the mountains of the sea, to hide him from the *Pequod's* fish-*spears*!''

This particular representation of cetology is further described to afford another jibe at Christian theology; another chance, allegorically, to pique God:

> His eyes, or rather the places where his eyes had been, were beheld. As strange misgrown masses gather in the knot-holes of the noblest oaks when prostrate, so from the points which the whale's eyes had once occupied, now pro-

truded blind bulbs, horribly pitiable to see. But pity there was none. For all his old age, and his one arm, and his blind eyes, he must die the death and be murdered, in order to light the gay bridals and other merry-makings of men, *and also to illuminate the solemn churches that preach unconditional inoffensiveness by all to all* [italics added]. Still rolling in his blood, at last he partially disclosed a strangely discolored bunch of protuberance, the size of a bushel, low down on the flank.

'A nice spot,' cried Flask; 'just let me prick him there once.'

'Avast!' cried Starbuck, 'theres no need of that!'

But humane Starbuck was too late. . . .

Although there is actually no need for adding other illustrations of Melville's fondness for taunting the Taunter, the importance of the correlation between the whaling activities and the Leviathan references in Job cannot be too strongly stressed. "I will not keep silence concerning his limbs," says Job's God. Neither will Melville keep silence: he describes how Stubb cuts the penis off the first whale he kills, and has penis steak for supper. "Who can strip off his outer garment?" asks Job's God. Melville describes the manner in which the foreskin of another whale is stripped off and tailored to make a jacket or "cassock" for the mincer who slices the blubber thin for trying out. He continues:

The mincer now stands before you invested in the full canonicals of his calling. Immemorial to all his order, this investiture alone will adequately protect him, while employed in the peculiar functions of his office.

That office consists in mincing the horse-pieces of blubber for the pots; an operation which is conducted . . . with a capacious tub beneath it, into which the minced pieces drop, fast as the sheets from a rapt orator's desk. Arrayed in decent black; occupying a conspicuous pulpit; intent on bible leaves; what a candidate for an *archbishoprick* [italics added], what a lad for Pope were this mincer.

In a footnote, Melville adds,

Bible leaves! Bible leaves! This is the invariable cry from the mates to the mincer. It enjoins him to be careful, and cut his work into as thin slices as possible. . . .

Again, Melville has provided his own exegesis. "Who shall come within his jaws? Who can open the doors of his face?" asks Job's God. Melville provides some highly illuminating *exempla,* by giving contrasted views of "The Right Whale's Head" and "The Sperm Whale's Head," exterior and interior.

For Melville's dark allegorical purposes, there are innumerable advantages in having a sperm whale serve as an emblem of God: the word "sperm" permits him to indulge his fondness for the extensions of word-play, sometimes quite indelicate, as in the archaic spelling of the word "archbishoprick," above. After all, sperm is the generative substance, and Melville's consciously incorrect interpretation of the word "spermaceti" enables him to associate the White Whale with the beginning of beginnings, particularly with Genesis. Removal of the sper-

maceti from the head of a slaughtered whale is described, after the reader is afforded the details as to how the whalemen open the doors of his face, pull his teeth, and cut a hole in the top. When Tashtego "retires" into one head, through such an aperture, and is in danger of drowning beneath spermaceti, Queequeg plunges in after him, and saves him by opening a womb-like door in the face, so that Tashtego may be born again! Then Ishmael supplies the theological application to the parable, in pertinent analogy. The sinister overtones hint at Melville's now disillusioned lumping of Platonic and Christian theology:

Now had Tashtego perished in that head, it had been a very precious perishing; smothered in the very whitest and daintiest of fragrant spermaceti; coffined, hearsed, and tombed in the secret inner chamber and sanctum sanctorum of the whale. Only one sweeter end can readily be recalled—the delicious death of an Ohio honey-hunter, who seeking honey in the crotch of a hollow tree, found such exceeding store of it, that leaning too far over, it sucked him in, so that he died embalmed. How many, think ye, have likewise fallen into Plato's honey head, and sweetly perished there.

Another correlation of what had now become for Melville the sickly sweetness of Platonism and the sickly sweetness of Christian optimism concerning life and death calls forth one of his most obvious stylistic displays of conscious overwriting for ironic effect. Specifically, he seems merely to let Ishmael describe the way in which the "sperm" has to be manipulated by the whalemen to process it. The reader is made to realize that the greasy task was obviously repellent to Ishmael, yet he pretends to praise what he disliked doing, thus heightening the burlesque of Christian baptism and brotherly love:

. . . A sweet and unctuous duty! No wonder that in old times sperm was such a favourite *cosmetic* [italics added; cf. use of "cosmetic" in "The Whiteness of the Whale"]. Such a clearer! such a sweetener! such a softener! such a delicious mollifier! After having my hands in it for only a few minutes, my fingers felt like eels, and began, as it were, to *serpentine* [italics added; he feels "devilish"] and spiralise.

As I sat there at my ease, cross-legged on the deck; after the bitter exertion at the windlass; under a blue tranquil sky; the ship under indolent sail, and gliding so serenely along; as I bathed my hands among those soft, gentle globules of infiltrated tissues, woven almost within the hour; as they richly broke to my fingers, and discharged all their opulence, like fully ripe grapes their wine; as I snuffed up that uncontaminated aroma,—literally and truly like the smell of spring violets; I declare to you, that for the time I lived as in a musky meadow; I forgot all about our horrible oath; in that inexpressible [unspeakable?] sperm, I washed my hands and my heart of it; I almost began to credit the old Paracelsan superstition that sperm is of rare virtue in allaying the heat of anger: while bathing in that bath, I felt divinely free from all ill-will, or petulance, or malice, of any sort whatsoever.

Squeeze! squeeze! squeeze! all the morning long; I squeezed that sperm till I myself almost melted into it; I squeezed that sperm till a strange sort of insanity came over me; and I found myself unwittingly squeezing my co-labourers' hands in it, mistaking their hands for the gentle globules. Such an abounding, affectionate, friendly, loving feeling did this avocation beget; that at last I was continually squeezing their hands, and looking up into their eyes sentimentally; as much as to say,—Oh! my dear fellow beings, why should we longer cherish any social acerbities, or know the slightest ill-humour or envy! Come; let us squeeze hands all round; nay, let us all squeeze ourselves into each other; let us squeeze ourselves universally into the very milk and sperm of kindness.

Would that I could keep squeezing that sperm for ever! For now, since by many prolonged, repeated experiences, I have perceived that in all cases man must eventually lower, or at least shift, his conceit of attainable felicity; not placing it anywhere in the intellect or the fancy; but in the wife, the heart, the bed, the table, the saddle, the fire-side, the country; now that I have perceived all this, I am ready to squeeze case eternally. In thoughts of the visions of the night, I saw long rows of angels in paradise, each with his hands in a jar of spermaceti.

That is pretty rough, and blessed are the pure in heart who can read it without noticing the accumulated off-color word-play. But it is quoted here for more pertinent reasons. Oddly, some interpreters have cited that passage as proof that the early Ishmael changes, until he parts company with the blasphemous Ahab; that here is a clean-cut turning point for Ishmael. Of course such interpreters insist on taking the passage at face value: Ishmael asserts that it was truly pleasant to sit with his hands in a tub of suggestive fat, all morning, and so he *must* mean *just* what he says! But there are several different forms of giveaway, in the passage, and they suggest a sardonic tone. Even the progression from the sweet stickiness of the spermaceti to the sweet stickiness of the "sentimentally" described emotions recalls certain saccharine Christian ideals of universal brotherhood. In short, a particular aspect of Christian doctrine is being ridiculed here, just as certainly as other Christian concepts are ridiculed from the beginning to the end of *Moby-Dick*. (pp. 214-19)

> *Lawrance Thompson, in his* Melville's Quarrel with God, *Princeton University Press, 1952, 475 p.*

MARIUS BEWLEY (essay date 1959)

[*Rebutting Thompson's contention that Melville attacks God in* Moby-Dick *(see excerpt dated 1952), Bewley argues that the novelist actually affirms the positive aspects of God and creation in his masterpiece. The whale provides the focus for this affirmation, in Bewley's opinion, functioning as both the "symbol of a good God" and an important indicator of Ishmael's reconciliation with creation. For further commentary on Melville's treatment of theology in* Moby-Dick, *see Thorp (1938), Thompson (1952), and Aiken (NCLC, Vol. 3). Critics who discuss symbolism in* Moby-Dick *include Lawrence (1923), Arvin (1950), Horsford (1962), Kulkarni (1970), Hillway (1979), and Mather, Lawrence, Mumford, Aiken, Winters, Sedgwick, Maugham, Auden, and*

Priestley (NCLC, Vol. 3). For additional commentary on the role of ontology in Moby-Dick, *see Thorp (1938), Horsford (1962), Zoellner (1973), Nechas (1978), Hillway (1979) and Aiken (NCLC, Vol. 3). For other critics who contrast Ahab's and Ishmael's view of the world, see the excerpts by Sedgwick (1942), Arvin (1950), Horsford (1962), Zoellner (1973), and Kazin (NCLC, Vol. 3).*]

In a recent book on Melville, *Melville's Quarrel with God,* Mr. Lawrance Thompson has undertaken to cast Melville in the role of God-hater. His position will provide a convenient foil for presenting its opposite. In *Moby Dick* Melville is not attacking God; he is attempting to rescue the idea of the good, to push back from his darkening consciousness that instinctive reaction of the disillusioned American: hatred of creation itself. . . . [A] good many of the insults against Christianity that Mr. Thompson uncovers are delivered at the level of the Calvinism preached by [the Dutch Reformed Church]. . . . The trouble with using Melville's attitude to that form of Calvinism as a touchstone by which to gauge his attitude to religion generally is simply that one is compelled to simplify disastrously. (pp. 192-93)

Mr. Thompson takes up the question of Ahab's name, which derives from the wicked King of Israel in the First Book of Kings. This is a crucial problem in any interpretation of *Moby Dick,* for it helps us guard against that romantic exaltation of Ahab which has resulted in missing Melville's point. A just appreciation of Melville's reasons for choosing this name, among all others, for his monomaniac captain, will reveal a great deal about his creative intentions. Mr. Thompson, in conformity with his general argument, sees in Melville's choice an instance of his habit of beguiling Christian readers:

> But there is one other correlation, far more interesting, between these two Ahabs. Each of them is seduced to his death by a prophet, and Captain Ahab's misleading prophet is Fedallah. . . . Consider, however, the hint in First Kings as to how it happened that King Ahab was similarly victimized: 'I saw the Lord sitting on his throne, and all the host of heaven standing by him, on his right hand and the left. And the Lord said, Who shall persuade Ahab, that he may go up and fall at Ramoth-gilead? . . . And there came forth a spirit, and stood before the Lord, and said, I will persuade him. And the Lord said unto him, Wherewith? And he said, I will go forth, and I will be a lying spirit in the mouth of all his prophets. And the Lord said, Thou shalt persuade him, and prevail also: go forth and do so.'

> For Melville's anti-Christian purposes, that passage lends itself nicely to a correlated series of insinuations that God is a malicious double-crosser, a deceiver, who is not above employing a 'lying spirit' . . . to lead a man to his death. . . .'

(p. 193)

The meaning of *Moby Dick* is, I think, in deep accord with a somewhat less 'sinister' reading of the scriptural chapter.

It may be recalled that as the chapter opens, King Jehosophat has arrived from Judah on a social visit to King Ahab of Israel. During an early conversation, Ahab raises the question of Ramoth-gilead, formerly a tributary city of his in the north, but for some time since, by the power of possession, in the hands of the King of Syria. Ahab wants it back, and persuades Je-hosophat to assist him in a military expedition. Being more devout than Ahab, Jehosophat insists that the prophets be officially consulted to insure that Jehovah's blessing rest on the undertaking. So at Jehosophat's insistence, Ahab summoned four hundred prophets—that is to say, four hundred of the clergy of the Established Church—to appear and prophesy before them in a public place. Two thrones were erected, and at the appointed time the two Kings in full royal regalia took their places. The four hundred prophets, passing before them, prophesied great success for their arms. . . . It is perfectly clear from the chapter as a whole that they were not unaware of the private expediency of their tack. In fact, ever since their day the clergies of most countries have not found it difficult to prophesy glory for the arms of their temporal sovereigns. But apparently Jehosophat was not deceived, for turning to King Ahab, he asked: 'Is there not here a prophet of the Lord besides, that we might enquire of him?' Why, yes: Ahab admitted that there was, but he never had anything agreeable to say. But Jehosophat would not be put off, and so Ahab had to send a messenger to summon the prophet Micaiah. But it is clear that he instructed his messenger to have a private talk with Micaiah, for coming before him the messenger said: 'Behold now, the words of the prophets declare good unto the King with one mouth; let thy word, I pray thee, be like the word of one of them, and speak that which is good.' . . . [As] an obedient subject of his temporal ruler, Micaiah obeyed. But Ahab understood well enough the way in which he had sealed the lips of his prophet. It is intriguing to speculate what compulsive drive led him to blurt out at the crucial moment, just when Micaiah had prophesied good as the King had commanded him to do through the messenger: 'How many times shall I adjure thee that thou tell me nothing but that which is true in the name of the Lord?' Nothing could be clearer than that this is an implicit confession that he hadn't believed the lying four hundred prophets in the first place. . . . Being thus adjured to speak, not in the name of his King but of his God, Micaiah prophesied the defeat of Ahab's army, and his death. Ahab's response to this, apart from putting Micaiah into prison, was to turn to Jehosophat and enquire: Didn't I tell you he would only speak evil about me? It is the perfect picture of a man who will not admit a truth that he knows to be true. It is, then, at this point, before being led away to gaol for having prophesied truly, that Micaiah turns to Ahab and speaks that passage about the 'lying spirit' and the four hundred prophets leading Ahab to destruction—the passage that leads Mr. Thompson to speak of God as a malicious double crosser, at least for the purposes of his critical argument. It is a little difficult to see how Mr. Thompson's reading can be accepted as plausible at any level of interpretation. Mr. Thompson has radically criticized the immaturity of meaning with which Melville invested Captain Ahab. Actually, Melville was as aware of the moral limitations of Ahab as Mr. Thompson, and a proof of it is that he chose the name Ahab for very different reasons than those Mr. Thompson attributes to him.

What, in fact, did Melville see in the Biblical King? So far from being a victim, King Ahab is one of the most petulant self-asserters among Israel's rulers. His God-defiance never really got above the level of a foot-stamping 'I won't!' Ahab didn't have a great will, but he had a leech-like will. Once he had fastened it to a purpose it was a little difficult to disengage it. With a blue-print of his own destruction in his hand he deliberately followed it to the last line and letter. He is one of the most remarkable delineations of a perverse will in sacred or profane literature, and what we see is not a Titan but a

weakling. Melville's Ahab is certainly not a weakling in the usual sense—but then the King was never more typical than when he insisted on going to war with the knowledge that he would be killed, and much of his army also. This, I think, was what influenced Melville in First Kings, chapter twenty-two. The flaw in the King and the Captain is identical. (pp. 194-96)

Another scriptural correspondence, also made in the interests of a God-hating Melville, seems equally unfortunate—at least in the way Mr. Thompson interprets it, for the correspondence itself is undeniable. Melville, according to this argument, hated God because God is the creator of evil as well as good, and Mr. Thompson argues that the White Whale is essentially a symbol of evil to Melville, though not an abstract, but a very specific, theological kind of evil that corrupts the universe. One of the great chapters of *Moby Dick* is the one in which Starbuck's whaling boat harpoons an old bull whale, crippled and enfeebled by age. . . . The scriptural correspondence of which I spoke a moment ago is the one which Mr. Thompson draws between the imagery of this chapter, describing the sufferings of the harpooned old whale, and the forty-first chapter of Job, in which Jehovah describes the impregnable attributes of Leviathan, thereby, as it were, taunting the afflicted man. According to Mr. Thompson, Melville's chapter is built up of concealed sarcasms at God's expense—a case of taunting the Taunter, dismembering the Dismemberer. The correspondence is there, but this reading of it promotes a sad falling off in Melville. Prefiguring the sufferings of Christ, the Psalmist cried: 'They have pierced my hands and feet, they have numbered all my bones.' This seems a better commentary on those chapters in *Moby Dick* in which we are presented with lengthy commentaries on the dismembering of the whales than the charge that Melville is insulting God thereby. Read from this point of view, we have in the image of the suffering Leviathan not only an image of the suffering God, but simultaneously the agonized whale, as a magnificent image of created nature, reveals the awful wrack in that creation which men themselves cause.

If the image of Leviathan can, at one level, be interpreted as the image of the suffering God, we would expect to find in the record of his afflictions some allusions to Christ. And I think we do. I would cite as a single instance at this point the passage which Mr. Thompson quotes as an example of Melville's concealed jibing against God—a passage which describes a harpooned whale attached by lines to three whaling-boats from the Pequod:

> Seems it credible that by three such thin threads the great Leviathan was suspended like the big weight to an eight day clock. Suspended? and to what? To three bits of board. Is this the creature of whom it was once so triumphantly said—'Canst thou fill his skin with barbed irons? or his head with fish-spears? The sword of him that layeth at him cannot hold, the spear, the dart, nor the habergeon: he esteemeth iron as straw; the arrow cannot make him flee; darts are counted as stubble; he laugheth at the shaking of a spear!' This the creature? this he? Oh! that unfulfilments should follow the prophets. For with the strength of a thousand thighs in his tail, Leviathan had run his head under the mountains of the sea, to hide him from the Pequod's fish-spears.

As one returns to this chapter with the whole of *Moby Dick* in mind, I think it not unreasonable to see something reminiscent of the three arms of the cross from which Christ hung in those three bits of wood from which Leviathan is suspended. 'Oh! that unfulfilments should follow the prophets!' It seems probable to me that this is a rhetorical exclamation calling attention to the fact that the old prophecies have indeed been fulfilled. The tormented Leviathan, running his head under the mountain of the sea, recalls Psalm 69, which is commonly accepted as prefiguring the sufferings of Christ and the malice of his persecutors:

> Save me, O God; for the waters are come in unto my soul.
>
> I sink in deep mire, where there is no standing: I am come into deep waters, where the floods overflow me.
>
> I am weary of my crying: my throat is dried: mine eyes fail while I wait for my God. . . .
>
> Deliver me out of the mire, and let me not sink: let me be delivered from them that hate me and out of the deep waters.
>
> Let not the waterflood overflow me, neither let the deep swallow me up, and let not the pit shut her mouth upon me.

The connection is at least not as tenuous as some Mr. Thompson proposes. And one might, to sustain the spirit of the counter-argument, surmise that since Christ was pierced by a spear, and since the Fish was an early symbol of Christ, it is possible that Melville's reference to the Pequod's fish-spears is, most deeply, at the expense of Ahab and his crew rather than at the expense of God. I am trying here to point to the function that this idea of the suffering Leviathan performs in the novel. It is a symbol in which Melville was not only able to express his growing horror of evil in the universe, but his positive affirmation of an indestructible good. It is a deeply tragic symbol redeemed by a yet profounder religious intuition. (pp. 196-98)

The White Whale is Melville's profoundest intuition into the nature of creation, and it is an intuition in which God and nature are simultaneously present and commenting on each other.

The evil of the world filled Melville with horror, and there is little doubt that because of that horror a Manichean element colours his sensibility. Many critics before Mr. Thompson have seen in the White Whale a symbol of God, and some of them have viewed that God as predominantly an evil one. And yet it seems to me that Melville makes some clear distinctions which, if not necessarily pointing towards a rigorously orthodox Christian God, exonerate the White Whale from that burden of malignancy that Ahab's own perverse will has projected into his image. I would point particularly to Chapter LIX entitled 'Squid'. It is one of the most imaginatively terrifying chapters in the novel, and also one of the most beautifully written. On a beautiful blue morning 'when the slippered waves whispered together as they softly ran on'—just such a morning as would banish any thought of evil from the mind—the crew of the Pequod is given a vision of pure evil, and at first they mistake it for the White Whale. From his lookout post on the mainmast, Daggoo, the harpooner, sights a huge rolling mass of white in the sea ahead, and cries out to those below, 'The White Whale, the White Whale!'

Instantly four boats and their crews are lowered in pursuit, but as they approach the floating mass it is not Moby Dick they see:

> Soon it went down, and while, with oars suspended, we were waiting its reappearance, lo! in the same spot where it sank, once more it slowly rose. Almost forgetting for the moment all thoughts of Moby Dick, we now gazed at the most wondrous phenomenon which the secret seas have hitherto revealed to mankind. A vast pulpy mass, furlongs in length and breadth, of a glancing cream colour, lay floating on the water, innumerable long arms radiating from its centre, and curling and twisting like a nest of anacondas, as if blindly to catch at any hapless object within reach. No perceptible face or front did it have; no conceivable token of either sensation or instinct; but undulated there on the billows, an unearthly, formless, chance-like apparition of life.

In Zoroastrianism, with which Melville, to some extent at least was familiar, the world is divided between a good and an evil principle, and they are twin brothers. In the end the good will triumph, but their conflict is for the length of time. The giant Squid was surely meant by Melville for his symbol of evil. It is, as one would expect, evil in a Manichean rather than in a Christian sense, but the Squid's horrid anaconda arms invoke the Christian serpent; and they also give an added meaning to a later reference to Captain Ahab as an anaconda of an old man—for he also has blindly caught at the hapless members of his crew, and carried them down to destruction. But what is most significant is the resemblance of this symbol of evil, when viewed at a little distance, to the White Whale. They are, as one might say, twin brothers. They resemble each other most in their whiteness and their facelessness, and both of these attributes signify the inscrutability of the divided yet impenetrable universe in which it is so difficult to distinguish good from evil. And as between the twin brothers of Zoroastrianism, so between the White Whale and the White Squid there is eternal enmity:

> . . . the spermaceti whale obtains his food in unknown zones below the surface; and only by inference is it that anyone can tell of what, precisely, that food consists. At times, when closely pursued, he will disgorge what are supposed to be the detached arms of the squid; some of them thus exhibited exceeding twenty and thirty feet in length. They fancy that the monster to which these arms belonged ordinarily clings by them to the bed of the ocean; and that the sperm whale, unlike other species, is supplied with teeth in order to attack it.

One of the most striking threads of imagery in *Moby Dick* is the 'feeding' imagery. What is fed upon becomes assimilated into the body of the feeder, and this idea sounds throughout *Moby Dick* as a deep and ominous note of resonance. In an oddly subterranean way it keeps the perception bubbling that, through all this mutual devouring, good and evil become inextricably confused with each other, assimilated into each other's being until it is impossible to distinguish between them. In its vulture or sharkish aspect, which reflects Melville's shocked recoil from the world he saw, it comes to a head in the devastating chapter called 'Shark Massacre', in which the sharks

. . . viciously snapped, not only at each other's disbowelments, but like flexible bows, bent around and bit their own, till those entrails seemed swallowed over and over again by the same mouth, to be oppositely voided by the gaping wound.

It is almost like *Maldoror;* but Melville, in the great orgy of cannibalism and inter-feeding that goes on throughout the novel, is searching for some sacramental essence of good that persists through all devourings.

Significant from this point of view is the opening sentence of Chapter LXV where the second mate, Stubb, has had the cook prepare a whale steak for him:

That mortal man should feed upon the creature that feeds his lamp, and, like Stubb, eat him by his own light, as you may say; this seems so outlandish a thing that one must needs go a little into the history and philosophy of it.

If the White Whale is a symbol of God, Melville's recurrent references to the light that is derived from his broken body are certainly important, and the metaphysical image of Stubb eating the whale by its own light is a sarcasm, not at God's expense, but at the expense of a hypocritical and savage world that, like the false four hundred prophets of King Ahab, uses the light of God for its own profit while lacerating the body of truth. The meaning of this image is enriched in what follows, for as Stubb eats the whale steak in his cabin, a ravenous shoal of sharks devour the body of the murdered whale that is tied to the side of the Pequod. When Stubb forces the old negro cook to preach a sermon to the sharks to quiet them down, before he goes onto the deck Stubb says to him: "'Here, take this lantern,'" snatching one from the sideboard: "'now, then, go and preach to them.'" So the old cook preaches over the ship's side to the sharks by the light of the whale they are devouring. No doubt it is an indictment of the perversions of Christianity in the world. But it is Christianity *in the world;* and it is the light of God, one might say by way of gloss, that reveals the horrors.

So far I may have seemed inconclusive in assuming, in opposition to Mr. Thompson's position, that the image of Leviathan is the symbol of a *good* God, although I have already given a number of reasons for taking such an attitude. The greatest chapter in **Moby Dick** is Chapter LXXXVII, 'The Grand Armada'. It is even more important than the chapter on the White Squid for determining what Leviathan meant for Melville. As the voyage of the Pequod approaches its end, the ship sails through the straits of Sunda in the China seas, and it is confronted there by an immense aggregation of sperm whales, by what seemed thousands and thousands of them. The lookout first becomes aware of them as a great semi-circle of spouting jets, 'a continuous chain . . . up-playing and sparkling in the noon-day air', and embracing one half of the level horizon. The Pequod sets off in pursuit, and the crew soon realizes that the crescent has come full circle, and that they are entirely surrounded by a vast circle of spouting jets—by what, as the chapter progresses, one feels might be called a heavenly host of whales. Three boats are lowered. The one in which Ishmael has his place fastens its harpoon in a whale which, plunging forward, heads into the heart of the great herd, drawing the boat behind it. There is something mystically portentous in the entry of Ishmael's whaling boat into the quiet centre of the circling whales:

. . . at last the jerking harpoon drew out, and the towing whale sideways vanished; then, with the tapering force of his parting momentum, we glided between two whales into the innermost heart of the shoal, as if from some mountain torrent we had slid into a serene valley lake. Here the storms in the roaring glens between the outermost whales, were heard but not felt. In this central expanse the sea presented a smooth satin-like surface. . . . Yes, we were now in that enchanted calm which they say lurks in the heart of every commotion. And still in the outer distance we beheld the tumults of the outer concentric circles, and saw successive pods of whales, eight or ten in each, swiftly going round and round, like multiplied spans of horses in a ring; and so closely shoulder to shoulder that a Titanic circus rider might easily have over-arched the middle ones, and so have gone round on their backs. . . .

Now, inconclusive of the occasional wide intervals between the revolving outer circles, and inconclusive of the spaces between the various pods in any one of those circles, the entire area at this juncture, embraced by the wide multitude, must have contained at least two or three square miles. At any rate . . . spoutings might be discovered from our low boat that seemed playing up almost from the rim of the horizon.

It seems obvious to me that the source (though probably the unconscious source) of this vision of circling whales is Canto XXVIII of the *Paradiso*. . . . In Canto XXVIII, it will be recalled, Dante, turning from Beatrice, beholds a point of intensest light around which spin the nine concentric circles of the angelic intelligences—great wheels of fire which, as they revolve, shoot forth sparkles. Visually, the circles of whales present a startlingly similar image to the imagination as their water-spouts catch the light of the sun in great concentric rings that are enclosed by the horizon only. The visual similarity is enhanced by the water imagery in which Dante describes the revolving angelic orders. Thus, he compares them to the luminous ring of vapour that sometimes surrounds the moon; and, again, he compares the reach of the circles with the rainbow's arc.

Beatrice, explaining to Dante the center of intense light about which the concentric circles eternally revolve, says: 'From that point doth hang heaven and all nature'. Now the question is, what did the Pequod's whaling boat, when it broke through the living circles into the enchanted calm, find there? It is here that Melville's writing achieved a beauty that he never surpassed, or equalled:

But far beneath this wondrous world upon the surface, another and still stranger world met our eyes as we gazed over the side. For, suspended in those watery vaults, floated the forms of the nursing mothers of the whales, and those that by their enormous girth seemed shortly to become mothers. The lake, as I have hinted, was to a considerable depth exceedingly transparent; and as human infants while suckling will calmly and fixedly gaze away from the breast, as if leading two different lives at the time; and while yet drawing mortal nourishment, be still spiritually feeding on some unearthly reminiscence;—even so did the young of these whales seem looking up towards us, as if we were but a bit of Gulf-weed in their new-born sight. Floating on their sides, the mothers also seemed quietly eyeing us. One of these little infants that from certain queer tokens seemed hardly a day old, might have measured some fourteen feet in length and some six feet in girth. He was a little frisky; though as yet his body seemed scarce yet recovered from that irksome position it had so lately occupied in the maternal reticule; where, tail to head, and all ready for the final spring, the unborn whale lies bent like a Tartar's bow. The delicate side fins, and the palms of his flukes still freshly retained the plaited crumpled appearance of a baby's ears newly arrived from foreign parts.

What we have here is a vision of the world in its primal innocence, an image of the life principle presented in an intuition so profound that it seems a part of God's being. The whale mother and her beautiful infant, still attached by the umbilical cord, is an image as tender and reverent, essentially as religious, as a Della Robbia Madonna and Child. The sheer loveliness of that 'enchanted calm' into which the whaling boat intrudes is such that, leaning over its side and looking down into the transparent depths wherein is reflected one of the most astonishing images of the purity and mystery of life ever conceived by an artist—the sheer loveliness of it is such that we almost say with Beatrice: From this point hangs heaven and all nature.

Leviathan is not the tyrant, and Melville would leave us in no doubt. (pp. 198-204)

In what I have said of the influence of Dante I have had no intention of suggesting that Melville is trying to use Leviathan as a kind of symbol for the Beatific Vision—but the emotional impact of Dante's Canto on Melville clearly seems to be an important element in the wonderful achievement represented by 'The Grand Armada'. And the significance of this for determining what Leviathan meant for Melville when he wrote *Moby Dick* can hardly, I think, be exaggerated. The image of God that Leviathan symbolizes is an image, certainly not beyond, but *outside* a *specific* theology. It represents a religious intuition of life itself in some of its most basic and positive affirmations. At the same time, it is essentially a tragic intuition, and Leviathan is a suffering God. If the image is not Christian, it is filled with Christian overtones, and they lend Leviathan a large part of his evocativeness. It is hardly too much to say that if we have seen Leviathan dismembered and his bones numbered by his enemies, we see him rise again after three days in Moby Dick's final victory over the Pequod at the end of the third day's chase.

Captain Ahab is the focus of attention in the novel, and as the symbolic embodiment of the representative nineteenth-century American the fate that overtakes him is an indication of Melville's own reaction to the American world of his day. [In] nothing is Ahab more representative (I use 'representative', of course, in this context not to indicate the average but the paradigmatic) than in the transition he illustrates between the American democratic acceptance of creation, and hatred of that creation. Ahab is sometimes mistakenly identified with Melville's viewpoint in the novel, and, indeed, to some extent he

represents a part of Melville's mind; and a much larger part if we consider the Melville of a year or so later. But it is Ishmael with whom we must identify Melville's viewpoint in the end; and this identification is essential if we are to discover a positive and coherent form in *Moby Dick*.

Leviathan, I have argued, represents the *good* in Melville's universe, but through Ahab's and Ishmael's eyes we are given two different visions of him. . . . But beyond that point of view we sense a universe of objective values in which moral action and direction are still possibilities, though difficult to achieve. That Ishmael *does* achieve them constitutes the formal justification of the novel. Ishmael's solitary survival at the end of the novel is, in a sense, the validation of his vision; and it represents Melville's momentary triumph in having introduced an element of moral order into his universe, in having reestablished, in the face of his growing doubts, the polarity of good and evil. I wish to consider here, as briefly as I may, the meaning of Ishmael's point of view. . . . For it is through Ishmael that Melville makes his positive affirmation.

The experiences in which Ishmael participates on the Pequod are, in a sense, his. They constitute a kind of passion play for him from which he is almost literally resurrected in the Epilogue into new life. The opening paragraph indicates the problem that faces Ishmael, and to which the action of the novel brings a cosmic solution:

> Whenever I find myself growing grim about the mouth; whenever it is a damp drizzly November in my soul; whenever I find myself involuntarily pausing before coffin warehouses, and bringing up the rear of every funeral I meet; and especially whenever my hypos get such an upper hand of me, that it requires a strong moral principle to prevent me from deliberately stepping into the street, and methodically knocking people's hats off—then, I account it high time to get to sea as soon as I can.

Though so casually expressed, Ishmael's malaise as described here represents the essence of that despair, though then greatly exaggerated, which overtook Melville in *Pierre* and *The Confidence Man*. But in *Moby Dick* there will be, as the opening paragraph indicates, no submission to it, but a vigorous resistance. The sea is the source of life in the world, and it is to the sea that Ishmael returns whenever he feels symptoms of this depression. Ishmael, then, hardly less than Ahab may be said to do, sets out on the voyage on a quest, but it is a different quest from Ahab's. It is a quest for spiritual health, a desire to enter into a new and deeper harmony with creation. Ishmael accepts the mystery of creation—particularly as embodied in Leviathan—which Ahab does not. Ishmael's attitude towards Moby Dick is one of respectful reverence and wonder, and although from time to time during the course of the Pequod's voyage Ishmael comes under the influence of Ahab's intellectual domination, such occasions are momentary.

From the very beginning, Moby Dick is not a symbol of evil to Ishmael, but a magnificent symbol of creation itself. Creation is not a pasteboard mask for Ishmael, to be broken through in some excess of spiritual pride, as it was for Ahab, whose attempt to penetrate visible creation, not through love but hatred, could only end in a material vision. The measure of Ishmael's contrast in this respect is given in the following passage. Ishmael is paying a visit to the whaling chapel in New Bedford:

Methinks that in looking at things spiritual, we are too much like oysters observing the sun through water, and thinking that thick water the thinnest air. In fact, take my body who will, take it, I say, it is not me. And therefore three cheers for Nantucket; and come a stove boat and stove my body when they will, for stave my soul Jove himself cannot.

We are sometimes inclined to lose sight of the elementary fact that the whole complex movement of *Moby Dick* originates in Ahab's inability to resign himself, after Ishmael's fashion as indicated here, to the loss of a leg. Ahab is guilty of that most democratic of sins—of denying hierarchy between the body and soul, eternal and temporal values. He can proceed from a severed limb to a condemned and guilty universe with the greatest of ease. (pp. 204-07)

The degrees of knowledge are the most important of all for they most directly reflect the degrees of order and value in the spiritual world. It is an important element in Ahab's comprehensive significance that, in Chapter CXVIII, 'The Quadrant', he symbolically destroys the instrument of knowledge by which he should determine his location—his place in creation, as it were:

> Then gazing at his quadrant, and handling, one after the other, its numerous cabalistical contrivances, he pondered again, and muttered: 'Foolish toy! babies' plaything of haughty Admirals, and Commodores, and Captains; the world brags of thee, of thy cunning and might; but what after all canst thou do, but tell the poor, pitiful point, where thou thyself happenst to be on this wide planet, and the hand that holds thee: no! not a jot more!'

The manner in which the official hierarchy of the navy is merged here with the ordered knowledge for which the quadrant stands, is worth noting. The importance of this chapter is generally recognized; but there is still reason to insist that it is not science as such that Ahab is rejecting here. Rather, it is the idea of degree. It is precisely Ahab's *place* in the universe which he does not wish, indeed refuses, to know. And it is only his *place* that the quadrant can tell, his place with reference to the sun. (pp. 207-08)

Ahab's attitude is the antithesis of life because it represents a rejection of creation. The analysis of this attitude forms the main substance of the novel, but its great formal achievement exists in the beautiful way that Melville placed the action in an evaluative perspective so that its final effect is one of positive affirmation.... [He achieved this by building] up the symbol of Leviathan, layer on layer, so that it became one of the most magnificent images in the language of the positive aspects of creation. Leviathan, especially in his greatest role of the White Whale, is the affirmation of all that Ahab denies. The impact of this recognition on the imagination is the greater because, if Melville leads one towards it irresistibly, we yet make the discovery in the midst of all the gargantuan suffering of the whaling ground. We learn the triumph of life that the White Whale represents only because we come to it through such seas of death. This is the most deeply Christian note that Melville ever strikes. (p. 208)

> *Marius Bewley, "Melville," in his* The Eccentric Design: Form in the Classic American Novel, *1959.*

Reprint by Columbia University Press, 1963, pp. 187-219.

HOWARD C. HORSFORD   (essay date 1962)

[*In the following discussion of the importance of ontology in* Moby-Dick, *Horsford first reviews contemporary attitudes toward the notion that God's nature is revealed through the physical world. Noting the influence of David Hume's theory that knowledge of the physical world cannot support metaphysical speculation, Horsford then contrasts this perspective with the views of such "traditionalists" as Ralph Waldo Emerson, who maintained that the world reveals the nature of God. In the critic's opinion,* Moby-Dick *challenges the traditional outlook, being an uncompromising artistic exploration of the implications of Hume's reasoning. Specifically, Horsford suggests that Melville employs symbolic methods in the novel to advance what is essentially an antisymbolist ontology. Ahab is thus interpreted as a man doomed by his dogmatic insistence on the symbolic nature of experience (in this case, his encounters with the White Whale), while Ishmael is considered a representative of the "desperate possibility of a universe simply meaningless, where all comforting analogies are only self-deceits." The role of ontology in* Moby-Dick *is also discussed by Thorp (1938), Bewley (1959), Zoellner (1973), Nechas (1978), Hillway (1979), and Aiken (NCLC, Vol. 3). For additional commentary on symbolism in* Moby-Dick, *see Lawrence (1923), Arvin (1950), Bewley (1959), Kulkarni (1970), Hillway (1979), and Mather, Lawrence, Mumford, Aiken, Winters, Sedgwick, Maugham, Auden, and Priestley (NCLC, Vol. 3). Other critics who contrast Ahab's and Ishmael's view of the world include Sedgwick (1942), Arvin (1950), Bewley (1959), Zoellner (1973), and Kazin (NCLC, Vol. 3).*]

It is not new to point to Melville's life-long concern with the relation between knowledge and belief, but we need to explore more fully his imaginative rendering of the implications of such a relationship—and its collapse—if we are to understand better our response to his fiction....

Melville grew up with the generations still wracked by the new theory of knowledge developed most fully by David Hume. In the face of the pious complacencies of the "Age of Reason," Hume had argued that nothing can be discovered by reasoning on the subjects with which metaphysics is concerned. Mere custom, only, stands warrant for our ideas of cause and effect; "belief" is not "knowledge" and "is more properly an act of the sensitive, than of the cogitative part of our natures." (p. 234)

[Those] young men of Emerson's and Melville's generations—those who thought about it all—sensed profoundly enough the desperate implications of Hume's skeptical epistemology. "Who is he that can stand up before him," the deeply troubled young Emerson asked his aunt, "& prove the existence of the Universe, & of its founders?"

This is the problem which for Melville so largely shapes the "ontological heroics" (the phrase is his) he passionately argued those years.... For Hume, in arguing the purely subjective, the illusory nature of knowledge, had struck at a rooted habit of thought, one conditioned by milleniums of tradition in the western religious world, one which had almost immemorially asserted the nature and providence of God on the material evidence of His handiwork. (pp. 235-36)

[Suppose] our "knowledge" of this universe, which presumably so manifests its Creator, should be, after all, only subjectively created illusion, delusory? The profound implications in this possibility were what so challenged the imagination of the returned young sailor just discovering the exciting world of the mind. And this is an America where ... the divinely benign influence of nature on the heroic new men of this new Eden was likely to be proclaimed in any editorial, in any patriotic oration, alike from the orthodox pulpit and the lyceum platform of the self-styled transcendentalists.

Thus, though they by no means define between them all the aspects then dominant in American faiths, Jonathan Edwards and Emerson may speak, the one for American Calvinism in its most intellectually rigorous form, the other for American transcendentalism in its most persuasive idiom. In any event, the impulse to assert symbolic identities between nature and its god was sufficiently universal for a young man to absorb anywhere. At no less a hallowed shrine than his mother's knee, Melville heard the Dutch Reformed Catechism proclaiming man could learn much of God through His created universe— "a most elegant book, wherein all creatures, great and small, are as so many characters leading us to contemplate the invisible things of God." . . .

[Even] the rigorous Edwards went much further in his thought. To him the "images" and "shadows" of the natural world were not merely useful for illustrations of divine truths; they were evidence of Truth itself. . . .

The success of Hume's destruction of the certainty of knowledge, together with all its devastating implications for thought generally, including religious belief, eventually set off what has been called a mania for epistemological investigation. Emerson, like his English and German fellows, was deeply shaken by the Scotch Goliath. But in the end, like them, he was able to reassert a faith, a confidence in the reading of the world as a symbol of God, founded on a depth of *intuitive* conviction beyond—or, at any rate, not susceptible to—rational argumentation or criticism.

At the same time, Emerson went beyond Edwards in denying the tragic possibilities of human error and suffering. It was the easy, cheerful benevolence of transcendentalism in its shallower reaches, as well as the complacent assurance in the myth of the new world paralleling it, which prompted . . . Melville's scorn. Melville, with far more direct experience of the world than Emerson, had found few Edens in the forecastle. (p. 236)

For the increasingly scornful Melville . . . , writers like Emerson or Goethe or Carlyle quickly became that "guild of self-impostors, with a preposterous rabble of Muggletonian Scots and Yankees, whose vile brogue still the more bestreaks the stripedness of their Greek or German Neoplatonical originals." His own "ontological heroics," of which he writes so often to Hawthorne in 1850-1851 while the whale was in his flurry, pursue the same questions of the nature of reality, the nature and existence of God, from a profoundly different vantage.

It would be absurd, of course, to make of *Moby-Dick* a systematic, discursive rebuttal of either Emersonian or more traditional ontological assumptions. Nonetheless, the represented experience of the novel is precisely that of the millennially old tradition viewed in a terrifying new perspective, of sensing faith and conviction disintegrate, so to speak, before one's eyes. We speak often, and with singular aptness, of the novel in metaphors of hunting, of questing, of going out to sea to "see"; what is seen and felt, what is projected here is that experience.

In Edwards and Emerson alike, the verb "see," once noticed, seems everywhere. . . . Yet what Edwards and even more Emerson "saw" they felt as reassurance about God's world. For Emerson, . . . the apparent faults of the world lay not in

the reality, but in our own imperfect vision. Life itself is an "angle of vision" and "man is measured by the angle at which he looks at objects." In *Nature* he disposes of evil and ugliness with the facility of a Shaftesbury or Pope: "The ruin or the blank that we see when we look at nature, is in our own eye"; "The Poet" finds that "the evils of the world are such only to the evil eye." But with Melville, . . . such passages provoked exasperated marginal comments. As against the bland pronouncement in "Spiritual Laws," "the good, compared to the evil which he sees, is as his own good to his own evil," Melville noted scathingly, "A perfectly good being, therefore, would see no evil.—But what did Christ see?—He saw what made him weep. . . .''

In the novel much of the hunt, of course, is after fair but much-pursued and slighter game like Biblical literalism, theological hair-splitting and apologetics, or practice versus preaching. The Biblical accounts of Jonah or Job, for example, are old familiar targets, and Melville is neither particularly original nor always at his best in heavy-handed irony and jocularity. Neither is this delighted hatchet-work altogether to the point, dealing as it does only with the engrafted fruit, not the roots of conviction.

The real triumph of the novel, both intellectually and esthetically, lies elsewhere; boldly, Melville adopted a symbolist esthetic—of the kind Emerson proclaimed in *Nature*—to express a vision of experience, with, at the same time, the profoundest questioning of its metaphysical premises. With a fuller sense of the radically symbolic quality of the mind's activity than any artist before him (Coleridge excepted), Melville created a great man tragically destroying himself because he assents fully and dogmatically to a symbolic interpretation of experience. Melville designed the tragedy of Ahab, the art of *Moby-Dick,* from material made to question the very foundation of that art.

It is the triumph of the novel that, as Thoreau would require, every natural fact is so intensely viewed it "flowers in a truth," even as that truth is questioned. Not Emerson himself could ask for a closer attention to the immediate, the familiar, the homely as the novel transmutes the grubby, greasy business of whaling into tragedy. But Emerson, in his determined effort to confront the divinity in the universe, had characteristically laid down the basis for his faith in a celebration of rural, pastoral nature. Melville, when he sent his searchers out to sea, confronted them with a nature vastly different. If, according to the young Thoreau, "Nature will bear the closest inspection"—because, according to Emerson, nature is "the present expositor of the divine mind"—we can suppose Melville sending his seekers out to widen their angle of vision, not by the dimension of a study window in Concord (or Northampton)—but from Ishmael's forecastle. (pp. 237-38)

When Emerson announced that the poet "disposes very easily of the most disagreeable facts," the fatuity of the remark prompted Melville's ironic "So it would seem. In this sense, Mr. E. is a great poet." The *Pequod's* search, far from disposing of the disagreeable, is exactly the attempt to face those facts, to ponder their significance. The land, with its comfortable securities, is kept only at the price of received opinion, of taking a part for the whole of experience, of seeing with too narrow an angle of vision. As in the familiar apostrophe concluding the abrupt dismissal of Bulkington,

> All deep, earnest thinking is but the intrepid
> effort of the soul to keep the open independence
> of her sea; while the wildest winds of heaven

and earth conspire to cast her on the treacherous, slavish shore. . . . as in landlessness alone
resides the highest truth, shoreless, indefinite
as God—so, better is it to perish in that howling
infinite, than be ingloriously dashed upon the
lee, even if that were safety! . . .   (p. 239)

The true whale hunter seeks the living, spouting whale, impatient with the stuffed and dessicated specimens, the inaccurate and misleading pictures offered ashore as representative
reality. So it is, too, in the search for illumination, only the
whale hunter "burns . . . the purest of oil, in its unmanufac-
tured, and, therefore, univitiated state . . . He goes and hunts
for his oil, so as to be sure of its freshness and genuineness. . . .''

This enforces one of the postulates of the whale hunt—an
endless process of hunt, capture, rendering, and hunting again.
The other is: "To grope down into the bottom of the sea after
them; to have one's hands among the unspeakable foundations,
ribs, and very pelvis of the world; this is a fearful thing." . . .
But wearying or terrifying, only in the search, in the unremitting, unblinking effort to face the disagreeable facts does
manhood realize itself.

To go to sea, to dive more deeply, to enlarge the vision—what
is it then that one sees? The Psalmist, St. Paul, the Bishops,
Edwards, or Emerson found the revelation of a just divinity.
In the novel we approach an immediate tactic (though not the
grand strategy) in Queequeg's exclamation of outraged pain
when the jaws of a dead shark reflexively snap on his hand.
"Queequeg no care what god made him shark . . . wedder
Fejee god or Nantucket god; but de god wat made shark must
be one dam Ingin." . . . The very first "Extract," with multiple
appropriateness from Genesis, reminds us that "God created
great whales," and though we are genially warned not to take
all "higgledy-piggledy whale statements" for "veritable gospel," we are all the same confronted immediately with the
classic logic of the syllogism: The creation, we have the highest
assurance, manifests the Creator; but this creation is notorious
for its suffering, its indifferent injustice, its ruthless energy
and merciless, predatory nature; therefore, such must be its
Creator.

Now this outraged conclusion is everywhere forced on our
attention in the novel—by Ahab. But properly to assess *Melville's* strategy, we must constantly observe the way he handles
the symbolizing mode of perception. The tradition of the symbolic connection between the creation and the creator, in all
of its many versions, is also everywhere in question here, but
most especially in its transcendental form. The strategic, the
fundamental, issue is coveniently though whimsically joined
in the mocking of the mast-head dreamer rapt in mystic communion. In an image which could have found an honored place
in Emerson's "Oversoul," Ishmael derides such a latter-day
Spinoza or Neoplatonist as he risks plunging to his destruction:
"lulled into such an opium-like . . . reverie is this absent-
minded youth by the blending cadence of waves with thoughts,
that at last he loses his identity; takes the mystic ocean at his
feet for the visible image of that deep, blue, bottomless soul,
pervading mankind and nature. . . .'' Yet in embodying elusive
thoughts in the dimly perceived, beautiful but elusive forms,
the dreamer loses his grip; only self-annihilation waits in that
mystic ocean.

All the same, it is by the full exploitation of the symbolizing
mode of perception that conclusions far other than those en-

tertained in Concord or Northampton are suggested. Persistently images of pastoral or domestic tranquility are juxtaposed
against the hidden dreadfulness of the sea. (pp. 239-41)

"The Gilder" chapter describes . . . [a day] when nature gilds
the surface with enchantment, and even the wary hunter has a
"land-like feeling towards the sea," regarding it as "so much
flowery earth," a "rolling prairie" where play-wearied children might sleep in the vales, and men, like colts, might roll
in new morning clover. But he who would argue benignity
ought in conscience to look beneath the memories of clovered
pastures beyond Concord and Walden.

Consider the subtleness of the sea; how its most
dreaded creatures glide under water, unappar-
ent for the most part, and treacherously hidden
beneath the loveliest tints of azure. Consider
also the devilish brilliance and beauty of
many . . . species of sharks. Consider, once
more, the universal cannibalism of the sea; all
whose creatures prey upon each other, carrying
on eternal war since the world began.

Consider all this; and then turn to this green,
gentle, and most docile earth; consider them
both, the sea and the land; and do you not find
a strange analogy to something in yourself? . . .

No longer do we see, with William Cullen Bryant, only "Nature's everlasting smile." All easy symbolizing analogies must
undergo a forcible revaluation. We must acknowledge the universal cannibalism in which sharks and men alike participate,
and we begin to see, in a wider angle of vision, all that to
which custom and convention on land had blindered us. Thoreau had travelled much in Concord, but a whaling ship was
Ishmael's Yale College and his Harvard. The vision of remorseless voracity beneath the deceiving surface is the experience of all genuine hunters for the oil of illumination. This
is what they have seen that makes *them* weep.

What Emerson would call the veils of Nature are to Ahab, as
he calls them in the famous passage, walls, pasteboard masks,
deceiving appearance through which he proposes to thrust at
the inscrutable malice he sees sinewing it from behind. To this,
then, has come for him the effort to confront the image of
divinity in the universe. . . . Ahab and Melville unquestionably
find a piously interpreted connection between nature and deity
no longer tenable; Ishmael and Melville are surely doubtful of
any other certainty resulting from a sea-search, but we ignore
the progressive thrust of the novel if we fail to recognize that
whatever doubts Ahab may entertain at points, by the end he
has acceded to a settled and violent conviction terribly but
merely the reverse of the traditional. (pp. 241-42)

He, too, insists on the symbolic connection between man and
god if only in the malice of destruction. (p. 242)

Ahab, though he has greatly dared beyond his landbound contemporaries in confronting a monstrous vision of the universe,
dared greatly in defying the malignant power so conceived,
yet not less than his contemporaries ashore does he hold the
creation to revolve egocentrically about himself. And in so
doing, like them he has only imposed his own solipsistic conception upon that world—a conception which has in no way
any greater warrant for its validity than that of the most egre-
giously complacent argument from design. Putatively, like Father Mapple, a seeking pilot of a ship's world, he is even more
like Father Mapple in being essentially convinced of his truth

before he begins; Ahab seeks not to discover what may be truth, but to prove his truth.

What this means in defining Ahab's tragedy, and how we are led to see his position as tragic, can be clarified by reconsidering the effect of Hume's ideas. . . . [Emerson] had at last to accommodate the new epistemology by identifying the creating mind of man with Providential purpose. Even as he discusses the "noble doubt" in *Nature,* Emerson adds, "It is a sufficient account of that Appearance we call the World, that God will teach a human mind . . . Whether nature enjoy a substantial existence without, or is only in the apocalypse of the mind, it is alike useful . . . to me." The assurance in this waiver is founded on the prior conviction, the "relation between the mind and matter is not fancied by some poet, but stands in the will of God . . ." Or as his contemporary journal adds, "The self of self creates the world through you." If by the 1840's, further experience had dampened this "Saturnalia of faith," he was still ready to describe "The Transcendentalist": "His thought—that is the Universe. . . . I—this thought which is called I—is the mould into which the world is poured like melted wax. The mould is invisible, but the world betrays the shape of the mould."

Carlyle's "The Universe is but one vast Symbol of God" or Emerson's equivalent "Nature is the symbol of spirit" assert, in effect, that the object and its significance are one. But for a mind not sharing the conviction of the radical correspondence of mind, matter, and God, such an epistemology must surely open appalling vistas. For if knowledge of the object may be merely illusion, then the avowed significance may be the wildest self-delusion. As Pierre will discover grimly not a year later, "Nature is not so much her own ever-sweet interpreter, as the mere supplier of that cunning alphabet, whereby selecting and combining as he pleases, each man reads his own peculiar lesson according to his own peculiar mind and mood." . . . This, at last, is the "metaphysical terror" contemplated by Ishmael, surpassing even Ahab's conviction in its fatal implications for the religious sensibility.

It is from this point of view, then, that Ahab may be considered as a re-viewed figure of the Emersonian, self-reliant, self-creating, self-destroying man, whose image of the "world, betrays the shape of the mould." (pp. 243-44)

The image which Ahab saw in the world is, finally, only what Narcissus saw—himself.

Modern psychological analysis of religious expression has familiarized us with the sense in which Calvins and Luthers transformed self-hates and guilts in their conceptions of deity. A hundred years ago Melville here creates the meaning of an equivalent insight. As the Calvinist finds wrathful justice in his ideas of the divine, as an Emerson finds his aspirations to benevolent serenity matched in the Concord landscape, so Ahab finds only his own hate and vengeful desire in what he takes to be the malice of the whale. . . .

The assertion of malevolent *intelligence* and *motivation* makes the same enormous leap into pure faith the orthodox and the transcendentalist have made. Ahab's "image" or "picture" of the whale has ultimately no more authenticity than the erroneous pictures found in incompetent books of "whale" lore, literally or metaphorically considered. The mad zealot Gabriel finds the incarnation of the Shaker God with as much or little warrant as Ahab. Ahab is destroyed—to this degree like his Biblical namesake—by establishing false idols of his own making. Ahab, who may long ago have begun by searching for

meaning and truth, has finally only succeeded, as Ishmael sees at length, in inverting delusion. (p. 245)

That we see both the magnificence and the peculiarly tragic nature of Ahab's "faith" is due, of course, to the angle of vision which Ishmael supplies. Once Ishmael, like the others, was caught up in the terrible grandeur of Ahab's vision. Once he, too, though with far more dubiety, could assert the "linked analogies"—"some certain significance lurks in all things, else all things are little worth, and the round world itself but an empty cipher. . . ." But the more Ishmael employs the analogical mode of perception, the more aware he becomes of its fatal deceptions.

For if, in a simple inversion of the orthodox view of reality, Ahab has made over the whale into an embodiment of all evil and malevolent purpose in the universe, Moby Dick comes eventually to suggest something quite different to Ishmael. . . . (pp. 246-47)

By a masterly balancing of image against image, Melville defines Ishmael's growing awareness of the desperate possibility of a universe simply meaningless, where all comforting analogies are only self-deceits. Not even malevolent, which would at least be personal, in some ways humanly apprehensible, but simply purposeless. Here is the dubiety in full consciousness— "all things *are* little worth, and the round world itself but an empty cipher," a Newtonian cryptogram without meaning, an empty zero.

We cannot fail to recognize in this chapter Melville's representation of Hume's implications; the dialectic of the material moves inexorably to the probable conclusion: all we can know, finally, of all the baffling phenomena presented by some possibly objective world is sheer illusion, a symbolic construct only of our own minds. From this appalling angle Ishmael must deny the certain validity of any "argument from design," orthodox, transcendental, or Satanic.

To affirm that either Edwards' or Emerson's God was still "the native of these bleak rocks" now seems to Ishmael a Laplandish superstition, as if one were looking at, seeing a very probably colorless world through deifying glasses. In one astonishing passage he sums up the implications of epistemological investigation from Locke to Hume:

> . . . is it, that as in essence whiteness is not so much a color as the visible absence of color, and at the same time the concrete of all colors . . . when we consider that other theory of the natural philosophers, that all other earthly hues— every stately or lovely emblazoning—the sweet tinges of sunset skies and woods; yea, and the gilded velvets of butterflies, and the butterfly cheeks of young girls; all these are but subtle deceits, not actually inherent in substances, but only laid on from without; so that all deified Nature absolutely paints like the harlot, whose allurements cover nothing but the charnel-house within; and when we proceed further, and consider that the mystical cosmetic which produces every one of her hues, the great principle of light, for ever remains white or colorless in itself, and if operating without medium upon matter, would touch all objects, even tulips and roses, with its own blank tinge—pondering all this, the palsied universe lies before us a leper; and like wilful travellers in Lapland, who re-

fuse to wear colored and coloring glasses upon their eyes, so the wretched infidel gazes himself blind at the monumental white shroud that wraps all the prospect around him. And of all these things the Albino whale was the symbol. . . .

Pointedly, the two chapters—"Moby Dick" for Ahab, "The Whiteness of the Whale" for Ishmael—are paired, barely one third of the way through the novel. The remainder of the novel takes all its significance from this differentiation. Now constantly borne in upon our attention, defining and shaping the impact of the novel upon our consciousness, are not only all those many images ambivalently linking pastoral tranquility and horror, but all the many overt statements, all the many images which point to a world neither benevolent nor malevolent, just icily, glacially cold, impersonal, indifferent, purposeless, meaningless. (pp. 247-48)

Beyond the veil, behind the mask, beneath the inscrutable whiteness may be—nothing. This is the terror which Ahab will not, at least for long, contemplate; but this is what the search for the white whale comes to signify for Ishmael. He had begun with the knowledge that to "have one's hands among the unspeakable foundations, ribs, and very pelvis of the world; this is a fearful thing." When he is at last among the ribs and pelvis of the skeleton in the Arsacides, he finds only—death. "I saw no living thing within; naught was there but bones." . . . With an equally grim jocularity, he finds he cannot make out the back parts, still less "how understand his head? much more, how comprehend his face, when face he has none?" . . . (p. 249)

With Ishmael's angle of vision Melville creates an insight transcending . . . Ahab. It is a view uncommitted to any dogmas, neither positively nor negatively theocentric; a view tentative and considerate of alternatives; one that seeks justly to evaluate and arrive at a sanely stable (if constantly provisional) understanding of the "truth of experience." "What plays the mischief with the truth," Melville wrote to Hawthorne late that memorable spring, "is that men will insist upon the universal application of a temporary feeling or opinion."

Without at all displacing Ahab as the dramatic center of the novel—in some sense of that slippery word, as "hero"—Ishmael develops a moral center and defining force, somewhat erratically, doubtless, in Melville's handling, and unsystematically, but nevertheless the indispensable perspective. It is shaped by the recognition at once of the "absurdity" of man's position in a purposeless universe, and yet the sober insistence, since this is all there is, there we must somehow make a life for ourselves. This is the other certainty. (pp. 249-50)

Hume undermined the notion that we can perceive even self as an objective entity, but at least, to be human is, precisely, to be aware of being human. One of the most insistently presented patterns in Ahab's tragic development is his progressive, wilful isolation from humanity and humane values. In defining contrast to this, again, is Ishmael's turning from his defiantly whimsical outcast mood to Queequeg. Between them grows what may inadequately be termed a "communion," undoctrinaire, based on no reference external to itself, transcending all differences of color, race, language, and nominal creed, not as sons of God, but as men. Queequeg's humanity, generosity and selflessness can exist irrespective of any institutionalized ethic, and despite the otherwise all too evident predatory nature of the world.

To be sure, this communion is represented perhaps rather too elaborately in the self-conscious analogy of the monkey-rope,

rather too graphically in the symbolic marriage at the Spouter Inn. Yet they together, Ishmael and Queequeg, shielded from the petrifying cold, are the "one warm spark in the heart of an arctic crystal." This is doubtless not an answer to the human predicament, but it is a necessary condition of existence. In one of its aspects it is passional love, just as the mating whales make the still center in the heart of the tornado of the Grand Armada. In its more general aspect it engages that the open independence of the sea and human interdependence, the never-ending self-reliant search and the concomitant responsibility of human love need not and must not be mutually exclusive. Against the weight of this moral center, Ahab is weighed, measured, and found wanting.

The tragic power of Ahab is the power of America's deepest cultural commitment, to the figure of the isolated, self-reliant individual, defining himself against both society and nature. The power of the novel is in the encompassing vision transcending this. What emerges is not a pious orthodoxy of belief and humility, nor yet solely the grandeur of Ahab's defiance, but a dynamic, unresolved tension between an experienced meaninglessness and the stubborn will to find meaning in experience, between the lonely grandeur of the lonely individual soul and the rights of human love. There is no *answer* here, only a vision of the conditions for the never-ending search in which mankind must forever engage—in the new world not less than in the old. Eden is not here, nor anywhere, but must forever be sought, worked for, with all of man's best energies and all his highest hopes, in all humility and in all the meaning of his humanity.

Here Melville has been beyond both piety and despair—not to some new cosmic moral revelation—but to the sobering proposition: If there is to be a moral order at all in this world, man—weak, flawed, fallible as he is—must somehow forge it himself out of his own human experience. (pp. 250-51)

> *Howard C. Horsford, "The Design of the Argument in 'Moby-Dick'," in* Modern Fiction Studies, *Vol. VIII, No. 3, Autumn, 1962, pp. 233-51.*

WARNER BERTHOFF (essay date 1962)

[In the following excerpt from The Example of Melville, *his study of Melville's artistry, Berthoff comments on two technical aspects of* Moby-Dick: *Ishmael's function and fitness as a first-person narrator and Melville's reliance on the short chapter as the basic unit of composition in the novel. Berthoff greatly admires Ishmael's narration. In particular, he emphasizes Ishmael's specificity, reliability, and absorption in his tale, noting the significant contributions that these qualities make toward controlling the pace of* Moby-Dick *and lending a consistent voice and style to the novel as a whole. The critic grants equal importance to Melville's handling of the numerous short chapters comprising the narrative. According to Berthoff, the chapters are the primary source of the novel's coherence, for in them Melville continually reinforces the story's unique conditions and perspectives. For additional commentary by Berthoff on Melville's treatment of settings and characterization in* Moby-Dick, *see NCLC, Vol. 3. The narrative point of view of the novel is discussed by Colcord (1922), Thompson (1952), and Nechas (1978). Nechas also provides further commentary on the structure of* Moby-Dick.]

Melville's particular skill in handling first-person narration may be illustrated by a comparison of two well-known passages from the American "classics," the first chapter of *Moby-Dick* and the first chapter of Washington Irving's *Sketch-Book*. . . . Their similarity goes well beyond their introductory function.

In each the effort is to establish the speaker in the character of the restless romantic voyager; and each moves directly on . . . to essentially the same corroborative image or scene, as well as to the implicit suggestion that the feelings described are such as any man of sense would experience in the same circumstances. Here is Irving's Geoffrey Crayon:

> This rambling propensity strengthened with my years. Books of voyages and travels became my passion, and in devouring their contents, I neglected the regular exercises of the school. How wistfully would I wander about the pier-heads in fine weather, and watch the parting ships, bound to distant climes; with what longing eyes would I gaze after their lessening sails, and waft myself in imagination to the ends of the earth!
>
> Further reading and thinking, though they brought this vague inclination into more reasonable bounds, only served to make it more decided. I visited various parts of my own country; and had I been merely a lover of fine scenery, I should have felt little desire to seek elsewhere its gratification, for on no country have the charms of nature been more prodigally lavished. Her mightly lakes, like oceans of liquid silver; her mountains, with their bright aërial tints; her valleys, teeming with wild fertility; her tremendous cataracts, thundering in their solitudes; her boundless plains, waving with spontaneous verdure; her broad deep rivers, rolling in solemn silence to the ocean; her trackless forests, where vegetation puts forth all its magnificence; her skies, kindling with the magic of summer clouds and glorious sunshine; no, never need an American look beyond his own country for the sublime and beautiful of natural scenery.
>
> But Europe held forth the charms of storied and poetical association. . . .

And here is Melville's Ishmael (who has already, in the book's opening paragraph, begun to turn attention off himself and his private reasons for going to sea):

> There now is your insular city of the Manhattoes, belted round by wharves as Indian isles by coral reefs—commerce surrounds it with her surf. Right and left, the streets take you waterward. Its extreme down-town is the battery, where that noble mole is washed by waves, and cooled by breezes, which a few hours previous were out of sight of land. Look at the crowds of water-gazers there.
>
> Circumambulate the city of a dreamy Sabbath afternoon. Go from Corlears Hook to Coenties Slip, and from thence, by Whitehall, northward. What do you see?—Posted like silent sentinels all around the town stand thousands upon thousands of mortal men fixed in ocean reveries. Some leaning against the spiles; some seated upon the pier-heads; some looking over the bulwarks of ships from China; some high aloft in the rigging, as if striving to get a still better seaward peep. But these are all lands-

men; of week days pent up in lath and plaster— tied to counters, nailed to benches, clinched to desks. How then is this? Are the green fields gone? What do they here?

> But look! here come more crowds, pacing straight for the water. . . .

(pp. 126-28)

[The contrast points up] the special abruptness and boldness with which, in *Moby-Dick,* the openings toward both audience and material are followed up. No sooner does Ishmael establish his personal character, in the first chapter, than he transforms it into a dramatic pose and promptly disappears into that. He makes his reader a positive accomplice—there now is *your* city, the streets take *you* waterward—the more effectively through the succession of commands and questions that follows: look, go, what do you see, why is it so, but look again! The device is transparent, and possibly risks impudence. What carries it off is the energetic particularity of the speaker's harangue, his quick attentiveness not only to "you" but to "them" and "it." The reader is caught up in specific names and images. The tour he is peremptorily summoned to go on is through concrete things, places, and events, with alternate possibilities. "Confidential" is from the first the word for Ishmael, but what is confided is not only a personal attitude but objective fact, observation, incident, aspect, enveloping condition. Without some such enthusiastic projection of self into material circumstances, this cheery familiarity of address would merely be impertinent and would cloy. It would have no natural function of disclosure, and we might well find ourselves preferring, over the long haul, the less overbearing company of a Geoffrey Crayon.

Characteristically, for Melville, the passage quoted proves itself most forcefully at its descriptive climaxes—in the exact kinesthetic hyperbole of "nailed to benches, clinched to desks," and in the expanding sympathy that builds to the image of landsmen mounting the rigging in their voiceless excitement. The note sounded, the gestures caught, are typical of Ishmael's witness. He is always something more than a figure of certain propensities and tastes who invites us to follow him around as he exercises them. He appears rather as a man attended—by "fate," he tells us, by a certain recklessness of inward temper; more decisively, as the teller of the story, by a capacity for being wholly absorbed into the images of his recollection. He does not stand on any private dignity. The range of his qualities is genuinely appealing: gaiety, compassion, a quick pleasure in the odd and the picturesque, a deeper elation of spirit in the presence of the really strange, a zest for sharing his enthusiasms (and for defining them), a self-awareness that is reassuringly self-deprecating, and then gusto, flippancy, gravity, sincerity, or awe, as the occasion warrants. As an observer and commentator he is discriminatingly alert to the way things happen in the world and especially to the conduct of men in it—an instance is the masterly series of sketches of the *Pequod's* mates (Chapters 26-27) and how each goes about his mortally hazardous work. As a chronicler of the adventure and the technology of whaling he holds easily to the human scale, yet he does not sentimentalize; he is as precisely sensitive to the "momentousness" of individual persons, including other writers, as to those "slidings and collidings of Matter" that Lawrence praised him for apprehending. Perhaps nothing is more ingratiating in Ishmael than the respectfulness of his appeal to older authorities—voyagers, chroniclers, scholars—in filling out his long narrative. We notice his interest, especially, in the testimony of "exact and reliable men"; it is as one such that he would wish himself to be known.

But these personal virtues of Ishmael's are really incidental to the imagination and voice, the authenticating turn of style, that sustain the whole bulky structure of *Moby-Dick*. For all the variety of the effects achieved, voice and style are consistent throughout the discursive mass of the book. They are fundamentally the same for its "larger, darker, deeper" concerns as for its representations of material fact. The standard of the "exact and reliable" holds for both kinds of exposition. It can sometimes make for rather elaborately adjectival writing, but even the most prodigal sequences of modifiers usually show a logic of conception as well as of sound and cadence. "A *wild, mystical, sympathetical* feeling was in me," Ishmael declares, in pledging himself to Ahab's purpose—and in due course devotes two magnificently detailed chapters, "Moby Dick" and "The Whiteness of the Whale," to confirming the simple accuracy of these high-flown epithets.

A sure instinct for when to hurry and when to take his time, for quick transition and for patient elaboration, is a major resource in Melville's art of spoken narrative. More than anything else, I think, it is his masterful control of the *pace* of Ishmael's exposition that secures for the narration in *Moby-Dick* the direct, continuing accent of reality. Chapter after chapter acts out rhetorically the conscious imaginative possession of what is there to be told. In writing of the emblematic Bulkington, for example, Ishmael does more than describe and represent; halfway along he positively rushes out to join him, as if to encourage the man in the behavior that makes him notable, as if he were real and alive and once more at that special parting of the ways marked out for him, and as if perceiving this about him suddenly enabled one to speak from an even further penetration into the whole "mortally intolerable truth" of things. ("Know ye now, Bulkington? Glimpses do ye seem to see . . .?") Of this control of the pace of disclosure and confirmation, this capacity to reproduce in meditative recollection the compounding rhythm of the whole conceived experience, the last paragraph of the important sixteenth chapter, "The Ship," provides another fine example. It comes just after Ishmael, now signed on for the *Pequod's* voyage but somewhat apprehensive about what is to come, has been absorbing from old Peleg a particularly wild barrage of hints and warnings concerning the ship's mysterious captain:

> As I walked away, I was full of thoughtfulness; what had been incidentally revealed to me of Captain Ahab, filled me with a certain wild vagueness of painfulness concerning him. And somehow, at the time, I felt a sympathy and a sorrow for him, but for I don't know what, unless it was the cruel loss of his leg. And yet I also felt a strange awe of him; but that sort of awe, which I cannot at all describe, was not exactly awe; I do not know what it was. But I felt it; and it did not disincline me towards him; though I felt impatience at what seemed like mystery in him, so imperfectly as he was known to me then. However, my thoughts were at length carried in other directions, so that for the present dark Ahab slipped my mind.

In such passages, in which the sequence of emotion in time past is given to us through the intense reflective emotion of the narrator's present—its strong pulse marked off by the short phrases and clauses, each built on one or two defining words—

the truth and the sufficiency of Ishmael's dramatic witness are not to be doubted. Yet we notice that there is no special appeal here to an established *character* in the speaker. The appeal is firmly to the quality of the event, and to the feeling of the moment. Ishmael's progressive withdrawal as a distinct character into the impersonal business of narration, a formal phenomenon which has bothered not a few of the book's critics, is only a step further, and a step that seems to me very efficiently prepared. Without these cultivated artifices of the first-person method, Melville's triumph in *Moby-Dick* is, strictly speaking, unimaginable. (pp. 128-32)

In all Melville's work through *Moby-Dick* the short chapter is the practical basis of the presentation. For the kind of documentary, episodic adventure-chronicle he was writing, it is the main ordering device. It becomes the simple means of piecing out the narrative, of moving easily from one thing to the next or of building quickly but with a sufficient illusion of suspense to some short-run climax. . . . A unit of discourse is also a unit of conception; and for the eager, opportunistic, quick-opening bursts of Melville's expanding imagination, a better compositional scheme than the loose string of relatively self-contained chapters is hard to think of. (p. 176)

With this as with most other phases of Melville's performance, *Moby-Dick* is the major instance. To look for the fullest development of a Melvillean signature, or indeed to think in general about the manner of his mastery as a writer, is (I find) to bring certain chapters and successions of chapters in *Moby-Dick* forcibly to mind. That is not to deny the book coherence as a whole. It is only to recognize certain facts about it: that its improvised practical structure is episodic and capitulatory, and that it finds its coherence not in the mechanism of its plot or in any other unitary (e.g., allegorical or speculative) scheme of presentation but in a continuous major harmony of apprehension—that is to say, in the sufficient assertion, each time anew, of a sufficient imaginative power to embrace, and so continue to create, the multiple connections it advances by. The chapter-episodes do, of course, have the advantage of a simple, stirring, naturally suspended main story; but without their continual re-enactment of that story's manifold conditions we would not be held by it as we are. . . . Certainly the drama of Ahab arouses, excitingly enough, a sympathetic curiosity. Certainly the rendering of it appeals very artfully to our readiness to salve our ignorance of the ultimate reason of things with explanatory parables. But it may be, I think, in individual chapters like "The Ship" or "Brit" or "The Grand Armada," that the quick of our consent is touched most compellingly. There Melville gives us plain and full that "sheer apprehension of the world," in D. H. Lawrence's fine words, which in one way or another particularly exacts from us (as we are capable) "a stillness in the soul, an awe" [see *NCLC,* Vol. 3].

Other chapters hardly less impressive might be named—and, properly, placed in context, quoted without abridgment, and delivered aloud in full voice like the eloquent recitatives and arias they function as. Certain ones cast in the book's best vein of genial hyperbole ("The Street," or "Nantucket," or—not everyone's choice—"Stubb's Supper," with its perhaps too easy footing in darky humor) would not go unmentioned; nor would those like "The Sermon," or "Moby Dick" and "The Whiteness of the Whale," or "The Try-Works," that are most frequently appealed to for interpretation of the book as a whole; or others, such as "The First Lowering" and the three chapters of the chase, in which the long narrative series bursts into its studied climaxes of tumultuous action; nor, finally, certain singularly vivid and moving short chapters as compact and resonant as great lyric poems—''The Albatross,'' ''The Pacific,'' ''The Symphony.'' (pp. 177-79)

[Each of these chapters] has become a touchstone for appreciation of Melville's art and for explanation of his ''meaning.'' For that reason it may be useful to look instead at one or two less spectacular chapters—chapters of the sort that, if accidentally left out in some reprinting, might not immediately be missed. One such is Chapter 110, ''Queequeg in His Coffin.'' It comes just at the beginning of the final rush toward the meeting with Moby Dick, and shares in the renewal of dramatic excitement already underway. And it starts, efficiently, from an incident of some importance to the main action—Ahab's prudential yielding to Starbuck's request to heave to and investigate a leakage of oil in the hold. At once we are deep in technical detail—''tierces,'' ''butts,'' ''casks,'' ''puncheons,'' ''shooks of staves'' and ''iron bundles of hoops''— and just as quickly this objective data opens out into metaphor; the now topheavy *Pequod* herself bobs ''like an air-freighted demijohn,'' or like ''a dinnerless student with all Aristotle in his head.'' All this is by way of introduction to the main episode of the chapter, which is Queequeg's strange illness and stranger recovery. . . . Typically this episode is launched in a one-sentence paragraph. And that in turn, also typically, opens with an irregular cadence which in its slight artificiality delicately points up the overform of the telling; for in the borrowing of an accent from the style of legend, or of Scripture, the way is prepared for the fable-rounded interlude, the story-within-the-story, which the main narrative pauses here to present: ''Now, at this time it was that my poor pagan companion, and fast bosom-friend, Queequeg, was seized with a fever, which brought him nigh to his endless end.'' The episode now moves along rapidly, but does not pass up its chances for underscoring. So Queequeg's falling ill after his sweated labor deep in the hold permits references, in quick succession, to the sea-going democracy of danger and job-responsibility, to the concrete severities of the ordinary chores of whaling, to the mysteries of body and soul in their joint course through life, and to all the further mysteries of life and death and of everything which, being ''truly wondrous and fearful in man, never yet was put into words or books.'' Queequeg, wasting away into a strange, soft mildness, orders a boat-like coffin made in preparation for certain legendary pagan rites of death; he lies in it, with harpoons, idol-god, and provisions for the last journey; Pip and Starbuck gather to comment, each according to his lights; but then Queequeg, as if by his own ''sovereign will and pleasure,'' decides that it is not really time to die yet, and promptly rallies—and upon his recovery sets about carving certain mystical hieroglyphs upon the coffin . . . which he himself cannot understand. So the chapter ends, but with a last emphasis—Ahab studying these hieroglyphs and crying out in anguish at the tantalizing mystery of them—which not only confirms the obvious correspondences between Queequeg's travail here and Ahab's in the main story but propels us violently back into that story; it is the momentous chapter, ''The Pacific,'' that now follows.

My other example of Melville's ordinary chapter-making in *Moby-Dick,* Chapter 57, has no part at all in the main action. Its title suggests its place in the book, and also the problem of composition it presents: ''Of Whales in Paint; in Teeth; in Wood; in Sheet-Iron; in Stone; in Stars.'' The last chapter in a group of three dealing with pictorial representations and images of the whale, it has the look of a repository for data that will not fit in anywhere else. The semicolons of the title almost

flaunt its casualness. But in just this respect it puts us in mind of Melville's most general problems of organization in *Moby-Dick,* for it exemplifies the kind of itemizing of random materials that the whole central mass of the book advances by and that without a determined exertion of imaginative control would have stalled it entirely. There is some point in noting, therefore, that the actual life and charm of this chapter derive in good part from the more than usually emphatic assertion of the narrator's own interposed presence. The chapter is of negligible importance in the over-all design of *Moby-Dick;* nevertheless the same voice speaks in it as in the book's most intensely compelling passages, and speaks as boldly. A mere survey of instances—a painting, the art of skrim-shander, savage carvings, roadside emblems, geological formations, the *trompe d' oeil* of natural shapes—rapidly takes on both the thick topicality and the spaciousness of the whole. So in a brief space there is easy reference to Tower-Hill and Wapping, and to all Christendom; one hears of what can be observed ''throughout the Pacific, and also in Nantucket, and New Bedford, and Sag Harbor''; a complex panorama of human types and conditions—Iroquois Indians, Hawaiian islanders, cannibals, Greek Achilles and Dutch Dürer, whaling forecastles and gable-roofed houses—is spread out, and succeeded by a complementary panorama of the whole physical earth, revealing fantastic rock-masses under grassy slopes, ''amphitheatrical heights'' of mountain, and remote and unknown island chains; until finally, ''expandingly lifted by your subject,'' you discover that the tallying of this data has become one with the naming of stars and constellations—Cetus and Argo Navis and the Flying Fish— and so has merged into the mythological origins of all narrative and all experience. The ending (in yet another one-sentence paragraph) is precisely in keeping: ''With a frigate's anchors for my bridle-bitts and fasces of harpoons for spurs, would I could mount that whale and leap the topmost skies, to see whether the fabled heavens with all their countless tents really lie encamped beyond my mortal sight.'' The mythical role Ishmael is roughly cast in being that of the free, versatile, curious, observant, adaptable, irrepressible, democratic everyman at home in all times, places and conditions—the man born, in the words of the nineteenth-century song, ''a hundred thousand years ago,'' whose report of all he has seen, and not seen, always shows him to be supremely the man upon whom nothing really discoverable has been lost—one cannot think of a fitter epitaph for him . . . than this casually magnificent little chapter. (pp. 179-82)

Warner Berthoff, in his The Example of Melville, *Princeton University Press, 1962, 218 p.*

LESLIE A. FIEDLER (essay date 1966)

[*An American critic, novelist, short story writer, essayist, poet, and editor, Fiedler is a commentator on American literature who has generated a great deal of controversy. Using primarily Marxist and Freudian perspectives, he attempts to uncover the origins of modern literature and show how myth is used in literature today. His critical works, which are often biographical and psychosexual in orientation, have been criticized for their sweeping generalizations. Though some have termed him ''the wild man of American literary criticism,'' Fiedler is frequently praised for his* Love and Death in the American Novel, *a landmark study of the distinguishing characteristics of the American novel. His reading of* Moby-Dick *in* Love and Death *is informed by his contention that evasion of heterosexual love and obsession with terror and violence are characteristic qualities of the American novel. Thus, he perceives a platonic homosexual ''marriage'' between Queequeg and Ishmael at the beginning of* Moby-Dick *(see excerpt below). Fiedler's elucidation of three mythic patterns in* Moby-Dick—*the Faust pattern, death and regeneration, and the slaying of the beast—is excerpted in NCLC, Vol. 3. For additional psychosexual interpretations of* Moby-Dick, *see Arvin (1950), Murray (1951), and Auden (NCLC, Vol. 3).*]

Ishmael, who begins as a comic character, somewhat green, more than a little pedantic, everybody's butt, plays in the account of his meeting with Queequeg the role of the sacred virgin. He seems quite improbably, to have no notions during his last days ashore of picking up a woman, visiting a brothel, even getting drunk. Indeed, he is something of a prohibitionist, prissy as well as timid; and it takes all of his energy and spirit simply to find a bed for the night. Ishmael reacts just as his joking landlord had foreseen at his first glimpse of the barbaric fellow with whom he must share his bed. Everything about Queequeg appalls him: his tattooing, the shrunken head he carries about for sale, the ugly, black idol—and especially his great, glowing tomahawk pipe, half symbol of peace, half weapon of assault: "this wild cannibal, tomahawk between his teeth, sprang into bed beside me. I sang out . . . and giving a grunt of astonishment he began feeling me . . ." It is an inauspicious enough beginning, and the maidenly Ishmael is terrified. . . . (pp. 372-73)

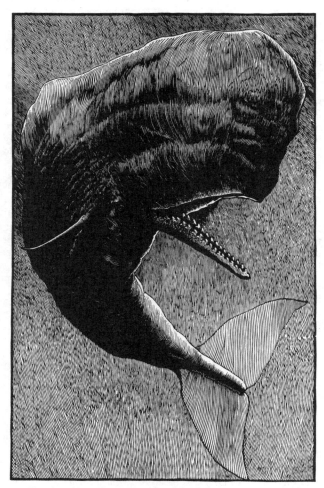

Woodcut from The University of California Press edition of Moby-Dick. *Copyright © 1979 by The Arion Press. All rights reserved. Reproduced by permission of The Arion Press.*

"Coffin, Angels! save me!" Ishmael cries, appealing to the landlord and to the powers above. He does not yet know (though Melville perhaps does) that Queequeg is his dark angel, and that on Queequeg's coffin he will escape death at the book's close. He sees only that his tattooed and savage bedmate, like an enlightened spouse, immediately ceases his attack, rolls over and away from him as much as to say—"I won't touch a leg of ye . . .''; and what began in fright ends in security: "I never slept better in my life." During Ishmael's peaceful sleep, matters have developed, however; and he awakens in the harpooner's embrace: "I found Queequeg's arm thrown over me in the most loving and affectionate manner. You had almost thought I had been his wife. . . ." It is worth noting that Ishmael tends to think of himself in the passive, the feminine role; but even more critical is his immediate sense of their relationship as a *marriage,* which is to say, a permanent commitment: the sort of indissoluble union, which he, as a detached wanderer, has presumably been fleeing. To be sure, it all seems quite comic and unreal, this bedroom scene with a Polynesian sailor— only a gross parody of marriage; and Ishmael reflects ironically on "the unbecomingness of hugging a male in that matrimonial style. . . ."

Yet he begins to grow a little disturbed, too, at the thought of being somewhat trapped. "For though I tried to . . . unlock his bridegroom clasp . . . he still hugged me tightly, as though naught but death should part us twain." The final words echo the marriage service, but in evoking the shadow of death, they also betray an access of panic, arising from an old association between sexual satisfaction and punishment. This suggestion is fortified by the recollection of a childhood nightmare, itself symbolic of rejection, paralysis, castration, and death. Somehow the pseudo-matrimonial aspects of his waking bring to Ishmael's mind memories of his stepmother: another unsuitable bedfellow, perhaps, who may once have "expostulated" with him on "the unbecomingness of hugging . . . in that matrimonial style," when he crawled in beside her for nighttime or morning comfort. The actual context in which he recalls her, however, has nothing to do with hugging; she is remembered as a legendary stepmother, a Bad Mother "who was all the time whipping me or sending me to bed supperless." (pp. 373-74)

It is tempting to read into Ishmael's little anecdote of crime and punishment a sense of guilt and powerlessness associated with the boy's special sin of masturbation. Certainly, it is the "hand" which plays a key role in the waking nightmare: "a phantom hand," "not daring to drag away my hand"; and in the larger pattern of Ishmael's experience, too, that word recurs in sensitive places. Not only does he describe his estrangement in terms of "his maddened hand" set against the "wolfish world"; but his reconciliation comes . . . in a chapter called "A Squeeze of the Hand," when he tells us that he has at last "washed my hands and heart," and cries out his appeal: "Come, let us squeeze hands all around. . . ."

In the childhood episode recalled in Queequeg's arms, the boy Ishmael was not as usual slippered, though he begged for that customary punishment. He was forced, instead, to remain in bed all through the longest day of the year: "sixteen entire hours must elapse before I could hope for a resurrection." He was, in effect, condemned to impotence and death; and to this condemnation his own unconscious subscribed, calling up the phantom hand that held him powerless, awake but involved still in nightmare terror. In his own fantasy, the sentence of a single, endless day had been extended through all eternity:

never, never (in either sense) to rise again! And for what crime had he presumably been punished—"some caper or other," about which he claims not to be sure, but which he thinks may have involved an attempt to climb up his mother's chimney. It is a fantasy more than a fact; and its interpretation suggests itself immediately, casts light on the meaning of chimneys for Melville in such a later story as **"I and My Chimney."**

Finding himself in a matrimonial deadlock with Queequeg, Ishmael feels again the old threat of impotence and death. But though he is in bed, in that forbidden hugging-place, he is not this time trying to crawl up his mother's chimney. He embraces no woman, no obvious surrogate for the banned mother, only another male, a figure patriarchal enough, in fact, to remind him of George Washington! Surely, the matrimonial hug of such a companion is innocent, only a joke, an accidental result of trying to find a room in an overcrowded town. And though the memory of the nightmare terror of childhood recurs, it recurs purged; for Ishmael has forgiven himself and is free at last to rise: "take away that awful fear, and my sensations . . . were very similar." Actually, he is free for a reconciliation with the tabooed mother; but this he will not know until the book's end, when, an orphan, he is picked up by "the devious cruising *Rachel*." His long sentimental re-education has now just begun.

Its first stage is represented by the disappearance of Ishmael's fear of Queequeg's tomahawk. That "wild pipe of his" becomes now only a peace pipe, "regularly passing between us . . ."; and their alliance can be regularly solemnized: "he pressed his forehead against mine, clasped me around the waist, and said that henceforth we were married." Ishmael hastens to add, of course, "meaning, in his country's phrase, that we were bosom friends"; for the innocence of their connection must be asserted continually. This is Platonism without sodomy, which is to say, marriage without copulation: the vain dream of genteel ladies fulfilled in a sailor's rooming-house by two men. Queequeg promises that "he would gladly die for me, if need should be"; and die he does, for there *is* need. Indeed, only by his self-sacrifice is Ishmael's sentence of death finally commuted; only in his symbolic body is Ishmael snatched from death.

But all this is not to be for a little while; more immediately, they divide between them Ishmael's worldly goods . . . and discuss the counter-claims of their rival religions. It is a scene half broadly comic, half subtly satiric: as Melville, on the one hand, gently parodies the problem of church allegiance in mixed marriages, and on the other, reflects in the style of *Typee* and *Omoo* on the insularity and rigidity of Protestant Christianity. Its real climax comes, however, with the kissing of the grotesque phallic idol, a bowing down before the less savory aspects of the natural and impulsive world which, for all its horror, seems to Melville the only source of love. And the chapter ends in bed, on a simple note of peace, never attained again in the rest of the book: "There, then, in our hearts' honeymoon, lay I and Queequeg—a cosy, loving pair." (pp. 374-76)

> *Leslie A. Fiedler, "The Failure of Sentiment and the Evasion of Love," in his* Love *and Death in the* American Novel, *revised edition, Stein and Day Publishers, 1966, pp. 337-90.**

BRIGID BROPHY, MICHAEL LEVEY, AND CHARLES OSBORNE (essay date 1967)

[*Brophy, Levey, and Osborne lampoon* Moby-Dick *in the following excerpt from the would-be heretics'* Fifty Works of English and American Literature We Could Do Without.]

[Moby Dick is not an] organic product of a true imagination. He's a mere inflated pretend-whale, inflated by the sheer wish that American literature should run to profundity.

The humblest claim made for Melville by his idolators is that he spins a good yarn: and he belies even that. Three-quarters of *Moby Dick* is a monument to Melville's inability to get down to telling his story at all. A hundred or so chapters elapse in dissertations, digressions, moralizings, symbolizings and chunks quoted from dictionaries and encyclopaedias before the narrative proper starts; and when it does, it turns out to be a slight little anecdote which comes too quickly and goes for almost nothing. Conrad, with all his technical cunning, would have been hard put to it to elaborate a short story out of the captain who, having lost a leg to the unique albino whale, seeks vengeance so monomaniacally and so recklessly as to lose his own life, his crew's and his ship. Melville is simply not up to the swift graphic narrative required by the externals of the tale. He muddies the action alternately with bathos and with would-be poeticisms and inversions: '. . . as if sucked into a morass, Moby Dick sideways writhed'; 'three of the oarsmen—who foreknew not the precise instant of the dart, and were therefore unprepared for its effects—these were flung out'. The internals, the psychology, Melville cannot even make a put at, since he cannot create Captain Ahab's obsession but can only refer to it. Indeed, the whole of *Moby Dick* is a gigantic memorandum, to the effect 'What a story this would make, if told by someone who knew how to tell stories'. Even that is a mis-estimate: it wouldn't.

Melville is not a novelist: he is an annotator and labeller. Throughout the superfluous hundred chapters before he appears, the white whale's shadow is cast at the reader in advance; and Melville, who is basically a lantern-lecturer (of the kind whose own chiaroscuro mannerisms provoke audiences to say 'What an actor he'd make'—again a mis-estimate: he wouldn't), constantly labels—but never *makes*—the shadow 'portentous'. Ishmael (that most confusing of narrators, since he narrates information he can't, within the terms of his own narrative, have possessed) hasn't so much as set foot on a whaler when he first calls a whale 'a portentous and mysterious monster'. In a sailors' lodging house he sees a painting of a whale which he twice in a paragraph describes as 'portentous'. By the time he's on board, even the appetites of the ship's company strike him as 'portentous'. The only item in the book that might be truly labelled portentous is Ishmael's own narrative manner. 'All these things are not without their meanings', he portentously says—without, however, saying what the meanings are, unless they lurk in the intellectual pretentiousness whereby he speaks of two dead whales' heads as 'Locke's head' and 'Kant's'. Sharks eating whale's corpses are pronounced by Ishmael 'a part of the universal problem of all things'. What, however, isn't?

Many novelists have tried to anticipate the critic's task by writing both narrative and a commentary alongside it pointing out the deeper beauties, profundities and significances of the narrative. Melville alone has supplied the commentary without supplying the narrative.

Moby Dick is shadow play by a Victorian-Gothic whale of papier-mâché. When he spouts, up comes a cacophonous false rhetoric ('meads and glades so eternally vernal that . . .'). When he sports, he is grotesque in his whimsy ('as when the red-cheeked, dancing girls, April and May, trip home'), obese in his facetiousness ('he was stopped on the way by a portly Sperm Whale, that begged a few moments' confidential business with him') and ungainly in his sprightliness ('The act of paying is perhaps the most uncomfortable infliction that the two orchard thieves entailed upon us'). He's worst of all when he fumbles for a metaphysical conceit in which to embody an emotional moment: 'Their hands met; their eyes fastened; Starbuck's tears the glue'.

Distended with hot air himself, Melville's whale can beget no progeny except wind eggs. One of them contained just life enough to hatch into the crocodile in *Peter Pan*. Otherwise, the whale is father to nothing but the dozens of novels which, with only the proper name altered, have repeated his burly opening sentence, 'Call me Ishmael', and the misconceptions that (*a*) the Great American Novel can be written by thinking about writing it instead of thinking about whatever it is about, (*b*) that it must be about brutality to animals, and (*c*) that brutality to animals, if pursued by men whose tears are the glue which fasten their eyes to the eyes of their fellow men, is manly and portentous. (Where did all the great white whales go? They went Hemingway.) *Moby Dick* is American literature's pseudo-founding-father, its false prophet in fake biblical prose, its Reproduction Antique ancient monument. American literature is now old enough and good enough to sell off the great white elephant. (pp. 73-5)

> *Brigid Brophy, Michael Levey, and Charles Osborne, "'Moby Dick',"* in their *Fifty Works of English and American Literature We Could Do Without, 1967. Reprint by Stein and Day Publishers, 1968, pp. 73-5.*

H. B. KULKARNI (essay date 1970)

[*Kulkarni is one of several critics, including Baird and Franklin (see Additional Bibliography), who have explored Melville's use of Oriental mythology in* Moby-Dick. *In the following excerpt from his* Moby-Dick: A Hindu Avatar, *in which he elucidates the Hindu aspects of the novel, Kulkarni discusses the mystic symbology of the doubloon that Ahab fastens to the* Pequod's *mast. The following critics also discuss the role of symbolism in* Moby-Dick: *Lawrence (1923), Arvin (1950), Bewley (1959), Horsford (1962), Hillway (1979), and Mather, Lawrence, Mumford, Aiken, Winters, Sedgwick, Maugham, Auden, and Priestley (see* NCLC, *Vol. 3).*]

Few have noted the symbolism of the doubloon, and those who have been drawn to it by its apparent mystery have disposed of it as something meaningless. John Seelye, however, recognizes its symbolic value, but his interpretation [in his essay "The Golden Navel: The Cabalism of Ahab's Doubloon"] seems to be inadequate. His difficulty stems from his notion that Pip and Ahab are both crazy, and that their talk is nothing but gibberish:

> Pip's gibberish brings the circle of interpretation full round; having commenced with the ravings of a monomaniac and ended with the babblings of a fool, the ring of prophecy that mirrors the roundness of the coin seems sealed with mad meaninglessness.

But Melville's genius, like that of Shakespeare, consists partly in expressing profound truths through the mouths of fools and madmen. If Pip appears to be cracked in the brain, it is necessary to remember that he was carried down to the wondrous depths of the sea, where "the miser-merman, Wisdom, revealed his hoarded heaps" and where "he saw God's foot upon the treadle of the loom." . . . Behind the crazy appearance of

Pip, therefore, there shines a wisdom which ought to be taken into account for a proper understanding of Melville. In fact, Pip, in his strange remarks, brings a philosophic perspective to things and makes them truly meaningful. In his "crazy-witty" way, he gives the doubloon a puzzling grammatical rendering and says: "I look, you look, he looks . . . they look." This is, indeed, a mystic grammar that lays down the law of man's understanding of truth, which seems to be always in terms of himself.

The doubloon, to which the members of the crew are mysteriously drawn, is riveted to the mast in such a way as to be constantly in view. Members of the *Pequod* are faintly aware that it carries some mystic significance beyond its monetary value and revere it as the "White Whale's talisman." The golden coin is "like a magician's glass to each and every man in turn but mirrors back his own mysterious self." But the seeing of each man is but a segment, which, when pieced together, will provide the full circle of the mystic meaning of the doubloon. Ahab sees himself in the coin, but knows that it is the image of the "rounder globe." He peers into the face of the sun, wheeling from storm to storm, equinox to equinox. Starbuck inspects the coin and reads in it the earthly symbol of God's Trinity. Stubb discovers in the doubloon "the life of man in one round chapter." If for Queequeg, it is "the sun in the thigh, . . . Sagittarius or the Archer," for Fedallah, it is the symbol of Fire, the god of his fanatic devotion. These interpretations are not just expressions of their separate egos, but have a significance that clarifies the purpose of the whale-hunt in relation to the human self and the world.

That the doubloon symbolizes an inner search for Truth and God is emphasized by the dominant image of the navel. Pip describes the coin as the ship's navel, but it is also the navel of the world: "This bright coin came from a country planted in the middle of the world, and beneath the great equator, and named after it." It is the navel of Vishnu, for it stands beneath the horse-shoe, signifying the sign of Leo or lion, which represents the avatar of Vishnu, the solar god of India. Finally, it is the navel of each one's self, which stands reflected in the coin, as in a magic mirror.

The random revelations that the doubloon offers to the different members of the crew stand united in the navel image, which operates on various levels, the individual, the universal, and the divine. The symbology of the navel forms an important part of the yogic philosophy of India. The navel is supposed to be the central and the most conspicuous part of Vishnu's being. He is, therefore, called "Padmanabha," i.e., a god who has a lotus navel. According to *Hatha-Yoga*, the human body contains seven nerve centers, storing within them tremendous potentiality of spiritual energy. Yoga describes Vishnu and the navel in identical terms: *nabhi-padma* (navel) and *padma-nabha* (Vishnu): for it identifies the navel with the solar plexus, which is believed to be the sun-center, containing seeds of mystic fire. It is the primary source of energy which provides the universe with its drive and creative force. When the navel opens like a lotus flower by yogic practice, it releases great spiritual power and expands man's consciousness to such an elevated state of vision that it gives him an insight into "the life of things." This expansion of spiritual consciousness which transforms the body into a powerhouse of energy is metaphorically described as the blossoming of the navel-lotus. It is in this sense that the word "unscrewed" should be understood. The Hindu story which is usually associated with the unscrewing of the navel is not a parody but a parable of the soul's release from its contact with the body. "The old story of the Hindu who spent a lifetime in contemplating his navel" is narrated by John Seelye thus:

> After careful consideration, the Hindu came to the conclusion that his umbilicus was purely ornamental, and calling a crowd of his fellow mystics together, he stood before them and carefully unscrewed the object of a lifetime's contemplation. At this point, naturally his backside fell to the ground.

This is a mystic parable which explains the unscrewing of the navel as the achievement of a lifetime of yogic practice, which releases the soul from the body to which it is screwed at birth and transforms it into pure spiritual energy.

It is in this mystic explanation that one may find the true meaning of the symbol stamped upon the doubloon. On three mountain summits, there are three pictures—a flame, a tower, and a crowing cock, balanced by the arch of the zodiac with the sun at the center. All the three figures are visually as well as symbolically united in the sun. The flame stands for the solar fire combining both destructive and creative powers. It is a destructive volcano and therefore has disastrous consequences. But it is also a creative symbol, complementary to the doubloon, "which is the sun in the thigh." The tower is a lookout, as Melville himself describes it in connection with the masthead. This idea of looking out in the distance is initiated in the very first chapter, which is significantly called "Loomings" and where Ishmael sees in his "inmost soul endless processions of the whale, and, midmost of them all, one grand hooded phantom, like a snow hill in the air." The word "looming" means an impressive, and large vision seen in the distance; it may also be understood in the sense of weaving and may be related to the well-laid out scheme prepared by the Fates for Ishmael and Ahab. The reference to the ocean reverie and the vision of the phantom is emphasized in the chapter "The Mast-Head" and symbolically presented in the doubloon and the pictures engraved upon it. The tower, in particular, symbolizes Pip's grammar of mystic insight and indicates the central meaning of *Moby-Dick* as man's search for Truth or God. The tower is related to the unscrewed navel, which is described in yogic literature as "the eye of the Lord." In the *Vedas*, it is stated that the sun is born of the eyes of *Purusha* (God). The doubloon, the navel, and the tower—all suggest the symbolism of the sun as the power of light and truth. As an inner principle it stands for man's understanding. What is laid out in the first chapter is symbolically worked out here again and illustrated fully in the whaling voyage. What is represented here is therefore the distant vision on the horizon one might get from the look-out of the tower and the masthead, which throws the observer into an ocean reverie from which he may be impelled to fling himself into the sea and be drowned. The image of the tower contains both the elements of the opportunity to visualize the truth and the danger involved in its pursuit. The crowing cock is equally two-sided in its symbolic direction. It is the scarecrow of death as feared by Pip; it is also "the courageous, the undaunted, and victorious fowl," as seen by Ahab. It indicates by the fusion of the two sides of its meaning an ultimate victory of life over death. The reference in the last part of the chapter to the resurrection is therefore significant: " . . . when they come to fish up this old mast and find a doubloon lodged in it, they will think it is "some old darkey's wedding ring." Whatever the doubloon might suggest to different people, the final impression which Melville intends to leave upon the read-

er's mind is that the symbolism of the unscrewing of the navel-doubloon is not the disaster of death but the triumph of creativity and harmony in resurrection.

Being the talisman of the White Whale and a worthy prize for Ahab's quest, the doubloon occupies a central place in the novel, as it does the central position in the ship and, symbolically, the world. This reminds us of another symbolic ship from which Father Mapple delivers his sermon. The identity between the ship and the church indicated clearly in the beginning of the novel was, perhaps, suggested to Melville by the etymological proximity of *nave* and *navis*. It is not too far-fetched to say that both these words may have the same Indo-European root in the Sanskrit word, *nabhi*, the navel. Starbuck thinks of the doubloon as "a sermon . . . writ in high heaven," and observes: "This coin speaks wisely, mildly, truly, but sadly to me." While delivering his sermon, Father Mapple refers to the pulpit as the masthead from which he would like to come down and learn what Jonah might teach him as "a pilot-prophet or speaker of the true things." The sermon that the coin preaches from the mast to which it is nailed and the message which Father Mapple delivers from the mast-like pulpit are alike central to the novel and emphasize the idea of whale-hunting as a spiritual experience. It has been indicated how the unscrewing of the navel signifies the freedom of the soul from the body to which it is nailed; even the chapter, "The Chapel," discusses the relation between the body and the soul and points out that death has no dominion over the soul: " . . . take my body who will, take it I say, it is not me . . . stave my soul, Jove himself cannot." Ishmael draws this philosophy even before he hears the sermon; we may say that this is the silent sermon that the Chapel preaches to those who come under its august influence. The chapel which is like a ship and the ship which is like a chapel both preach the same sermon and point to the spiritual significance underlying the quest for the white whale.

In the context of this explanation, Pip's cryptic observations and his grammatical declension of the verb "look" cannot be the babblings of a fool. The wisdom of his remarks here and elsewhere makes his name significant. Pip, however small he might be, represents the very seed of the novel, in whose statements the meaning of the hunt lies compact. Ahab and his crew had been looking at the doubloon every day, but only on this particular day, the coin seems to have unlocked its mysteries to them. Is it because their navels had suddenly bloomed open and their spiritual eyes were peeled, as it were, that they were able to understand the true significance of the doubloon and the purpose of their voyage into these "ultimate seas of God"? Ahab has offered the gold coin to whosoever might raise the whale by saying: "It's a white whale. I say, . . . a white whale. Skin your eyes for him, men; look sharp for white water; if you see but a bubble sing out." While binding all members to an "indissoluble league" for hunting the whale, Ahab invokes them not to measure his enterprise in terms of money but learn to *look* at the "lower layer" of things. Now the crew really "looks" and gets a genuine glimpse of the lower layer of significance and understands the prize of its enterprise: to be nothing less than an insight into the nature of self and God.

The navel image, therefore, should be understood in terms of yogic significance attached to it in Hindu philosophy and its relation to Vishnu and the sun-principle. This makes the doubloon a symbol of the zodiac which arches over it on the ship's mast. Thus the nave, the sun, and the myth of Vishnu's *avatars*, which is based on the zodiac, not only explain man's adoration of the sun in ancient times, but provide a philosophic perspective to **Moby-Dick**. The relation between Vishnu and Moby Dick is symbolically enlarged from the physical and mythological to its philosophical and mystic dimensions and turns the whale-hunt into a quest for truth about the self, the world, and God. (pp. 21-6)

H. B. Kulkarni, in his "Moby-Dick," a Hindu Avatar: A Study of Hindu Myth and Thought in "Moby-Dick," Utah State University Press, 1970, 70p.

ROBERT ZOELLNER   (essay date 1973)

[*Zoellner asserts that through a gradual transformation in his perceptions, Ishmael humanizes the whale in* Moby-Dick *and thereby avoids an Ahabian or nihilistic view of the cosmos. The critic cites three major encounters with whales—respectively referred to as "Stubb's Whale," the "Gerontological" or "Medicare Whale," and the "Social Whale"—as primary evidence for his contention. Zoellner also challenges epical and mythological interpretations of* Moby-Dick, *arguing partly on the grounds that the vulnerable, lovable creature presented in the novel is an unfit object for either heroic conquest or transcendent symbology. Other critics who contrast Ahab's and Ishmael's view of the world include Sedgwick (1942), Arvin (1950), Bewley (1959), Horsford (1962), and Kazin (see* NCLC, *Vol. 3). Additional criticism of the role of ontology in* Moby-Dick *is provided by Thorp (1938), Bewley (1959), Horsford (1962), Nechas (1978), Hillway (1979), and Aiken (see* NCLC, *Vol. 3). Further commentary on the epic qualities of the novel is available in the excerpts by Chase (1949) and Brooks, Winters, Arvin, and Kazin (see* NCLC, *Vol. 3). See the excerpts by Mumford (1929), Chase (1949), and Freeman, Arvin, Camus, and Fiedler (*NCLC, *Vol. 3) for further discussion of the mythic properties of* Moby-Dick.]

In 1923, in the brilliant *Studies in Classic American Literature*, D. H. Lawrence asserted that the Leviathan of **Moby-Dick** is "warm-blooded and lovable, . . . a mammal. And hunted, hunted down." Never given to explaining his oracularities, Lawrence did not develop his "lovable" whale, and subsequent criticism has been little influenced by it. Early readings of the Melville revival accepted Ahab's version of the whale as "evil." More recent interpretations have either mythologized the whale into pure idea and transcendent archetype, or made him neutral, indifferent, naturalistically unaware, at best distantly benign, akin to Emerson's "commodity" in his usefulness to man. Since Lawrence, it has seldom been suggested that Melville's alien monster is sufficiently *human* to be an appropriate object for affectionate regard—and yet that he is in fact both loving and lovable is the most significant of the "special leviathanic revelations" . . . made to Ishmael in the course of **Moby-Dick**. While this humanizing often consists of almost imperceptible shifts in Ishmaelian apprehension, three encounters with Leviathan can be taken as typical of the entire process. Two of these have to do with a pair of whales actually killed and butchered by the *Pequod's* crew. The first is *Stubb's Whale*. The second is the *Gerontological* or *Medicare Whale*. The third is the *Social Whale* as he reveals himself in the massed thousands of that immense whalepod, the Grand Armada. (pp. 166-67)

It is not until Chapter 61, "Stubb Kills a Whale," that Ishmael, standing his turn at the mast-head, starts abruptly from a brief doze to find the fabulous creature he has never seen, and which he has come so far to see, floating hardly an arm's length away. "And lo! close under our lee, not forty fathoms off, a gigantic Sperm Whale lay rolling in the water like the capsized hull of a frigate, his broad, glossy back, of an Ethiopian hue, glistening in the sun's rays like a mirror.'' Caught off his guard, one might expect that Ishmael would describe this frigate-sized and sudden Leviathan in the Ahabian terms of earlier chapters. Instead, his first spontaneous impression is one of ponderous and corpulent *placidity*. "But lazily undulating in the trough of the sea, and ever and anon tranquilly spouting his vapory jet, the whale looked like a portly burgher smoking his pipe of a warm afternoon.'' . . . With this anthropomorphic analogy, the humanizing of the whale begins.

It is the *pipe* this Leviathanic burgher smokes which expresses the essential equivalence between man and whale. For Melville, pipe-smoking is emblematic of the on-going life-processes which unite all sentient beings. Babbalanja of **Mardi** asserts that "life itself is a puff and a wheeze. Our lungs are two pipes which we constantly smoke." . . . The pipe also connotes humanity and fraternal identity. It is as a consequence of Ishmael's having proposed a "social smoke" that he and Queequeg become friends. (pp. 167-68)

It is no accident, then, that Stubb, during the interval when the whale sounds, lights a pipe to match the one of the "portly burgher'' he is pursuing. In the subsequent chase, Ishmael returns to Stubb's pipe with repetitive frequency. The whale, his sounding out, rises "in advance of the smoker's boat.'' When the whale tries to escape, Stubb, "still puffing at his pipe, . . . cheered on his crew to the assault." "Start her, start her, my men!'' he shouts, "spluttering out the smoke as he spoke.'' As the boat comes within harpoon-range, he encourages the men to even greater efforts, "all the while puffing the smoke from his mouth.'' When the harpoon is thrown and the whale dives, Stubb wraps the whale-line around the boat's loggerhead, "whence, by reason of its increased rapid circlings, a hempen blue smoke now jetted up and mingled with the steady fumes from his pipe.'' Ishmael clearly is after a meaning. What that meaning is becomes clear as the whale, harpooned and lanced, fights for life. "And all the while, jet after jet of white smoke was agonizingly shot from the spiracle of the whale, and vehement puff after puff from the mouth of the excited headsman.'' Stubb and his whale are not totally alien antagonists. They are both pipe-smokers. The fact that one is butchering the other cannot obliterate this symbolic identity. Finally, the whale goes into his flurry, "surging from side to side; spasmodically dilating and contracting his spout-hole, with sharp, cracking, agonized respirations. At last, gush after gush of clotted red gore . . . shot into the frighted air; and falling back again, ran dripping down his motionless flanks into the sea. His heart had burst!'' At this climax, the tragic identity of pursuer and pursued is stated by Stubb himself who, here as elsewhere, is not nearly so unaware as he often pretends to be. "He's dead, Mr. Stubb," Tashtego announces. "Yes; both pipes smoked out!'' Stubb responds, and, "withdrawing his own from his mouth, [he] scattered the dead ashes over the water; and, for a moment, stood thoughtfully eyeing the vast corpse he had made.'' . . .

The pipe-figure is important because it measures Ishmael's capacity for empathic identification. Ahab regards the whale as "prey,'' and pursues him "with tornado brow, and eyes of red murder, and foam-glued lips'' . . . , but Ishmael cannot. Leviathan may be the salt-sea mastodon, an utterly alien creature from those regions of the natural world least familiar to man. Nevertheless, as the butchery proceeds, Ishmael feels *with* the whale rather than *against* the whale. In a definitive instance of the moral power of the creative lamp-mind, he projects his own humanity out upon that alien *other*, that inconceivable and unimaginable *not-me* which is Leviathan. Indeed, Ishmael suffers nearly as much as the whale during this first confrontation. He is unable to muster the methodical and dispassionate distance of the professional butcher. Words like *horrible, agonizing,* and *unspeakable* suggest what he is feeling. (pp. 168-69)

The nightmare comes to a climax as Stubb employs his lance with surgical deliberation:

> "Pull up—pull up!" he now cried to the bowsman, as the waning whale relaxed in his wrath. "Pull up!—close to!" and the boat ranged along the fish's flank. When reaching far over the bow, Stubb slowly churned his long sharp lance into the fish, and kept it there, carefully churning and churning, as if cautiously seeking to feel after some gold watch that the whale might have swallowed, and which he was fearful of breaking ere he could hook it out. But that gold watch he sought was the innermost life of the fish. And now it is struck; for, starting from his trance into that unspeakable thing called his "flurry," the monster horribly wallowed in his blood, overwrapped himself in impenetrable, mad, boiling spray, so that the imperilled craft, instantly dropping astern, had much ado blindly to struggle out from that phrensied twilight into the clear air of the day....

But Ishmael is not in the clear air of day. He is engulfed in horror, a horror which initiates the redemptive process he must undergo. (pp. 169-70)

This first encounter proves that the whale is vulnerable to man as for eons of time the deer, the buffalo, and the bear have been vulnerable, suffering in the unique crisis of death as man suffers. But there is little in the incident to suggest any further identity. Had the voyage of the *Pequod* been terminated at this point, the whale would have remained one of those raptly mythic figures from the natural world with which man has for centuries adorned his cave-walls, his hogans, and his domestic artifacts—wistful images of an animalistic integrity, of an organically flawless relationship with the external world, which sundered and distracted man perpetually seeks and never finds. Many interpretations of *Moby-Dick* develop Leviathan in just these terms—and thus miss one of Melville's major meanings.

That Ishmael's Leviathan is much more than a conventionally mythopoeic figure becomes clear twenty chapters after the slaughter of the pipe-smoking burgher. As the *Pequod* gams with the German whaler *Jungfrau*, whales are sighted simultaneously from both mastheads. The main pod of young and vigorous whales proves too swift for the pursuing boats, but wallowing helplessly in their rear, unable to keep up with his juniors, is a bull whale whose condition alters decisively Ishmael's perception of Leviathanic reality:

> Full in [the] rapid wake [of the younger whales], and many fathoms in the rear, swam a huge, humped old bull, which by his comparatively slow progress, as well as by the unusual yellowish incrustations over-growing him, seemed afflicted with the jaundice, or some other infirmity.... His spout was short, slow, and laborious; coming forth with a choking sort of gush, and spending itself in torn shreds, fol-

lowed by strange subterranean commotions in him, which seemed to have egress at his other buried extremity, causing the waters behind him to upbubble.

> "Who's got some paregoric?" said Stubb, "he has the stomach-ache, I'm afraid. Lord, think of having half an acre of stomach-ache! Adverse winds are holding mad Christmas in him, boys. It's the first foul wind I ever knew to blow from astern." . . .

Old and tired, dyspeptic and flatulent, jaundiced and short of breath: this is hardly the whale of mythic or archetypal affirmation, nor the Leviathan of transcendental indomitability. This ancient and infirm whale, feebly struggling to escape the *Pequod's* boats, brings Ishmael to the redemptive realization that the largest and most powerful creature on the face of the earth is, like man, subject to all the ills that flesh is heir to. That this is Melville's meaning becomes clear as the whale, in his frantic efforts to escape, rolls from one side to the other:

> As an overladen Indiaman bearing down the Hindostan coast with a deck load of frightened horses, careens, buries, rolls, and wallows on her way; so did this old whale heave his aged bulk, and now and then partly turning over on his cumbrous rib-ends, expose the cause of his devious wake in the unnatural stump of his starboard fin. Whether he had lost that fin in battle, or had been born without it, it were hard to say.

> "Only wait a bit, old chap, and I'll give ye a sling for that wounded arm," cried cruel Flask, pointing to the whale-line near him. . . .

(pp. 170-71)

The Medicare Whale thus joins that gallery of human characters in *Moby-Dick* who, having been thumped by natural process, carry forevermore as emblem of their affliction, a mutilated extremity. Captain Ahab is missing a leg. Captain Boomer is missing an arm.... And Perth, the *Pequod's* blacksmith, victim of alcoholism and frostbite, yaws his way through life bereft of the better part of both feet.... And so the whale. One of the great ironies of *Moby-Dick* is that although Ahab here encounters a whale of hundred-barrel ponderosity who has been "dismasted" and "razeed" just as he has been . . . , the *Pequod's* Captain is unable to detect the redemptive analogy or draw the saving parallel which the Medicare Whale represents.

What Ahab misses, however, Ishmael sees. As the *Pequod's* boats draw near, the tragic debility of so stupendous a creature generates a compassionate horror which marks decisively the beginning of Ishmael's separation from Ahab:

> It was a terrific, most pitiable, and maddening sight. The whale was now going head out, and sending his spout before him in a continual tormented jet; while his one poor fin beat his side in an agony of fright. Now to this hand, now to that, he yawed in his faltering flight, and still at every billow that he broke, he spasmodically sank in the sea, or sideways rolled towards the sky his one beating fin. So have I seen a bird with clipped wing, making affrighted broken circles in the air, vainly striving to escape the piratical hawks. But the bird has

a voice, and with plaintive cries will make known her fear; but the fear of this vast dumb brute of the sea, was chained up and enchanted in him; he had no voice, save that choking respiration through his spiracle, and this made the sight of him unspeakably pitiable; while still, in his amazing bulk, portcullis jaw, and omnipotent tail, there was enough to appal the stoutest man who so pitied. . . .

[Ishmael] has already told us that however much others may "thump and punch" him about, he nevertheless has "the satisfaction of knowing that it is all right; that everybody else is one way or other served in much the same way—either in a physical or metaphysical point of view, that is; and so the universal thump is passed round." . . . The Medicare Whale makes it clear that the "everybody else" Ishmael speaks of includes the great whale himself. As Ahab has been served, so is Leviathan served. It follows that Ahab's conception of the whale as transcendent and untrammeled power is false.

That the Medicare Whale initiates such a repudiation of the Ahabian version of Leviathan becomes apparent when the whale desperately sounds to escape his pursuers:

Not eight inches of perpendicular rope were visible at the bows. Seems it credible that by three such thin threads the great Leviathan was suspended like the big weight to an eight day clock. Suspended? and to what? To three bits of board. Is this the creature of whom it was once so triumphantly said—"Canst thou fill his skin with barbed irons? or his head with fish-spears? The sword of him that layeth at him cannot hold, the spear, the dart, nor the habergeon: he esteemeth iron as straw; the arrow cannot make him flee; darts are counted as stubble; he laugheth at the shaking of a spear!" [Job 41:7, 26-29]. This the creature? this he? Oh! that unfulfilments should follow the prophets. For with the strength of a thousand thighs in his tail, Leviathan had run his head under the mountains of the sea, to hide him from the Pequod's fish-spears! . . .

It is appropriate that Ishmael should quote from Job, since much more is being dismissed here than Ahab's whale. In a more general way, the triumphalism and arrogant transcendentalism of traditional Christian theism are also being repudiated. Ishmael here rejects not only the Leviathan of Job, of Jonah, and of Father Mapple; he also implicitly rejects the overkill, megaton God which all three presuppose. This is what he means when he speaks of the "unfulfilments" which "follow the prophets." The shift is crucial. Ishmael could never learn to love Omnipotent Leviathan, much less what Omnipotent Leviathan might represent. But he can learn to love—in the sense suggested by D. H. Lawrence—a Leviathan as humanly vulnerable as he is himself. And if Ishmael can learn to love the whale, he can learn to love the immense cosmos of which the whale is symbol. (pp. 171-73)

Nothing could better express the tragic vulnerability of great Leviathan than the ulcerated growth which the struggles of the Medicare Whale reveal. "Still rolling in his blood, at last he partially disclosed a strangely discolored bunch or protuberance, the size of a bushel, low down on the flank." Insensitive Flask cannot resist: "A nice spot," he exclaims; "just let me

prick him there once." Starbuck tries to intervene: "Avast!" he cries, "there's no need of that!":

But humane Starbuck was too late. At the instant of the dart an ulcerous jet shot from this cruel wound, and goaded by it into more than sufferable anguish, the whale now spouting thick blood, with swift fury blindly darted at the craft, bespattering them and their glorying crews all over with showers of gore, capsizing Flask's boat and marring the bows. It was his death stroke. For, by this time, so spent was he by loss of blood, that he helplessly rolled away from the wreck he had made; lay panting on his side, impotently flapped with his stumped fin, then over and over slowly revolved like a waning world; turned up the white secrets of his belly; lay like a log, and died. It was most piteous, that last expiring spout. . . .

Thus does the Medicare Whale become a symbol of the tragic condition of all sentient beings, and of the universal suffering which can—or should—draw all sentient beings together in brotherhood. (p. 174)

The killing of the Medicare Whale provides an opportunity to attend to the problem—so far ignored—of whether Melville intended to write a cetological *epic*. The question is important because the answer to it will determine the light in which the reader regards the killing of the various whales the *Pequod* encounters, as well as the attack on Moby Dick himself. At first glance, there would seem to be considerable sanction for an epic-heroic reading. Chapter 82, "The Honor and Glory of Whaling," which immediately follows the killing of the Medicare Whale, appears to develop the epic qualities of the fisheries:

The more I dive into this matter of whaling, and push my researches up to the very springhead of it, so much the more am I impressed with its great honorableness and antiquity; and especially when I find so many great demi-gods and heroes, prophets of all sorts, who one way or other have shed distinction upon it, I am transported with the reflection that I myself belong, though but subordinately, to so emblazoned a fraternity. . . .

Ishmael leads off his fraternity roster with the intrepid Perseus, who rescued Andromeda from a coastal rock just as Leviathan was about to carry her off. "It was an admirable artistic exploit," he dryly observes, "rarely achieved by the best harpooneers of the present day; inasmuch as this Leviathan was slain at the very first dart." With a similar air of droll earnestness, he cites the story of St. George and the Dragon, "which dragon I maintain to have been a whale":

Let not the modern paintings of this scene mislead us; for though the creature encountered by that valiant whaleman of old is vaguely represented of a griffin-like shape, and though the battle is depicted on land and the saint on horseback, yet considering the great ignorance of those times, when the true form of the whale was unknown to artists; and considering that as in Perseus' case, St. George's whale might have crawled up out of the sea on the beach; and considering that the animal ridden by St. George might have been only a large seal, or sea-horse; bearing all this in mind, it will not appear altogether incompatible with the sacred legend . . . to hold this so-called dragon no other than the great Leviathan himself. . . .

The dragon a whale; the whale an amphibian; the horse a seal; and the sea the land: is sly Ishmael once again pulling the reader's leg? Such a possibility becomes a probability when Hercules is added to the epic roster because he was "swallowed down and thrown up by a whale." Ishmael admits that this is not the usual way one becomes a whaleman, or an epic hero for that matter. "Nevertheless, [Hercules] may be deemed a sort of involuntary whaleman; at any rate the whale caught him, if he did not the whale. I claim him for one of our clan." (pp. 175-76)

It is distressing to discover that this arrant Ishmaelian nonsense has been used as the foundation for readings of *Moby-Dick* almost certainly at odds with what Melville actually intended. Alfred Kazin, for example, regards *Moby-Dick* as "an epic, a long poem on a heroic theme" [see *NCLC*, Vol. 3], and Warner Berthoff characterizes the novel as "a meditative-heroic poem on the honor and glory, and practical enterprise, of whaling." There is no way to disprove categorically such readings, but certain facts should give us pause. It is striking, for example, that Ishmael juxtaposes the Homeric simile with the brutal butchery of the Medicare Whale. Five times in seven pages he resorts to this formalistic and hyperliterary device, with all its epic and heroic associations. The five instances are worth listing in sequence:

> As an overladen Indiaman bearing down the Hindostan coast with a deck load of frightened horses, careens, buries, rolls, and wallows on her way; so did this old whale heave his aged bulk, and now and then partly turning over on his cumbrous rib-ends, expose the cause of his devious wake in the unnatural stump of his starboard fin. . . .

And the second:

> Now to this hand, now to that, he yawed in his faltering flight, and still at every billow that he broke, he spasmodically sank in the sea, or sideways rolled towards the sky his one beating fin. So have I seen a bird with clipped wing, making affrighted broken circles in the air, vainly striving to escape the piratical hawks. . . .

And the third:

> Yet so vast is the quantity of blood in [the whale], and so distant and numerous its interior fountains, that he will keep thus bleeding and bleeding for a considerable period; even as in a drought a river will flow, whose source is in the well-springs of far-off and undiscernible hills. . . .

And the fourth:

> As strange misgrown masses gather in the knotholes of the noblest oaks when prostrate, so from the points which the whale's eyes had once occupied, now protruded blind bulbs, horribly pitiable to see. . . .

And the fifth:

> As when by unseen hands the water is gradually drawn off from some mighty fountain, and with half-stifled melancholy gurglings the spray-column lowers and lowers to the ground—so the last long dying spout of the whale. . . .

(p. 176)

Once again, Ishmael is after a meaning. He employs the Homeric simile to express, not the epic aspects of whaling, but rather the counter-epic aspects. There is immense irony in the fact that the "antagonist" of Chapter 81 is not a many-headed hydra breathing fire and destruction, nor a cyclops able to tear up trees by the roots. It is not even Fabulous Leviathan in all the vast brawn of his cetacean prime. It is instead the Medicare Whale, wheezing, flatulent, and terrified. Where Ishmael launches into Homeric simile, the matter of comparison is not the indomitable might of Leviathan, but rather his age, his helplessness, his blindness, his tragic blood-vulnerability. In Chapter 81, the crew of the *Pequod* attacks and kills a helpless cripple. No amount of critical transmogrification can elevate this brutal enounter into the epic mode. Moreover, to do so would be to distort the ultimate meanings of *Moby-Dick*. The redemption of Ishmael and the resolution of his hypos depend upon his learning to *love Leviathan,* the alien, the cosmic, other. The epic frame of mind can only retard this redemptive process. The one universal emotion which has no place in the epic idiom is *love* for the antagonist which the hero must encounter and conquer by feats of derring-do. (pp. 176-78)

Stubb's Whale and the Medicare Whale are, however, only prelusive to the encounter of Ishmael with the Social Whale of Chapter 87, "The Grand Armada." Sailing through the Straits of Sunda, the *Pequod* overtakes and pursues an "immense caravan" consisting of "thousands on thousands" of Sperm Whales. As they emerge upon the China Seas, three keels are lowered and the chase continued by oar for several hours, when suddenly and inexplicably the entire herd *gallies,* which Ishmael defines as "to confound with fright." . . . That these thousands of the great Sperm Whale should gally, victims of blind panic, vitiates further the Ahabian and Biblical version of "indomitable" Leviathan. The point is not lost on Ishmael. "Had these leviathans been but a flock of simple sheep," he dryly observes, "pursued over the pasture by three fierce wolves, they could not possibly have evinced such excessive dismay." But whales are, after all, only "herding creatures," and like all such animals, given to "occasional timidity." Such timidity is touchingly human, and especially so when it appears in so vast an animal. . . . (pp. 179-80)

Ishmael's initiation into the secret life of Leviathan begins when Queequeg harpoons a lone whale on the outskirts of the shoal, whereupon "the stricken fish darted blinding spray in our faces, and then running away with us like light, steered straight for the heart of the herd." At precisely the right moment, the harpoon pulls free, and the translation—it is really an epistemological voyage covering immense conceptual distances—is complete: ". . . we glided between two whales into the innermost heart of the shoal, as if from some mountain torrent we had slid into a serene valley lake." It is a movement from active pursuit to contemplative stasis: "Here the storms in the roaring glens between the outermost whales, were heard but not felt." In a culminating instance of the metaphor of reflective transparency, Ishmael, like Narcissus, is presented with a water-mirror he can both gaze at and gaze through: "In this central expanse the sea presented that smooth satin-like surface, called a sleek, produced by the subtle moisture thrown off by the whale in his more quiet moods.'' He thus enters a magic realm. ''Yes, we were now in that enchanted calm which they say lurks at the heart of every commotion.'' The whales in this ''innermost fold'' inhabit a ''wondrous World''; floating in their ''enchanted pond,'' they seem to be ''entranced,'' ''becharmed,'' under a ''spell.'' Ishmael is now immured in Leviathanism, swallowed up by the Sperm Whale herd just as Jonah was swallowed by a single whale. (p. 180)

What Ishmael has been brought here to see is the Social Whale, secretly leading a domestic life much like man's. The first significant consequence is a change in Ishmael's perception of the whale as sheer size, overweening bulk, untrammeled power. This shift is accomplished by a re-articulation of Leviathanism . . . in feminine and infantile modes. Ishmael perceives that the ''cows and calves'' of the herd ''had been purposely locked up in this innermost fold.'' He immediately humanizes them. They are ''the women and children of this routed host,'' placed at the protected center because they are ''so young, unsophisticated, and every way innocent and inexperienced.'' Viewed from another vantage-point, great Leviathan becomes not very different from the domestic cat purring on the hearthstone, or the dog nuzzling our hand, importunate to be patted and spoken to:

> . . . these smaller whales—now and then visiting our becalmed boat from the margin of the lake—evinced a wondrous fearlessness and confidence, or else a still, becharmed panic which it was impossible not to marvel at. Like household dogs they came snuffling round us, right up to our gunwales, and touching them; till it almost seemed that some spell had suddenly domesticated them. Queequeg patted their foreheads; Starbuck scratched their backs with his lance. . . .

The profoundly human process underlying this perceptual and conceptual shift is identical with that which shapes other pages of *Moby-Dick.* Following Tashtego's plunge into the Heidelberg Tun, death was *honeyized* in the analogue of the Ohio honey-hunter. . . . Similarly, the annihilative power of the Sperm Whale's tail was *aestheticized* in crescentic ''lines of beauty.'' . . . So now, the vastness of Leviathan is *femininized* and *infantilized.* (pp. 180-81)

In a consummate elaboration of the protometaphor which shapes all of *Moby-Dick,* [Ishmael] is now permitted a glimpse of the most intimate interiorities of Leviathanic life. ''But far beneath this wondrous world upon the surface,'' he continues, ''another and still stranger world met our eyes as we gazed over the side.'' Beneath the perceptual interface, in that pallidly noumenal world which up to this point has been populated only with terrifying primal forms such as the shark and the squid, another and quite opposite aspect of natural process is revealed. . . . Ishmael has been haunted by the fear that the surface of nature was a deceitful array of harlot colors, and that were he ever permitted to pierce the phenomenal derma, he would find a ghastly ''charnel-house'' of noumenal horror. . . . In ''The Grand Armada'' he is permitted such a perceptual dive. What greets his eyes is not a charnel-house, but rather a house of life, a fecund and proliferant realm of ''submarine bridal chambers and nurseries'':

> For, suspended in those watery vaults, floated the forms of the nursing mothers of the whales, and those that by their enormous girth seemed shortly to become mothers. The lake . . . was to a considerable depth exceedingly transparent; and as human infants while suckling will calmly and fixedly gaze away from the breast, as if leading two different lives at the [same] time; and while yet drawing mortal nourishment, be still spiritually feasting upon some unearthly reminiscence;—even so did the young of these whales seem looking up towards us, but not at us, as if we were but a bit of Gulfweed in their new-born sight. . . .

Cetacean infants and human infants: they are strikingly similar, one as much as the other trailing clouds of glory. The scene is redolent with a vast maternal placidity: ''Floating on their sides, the mothers also seemed quietly eyeing us.'' Utterly fascinated, Ishmael returns to the paradox which infantile Leviathanism represents:

> One of these little infants, that from certain queer tokens seemed hardly a day old, might have measured some fourteen feet in length, and some six feet in girth. He was a little frisky; though as yet his body seemed scarce yet recovered from that irksome position it had so lately occupied in the maternal reticule; where, tail to head, and all ready for the final spring, the unborn whale lies bent like a Tartar's bow. The delicate side-fins, and the palms of his flukes, still freshly retained the plaited crumpled appearance of a baby's ears newly arrived from foreign parts. . . .

Ishmael describes [the day-old whale pup] empirically: he is fourteen feet long and six feet around. One wishes that Ishmael had added that datum which so concerns human mothers: the baby's probable weight. Surely we have here an infant tipping the scales at over a ton. If this is the case, the baby whale might stand as a supreme example of what I have called the ''empirical bogey,'' that dispiriting sense of the vast *size,* the outrageous *extension,* of most aspects of the cosmos in relation to puny man. But Ishmael is not dispirited by this incredible specimen of infantile ponderosity. Rather, he is charmed, fascinated, delighted. The reason has that simplicity which characterizes all metaphysical subtleties. This baby Leviathan is not, for Ishmael, a ton of whale. Rather, he is a *ton of baby.* As a consequence, the humane and humanizing emotions which all babies naturally generate have, simply, a much more ample field in which to play. For the first time in *Moby-Dick,* Ishmael achieves a mode of apprehension forever closed to Ahab: he is able to take delight in immensity, pleasure in size. The baby whale is much more than a sentimental diversion. He is ontologically significant, representing for Ishmael the definitive obliteration of the empirical bogey.

It is characteristic of the Ishmaelian sensibility that this humanizing of the Grand Armada should reach its fullest development in a series of sexual analogues. . . . ''We saw young Leviathan amours in the deep,'' he blurts out, and then, chafing under the constraints of conventional expression, he drops into the relative inconspicuousness of a footnote:

> The sperm whale, as with all other species of the Leviathan, but unlike most other fish, breeds indifferently at all seasons; after a gestation which may probably be set down at nine months, producing but one at a time; though in some

few known instances giving birth to an Esau and Jacob:—a contingency provided for in suckling by two teats, curiously situated, one on each side of the anus; but the breasts themselves extend upwards from that. When by chance these precious parts in a nursing whale are cut by the hunter's lance, the mother's pouring milk and blood rivalingly discolor the sea for rods. The milk is very sweet and rich; it has been tasted by man; it might do well with strawberries. When overflowing with mutual esteem, the whales salute *more hominum.* . . .

Year-round sexual activity; a nine-month gestation period; occasional twins and teats to match; mother's milk worthy of human consumption; and . . . an ability to copulate and a way of going about it, both of which are distinctly human, differentiating the whale not only from other fish, which do not copulate, but also from mere quadrupedal mammals, which do. Such analogues derived from cetacean sexuality round out the humanizing similarities between man and this most alien of sea-creatures. (pp. 181-84)

In Chapter 58, "Brit," Ishmael assured us that "you can hardly regard any creature of the deep with the same feelings that you do those of the shore." Historically, he added, "the native inhabitants of the seas have ever been regarded with emotions unspeakably unsocial and repelling." . . . Through a crucial span of thirty chapters, . . . Ishmael changes his mind. He discovers that Leviathan is *not* like other sea-creatures, is indeed like man, and must stand as a redemptive exception to his own rule. It is this pivotal shift in Ishmaelian perception which provides the dramatic justification for the accumulations of factual data on cetacean physiology and behavior scattered through *Moby-Dick*. The humanizing of the whale, while imaginative in thrust and effect, is solidly scientific in basis. Ishmael discovers, or comes to realize, that vast Leviathan is, like man, a placental mammal. This makes him a congener of man, with all the manifold and intimate identities such a scientific relationship implies. The consequence is that growing feeling of *fraternal congenerity* regarding the whale which Ishmael exhibits, and which leads in turn to more subtle feelings of tragic affinity and metaphysical consanguinity with this unbelievably vast taxonomic relative. Leviathan is not, after all, an alien. Rather, and in literal scientific fact, he is a brother.

Ishmael prepares for this change in perception of Leviathanic reality between Chapters 58 and 87 by rejecting all exaggerated and fabulous versions of the whale. In Chapter 55, "Of the Monstrous Pictures of Whales," he cannot too much deprecate illustrations in which Leviathan is represented with a "distended tusked mouth into which the billows are rolling," or where "whales, like great rafts of logs, are represented lying among ice-isles, with white bears running over their living backs." . . . Worst of all, however, are those wildly exaggerated whales encountered in any American city:

> As for the sign-painters' whales seen in the streets hanging over the shops of oil-dealers, what shall be said of them? They are generally Richard III. whales, with dromedary humps, and very savage; breakfasting on three or four sailor tarts, that is whaleboats full of mariners: their deformities floundering in seas of blood and blue paint. . . .

Such deprecation of Fabulous Leviathan is important for two reasons. First, Ahab's whale is very much a Richard III whale.

Implicit in Chapter 55 is a repudiation of Ahab's version of Moby Dick as a creature of "outrageous strength" and "inscrutable malice," a veritable breakfaster on sailor tarts. Second, Ishmael's rejection of Fabulous Leviathan is helpful in arriving at a proper perspective on *Moby-Dick* as a whole. Almost without exception, commentators on the novel have been unable to resist the temptation to mythologize (and in the process, dehumanize) Leviathan. It is difficult to reconcile such an approach with Ishmael's persistent efforts, from Chapter 55 on, at *de*mythification.

Such demythification is necessary because Fabulous Leviathan cannot at the same time be Brotherly Leviathan. The two are irreconcilable. So Ishmael sets to work, using cetology as his tool, to minimize the strange and maximize the familiar in the whale. . . . [In Chapter 85, he returns to the cetological fact mentioned in Chapter 68, that the whale has "regular lungs, like a human being's."] He notes that the whale cannot remain under the surface indefinitely as a gilled fish can. Instead, at hourly intervals he must return to the upper air and oxygenate his blood through his spout-hole. Nor is this process susceptible of variation: he must "have his spoutings out," achieving full aeration before returning to the bottom. This fact gives the whale-hunter his advantage. "For not by hook or by net could this vast leviathan be caught, when sailing a thousand fathoms beneath the sunlight. *Not so much thy skill, then, O hunter, as the great necessities, that strike the victory to thee!*" . . . Fabulous Leviathan could not, in the nature of things, be subject to the "great necessities" of life, and still be fabulous. Mythic and transcendental figures are not necessitarian figures. But flesh-and-blood Leviathan, tragically subject to ineluctable necessity, thus achieves identity with man on philosophical as well as physiological grounds.

The consequence of such philosophical cetology is a persistent humanizing of the whale not only in set scenes such as those dealing with the Medicare Whale and the Grand Armada, but in isolated paragraphs and passing references scattered through the latter half of *Moby-Dick*. There are young whales, for example, "in the highest health, and swelling with noble aspirations, . . . in the warm flush and May of life, with all their panting lard about them[,] . . . brawny, buoyant heroes." There are old whales, "broken-hearted creatures, their pads of lard diminished and all their bones heavy and rheumatic." . . . Forty-barrel bulls are "Like a mob of young collegians, . . . full of fight, fun, and wickedness, tumbling round the world at such a reckless, rollicking rate, that no prudent underwriter would insure them any more than he would a riotous lad at Yale or Harvard." . . . Brother Whale even progresses through something very like the seven ages of man. Ishmael remarks that a pod of female whales is almost always accompanied by a "Grand Turk" or "Bashaw." "In truth, this gentleman is a luxurious Ottoman, swimming about over the watery world, surroundingly accompanied by all the solaces and endearments of the harem." . . . But such "omnivorous roving lovers" come to a very human end:

> In good time, . . . as the ardor of youth declines; as years and dumps increase; as reflection lends her solemn pauses; in short, as a general lassitude overtakes the sated Turk; then a love of ease and virtue supplants the love for maidens; our Ottoman enters upon the impotent, repentant, admonitory stage of life, forswears, disbands the harem, and grown to an exemplary, sulky old soul, goes about all alone among the

meridians and parallels saying his prayers, and
warning each young Leviathan from his amorous errors. . . .

It is in precisely these terms that Captain Boomer of the *Samuel
Enderby,* who has lost an arm to Moby Dick, perceives the
great White Whale. Moby Dick is to him, not a monster, but
simply "this old great-grandfather." . . . Such capacity for
humanizing vision makes it possible for Captain Boomer to
survive, his sense of humor intact, that same experience which
destroys Captain Ahab.

Among the various Yankee simplicities which lie at the heart
of *Moby-Dick,* one of the most important is that insight toward
which the humanizing of Leviathan tends: Ishmael's realization
that even the great whale, the mightiest creature of the living
earth, is part of a tragic continuum from which *nothing* is free.
He makes this point as the whitened corpse of Stubb's Whale,
peeled of its blubber and cast loose from the ship, floats away
to the horizon:

> There's a most doleful and most mocking fu-
> neral! The sea-vultures all in pious mourning,
> the air-sharks all punctiliously in black or
> speckled. In life but few of them would have
> helped the whale, I ween, if peradventure he
> had needed it; but upon the banquet of his fu-
> neral they most piously do pounce. *Oh, hor-
> rible vulturism of earth! from which not the
> mightiest whale is free. . . .*

The universal thump is just that: universal. *All* nature suffers.
This is an insight forever denied to Ahab. His pervasively
Christian outlook, his deicidal envy, and his consequent sense
of nature as antagonist, make it inevitable that he will detect
an element of transcendental indomitability in natural process.
Ishmael, through the humanizing of the whale, avoids this
tragic mistake. As a result, Leviathan, which began as a focus
of terror and despair for Ishmael, becomes in the end a source
of hope. In Chapters 42 and 51, "The Whiteness of the Whale"
and "The Spirit-Spout," the whale and his spout became emblematic of the noumenal world which Ishmael believed lay
hidden under the chromatic richness of sensuous nature. Both
were albescent forms suggestive of a "colorless all-color of
atheism." Now, in a crucial turnabout, the whale—and his
spout—are suddenly integrated with the *rainbow,* that prismatic
color-array which Ishmael has explicitly associated with "hope
and solace" . . . :

> And how nobly it raises our conceit of the
> mighty, misty monster, to behold him solemnly
> sailing through a calm tropical sea; his vast,
> mild head overhung by a canopy of vapor . . .
> and that vapor . . . glorified by a rainbow, as
> if Heaven itself had put its seal upon his thoughts.
> For, d'ye see, rainbows do not visit the clear
> air; they only irradiate vapor. And so, through
> all the thick mists of the dim doubts in my
> mind, divine intuitions now and then shoot,
> enkindling my fog with a heavenly ray. And
> for this I thank God; for all have doubts; many
> deny; but doubts or denials, few along with
> them, have intuitions. Doubts of all things
> earthly, and intuitions of some things heavenly;
> this combination makes neither believer nor in-
> fidel, but makes a man who regards them both
> with equal eye. . . .

The rainbow imagery of this passage—a compelling instance
of the metaphor of illumination—gives us for the first time a
whale endowed with *philosophical chromaticity.* Such a Rainbow Leviathan, such a Tingent Whale, suggests that Ishmael,
having plunged in despair to the antipodes of the anteperceptual
realm, is now on his way back to the polychrome world of
sensuous apprehension—and is bringing his newly-found cetacean brother with him. Ishmael here stands poised on a knife-
edge. If he is not a believer, neither is he now the "wretched
infidel" of the "Whiteness" chapter, nor the haunted man
insinuating the possible "propriety of devil-worship" during
Stubb's supper. Rainbow intuitions of "things heavenly,"
brought to him by the whale and the whale's irradiated spout,
have acted as counterpoise. For the first time viewing all things
with "equal eye," Ishmael is now ready for—indeed, is already involved in—a series of insights which will profoundly
alter his despairing view of cosmic reality. (pp. 186-90)

> *Robert Zoellner, in his* The Salt-Sea Mastodon: A
> Reading of Moby-Dick, *University of California
> Press, 1973, 288 p.*

JAMES WILLIAM NECHAS   (essay date 1978)

[In Nechas's opinion, Moby-Dick *is informed by Melville's belief
that ontological inquiry is solipsistic, limiting understanding of
the nature of reality to individual self-knowledge. Moby Dick is
thus depicted as the object of intense but solipsistic inquiry as a
symbol of nature, with Ishmael functioning in the role of an ontological hero who "refuses to accept as true and complete any
single interpretation of Moby Dick, . . . [placing] such interpretive
assurance outside of human knowledge." The critic identifies
Ishmael's "balanced" consciousness as the major thematic vehicle in* Moby-Dick *and traces its manifestations in the structural
and linguistic multiplication of meaning in the novel. Other critics
who discuss the ontological aspects of the novel include Thorp
(1938), Bewley (1959), Horsford (1962), Zoellner (1973), Hillway
(1979), and Aiken (see* NCLC, *Vol. 3). The narrative point of
view of the book is also discussed by Colcord (1922), Thompson
(1952), and Berthoff (1962). For further commentary on Melville's prose style in* Moby-Dick, *see the excerpts by Sir Nathaniel
(1853), MacMechan (1899), Winters (1938), Wilder (1952), and
Matthiessen (*NCLC, *Vol. 3). Berthoff (1962) provides additional
discussion of the novel's structure.]*

Melville attempted to use his awareness of man's metaphysical
presumption to escape its tyranny in his presentation of the
White Whale in *Moby-Dick.* Indeed, the fact that the Whale,
as a symbol of Nature, means different things to different
people controls every element of Melville's art. To escape the
egocentrism inherent in man, Melville pieced together his vast
picture of the White Whale from the fragmentary evidence of
a multitude of different view points, a multitude of individual
perspectives. Although eventually visible everywhere in the
novel, this tactic is most obvious in the handling of characterization. The Whale means something unique to each member
of the *Pequod's* crew and to each sailor the ship encounters
on her various gams. The final shifting and ambiguous picture
of the Whale that emerges from *Moby-Dick* is the artificial sum
of these different view points. The characters exist primarily
as embodiments of conflicting attitudes toward the Whale, and,
as Melville allows each to speak of Moby Dick, another shade
of meaning is added to his mottled back. Ahab sees the Whale
as the irresistible, man-devouring Evil of a malignant God . . . ;
Starbuck sees him as a dumb brute who is the agent of a
Christian evil which must be faced and overcome to win the
material rewards of life . . . ; to Queequeg the Whale is the

sign of a pagan diabolism in the world which must be placated and avoided . . . ; and to crazy Gabriel he is cryptically "the Shaker God incarnated," a stern and violent God not to be opposed as Ahab presumes to do. . . . On the other hand, to Stubb the White Whale is merely an industrial commodity to be chased, slain, and boiled . . . , while to little Flask he is "but a species of magnified mouse, or at least water-rat" to be killed for sport. . . . This aspect of *Moby-Dick* is epitomized in the chapters "Knights and Squires" and "the Doubloon." In these chapters, Melville brings forth the various crew members in formal juxtaposition to interpret the White Whale in voices which are weighted and respected. In their turns, the *Pequod*'s "isolatoes" speak of the Whale's meaning for them and thus reveal their own particular blindnesses. The attitudes of the crew members toward the Whale remain fairly static throughout the novel. Only Ishmael's view of Moby Dick is seen to change. This is true, because only Ishmael is allowed to escape the limitation of human blindness; Ishmael's consciousness is an artificial composite of the novel's many perspectives on the Whale. For a time, the Whale is merely a formless "phantom" which haunts Ishmael's imagination. Then he falls under Ahab's quarter-deck spell and begins to see the Whale as cosmic evil. As the frenzy of the moment passes, the Whale becomes even more horrible to Ishmael; he comes to represent cosmic indifference and meaninglessness. Finally, the conflict of these various attitudes produces in him a "balanced" view of the Whale; he refuses to accept as true and complete any single interpretation of Moby Dick, and he places such interpretive assurance outside of human knowledge. Ishmael ultimately achieves the position of the *Pequod* itself, burdened but "balanced" by the two whale heads hung at its sides. Ishmael's foundering mind is trimmed by hoisting up "Locke's head" in opposition to "Kant's" . . . , by opposing the mere acceptance of a meaningless empirical reality to a faith in a transcendent reality. He learns that those who view the Whale as a purely objective creature are exactly "balanced" by those who argue for some cryptic significance in him. . . . The many-faceted but "balanced" nature of Ishmael's consciousness thus makes him a good deal more than just the narrator of *Moby-Dick* or Melville's representative in the novel. It is Ishmael's composite intelligence which contains the theme of *Moby-Dick* and produces the structure and language. Ishmael is the sign of the artistic and philosophical impulse which controls the creation of *Moby-Dick*. (pp. 29-31)

Structurally, the microcosmic quality of the *Pequod*'s crew is paralleled by the . . . series of "digressions" on the natural and unnatural history of the great sperm whale. . . . Superfluous and contradictory though they at first appear, they represent a method for at once presenting and masking the philosophical complexity of the universal Whale. Each so-called digression, like each of the novel's characters, considers the Whale from a different perspective, presents him from within another frame of reference. Thus, in successive chapters, the history, anthropology, and mythology of the Whale are discussed, his artistic and biological profiles are contrasted, and, overall, his industrial and economic importance is projected. These perspectives which collectively structure much of *Moby-Dick* are, of course, what Guetti refers to as its different "languages" and "vocabularies" [see Additional Bibliography]. They are representations and redefinitions of the reality of the Whale which work in the same way as Melville's speculations on the Jonah story in chapter 83; they continually restate its meaning in fresh terms. Melville provides a schematization of the structural principles which govern *Moby-Dick*'s "cetological center" in the "Extracts" sections of the novel. There, different

and often mutually exclusive formulations of the reality of the Whale . . . are placed side by side without comment or qualification. These formulations are not offered as "gospel cetology" but as the "higgledy-piggledy" beginning of "a glancing bird's eye view of" him—that is, a view with a widely shifting perspective. . . . (pp. 31-2)

The structural rhythm of *Moby-Dick*—the interplay of the various definitions and formulations of the reality of the Whale—creates in the reader of the novel an attitude toward the White Whale which is similar to Ishmael's "balanced" view of him. As the meaning of the Whale is stated and restated, the monster accumulates symbolic significance. But even as these layers of meaning pile up, they begin to qualify and undercut one another. For instance, the view of the Whale as the immortal monster of forecastle mythology is contradicted and, for a moment, cancelled by the view of him as a victim of his own biology in the vicissitudes of the chase—the "inexplicable obstinacy of the leviathan in having his spoutings out" continually exposes him to the whaleman's lance. . . . This fantastic texture of contradiction and contrast produces a delicate tension in the reader's image of the Whale; he struggles to resolve the ambiguity of the monster but finds it impossible. His only recourse is to turn this tension into Ishmael's "balanced" view of the Whale: he must decide that the Whale is, at some time, all of these things. Each definition of the Whale is, for the time it is on the stage, adequate, but it is impossible finally to know his complete meaning.

It is Ishmael's voice and language, quite naturally, which account for the "balanced" acceptance of the diverse formulations of the Whale's meaning in *Moby-Dick*. His careful modulation and intimate tone give meaningful expression and weight to each definition of the Whale and defy the formulation of a rigid system or priorities. Just as the theme of *Moby-Dick* demanded that Melville provide a structure which would hold the various realities of the Whale in juxtaposition and equilibrium, this theme demanded that he provide a language which was capable of developing a similar balance and tension. Working, of course, with smaller units of meaning, Melville used the language of *Moby-Dick*, as he used structure, to phrase and rephrase the thematic or symbolic meaning of a particular event, object, or character in a variety of lexically, syntactically, and logically balanced ways. Thus, if the "Extracts" section of the novel is accepted as a schematization of its structural techniques, the "Etymology" section may be seen as the model for its linguistic devices. This list of words meaning "Whale" in several languages . . . reflects the fact that the Whale is called by many names, that he means something different to each man who beholds him. This section is a catalogue of duplication, and it provides the pattern from which the language of *Moby-Dick* is developed. . . . [The] hallmark of the language of *Moby-Dick* is semantic multiplication, a very deepseated tendency toward repetition. This tendency is produced by the desire to give expression to a world which offers many clues to meaning but no final assurance of meaning.

The techniques of semantic multiplication in *Moby-Dick* may be broken down into three major categories of language use: synonymy, repetition, and restatement. In the language of the three categories, some form of duplication or redefinition of the meaning of a particular thematic referent takes place. In each case also, the various semantic formulations which result from the specific type of duplication or multiplication are bound together and held in suspension by a system of linguistic ties. In other words, their philosophical (or semantic) interrelation is supported by their linguistic (or physical) interrelation. These linguistic ties may take the form of syntactic parallelisms, phonological echoing, lexical repetition or variation, or any of a number of similar devices. Collectively these multiplications, both semantic and linguistic, produce the ambiguous texture of contrast and conflict which forces the reader of **Moby-Dick** to accept Ishmael's "balanced" view of the White Whale.

Synonymy, the principle upon which the "Etymology" section of the novel is based, is the use of words with the same or similar meanings in connection with the same referent; it is a process of enumeration wherein the qualities of the referent are catalogued in the list of synonyms. There are three basic types of synonymy in **Moby-Dick:** transparent synonymy, oblique synonymy, and artificial synonymy. To make the preliminary identification of each type easier, it seems best to choose examples from only one category of language usage in the novel. Accordingly, the examples here are all instances of what might be called the synonymous word pair—two words usually joined by the conjunction "and" which mean or come to mean virtually the same thing.

The first and simplest type of synonymy makes use of words which have the same (or again, nearly the same) dictionary meaning or denotation. This type of synonymy is transparent, and its effect is unavoidable. This type of synonymy may be seen in the following phrases picked at random and presented in the order in which they appear in the novel:

> most young candidates for the *pains* and *penalties* of whaling . . .

> Such unaccountable manner of *shades* and *shadows* . . .

> he treated me with so much *civility* and *consideration* . . .

> a determined rushing sort of *energy* and *vigor* . . .

> I *laugh* and *hoot* at ye . . .

> mere unaided *virtue* or *right mindedness* . . .

> the object of trembling *reverence* and *awe* (. . . ; italics added throughout)

In these examples, note that all the italicized pairs have roughly the same dictionary meaning; in most cases, the paired words could be used interchangeably. Note also, however, that Melville gains something by using both words; he gains an important new dimension in meaning by adding the second word. His meaning becomes richer because he adds a slightly different quality with each new word. The word "penalties" is not strong enough to express the disadvantages of whaling—considered both professionally and metaphysically—so Melville adds "pains." There is pain in reaching for the truth of the Whale and physical discomfort in whaling. Similarly, "shadows" alone would adequately describe the besmirched quality of the whale painting in the Spouter Inn, but Melville did not want a simple physical description of the picture. Consequently, he added the meaning associated with the great Whale in "Loomings;" there is death in confronting him. And this same semantic strategy is present in each example. Each member of the synonymous pair mentions a different but related quality of the referent. "Civility" could be mere hollow politeness, but Melville heightens his description of Queequeg's humanity with the more specific and active "consideration." Starbuck's "virtue" is made all the more impotent in the face of Ahab's power with the addition of "right mindedness" and the elimination of action carried in that word. And the awesome "White Steed of the Prairies" is made even more horrible

when "reverence"—with its connotations of devoted and comfortable respect—is shaded into "awe"—with its connotations of fearful and forced respect.

The second type of synonymy, oblique synonymy, consists of words whose meanings are only obliquely similar, whose connotations overlap at some point. Once again, the presence of this type of synonymy is fairly obvious. The second type of synonymy may be seen in the following phrases:

> It came in as a sort of brief *interlude* and *solo* . . .

> a nature in which there lurked no civilized *hypocrisies* and *bland deceits*. . . .

> some time of general *drought* and a *sorrow* for him . . .

> the hardly tolerable *constraint* and nameless invisible *domineerings* . . .

> all manner of morbid *hints* and half-formed-foetal *suggestions* of supernatural agencies . . .

> in the earthly *make* and incontestable *character* of the monster . . .

> he was all the better *qualified* and *set* on *edge,* for a pursuit so full of *rage* and *wildness* as the bloody hunt of whales (. . . ; italics added throughout)

The second type of synonymy works in the same way that the first type does. It enumerates (in these cases) two slightly different but interrelated qualities of a particular referent by applying words which are semantically similar to it. The only difference between the first and second types is that the words Melville employed in the second type are not interchangeable in all cases. In most cases, one of the linked words is a specialized or more specific example of the other, hence the coupling of "interlude" and "solo," "hypocrisy" and "deceit," "drought" and "famine." And Melville's motive in this second type of synonymy is the same as the first. In each case he is augmenting the meaning of his phrase by using the synonymous pair. When Ishmael adds "sorrow" to "sympathy" in his list of feelings for Ahab, he expands his ties to the captain. Even though he is attracted to Ahab, even though he appreciates the urge which drives him, it is clear that Ishmael pities Ahab. In the same way, Melville changes the mild "constraint" of the captain's table into sinister "domineerings" and suggests that to be "qualified" for the hunt of whales, the sailor must be "set on edge;" he must be somehow changed, somehow abnormal.

The third type of synonymy, artificial synonymy, is unlike the other two because it involves an artificial process and is therefore relatively exotic and elusive. The words used in this category are not generally equated or even related semantically. They are, however, forced into synonymy by being repeatedly used within the confines of a very narrow context. In this process, the words become physically linked through their place within the common context and through their common referent. Moreover, this is a kind of metaphorical synonymy: the synonymous words become physical symbols, through repetition within a specific context, for a highly specialized body of knowledge, and they immediately bring the knowledge to mind whenever they are used. In turn, as the process continues, these words help to identify and call attention to the particular contexts and referents they represent. Thus, an interchange takes place between the individual words and contexts involved in this process; the dictionary meanings of the words add objective variety to their related contexts, and the contexts, in turn, add symbolic significance to the words. The third type of synonomy is created in two ways. It can occur in a single sentence or phrase when two totally unrelated words are forced to express the same thing about a referent through context. It can occur over large areas of the novel when various semantically dissimilar words are brought together by repeated association with the same referent and/or context. The third type of synonomy occurs very rarely in sentences or phrases. Its enforced synonomy requires time and the frequent repetition of the keyword (or words) in carefully related but separate contexts to be accomplished. However, it may be seen in the following phrases:

my own unbiased *free will* and discriminating *judgment* . . .

my splintered *heart* and maddened *hand* . . .

battled with virgin *wonders* and *terrors* . . .

Man may seem detestable as *joint stock companies* and *nations* (. . . ; italics added throughout)

In each case, Ishmael equates two different things in their peculiar relationship to a common referent: "The invisible police officer of the Fates" negates both "free will" and "judgment;" the soothing savageness of Queequeg quiets both the "heart" and "hand" of Ishmael, his fevered mind and jittery body; the explorer of the sea-world meets many stupifying "wonders," but he soon learns that these "wonders" are also absolute "terrors;" and men are ignoble when they band together because, no matter what body they form, the bonding principle is always greed, the unifying principle of "joint stock companies" and "nations."

The effect of the third type of synonomy is created over large areas of the novel. Words which are repeated often in *Moby-Dick*—the "staple" words of the novel—are separately associated with the same referent and thus eventually become symbolically or metaphorically synonymous. This type of synonomy is too complicated to be adequately demonstrated. . . . However, its outlines can be suggested. Beginning nearly at once, but starting practically with the chapter, "The Whiteness of the Whale," the words, "white," "mild," "calm," and "serene" are all repeatedly associated with the metaphysical meaning of the Whale. They denote the quiet and unconscious but potentially horrific power of many of his appearances in the novel. Similarly, the words "terror," "horror," and "black" become synonymous in their attachment to the violent and destructive aspects of the sea and the Whale. And because both sets of seemingly opposed words are related to the same referent and context, "mild" and "horror" eventually become synonymous in the novel. The White Whale of *Moby-Dick* is both mild and horrible, and it is impossible to say which quality is dominant in him.

The synonymic word groups of *Moby-Dick* of whatever type are, in their re-naming function, symbols of the many-faceted ambiguity of the Whale, that quality which causes him to appear different to different men. The synonymic groups of the novel, like all of its linguistic devices, catalogue the multiple meanings of their referent, whether it be the Whale or some surrogate. And because these synonymic equations are never perfect—no two or three words are ever exactly interchangeable—they produce the characteristic aggrandizement of meaning and its subsequent pattern of contrast and contradiction which result in a "balanced" view of the Whale.

Repetition, the second broad category of linguistic technique in *Moby-Dick,* is the verbatim reuse of a specific language element—a word, a phrase, a clause, or a sound. Repetition may or may not occur within the same syntactic or structural unit. Indeed, if an element is repeated often enough early in the novel, its later appearances may be widely separated and remain effective. But in either case, the process involved is the same: the two or more contexts in which the repetitions occur are physically bound together. Repetition, like synonomy, moreover, calls attention to itself, and thus the contexts which are physically drawn together tend to become semantically identified, semantically interchangeable. The meaning of one is associated with, and begins to shed light on, the other. And because this process of interchange most often takes place between contexts which are thematically similar, the repeated unit becomes the physical symbol of the interchange; it becomes encrusted with the separate significance of each of the contexts in which it appears and emerges as a representative of the collective meaning of them all. The repeated unit, in fact, becomes a linguistic symbol of the Whale, for its meaning has undergone a layering of meaning and a period of confusion and conflict which produce for it a "balanced" and ambiguous value. . . . [The] mechanics of repetition produce the favorite or "staple" words of *Moby-Dick*. Because Melville found words such as "white" and "mild," "horror" and "lurk," "level" and "lee" so expressive of particular aspects of his theme he repeated them again and again. And because he repeated them, these words build up complicated and rich meanings as the novel is read. For instance, in the chapter, "The Lee-Shore," the lee-shore is to be avoided; it is comfort and security and the denial of metaphysical meaning in the Whale; to seek its comfort is to deny half of life. However, the lee-shore is also insidious; its blandishments are forever attractive to man. And thus, as the novel continues, the meaning of the word "lee" changes. All the whales sighted by the sailors of the *Pequod* appear off its lee side, its side away from the wind, and each time Moby Dick escapes Ahab, he swims to the lee. By repeating the word "lee" in these particular situations, Melville is forcing his reader to see that the confrontation with the Whale is unavoidable. Even if man chooses the security of the lee-shore, he will be confronted with the potential evil and horror of life. Melville also uses the mechanics of repetition to produce the negative affix words of *Moby-Dick*. He repeatedly describes the Whale with words which employ the *im-*, *in-*, *il-*, and *ir-* prefixes and the *-less* suffix, such as "inscrutable," "unknowable," "unfathomable," "meaningless." Because he does so, he makes apparent that no final explanation of the Whale is possible. The Whale can be known only in negative terms, in terms of what he is not.

Restatement, the third major category of usage in *Moby-Dick,* is directly related to synonomy and indirectly related to repetition. Restatement is fundamentally the principle of synonomy embodied in a larger form, that of the phrase, clause, or sentence; it is the recasting and rephrasing of an idea in several connected or even unconnected syntactic units. As in synonomy, the semantic values of the separate restatements are never entirely equal, and the resulting aggregation of individual meanings (or reinterpretations) becomes an indication of the Whale. This symbolic accumulation of meaning—when it takes place in one syntactic unit—is usually accompanied by one or more forms of repetition. Repetition, either of word or sound, within a system of restatement serves both to separate and physically link the various elements of that system. At the same time, it identifies each element as an independent reinterpretation of the referent and prevents it from being valued over any of the others; repetition within a system of restatement, like all of the linguistic devices of *Moby-Dick,* works toward the achievement of a semantic "balance." The most important examples of restatement in the novel are the epithets applied to various characters and objects. It is a commonplace that to name something is to know it, but for Melville Nature was ultimately unknowable. As a result, the Whale and the many people and things which make up Nature in *Moby-Dick* are ultimately unnamed; no one name can contain them. The many epithets which are applied to the Whale, to the *Pequod*, and to Ahab, correspond with the many coexistent truths of their existences. Thus, the *Pequod* is called:

rare old *Pequod* . . .

a ship of the old school . . .

a cannibal of a craft . . .

a noble craft . . .

a most melancholy craft . . .

the unceasingly advancing keel . . .

our urn-like prow . . .

a thing appointed to desolation . . .

the ivory *Pequod* . . .

the circumnavigating *Pequod* . . .

the sometimes madly merry and predestined craft . . .

Some of these epithets portray the *Pequod* in a purely objective manner, while others make her a gloomy microcosm of a desolate world. On one hand, she is merely an industrial vessel in search of her livelihood, and on the other hand she is an "urn," the symbol of a death-laden world. The *Pequod* is none of these things exclusively and all of them. By constantly restating the ship's meaning with contradictory epithets, Melville forces his reader to take a "balanced" view of her significance: he denies the reader a final meaning for the ship. (pp. 33-41)

[The topics] discussed here have been chosen because together they demonstrate Melville's peculiar attitude toward the word as a unit of meaning. Melville did not see the word as simply the sign of a single objective denotation. He saw it as a cluster of many subjective connotations as well. In using words, he attempted to force into his reader's comprehension as many of these connotations as possible—or as were appropriate to his immediate objective. This is what he is doing when playing with the several meanings of "call" and "substitute" in the first paragraph of *Moby-Dick,* and this is what he attempts to do with the word "counterpane" in chapter four. Throughout the novel he constantly stretches the semantic limits of his words in many ways. . . . The constant repetition of a word in a novel causes the reader to look at it from the perspectives provided by a number of different contexts; in this way the reader is forced to acknowledge its many different connotations as each new context calls forth a slightly different meaning from the repeated word. In the case of *Moby-Dick,* because each of these repeated words is purposely negated, the reader must conclude that the final meaning of these words and their contexts—and the Whale and his sea-world—is negative or unknowable. (pp. 49-50)

James William Nechas, in his Synonymy, Repetition, and Restatement in the Vocabulary of Herman Melville's "Moby-Dick," *Norwood Editions, 1978, 286 p.*

TYRUS HILLWAY   (essay date 1979)

[*Hillway is a respected Melville scholar and the founder of the Melville Society. In the course of the following excerpt he makes several assertions concerning what the author did—and did not—intend to convey in* Moby-Dick. *Significantly, Hillway rejects a host of "elaborate allegorical interpretations" of the Ahab/Moby Dick conflict, maintaining that Ahab clearly represents a self-proclaimed sovereign individual who defies human limitations in searching for insight into the mystery of the universe. The author's intent, according to Hillway, is to condemn Ahab's assumption of social superiority and to convey the conviction that, "on the one hand, pursuit of the Absolute leads to frustration and madness; on the other, arrogance in the search is inherently self-destructive." Hillway also asserts that Melville neither denies the existence of God nor depicts God as an enemy in the novel. Rather, claims the critic, "*Moby-Dick *declares allegorically . . . total independence of subservience to any established religious or philosophical explanation of man's role in the universal order. It stands, however dangerously, as a declaration of man's freedom to control his own spiritual destiny." For further commentary on Melville's treatment of religion in* Moby-Dick, *see the excerpts by Auden (1950), Murray (1951), and Thompson (1952). The role of allegory in the novel is also discussed by Colcord (1922), and the symbolism of* Moby-Dick *is further elucidated in the excerpts by Lawrence (1923), Arvin (1950), Bewley (1959), Horsford (1962), Kulkarni (1970), and Mather, Lawrence, Mumford, Aiken, Winters, Sedgwick, Maugham, Auden, and Priestley (see NCLC, Vol. 3). For further discussion of Melville's treatment of theology in the novel, see the excerpts by Thorp (1938), Thompson (1952), Bewley (1959), and Aiken (NCLC, Vol. 3). Additional commentary on the role of ontology in* Moby-Dick *is provided in the criticism of Thorp (1938), Bewley (1959), Horsford (1962), Zoellner (1973), Nechas (1978), and Aiken (see NCLC, Vol. 3).*]

What were Ahab's true motives for the pursuit of Moby Dick? This is the key that unlocks the main mystery. Failure to answer this question correctly means misunderstanding the theme of Melville's masterpiece. Attempts to interpret *Moby-Dick* as a carefully constructed allegory have resulted in the proposal of different answers by different critics, but, in the long run, they have proved mainly how difficult has been the task of reading Melville's intentions through his profusion of symbols. Obviously, all the proposed interpretations cannot be right. How, then, can the reader determine which one is correct—which answer Melville himself would have given to the question of Ahab's motives?

Fortunately, Melville has provided clear guidelines in the story, though some critics have displayed a tendency to ignore them. Tempted by the rampant symbolism in the book to indulge themselves in a free play of the imagination, readers have been able to invent various interesting and sometimes elaborate allegorical interpretations, internally consistent, that fit the story fairly well. Almost any reader can find an interpretation that suits his own line of thinking. It is possible, for example, to argue, on the basis of a Freudian psychology, that the White Whale represents Melville's Puritan conscience, against which his ego is engaged in a life-or-death struggle. Others may prefer the theory that the whale stands for evil and Ahab for a modern Christ or Prometheus resisting its power. Still others equate the whale with religion and Ahab with liberal thought. The contest may even suggest a struggle between individualism and social convention, or between Marxism and capitalism, or between science and nature, or any one of a dozen plausible combinations, none of which Melville had in mind. A case can be made for almost any set of ideas which the reader sees to be in conflict in human life; and apparently, once a person has convinced himself that his particular interpretation of the story is possible, no one can dissuade him from believing it to be the only right one.

But Melville makes no insuperable mystery of the matter. If he had, the book would certainly have to be considered an intellectual failure. Not only does Ahab recognize his own motives (as well as his madness), but he clearly states them. Ahab is—as Melville once admiringly described his friend Hawthorne—"a man who, like Russia or the British Empire, declares himself a sovereign nature (in himself) amid the powers of heaven, hell, and earth. He may perish; but so long as he exists he insists upon treating with all Powers upon an equal basis. If any of those other Powers choose to withhold certain secrets, let them; that does not impair my sovereignty in myself; that does not make me tributary. And perhaps, after all, there is *no* secret." Ahab, too, declares his individual sovereignty, and in doing so he commits the unpardonable sin of thinking himself superior to the rest of mankind. He "would be," says Starbuck, "a democrat to all above; [but] look, how he lords it over all below."

What Ahab seeks—if the reader takes him at his word—is not the actual whale but a symbolical whale—the ultimate mystery of the universe. Being highly educated and a Kantian as well, Ahab acknowledges the limitation of man's power to know God through his intellect; yet, instead of submitting to his weakness, he hopes to transcend it by sheer defiance. His relentless determination to pierce the mystery is precisely that of Taji in *Mardi*. To do so, he believes that he must somehow strike through the "pasteboard mask" of nature; he must reason beyond the emblems of reality. But his puny powers, when matched against the forces of nature and fate, inevitably entrap him. "The painfullest feeling," writes Teufelsdrockh [in Thomas Carlyle's *Sartor Resartus*], "is that of your own Feebleness *(Unkraft);* ever, as the English Milton says, to be weak is the true misery."

Ahab, although boldly announcing himself a sovereign individual in the spiritual sense, equal in importance if not in strength of mind and body to any other sovereign individual in the universe—"I would strike the sun if he offended me"—is, however, the prisoner of his human form and human limitations. His mind fails in its attempts to pierce the wall of symbol, and his response to the failure is anger both at fate and at his own weakness. He strikes back blindly, even when aware of his doom. For "[h]ow can the prisoner reach outside except by thrusting through the wall?" Braving destruction, he is driven by the desperate urge to know into open defiance of the Power that bound him into weakness and the Mind that remains forever hidden behind the emblematic mask. "Sometimes," he comments bitterly, "I think there's naught beyond." And here he reiterates Melville's own blasphemy: "And perhaps, after all, there is *no* secret."

To argue from this that Melville denied the existence of God or that he regarded God as an enemy is going further than the evidence warrants. While raising serious questions about the inscrutable ways of God and the frustrating mystery of man's place in the universe, Melville took pains to reveal the futility of Ahab's posture of defiance. The appealing thing about Ahab is his courage—though perhaps *foolhardiness* would be a more accurate word—in playing for high stakes with a stacked deck. In his courage to disobey he resembles Prometheus, but there the resemblance ends. In no true sense can he be said to speak or act consistently for Melville, and his example is not recommended for imitation. Again and again in the story the reader is reminded of Ahab's utter madness—the "madness of

strength." There is another madman, but quite a different one, in the book. Pip, the pathetic little Negro boy driven insane after being heartlessly abandoned for a time on the open ocean, possesses the "madness of weakness." He never bewails or defies his fate. Yet he, not Ahab, glimpses in a sudden flash, at the instant of losing sanity, the true nature of the universe. Melville certainly means to convey in *Moby-Dick* the conviction—forced upon him by his own philosophical inquiries—that, on the one hand, pursuit of the Absolute leads to frustration and madness; on the other, arrogance in the search is inherently self-destructive.

Ahab's great error, like Taji's, is failure to accept human limitations. In assuming the possibility of learning final truth, he puts himself in effect on a plane of equality with God. Thus he is not only unrealistic but guilty of the fatal sin of pride; for, like Ethan Brand in Hawthorne's tale, he believes himself above and apart from other men. This attitude, though heroic, Melville plainly condemns. While the climax of *Moby-Dick* seems to come at the moment when Ahab steps into the whaleboat for the final confrontation of his nemesis, it really occurs earlier, in the chapter entitled "The Symphony." In that chapter Ahab for a time recovers his humanity; he nearly allows himself to be persuaded by the sympathetic Starbuck to relinquish his vengeful pursuit of Moby Dick and Fate and to resign himself to the common lot of mankind in an imperfect world. The attractions of brotherhood and peace momentarily conquer his insane desire to storm heaven. But his good resolves disappear, and he determines to press on in the chase. Unable to resist the urge to strike at Fate and, by striking, to probe the universal mystery, he dooms himself.

Ahab as captain of the *Pequod* acts as moral and intellectual leader of a crew representing every aspect of human life. Among the strangely assorted collection of characters are primitive savages like Daggoo and Queequeg, sailors from all the countries of Europe, young innocents like Pip and Ishmael, wise old seafarers, men of different religious faiths, good men and bad men. Some, like Stubb, laugh at life; others, like Starbuck, prize devotion to duty. The ship meets in the course of its voyage a great many other whaling ships bound on their own courses and intent on their own concerns. The meetings at sea provide interesting interludes in the story, sometimes humorous and sometimes tragic, but they also serve to shed the light of numerous and varying points of view on Ahab's quest. One such meeting demonstrates Ahab's loss of humanity. When the *Rachel* asks for aid in the search for a lost whaleboat which contains the captain's only son, Ahab, now close on the trail of Moby Dick, unfeelingly refuses.

One of the minor characteristics of the book that modern readers may regard as a defect is the use of melodramatic devices to inspire fear or wonder. Although Melville's literary principles in 1850 were edging more and more toward scientific realism, he introduced into the story, either through habit or in a bid for popularity, such relics of eighteenth-century taste as the Parsee Fedallah and his mysterious companions. These odd creatures, having for no apparent reason stolen aboard the ship secretly and in the darkness, remain hidden for months below decks and are not seen until called out as the special crew of the captain's whaleboat after the White Whale has been sighted. While the reason for Fedallah's presence in the book may lie, as Thorp suggests, in the fact that he symbolizes the evil which Ahab has created for himself—an evil spawned by single-minded hatred—yet as an actor in the drama he is nearly unbelievable. He must be considered a throwback to the phantom figures that haunt the shadowy stairways of gothic horror tales, or the grim underlings of Milton's fallen Satan. (pp. 87-92)

When the frantic struggle to finish *Moby-Dick* and see it through the press was finally ended, Melville confessed to his friend Hawthorne: "I have written a wicked book and feel spotless as the lamb." While readers today might not consider the work "wicked," nineteenth-century Christianity would clearly regard it so because the chief character openly questions the goodness of God. In his moments of despair Ahab even doubts the existence of a just Creator. Like Satan, he refuses to accept the fact of his inferiority and weakness and generally sees the universe as having been "formed in fright." Melville, in spite of having created such a character and expressed through him some of his own religious and philosophical doubts, could feel personally "spotless" and innocent because as author he could hold himself aloof from the madness of Ahab and because he had shown the defiance of heaven to be ultimately self-destructive.

In summation, one may say that the several different levels of meaning on which Melville speaks in *Moby-Dick,* baffling as they were to many readers of the nineteenth century, have today been fairly well defined. On one level Melville presents an exciting narrative of adventure at sea; on another, a remarkably accurate account of the American whale fisheries and the whaleman's life. On a deeper level he explores human psychology—still deeper, man's moral nature and his relationship to his universe. To the last-named problem he offers no clear-cut solution but only a powerful *No* to ready-made philosophies and creeds. From the supposition that Ahab in some degree depicts the spiritual autobiography of his creator (though young Ishmael and not Ahab is the actual narrator of the story and thus more closely relates to Melville), one may infer Melville's arrival in 1850 at the "Everlasting No" in the development of a personal philosophy. *Moby-Dick* declares allegorically (as its author did more directly in his letters to Hawthorne) total independence of subservience to any established religious or philosophical explanation of man's role in the universal order. It stands, however dangerously, as a declaration of man's freedom to control his own spiritual destiny. The risks are understood and accepted: "Make it an utter wreck, if wreck I must!" Melville's admiration for Hawthorne as a "Nay-sayer" indicates his own leanings in this direction:

> He says No! in thunder; but the Devil himself cannot make him say *yes.* For all men who say *yes,* lie; and all men who say *no,*—why, they are in the happy condition of judicious, unincumbered travellers in Europe; they cross the frontiers into Eternity with nothing but a carpet-bag—that is to say, the Ego. Whereas those *yes*-gentry, they travel with heaps of baggage, and damn them! they will never get through the Custom House.

To his deep disquiet, however, as the perspicacious Hawthorne was to observe later, Melville never could be comfortable in his unbelief. To describe the state of his mind revealed in *Moby-Dick,* one may use the words he applied in his famous review of *Mosses from an Old Manse* to the author of that collection of thoughtful tales and call him "a seeker, not a finder yet." (pp. 92-3)

> *Tyrus Hillway, in his* Herman Melville, *revised edition, Twayne Publishers, 1979, 177 p.*

JANE MUSHABAC   (essay date 1981)

[*In the following source study, Mushabac proposes that such eminent European writers as François Rabelais, Robert Burton, Laurence Sterne, Thomas De Quincey, and Charles Lamb provided Melville with models for the "frontier" humor in* Moby-Dick. *American culture helps shape the novel's humor, in her opinion, but not to the extent suggested by Chase (1949). The American properties of* Moby-Dick *are also discussed by MacMechan (1899), Olson (1947), Wilder (1952), and Rourke (see Additional Bibliography).*]

Part of the sustained achievement of *Moby-Dick* is that Melville has not only found exactly the subject to talk about, but a way of talking about it. One of his distractions in earlier novels was finding a form when available ones such as the travel narrative and the sentimental novel were wrong—unresilient and constricting. Richard Chase has suggested forms and motifs which Melville found in American folklore; these indeed were instrumental in liberating Melville's humor by providing him a way to talk about his very American subject. I suggest, however, that American folklore is only one part, the final part, of what Melville was absorbing and building upon. This was the whole tradition of prose humorists who, from the Renaissance on, played with the excitement of the opening of the frontier, of land and knowledge, of the new man of infinite potentials. Indeed, Melville is not only relieved to find available to him all the forms of the past, but even seems to enjoy the showmanship of incorporating and building upon all the male frontier monologues he knew and admired: the Renaissance tall tale of Rabelais; the melancholy anatomy of Burton; the humorous novel of sensibility/cock-and-bull story of Sterne; the humorous essay of sensibility of Lamb, De Quincey, and Irving; and finally the periodical tall tale or twister of popular American culture.

In his extravaganza, Rabelais gave Melville a way of spelling out the feeling of prodigiousness and bounty that is at the heart of frontier humor. Rabelais created Gargantua and Pantagruel, giants of body, mind, and heart who are described in an affectionate extravagant vernacular and sprung from native folk legend. Like Pantagruel, the whale in Melville's book is a vast creature, described and admired in a spirited colloquial tongue, one who as an infant consumes in a day thousands of gallons of milk, and as an adult, travelling whither he pleases and turning up everywhere, takes the whole world for his province. Moby Dick, in addition, as one particular whale, is sprung very consciously from native legend and, like Pantagruel, is male, important, and importantly dressed in white. Gargantua's enterprising love of learning and independent thinking meanwhile has encouraged Ishmael's bragging, central to *Moby-Dick,* of the grand sweep and scope of his research and knowledge. And so contagious is the love of learning in Rabelais's book that even Panurge, obscene practical joker that he is, first wins Pantagruel's heart in the beginning of their long friendship by saying that he is hungry in thirteen languages. Is this perhaps why Ishmael in his overture to his reader translates *whale* into thirteen languages? (pp. 89-90)

That Melville had Rabelais in mind . . . is clear from a crucial chapter that he borrowed from Rabelais, the whiteness chapter—about Pantagruel wearing, and Moby Dick being, white. The business of these chapters is a theatrical redefinition of the word *white,* Rabelais and Melville each ceremoniously rejecting meanings from the past, insisting upon his own interpretation of things, and officiously cataloguing all the evidence supporting his view. If Melville emphasizes dread to Rabelais's joy, we should keep in mind that Rabelais in that chapter tells us that the "lion, who with his only cry and roaring affrights all beasts, dreads and feareth only a white cock," and ends by speaking of white as the color of a joy so extreme you could die from it. Similarly Melville in his milk-white steed gives us a creature of royal magnificence which, like that of the Milky Way itself, affrights us, but only by being the greatest of spectacles of this universe. It is certainly true that Rabelais never emphasizes the dread which haunts Melville's novel, that atheism to Rabelais never seems the truly terrifying spectre it does to Melville, that Melville in turn takes Rabelais's catalogue of the previous meanings of white up past Rabelais, through Coleridge (and Poe) to his own. We do have a contrast in tone and fable between the two books. But in some basic concept of the bounty of the universe and of the sociability of friendships like those of Pantagruel and Panurge, Gargantua and Pantagruel, in the excitement of gigantic man as a New World creature of possibilities, and the bounty of nature's gallons of milk, white and endless—Melville found a great source in Rabelais.

[In his *The Anatomy of Melancholy,*] Robert Burton gave **Moby-Dick** not just the form of the anatomy, but his subject and a purpose, to cure his own melancholy by writing. "When I first took this task in hand," Democritus, Jr. writes, "this I aimed at: to ease my mind by writing, for I had a heavy heart and an ugly head, a kind of imposthume in my head, which I was very desirous to be unladen of, and could imagine no fitter evacuation than. Besides I might not well refrain, for one must needs scratch where it itches." Ishmael goes to sea for the same reason: "It is a way I have of driving off the spleen, and regulating the circulation. Whenever I find myself growing grim about the mouth: whenever it is a damp, drizzly November in my soul . . . especially whenever my hypos get such an upper hand of me. . . . This is my substitute for pistol and ball. With a philosophical flourish Cato throws himself upon his sword; I quietly take to the ship." . . . One for his anatomy, the other for his journey, the purpose is the same, to drive off the spleen, the ugliness in the head, the haziness around the eyes, the heaviness of the heart. Indeed in **Moby-Dick,** as in *The Anatomy of Melancholy,* the imposthume of the head is a central obsession; it is not incidental that Ishmael, while he turns to other things, enjoys leaving the sperm whale's prodigious head hanging on the *Pequod*'s side for, as in Burton, the story begins with a prodigious head (the persona's) caught, suspended, and turned into a helpless monstrosity waiting upon its master. "Too many heads" . . . , says the landlord of the Spouter Inn, and Melville loves to let us see the steam rising both from whale's heads and philosophers'. (pp. 91-3)

The cure for the imposthume in the head is much the same in both works. Ishmael, like Democritus, Jr., consoles himself with absorption in some monumental all-defying project; it hardly matters that one uses a voyage at sea and the other a voyage of the mind. . . . The important thing about the cure is that neither the wonders of travel nor the spectacles of the extravaganza anatomy are mere curatives to the disease, but its cause to begin with. In a popular American song, a doctor prescribes lime and coconut for the patient who is sick from drinking lime and coconut. The madness itself is a product of the original excitability. What Melville borrows from Burton is the underlying preposterousness of the cure. Burton cites Felix Plater, who went on a seven-year voyage to rid himself of the chattering Aristophanic frogs in his belly, but what are Burton's *Anatomy* and Melville's **Moby-Dick** but more frogs chanting splendid impossible "wicked" nonsense, . . . a fine

promiscuity of erudition and jabber, of fancy scientific words and slang. (pp. 93-4)

Comparing Burton's central proof that all men are mad with Melville's that whaling is noble gives us a concrete image of how all this works out through the two books. Just as Burton makes up an absurd list of exceptions to prove the rule, such as Monsieur Nobody and the Stoics who must be mad for not being so, Ishmael as the "advocate" conjures up a great melodramatic courtroom scene in which, to vindicate the nobility of whaling, a hodgepodge of absurd logic, grandiose allusion, and general fast-talking is thrown at the reader while the speaker works himself into a frenzy of assertion. Burton's frenzy is quieter and more archaic in its tone, but he is doing the same thing.

> *No dignity in whaling?* The dignity of our calling the very heavens attest. Cetus is a constellation in the South! No more! Drive down your hat in presence of the Czar, and take it off to Queequeg! No more! I know a man that, in his lifetime, has taken three hundred and fifty whales. I account that man more honorable than that great captain of antiquity who boasted of taking as many walled towns. . . .

The odd thing is that while the rowdy exaggeration would seem to undermine the argument, the more it parodies itself, the more it nonetheless convinces us. Say no more, indeed! All men are mad! Whaling is noble! Can we possibly disagree? Can we possibly not submit to the acataleptic fervor? . . . The whole of **Moby-Dick,** with its perpetual fossil whales, cetologies, and masthead exhaustive researches, endlessly anatomizes the whale, the whaleship, and this watery world.

Laurence Sterne's *Tristram Shandy* . . . gave Melville another handle for **Moby-Dick.** That Tristram writes in the same vein as Democritus, Jr. is clear. "If 'tis wrote against anything,—'tis wrote," Tristram says of his book, "against the spleen." Sterne, however, has made several shifts. Dropping Burton's discreetness, he has revived Rabelais's open sexual and religious teasing in time to encourage Melville to do the same. In addition, Sterne has turned Burton's dignified melancholic philosopher into the domesticated pathetic men of the Shandy household, who are as infatuated with learning as Democritus, Jr. ever was but, in addition, ceremoniously castrated and mechanized, deprived of their noses and names. (pp. 94-5)

Sterne has tightened Burton's unwieldy extravaganza *consolatio* to the form at its core, the novel of sensibility/cock-and-bull story. . . . It is most of all the form of Sterne's novel that Melville has worked from; for Sterne's book, unlike Burton's, devotes itself to a series of plotted splenetic events. . . . *Tristram Shandy*'s plot itself is hardly more than a series of disconnections and exasperations.

It is in this conceptual sense that Melville's book is a novel of sensibility. The author is not only willing to dispel his own hypos—morbid blues—but to expiate them, not with a plot built upon a series of frustrations, but with a plot centered on one major exasperation. Indeed the word *exasperation* occurs regularly in the book, like a chime, beginning with the picture of the exasperated whale impaling itself upon the dismantled masts of a ship, like Cato upon his sword. . . . [This] is the humorist's perspective, establishing from the start a vision of man as a creature beset by hypos and exasperations, and needing continually to get himself from one to the next. (pp. 95-6)

Melville's humor is grounded in a way that Sterne's is never intended to be; Melville is utterly determined to take the hypo, spleen, and exasperation to their sharpest, so that we most need the humor that is the staple of the book, so that it is in no way gratuitous. Nonetheless, there is a certain similarity that is important, not just incidental. The final thing we must say about Ahab is astonishing to come upon. We have seen him described as one sullen animal after another—all comparisons that are grim jokes on man's idealization of his misery. Even further, however, what we must come to terms with is the hum: "While the mate was getting the hammer, Ahab, without speaking, was slowly rubbing the gold piece against the skirts of his jacket, as if to heighten its lustre, and without using any words was meanwhile lowly humming to himself, producing a sound so strangely muffled and inarticulate that it seemed the mechanical humming of the wheels of his vitality in him." . . . (pp. 96-7)

[This is close to] Henri Bergson's mechanical man at the root of all humor. This is related to Walter Shandy's winding up the clock and his marital relations the same one night a month at the opening of Sterne's book. Ishmael too will become the mechanical man of warp and woof, the mere shuttle in "The Mat-Maker," as does the carpenter at the end of the book in a short, brilliant sketch. Finally Moby Dick also in the last moment before Ahab's death: "Suddenly the waters around them slowly swelled in broad circles; then quickly upheaved, as if sideways sliding from a submerged berg of ice, swiftly rising to the surface. A low rumbling sound was heard; a subterraneous hum; and then all held their breaths; as bedraggled with trailing ropes, and harpoons, and lances, a vast form shot lengthwise, but obliquely from the sea." . . . Melville's mechanical exasperated creature—man or beast, cock and bull— is a creature of sensibility and grim humor. Melville takes the joke of the hypo absolutely and deliberately to its limit, but the pattern in which he does so is the novel of sensibility/cock-and-bull story.

It was in Thomas De Quincey's book [*Confessions of an English Opium Eater*] that Melville found this sensibility gone to seed. Indeed, De Quincey often uses the word *sensibility* to describe the extreme hypos which pushed him to his own extreme remedy, opium addiction. The braggadocio of extremism, the determination to encounter the worst, provided a model, a novel of grim humor, which we cannot be surprised that Melville found "wondrous" in 1849. (p. 97)

It is in Melville's chapter 35 that De Quincey's opium is introduced. Ishmael tells us riding in the masthead produced a trance very much like that produced by opium. The trance in turn produces a giddy, wry monologue with historical, philosophical, and emotional commentary upon mastheads; with a mock earnestness cataloguing all possible entrants in that category; teasing pious narrators like Scoresby; and above all celebrating the snugness of this cold, vulnerable, lonely perch which might easily throw a man to his watery death hundreds of feet below. The masthead, indeed, with its opiumlike trance, is Melville's De Quinceyan cottage of happiness par excellence, perfectly fit out to supply the theory of happiness. Here we not only deny ourselves fire, counterpane, and tea . . . , but windows, walls, and roof.

Indeed, finally here is the difference between De Quincey's and Melville's wry humor of vast vulnerability . . .—that De Quincey actually takes a drug to induce his giddy wryness, whereas Ishmael induces his own without help from any of the beverages which humorists have so depended upon to soothe

their melancholy souls. In *Moby-Dick,* Melville leaps from the standard humorists' ploy of drinking a beverage to mentally fixating on one. The liquid in *Moby-Dick* is water, but instead of physically drinking it, Ishmael mentally takes it in and becomes obsessed with it, as if he has taken the whole "watery world" and got drunk on it. In contrast to De Quincey, because his trance is only opium-like, and not actually opium-induced, Melville has all the freedom of its intense vision and all the depths of its vulnerability which are the realm of the humorist, but none of the disadvantages. . . . [Neither] Melville as author nor Ishmael as narrator-humorist is forced into the bondage produced by a chemical actually in the blood. Thus the fine wryness that is so spotty in De Quincey—as in the footnote in which he earnestly discusses whether a druggist may "evanesce," or tosses off a thought about it being a disagreeable thing to die—is intrinsic to Melville's work and steady in it. (pp. 98-9)

Much more in control than De Quincey, although turning the game from deliberately confronting to deliberately evading the extremes of human vulnerability, is Charles Lamb. Elia [the fictive author of Lamb's "Elia" essays] is an important source for Ishmael. Elia is male, a bachelor, melancholy, domesticated, all oddities and quirks, and pleasures and displeasures, yet overridingly sociable and amiable, with affection especially for other ornery types like his grumbling housekeeper. Elia besides is a customshouse thrall, "poor Elia," who is continuously drawing our attention to the pathetic distance between man's illusion of mental control and the actuality of dependency and slavery, between theory and practice: "My theory is to enjoy life, but the practice is aginst it." Elia, all sensibility, consoles himself with the joys of roast pig and plum pudding. Sympathetically he pokes fun at our Caledonian earnestness. Indulgently he lets himself out for wandering in the "twilight of dubiety" where he will "cry halves" for the bits of truth that he may find, allowing himself only "hints and glimpses," "crude essays at a system," "wanderings" in the maze of possibilities, for "truth presents no full face," a "feature or side face at most."

Ishmael, like Elia, is male, a bachelor, in his own way on board ship domesticated, puttering about among the try-pots and all his likes and dislikes, making friends with other isolatoes—those ornery and intimidating, but ultimately most affectionate, types. Ishmael, too, tells us his foibles and his loves: for whaling, chowder, forbidden seas, cannibals, following funerals, the whale as a dish, confidential chats, dipping his biscuit, holding mock debates, unraveling parodic dissertations and anatomies upon the whale who never shows his face, and turning over his endless thinking as neither infidel nor believer. Ishmael, the whaleship thrall, takes up Lamb's crude "essay" in both its meanings. Duyckinck was one critic to notice the essayistic quality of many of *Moby-Dick*'s chapters, and indeed in this perspective we may recognize them as fine examples of humorous essays—monologue bits in the method of Lamb, Hazlitt, De Quincey, and Irving. (pp. 100-01)

Washington Irving was another humorist essayist who seems to have been in Melville's mind during the writing of *Moby-Dick*. . . . Irving's pathetic schoolmaster Ichabod Crane, as well as the Burtonesque bachelor Geoffrey Crayon, provided humorous prototypes for Ishmael; and the tyrannical peglegged Peter Stuyvesant provided one for Ahab. We must say immediately, of course, that Irving's tyrant turns out to be most kindhearted after all, and Irving's pathetic types are often thin in their appeal, resting too much upon their settings, or rallying a bit too easily after all. Ichabod, for instance, after the headless horseman fright, goes to the city and becomes, within sentences, a successful businessman. Nonetheless, Irving seems to have been in Melville's mind as a novice of an artist. It is as if Melville becomes Irving and survives him, becomes him and transcends him. In "Bartleby," we may see the relationship between the two authors more clearly. For the moment, let us simply note that it must have been important to Melville to find an American working the Democritan extravaganza vein of humor in its romantic essay form. (p. 103)

[No] one questions the essential Americanness of *Moby-Dick*. . . . The question is exactly what did Melville take from developing American humor to flesh out the Americanness of his book, and to develop his own humor to its quickest, brightest level.

Richard Chase makes some important suggestions along these lines. He points out that Melville borrows American folk figures—Ishmael, for example, being a composite of the Yankee, the frontiersman, the comic Promethean demigod of a trickster, the jack-of-all-trades like Sam Slick, and finally the elusive soliloquizing yarn-spinner. Stubb is a typically American screamer, using the standard techniques of the American trickster, razzing Negroes and gulling Europeans; and finally out of the comic realm, Ahab is the ultimate screamer, a folkloric embodiment of Manifest Destiny, an American Prometheus. For both his central fable and its spin-offs, Melville also uses, Chase tells us, the American predilection for comic metamorphosis, an instantaneous transformation back and forth that makes the whale into an albino and then into a god; the story's heroes into titans, beasts, and machines; men into animals and back again, as Ahab is made into a grizzly and Ishmael into a May grasshopper. It is only the beginning to recall that Crockett, for one, was half-horse, half-alligator, and half-man, or that he went so far as to call himself an entire zoological institute. Chase shows that in *Moby-Dick*, Melville was working from a grab bag of standard American tall tales built upon exaggeration, sudden or eventual violation of the laws of nature, or the whimsy that shows the utter impracticality of human endeavor.

Within this typically American flight of fantasy, Chase finds a very American emphasis on and undercurrent of fact and practicality, so strong that it sometimes camouflages the fantasy. . . . This underlying bias toward fact is as responsible for the workings of the central fable as it is for the book's whole style. This style has its roots in P. T. Barnum showmanship, American magniloquent oratory, and the theatre of the 1830s and 1840s in which a blank mask, omnipresent from the Yankee pedlar, allows the tale-teller to move freely back and forth from sales pitch to scientific razzmatazz to dramatic action.

Two problems arise with the suggestions Chase made in 1949. To begin with, it was Chase's ultimate point about all this material that Melville exploits Americana to provide a fabric for his historical-tragic allegory, the comic material giving a "low enjoying power" to the higher stuff as Melville transmutes "the language of the screamer" into an apostrophe "to space and freedom." The P. T. Barnum hoax, Chase says, Melville turns inside out. Barnum was exploiting the desire of the audience to be comforted by the destruction of any fierce emotion. Melville, on the contrary, uses his hoax to insist on that emotion. When Melville neither transmutes nor turns inside out the Americana, Chase feels its tastelessness needs apology. For example, regarding Stubb's callous gulling of Fleece, Chase explains that, unpleasant as this sort of play may be, we must accept it as cultural fact.

The main problem with Chase's analysis, however, is that most of what Chase refers to as distinctly American is simply essentially humorous. The American folk tradition, we should realize, is only one part of the background of the comic trickster Prometheus. The European literature which Melville read was full of comic Prometheuses and demigods, like Pantagruel inventing his omnipotent Pantagruelion, Panurge inventing his *libertin* tricks, or de Bergerac inventing his moon machine and calling himself a Prometheus as a result. The literature was full as well of pure rogues and tricksters, from Lazarillo to Volpone to Mosca. For sources of Ishmael as a soliloquizing monologuist, we have already said much here of his literary paternity—Alcofrybas, Democritus, Jr., Tristram Shandy, Elia, and Geoffrey Crayon. The comic metamorphosis, too, is only partially American. We have not only the tall tale of Renaissance humor to cite, but the humorist's whole game of *what I desire I am*. Humor depends upon continuous expansions and contractions, continually thrown back to back. Democritus, Jr. is a free man and a slave, Panurge a giant of desire and cowardice—and later Alice in Wonderland will be a giant, then after a sip of "Drink Me," a mite. The only particularly American characteristic of Melville's metamorphoses may be the predominance of animals in the transformations. Otherwise, the shuffling back and forth is simply the humorist's insistence on writing as he pleases, showing he is boss, submitting to no logic or dogma, continually indulging his fantasies.

Finally to recognize that the showmanship of a literary-scientific extravaganza is not merely American, we need only mention *Gargantua and Pantagruel, The Anatomy of Melancholy,* and *The Historical and Critical Dictionary*. In each of those works of peremptory showmanship, the author is, above all, determined to outdo anything prior in scope and method, as well as to suggest continually the farce of this sort of determination. This is what makes it so important to see beyond the Barnum roots of Melville's humor; while with Chase we may condemn the ultimately shabby artistry of a P. T. Barnum, we may respect and admire the shaggy dog encyclopedias of such great writers as Rabelais, Burton, and Bayle. Their hoaxes need not be turned inside out; their humor needs no "transmuting." The actually literary literary-scientific extravaganza is built upon a fundamental bleakness and the "fierce emotion" it can inspire. It is built upon the uncertainty that Panurge faces, the slippery road on which the patriarchs walk, the bleak lot of a Lazarillo, the whiteness of acatalepsy, the all pervasiveness of mad melancholy, and the trance, finally, of opium. It is always there, that atheistical whiteness. In short, . . . humor need not be, and in fact is not, a stepping-off point for this book. It is its center.

Still, once we have recognized that American humor only added one more element to the humor that is central to *Moby-Dick*, let us see what that element is. First of all, America provided the allusive materials for many of Melville's exaggerations and reversals. As a white American, Ishmael need not spell out that he is a free man born, but may jump ahead to the turnaround of "who aint a slave?" So, too, while the squire and Lazarillo or Volpone and Mosca, as master and servant types appropriate to their era, gull each other by turns, it is only fitting that in America, the two parties turning tables on each other—the Cabin Table, for one—should be white and black, or American and European, or Lakeman and Vineyarder. It is fitting also that Melville's metamorphoses jump back and forth not only from erudition to slang, or from rhapsody to the thump, or from piety to phallicism, but from man to animal; America was a land in which the animals were only then in the process of being subdued, conquered, and exterminated. In addition to the incidentals, however, American humor did indeed provide a grab bag of yarns and twisters to help Ishmael, a sort of King Midas, transform details into braggadocio. More importantly, the yarn helped Melville shape the central fable as a fish story of one man hunting down one particularly monstrous fish. Melville uses the yarn to transform and tighten the spacious voyage of Rabelais, the anatomy of Burton, the encyclopedia of Bayle, the rambling novel of Sterne; and he uses it to open up the small essay of sensibility, the melancholic sketch of De Quincey, Lamb, and Irving.

But beyond the paraphernalia for the quick allusiveness which humor always demands, and beyond the form both peripheral and central of the yarn or twister, Melville gets something which is distinctively American, a game of immediacy. The American hallmark of *Moby-Dick*'s humor is a certain journalistic predilection that moves us from Rabelais's fantasy of the giant Pantagruel drinking thousands of pails of milk a day to the actuality of a whale sucking that much from its dam; from Rabelais's fantasy of Pantagruel's arch of triumph to the actual six-foot-long pride of the whale. Chase had hinted at this essentially American aspect when he spoke of the particularly American reliance on fact and practicality. Practicality is too broad because all humor depends upon the play between the lofty and the banal, the theory and the practice, the soaring desire and the menial actuality. The fact part is right, however, and crucial. In the Renaissance frontier humor springing from the explorations of that era, the New World is very much in people's minds and very strong in creating the braggadocio and self-parody of that literature, but the authors themselves are not actually *in* the New World. With the earlier non-American humorists, the idea of the frontier is what sets them going, but with those in America, it is as if the joke has been suddenly accelerated and escalated into actuality. In American humor, we are not just given the remote idea or the willful fantasy, but the literal physical frontier, the experience of the land, the Indians, the animals, and the sea.

It is the periodical journalistic aspect which Melville borrowed most from American humor, a certain literal-mindedness, a stubbornness of the persona's insistence on having been here. *And I only am escaped to tell you* is part of the song: I alone was there and saw it with my own eyes. That the almanac, periodical book of timely and pragmatic knowledge as well as of humor and entertainment, was the standard American household book is not surprising, nor is it that the humor there is that of factual experience and deposition braggadocio. . . . To see that Melville was responding to this spirit, we may look at central chapters like "The Affidavit," which reveal the book as the bragging deposition that it is. Ishmael calls himself at one point "a veritable witness" . . . ; at another he speaks of procuring for every snow crystal "a sworn affidavit." . . . I cannot help thinking that, finally, part of the fun of the title *Moby-Dick* was that the word *dick* in the slang of Melville's day—not yet into the explicitness of our own time—not only signaled fellow (as in Tom, Dick, and Harry), and the dictionary, but declaration or affidavit. *Moby-Dick* is Ishmael's wordy bragging, in effect, "I was there, ladies and gentlemen, this man was there and saw all this with his own eyes."

Although as a doctor, Rabelais teases us with a lot of close-up physicality, he has a certain distance from the low life he describes. Burton, one feels, has isolated himself in his study. Even Sterne and the Romantic essayists have a certain remove. In Melville's humor, however, if only to be able to brag that

you were there in the most complete fashion, you are forever "putting your hand into the tarpot" . . . ; *Moby-Dick* is a total immersion in universal social, economical, political, and physical realities. The central conflict gives us all the innards of fish cleaning and fish stories, while it plays off a history of the peaking of one of America's first extraordinarily successful commercial enterprises. Melville's Ishmael, too, is not only directly at the masthead watching over all the watery world, not only at the helm once with the entire survival of the ship at his hand, not only in the whaleboat privy to the inner circles of the whales copulating and giving suck, but in chapter after chapter on board ship wresting the oil from the captured whale, at the end of the monkey rope, and with his hands, his whole body immersed in the smell and realities of the whale. Indeed the humor of "A Squeeze of the Hand" is that the exultant image of the felicitous brotherhood of mankind is pinned to the most physical and inane of immersions.

Melville is never afraid of getting his hands wet or dirty. His very American humor not only anatomizes the world and presents a melancholic idiosyncratic persona, but gets "these visible hands" . . . into the actual physicalities of the whale—and squeezes. Yet, and this is important too, for it makes the whole difference, American as Melville was in his deposition, in his bragging journalistic immersion, at the same time, by his leaning on and listening to earlier and highly literary voices, he avoids the reductionism, provinciality, and claustrophobia of American periodical and almanac humor, whose joke of literalness and insistence on petty regionalist rivalry can quickly begin to pall.

Finally, then, *Moby-Dick*'s giddy sense of triumph evolves out of Melville's building upon a tradition of the giddy sense of triumph. It rests upon his awareness that he is building upon other humorous literature that has gone before, quickening the European fantasy with an American eye for physical and economic realities, sustaining the American quick turn of periodical humor by giving it a longer form and a substantial vision, broadening the American game of provincial literalness with a truly literary and catholic teasing and sense of play. Besides, however, doing all of this, we may ask if Melville adds anything to the long line of developing humor, or whether his whole achievement lies simply in impersonating and stretching. To be sure, the building itself is characteristically Melville's. That he takes everything he looks at into the superlative of the modern, and metamorphoses all that he has read into the present, is itself the game of his humor. In addition, however, it is the intensity of the hug which brings all of Melville's book into focus and distinctively shapes his originality. Against a frame of absolute universality, Melville opens up what he calls the "spheres" of "fright" and "love" . . . to two sustaining hugs, Ishmael and Queequeg at one end, Ahab and Moby Dick at the other. To transform the humorous male monologues of the past into his present, and impose upon them the preposterous hug: here is the achievement of Melville's humor in *Moby-Dick*. (pp. 103-10)

Jane Mushabac, in her Melville's Humor: A Critical Study, *Archon Books, Hamden, CT, 1981, 199 p.*

ADDITIONAL BIBLIOGRAPHY

Adams, Michael Vannoy. "Ahab's Jonah-and-the-Whale Complex: The Fish Archetype in *Moby-Dick*." *ESQ* 28, No. 3 (3rd Quarter 1982): 167-82.

Uses Carl Jung's concept of the "Jonah-and-the-Whale complex" to elucidate the meaning of Ahab's conflict with Moby Dick.

Ament, William S. "Bowdler and the Whale: Some Notes on the First English and American Editions of *Moby-Dick.*" *American Literature* 4 (1932-1933): 39-46.
Briefly notes the bowdlerizations that Melville's English publisher performed on his original text, which was published unexpurgated in the first American edition of the work.

Anderson, Charles Roberts. "Outward Bound." In his *Melville in the South Seas*, pp. 11-65. New York: Columbia University Press, 1939.
Sheds light on Melville's compositional technique by investigating the connection between *Moby-Dick* and Melville's experience and knowledge of the South Seas.

Baird, James. *Ishmael*. Baltimore: Johns Hopkins Press, 1956, 445 p.
Treats Melville as the chief exemplar of modern authentic primitivism, citing the example of *Moby-Dick* throughout. In addressing the issue of Melville's symbolism, Baird maintains that the writer was "engaged in the act of making new symbols to replace the 'lost' symbols of Protestant Christianity," and that the symbols he created are more closely related to Eastern than to Western symbology.

Barnett, Louise K. "Speech in *Moby-Dick.*" *Studies in American Fiction* 11, No. 2 (Autumn 1983): 139-51.
Analyzes the dynamics of verbal communication in *Moby-Dick*. Barnett focuses on Ahab, whose language is "primarily [an instrument] of self-assertion and self-validation, not . . . a means of establishing connections with other men or exploring the world."

Bell, Millicent. "Pierre Bayle and *Moby-Dick.*" *PMLA* LXVI, No. 5 (September 1951): 626-48.
Describes Pierre Bayle's *Dictionnaire historique et critique* as an important source of philosophy and rhetorical style in *Moby-Dick*.

Blackmur, R. P. "The Craft of Herman Melville: A Putative Statement." In his *The Expense of Greatness*, pp. 139-66. New York: Arrow Editions, 1940.
Uses the examples of *Pierre; or, The Ambiguities* and *Moby-Dick* to support the contention that Melville's work "nowhere showed conspicuous mastery of the formal devices of fiction which he used."

Bowen, Merlin. *The Long Encounter: Self and Experience in the Writings of Herman Melville*. Chicago: University of Chicago Press, 1960, 282 p.
Discusses the role of selfhood in *Moby-Dick* and other works by Melville.

Branch, Watson G., ed. *Melville: The Critical Heritage*. The Critical Heritage Series, edited by B. C. Southam. London: Routledge & Kegan Paul, 1974, 444 p.
Reprints selected nineteenth-century reviews and notices of *Moby-Dick*.

Braswell, William. "Accuser of the Deity." In his *Melville's Religious Thought: An Essay in Interpretation*, pp. 57-73. New York: Pageant Books, 1959.
Interprets Ahab's defiance of God as a projection of Melville's heretical religious views.

Brodhead, Richard H. "The Uncommon Long Cable: *Moby Dick.*" In his *Hawthorne, Melville, and the Novel*, pp. 134-62. Chicago: University of Chicago Press, 1976.
Proposes that *Moby-Dick* presents and is founded on an opposition between two views concerning the nature of the world; namely, "a sense of reality as something inhuman that lies beyond the actual and apparent and a sense of it as something visible, tangible, and finally supportive of human scrutiny."

Brodtkorb, Paul, Jr. *Ishmael's White World: A Phenomenological Reading of "Moby Dick."* Yale Publications in American Studies, edited by David Horne, no. 9. New Haven: Yale University Press, 1965, 170 p.

A comprehensive phenomenological analysis of Ishmael's consciousness. The critic uses his findings to elucidate such concerns as the presence of inconsistencies in narrative point of view and the role of allegory in the novel.

Cameron, Sharon. "Identity and Disembodiment in *Moby-Dick.*" In her *The Corporeal Self: Allegories of the Body in Melville and Hawthorne*, pp. 15-75. Baltimore: Johns Hopkins University Press, 1981.
Focuses on Melville's treatment of the relationship between the self, the body, and the outside world in *Moby-Dick*.

Chase, Richard. "Melville and *Moby-Dick.*" In his *The American Novel and Its Tradition*, pp. 89-115. Garden City, N.Y.: Doubleday & Co., Doubleday Anchor Books, 1957.*
A summary discussion of the novel's composition, form, and meaning.

Cohen, Hennig, and Cahalan, James, eds. *A Concordance to Melville's "Moby-Dick."* 3 vols. Glassboro, N.J.(?): The Melville Society, 1978.
An index to the principal words in *Moby-Dick*.

Dryden, Edgar A. "Ishmael as Teller: Self-Conscious Form in *Moby-Dick.*" In his *Melville's Thematics of Form: The Great Art of Telling the Truth*, pp. 83-113. Baltimore: Johns Hopkins Press, 1968.
Maintains that, through Ishmael's agency as narrator, *Moby-Dick* is "always moving away from the objective or factual world and persistently calling attention to itself as fiction." Dryden regards this "literary" stance as an implicit admission and reminder of mankind's inability to impose order on the real world.

Feidelson, Charles, Jr. *Symbolism and American Literature*. 1953. Reprint. Chicago: Phoenix Books, 1959, 356 p.*
Outlines the emergence of an "American symbolist movement" in the works of Hawthorne, Poe, Whitman, and Melville. *Moby-Dick* figures prominently in Feidelson's discussion of Melville's contribution to the movement.

Franklin, H. Bruce. "*Moby-Dick*: An Egyptian Myth Incarnate." In his *The Wake of the Gods: Melville's Mythology*, pp. 53-98. Stanford: Stanford University Press, 1963.
Discusses the role of mythology in *Moby-Dick*. Franklin's central contention is that Melville based Ahab's conflict with the White Whale on the Egyptian Osiris-Typhon myth.

Green, Martin. "Melville and the American Romance." In his *Re-Appraisals: Some Commonsense Readings in American Literature*, pp. 87-112. New York: W. W. Norton & Co., 1967.
Argues that much of *Moby-Dick* belongs to either the genre of the epic or that of the romance, and that "the romance parts fail as clearly as the epic parts succeed." Green offers his commentary as a response to critics who contend that the romance is the foundation of the American fictional tradition.

Guetti, James. "The Languages of *Moby-Dick.*" In his *The Limits of Metaphor: A Study of Melville, Conrad, and Faulkner*, pp. 12-45. Ithaca, N.Y.: Cornell University Press, 1967.
Maintains that *Moby-Dick* is informed by a fundamental concern with the limitations of language as an instrument for ordering experience. According to Guetti, Ishmael's inconclusiveness as a narrator is one of several elements in the novel reinforcing the notion that language is artificial and reality sometimes ineffable.

Harrison, Hayford, and Parker, Hershel, eds. "*Moby-Dick*": An Authoritative Text, Reviews and Letters by Melville, Analogues and Sources, Criticism, by Herman Melville and others. New York: W. W. Norton & Co., 1967, 728 p.
A highly regarded critical edition of *Moby-Dick*.

Herbert, T. Walter, Jr. *"Moby-Dick" and Calvinism: A World Dismantled*. New Brunswick, N.J.: Rutgers University Press, 1977, 186 p.
Traces Melville's struggle with contemporary theological ideas and explores how the author reworks those ideas in *Moby-Dick*. In Herbert's opinion, the novel dramatizes and illuminates the conditions that attended the advent of the modern secular consciousness.

Hillway, Tyrus, and Mansfield, Luther S., eds. *"Moby-Dick" Centennial Essays*. Dallas: Southern Methodist University Press, 1953, 182 p.
> A collection of essays honoring the centennial of *Moby-Dick*'s publication. The anthology includes criticism by Perry Miller, Walter Bezanson, and other prominent scholars.

Hirsch, David H. "*Hamlet, Moby-Dick,* and Passional Thinking." In *Shakespeare: Aspects of Influence,* edited by G. B. Evans, pp. 135-62. Harvard English Studies, no. 7. Cambridge: Harvard University Press, 1976.*
> Argues that Melville adopted a "Shakespearean-biblical meditative style" in *Moby-Dick,* thus achieving an "astonishing grandeur" unmatched in nineteenth-century English-language literature.

Hoffman, Daniel G. "Melville." In his *Form and Fable in American Fiction,* pp. 221-313. New York: Oxford University Press, 1961.
> A comprehensive discussion of Melville's use of myth, folklore, and metaphor in *Moby-Dick.*

Homans, George C. "The Dark Angel: The Tragedy of Herman Melville." *The New England Quarterly* V, No. 4 (October 1932): 699-730.
> Treats *Mardi: And a Voyage Thither, Moby-Dick,* and *Pierre* as a three-act tragedy dramatizing Melville's search for the secret of the universe.

Howard, Leon. "Melville's Struggle with the Angel." *Modern Language Quarterly* 1, No. 2 (June 1940): 195-206.
> Attributes Melville's technical improvement in *Moby-Dick* to the artistic influence of Shakespeare and Hawthorne.

————. *Herman Melville: A Biography*. Berkeley: University of California Press, 1951, 354 p.
> A respected modern biography.

Irwin, John T. "Melville." In his *American Hieroglyphics: The Symbol of the Egyptian Hieroglyphics in the American Renaissance,* pp. 285-349. New Haven: Yale University Press, 1980.
> Identifies and elucidates hieroglyphic and related mythic motifs in *Moby-Dick.*

Leverenz, David. "Moby-Dick." In *Psychoanalysis and Literary Process,* edited by Frederick Crews, pp. 66-117. Cambridge, Mass.: Winthrop Publishers, 1970.
> A close psychoanalytic reading of the novel.

Levin, Harry. "The Jonah Complex." In his *The Power of Blackness: Hawthorne, Poe, Melville,* pp. 201-37. New York: Alfred A. Knopf, 1958.
> Studies the theme of darkness in *Moby-Dick.*

Lewisohn, Ludwig. "The Troubled Romancers." In his *Expression in America,* pp. 153-93. New York: Harper & Brothers, 1932.*
> Argues that Melville is "not even a minor master" of literature and that *Moby-Dick* cannot validly be considered a masterpiece.

Leyda, Jay. *The Melville Log: A Documentary Life of Herman Melville, 1819-1891*. 2 vols. 1951. Reprint. New York: Gordian Press, 1969.
> A collection of documents, including journal entries, credit statements, letters, marginalia, and other materials, illuminating Melville's career on a day-to-day basis.

Marx, Leo. "Two Kingdoms of Force." In his *The Machine in the Garden: Technology and the Pastoral Ideal in America,* pp. 227-353. New York: Oxford University Press, 1964.*
> Probes the relationship between *Moby-Dick* and American pastoralism. Marx concludes that Melville endorses Ishmael's view of life, defined here as a "complex pastoralism in which the ideal is inseparably yoked to its opposite."

Miller, James E., Jr. "*Moby-Dick:* The Grand Hooded Phantom." In his *A Reader's Guide to Herman Melville.* pp. 75-117. New York: Farrar, Straus and Giroux, 1962.
> A reading of *Moby-Dick* that provides a comprehensive critical introduction to the novel.

Olson, Charles. "*Lear* and *Moby-Dick.*" *Twice a Year,* No. 1 (Fall-Winter 1938): 165-89.
> Evaluates the influence of Shakespeare's plays—particularly *King Lear*—on *Moby-Dick.*

Parker, Hershel, and Hayford, Harrison, eds. *"Moby-Dick" as Doubloon: Essays and Extracts (1851-1970)*. New York: W. W. Norton & Co., 388 p.
> A collection which "displays the range of approaches, interpretations and judgments of the first century-and-a-quarter of *Moby-Dick* criticism." The work includes seventy reviews of the novel written by Melville's contemporaries.

Phelps, Leland R., and McCullough, Kathleen. *Herman Melville's Foreign Reputation: A Research Guide*. A Reference Publication in Literature, edited by Hershel Parker. Boston: G. K. Hall & Co., 331 p.
> A bibliography of foreign language translations and criticism of Melville's works.

Rogin, Michael Paul. *Subversive Genealogy: The Politics and Art of Herman Melville*. New York: Alfred A. Knopf, 1983, 354 p.
> Discusses the political origins of Melville's fiction, emphasizing the influence of his family's political history on the author's works. As part of his study, Rogin examines the connection between *Moby-Dick* and contemporary political events.

Rosenberry, Edward H. "Consummation." In his *Melville and the Comic Spirit,* pp. 93-138. Cambridge: Harvard University Press, 1955.
> Hails *Moby-Dick* as the acme of Melville's comic artistry. Rosenberry comments extensively on four types of comedy in the novel: the "jocular-hedonic," the "imaginative-critical," the "philosophical-psychological," and the "dramatic-structural."

Rourke, Constance. "I Hear America Singing." In her *American Humor: A Study of the National Character,* pp. 133-62. Garden City, N.Y.: Doubleday & Co., Doubleday Anchor Books, 1931.*
> Posits an integral connection between *Moby-Dick* and two American traditions: legend-making and popular comedy. Rourke also underscores Melville's achievement in transmuting his native materials into an epic confrontation "between gods and men."

Slochower, Harry. "*Moby-Dick:* The Myth of Democratic Expectancy." *American Quarterly* II, No. 3 (Fall 1950): 259-69.
> Explicates *Moby-Dick* as a transmutation of American mythology that reveals Melville's serious reservations concerning the societal changes taking place in the United States during industrialization.

Smith, Henry Nash. "The Madness of Ahab." In his *Democracy and the Novel: Popular Resistance to Classic American Writers,* pp. 35-55. New York: Oxford University Press, 1978.
> Investigates the ways in which Ahab's insanity serves to qualify or elaborate his proposition that the universe is controlled by an evil power.

Stern, Milton R. "The Fin of the Whale." In his *The Fine Hammered Steel of Herman Melville,* pp. 240-50. Urbana: University of Illinois Press, 1968.
> Interprets "The Try-Works" as an expression of Melville's opposition to cosmic and artistic idealism.

————, ed. *Discussions of "Moby-Dick."* Discussions of Literature, edited by Joseph H. Summers. Boston: D. C. Heath and Co., 1960, 134 p.
> A collection of essays that includes discussions of contemporary reaction to the novel, the significance of Ahab's perception of evil, and other pertinent topics.

Stewart, George R. "The Two *Moby-Dicks.*" *American Literature* XXV, No. 4 (January 1954): 417-48.
> Suggests that Melville changed his conception of *Moby-Dick* while writing the novel. According to Stewart, the book in its final form comprises an "original story, very slightly revised" (chapters I-XV); the "original story with a certain amount of highly important revision" (chapters XVI-XXII); and "the story as it was written after Melville reconceived it" (chapters XX through the epilogue).

Vincent, Howard P. *The Trying Out of "Moby-Dick."* Boston: Houghton Mifflin Co., 1949, 400 p.

A chapter-by-chapter analysis that "combines a study of the whaling sources of *Moby-Dick* with an account of its composition, and suggestions concerning interpretation and meaning."

————, ed. *The Merrill Studies in "Moby-Dick."* Columbus, Ohio: Charles E. Merrill Publishing Co., 1969, 163 p.

An anthology of commentary on *Moby-Dick* ranging from contemporary reviews to modern appraisals. The editor includes discussions by Emilio Cecchio, Cesare Pavese, Auden, and Bewley in an effort to represent international reaction to the novel.

Watters, R. E. "Melville's 'Isolatoes'." *PMLA* LX, No. 4 (December 1945): 1138-48.

Discusses Melville's treatment of the theme of individual isolation in *Moby-Dick* and other works.

Weaver, Raymond M. *Herman Melville: Mariner and Mystic*. New York: George H. Doran Co., 1921, 399 p.

The biography central to the Melville revival of the 1920s. This work was extremely influential in establishing Melville's reputation as an author of world importance.

Young, John W. "Ishmael's Development as Narrator: Melville's Synthesizing Process." *College Literature* IX, No. 2 (Spring 1982): 97-111.

Examines Melville's strategies for making Ishmael's shifting points of view credible to the reader.

Francis Parkman

1823-1893

American historian, travel sketch writer, and essayist.

Parkman is considered the foremost exponent of the romantic movement in nineteenth-century American historiography. His importance rests on his *France and England in North America*, a series of seven works that describes the contest between England and France for control of North America as well as the struggles both nations faced with the North American Indians. Like his fellow members of the romantic school, Parkman believed that historical composition was an art, and he took great pains to ensure the literary quality of *France and England in North America*. Yet critics note that the series rests on a solid basis of scholarship not displayed in the works of other romantic historians. Apart from its significance as history, *France and England in North America* represents a heroic personal accomplishment; for over thirty years, Parkman battled a variety of illnesses in order to complete his project. Despite the critical acclaim accorded Parkman's histories, modern readers have exhibited little interest in them. Ironically, his most popular work today is *The Oregon Trail*, a travel narrative that he regarded as tangential to his main purpose.

Parkman decided upon his lifework at an early age. Born into a wealthy Boston Brahmin family with an illustrious Puritan heritage, he had a personal interest in America's past. Parkman spent much of his childhood roaming the Middlesex Fells, a rocky, wooded region located near his grandfather's farm in Medford, Massachusetts. It was here that he developed his lifelong love of the wilderness and his fascination with Indian artifacts. From this time on Parkman had, as he called it, a case of "Injuns on the brain." During his sophomore year at Harvard, he resolved to write a history of the Seven Years' War, but soon expanded this plan to include the whole course of the struggle between England and France for dominance in North America. As an undergraduate and later as a law student at Harvard, Parkman sought every opportunity to extend his knowledge of this topic. In addition to studying a wide variety of primary documents, he spent his summer vacations in the forests of New England and Canada, following Indian paths and tracing the routes of the French trappers.

After his graduation from law school in 1846, Parkman devoted his energies to compiling information on his historical topic. In the spring of that year, he embarked on a strenuous expedition to the Far West, where he lived for several weeks with a Sioux tribe in order to increase his knowledge of the Indian way of life. Although Parkman gained valuable information, the exhausting journey ruined his health. Shortly after he returned to Boston in 1847, he suffered a complete nervous and physical collapse and remained a semi-invalid for the rest of his life. The exact nature of Parkman's illness is still debated, but most commentators agree that an extreme nervous disorder caused his severe headaches and partial blindness as well as recurring attacks of mental confusion, insomnia, and arthritis.

Parkman remained undaunted by "the Enemy," as he referred to his numerous ailments, for several years. Incapable of writing because of his poor eyesight, he dictated his first and most famous book, *The California and Oregon Trail: Being Sketches*

of Prairie and Rocky Mountain Life, to his cousin Quincy Adams Shaw. A vivid account of his trip west, this work was originally published serially in the *Knickerbocker Magazine* in 1847 and later reissued as *The Oregon Trail*. By 1851, he had completed *History of the Conspiracy of Pontiac, and the War of the North American Tribes against the English Colonies after the Conquest of Canada*, a brief outline of the American contest between England and France and a description of the Indian wars of the mid-1760s. Parkman intended *Pontiac* as a prelude to his vast history, but some critics treat it as part of *France and England in North America*. Most scholars, however, do not include it in the series.

In 1853, "the Enemy" struck Parkman with renewed virulence, forcing him to abandon his project for almost a decade. To occupy himself during his illness, he wrote *Vassall Morton*, a semi-autobiographical novel that has been virtually ignored by critics. Parkman also turned to the study of horticulture. His interest in the subject resulted in *The Book of Roses*, which is generally considered an excellent guide to the cultivation of the flower.

Parkman's condition gradually improved during the early 1860s, enabling him to dedicate the last thirty years of his life to his great history. When his health permitted, he traveled to France and Canada in search of documentary materials and made excursions to the sites described in his narratives. Parkman's poor eyesight made composition difficult; he employed assistants to read aloud from his sources and used a wire grid that enabled him to write with his eyes closed. Nevertheless, the separate volumes of *France and England in North America* were published at fairly regular intervals between 1865 and 1892. In the first three works in the series—*Pioneers of France in the New World, The Jesuits in North America in the Seventeenth Century,* and *The Discovery of the Great West* (later reissued in revised form as *La Salle and the Discovery of the Great West*)—Parkman focused on the Jesuits' missionary enterprises and on French explorations in Florida and the Mississippi Valley during the fifteenth, sixteenth, and seventeenth centuries. In the succeeding volumes of his history—*The Old Régime in Canada, Count Frontenac and New France under Louis XIV, Montcalm and Wolfe,* and *A Half-Century of Conflict*—he described the feudal government of French Canada and carried the clash between England and France to its conclusion, the signing of The Treaty of Paris in 1763. Except for the last two works, the series was written in chronological sequence. Parkman wrote *Montcalm and Wolfe,* the climax of his history, before *A Half-Century of Conflict,* which covers the years 1700-50, because he was afraid he would not live to finish the project. A year after completing his vast work, Parkman died of peritonitis.

In his histories, Parkman depicts England's victory over France as the triumph of progressive over reactionary forces. He repeatedly contrasts English democracy with French absolutism, relying on documentary materials to emphasize the differences between the two. Yet Parkman does not merely present the findings of his research. He believed that a historian should use his source materials, personal observation, and imagination to reconstruct and animate the past. In his preface to *Pioneers,* Parkman outlines his theory of historical writing: "Faithfulness to the truth of history involves far more than a research, however patient and scrupulous, into special facts. . . . The narrator must seek to imbue himself with the life and spirit of the time." In praise of Parkman's artistry, critics frequently note that *France and England in North America* reads like good fiction; he relates the story in a vivid, straightforward prose style that heightens its dramatic interest, and the characters act against a backdrop of picturesque wilderness scenes.

Parkman's popular appeal with modern audiences rests almost entirely on *The Oregon Trail,* which is one of the most widely read travel narratives in American literature. Although critics unanimously praise the work as a fast-paced and exciting record of Parkman's western experience, it has inspired controversy in two specific areas: his description of Indians and his treatment of the American westward movement. The focus of nineteenth-century reviews was greatly determined by Parkman's preface, in which he contrasted his realistic depiction of Indian life with earlier writers' idealized representations. Contemporary commentators aligned themselves in two camps on this issue, with some applauding Parkman for debunking the noble savage myth and others, most notably Herman Melville, arguing that he judged the Indian too harshly. This dispute gave way in the twentieth century to a debate over Parkman's failure to discuss the American westward migration. His detractors maintained that this omission greatly reduced the value of *The Oregon Trail* as a historical study. However, other critics defended Parkman against this charge, pointing out that he considered the work a collection of travel sketches rather than an authoritative account of the westward movement.

Most commentators agree that the hallmark of Parkman's histories is their fusion of factual information and literary artistry. Since the mid-nineteenth century, his thorough methods of documentation and efforts to recapture the spirit of past events have earned the admiration of both literary scholars and historians. Parkman's fame reached its height in the late 1800s, when several critics labeled his histories the "last word" on the subject of New France. One of Parkman's contemporaries, the leading American historian and philosopher John Fiske, enthusiastically ranked his works with those of Herodotus, Thucydides, and Edward Gibbon. Parkman no longer holds this place of eminence, largely because standards in historical writing have changed. Critics note that two schools of American historiography emerged during Parkman's era: the romantic school—also called the narrative or literary school—and the scientific school. The writers of the romantic school, who prevailed for most of the nineteenth century, looked to literature for narrative technique and chose subjects rich in dramatic potential. Members of the scientific school, a movement that took hold in the late 1800s, assiduously collect documentary materials, but display little concern for literary style. Parkman's twentieth-century critics have concentrated on establishing his relationship to these two movements. Because he was primarily interested in exploiting the artistic possibilities of his subject, Parkman is generally assigned to the romantic school. Yet because of his careful compilation of source materials, critics emphasize that his approach shows evidence of the scientific method. Most scholars cite the dominance of the scientific school as the greatest reason for the decline in Parkman's reputation.

In the twentieth century, Parkman's histories are considered the best-documented among those of the romantic school, but a number of critics have detected inaccuracies in *France and England in North America.* They particularly object to Parkman's alleged pro-English bias, which led him to distort and suppress facts in order to denigrate the French and the Indians. Modern historians also point out that he grossly underrated the role of economic factors in determining the outcome of the clash between England and France. Despite these flaws, Parkman is respected for his tireless devotion to his project and for infusing history with more life than did his romantic rivals George Bancroft, William Hickling Prescott, and John Lothrop Motley. Since the 1950s, Parkman's literary technique has been the subject of several studies. Critics especially praise his use of visual imagery to create a sense of immediacy, his sensitivity to landscapes, and what Edmund Wilson termed his "disciplined, dynamic prose." In addition, the publication of the Library of America edition of *France and England in North America* attests to Parkman's continuing importance as a literary figure. Mason Wade reflects the opinion of most modern critics in his estimation of Parkman's contribution to American literature: "There is no other explanation but sheer genius for his ability to reduce the conclusions of years of study of dusty documents and garbled accounts to a narrative of remarkable clarity and vigor."

PRINCIPAL WORKS

The California and Oregon Trail: Being Sketches of Prairie and Rocky Mountain Life   (travel sketches)   1849; also published as *The Oregon Trail,* 1872
History of the Conspiracy of Pontiac, and the War of the North American Tribes against the English Colonies after the Conquest of Canada   (history)   1851

Vassall Morton   (novel)   1856
*Pioneers of France in the New World   (history)   1865
The Book of Roses   (handbook)   1866
*The Jesuits in North America in the Seventeenth Century
        (history)   1867
*The Discovery of the Great West   (history)   1869; also
        published in revised form as *La Salle and the Discovery
        of the Great West,* 1878
*The Old Régime in Canada   (history)   1874
*Count Frontenac and New France under Louis XIV
        (history)   1877
*Montcalm and Wolfe   (history)   1884
*A Half-Century of Conflict   (history)   1892
The Journals of Francis Parkman. 2 vols.   (journals and
        notebooks)   1947
Letters of Francis Parkman. 2 vols.   (letters)   1960
France and England in North America. 2 vols.   (histories)
        1983

*These works are collectively referred to as *France and England in
North America.* They were first published under this title in *The Works
of Francis Parkman* in 1897-98.

FRANCIS PARKMAN, JR.   (essay date 1849)

[*In the following excerpt from his preface to* The Oregon Trail,
*Parkman asserts that his portrayal of Indian life is more accurate
than earlier writers' idealized representations of it. Parkman's
rejection of the noble savage myth is a frequent subject of critical
commentary.*]

The journey which [*The California and Oregon Trail*] describes
was undertaken on the writer's part with a view of studying
the manners and character of Indians in their primitive state.
Although in the chapters which relate to them, he has only
attempted to sketch those features of their wild and picturesque
life which fell, in the present instance, under his own eye, yet
in doing so he has constantly aimed to leave an impression of
their character correct as far as it goes. In justifying his claim
to accuracy on this point, it is hardly necessary to advert to
the representations given by poets and novelists, which, for
the most part, are mere creations of fancy. The Indian is certainly entitled to a high rank among savages, but his good
qualities are not those of an Uncas or an Outalissi.

> *Francis Parkman, Jr., in a preface to his* The Cal-
> ifornia and Oregon Trail: Being Sketches of Prairie
> and Rocky Mountain Life, *1849. Reprint by Time-
> Life Books, 1983, p. v.*

[HERMAN MELVILLE]   (essay date 1849)

[*A novelist, short story writer, poet, and critic, Melville was one
of the major American literary figures of the nineteenth century.
He is best known for* Moby-Dick, *his complex metaphysical novel
of the quest for the white whale. Melville's review of* The Oregon
Trail *is mixed. He praises the work's straightforward style, but
censures Parkman's contemptuous attitude toward the Indians.*]

Though without literary pretension, [*The California and Oregon
Trail*] is a very entertaining work, straightforward and simple
throughout, and obviously truthful. . . .

In a brief and appropriate preface Mr. Parkman adverts to the
representations of the Indian character given by poets and novelists, which he asserts are for the most part mere creations of
fancy. He adds that "the Indian is certainly entitled to a high
rank among savages, but his good qualities are not those of an
Uncas or Outalissa" [see excerpt dated 1849]. Now, this is
not to be gainsaid. But when in the body of the book we are
informed that it is difficult for any white man, after a domes-
tication among the Indians, to hold them much better than
brutes; when we are told, too, that to such a person, the slaughter of an Indian is indifferent as the slaughter of a buffalo; with
all deference, we beg leave to dissent.

It is too often the case, that civilized beings sojourning among
savages soon come to regard them with disdain and contempt.
But though in many cases this feeling is almost natural, it is
not defensible; and it is wholly wrong. Why should we contemn
them? Because we are better than they? Assuredly not; for
herein we are rebuked by the story of the Publican and the
Pharisee. Because, then, that in many things we are happier?
But this should be ground for commiseration, not disdain. . . .
When we affect to contemn savages, we should remember that
by so doing we asperse our own progenitors; for they were
savages also. . . . We are all of us—Anglo-Saxons, Dyaks, and
Indians—sprung from one head, and made in one image. And
if we regret this brotherhood now, we shall be forced to join
hands hereafter. A misfortune is not a fault; and good luck is
not meritorious. The savage is born a savage; and the civilized
being but inherits his civilization, nothing more.

Let us not disdain, then, but pity. And wherever we recognise
the image of God, let us reverence it, though it hung from the
gallows. . . .

Mr. Parkman's sole object, he tells us, in penetrating into the
Land of Moccasins, was to gratify a curiosity he had felt from
boyhood, to inform himself accurately of Indian life. And it
may well be expected that, with such an object in view, the
travels of an educated man should, when published, impart to
others the knowledge he himself sought to attain: and this holds
true concerning the book before us. As a record of gentlemanly
adventure among our Indian tribes, it is by far the most pleasant
book which has ever fallen in our way. The style is easy and
free, quite flowingly correct. There are no undue sallies of
fancy, and no attempts at wit which flash in the pan. (p. 291)

The book, in brief, is excellent, and has the true wild-game
flavor. And amazingly tickled will all their palates be, who
are so lucky as to read it. (p. 292)

> [*Herman Melville*], "Mr. Parkman's Tour," in The
> Literary World, *Vol. IV, No. 113, March 31, 1849,
> pp. 291-93.*

THE NORTH AMERICAN REVIEW   (essay date 1849)

[*This anonymous critic admires* The Oregon Trail's *faithful descriptions of Indian life and its "moral interest," which derives
from Parkman's courageous struggle against illness. In declaring
that* The Oregon Trail "*has all the air of truth with the attractiveness of fiction," the reviewer singles out what critics consider
the leading characteristics of Parkman's writings: they are both
factual and artistic.*]

[The popularity of the serial publication of *The California and
Oregon Trail* was well deserved, for since the publication of
Mr. Irving's "Tour on the Prairies,"] we have seen no more
pleasing and truthful sketches than these of buffalo hunting,

camping out, encounters with the Indians, and the other incidents which usually lend variety and interest to a journey to the Rocky Mountains. Mr. Parkman writes with much vivacity and good taste, and his story has all the air of truth with the attractiveness of fiction. It has a moral interest, also, from the fortitude and strength of mind shown by the author under very trying circumstances; for he was attacked by a tedious and wasting disease when far out in the wilderness, exposed to many privations and hardships, with only Indians and half-breeds around him, who, it seemed probable for several weeks, would soon be obliged to prepare his grave. His situation was one to tax all the energies of a man in the prime of life and the full enjoyment of his strength; and he was but a youth of gentle nurture and delicate habits, who had but recently left college, and was now completely prostrated by illness. Few would be able to bear up with a stout heart under such depressing circumstances, to choose with a clear judgment the best course to be adopted, and to act upon it with decision and energy; and in no position, we may add, are such high traits of character more likely to be developed than amid the various casualties of the traveller's progress over our great western desert. (p. 177)

Mr. Parkman's chief object . . . was to study the character and manners of the Indians who had been least contaminated by intercourse with the whites. He says little, therefore, of the straggling savages whom he met while still near the settlements; for most of them were feeble and besotted wretches, who retained only the worst characteristics of their race. But near Fort Laramie he encountered several bands of the Dahcotahs, who still showed some of the nobler traits of the true children of the desert. With a quick perception of their peculiarities,

Parkman at the age of twenty.

and much tact in adapting himself to their humor, he seems to have gained their confidence and good will; and his sketches of them being drawn from abundant opportunities for observation, appear as faithful as they are entertaining. He has resisted the common propensity to exaggeration in describing either the bright or the dark traits of the Indian character; and there is no reason to believe, that his picture of them is darkened either by alarm or prejudice. He was for weeks an inmate of one of their villages, with no other white companions than two stupid Canadians. He studied their language, made himself at home in their lodges, accompanied them in their hunting excursions, and took an active share in their other labors and amusements. The most striking scenes of Indian life thus came under his observation, and he describes them with much graphic effect, and singular spirit and beauty of language. (pp. 188-89)

> *"Adventures on the Prairies," in* The North American Review, *Vol. LXIX, No. 144, July, 1849, pp. 175-96.**

FRANCIS PARKMAN   (essay date 1851)

[*Parkman's preface to the 1851 edition of* Pontiac, *excerpted below, provides insight into his method as a historian. He explains that he became familiar with the events related in* Pontiac *by both visiting the scenes of his narrative and carefully studying a wide variety of primary sources. Parkman's preface to* Pioneers (*see excerpt dated 1865) contains further commentary on his historical method.*]

The conquest of Canada was an event of momentous consequence in American history. It changed the political aspect of the continent, prepared a way for the independence of the British colonies, rescued the vast tracts of the interior from the rule of military despotism, and gave them, eventually, to the keeping of an ordered democracy. Yet to the red natives of the soil its results were wholly disastrous. Could the French have maintained their ground, the ruin of the Indian tribes might long have been postponed; but the victory of Quebec was the signal of their swift decline. Thenceforth they were destined to melt and vanish before the advancing waves of Anglo-American power, which now rolled westward unchecked and unopposed. They saw the danger, and, led by a great and daring champion, struggled fiercely to avert it. The history of that epoch, crowded as it is with scenes of tragic interest, with marvels of suffering and vicissitude, of heroism and endurance, has been, as yet, unwritten, buried in the archives of governments, or among the obscurer records of private adventure. To rescue it from oblivion is the object of the following work. It aims to portray the American forest and the American Indian at the period when both received their final doom.

It is evident that other study than that of the closet is indispensable to success in such an attempt. Habits of early reading had greatly aided to prepare me for the task; but necessary knowledge of a more practical kind has been supplied by the indulgence of a strong natural taste, which, at various intervals, led me to the wild regions of the north and west. Here, by the camp-fire, or in the canoe, I gained familiar acquaintance with the men and scenery of the wilderness. In 1846, I visited various primitive tribes of the Rocky Mountains, and was, for a time, domesticated in a village of the western Dahcotah, on the high plains between Mount Laramie and the range of the Medicine Bow.

The most troublesome part of the task was the collection of the necessary documents. These consisted of letters, journals, reports, and dispatches, scattered among numerous public of-fices, and private families, in Europe and America. When brought together, they amounted to about three thousand four hundred manuscript pages. Contemporary newspapers, mag-azines, and pamphlets have also been examined, and careful search made for every book which, directly or indirectly, might throw light upon the subject. I have visited the sites of all the principal events recorded in the narrative, and gathered such local traditions as seemed worthy of confidence. (pp. xxxi-xxxii)

The crude and promiscuous mass of materials presented an aspect by no means inviting. The field of the history was uncultured and unreclaimed, and the labour that awaited me was like that of the border settler, who, before he builds his rugged dwelling, must fell the forest-trees, burn the under-growth, clear the ground, and hew the fallen trunks to due proportion.

Several obstacles have retarded the progress of the work. Of these, one of the most considerable was the condition of my sight, seriously, though not permanently, impaired. For about three years, the light of day was insupportable, and every attempt at reading or writing completely debarred. Under these circumstances, the task of sifting the materials and composing the work was begun and finished. The papers were repeatedly read aloud by an amanuensis, copious notes and extracts were made, and the narrative written down from my dictation. This process, though extremely slow and laborious, was not without its advantages; and I am well convinced that the authorities have been even more minutely examined, more scrupulously collated, and more thoroughly digested, than they would have been under ordinary circumstances. (p. xxxiii)

> *Francis Parkman, in a preface to his* The Conspiracy of Pontiac and the Indian War after the Conquest of Canada, *Vol. I, E. P. Dutton & Co., 1908, pp. xxxi-xxxiii.*

[FRANCIS BOWEN]   (essay date 1851)

[*Bowen praises both the style and content of* Pontiac, *arguing that it is an entertaining, original, and well-documented contribution to the study of the American Indian.*]

We are glad that the task of writing one important chapter in [the American Indian's] history has fallen into so competent hands as those of Mr. Parkman. [*History of the Conspiracy of Pontiac*] has been to him a labor of love, and he has devoted himself to it with untiring zeal and assiduity, leaving no source of information unexplored, and no means of illustrating his subject untried. (p. 499)

The task of collecting the necessary documents, both in print and manuscript, to elucidate the chapter of Indian history which is here written, was a long and laborious one, and it has been faithfully performed. The author's researches have been ex-tended through many public offices and private collections, both in Europe and America; and the contemporaneous ac-counts, in ephemeral publications, have been carefully brought together, and diligently compared and sifted. The collection thus formed, we are told in the preface, ''amounted to about three thousand four hundred manuscript pages'' [see excerpt by Parkman dated 1851]. It has been used with excellent judg-ment and taste, not to supersede the necessity of writing out the history in the author's own words by supplying the means for a patchwork compilation of undigested authorities, but to afford the foundation of the narrative, which is written with

great animation and freshness, and bears a distinct impress throughout of the writer's own mind. History often purports to have been composed from hitherto unedited materials and original sources of information; but this pretension is seldom borne out so fully as in Mr. Parkman's work, which may fairly be called the contribution of a new chapter to the annals of the aborigines of America. It gives a more complete and accurate picture of Indian character and life, and of Indian warfare such as it was a century ago, than has yet appeared in print. And it is written with so much spirit and picturesque effect that it is as entertaining as a nursery tale. (p. 500)

The portion of Indian history which Mr. Parkman has selected for the subject of the present work is well adapted to his pur-pose, both of illustrating a portion of the general history of the country which has been but imperfectly treated by former writ-ers, and of throwing a bold light upon those peculiarities in the character and condition of the native tribes at this epoch which led to the formation of a great confederacy among them, and to an obstinate contest with the English colonies. (pp. 501-02)

The work performs more than it promises; it is not a mere history of the conspiracy of Pontiac, and the subsequent war; it presents, also, a broad picture of the condition of the ab-origines in the middle of the last century, of their relations with the French, the English, and the settlers on the frontiers, and of their modes of life and customs in war. The whole is drawn with so much spirit and minuteness of detail, and colored so highly with the author's personal observation of life in the forest, on the prairie, and in the Indian village, and it has all the interest of romance, while fidelity to truth and nature is scrupulously preserved. The work is, therefore, a valuable con-tribution to the general history of the native tribes of this con-tinent; the descriptive portions of it, even where they seem highly colored by the imagination, are as strictly historical as the narrative proper. The costume is as faithful, and as nec-essary to the completeness of the resemblance, as the limbs and features of the statue. (pp. 502-03)

[Mr. Parkman] has happily avoided the easily besetting sin of those who have labored with enthusiasm upon the biography of an individual or a people,—that of falling in love with the subject, and portraying it in colors rather of fond association and friendship, than of a clear perception and strict argument. (p. 503)

Mr. Parkman gives an animated and picturesque sketch of the principal events of [the struggle between France and England for possession of colonial America], chiefly with a view to show what part the Indians bore in the struggle, and how they were affected by its termination. Often as the story of Brad-dock's defeat, of the battles near Lake George, of the repulse of Ticonderoga, and of Wolfe's victory has been repeated, it was never told with more liveliness and effect, or with stricter regard to accuracy in all the details, than in this volume. (p. 510)

[*History of the Conspiracy of Pontiac*] seems to furnish a more perfect sketch of the habits and character of the aborigines of this continent, and of a remarkable epoch in their history, than has yet appeared in print. As the curious materials which the author has amassed with so much industry and zeal cannot yet be exhausted, we hope soon to learn that he is engaged upon the preparation of another and more elaborate work, to which the present one may be regarded only as an introduction. (p. 529)

> [*Francis Bowen*], ''Parkman's History of Pontiac's War,'' *in* The North American Review, *Vol. LXXIII, No. 153, October, 1851, pp. 495-529.*

THE ATHENAEUM   (essay date 1851)

[*This anonymous critic ranks* Pontiac *highly among contemporary American historical works, but faults its style as frequently unsuited to its subject matter.*]

[*History of the Conspiracy of Pontiac*] is one of the best written histories that has been produced by the recent literary talent of America. The American chief Pontiac, indeed, does not make so grand a figure as the author promises, and on the whole the attempt to make an interesting hero of this greatest of the Red Skins is a failure; but the narrative of the protracted and desultory wars with the Indians, by which the Anglo-Saxon fathers of the present American nation had to make good every mile of their advance into that amazing country which now teems with the evidences of civilization, is of interest in itself and is admirably conducted. Here we have, in the form of authentic and detailed record, exactly such incidents as make the materials in the most delightful of Cooper's novels. The only fault we have to find with the author is, that his style is often too grandiose for his subject. The balanced cadence and verbal ornateness of some of his sentences seem out of keeping with the rough set of beings whose forest life he is describing. We do not object so much to his elaborate descriptions of forest scenery, which are sometimes fine to the verge of poetry, as to his want of the refreshing homeliness of style which is appropriate in describing actions of minor historic importance done amid such scenes. Pontiac was not a Pericles,—and his history cannot be told in Attic periods. But this fault proceeds from what is a merit in the writer—extreme care to write from beginning to end as well as possible; and if Mr. Parkman should enter on higher and more civilized fields of historic research, this quality will doubtless contribute to the value of his compositions.

A review of "History of the Conspiracy of Pontiac, and the War of the North American Tribes against the English Colonies after the Conquest of Canada," in The Athenaeum, *No. 1257, November 29, 1851, p. 1252.*

THEODORE PARKER   (letter date 1851)

[*Parker was a prominent Unitarian clergyman who became widely known in the United States during the 1840s and 1850s for his espousal of Transcendentalism and for his outspoken opposition to slavery. In the following excerpt from a letter to Parkman, Parker offers constructive criticism on the content, organization, and style of* Pontiac. *First, he cautions Parkman against highlighting the savagery of the Indians, pointing out that the English and French behaved similarly. Parker then suggests ways in which* Pontiac's *structure might be altered to increase its dramatic unity. Last, he advises Parkman that his descriptions of persons and places lack sufficient detail.*]

I have lately read [*History of the Conspiracy of Pontiac*] with much pleasure. I have gained a good deal of information from the book which relates to a period and place where I had not studied the Indians much. On the whole, it seems to me the book is highly creditable to you—to your industry and your good sense. But you will be likely to get mere praise enough, and asked me to speak discriminatingly of the work, so I will write down things which occurred to me in reading the book, and in studying some parts of it. I will speak of the substance, the arrangement and the style; of the *timber,* the *plan,* and the *finish* of it.

I. Of the *substance,* that is the *sentiments* and *ideas.* You evidently have a fondness for the Indian—not a romantic fondness, but one that has been tempered by sight of the fact. Yet I do not think you do the Indian quite justice; you side rather too strongly with the white man and against the red. I think you bring out the vices of the Indian into more prominence than those of the European—which were yet less excusable. The treachery which you censure in the Indian was to him no more a violation of any sentiment or idea that he felt or knew than it was to a Briton to fight with powder and balls. This treachery is not specific of Indians; but generic of all races in a low state of development. It seems to me Pontiac was much more excusable than the Paxton men, the Owens, and the like. It seems to me that the whites are not censured so much as they deserve for their conduct toward the Indians in three particulars:

1. In the matter of *rum,* which the Christian brought to the Savage.

2. In the matter of *women*—whom the Christian took from the Savage as concubines and then deserted when the time came.

3. In the matter of *treachery* and *cruelty* which the whites too often displayed.

I have thought you were a little unjust to the Quakers. But here I have so little direct and positive knowledge that I hesitate in my judgment.

One thing is curious in history:—the Teutonic Race in all its three great divisions,—the Goths, Germans, and Scandinaviana—is naturally exclusive, and loves to exterminate the neighboring tribes. On the other side, the Celts and Greco-Italian stock assimilate with other tribes. The history of America shows the same thing in the conduct of the English and the French toward the Indians. It would have enriched your book a little to have called attention to that fact—not generally known. It always enriches a special history to drop into it universal laws or any general rules of conduct which distinguish one nation from another.

The facts of history which you set down seem generally well chosen. The historian cannot tell all. He must choose such as, to him, most clearly set forth the Idea of the nation—or man—he describes. (pp. 374-75)

So much for the material—which is mainly good *timber,*—now a word of the frame and plan. So

II. Of the distribution of the parts. The title indicates that the conspiracy of Pontiac is the chief theme. But in the book itself it seems to me this is not exactly so, that other things are not quite enough subordinated to the main theme, so as to give unity to the whole book. The *barn* is a little too near the house and the *shed* a little too prominent for the general effect of the house itself. This appears as you look over the table of contents, when Pontiac and his scheme are not the central object about which the rest is grouped. So the book lacks the dramatic unity which is necessary for the artistic treatment of such a subject. Pontiac does not appear so important in the titles of the chapters as the title-page seems to demand. Then the book lacks a sufficient conclusion, and ends abruptly. You do not tell the effect which his death has on Indian affairs. A special history like this requires at the end a general summary with the philosophical reflections which have grown out of the historical treatment of the theme.

It seems to me it would have been better to have divided the matter something after this line:

Introduction. Containing all the general matter relative to the Indians, their origin, geographical distribution, language, arts, agriculture, domestic, political and religious institutions. This is now too much scattered about in the book.

Book I. History of the Indians in the connection with the Europeans up to the time of the general rising.

Book II. History of Pontiac and his efforts to overcome the Europeans.

Book III. Result of the movement on the Indian people, and its effect on their subsequent history. Then it seems to me there should have been more and more obvious unity in the book; now it seems as if the materials have been collected without a definite aim, and that the plan was not quite complete until the book was done. So much of the *plan* and *frame*. Now a word of the *finish*.

III. Of the style of the book. Some passages in it are very well written; in general the style is good, simple, natural, easy. But there is a general lack of severity of style, for which the great Master of Roman history is so remarkable. Some passages remind me of Melville and Headley—whom you would not like to be like. There is a lack of what is characteristic. This appears—

1. In the *description of places.* You do not tell what kind of trees, etc., there were, only trees—leaving us to guess whether they were pines or palms, bushes or tall trees.

2. In the description of persons, the book lacks portraits. Wolfe is well done, so is Montcalm (the account of Braddock is well done). But the picture of Pontiac is not adequate to his important place in the history. It strikes me that Johnson is not very well done. Some passages are left too imperfect. It seems as if you got vexed with the thing and struck out a little recklessly, to hit or miss as it might happen. The style of the book often indicates haste—as do almost all American books—like everything else we do.

There, sir, is not there a list of faults for you? Yes, more than all your critics in the reviews, I suppose, have found with you. But if I did not expect you and think you capable of better things than you have done yet, I should not go to the trouble of pointing out all these faults. You seem to have chosen literature for your profession, and history for your special department thereof, and I do so love to see literary conscientiousness applied to explain the meaning of human history and convey its lesson to mankind, that I have taken the pains to point out particular things in which your book might have been made better. You have already received so much commendation that it is not necessary I should go into the pleasanter business of telling you how many things I like in the book. (pp. 376-78)

Theodore Parker, in a letter to Francis Parkman on December 22, 1851, in A Life of Francis Parkman *by Charles Haight Farnham, Little, Brown and Company, 1900, pp. 374-78.*

FRANCIS PARKMAN (essay date 1865)

[*In this excerpt from his preface to* Pioneers, *Parkman states that the work is the first in a projected series of histories describing France's attempt to colonize North America. He adds that the completion of* Pioneers *was slowed by both his poor health and* the inaccessibility of most documentary materials on his subject. Parkman stresses, however, that the writing of history entails more than exhaustive research and the recital of facts: the historian must use his source materials, personal observation, and imagination to reconstruct and animate the past. Parkman's preface to* Pontiac (*see excerpt dated 1851*) *also contains information on his method as a historian.*]

The subject to which [my proposed series of histories] will be devoted is that of "France in the New World,"—the attempt of Feudalism, Monarchy, and Rome to master a continent. . . . (p. xix)

This memorable but half-forgotten chapter in the book of human life can be rightly read only by lights numerous and widely scattered. The earlier period of New France was prolific in a class of publications which are often of much historic value, but of which many are exceedingly rare. The writer, however, has at length gained access to them all. Of the unpublished records of the colonies, the archives of France are of course the grand deposit; but many documents of important bearing on the subject are to be found scattered in public and private libraries, chiefly in France and Canada. The task of collection has proved abundantly irksome and laborious. (p. xxiii)

In this, and still more must it be the case in succeeding volumes, the amount of reading applied to their composition is far greater than the citations represent, much of it being a collateral and illustrative nature. This was essential to a plan whose aim it was, while scrupulously and rigorously adhering to the truth of facts, to animate them with the life of the past, and, so far as might be, clothe the skeleton with flesh. If, at times, it may seem that range has been allowed to fancy, it is so in appearance only; since the minutest details of narrative or description rest on authentic documents or on personal observation.

Faithfulness to the truth of history involves far more than a research, however patient and scrupulous, into special facts. Such facts may be detailed with the most minute exactness, and yet the narrative, taken as a whole, may be unmeaning or untrue. The narrator must seek to imbue himself with the life and spirit of the time. He must study events in their bearings near and remote; in the character, habits, and manners of those who took part in them. He must himself be, as it were, a sharer or a spectator of the action he describes.

With respect to that special research which, if inadequate, is still in the most emphatic sense indispensable, it has been the writer's aim to exhaust the existing material of every subject treated. While it would be folly to claim success in such an attempt, he has reason to hope that, so far at least as relates to the present volume, nothing of much importance has escaped him. With respect to the general preparation just alluded to, he has long been too fond of his theme to neglect any means within his reach of making his conception of it distinct and true.

To those who have aided him with information and documents, the extreme slowness in the progress of the work will naturally have caused surprise. This slowness was unavoidable. During the past eighteen years, the state of his health has exacted throughout an extreme caution in regard to mental application, reducing it at best within narrow and precarious limits, and often precluding it. Indeed, for two periods, each of several years, any attempt at bookish occupation would have been merely suicidal. A condition of sight arising from kindred sources has also retarded the work, since it has never permitted reading or writing continuously for much more than five minutes, and often has not permitted them at all. A previous work, *The Conspiracy of Pontiac,* was written in similar circumstances.

The writer means, if possible, to carry the present design to its completion. Such a completion, however, will by no means be essential as regards the individual volumes of the series, since each will form a separate and independent work. (pp. xxiv-xxv)

> *Francis Parkman, in an introduction to his* Pioneers of France in the New World: France and England in North America, Part First, *1865. Reprint by Little, Brown and Company, 1903, pp. xix-xxv.*

[HENRY JAMES] (essay date 1867)

[*James was an American-born English novelist, short story writer, critic, and essayist of the late nineteenth and early twentieth centuries. He is regarded as one of the greatest novelists of the English language and a lucid and insightful critic. In the following excerpt from his review of* The Jesuits, *James describes the work as both interesting and instructive. He also briefly discusses Parkman's use of documentary materials and portrayal of the Indians.*]

Mr. Parkman gives in [*The Jesuits in North America in the Seventeenth Century*] the second part of his history of the short-lived French dominion in North America. His first volume [*Pioneers of France in the New World*] describes the abortive attempt of the Huguenots to establish themselves in Florida, the cruel destruction of their colony by the Spaniards, and the vengeance wrought upon them in turn by the Frenchman de Jourgue, together with a narrative of the gallant and useful career of Samuel de Champlain, the founder of Quebec. His third volume is to be devoted to [the] French exploration of the Valley of the Mississippi. . . . But whatever may be the interest of these narratives, and the importance of the facts on which they rest, it is certain that this touching story of the Jesuit missions in Canada is no less dramatic and instructive. It has peculiar and picturesque interest from the fact that the enterprise was, in a great measure, a delusion and a failure— a delusion consecrated by the most earnest conviction and the most heroic effort, a failure redeemed by the endurance of incalculable suffering. The Jesuit undertaking as it stands described in Mr. Parkman's pages has an indefinably factitious look—an expression intensely *subjective,* as we call it nowadays. . . .

Mr. Parkman's narrative is founded chiefly on the reports regularly transmitted to France by the active members of the [Jesuit] order, and from which, frequent as are his citations, we cannot help wishing that he had given more copious extracts. . . . Mr. Parkman gives a very vivid picture of the state of the savage populations at the time of the early settlements— a picture beside which the old-fashioned portrait of the magnanimous and rhetorical red man is a piece of very false coloring. Mr. Parkman knows his subject, and he mentions no single trait of intelligence, of fancy, or of character by which the Indian should have a hold on our respect or his fate a claim to our regret. (p. 450)

> [*Henry James*], *in a review of "The Jesuits in North America in the Seventeenth Century," in* The Nation, *Vol. IV, No. 101, June 6, 1867, pp. 450-51.*

W. D. HOWELLS (essay date 1874)

[*Howells was the chief progenitor of American realism and an influential American literary critic during the late nineteenth and early twentieth centuries. Although he wrote nearly three dozen novels, few of them are read today. Despite his eclipse, however, he stands as one of the major literary figures of the late nineteenth century; having successfully weaned American literature from the sentimental romanticism of its infancy, he earned the popular sobriquet "the Dean of American Letters." Howells's review of Parkman's histories, excerpted below, focuses on* The Old Régime. *He argues that in this book Parkman best expresses the dominant theme of his writings on New France: the evil of religious and political despotism. Howells also praises* The Old Régime's *unpretentious style, vivid descriptions, and thorough documentation, concluding that this work, as well as Parkman's other histories, will not be surpassed.*]

[Each of Mr. Parkman's historical narratives of France and England in North America] is complete in itself, and in spite of their irregular and unsequent production, there is a perfect unity of intention in them, and from first to last the author is more and more fortunate in fulfilling his purpose of giving a full view of the French dominion in North America. One moral is traced from beginning to end,—that spiritual and political despotism is so bad for men that no zeal, or self-devotion, or heroism can overcome its evil effects; one lesson enforces itself throughout,—that the state which persistently meddles with the religious, domestic, and commercial affairs of its people, dooms itself to extinction. In Canada the Jesuit realized his dream of a church untroubled by a heretic, obedient, faithful, devoted; in Canada the monarchist realized his dream of subjects paternally governed even to the intimate details of social and family life; and these dreams were such long nightmares to the colonists that the English conquest, and the perpetual separation of the colony from the mother-country, was a blessing instinct with life, freedom, and prosperity.

It is in Mr. Parkman's [*Canada under the Old Régime*] that these facts, tacitly or explicitly presented in all his books on Canada, are most vividly stated; and we do not know where else one should find any part of the past more thoroughly restored in history. In all this fullness of striking and significant detail, one is never conscious of the literary attitude, and of the literary intent to amuse and impress; Mr. Parkman soberly and simply portrays the conditions of that strange colony of priests, lawyers, and soldiers, without artificial grouping, and reserves his own sense of the artistic charm which the reader will be sure to feel in the work. (pp. 602-03)

In his notices of that picturesque offshoot of the Canadian civilization, the coureur de bois, Mr. Parkman has given a picture of the wilderness which affects us like a vigorous sketch made by some quick-eyed, sure-handed painter in the presence of the scene; the desert breathes from it; the canvas has the very light and darkness of the primeval woods on it. . . . (p. 607)

[We] commend specially to the reader's notice [the chapters relating to the feudal system in Canada]. There is also a most delightful chapter on the morals and manners of the colonists. . . . (p. 609)

[*Canada under the Old Régime*] leaves untouched no point of interest or significance in [the old colonial life of Canada], and we must again praise the excellent taste of the whole work. If one will think with what good sense and discretion the rich material is managed, in a time when there has been so much meretricious historical writing, disfigured by the wretched egotisms of the writers, and falsified by their literary posturing and their disposition to color whole epochs from a single picturesque event,—in a time when, to say it briefly, Hepworth Dixon has descended directly, however illegitimately, from Thomas Carlyle,—one will be the more grateful to the author who has given us this valuable and charming book. There is material enough in it for innumerable romances, for many volumes of historical sketching, eked out as such things are with plausible conjecture and conscious comment. Mr. Parkman—one readily sees it—does not lack at any moment due sense of the strangeness of the situation he depicts; a lurking smile lights up the gravity of his narrative at times; and it all glows from an imagination which the sublime and poetic facts never fail to kindle. But he addresses himself with direct simplicity to the business of making the reader understand him and discern the characters and events; this accomplished, he leaves the story to the possession of the delighted fancy.

Mr. Parkman has been most fortunate, of course, in his subject. The period which he presents lies comparatively near at hand; its outlines are distinctly marked; its characteristic traits are broad and clear. If his researches have not exhausted the whole material, they have explored everything that was attainable in Canada and France, and they have developed so much fact that the reader may feel full security that nothing essential is lacking. It seems to us that it must be the last word on the subject—except, of course, from those Catholic critics who will disagree with Mr. Parkman's opinions and inferences, and from whom he will probably not soon hear the last word. But here—we

A depiction of a buffalo hunt in the American West. This Frederic Remington illustration appeared in an 1892 edition of The Oregon Trail.

comfort ourselves in a world which is continually rebuilding—seems really to be work that need not be done over again.

We have this feeling in regard to Mr. Parkman's other histories. He would probably be the last to allow that his efforts had left nothing for future workers in the same field to do; but we believe that whatever may be added to his labors, they will remain undisturbed as thorough, beautiful, and true. (pp. 609-10)

If we have objected to nothing in these histories, it is because we have no fault to find with them. They appear to us the fruit of an altogether admirable motive directing indefatigable industry, and they present the evidences of thorough research and thoughtful philosophization. We find their style delightful always. (p. 610)

> W. D. Howells, "Mr. Parkman's Histories," in The Atlantic Monthly, *Vol. XXXIV, No. 5, November, 1874, pp. 602-10.*

[HENRY ADAMS]　(essay date 1875)

[Adams was an American autobiographer, historian, essayist, and novelist. His work is less pertinent to the history of literature than it is to the history of ideas. In the latter context, he embodies for many a particularly modern viewpoint, one which sees the world becoming less stable and coherent and which predicts that this trend will continue unabated. Adams developed this doctrine most thoroughly in his best-known work, the autobiography The Education of Henry Adams. *As a historian, Adams is chiefly remembered for his* History of the United States of America during the Administrations of Thomas Jefferson and James Madison. *This nine-volume work continues to be valued as an insightful analysis of the period and is ranked with the histories of Edward Gibbon and Thomas Macaulay. Here, Adams reviews* The Old Régime, *which he considers an admirable description of New France under the paternalistic rule of Louis XIV. Unlike Parkman's earlier writings on New France, the critic notes,* The Old Régime *treats philosophical issues. Adams maintains that this feature of the work entitles it to rank highest among Parkman's histories.]*

In the series of works which have placed Mr. Parkman among the first of American historical writers, [*The Old Régime in Canada*] deserves to rank highest. This is to be understood, however, as the estimate of a literary critic only, not as that of the public. That book will of course have the most readers which interests or amuses the largest number, and it is very possible that more than one of Mr. Parkman's previous volumes have a more absorbing and more consecutive interest than this. By natural inclination and cast of mind Mr. Parkman has an objective way of dealing with history. He prefers to follow action rather than to meditate upon it, to relate rather than to analyze, to describe the adventures of individuals rather than the slow and complicated movements of society. This lends to his books a freshness and a simplicity of structure which are very agreeable, and which in turn suit well the general subject he has chosen. In following out this subject, he has now, however, entered a wider field of thought. The present volume deals with matters which, if not themselves of the highest philosophical interest, are still on one side at least illustrative of great and permanent principles in political science. The story he tells is curious and unusual. . . . Mr. Parkman describes the colony [of New France as Louis XIV.] ruled it. A line of dwellings ranged along the river-shores, with the dense wilderness behind them, and at Quebec a cluster of some seventy houses, contained the population which was to form the future state. A population so situated, exposed on every side to the temptations of savage life, and pushed by many motives to the wildest sort of liberty, was considered and treated by Louis as though it were a model farm within the park of Versailles. The theories of paternal government and the facts of natural liberty never came into sharper contrast. Mr. Parkman has drawn these contrasts with great skill; his work is that of an artist. On the one side he collects all the curious details which an elaborate search through the French archives and elsewhere has brought to light, in regard to the king's care for the colony; his lavish expenditure; his minute instructions to the royal officials; and his religious zeal for the eternal welfare of those who were so peculiarly dependent on his bounty. On the other side are described in strong colors the natural forces which were unceasingly in action to neutralize the king's efforts and to undo his work. (pp. 175-76)

One must judge a creation to some extent by the objects of its authors. The first object of the French monarch appears to have been to found a French society in the New World, which should reflect and support his ideas of obedience and docility in politics and religion. Commercial and military success belonged more peculiarly to the government at home. In spite of the difficulties he encountered, in spite of *coureurs de bois,* drunkenness, the climate, the English, and all economical laws, it cannot be said that the experiment failed. On the contrary, its remarkable and permanent success is the very point which makes it worth studying at all. One cannot deny that the character stamped by Louis upon this favorite political creation has been on the whole the most permanent of all the achievements of that once great monarch. The exciting adventures which Mr. Parkman loves to relate, and which gain so much under his touch, the daring exploits of Jesuits and *gentilshommes,* the vices and lawlessness of the *coureurs de bois,* were but the more or less inevitable consequences, the appendages, and one might almost say the dramatic *mise en scène,* which introduced the new society to existence. The real subject of interest, which survived Jesuits, Indians, and all the external forms of its original foundation, which survived conquest itself, and has proved the solidity of its foundation by preserving the stamp of Louis XIV. through all the vicissitudes of a century of alien rule, the true core of Canadian history is of necessity the quiet and industrious part of the colony, whose manners and mode of life are admirably described in this volume. (pp. 177-78)

As the colony itself is the centre of interest, so the public life of the colony is the principal object of study, as showing how the desired results were obtained. And here the industry of Mr. Parkman has left little to be asked. Every detail is presented that can throw light on the actions and motives of the actors. Necessarily one great factor of interest is wanting, since the people neither had nor claimed any share in the management of their affairs. The colony was an experiment destined to prove that the Crown and the Church were more capable of conducting a good government than the people could be. It must be allowed that both the Crown and the Church did their duty faithfully and on the whole successfully. (pp. 178-79)

Of the episodes of adventure with which the volume abounds, less need be said. The public is familiar with Mr. Parkman's skill as a *raconteur.* But the reader's interest can only increase as Mr. Parkman goes on to give the public, as he alone can do, an account from the Canadian standpoint of those bloody wars with the English colonies, which, carried on as they were under great disadvantages of numbers and resources, can hardly fail to excite wonder and deep interest at Canadian energy and enterprise. (p. 179)

[*Henry Adams*], ''Parkman's 'Old Régime in Canada','' in The North American Review, *Vol. CXX, No. 246, January, 1875, pp. 175-79.*

GEORGE BANCROFT   (letter date 1884)

[*Bancroft was a leading nineteenth-century American historian. Like Parkman, he is generally assigned to the romantic school, and critics often compare his masterpiece, the twelve-volume* History of the United States, *to Parkman's* France and England in North America. *In the letter to Parkman excerpted below, Bancroft responds favorably to* Montcalm and Wolfe *and enthusiastically describes the qualities that make Parkman a good historian.*]

I am delighted at receiving from you under your own hand these two new volumes [entitled ***Montcalm and Wolfe***] with which you delight your friends and instruct readers in both worlds. You belong so thoroughly to the same course of life which I have chosen that I follow your career as a fellow soldier, striving to promote the noblest ends, and I take delight in your honors as much or more than I should my own. You have just everything which go to make an historian—persistency in collecting materials, indefatigable industry in using them, swift discernment of the truth, integrity and intrepidity in giving utterance to truth, a kindly humanity which is essential to the true historian, and which gives the key to all hearts, and a clear and graceful and glowing manner of narration.

George Bancroft, in a letter to Francis Parkman on November 28, 1884, in Francis Parkman *by Henry Dwight Sedgwick, Houghton, Mifflin and Company, 1904, p. 258.*

HENRY ADAMS   (letter date 1884)

[*In this excerpt from a letter to Parkman, Adams states that* Montcalm and Wolfe *ensures his place among the* ''front rank of living English historians.'']

Your two volumes on Montcalm and Wolfe deserve much more careful study than I am competent to give them, and so far as I can see, you have so thoroughly exhausted your sources as to leave little or nothing new to be said. [***Montcalm and Wolfe***] puts you in the front rank of living English historians, and I regret only that the field is self-limited so that you can cultivate it no further. Your book is a model of thorough and impartial study and clear statement. Of its style and narrative the highest praise is that they are on a level with its thoroughness of study. Taken as a whole, your works are now dignified by proportions and completeness which can be hardly paralleled by the ''literary baggage'' of any other historical writer in the language known to me to-day.

Henry Adams, in a letter to Francis Parkman on December 21, 1884, in Francis Parkman *by Henry Dwight Sedgwick, Houghton, Mifflin and Company, 1904, p. 255.*

HENRY JAMES   (letter date 1885)

[*The following comments on* Montcalm and Wolfe *are drawn from a letter James wrote to Parkman. James lavishly praises the work, calling it* ''truly a noble book'' *and stating that he was overcome with emotion while reading it.*]

This is only three lines, because I cannot hold my hand from telling you, as other people must have done to your final weariness, with what high appreciation and genuine gratitude I have been reading your ''Wolfe and Montcalm.'' (You see I am still so overturned by my emotion that I can't even write the name straight.) I have found the right time to read it only during the last fortnight, and it has fascinated me from the first page to the last. You know, of course, much better than any one else how good it is, but it may not be absolutely intolerable to you to learn how good still another reader thinks it. The manner in which you have treated the prodigious theme is worthy of the theme itself, and that says everything. It is truly a noble book, my dear Parkman, and you must let me congratulate you, with the heartiest friendliness, on having given it to the world. So be as proud as possible of being the author of it, and let your friends be almost as proud of possessing his acquaintance. Reading it here by the summer smooth channel with the gleaming French coast, from my windows, looking on some clear days only five miles distant, and the guns of old England pointed seaward, from the rambling, historic castle, perched above me upon the downs; reading it, I say, among these influences, it has stirred all sorts of feelings—none of them, however, incompatible with a great satisfaction that the American land should have the credit of a production so solid and so artistic. (pp. 256-57)

> *Henry James, in a letter to Francis Parkman on August 24, 1885, in* Francis Parkman *by Henry Dwight Sedgwick, Houghton, Mifflin and Company, 1904, pp. 256-57.*

THE SPECTATOR (essay date 1886)

[*This English reviewer enthusiastically greets a British edition of Parkman's collected works.*]

Until that striking book, **Montcalm and Wolfe,** . . . was published in England . . . , the name of Francis Parkman was almost unknown on this side of the Atlantic, and his writings were a veritable *terra incognita.* It is, no doubt, the cordial reception given to **Montcalm and Wolfe** which has led to the [British publication of a complete edition of Mr. Parkman's writings entitled **The Works of Francis Parkman**]. It is, therefore, with a feeling akin to shame that one sees ''twentieth edition'' and ''twenty-third edition'' on the title-pages of some of these volumes, and observes that the *Oregon Trail,* which is the only one of them that is not historical, gives an account of a personal expedition to the Rocky Mountains forty years ago; for if there is any American writer of the day who ought to have been popular here, both on account of his subject and of his style, it is Mr. Parkman. Readability is the characteristic of his literary work; it is, indeed, both his strength and his weakness. He traverses the ground, and is instinct with the spirit of Fenimore Cooper; while, under the flow of his style, as under the flow of Mr. Green's, one perceives the steady current of vigorous humanity if not of democratic humanitarianism. The subject, moreover, of Mr. Parkman's works, taken as a whole, is one that ought to be specially fascinating to Englishmen who frequent ''the ordinary of literature,'' as Coleridge terms the circulating library, and who, it must be allowed, are a trifle sentimental, if not Jingoish. If there is any struggle which ought to inspire us with pride of race, it is that which ended in the placing of the North American Continent at the feet of Great Britain. In that struggle, the patient, solid, often stolid, Anglo-Saxon is seen triumphing over the most formidable of Red, and the most brilliant and dangerous of White, rivals. It is true, indeed, that Mr. Parkman deals more with the French than with the English aspect of the conflict for

empire in America. But the fact should make his writings all the more interesting. He shows what it was that our grandfathers had to cope with,—the most pertinacious and remorseless of religious organisations, and the most brilliant of aristocratic societies, that sought, after its own fashion, too, to make the New World reproduce afresh the *ancien régime,* which was, and felt itself to be, moribund.

There is no excuse now, however, for not knowing who Mr. Parkman is, and of what stuff as a historian he is made. Of the ten works which compose [**The Works of Francis Parkman**], only two, **Montcalm and Wolfe** and **The Conspiracy of Pontiac,** reach two volumes. Of the single-volume books, **The Oregon Trail** must be dismissed with a very few words. As already said, it gives an account of a journey Mr. Parkman undertook to the Rocky Mountains in 1846. It is delightfully written; Mr. Parkman's literary undress is quite as becoming as his historical full-dress. It is, perhaps, most interesting as showing how Mr. Parkman made the intimate acquaintance of the Indians of his own time, and through them of the nature of the Red Man generally,—a knowledge which must have been invaluable to him when engaged in his purely historical investigations. The other one-volume works in Mr. Parkman's series, **The Pioneers of France in the New World, The Jesuits in North America, The Old Régime in Canada, La Salle and the Discovery of the Great West, Count Frontenac and New France,** give the best picture that exists of the France that rose and flourished in Canada, only to fall before the sword of Wolfe, the genius of the elder Pitt, and the superior colonising capacity of the English people. . . . [It] is a remarkable panorama that Mr. Parkman places before us, and we find it difficult to say whether we admire more the patient industry with which he has set forth the economic and social causes of French failure in the New World, or his love of the picturesque, which makes him (and with him his readers) equally at home in the solitudes of Nature and the artificialities of Franco-Canadian society, in the wigwam of the Indian and in the hut of a Jesuit martyr by mistake. Mr. Parkman is, all things considered, at his best when he deals with the adventurous and the romantic, and there is beyond question enough of both in his volumes. (p. 205)

> *A review of ''The Works of Francis Parkman,'' in* The Spectator, *Vol. 59, No. 3006, February 6, 1886, pp. 205-06.*

THEODORE ROOSEVELT (letter date 1888)

[*Roosevelt was active in American politics during the late nineteenth and early twentieth centuries, serving as assistant secretary of the navy and vice-president of the United States before succeeding William McKinley as president in 1901. One of Parkman's greatest admirers, Roosevelt was intensely interested in American history and wrote a number of books on the subject, most notably* The Winning of the West. *Excerpted below is a letter in which he requests Parkman's permission to dedicate this work to him.*]

I suppose that every American who cares at all for the history of his own country feels a certain personal pride in your work— it is as if Motley had written about American instead of European subjects, and so was doubly our own; but those of us who have a taste for history, and yet have spent much of our time on the frontier, perhaps realize even more keenly than our fellows that your works stand alone, and that they must be models for all historical treatment of the founding of new communities and the growth of the frontier here in the wilderness. This—even more than the many pleasant hours I owe you—must be my excuse for writing.

I am engaged on a work of which the first part treats of the extension of our frontier westward and southwestward during the twenty odd years from 1774 to 1796. . . . [It] will be in two volumes, with some such title as ''The Winning of the West and Southwest.'' . . .

I should like to dedicate this to you. Of course I know that you would not wish your name to be connected, in even the most indirect way, with any but good work; and I can only say, that I will do my best to make the work creditable. (pp. 259-60)

> *Theodore Roosevelt, in a letter to Francis Parkman on April 23, 1888, in* Francis Parkman *by Henry Dwight Sedgwick, Houghton, Mifflin and Company, 1904, pp. 259-60.*

JAMES RUSSELL LOWELL   (essay date 1891)

[*Lowell was a celebrated nineteenth-century American poet, critic, essayist, and editor of two leading journals: the* Atlantic Monthly *and the* North American Review. *He is noted today for his satirical and critical writings, including* A Fable for Critics, *a book-length poem featuring witty critical portraits of his contemporaries. Here, Lowell attributes the appeal of Parkman's histories to their combination of factual information and picturesque detail. This essay was written in 1891 and left unfinished at Lowell's death.*]

It is rare, indeed, to find, as they are found in [Mr. Parkman], a passion for the picturesque and a native predilection for rapidity and dash of movement in helpful society with patience in drudgery and a scrupulous deference to the rights of facts, however disconcerting, as at least sleeping-partners in the business of history. Though never putting on the airs of the philosophic historian, or assuming his privilege to be tiresome, Mr. Parkman never loses sight of those links of cause and effect, whether to be sought in political theory, religious belief, or mortal incompleteness, which give to the story of Man a moral, and reduce the fortuitous to the narrow limits where it properly belongs. . . .

It is a great merit in Mr. Parkman that he has sedulously culled from his ample store of documents every warranted piece of evidence . . . that could fortify or enliven his narrative, so that we at least come to know the actors in his various dramas as well as the events in which they shared. And thus the curiosity of the imagination and that of the understanding are together satisfied. We follow the casualties of battle with the intense interest of one who has friends or acquaintance there. Mr. Parkman's familiarity also with the scenery of his narratives is so intimate, his memory of the eye is so vivid, as almost to persuade us that ourselves have seen what he describes. We forget ourselves to swim in the canoe down rivers that flow out of one primeval silence to lose themselves in another, or to thread those expectant solitudes of forest . . . that seem listening with stayed breath for the inevitable ax, and then launch our birchen eggshells again on lakes that stretch beyond vision into the fairyland of conjecture. The world into which we are led touches the imagination with pathetic interest. It is mainly a world of silence and of expectation, awaiting the masters who are to subdue it and to fill it with the tumult of human life, and of almost more than human energy.

One of the convincing tests of genius is the choice of a theme, and no greater felicity can befall it than to find one both familiar and fresh. All the better if tradition, however attenuated, have made it already friendly with our fancy. In the instinct that led him straight to subjects that seemed waiting for him so long,

Mr. Parkman gave no uncertain proof of his fitness for an adequate treatment of them. (p. 45)

> *James Russell Lowell, ''Francis Parkman,'' in* The Century, *Vol. XLV, No. 1, November, 1892, pp. 44-5.*

OLIVER WENDELL HOLMES   (poem date 1893)

[*Holmes was a prominent physician, scientist, poet, essayist, and novelist of the nineteenth century. Today, his poetry is valued primarily for its social commentary as well as its influential tone and language. Holmes's poem commemorating Parkman's death was read at a special meeting of the Massachusetts Historical Society held on November 21, 1893. The poem contains references to two other Boston historians: Prescott (stanzas one, two, and three) and Motley (stanzas one, four, five, and six).*]

> He rests from toil; the portals of the tomb
>   Close on the last of those unwearying hands
> That wove their pictured webs in History's loom,
>   Rich with the memories of three mighty lands.
>
> One wrought the record of the Royal Pair
>   Who saw the great Discoverer's sail unfurled,
> Happy his more than regal prize to share,
>   The spoils, the wonders of the sunset world.
>
> There, too, he found his theme; upreared anew,
>   Our eyes beheld the vanished Aztec shrines,
> And all the silver splendors of Peru
>   That lured the conqueror to her fatal mines.
>
> Nor less remembered he who told the tale
>   Of empire wrested from the strangling sea;
> Of Leyden's woe, that turned his readers pale,
>   The price of unborn freedom yet to be;
>
> Who taught the New World what the Old could teach;
>   Whose silent hero, peerless as our own,
> By deeds that mocked the feeble breath of speech
>   Called up to life a State without a Throne.
>
> As year by year his tapestry unrolled,
>   What varied wealth its growing length displayed!
> What long processions flamed in cloth of gold!
>   What stately forms their flowing robes arrayed!
>
> Not such the scenes our later craftsman drew;
>   Not such the shapes his darker pattern held;
> A deeper shadow lent its sober hue,
>   A sadder tale his tragic task compelled.
>
> He told the red man's story; far and wide
>   He searched the unwritten annals of his race;
> He sat a listener at the Sachem's side,
>   He tracked the hunter through his wildwood chase.
>
> High o'er his head the soaring eagle screamed;
>   The wolf's long howl rang nightly; through the vale
> Tramped the lone bear; the panther's eyeballs gleamed;
>   The bison's gallop thundered on the gale.
>
> Soon o'er the horizon rose the cloud of strife,—
>   Two proud, strong nations battling for the prize,
> Which swarming host should mould a nation's life;
>   Which royal banner flout the western skies.
>
> Long raged the conflict; on the crimson sod
>   Native and alien joined their hosts in vain;

The lilies withered where the Lion trod,
  Till Peace lay panting on the ravaged plain.

A nobler task was theirs who strove to win
  The blood-stained heathen to the Christian fold,
To free from Satan's clutch the slaves of sin;
  Their labors, too, with loving grace he told.

Halting with feeble step, or bending o'er
  The sweet-breathed roses which he loved so well,
While through long years his burdening cross he bore,
  From those firm lips no coward accents fell.

A brave, bright memory! his the stainless shield
  No shame defaces and no envy mars!
When our far future's record is unsealed,
  His name will shine among its morning stars.

                                        (pp. 360-61)

*Oliver Wendell Holmes, in a poem commemorating
Francis Parkman, in* Proceedings of the Massachusetts Historical Society, *n.s. Vol. VIII, 1892-1894,
pp. 360-61.*

BARRETT WENDELL   (essay date 1894)

[*Wendell was a friend of Parkman and a prominent Harvard
educator during the late nineteenth and early twentieth centuries.
In the essay excerpted below, he labels Parkman the most modern
of New England's romantic historians, citing the broad scope of
his series of works on New France, his nationalistic theme, and
his vivid, straightforward prose. In addition, he underscores the
significance of Parkman's historical topic while acknowledging
that the wealth of descriptive detail often obscures the works'
deeper import. Wendell does offer one criticism of the histories:
concerning whether Parkman's illness affected his abilities, Wendell states that "his infirmities forbade him sustained intensity of
thought." This essay was written in 1894.*]

Mr. Parkman was the last and in many respects the ripest of
the romantic historians who for more than half a century gave
distinction to the literary life of New England. Younger than
the others, surviving them all in spite of his prolonged years
of illness, and doing his best work toward the end of his life,
he seems to-day a far more modern figure than Prescott, or
Ticknor, or Motley. More than theirs, too, his work concerned
our own country. The chief centre of his interest, from the
beginning, was the frontier of that British civilization in America from which has sprung the United States. (p. 438)

This constantly national purpose, none the less profoundly patriotic that with [open sincerity] . . . he disdained to neglect or
to deny our errors and our dangers, makes his work peculiarly
ours. The literary sensitiveness, too, with which his style changed
from what now seems the somewhat excessive floridity, or at
least the figurative formality, of half a century ago, to the
direct, fluent simplicity of the best modern English, makes him
above most men of letters steadily contemporary. Besides this,
his unswerving tenacity of purpose makes his work singularly
complete. In the first six chapters of *The Conspiracy of Pontiac*
. . . he sketched what may broadly be called the whole scheme
of his historical writing. For forty years of enthusiastic study,
in the course of which he sought out every available authority,
he busied himself in finishing, on the grand scale, the picture
thus sketched. In its own way, then, his work probably stands
among the most permanent that has been done by American
hands.

Perhaps its most salient trait is its unbroken vitality. His imagination was very vivid. To him men were always alive,—
thinking, feeling, acting, stirring, in the midst of a living Nature. To him a document of whatever kind—a state paper, a
Jesuit "Relation," the diary of a Provincial soldier, the record
of a Yankee church—was merely the symbol of a fact which
had once been as real as his own hardships among the Western
Indians, or as the lifetime of physical suffering which never
bent his will. In turning from *The Oregon Trail*—the single
volume which records experience of his own—to the series of
volumes which record the expression of men who have been
dead for generations, one feels strangely little difference. Both
alike are records of actual human existence.

This constant vitality is generally recognized. By those who
know his work well, indeed, it is by and by assumed, in a
mood akin to that in which the great generalizations of human
wisdom are accepted by posterity as commonplace. If much
remarked, it is spoken of as notable in view of the maladies
which kept him so long a cripple or an invalid. These, it is
said, in no way impaired his scholarly and artistic vigor. To
a great extent, the remark is true. More vivid writing than his
is hard to find; nothing could be further from what he called
"the pallid and emasculate scholarship of which New England
has already had too much."

For all this vitality, there is an aspect of his work which thorough criticism cannot neglect. Here and there one sometimes
hears from people who cordially admire his writings an occasional expression of regret that he did not devote his exceptional powers to the execution of a task in itself more important.
After all, these critics say, he has only told us—incomparably,
to be sure—how European missionaries and pioneers penetrated and tamed the American wilderness, and how in the end
the provinces that used to be French became subject to the
Crown of England. Full of vigorous interest as all this is, it
sometimes seems—in this age of grave constitutional and philosophic study—just a shade puerile. Boys like to read it. Nowadays this is often reason enough for grown people to think it
a bit the less worth their attention.

In this criticism there is some apparent truth. Undoubtedly Mr.
Parkman's first youthful purpose was, in his own words, to
write "the history of the American forest," which incidentally
should include the long struggle between France and England.
Undoubtedly his love for the woods pervaded his fancy to the
last. Undoubtedly, in comparison with much that has happened
on earth, these matters seem at first glance rather picturesque
than notable, of romantic interest rather than of historic. To
assert that they are really so, however, is not to understand
them. A little consideration reveals them in a different light.
Historical phenomena of any kind must be the result of historical forces; and though here the historical phenomena may
sometimes seem trivial, the historical forces that underlie them
prove before long to be of prime importance. In the first place,
we have European civilization inevitably, unwittingly overpowering the barbarism of savage America. In the second place,
far nearer to ourselves, we have the absolutism of the old
French monarchy struggling to the death for the dominion of
a conquered continent with that firmest known system of human
rights,—the common law of England. All this, too, we have
implied in Mr. Parkman's own pages; to feel it so that we may
philosophize about it to our hearts' content, we need only turn
to him. The matters he deals with, then, are really matters
grave enough for anybody.

The fact that the seriousness of his work is not to all readers instantly apparent, however, is in itself significant. Here, and only here, I think, is revealed the superficiality of that commonplace criticism which declares that his illness in no way affected his achievement. Whoever knew him, at least in his later years, must have felt that the man himself was as far removed as possible from that delightful but unimportant personage, the mere teller of stories. You could not talk with him for five minutes without feeling that he not only knew things, but thought about them too; that, to a rare degree, he was a critic of life. In his historical work, however, this trait, though by no means absent if one will but search for it, is not quite obvious. In his later books, to be sure, it is more apparent than in his earlier; implicitly, after a while, one finds it everywhere; but to find it one must sometimes search. To a superficial reader, in fact, the luxuriant profusion of his detail—a trait which would naturally result from the circumstances under which his illness compelled him to work—must sometimes obscure the principles which any one who knew him knows that he constantly realized to underlie the facts and the people he has made so vividly real. A deliberate practice of his, too, gives color to the superficial criticism. He was very sparing of generalization, of philosophic comment. For this he had good reason. To philosophize with certainty of conviction means to think long and hard; to philosophize flippantly means not to realize the responsibility which lies on whoever dares to leave written records behind him. This responsibility Mr. Parkman fully realized; from the beginning of his life to the end his infirmities forbade him sustained intensity of thought. To them, I believe, and only to them, we may attribute our misfortune in that this gentlest and ripest of our historical writers has not left us books that should instantly show him beyond question the gravest of our historical thinkers. (pp. 438-41)

Barrett Wendell, "Francis Parkman," in Proceedings of the American Academy of Arts and Sciences, *Vol. XXIX, May, 1893-May, 1894, pp. 435-47.*

JOHN FISKE (essay date 1897)

[*Fiske was one of the leading intellectual figures in the United States during the late nineteenth century. He is best known for his works on early American history and for his philosophical essays, which helped to popularize the theory of evolution developed by Charles Darwin and Herbert Spencer. Here, Fiske lavishly praises* France and England in North America, *ranking Parkman's series with the works of Herodotus, Thucydides, and Edward Gibbon. Arguing that the events in North America merit attention by historians, Fiske labels Parkman "a master in the field of history" for recognizing both the scholarly and dramatic interest of his topic. Fiske especially admires Parkman's realistic depiction of the Indians. This essay was written in 1897.*]

In the summer of 1865 I had occasion almost daily to pass by the pleasant windows of Little, Brown & Co., in Boston. . . . Among the freshest novelties there displayed were to be seen Lord Derby's translation of the "Iliad," Forsyth's "Life of Cicero," Colonel Higginson's "Epictetus," a new edition of Edmund Burke's writings, and the tasteful reprint of Froude's "History of England." . . . One day, in the midst of such time-honoured classics and new books on well-worn themes, there appeared a stranger that claimed attention and aroused curiosity. It was . . . *Pioneers of France in the New World.* The author's name was not familiar to me, but presently I remembered having seen it upon a stouter volume labelled *The Conspiracy of Pontiac.* . . . This older book I had once taken down from its shelf, just to quiet a lazy doubt as to whether Pontiac

might be the name of a man or a place. Had that conspiracy been an event in Merovingian Gaul or in Borgia's Italy, I should have felt a twinge of conscience at not knowing about it; but the deeds of feathered and painted red men on the Great Lakes and the Alleghanies, only a century old, seemed remote and trivial. Indeed, with the old-fashioned study of the humanities, which tended to keep the Mediterranean too exclusively in the centre of one's field of vision, it was not always easy to get one's historical perspective correctly adjusted. Scenes and events that come within the direct line of our spiritual ancestry, which until yesterday was all in the Old World, thus become unduly magnified, so as to deaden our sense of the interest and importance of the things that have happened since our forefathers went forth from their homesteads to grapple with the terrors of an outlying wilderness. (pp. 187-88)

But as we learn to broaden our horizon, the perspective becomes somewhat shifted. It begins to dawn upon us that in New World events, also, there is a rare and potent fascination. Not only is there the interest of their present importance, which nobody would be likely to deny, but there is the charm of an historic past as full of romance as any chapter whatever in the annals of mankind. The Alleghanies as well as the Apennines have looked down upon great causes lost and won, and the Mohawk Valley is classic ground no less than the banks of the Rhine. To appreciate these things thirty years ago required the vision of a master in the field of history; and when I carried home and read [*The Pioneers of France,*] I saw at once that in Francis Parkman we had found such a master. The reading of the book was for me, as doubtless for many others, a pioneer experience in this New World. It was a delightful experience, repeated and prolonged for many a year, as those glorious volumes came one after another from the press, until the story of the struggle between France and England for the possession of North America was at last completed. It was an experience of which the full significance required study in many and apparently diverse fields to realize. By step after step one would alight upon new ways of regarding America and its place in universal history.

First and most obvious, plainly visible from the threshold of the subject, was its extreme picturesqueness. It is a widespread notion that American history is commonplace and dull; and as for the American red man, he is often thought to be finally disposed of when we have stigmatized him as a bloodthirsty demon and grovelling beast. It is safe to say that those who entertain such notions have never read Mr. Parkman. In the theme which occupied him his poet's eye saw nothing that was dull or commonplace. (pp. 189-90)

What was an uncouth and howling wilderness in the world of literature he has taken for his own domain, and peopled it forever with living figures, dainty and winsome, or grim and terrible, or spritely and gay. Never shall be forgotten the beautiful earnestness, the devout serenity, the blithe courage, of Champlain; never can we forget the saintly Marie de l'Incarnation, the delicate and long-suffering Lalemant, the lion-like Brébeuf, the chivalrous Maisonneuve, the grim and wily Pontiac, or that man against whom fate sickened of contending, the mighty and masterful La Salle. These, with many a comrade and foe, have now their place in literature as permanent and sure as Tancred or St. Boniface, as the Cid or Robert Bruce. As the wand of Scott revealed unsuspected depths of human interest in Border castle and Highland Glen, so it seems that North America was but awaiting the magician's touch that should invest its rivers and hillsides with memories of great days gone by. Parkman's sweep has been a wide one, and many are the spots that his wand has touched, from the cliffs of the Saguenay to the Texas coast, and from Acadia to the western slopes of the Rocky Mountains.

I do not forget that earlier writers than Parkman had felt something of the picturesqueness and the elements of dramatic force in the history of the conquest of our continent. In particular, the characteristics of the red men and the incidents of forest life had long ago been made the theme of novels and poems, such as they were; I wonder how many people of to-day remember even the names of such books as "Yonnondio" or "Kabaosa"? All šuch work was thrown into the shade by that of Fenimore Cooper, whose genius, though limited, was undeniable. But when we mention Cooper we are brought at once by contrast to the secret of Parkman's power. It has long been recognized that Cooper's Indians are more or less unreal; just such creatures never existed anywhere.... [You] cannot introduce unreal Indians as factors in the development of a narrative without throwing a shimmer of unreality about the whole story. It is like bringing in ghosts or goblins among live men and women: it instantly converts sober narrative into fairy tale; the two worlds will no more mix than oil and water.... When any unsound element enters into a narrative, the taint is quickly tasted, and its flavour spoils the whole.

We are then brought, I say, to the secret of Parkman's power. His Indians are true to the life. In his pages Pontiac is a man of warm flesh and blood, as much so as Montcalm or Israel Putnam. This solid reality in the Indians makes the whole work real and convincing. Here is the great contrast between Parkman's work and that of Prescott, in so far as the latter dealt with American themes. In reading Prescott's account of the conquest of Mexico, one feels one's self in the world of the "Arabian Nights." ... (pp. 191-94)

[Prescott's] Montezuma is a personality like none that ever existed beneath the moon. This is because Prescott simply followed his Spanish authorities not only in their statements of physical fact, but in their inevitable misconceptions of the strange Aztec society which they encountered; the Aztecs in his story are unreal, and this false note vitiates it all. (pp. 194-95)

Now it was Parkman's good fortune at an early age to realize that in order to do his work it was first of all necessary to know the Indian by personal fellowship and contact.... [In 1846], young Parkman had a taste of the excitements of savage life.... In the chase and in the wigwam, in watching the sorcery of which their religion chiefly consisted, or in listening to primitive folk tales by the evening camp fire, Parkman learned to understand the red man, to interpret his motives and his moods. With his naturalist's keen and accurate eye and his quick poetic apprehension, that youthful experience formed a safe foundation for all his future work. From that time forth he was fitted to absorb the records and memorials of the early explorers, and to make their strange experiences his own.

The next step was to gather these early records from government archives, and from libraries public and private, on both sides of the Atlantic,—a task, as Parkman himself called it, "abundantly irksome and laborious" [see excerpt dated 1865]. It extended over many years and involved several visits to Europe. It was performed with a thoroughness approaching finality. (pp. 195-96)

This elaborateness of preparation had its share in producing the intense vividness of Parkman's descriptions. Profusion of detail makes them seem like the accounts of an eyewitness. The realism is so strong that the author seems to have come in person fresh from the scenes he describes, with the smoke of the battle hovering about him and its fierce light glowing in his eyes. Such realism is usually the prerogative of the novelist rather than of the historian, and in one of his prefaces Parkman recognizes that the reader may feel this and suspect him. "If at times," he says, "it may seem that range has been allowed to fancy, it is so in appearance only, since the minutest details of narrative or description rest on authentic documents or on personal observation" [see excerpt dated 1865].

This kind of personal observation Parkman carried so far as to visit all the important localities, indeed well-nigh all the localities, that form the scenery of his story, and study them with the patience of a surveyor and the discerning eye of a landscape painter. His strong love of nature added keen zest to this sort of work.... His books fairly reek with the fragrance of pine woods. (pp. 198-99)

[Parkman] had the kind of temperament that could look into the Indian's mind and portray him correctly. But for this inborn temperament all his microscopic industry would have availed him but little. To use his own words: "Faithfulness to the truth of history involves far more than a research, however patient and scrupulous, into special facts. Such facts may be detailed with the most minute exactness, and yet the narrative, taken as a whole, may be unmeaning or untrue" [see excerpt dated 1865]. These are golden words for the student of the historical art to ponder. To make a truthful record of a vanished age patient scholarship is needed, and something more. Into the making of a historian there should enter something of the philosopher, something of the naturalist, something of the poet. In Parkman this rare union of qualities was realized in a greater degree than in any other American historian. Indeed, I doubt if the nineteenth century can show in any part of the world another historian quite his equal in respect of such a union.

There is one thing which lends to Parkman's work a peculiar interest, and will be sure to make it grow in fame with the ages. Not only has he left the truthful record of a vanished age so complete and final that the work will never need to be done again, but if any one should in future attempt to do it again he cannot approach the task with quite such equipment as Parkman. In an important sense, the age of Pontiac is far more remote from us than the age of Clovis or the age of Agamemnon. When barbaric society is overwhelmed by advancing waves of civilization, its vanishing is final; the thread of tradition is cut off forever with the shears of Fate. Where are Montezuma's Aztecs? Their physical offspring still dwell on the table-land of Mexico, and their ancient speech is still heard in the streets, but that old society is as extinct as the trilobites, and has to be painfully studied in fossil fragments of custom and tradition. So with the red men of the North: it is not true that they are dying out physically, as many people suppose, but their stage of society is fast disappearing, and soon it will have vanished forever. (pp. 200-01)

Now the study of comparative ethnology has begun to teach us that the red Indian is one of the most interesting of men. He represents a stage of evolution through which civilized men have once passed,—a stage far more ancient and primitive than that which is depicted in the Odyssey or in the Book of Genesis. When Champlain and Frontenac met the feathered chieftains of the St. Lawrence, they talked with men of the Stone Age face to face. Phases of life that had vanished from Europe long before Rome was built survived in America long enough to be

Henry Chatillon, Parkman's Oregon Trail guide, as depicted by Frederic Remington.

seen and studied by modern men. Behind Mr. Parkman's picturesqueness, therefore, there lies a significance far more profound than one at first would suspect. He has portrayed for us a wondrous and forever fascinating stage in the evolution of humanity. We may well thank Heaven for sending us such a scholar, such an artist, such a genius, before it was too late. As we look at the changes wrought in the last fifty years, we realize that already the opportunities by which he profited in youth are in large measure lost. He came not a moment too soon to catch the fleeting light and fix it upon his immortal canvas.

Thus Parkman is to be regarded as first of all the historian of Primitive Society. No other great historian has dealt intelligently and consecutively with such phases of barbarism as he describes with such loving minuteness. . . . Parkman's minute and vivid description of primitive society among red men is full of lessons that may be applied with profit to the study of preclassic antiquity in the Old World. No other historian has brought us into such close and familiar contact with human life in such ancient stages of its progress. In Parkman's great book we have a record of vanished conditions such as hardly exists anywhere else in literature.

I say his great book, using the singular number; for, with the exception of that breezy bit of autobiography, *The Oregon Trail,* all Parkman's books are the closely related volumes of a single comprehensive work. From the adventures of *The Pioneers of France* a consecutive story is developed through *The Jesuits in North America* and *The Discovery of the Great West.* In *The Old Régime in Canada* it is continued with a masterly analysis of French methods of colonization in this their greatest colony, and then from *Frontenac and New France under Louis XIV.* we are led through *A Half-Century of Conflict* to the grand climax in the volumes on *Montcalm and Wolfe,* after which *The Conspiracy of Pontiac* brings the long narrative to a noble and brilliant close. In the first volume we see the men of the Stone Age at that brief moment when they were

disposed to adore the bearded newcomers as Children of the Sun; in the last we read the bloody story of their last and most desperate concerted effort to loosen the iron grasp with which these palefaces had seized and were holding the continent. It is a well-rounded tale, and as complete as anything in real history, where completeness and finality are things unknown. (pp. 202-06)

Nowhere can we find a description of despotic government more careful and thoughtful, or more graphic and lifelike, than Parkman has given us in his volume on *The Old Régime in Canada.* Seldom, too, will one find a book fuller of political wisdom. The author never preaches like Carlyle, nor does he hurl huge generalizations at our heads like Buckle; he simply describes a state of society that has been. But I hardly need say that his description is not—like the Dryasdust descriptions we are sometimes asked to accept as history—a mere mass of pigments flung at random upon a canvas. It is a picture painted with consummate art; and in this instance the art consists in so handling the relations of cause and effect as to make them speak for themselves. These pages are alive with political philosophy, and teem with object lessons of extraordinary value. It would be hard to point to any book where History more fully discharges her high function of gathering friendly lessons of caution from the errors of the past.

Of all the societies that have been composed of European men, probably none was ever so despotically organized as New France, unless it may have been the later Byzantine Empire, which it resembled in the minuteness of elaborate supervision over all the pettiest details of life. In Canada the protective, paternal, socialistic, or nationalistic theory of government—it is the same old cloven hoof, under whatever specious name you introduce it—was more fully carried into operation than in any other community known to history except ancient Peru. (pp. 210-11)

Such was the community whose career our historian has delineated with perfect soundness of judgment and wealth of knowledge. The fate of this nationalistic experiment, set on foot by one of the most absolute of monarchs and fostered by one of the most devoted and powerful of religious organizations, is traced to the operation of causes inherent in its very nature. The hopeless paralysis, woeful corruption, the moral torpor, resulting from the suppression of individualism, are vividly portrayed; yet there is no discursive generalizing, and from moment to moment the development of the story proceeds from within itself. It is the whole national life of New France that is displayed before us. Historians of ordinary calibre exhibit their subject in fragments, or they show us some phases of life and neglect others. Some have no eyes save for events that are startling, such as battles and sieges; or decorative, such as coronations and court balls. Others give abundant details of manners and customs; others have their attention absorbed by economics; others again feel such interest in the history of ideas as to lose sight of mere material incidents. Parkman, on the other hand, conceives and presents his subject as a whole. He forgets nothing, overlooks nothing; but whether it is a bloody battle, or a theological pamphlet, or an exploring journey through the forest, or a code for the discipline of nunneries, each event grows out of tis context as a feature in the total development that is going on before our eyes. It is only the historian who is also philosopher and artist that can thus deal in block with the great and complex life of a whole society. The requisite combination is realized only in certain rare and high types of mind, and there has been no more brilliant illustration of it than Parkman's volumes afford.

The struggle between the machine-like socialistic despotism of New France and the free and spontaneous political vitality of New England is one of the most instructive object lessons with which the experience of mankind has furnished us. The depth of its significance is equalled by the vastness of its consequences. Never did Destiny preside over a more fateful contest; for it determined which kind of political seed should be sown all over the widest and richest political garden plot left untilled in the world. Free industrial England pitted against despotic militant France for the possession of an ancient continent reserved for this decisive struggle, and dragging into the conflict the belated barbarism of the Stone Age,—such is the wonderful theme which Parkman has treated. When the vividly contrasted modern ideas and personages are set off against the romantic though lurid background of Indian life, the artistic effect becomes simply magnificent. Never has historian grappled with another such epic theme, save when Herodotus told the story of Greece and Persia, or when Gibbon's pages resounded with the solemn tread of marshalled hosts through a thousand years of change. (pp. 212-14)

Great in his natural powers and great in the use he made of them, Parkman was no less great in his occasion and in his theme. Of all American historians he is the most deeply and peculiarly American, yet he is at the same time the broadest and most cosmopolitan. The book which depicts at once the social life of the Stone Age, and the victory of the English political ideal over the ideal which France inherited from imperial Rome, is a book for all mankind and for all time. The more adequately men's historic perspective gets adjusted, the greater will it seem. Strong in its individuality, and like to nothing else, it clearly belongs, I think, among the world's few masterpieces of the highest rank, along with the works of Herodotus, Thucydides, and Gibbon. (p. 254)

John Fiske, "Francis Parkman," in his A Century of Science and Other Essays, *The Riverside Press, 1902, pp. 187-254.*

JOHN SPENCER BASSETT   (essay date 1902)

[*Bassett was an American historian who specialized in United States history. In the following discussion of* France and England in North America, *he faults Parkman's frequently biased approach and points out that his knowledge of history was limited to Canadian topics. Despite these reservations, Bassett contends that Parkman was a "great historian" who created works of unparalleled scholarly and dramatic interest.*]

[Parkman loved one thing] better than the wilderness: it was the writing of its history and of the history of the wild Indians and of the hardly less wild white men who moved through the wilderness. If there is any feeling which can deaden the pain of the tortured body, it is the joy of creating an honest sentence in an honest narrative, as every lover of historical research must know. Parkman himself thought that the habit of writing slowly, completing sentence by sentence the short task of the day, had the good effect of making him more careful about his words. It perhaps restrained his mind from philosophizing and gave his chapters that strictly narrative form which made them so unlike most of the history the world was used to reading before his day. Fortunately, it is less in style to-day than formerly to deliver sermons between the lines in our histories.

The education of Parkman was, perhaps, too highly specialized. From the time when as a Harvard Sophomore he determined on his life work he gave all his study to accomplishing that end. He practically took his education into his own hands. He read much literature, and he even attempted poetry; but gradually his chosen object supplanted all other claims. His disease, no doubt, facilitated this process by taking so much of his time that he felt impelled to use all his working opportunity in following his one task. As a result he knew no other field of history than that which related to Canada. This unquestionably meant a loss in breadth of view. Back of a specialization should be an honest knowledge of the general field. Parkman's feeling sometimes made his work less reliable than it would otherwise have been. There is no doubt that his lack of sympathy with so mystical a religious organization as the Quakers led him to underestimate the position they played in Pennsylvania, and that this produced the strictures against them which is one of the objectionable features of *The Conspiracy of Pontiac*. The same may be said in regard to his treatment of the New England Puritans, for whom he had no sympathy.

And yet neither the one-sidedness of his education nor the intensity of his feelings prevented Parkman from being a great historian. No other American of his day, save George Bancroft, had been confronted by so large a task; and no other, not even Bancroft himself, performed that task better. The subject had peculiar difficulties. The materials were to be found in a hundred scattered reports, or monographs, many of which had never been printed. To get at them it was necessary to pass weary months in France, going from Paris to some provincial town, and back again, and after that as long again in Canada. He was not satisfied till he had got at the last accessible fact. How much pain it cost him will never be known. He was not satisfied to write until he had personally gone over the scene of the events about which he proposed to write. Moreover, he had the disadvantage of presenting the subject from the standpoint of the French and the Indians. Former treatments had continually treated it from the standpoint of the English colonies which had suffered from the French. To them the Indian attacks had been but the torturing raids of demons; to Parkman the subject appeared as the shock of two great forces which contended for a continent. When his work appeared in the white light of scientific inquiry the public, who had been educated in the old school, was disappointed. Scholars quickly recognized the superiority of the treatment, however, and the public gradually came around to the new way of thinking. In fact, this very spirit got so strong a hold on the mind of the public that scholarly investigation received from it a powerful impetus.

Parkman was essentially a man of action, and his books are the histories of life. He always loved a hero. He told his story best and found most interest in it when it had some central figures to absorb his interest. Thus he took but little interest in *The Old Régime*, which had to do with the institutions of Canada. But for Frontenac, and Pontiac, and, most of all, for La Salle, he had the greatest interest. The stories which he built up around these men are unsurpassed in the realm of history for dramatic, accurate, and vivid treatment. They appeal to the reader, boy or man, like a novel. As one reads them he is apt to sigh: "Why is not all history written in this way?" Ah! why is it not so written? The answer is plain: Not all historians are Parkmans. It will be many a day before there comes to our country another who is so complete a master of the real as he, and withal so clear a lover of truth. (pp. 297-99)

John Spencer Bassett, "Francis Parkman, the Man," in The Sewanee Review, *Vol. X, No. 3, July, 1902, pp. 285-301.*

CLARENCE WALWORTH ALVORD (essay date 1923)

[*Arguing that* France and England in North America *is a supreme artistic achievement but limited as history, Alvord assigns Parkman to the romantic school, or "Middle Group," of American historians. According to Alvord,* France and England in North America *is marred as a historical study because Parkman neglected to discuss a number of important events, overemphasized the significance of others, and allowed his partiality toward the English colonists to color his judgment. Alvord attributes these flaws to Parkman's preoccupation with New England history and to his belief in Anglo-Saxon superiority.*]

Francis Parkman, by the dates of his birth and death, 1823-1893, belongs in what is known as the "Middle Group of American historians," which occupied the stage from after the War of 1812 to about 1884 when the new critical spirit in historical studies, largely a product of the German seminars and nurtured by our graduate schools, seized the leadership in the field of historical research. . . . Professor John Bassett, who has written learnedly and interestingly of the middle group, prefers to assign Parkman to [the] new school, because, "while he wrote with that fine appreciation of style which was characteristic of Bancroft and the literary historians, his industry, his research among documents, and especially his detachment seem to place him among the men of today."

This opinion of Professor Bassett is a weighty one and should not be lightly disregarded, yet with some mental reservations it seems better to place Parkman squarely within the period wherein he passed his life and explain any superiority over his contemporaries he may have possessed as emanations from his genius and not as anticipations of a period to which he did not belong and within which he would have found himself very uncomfortable. (p. 394)

Viewed under the light of modern research with its greater understanding of the fundamental forces of society, its wider field of interpretation, and its more comprehensive search for information Parkman's histories seem very sketchy, his understanding of past events very superficial. Before him as he worked lay hundreds of problems which he never even saw and other hundreds of which he touched only the fringes. A few years ago my own investigations forced me to read all his volumes in rapid succession, on an average one every two days. It was, I acknowledge, a severe test and therefore my immediate reaction was not trustworthy. Still I give it for what it is worth. After the test was completed, my thought was: "This is not history, this is romance, pageantry, story writing."

What was it in Parkman's writing which produced this result? First of all the events which interested him no longer play so important a part in the historical viewpoint of the present day. After reading Monro's "Seignorial System in Canada," it is difficult to understand the contemporary enthusiasm over Parkman's *Ancient Regime.* It is really surprising how relatively few pages of the volume are devoted to an analysis of Canadian society under the French. Or, consider how few of the subjects discussed in Beer's "British Colonial Policy, 1754-1765," are to be found even mentioned in Parkman's *Montcalm and Wolfe.* Parkman devotes many pages to Sir William Johnson as general and leader of the Indians in war, but only a line in two places to remind the reader that this same Johnson held the more important newly created imperial office of superintendent of Indians in the northern department. Parkman quotes two letters from Governor Dinwiddie of Virginia to his friend the financier Hanbury of London, but fails to picture in high light the land

speculations of these two worthies and their associates which were the immediate occasion of the French and Indian War. George Washington in his first romantic mission to the West to protest against the French occupation of the Upper Ohio Valley is not so much the representative of imperial Britain as the voice of the land speculators of the Old Dominion. Parkman's detailed description of that journey does not leave such an impression on the mind of the reader.

The enthusiastic study of Western American history of late years has revealed many gaps in the narrative of the discovery and occupation of the Mississippi Valley as related by Parkman; yet the discovery of new documents and the more careful examination of known ones do not explain satisfactorily the spotted thinness of his story. This must be attributed in part to his New Englandism, a disease not easily cured even by absence for many years, even generations, from the charmed territory. To Parkman as to the many other New England historians the happenings in their home land, so well known, so carefully studied, loom large on their horizon hiding a view of more distant scenes. The massacre of Deerfield becomes for Parkman an event of such stupendous importance that all the gory details even to the tomahawking and scalping of Tom, Dick, and Harry, and the daily sufferings of Susan on her forced excursion to Canada must be narrated at the expense of curtailing the story of more important but distant events.

The truth of the matter is that Parkman knew intimately only two short periods of Western history, that of the explorations and business enterprise of La Salle and that of the Conspiracy of Pontiac, the Alpha and Omega of his whole work. Of what falls between these his knowledge was not intensive or comprehensive. Of Louisiana he knew relatively little outside of its romantic beginnings; he never understood the importance, and his successors have also missed it, to the southern English colonies that their traders had cemented friendly relations with the Indians of the Old Southwest before the French, thus preventing a control by the latter in this region.

There is one further limitation to Parkman's historical interpretation which should be mentioned. He did his research in the generation which created the religion of Anglo-Saxonism, whose high priest, Edward A. Freeman, traced the apostolic succession of the Anglo-Saxon institutions from their German origin—God save the mark! for the doctrine was a Hun atrocity and was "made in Germany"—down through the ages of English history. It was these same Teutonic institutions that were brought to America and laid the foundations of glorious freedom. Compared with the states founded upon this solid rock of the Anglo-Saxon faith, all other states are like unto Sodom and Gomorrah.

This Anglo-Saxon superiority complex forms the warp and woof of Parkman's thought, and also that of his readers of that time, whose hearts beat responsively to these words of Parkman's announcement of his purpose to write a series of histories devoted to "the attempt of Feudalism, Monarchy, and Rome to master a continent, where at this hour (1865) half a million bayonets are vindicating the ascendancy of a regulated freedom. Many modern American historians may still cling to the belief thus voiced by Parkman fifty years ago, but no one of them would dare be so candidly chauvinistic. Parkman has been universally praised by Protestants, frequently but not universally by Catholics, for his impartial treatment of an alien race with an alien religion; and I think from the religious viewpoint the praise is merited. Being a consistent and conscientious agnostic he strove to be impartial in his attitude toward both

Catholic and Puritan; but from the beginning to the end of his career as an historian he clung to his faith in the Anglo-Saxon cult, and thus impaired his own achievement.

But enough of this negative discussion. In celebration of his centenary we want to know what Francis Parkman did accomplish. . . . (pp. 394-95)

The development of the American school of history which is called the "Middle Group" would appear inexplicable in consideration of the barrenness of research in kindred fields, were it not that a similar phenomenon was taking place in Europe. It was the natural consequence there as here of the literary and artistic movement known as Romanticism. The same idealistic view of the past which produced Scott's novels inspired Cooper in America. The same forces underlying the work of Von Ranke, Thierry, and Freeman moved the literary and scientific circles in America and drove to their labors Bancroft, Irving, Prescott, Ticknor and was still effective in the lives of their younger friends, Motley and Parkman.

The romantic school, whether German, English, or American, visualized its subject as did the contemporary sculptors or painters; it must be grand in character, a particular event of stupendous import in the history of humanity, wherein were displayed all the complex forces of human nature working themselves out to a dramatic denouement. Thus the inherent artistic possibilities of the subject to be chosen were a matter of deep consideration. Prescott in his conquests of Mexico and Peru, Motley in the struggle of the Dutch against the tyranny of Spain had made happy choices. All the elements of historical drama suited to literary treatment lay in their subjects.

The genius of Parkman consisted in perceiving when still in college that the same qualities existed in the struggle between England and France for the North American continent. And the still greater genius of perseverance was exhibited in continuing his work under the severest handicaps of ill health until it was completed in his sixty-ninth year.

Never has subject been so well fitted to the genius of an historian. Parkman was one of those happy artists chosen by Nature to perform a particular piece of work. He does it as naturally as his garden produced its roses, as a bird sings, or a Raphael paints a Madonna. This naturalness, this production without evidence of effort, is one of the signs of a supreme artist and Parkman was certainly that. He may be happily compared to the ideal Greek who looked out upon his environment, uncontaminated by the thought or products of older artists or philosophers, and joyfully attacked with the freshness of youth the knotty problems of life. The freshness of youth remained with Parkman until the end and gives to all his books charm. (pp. 395-96)

From 1865 began the steady flow from the press of those histories which remain even today the greatest achievement of any American historian. . . .

What a picture they present! How they grip the imagination! You may acknowledge, as you must, that there is too much of the fife and the drum, of the tomahawk and the scalping knife, too little of other human activities; you may concede that there is no organic connection between the beautiful scenes he depicts and the participants in the battle: concede all this and still the artistry of it remains; his books have all the force of a Grecian drama. The story is told, and the means he employs are fitted to the end he has in view. It is great literature and within its limits it is great history. (p. 396)

Clarence Walworth Alvord, "Francis Parkman," in The Nation, *Vol. CXVII, No. 3040, October 10, 1923, pp. 394-96.*

JOSEPH SCHAFER (lecture date 1923)

[*Schafer judges* France and England in North America *according to prevailing standards of historical writing. He praises Parkman's vivid descriptions of scenery and realistic characters, but states that* France and England in North America *suffers from its romantic elements and, especially, from its inadequate treatment of economic issues. Schafer's comments were originally presented to the Mississippi Valley Historical Association on December 28, 1923.*]

Though we concede that [Parkman] was a well-equipped worker, of sound critical insight and the highest ideals as a researcher, and recognize in him a literary genius calculated to glorify any subject which might engage his pen, the question remains, was the theme of his series rightly conceived? Parkman thought of it somewhat vaguely as "the history of the American forest," but he does not by any means range through the entire forested area of North America. A history of the conflict between French and British for the mastery of eastern North America would be a more accurate description of what he achieved. In this, as others have pointed out, he made himself the "Herodotus of Our Western World" [in the words of Edward Gaylord Bourne (see Additional Bibliography)], though in his case, unlike that of the Greek original, a convinced friendliness to the principles of one contestant did not color his interpretation of evidence to the disadvantage of the other. Parkman's Anglo-Saxonism, so far as its effect on the books was concerned, constituted a somewhat pervading atmosphere, but little more. The French governors, priests, habitants, and *coureurs de bois* receive full credit for motive and achievement, notwithstanding the author's skepticism concerning both the political and religious systems of which they were exponents and, in his view, victims. (pp. 357-58)

When all is said, the series must be considered somewhat episodical. Parkman selected for treatment those features of the French-British-Indian story which appealed to him as most worth while. . . . It was wilderness drama that intrigued him, the scouting party rather than the emigrants' cavalcade, the fur-trader instead of the tidewater merchant, the missionary who lost his scalp, not the prophet of a new religious movement. Save in *The old régime* one finds only incidental attention given to those institutional, social, and economic phases of history which to-day are so generally stressed, but his excursion into that field in *The old régime* proves that this omission was due to conscious choice, not to unconscious neglect. He demonstrated in that volume his ability to treat social groupings, trade and commerce, governmental organization, feudal relations, monopoly, and the influence of the backwoods on tidewater society equally with the stories of bivouacs, ambuscades, sorties, and sieges with which his pages thrill the reader. But he felt no compulsion to present extended institutional or social studies in other sections of his field. His neglect to do so may have been subconsciously related to an intense ambition for literary success. At all events, no reader of the series can fail to perceive the difference in dramatic quality, and hence in popularity, between the other works and *The old régime*, admirable as the latter is in its own way. Wedded to the arts of narrative and description, our author may also have found the requirements of the tamer style of exposition more or less irksome. But he probably judged the course of events as narrated, with many brief explanatory "asides," to be adequately interpreted. On that question there are bound to be differences of opinion among present-day historians, most of them leaning more strongly toward the type of history that aims to interpret through economics, in its broader sense, than Parkman did. It is easy to overstate his limitation from that point of view, yet a limitation there undoubtedly was, as modern research reveals, and here Parkman is destined to yield most ground to others. It is desirable that the best scholarship along these lines should be incorporated in new editions of his works.

Whatever our judgment as regards Parkman's interpretation through economics, there can hardly be two opinions about his success in the equally important and often neglected domain of psychological interpretation. Here, certainly, he does not suffer by comparison with present-day writers. The power to delineate character is rightly accounted one of the chief gifts of the dramatist and that gift Parkman possessed in high perfection. His leading figures, like Frontenac, La Salle, and Wolfe, are as strongly drawn as the characters in Tacitus, though Parkman always drew them from the evidence and not, as the great Roman did, under the play of subjective impulses. A few strokes, bold and sure, sketch for us the outline of a Sir William Johnson, a Bouquet, a Shirley, a Loudon, a Lord Howe; a Laval, a Talon, a Bigot, or a Vaudrueil. The detail is added deftly, an inference from this record, a quotation from that, a bit of gossip, a touch of humor, until these heroes, near heroes, and nonheroes move through the story as lifelike as the creations of great fictionists.

Irony and satire are ready instruments of the caricaturist and these Parkman used sparingly, but some of his good-natured hits are classic. Thus Vaudrueil, who was "courageous except in the immediate presence of danger, and failed only when the crisis came," was further delineated in a quotation from Bougainville, beginning: "When V. produces an idea he falls in love with it, as Pygmalion did with his statue. I can forgive Pygmalion, for what he produced was a masterpiece." Parkman appreciated the solid virtues of the city of brotherly love, "home of order and thrift. It took its stamp from the Quakers, its original and dominant population, set apart not only in character and creed, but in the outward symbols of a peculiar dress and a daily sacrifice of grammar on the altar of religion." Even the New Englanders do not escape, in as much as the diary of Dr. Caleb Rae, of Cleaveland's regiment in the old French war, enables him to describe their camp, under Rae's stimulation of psalm singing, as having become "vocal with rustic harmony, sincere if somewhat nasal."

His keenest barbs were reserved for those who respected more the tomahawk and scalping knife. Who can forget those unhappy Onondaga, tricked by their would-be French victims into accepting the *festin à manger tout*, "the eat-all ceremony," who, after the feast was over were left sitting "helpless as a conventicle of gorged turkey buzzards without the power possessed by those unseemly birds to rid themselves of the burden." (pp. 358-60)

Parkman's works have been illustrated only with maps and a few portraits. The publishers, wisely in this case, have denied themselves the coöperation of the camera-man and the landscape painter; so that, under the author's stimulation and guidance, the reader is privileged to exercise the heaven-bestowed gift of imagination in restoring, from the text, the diverse scenes of a colossal wilderness drama. How he etches those scenes on the mind! A *coup d'œil* is all that is needed to impart to them the color and movement of actuality. The attentive reader of **Montcalm and Wolfe** might be led blindfolded to the citadel of Quebec and, with vision momentarily restored, he would gaze south, east, and west upon landscapes to him perfectly familiar though perceived for the first time by the physical sense. He could go to Louisbourg, Detroit, Lake George, or Ticonderoga with the same result. Starved Rock on the Illinois river is probably more real to readers of **La Salle** than if it had been photographed from every distinct angle.

Images projected from the dramatic life of long ago are equally clear, endowed moreover with the ghostly quality of haunting the memory whether on or off their native stage. In this sense Braddock's white charger, seen in Indian hands nine years after his master's tragic death, still ranges the forest trails, goaded by his savage captor; the howling of the "red devils" at the Deerfields, William Henrys and Mackinacs of the imagination still terrifies in the hours of darkness; the heroic suffering of a tortured Father Jogues wrings tears of pity from the tenderhearted.

Parkman's subject, to most writers, would have constituted an overmastering temptation to melodrama, but his artistic eye avoided that pitfall. The sanity of judgment, humor, and complete absence of sentimentality with which he narrates the most tragic incidents, enable the reader to maintain an objective attitude through the harrowing episodes that fall so thickly in some of the books. And here again literary genius asserts itself. His incomparable descriptions occasionally appear to be open to the criticism of redundancy. It is undeniable that they sometimes have little relation to the theme immediately in hand, but, like his sallies of wit or rapier thrusts of satire, they also serve the dramatic object of redirecting the thought and relieving the strain on the emotions. Fortunately, life as depicted by him with rare fidelity, even in times of distress and conflict, presents some of the saving human qualities of tenderness, humor, good faith, and devoted friendship. And when the end of his theme draws near, with the rendition of the captives taken in Pontiac's war, the fringe of the panoramic picture is momentarily touched with rainbow tints.

Unrivaled among American historical writers of his own age, Parkman leans too strongly in the direction of romance to be accepted by ours as fulfilling the very highest ideal. Yet his professional character is clear of serious blemishes. An occasional hint of imperfect sympathy; at infrequent intervals a judgment marred by impatient harshness—these are slight defacements of his monumental work, so nearly perfect in execution and of such exquisite symmetry and grace. Doubtless his books, more and more, will reveal those inherent shortcomings which arise, as already pointed out, from the author's acceptance of a restricted view of the historian's function. Nevertheless, it seems probable that they are destined to be supplemented at a number of points rather than superseded in their main design. Perhaps a century hence historians may still congratulate themselves, as we do now, on having so much of American history as is comprised in Parkman's eleven beautiful volumes done with an honest thoroughness and in a form to make it "a possession forever." (pp. 362-64)

Joseph Schafer, "Francis Parkman, 1823-1923," in The Mississippi Valley Historical Review, *Vol. X, No. 4, March, 1924, pp. 351-64.*

BLISS PERRY (essay date 1924)

[*Perry's appreciative assessment of Parkman's works is biographical in approach. He first examines the influence of Parkman's early years on his writings, focusing on his interest in Romantic literature and his frontier expedition. Perry then discusses Parkman's illness and its effect on his writings.]*

Enough has been made of Parkman's boyish passion for the woods as related to his later development, but not enough has been made of his early reading in its relation to his task as a historian. The young Parkman was a Romantic. He tells us in an autobiographical sketch that his first ambition was to be a poet, then a novelist, and that he turned to history as a third choice. He read Byron, Scott, Chateaubriand, Cooper. I find the trace of Byron everywhere in his earliest books, such as **The Oregon Trail** and **Vassall Morton**. . . . In **The Oregon Trail** and **Vassall Morton** you will find the very image of the Byronic wanderer and outlaw, the Byronic clash of the Primitive against the Civilized. Doubtless the middle-aged Parkman felt that there was too much Byronic rebellion and self-revelation in **Vassall Morton,** and was glad to suppress his unsalable novel. But Byron had taught him much. I have the greatest respect for the certificated professional historians of the present day, but I submit that some of them might still learn a little something from the art of the great poets and novelists.

One scarcely needs to say how much Parkman owed to Sir Walter Scott. Here was his pattern for portrait-making, for picturesque grouping, for dramatic narrative. From **The Oregon Trail** to the **Half-Century of Conflict** how many a forceful personage, how many a march, a bivouac, an attack, are painted in the Scott manner! But I think that Parkman learned from Scott a more significant historical lesson than the mere art of picturesque narrative; namely, the secret of dispassionate fairness. For the Wizard of the North was a very soundly documented wizard; an antiquarian who knew the value of personal narrative and family papers and government archives; a lawyer who could sift evidence; a historian who could weigh Jacobites and Presbyterians, kings and commoners, in the scales of equal justice. When Parkman came to his extraordinarily delicate task of comparing English and French civilizations, of appraising the merits of Jesuit and Puritan, of explorer and soldier, I think his judgment was all the more finely balanced, his sense of human values all the more penetrating, for his early training in Sir Walter's school. If you and I are ever tried for murder, we may well wish to have a Parkman and a Scott upon the jury; for if these gentlemen vote that we deserve hanging, we should be quite content to be hanged.

But Francis Parkman was far other than a mere reader of books. More than most historians, he coveted first-hand experience. He must see for himself. . . . To understand how his personal qualities affected his literary methods, the indispensable document is **The Oregon Trail,** dictated when he was twenty-three. He wanted a key to that "history of the American forest" to which he had already devoted himself, and he found it in the Far West of 1846. That journey gave him the clue to the Indian character, to the hunter, the bushranger, the pioneer. . . . Long days of enforced idleness in Dakota wigwams helped him to understand the Jesuit Relations and the French archives. Henceforth he could check up his sources by what his own eyes had seen. That journey to the Black Hills may have fatally impaired his health, but its wholesome influence upon his mind can be traced in every one of his later books. Just as Charles Dickens's boyhood gave him the key of the London streets, Parkman's boyhood gave him the key of the wilderness.

The name of Dickens suggests another curious parallel between a writer's physical endowment and his chosen theme. The bodily and mental restlessness of Dickens, his sense of life as

motion, as struggle, gives his novels their flashing, pulsing energy. Parkman's physical and mental energy was subjected to a more rigid control, for he was told that his sanity and even his life depended upon mastery of his emotions, and he never failed to keep himself in hand. It was the irony of his career that his disease increased this inner urge to action, while forbidding—often for years at a time—any real mental or physical exertion. . . . [His malady] intensified his abnormal inner excitement in the presence of his material. He wanted to tell the thrilling story of the struggle of two empires for the control of a continent—a struggle typified by racing ships, forced marches, Indian raids, swift reversals of fortune—the drama of clashing, changing civilizations. That his drama was enacted in the lonely forest only increased its fascination to a man who knew, as Parkman did, the secret of the woods. That secret is *expectancy.* You have in the woods, even more than in the great cities, the sense of "something evermore about to be."

The motion-picture was unknown in Parkman's day, but this new art of our time suggests something of the fashion in which that restless forest-drama unrolled itself before his picture-making, his story-weaving imagination. If you can fancy a "movie" without sentimentality, a "movie" firmly documented, unwaveringly just, with every landscape sharply focussed, every portrait clear, every action motivated, then I submit that you would have something like the effect which Parkman's twelve volumes convey. And his nerves paid the price of his self-absorption in his theme. "The poet writes the history of his own body," said Thoreau. But so does the historian, and every artist who puts himself into his books. . . . Parkman lived passionately with his characters for fifty years. With every instinct urging him to a life of action rather than contemplation, he was forced to sit for long years in his wheel-chair and see that splendid swift procession of his heroes pass—priests and soldiers, statesmen and savages, against a background of eternally living Nature where the woods break into leaf and then turn to gold or scarlet, where the pitiless rains fall and the snow-drifts melt into the floods of spring—pageantry all, passing, passing, with men withering like leaves and newer generations pressing on, pageantry and heroism and martyrdom and dreams of empire, until that stormy September morning upon the Plains of Abraham when the dying General Wolfe knew that he had won.

To have had his first glimpse of that unforgettable story-picture in boyhood, to keep it steadily in focus through the tortured years of manhood, patiently adding his pitiful five or six lines a day, but never yielding to despair, never abandoning his theme—I maintain that that achievement of a motor-minded cripple was as gallant and glorious an exploit as anything achieved by any of Parkman's heroes. (pp. 443-47)

[It may] be true that Parkman would be deaf to some of the finer voices of the twentieth century, as he was certainly deaf to the more spiritual accents of seventeenth-century mysticism. It would have been hard for him to think internationally, for he had, I imagine, less faith in World Courts and Leagues of Nations than he had in the sword, held by firm and able hands. Parkman was a Stoic, in philosophy as in life. He would perhaps retort that his life-work was not to dream of a new heaven and a new earth, but to give the actual record of the American wilderness. And we may say for him, what he would have been too modest—or too proud!—to say for himself, that he told that story as no other man could have told it, and that he served his generation best by living—as the dying Henry Thoreau said quietly—in "one world at a time." (p. 448)

Bliss Perry, ''Some Personal Qualities of Francis Parkman,'' in The Yale Review, Vol. XIII, No. 3, April, 1924, pp. 443-48.

WILBUR L. SCHRAMM (essay date 1938)

[*Schramm analyzes Parkman's theory of historical writing as revealed in his critical reviews of contemporary historical works. He also discusses the various influences that informed Parkman's approach. According to Schramm, Parkman drew his rationalism from the Federalists, his literary style from the romantic historians, and his methods of research from the scientific historians.*]

With his admirable resolution to write history, not write *about* it, Francis Parkman never recorded in any eassy, criticism, or apologia his theory of how history should be written. Yet anyone who is familiar with Parkman's works can guess what that theory must have been. It must have been compounded of two passions: a passion for *the truth* (and Parkman meant the whole truth and nothing but the truth, about whatever subject may have been under consideration); and a passion for clear, realistic expression of that truth, in a manner dignified but vivid. This was the recipe he used for his own books, and it must have been the recipe he would have recommended to others.

But ''must have been'' is shifting sand on which to reconstruct a man's belief. We can do better than that by examining the prefaces to Parkman's books, his occasional critical comments, and his reviews. The last, especially, deserve our attention. It has almost been forgotten that Parkman reviewed new historical books for at least four Eastern periodicals [*Christian Examiner, Atlantic Monthly, North American Review,* and *Nation*] from his twenties until the last few years of his life. Many of these reviews are excellent in themselves, and all are important for their bearing on Parkman's thought and taste. By examining these reviews, side by side with other important pronouncements, and by isolating the characteristics which Parkman approved of and those he did not approve of, it is possible to formulate Parkman's theory of historical writing almost entirely in his own words.

While Parkman would doubtless have been the last man to insist that an historian should write only the history of his own country, there is a significant nationalism in his comments about subject matter. He praised Cooper because his work springs from the ''deep rich soil'' of America. He lamented that ''the highest civilization of America is communicated from without instead of being developed from within, and is therefore nerveless and unproductive.'' The tone of the fine review of Cooper and the emphasis on knowledge of the subject and background in all the reviews implied plainly that Americans should write of America. And although Parkman justly praised Prescott and Motley, his own choice of an American theme is significant in view of the well-known fact that Prescott purposely shied away from such a theme. Parkman was thus inclined probably not because of any militant nationalism, but because of his insistence on accuracy and exact information. A man can write a better history of a country if he is familiar with its people, its geography, customs, and traditions. One should write about what he knows best.

In *The Book of Roses* Parkman gave horticulturists a piece of advice which he might also have applied to historians: ''Never attempt to do any thing which you are not prepared to do thoroughly. A little done well is far more satisfactory than a great deal done carelessly and superficially.'' (pp. l-lii)

Parkman's own pursuit of historical sources [was almost fanatical in character]. It is not surprising, therefore, that his first attack on the books he reviews should concern the adequacy of their documentation. He was glad to report that ''M. Girouard has been untiring in research.'' He admired H. H. Bancroft's herculean work in collecting native material from the Pacific slopes. Charlevoix's research was ''thorough and tolerably exact.'' In another case, the author was ''very zealous, and no less successful, in collecting material.''

How much does the author know of his subject? was always his first question. He took pains, of course, to be sure that the author had used first-hand sources. He exceedingly regretted M. Rameau's ''use of second-hand sources.'' And in his own research he accepted the statements of secondary sources only when they conformed to carefully weighted primary sources.

Another requirement is that the author imbue himself with the spirit of the times, become like a spectator or a participant. This will often require more than book knowledge. It will require personal inspection of the places he writes about and personal experience with the kind of life he writes about. ''The subject has been studied as much from life and in the open air as at the library table,'' he said of one of his own books.

One of Parkman's own greatest problems was to digest the enormous mass of source material he gathered and combine it into a harmonious whole. In this he was highly successful, and he required the same success of others. Thus he admired M. Gravier's ''careful analysis'' of a difficult mass of material, and he wished that a well-known author had ''digested his material, and given it to us in a more compact form.''

Parkman's own works are examples of full but unpedantic annotation. Of books under review he always asked the question, Where did you learn this? He regretted exceedingly that Margry's first volume had no notes, and he complimented the translator of a famous work because, although ''Charlevoix rarely gives his authorities,'' the translator has gone through the book and supplied the lack. Bancroft's book, he said, ''is a storehouse of facts, gathered with admirable industry and care, arranged with skill and judgment, and sustained, at all points, by copious reference to the sources whence they were drawn.''

Once the source material is gathered and digested, the duty of the historian is to give a truthful interpretation of it. Parkman was adamant in his stand on this point. He was lukewarm toward Longfellow's poetry because Longfellow sentimentalized the Acadian peasant and the Indian. He vigorously criticized Rameau: ''He is the bravest of generalizers; snatches at a detached fact and spreads it over as much ground as his theories require.... [His] book is a curious example of the manner in which a man of confused brain and weak judgment, eager to see things in his own way, will distort some facts, overlook others, magnify others that are trifling into gigantic proportion, and all with no apparent intention to deceive anybody.'' Parkman even objected to the grammatical revision of source materials.... The unvarnished truth was always Parkman's goal. ''Describe them just as they are,'' he once advised Farnham, ''and let the reader philosophize as much as he likes.''

This devotion to truth was certain, sooner or later, to cause him trouble. He admitted that when he was writing on the history of the Catholic Church in America he was on ''delicate ground,'' and he regretted the nature of some of his findings because ''they cannot be agreeable to persons for whom I have a very cordial regard.'' But he told the truth as he saw it, and

An illustration from The Oregon Trail *depicting battling Indians.*

let the chips fall where they might. He was always ready to recant when he was proved wrong, and at the time of his death he was still revising and enlarging on the basis of new information. As a result, he could say of his most bitterly attacked book, "so far as I know, none of the statements of fact contained in it have been attacked by evidence, or even challenged."

The highest praise he could give the content of a book he reviewed was to say that it showed "the results of a genuine research concentrated on an object truly historic, and producing results of a real interest and value."

Oftener than any other quality except documentation and truth in the books he criticized, Parkman chose to speak of their sense of proportion. He accused his good friend Casgrain of lacking a sense of proportion, when the Abbé objected to Parkman's treatment of the Roman church. He criticized the heterogeneity of Girouard's book, which "fills whole pages with the names of the *habitants,* or peasants, of La Chine, to the exclusion of more important matter." Of another book he wrote: "If Mr. Hole could contain his vivacity within reasonable bounds, curtail his anecdotes, suppress his Greek, Latin, and French, and spare us the occasional butt end of a sermon inserted as a counterpoise to his jokes, his book would be more useful." He expected writers "when so much that is trivial, crude, and superficial is daily thrust before the public" to know what material is important and what is not.

Knowing Parkman's own style, we might expect him to be critical of the styles of others. And indeed he was. Crudities in style he hated. He mentioned the abundant grammatical

errors in the writing of Gerald E. Hart, and suggested that the Society for Historical Studies, of which Hart was president, restrain the literary activities of its chief officer. He admired the "manly directness" of Cooper's style, and commended its "freedom from those prettinesses, studied turns of expression, and petty tricks of rhetoric, which are the pride of less masculine writers." On the other hand, he regretted that Cooper's style had no "glow."

In order to understand what Parkman meant by "glow" and by "manly," "direct," and "vigorous," turn to his books, and read the description of the coureur de bois in *The Old Régime,* of Frontenac's expedition in *Pontiac,* and of Fort Duquesne in *Montcalm and Wolfe.* Such pages as these have been far better teachers for young writers than any essay on literary theory Parkman might have left.

Akin to his demand for truth was his demand for real and living characters and scenes. This was one of the main reasons for his painstaking research, for his far traveling, for his seeking to imbue himself with the spirit of the period he wrote about. But to this basic material, he realized, the writer must add imagination—not to create a fiction but to make the truth live. . . . Parkman noticed that "Mrs. Grant's facts . . . have an air of fiction; while Cooper's fiction wears the aspect of solid fact." He admires the vividness of Cooper's descriptions of forests and battles, although he thought that Cooper's white women and Indians were unreal. The secret of the vividness of the battles and forests, he says, is in "their fidelity, in the strength with which they impress themselves upon the mind, and the strange tenacity with which they cling to the memory." Even Parkman's enemies admitted the vividness and the realism of his own characters and his own narration. La Salle, Joliet, Menéndez, Frontenac, Wolfe, Montcalm—all seem to live again in Parkman's pages; and the person who reads **Montcalm and Wolfe** can see the heights of Quebec flame with French guns and hear the cannon balls whistle over his head. (pp. lii-lviii)

If we want to put Parkman's theory of historical writing in a few words, we can say this:

He advises the choice of a subject which the writer is readily qualified to handle, preferably a national subject. Then he insists upon the most meticulous search for all the facts bearing upon that subject—utilizing first-hand sources whenever possible, observing as well as reading, striving to imbue oneself with the spirit of the period. Then this material must be digested into a harmonious whole, annotated punctiliously with the sources of the information. The goal of all this work is to create the basis of a truthful interpretation of all the known facts; integrity is perhaps the most important requirement of good history. There remains, then, the question of how the interpretation and its supporting facts shall be written. Parkman says that, first of all, the writer should show a sense of proportion in arranging and discarding. Secondly, he should write in a direct, manly, vigorous, glowing style. Finally, he should make his characters and events live again in the pages of the book. (pp. lix-lx)

When Parkman chose his career to new currents were powerfully altering the course of history. One was the romantic contemplation of the glories of the past, a movement which looked to literature for its inspiration in the historical novels of Scott and the romances of Chateaubriand, and in America the novels of Cooper and the stories of Irving. The other was the inductive, critical, and scientific approach to the remnants of the past, which was typified by the beginnings of scientific philology in Germany and the new historical writing of Wolf and Niebuhr, and which was brought across the Atlantic by American students from Göttingen: Ticknor, Bancroft, Hedge, Everett, and others. Both currents were offshoots of the Romantic Movement and its respect for the past. One led historians to become intensely interested in some portions of the past which, less than a century before, had seemed wholly uninteresting. The other led historians to build their generalizations inductively from evidence painstakingly gathered and weighted.

From the one current Parkman took his love for the picturesque and dramatic, his vivid style; from the other he took his respect for sources and their honest, accurate interpretation. The rational, inductive method of the one he combined with the penetrating flashes of the other, and his whole structure was built on the solid rock of almost fanatical research and preparation.

Thus Parkman stood between the older group of American moralist-historians—represented a century before by Cotton Mather and his righteous *Magnalia* and in Parkman's own time by Jared Sparks with his twelve volumes of *Washington*—and the new hybrid history of the social scientists, represented in our time by Charles A. Beard, Frederick Jackson Turner, and Vernon L. Parrington. The older group, like Parson Weems, put hatchets in George Washington's hand and then expounded the moral at great length. . . . The younger group, strangely indoctrinary in their own tendency, have been trained to regard history as a science, the rules for which may be learned through accurate investigation, and the whole of which may be interpreted by means of these fundamental rules. (pp. cviii-cx)

From the moralist, Parkman borrowed the vigor, left the moral. To the later historians he left his strenuous ideal of documentation and his fervid respect for the truth, without anticipating their interest in the social and economic aspects of the story. He achieved an objectivity to which the moralists had never attained, and he left a living, dramatic style which his followers have never equaled. (p. cx)

Given a few wishes, we could wish many differences in Parkman's history: more unity in the individual books and in the series, for instance, more attention to social and economic questions, greater sympathy for beliefs foreign to his own. But there is no doubt that he succeeded in his object and that the history he has written is firm and enduring, as well as vivid and dramatic. He himself, with his regard for achievement, would have considered that of much greater importance than the result of the process of relativity by which critics have for years, and almost with one voice, named him the greatest of American historians.

Born into the Romantic Movement, writing his greatest books in the Age of Realism, Francis Parkman declined allegiance to either and gave it rather to the rational Federalism of the age before. . . . Romantic sentimentalism sickened him; what he chose to call "romantic eccentricities"—transcendentalism, individualism, utopianism, humanitarianism, back-to-Nature-ism—disgusted him. He would have argued with Emerson the sources of knowledge and the problem of evil. He disliked Thoreau's eccentric nature. He had no sympathy for Longfellow's mellow sentiment. He was deaf to the pleas of the abolitionists, and thought union more important than freedom of the Negroes. Himself a lover of nature, he stood at sword's points with the whole Romantic Movement over the meaning of nature and over the concept of the natural man. And although he is not known to have expressed himself at length on the literature of realism, he repeatedly took his stand against the materialism of the postwar years. He feared that materialism would throttle out art itself. "The present condition and prospects of American Literature are not very flattering," he said in 1875. "A score or more of years ago there seemed a fair hope that the intellectual development of the country would not be absolutely disproportioned to its material growth; but thus far the hope has not been fulfilled, and, relatively to our vast increase in wealth and population, the value, though not the volume, of literary products is less than before."

From each age he took what he wanted. From the romantic age in general he heard the call to an investigation of the past, although he never chose to look at the past through nostalgic spectacles. From the scientific German scholars of the age he took a method of investigating the past. From the romantic novelist Scott and others he learned the value of vivid pages. If he gained anything from the realists it was support for his realistic attitude toward facts. From the Federalists he drew his political viewpoint and his rationalism. "Yet through the rock and iron of his character, there ran, known to but few, a delicate vein of poetic feeling."—this characterization of one of the figures in *Vassall Morton* might have been applied to Parkman himself. The rock and iron—evident in his stern vigor, his demand for justice, his uncompromising attitude—came from his ancestral Puritanism reinforced by his Federalistic training; the poetic feeling—evident in the glamour of his pages and in his eye for nature—was in key with the Romantic Movement.

His books are a compromise between his contemporary inclination to romanticize and the restraint he learned from Puritan and rationalist teachers. A very few pages will show a reader that he might have liked to romanticize the Indian as Cooper did and to glorify wild natural scenes as Scott did; but he resisted the temptation. (pp. cxii-cxiv)

He was too big for a pigeonhole, and yet if we have to pigeonhole him we must call him a romantic. Basically his history was romantic: stirring events in a setting of great natural vigor (an unknown continent, mysterious forests, rivers, mountains, and savages), and the whole story told in a colorful and dramatic style. That was Prescott's formula, and Motley's, and we have seen that it was also Parkman's—up to a certain point. But the limitations of the name ''romantic'' are nowhere more glaringly evident than when the name is used to define the writing of Parkman.

In American literary thought he stands as the apostle of liberty, opposed to both license and absolutism; as the representative of rationalism against both natural inspiration and supernatural inspiration; as the representative of Spartan and Stoic virtues amidst an age of natural goodness and materialistic laissez faire; as a realist, searching uncompromisingly for truth, as a thinker of unusual stability who could make up his mind on the fundamental questions by the time he reached his middle twenties and plan a course of action to last throughout the rest of his life; as a man of unusual moral fibre who could early choose an object in life and pursue that object over almost insurmountable obstacles to a successful conclusion.

His books join with the Federalist papers, the best American state papers, and the works of a few other historians in triumphant proof that the literature of knowledge can be literature. For the great individual triumph of Parkman is in using—and still hiding—his vast scholarship in books that are as exciting as Cooper's, as true as Howells's, as dramatic as Melville's, books that because of the character of their thought and method belong in the American tradition as surely as do *The Deerslayer, The Rise of Silas Lapham,* and *Moby Dick.*

Since Parkman's time only a few historians have been admitted without question to American literature, one—Henry Adams—more for his autobiography and a book of interpretation that is almost autobiography than for his history, and another—John Fiske—as much for his work on science as his work on history. Modern historians have kept Parkman's scholarship but, it seems, lost the tragic elixir for which De Soto searched and which every great author has—the priceless formula which keeps men and their actions forever alive. (pp. cxiv-cxvi)

> *Wilbur L. Schramm, in an introduction to* Francis Parkman: Representative Selections *by Francis Parkman, edited by Wilbur L. Schramm, American Book Company, 1938, pp. xiii-cxvi.*

MASON WADE (essay date 1942)

[*The following appreciative assessment of Parkman's career is drawn from Wade's* Francis Parkman: Heroic Historian, *which is considered a leading twentieth-century study of the author; he also edited* The Journals of Francis Parkman. *In addition to discussing the artistic and cultural influences that inform Parkman's writings, Wade comments on his method, style, and relationship to his contemporaries and successors.*]

The passing of nearly half a century since Parkman's death has both clarified and obscured his greatness. His books are more widely read than those of any other American historian of his period, and the historical value of his work has suffered little in the light of fifty years' research. Yet the triumph of the scientific school of historiography over the romantic and rhe-

torical has tended to place him in the shade, along with Motley and Prescott, in the minds of those who are not especially concerned with his field. He died at the summit of his career, and he was mourned almost fulsomely by his contemporaries, who saw in his passing the close of New England's great age. Those who came after have been suspicious of the critical verdicts of that age, and in the main justly so, for in instance after instance time has made radical changes in them. Despite the fact that Parkman's reputation has weathered the years with less loss of luster than has fallen to the lot of most of the great American names of the nineteenth century, it is by no means unnecessary today to point out once more his achievement and its nature.

As we look back over the period from the vantage point of today, it is difficult to avoid the foreshortening effect of our perspective; it is hard to grasp how original and how fresh Parkman's work was in its own day, and how nearly it approximated our modern notion of how history should be written.... [During the mid-1800s, the] average American had no interest in his heritage, certainly none in the period before the Revolution, whose story had grown familiar to him through many retellings in the eagle-screaming orations which were long the core of Fourth of July celebrations. The American of the middle years of the nineteenth century still looked across the Atlantic, if he were of a literary or a scholarly turn of mind; in many respects his point of view was European. His taste in history was for works that made him more familiar with the European tradition. Parkman was the first to see the importance of the wilderness struggles which made America; the first to recognize that they were not mere backwoods skirmishes but conflicts of more than local importance and with considerable influence on the course of events in the European world. And to the task of chronicling this forgotten chapter of history he brought great gifts and a new historical method. (pp. 446-47)

It is no longer the fashion to write history in terms of great men, and to confine oneself to the chronicling of political and military events. But Parkman was writing the history of a colony whose destinies were absolutely controlled by a handful of men, and so his tendency to think of history in terms of individuals rather than masses and forces did not mislead him. To a very great extent New France was Champlain, La Salle, Frontenac, Laval, Bigot, or Montcalm in the several periods of those men's power. A decade before the effect of the new German school of history was felt in America, Parkman was devoting a whole book to the economic and social factors in the history of New France, and in his other works he did not neglect the effect of such economic factors as the fur trade on Canadian life. For a pioneer he did a remarkably thorough, detailed, and well-rounded piece of work, whose general outlines have not been changed and whose details have been corrected in only a few instances by later historians working in a different spirit and with a broader view of their subject. And his personal experiences enabled him to vitalize his accounts of such dry matters as tribal divisions and land tenure in a way that is seldom encountered today. (pp. 448-49)

Parkman had one great literary advantage over the modern historian: in his day history was not regarded as the record of all man's activities. Economic, social, and cultural events were not given the same importance that they are today in connection with political and military occurrences. Parkman did not face the problem of composing a chronological narrative which would unite and relate the advances and declines in many different fields. And though his talent for construction was great, it is clear from the evidence of **The Old Regime** that he would have shared the modern historian's inability to solve the problem satisfactorily. Even though he generally confined himself to political and military events, he needed a central figure around which to build his narrative. When such a protagonist was lacking, as in **A Half-Century of Conflict,** his work lost unity and clear and logical structure. His tendency to think of history in terms of eras dominated by one individual was one great literary asset; another asset was his physical handicap. Debarred from making much use of his eyes, he had to digest his materials thoroughly and arrange them in his mind before beginning to write. Without a preconceived outline, the tortoise-like method of composition forced upon him would soon have involved him in hopeless confusion. But driven as he was by a passion for his subject which ruled out almost all other considerations, and possessed of great mental energy, he used his enforced solitude and sleepless nights for mental composition, so that when he began to dictate a book, he was able to do so without halts for reference and in such finished form that few corrections were required. While his powers of memory were not those of Prescott, who could keep sixty pages in his head for several days, they were remarkable enough; for it was his practice to digest materials and take mental notes years before he wrote the books based upon them, and yet he used hardly any written notes or outlines. Generally his documents and reference works are annotated only with symbols calling attention to various important points, and again with a mark indicating that the material has been used. All the modern historian's cumbersome apparatus of filing cards and cabinets has produced no more accurate or detailed results.

Parkman also had the personal and literary qualifications for being a great writer of history. He believed so thoroughly in himself that he did not feel it necessary to parade all the factors that went into the making of his conclusions, though he was always ready to reveal them to fellow-students concerned about some point. After **Pontiac,** his first historical work, he did not load down his books with presentations of all his data and citations of all his authorities. He merely made it clear that he had been at great pains to ascertain all the facts, mentioned his chief sources of information, and then assumed the reader's confidence in his thoroughness and integrity, without continually producing his raw materials as so many modern pedants feel obliged to do. He had the literary taste to know when a quotation from a source would increase the flavor and color of his narrative, and when it was better presented in digested form. He was artist enough to be able to cloak his facts with the life that makes them stick in the reader's mind. A comparison of passages on the same topic from George Bancroft and from Parkman reveals the great difference between the historical pedant and the historical artist. In Bancroft most of the facts are to be found and the style is correct enough, but the narrative is lifeless; in Parkman the facts take on new meaning and become memorable through the warm life with which they are infused. Yet Parkman is a far more reliable historian, factually, than Bancroft.

In one respect Parkman fell short of the highest level of historical writing. **France and England in North America,** as a whole, lacks the sweep and majestic perspective of a whole period which such a masterwork as Gibbon's **Decline and Fall** possesses. The criticism may be unjustified, since Parkman was conscious of the necessity of tying the whole work together . . . , and was only prevented from doing so by ill health and death. But it remains dubious whether he could ever have accomplished his object, even if he had had the opportunity.

History may be "a compound of innumerable biographies," as Parkman undoubtedly felt that it was, but he lacked both the philosophical equipment to concoct that compound on a large scale and the interpretive ability to draw general conclusions from it once it was made. Devoted to the great-man theory of history, he could hardly be expected to sense the laws of social evolution, to see, as Spencer put it, "that the forces which mold society work out their results apart from, and often in spite of, the aims of the leading men." He was an artist, not a sociologist, and he viewed his subjects pictorially, in much the same manner as the sculptors and painters of the period did theirs.

Parkman is notable for his detachment among his historical contemporaries, but he would hardly be considered the model of the impartial historian today. He was a New Englander of New Englanders, and his heritage marked his opinions and ways of thought irrevocably. He was also a product of the romantic era, and though he shed some of his early Byronic romanticism as he grew older, he never lost it entirely. He began his work in the conscious belief that the story of New France demonstrated the innate superiority of the civilization of Protestant England over that of Catholic France, and such remained his view at the close of his career, though he had penned passages which indicate more than a little doubt about the principle in certain instances. **The Oregon Trail** shows how little capable this New Englander was of understanding the West of his own day, and there are evidences of such astigmatism in his treatment of western topics in the histories. Parkman cherished his ideal of the Indian and of the frontiersman and of the life they led, but his environment made him recoil before the reality. Conscious supporter that he was of the doctrine of Anglo-Saxonism, of the innate superiority of the plain man of English blood and Protestant faith to men of another race and creed, his own tastes made him sympathize with those of his characters who displayed the aristocratic virtues, who represented a mature European civilization rather than a raw and callow American one, despite their Latin blood and religion. Puritan that he was, he disliked the Puritans most cordially; republican that he was, he loathed democracy and fought its growing influence. For all the insight that his lifetime's labor gave him into the making of American democracy, he remained a Brahmin, shocked and grieved in his later years by the course that the country was following. Long buried in his work and isolated by his illness and his means, at his death he was already a monument to a vanished era and an anachronism. He was the last of the Brahmins; the last of that goodly company who did so much to make the name of Boston as the cultural capital of a young country and as the center of a civilization which was not to be that of the country as a whole. The enduring worth of the books he left behind him is such as to entitle him to recognition not only as the last but the greatest of that caste which has set its stamp upon our way of life. (pp. 449-52)

> *Mason Wade, in his* Francis Parkman: Heroic Historian, *The Viking Press, 1942, 466 p.*

BERNARD DeVOTO (essay date 1943)

[*An editor of the* Saturday Review of Literature *and longtime contributor to* Harper's Magazine, *DeVoto was a highly controversial literary critic and historian. A man whose thought enraged much of America's literary establishment during the 1930s and 1940s, he was frequently motivated by anger at authors he considered ignorant of American life and history. DeVoto was par-*

ticularly interested in the history of the American West and wrote several books on the subject, notably the Pulitzer Prize-winning Across the Wide Missouri. *As a critic, he admired mastery of form and psychological subtlety in literature. His own works are praised for their scholarly thoroughness and vigorous style. DeVoto's discussion of* The Oregon Trail *is drawn from his* The Year of Decision: 1846, *in which he chronicles the frontier experiences of Parkman and other travelers who journeyed to the West during 1846, when the expansionist movement gained its greatest momentum. DeVoto contends that* The Oregon Trail *is flawed as a historical study, arguing that Parkman was a narrow-minded Brahmin whose prejudices prevented him from recognizing the significance of the westward movement.*]

[Parkman went West in 1846 primarily] to study the Indians. He intended to write the history of the conflict between imperial Britain and imperial France, which was in great part a story of Indians. *The Conspiracy of Pontiac* had already taken shape in his mind; beyond it stretched out the aisles and transepts of what remains the most considerable achievement by an American historian. So he needed to see some uncorrupted Indians in their native state.

It was Parkman's fortune to witness and take part in one of the greatest national experiences, at the moment and site of its occurrence. It is our misfortune that he did not understand the smallest part of it. No other historian, not even Xenophon, has ever had so magnificent an opportunity: Parkman did not even know that it was there, and if his trip to the prairies produced one of the exuberant masterpieces of American literature [*The Oregon Trail*], it ought instead to have produced a key work of American history. But the other half of his inheritance forbade. It was the Puritan virtues that held him to the ideal of labor and achievement and kept him faithful to his goal in spite of suffering all but unparalleled in literary history. And likewise it was the narrowness, prejudice, and mere snobbery of the Brahmins that insulated him from the coarse, crude folk who were the movement he traveled with, turned him shuddering away from them to rejoice in the ineffabilities of Beacon Hill, and denied our culture a study of the American empire at the moment of its birth. Much may rightly be regretted, therefore. But set it down also that, though the Brahmin was indifferent to Manifest Destiny, the Puritan took with him a quiet valor which has not been outmatched among literary folk or in the history of the West. (p. 115)

> Bernard DeVoto, "Equinox," in his The Year of Decision: 1846, *1943. Reprint by Houghton Mifflin Company, 1950, pp. 102-15.**

GRAHAM GREENE (essay date 1949)

[*An English man of letters, Greene is generally considered the most important contemporary Catholic novelist. In his major works, he explores the problems of spiritually and socially alienated individuals living in the corrupt and corrupting societies of the twentieth century. Formerly a book reviewer for the* Spectator, *Greene is deemed a shrewd literary critic with a taste for the works of neglected authors. His review of* The Journals of Francis Parkman, *from which the following excerpt is drawn, first appeared in the* New Statesman & Nation *on August 20, 1949. Greene praises Parkman's tireless devotion to his historical project and proposes that the journals are an important record of his artistic development.*]

'My 23rd Birthday. Nooned at a mud puddle.' So Parkman noted in his journal in 1846 and we shall look far for any comparable passage in the diaries of a creative artist. Certainly the wind has never played quite so freely at a historian's birth.

The smell of documents, the hard feel of the desk chair, are singularly absent. . . . Surely no other historian has planned his life work so young nor learned to write so hard a way. At the age of eighteen the whole scheme of his great work *France and England in North America* had captured his consciousness; there remained only to gather his material and to begin. One remembers the immense importance that Gibbon's biographers have attributed to his gentlemanly service in the Hampshire Militia, but what are we to think of a young historian who before starting to write his first volume, *The Conspiracy of Pontiac*, finds it necessary to make the long journey to Europe and Rome, there to stay in a Passionist monastery so that he may attain some imaginative sympathy with the Catholic missionaries who are the heroes of his second volume . . . and after that to undertake his journey along the Oregon trail in quest of Indian lore, thus ruining his health for a lifetime in the mere gathering of background material?

Parkman was an uncertain stylist . . . , but his errors of taste are carried away on the great drive of his narrative, much as they are in the case of Motley and in our own day Mr. Churchill. He had ridden off through the dangerous wilderness with a single companion, like one of the heroes of his epic or a character in Fenimore Cooper, who had woken his genius, he had eaten dog with the Indians and stayed in their moving villages, he had watched the tribes gather for war and heard the news of traders' deaths brought in. He had listened to Big Crow's own account of his savagery—'he has killed 14 men; and dwells with great satisfaction on the capture of a Utah, whom he took personally; and, with the other Sioux, scalped alive, cut the tendons of his wrist, and flung, still alive, into a great fire.' Since the seventeenth century no historian has so lived and suffered for his art. Like Prescott he all but lost his sight, so that he was forced to use a wire grid to guide his pencil, he suffered from misanthropy and a melancholia that snaps out like a dog even from his early journals ('the little contemptible faces—the thin, weak tottering figures—that one meets here on Broadway, are disgusting. One feels savage with human nature'). The work planned at eighteen, begun at twenty-eight, was only finished at [sixty-nine], in the year before his death, by working against time and his own health. This was a poet's vocation, followed with a desperate intensity careless of consequences, and [*The Journals of Francis Parkman*] are as important in tracing the course of the creative impulse as the journals of Henry James. (pp. 121-22)

For the general reader the most interesting [find made by Mr. Mason Wade, who discovered and edited *The Journals of Francis Parkman*,] is Parkman's journal of the Oregon Trail which Mr. Wade rightly prefers to the work based on it—Parkman's first and most popular book, popular perhaps because of the way in which it was adulterated to suit the fashion of the time by his friend Charles Eliot Norton, 'carefully bowdlerized of much anthropological data and many insights into Western life which seemed too crude to his delicate taste.' Mr. Wade quotes several examples of these changes from the vivid fluid journal to the stilted literary tones—the false Cooperisms—of the book. These Cooperisms, still evident in *The Conspiracy of Pontiac*, Parkman gradually shed. Life and literature at the beginning lay uneasily with a sword between them, so that nothing in the early books has the same sense of individual speech and character that we find in the journals. (p. 123)

Only with his third book—*The Jesuits in North America*—did the marriage satisfactorily take place. In the deeply moving *Relations* of the Jesuits that form the greater part of his material he found again the power of characteristic speech: the tortured priest Bressani who wrote with bitter humour to his Superior, 'I could not have believed that a man was so hard to kill,' and in another letter of ironic apology to the Jesuit General in safe Rome: 'I don't know if your Paternity will recognize the hand-writing of one whom you once knew very well. The letter is soiled and ill-written; because the writer had only one finger of his right hand left entire, and cannot prevent the blood from his wounds, which are still open, from staining the paper. His ink is gunpowder mixed with water and his table is the earth.'

By this time, too, Parkman had learned the value of bald narrative:

> Noel Chabanel came later to the mission; for he did not reach the Huron country until 1643. He detested the Indian life—the smoke, the vermin, the filthy food, the impossibility of privacy. He could not study by the smoky lodge-fire, among the noisy crowd of men and squaws, with their dogs, and their restless, screeching children. He had a natural inaptitude to learning the language, and laboured at it for five years with scarcely a sign of progress. The Devil whispered a suggestion into his ear: Let him procure his release from these barren and re-volting toils, and return to France, where con-genial and useful employments awaited him. Chabanel refused to listen; and when the temp-tation still beset him he bound himself by a solemn vow to remain in Canada to the day of his death.

And to complete the marriage Parkman had learned to control on occasion his poetic prose with fine effect as in this picture of Indian immortality:

> In the general belief, however, there was but one land of shades for all alike. The spirits, in form and feature as they had been in life, wended their way through dark forests to the villages of the dead, subsisting on bark and rotten wood. On arriving they sat all day in the crouching posture of the sick, and when night came, hunted the shades of animals, with the shades of bows and arrows, among the shades of trees and rocks; for all things, animate and inanimate, were alike immortal, and all passed together to the gloomy country of the dead.

The last notebook Parkman kept contains an account of his desperate final battle against insomnia—the amount of sleeping draught, the hours of sleep gained. One column, *A Half-Century of Conflict,* had to be finished and inserted in its place to complete the great scheme. The hours of sleeping dropped as low as three and a half and only once in the three-year record rose above eight. In that bare mathematical catalogue there is something of the spirit of Chabanel. The historian had made his vow [fifty] years before and it was kept. (pp. 124-25)

> Graham Greene, "Francis Parkman," in his The Lost Childhood and Other Essays, *The Viking Press, 1952, pp. 121-25.*

HENRY STEELE COMMAGER   (essay date 1949)

[*Commager is an American historian and editor who specializes in the history of the United States. In his introduction to* The Oregon

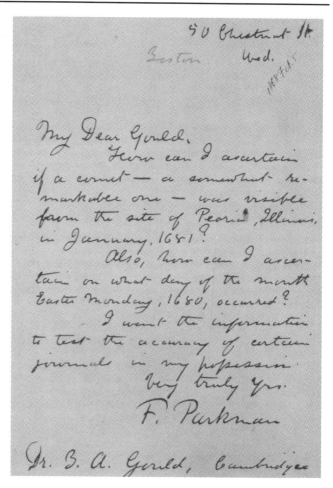

A letter in which Parkman consults a leading astronomer in order to verify the authenticity of some of his documentary materials for France and England in North America.

Trail, *excerpted below, he points out that Parkman intended the work as a collection of travel sketches and faults critics for judging it as a historical study. To Commager, the chief interest of* The Oregon Trail—*and the source of its immortality—is its "youth-fulness and spontaneity."*]

It is just over a century now since Parkman set out from West-port over the Oregon Trail, but the West that emerges from his lively pages seems as distant to us as the world of Ulysses or of King Arthur. Even as Parkman and his friends pushed along the banks of the Platte and the Arkansas they could note evidences of those changes which were so soon to tame the Wild West. Eighteen forty-six was, indeed, the year of deci-sion—the year of the Mexican War, of the Bear Flag Revolt, of the acquisition of Oregon. The advance guard of the great migration to the West was already under way: pioneers headed for the banks of the Willamette, Mormons seeking the Promised Land around the inhospitable shores of the Great Salt Lake, fortune hunters on the old Santa Fe Trail, dragoons heading for Mexico to help win the great Southwest for the United States. Some realization of the change that was under way can be read between the lines of this narrative, for though the youthful Parkman missed much, he did not miss the signifi-cance of the white invasion of the prairies. He looked upon this invasion—and upon the invaders as well—with jaundiced eye, for he preferred his West unspoiled. (p. x)

Parkman was fortunate—as are we—that he saw the prairies and the mountains, the Indian and the buffalo, before the emigrant and the locomotive transformed it all, and he was fortunate, too, that through the good offices of [his guide] Henry Chatillon he was able to know it all so intimately, to understand Indian character better than any other American historian. He attached himself to a straggling village of the Sioux—he called them Dacotah—shared their privations and their triumphs, ate dog stew and the mixture of wild cherries and grease which was one of their delicacies, slept in their lodges with little Indian children curled up against him, hunted buffalo and antelope, prepared even to fight alongside them against their traditional enemy the Snakes. The experience impaired his health, but he never regretted it or counted the cost too high. "My business," he wrote later, "was observation, and I was willing to pay dearly for the opportunity of exercising it."

And no one ever exercised it better. Later historians—Bernard De Voto and Mason Wade, for example—have lamented that Parkman missed so much [see excerpts dated 1943 and 1942]. "No other historian, not even Xenophon," says De Voto with some exaggeration, "ever had so magnificent an opportunity; Parkman did not even know it was there, and if his trip to the prairies produced one of the exuberant masterpieces of American literature, it ought instead to have produced a key work of American history." But a key work of American history is a great deal to ask of a young man of twenty-three, and no one will deny that Parkman made up later for any historical inadequacies in *The Oregon Trail*. It is true that Parkman lacked the wisdom and the insight of later historians, that he was a Brahmin, fastidious and aloof, that he failed to appreciate the significance of the Westward movement or to see democracy (he had no use for democracy, then or later) in the Pikers and the Suckers and the Mormons who so offended him by their push and brag. But he was not writing history; he was writing "sketches of Prairie and Rocky Mountain life."

Those who complain that Parkman's account of the Oregon Trail was personal and irrelevant, and that he missed the significance of what he saw, themselves miss what is most valuable in *The Oregon Trail*. For what is it that gives enduring fame to this book? It is not the historical content. That is important, to be sure, for with Garrard's *Wah-To-Yah* it is the best of the documents for this year of decision. Yet we could reconstruct the westward movement of that year without Parkman. It is not the portrayal of the Indian; Parkman's Indians are wonderfully real and impressive, but they are without benefit of ethnology, and, again, we look elsewhere for our knowledge of the Indian. It is not even what it tells us of Parkman himself; everything about the greatest of our historians is valuable, but biographically the Journals are more interesting than the formal narrative.

No, it is not these qualities, but precisely youthfulness and spontaneity that endues *The Oregon Trail* with its charm, that assures it an immortality denied to more learned or more thoughtful books. Parkman was a very mature young man at twenty-three, but he was, for all that, a very young man, with all the zest for adventure that we associate with youth. It is youthfulness that breaks through on every page, the tingling excitement, the delight in action and in adventure. No other travel book in our literature, unless it is Melville's *Typee*, has such delicious freshness; *The Oregon Trail* belongs not so much with the self-consciously romantic literature of the forties as with those Elizabethan narratives that Hakluyt collected two and a half centuries earlier.

This assuredly is what most readers remember from *The Oregon Trail*—the boyish delight in the beauty and majesty of nature, in the Indians, the buffalo hunt, the displays of horsemanship and of marksmanship. Who, that has once read these pages, can forget the description of the magnificent thunderstorms in the Black Hills, the prairie fires, the icy streams that like Alph, the sacred river, ran through caverns measureless to man, the rattlesnakes and prairie dogs, the antelope and the elk? Who has not relived, in imagination, those idyllic days under the giant cottonwood tree on the bank of the brawling Laramie Creek, waiting for The Whirlwind to come up on his way to La Bonté's camp? Who does not recall the stirring picture of Smoke's village fording Laramie Creek, naked men and boys splashing through the shallow water, horses dragging *traineaux* loaded down with domestic utensils, black-eyed babies, howling dogs and whining puppies. . . . Or who can fail to respond to the excitement of the great buffalo hunt, Parkman himself, almost dead from dysentery, in the midst of it:

> Looking up I saw the whole body of Indians full an hundred yards in advance. I lashed Pauline in pursuit and reached them just in time; for, at that moment, each hunter, as if by a common impulse, violently struck his horse, each horse sprang forward, and, scattering in the charge in order to assail the entire herd at once, we all rush headlong upon the buffalo. We were among them in an instant. Amid the trampling and the yells I could see their dark figures running hither and thither through clouds of dust, and the horsemen darting in pursuit. . . . The uproar and confusion lasted but a moment. The dust cleared away, and the buffalo could be seen scattering as from a common center, flying over the plain singly, or in long files and small compact bodies, while behind them followed the Indians, riding at furious speed, and yelling as they launched arrow after arrow into their sides.

(pp. xi-xiv)

It is this picturesqueness, this racy vigor, this poetic eloquence, this unconquerably youthful quality which give [*The Oregon Trail*] its perennial charm, recreating for us, as perhaps no other book in our literature, the wonder and beauty and intensity of life in a new world that is now old and but a memory. (p. xiv)

Henry Steele Commager, in an introduction to The Oregon Trail: Sketches of Prairie and Rocky-Mountain Life *by Francis Parkman, The Modern Library, 1949, pp. vii-xiv.*

OTIS A. PEASE   (essay date 1953)

[*The following excerpt is drawn from Pease's book-length study of Parkman's literary technique. Pease first argues that Parkman creates a sense of immediacy by rendering historical concepts "in terms of sensations rather than in terms exclusively intellectual." He then examines Parkman's method of recreating historical facts through the use of four types of visual imagery: panoramic wilderness scenes; metaphoric and symbolic passages that describe broad historical movements in simple, graphic language; pictorial accounts of wilderness conditions that vivify battle scenes; and symbolic incidents that contrast the permanence of the wilderness with the transience of human life.*]

In his preface to **The Jesuits** Parkman stated that his care in writing history was "to secure the greatest possible accuracy of statement, and to reproduce an image of the past with photographic clearness and truth." Allusions to visual sense and metaphors that invoke light, appearance, or seeing occur continually through his books. His most compelling writing, in fact, literally describes; at the same time it is seldom static. [In his preface to **Pioneers** he said:] "The narrator must seek to imbue himself with the life and spirit of the times. He must study events in their bearings near and remote; in the character, manner, and habits of those who took part in them. *He must himself be, as it were, a sharer or a spectator of the action he describes*" [see excerpt dated 1865].

Parkman rendered movement and action in words of force and elemental simplicity. He stripped his style of phrases that intellectualize or that tend to obstruct one's direct experiencing of what he wished to show. Consequently his style enables his own apprehension of the experience to become that of his readers, who thereby share in the event to the extent which he did. Even in expository prose, analyzing or summarizing, his imagery tends to reduce itself to a universal frame of reference, of things seen, felt, or thought which are common to a wide class of readers. To talk of a distinction between intellect and sensation is precarious, since the two are ultimately inseparable, but it may clarify the nature of Parkman's prose to suggest that in countless instances it renders the complex issues of a historical trend, normally understood as abstractions and concepts which make sense only through intellectual effort, in terms of sensations rather than in terms exclusively intellectual. If as a result his writing loses in accuracy and qualification, if it occasionally tends dangerously toward generalization, it nevertheless gains immense force and swiftness of movement. It enabled him to convey a broad movement of history in brief, tangible images which express what he saw to have been the essential character of the past. The reader experiences its character from the image, even while he grasps it with his mind. As long as he may rely on Parkman's ability to comprehend what actually did occur, he finds in the image a quality of truth, conveyed to him as a visual experience.

The simplest visual experience occurs in Parkman's panoramas. The scenes so described are generally based on original documents, but in the process of rendering them Parkman relied mostly on his own direct observations, and the wording was his own. A panorama suggests movement or unfolding, and this was precisely his technique of presentation. The wilderness changes and slips slowly by as the reader moves through it. The account of the Mississippi written by Joliet and Marquette was the first of an infinite series of descriptions of that river to occur in literature, and Parkman presents it with the authenticity of his own vision. They

> glided through an endless growth of wild rice.... On either hand rolled the prairie, dotted with groves and trees ... thickets and marshes and broad bare sand-bars.... In the morning the mist hung on the river like a bridal veil, then melted before the sun.... A torrent of yellow mud rushed furiously athwart the calm blue current of the Mississippi, boiling and surging and sweeping in its course logs, branches, and uprooted trees. They had reached the mouth of the Missouri.... The sun glowed through the hazy air with a languid stifling heat....

This hazardous adventure included hunting, exploring, Indian feasts, and disease, and ultimately resulted in death for one of the two men; action and scenic movement alternate, and one catches in both the elemental exploits of men facing a wilderness.

In another instance the reader stands on the south shore of the Lower St. Lawrence in the late autumn of the 1680's.

> A ship from France, the last of the season, holds her way for Quebec.... Swelling her patched and dingy sails, she glides through the wilderness and the solitude where there is nothing but her to remind you of the great troubled world behind and the little troubled world before. On the far verge of the ocean-like river clouds and mountains mingle in dim confusion. Fresh gusts from the north dash waves against the ledges, sweep through the quivering spires of stiff and stunted fir-trees....

A local French curé rounds a point in his tiny canoe; he is on a trip through his parish, which extends sixty miles in a thin strip along the river bank. The reader follows the curé and is made aware, as if having followed him for a year, of the life he lives and the things he sees.

Or again, Parkman places the reader on an incoming ship and gives him the sensations of a new settler. Passing Quebec he moves up the river to Montreal and slowly down again as the narrator points out to him what is virtually the entire colony of New France (1670), the houses, feudal farms, cabins, huts, forests, and docks. Parkman made of this view of Quebec from a slowly approaching vessel a leitmotiv that binds together a century and a half of drama. The reader sees what Champlain first saw; later, the view from Phips' fleet off the rock, in 1690. One may follow various governors—Tracy, Frontenac, Montcalm—as they disembark from France and climb, "breathing heavily," the long steep path to the Upper Town, their new home. Finally one arrives with Wolfe in 1759 and stares at the same natural wonder, noting this time the redoubts, entrenchments, and especially the sheer impregnability of the cliff walls. Yet the cliff was breached, and Quebec, wracked for weeks by naval cannon, battered by invasion in its final hours, fell to the English; one enters the town with them and moves through its streets. In another few weeks only the occupation troops and civilian inhabitants remain.

> The fleet was gone; the great river was left a solitude; and the chill days of a fitful November passed over Quebec in alternations of rain and frost, sunshine and snow.... The Lower Town was a wilderness of scorched and crumbling walls.... On the right was a skeleton of tottering masonry, and the buildings on the left were a mass of ruin, where ragged boys were playing at see-saw among the fallen planks and timbers.... The Cathedral was burned to a shell.... The bombshells that fell through the roof had broken into the pavement, and as they burst had thrown up the bones and skulls of the dead from the graves beneath.

If there is any quality of visual truth which renders history timeless it is the impact of such a scene on those who have recently stood in the market square of Caen or by the river in Liège or in any nameless town on the Rhine, the Dnieper, the Vistula, or the Po. Ragged boys were playing see-saw in Babylon and Rome and will continue their game long after men have ceased turning their cities into wildernesses.

There are a score of other scenes through which Parkman conducts his reader: the coast line of Louisbourg and the islands off the Acadian peninsula, the wilderness west of Fort Cumberland when Braddock's army cut its way through, the Black Hills and the Platte River Valley, as backdrop for the expedition of La Vérendrye in the 1740's, but seen and described and preserved by Parkman in his own notebook a century later. Perhaps the most striking panorama of all is of an aerial flight over the wilderness battleground from Albany to Montreal. A prelude to the final years of the war it combines ingeniously a sense of over-all geography with the reality of a specific scene. The reader moves with a flock of wild fowl north in the spring, and the land moves under him "like a map"; frontier posts along the Hudson, the "geometric lines of Fort Edward"; then "the lake stretched northward, like some broad river, trenched between mountain ranges still leafless and gray.... Ticonderoga, with the flag of the Bourbons, like a flickering white speck, waving on its ramparts.... On the left the mountain wilderness of the Adirondacks, like a stormy sea congealed." The land slips beneath in utter solitude, and one feels detached from it even while caught up in it. Parkman's eye and controlled imagination served him so well that today one could scarcely improve the authenticity of his aerial perspective.

One finds a second and more difficult type of "visual" characterization in some of Parkman's expository writing. A broad historical movement is reduced to graphic terms, metaphorically or through the medium of human symbols, not because he sought to render history more accurate thereby but because such sketches afford glimpses of the structural background to more important or immediate matters; full, qualified accuracy would have made them interminable. Parkman's flair for imagery often enabled him to suggest the essential core of an idea where an analytical treatise would have put one no closer to it. One may dislike having to trust so absolutely a historian's ability to generalize.... But in matters where he had made himself expert his general conclusions have gone unchallenged; in any event his conclusion would be irrelevant in appraising his technique of visual characterization.

Consider, for example, this passage: "It was the nature of French colonization to seize upon detached strategic points, and hold them by the bayonet, forming no agricultural basis, but attracting the Indians by trade, and holding them by conversion. A musket, a rosary, and a pack of beaver skins may serve to represent it, and in fact it consisted of little else." In the first sentence five active verbs, balanced in two parts, establish a vision of military movement. Here the verbs require people as their subjects: the action is made personal because the reader "sees" people in action. The action, however, is reported impersonally and objectively, for the sentence focuses on "colonization," and its function is to contrast French colonization with what had been said about English colonization in a preceding paragraph. Parkman reduced nearly every element in this exposition to simple terms: point, bayonet, conversion, trade. One's understanding is further reinforced by his use of emblematic objects, which reduces to even simpler terms the "nature" of colonization. Yet in reduction one has not lost a sense of details, for the emblems stand not only for what they mean to us—and this is graphic enough—but for what has preceded them in the story.

Earlier in the series Parkman attempted a complex comparison of French and Canadian feudalism to show how the latter evolved from the former. In France the older feudal lords had gradually lost their power to the central monarchy. This plainly involved administrative and local political problems, for power must reside in people who deal with such problems, and power does not simply "change" without reference to people. Parkman described it in terms of the key person, the intendant, whom, in characterizing, he made use of to suggest the nature and quality of the change in government.

> He was the King's agent; of modest birth, springing from the legal class; owing his present to the King, and dependent on him for his future; learned in the law and trained to administration. It was by such instruments that the powerful centralization of the monarchy enforced itself throughout the kingdom, and, penetrating beneath the crust of old prescriptions, supplanted without seeming to supplant them. The courtier noble looked down in the pride of rank on the busy man in black at his side; but this man in black, with the troop of officials at his beck, controlled finance, the royal courts, public works, and all the administrative business of the province.

A visual experience conveys the entire nature of an institutional evolution.

To be sure Parkman often overpainted; in his desire to savor every ounce of romance in these vast historic movements he sometimes lapsed into the empty rhetoric of mid-century oratory: "Years rolled on. France [in 1543], long tossed among the surges of civil commotion, plunged at last into a gulf of fratricidal war. Blazing hamlets, sacked cities, fields streaming with slaughter, profaned altars, and ravished maidens, marked the track of the tornado." Almost as florid was his reflection upon Pitt's coming to head the king's government: "As Nature, languishing in chill vapors and dull smothering fogs, revives at the touch of the sun, so did England spring into fresh life under the kindling influence of one great man." Much of his earlier style defeats itself in a plethora of "sullen," "gloomy," "groaning," "solemn," "sluggish," "portentous"—all to characterize natural phenomena. But in his last two books he pared his phrases to the bone, and his words seem to hit with the impact of their original freshness.

"He must be a sharer or a spectator of the action he describes," Parkman wrote of the historian. One finds yet another, and most dramatic, type of visual characterization in the many accounts of small border raids and partisan exploits of small bands of men in the wilderness.... Not only had [Parkman] experienced the wilderness environment; his own temperament seemed to reflect the feelings and moods of the men who took part in them. What the records did not reveal he could supply. The re-creation of these exploits may well be considered the most convincing and permanent of his writings.

The striking element in them is the presence of the wilderness. It pervades every action. The miseries of weather and warfare occur in any military campaign, and will likewise appear in military histories. To the weather and the savagery Parkman added a greater note of drama: the struggle between man and an indifferent wilderness. Whenever men stepped off the edge of society and hacked a trail through the swamps, rocks, and windfalls they committed every nerve and sense to the elemental act of survival. To fail to move, to fail to act, was to lose ground. Only a few ever expected to make their living in the wilderness; the Indians did and the trappers did, but for the rest (including Parkman) the wilderness was a foreign environment in which to transact one's business or pleasure and get out. Man struggled to destroy it, to tame it, to enjoy it, as the case warranted. The stumbling forms of men whom Parkman in his imagination accompanied on their exploits did not adapt themselves permanently to the forest; they moved through it because to accomplish their purpose they could not avoid doing so. The wilderness formed a backdrop and a set of conditions imposed on those who waged border warfare. Describe the backdrop, convey the actual impact of elemental conditions, and the warfare becomes real. Parkman's style functioned not to recapture the subjective moods of other men but to re-create the all-coercive sensations of weather, forest, color, and movement, adding to them the dimension of personal experience. So well did he succeed that his readers, sensing the wilderness firsthand, move along with the men and react as they did.

A simple illustration of Parkman's re-creation may be had by comparing one of his descriptive paragraphs with that part of the original document on which the description is based. The annual report of Jesuit missionary activities for the year 1639 contained a firsthand account of the winter trip of two priests, Garnier and Jogues, through the forest to the Erie villages:

> In the middle of the journey, being unable to find a certain detour which would have led us to some cabins which are a little isolated, we were overtaken by night in a fir grove; we were in a damp place and could not find a drier one; we had great difficulty gathering a few pieces of wood to make a little fire, and a few dry branches for us to lie upon; the snow was threatening to put out our fire, but it ceased suddenly. God be praised, we passed the night very well.

From this bare account Parkman built the following picture.

> The forests were full of snow; and the soft, moist flakes were still falling thickly, obscuring the air, beplastering the gray trunks, weighing to the earth the boughs of spruce and pine, and hiding every footprint of the narrow path. The Fathers missed their way, and toiled on till night, shaking down at every step from the burdened branches a shower of fleecy white on their black cassocks. Night overtook them in a spruce swamp. Here they made a fire with great difficulty, cut the evergreen boughs, piled them for a bed, and lay down. The storm presently ceased; and, "praised be God," writes one of the travelers, "we passed a very good night."

Implicit in Parkman's rendering of the Jesuits' account was the historian's assumption of the continuity of experience. His imagination supplied the document with details that are valid in experience; and these details, completely consistent with the known facts, bring the reader closer to the event than does the original document. Parkman's version is not only truthful; it is memorably pictorial. Its qualities of color and mood transcend the facts to present an artistically valid version of the facts. It is history re-created.

A more sweeping scene of action enabled Parkman to employ a more complex visual technique. In the dead of winter, 1666, a war party of five hundred Frenchmen moved out over the "solid floor" of the St. Lawrence highway to attack the Dutch outpost of Schenectady. Their "snowshoes tied at their backs, [they] walked with difficulty and toil over the bare and slippery ice. A keen wind swept the river, and the fierce cold gnawed them to the bone.... Some fell in torpor and were dragged on by their comrades to the shivering bivouac." Here is a near view. But the scenes now alternate between a vast panorama and the detailed close-up, giving, as in a film, the dual awareness both of the event and of the men.

> Lake Champlain lay glaring in the winter sun, a sheet of spotless snow; and the wavy ridges of the Adirondacks bordered the dazzling landscape with the cold gray of their denuded forests. The long procession of weary men crept slowly on under the lee of the shore; and when night came they bivouacked by squads among the trees, dug away the snow with their snowshoes, piled it in a bank around them, built their fire in the middle, and crouched about it on beds of spruce or hemlock—while, as they lay close packed for mutual warmth, the winter sky arched them like a vault of burnished steel, sparkling with the cold diamond lustre of its myriads of stars.

The visual immediacy places the reader among the men. In seeing them simultaneously from a distance one maintains an objective detachment. The mood of the men is reflected by the impact of the wilderness on them. And all the while one is aware of the impersonal and awful vastness of the scene itself. Though the scenic description is from Parkman's own experience, the record of camping was a historical fact. To it Parkman added a quality of art which lifts both scene and event into a universal experience, suggestive of the qualities in history which he valued most.

In numerous other incidents the numbing terror of winter seems to sweep through the reader. One example is the account of the raid on Deerfield in 1704 and the subsequent fate of the prisoners. Such incidents comprised only a few out of hundreds which frontier settlers endured year by year for a generation. Parkman described the winter trek, three hundred miles to Montreal, in terse, subdued prose, relentless in pace. The terrible realism of the scene conveys a wintry horror all its own, drawing its power less from descriptive virtuosity than from a tension between word and event. The reader is told less than the facts but immediately perceives more.

> They came soon after to Green River, a stream then about knee-deep, and so swift that the water had not frozen. After wading it with difficulty, they climbed a snow-covered hill beyond. The minister, with strength almost spent, was permitted to rest a few moments at the top; and as the other prisoners passed by in turn, he questioned each for news of his wife. He was not left long in suspense. She had fallen from weakness in fording the stream, but gained her feet again, and, drenched in the icy current, struggled to the farther bank, when the savage who owned her, finding that she could not climb the hill, killed her with one stroke of his hatchet. Her body was left on the snow....

The details are presented stripped bare. Implicit in the prose is the impact of those same details as they are told to the minister. The serene detachment of the words establishes the minuteness of the incident amid a large sweep of time. But the incident engulfs the reader's sensations, for an instant completely involved in the shock and the tension. Events strange and remote, microscopic details of history, suddenly loom larger than life. Parkman has transfixed in one event part of the history of the New England border.

Other scenes reveal similar qualities. The midwinter attack on Grand Pré: a body of English occupation troops asleep in dry rooms, while sixty miles through the Acadian forest amid a white-swirling blizzard moved a band of young French partisans, "galants" and adventurers. Parkman clearly approved of them and admired their courage and military dash. The fight was bloody, the snow hampered movement, but when the surprised English surrendered, the two sides mingled (the officers did) in feasting and drinking while the snow continued to fall outside. Compared with these tales the fabulous exploits of Rogers and his Rangers are often overwritten. The details of fighting, raiding, and prisoner catching somehow dilute the immediacy and the visual identification displayed better elsewhere. The account of Rogers' defeat in 1758 in a winter ambush, nevertheless, is a masterful description of partisan warfare, and the subsequent story of the band lost in the forest with a delirious guide assumes significance and atmosphere of peculiar intensity. With careful objectivity Parkman suppressed all extraneous "subjective" speculation of whatever kind, though he permitted details from his own experience to fill out the structure. The fidelity of such accounts is the fidelity of documentary sources. The quality of visual "experiencing" is Parkman's.

One finds scattered through the history a few small incidents of unmistakably symbolic quality. They often center in some particular image or emblem, such as the cliffs of Quebec. . . . Their combined import suggests an awareness of the insignificance of men's efforts face to face with a wilderness which they have the audacity to proclaim as their own. It is by no means certain that Parkman determined in advance to present such a thread of poetic symbolism. Yet when the individual situations suggested themselves he was perceptive enough to grasp their deeper possibilities. One instance occurs in the first book of the series. By 1620 Quebec had been well settled as a military and trading post and a mission. There was only one agriculturally minded settler, a man named Hébert, who, with his wife, cultivated a vegetable garden. Years passed. The colony grew, trade prospered, Champlain envisaged an empire. But the brief invasion of an English fleet toppled the structure. The colony virtually disappeared, until, in 1632, Champlain returned with his men and found—"the stone cottage of the Héberts, surrounded with its vegetable gardens—the only thrifty spot amid a scene of neglect." In a later book, Parkman subtly needled the pretensions of the political animal when faced with an empty continent. The minions of His Most Christian Majesty paddled down the Ohio in 1749 and, in the presence of the astonished Indians who lived there, buried leaden plates in the soil, spoke before savage council fires, and departed having hoped thereby to prevent the English (or even the Indians) from seizing the land from its rightful owner. The most ironic scene of this nature depicts La Salle's party at the mouth of the Mississippi. "The broad bosom of the great Gulf opened on his sight, tossing its restless billows, limitless, voiceless, lonely as when born of chaos, without a sail, without a sign of life." They prepared a large pole bearing the arms and title of Louis the Great. While the Indians of the party looked on, the French chanted a *Te Deum* and La Salle proclaimed possession of the

river. The pole, a leaden plate, and a cross were planted on the sandy marshland. Renewed shouts and praises rang from their throats. Parkman added, "On that day the realm of France received on parchment a stupendous accession. The fertile plains of Texas; the vast basin of the Mississippi . . . a region of savannas and forests, sun-cracked deserts, and grassy prairies, watered by a thousand rivers, ranged by a thousand war-like tribes, passed beneath the sceptre of the Sultan of Versailles; and all by the virtue of a feeble human voice, inaudible at half a mile." Here is surely the essence of the dual focus in Parkman's writing—the vast panorama and the individual exploit; the one is a permanent feature, impersonal, meaningless; the other insignificantly tiny, personalized, yet the raw material of history. La Salle looms larger than any other figure in Parkman's works, and the scene at the river's mouth climaxes his career. But with superb irony Parkman contrasts the permanence of things with the feebleness of individuals, as if to say that for all of man's recorded exploits he makes no history by himself, and that one obtains little understanding of historical events except as one focuses his vision on the deeds, acts, and surroundings of men and not on the men themselves. In just these terms Parkman's artistry has made history and its meanings "real" for his readers. (pp. 53-67)

Otis A. Pease, in his Parkman's History: The Historian as Literary Artist, *Yale University Press, 1953, 86 p.*

SAMUEL ELIOT MORISON   (essay date 1955)

[*Morison was a prominent American historian whose most important works include the Pulitzer Prize-winning maritime histories* Admiral of the Ocean Sea *and* John Paul Jones. *In the following discussion of* The Oregon Trail, *Morison defends Parkman against the charge that his aristocratic sympathies blinded him to the importance of the American westward migration. Morison counters that Parkman went west to hunt and study Indians; the westward movement "was simply not his dish."*]

The Oregon Trail and its author have found detractors in recent years because Parkman was not interested in the American westward migration, in the thick of which he found himself; so he has been labeled a "Boston Brahmin," a "Harvard snob," "Federalist oligarch," "Proper Bostonian," and victim of "Anglo-Saxon superiority complex." Now, although any attempt to label, ticket or otherwise account for an individual like Francis Parkman is vain, and although nobody properly described by one of the above labels even thought of doing as he did, there is no doubt that he was a gentleman; and, even in the best sense of a much-abused word, an aristocrat. "My political faith," he wrote in 1875, "lies between two vicious extremes, democracy and absolute authority, each of which I detest, the more because it tends to react into the other." Like most gentlemen, he disliked equally the newly rich and democrats of the envious and pushing type; but like a true sportsman he loved primitive people like Indians and trappers and rough-and-ready white folk who were not trying to put on airs. (pp. 15-16)

It is true that Parkman was not interested in the westward movement; it was simply not his dish. He went West to hunt buffalo, view the scenery and study the Indians—which is what he did. Everyone praises Parkman for seeing through that eighteenth-century myth of the Noble Savage; why, then, scold him for not supporting the nineteenth-century myth of the Noble Democrat, or the twentieth-century myth of the Noble Western Pioneer? His guide Chatillon once remarked that "gentlemen of the right sort" could stand hardship better than ordinary people; and if Parkman had not been that kind of gentleman, he could never have surmounted his physical infirmities and we should have had no great history from his pen. (pp. 16-17)

Samuel Eliot Morison, in an introduction to The Parkman Reader *by Francis Parkman, edited by Samuel Eliot Morison, Little, Brown and Company, 1955, pp. 3-24.*

DAVID LEVIN   (essay date 1959)

[*The following excerpt is drawn from Levin's comparative study of the romantic literary conventions employed by Bancroft, Prescott, Motley, and Parkman. Focusing on Bancroft's* History of the United States, *Prescott's* The Conquest of Mexico, *Motley's* The Rise of the Dutch Republic, *and Parkman's* Montcalm and Wolf, *Levin argues that all four writers viewed historical composition as a literary art; in addition, they shared an interest in heroic historical figures, a belief in the inevitability of progress, and an enthusiasm for nature and the past. Here, Levin illustrates that the structure, characterization, and style of* Montcalm and Wolfe *place it "squarely" in the romantic tradition. Levin maintains that the structure of the work is "clearly dramatic" and can be divided into five acts, each of which highlights important historical events. Rather than focusing the history on one dominant hero, the critic notes, Parkman portrayed many characters whose exploits dramatize the differences between French absolutism and English liberty. In Levin's opinion, the best passages in* Montcalm and Wolfe *are those in which Parkman describes specific geographic sites and historical facts in simple, precise language; accordingly, "Parkman's best method of characterization was to reveal conventional contrasts by combining factual and unpretentious, abstract language with documents and with a careful arrangement of the action."*]

Montcalm and Wolfe, published more than forty years after *The Conquest of Mexico* and almost thirty years after *The Rise of the Dutch Republic,* represents the culmination not only of Parkman's history of *France and England in North America,* but of his long career. It seems at first, therefore, to be the least clearly "romantic" of all the major histories. By 1884 some of the more obviously conventional language had gone out of fashion. Even the ageless Bancroft, having brought his history down to 1789, was preparing to condense his twelve-volume work into six volumes from which much of his "nauseous grandiloquence" would be removed—and Parkman had learned to minimize the tritest of his own rhetoric. The impression is strengthened, too, by Parkman's emphasis on geographical precision and by his increased reliance on letters and journals to carry parts of his narrative. But the impression is misleading. In theme, in construction, in characterization, and even in style, Parkman's masterpiece stands squarely in the New England romantic tradition, and both its merits and its defects need to be examined in that context.

The subject itself offers a perfect conclusion to Parkman's work. In one decisive conflict it brings together all the racial, moral, and natural forces depicted in his earlier volumes. The issue is decided in action by a mortal battle between the two most admirably representative soldiers of France and England; in principle, by the torpid corruption of the worst representatives of "Absolutism" and the "vigorous" patriotism of the best representative of Liberty. Unstable Indians, sought as allies by both sides and "hounded on" at times by intriguing Catholic priests, vacillate, murder indiscriminately, and at last choose to help the country most clearly opposed to their own

true interests. Furthermore, this first major European war to originate in America begins with a frontier skirmish that introduces the hero of the American Revolution, and it also makes the Revolution inevitable. It opens the West to colonization; it ruins France as a world power; it establishes Britain as the "mother of nations" and Prussia as the foundation of modern Germany.... By thus giving immense political significance to the volumes that dramatize the results of Parkman's major themes, it deepens the meaning of his entire series.

Parkman recognized these advantages, and he used them to achieve a remarkable literary feat. Without the help of great prose, without achieving a single great characterization, he wrote the most completely successful of all the romantic histories. He controlled masterfully a much more complex narrative than *The Conquest of Mexico,* and avoided the worst of Motley's interpretative errors. And although he failed to control his inadequate rhetoric when faced with certain kinds of character and scenery, he exploited his documents, his precise sense of place, and the point of view to give events and some characters an immediacy that is rare in any general history.

Although Parkman did not divide *Montcalm and Wolfe* into books with separate titles, he did give it a clearly dramatic structure, which invites subdivision into a prologue and five acts. The prologue (chaps. 1-6) introduces "the combatants," states the theme, and moves to the departure of French and British armies for America. The first act (chaps. 7-10) follows Braddock's and Shirley's unsuccessful campaign against four French objectives. Act II (chaps. 11-17) moves from Montcalm's successes to the fall of Newcastle's government in England; Act III (chaps. 18-23), from the accession of Pitt to the "brink" of Canadian "ruin" after the loss of Fort Duquesne; Act IV (chaps. 24-28), from Wolfe's appointment as commanding general to the fall of Quebec; and the last act, to the Peace of Paris. (pp. 210-11)

The beauty of this structure ... lies less in Parkman's recognition of neatly placed crises than in the usefulness of these divisions to his conventions and his theme. He regarded this battle of "past against future," "united few" against "divided many," "moral torpor" against "moral vigor," as a test of principles, institutions, and national character. He had little doubt that France's failure in all three of these had caused her to waste the heroism that had been lavished on New France, and he designed *Montcalm and Wolfe* to dramatize the importance of those faults. Each of his major divisions is based not only on important events, but on contrasts in character that represent the essential contrast.

The prologue demonstrates through character and action that both countries are "weak in leadership" ... and that neither knows its own true interests. If the "effeminate libertine" king of France can give political control to "Jane Fish" Pompadour ..., the "dull, languid" England of 1750 is capable of trusting Newcastle. Especially in his prologue, Parkman establishes a balance between such characters, and, after beginning with a discussion of France and England, he extends this symmetry to America. There the jealous niggardliness of English colonial legislatures almost negates good leadership, and it becomes more damaging, for the moment, than the "heartless" fanaticism of French missionaries and the corruption of Canadian officials. As he turns from Europe to America and from the site of Pittsburgh in the West to Acadia in the East, Parkman can therefore set French "celerity" ... against English slowness; he can show that England temporarily lost the West because the provincial assemblies hindered Washington and Dinwiddie while the Canadian government encouraged Fathers Piquet and Le Loutre to foment Indian war. In the last chapter of this section he returns to Europe to focus once more on Newcastle, "a fantastic political jobber" . . . , and on Madame de Pompadour during the mutually deceitful preparations for war.

This entire section has a comic quality, for Parkman dramatizes the inefficiency, corruption, or villainy of all the "combatants": France, England, Canada and the British colonies. In his last chapter, moreover, he quotes satirical anecdotes from Horace Walpole's *George II* and Smollett's *Humphry Clinker* to illustrate Newcastle's incompetence, and he declares that at this time neither army had a great general. It is against this background that the naval phase of the European fighting begins—with a treacherous British attack on a French ship—and the stage is prepared for the "gallant bulldog" . . . , General Braddock.

The first act curtain rises on Braddock, whose march to Fort Duquesne opens a four-point campaign against French positions, and in peacetime. This action begins in foolish inefficiency and ends in disgraceful retreat. Braddock's stubbornness, the provincial assemblies' stinginess, and Dunbar's

cowardice leave the frontier completely unguarded. . . . True to his principles of balanced contrast, Parkman turns then to Acadia, where the faults of French character are equally costly. Vergor, the French commandant at Beauséjour, is a corrupt political appointee, whose cowardice offsets the fanatical vigor of Father Le Loutre. He surrenders even before the British have placed their cannon . . . , and Le Loutre's aggressive intrigues gain nothing but suffering for the Acadians, whom the British feel obliged to expel. In the rest of this act Parkman follows the same principles, showing that in the attack on Crown Point British leadership caused a "failure" that was "disguised under an incidental success" . . . and that all the British faults combined to defeat the fourth part of the original plan. . . . At the end British fortunes approach their nadir as the incompetent Loudon and Abercromby take over the army, and the French send murdering Indians all along the frontier. After one brief glimpse of Washington standing almost alone against this invasion . . . , Parkman devotes the last pages of this act to the Quakers' opposition to appropriations for defending the frontier. And in this British crisis the French accidentally find their best leader.

Here Parkman has deliberately passed by the declaration of war and Montcalm's victory at Oswego in order to give the

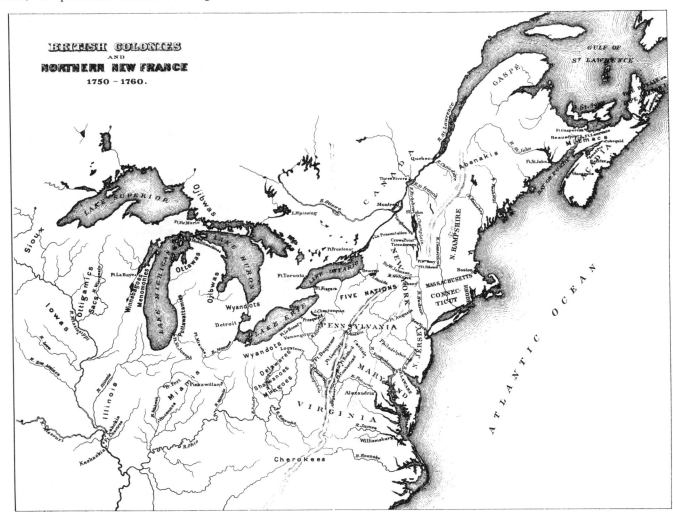

A map from Montcalm and Wolfe *that shows Northern New France and the British colonies as they existed between 1750 and 1760.*

French hero a more emphatic position and to avoid interrupting his account of the four-point British campaign. Montcalm, representing the best of French nobility, dominates Parkman's second act, but Parkman takes care to magnify his virtues by setting them against the French weaknesses that destroy New France. Opening this act in Europe with the formal declaration of war, Parkman sets the manly Frederick against Maria Theresa and Madame de Pompadour, whose "infatuated" policy neglects Canada; only then does he introduce Montcalm, who owes his appointment to the unwillingness of any court favorites to accept "a command in the backwoods." . . . Before dramatizing Montcalm's victories, Parkman also uses his arrival in New France as the occasion for describing Governor Vaudreuil, the boastful, jealous, indecisive provincial whose faults will prove so important at the climax. The action occurs in this context. Montcalm destroys Oswego while the British ministry delays assigning a new commander; and when Loudon (the choice of Newcastle) does come, he proves incompetent. In spite of the difficulties presented by Vaudreuil, Montcalm and his "man-eating savages" also destroy Fort William Henry, because Loudon has foolishly drawn British troops off the mainland for an abortive attack on Louisbourg. After these French successes, however, Parkman uses Montcalm's letters during the ensuing "winter of discontent" to give his first full report of Canadian official corruption. As he entitled his opening chapter **"Montcalm,"** he names his concluding chapter for the "sinister" Intendant, Bigot. By focusing here on this colossally representative peculator, he reveals Canada's "desperate" financial condition and prepares at the same time for the accession of William Pitt.

The critical third act restores England and France to a temporary balance and then swings toward the inevitable result. In the opening chapter on Pitt, Parkman returns again to Europe for his most energetic picture of Frederick—the incarnation, here, of indomitable Will. . . . Then, as "silken" King Louis dismisses the best two French ministers, the English middle class, sick of Newcastle, find in Pitt "a leader after their own heart." Parkman considers this change so important that he compares Pitt's influence to that of Nature: "as Nature, languishing in chill vapors and dull smothering fogs, revives at the touch of the sun, so did England spring into fresh life under the kindling influence of one great man." . . . Under Pitt's "robust impulsion" tough British sailors, who resemble Motley's Beggars of the Sea, win a series of naval victories, and in the first action of Pitt's three-point attack on New France the "ardent" General Wolfe . . . helps to take Louisbourg.

But even in this grand British victory one can see the balance of the two powers. This is the kind of battle Parkman loves, for besides occurring in a sublime natural setting, it reveals the best qualities of both countries. The officers and men on both sides of the walls prove to be good fellows, and the British win only by overcoming a "gallant defence." (pp. 211-14)

The fourth act curtain rises on Wolfe, for Parkman has decided to devote the entire act to the decisive battle for Quebec. Having reserved Wolfe's portrait and biography for this position, he is able to reveal the triumphant "spirit" just before Wolfe's greatest achievement. He brings Wolfe to Quebec, dramatizes the siege and the failure of Wolfe's first assault on the city, and then, as Vaudreuil boasts vainly once again, turns to the methodical Amherst's failure to mount a diversionary attack after capturing Niagara. This device accomplishes more than an increase in suspense, for it offers another contrast in character, and it demonstrates that Wolfe must now rely on himself alone if he wants to take Quebec before winter.

The climax, one of the best-known episodes in our literature, needs no rehearsal here, but one must notice that Parkman takes advantage of every opportunity to make it depend on the fundamental contrasts that are so important to his theme. Wolfe's only hope lies "in the composition of Montcalm's army" . . . , and although the "difficulties" of the assault seem "insurmountable," Wolfe's own indomitable spirit is aided by something more than chance. Captain of the slovenly guard at the point where Wolfe climbs the heights is none other than Vergor, the coward of Beauséjour, who has been acquitted of misconduct there only because Bigot and Vaudreuil have interceded for him. Vaudreuil, moreover, fails to send Montcalm the necessary reinforcements after the British have been discovered. And Montcalm himself indulges his French "impetuosity" . . . in attacking the firm British line. In this crucial battle, on the other hand, it is British "discipline" that wins, as the silent Redcoats hold their fire until the shouting French have rushed into confusion. At last, with Montcalm dying and Wolfe dead, Vaudreuil shamefully abandons Quebec, only to be persuaded too late that it might be defended. "The funeral of Montcalm" (who is buried in a shell-hole under a chapel) becomes "the funeral of New France" . . . ; and at the end of this act Vaudreuil tries to save himself by "belittling [Montcalm's] achievements and blackening his name." (p. 215)

Even the short fifth act, though it chronicles the decline of action, depends on conventional contrasts of character. Parkman raises the curtain on quiet scenes that depict not only the ruin of Quebec but the virtues of English troops, whom French nuns call "the most moderate of conquerors." . . . British "humanity" rescues a dying French soldier and the deed is rewarded by a warning of surprise attack; then a temporary French victory allows Indian converts to "murder, scalp, and mangle" most of the English wounded . . . ; and soon afterward a British commander prevents his unconverted Indian allies from scalping French prisoners. General Amherst, mobile at last after a ponderous start, is an ideal representative of the methodical British strength that would eventually have crushed New France in any case; and he also represents British moral indignation when he denies the Montreal garrison "the honors of war" because of "the infamous [Indian] barbarities" tolerated by French officers throughout the war. . . . As the American action ends, moreover, Parkman allows New England ministers to pronounce the final speeches: on future prosperity and the conversion of the wilderness from a trapper's paradise to "the glory and joy of the whole earth." (pp. 215-16)

Nor can the drama end before the Canadian peculators have been tried or before Pitt and Frederick have fought their battles to the end. Telescoping the European war as he has throughout the history, Parkman focuses on the two heroes in his last chapter of action—as Frederick barely avoids destruction and as George III's tyrannical jealousy forces Pitt, the people's "representative," to resign. . . . It is by bringing these two titans to rest that Parkman restores Europe to the moral lassitude of 1750. Although British armies and navies still feel "the impulsion" of Pitt's "imperial hand" and "the unconquerable spirit that he had aroused," the government is returned to "weak and unwilling hands." . . . And Frederick learns to restrain his insults and to live at peace with new tyrants. . . . Thus, before Parkman issues his final challenge to American leadership, he has painted his two exhausted heroes as examples: Frederick, deserted by England, but fighting on and rewarded at last "as by a miracle"; Pitt, carried to Parliament to thunder one last protest against an excessively generous peace treaty.

It is against these images, and the more remote ones of Mont-calm and Wolfe, that Parkman's last challenge must be read. His demand that democracy give the world "types of manhood as lofty and strong" as those of other systems does not pay mere "lip-service" to progress. It concludes a history orga-nized from beginning to end around contrasts that demonstrate his implicit faith in conventional ideas of progress.

Parkman's organization, then, is remarkably economical. While he exploits the genuinely dramatic arrangement that the course of the war invited him to fashion, he uses his characters with equal skill. Far from being embarrassed by the lack of a dom-inant hero for the entire history, he repeatedly brings forward the right man at the right time, dramatizing the merits and defects of both countries at appropriate moments of victory and defeat. Nor does his final evaluation of French and British institutions prevent him from sympathizing with both sides, for he does not need to deal directly with the absolute moral cleavage that divides Motley's history, and he has within the French lines a hero from whose pathetic, thoroughly moral point of view he can reveal the worst effects of bad government. This last technique serves him especially well during the winter after each of Montcalm's campaigns—an occasion for filling in the narrative with the observations on Canadian society and official corruption that Montcalm wrote during the long months in Montreal and Quebec. In this way Parkman describes the society without seeming to interrupt his narrative of military action, and he uses the same kind of device to provide important information about the English colonies. Besides making his military narrative reveal the complex relationship between colonial legislatures and governors, he often advances his nar-rative by using contemporary journals that illustrate the man-ners of provincial soldiers, the methods of recruiting, the perils of life on the frontier.

Parkman's acute awareness of geography also affects his or-ganization. Besides arranging his acts so that he can summarize European events at the beginning or end of every one of them, he keeps always before the reader some sense of the vast con-tinent for which the two nations fought. His first paragraph on America emphasizes the "boundless interior" controlled by the French posts from Canada to Louisiana . . . , and his final paragraph on France points out the "two island rocks . . . that the victors had given her for drying her codfish." . . . In the drama that he enacts between these opposite pictures he moves periodically from western to eastern campaigns while centering most of the action in the recurrent battles along the short line from Albany to Montreal. Regularly, moreover, he takes the reader inside a raiding party or an army—often as it marches over wild country that has already been "won" by one side or the other—and he thus communicates a sense not only of immediacy but of the terror and futility of military conquest in the forest. . . . The first British success at Crown Point and Montcalm's victories at Oswego, Fort William Henry, and Ticonderoga are all equally barren. Soon after each one of them the scene becomes a "wild solitude" again. (pp. 216-17)

The characterization in *Montcalm and Wolfe* needs little de-tailed analysis . . . , for its chief literary value lies in the skill with which Parkman built the conventional contrasts into his dramatic structure. Although he chose to tell the story in only half the space that Motley had used in *The Rise of the Dutch Republic*, he was obliged to portray almost as many characters, and most of them were well known even through American histories before he started to write *Montcalm and Wolfe*. Like Prescott, moreover, he was interested in the influence and

experience of the individual character without having either the desire or the ability to communicate more than the broad outlines of a few traits. For these reasons, and because he had no dominant hero, he did not devote as much space to any one person as Motley and Prescott had given to each of several figures. He relied on concise summaries and action itself to portray most of his cast, and for the few characters whom he considered most important he employed more of the conven-tional rhetoric and more extensive quotations from their letters. If these techniques prevented him from achieving more than one distinguished portrait, they also spared him the worst dis-tortions of Motley and Prescott, and they focused attention on his theme and the developing action. Only when he trusted his most "elevated" rhetoric did the method fail him.

The line of characters projected in *Montcalm and Wolfe* in-cludes nearly every type to be found in the romantic histories. Vigorous English, French, and American aristocrats represent the natural, the normal; Wolfe, Pitt, Howe, Montcalm, and Washington stand at the center. To their right extends a row of increasingly less natural characters: the sturdy governors Dinwiddie and Shirley; the typical generals, from Braddock the "bulldog" and Amherst the slow mover to the competent French officers and the incompetent Loudon and Abercromby; the fanatical priests and the dishonest Canadian officials; and, at the extreme, Newcastle, George III, Louis XV and his Pom-padour. On the left the file includes fewer distinct individuals, but the progression from Rogers "the woodsman" to the few good Indians and the crowds of "man-eating savages" is per-fectly clear. (pp. 217-18)

Parkman's interest centers less on the complexity of individual character than on a few qualities relevant to his own situation and to his conventional interpretation of the war. He seems, moreover, to concentrate primarily on communicating a sense of the character's experience, and on a particular kind of ex-perience. From Frederick Post and a nameless pioneer "buried in the woods . . . in an appalling loneliness" . . . to Frederick the Great and Montcalm and Wolfe themselves, he focuses repeatedly on lonely effort in the midst of terrifying danger, overwhelming physical difficulties, incompetent support, im-placable enemies. He communicates these and other qualities most effectively when he stays close to the documents and the specific fact and when he uses his least inflated language.

When he turns to Pitt, Frederick, and Washington . . . the inadequacy of his rhetoric becomes . . . damaging, for in these characterizations he must stand farther away from the docu-ments, and the kind of pose in which he wants to display these men persuades him to use an energetic language that often escapes his control. Parkman's forceful rhythm, his occasion-ally consistent imagery . . . , and the energy of the historical characters save him from complete failure in these passages, but trite, inconsistent imagery, and shoddy diction repeatedly betray him. (pp. 220-21)

Although the faults [of Parkman's prose style] cannot be blamed entirely on the kind of characters that provoked them, they usually occur when Parkman expresses strong feeling—his own or that of his characters. In moments of extreme crisis for his Byronic heroes his diction becomes extremely unreliable. Just as a crucial test of La Salle's endurance and a Northern defeat in the Civil War had led Parkman to write two of the worst paragraphs he ever published, so in *Montcalm and Wolfe* his worst passages describe Frederick and Pitt; and his diction also betrays him in some of Wolfe's moments of decision. When he says, "Here was Wolfe's best hope. This failing, his only chance was audacity. The game was desperate; but, intrepid gamester as he was in war, he was a man, in the last resort, to stake everything on the cast of the dice'' . . . , his combination of short sentences, heroic rhythm, and periodic construction only calls attention to the triteness of his figures. When he describes the battle itself, however, his quotations and his intense interest in the facts and the experience help him to avoid this kind of error.

One must conclude, then, that Parkman's best method of characterization was to reveal conventional contrasts by combining factual and unpretentious, abstract language with documents and with a careful arrangement of the action. He simply did not have Motley's talent for conveying visual images of character. (pp. 221-22)

If the weakness of Parkman's prose lies in his most self-consciously heroic diction and his trite imagery, its great strength comes from his acute sense of specific place and specific fact, and from his brilliant control of the pace of his narrative. In spite of his embarrassing faults, Parkman was indeed a good writer. Much of his prose does have a "hard grace," but his most "energetic" prose is often his least precise. His best prose is his ordinary exposition, his least pretentious narrative—those relatively unadorned passages which, dominating most of the two volumes, communicate social information, analyze the opposing nations' arguments . . . , prepare the reader carefully for a particular action, bring the reader inside one camp or another; those passages which, by joining specific fact to general action, give the narrative its admirable order.

One can see the value of this kind of prose by examining Parkman's account of a single battle, Sir William Johnson's defeat of Baron Dieskau on the site of Fort William Henry. Parkman approaches the action by describing not only the terrain but each of the two armies. Since this is the first battle involving New England militia, he wants to describe Johnson's "crude" army with some care, while remaining true to his principle of narrative economy. He chooses, therefore, to depict the army as it waits nervously for supplies. He begins with a paragraph on some of the colonial officers, including future heroes of the Revolution, and then he describes the men:

> The soldiers were no soldiers, but farmers and farmers' sons who had volunteered for the summer campaign. One of the corps had a blue uniform faced with red. The rest wore their daily clothing. Blankets had been served out to them by the several provinces, but the greater part brought their own guns; some under the penalty of a fine if they came without them, and some under the inducement of a reward. They had no bayonets, but carried hatchets in their belts as a sort of substitute. At their sides were slung powder-horns, on which, in the leisure of the camp, they carved quaint devices with the points of their jack-knives. They came chiefly from plain New England homesteads,— rustic abodes, unpainted and dingy, with long well-sweeps, capacious barns, rough fields of pumpkins and corn, and vast kitchen chimneys, above which in winter hung squashes to keep them from frost, and guns to keep them from rust.
>
> (pp. 223-24)

This paragraph illustrates Parkman's most effective description. He does not paint a detailed picture, but instead names

significant objects. The short sentences that set the one uniform against daily clothing; the moderate alliteration, the repetition, the simple diction, and the forceful rhythm gained from balanced constructions and periodic emphasis—these function as well as *farmers, plain homesteads, rustic abodes,* and the final picture to emphasize the naturalness of the men. Some of the objects and statements, moreover, clearly suggest a double significance. The contrast between "fine" and "reward" suggests the niggardliness and lack of concert that Parkman has just been deploring in English colonial legislatures; the quaint devices carved on the powder horns with jacknives imply both rude individuality and the boredom of waiting in camp; the guns above the chimneys suggest self-reliance and constant preparedness for danger.

But the full value of this paragraph becomes clear only as one sees its place in the narrative. Parkman stays with Johnson's force until it has finally moved to Lake George, and then, as the British sentries are posted, he turns to the French army. He establishes the moral contrast simply by paraphrasing Baron Dieskau's order telling the Indians "not to amuse themselves by taking scalps till the enemy is entirely defeated, since they can kill ten men in the time required to scalp one." And he drives home the point by quoting from a letter of Dieskau's:

> "They drive us crazy," he says, "from morning till night. There is no end to their demands. They have already eaten five oxen and as many hogs, without counting the kegs of brandy they have drunk. In short, one needs the patience of an angel to get on with these devils; and yet one must always force himself to seem pleased with them."
>
> (p. 224)

This idiomatic translation of Dieskau's letter exemplifies the great merit of Parkman's narrative technique. His short sentences name things and concentrate attention on the participant's point of view, stressing the problems of a competent officer faced with difficulties beyond his control. Since the Indians' irresponsibility is the main cause of Dieskau's eventual defeat . . . , their inferiority to the New England farmers has particular significance here, and Dieskau's allusion to devils justifies the imagery that Parkman himself applies to fighting savages. It is through the Indians, moreover, that Parkman, in the next sentence, again sets his narrative in motion. Reluctant even to "go out as scouts," they finally do bring in an English captive whose "patriotic falsehood" persuades Dieskau to march against the British.

The same kind of technique leads one to the action itself. Since the first engagement is a French-Indian ambush that drives the English back to their camp, Parkman follows the French and Indian army to the "snare," leaving them only after he has stationed "a Canadian or a savage, with gun cocked and ears intent," behind "every bush." . . . Then, having created the desired suspense, he uses English documents to place the reader inside the vanguard who march into the trap. He dramatizes both Johnson's "complete misconception" of the size of the French force, and the eloquent warning of the Mohawk chief Hendrick, the noblest Indian of the entire history, against marching out to meet the French. And he quotes from the hasty letter of a New England officer who will be killed in the ambush. (pp. 224-25)

After this remarkable preparation neither the skirmish nor the decisive battle requires "elevated" prose. One sees "some sign of an enemy'' through ''the sharp eye of old Hendrick,'' and the firing begins ''at that instant.'' With a fine sense of drama Parkman recognizes that the best way he can suggest the suddenness of injury or death is to rely on flat statements of fact: ''Hendrick's horse was shot down, and the chief was killed with a bayonet as he tried to rise. [Colonel] Williams, seeing a rising ground on his right, made for it, calling on his men to follow; but as he climbed the slope, guns flashed from the bushes, and a shot through the brain laid him dead.'' (p. 225)

When he comes to the climax of the ensuing battle, Parkman achieves an artistic triumph by combining all these methods, for he concentrates once again on Dieskau. At the moment when an attack would surely have succeeded, the ''French Indians'' and Canadians had refused to obey, and some of the Indians had then been ''driven off by a few shells dropped among them.'' With plain statement and Dieskau's own words, then, Parkman impels one to look more closely at the particular action and its meaning than any of the other historians can manage to do:

> At length Dieskau, exposing himself within short range of the English line, was hit in the leg. His adjutant, Montreuil, himself wounded, came to his aid, and was washing the injured limb with brandy, when the unfortunate commander was again hit in the knee and thigh. He seated himself behind a tree while the Adjutant called two Canadians to carry him to the rear. One of them was instantly shot down. Montreuil took his place; but Dieskau refused to be moved, bitterly denounced the Canadians and Indians, and ordered the Adjutant to leave him and lead the regulars in a last effort against the camp.
>
> It was too late. Johnson's men, singly or in small squads, were already crossing their row of logs; and in a few moments the whole dashed forward with a shout, falling upon the enemy with hatchets and the butts of their guns. The French and their allies fled. The wounded General still sat helpless by the tree, when he saw a soldier aiming at him. He signed to the man not to fire; but he pulled the trigger, shot him across the hips, leaped upon him, and ordered him in French to surrender. ''I said,'' writes Dieskau, '' 'You rascal, why did you fire? You see a man lying in his blood on the ground, and you shoot him!' He answered: 'How did I know that you had not got a pistol? I had rather kill the devil than have the devil kill me.' 'You are a Frenchman?' I asked. 'Yes,' he replied; 'it is more than ten years since I left Canada'; whereupon several others fell on me and stripped me. I told them to carry me to their general, which they did. On learning who I was, he sent for surgeons, and, though wounded himself, refused all assistance till my wounds were dressed.''

Here Parkman comes almost as near as Mark Twain and Stephen Crane to the kind of plain statement in which Ernest Hemingway describes violent action. Dieskau does not, like Frederic Henry, put his hand into the hole where his knee has been, but one sees his helplessness just as clearly; not only the picture of the man sitting down, but the numerous blunt sentences and the naked, monosyllabic statement of fact suggest the incoherence and awful tension of the action. As Dieskau's position suffices to reveal his helplessness, so his point of view, his first-hand report, and Parkman's blunt assertion of other facts (''The French and their allies fled.'') communicate the meaning of the episode.

Although Parkman concentrates his simplest language in these climactic paragraphs, scarcely a line in the twenty-six-page chapter departs from the relatively simple diction and plain statement that make them so admirably effective. Throughout the chapter Parkman subordinates rhetoric to fact, and his selection and placement of facts—from the description of Johnson's soldiers to Johnson's restraint of the Mohawks who want to torture Dieskau—express his judgment much more effectively than his few figurative efforts can express it. (pp. 225-26)

> *David Levin, '' 'Montcalm and Wolfe','' in his* History as Romantic Art: Bancroft, Prescott, Motley, and Parkman, *Stanford University Press, 1959, pp. 210-26.*

BRUCE CATTON   (essay date 1960)

[*Catton was a popular American historian who wrote extensively on the Civil War. Here, he reviews* Letters of Francis Parkman, *which he considers a valuable account of the author's dogged determination to complete his historical project.*]

One of the benefits that come from the study of history, which after all is nothing more than the examination of assorted human lives, is the recurrent discovery that the human spirit is basically unconquerable.... Simple strength of will can win over the longest odds. Wish hard enough and what you wish for can come true. Possibly the moral, if a moral must be looked for, is that the dreams we serve had better be lofty; some day they may turn into realities.

One is bound to indulge in some such reflections when one examines the career of the greatest of all American historians, Francis Parkman. This man, who combined the very best in professional capacity and dedication with the talents of a superlative literary craftsman, pulled himself up by his own bootstraps. He had all the gifts a historian could wish for, but he also had handicaps enough to destroy all that had been given him. What finally made him and his work imperishable was nothing less than strength of will. Sheer determination beat the odds.

A good way to see what this man was like, and to understand how he did the splendid things he did, is to read the assembled *Letters of Francis Parkman.* ... Covering the long span from his late teens in 1841 to the autumn of his death in 1893, these letters show Parkman driving on relentlessly to do, finally, what he set out to do—to describe the conflict in colonial America of English, French, and Indians which laid the foundation for the American nation, and to do it so accurately and with such narrative skill that no one since then has had to cover the same ground. (p. 109)

He had certain advantages. He was born a Boston Brahmin, heir to a comfortable fortune. He got, at Harvard, as good an education as the America of that day could provide—he became master of five languages, studied history under the stimulating Jared Sparks, got an excellent grounding in the classics, and all in all was as well prepared for the historian's task as any young man could hope to be.

But he had problems. Over and over, his letters refer to his unending struggle with "the enemy"—his own atrocious health; and here he had troubles enough to overthrow all of his advantages. . . . The enemy was always with him, and this enemy was powerful enough to make any ordinary mortal abandon forever the demanding tasks of unending research and careful writing.

Parkman, of course, was not an ordinary man. He made himself do the things he wanted to do, overriding his physical handicaps by simple determination; and he was finally able to write, "If I had my life to live over again I would follow exactly the same course again, only with less vehemence." The qualifying note should not, perhaps, be taken seriously; the vehemence was at the heart of the matter, and with less of it he probably could not have succeeded. (pp. 109-10)

In his introduction to this collection of letters Mr. Jacobs remarks that the main figures in Parkman's books—Pontiac, Frontenac, La Salle, Wolfe, Montcalm, and the rest—"are not remembered primarily because of their accomplishments but because Parkman wrote about them" [see Additional Bibliography]. True enough; but what a struggle it took to produce those books! The determination that took a sick man into the Indian wilds, and that kept an almost blind man burrowing about year after year in dusty books on the unending quest for facts, seems fully as remarkable and as admirable as the artistic skill that produced enduring classics. (p. 110)

> *Bruce Catton, "Defeating the Enemy," in* American Heritage, *Vol. XII, No. 1, December, 1960, pp. 109-10.*

W. J. ECCLES (essay date 1961)

[*Eccles condemns* France and England in North America *as historically inaccurate. According to the critic, Parkman presented a biased interpretation of New France's history, one that conformed to his belief in the inevitability of progress. Because he viewed the French, the Indians, absolutism, and Catholicism as stumbling blocks to progress, Eccles writes, Parkman often distorted and suppressed facts in order to portray them as evil.*]

Between the years 1851 and 1892 Francis Parkman wrote his epic series, *France and England in North America.* From the date of their first appearance these eight volumes have continued to influence the interpretation of the early history of Canada. Recently, however, some few historians have begun to study the history of New France, not in the works of Parkman, but in the original documents, and their depictions of events and portrayals of the more important personages are markedly at variance with his. This departure cannot be accounted for by the discovery of much new evidence, rather, it arises from the fact that the historian today selects and evaluates historical evidence in the light of values and basic assumptions that differ from those in vogue in Parkman's time.

For example: Parkman, in company with the other Whig historians, always used the concept of Progress to judge the past. He was convinced that the onward march of Progress was inevitable; it might be hindered by reactionary forces, but eventually all opposition would be overcome. It seemed to him that this was as natural a law as that water must run downhill; a river might have to twist and turn, seep slowly through swamps, or it might be dammed, but its onward course could not be halted for long. This was the basic premise that underlay his study of the history of New France. To him it was simply a conflict between the forces of light and the forces of darkness,

between the nation of Progress and the nation that stood opposed to it; between Anglo-Saxon Protestant liberty—which was the hallmark of Progress—and French Roman Catholic absolutism. (p. 163)

Though his basic theme is, to say the least, debatable, it did enable him to select and organize his material in a simple, coherent framework which makes the completed works very readable. As literature they rate very highly indeed. By means of this device they are endowed with the epic qualities of Greek tragedy. We have the colony of New France, an outpost of French absolutism, struggling heroically against tremendous odds, coming very close to final victory, but eventually, and inevitably, brought low because it has been foreordained that Progress will win out. In the final analysis, French Catholic absolutism cannot, by the very nature of things, prevail against Anglo-Saxon Protestant liberty. As history, however, Parkman's works are of considerably less value because, owing to this frame of reference, his approach was essentially uncritical. There was no need to seek very far to discover why New France was defeated, the reasons were obvious. Nor was there need to discover what society was really like in New France, enough to indicate that it compared very unfavorably with that of the English colonies.

In his description of Canadian society Parkman made extensive use of his source material, relating incidents from the original documents which convey a clear, albeit superficial and distorted impression of the social environment. He also used commendable critical judgment on occasion, rejecting, for example, the rather scurrilous tales of La Hontan concerning the morals of the emigrant girls sent to Canada. It is clear, however, that his opinion of this society was strongly influenced by the prevailing concept of his own day, that of Social Darwinism. Thus he wrote: "One of the faults of his [Louis XIV's] rule is the excess of his benevolence; for not only did he give money to support parish priests, build churches, and aid the seminary, the Ursulines, the missions, and the hospitals; but he established a fund destined, among other objects, to relieve indigent persons, subsidized nearly every branch of trade and industry, and in other instances did for the colonists what they would far better have learned to do for themselves." The latter-day historian, accustomed to the social philosophy of the welfare state, would, of course, be less likely to see anything wrong with all this.

Again, in commenting on justice Parkman stated that it "seems to have been administered on the whole fairly; and judges of all grades often interposed in their personal capacity to bring parties to an agreement without a trial. From head to foot, the government kept its attitude of paternity." Intervention by the intendant to protect the habitants from extortion by their seigneurs he described as "well-meaning despotism." Similarly, Canadian economic activity suffered from the inexcusable lack of nineteenth-century laissez-faire concepts: "The besetting evil of trade and industry in Canada was the habit they contracted, and were encouraged to contract, of depending on the direct aid of government. Not a new enterprise was set on foot without a petition to the King to lend a helping hand." This last statement was pure supposition on Parkman's part; it may be true, but he could never have proved it. Moreover, although there can be no doubt that Canadian economic activity was nowhere near as flourishing as that of the English colonies, less state aid would not have caused it to thrive; just the reverse, more likely. In any event, this particular yardstick gives very inaccurate measurements.

Parkman's belief in the inevitability of Progress also explains, in large measure, his Olympian style of writing. He had only to select the evidence to prove the obvious; he was never beset with doubts in his interpretation of the evidence; there are none of those cautious, qualifying phrases which are the crutches of many latter-day historians who fear the hostile reviewer. The absence of such weakening phrases gives Parkman's writing strength and clarity, lends it the ring of conviction. This is, of course, greatly strengthened by his use of primary source material. His familiarity with the documents is most praiseworthy; unfortunately, however, lengthy sections of his volumes were put together with scissors and paste, being little more than translations of long passages from the documents. This is particularly true of *The Jesuits in North America* and the two volumes of the inaptly titled *A Half Century of Conflict*. Both works would have been much improved by the liberal use of a blue pencil.

In his treatment of the clergy in New France, it is quite apparent that he was anticlerical, and more particularly, anti-Jesuit; but his prejudice was based squarely on political grounds. That it was what the clergy represented that caused him to go to extremes is evidenced by his denunciation of the Puritan regime in New England in terms almost as strong as those used against the Jesuits, accusing the Puritans of having established ''one of the most detestable theocracies on record.'' The clergy in both New France and New England were the enemies of liberty of conscience, of Progress. This was their mortal sin. The Jesuits were, he was convinced, far more the political agents of French and Papal absolutism than they were the agents of God. He had great admiration for them as men; their fortitude in the face of terrible hardship and their superhuman courage when tortured by the Iroquois he depicted in glowing passages, but he could never forget that they espoused the wrong cause. (pp. 164-66)

The aims of the Jesuits he succinctly described as: ''The Church to rule the world; the Pope to rule the Church; the Jesuits to rule the Pope,—such was and is the simple programme of the Order of Jesus. . . .'' Thus, when discussing the choice of Laval as bishop at Quebec, he made the appointment appear to be a sinister Jesuit plot, stating: ''The Jesuits, adepts in human nature, had made a sagacious choice when they put forward this conscientious, zealous, dogged and pugnacious priest to fight their battles. Nor were they ill pleased that, for the present, he was not Bishop of Canada, but only vicar apostolic; for such being the case, they could have him recalled if on trial they did not like him, while an unacceptable bishop would be an evil past remedy.'' Parkman cited no evidence to support the imputing of these motives to the Jesuits; it was pure supposition on his part. The nature of the evidence, however, lent itself to such hostile interpretations. Since Colbert was notably anticlerical and particularly so of the Jesuits, those in the colony who wished to pay their court to the great minister found a receptive audience when they accused the Jesuits of all manner of crimes. In the letters and dispatches of Jean Talon, Frontenac, La Salle, and La Mothe Cadillac, Parkman found much ammunition, and he invariably accepted their statements at face value. Those of the Jesuits and Bishop Laval, on the other hand, he regarded as inadmissible. Not satisfied with all this, however, he quoted from a sermon delivered by a Jesuit in Montreal on November 1, 1872, to condemn the Jesuits of two centuries earlier. This, one is inclined to think, is carrying prejudice a little too far.

An illustration from Montcalm and Wolfe *depicting the city of Quebec at the time of the English conquest.*

In his characterization of Bishop Laval also, Parkman used rather dubious methods. To introduce this "tool of the Jesuits" he first of all devoted over five pages to the Hermitage at Caen where Laval resided for a time. The description, dwelling at great length on the religious fanaticism of the inmates, was well calculated to stimulate revulsion in the reader. Having thus damned Laval with guilt by association, he rather lamely concluded that although the excesses described "took place after Laval had left the Hermitage, they serve to characterize the school in which he was formed; or, more justly speaking, to show its more extravagant side." Unfortunately, the character of Laval established in the unwary reader's mind by the preceding five pages of vivid description would not likely be altered by this last brief, qualifying statement. Moreover, Parkman went on to negate this qualification by stating: "In vindicating the assumed rights of the Church, he invaded the rights of others, and used means from which a healthy conscience would have shrunk. . . . He was penetrated by the poisonous casuistry of the Jesuits, based on the assumption that all means are permitted when the end is the service of God. . . ." The Jesuits Parkman could admire as men, but in Laval he could find no redeeming features. Laval had never endured the hardship of life in an Indian village, or withstood torture at the hands of the Iroquois as the Jesuits had. He represented clerical absolutism incarnate, the worst of all the enemies of Progress. Laval, he wrote, "was one of those who by nature lean always to the side of authority; and in the English Revolution he would inevitably have stood for the Stuarts; or, in the American Revolution for the Crown. . . . His life was one long assertion of the authority of the Church, and this authority was lodged in himself." There can be no doubt that Laval was possessed of a strong character—and considering the magnitude of his task, he needed it—but the evidence will not sustain the Laval depicted by Parkman; there are no shades of gray in this portrait, it is all black; in fact it is nothing more than a very hostile caricature.

Parkman's delineation of lay figures is also colored, to a considerable degree, by the theme of Progress; but there are other influences at work as well. He fully subscribed, as one would expect, to the Great Man concept of history—witness his eulogies of Pitt, Frederick II, and Washington—and the romantic outlook is also much in evidence. His two full-length studies of outstanding figures, Frontenac and La Salle, illustrate these influences very clearly. There were other men in the history of New France of equal or even greater stature than either of these: Champlain, Charles le Moyne, Iberville, Maisonneuve, Gilles Hocquart, Champigny, to mention a few. Perhaps the main reason why he chose Frontenac and La Salle was that there was so much evidence readily available. La Salle's supporters were prolific writers, and Frontenac was certainly a very skilled advocate on his own behalf. They had, in fact, virtually written the books for Parkman; he had merely to edit them. Moreover, both men had fought persistently against the clergy in New France; therefore, if they were not exactly on the side of the Angels of Progress, they at least were lending them a hand. Both men had suffered adversity, both had occupied the center of the stage, the one in New France, the other in the West. They were made to order for Parkman. All that was needed, then, was to accept at face value what Frontenac and La Salle said of themselves and refute or disregard evidence that conflicted with their statements. Thus it is that in these volumes Parkman was at his weakest as a historian and at his best as a writer of romantic epic literature.

Frontenac was on one occasion actually made to appear as an apostle of Progress. Of his convoking of the meeting of the four estates at Quebec, Parkman declared: "Like many of his station, Frontenac was not in full sympathy with the centralizing movement of the time, which tended to level ancient rights, privileges, and prescriptions under the ponderous roller of the monarchical administration. He looked back with regret to the day when the three orders of the State—clergy, nobles, and commons—had a place and a power in the direction of national affairs." There is not a shred of evidence to support this statement; in fact, Frontenac specifically denied that he had ever had any such intention, but Parkman chose to ignore evidence not in accord with his views. Similarly, when Frontenac was finally dismissed from his post and recalled to France in disgrace, Parkman claimed: "he left behind him an impression, very general among the people, that, if danger threatened the colony, Count Frontenac was the man for the hour." On the contrary, he left just the reverse impression, and Parkman was clearly ignoring all the evidence. Worse still, the reader is led to believe that since Frontenac did return to New France when the colony was in grave danger, he was sent back to retrieve the situation. Though the evidence denies any such conclusion, several eminent historians have stumbled blindly into the pitfall set by Parkman; and so the myth of Frontenac, the Savior of New France, has been perpetuated. In his final estimate of Frontenac, however, it is clear that it was the turbulent Governor's colorful character that most appealed to him; despite the fact that he had consistently depicted Frontenac as a great man, he declared at the end that "greatness must be denied him." Why this should be, he does not explain. One can guess that it was because Frontenac had been engaged on the wrong side in the struggle between absolutism and Progress, and in the final analysis Parkman could not condone this.

In the volume on La Salle, however, Parkman's sympathies were completely engaged for his subject. Any evidence that might have detracted from the luster of this "great man" was swept aside. Perhaps it would be demanding too much to expect Parkman to have ferreted out all the evidence concerning La Salle's connection with the Bernou, Renaudot, Villermont clique of court intriguers, as Jean Delanglez was later to do so admirably, but one could expect him to take into account the obvious. And the most obvious thing about La Salle was that he was mentally deranged; moreover, his malady grew markedly worse toward the end of his career. Indeed, the evidence for this is so strong that even Parkman was obliged to mention it, but he did so as the only alternative to admitting that La Salle was a scoundrel. After describing La Salle's actions, which had convinced those associated with him that he must be mad, Parkman stated: "It is difficult not to see in all this the chimera of an overwrought brain, no longer able to distinguish between the possible and the impossible." With this matter dismissed, La Salle was thereafter treated as though no doubts as to either his sanity or his probity had ever existed. La Salle, in Parkman's final assessment, was possessed of the "Roman virtues" and, "beset by a throng of enemies, he stands, like the King of Israel, head and shoulders above them all." There is the Great Man concept; and along with it goes the final and even greater tribute: "America owes him an enduring memory; for in this masculine figure she sees the pioneer who guided her to the possession of her richest heritage." Here, in the eyes of Parkman, lies the true greatness of La Salle for which all else must be forgiven. He was, after all, the herald of Progress.

In his attitude toward the North American Indians, however, Parkman shed all his romanticism. . . . To Parkman the Indian was not the noble savage, but a treacherous, murdering, fiend incarnate, existing in filth and squalor—an opinion perhaps influenced by his close contacts with the Plains Indians at a time when the Americans were bent on exterminating the remnants of this Stone Age civilization. But there is more to it than that. To Parkman the Indians were nothing more than a stumbling block in the path of Progress. (pp. 167-72)

In depicting the raids by the Canadians and their Indian allies on the frontiers of the English colonies, Parkman gave us his most vivid writing. Reading his description of the Deerfield massacre, or the attacks on the western frontier during the Seven Years' War, makes one feel almost as though he were a participant—but always on the English side. These raids were invariably treated as savage, unprovoked aggression against innocent English colonial settlers, and gory details were presented to strengthen the case; to the Deerfield raid alone he devoted thirty-nine pages. He was quite unable to conceive that the Indian tribes were fighting desperately against overwhelming odds to retain their ancient hunting grounds in the face of English encroachment. He could not view the struggle from the other camp, that of the Indian. Nor did he ever ask himself why the Indians should have been expected to fight according to European rules of warfare. That it may, at bottom, have been the English colonials who were the aggressors and the Indians, the victims never occurred to him. They had dared to stand in the path of Progress; this made their eradication both essential and inevitable.

If Parkman was, to say the least, severe in his judgment on the Indians, he was virulent in his condemnation of the French for aiding and inciting them against the English colonies. That these same colonies incited the Iroquois against New France was of no account. And when the French most directly concerned happened to be priests as well, the acts committed were clearly beyond the pale. (pp. 172-73)

The final picture of New France that emerges from a reading of this series is one that is not altogether unsympathetic. Parkman frequently paid tribute to qualities that he found admirable in the Canadians, although in a rather patronizing manner. He admired, for example, their courage, their fortitude, and the romantic aura of this frontier breed. But he could never really forgive them for being so obstinately French, Roman Catholic, and subjects of a supposedly absolute monarch. "As a bold and hardy pioneer of the wilderness," he wrote, "the Frenchman in America has rarely found his match. [But] his civic virtues withered under the despotism of Versailles, and his mind and conscience were kept in leading-strings by an absolute Church. . . ."

Parkman brought to his task the gifts of historical imagination, the willingness to consult all the available source material, and considerable talent as a writer. Thus he was able to create very vivid pictures in the mind's eye of the reader and to enable him to live in the past for a brief spell; but the reader always views this past through Parkman's own Whig-colored spectacles. Most of his faults were the faults of his age and these must be forgiven him; but this does not mean that they must be overlooked. His works have served us well, for perhaps too many years. In fact, it might almost be said that he performed his task too well, and the consequences have been disastrous for the study of the history of Canada. It gave rise to the belief, amongst English-speaking historians at least, that Parkman had said all that needed to be said about the history of New France, and that there was no need to do any further research. Clearly, this condition cannot endure much longer. It is to be hoped that before too many years have passed, Parkman's works will be relegated to the same shelf as those of his contemporaries, George Bancroft, William Prescott, and John Motley, where they will be consulted more by the student of American literature or historiography than by the student of history. (pp. 174-75)

> W. J. Eccles, "The History of New France According to Francis Parkman," in The William and Mary Quarterly, *third series, Vol. XVIII, No. 2, April, 1961, pp. 163-75.*

KENNETH REXROTH   (essay date 1961)

[*Rexroth interprets* France and England in North America *as an autobiographical account of Parkman's conflicting attitudes toward the Puritan ethic.*]

Samuel Eliot Morison, as one might guess from his name alone, is a product of the same milieu as Parkman. He shares many of his prejudices, and is as unaware of them. If there has to be a *Parkman Reader,* he is certainly as good a man as any to put it together. It is necessary, however, to take his preface with a grain of salt [see excerpt dated 1955]. He speaks of Parkman as a literary stylist worthy of respect. As a matter of fact, only when he was caught up in the circumstantial rush of his narrative did Parkman write well. His set pieces on the beauties of the forest primeval, the savagery of an Indian war dance or the vices of the little provincial court at Montreal are rather comic reading today. Although he set out to deflate the legend of the noble savage, whole pages might well have come from Chateaubriand's *Atala*—illustrated by Gustave Doré.

John Fiske, who introduced the last collected edition [see excerpt dated 1897], speaks of Parkman's people as being far more real than Prescott's. Morison shares this view. Prescott's Mexico and Montezuma resemble *The Arabian Nights,* it is true. But this is realism. They really were like that. Parkman's heroes are moved by the highly stereotyped motives of a sort of Puritan Ivanhoe.

Again, Morison speaks of Parkman as a gentleman and an aristocrat. He may have been a gentleman, but he was certainly not an aristocrat. He was a bourgeois valetudinarian. Whether it be Procopius, H. G. Wells or Motley, the historian usually injects much of himself between the lines of his history. But Parkman comes close to having written a fourteen-volume invisible autobiography. He came from a rich, upper-middle-class family of Boston Brahmins. He seems to have been thoroughly indoctrinated in the liberal but nonetheless "puritan" Puritanism of Unitarianism and advanced Congregationalism. He was expected to make his way in the world, but early in youth he started going off to the woods. In college days he took several long trips in the New England and New York backwoods; then a walking trip across Sicily and much of Italy as the beginning of a year on the Grand Tour; then a trip far out on the Oregon Trail, where he traveled as a guest with the Sioux.

In later life Parkman was to attribute his variously described incapacitating illness to incidents on all three of these excursions. One way or another he always blamed his poor health on the strenuous life of his youth. What seems to have happened is that, first casually in Sicily and Naples, and then in all its glory at the headwaters of the Missouri, he met his Id, and it was too much for him. The memory of the abandoned, dark-eyed *signorine* by the Porta Capuana and the naked Sioux belles disporting themselves in the waters of the Missouri prostrated him for the rest of his life. For forty years he devoted himself to justifying the triumph of anal over oral sexuality—or, in the words of another great Puritan, the ways of God to man.

The thesis of *France and England in North America* is that drinking, running around with women, rising late and loafing in the woods must go down to disaster before the righteous onslaught of the forty-eight-hour day, the well-kept savings account, patriarchal domesticity, well-shined shoes and cold baths. During the nineteenth century this was probably true, but the nineteenth century is a very brief period in the long history of man. It is doubtful if this moral struggle had much to do with the defeat of France in the New World. French America was lost in Europe.

Parkman was not horrified and fascinated only by Frenchmen. He speaks of the quasi-aristocratic Dutch on the upper Hudson as boors (aristocrats, of course, are always pretty boorish in the eyes of merchants). That thoroughly feudal personality of his period, Sir William Johnson, the "Father of the Iroquois," he looks on as nothing but a rascal. He never mentions the Quakers without losing his temper over their obstinacy and pacifism. The type that wins is the go-getter. Now that New England is a dying land gradually filling up with Poles and French Canadians, we forget that once almost everyone who lived there was a go-getter.

Recently we have seen in American history "the rehabilitation of the Business Community." The Business Community is the avowed hero of Parkman's history. In his pages appear the archetypes of the nineteenth-century robber barons and the twentieth-century hypomanics who grace the covers of the newsweeklies and who, alas, to judge by the newsweeklies, rule America.

But Parkman didn't break down and become a lifelong neurotic because he was a good businessman. He was a man in profound conflict with himself. As with Milton, his heroes are unconvincing and his villains are heroic. Except at the top, where no sane men want to be, it is doubtful if the Puritan tradition has really been as determinative in American culture as the scholars of Yale and Harvard would like us to believe.

All Americans are not those monsters portrayed by Artzybasheff who rise at 4 A.M. and bring home a brief case full of homework at 3 A.M. the next morning. The systematic conquest of the old Northwest by red-coated soldiers and land speculators has moved few boyish hearts, even in New England. But the story of the boats of Champlain poking their way into the dark, leafy wilderness, the heroic death of Father Jorgues, the pathetic death of La Salle, the joyful portages of Marquette and Joliet—even the cognac, riot and abandoned women in besieged Montreal—are as moving as the tribulations and defiance of Milton's Satan. And these traditions are still powerful, however quiet, in the land.

It is the spiritual conflict in the author, as well as his reading of history as a war between two basic types of personality, which gives Parkman's work its power. The archetypal struggle gives it epic character. The personal conflict gives it the intricacy and ambiguity of a psychological novel. The real subject and background—redskins, redcoats and chevaliers—give it the fanfare of high romance.

Parkman is very far from being Homer or Proust or even Scott, but he does combine—perhaps in cheaper colors but on a canvas of tremendous scope—the virtues of all three. I first read Parkman with a chill along my scalp when I was but in skirts—or at least in short pants—and I've read him all several times since. Opening Morison's reader to the map of Quebec and seeing the words "The Plains of Abraham," and then rereading the words of Montcalm and Wolfe, the same old chill comes back.

Near the end of the last volume, *The Conspiracy of Pontiac*, in lines that echo Melville, Parkman sums up the real, not the putative, moral of his life work:

> . . . To him who has once tasted the reckless independence, the haughty self-reliance, the sense of irresponsible freedom, which the forest life engenders, civilization thenceforth seems flat and stale. Its pleasures are insipid, its pursuits wearisome, its conventionalities, duties, and mutual dependence alike tedious and disgusting. The entrapped wanderer grows fierce and restless, and pants for breathing-room. His path, it is true, was choked with difficulties, but his body and soul were hardened to meet them; it was beset with dangers, but these were the very spice of his life, gladdening his heart with exulting self-confidence, and sending the blood through his veins with a livelier current. The wilderness, rough, harsh, and inexorable, has charms more potent in their seductive influence than all the lures of luxury and sloth. And often he on whom it has cast its magic finds no heart to dissolve the spell, and remains a wanderer and an Ishmaelite to the hour of his death.

Mr. Morison does not include this passage or anything like it in his selection. (pp. 175-79)

> *Kenneth Rexroth, "Notes on Historians," in his* Assays, *New Directions, 1961, pp. 175-83.**

EDMUND WILSON   (essay date 1964)

[*Wilson is generally considered America's foremost man of letters in the twentieth century. A prolific reviewer, creative writer, and social and literary critic endowed with formidable intellectual powers, he exercised his greatest literary influence in* Axel's Castle, *a seminal study of literary symbolism, and in widely read reviews and essays in which he introduced the best works of modern literature to the reading public. In the excerpt below, Wilson attributes the success of Parkman's histories to their vigorous prose and concrete descriptions of frontier life. Although Wilson notes that* France and England in North America *becomes less interesting midway through the series, he considers this flaw less a function of Parkman's limitations than an inevitable consequence of the subject matter.*]

At the time Parkman's [*France and England in North America*] was appearing—the sixties, seventies, eighties, and nineties of the last century—it presented itself as a project of an almost wholly novel kind. Parkman gave it as secondary title "A History of the American Forest," and nobody had written before a chronicle of recent history which, instead of dealing almost exclusively with parliaments and chancellors and treaties, with organized armies and strategic wars, tried to follow the movements of white pioneers invading a continent of primitive peoples and unsurveyed wildernesses. No one in the United States had apparently been interested in this subject, had thought of it as an object for serious study. Such records of those times as survived had more or less the aspect of old debris in the back yard of American progress, of cherished family legends that might be handed down in the household but that nobody had had an interest in checking and relating to one another. But Parkman spent years of research among published and unpublished personal records, letters that had been somehow preserved yet never examined as evidence, state papers stowed away in the archives of London and Paris, the two Canadas, and the United States. (pp. 72, 74)

How was it possible to construct a narrative which, never resorting to the methods of nineteenth-century romantic fiction, would carry along the reader through volume after volume, out of incidents and chains of events so scattered and disconnected, the doings of small settlements so isolated, the skirmishes and takings-of-possession so inconsecutive, sporadic, and confused? One has to read about so many sieges, so many bleak and lethal marches, so many palavers with the Indians, so many spiteful intrigues for position among exiled and discontented colonial officials. The genius of Parkman is shown not only in his disciplined, dynamic prose but in his avoidance of generalizations, his economizing of abstract analysis, his sticking to concrete events. Each incident, each episode is different, each is particularized, each is presented, when possible, in sharply realistic detail, no matter how absurd or how homely, in terms of its human participants, its local background, and its seasonal conditions. But a knowledge of all this could not wholly be drawn from the written sources, especially such inadequate documents as those with which Parkman had sometimes to work. He had already spent five months in the West, mostly living with the Sioux Indians, in order to get some first-hand knowledge of the peoples with whom the white men at first had had to share the continent, and he afterward went to much trouble to travel to even the most distant sites of the happenings he had to describe—wild spots which were often still scarcely or not at all changed from the time when these events had taken place. He had a special sensitivity to landscape and terrain, a kind of genius unequalled, so far as I know, on the part of any other important historian, without which such a story could hardly have been told.

It was all right for the urban Gibbon to build up a description of Constantinople—and an extraordinary description it is, which even creates a kind of suspense—without ever having visited the city, but for America, as yet unconstructed, this method would never do. There were no models to follow for America. The historian must himself go to see what was seen for the first time by the immigrants. Lake George in winter: "In the morning they marched again, by icicled rocks and ice-bound waterfalls, mountains gray with naked woods and fir trees bowed down with snow. . . . When clouds hang low on the darkened mountains, and cold mists entangle themselves in the tops of the pines." In summer and autumn: "Embarked in whaleboats or birch canoes they glided under the silent moon or in the languid glare of a breathless August day when islands floated in dreamy haze, and the hot air was thick with odors of the pine; or in the bright October, when the jay screamed from the woods, squirrels gathered their winter hoard, and congregated blackbirds chattered farewell to their summer haunts; when gay mountains basked in light, maples dropped leaves of rustling gold, sumachs glowed like rubies under the dark green of the unchanging spruce, and mossed rocks with all their painted plumage lay double in the watery mirror." But it would take too many quotations to illustrate the variety of this master of prose: The desolate plains of the West, "half-covered with snow and strewn with the skulls and bones of buffalo;" Starved Rock, on the Illinois, from the trunk of

whose "stunted cedar that leans forward from the brink, you may drop a plummet into the river below, where the cat-fish and the turtles may plainly be seen gliding over the wrinkled sands of the clear and shallow current;" the forests of Maine, dense and daunting—matted bushes, saplings choked to death, perishing by their very abundance. How he gives to this forest of Maine a teeming and tangled life quite distinct from that of any of his other forests! Yet he is scrupulous in never inventing. If some picturesque detail in Parkman may suggest for a moment indulgence in the fantasies of fictionalized history, you will find it is an actual impression recorded by one of his pioneers. (pp. 74, 77-8)

The clarity, the momentum, and the color of the first volumes of Parkman's narrative are among the most brilliant achievements of the writing of history as an art. After this, although his powers never fail him for presenting any aspect of his subject, the nature of the material itself sometimes obstructs the artist. In the middle of the step-by-step chronicle, the momentum a little flags. The French cities have by this time become big enough, with a society sufficiently developed, to demand the historian's analysis, and in the volume *The Old Régime in Canada* he gives us this analysis at length; but these centers, in spite of their apings of the society of the old regime in France, are still rather meagre and second-rate, and the rivalries and schemings and liaisons of the governors and priests and generals do become a trifle tedious when treated on a scale comparable with the more novel events that have gone before. One continues to read eagerly in order to find out what will happen to the white man adventuring in a world of whose inhabitants he has never before héard and whose geography he has still to discover; but the drawing rooms and convents of Montreal cannot excite an equal interest. And then Louisbourg—irreducible historical fact—is taken and retaken too many times; the sieges become rather monotonous. They may have bored Parkman, too, for—fearing that he might not live to finish his story—he skipped ahead to write the volume *Montcalm and Wolfe,* then returned to *A Half-Century of Conflict.* The suspense of the whole adventure, as an artistically created effect, is itself somewhat weakened by the explicitness of Parkman in telling us in his introduction exactly what the upshot is going to be and exactly what this upshot will prove. Not that he writes an obvious morality play; he never deals in heroes or villains. The objectivity that Parkman achieves is the product of a never-remitting discipline, which almost makes him lean over backward in admiring the nobility of the French, the chivalrous virtues of their soldiers and the grandiose ambitions of their leaders, and in rather playing down the more prosaic virtues of the New Englanders, Pennsylvanians, and New Yorkers. But he has made it quite clear that the French, for all their visions and their efforts in this arduous new world, so different from anything they have known at home, are to be crushed "under the exactions of a grasping hierarchy," stifled "under the curbs and trappings of a feudal monarchy," whereas the Protestant English, already recalcitrant against their king and his church, "a busy multitude, each in his narrow circle toiling for himself, to gather competence or wealth," were in a position to build up independent industries and to establish enduring commonwealths. New France, though so far from home, had to suffer from the corruption of old France, from its selfish inefficiency and extravagance, and it was let down by Louis XV when it most needed his help to survive. No ray of the Enlightenment reached it during the ferment of the eighteenth century; the revolution that overthrew the Bourbons and exalted the Goddess of Reason left French Canada Catholic and feudal, abandoned and yet unchanged. But New

England was already the Revolution. It was bound to win against the British Tories, especially the second-rate officials that were usually sent out to the colonies. A good many of these fled to Canada, where they still had their Crown to back them, as the French no longer had theirs. Since most of this has already been told us at the very beginning of the story, the defeat of Montcalm by Wolfe comes as something of a Q.E.D.

The historical point being made—if we strip away the forests and the Indians—may then appear rather simple, and if Parkman does fall short in interest of the greatest of the European historians, such as Gibbon and Michelet, it is because he does not give us, cannot give us, in view of the limited resources with which his human materials supply him, the same sense of looking on at the whole destiny of Western man, of being made to confront his great problems and to speculate as to what will be his future. Of course, Michelet and Gibbon cover many centuries, and they can range over the varied societies of a more or less civilized Europe, whereas Parkman extends over little more than two centuries and a half and deals mainly with a sparsely peopled wilderness. Yet the rough conflicts between small bands of men are significant because, though lost in this wilderness, they will eventually be seen to have contributed to the settling of important issues. One has somewhat to readjust one's sights to appreciate the drama of early America. The scale of humanity is so reduced, compared to that of denser societies, that it may not at once be obvious that great questions of Church or State may actually be at stake in a skirmish, a feud, or a duel. And it is a history of such encounters that Parkman has written here. (pp. 78, 80, 82)

> Edmund Wilson, "O Canada: An American's Notes on Canadian Culture—I," in The New Yorker, Vol. XL, No. 39, November 14, 1964, pp. 63-140.*

ALLAN NEVINS (essay date 1965)

[Nevins faults the structure of France and England in North America, arguing that the series' greatest weakness is its sketchy coverage of the years 1700-50 in A Half-Century of Conflict. In this work, Nevins argues, Parkman attempted to cover too many events; consequently, it lacks the "vigor, energy, and scholarly thoroughness" of his other histories.]

Parkman did not carefully plan [France and England in North America] as a whole, and in detail; he simply plotted in a general way, and then allowed it to grow. He wrote the Montcalm and Wolfe before he composed the Half Century of Conflict, which chronologically precedes it. If we look at his seven books as a general history either of New France or of the conflict between the French and the English, its design is in various ways radically defective. Some parts of the story are given excessive emphasis; some parts are improperly slighted. Perhaps the work is best described as a history of French Canada which expands, when the year 1690 is reached, into a history of the struggle between the French and British for dominion in America. But even regarded in this light, the narrative is not altogether well-proportioned or well arranged.

It was assuredly a mistake, viewing the series as a whole, to give almost half the first volume, Pioneers of France in the New World, to an account of the abortive attempt of Ribaut, Laudonnière, and others to establish a French colony in Florida. That attempt, and the conflict with Spain which it provoked, is an interesting little tale, but it had no lasting significance whatever, it is connected neither with the history of French Canada nor that of the Anglo-French conflict, and it stands as

a detached and rather pointless historical essay. It would have been better had Parkman, beginning with Jacques Cartier's voyages of 1534-35, alloted more space to them and the French fishing and fur-trading enterprises in Canada which preceded the advent of Samuel de Champlain in 1603. Later on, Parkman grossly neglects the activities of the French in the Ohio and Mississippi Valleys, and at points farther West; that is, he neglects this subject in the sense of giving it quite inadequate study and space. He tells most nobly the story of Marquette, La Salle, and Joliet. He is fairly satisfactory in [his] treating of Detroit, if not of Michillimackinac.

But the whole history of Louisiana from its beginnings in 1697 down to the year 1750 receives only one chapter (in Half Century of Conflict), which does not extend to thirty pages. The account of the establishment and maintenance of the chain of posts with which France, in the first half of the eighteenth century, joined her colony in Canada to her colony in Louisiana, is equally thin and unsatisfactory. And the history of the trans-Mississippi explorations of La Vérendrye and others is not only inaccurate from the modern point of view, but is allotted insufficient space and emphasis. The West was of crucial importance in the conflict of France and Britain in the New World. Able leaders on both sides began to see as early as 1700 that the control of the interior was the vital point on which all else depended. Yet such is Parkman's apportionment of space that readers of his seven books would not readily grasp the fact.

The fact is that Parkman ought to have written nine different books, and perhaps even ten, rather than seven. He begins well. The first epoch in the history of French Canada is that period of thirty-five or forty years paralleling the career of Champlain. He sailed up the St. Lawrence in 1603. He helped next year to found Port Royal (Annapolis) in Nova Scotia. Until his death in 1635 he labored to develop Canada as a French colony; to spur on the work of exploration, he himself reaching Lakes Champlain, Ontario, and Huron; and to make the fur trade profitable.

The second era in the history of French Canada is that of the missionary activities conducted by the Franciscans, the Recollets, the Ursulines, and above all the Jesuits; an era which began to end when in 1649 the Iroquois virtually wiped out the Huron tribesmen among whom the Jesuits had met the greatest success. Commercially also the colony was a failure in these years. The year 1660 found not more than 2,000 French people settled in the whole land. Parkman treats this heroic but by no means fruitful or triumphant period admirably in The Jesuits in North America.

Then came a third era. A new company was formed—The Company of the West Indies—to develop the colony; Louis XIV began to show a personal interest in it; fresh shiploads of colonists were sent out; New France became a royal province. A young churchman arrived at Quebec in 1659, François Xaxier de Montmorency-Laval who had resolved that Canada should be ruled by the church, and under a regime as strict and austere as that of the Puritan theocracy in New England. Laval's mark is still upon Quebec's life. He came into conflict with governor after governor, but usually he had his own way. This is the era of which Parkman treats, again admirably, in The Old Régime, a volume remarkable for its political insight and economic analysis. At the same time, in the twenty years 1659-1682, the explorers were busy in the Far West—Radisson, Groseilliers, Joliet, Marquette, and above all La Salle. To some of them Parkman has devoted one of the most fascinating of his books—*La Salle and the Discovery of the Great West.*

The fourth era was ushered in by the arrival of the Comte de Frontenac, in 1672, as governor of New France. He was a man of determination and iron strength. He asserted the dominance of the civil authorities over the church in administering the province; he broke the strength of the Iroquois; he fought off Sir William Phips's expedition against Quebec in King William's War; and before he died at the close of the century he had begun preparing New France for the desperate struggle which all men of vision saw must be fought out with the British. This story could not be better told than in Parkman's *Count Frontenac and New France under Louis XIV.*

So far, in his first five books, Parkman has done admirably. The *Pioneers of New France* lacks unity, but that fault, arising from the attempt to treat both the Florida colony and Champlain's work, is the only notable defect. But Parkman, after giving five volumes to the first century of New France, 1603-1698, essayed to cover the ensuing half-century of Anglo-French history in America, crowded with events, in the two volumes which he gave the most colorless and vague of his titles. Comprehending so much history, the *Half Century of Conflict* lacks unity, sprawling as does no other of Parkman's works. But its chief weakness lies in its want of vigor, energy, and scholarly thoroughness. It contains fine elements, but too much action and too many leaders had to be brought within the covers of one not very long work.

Here interesting personalities are depicted—Cadillac, Bienville, Vaudreuil, Iberville, and Charlevoix on the French side; Shirley, Pepperrell, and Drummer on the English. Here are two bloody wars, those of the Spanish Succession and the Austrian Succession, with sieges, battles, and sickening border massacres. Here we find the establishment of two potentially great cities, Detroit and New Orleans, and the rise of the colony of Louisiana. Here are fresh administrative changes in New France, and additional conflicts between church and civil authorities; here is the development of Canadian agriculture as well as the fur trade, with 50,000 or 60,000 French colonists finally settled in the valley of the St. Lawrence and the maritime areas; here are the capture of Louisbourg, the deportation of the Acadians, the founding of Halifax, and the colonization of Nova Scotia; here are the establishment of the chain of posts reaching from Niagara down the Mississippi, and the Far Western explorations already mentioned. The half-century offers matter enough for two books. Had Parkman, the sands of whose life were now ebbing away, written those two books—had he closed the first with the Treaty of Utrecht and its immediate sequels, and opened the second with the outbreak of King George's War, making each book full and thorough—his great series would be without the one glaring weakness which it now shows.

But this one defect ought not to diminish our admiration for the volumes which precede the *Half Century of Conflict*, or for the masterly work on Montcalm and Wolfe which follows it. Parkman's search for materials was so painstaking, his use of it was so impartial, and the alembic of his concise but eloquent style is so magical, that his best works are perdurable. They are truly made—as Carlyle said permanent books would have to be—of asbestos. (pp. xii-xvii)

Allan Nevins, "The Achievement of Francis Parkman," in France and England in North America: Pioneers of France in the New World, *Vol. I by*

Francis Parkman, Frederick Ungar Publishing Co., 1965, pp. v-xxvi.

RICHARD C. VITZTHUM   (essay date 1974)

[*The following excerpt is drawn from Vitzthum's* The American Compromise: Theme and Method in the Histories of Bancroft, Parkman, and Adams. *In this study, Vitzthum proposes that the works of Bancroft, Parkman, and Adams constitute a distinct tradition in nineteenth-century American historiography and share an approach that is characterized by the motto "e pluribus unum." Vitzthum defines this approach as one that broadly interprets early American history as a compromise between polarities, with "anarchy, or complete diffusion and decentralization, at one extreme and tyranny—complete subordination and centralization—at the other." The critic here examines Parkman's treatment of the conflict between centralization and decentralization in France and England in North America. He also briefly compares the series with Bancroft's* History of the United States. *In Parkman's histories, Vitzthum argues, New France signifies complete centralization, or tyranny, while the American wilderness symbolizes complete decentralization, or anarchy. According to Vitzthum, "the English colonies with their tradition of 'ordered liberty' represent a tough and . . . desirable compromise" between these two polar extremes.*]

[Nature and civilization] each have a primary connotation in *France and England* that establishes them as poles between which the whole work develops. The basic connotation of nature, or the American wilderness, is personal freedom, or license; the basic connotation of civilization, or the French and the English colonies, is union, self-sacrifice to the group, centralization. Yet Parkman distinguishes between the civilization of the French and the English colonies. New France emerges as the polar extreme of centralization, opposite the polar extreme of anarchic freedom connoted by the wilderness, while the English colonies with their tradition of "ordered liberty" represent a tough and, in Parkman's eyes, desirable compromise between the two. As Doughty shows, however, neither nature nor civilization is to Parkman altogether good or altogether bad. Correspondingly, the freedom of the wilderness emerges from *France and England* as both desirable and undesirable, similarly ambiguous in this respect to its opposite number, the absolutism of New France. Even the compromise system lying symbolically between them, that of the seaboard British colonies, reveals weaknesses as well as strengths. It is in the self-control, self-discipline, and moral strength of individual men and women that Parkman finds a denominator not only common to the wilderness, the English colonies, and New France but sufficiently stable and universal to serve as a moral criterion valid for the whole range of human experience they embrace. (p. 89)

[The] negative side of the freedom that the wilderness always connotes to Parkman is its anarchy. The woods are often pictured in terms of jungle war, with the fittest alone surviving and they themselves succumbing at last to the inexorable cycle of birth, growth, death, and decay. At one point in *A Half-Century of Conflict* the forest is described as full of "[y]oung seedlings . . . , [which are] rich with the decay of those that had preceded them, crowding, choking and killing each other" and which "survive by blighting those about them. They in turn, as they grow, interlock their boughs, and repeat in a season or two the same process of mutual suffocation." Immediately afterward, Parkman half-playfully connects this carnage with democracy: "Not one infant tree in a thousand lives to maturity; yet these survivors form an innumerable host, pressed together in struggling confusion, squeezed out of symmetry and robbed of normal development, as men are said to be in the level sameness of democratic society." Although his needling of extreme egalitarians here is tongue in cheek, his linking of democracy with the chaos of raw nature reflects one of the basic ideas of *France and England.* The wilderness functions throughout as a metaphor for complete social diffusion and individualism—that is, for extreme democracy. Correspondingly, it is enervating and meaningless. When the first explorers reach the site of Quebec, they are surrounded by "nameless barbarism"; repeatedly Parkman describes the entire continent as wrapped in "savage slumber"; when La Salle penetrates the Mississippi Valley, he finds a "dark domain of solitude and horror" and, at the mouth of the Mississippi, the "limitless, voiceless" Gulf of Mexico, "lonely as when born of chaos, without a sail, without a sign of life." The history of the continent before the arrival of European civilization is described as "gloomy and meaningless" and Parkman is more than content that in face of the French and English the "long and gloomy reign of barbarism was drawing near its close." Insofar as the wilderness remains without order or discipline of any kind it is a perfect image, in Parkman's eyes, of the lethargy, brutishness, and irrationality of man in the state of nature. (pp. 91-2)

Yet while the wilderness always connotes a fundamentally dangerous freedom in *France and England,* it also connotes refreshment and invigoration. If one opens *France and England* and reads a few pages, he is likely to find evidence of the fascination with woodsmanship and wilderness scenery that distinguishes it from the work of every other nineteenth-century American historian except Theodore Roosevelt, who of course drew much of his inspiration for his *Winning of the West . . .* from *France and England* and dedicated the work to Parkman [see excerpt dated 1888]. Parkman's narrative is regularly punctuated with lush descriptions of natural setting drawn from his own observations. His books shimmer with forest sunrises and sunsets, panoramas of coastlines, mountains, and prairies, and light sparkling from countless rivers and lakes. Storms of rain, snow, and wind whip through his pages with almost visceral force. We smell the frozen air of winter and the hot perfumes of summer. Repeatedly, he suggests that leaving civilization and immersing one's self in nature for a while is excellent spiritual and physical tonic. (p. 95)

It was as a challenge to the moral strength and technical skill of the civilized man that Parkman seems to have valued the wilderness most highly. The wilderness tends to bring out the best in his strong-willed, masculine heroes and at least certain good qualities in those who, like the *coureurs de bois,* live a more or less savage life. The *coureurs de bois* are "white Indians, without discipline, and scarcely capable of it, but brave and accustomed to the woods." As "excellent woodsmen, skillful hunters, and perhaps the best bushfighters in all Canada," they exhibit, like one of their most well-known members, Du Lhut, "a persistent hardihood" born of lives spent "exploring, trading, fighting." The wilderness teaches them and the nobler representatives of civilization who enter it lessons of courage, self-discipline, and resourcefulness unavailable in civilized life yet as useful there, Parkman hints, as in the woods. The process of mastering the wilderness usually implies for Parkman a process of self-toughening and self-improvement, so that the value of contact with it is not only to clear one's brain of the cobwebs of civilization but to strengthen one's moral fiber.

At the opposite extreme from the anarchy of wild nature in *France and England* stands the paternalism and despotism of New France. Although Parkman's repeated contrast of what he calls the absolutism of the French colony with the liberty of the English colonies is a central organizing principle of the nine volumes, it reflects an opposition that on the English side lies inside his more comprehensive contrast between New France and the wilderness. The liberty of the English colonies is of the regulated or ordered variety, as has already been mentioned and will be further analyzed, which represents a compromise between the true political poles of wilderness freedom and absolutist centralization in Parkman's work as a whole. (pp. 97-8)

[As] with wilderness freedom, Parkman sees French-Canadian centralization as representing an undesirable extreme. Its worst flaw, the one Parkman sees as the key to the ultimate collapse of the colony, was its repression of individual initiative and, correspondingly, of self-reliance and self-discipline. Yet while Parkman sees the repressiveness of French absolutism as chiefly to blame for Canada's woes, he also suggests there was a ludicrous, quixotic quality about the whole Canadian venture that should limit the seriousness with which we take the repressiveness. It is in the areas of religion and politics that he takes the despotism of New France most to task.

Like Bancroft, though not so strongly, he argues that the religious despotism of New France contrasted with the religious freedom of the English colonies. "To plant religious freedom on this Western soil," he says, "was not the mission of France. It was for her to rear in Northern forests the banner of Absolutism and of Rome; while, among the rocks of Massachusetts, England and Calvin fronted her in dogged opposition." The main force behind this papist thrust, of course, was Jesuitism, which Parkman interprets as the incarnation of a totally hierarchical and authoritarian view of the universe. The Jesuits "would act or wait, dare, suffer, or die, yet all in unquestioning subjection to the authority of the Superiors, in whom they recognized the agents of Divine authority itself." As the Iroquois was Indian *par excellence,* the Jesuit was priest *par excellence,* "rank," says Parkman, with the "instinct of domination" which, unchecked, "has always been the most mischievous of tyrannies." Yet Parkman argues that the Jesuit was not so much ambitious for himself as "for the great corporate power in which he had merged his own personality." He uses this argument to explain, for example, why the Jesuits encouraged only nuns to support the Canadian mission: "We hear of no zeal for the mission among religious communities of men. The Jesuits regarded the field as their own, and desired no rivals. . . . It was to the combustible hearts of female recluses that the torch was most busily applied." Self-abasement to jealous, despotic power is what Parkman finds most deplorable in the Jesuit system. (pp. 98-9)

Parkman finds Canada's religious despotism inseparable from its political. The one fueled the other. Behind them both stood French monarchism, epitomized for Parkman by Louis XIV: "He was a devout observer of the forms of religion. . . . Above all rulers of modern times, he was the embodiment of the monarchical idea." Summing up the meaning of Louis' career, Parkman emphasizes its repressiveness: "Crushing taxation, misery, and ruin followed, till France burst out at last in a frenzy, drunk with the wild dreams of Rousseau. Then came the Terror and the Napoleonic wars, and reaction on reaction, revolution on revolution, down to our own day." Here Parkman extends the repressing-binge syndrome of French Canada to

A photograph of Parkman in his garden. The Bettmann Archive, Inc.

the entire history of modern France, warning that excessive political constraint always engenders its opposite number. Virtually all of **The Old Regime** is devoted to describing the particulars of Louis' paternalism in New France, which is said to have bound the government of the colony "from head to foot": "Seignior, *censitaire*, and citizen were prostrate alike in flat subjection to the royal will." (pp. 100-01)

And yet, like the wilderness, New France also symbolizes certain values that Parkman admires. Though basically undesirable, its drive toward religious, political, military, and social centralization is in Parkman's eyes not simply an unavoidable ingredient in human nature but in some ways a commendable one. In the first place, he sees it as tending to inspire loyalty to great central ideas or organizational systems. For example, despite its "horrible violence to the noblest qualities of manhood," the Jesuit order "has numbered among its members men whose fervent and exalted natures have been intensified, without being abased, by the pressure to which they have been subjected" during their indoctrination. It produced in Canada that "marvellous *espirit de corps,* that extinction of self, and absorption of the individual in the Order, which has marked the Jesuits from their first existence as a body," a faithfulness and selflessness "no less strong than the self-devoted patriotism of Sparta or the early Roman Republic." The loyalty, the sense of duty, the willingness to sacrifice oneself for a higher cause, which Parkman believes characterized the feudal ideal from which modern Catholicism and monarchy developed, attract him powerfully, and throughout **France and England** he pays a real if qualified tribute to these virtues.

In addition, he praises the military efficiency that centralization gave Canada. He finds the whole military atmosphere of Canada bracing. When he says in the introduction to **Pioneers** that the "story of New France is, from the first, a story of war," he invites us to share his own fascination with it. In his sympathetic portrayal of the Canadians as a military people, he balances their willingness and ability to fight against the torpor other forms of paternalistic centralization produced. (pp. 103-04)

Finally and perhaps most important, absolutist habits of thought produced in the leaders and explorers of New France a largeness and boldness of imagination missing in the English colonies. Although ultimately vain, the growth of New France "was the achievement of a gigantic ambition striving to grasp a continent." Parkman is usually critical, as here, of the quixotism of French schemes, yet he admires their breadth and associates them in a sympathetic way with the aristocratic, absolutist temper of French-Canadian culture. "In the French colonies," he says, "the representatives of the Crown were men bred in an atmosphere of broad ambition and masterful and far-reaching enterprise. Achievement was demanded of them." The most striking embodiment of this spirit was La Salle, in whose exploits Parkman sees "a grand type of incarnate energy and will." While the English colonists "plodded at their workshops, their farms, or their fisheries," New France strove behind the "patient gallantry of her explorers, the zeal of her missionaries, the adventurous hardihood of her bushrangers" to realize mighty dreams. Her willingness to gamble for high stakes impresses Parkman as one of the great contributions of her system to American civilization.

At heart, however, Parkman, like Bancroft, is a believer in compromise. Though the extremes of wilderness freedom and Canadian unity attract him in several ways, he never seriously questions that the Anglo-American tradition of "regulated freedom," despite its imperfections, is the best solution available to mankind of the existential contradictions symbolized in New France and the wilderness. The imperfections in the English colonies, . . . are not only similar to those which Bancroft argues became evident during the revolutionary era but are, like Bancroft's, the result of too great a tendency to freedom. The three Parkman stresses are economic greed, military inefficiency, and political disunity.

He implies that greed for wealth will always be a danger in an industrial democracy like America's. In his famous charge to America at the end of ***Montcalm and Wolfe,*** he asserts that the country must "rally her powers from the race for gold and the delirium of prosperity to make firm the foundations on which that prosperity rests." At the beginning of the same book he condemns the Puritans for their "excess in the pursuit of gain," and in ***Count Frontenac*** he equates the materialism of democracy with military weakness: "The conditions of [Massachusetts'] material prosperity were adverse to efficiency in war. A trading republic, without trained officers, may win victories; but it wins them either by accident or by an extravagant outlay in money and life." Hints of Parkman's distaste for the scramble for money which he feels threatens American democracy can be heard throughout ***France and England,*** and the hints are all connected with his belief that economic selfishness, like other kinds, smacks of the tooth-and-claw savagery of the primeval forest. The man struggling blindly for fortune is like the tree, the animal, or the Indian struggling blindly for existence. Parkman deplores the hucksterism, especially in America, of what he elsewhere favorably calls "the self-relying energies of modern practical enterprise."

The military inefficiency of the British colonies is presented in ***France and England*** as one of their chief problems from the beginning of hostilities with New France in the 1680's to Pitt's rise to power in 1757. Parkman introduces the seventy-year struggle between the colonies by excoriating "the bungling inefficiency which marked the military management of the New England governments from the close of Philip's war to the peace of Utrecht." At Fort Pemaquid in 1696 the Massachusetts government acts "with its usual military fatuity." Summarizing the military differences between New France and the English colonies, he says the conflict consisted of "a compact military absolutism confronting a heterogeneous group of industrial democracies, where the force of numbers was neutralized by diffusion and incoherence."

The military shortcomings of the English colonies were only a symptom of what Parkman sees as a deeper political malaise: the political disorder and disunity both within the individual colonies and among them as a whole. Although he sees the New England colonies as relatively stable, the others, especially New York, are pictured as little patchwork kingdoms not far from anarchy. In 1700, he says, "New York was a mixture of races and religions not yet fused into a harmonious body politic, divided in interests and torn with intestine disputes." In the 1750's, Pennsylvania's population, like New York's, was "heterogeneous." Yet the disunity within individual colonies was insignificant compared to their lack of mutual cooperation. . . . Parkman's view of their situation on the eve of the French and Indian War is a good deal bleaker than Bancroft's. While Bancroft sees them as consciously—

and successfully—striving for unity, Parkman argues that results along this line

> had been most discouraging. . . . They were all subject to popular legislatures, through whom alone money and men could be raised; and these elective bodies were sometimes factious and selfish, and not always either far-sighted or reasonable. Moreover, they were in a state of ceaseless friction with their governors, who represented the king, or, what was worse, the feudal proprietary.

In terms of his major freedom-order symbols, Parkman argues that the English colonies had to move closer to New France, farther from the wilderness, to become politically sound.

Yet there is never any more question in Parkman's mind than in Bancroft's that despite their economic, military, or political flaws the English colonies, with their tradition of "ordered freedom" midway between the extremes of repression and license, were more than equal to the task. They eventually coalesced into the United States, the "eldest and greatest" of Britain's offspring, thereby justifying their wilderness vigor—their "liberty, crude, incoherent, and chaotic, yet full of prolific vitality." Their drive toward order, Parkman implies, diverted their drive toward freedom into productive channels, while the freedom kept the order from becoming "barren and absolutist." Yet unlike Bancroft, Parkman sees nothing predestined or inevitable about the spread of democracy throughout the earth. "The air of liberty," he says, "is malaria to those who have not learned to breathe it. The English colonists throve in it because they and their forefathers had been trained in a school of self-control and self-dependence; and what would have been intoxication for others, was vital force to them." Here as elsewhere he stresses the centuries of growth and experience that produced the English concept of freedom and successfully transplanted it to America. Whereas the French-American, suddenly exposed in the New World to a wilderness freedom his background had not prepared him for, either went native or remained the passive tool of monarchy and Catholicism, the Anglo-American, inured to the temptations of freedom through long experience with it, calmly confronted and mastered the wilderness.

Parkman offers another, related, explanation for the success of the British colonies. English colonization was open and voluntary, while French colonization was state controlled. "British America," he says,

> was an asylum for the oppressed and the suffering of all creeds and nations, and population poured into her by the force of a natural tendency. France, like England, might have been great in two hemispheres, if she had placed herself in accord with this tendency, instead of opposing it; but despotism was consistent with itself, and a mighty opportunity was for ever lost.

In other words, the success of the English colonies was due no more to a political tradition innate in their settlers than to a single enormous mistake in French policy which followed naturally from France's absolutism. France's failure was inevitable only in the sense that she held doggedly to her error. Providence played little part in the affair.

Yet the result, according to Parkman, was to introduce into English America a population hardened by the fires of persecution and extremely jealous of its rights and freedoms. Whatever the English colonists achieved was the result of their own choice and their own personal sacrifice. They were not coddled, argues Parkman, by a paternalistic government, nor did they come to North America to renounce the world. The Puritans, for example, "thought that a reward on earth as well as in heaven awaited those who were faithful to the law," and although this hardheaded practicality encouraged selfishness it was "manly, healthful, and invigorating" in a way that the religious asceticism of New France, with its constant harping on "the nothingness and the vanity of life," was not. The motivation for the Puritan exodus came from within: "In their own hearts, not in the promptings of a great leader or the patronage of an equivocal government, their enterprise found its birth and its achievement." In episode after episode Parkman repeats this idea, as when he says of Massachusetts' sacrifices for the war in 1758 that her "contributions of money and men were not ordained by an absolute king, but made by the voluntary act of a free people." He sees a spirit of self-reliance and self-motivation pervading not only New England but all the English colonies, and it is this spirit which for him lies at the heart of the Anglo-American compromise between freedom and order. Discipline and control of one's self is the key to the highest civilization. Each man must master his own appetites for license and for tyranny—for the wilderness and for New France—before he can be said to be truly civilized. Freedom and restraint are ultimately internal contradictions to be fought out on the battlefield of each man's soul.

Consequently, the portrayal of heroic character emerges as one of the most important purposes of *France and England.* That heroism would be a key to all the volumes was made clear in the introduction to the first, *Pioneers,* where Parkman says that in the early history of North America "men, lost elsewhere in the crowd, stand forth as agents of Destiny." His point is not that individuals control history but that much of the meaning of his own historical narratives lies in the examples of heroic character they depict. He clinches the point in the last sentence of the book when, having just concluded the account of his first major hero, Champlain, he comments that "[h]eroes of another stamp succeed; and it remains to tell hereafter the story of their devoted lives, their faults, their follies, and their virtues." In *France and England* as a whole Parkman attributes heroism to what at one point he calls "that height and force of individual development which is the brain and heart of civilization"—that is, to the self-discipline and self-motivation of each and every man. All his heroes reveal some combination of these essential virtues. The capacity to generate and sustain not merely the drive but also the self-regulation necessary to achieve heroic ends is in Parkman's eyes the monopoly neither of England nor of France. If anything, France produced more individual heroism in North America than did England. The aristocratic, semi-feudal society of France and New France encouraged the "highest growth of the individual" more than the English colonies, at least among its upper classes. On the other hand, individual freedom and initiative were much more widely diffused in England's society. Her colonies took root and flourished because of "the historical training of her people in habits of reflection, forecast, industry, and self-reliance,—a training which enabled them to adopt and maintain an invigorating system of self-rule, totally inapplicable to their rivals." (pp. 104-11)

Parkman's concept of character and heroism differs widely from Bancroft's. Bancroft argues that the ideal leader follows or embodies the will of the masses, which is by definition, because it rests on their intuitive perception of divine truth, infallible. Parkman argues that the masses are no better than the self-discipline each one of them has individually achieved. Leaders are ultimately interesting to him not as individuals to venerate but as examples of a self-mastery all men must strive to win. Bancroft's whole system rests on the idea that to follow the common will is to realize the will of God; Parkman's rests on the idea that there is no improvement beyond self-improvement. "There are no political panaceas," he asserts, "except in the imagination of political quacks. . . . Freedom is for those who are fit for it. The rest will lose it, or turn it to corruption." The rulers of New France erred, he goes on, not in exercising authority but in exercising "too much of it, and, instead of weaning the child to go alone, [keeping] him in perpetual leading-strings, making him, if possible, more and more dependent, and less and less fit for freedom." Parkman's social views are aristocratic only in the sense that he denies Bancroft's faith in the innate goodness of man. He everywhere implies it is the duty of each man, no matter what his station in life, to civilize his own internal wilderness.

Yet this process of self-cultivation implies the whole task of compromise that is suggested in his narrative of the taming of the historical North America. The individual must be subordinate enough to organzied society and the restrictions it imposes on him for the commonweal to honor "the true foundations of a stable freedom,—conscience, reflection, faith, patience, and public spirit." Yet at the same time he must be independent enough—imbued enough with the lawless spirit of the wilderness—not to have, as was the case in Canada, his "volition enfeebled" or his "self-reliance paralyzed." "A man, to be a man," says Parkman, "must feel that he holds his fate, in some good measure, in his own hands." In some good measure. Not entirely, but in some good measure. Parkman never tries to define the formula precisely but instead dramatizes it in dozens of case histories of heroism and in his symbolization of the extremes of the wilderness and New France, with the English colonies lying roughly midway between. Another important and related set of poles is "the modern world of practical study and practical action" which La Salle embodied and the medieval world of knighthood, chivalry, and religious faith which produced its own peculiar strengths and weaknesses. Among all these coordinates Parkman would have us chart the true path of individual character. The liberty of primeval nature and the restraint of New France, and the English compromise between them, are only the most important. (pp. 111-13)

Richard C. Vitzthum, "The Wilderness, New France, and English Liberty," in his The American Compromise: Theme and Method in the Histories of Bancroft, Parkman, and Adams, *University of Oklahoma Press, 1974, pp. 77-113.**

WILLIAM P. TAYLOR (essay date 1983)

[*Excerpted below is a review of the Library of America edition of* France and England in North America. *Taylor attempts to explain the continuing appeal of the series in light of its historical inaccuracy. He focuses on narrative voice, for he sees Parkman's authorial persona as one that unifies and gives dramatic suspense to a vast body of diverse material. More importantly, Taylor argues, Parkman injected his ambivalent attitudes toward the seventeenth and nineteenth centuries into his histories, thereby infusing them with the same "troubled vision of the future" that characterizes such American classics as Henry Thoreau's* Walden, *Henry Adams's* The Education of Henry Adams, *and Thorstein Veblen's* The Theory of the Leisure Class.]

Francis Parkman's seven-part history, *France and England in North America,* the consuming work of the last twenty-seven years of his life, has now been made available by the Library of America to readers of the 1980s. There is little doubt that its publication will raise the question of Parkman's standing both as a historian and as an imaginative writer. . . .

It is easy to forget that by the 1880s, when he published the climactic volume of his history, *Montcalm and Wolfe,* Parkman's reputation as a writer probably equaled or exceeded that of many of the major nineteenth-century novelists. But as fiction emerged as the predominant literary form, historical writing declined as a literary genre. With the rise of professional, monographic historical writing at the close of Parkman's life, those who wrote history were separated from those who studied and taught literature.

Parkman suffered, ironically, from the very success of his own efforts, as generations of students swarmed into the vast territory that he and other historian archivists had charted, staked out their claims, and brought his conclusions into question. I doubt very much that anyone today reads Parkman to find out about French Canada. His work has been relegated, instead, to a few pages in anthologies of American literature, together with his less interesting predecessors William Prescott, J. L. Motley, and George Bancroft.

If Parkman has enjoyed a popular following at all, it has been as the author of *The Oregon Trail.* . . . It is one of those engaging nineteenth-century tales, like *Two Years Before the Mast,* that describe cultivated young men enduring physical hardship in far-off, exotic places. *The Oregon Trail* has many fine moments, but it is the work of a young man just out of college and has little of the quality and complexity of the writings of some eighteen years later. To know Parkman only as the author of *The Oregon Trail,* as most American readers have, is a little like knowing Melville only as the author of *Typee.*

Twenty-five years ago not one volume of Parkman's great history was in print, although editions of his letters, his notebooks, and several biographies were available. Although recently several of the histories were published separately and, in 1969, a limited facsimile edition of the entire history, Parkman has not had the readers he deserves. . . .

Parkman's historical conclusions had proved controversial from the time of publication, especially among Canadian contemporaries who quickly detected his anti-French and anti-Jesuit bias. His standing as a historian continued to be examined critically throughout the 1960s. In perhaps the most comprehensive conventional reassessment of his work, "The History of New France According to Francis Parkman," the Canadian historian W. J. Eccles concluded that very little of the edifice that Parkman had constructed remained intact [see excerpt dated 1961]. . . .

Parkman's need for heroes led him to single out men whose historical importance has subsequently been questioned. He appears, for example, to have accepted uncritically the clever, self-promoting accounts of the leadership left behind by Frontenac, Louis XIV's governor of New France, even while neglecting important figures like Champlain, who could be rightly called the founder and first colonizer of the new France. In his determination to find a selfless hero in the explorer La Salle,

furthermore, Parkman overlooked La Salle's involvement in court intrigue and played down his growing mental derangement. Most serious of all, according to Eccles, was Parkman's tendency to see the Indian as little more than a pawn in the battle between Frenchman and Englishman. To Parkman the Indian, at his best, was a white man with brown skin, as in the opening chapter of *A Half-Century of Conflict;* at his worst, he was a savage beast venting his senseless rage on innocent settlers, as in the horrifed account of the Deerfield massacre.

The authoritativeness of Parkman's interpretation of events has been further undermined in recent studies that focus on Amerind cultures and on the North American environment as active force in shaping events. In Parkman the Indian hardly seems to figure as much more than a colorful backdrop against which to stage a drama of European cultures in conflict. (p. 35)

In the light of such criticism, it is hard to explain the extraordinary power these histories still retain. Rereading them today, even with these limitations in mind, we are caught up in them afresh. They have, to begin with, something of the quality one associates with what anthropologists call "contact history," those arresting, enigmatic descriptions of the first encounters between a native population and outsiders who come to conquer or study them. Beyond that they take on some of the character of historical fiction, of novels such as *The Scarlet Letter* or *A Tale of Two Cities,* constructs of a past framed in a later time and shaped by its values. Then, too, we are held by the tension between Parkman's wish to reenter the seventeenth-century world, which is at the center of his histories, and his nineteenth-century mind at work deciphering vestiges of that past.

The 1980s, for a number of reasons, should provide a more receptive climate for Parkman's work than any other period since his death. The recent revival of interest in narrative history, in both its theory and its practice, the fresh attention given by art historians to the landscape paintings of Parkman's contemporaries, and a renewed critical interest in nonfiction texts— to name only the more obvious reasons—suggest that Parkman will be examined by readers more sympathetic with his achievement. (pp. 35-6)

The ways in which Parkman elaborated the narrative history of his predecessors, changing both its methods and its substance, help to explain why he was its last great practitioner. For by bringing new concerns and strategies to his history, Parkman created tensions that were to tear narrative history apart. . . .

In a way, Parkman succeeded in doing with narrative history what James was doing with the novel, complicating its formal character and turning it inward toward the historical equivalent of the *roman psychologique,* transforming its sources and its personal judgments and observations into felt experience. Parkman introduced into the narrative voice an implicit moral consciousness that replaced the moralism of previous historians such as Jared Sparks and J. L. Motley. It was this voice— judging, evoking, distancing, ironic, and empathetic by turns— that James must have singled out as Parkman's "manner" [see excerpt dated 1885]. (p. 36)

Parkman's vision of French feudal power held at bay in the American wilderness altered the perspective historians had traditionally taken. Following Voltaire and Gibbon and even earlier writers, other historians had worked with settings close to the centers of power, in court or ecclesiastical domain. Parkman was among the first to follow the lines of power to the periphery of empire. It is this perspective that gives his history particular interest today. Unlike his fellow Bostonian Prescott, whose histories of the conquest of Mexico and Peru, though set in these countries, had placed a triumphant Spain in the foreground, and unlike both Bancroft and Motley, who had traced the rise of national sentiment domestically in the United States and in the Dutch republic, Parkman centered his histories on the course of French power as viewed from the colonial outposts in North America. The French monarchy and events in metropolitan France were portrayed and characterized by the way they were seen from afar. Only occasionally, as in the opening chapter of *Montcalm and Wolfe,* does Parkman describe the French court or events on the Continent in terms that would have proved familiar to Voltaire or Gibbon. The Seven Years' War is seen, instead, through the wrong end of a telescope, as colonial eyes might have perceived it. . . .

Modern readers will no doubt see in the Frenchmen Parkman described in the 1880s the French in Indochina sixty or seventy years later. If the historical line runs forward to Dien Bien Phu and the Algerian War, the literary line runs through modern writers from Kipling and Conrad to Orwell and Graham Greene, other writers who have subsequently taken the pulse of empire in jungle places.

No other history illustrated Parkman's mature "manner" as fully as *La Salle and the Discovery of the Great West,* a work which contains almost all the qualities of Parkman's historical work, and because it concerns itself largely with a single figure, it possesses the greatest coherence and dramatic force. It is a story of miscalculation and mischance, with ironies abounding. Nowhere else I know of is the almost insane grandiosity of French colonial ambition more apparent, and nowhere else, partly because of the close identity Parkman appears to have felt with La Salle, is its tragic failure more affectingly portrayed.

La Salle and the Discovery of the Great West was published in its final form in 1879 at the midpoint in the histories, its central epoch France under Louis XIV. The "Great West" of the title was the vast continental expanse between the Allegheny and Rocky mountains and between Canada and the Gulf of Mexico, the "Louisiana" claimed by La Salle in the name of his monarch. The unity of Parkman's histories has in part to do with their preoccupation with the exploration and pre-emption of this domain by La Salle and others. The very language used by these explorers in describing this territory and claiming it for France provided Parkman with the basis for his graphic portrayal of the times. All the diverse aspects of this saga— the narratives of French exploit, the portrayals of Indian life, the descriptions of landscape and wildlife—are thus fused into an imaginative act of repossession, as if for his time and for his country. (p. 37)

La Salle also reveals . . . the relationship that Parkman, at his best, expresses between the seventeenth century and his own nineteenth-century world. In a chapter entitled **"La Salle Painted by Himself,"** Parkman, working from an interview La Salle once gave in Paris and biographical sketches from other sources, draws a complex psychological portrait of introverted ambition which depends almost entirely on seventeenth-century documents. But if the language is from another time, its selection and conceptual frame are from Parkman's. Behind La Salle's outer reserve, Parkman's quotations from these documents suggest, was his determination neither to succumb to temptations, whether of worldly ambition or material comfort, nor to be defeated by physical pain or hardship. La Salle is perceived as having been able to hold the judgments of others at a distance

without wholly disregarding them, as having an almost instinctive distrust of any but his most intimate associates. La Salle is quoted as claiming for himself "a timidity which is natural to me," and to it he attributes his preference for solitary pursuits.

While these traits apply to the historical La Salle, they also seem part of an act of projection in which Parkman revealed his own character across a long span of history and in the language of another society and age. In his portrait of La Salle Parkman himself emerges as a figure torn between two centuries. While he was convinced that something of great value, unblemished forests and in men "hardihood," had been lost in bringing his nineteenth-century American world into being, Parkman was impatient and contemptuous, like La Salle himself, of much that he found in the seventeenth century, its cruelties and its religious superstition most of all.

The closing chapter of *Montcalm and Wolfe* even more powerfully dramatizes Parkman's uncertainty whether the victory of bourgeois commercial society in America represents an advance over what it had replaced, whether, to quote his final sentence.

> the rule of the masses is consistent with the highest growth of the individual; [whether] democracy can give the world a civilization as mature and pregnant, ideas as energetic and vitalizing, and types of manhood as lofty and strong, as any of the systems which it boasts to supplant.

Parkman's desk at his home in Boston and the wire "gridiron" he used when he could not see to write. Elizabeth Cordner Collection.

Throughout, with his ambivalence toward the past and the present, his histories express an uncomfortable equilibrium between the seventeenth and the nineteenth centuries.

Parkman's voluminous notes in *Montcalm and Wolfe* and elsewhere reveal a mind in marked contrast to that of the characters he describes in his narrative: a nineteenth-century skeptical and scientific mind schooled in exactitude of description and measurement, and rigorously insistent on accuracy and the detailed verification of claims made by others. He closely scrutinizes the chronicles of explorers, checking whether their accounts of their travels are plausible. (p. 38)

Parkman is just as rigorous with himself. Often, if he has translated a statement made by a historical figure, he will quote the original French in a note. This counterpoint to the narrative events themselves, when it is continued over thousands of pages, results in an effect very different from the monolinear narrative thread that Parkman announces as his intention. His histories are crammed with what might appear to be digressions, anecdotes, descriptions of natural life, ethnographic detail, topographic annotations, and analyses of illustrations from the period. Literally hundreds of historical figures are singled out by name, a great many of them characterized, some of them at length. In sum, Parkman's histories are a vast miscellany that would have shattered into fragments in the hands of other historians with a less certain purpose.

The voices that Parkman employs in his narration can seem almost as numerous as his details. They are sometimes (often only potentially) dissonant or conflicting. There are long stretches in which Parkman synthesizes the conclusions drawn by other contemporary historians, like Jared Sparks, that read like stylish versions of present-day textbook history, as in the opening chapter of *Montcalm and Wolfe.* Sometimes such passages are followed by the kind of subtle psychological characterizations that are contained in his *La Salle,* or by verbal landscapes of closely observed detail. Paragraphs of unsurpassed lyricism and great literary complexity are followed by others that seem little more than routine paraphrases of sources. There are clear lapses now and then in rhetoric, and the use of detail often verges upon clutter, but the remarkable feature of the histories is the degree to which, diverse and disparate though they seem, they cohere, and can be experienced as a whole.

How did he achieve this? A recent study by Richard Vitzhum compares Parkman's methods to those of George Bancroft and Henry Adams, pointing out that while Parkman's method was scarcely different from Bancroft's, no one would claim for Bancroft the kind of literary power that Parkman's histories possess. The source of that power seems to me to lie in the cadenced voice that runs throughout the work, setting a pace that varies but never slackens, and that sustains the momentum of the background story through many digressions and asides by keeping the reader in suspense.

At the same time the voice has a quality of omniscience that gives unity to diverse material and makes the reader feel that the narrator is masterfully unfolding very different kinds of knowledge as his story moves forward, as in the long "detours" from his account of La Salle's discoveries in which parallel accounts of discoveries by Hennepin and others add suspense and meaning to the central narrative. Parkman can also hold up narrative action while building suspense, as when, within the narrative, he meticulously examines and rejects claims made by the family of La Salle that he had first discovered the Mississippi, and he gives brilliant descriptions of the landscape that other explorers saw, descriptions that invariably become charged with human significance. Although Parkman claimed not to read novels himself and experienced literature mostly from being read to by his sister and others close to him, the narrative cadence of his work seems to me to owe much to the tone of the nineteenth-century novel. Indeed, it is Parkman's ability to maintain the narrative that seems central to his achievement. His painstaking work on thousands of sources and authorities comes to us through a calmly authoritative persona that remains at the imaginative center of his histories, modulating their tone, arbitrating their shifts in strategy, carrying the reader forward less by explicit argument than by using again and again the same modes of storytelling. The narrative voice transforms the sources it works from, even when it cites them verbatim, as in the portrayal of La Salle. (p. 39)

[Many major figures of Parkman's time] seem preoccupied with the affinities between the seventeenth and nineteenth centuries. It was not just that the discovery of the mysterious and unique New World set Western evolutionary and historical thought in motion, changing forever the cultural and natural environment both in Europe and America in ways that only began to become clear in the nineteenth century. What was also taking place was a kind of colonization of nineteenth-century culture by the literary rhetorical modes of the seventeenth, a process one can imagine at work as Parkman pored over the *Jesuit Relations* and other chronicles of two centuries before.

The involvement of nineteenth-century Americans with the culture of seventeenth-century England, the rediscovery of Puritanism quite apart, seems incontrovertible. . . . The rhythms of Shakespeare and the Bible, no one now needs to be reminded, can be heard throughout American literature during much of the nineteenth-century. In this Parkman was no exception. His devices of listing and naming, as in the passage I have quoted, echo Biblical rhythms as he tries to recover in America's wild and virgin landscape a lost seventeenth-century world that no historical mind could fully recapture.

To recover was to repossess. What drove Parkman to elaborate the form of narrative history was the need to perform such an act of repossession. In this quest he had allies in other historical thinkers and many of the major theorists of the day. Where some turned to theory, Parkman resorted to his version of the historical narrative. They were all aware that the social changes that had taken place since the seventeenth century were of a magnitude difficult to comprehend. We now tend to forget that their writings and speculations spoke less to the secure conviction that society was evolving in an orderly way than to a sense of the unsettling mystery of what had passed. For on that mystery depended an even more uncertain future. The conundrum invited ambitious forays into the past, such as those Parkman undertook.

It is important to realize how singular Parkman was in his time. The speculative temper of Marx, or even of John Fiske, was foreign to his nature. Half verbal artist, half naturalist—he sometimes referred to his work as "a history of the American forest"—Parkman was denied an explanation to the problem of anomalous historical change that plagued him and his age. In everything he wrote the exactions of a scientific temperament pressed hard upon him, separating him both psychologically and stylistically from the events and the historical figures that were his lifelong preoccupation. Parkman, believing as he did in the inevitability of progress, must have sensed as he worked through the closing years of his life, battered by illness, that his great work was, in a certain way, as doomed as the French domain in America.

This premonition, I suspect, will soon prove unwarranted. The republication of the histories should assure them a place among such classics as *Walden, The Education of Henry Adams*, and *The Theory of the Leisure Class*, maverick works whose idiosyncratic voice and troubled vision of the future have characterized the main tradition of American letters. (p. 40)

William P. Taylor, "Repossessing America," in The New York Review of Books, *Vol. XXX, No. 15, October 13, 1983, pp. 35-40.*

ADDITIONAL BIBLIOGRAPHY

Bourne, Edward Gaylord. "Francis Parkman." In his *Essays in Historical Criticism*, pp. 277-87. 1901. Reprint. Freeport, N.Y.: Books for Libraries Press, 1967.

    Assigns Parkman to the narrative school of historians and predicts that his works will outlive those of Prescott, Motley, and Bancroft.

Brooks, Van Wyck. "Francis Parkman." In his *New England: Indian Summer, 1865-1915*, pp. 169-83. New York: E. P. Dutton & Co., 1940.

    Appraises *France and England in North America*. Although Brooks criticizes Parkman's harsh treatment of the Indians, he contends that, on the whole, the historian brought insight and understanding to his study of New France.

Doughty, Howard. *Francis Parkman*. New York: Macmillan Co., 1962, 414 p.

    A highly regarded biographical and critical study. Doughty provides a detailed analysis of theme, structure, characterization, and style in Parkman's histories. Of particular interest to the critic is Parkman's blending of factual authenticity and literary artistry.

Farnham, Charles Haight. *A Life of Francis Parkman*. Boston: Little, Brown and Co., 1900, 394 p.

    The first book-length biography, by Parkman's secretary. Farnham is faulted by modern scholars for misrepresenting Parkman's life as "solitary" and "pathetic."

Frothingham, O. B. "Memoir of Francis Parkman, LL.D." In *Proceedings of the Massachusetts Historical Society*, Second Series Vol. VIII, pp. 520-62. Boston: Massachusetts Historical Society, 1894.

    A eulogistic sketch of Parkman's life, largely based on personal reminiscences.

Gale, Robert L. *Francis Parkman*. Twayne's United States Authors Series, edited by Sylvia E. Bowman, no. 220. New York: Twayne Publishers, 1973, 204 p.

    Combines biographical information with a thorough examination of Parkman's literary technique. Gale provides a detailed analysis of style and structure in Parkman's histories as well as in *The Oregon Trail* and *Vassall Morton*.

Gohdes, Clarence. "The Challenge of Social Problems and of Science." In *The Literature of the American People: An Historical and Critical Survey*, edited by Arthur Hobson Quinn, pp. 763-89. New York: Appleton-Century-Crofts, 1951.*

    A commendatory overview of Parkman's life and career. Gohdes admires *France and England in North America* for both its scholarly and artistic value, arguing that "with all its scrupulous dependence on documents, the narrative often spills forth with the liveliness of fiction."

Griffin, David E. "'The Man for the Hour': A Defense of Francis Parkman's *Frontenac*." *The New England Quarterly* XLIII, No. 4 (December 1970): 605-20.

    Challenges W. J. Eccles's contention that Parkman's *Frontenac* is historically inaccurate.

Jacobs, Wilbur R. "Some Social Ideas of Francis Parkman." *American Quarterly* IX, No. 4 (Winter 1957): 387-97.

    Analyzes Parkman's attitudes toward democracy, universal suffrage, and Catholicism as evidenced in his historical writings.

————. "Some of Parkman's Literary Devices." *The New England Quarterly* XXXI, No. 2 (June 1958): 244-52.

    Examines Parkman's methods of creating dramatic suspense in his historical narratives.

————. Introduction to *Letters of Francis Parkman*, Vol. I, by Francis Parkman, edited by Wilbur R. Jacobs, pp. xxix-lix. Norman: University of Oklahoma Press, 1960.

    An account of Parkman's life and career that relies heavily on his correspondence.

Jordy, William. "Henry Adams and Francis Parkman." *American Quarterly* III, No. 1 (Spring 1951): 52-68.*

    Contrasts Parkman's literary approach to history with Adams's scientific approach.

Kraus, Michael. "Francis Parkman." In his *A History of American History*, pp. 272-90. New York: Farrar & Rinehart, 1937.

    An introductory discussion of Parkman's works. Kraus briefly summarizes the material covered in the separate volumes of *France and England in North America*.

Levin, David. "Francis Parkman: The Oregon Trail." In *Landmarks of American Writing*, edited by Hennig Cohen, pp. 79-89. New York: Basic Books, Publishers, 1969.

    Praises *The Oregon Trail*'s picturesqueness, but faults Parkman's condescending view of the Indians.

Lewis, R.W.B. "The Function of History: Bancroft and Parkman." In his *The American Adam: Innocence, Tragedy, and Tradition in the Nineteenth Century*, pp. 159-73. Chicago: University of Chicago Press, 1966.*

    Examines the relationship between Parkman's attitude toward the American forest and his attitude toward history. According to Lewis, Parkman was "dispassionate" about the outcome of the struggle between France and England in North America because he regretted the triumph of civilization and the disappearance of the forest.

Lodge, Henry Cabot. "Francis Parkman." In *Hero Tales from American History*, by Henry Cabot Lodge and Theodore Roosevelt, pp. 161-70. New York: Century Co., 1919.

    Describes Parkman's "heroic" triumph over his various illnesses.

————. "Francis Parkman." In *Proceedings of the Massachusetts Historical Society: October, 1922—June, 1923*, Vol. LVI, pp. 319-35. Boston: Massachusetts Historical Society, 1923.

    Ranks *France and England in North America* with the histories of Herodotus, Thucydides, Tacitus, and Edward Gibbon.

Morison, Samuel Eliot. "Bibliography." In *The Parkman Reader*, by Francis Parkman, edited by Samuel Eliot Morison, pp. 519-24. Boston: Little, Brown and Co., 1955.

    A bibliography of Parkman's historical works valuable for its listing of revised editions.

Parkman Centenary Celebration at Montreal: 13th November, 1923. McGill University Publications, series I, no. 6. Montreal: Parkman Centenary Sub-committee and McGill University, 1924, 40 p.

    Prints speeches delivered at a meeting held in Montreal to commemorate the centenary of Parkman's birth. The collection includes addresses given by Bliss Perry, Aegidius Fauteux, and Arthur Currie.

Parrington, Vernon Louis. "The Mind of New England: Other Aspects of the New England Mind, The Reign of the Genteel." In his *Main Currents in American Thought: 1800-1860, The Romantic Revolution in America*, Vol. II, pp. 427-33. New York: Harcourt Brace Jovanovich, 1927.*

    Assigns Parkman, Prescott, and Motley to the romantic school of historians and briefly discusses their works within the context of their Brahmin heritage.

Pritchett, V. S. "Injun Mad." *New Statesman* LXIII, No. 1624 (27 April 1962): 598-99.

Attributes Parkman's lack of interest in the American westward migration of the 1840s to his passion for the untamed wilderness.

Schramm, Wilbur L. "Parkman's Novel." *American Literature* 9, No. 2 (May 1937): 218-27.

Discusses the autobiographical nature of *Vassall Morton*.

Sedgwick, Henry Dwight. *Francis Parkman*. American Men of Letters. Boston: Houghton, Mifflin and Co., Riverside Press, 1904, 345 p.

A detailed account of Parkman's life focusing on his travels as described in *The Oregon Trail* and *France and England in North America*. Sedgwick's biography contains numerous extracts from Parkman's correspondence and journals.

Smith, Joe Patterson. "Francis Parkman." In *The Marcus W. Jernegan Essays in American Historiography*, edited by William T. Hutchinson, pp. 43-59. Chicago: University of Chicago Press, 1937.

Attributes Parkman's success as a historian to his skillful character delineation, impartial presentation of facts, extensive use of primary sources, and detailed descriptions of historical sites.

Sonderegger, Richard. *Francis Parkman*. Historiadores de America, no. 8. Mexico: Instituto Panamericano de Geografia e Historia, 1951. 41 p.

A brief introduction to Parkman's life and career. Sonderegger emphasizes that Parkman's historical approach encompasses both the literary and scientific methods.

Taylor, William R. "Francis Parkman." In *Pastmasters: Some Essays on American Historians,* edited by Marcus Cunliffe and Robin W. Winks, pp. 1-38. New York: Harper & Row, Publishers, 1969.

A biographical and critical overview. Taylor first examines Parkman's social and political beliefs within the context of the intellectual climate in Boston during the nineteenth century. The critic then discusses the influence of these beliefs on Parkman's historical method, particularly as evidenced in *La Salle*.

Tonsor, Stephen. "The Conservative as Historian: Francis Parkman." *Modern Age* 27, Nos. 3-4 (Summer-Fall 1983): 246-55.

Contends that *France and England in North America* is informed by Parkman's conservative social and political views.

Van Doren, Mark. Introduction to *The Oregon Trail*, by Francis Parkman, pp. vii-xiii. New York: Holt, Rinehart and Winston, 1969.

A laudatory account of Parkman's journey on the Oregon Trail and his stay with the Ogillallah Indians.

Van Tassel, David D. "Rise of the Romantic Nationalists, 1830-60." In his *Recording America's Past: An Interpretation of the Development of Historical Studies in America, 1607-1884,* pp. 111-20. Chicago: University of Chicago Press, 1960.*

Examines Parkman's contribution to the development of American historiography. Van Tassel likens Parkman's style and subject matter to those of the romantic historians Bancroft, Prescott, and Motley. However, Van Tassel also points out that Parkman's historical method, which was characterized by an emphasis on factual information, relates him to the scientific school of American historians.

Wheelwright, Edward. "Memoir of Francis Parkman, LL.D." In *Publications of the Colonial Society of Massachusetts: Transactions, 1892-1894,* Vol. I, pp. 304-50. Boston: Colonial Society of Massachusetts, 1895.

A detailed biographical sketch based on personal memories. Wheelwright was one of Parkman's Harvard classmates.

Winsor, Justin. "Francis Parkman: I." *The Atlantic Monthly* LXXIII, No. CCCCXXXIX (May 1894): 660-64.

Praises the historical accuracy of Parkman's writings. In addition, Winsor briefly assesses Parkman's debt to the American historians Bancroft, Prescott, Motley, and Sparks.

Woodward, C. Vann. "Obsessed with the Conquest of a Continent." *The New York Times Book Review* (3 July 1983): 3, 18.

An appreciative review of the Library of America edition of *France and England in North America*. Woodward praises Parkman's dedication to his historical project and confidently states that this new collection of his works will enjoy widespread popularity.

Wrong, George M. "Francis Parkman." *The Canadian Historical Review* IV, No. 4 (December 1923): 289-303.

A biographical and critical sketch commemorating the centenary of Parkman's birth. Wrong applauds the unity, dramatic power, and accuracy of Parkman's historical writings, but faults him for belittling the methods used by the French in their attempt to colonize North America.

William Wordsworth

1770-1850

English poet, critic, essayist, and dramatist.

Wordsworth is considered the greatest and most influential English Romantic poet. For his perceptive use of nature, for his earnest exploration of philosophical ideas, and for his original poetic theories, critics regard Wordsworth as a key figure in English literature. Asserting in the Preface to his *Lyrical Ballads, with a Few Other Poems* that poetry should consist of "language really used by men," Wordsworth challenged the prevailing eighteenth-century notion of formal poetic diction and thereby profoundly affected the course of modern poetry. His major work, *The Prelude, or Growth of a Poet's Mind: Autobiographical Poem,* a study of the role of the imagination and memory in the formation of poetic sensibility, is now viewed as one of the most seminal long poems of the nineteenth century. The freshness and emotional power of Wordsworth's poetry, the keen psychological depth of his characterizations, and the urgency of his social commentary ensure his present stature as one of the most important writers in English.

Wordsworth was born in Cockermouth, England, the second son of John and Anne Cookson Wordsworth. An attorney for a prominent local aristocrat, John Wordsworth provided a secure and comfortable living for his family. But with his wife's death in 1778, the family dispersed: the boys were enrolled at a boarding school in Hawkeshead, and Wordsworth's sister, Dorothy, was sent to live with cousins in Halifax. In the rural surroundings of Hawkeshead, situated in the lush Lake District, Wordsworth early learned to love nature, including the pleasures of walking and outdoor play. He also enjoyed his formal education. The school curriculum included the works of Edmund Spenser, William Shakespeare, John Milton, James Beattie, and Thomas Chatterton, which Wordsworth supplemented with such authors as Henry Fielding and Miguel de Cervantes. In addition, Wordsworth demonstrated a talent for writing poetry and received encouragement from his teachers. However, the tranquility of his years at Hawkeshead was marred by the death of his father in 1783. Left homeless, the Wordsworth children spent their school vacations with various relatives, many of whom regarded them as nothing more than a financial burden. Biographers have pointed out that Wordsworth's frequently unhappy early life contrasts sharply with the idealized portrait of childhood he presented in his poetry.

Leaving his beloved Lake District in 1787, Wordsworth commenced study at St. John's College, Cambridge. His guardians hoped that he would choose the ministry, thus freeing them from their obligation to support him, yet Wordsworth scorned academics. The highlight of his college years, he later wrote, was a walking tour through France and Switzerland undertaken with his friend Robert Jones. Graduating in 1791, but restless and without definite career plans, Wordsworth lived for a short time in London and Wales and then traveled to France. The French Revolution was in its third year, and although he previously had shown little interest in politics, he quickly came to advocate its goals. Along with a heightened political consciousness, he experienced an emotional awakening, the details of which were kept a family secret until the early twentieth

century. During his stay in France he fell in love with a Frenchwoman, Annette Vallon, and in 1792 they had a child, Anne-Caroline. Too poor to marry and forced by the outbreak of civil war to flee France, Wordsworth reluctantly returned to England in 1793.

The next several years proved a time of great disequilibrium for the poet. England's official declaration of war on France a few months after his return precipitated Wordsworth's spiritual crisis. In addition to being apprehensive about the safety of Annette and Anne-Caroline, he felt deeply troubled by the conflict between his patriotism and his sympathy with the French Revolution. Moreover, like many of his contemporaries, Wordsworth was shocked by the degeneration of the idealistic spirit of the Revolution and by its aftermath, the Reign of Terror. For a time he sought consolation in the philanthropic doctrine of the English philosopher William Godwin, but he eventually became disenchanted with his emphasis on reason rather than emotion. However, Godwin, who had befriended the young Wordsworth, remained one of the most enduring influences on his thought. In addition to his reading of Godwin, several other events helped to raise Wordsworth's spirits in 1793. The first was the publication of his two volumes of poetry, *Descriptive Sketches* and *An Evening Walk: An Epistle in Verse*. Written in a conventional eighteenth-century style, the collections did not fare well critically. Later that year, his friend William Calvert invited Wordsworth to accompany him on a trip through the west of England. Shortly after returning, Wordsworth received a small legacy from a friend that enabled him to concentrate entirely on writing.

Following a brief sojourn in London, Wordsworth settled with his sister, Dorothy, at Racedown in 1795. Living modestly but contentedly, he now spent much of his time reading contemporary European literature and writing verse. An immensely important contribution to Wordsworth's success was Dorothy's lifelong devotion: she encouraged his efforts at composition and looked after the details of their daily life. During the first year at Racedown, Wordsworth wrote *The Borderers,* a verse drama based on the ideas of Godwin and the German Sturm und Drang writers. The single most important event of his literary apprenticeship occurred in 1797 when he met the poet Samuel Taylor Coleridge. The two had corresponded for several years, and when Coleridge came to visit Wordsworth at Racedown, their rapport and mutual admiration were immediate. Many critics view their friendship as one of the most extraordinary in English literature. The Wordsworths soon moved to Nether Stowey in order to be near Coleridge. In the intellectually stimulating environment he and Coleridge created there, Wordsworth embarked on a period of remarkable creativity. Coleridge's influence on Wordsworth during this time was immense, and his astute critiques gave the young poet direction and fostered his artistic growth. Coleridge strove particularly to encourage Wordsworth's development as a visionary thinker capable of writing philosophical poetry. To that end, he introduced him to the writings of the philosopher David Hartley, whose theories had a profound effect on Wordsworth's poetry.

In 1798, the two friends collaborated on and anonymously published *Lyrical Ballads,* a collection of experimental poems. The majority of the pieces were written by Wordsworth, including the now-famous Preface. There, he emphasized the importance of an unadorned style; his distaste for the "gaudiness" of eighteenth-century poetic diction even led Wordsworth to make the revolutionary claim that there exists no "*essential* difference between the language of prose and metrical composition." Applying the principles he outlined in the Preface, Wordsworth concentrated in his poetry on subjects derived from "humble and rustic life." Writing in a deliberately simple and powerfully direct style, he depicted social outcasts, country folk, and the poor. Wordsworth's most striking contribution to the collection was "Tintern Abbey." One of his strongest poems, it explores the relationship between nature and infinity in the descriptive-meditative style most closely associated with Wordsworth.

The appearance of *Lyrical Ballads,* with its controversial technique and subject matter, firmly established Wordsworth in the public eye. With the profits from the book, he, Coleridge, and Dorothy journeyed to Germany in 1798-99 to learn the language and attend university lectures. There Wordsworth composed the pieces that are collectively called the "Lucy" poems, as well as the first two books of *The Prelude.* Upon their return to England, he composed many new poems and revised and expanded *Lyrical Ballads,* refining his theories in the 1800, 1802, and 1805 editions.

In 1802, Wordsworth married Mary Hutchinson, a childhood friend. Realizing that Wordsworth now required a more steady source of income, Coleridge introduced him to Sir George Beaumont, a wealthy art patron who became Wordsworth's benefactor and friend. Beaumont's kindness and support saw Wordsworth through the difficult period following his brother

John's death at sea in 1805 and facilitated the publication of the *Poems* of 1807. In that collection, Wordsworth once again displayed his extraordinary talent for nature description; but further, he displayed his characteristic technique of transmuting musings about everyday subjects into meditations about humanity's place in the universe. By infusing an element of mysticism into ordinary experience, Wordsworth celebrated the imagination and its transcendent power. Always fascinated by human psychology, he also stressed the influence of childhood experiences and memory on adult attitudes and actions, summarizing his view in the phrase "The Child is father of the Man." Critical reception of the *Poems* as a whole was mixed, but most reviewers singled out "Ode: Intimations of Immortality from Recollections of Early Childhood" as perhaps Wordsworth's greatest production.

The remaining years of Wordsworth's career are generally viewed as a decline from the revolutionary and experimental fervor of his youth. He condemned French imperialism in the period after the Revolution, and his nationalism became more pronounced. The pantheism of his early nature poetry, too, gave way to orthodox religious sentiment in the later works. When Wordsworth accepted a post as distributor of stamps for Westmorland county, a political appointment that ensured his prosperity, his transformation seemed complete. Such admirers as Percy Bysshe Shelley, who formerly had respected Wordsworth as a reformer of poetic diction, now regarded him with scorn and a sense of betrayal. Whether because of professional jealousy or because of alterations to his personality caused by prolonged drug use, Coleridge grew estranged from Wordsworth after 1810. Wordsworth continued to write and published *The Excursion, Being a Portion of The Recluse* in 1814. *The Recluse* was Wordsworth's projected philosophical poem, the masterwork which would comprise all the poetry he ever wrote. He left a careful record of its plan, although he never completed it.

Wordsworth continued to write prolifically in his later years. Of these works, the most important are the *Poems* of 1815 and three long narrative poems—*The White Doe of Rylstone; or, The Fate of the Nortons, Peter Bell: A Tale in Verse,* and *The Waggoner*. Two additional works, *Yarrow Revisited and Other Poems* and *The Sonnets of William Wordsworth,* received critical accolades upon their publication and evoked comparisons of Wordsworth's sonnets with those of Shakespeare and Milton. Having become a highly respected literary figure during the 1830s, Wordsworth was awarded honorary degrees from the University of Durham and Oxford University, and in 1843 won the distinction of being named Poet Laureate. After receiving a government pension in 1842, he lived in retirement in Rydal. Only the death of his daughter Dora in 1847 and Dorothy's illness impinged on the serenity of his last years. When he died in 1850, he was one of England's best-loved poets.

Wordsworth's greatest work, *The Prelude,* was published shortly after his death. Begun some fifty years earlier, the poem was completed in 1805 and then drastically revised over time. Greeted with uneven praise at its first appearance, the poem is now hailed as Wordsworth's greatest work. Critics laud *The Prelude*'s blending of autobiography, history, and epic, its theme of loss and gain, its mythologizing of childhood experience, and its affirmation of the imagination.

Critics of Wordsworth's works have made his treatment of nature, his use of diction, and his critical theories the central focus of their studies. Early response to his poetry begins with

Francis Jeffrey's concerted campaign to thwart Wordsworth's poetic career. His reviews of the works of the Lake poets, and of Wordsworth's poetry in particular, were so vitriolic that they stalled public acceptance of the poet for some twenty years but brought many critics to his defense. To Jeffrey, Wordsworth's poetic innovations were in "open violation of the established laws of poetry," his compassionate depictions of social outcasts merely "splenetic and idle discontent with existing institutions in society." He described Wordsworth's stylistic simplicity as affectation and his focus on ordinary people and events as bathos. Despite Jeffrey's comments, considered unprecedented in their systematic malice, Wordsworth's poetry eventually gained acceptance. By the 1830s, Wordsworth was England's preeminent poet, and he retained that honor until the 1860s, when his fame briefly waned. Critical debate on Wordsworth resumed in the 1870s with Leslie Stephen's laudatory essay on the poet's philosophical doctrine and Matthew Arnold's famous reply. A Wordsworthian himself, Arnold suggested that indiscriminate praise of Wordsworth's poetry and schematization of his ideas might diminish his importance, establishing him as the leader of a clique rather than as an author with universal appeal.

The modern resurgence of interest in Wordsworth's poetry manifested itself in specialized studies of his ideas. Many critics in the early twentieth century concentrated on Wordsworth's view of nature. Walter Raleigh and Alfred North Whitehead examined Wordsworth's attitude toward scientific thought, noting his techniques of describing the particular in terms of the universal and emphasizing his visionary view of the unity of the universe. Discussing Wordsworth's view of the development of the mind in relation to nature, Arthur Beatty observed that the poet understood nature to be the ultimate repository of truth, reason, and the imagination. In an often-rebutted essay on Wordsworth's benign concept of nature, Aldous Huxley accused the poet of falsifying the realities of the natural world to support his tame representation of the universe. Joseph Warren Beach, on the other hand, focused on the tenets and evolution of Wordsworth's religion of naturalism, his underlying belief in a providentially ordered cosmos, and the gradual shift to intuitionism and belief in the soul that heralded his later religious orthodoxy.

In addition to delving into Wordsworth's view of nature, critics have explored his philosophical ideas. Newton Stallknecht discussed the relationship between Wordsworth's political views and his style: commenting on the importance of the concept of liberty in Wordsworth's writings, he theorized about the poet's succumbing to what Stallknecht termed the "democratic fallacy." Stressing the role of moral vision in Wordsworth's poetry, David Perkins probed his sincerity and its stylistic and thematic implications. Wordsworth's philosophy as it is embodied in *The Prelude* is the subject of an important and influential study by Raymond Dexter Havens. Like Havens, Robert Langbaum evaluated Wordsworth's contributions to the Romantic concept of personal identity in *The Prelude*, tracing his modifications of the Lockean epistemological model.

Wordsworth's poetic theory has been an area of dispute among scholars ever since the publication of *Lyrical Ballads*. Although Jeffrey considered its Preface an anarchical manifesto, later critics have come to regard it as a milestone in nineteenth-century poetics and, according to Perkins, as "one of the finest critical achievements in English." Paradoxically, it was Coleridge who both clarified the merits of Wordsworth's poetic principles and, at the same time, most pointedly identified their defects. In writing about Wordsworth's theories in his *Biographia Literaria*, Coleridge praised his originality, "sane sentiments," and the "perfect appropriateness of the words to the meaning" in his works. Disagreeing with Wordsworth's preference for a poetic "language really used by men," Coleridge challenged his friend's assumption that humble diction and ordinary subjects were inherently superior to formal ones. He reasoned further that various poetic moods necessitate a wide range of styles and pointed out instances of elevated language in Wordsworth's own poetry. By doing so, Coleridge hoped to discourage Wordsworth from his "laborious minuteness" in describing rustic subjects and to encourage him instead to concentrate on meditative poetry. Such subsequent critics as Thomas De Quincey and George Saintsbury, like Coleridge, stated that Wordsworth fettered his genius by insisting on extreme simplicity of style. Wordsworth's views in the Preface were quite radical in their time, and twentieth-century critics, notably M. H. Abrams, have come to acknowledge the modernity of Wordsworth's theories; however, they also cite his debt to eighteenth-century thought.

In addition to discussions of Wordsworth's ideas, debate also continues about the effectiveness and intrinsic merit of his style. Early reviewers objected to the didactic element they discerned in Wordsworth's poetry, particularly in his longer narrative works. But given his plea "to be considered as a teacher or as nothing," this tendency to instruct has been accepted as one of the hallmarks of his style. Like Coleridge, William Hazlitt and Walter Pater greatly furthered the public's appreciation of Wordsworth's works. Hazlitt stressed the poet's democratic impulse as embodied in his "vernacular" style and called him the "most original poet now living." Emphasizing that "impassioned contemplation" is one of the most important features of Wordsworth's style, Pater was among the first critics to explore sensuousness and duality in his poetry. The comments of such later scholars as James Russell Lowell, A. C. Bradley, and Helen Darbishire, on the other hand, typify the school of critics who value Wordsworth's naturalness, simplicity, and boldness above all his other stylistic traits. Yet Bradley maintained that Wordsworth's mysticism figures equally prominently in his poetry, echoing Pater's observation that in Wordsworth's works, one senses the presence of "a power not altogether his own, or under his control." Some critics have noted, too, that Wordsworth's simplicity can produce a soporific effect and lead to narrowness of perspective, while others have argued that his philosophical digressions in some instances undermine the unity of his works.

In the twentieth century, many commentators have concentrated on analyzing Wordsworth's symbolism. Frederick Pottle, for instance, examined the process by which Wordsworth transforms real images into symbols. In his groundbreaking study, Geoffrey Hartman inquired into the connection between consciousness, symbolism, and identity in Wordsworth's poetry. In an article on the "Intimations" ode that is considered by many scholars the most important individual essay on Wordsworth, Lionel Trilling examined the poem's themes and imagery, overturning the formerly accepted notion that the ode documents the diminishment of Wordsworth's artistic power.

Whether critics focus on the "simple" Wordsworth of the nature poems and the early lyrics, the "philosophical" Wordsworth of the meditative poetry, or the "innovative" Wordsworth of the *Lyrical Ballads*, they continue to be stimulated by the richness of Wordsworth's poetry. His wide-ranging intellect and originality in shaping a new poetic tradition have assured him a central place in English literature, and his joyous celebration of the imagination has engaged the interest and admiration of each new generation of readers. The appeal of Wordsworth's poetry is perhaps best summarized in these lines from Arnold's memorial tribute:

> Others will strengthen us to bear—
> But who, ah who, will make us feel?

PRINCIPAL WORKS

Descriptive Sketches (poetry) 1793
An Evening Walk: An Epistle in Verse (poetry) 1793
Lyrical Ballads, with a Few Other Poems [with Samuel Taylor Coleridge] (poetry) 1798; also published in revised form as *Lyrical Ballads, with Other Poems*, 1800, 1802, 1805
Poems (poetry) 1807
The Excursion, Being a Portion of The Recluse (poetry) 1814
Poems (poetry) 1815
The White Doe of Rylstone; or, The Fate of the Nortons (poetry) 1815
Peter Bell: A Tale in Verse (poetry) 1819
The Waggoner (poetry) 1819
The River Duddon: A Series of Sonnets, Vaudracour and Julia, and Other Poems (poetry) 1820
Ecclesiastical Sketches (poetry) 1822
Memorials of a Tour on the Continent, 1820 (poetry) 1822
Yarrow Revisited and Other Poems (poetry) 1835
The Sonnets of William Wordsworth (poetry) 1838
*Poems, Chiefly of Early and Late Years; Including The Borderers. 4 vols. (poetry and drama) 1842-54
**The Prelude, or Growth of a Poet's Mind: Autobiographical Poem (poetry) 1850
The Recluse (unfinished poem) 1888
The Letters of William and Dorothy Wordsworth. 6 vols. (letters) 1935-39; also published in revised form as *The Letters of William and Dorothy Wordsworth.* 6 vols. to date. 1967-
Poetical Works of William Wordsworth. 5 vols. (poetry) 1940-49
The Prose Works of William Wordsworth (prose) 1974
The Cornell Wordsworth. 12 vols. to date. (poetry, prose, and drama) 1975-

*The Borderers was written in 1795.

**This work was written in 1799-1805.

[THOMAS HOLCROFT] (essay date 1793)

[*In this brief review, Holcroft disparages "descriptive poetry" in general and Wordsworth's* Descriptive Sketches *in particular. Holcroft criticizes what he perceives as a lack of clarity and logical thought in the poems, especially in Wordsworth's conception of nature.*]

More descriptive poetry! . . . Have we not yet enough? Must eternal changes be rung on uplands and lowlands, and forests, and brooding clouds, and cells, and dells, and dingles? Yes; more, and yet more: so it is decreed.

Mr. Wordsworth begins his [*Descriptive Sketches*] with the following exordium:

> Were there, below, a spot of holy ground,
> By Pain and her sad family *un*found,
> Sure, Nature's God that spot to man had giv'n,
> Where murmuring *rivers join* the song of *ev'n!*
> Where *falls* the purple morning far and wide
> *In flakes* of light upon the mountain side;
> Where summer suns in ocean sink to rest,
> Or moonlight upland lifts her hoary breast;
> Where Silence, on her night of wing, o'er-broods
> Unfathom'd dells and undiscover'd woods;
> Where rocks and groves the *power* of waters *shakes*
> In cataracts, or sleeps in quiet lakes.

May we ask, how it is that rivers join in the song of ev'n? or, in plain prose, the evening! but, if they do, is it not true that they equally join the song of morning, noon, and night? The *purple morning falling in flakes* of light is a bold figure: but we are told, it falls far and wide—Where?—On the mountain's *side*. We are sorry to see the purple morning confined so like a maniac in a straight waistcoat. What the night of wing of silence is, we are unable to comprehend: but the climax of the passage is, that, were there such a spot of holy ground as is here so sublimely described, *unfound* by Pain and her sad family, Nature's God had surely given that spot to man, though its *woods* were *undiscovered*.

Let us proceed,

> But *doubly* pitying Nature loves to show'r
> Soft on his *wounded heart* her healing pow'r,
> Who *plods* o'er hills and vales his road *forlorn*,
> Wooing her varying charms from eve to morn.
> *No sad vacuities* his heart *annoy*,
> *Blows* not a Zephyr but it *whispers joy*;
> For him *lost* flowers their *idle* sweets *exhale*;
> He *tastes* the meanest *note* that swells the gale;
> For him sod-seats the cottage-door adorn,
> And *peeps* the far-off *spire*, his evening bourn!
> Dear is the forest *frowning* o'er his head,
> And dear the green-sward to his *velvet tread*;
> Moves there a *cloud* o'er mid-day's flaming eye?
> Upwards he looks—and calls it luxury;
> Kind Nature's *charities* his steps attend,
> In every babbling brook he finds a friend.

Here we find that *doubly* pitying Nature is very kind to the traveller, but that this traveller has a *wounded heart* and *plods* his road *forlorn*. In the next line but one we discover that—

> No *sad vacuities* his heart *annoy*;
> Blows not a Zephyr but it whispers *joy*.

The flowers, though they have lost themselves, or are lost, exhale their idle sweets for him; the *spire peeps* for him; sod-seats, forests, clouds, nature's charities, and babbling brooks, all are to him luxury and friendship. He is the happiest of mortals, and plods, is forlorn, and has a wounded heart. How often shall we in vain advise those, who are so delighted with their own thoughts that they cannot forbear from putting them into ryhme, to examine those thoughts till they themselves understand them? No man will ever be a poet, till his mind be sufficiently powerful to sustain this labour. (pp. 216-18)

> [*Thomas Holcroft*], *in a review of "'Descriptive Sketches', in Verse," in* The Monthly Review, *London, Vol. XII, October, 1793, pp. 216-18.*

[THOMAS HOLCROFT]   (essay date 1793)

[*In the following excerpt from his review of* An Evening Walk, *Holcroft censures Wordsworth's imagery—"figures which no poetical license can justify"—but concedes that the collection shows promise.*]

[In *An Evening Walk*], the subject and the manner of treating it vary but little from [*Descriptive Sketches.*] We will quote four lines from a passage which the author very sorrowfully apologizes for having omitted:

> Return delights! with whom my road beg*un,*
> When *Life-rear'd* laughing *up her* morning *sun;*
> When Transport kiss'd away my April tear,
> Rocking as in a dream the tedious year.

Life *rearing* up the sun! Transport kissing away an *April* tear and *rocking* the year as in a dream! Would the cradle had been specified! Seriously, these are figures which no poetical license can justify. If they can possibly give pleasure, it must be to readers whose habits of thinking are totally different from ours. Mr. Wordsworth is a scholar, and, no doubt, when reading the works of others, a critic. There are passages in his poems which display imagination, and which afford hope for the future: but, if he can divest himself of all partiality, and will critically question every line that he has written, he will find many which, he must allow, call loudly for amendment.

[*Thomas Holcroft*], *in a review of "An Evening Walk," in* The Monthly Review, *London, Vol. XII, October, 1793, p. 218.*

[ROBERT SOUTHEY]   (essay date 1798)

[*An English poet, historian, biographer, essayist, short story writer, and editor, Southey was a prominent literary figure of the late eighteenth and early nineteenth centuries and a key member of the Lake School of poetry. While critics of his era generally applauded his prose writings, his verse received little favorable attention and its merits are still debated. Southey is chiefly remembered today for his association with the early Romantics and for his literary and social criticism. Scholars agree that his distinction may lie in being a quintessential working man of letters rather than a great artist. In this excerpt from his review of* Lyrical Ballads, *Southey writes that "every piece discovers genius," but deems "The Idiot Boy" and "Tintern Abbey" the most important poems in the collection. Though he ranks Wordsworth among the best contemporary poets, Southey judges his poetic experiment a failure owing to the inherently "uninteresting" subject matter of the poems.*]

The majority of [*Lyrical Ballads*], we are informed in the advertisement, are to be considered as experiments.

> They were written chiefly with a view to ascertain how far the language of conversation in the middle and lower classes of society is adapted to the purposes of poetic pleasure.

Of these experimental poems, the most important is the **"Idiot Boy."** (pp. 197-98)

No tale less deserved the labour that appears to have been bestowed upon this. It resembles a Flemish picture in the worthlessness of its design and the excellence of its execution. . . .

The other ballads of this kind are as bald in story, and are not so highly embellished in narration. With that which is entitled the **"Thorn"** we were altogether displeased. The advertisement

says, it is not told in the person of the author, but in that of some loquacious narrator. The author should have recollected that he who personates tiresome loquacity, becomes tiresome himself. The story of a man who suffers the perpetual pain of cold, because an old woman prayed that he never might be warm, is perhaps a good story for a ballad, because it is a well-known tale: but is the author certain that it is *'well authenticated?'* and does not such an assertion promote the popular superstition of witchcraft? (p. 200)

With pleasure we turn to the serious pieces, the better part of the volume. The **"Softer-Mother's Tale"** is in the best style of dramatic narrative. **"The Dungeon,"** and the **"Lines upon the Yew-tree Seat,"** are beautiful. **"The Tale of the Female Vagrant"** is written in the stanza, not the style, of Spenser. (p. 201)

Admirable as this poem is, the author seems to discover still superior powers in the **"Lines written near Tintern Abbey."** On reading this production, it is impossible not to lament that he should ever have condescended to write such pieces as the **"Last of the Flock,"** the **"Convict,"** and most of the ballads. In the whole range of English poetry, we scarcely recollect anything superior to [it]. . . . (p. 203)

The 'experiment,' we think, has failed, not because the language of conversation is little adapted to 'the purposes of poetic pleasure,' but because it has been tried upon uninteresting subjects. Yet every piece discovers genius; and, ill as the author has frequently employed his talents, they certainly rank him with the best of living poets. (p. 204)

[*Robert Southey*], *in a review of "Lyrical Ballads, with a Few Other Poems," in* The Critical Review, *n.s. Vol. XXIV, October, 1798, pp. 197-204.*

[CHARLES BURNEY]   (essay date 1799)

[*The father of novelist Fanny Burney, Charles Burney was a distinguished music scholar of the late eighteenth and early nineteenth centuries. Although he praises the "fancy" and "facility" of the* Lyrical Ballads, *Burney considers their simple diction and style regressive. Expressing mixed opinions about the individual poems, he hopes that Wordsworth's talents will in the future be employed in treating more lofty and cheerful subjects.*]

Though we have been extremely entertained with the fancy, the facility, and (in general) the sentiments, of [*Lyrical Ballads*], we cannot regard them as *poetry,* of a class to be cultivated at the expence of a higher species of versification, unknown in our language at the time when our elder writers, whom this author condescends to imitate, wrote their ballads.—Would it not be degrading poetry, as well as the English language, to go back to the barbarous and uncouth numbers of Chaucer? Suppose, instead of modernizing the old bard, that the sweet and polished measures, on lofty subjects, of Dryden, Pope, and Gray, were to be transmutted into the dialect and versification of the xivth century? Should we be gainers by the retrogradation? *Rust* is a necessary quality to a counterfeit old medal: but, to give artificial rust to modern poetry, in order to render it similar to that of three or four hundred years ago, can have no better title to merit and admiration than may be claimed by any ingenious forgery. None but savages have submitted to eat acorns after corn was found. (pp. 202-03)

We have had pleasure in reading the *reliques of ancient poetry,* because it was antient; and because we were surprised to find so many beautiful thoughts in the rude numbers of barbarous times. These reasons will not apply to *imitations* of antique versification.—We will not, however, dispute any longer about names; the author shall style his rustic delineations of low-life, *poetry*, if he pleases, on the same principle on which Butler is called a poet, and Teniers a painter: but are the doggrel verses of the one equal to the sublime numbers of a Milton, or are the Dutch boors of the other to be compared with the angels of Raphael or Guido?—When we confess that our author has had the art of pleasing and interesting in no common way by his natural delineation of human passions, human characters, and human incidents, we must add that these effects were not produced by the *poetry:*—we have been as much affected by pictures of misery and unmerited distress, in *prose*. The elevation of soul, when it is lifted into the higher regions of imagination, affords us a delight of a different kind from the sensation which is produced by the detail of common incidents. . . .

Having said thus much on the *genus*, we now come more particularly to the *species*. (p. 203)

"The Dramatic Fragment," if it intends anything, seems meant to throw disgrace on the savage liberty preached by some modern *philosophes*.

The **"Yew-Tree"** seems a seat for *Jean Jaques;* while the reflections on the subject appear to flow from a more pious pen.

"The Nightingale" sings a strain of true and beautiful poetry;—Miltonic, yet original; reflective, and interesting, in an uncommon degree. (p. 204)

"The Female Vagrant" is an agonizing tale of individual wretchedness; highly coloured, though, alas! but too probable. Yet, as it seems to stamp a general stigma on all military transactions, which were never more important in free countries than at the present period, it will perhaps be asked whether the hardships described never happen during revolution, or in a nation subdued? The sufferings of individuals during the war are dreadful: but it is not better to try to prevent them from becoming general, or to render them transient by heroic and patriotic efforts, than to fly to them for ever?

Distress from poverty and want is admirably described, in . . . ["Goody Blake, and Harry Gill"]: but are we to imagine that Harry was bewitched by Goody Blake? The hardest heart must be softened into pity for the poor old woman;—and yet, if all the poor are to help themselves, and supply their wants from the possessions of their neighbours, what imaginary wants and real anarchy would it not create? Goody Blake should have been relieved out of the *two millions* annually allowed by the state to the poor of this country, not by the plunder of an individual.

"Lines on the first mild day of March" abound with beautiful sentiments from a polished mind.

"Simon Lee, the old Huntsman," is the portrait, admirably painted, of every huntsman who, by toil, age, and infirmities, is rendered unable to guide and govern his canine family.

"Anecdote for Fathers." Of this the dialogue is ingenious and natural: but the object of the child's choice, and the inferences, are not quite obvious.

"We are seven."—innocent and pretty infantine prattle.

On an **["Early Spring"]**. The first stanza of this little poem seems unworthy of the rest, which contain reflections truly pious and philosophical.

"The Thorn." All our author's pictures, in colouring, are dark as those of Rembrandt or Spanioletto.

"The last of the Flock" is more gloomy than the rest. We are not told how the wretched hero of this piece became so poor. He had, indeed, ten children: but so have many cottagers; and ere the tenth child is born, the eldest begin to work, and help, at least, to maintain themselves. No oppression is pointed out; nor are any means suggested for his relief. If the author be a wealthy man, he ought not to have suffered this poor peasant to part with *the last of the flock*. What but an Agrarian law can prevent poverty from visiting the door of the indolent, injudicious, extravagant, and, perhaps, vicious? and is it certain that rigid equality of property as well as of laws could remedy this evil?

"The Dungeon." Here candour and tenderness for criminals seem pushed to excess. Have not jails been built on the humane Mr. Howard's plan, which have almost ruined some counties, and which look more like palaces than habitations for the perpetrators of crimes? Yet, have fewer crimes been committed in consequence of the erection of those magnificent structures, at an expence which would have maintained many in innocence and comfort out of a jail, if they have been driven to theft by want?

"The mad Mother"; admirable painting! in Michael Angelo's bold and masterly manner.

"The Idiot Boy" leads the reader on from anxiety to distress, and from distress to terror, by incidents and alarms which, though of the most mean and ignoble kind, interest, frighten, and terrify, almost to torture, during the perusal of more than a hundred stanzas.

"Lines written near Richmond"—*literally "most musical, most melancholy!"*

"Expostulation and Reply." The author tells us that 'these lines, and those which follow, arose out of conversation with a friend who was somewhat unreasonably attached to modern books of moral philosophy.' These two pieces will afford our readers an opportunity of judging of the author's poetical talents, in a more modern and less gloomy style than his Ballads. . . . (pp. 206-08)

"The Old Man travelling, a Sketch," finely drawn: but the termination seems pointed against the war; from which, however, we are now no more able to separate ourselves, than Hercules was to free himself from the shirt of Nessus. The old traveller's son might have died by disease.

Each ballad is a tale of woe. The style and versification are those of our antient ditties: but much polished, and more constantly excellent. In old songs, we have only a fine line or stanza now and then; here we meet with few that are feeble:—but it is *poesie larmoiante*. The author is more plaintive than Gray himself.

"The Complaint of a forsaken Indian Woman:" another tale of woe! of the most afflicting and harrowing kind. The want of humanity here falls not on wicked Europeans, but on the innocent Indian savages, who enjoy unlimited freedom and liberty, unbridled by kings, magistrates, or laws.

"*The Convict.*" What a description! and what misplaced commiseration, on one condemned by the laws of his country, which he had confessedly violated! We do not comprehend the drift of lavishing that tenderness and compassion on a criminal, which should be reserved for virtue in unmerited misery and distress, suffering untimely death from accident, injustice, or disease.

"*Lines written near Tintern Abbey.*"—The reflections of no common mind; poetical, beautiful, and philosophical: but somewhat tinctured with gloomy, narrow, and unsociable ideas of seclusion from the commerce of the world: as if men were born to live in the woods and wilds, unconnected with each other! Is it not to education and the culture of the mind that we owe the raptures which the author so well describes, as arising from the view of beautiful scenery, and sublime objects of nature enjoyed in tranquillity, when contrasted with the artificial machinery and "busy hum of men" in a city? The savage sees none of the beauties which this author describes. The convenience of food and shelter, which vegetation affords him, is all his concern; he thinks not of its picturesque beauties, the course of rivers, the height of mountains, &c. He has no *dizzy raptures* in youth; nor does he listen in maturer age "to the still sad music of humanity."

So much genius and originality are discovered in this publication, that we wish to see another from the same hand, written on more elevated subjects and in a more cheerful disposition. (pp. 209-10)

> [*Charles Burney*], *in a review of "Lyrical Ballads, with a Few Other Poems," in* The Monthly Review, *London, Vol. XXIX, June, 1799, pp. 202-10.*

WILLIAM WORDSWORTH (essay date 1802)

[*In this excerpt from his Preface to the 1802 edition of* Lyrical Ballads, *Wordsworth outlines the principles of his poetic experiment in that collection. Describing the main features of his highly controversial theory of diction, Wordsworth also comments on the nature of poetry and on the role of the poet. For other views on Wordsworth's critical theory, see the excerpts by Coleridge (1817), De Quincey (1845), Saintsbury (1896), and Abrams (1953).*]

The principal object . . . proposed in these Poems was to choose incidents and situations from common life, and to relate or describe them, throughout, as far as was possible in a selection of language really used by men, and, at the same time, to throw over them a certain colouring of imagination, whereby ordinary things should be presented to the mind in an unusual aspect; and, further, and above all, to make these incidents and situations interesting by tracing in them, truly though not ostentatiously, the primary laws of our nature; chiefly, as far as regards the manner in which we associate ideas in a state of excitement. Humble and rustic life was generally chosen, because, in that condition, the essential passions of the heart find a better soil in which they can attain their maturity, are less under restraint, and speak a plainer and more emphatic language; because in that condition of life our elementary feelings co-exist in a state of greater simplicity, and, consequently, may be more accurately contemplated, and more forcibly communicated; because the manners of rural life germinate from those elementary feelings, and, from the necessary character of rural occupations, are more easily comprehended, and are more durable; and lastly, because in that condition the passions of men are incorporated with beautiful and permanent forms of nature. The language, too, of these men has been adopted (purified indeed from what appear to be its real defects, from all lasting and rational causes of dislike or disgust) because such men hourly communicate with the best objects from which the best part of language is originally derived; and because, from their rank in society and the sameness and narrow circle of their intercourse, being less under the influence of social vanity, they convey their feelings and notions in simple and unelaborated expressions. Accordingly, such a language, arising out of repeated experience and regular feelings, is a more permanent, and a far more philosophical language, than that which is frequently substituted for it by Poets, who think that they are conferring honour upon themselves and their art, in proportion as they separate themselves from the sympathies of men, and indulge in arbitrary and capricious habits of expression, in order to furnish food for fickle tastes, and fickle appetites, of their own creation.

I cannot, however, be insensible to the present outcry against the triviality and meanness, both of thought and language, which some of my contemporaries have occasionally introduced into their metrical compositions. . . . From such verses the Poems in these volumes will be found distinguished at least by one mark of difference, that each of them has a worthy *purpose.* Not that I always began to write with a distinct purpose formally conceived; but habits of meditation have, I trust, so prompted and regulated my feelings, that my descriptions of such objects as strongly excite those feelings, will be found to carry along with them a *purpose.* If this opinion be erroneous, I can have little right to the name of a Poet. For all good poetry is the spontaneous overflow of powerful feelings: and though this be true, Poems to which any value can be attached were never produced on any variety of subjects but by a man who, being possessed of more than usual organic sensibility, had also thought long and deeply. (pp. 115-16)

It may be safely affirmed, that there neither is, nor can be, any *essential* difference between the language of prose and metrical composition. We are fond of tracing the resemblance between Poetry and Painting, and, accordingly, we call them Sisters: but where shall we find bonds of connection sufficiently strict to typify the affinity betwixt metrical and prose composition? They both speak by and to the same organs; the bodies in which both of them are clothed may be said to be of the same substance, their affections are kindred, and almost identical, not necessarily differing even in degree; Poetry sheds no tears 'such as Angels weep,' but natural and human tears; she can boast of no celestial ichor that distinguishes her vital juices from those of prose; the same human blood circulates through the veins of them both. (pp. 119-20)

What is a poet? To whom does he address himself? And what language is to be expected from him?—He is a man speaking to men: a man, it is true, endowed with more lively sensibility, more enthusiasm and tenderness, who has a greater knowledge of human nature, and a more comprehensive soul, than are supposed to be common among mankind; a man pleased with his own passions and volitions, and who rejoices more than other men in the spirit of life that is in him; delighting to contemplate similar volitions and passions as manifested in the goings-on of the Universe, and habitually impelled to create them where he does not find them. To these qualities he has added a disposition to be affected more than other men by absent things as if they were present; an ability of conjuring up in himself passions, which are indeed far from being the same as those produced by real events, yet (especially in those parts of the general sympathy which are pleasing and delightful) do more nearly resemble the passions produced by real events, than anything which, from the motions of their own minds merely, other men are accustomed to feel in themselves:— whence, and from practice, he has acquired a greater readiness and power in expressing what he thinks and feels, and especially those thoughts and feelings which, by his own choice, or from the structure of his own mind, arise in him without immediate external excitement. (p. 121)

The obstacles which stand in the way of the fidelity of the Biographer and Historian, and of their consequent utility, are incalculably greater than those which are to be encountered by the Poet who comprehends the dignity of his art. The Poet writes under one restriction only, namely, the necessity of giving immediate pleasure to a human Being possessed of that information which may be expected from him, not as a lawyer, a physician, a mariner, an astronomer, or a natural philosopher, but as a Man. Except this one restriction, there is no object standing between the Poet and the image of things; between this, and the Biographer and Historian, there are a thousand. (pp. 122-23)

What then does the Poet? He considers man and the objects that surround him as acting and re-acting upon each other, so as to produce an infinite complexity of pain and pleasure; he considers man in his own nature and in his ordinary life as contemplating this with a certain quantity of immediate knowledge, with certain convictions, intuitions, and deductions, which from habit acquire the quality of intuitions; he considers him as looking upon this complex scene of ideas and sensations, and finding every where objects that immediately excite in him sympathies which, from the necessities of his nature, are accompanied by an overbalance of enjoyment. (p. 123)

I have said that poetry is the spontaneous overflow of powerful feelings: it takes its origin from emotion recollected in tranquility: the emotion is contemplated till, by a species of reaction, the tranquility gradually disappears, and an emotion, kindred to that which was before the subject of contemplation, is gradually produced, and does itself actually exist in the mind. In this mood successful composition generally begins, and in a mood similar to this it is carried on; but the emotion, of whatever kind, and in whatever degree, from various causes, is qualified by various pleasures, so that in describing any passions whatsoever, which are voluntarily described, the mind will, upon the whole, be in a state of enjoyment. If Nature be thus cautious to preserve in a state of enjoyment a being so employed, the Poet ought to profit by the lesson held forth to him, and ought especially to take care, that, whatever passions he communicates to his Reader, those passions, if his Reader's mind be sound and vigorous, should always be accompanied with an overbalance of pleasure. (pp. 128-29)

> *William Wordsworth, "Preface to 'Lyrical Ballads'," in his* Wordsworth's Preface to "Lyrical Ballads," *edited by W.J.B. Owen, Rosenkilde and Bagger, 1957, pp. 111-33.*

AMERICAN REVIEW, AND LITERARY JOURNAL (essay date 1802)

[*Admitting Wordsworth's merits as a poet of nature and the emotions, the author of the following excerpt posits that the "humble" style and sentiment in the* Lyrical Ballads *deprives the poems of their potential impact.*]

Mr. W. endeavours to maintain, that between poetry and prose there neither is nor can be any essential difference; that some of the most interesting parts of the best poems will be found to be strictly the language of prose when prose is well written. . . . To prove the truth of this theory by his own practice, the author excludes from his poetry all personifications of abstract ideas, as not making any regular or natural part of the language of men, and for the same reason he employs very little of what is called *poetic diction,* consisting of phrases and figures of speech, which, he observes, "from father to son have been regarded as the common inheritance of poets" [see excerpt dated 1802]. This is indeed stripping poetry at once of half her plumage, and condemning her to skim along the vale, without daring to soar into the sublime regions of fancy. The laws prescribed by Mr. W. may suit a particular species of poetry like his own, but we apprehend that their authority will not be acknowledged by the lovers of poetry in general.

As the author has drawn his subjects from the incidents of common life, for the purpose of tracing in them without ostentation the primary laws of our nature, he has chosen a style imitative of the language of ordinary conversation in the middle classes of society. On this plan we think he has made some successful experiments. As the poems are almost entirely free from intricacy of thought or expression, they may be read by the simplest swain without difficulty. Some of them appear to us too humble both in style and sentiment to be generally interesting. Many of the pieces display a lively sensibility to the beauties of rural scenery; but they are particularly distinguished for the delicate and affecting manner of pourtraying the sensations of the mind, when agitated, as the author expresses it, by the great and simple affections of our nature;— of nature, however, as she appears in the walks of low and rustic life. (pp. 118-19)

> *A review of "Lyrical Ballads," in* American Review, and Literary Journal, *Vol. II, No. 1, January-March, 1802, pp. 118-19.*

DOROTHY WORDSWORTH (journal date 1802)

[*Critics generally agree that Dorothy Wordsworth's role was a crucial one in encouraging and nurturing her brother's poetic endeavors. Moreover, her various journals and letters provide valuable information about the origin and composition of Wordsworth's poems. Biographers have noted that Wordsworth often relied heavily on his sister's descriptions of nature and sometimes incorporated them into his poems. The excerpt below, taken from Dorothy's Grasmere journal and dated April 15, 1802, describes the scene which became the subject of Wordsworth's "I Wandered Lonely as a Cloud" (see excerpt dated 1804).*]

[*April*] *15th, Thursday.* It was a threatening, misty morning, but mild. We set off after dinner from Eusemere. . . . When we were in the woods beyond Gowbarrow Park we saw a few daffodils close to the water-side. We fancied that the lake had floated the seeds ashore, and that the little colony had so sprung up. But as we went along there were more and yet more; and at last, under the boughs of the trees, we saw that there was a long belt of them along the shore, about the breadth of a country turnpike road. I never saw daffodils so beautiful. They grew among the mossy stones about and about them; some rested their heads upon these stones as on a pillow for weariness; and the rest tossed and reeled and danced, and seemed as if they verily laughed with the wind, that blew upon them over the lake; they looked so gay, ever glancing, ever changing. This wind blew directly over the lake to them. There was here and there a little knot, and a few stragglers a few yards higher up; but they were so few as not to disturb the simplicity, unity, and life of that one busy highway. (pp. 192-93)

Dorothy Wordsworth, in a journal entry of April 15, 1802, in Home at Grasmere by Dorothy Wordsworth and William Wordsworth, edited by Colette Clark, 1960. Reprint by Penguin Books, 1978, pp. 192-94.

[FRANCIS JEFFREY] (essay date 1802)

[*Jeffrey was a founder and editor (1803-1829) of the* Edinburgh Review, *one of the most influential magazines in early nineteenth-century England. A liberal Whig and a politician, Jeffrey often allowed his political beliefs to color his critical opinions. His literary criticism, perhaps the most characteristic example of "impressionistic" critical thought dominant during the first half of the nineteenth century, stressed a personal approach to literature. Jeffrey felt that literature should be judged by his own conception of beauty (a beautiful work being that which inspires sensations of tenderness or pity in the reader), rather than by such Neoclassical criteria as restraint, clarity, order, balance, and proportion. Seeking a universal standard of beauty and taste, Jeffrey exhorted artists to "employ only such subjects as are the natural signs, or the inseparable concomitants of emotions, of which the greater part of mankind are susceptible." In addition, Jeffrey wanted literature to be realistic and to observe standards of propriety. Though he became famous for his harsh criticism of the Lake poets (Samuel Taylor Coleridge, Robert Southey, and Wordsworth), Jeffrey was an exponent of moderate Romanticism and praised the work of John Keats, Lord Byron, and Walter Scott. Jeffrey was widely influential throughout his lifetime and helped to raise the status of periodical reviewing in nineteenth-century England. Wordsworth's poetry was to become the central focus of Jeffrey's vehement and prolonged attack on the Lake poets and forms a brief but important chapter in literary history. The following excerpt from his review of Southey's* Thalaba *marks the beginning of Jeffrey's systematic campaign against Wordsworth. Arguing that the modern poets' simple diction was, in fact, "affectation" and that it produced "meanness and insipidity," Jeffrey contends that the style of this school debases poetry. Further, he emphasizes that Wordsworth's adherence to the simple style is inconsistent. He concludes by censuring the modern poets for their "splenetic and idle discontent" with social institutions. For additional commentary by Jeffrey on Wordsworth's poetry, see the excerpts dated 1807, 1814, 1815, and 1822.*]

[The modern poets] have, among them, unquestionably, a very considerable portion of poetical talent, and have, consequently, been enabled to seduce many into an admiration of the false taste (as it appears to us) in which most of these productions are composed. They constitute, at present, the most formidable conspiracy that has lately been formed against sound judgement in matters poetical; and are entitled to a larger share of our censorial notice, than could be spared for an individual delinquent. (p. 64)

Their most distinguishing symbol, is undoubtedly an affectation of great simplicity and familiarity of language. They disdain to make use of the common poetical phraseology, or to ennoble their diction by a selection of fine or dignified expressions. There would be too much *art* in this, for that great love of nature with which they are all of them inspired; and their sentiments, they are determined, shall be indebted, for their effect, to nothing but their intrinsic tenderness or elevation. There is something very noble and conscientious, we will confess, in this plan of composition; but the misfortune is, that there are passages in all poems that can neither be pathetic nor sublime; and that, on these occasions, a neglect of the establishments of language is very apt to produce absolute meanness and insipidity. The language of passion, indeed, can scarcely

be deficient in elevation; and when an author is wanting in that particular, he may commonly be presumed to have failed in the truth, as well as in the dignity of his expression. The case, however, is extremely different with the subordinate parts of a composition; with the narrative and description, that are necessary to preserve its connexion; and the explanation, that must frequently prepare us for the great scenes and splendid passages. In these, all the requisite ideas may be conveyed, with sufficient clearness, by the meanest and most negligent expressions; and, if magnificence or beauty is ever to be observed in them, it must have been introduced from some other motive than that of adapting the style to the subject. It is in such passages, accordingly, that we are most frequently offended with low and inelegant expressions; and that the language, which was intended to be simple, and natural, is found oftenest to degenerate into mere slovenliness and vulgarity. It is in vain, too, to expect that the meanness of those parts may be redeemed by the excellence of others. A poet, who aims at all sublimity or pathos, is like an actor in a high tragic character, and must sustain his dignity throughout, or become altogether ridiculous. We are apt enough to laugh at the mock-majesty of those whom we know to be but common mortals in private; and cannot permit Hamlet to make use of a single provincial intonation, although it should only be in his conversation with the grave-diggers.

The followers of simplicity are, therefore, at all times in danger of occasional degradation; but the simplicity of this new school seems intended to ensure it. *Their* simplicity does not consist, by any means, in the rejection of glaring or superfluous ornament,—in the substitution of elegance to splendour,—or in that refinement of art which seeks concealment in its own perfection. It consists, on the contrary, in a very great degree, in the positive and *bona-fide* rejection of art altogether, and in the bold use of those rude and negligent expressions, which would be banished by a little discrimination. One of their own authors, indeed, has very ingenuously set forth, (in a kind of manifesto that preceded one of their most flagrant acts of hostility [the **Lyrical Ballads**]), that it was their capital object 'to adapt to the uses of poetry, the ordinary language of conversation among the middling and lower orders of the people.' What advantages are to be gained by the success of this project we confess ourselves unable to conjecture. The language of the higher and more cultivated orders may fairly be presumed to be better than that of their inferiors: at any rate, it has all those associations in its favour, by means of which a style can ever appear beautiful or exalted, and is adapted to the purposes of poetry, by having been long consecrated to its use. The language of the vulgar, on the other hand, has all the opposite associations to contend with; and must seem unfit for poetry, (if there were no other reason) merely because it has scarcely ever been employed in it. A great genius may indeed overcome these disadvantages; but we scarcely conceive that he should court them. We may excuse a certain homeliness of language in the productions of a ploughman or a milkwoman; but we cannot bring ourselves to admire it in an author, who has had occasion to indite odes to his college-bell, and inscribe hymns to the Penates.

But the mischief of this new system, is not confined to the depravation of language only; it extends to the sentiments and emotions, and leads to the debasement of all those feelings which poetry is designed to communicate. It is absurd to suppose, that an author should make use of the language of the vulgar, to express the sentiments of the refined. His professed object, in employing that language, is to bring his compositions nearer to the true standard of nature; and his intention to copy the sentiments of the lower orders, is implied in his resolution to make use of their style. Now, the different classes of society have each of them a distinct character, as well as a separate idiom; and the names of the various passions to which they are subject respectively, have a signification that varies essentially, according to the condition of the persons to whom they are applied. The love, or grief, or indignation of an enlightened and refined character, is not only expressed in a different language, but is in itself a different emotion from the love, or grief, or anger of a clown, a tradesman, or a market-wench. The things themselves are radically and obviously distinct; and the representation of them is calculated to convey a very different train of sympathies and sensations to the mind. The question, therefore, comes simply to be—Which of them is the most proper object for poetical imitation? It is needless for us to answer a question, which the practice of all the world has long ago decided irrevocably. The poor and vulgar may interest us, in poetry, by their *situation;* but never, we apprehend, by any sentiments that are peculiar to their condition, and still less by any language that is characteristic of it. The truth is, that it is impossible to copy their diction or their sentiments correctly, in a serious composition; and this, not merely because poverty makes men ridiculous, but because just taste and refined sentiment are rarely to be met with among the uncultivated part of mankind; and a language fitted for their expression, can still more rarely form any part of their 'ordinary conversations.'

The low-bred heroes, and interesting rustics of poetry, have no sort of affinity to the real vulgar of this world; they are imaginary beings, whose characters and language are in contrast with their situation; and please those who can be pleased with them, by the marvellous, and not by the nature of such a combination. In serious poetry, a man of the middling or lower order *must necessarily* lay aside a great deal of his ordinary language; he must avoid errors in grammar and orthography; and steer clear of the cant of particular professions, and of every impropriety that is ludicrous or disgusting: nay, he must speak in good verse, and observe all the graces in prosody and collocation. After all this, it may not be very easy to say how we are to find him out to be a low man, or what marks can remain of the ordinary language of conversation in the inferior orders of society. If there be any phrases that are not used in good society they will appear as blemishes in the composition, no less palpably than errors in syntax or quantity; and if there be no such phrases, the style cannot be characteristic of that condition of life, the language of which it professes to have adopted. All approximation to that language, in the same manner, implies a deviation from that purity and precision, which no one, we believe, ever violated spontaneously.

It has been argued, indeed, (for men will argue in support of what they do not venture to practice), that as the middling and lower orders of society constitute by far the greater part of mankind, so, their feelings and expressions should interest more extensively, and may be taken, more fairly than any other, for the standards of what is natural and true. To this, it seems obvious to answer, that the arts that aim at exciting admiration and delight, do not take their models from what is ordinary, but from what is excellent; and that our interest in the representation of any event, does not depend upon our familiarity with the original, but on its intrinsic importance, and the celebrity of the parties it concerns. The sculptor employs his art in delineating the graces of Antinous or Apollo, and not in the representation of those ordinary forms that belong to the crowd

of his admirers. When a chieftain perishes in battle, his followers mourn more for him, than for thousands of their equals that may have fallen around him.

After all, it must be admitted, that there is a class of persons (we are afraid they cannot be called *readers*), to whom the representation of vulgar manners, in vulgar language, will afford much entertainment. We are afraid, however, that the ingenious writers who supply the hawkers and ballad-singers, have very nearly monopolized that department, and are probably better qualified to hit the taste of their customers, than Mr. Southey, or any of his brethren can yet pretend to be. To fit them for the higher task of original composition, it would not be amiss if they were to undertake a translation of Pope or Milton into the vulgar tongue, for the benefit of those children of nature.

There is another disagreeable effect of this affected simplicity, which, though of less importance than those which have been already noticed, it may yet be worth while to mention: This is, the extreme difficulty of supporting the same low tone of expression throughout, and the inequality that is consequently introduced into the texture of the composition. To an author of reading and education, it is a style that must always be assumed and unnatural, and one from which he will be perpetually tempted to deviate. He will rise, therefore, every now and then, above the level to which he has professedly degraded himself; and make amends for that transgression by a fresh effort of descension. His composition, in short, will be like that of a person who is attempting to speak in an obsolete or provincial dialect; he will betray himself by expressions of occasional purity and elegance, and exert himself to efface that impression, by passages of unnatural meanness or absurdity. (pp. 64-8)

The *style* of our modern poets, is that, no doubt, by which they are most easily distinguished: but their genius has also an internal character; and the peculiarities of their taste may be discovered, without the assistance of their diction. Next after great familiarity of language, there is nothing that appears to them so meritorious as perpetual exaggeration of thought. There must be nothing moderate, natural, or easy, about their sentiments. There must be a 'qu'il mourut,' and a 'let there be light,' in every line; and all their characters must be in agonies and ecstasies, from their entrance to their exit. To those who are acquainted with their productions, it is needless to speak of the fatigue that is produced by this unceasing summons to admiration, or of the compassion which is excited by the spectacle of these eternal strainings and distortions. Those authors appear to forget, that a whole poem cannot be made up of striking passages; and that the sensations produced by sublimity, are never so powerful and entire, as when they are allowed to subside and revive, in a flow and spontaneous succession. It is delightful, now and then, to meet with a rugged mountain, or a roaring stream; but where there is no sunny slope, nor shaded plain, to relieve them—where all is beetling cliff and yawning abyss, and the landscape presents nothing on every side but prodigies and terrors—the head is apt to grow giddy, and the heart to languish for the repose and security of a less elevated region.

The effect even of genuine sublimity, therefore, is impaired by the injudicious frequency of its exhibition, and the omission of those intervals and breathing places, at which the mind should be permitted to recover from its perturbation or astonishment: but, where it has been summoned upon a false alarm, and disturbed in the orderly course of its attention, by an impotent attempt at elevation, the consequences are still more disastrous. There is nothing so ridiculous (at least for a poet) as to fail in great attempts. If the reader foresaw the failure, he may receive some degree of mischievous satisfaction from its punctual occurrence; if he did not, he will be vexed and disappointed; and, in both cases, he will very speedily be disgusted and fatigued. It would be going too far, certainly, to maintain, that our poets have never succeeded in their persevering endeavours at elevation and emphasis; but it is a melancholy fact, that their successes bear but a small proportion to their miscarriages; and that the reader who has been promised an energetic sentiment, or sublime allusion, must often be contented with a very miserable substitute. Of the many contrivances they employ to give the appearance of uncommon force and animation to a very ordinary conception, the most usual is, to wrap it up in a veil of mysterious and unintelligible language, which flows past with so much solemnity, that it is difficult to believe it conveys nothing of any value. Another device for improving the effect of a cold idea, is, to embody it in a verse of unusual harshness and asperity. Compound words, too, of a portentous sound and conformation, are very useful in giving an air of energy and originality; and a few lines of scripture, written out into verse from the original prose, have been found to have a very happy effect upon those readers to whom they have the recommendation of novelty.

The qualities of style and imagery, however, form but a small part of the characteristics by which a literary faction is to be distinguished. The subject and object of their compositions, and the principles and opinions they are calculated to support, constitute a far more important criterion, and one to which it is usually altogether as easy to refer. Some poets are sufficiently described as the flatterers of greatness and power, and others as the champions of independence. One set of writers is known by its antipathy to decency and religion; another, by its methodistical cant and intolerance. Our new school of poetry has a moral character also; though it may not be possible, perhaps, to delineate it quite so concisely.

A splenetic and idle discontent with the existing institutions of society, seems to be at the bottom of all their serious and peculiar sentiments. Instead of contemplating the wonders and the pleasures which civilization has created for mankind, they are perpetually brooding over the disorders by which its progress has been attended. They are filled with horror and compassion at the sight of poor men spending their blood in the quarrels of princes, and brutifying their sublime capabilities in the drudgery of unremitting labour. For all sorts of vice and profligacy in the lower orders of society, they have the same virtuous horror, and the same tender compassion. While the existence of these offences overpowers them with grief and confusion, they never permit themselves to feel the smallest indignation or dislike towards the offenders. The present vicious constitution of society alone is responsible for all these enormities: the poor sinners are but the helpless victims or instruments of its disorders, and could not possibly have avoided the errors into which they have been betrayed. Though they can bear with crimes, therefore, they cannot reconcile themselves to punishments; and have an unconquerable antipathy to prisons, gibbets, and houses of correction, as engines of oppression, and instruments of atrocious injustice. While the plea of moral necessity is thus artfully brought forward to convert all the excesses of the poor into innocent misfortunes, no sort of indulgence is shown to the offences of the powerful and rich. Their oppressions, and seductions, and debaucheries, are the theme of many an angry verse; and the indignation and

abhorrence of the reader is relentlessly conjured up against those perturbators of society, and scourges of mankind. (pp. 69-71)

[Francis Jeffrey], "Southey's 'Thalaba'," in The Edinburgh Review, *Vol. I, No. I, October, 1802, pp. 63-83.**

WILLIAM WORDSWORTH   (poem date 1804)

[Wordsworth's famous poem "I Wandered Lonely as a Cloud," written in 1804, bears a debt to the insight of his sister Dorothy. Here is his rendition of a scene described by Dorothy in her Grasmere journal (see excerpt dated 1802).]

> I wandered lonely as a cloud
> That floats on high o'er vales and hills,
> When all at once I saw a crowd,
> A host, of golden daffodils;
> Beside the lake, beneath the trees,
> Fluttering and dancing in the breeze.
>
> Continuous as the stars that shine
> And twinkle on the milky way,
> They stretched in never-ending line
> Along the margin of a bay:
> Ten thousand saw I at a glance,
> Tossing their heads in sprightly dance.
>
> The waves beside them danced; but they
> Out-did the sparkling waves in glee:
> A poet could not but be gay,
> In such a jocund company:
> I gazed—and gazed—but little thought
> What wealth the show to me had brought:
> For oft, when on my couch I lie
> In vacant or in pensive mood,
> They flash upon that inward eye
> Which is the bliss of solitude;
> And then my heart with pleasure fills,
> And dances with the daffodils.
>
>   (pp. 216-17)

William Wordsworth, "I Wandered Lonely as a Cloud," in his The Poetical Works of William Wordsworth, *edited by E. de Selincourt, Oxford at the Clarendon Press, Oxford, 1944, pp. 216-17.*

[LORD BYRON]   (essay date 1807)

[Byron was an English poet and dramatist who is now considered one of the most important poets of the nineteenth century. Because of the satiric nature of much of his work, Byron is difficult to place within the Romantic movement. His most notable contribution to Romanticism is the Byronic hero: a melancholy man, often with a dark past, who eschews societal and religious strictures, seeking truth and happiness in an apparently meaningless universe. Although Byron often expressed contempt for Wordsworth, whom he sometimes referred to as "Wordswords" and "Turdsworth," in this excerpt from his review of the Poems *of 1807 he praises his natural and fluid style. However, he criticizes Wordsworth's occasional "puerile" language and disdains his "trifling" subject matter. Byron's review, published anonymously, originally appeared in July, 1807, in* Monthly Literary Recreations.]

The characteristics of Mr. Wordsworth's muse are simple and flowing, though occasionally inharmonious verse; strong, and sometimes irresistible appeals to the feelings, with unexcep-

Wordsworth's birthplace in Cockermouth, Cumberland.

tionable sentiments. Though [*Poems*] may not equal his former efforts, many of the poems possess a native elegance, natural and unaffected, totally devoid of the tinsel embellishments and abstract hyperboles of several contemporary sonneteers. (p. 341)

The song at the "**Feast of Brougham Castle,**" the "**Seven Sisters,**" the "**Affliction of Margaret —— of ——,**" possess all the beauties, and a few of the defects, of the writer. . . .

The pieces least worthy of the author are those entitled "**Moods of my own Mind.**" We certainly wish these "**Moods**" had been less frequent, or not permitted to occupy a place near works which only make their deformity more obvious; when Mr. W. ceases to please, it is by "abandoning" his mind to the most commonplace ideas, at the same time clothing them in language not simple, but puerile. What will any reader or auditer, out of the nursery, say to such namby-pamby as "**Lines written at the Foot of Brother's Bridge**"? (p. 342)

"**The ploughboy is whooping anon anon,**" etc., etc., is in the same exquisite measure. This appears to us neither more nor less than an imitation of such minstrelsy as soothed our cries in the cradle, with the shrill ditty of

> Hey de diddle,
> The cat and the fiddle:
> The cow jump'd over the moon,
> The little dog laugh'd to see such sport,
> And the dish ran away with the spoon.

On the whole, however, with the exception of the above, and other INNOCENT odes of the same cast, we think these volumes display a genius worthy of higher pursuits, and regret that Mr. W. confines his muse to such trifling subjects. We trust his motto will be in future "Paulo majora canamus." Many, with inferior abilities, have acquired a loftier seat on Parnassus, merely by attempting strains in which Wordsworth is more qualified to excel. (pp. 342-43)

> [Lord Byron], "*Review of Wordsworth's 'Poems',*" *in his* The Works of Lord Byron: Letters and Journals, Vol. I, *edited by Rowland E. Prothero, revised edition, Charles Scribner's Sons, 1922, pp. 341-43.*

[FRANCIS JEFFREY]   (essay date 1807)

> [*Stating that his harsh evaluation of Wordsworth's style in the* Lyrical Ballads *is confirmed by his reading of the* Poems *of 1807, Jeffrey faults Wordsworth's use of unelevated subjects and "peculiarities" of diction. However, he praises Wordsworth's sonnets, from which he surmises that Wordsworth is indeed capable of writing well. Jeffrey adds that he hopes Wordsworth will in the future cease his "open violation of the established laws of poetry." For additional commentary by Jeffrey on Wordsworth's poetry, see the excerpts dated 1802, 1814, 1815, and 1822.*]

[Wordsworth] is known to belong to a certain brotherhood of poets, who have haunted for some years about the Lakes of

Cumberland; and is generally looked upon, we believe, as the purest model of the excellences and peculiarities of the school which they have been labouring to establish. (p. 214)

The *Lyrical Ballads* were unquestionably popular; and, we have no hesitation in saying, deservedly popular; for in spite of their occasional vulgarity, affectation, and silliness, they were undoubtedly characterised by a strong spirit of originality, of pathos, and natural feeling; and recommended to all good minds by the clear impression which they bore of the amiable dispositions and virtuous principles of the author. By the help of these qualities, they were enabled, not only to recommend themselves to the indulgence of many judicious readers, but even to beget among a pretty numerous class of persons, a sort of admiration of the very defects by which they were attended. It was upon this account chiefly, that we thought it necessary to set ourselves against this alarming innovation. Childishness, conceit, and affectation, are not of themselves very popular or attractive; and though mere novelty has sometimes been found sufficient to give them a temporary currency, we should have had no fear of their prevailing to any dangerous extent, if they had been graced with no more seductive accompaniments. It was precisely because the perverseness and bad taste of this new school was combined with a great deal of genius and of laudable feeling, that we were afraid of their spreading and gaining ground among us, and that we entered into the discussion with a degree of zeal and animosity which some might think unreasonable towards authors, to whom so much merit had been conceded. There were times and moods indeed, in which we were led to suspect ourselves of unjustifiable severity, and to doubt, whether a sense of public duty had not carried us rather too far in reprobation of errors, that seemed to be atoned for, by excellences of no vulgar description. At other times, the magnitude of these errors—the disgusting absurdities into which they led their feebler admirers, and the derision and contempt which they drew from the more fastidious, even upon the merits with which they were associated, made us wonder more than ever at the perversity by which they were retained, and regret that we had not declared ourselves against them with still more formidable and decided hostility.

In this temper of mind, we read the *annonce* of Mr Wordsworth's [*Poems*] with a good deal of interest and expectation, and opened his volumes with greater anxiety, than he or his admirers will probably give us credit for. We have been greatly disappointed certainly as to the quality of the poetry; but we doubt whether the publication has afforded so much satisfaction to any other of his readers:—it has freed us from all doubt or hesitation as to the justice of our former censures, and has brought the matter to a test, which we cannot help hoping may be convincing to the author himself.

Mr Wordsworth, we think, has now brought the question, as to the merit of his new school of poetry, to a very fair and decisive issue. The volumes before us are much more strongly marked by all its peculiarities than any former publication of the fraternity. In our apprehension, they are, on this very account, infinitely less interesting or meritorious; but it belongs to the public, and not to us, to decide upon their merit, and we will confess, that so strong is our conviction of their obvious inferiority, and the grounds of it, that we are willing for once to wave our right of appealing to posterity, and to take the judgment of the present generation of readers, and even of Mr Wordsworth's former admirers, as conclusive on this occasion. (pp. 214-15)

The end of poetry, we take it, is to please—and the name, we think, is strictly applicable to every metrical composition from which we receive pleasure, without any laborious exercise of the understanding. This pleasure, may, in general, be analyzed into three parts—that which we receive from the excitement of Passion or emotion—that which is derived from the play of Imagination, or the easy exercise of Reason—and that which depends on the character and qualities of the Diction. The two first are the vital and primary springs of poetical delight, and can scarcely require explanation to anyone. The last has been already overrated and undervalued by the professors of the poetical art, and is in such low estimation with the author now before us and his associates, that it is necessary to say a few words in explanation of it.

One great beauty of diction exists only for those who have some degree of scholarship or critical skill. This is what depends on the exquisite *propriety* of the words employed, and the delicacy with which they are adapted to the meaning which is to be expressed. Many of the finest passages in Virgil and Pope derive their principal charm from the fine propriety of their diction. Another source of beauty, which extends only to the more instructed class of readers, is that which consists in the judicious or happy application of expressions which have been sanctified by the use of famous writers, or which bear the stamp of a simple or venerable antiquity. There are other beauties of diction, however, which are perceptible by all—the beauties of sweet sound and pleasant associations. The melody of words and verses is indifferent to no reader of poetry; but the chief recommendation of poetical language is certainly derived from those general associations, which give it a character of dignity or elegance, sublimity or tenderness. Every one knows that there are low and mean expressions, as well as lofty and grave ones; and that some words bear the impression of coarseness and vulgarity, as clearly as others do of refinement and affection. We do not mean, of course, to say anything in defence of the hackneyed common-places of ordinary versemen. Whatever might have been the original character of these unlucky phrases, they are now associated with nothing but ideas of schoolboy imbecility and vulgar affectation. But what we do maintain is, that much of the most popular poetry in the world owes its celebrity chiefly to the beauty of its diction; and that no poetry can be long or generally acceptable, the language of which is coarse, inelegant, or infantine.

From this great source of pleasure, we think the readers of Mr Wordsworth are in great measure cut off. His diction has no where any pretensions to elegance or dignity; and he has scarcely ever condescended to give the grace of correctness or melody to his versification. If it were merely slovenly and neglected, however, all this might be endured. Strong sense and powerful feeling will ennoble any expressions; or, at least, no one who is capable of estimating those higher merits, will be disposed to mark these little defects. But, in good truth, no man, now-a-days, composes verses for publication with a slovenly neglect of their language. It is a fine and laborious manufacture, which can scarcely ever be made in a hurry; and the faults which it has, may, for the most part, be set down to bad taste or incapacity, rather than to carelessness or oversight. With Mr Wordsworth and his friends, it is plain that their peculiarities of diction are things of choice, and not of accident. They write as they do, upon principle and system; and it evidently costs them much pains to keep *down* to the standard which they have proposed to themselves. They are, to the full, as much mannerists, too, as the poetasters who ring changes on the common-places of magazine versification; and all the difference between them is, that they borrow their phrases from a different and a scantier *gradus ad Parnassum*. If they were, indeed, to discard all imitation and set phraseology, and to bring in no words merely for show or for metre,—as much, perhaps, might be gained in freedom and originality, as would infallibly be lost in allusion and authority; but, in point of fact, the new poets are just as great borrowers as the old; only that, instead of borrowing from the more popular passages of their illustrious predecessors, they have preferred furnishing themselves from vulgar ballads and plebeian nurseries.

Their peculiarities of diction alone, are enough, perhaps, to render them ridiculous; but the author before us really seems anxious to court this literary martyrdom by a device still more infallible,—we mean, that of connecting his most lofty, tender, or impassioned conceptions, with objects and incidents, which the greater part of his readers will probably persist in thinking low, silly, or uninteresting. Whether this is done from affectation and conceit only, or whether it may not arise, in some measure, from the self-illusion of a mind of extraordinary sensibility, habituated to solitary meditation, we cannot undertake to determine. It is possible enough, we allow, that the sight of a friend's garden-spade, or a sparrow's nest, or a man gathering leeches, might really have suggested to such a mind a train of powerful impressions and interesting reflections; but it is certain, that, to most minds, such associations will always appear forced, strained, and unnatural; and that the composition in which it is attempted to exhibit them, will always have the air of parody, or ludicrous and affected singularity. All the world laughs at Elegiac stanzas to a sucking-pig—a Hymn on Washing-day—Sonnets to one's grandmother—or Pindarics on gooseberry-pye; and yet, we are afraid, it will not be quite easy to convince Mr Wordsworth, that the same ridicule must infallibly attach to most of the pathetic pieces in these volumes. (pp. 216-18)

The first [poem in the collection] is a kind of ode . . . ["**To the Daisy**,"]—very flat, feeble, and affected; and in a diction as artificial, and as much encumbered with heavy expletives, as the theme of an unpracticed schoolboy. (p. 218)

The scope of the piece is to say, that the flower is found everywhere; and that it has suggested many pleasant thoughts to the author—some chime of fancy *'wrong or right'*—some feeling of devotion *'more or less'*—and other elegancies of the same stamp.

The next is called "**Louisa**," and begins in this dashing and affected manner.

> I met Louisa in the shade;
> And, having seen that lovely maid,
> *Why should I fear to say*
> That she is ruddy, fleet, and *strong;*
> *And down the rocks can leap* along,
> Like rivulets in May?

Does Mr Wordsworth really imagine that this is at all more natural or engaging than the ditties of our common song writers?

A little farther on we have another original piece, entitled, "**The Redbreast and the Butterfly**." . . . (p. 219)

This, it must be confessed, is 'Silly Sooth' in good earnest. The three last lines seem to be downright raving.

By and by, we have a piece of namby-pamby "**To the Small Celandine**," which we should almost have taken for a professed imitation of one of Mr Philips's prettyisms. (pp. 219-20)

After this come some more manly lines on "**The Character of the Happy Warrior**," and a chivalrous legend on "**The Horn of Egremont Castle**," which, without being very good, is very tolerable, and free from most of the author's habitual defects. Then follow some pretty, but professionally childish verses, on a kitten playing with the falling leaves. There is rather too much of Mr Ambrose Philips here and there in this piece also; but it is amiable and lively. Further on, we find an "**Ode to Duty**," in which the lofty vein is unsuccessfully attempted. This is the concluding stanza.

> Stern lawgiver! yet thou dost wear
> The Godhead's most benignant grace;
> Nor know we any thing so fair
> As is the smile upon thy face;
>
> Flowers laugh before thee on their beds;
> And fragrance in thy footing treads;
> Thou dost preserve the stars from wrong;
> And the most ancient heavens through thee are fresh
>   and strong.

The two last lines seem to be utterly without meaning; at least we have no sort of conception in what sense *Duty* can be said to keep the old skies *fresh*, and the stars from wrong.

The next piece, entitled "**The Beggars**," may be taken, we fancy, as a touchstone of Mr Wordsworth's merit. There is something about it that convinces us it is a favourite of the author's; though to us, we will confess, it appears to be a very paragon of silliness and affectation. (pp. 220-21)

[In the second volume] there is a "**Minstrel's Song, on the Restoration of Lord Clifford the Shepherd**," which is in a very different strain of poetry; and then the volume is wound up with an "**Ode**" with no other title but the motto, *Paulo majora canamus*. This is, beyond all doubt, the most illegible and unintelligible part of the publication. We can pretend to give no analysis or explanation of it. . . . (p. 227)

We have thus gone through this publication, with a view to enable our readers to determine, whether the author of the verses which have now been exhibited, is entitled to claim the honours of an improver or restorer of our poetry, and to found a new school to supersede or new-model all our maxims on the subject. If we were to stop here, we do not think that Mr Wordsworth, or his admirers, would have any reason to complain; for what we have now quoted is undeniably the most peculiar and characteristic part of his publication, and must be defended and applauded if the merit or originality of his system is to be seriously maintained. In our own opinion, however, the demerit of that system cannot be fairly appreciated, until it be shown, that the author of the bad verses which we have already extracted, can write good verses when he pleases; and that in point of fact, he does always write good verses, when, by any accident, he is led to abandon his system, and to transgress the laws of that school which he would fain establish on the ruin of all existing authority. (p. 228)

All English writers of sonnets have imitated Milton; and, in this way, Mr Wordsworth, when he writes sonnets, escapes . . . from the trammels of his own unfortunate system; and the consequence is, that his sonnets are as much superior to the greater part of his other poems, as Milton's sonnets are superior to his. (p. 230)

[When we look at such poems as "**On the Extinction of the Venetian Republic**"] and many still finer passages, in the writings of this author, it is impossible not to feel a mixture of indignation and compassion, at that strange infatuation which has bound him up from the fair exercise of his talents, and withheld from the public the many excellent productions that would otherwise have taken the place of the trash now before us. Even in the worst of these productions, there are, no doubt, occasional little traits of delicate feeling and original fancy; but these are quite lost and obscured in the mass of childishness and insipidity with which they are incorporated; nor can anything give us a more melancholy view of the debasing effects of this miserable theory, than that it has given ordinary men a right to wonder at the folly and presumption of a man gifted like Mr Wordsworth, and made him appear, in his second avowed publication, like a bad imitator of the worst of his former productions.

We venture to hope, that there is now an end of this folly; and that, like other follies, it will be found to have cured itself by the extravagances resulting from its unbridled indulgence. In this point of view, the publication of the volumes before us may ultimately be of service to the good cause of literature. Many a generous rebel, it is said, has been reclaimed to his allegiance by the spectacle of lawless outrage and excess presented in the conduct of the insurgents; and we think there is every reason to hope, that the lamentable consequences which have resulted from Mr Wordsworth's open violation of the established laws of poetry, will operate as a wholesome warning to those who might otherwise have been seduced by his example, and be the means of restoring to that antient and venerable code its due honour and authority. (p. 231)

> [*Francis Jeffrey*], "'Poems' by W. Wordsworth," in The Edinburgh Review, *Vol. XI, No. XXII, October, 1807, pp. 214-31.*

THE EDINBURGH ANNUAL REGISTER   (essay date 1808)

[*In the excerpt below, the reviewer points out that Wordsworth's poetic system, described here as "rude in diction and trivial in narrative," hinders his poetry and that one of his greatest errors is that of attributing importance to "common and unimportant incidents." The critic attributes this flaw to the poet's secluded life—an inference echoed by many later writers.*]

Although hitherto an unsuccessful competitor for poetical fame, as far as it depends upon the general voice of the public, no man has ever considered the character of the poet as more honourable, or his pursuits as more important [than Wordsworth]. We are afraid he will be found to err on the opposite side, and, with an amiable Quixotry, to ascribe to those pursuits, and to that character, a power of stemming the tide of luxury, egotism, and corruption of manners, and thus of reforming an age, which we devoutly believe can be reformed by nothing short of a miracle. But in this, as in other particulars, the poetry of Mr Wordsworth accords strikingly with his character and habits.... It might have been supposed, that, surrounded by romantic scenery, and giving his attention only to poetical imagery, and to the objects by which they were best suggested, the situation he had chosen was the most favourable for his studies; and that such a happy coincidence of leisure, talents, and situation, ought to have produced poetry more generally captivating than that of Mr Wordsworth has hitherto proved. But we have constant reason to admire the caprices of human intellect. This very state of secluded study seems to have produced effects upon Mr Wordsworth's genius unfavourable to its popularity. In the first place, he who is constantly surrounded by the most magnificent natural subjects of description, becomes so intimately acquainted with them, that

he is apt to dwell less upon the broad general and leading traits of character which strike the occasional visitor, and which are really their most poetical attributes, than upon the more detailed and specific particulars in which one mountain or valley differs from another, and which, being less obvious to the general eye, are less interesting to the common ear. But the solitude in which Mr Wordsworth resides has led to a second and more important consequence in his writings, and has affected his mode of expressing moral truth and feeling, as well as his turn of natural description. He has himself beautifully described the truths which he teaches us, as being

>——The harvest of a quiet eye
>That broods and rests on his own heart.

A better heart, a purer and more manly source of honourable and virtuous sentiment beats not, we will say it boldly, within Britain. But the observation of a single subject will not make a skilful anatomist, nor will the copying one model, however beautiful, render a painter acquainted with his art. To attain that knowledge of the human bosom necessary to moral poetry, the poet must compare his own feelings with those of others; he must reduce his hypothesis to theory by actual experiment, stoop to sober and regulated truth from the poetic height of his own imagination, and observe what impulse the mass of humanity receive from those motives and subjects to which he is himself acutely alive. It is the want of this observation and knowledge of the world which leads Wordsworth into the perpetual and leading error of supposing, that trivial and petty incidents can supply to mankind in general that train of reflection which, in his speculative solitude, he himself naturally attaches to them. (pp. 428-29)

[The] impressions made upon the susceptible mind of the solitary poet by common and unimportant incidents; and the train of "sweet and bitter fancies" to which they give rise are, in the eye of the public, altogether extravagant and disproportioned to their cause. We mark this with sincere regret; for though Mr Wordsworth, to the affectation of rude and bald simplicity, which we have censured in Southey and Coleridge, adds that of harsh and rugged versification, often reduced in harmony several steps below well-written prose, yet his power of interesting the feelings is exquisite, and we do not envy the self-possession of those who can read his beautiful pastorals, **"The Brothers"** and **"Michael,"** without shedding tears; for it may be said of such, that they have no interest in humanity, "no part in Jacob, and no inheritance in Israel." It is therefore to be lamented, that Wordsworth should be, upon system, rude in diction and trivial in narrative; and that he should continue to exhibit traits of feeling bordering upon extravagance, and so metaphysically subtile that they are a stumbling block to the ignorant, and foolishness to the learned. But his muse is, we fear, irreclaimable, and pleads the freedom of a Cumbrian mountaineer:—

>Oer rough and smooth she trips along,
>   And never looks behind;
>And sings a solitary song
>   That whistles in the wind.

>   (pp. 429-30)

> "General View of Literature, of the Living Poets of Great Britain," in The Edinburgh Annual Register, *Vol. I, 1808, pp. 417-43.*

[CHARLES LAMB AND WILLIAM GIFFORD]   (essay date 1814)

[*An essayist, critic, and poet, Lamb is credited with initiating the revival of interest in Elizabethan and Restoration drama in nine-*

teenth-century England. His critical comments on the plays of John Webster, Jeremy Taylor, Thomas Haywood, and John Ford, recorded in the form of notes to his anthology, Specimens of the English Dramatic Poets Who Lived About the Time of Shakespeare, *demonstrate a literary taste and refinement new in his time. Unlike some of his contemporaries, Lamb never tried to construct an all-embracing, systematic critical theory. Instead, his method was to point out fine passages in particular works and convey his enthusiasm to his readers. Lamb is chiefly remembered, however, for his* Essays of Elia, *a series of familiar essays which are admired for their breadth, quaint style, and intimate tone. Gifford, less well known than Lamb, was an English editor, poet, and literary critic. In their review of* The Excursion, *excerpted below, the critics praise Wordsworth's depiction of nature and assert that he has not achieved popularity because of the "boldness" and seriousness of his poetry. They conclude by defending the suitability of Wordsworth's choice of a pedlar as a spokesman in the work, countering the argument of other critics that Wordsworth's themes and diction were too humble to comprise serious poetry.]*

[*The Excursion,*] as we learn from the Preface, is 'a detached portion of an unfinished poem, containing views of man, nature, and society;' to be called the **Recluse,** as having for its principal subject the 'sensations and opinions of a poet living in retirement;' and to be preceded by a 'record in verse of the origin and progress of the author's own powers, with reference to the fitness which they may be supposed to have conferred for the task.' To the completion of this plan we look forward with a confidence which the execution of the finished part is well calculated to inspire.—Meanwhile, in what is before us there is ample matter for entertainment: for the **Excursion** is not a branch (as might have been suspected) prematurely plucked from the parent tree to gratify an overhasty appetite for applause; but is, in itself, a complete and legitimate production. (p. 100)

[The] poem is of a didactic nature, and not a fable or story; yet it is not wanting in stories of the most interesting kind,— such as the lovers of Cowper and Goldsmith will recognise as something familiar and congenial to them. We might instance the **"Ruined Cottage,"** and the Solitary's own story, in the first half of the work; and the second half, as being almost a continued cluster of narration. But the prevailing charm of the poem is, perhaps, that, conversational as it is in its plan, the dialogue throughout is carried on in the very heart of the most romantic scenery which the poet's native hills could supply; and which, by the perpetual references made to it either in the way of illustration or for variety and pleasurable description's sake, is brought before us as we read. We breathe in the fresh air, as we do while reading Walton's *Complete Angler;* only the country about us is as much bolder than Walton's, as the thoughts and speculations, which form the matter of the poem, exceed the trifling pastime and low-pitched conversation of his humble fishermen. (p. 101)

To a mind constituted like that of Mr. Wordsworth, the stream, the torrent, and the stirring leaf—seem not merely to suggest associations of deity, but to be a kind of speaking communication with it. He walks through every forest, as through some Dodona; and every bird that flits among the leaves, like that miraculous one in Tasso, but in language more intelligent, reveals to him far higher love-lays. In his poetry nothing in Nature is dead. Motion is synonymous with life. (pp. 102-03)

To such a mind, we say—call it strength or weakness—if weakness, assuredly a fortunate one—the visible and audible things of creation present, not dim symbols, or curious emblems, which they have done at all times to those who have

been gifted with the poetical faculty; but revelations and quick insights into the life within us, the pledge of immortality.... (p. 103)

The causes which have prevented the poetry of Mr. Wordsworth from attaining its full share of popularity are to be found in the boldness and originality of his genius. The times are past when a poet could securely follow the direction of his own mind into whatever tracts it might lead. A writer, who would be popular, must timidly coast the shore of prescribed sentiment and sympathy. He must have just as much more of the imaginative faculty than his readers, as will serve to keep their apprehensions from stagnating, but not so much as to alarm their jealousy. He must not think or feel too deeply.

If he has had the fortune to be bred in the midst of the most magnificent objects of creation, he must not have given away his heart to them; or if he have, he must conceal his love, or not carry his expressions of it beyond that point of rapture, which the occasional tourist thinks it not overstepping decorum to betray, or the limit which that gentlemanly spy upon Nature, the picturesque traveller, has vouchsafed to countenance. He must do this, or be content to be thought an enthusiast.

If from living among simple mountaineers, from a daily intercourse with them, not upon the footing of a patron, but in the character of an equal, he has detected, or imagines that he has detected, through the cloudy medium of their unlettered discourse, thoughts and apprehensions not vulgar; traits of patience and constancy, love unwearied, and heroic endurance, not unfit (as he may judge) to be made the subject of verse, he will be deemed a man of perverted genius by the philanthropist who, conceiving of the peasantry of his country only as objects of a pecuniary sympathy, starts at finding them elevated to a level of humanity with himself, having their own loves, enmities, cravings, aspirations, &c., as much beyond his faculty to believe, as his beneficence to supply.

If from a similar observation of the ways of children, and much more from a retrospect of his own mind when a child, he has gathered more reverential notions of that state than fall to the lot of ordinary observers, and, escaping from the dissonant wranglings of men, has tuned his lyre, though but for occasional harmonies, to the milder utterance of that soft age,— his verses shall be censured as infantile by critics who confound poetry 'having children for its subject' with poetry that is 'childish,' and who, having themselves perhaps never been *children,* never having possessed the tenderness and docility of that age, know not what the soul of a child is—how apprehensive! how imaginative! how religious!

We have touched upon some of the causes which we conceive to have been unfriendly to the author's former poems. We think they do not apply in the same force to the one before us. There is in it more of uniform elevation, a wider scope of subject, less of manner, and it contains none of those starts and imperfect shapings which in some of this author's smaller pieces offended the weak, and gave scandal to the perverse. It must indeed be approached with seriousness. It has in it much of that quality which 'draws the devout, deterring the profane.' Those who hate the *Paradise Lost* will not love this poem. The steps of the great master are discernible in it; not in direct imitation or injurious parody, but in the following of the spirit, in free homage and generous subjection.

One objection it is impossible not to foresee. It will be asked, why put such eloquent discourse in the mouth of a pedlar? It might be answered that Mr. Wordsworth's plan required a

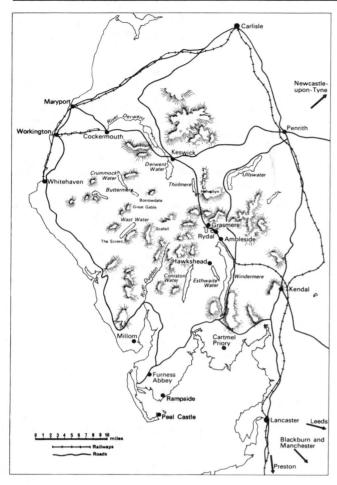

A map of Wordsworth's Lake District in about 1845.

character in humble life to be the organ of his philosophy. It was in harmony with the system and scenery of this poem. We read Pier's Plowman's Creed, and the lowness of the teacher seems to add a simple dignity to the doctrine. Besides, the poet has bestowed an unusual share of education upon him. Is it too much to suppose that the author, at some early period of his life, may himself have known such a person, a man endowed with sentiments above his situation, another Burns; and that the dignified strains which he has attributed to the Wanderer [in *The Excursion*] may be no more than recollections of his conversation, heightened only by the amplification natural to poetry, or the lustre which imagination flings back upon the objects and companions of our youth? After all, if there should be found readers willing to admire the poem, who yet feel scandalized at a *name,* we would advise them, wherever it occurs, to substitute silently the word *Palmer,* or *Pilgrim,* or any less offensive designation, which shall connect the notion of sobriety in heart and manners with the experience and privileges which a wayfaring life confers. (pp. 110-11)

> [*Charles Lamb and William Gifford*], "Wordsworth's 'Excursion'," in The Quarterly Review, Vol. XII, No. XXIII, October, 1814, pp. 100-11.

[FRANCIS JEFFREY] (essay date 1814)

[*In this excerpt from his well-known review of* The Excursion, *Jeffrey concludes that the poem is Wordsworth's weakest to date.*

He particularly criticizes the poet's "profuse and irrepressible wordiness," the lack of action, the didacticism, the overly simple theme, and the use of a pedlar as hero. Even the nature descriptions are stylized and exaggerated, Jeffrey notes. He laments the "perversion" of Wordsworth's talent, but declares that "The case of Mr. Wordsworth, we perceive, is now manifestly hopeless." For additional commentary by Jeffrey on Wordsworth's poetry, see the excerpts dated 1802, 1807, 1815, and 1822.]

This will never do. [*The Excursion*] bears no doubt the stamp of the author's heart and fancy; but unfortunately not half so visibly as that of his peculiar system. His former poems were intended to recommend that system, and to bespeak favour for it by their individual merit;—but this, we suspect, must be recommended by the system—and can only expect to succeed where it has been previously established. It is longer, weaker, and tamer, than any of Mr Wordsworth's other productions; with less boldness of originality, and less even of that extreme simplicity and lowliness of tone which wavered so prettily, in the *Lyrical Ballads,* between silliness and pathos. We have imitations of Cowper, and even of Milton here, engrafted on the natural drawl of the Lakers—and all diluted into harmony by that profuse and irrepressible wordiness which deluges all the blank verse of this school of poetry, and lubricates and weakens the whole structure of their style.

Though it fairly fills four hundred and twenty good quarto pages, without note, vignette, or any sort of extraneous assistance, it is stated in the title—with something of an imprudent candour—to be but 'a portion' of a larger work; and in the preface, where an attempt is rather unsuccessfully made to explain the whole design, it is still more rashly disclosed, that it is but 'a part of the second part of a *long* and laborious work'—which is to consist of three parts.

What Mr Wordsworth's ideas of length are, we have no means of accurately judging; but we cannot help suspecting that they are liberal, to a degree that will alarm the weakness of most modern readers. As far as we can gather from the preface, the entire poem—or one of them, for we really are not sure whether there is to be one or two—is of a biographical nature; and is to contain the history of the author's mind, and of the origin and progress of his poetical powers, up to the period when they were sufficiently matured to qualify him for the great work on which he has been so long employed. Now, the quarto before us contains an account of one of his youthful rambles in the vales of Cumberland, and occupies precisely the period of three days; so that, by the use of a very powerful *calculus,* some estimate may be formed of the probable extent of the entire biography.

This small specimen, however, and the statements with which it is prefaced, have been sufficient to set our minds at rest in one particular. The case of Mr Wordsworth, we perceive, is now manifestly hopeless; and we give him up as altogether incurable, and beyond the power of criticism. We cannot indeed altogether omit taking precautions now and then against the spreading of the malady;—but for himself, though we shall watch the progress of his symptoms as a matter of professional curiosity and instruction, we really think it right not to harass him any longer with nauseous remedies,—but rather to throw in cordials and lenitives, and wait in patience for the natural termination of the disorder. In order to justify this desertion of our patient, however, it is proper to state why we despair of the success of a more active practice.

A man who has been for twenty years at work on such matter as is now before us, and who comes complacently forward with a whole quarto of it after all the admonitions he has received, cannot reasonably be expected to 'change his hand, or check his pride,' upon the suggestion of far weightier monitors than we can pretend to be. Inveterate habit must now have given a kind of sanctity to the errors of early taste; and the very powers of which we lament the perversion, have probably become incapable of any other application. The very quantity, too, that he has written, and is at this moment working up for publication upon the old pattern, makes it almost hopeless to look for any change of it. All this is so much capital already sunk in the concern; which must be sacrificed if it be abandoned: and no man likes to give up for lost the time and talent and labour which he has embodied in any permanent production. We were not previously aware of these obstacles to Mr Wordsworth's conversion; and, considering the peculiarities of his former writings merely as the result of certain wanton and capricious experiments on public taste and indulgence, conceived it to be our duty to discourage their repetition by all the means in our power. We now see clearly, however, how the case stands;—and, making up our minds, though with the most sincere pain and reluctance, to consider him as finally lost to the good cause of poetry, shall endeavour to be thankful for the occasional gleams of tenderness and beauty which the natural force of his imagination and affections must still shed over all his productions,—and to which we shall ever turn with delight, in spite of the affectation and mysticism and prolixity, with which they are so abundantly contrasted.

Long habits of seclusion, and an excessive ambition of originality, can alone account for the disproportion which seems to exist between this author's taste and his genius; or for the devotion with which he has sacrificed so many precious gifts at the shrine of those paltry idols which he has set up for himself among his lakes and his mountains. Solitary musings, amidst such scenes, might no doubt be expected to nurse up the mind to the majesty of poetical conception,—(though it is remarkable, that all the greater poets lived, or had lived, in the full current of society):—But the collision of equal minds,—the admonition of prevailing impressions—seems necessary to reduce its redundancies, and repress that tendency to extravagance or puerility, into which the self-indulgence and self-admiration of genius is so apt to be betrayed, when it is allowed to wanton, without awe or restraint, in the triumph and delight of its own intoxication. . . . [If] Mr Wordsworth, instead of confining himself almost entirely to the society of the dalesmen and cottagers, and little children, who form the subjects of his book, had condescended to mingle a little more with the people that were to read and judge of it, we cannot help thinking, that its texture would have been considerably improved: At least it appears to us to be absolutely impossible, that any one who had lived or mixed familiarly with men of literature and ordinary judgment in poetry, (of course we exclude the coadjutors and disciples of his own school), could ever have fallen into such gross faults, or so long mistaken them for beauties. (pp. 1-4)

[*The Excursion*], if we were to describe it very shortly, we should characterize as a tissue of moral and devotional ravings, in which innumerable changes are rung upon a few very simple and familiar ideas:—but with such an accompaniment of long words, long sentences, and unwieldy phrases—and such a hubbub of strained raptures and fantastical sublimities, that it is often extremely difficult for the most skillful and attentive student to obtain a glimpse of the author's meaning—and altogether impossible for an ordinary reader to conjecture what he is about. Moral and religious enthusiasm, though undoubt-

edly poetical emotions, are at the same time but dangerous inspirers of poetry; nothing being so apt to run into interminable dulness or mellifluous extravagance, without giving the unfortunate author the slightest intimation of his danger. His laudable zeal for the efficacy of his preachments, he very naturally mistakes for the ardour of poetical inspiration;—and, while dealing out the high words and glowing phrases which are so readily supplied by themes of this description, can scarcely avoid believing that he is eminently original and impressive:—All sorts of commonplace notions and expressions are sanctified in his eyes, by the sublime ends for which they are employed; and the mystical verbiage of the methodist pulpit is repeated, till the speaker entertains no doubt that he is the elected organ of divine truth and persuasion. But if such be the common hazards of seeking inspiration from those potent fountains, it may easily be conceived what chance Mr Wordsworth had of escaping their enchantment,—with his natural propensities to wordiness, and his unlucky habit of debasing pathos with vulgarity. The fact accordingly is, that in this production he is more obscure than a Pindaric poet of the seventeenth century; and more verbose 'than even himself of yore;' while the willfulness with which he persists in choosing his examples of intellectual dignity and tenderness exclusively from the lowest ranks of society, will be sufficiently apparent, from the circumstance of his having thought fit to make his chief prolocutor in this poetical dialogue, and chief advocate of Providence and Virtue, *an old Scotch Pedlar*—retired indeed from business—but still rambling about in his former haunts, and gossiping among his old customers, without his pack on his shoulders. The other persons of the drama are, a retired military chaplain, who has grown half an atheist and half a misanthrope—the wife of an unprosperous weaver—a servant girl with her infant—a parish pauper, and one or two other personages of equal rank and dignity.

The character of the work is decidedly didactic; and more than nine tenths of it are occupied with a species of dialogue, or rather a series of long sermons or harangues which pass between the pedlar, the author, the old chaplain, and a worthy vicar, who entertains the whole party at dinner on the last day of their excursion. The incidents which occur in the course of it are as few and trifling as can be imagined;—and those which the different speakers narrate in the course of their discourses, are introduced rather to illustrate their arguments or opinions, than for any interest they are supposed to possess of their own.—The doctrine which the work is intended to enforce, we are by no means certain that we have discovered. In so far as we can collect, however, it seems to be neither more nor less than the old familiar one, that a firm belief in the providence of a wise and beneficent Being must be our great stay and support under all afflictions and perplexities upon earth—and that there are indications of his power and goodness in all the aspects of the visible universe, whether living or inanimate—every part of which should therefore be regarded with love and reverence, as exponents of those great attributes. We can testify, at least, that these salutary and important truths are inculcated at far greater length, and with more repetitions, than in any ten volumes of sermons that we ever perused. It is also maintained, with equal conciseness and originality, that there is frequently much good sense, as well as much enjoyment, in the humbler conditions of life; and that, in spite of great vices and abuses, there is a reasonable allowance both of happiness and goodness in society at large. If there be any deeper or more recondite doctrines in Mr Wordsworth's book, we must confess that they have escaped us;—and, convinced as we are of the truth and soundness of those to which we have alluded, we cannot help thinking that they might have been enforced with less parade and prolixity. His effusions on what may be called the physiognomy of external nature, or its moral and theological expression, are eminently fantastic, obscure, and affected. (pp. 4-6)

Nobody can be more disposed to do justice to the great powers of Mr Wordsworth than we are; and, from the first time that he came before us, down to the present moment, we have uniformly testified in their favour, and assigned indeed our high sense of their value as the chief ground of the bitterness with which we resented their perversion. That perversion, however, is now far more visible than their original dignity; and while we collect the fragments, it is impossible not to lament the ruins from which we are condemned to pick them. If any one should doubt of the existence of such a perversion, or be disposed to dispute about the instances we have hastily brought forward, we would just beg leave to refer him to the general plan and the characters of the poem now before us.—Why should Mr Wordsworth have made his hero a superannuated Pedlar? What but the most wretched and provoking perversity of taste and judgment, could induce any one to place his chosen advocate of wisdom and virtue in so absurd and fantastic a condition? Did Mr Wordsworth really imagine, that his favourite doctrines were likely to gain anything in point of effect or authority by being put into the mouth of a person accustomed to higgle about tape, or brass sleeve-buttons? Or is it not plain that, independent of the ridicule and disgust which such a personification must give to many of his readers, its adoption exposes his work throughout to the charge of revolting incongruity, and utter disregard of probability or nature? For, after he has thus willfully debased his moral teacher by a low occupation, is there one word that he puts into his mouth, or one sentiment of which he makes him the organ, that has the most remote reference to that occupation? Is there any thing in his learned, abstracted, and logical harangues, that savours of the calling that is ascribed to him? Are any of their materials such as a pedlar could possibly have dealt in? Are the manners, the diction, the sentiments, in any, the very smallest degree, accommodated to a person in that condition? or are they not eminently and conspicuously such as could not by possibility belong to it? A man who went about selling flannel and pocket-handkerchiefs in this lofty diction, would soon frighten away all his customers; and would infallibly pass either for a madman, or for some learned and affected gentleman, who, in a frolic, had taken up a character which he was peculiarly ill qualified for supporting.

The absurdity in this case, we think, is palpable and glaring; but it is exactly of the same nature with that which infects the whole substance of the work—a puerile ambition of singularity engrafted on an unlucky predilection for truisms; and an affected passion for simplicity and humble life, most awkwardly combined with a taste for mystical refinements, and all the gorgeousness of obscure phraseology. His taste for simplicity is evinced, by sprinkling up and down his interminable declamations, a few descriptions of baby-houses, and of old hats with wet brims; and his amiable partiality for humble life, by assuring us, that a wordy rhetorician, who talks about Thebes, and allegorizes all the heathen mythology, was once a pedlar—and making him break in upon his magnificent orations with two or three awkward notices of something that he had seen when selling winter raiment about the country—or of the changes in the state of society, which had almost annihilated his former calling. (pp. 29-30)

[*Francis Jeffrey*], "Wordsworth's 'Excursion'," in *The Edinburgh Review, Vol. XXIV, No. XLVII, November, 1814, pp. 1-30.*

[FRANCIS JEFFREY] (essay date 1815)

[*Contending that* The White Doe of Rylstone *is "the very worst poem we ever saw imprinted in a quarto volume," Jeffrey describes the work as a dull, wordy production that reads like a parody of the Lake poets' style. Yet he concedes that the story line is good and might have been well developed by another writer. For additional commentary by Jeffrey on Wordsworth's poetry, see the excerpts dated 1802, 1807, 1814, and 1822.*]

[*The White Doe of Rylstone*] we think, has the merit of being the very worst poem we ever saw imprinted in a quarto volume; and though it was scarcely to be expected, we confess, that Mr Wordsworth, with all his ambition, should so soon have attained to that distinction, the wonder may perhaps be diminished, when we state, that it seems to us to consist of a happy union of all the faults, without any of the beauties, which belong to his school of poetry. It is just such a work, in short, as some wicked enemy of that school might be supposed to have devised, on purpose to make it ridiculous; and when we first took it up, we could not help fancying that some ill-natured critic had taken this harsh method of instructing Mr Wordsworth, by example, in the nature of those errors, against which our precepts had been so often directed in vain. We had not gone far, however, till we felt intimately, that nothing in the nature of a joke could be so insupportably dull;—and that this must be the work of one who honestly believed it to be a pattern of pathetic simplicity, and gave it out as such to the admiration of all intelligent readers. In this point of view, the work may be regarded as curious at least, if not in some degree interesting; and, at all events, it must be instructive to be made aware of the excesses into which superior understandings may be betrayed, by long self-indulgence, and the strange extravagances into which they may run, when under the influence of that intoxication which is produced by unrestrained admiration of themselves. This poetical intoxication, indeed, to pursue the figure a little farther, seems capable of assuming as many forms as the vulgar one which arises from wine; and it appears to require as delicate a management to make a man a good poet by the help of the one, as to make him a good companion by means of the other. In both cases, a little mistake as to the dose or the quality of the inspiring fluid may make him absolutely outrageous, or lull him over into the most profound stupidity, instead of brightening up the hidden stores of his genius: And truly we are concerned to say, that Mr Wordsworth seems hitherto to have been unlucky in the choice of his liquor—or of his bottle holder. In some of his odes and ethic exhortations, he was exposed to the public in a state of incoherent rapture and glorious delirium, to which we think we have seen a parallel among the humbler lovers of jollity. In the *Lyrical Ballads,* he was exhibited, on the whole, in a vein of very pretty deliration; but in the poem before us, he appears in a state of low and maudlin imbecility, which would not have misbecome Master Silence himself, in the close of a social day. Whether this unhappy result is to be ascribed to any adulteration of his Castalian cups, or to the unlucky choice of his company over them, we cannot presume to say. It may be, that he has dashed his Hippocrene with too large an infusion of lake water, or assisted its operation too exclusively by the study of the ancient historical ballads of 'the north countrie.' That there are palpable imitations of the style and manner of those venerable compositions in the work before us, is indeed undeniable; but it unfortunately happens, that while the hobbling versification, the mean diction, and flat stupidity of these models are very exactly copied, and even improved upon, in this imitation, their rude energy, manly simplicity, and occasional felicity of expression, have totally disappeared; and, instead of them, a large allowance of the author's own metaphysical sensibility, and mystical wordiness, is forced into an unnatural combination with the borrowed beauties which have just been mentioned.

The story of the poem, though not capable of furnishing out matter for a quarto volume, might yet have made an interesting ballad; and, in the hands of Mr Scott, or Lord Byron, would probably have supplied many images to be loved, and descriptions to be remembered. (pp. 355-56)

> [Francis Jeffrey], "Wordsworth's 'White Doe'," in The Edinburgh Review, *Vol. XXV, No. L, October, 1815, pp. 355-63.*

THE MONTHLY REVIEW, LONDON   (essay date 1815)

[*The author of this brief review of the* Poems *of 1815 focuses on Wordsworth's preface to that volume. Disapproving of his "pompous classification of trifles," the critic points out that the "silliness" of the poems themselves serves as an antidote to Wordsworth's intimidating tone in the preface.*]

After all that the public has known of the productions of Mr. Wordsworth, and all that we have said concerning them, it is scarcely necessary for us now to observe that the sum and substance of his poetical character may be comprehensively described under one quality; viz. a strong admiration of the beauties of external nature. Accustomed to visit rocks and mountains rather than cities or market-towns, and cherishing a strict intimacy with the plants and flowers of his neighbourhood while he has maintained, comparatively, but little converse with men and women, he has contracted such habits of composition as were the natural consequence of so recluse and peculiar a mode of life. This simple explanation of a series of phaenomena intitled *Poems*, and scientifically distributed by the author into classes of 'Imagination,' 'Fancy,' 'Affections,' 'Sentiment and Reflection,' &c. &c. will probably give little satisfaction to that author himself, or to his few though ardent votaries: but the "*raison suffisante*" for *all* Mr. Wordsworth's writings is nevertheless to be found in his "local habitation;" where he has long been giving "a name to airy nothings," and, with much, very much indeed, of the real genius of a poet, has been wasting that genius on unworthy though innocent subjects, and displaying every variety of a whimsical and inveterately perverted taste which it is possible to conceive.

In a preface to the *Poems* before us, which is not remarkable for clearness of idea nor for humility of tone, a fresh attempt is made to give that air of invention and novelty to Mr. W.'s writings which it seems to be his main object to claim. He wishes to be the founder of a school or system in poetry; and he endeavours to refer all his chance-effusions, all his walking thoughts, suggested by the stocks and stones or the old men and children that he encounters, to some particular class of composition, in which this or that faculty of the human mind has been appropriately exercised. Thus in the present volumes we have a poem belonging to the class of 'Fancy,' with no possible distinguishing characteristic from another in the class of 'Imagination;' 'the Affections' lay claim to a third, which might as well have been ranked under the head of 'Sentiment and Reflection;' and, in short, we have here such a pompous

classification of trifles, for the most part obvious and extremely childish, that we do not remember to have ever met with so "Much Ado about Nothing" in any other author. (pp. 225-26)

We are so thoroughly overwhelmed by the high and mighty tone of this author's prose [in the preface] that we really must have immediate recourse to his verse, in order to get rid of the painful humiliation and sense of inferiority which he inflicts on his readers. There, (*Dieu merci!*) we are comforted by silliness instead of system; by want of harmony instead of abundance of pride; by downright vacancy instead of grandeur and presumption. Will any one believe that the critic who speaks so contemptuously of other severe critics, and yet is very gall and vinegar himself,—and the poet,—are the same person? (pp. 230-31)

> "Wordsworth's 'Poems'," *in* The Monthly Review, *London, Vol. LXXVIII, November, 1815, pp. 225-34.*

PERCY BYSSHE SHELLEY   (essay date 1816)

[*Regarded as a major English poet, Shelley was a leading figure in the English Romantic movement. His so-called "defense of poetry," in which he investigated poetry's relation to the history of civilization, was an important contribution to nineteenth-century aesthetics. Influenced by the French philosopher Jean-Jacques Rousseau and the German poet and pre-Romanticist Johann Gottfried Herder, Shelley viewed poetry, like human society, as a continuing evolution of ideas—in his words, as a "fountain forever overflowing with the waters of wisdom and delight," which when exhausted by one age, "another and yet another succeeds and new relations are ever developed." He argued that poetry was like a mirror to its age, the history of its manners, and as such he labeled all poets "legislators and prophets" who, even unconsciously or when in least prominence, as in the English Restoration, contributed to the spiritual and political evolution of humankind. A great admirer of Wordsworth, Shelley wrote this sonnet as a tribute to the older poet. However, Shelley grew increasingly more uncomfortable with Wordsworth's orthodoxy, and his high estimate gradually waned. The sonnet was first published in* Alastor, or, the Spirit of Solitude *in 1816.*]

Poet of Nature, thou hast wept to know
That things depart which never may return:
Childhood and youth, friendship and love's first glow,
Have fled like sweet dreams, leaving thee to mourn.
These common woes I feel. One loss is mine
Which thou too feel'st, yet I alone deplore.
Thou wert as a lone star, whose light did shine
On some frail bark in winter's midnight roar:
Thou hast like to a rock-built refuge stood
Above the blind and battling multitude:
In honoured poverty thy voice did weave
Songs consecrate to truth and liberty,—
Deserting these, thou leavest me to grieve,
Thus having been, that thou shouldst cease to be.

> Percy Bysshe Shelley, "To Wordsworth," *in his* The Complete Poetical Works of Percy Bysshe Shelley, *edited by Thomas Hutchinson, Oxford University Press, 1956, p. 526.*

SAMUEL TAYLOR COLERIDGE   (essay date 1817)

[*An English poet and critic, Coleridge was central to the English Romantic movement and is considered one of the greatest literary critics in the English language. Besides his poetry, his most important contributions include his formulation of Romantic theory, his introduction of the ideas of the German Romantics to England,*

and his Shakespearean criticism, which overthrew the last rem-
nants of the Neoclassical approach to Shakespeare and focused
on Shakespeare as a masterful portrayer of human character.
Coleridge and Wordsworth were best friends at the time of their
collaboration on the Lyrical Ballads, *and their influence on each*
other proved crucial to the career of each poet. In the following
excerpt from his seminal critical work, the Biographia Literaria
(originally published in 1817), Coleridge presents one of the most
important appraisals of his friend's poetry. The first section of
his critique focuses on Wordsworth's experiment with diction.
Though he contends that it deserves praise, Coleridge challenges
certain assumptions inherent in the experiment. The language of
men in "low and rustic life" is not necessarily more pure than
other kinds of language, he argues, and natural diction is not
appropriate in all situations. In the second section, Coleridge
offers general commentary on the shortcomings and strengths of
Wordsworth's style. Wordsworth's theory is different from his
practice, Coleridge asserts: the style of his poems is inconsistent
and his imagery is sometimes too complex. Further, Wordsworth's
poetry tends to be wordy, repetitive, and overly dramatic. How-
ever, Coleridge goes on to compliment his friend on his powerful
descriptions, "meditative pathos," and original style. He con-
cludes by stating that those critics who dismiss Wordsworth as a
"simple" poet do him more of a disservice than those who berate
him "for vulgarity of style." For other views on Wordsworth's
critical theory, see the excerpts by Wordsworth (1802), De Quin-
cey (1845), Saintsbury (1896), and Abrams (1953).]

As far . . . as Mr Wordsworth in his preface contended, and
most ably contended, for a reformation in our poetic diction,
as far as he has evinced the truth of passion, and the dramatic
propriety of those figures and metaphors in the original poets
which, stript of their justifying reasons and converted into mere
artifices of connection or ornament, constitute the characteristic
falsity in the poetic style of the moderns; and as far as he has,
with equal acuteness and clearness, pointed out the process by
which this change was effected and the resemblances between
that state into which the reader's mind is thrown by the pleasurable confusion of thought from an unaccustomed train of
words and images and that state which is induced by the natural
language of impassioned feeling, he undertook a useful task
and deserves all praise, both for the attempt and for the execution. (p. 188)

My own differences from certain supposed parts of Mr Wordsworth's theory ground themselves on the assumption that his
words had been rightly interpreted, as purporting that the proper
diction for poetry in general consists altogether in a language
taken, with due exceptions, from the mouths of men in real
life, a language which actually constitutes the natural conversation of men under the influence of natural feelings. My objection is, first, that in any sense this rule is applicable only
to certain classes of poetry; secondly, that even to these classes
it is not applicable, except in such a sense as hath never by
any one (as far as I know or have read) been denied or doubted;
and, lastly, that as far as, and in that degree in which it is
practicable, it is yet as a *rule* useless, if not injurious, and
therefore either need not or ought not to be practised. The poet
informs his reader that he had generally chosen low and rustic
life, but not *as* low and rustic, or in order to repeat that pleasure
of doubtful moral effect which persons of elevated rank and
of superior refinement oftentimes derive from a happy imitation
of the rude unpolished manners and discourse of their inferiors.
For the pleasure so derived may be traced to three exciting
causes. The first is the naturalness, in fact, of the things represented. The second is the apparent naturalness of the representation, as raised and qualified by an imperceptible infusion
of the author's own knowledge and talent, which infusion does

indeed constitute it an imitation, as distinguished from a mere
copy. The third cause may be found in the reader's conscious
feeling of his superiority, awakened by the contrast presented
to him; even as for the same purpose the kings and great barons
of yore retained sometimes actual clowns and fools, but more
frequently shrewd and witty fellows in that character. These,
however, were not Mr Wordsworth's objects. *He* chose low
and rustic life, 'because in that condition the essential passions
of the heart find a better soil in which they can attain their
maturity, are less under restraint, and speak a plainer and more
emphatic language; because in that condition of life our elementary feelings co-exist in a state of greater simplicity and
consequently may be more accurately contemplated and more
forcibly communicated; because the manners of rural life germinate from those elementary feelings, and from the necessary
character of rural occupations are more easily comprehended
and are more durable; and lastly, because in that condition the
passions of men are incorporated with the beautiful and permanent forms of nature.'

Now it is clear to me that in the most interesting of the poems
in which the author is more or less dramatic, as the **"Brothers,"**
"Michael," "Ruth," the **"Mad Mother,"** etc., the persons
introduced are by no means taken from low or rustic life in
the common acceptation of those words; and it is not less clear
that the sentiments and language, as far as they can be conceived to have been really transferred from the minds and
conversation of such persons, are attributable to causes and
circumstances not necessarily connected with "their occupations and abode.' The thoughts, feelings, language and manners
of the shepherd-farmers in the vales of Cumberland and Westmoreland, as far as they are actually adopted in those poems,
may be accounted for from causes which will and do produce
the same results in every state of life, whether in town or
country. As the two principal I rank that independence which
raises a man above servitude or daily toil for the profit of
others, yet not above the necessity of industry and a frugal
simplicity of domestic life, and the accompanying unambitious,
but solid and religious education which has rendered few books
familiar but the bible and the liturgy or hymn book. To this
latter cause indeed, which is so far accidental that it is the
blessing of particular countries and a particular age, not the
product of particular places or employments, the poet owes the
show of probability that his personages might really feel, think
and talk with any tolerable resemblance to his representation.
(pp. 189-91)

The characters of the vicar and shepherd-mariner in the poem
of the **"Brothers,"** those of the Shepherd of Green-head Gill
in the **"Michael,"** have all the verisimilitude and representative
quality that the purposes of poetry can require. They are persons
of a known and abiding class, and their manners and sentiments
the natural product of circumstances common to the class. (pp.
192-93)

On the other hand, in the poems which are pitched at a lower
note, as the **'Harry Gill," "Idiot Boy,"** etc., the feelings are
those of human nature in general; though the poet has judi-
ciously laid the scene in the country, in order to place himself
in the vicinity of interesting images without the necessity of
ascribing a sentimental perception of their beauty to the persons
of his drama. In the **"Idiot Boy,"** indeed, the mother's character is not so much a real and native product of a 'situation
where the essential passions of the heart find a better soil, in
which they can attain their maturity and speak a plainer and
more emphatic language,' as it is an impersonation of an in-

stinct abandoned by judgement. Hence the two following charges seem to me not wholly groundless; at least, they are the only plausible objections which I have heard to that fine poem. The one is that the author has not, in the poem itself, taken sufficient care to preclude from the reader's fancy the disgusting images of ordinary, morbid idiocy, which yet it was by no means his intention to represent. He has even by the 'burr, burr, burr,' uncounteracted by any preceding description of the boy's beauty, assisted in recalling them. The other is that the idiocy of the boy is so evenly balanced by the folly of the mother as to present to the general reader rather a laughable burlesque on the blindness of anile dotage than an analytic display of maternal affection in its ordinary workings.

In the **"Thorn,"** the poet himself acknowledges in a note the necessity of an introductory poem in which he should have pourtrayed the character of the person from whom the words of the poem are supposed to proceed: a superstitious man moderately imaginative, of slow faculties and deep feelings, 'a captain of a small trading vessel, for example, who, being past the middle age of life, had retired upon an annuity, or small independent income, to some village or country town of which he was not a native, or in which he had not been accustomed to live. Such men, having nothing to do, become credulous and talkative from indolence.' But in a poem, still more in a lyric poem (and the Nurse in Shakespeare's *Romeo and Juliet* alone prevents me from extending the remark even to dramatic poetry, if indeed the Nurse itself can be deemed altogether a case in point), it is not possible to imitate truly a dull and garrulous discourser without repeating the effects of dulness and garrulity. However this may be, I dare assert that the parts (and these form the far larger portion of the whole) which might as well or still better have proceeded from the poet's own imagination, and have been spoken in his own character, are those which have given, and which will continue to give, universal delight; and that the passages exclusively appropriate to the supposed narrator, such as the last couplet of the third stanza, the seven last lines of the tenth, and the five following stanzas, with the exception of the four admirable lines at the commencement of the fourteenth, are felt by many unprejudiced and unsophisticated hearts as sudden and unpleasant sinkings from the height to which the poet had previously lifted them, and to which he again re-elevates both himself and his reader.

If then I am compelled to doubt the theory by which the choice of characters was to be directed, not only *a priori*, from grounds of reason, but both from the few instances in which the poet himself need be supposed to have been governed by it, and from the comparative inferiority of those instances; still more must I hesitate in my assent to the sentence which immediately follows the former citation, and which I can neither admit as particular fact or as general rule. 'The language too of these men is adopted (purified indeed from what appear to be its real defects, from all lasting and rational causes of dislike or disgust) because such men hourly communicate with the best objects from which the best part of language is originally derived; and because, from their rank in society and the sameness and narrow circle of their intercourse, being less under the action of social vanity they convey their feelings and notions in simple and unelaborated expressions.' To this I reply: that a rustic's language, purified from all provincialism and grossness, and so far re-constructed as to be made consistent with the rules of grammar (which are in essence no other than the laws of universal logic applied to psychological materials), will not differ from the language of any other man of common-

sense, however learned or refined he may be, except as far as the notions which the rustic has to convey are fewer and more indiscriminate. This will become still clearer if we add the consideration (equally important though less obvious) that the rustic, from the more imperfect development of his faculties and from the lower state of their cultivation, aims almost solely to convey insulated facts, either those of his scanty experience or his traditional belief; while the educated man chiefly seeks to discover and express those connections of things, or those relative bearings of fact to fact, from which some more or less general law is deducible. For facts are valuable to a wise man chiefly as they lead to the discovery of the indwelling law which is the true being of things, the sole solution of their modes of existence and in the knowledge of which consists our dignity and our power.

As little can I agree with the assertion that from the objects with which the rustic hourly communicates the best part of language is formed. For first, if to communicate with an object implies such an acquaintance with it as renders it capable of being discriminately reflected on, the distinct knowledge of an uneducated rustic would furnish a very scanty vocabulary. The few things and modes of action requisite for his bodily conveniences would alone be individualized; while all the rest of nature would be expressed by a small number of confused general terms. Secondly, I deny that the words and combinations of words derived from the objects with which the rustic is familiar, whether with distinct or confused knowledge, can be justly said to form the best part of language. It is more than probable that many classes of the brute creation possess discriminating sounds by which they can convey to each other notices of such objects as concern their food, shelter or safety. Yet we hesitate to call the aggregate of such sounds a language otherwise than metaphorically. . . . When therefore Mr Wordsworth adds, 'accordingly such a language' (meaning, as before, the language of rustic life purified from provincialism), 'arising out of repeated experience and regular feelings is a more permanent and a far more philosophical language than that which is frequently substituted for it by poets, who think they are conferring honor upon themselves and their art in proportion as they indulge in arbitrary and capricious habits of expression'; it may be answered that the language which he has in view can be attributed to rustics with no greater right than the style of Hooker or Bacon to Tom Brown or Sir Roger L'Estrange. Doubtless, if what is peculiar to each were omitted in each, the result must needs be the same. Further, that the poet who uses an illogical diction, or a style fitted to excite only the low and changeable pleasure of wonder by means of groundless novelty, substitutes a language of folly and vanity, not for that of the rustic, but for that of good sense and natural feeling.

Here let me be permitted to remind the reader that the positions which I controvert are contained in the sentences—'a selection of the real language of men';—'the language of these men (i.e. men in low and rustic life) I propose to myself to imitate, and as far as possible to adopt the very language of men.' 'Between the language of prose and that of metrical composition there neither is, nor can be any essential difference.' It is against these exclusively that my opposition is directed.

I object, in the very first instance, to an equivocation in the use of the word 'real.' Every man's language varies according to the extent of his knowledge, the activity of his faculties and the depth or quickness of his feelings. Every man's language has, first, its individualities; secondly, the common properties of the class to which he belongs; and thirdly, words and phrases of universal use.... For 'real' therefore we must substitute *ordinary,* or *lingua communis.* And this, we have proved, is no more to be found in the phraseology of low and rustic life than in that of any other class. Omit the peculiarities of each, and the result of course must be common to all. And assuredly the omissions and changes to be made in the language of rustics before it could be transferred to any species of poem, except the drama or other professed imitation, are at least as numerous and weighty as would be required in adapting to the same purpose the ordinary language of tradesmen and manufacturers. Not to mention that the language so highly extolled by Mr Wordsworth varies in every county, nay in every village, according to the accidental character of the clergyman, the existence or nonexistence of schools; or even, perhaps, as the exciseman, publican or barber happen to be, or not to be, zealous politicians and readers of the weekly newspaper *pro bono publico.* Anterior to cultivation the *lingua communis* of every country, as Dante has well observed, exists everywhere in parts and nowhere as a whole.

Neither is the case rendered at all more tenable by the addition of the words 'in a state of excitement.' For the nature of a man's words, when he is strongly affected by joy, grief or anger, must necessarily depend on the number and quality of the general truths, conceptions and images, and of the words expressing them, with which his mind had been previously stored. For the property of passion is not to *create,* but to set in increased activity. At least, whatever new connections of thoughts or images, or (which is equally, if not more than equally, the appropriate effect of strong excitement) whatever generalizations of truth or experience the heat of passion may produce, yet the terms of their conveyance must have pre-existed in his former conversations, and are only collected and crowded together by the unusual stimulation. It is indeed very possible to adopt in a poem the unmeaning repetitions, habitual phrases and other blank counters which an unfurnished or confused understanding interposes at short intervals in order to keep hold of his subject which is still slipping from him, and to give him time for recollection; or in mere aid of vacancy, as in the scanty companies of a country stage the same player pops backwards and forwards, in order to prevent the appearance of empty spaces, in the procession of *Macbeth* or *Henry VIIIth.* But what assistance to the poet or ornament to the poem these can supply, I am at a loss to conjecture. Nothing assuredly can differ either in origin or in mode more widely from the apparent tautologies of intense and turbulent feeling in which the passion is greater and of longer endurance than to be exhausted or satisfied by a single representation of the image or incident exciting it. Such repetitions I admit to be a beauty of the highest kind; as illustrated by Mr Wordsworth himself from the song of Deborah. 'At her feet he bowed, he fell, he lay down: at her feet he bowed, he fell: where he bowed, there he fell down dead.' (pp. 193-200)

[It] is high time to announce decisively and aloud, that the supposed characteristics of Mr Wordsworth's poetry, whether admired or reprobated; whether they are simplicity or simpleness; faithful adherence to essential nature or wilful selections from human nature of its meanest forms and under the least attractive associations: are as little the real characteristics of his poetry at large as of his genius and the constitution of his mind.

In a comparatively small number of poems he chose to try an experiment; and this experiment we will suppose to have failed. Yet even in these poems it is impossible not to perceive that the natural tendency of the poet's mind is to great objects and elevated conceptions. The poem entitled **'Fidelity'** is for the greater part written in language as unraised and naked as any perhaps in [Wordsworth]. Yet take the following stanza and compare it with the preceding stanzas of the same poem:

> There sometimes does a leaping fish
> Send through the tarn a lonely cheer;
> The crags repeat the raven's croak
> In symphony austere;
> Thither the rainbow comes—the cloud,
> And mists that spread the flying shroud;
> And sunbeams; and the sounding blast,
> That if it could would hurry past,
> But that enormous barrier holds it fast.

Or compare the four last lines of the concluding stanza with the former half:

> Yes, proof was plain that since the day
> On which the traveller thus had died,
> The dog had watched about the spot,
> Or by his master's side:
> *How nourished here for such long time*
> *He knows who gave that love sublime,*
> *And gave that strength of feeling, great*
> *Above all human estimate.*

Can any candid and intelligent mind hesitate in determining which of these best represents the tendency and native character of the poet's genius? Will he not decide that the one was written because the poet *would* so write, and the other because he could not so entirely repress the force and grandeur of his mind, but that he must in some part or other of every composition write otherwise? In short, that his only disease is the being out of his element; like the swan, that having amused himself for a while with crushing the weeds on the river's bank soon returns to his own majestic movements on its reflecting and sustaining surface. Let it be observed that I am here supposing the imagined judge to whom I appeal to have already decided against the poet's theory, as far as it is different from the principles of the art generally acknowledged. (pp. 246-47)

The first characteristic, though only occasional defect, which I appear to myself to find in these poems is the inconstancy of the style. Under this name I refer to the sudden and unprepared transitions from lines or sentences of peculiar felicity (at all events striking and original) to a style not only unimpassioned but undistinguished. He sinks too often and too abruptly to that style which I should place in the second division of language, dividing it into the three species: first, that which is peculiar to poetry; second, that which is only proper in prose; and third, the neutral or common to both.... There is something unpleasant in the being thus obliged to alternate states of feeling so dissimilar, and this too in a species of writing the pleasure from which is in part derived from the preparation and previous expectation of the reader. (p. 248)

But it would be unjust not to repeat that this defect is only occasional. From a careful reperusal of the two volumes of poems I doubt whether the objectionable passages would amount in the whole to one hundred lines; not the eighth part of the number of pages. In the *Excursion* the feeling of incongruity is seldom excited by the diction of any passage considered in itself, but by the sudden superiority of some other passage forming the context.

The second defect I could generalize with tolerable accuracy if the reader will pardon an uncouth and new coined word. There is, I should say, not seldom a *matter-of-factness* in certain poems. This may be divided into, first, a laborious minuteness and fidelity in the representation of objects and their positions as they appeared to the poet himself; secondly, the insertion of accidental circumstances, in order to the full explanation of his living characters, their dispositions and actions: which circumstances might be necessary to establish the probability of a statement in real life, where nothing is taken for granted by the hearer, but appear superfluous in poetry, where the reader is willing to believe for his own sake. To this accidentality I object, as contravening the essence of poetry, which Aristotle pronounces to be . . . the most intense, weighty and philosophical product of human art; adding, as the reason, that it is the most catholic and abstract. (p. 251)

It must be some strong motive (as, for instance, that the description was necessary to the intelligibility of the tale) which could induce me to describe in a number of verses what a draftsman could present to the eye with incomparably greater satisfaction by half a dozen strokes of his pencil, or the painter with as many touches of his brush. Such descriptions too often occasion in the mind of a reader who is determined to understand his author a feeling of labour, not very dissimilar to that with which he would construct a diagram, line by line, for a long geometrical proposition. It seems to be like taking the pieces of a dissected map out of its box. We first look at one part, and then at another, then join and dove-tail them; and when the successive acts of attention have been completed, there is a retrogressive effort of mind to behold it as a whole. The poet should paint to the imagination, not to the fancy. . . . (p. 252)

A portrait of Dorothy Wordsworth in 1833, aged sixty-one.

The second division respects an apparent minute adherence to matter-of-fact in character and incidents; a biographical attention to probability, and an anxiety of explanation and retrospect. Under this head I shall deliver, with no feigned diffidence, the results of my best reflection on the great point of controversy between Mr Wordsworth and his objectors; namely, on the choice of his characters. I have already declared, and I trust justified, my utter dissent from the mode of argument which his critics have hitherto employed. To their question, why did you chuse such a character, or a character from such a rank of life? the poet might, in my opinion, fairly retort: why with the conception of my character did you make wilful choice of mean or ludicrous associations not furnished by me but supplied from your own sickly and fastidious feelings? (p. 253)

But yet I object nevertheless, and for the following reasons. First, because the object in view, as an immediate object, belongs to the moral philosopher, and would be pursued not only more appropriately, but in my opinion with far greater probability of success, in sermons or moral essays than in an elevated poem. It seems, indeed, to destroy the main fundamental distinction, not only between a poem and prose, but even between philosophy and works of fiction, inasmuch as it proposes truth for its immediate object instead of pleasure. Now till the blessed time shall come when truth itself shall be pleasure, and both shall be so united as to be distinguishable in words only, not in feeling, it will remain the poet's office to proceed upon that state of association which actually exists as general; instead of attempting first to make it what it ought to be, and then to let to the pleasure follow. But here is unfortunately a small *hysteron-proteron*. For the communication of pleasure is the introductory means by which alone the poet must expect to moralize his readers. Secondly: though I were to admit, for a moment, this argument to be groundless; yet how is the moral effect to be produced by merely attaching the name of some low profession to powers which are least likely, and to qualities which are assuredly not more likely, to be found in it? The poet, speaking in his own person, may at once delight and improve us by sentiments which teach us the independence of goodness, of wisdom, and even of genius, on the favors of fortune. (p. 254)

Is there one word, for instance, attributed to the pedlar in the *Excursion* characteristic of a pedlar? One sentiment that might not more plausibly, even without the aid of any previous explanation, have proceeded from any wise and beneficent old man of a rank or profession in which the language of learning and refinement are natural and to be expected? Need the rank have been at all particularized, where nothing follows which the knowledge of that rank is to explain or illustrate? (p. 257)

For all the admirable passages interposed in [the] narration might, with trifling alterations, have been far more appropriately and with far greater verisimilitude told of a poet in the character of a poet; and without incurring another defect which I shall now mention, and a sufficient illustration of which will have been here anticipated.

Third: an undue predilection for the dramatic form in certain poems, from which one or other of two evils result. Either the thoughts and diction are different from that of the poet, and then there arises an incongruity of style; or they are the same and indistinguishable, and then it presents a species of ventriloquism, where two are represented as talking while in truth one man only speaks.

The fourth class of defects is closely connected with the former; but yet are such as arise likewise from an intensity of feeling disproportionate to such knowledge and value of the objects described as can be fairly anticipated of men in general, even of the most cultivated classes; and with which therefore few only, and those few particularly circumstanced, can be supposed to sympathize: in this class I comprize occasional prolixity, repetition and an eddying instead of progression of thought. . . .

Fifth and last: thoughts and images too great for the subject. This is an approximation to what might be called *mental* bombast, as distinguished from verbal; for as in the latter there is a disproportion of the expression to the thoughts, so in this there is a disproportion of thought to the circumstance and occasion. This, by the bye, is a fault of which none but a man of genius is capable. It is the awkwardness and strength of Hercules with the distaff of Omphale. (p. 258)

To these defects which, as appears by the extracts, are only occasional I may oppose with far less fear of encountering the dissent of any candid and intelligent reader the following (for the most part correspondent) excellencies. First, an austere purity of language both grammatically and logically; in short a perfect appropriateness of the words to the meaning. (p. 263)

The second characteristic excellence of Mr. W.'s works is: a correspondent weight and sanity of the thoughts and sentiments—won, not from books, but—from the poet's own meditative observation. They are fresh and have the dew upon them. His muse, at least when in her strength of wing and when she hovers aloft in her proper element,

> Makes audible a linked lay of truth,
> Of truth profound a sweet continuous lay,
> Not learnt, but native, her own natural notes! . . .

Even throughout his smaller poems there is scarcely one which is not rendered valuable by some just and original reflection. (p. 265)

Both in respect of this and of the former excellence, Mr Wordsworth strikingly resembles Samuel Daniel, one of the golden writers of our golden Elizabethan age, now most causelessly neglected: Samuel Daniel, whose diction bears no mark of time, no distinction of age, which has been and, as long as our language shall last, will be so far the language of the to-day and for ever, as that it is more intelligible to us than the transitory fashions of our own particular age. A similar praise is due to his sentiments. No frequency of perusal can deprive them of their freshness. For though they are brought into the full daylight of every reader's comprehension, yet are they drawn up from depths which few in any age are priviledged to visit, into which few in any age have courage or inclination to descend. If Mr Wordsworth is not equally with Daniel alike intelligible to all readers of average understanding in all passages of his works, the comparative difficulty does not arise from the greater impurity of the ore but from the nature and uses of the metal. A poem is not necessarily obscure because it does not aim to be popular. It is enough if a work be perspicuous to those for whom it is written, and

> Fit audience find, though few.
>
> (p. 267)

Third (and wherein he soars far above Daniel) the sinewy strength and originality of single lines and paragraphs: the frequent *curiosa felicitas* of his diction of which I need not here give specimens, having anticipated them in a preceding page. This beauty, and as eminently characteristic of Wordsworth's poetry, his rudest assailants have felt themselves compelled to acknowledge and admire.

Fourth: the perfect truth of nature in his images and descriptions as taken immediately from nature, and proving a long and genial intimacy with the very spirit which gives the physiognomic expression to all the works of nature. Like a green field reflected in a calm and perfectly transparent lake, the image is distinguished from the reality only by its greater softness and lustre. Like the moisture or the polish on a pebble, genius neither distorts nor false-colours its objects; but on the contrary brings out many a vein and many a tint which escape the eye of common observation, thus raising to the rank of gems what had been often kicked away by the hurrying foot of the traveller on the dusty highroad of custom. (pp. 268-69)

Fifth: a meditative pathos, a union of deep and subtle thought with sensibility; a sympathy with man as man; the sympathy indeed of a contemplator, rather than a fellow-sufferer or co-mate *(spectator, haud particeps),* but of a contemplator from whose view no difference of rank conceals the sameness of the nature; no injuries of wind or weather, of toil or even of ignorance, wholly disguise the human face divine. The superscription and the image of the Creator still remain legible to him under the dark lines with which guilt or calamity had cancelled or cross-barred it. Here the man and the poet lose and find themselves in each other, the one as glorified, the latter as substantiated. In this mild and philosophic pathos Wordsworth appears to me without a compeer. Such he is: so he writes. (p. 270)

Lastly, and pre-eminently, I challenge for this poet the gift of imagination in the highest and strictest sense of the word. In the play of fancy Wordsworth, to my feelings, is not always graceful, and sometimes recondite. The likeness is occasionally too strange, or demands too peculiar a point of view, or is such as appears the creature of predetermined research rather than spontaneous presentation. Indeed his fancy seldom displays itself as mere and unmodified fancy. But in imaginative power he stands nearest of all modern writers to Shakespeare and Milton; and yet in a kind perfectly unborrowed and his own. To employ his own words, which are at once an instance and an illustration, he does indeed to all thoughts and to all objects—

> add the gleam,
> The light that never was on sea or land.
> The consecration, and the poet's dream.
>
> (p. 271)

What Mr Wordsworth *will* produce it is not for me to prophesy: but I could pronounce with the liveliest convictions what he is capable of producing. It is the FIRST GENUINE PHILOSOPHIC POEM.

The preceding criticism will not, I am aware, avail to overcome the prejudices of those who have made it a business to attack and ridicule Mr Wordsworth's compositions.

Truth and prudence might be imaged as concentric circles. The poet may perhaps have passed beyond the latter, but he has confined himself far within the bounds of the former in designating these critics as too petulant to be passive to a genuine poet, and too feeble to grapple with him: 'men of palsied imaginations, in whose minds all healthy action is languid; who therefore feel as the many direct them, or with the many are greedy after vicious provocatives.' (p. 275)

So much for the detractors from Wordsworth's merits. On the other hand, much as I might wish for their fuller sympathy, I dare not flatter myself that the freedom with which I have declared my opinions concerning both his theory and his defects, most of which are more or less connected with his theory either as cause or effect, will be satisfactory or pleasing to all the poet's admirers and advocates. More indiscriminate than mine their admiration may be: deeper and more sincere it cannot be. But I have advanced no opinion either for praise or censure other than as texts introductory to the reasons which compel me to form it. Above all, I was fully convinced that such a criticism was not only wanted; but that, if executed with adequate ability, it must conduce in no mean degree to Mr Wordsworth's reputation. His fame belongs to another age, and can neither be accelerated nor retarded. How small the proportion of the defects are to the beauties I have repeatedly declared; and that no one of them originates in deficiency of poetic genius. Had they been more and greater, I should still, as a friend to his literary character in the present age, consider an analytic display of them as pure gain; if only it removed, as surely to all reflecting minds even the foregoing analysis must have removed, the strange mistake so slightly grounded yet so widely and industriously propagated of Mr Wordsworth's turn for simplicity! I am not half as much irritated by hearing his enemies abuse him for vulgarity of style, subject and conception, as I am disgusted with the gilded side of the same meaning, as displayed by some affected admirers with whom he is, forsooth, a sweet, simple poet! (pp. 276-77)

> *Samuel Taylor Coleridge, "Examination of the Tenets Peculiar to Mr Wordsworth" and "The Characteristic Defects of Wordsworth's Poetry," in his* Biographia Literaria; or, Biographical Sketches of My Literary Life and Opinions, *edited by George Watson, revised edition, Dutton, 1965, pp. 188-200, 246-78.*

JOHN KEATS (letter date 1818)

[*Keats is considered a key figure in the English Romantic movement and one of the major poets in the English language. Critics note that though his creative career spanned only four years, he achieved remarkable intellectual and artistic development. His poems, notably those contained in the collection* Lamia, Isabella, The Eve of St. Agnes, and Other Poems, *are valued not only for their sensuous imagery, simplicity, and passionate tone, but also for the insight they provide into aesthetic and human concerns, particularly the conflict between art and life. In this excerpt from Keats's well-known "Mansion of Many Apartments" letter, written on May 3, 1818 and addressed to John Hamilton Reynolds, he discusses the idea that poetry can be a consolation in life and speculates on the state of mind which led Wordsworth to write "Tintern Abbey."*]

[I have nothing but surmises about] whether Wordsworth has in truth epic passion, and martyrs himself to the human heart, the main region of his song. In regard to his genius alone—we find what he says true as far as we have experienced and we can judge no further but by larger experience—for axioms in philosophy are not axioms until they are proved upon our pulses. We read fine things, but never feel them to the full until we have gone the same steps as the Author. (p. 154)

[To return to] whether or no he has an extended vision or a circumscribed grandeur—whether he is an eagle in his nest, or on the wing. And to be more explicit and to show you how tall I stand by the giant, I will put down a simile of human life as far as I now perceive it; that is, to the point to which I

say we both have arrived at. Well—I compare human life to a large Mansion of Many Apartments, two of which I can only describe, the doors of the rest being as yet shut upon me. The first we step into we call the infant or thoughtless Chamber, in which we remain as long as we do not think. We remain there a long while, and notwithstanding the doors of the second Chamber remain wide open, showing a bright appearance, we care not to hasten to it; but are at length imperceptibly impelled by the awakening of the thinking principle within us—we no sooner get into the second Chamber, which I shall call the Chamber of Maiden-Thought, than we become intoxicated with the light and the atmosphere, we see nothing but pleasant wonders, and think of delaying there for ever in delight. However among the effects this breathing is father of is that tremendous one of sharpening one's vision into the heart and nature of Man—of convincing one's nerves that the world is full of Misery and Heartbreak, Pain, Sickness and oppression—whereby this Chamber of Maiden Thought becomes gradually darken'd and at the same time on all sides of it many doors are set open—but all dark—all leading to dark passages. We see not the ballance of good and evil. We are in a Mist. *We* are now in that state—We feel the 'burden of the Mystery'. To this point was Wordsworth come, as far as I can conceive when he wrote **'Tintern Abbey'** and it seems to me that his Genius is explorative of those dark Passages. Now if we live, and go on thinking, we too shall explore them. He is a Genius and superior [to] us, in so far as he can, more than we, make discoveries, and shed a light in them. Here I must think Wordsworth is deeper than Milton, though I think it has depended more upon the general and gregarious advance of intellect, than individual greatness of Mind. (pp. 155-56)

> *John Keats, in a letter to John Hamilton Reynolds on May 3, 1818, in his* The Letters of John Keats, Vol. I, *edited by Maurice Buxton Forman, Oxford University Press, London, 1931, pp. 151-58.*

[JOHN WILSON] (essay date 1818)

[*A Scottish critic, essayist, novelist, poet, and short story writer, Wilson is best known as Christopher North, the name he assumed when writing for* Blackwood's Edinburgh Magazine, *a Tory periodical to which he was a principal contributor for over twenty-five years. He is chiefly famous for his* Noctes Ambrosianae, *a series of witty dialogues originally published in* Blackwood's *between 1822 and 1835 in which contemporary issues and personalities are treated at once with levity, gravity, and pungent satire. Wilson is not recognized as a great critic. His criticism, which was frequently written in haste, is often deficient in sagacity, analysis, and finish. He could be severe and stinging, and he reserved his harshest words for gifted young writers whom he sincerely wanted to help by objectively analyzing their work. His other critical opinions are largely regarded as the projections of his varying moods; his conflicting assessments of Wordsworth's poetry, for instance, are often cited as evidence of his subjectivity. Indiscriminate benevolence, on the other hand, led him to equate such authors as Joanna Baillie and William Shakespeare. In this excerpt from his review of* The White Doe of Rylstone, *Wilson praises characterization and imagery in the poem, arguing that it is written "with a power and pathos that have not often been excelled in English poetry." He acknowledges, nevertheless, that many readers will not appreciate* The White Doe's *excellence.*]

[**The White Doe of Rylstone** is] a poem which exhibits in perfection many of Wordsworth's peculiar beauties, and, it may be, some of his peculiar defects. (p. 372)

It will be soon seen, by those who have not read this Poem, that in it Mr Wordsworth has aimed at awakening the feelings and affections through the medium of the imagination. There are many readers of Poetry who imperiously demand strong passion and violent excitement, and who can perceive little merit in any composition which does not administer to that kind of enjoyment. Such persons will probably consider this Poem feeble and uninteresting, as they will do numerous productions that have, nevertheless, established themselves in the literature of our country. But it is owing to a defect of imagination that the beauty, apparent and delightful to others, shines not upon them. All those magical touches, by which a true Poet awakens endless trains of thought in an imaginative mind, are not felt at all by persons of such character. It is wonderful what influence a delicate tune, or shade, or tone, may have over the poetical visions of a poetical reader. In poetry, as in painting, gentle lineaments, and sober colouring, and chastened composition, often affect and delight the mind of capable judges more than even the most empassioned efforts of the art. But, to the vulgar,—and even to minds of more power than delicacy or refinement, such delineations carry with them no charm— no authority. Many persons, in some things not only able but enlightened, would look with untouched souls on the pictures of Raphael,—and turn, undelighted, from the countenance and the eyes of beings more lovely than human life,—to the rapturous contemplation of mere earthly beauty. If we do not greatly err, the Poem we have now been analyzing possesses much of the former character, and will afford great delight on every perusal,—new and gentle beauties stealing and breathing from it like fragrance from perennial flowers.

Indeed, the tradition on which the Poem is founded must, to an unimaginative mind, appear childish and insignificant; but to purer spirits, beautifully adapted to the purposes of Poetry. The creature, with whose image so many mournful and sublime associations are connected, is by nature one the loveliest— wildest—of the lower orders of creation. All our ordinary associations with it are poetical. (p. 380)

Of Emily . . . little need be said. From the first moment she is felt to be orphaned,—all her former happiness is to us like a dream,—all that is real with her is sorrow. In one day she becomes utterly desolate. But there is no agony, no convulsion, no despair: profound sadness, settled grief, the everlasting calm of melancholy, and the perfect stillness of resignation. All her looks, words, movements, are gentle, feminine, subdued. Throughout all the Poem an image of an angelical being seems to have lived in the Poet's soul,—and without effort, he gives it to us in angelical beauty.

The character and situation of Francis, the eldest brother, are finely conceived, and coloured in the same calm and serene style of painting. He is felt to be a hero, though throughout branded with the name of coward. It required some courage in a Poet to describe a character so purely passive. There is, we think, a solemnity, and piety, and devotion, in the character that becomes truly awful, linked, as they are, throughout, with the last extremities of human suffering and calamity.

But we must conclude,—and we do so with perfect confidence, that many who never have read this Poem, and not a few who may have read extracts from it with foolish and unbecoming levity, will feel and acknowledge . . . that the **White Doe of Rylstone** is a tale written with singularly beautiful simplicity of language, and with a power and pathos that have not been often excelled in English Poetry. (p. 381)

[John Wilson], "Essays on the Lake School of Poetry, No. I: Wordsworth's 'White Doe of Rylstone'," in Blackwood's Edinburgh Magazine, Vol. III, No. XVI, July, 1818, pp. 369-81.

THE MONTHLY REVIEW, LONDON   (essay date 1819)

[The author of this scathing review of Peter Bell refers to Wordsworth as a "buffoon of Nature herself," and to the poem's style as a parody of "all that is good poetry."]

[**Peter Bell**] is dedicated to Robert Southey, Esq. *P.L.* or Poet Laureate, by William Wordsworth, Esq. *L.P.* or Lake Poet. It is, in truth, "a right merry and conceited" small production; worthy of the bard to whom it is offered, and worthy of him also by whom it is produced. All past, present, and (probably) future performances, by the same author, must sink into nothing before **Peter Bell**. No lisping was ever more distinctly lisped than the versification of this poem; and no folly was ever more foolishly boasted than that of the writer, whether in style or subject-matter. (pp. 419-20)

Can Englishmen write, and Englishmen read, such drivel,— such daudling, impotent drivel,—as this! . . . Weak indeed must be the mind that, by any process of sophistry, or long practice of patience, can be reconciled to the aforesaid drivel. We feel the force of custom to be *almost* omnipotent: but, however *dulled* and *deadened* our sense of propriety, our sense of poetry, or sense of every kind may have been by the eternal repetition of similar imbecilities, we *should* have thought that, until the very brains were extracted, no head could hold such unmeaning prittle-prattle as the above;—no tongue, we *are* persuaded, tied by the thinnest silk of shame, would ever have poured it forth.—We really waste *words*, however, on what is scarcely *Word's-worth;* and, suffering this infatuated poetaster to condemn himself out of his own mouth, we shall intersperse very few farther remarks with his modicums of matchless vanity.

Some well-meaning, and, in one case, witty individuals have published parodies of *Peter Bell,* the potter, and of his brother, the Waggoner. We shall be required briefly to notice these parodies, as well as their originals: but in fact the originals themselves are the parodies, or rather the gross burlesques of all that is good in poetry. . . . Nay, he is the buffoon of Nature herself; and, by lowering her grand and general associations of physical and moral beauty into petty pastry-cook details of fruit and flowers, he presents to some a *ludicrous,* and to all an *unfaithful* portrait of his pretended original. We say pretended; for in fact it is not Nature, but his own narrow, whimsical, unpoetical idea of Nature, which this strange writer worships. It is, however, true that rays of reason escape through these hallucinations. . . . (p. 421)

Yet what is [**Peter Bell**] about? About a man who was reading in his room at midnight, when all grew suddenly dark, and on the paper, in letters of light, was formed a *word—too* something or other to be mentioned!!! Oh dear! Oh dear! and this is written for full-grown men and women! We can only say that, if a nurse were to talk to any of their children in this manner, a sensible father and mother would be strongly disposed to dismiss her without a character.

Peter sees a number of strange things in the water, the product of his own guilty fancy. . . . Among other scenes is the following:

Is it a party in a parlour?
Cramm'd just as they on earth were cramm'd—
Some sipping punch, some sipping tea,
But, as you by their faces see,
All silent and all damn'd!

Fie, fie, Mr. Wordsworth! (p. 422)

> *"Wordsworth's 'Peter Bell',"* in The Monthly Review, *London, n.s. Vol. LXXXIX, August, 1819, pp. 419-22.*

THE LONDON LITERARY GAZETTE   (essay date 1822)

[*In the following excerpt from a largely negative review of* Ecclesiastical Sketches, *the reviewer terms Wordsworth's subject "intractable," his poetic style "prosaic," and his overall scheme for the collection "absurd."*]

The disease of the mind which manifests itself in eruptions of poetry, is certainly an extraordinary phenomenon, and as likely to puzzle the acumen of the critic as the symptoms of the plague are calculated to perplex the skill of the physician. With Mr. Wordsworth it is evidently chronic, and assumes very different appearances at different periods. In his Excursions he seems occasionally to respire a pure atmosphere, as he breathes the healthful country air; with Peter Bell we find only the atrophious invalid transported per Waggoner to the nearest hospital; on the Duddon, braced again by mountain breeze and laving stream, he revives in genuine song; and now, cloistered up with dull, monotonous association, he sinks once more into weakness and doating. Indeed these **Ecclesiastical Sketches** are less to our taste than even the **Peter Bell** class of the author's performances, inasmuch as a solemn ass is less amusing than a whimsical fool. It is astonishing to see a man of genius so far delude himself as to fancy he can render any thing popular, no matter how untractable the subject, how prosaic the verse, and how absurd the plan. Nothing short of such delusion could have led Mr. Wordsworth to choose a theme unsusceptible of poetry; and give us the baldest historical sketches in all the form and pretension of the most imaginative composition. It seems as if he were determined to contest the cap and bells with his friend Southey's *Vision of Judgment*, or with Byron's dramas, determined, like them, to shun what he can do admirably, and turn either to that for which he has no talent, or to that which no talent can render acceptable. Such is our opinion of the present work. The design is radically unpropitious, and where we discover poetical beauties (of which no effusion of Mr. Wordsworth can be destitute,) they appear like flowers in a desert, and we wonder more how the soil could produce and the climate nourish them, than feel relieved from the uniformity of the dreary waste. (p. 191)

The sum of the impression made upon us by this volume is, that we have to wade through too much of the tiresome for the value of the pleasing; the chaff is out of all proportion to the grains. (p. 192)

> *A review of "Ecclesiastical Sketches,"* in The London Literary Gazette, *No. 271, March 30, 1822, pp. 191-92.*

[FRANCIS JEFFREY]   (essay date 1822)

[*In this excerpt from his last review of Wordsworth's poetry, Jeffrey declares the Lake School of poetry "pretty nearly extinct." He derides the poet's growing conservatism and its effect on his work. For additional commentary by Jeffrey on Wordsworth's poetry, see the excerpts dated 1802, 1807, 1814, and 1815.*]

The Lake School of Poetry, we think, is now pretty nearly extinct. . . . The contact of the Stamp-office appears to have had [a] bad effect on Mr Wordsworth. His *Peter Bell* and his *Waggoner* put his admirers, we believe, a little to their shifts; but since he has openly taken to the office of a publican, and exchanged the company of leech-gatherers for that of tax-gatherers, he has fallen into a way of writing which is equally distasteful to his old friends and his old monitors—a sort of prosy, solemn, obscure, feeble kind of mouthing,—sadly garnished with shreds of phrases from Milton and the Bible—but without nature and without passion,—and with a plentiful lack of meaning, compensated only by a large allowance of affectation and egotism. This is the taste in which a volume of Sonnets to the river Duddon is composed—and another which he calls *Ecclesiastical Sketches,* and these precious [*Memorials of a Tour on the Continent*]. (pp. 449-50)

The great characteristic of these works is a sort of emphatic inanity—a singular barrenness and feebleness of thought, disguised under a sententious and assuming manner and a style beyond example verbose and obscure. Most of the little pieces of which they are composed begin with the promise of some striking image or deep reflection; but end, almost invariably, in disappointment—having, most commonly, no perceptible meaning at all—or one incredibly puerile and poor—and exemplifying nothing but the very worthless art of saying ordinary things in an unintelligible way—and hiding no meaning in a kind of stern and pompous wordiness. (p. 450)

> [*Francis Jeffrey*], *"Wordworth's 'Tour',"* in The Edinburgh Review, *Vol. XXXVII, No. LXXIV, November, 1822, pp. 449-56.*

WILLIAM HAZLITT   (essay date 1825)

[*One of the most important commentators of the Romantic age, Hazlitt was an English critic and journalist. He is best known for his descriptive criticism in which he stressed that no motives beyond judgment and analysis are necessary on the part of the critic. A critic must start with a strong opinion, Hazlitt asserted, but must also keep in mind that evaluation is the starting point— not the object—of criticism. Hazlitt's often recalcitrant refusal to engage in close analysis, however, led other critics to wonder whether in fact he was capable of close, sustained analysis. Characterized by a tough, independent view of the world, by his political liberalism, and by the influence of Samuel Taylor Coleridge and Charles Lamb, Hazlitt's style is particularly admired for its wide range of reference and catholicity of interests. Though he wrote on many diverse subjects, Hazlitt's most important critical achievements are his typically Romantic interpretation of characters from William Shakespeare's plays, influenced by the German critic August Wilhelm Schlegel, and his revival of interest in such Elizabethan dramatists as John Webster, Thomas Haywood, and Thomas Dekker. Hazlitt commences his evaluation of Wordsworth's poetry by emphasizing that the poet's genius perfectly expresses the spirit of his age. His style is "vernacular" and democratic, and he successfully exposes and eliminates the trappings of poetry. In addition, Hazlitt extols Wordsworth's strikingly innovative way of presenting nature, concluding that "in this sense (he) is the most original poet now living." To Hazlitt, Wordsworth's later, more philosophical poetry is less effective than his earlier, lyrical poetry. Addressing Wordsworth's ten-*]

dency to self-aggrandizement, Hazlitt theorizes that he may be viewed as "the spoiled child of disappointment" and that his defensiveness may have been caused by the inordinately harsh criticism he received early in his career. Other critics who consider Wordsworth's style include Pater (1874), Lowell (1875), Bradley (1909), Darbishire (1949), Pottle (1950), and Hartman (1964).]

Mr. Wordsworth's genius is a pure emanation of the Spirit of the Age. Had he lived in any other period of the world, he would never have been heard of. As it is, he has some difficulty to contend with the hebetude of his intellect and the meanness of his subject. With him 'lowliness is young ambition's ladder': but he finds it a toil to climb in this way the steep of Fame. His homely Muse can hardly raise her wing from the ground, nor spread her hidden glories to the sun. He has 'no figures nor no fantasies, which busy *passion* draws in the brains of men': neither the gorgeous machinery of mythologic lore, nor the splendid colours of poetic diction. His style is vernacular: he delivers household truths. He sees nothing loftier than human hopes, nothing deeper than the human heart. This he probes, this he tampers with, this he poises, with all its incalculable weight of thought and feeling, in his hands, and at the same time calms the throbbing pulses of his own heart by keeping his eye ever fixed on the face of nature. If he can make the life-blood flow from the wounded breast, this is the living colouring with which he paints his verse: if he can assuage the pain or close up the wound with the balm of solitary musing, or the healing power of plants and herbs and 'skyey influences,' this is the sole triumph of his art. He takes the simplest elements of nature and of the human mind, the mere abstract conditions inseparable from our being, and tries to compound a new system of poetry from them; and has perhaps succeeded as well as any one could. *'Nihil humani a me alienum puto'* is the motto of his works. He thinks nothing low or indifferent of which this can be affirmed: every thing that professes to be more than this, that is not an absolute essence of truth and feeling, he holds to be vitiated, false and spurious. In a word, his poetry is founded on setting up an opposition (and pushing it to the utmost length) between the natural and the artificial, between the spirit of humanity and the spirit of fashion and of the world.

It is one of the innovations of the time. It partakes of, and is carried along with, the revolutionary movement of our age: the political changes of the day were the model on which he formed and conducted his poetical experiments. His Muse (it cannot be denied, and without this we cannot explain its character at all) is a levelling one. It proceeds on a principle of equality, and strives to reduce all things to the same standard. It is distinguished by a proud humility. It relies upon its own resources, and disdains external show and relief. It takes the commonest events and objects, as a test to prove that nature is always interesting from its inherent truth and beauty, without any of the ornaments of dress or pomp of circumstances to set it off. Hence the unaccountable mixture of seeming simplicity and real abstruseness in the *Lyrical Ballads*. Fools have laughed at, wise men scarcely understand, them. He takes a subject or a story merely as pegs or loops to hang thought and feeling on; the incidents are trifling, in proportion to his contempt for imposing appearances; the reflections are profound, according to the gravity and aspiring pretensions of his mind.

His popular, inartificial style gets rid (at a blow) of all the trappings of verse, of all the high places of poetry: 'the cloud-capt towers, the solemn temples, the gorgeous palaces,' are swept to the ground, and 'like the baseless fabric of a vision, leave not a wreck behind.' All the traditions of learning, all the superstitions of age, are obliterated and effaced. We begin *de novo* on a *tabula rasa* of poetry. The purple pall, the nodding plume of tragedy are exploded as mere pantomime and trick, to return to the simplicity of truth and nature. Kings, queens, priests, nobles, the altar and the throne, the distinctions of rank, birth, wealth, power, 'the judge's robe, the marshal's truncheon, the ceremony that to great ones 'longs,' are not to be found here. The author tramples on the pride of art with greater pride. The Ode and Epode, the Strophe and the Antistrophe, he laughs to scorn. The harp of Homer, the trump of Pindar and of Alcaeus, are still. The decencies of costume, the decorations of vanity are stripped off without mercy as barbarous, idle, and Gothic. The jewels in the crisped hair, the diadem on the polished brow, are thought meretricious, theatrical, vulgar; and nothing contents his fastidious taste beyond a simple garland of flowers. Neither does he avail himself of the advantages which nature or accident holds out to him. He chooses to have his subject a foil to his invention, to owe nothing but to himself.

He gathers manna in the wilderness; he strikes the barren rock for the gushing moisture. He elevates the mean by the strength of his own aspirations; he clothes the naked with beauty and grandeur from the stores of his own recollections. No cypress grove loads his verse with funeral pomp: but his imagination lends 'a sense of joy

> To the bare trees and mountains bare,
> And grass in the green field.

No storm, no shipwreck startles us by its horrors: but the rainbow lifts its head in the cloud, and the breeze sighs through the withered fern. No sad vicissitude of fate, no overwhelming catastrophe in nature deforms his page: but the dew-drop glitters on the bending flower, the tear collects in the glistening eye.

> Beneath the hills, along the flowery vales,
> The generations are prepared; the pangs,
> The internal pangs are ready; the dread strife
> Of poor humanity's afflicted will,
> Struggling in vain with ruthless destiny.

As the lark ascends from its low bed on fluttering wing, and salutes the morning skies, so Mr. Wordsworth's unpretending Muse in russet guise scales the summits of reflection, while it makes the round earth its footstool and its home!

Possibly a good deal of this may be regarded as the effect of disappointed views and an inverted ambition. Prevented by native pride and indolence from climbing the ascent of learning or greatness, taught by political opinions to say to the vain pomp and glory of the world, 'I hate ye,' seeing the path of classical and artificial poetry blocked up by the cumbrous ornaments of style and turgid *common-places*, so that nothing more could be achieved in that direction but by the most ridiculous bombast or the tamest servility, he has turned back, partly from the bias of his mind, partly perhaps from a judicious policy—has struck into the sequestered vale of humble life, sought out the Muse among sheep-cotes and hamlets, and the peasant's mountain-haunts, has discarded all the tinsel pageantry of verse, and endeavoured (not in vain) to aggrandise the trivial, and add the charm of novelty to the familiar. No one has shown the same imagination in raising trifles into importance: no one has displayed the same pathos in treating of the simplest feelings of the heart. Reserved, yet haughty, having no unruly or violent passions (or those passions having been early suppressed), Mr. Wordsworth has passed his life in solitary musing or in daily converse with the face of nature. He exemplifies in an eminent degree the *association;* for his poetry has no other source or character. He had dwelt among pastoral scenes, till each object has become connected with a thousand feelings, a link in the chain of thought, a fibre of his own heart. Every one is by habit and familiarity strongly attached to the place of his birth, or to objects that recal the most pleasing and eventful circumstances of his life.

But to the author of the *Lyrical Ballads* nature is a kind of home; and he may be said to take a personal interest in the universe. There is no image so insignificant that it has not in some mood or other found the way into his heart: no sound that does not awaken the memory of other years.—

> To him the meanest flower that blows can give
> Thoughts that do often lie too deep for tears.

The daisy looks up to him with sparkling eye as an old acquaintance: the cuckoo haunts him with sounds of early youth not to be expressed: a linnet's nest startles him with boyish delight: an old withered thorn is weighed down with a heap of recollections: a grey cloak, seen on some wild moor, torn by the wind or drenched in the rain, afterwards becomes an object of imagination to him: even the lichens on the rock have a life and being in his thoughts. He has described all these objects in a way and with an intensity of feeling that no one else had done before him, and has given a new view or aspect of nature. He is in this sense the most original poet now living, and the one whose writings could the least be spared: for they have no substitute elsewhere. The vulgar do not read them; the learned, who see all things through books, do not understand them; the great despise. The fashionable may ridicule them: but the author has created himself an interest in the heart of the retired and lonely student of nature, which can never die.

Persons of this class will still continue to feel what he has felt: he has expressed what they might in vain wish to express, except with glistening eye and faltering tongue! There is a lofty philosophic tone, a thoughtful humanity, infused into his pastoral vein. Remote from the passions and events of the great world, he has communicated interest and dignity to the primal movements of the heart of man, and ingrafted his own conscious reflections on the casual thoughts of hinds and shepherds. Nursed amidst the grandeur of mountain scenery, he has stooped to have a nearer view of the daisy under his feet, or plucked a branch of white-thorn from the spray: but, in describing it, his mind seems imbued with the majesty and solemnity of the objects around him. The tall rock lifts its head in the erectness of his spirit; the cataract roars in the sound of his verse; and in its dim and mysterious meaning the mists seem to gather in the hollows of Helvellyn, and the forked Skiddaw hovers in the distance. There is little mention of mountainous scenery in Mr. Wordsworth's poetry; but by internal evidence one might be almost sure that it was written in a mountainous country, from its bareness, its simplicity, its loftiness and its depth!

His later philosophic productions have a somewhat different character. They are a departure from, a dereliction of, his first principles. They are classical and courtly. They are polished in style without being gaudy, dignified in subject without affectation. They seem to have been composed not in a cottage at Grasmere, but among the half-inspired groves and stately recollections of Cole-Orton. (pp. 117-22)

Mr. Wordsworth's philosophic poetry, with a less glowing aspect and less tumult in the veins than Lord Byron's on similar occasions, bends a calmer and keener eye on mortality; the impression, if less vivid, is more pleasing and permanent; and we confess it (perhaps it is a want of taste and proper feeling) that there are lines and poems of our author's, that we think of ten times for once that we recur to any of Lord Byron's. Or if there are any of the latter's writings, that we can dwell upon in the same way, that is, as lasting and heart-felt sentiments, it is when laying aside his usual pomp and pretension, he descends with Mr. Wordsworth to the common ground of a disinterested humanity. It may be considered as characteristic of our poet's writings, that they either make no impression on the mind at all, seem mere *nonsense-verses,* or that they leave a mark behind them that never wears out. They either

> Fall blunted from the indurated breast—

without any perceptible result, or they absorb it like a passion. To one class of readers he appears sublime, to another (and we fear the largest) ridiculous. He has probably realised Milton's wish,—'and fit audience found, though few': but we suspect he is not reconciled to the alternative.

There are delightful passages in the *Excursion,* both of natural description and of inspired reflection (passages of the latter kind that in the sound of the thoughts and of the swelling language resemble heavenly symphonies, mournful *requiems* over the grave of human hopes); but we must add, in justice and in sincerity, that we think it impossible that this work should ever become popular, even in the same degree as the *Lyrical Ballads.* It affects a system without having any intelligible clue to one, and, instead of unfolding a principle in various and striking lights, repeats the same conclusions till

A reputed portrait of Annette Vallon.

they become flat and insipid. Mr. Wordsworth's mind is obtuse, except as it is the organ and the receptacle of accumulated feelings: it is not analytic, but synthetic; it is reflecting, rather than theoretical. The *Excursion,* we believe, fell still-born from the press. There was something abortive, and clumsy, and ill-judged in the attempt. It was long and laboured. The personages, for the most part, were low, the fare rustic; the plan raised expectations which were not fulfilled; and the effect was like being ushered into a stately hall and invited to sit down to a splendid banquet in the company of clowns, and with nothing but successive courses of apple-dumplings served up. It was not even *toujours perdrix*! (pp. 123-24)

[If] Mr. Wordsworth had been a more liberal and candid critic, he would have been a more sterling writer. If a greater number of sources of pleasure had been open to him, he would have communicated pleasure to the world more frequently. Had he been less fastidious in pronouncing sentence on the works of others, his own would have been received more favourably, and treated more leniently. The current of his feelings is deep, but narrow; the range of his understanding is lofty and aspiring rather than discursive. The force, the originality, the absolute truth and identity, with which he feels some things, makes him indifferent to so many others. The simplicity and enthusiasm of his feelings, with respect to nature, render him bigoted and intolerant in his judgments of men and things. But it happens to him, as to others, that his strength lies in his weakness; and perhaps we have no right to complain. We might get rid of the cynic and the egotist, and find in his stead a common-place man. We should 'take the good the Gods provide us': a fine and original vein of poetry is not one of their most contemptible gifts; and the rest is scarcely worth thinking of, except as it may be a mortification to those who expect perfection from human nature, or who have been idle enough at some period of their lives to deify men of genius as possessing claims above it. But this is a chord that jars, and we shall not dwell upon it.

Lord Byron we have called, according to the old proverb, 'the spoiled child of fortune': Mr. Wordsworth might plead, in mitigation of some peculiarities, that he is 'the spoiled child of disappointment.' We are convinced, if he had been early a popular poet, he would have borne his honours meekly, and would have been a person of great *bonhomie* and frankness of disposition. But the sense of injustice and of undeserved ridicule sours the temper and narrows the views. To have produced works of genius, and to find them neglected or treated with scorn, is one of the heaviest trials of human patience. We exaggerate our own merits when they are denied by others, and are apt to grudge and cavil at every particle of praise bestowed on those to whom we feel a conscious superiority. In mere self-defence we turn against the world when it turns against us, brood over the undeserved slights we receive; and thus the genial current of the soul is stopped, or vents itself in effusions of petulance and self-conceit. Mr. Wordsworth has thought too much of contemporary critics and criticism, and less than he ought of the award of posterity and of the opinion, we do not say of private friends, but of those who were made so by their admiration of his genius.

He did not court popularity by a conformity to established models, and he ought not to have been surprised that his originality was not understood as a matter of course. He has *gnawed too much on the bridle,* and has often thrown out crusts to the critics, in mere defiance or as a point of honour when he was challenged, which otherwise his own good sense would have

withheld. We suspect that Mr. Wordsworth's feelings are a little morbid in this respect, or that he resents censure more than he is gratified by praise. Otherwise, the tide has turned much in his favour of late years. He has a large body of determined partisans, and is at present sufficiently in request with the public to save or relieve him from the last necessity to which a man of genius can be reduced—that of becoming the God of his own idolatry! (pp. 127-29)

William Hazlitt, "Mr. Wordsworth," in his The Spirit of the Age; or, Contemporary Portraits, *1825. Reprint by Oxford University Press, 1947, pp. 117-29.*

WILLIAM BLAKE   (essay date 1826)

[*Critics view Blake, an English poet and artist, as one of the most important literary figures of the nineteenth century. His works are esteemed for their dense thematic texture, for the compression and allusiveness of his style, for the original system of mythology he created, and for the impassioned, prophetic tone which characterizes all his works. Blake's early poetry demonstrates the influence of the Swedish theologian Emanuel Swedenborg, but the poet later rebelled against his teachings and against all forms of quantifying and systematizing reality. Since all reality is a mental construct, Blake believed, the only path to achieving salvation lies in the full awakening of the imagination. Blake stressed this theme in all of his works, emphasizing that, because he was a visionary, his drawings were copied from and his poetry dictated by a higher power. Virtually unknown and often dismissed as a lunatic in his own time, Blake is still considered the most extreme of the English Romantic writers, but critics today acknowledge his stature as one of the greatest poets of his age. The following comment is taken from Blake's brief annotation to Wordsworth's "Poems Referring to the Period of Childhood." It was written in 1826.*]

I see in Wordsworth the Natural Man rising up against the Spiritual Man Continually, & then he is No Poet but a Heathen Philosopher at Enmity against all true Poetry or Inspiration. (p. 782)

William Blake, "Annotations to 'Poems' by William Wordsworth," in his The Complete Writings of William Blake, *edited by Geoffrey Keynes, 1957. Reprint by Oxford University Press, London, 1966, pp. 782-83.*

SIR WALTER SCOTT   (journal date 1827)

[*Scott was a Scottish novelist, poet, historian, biographer, and critic of the Romantic period who is best known for his popular historical novels. In this excerpt from a journal entry dated January 1, 1827, Scott disapproves of Jeffrey's negative evaluation of Wordsworth's "Matthew," but acknowledges that Wordsworth prompts such criticism by choosing unsympathetic subjects.*]

[The effect of grief upon those of us who] are highly susceptible of humour, has, I think, been finely touched by Wordsworth in the character of the merry village teacher Matthew, whom Jeffrey profanely calls the hysterical schoolmaster. But, with my friend Jeffrey's pardon, I think he loves to see imagination best when it is bitted and managed and ridden upon the *grand pas*. He does not make allowance for starts and sallies and bounds when Pegasus is beautiful to behold, though sometimes perilous to his rider. Not that I think the amiable bard of Rydal shows judgment in choosing such subjects as the popular mind cannot sympathise in. It is unwise and unjust to himself. I do not compare myself, in point of imagination, with Wordsworth—far from it; for [his] is naturally exquisite, and highly cultivated by constant exercise. But I can see as many castles in the clouds as any man, as many genii in the curling smoke of a steam engine, as perfect a Persepolis in the embers of a sea-coal fire. My life has been spent in such day-dreams. But I cry no roast-meat. There are times a man should remember what Rousseau used to say: *Tais-toi, Jean-Jacques, car on ne t'entend pas!*

> *Sir Walter Scott, in a journal entry of January 1, 1827, in his* The Journal of Sir Walter Scott, *edited by David Douglas, 1890. Reprint by Harper & Brothers, 1891, p. 217.*

[WILLIAM MAGINN] (essay date 1832)

[*One of the most prominent journalists in England during the first half of the nineteenth century, Maginn wrote prolifically for a variety of English periodicals. His articles range from burlesques in verse to literary criticism and contain a rich blend of farcical humor, classical allusions, and political commentary. The following excerpt was drawn from the popular* Gallery of Illustrious Literary Characters, *a series of brief biographical sketches on prominent literary figures that appeared in* Fraser's Magazine *between 1830 and 1838. Here, Maginn asserts that no other contemporary poet was "so much praised and abused" as Wordsworth. While objecting to the "Edinburgh reviewers'" campaign against Wordsworth, Maginn also admits that Wordsworth's defensive stance was too often uncompromising.*]

No man of his generation has been so much praised and abused [as Wordsworth]. He truly prophesied, in his preface to *Lyrical Ballads,* that these poems would be enthusiastically admired, or consigned to the uttermost contempt. Not long after their publication, the cackling brood of the Edinburgh reviewers came into existence, and they were determined to crow down Wordsworth. . . . Accordingly, the *Lyrical Ballads,* and all that ever fell from Wordsworth's muse, were decried as the most unmeaning nonsense that ever emanated from the brain of a driveller; and though they fought their way gallantly up in the world, in the teeth of this adverse criticism, and much more founded upon it (for of back critics it is true, as of dogs, that the filth of one acts as an incentive to the filth of another), yet, to the very last of Jeffery's career, Wordsworth was set down as an ass, great as that belaboured by Peter Bell. . . .

Any man of common sense in half an hour would, by blotting a couple of dozen pages from Wordsworth's works, render them secure from criticism; but these very couple of dozen are the pages which he would most strenuously insist on retaining, stunning you with oratory to prove them the most superb things ever composed.

For the rest, he is a good sturdy Tory, a most exemplary man in all the relations of life, and a stamp-master void of reproach.

> [*William Maginn*], "Gallery of Literary Characters, No. XXIX: William Wordsworth, Esq.," in Fraser's *Magazine, Vol. VI, No. XXXIII, October, 1832, p. 313.*

THE EXAMINER (essay date 1838)

[*The writer of the following excerpted review of* The Sonnets of William Wordsworth *characterizes Wordsworth's sonnets as equal to Milton's, but objects to the poet's choice of style and subject matter in "Protest against the Ballot."*]

This delightful volume will be its own best recommendation to every lover of true poetry. Wordsworth's sonnets have long since, by common consent, been placed beyond the reach of

criticism. It is admitted by every one in any way conversant with the subject, that in the construction of that sort of poem, our great comtemporary has surpassed all previous writers of every age and nation. Even Milton, with his dozen perfect sonnets of grandeur and grace and tenderness, must in this respect yield the palm [Wordsworth], in number between four and five hundred, and in quality not inferior to *his.* It is astonishing to see all of them thus, as in this beautiful little volume, brought under the eye at once, sparkling with such exquisite, such various, such inexhaustible riches, of fancy, imagination, morality, and wisdom. We may question the propriety of any poet, so capable of greater things, willingly submitting himself, to such an extent, to the fetters of fourteen lines; but we cannot deny the music he makes in them, or say that it is not wonderful indeed.

"My admiration of some of the sonnets of Milton," it is observed by Mr. Wordsworth, in a short advertisement to the volume, "first tempted me to write in that form. The fact is not mentioned from a notion that it will be deemed of any importance by the reader, but merely as a public acknowledgment of one of the innumerable obligations, which, as a poet and a man, I am under to our great fellow countryman." Let us be allowed, then, to express our surprise that, with such a high and estimable feeling as this in his heart, the same writer could have descended to the absurdity of foisting into the middle of his volume (whose general loftiness of sentiment and tone should indeed have been its own safeguard from such a profanation), the ["**Protest against the Ballot**"]. . . . The starved absurdity of the thought is here wonderfully matched by a ridiculous and most schoolboy-like magniloquence of expression. No doubt Lord Londonderry or Mr. Borthwick, at the time of writing it, had completely elbowed the spirit of Milton out of Wordsworth's mind. Happily, they had also elbowed out everything that in any way resembled his genius. We look upon the lines at the same time, as no bad argument in favour of the thing they protest against. It is much to say for the ballot that such an assailant was obliged to adapt himself to the business he had in hand, by exchanging the reason and wisdom of his genius for a confused schoolboy drivel about the box of Pandora and Saint George and the Dragon!

> *A review of "The Sonnets of William Wordsworth,"* in The Examiner, *No. 1589, July 15, 1838, p. 436.*

THOMAS DE QUINCEY (essay date 1845)

[*An English critic and essayist, De Quincey used his own life as the subject of his best-known work,* Confessions of an English Opium Eater, *in which he chronicled his addiction to opium. De Quincey contributed reviews to a number of London journals and earned a reputation as an insightful if occasionally long-winded literary critic. At the time of De Quincey's death, his critical expertise was underestimated, though his talent as a prose writer had long been acknowledged. In the twentieth century, some critics still disdain the digressive qualities of De Quincey's writing, yet others find that his essays display an acute psychological awareness. In the excerpt below, De Quincey maintains that Wordsworth's Preface to the 1800 edition of* Lyrical Ballads *was "injurious" to his reputation, and he argues against Wordsworth's theory of using common subjects and diction. Exploring the emotional content of Wordsworth's works, De Quincey observes that although he deals with passion indirectly, Wordsworth's poetry "appeals to what is deepest in man." For other views on Wordsworth's critical theory, see the excerpts by Wordsworth (1802), Coleridge (1817), Saintsbury (1896), and Abrams (1953).*]

[Amongst] all works that have illustrated our own age, none can more deserve an earnest notice than those of the Laureate [Wordsworth], and on some grounds, peculiar to themselves, none so much. Their merit in fact is not only supreme but unique; not only supreme in their general class, but unique as in a class of their own. And there is a challenge of a separate nature to the curiosity of the readers, in the remarkable contrast between the first stage of Wordsworth's acceptation with the public and that which he enjoys at present. One original obstacle to the favourable impression of the Wordsworthian poetry, and an obstacle purely self-created, was his theory of poetic diction. The diction itself, without the theory, was of less consequence; for the mass of readers would have been too blind or too careless to notice it. But the preface to the second edition of his Poems, . . . compelled them to notice it. Nothing more injudicious was ever done by man. An unpopular truth would, at any rate, have been a bad inauguration, for what, on *other* accounts, the author had announced as "an experiment." His poetry was already an experiment as regarded the quality of the subjects selected, and as regarded the mode of treating them. That was surely trial enough for the reader's untrained sensibilities, without the unpopular truth besides, as to the diction. But, in the mean time, this truth, besides being unpopular, was also, in part, false: it was true, and it was *not* true. And it was not true in a double way. Stating broadly, and allowing it to be taken for his meaning, that the diction of ordinary life, in his own words, "the very language of man," was the proper diction for poetry, the writer meant no such thing; for only a *part* of this diction, according to his own subsequent restriction, was available for such a use. And, secondly, as his own subsequent practice showed, even this part was available only for peculiar classes of poetry. In his own exquisite **"Laodamia,"** in his *Sonnets,* in his *Excursion,* few are his obligations to the idiomatic language of life, as distinguished from that of books, or of prescriptive usage. . . . [In meditative poetry, the] gamut of ideas needs a corresponding gamut of expressions; the scale of the thinking, which ranges through *every* key, exacts, for the artist, an unlimited command over the entire scale of the instrument which he employs. (pp. 545-46)

[Whosoever] looks searchingly into the characteristic genius of Wordsworth, will see that he does not willingly deal with a passion in its direct aspect, or presenting an unmodified contour, but in forms more complex and oblique, and when passing under the shadow of some secondary passion. Joy, for instance, that wells up from constitutional sources, joy that is ebullient from youth to age, and cannot cease to sparkle, he yet exhibits in the person of Matthew, the village schoolmaster, as touched and overgloomed by memories of sorrow. In the poem of **"We are Seven,"** which brings into day for the first time a profound fact in the abysses of human nature, namely, that the mind of an infant cannot admit the idea of death, any more than the fountain of light can comprehend the aboriginal darkness, . . . the little mountaineer, who furnishes the text for this lovely strain, she whose fulness of life could not brook the gloomy faith in a grave, is yet (for the effect upon the reader) brought into connexion with the reflex shadows of the grave: and if she herself has *not,* the reader *has,* the gloom of that contemplation obliquely irradiated, and raised in relief upon his imagination, even by *her.* Death and its sunny antipole are forced into connexion. (p. 547)

A volume might be filled with . . . glimpses of novelty as Wordsworth has first laid bare, even to the apprehension of the *senses.* For the *understanding,* when moving in the same

track of human sensibilities, he has done only not so much. How often (to give an instance or two) must the human heart have felt that there are sorrows which descend far below the region in which tears gather; and yet who has ever given utterance to this feeling until Wordsworth came with his immortal line—

Thoughts that do often lie too deep for tears?

This sentiment, and others that might be adduced, (such as "The child is father of the man,") have even passed into the popular mind, and are often quoted by those who know not *whom* they are quoting. Magnificent, again, is the sentiment, and yet an echo to one which lurks amongst all hearts, in relation to the frailty of merely human schemes for working good, which so often droop and collapse through the unsteadiness of human energies,—

——foundations must be laid
In Heaven.

How? Foundations laid in realms that are *above?* But *that* is at war with physics;—foundations must be laid *below.* Yes; and even so the poet throws the mind yet more forcibly on the hyperphysical character—on the grandeur transcending all physics—of those shadowy foundations which alone are enduring.

But the great distinction of Wordsworth, and the pledge of his increasing popularity, is the extent of his sympathy with what is *really* permanent in human feelings, and also the depth of this sympathy. Young and Cowper, the two earlier leaders in the province of meditative poetry, are too circumscribed in the range of their sympathies, too exclusive, and oftentimes not sufficiently profound. Both these poets manifested the quality of their strength by the quality of their public reception. Popular in some degree from the first, they entered upon the inheritance of their fame almost at once. Far different was the fate of Wordsworth; for, in poetry of this class, which appeals to what lies deepest in man, in proportion to the native power of the poet, and his fitness for permanent life, is the strength of resistance in the public taste. Whatever is too original will be hated at the first. It must slowly mould a public for itself; and the resistance of the early thoughtless judgments must be overcome by a counter resistance to itself, in a better audience slowly mustering against the first. Forty and seven years it is since William Wordsworth first appeared as an author. Twenty of those years he was the scoff of the world, and his poetry a byeword of scorn. Since then, and more than once, senates have rung with acclamations to the echo of his name. Now at this moment, whilst we are talking about him, he has entered upon his seventy-sixth year. For himself, according to the course of nature, he cannot be far from his setting; but his poetry is but now clearing the clouds that gathered about its rising. Meditative poetry is perhaps that which will finally maintain most power upon generations more thoughtful; and in this department, at least, there is little competition to be apprehended by Wordsworth from any thing that has appeared since the death of Shakspere. (p. 554)

Thomas De Quincey, "On Wordsworth's Poetry," in Tait's Edinburgh Magazine, *Vol. XII, No. CXLI, September, 1845, pp. 545-54.*

TAIT'S EDINBURGH MAGAZINE   (essay date 1850)

[In the excerpt below, the reviewer maintains that The Prelude *is hampered by its excessive length, occasional wordiness, and mun-*

dane themes. Yet the charm of the poetry, the critic contends, compensates for its lack of intensity. Referring to Wordsworth's explanation of his sympathy with the French Revolution, the critic remarks that "his love of right led to treason to his nationality."]

As *The Prelude* is not, nor pretends to be, a tale of stirring interest, and as it is also of very considerable length, it necessarily requires all legitimate aids of poetic art to sustain the continued attention of the reader. Unfortunately, Wordsworth never attributed to these their just importance; and, accordingly, in *The Prelude,* as in all his longer pieces, we cannot conceal from ourselves that the bard is sometimes prolix, and sometimes careless, in the selection of his phrase, and still more often we find his humbler themes become almost trivial from his want of that nameless tact possessed in so high a degree by Addison and Cowper.

Having thus warned the reader that *The Prelude* is not "a faultless monster," we may betake ourselves to the more agreeable task of giving a sketch of the very delightful volume before us. (p. 521)

[*The Prelude*] will be a charm and a solace to tens of thousands. Egotism is, of course, to be expected in every autobiography; nay, it were idle to complain of its appearance in works specially destined to record the thoughts and actions of the writers. It is only when it appears deformed with selfishness or absurd vanity that it becomes repulsive. From these it is superfluous to say that Wordsworth and his writings are entirely exempt. Whether, on the one hand, he did not err in judgment, both as to the functions of a poet and his own capability to fulfil them, may be doubted. . . . The walk which Wordsworth selected was very limited, though by no means unworthy. He is the poet of the external phases of Nature, but only in her milder moods. He cannot make, as Byron did, "the live thunder leap from crag to crag," but he serenely gazes with artless joy on the sun sinking behind the dark outline of a Cumbrian fell, and his soul hovers in rapture over the silvery mist that fills the vale at daybreak. In dealing with human passions, the noblest, in fact the only real theme of song (for the external imageries of the visible are but accessories deriving their interest only from their relation to the sentient soul of man), the power of Wordsworth is voluntarily confined to tales of simple pathos and subdued sorrow, or tranquil enjoyment. The texture of his compositions is in general eminently artless. From multiplicity he shrinks as from confusion; and in no instance does he summon thoughts and feelings from various regions to converge like troops in a campaign, and to bear with irresistible effect on a point long since predetermined. His is the ripple of the brook, and not the collective might of waters slowly gathering to break in one huge billow on the shore.

There is, however, a charm about Wordsworth that amply compensates for the absence of those vivid and passionate passages which stir us powerfully in more vigorous poets. Much of our life is work-a-day and weary; we are daily racked by the apprehension of real calamities, and in our struggles to avoid them our moral nature has a tendency to become soured and perverted from very suffering. It is in these phases of mind that Wordsworth's gentle pages cast a soothing influence upon the troubled spirit, and supply that invigorating repose which enables us to withstand the recurring fever of life's turmoil. In this respect *The Prelude* . . . , a tale of childhood, boyhood, and youth, tranquil, happy, and innocent, will minister to minds diseased as effectively as its predecessors have done.

We cannot, however, dismiss the poem before us without noticing the marked deviation from Wordsworth's usually tranquil flow of feeling which it exhibits in his allusion to the French Revolution. That a kindly mind like his should be so stirred up and exasperated as to rejoice when thousands of his fellow-countrymen were slain, is a moral phenomenon which in these days seems hardly credible. But for his deep conviction that the English armies were sustaining the cause of unmitigated wrong, such a sentiment might be summarily condemned as shocking and revolting to the last degree; even as it is we can hardly reconcile ourselves to its justification. There is no stronger instinct in our nature than the sympathy which we feel for the fortunes of men of our own race and country; and even the school-boy turns with pain from tales of national discomfiture, whatever may be the justice of the cause maintained by English armaments. After all, however, in a true and earnest heart, everything must give way to the great principle of "Fiat Justitia," be the sacrifice what it may; and the pages before us bear evidence that with Wordsworth it was not a slight one. It was with pain and grief that he examined his inmost feelings, and discovered that his love of right led to treason to his nationality. Up to the last moment of his life it does not appear that he repented of having entertained these sentiments, though he still looked back with sorrow upon the events that occasioned them; and at no period, notwithstanding the untoward fate of nations during the last half century, did he swerve from the hopeful faith that, under Providence, the different peoples of Europe would work out institutions in accordance with the proper rights of humanity. (pp. 526-27)

> *A review of "The Prelude," in* Tait's Edinburgh Magazine, *Vol. XVII, No. CCI, September, 1850, pp. 521-27.*

THE NORTH AMERICAN REVIEW   (essay date 1851)

[*Praising* The Prelude's *style in general, the author of the following excerpt deems it "one of the best studies for the psychologist."*]

The complete history of the growth of any mind would be a work of universal and most intense interest, could it ever be written; and the story of the growth of such a mind as Wordsworth's,—however imperfectly, from the necessity of the case, it must be told,—cannot but be welcomed with delight and studied with advantage. The author attempts no unachievable portrait of all the myriad, multiform emotions of the soul, nor does he undertake "to parcel out his intellect by geometric rules;" but he has a full sense of the difficulty of his high argument,—often prompting "breathings for incommunicable powers." He has succeeded, however, in presenting a vivid picture of the scenes of his early life, with many delicate delineations of the influences, subtle or direct, by which his mind was moulded; thus giving a general view of the progress of his mental growth. This poem, in connection with the other works of its author, presents one of the best studies for the psychologist which literature anywhere affords, and is perhaps as complete and valuable an exposition of the mysterious development of a mighty intellect as will ever be given to the world.

Like most works of genius, the *Prelude* is read with an interest heightening on each successive perusal. The style is simple, but elegant, often flowing along in a quiet philosophic strain, but rising ever and anon into glowing eloquence; and the reader's admiration is constantly excited by felicitous expression or elevated sentiment. (pp. 484-85)

"The Life and Poetry of Wordsworth," in The North American Review, *Vol. LXXIII, No. 153, October, 1851, pp. 473-95.*

JOHN STUART MILL (essay date 1853-54)

[*An English essayist and critic, Mill is regarded as one of the greatest philosophers and political economists of the nineteenth century. At an early age, Mill was recognized as a leading advocate of the utilitarian philosophy of Jeremy Bentham, and he was a principal contributor to the* Westminster Review, *an English periodical founded by Bentham that later merged with the* London Review. *During the 1830s, after reading the works of Wordsworth, Samuel Taylor Coleridge, and Auguste Comte, Mill gradually diverged from Bentham's utilitarianism and acknowledged the importance of intuition and feelings, attempting to reconcile them with his rational philosophy. As part owner of the* London and Westminster Review *from 1835-40, Mill was instrumental in modifying the periodical's utilitarian stance. He is considered a key figure in the transition from the rationalism of the Enlightenment to the renewed emphasis on mysticism and the emotions of the Romantic era. In the excerpt below from his* Autobiography, *Mill recounts the experience of reading Wordsworth's poetry for the first time, during a period of severe depression. Mill recalls the great impact of Wordsworth's expression of "states of feeling, and of thought colored by feeling" and credits his influence with helping him to emerge from a mental crisis. Mill's* Autobiography *was written in 1853-54.*]

[The] state of my thoughts and feelings made the fact of my reading Wordsworth for the first time . . . an important event in my life. I took up the collection of his poems from curiosity, with no expectation of mental relief from it, though I had before resorted to poetry with that hope. In the worst period of my depression I had read through the whole of Byron (then new to me) to try whether a poet, whose peculiar department was supposed to be that of the intenser feelings, could rouse any feeling in me. . . . But while Byron was exactly what did not suit my condition, Wordsworth was exactly what did. I had looked into the *Excursion* two or three years before, and found little in it; and should probably have found as little, had I read it at this time. But the miscellaneous poems, in the two-volume edition of 1815 (to which little of value was added in the latter part of the author's life), proved to be the precise thing for my mental wants at that particular juncture.

In the first place, these poems addressed themselves powerfully to one of the strongest of my pleasurable susceptibilities, the love of rural objects and natural scenery; to which I had been indebted not only for much of the pleasure of my life, but quite recently for relief from one of my longest relapses into depression. In this power of rural beauty over me, there was a foundation laid for taking pleasure in Wordsworth's poetry; the more so, as his scenery lies mostly among mountains, which, owing to my early Pyrenean excursion, were my ideal of natural beauty. But Wordsworth would never have had any great effect on me, if he had merely placed before me beautiful pictures of natural scenery. Scott does this still better than Wordsworth, and a very second-rate landscape does it more effectually than any poet. What made Wordsworth's poems a medicine for my state of mind, was that they expressed, not mere outward beauty, but states of feeling, and of thought coloured by feeling, under the excitement of beauty. They seemed to be the very culture of the feelings, which I was in quest of. In them I seemed to draw from a source of inward joy, of sympathetic and imaginative pleasure, which could be shared in by all human beings; which had no connexion with struggle or imperfection, but would be made richer by every improvement in the physical or social condition of mankind. From them I seemed to learn what would be the perennial sources of happiness, when all the greater evils of life shall have been removed. And I felt myself at once better and happier as I came under their influence. There have certainly been, even in our own age, greater poets than Wordsworth; but poetry of deeper and loftier feeling could not have done for me at that time what his did. I needed to be made to feel that there was real, permanent happiness in tranquil contemplation. Wordsworth taught me this, not only without turning away from, but with a greatly increased interest in, the common feelings and common destiny of human beings. And the delight which these poems gave me, proved that with culture of this sort, there was nothing to dread from the most confirmed habit of analysis. At the conclusion of the *Poems* came the famous Ode, falsely called Platonic, "**Intimations of Immortality**": in which, along with more than his usual sweetness of melody and rhythm, and along with the two passages of grand imagery but bad philosophy so often quoted, I found that he too had had similar experience to mine; that he also had felt that the first freshness of youthful enjoyment of life was not lasting; but that he had sought for compensation, and found it, in the way in which he was now teaching me to find it. The result was that I gradually, but completely, emerged from my habitual depression, and was never again subject to it. I long continued to value Wordsworth less according to his intrinsic merits, than by the measure of what he had done for me. Compared with the greatest poets, he may be said to be the poet of unpoetical natures, possessed of quiet and contemplative tastes. But unpoetical natures are precisely those which require poetic cultivation. This cultivation Wordsworth is much more fitted to give, than poets who are intrinsically far more poets than he. (pp. 88-90)

> *John Stuart Mill, "A Crisis in My Mental History: One Stage Onward," in his* Autobiography and Other Writings, *edited by Jack Stillinger, Houghton Mifflin Company, 1969, pp. 80-110.**

W[ALTER] B[AGEHOT] (essay date 1864)

[*Bagehot is regarded as one of the most versatile and influential authors of mid-Victorian England. In addition to literary criticism, he wrote several pioneering works in the fields of politics, sociology, and economics. As editor of the London* Economist, *he was instrumental in shaping the financial policy of his generation. Despite their diverse subject matter, Bagehot's works are unified by his emphasis on factual information and his interest in the personalities of literary figures, politicians, and economists. Many modern commentators contend that it is partially because of the readable quality of his prose that Bagehot's writings, which were primarily composed as journalistic pieces, are still enjoyed today. In this brief evaluation of Wordsworth's poetic manner, Bagehot emphasizes his stylistic purity, compression, and self-effacement.*]

The English literature undoubtedly contains much impure literature; impure in its style if not in its meaning: but it also contains one great, one nearly perfect, model of the pure style in the literary expression of typical *sentiment;* and one not perfect, but gigantic and close approximation to perfection in the pure delineation of objective character. Wordsworth, perhaps, comes as near to choice purity of style in sentiment as is possible. . . . (p. 39)

Of course no individual poem embodies this ideal perfectly; of course every human word and phrase has its imperfections, and if we choose an instance to illustrate that ideal, the instance has scarcely a fair chance. By contrasting it with the ideal we suggest its imperfections; by protruding it as an example, we turn on its defectiveness the microscope of criticism. Yet [Wordsworth's sonnets **"The Trosachs"** and **"Composed Upon Westminster Bridge, Sept. 3, 1802"**] may be fitly read in this place, not because they are quite without faults, or because they are the very best examples of their kind of style; but because they are *luminous* examples; the compactness of the sonnet and the gravity of the sentiment, hedging in the thoughts, restraining the fancy, and helping to maintain a singleness of expression. (pp. 39-40)

Instances of barer style . . . may easily be found, instances of colder style—few better instances of purer style. Not a single expression . . . can be spared, yet not a single expression rivets the attention. . . . The great subjects of the two sonnets, the religious aspect of beautiful but grave nature—the religious aspect of a city about to awaken and be alive, are the only ideas left in our mind. To Wordsworth has been vouchsafed the last grace of the self-denying artist; you think neither of him nor his style, but you cannot help thinking of—you *must* recall—the exact phrase, the *very* sentiment he wished. (pp. 40-1)

> W[alter] B[agehot], "Wordsworth, Tennyson, and Browning; or, Pure, Ornate, and Grotesque Art in Poetry," in The National Review, *London, n.s. Vol. 19, No. 1, November, 1864, pp. 27-67.**

THOMAS CARLYLE   (essay date 1867)

[*A noted nineteenth-century essayist, historian, critic, and social commentator, Carlyle was a central figure of the Victorian age in England and Scotland. In his writings, Carlyle advocated a Christian work ethic and stressed the importance of order, piety, and spiritual fulfillment. Known to his contemporaries as the "Sage of Chelsea," Carlyle exerted a powerful moral influence in an era of rapidly shifting values. In this excerpt from his* Reminiscences, *first published in 1867, Carlyle focuses on Wordsworth's poetic and philosophic limitations. While admiring his "limpid" style, Carlyle deprecates Wordsworth's theoretical "unfathomabilities."*]

[Wordsworth's] works I knew, but never considerably reverenced; could not, on attempting it. A man recognizably of strong intellectual powers, strong character; given to meditation, and much contemptuous of the unmeditative world and its noisy nothingnesses; had a fine limpid style of writing and delineating, in his small way; a fine limpid vein of melody too in him (as of an honest rustic fiddle, good, and well handled, but wanting two or more of the strings, and not capable of much!). In fact, a rather dull, hard-tempered, unproductive, and almost wearisome, kind of man; not adorable, by any means, as a great poetic genius, much less as the Trismegistus of such; whom only a select few could ever read, instead of misreading, which was the opinion his worshippers confidently entertained of him! Privately I had a real respect for him withal, founded on his early biography . . . "Poverty and Peasanthood! Be it so! but we consecrate ourselves to the Muses, all the same, and will proceed on those terms, Heaven aiding!" This, and what of faculty I did recognize in the man, gave me a clear esteem of him, as of one remarkable and fairly beyond common; not to disturb which, I avoided speaking of him to his worshippers; or, if the topic turned up, would listen with an acquiescing air. But to my private self his divine reflections and unfathomabilities seemed stinted, scanty, palish, and uncertain—perhaps in part a feeble reflex (derived at second hand

through Coleridge) of the immense German fund of such—and I reckoned his poetic store-house to be far from an opulent or well-furnished apartment. (pp. 331-32)

> *Thomas Carlyle, "Appendix: Southey, Wordsworth," in his* Reminiscences, *edited by James Anthony Froude, Harper & Brothers, 1881, pp. 321-37.**

WALTER PATER   (essay date 1874)

[*A nineteenth-century essayist, novelist, and critic, Pater is regarded as one of the most famous proponents of aestheticism in English literature. Distinguished as the first major English writer to formulate an explicitly aesthetic philosophy of life, he advocated the "love of art for art's sake" as life's greatest offering, a belief which he exemplified in his influential* Studies in the History of the Renaissance *and elucidated in his novel* Marius the Epicurean *and other works. Pater's essay on Wordsworth, excerpted below, is considered seminal because of its sustained and cogent analysis. He commences by highlighting the mixture of sincerity and "conventional sentiment," and of elevated and prosaic moods in Wordsworth's poetry that occasionally mar his work. Stressing the sensuousness of Wordsworth's imagery, he also explores his relationship with nature and emphasizes that his poetry is not devoid of passion. His nature descriptions, Pater observes, have the effect of "clearing the scene for the great exhibitions of emotion," while his meter acts as a "sedative" for the language of his poetry. Pater also senses in the poet "a power not altogether his own, or under his control." In describing the philosophic strain in Wordsworth's poetry, Pater commends his mental boldness and agility and affirms that "impassioned contemplation" as an end in itself is the chief lesson that Wordsworth can teach his readers. This essay was written in 1874. Other critics who consider Wordsworth's style include Hazlitt (1825), Lowell (1875), Bradley (1909), Darbishire (1949), Pottle (1950), and Hartman (1964).*]

[Nowhere] is there so perplexed a mixture as in Wordsworth's own poetry, of work touched with intense and individual power, with work of almost no character at all. He has much conventional sentiment, and some of that insincere poetic diction, against which his most serious critical efforts were directed: the reaction in his political ideas, consequent on the excesses of 1795, makes him, at times, a mere declaimer on moral and social topics; and he seems, sometimes, to force an unwilling pen, and write by rule. By making the most of these blemishes it is possible to obscure the true aesthetic value of his work, just as his life also, a life of much quiet delicacy and independence, might easily be placed in a false focus, and made to appear a somewhat tame theme in illustration of the more obvious parochial virtues. And those who wish to understand his influence, and experience his peculiar savour, must bear with patience the presence of an alien element in Wordsworth's work, which never coalesced with what is really delightful in it, nor underwent his special power. Who that values his writings most has not felt the intrusion there, from time to time, of something tedious and prosaic? Of all poets equally great, he would gain most by a skilfully made anthology. Such a selection would show, in truth, not so much what he was, or to himself or others seemed to be, as what, by the more energetic and fertile quality in his writings, he was ever tending to become. And the mixture in his work, as it actually stands, is so perplexed, that one fears to miss the least promising composition even, lest some precious morsel should be lying hidden within—the few perfect lines, the phrase, the single word perhaps, to which he often works up mechanically through a poem, almost the whole of which may be tame enough. He who thought that in all creative work the larger part was *given* passively, to the recipient mind, who waited so dutifully upon the gift, to whom so large a measure was sometimes given, had his times also of desertion and relapse; and he has permitted the impress of these too to remain in his work. And this duality there—the fitfulness with which the higher qualities manifest themselves in it, gives the effect in his poetry of a power not altogether his own, or under his control, which comes and goes when it will, lifting or lowering a matter, poor in itself; so that that old fancy which made the poet's art an enthusiasm, a form of divine possession, seems almost literally true of him.

This constant suggestion of an absolute duality between higher and lower moods, and the work done in them, stimulating one always to look below the surface, makes the reading of Wordsworth an excellent sort of training towards the things of art and poetry. It begets in those, who, coming across him in youth, can bear him at all, a habit of reading between the lines, a faith in the effect of concentration and collectedness of mind in the right appreciation of poetry, an expectation of things, in this order, coming to one by means of a right discipline of the temper as well as of the intellect. He meets us with the promise that he has much, and something very peculiar, to give us, if we will follow a certain difficult way, and seems to have the secret of a special and privileged state of mind. And those who have undergone his influence, and followed this difficult way, are like people who have passed through some initiation, a *disciplina arcani*, by submitting to which they become able constantly to distinguish in art, speech, feeling, manners, that which is organic, animated, expressive, from that which is only conventional, derivative, inexpressive.

But although the necessity of selecting these precious morsels for oneself is an opportunity for the exercise of Wordsworth's peculiar influence, and induces a kind of just criticism and true estimate of it, yet the purely literary product would have been more excellent, had the writer himself purged away that alien element. How perfect would have been the little treasury, shut between the covers of how thin a book! (pp. 40-2)

An intimate consciousness of the expression of natural things, which weighs, listens, penetrates, where the earlier mind passed roughly by, is a large element in the complexion of modern poetry. . . . Of this new sense, the writings of Wordsworth are the central and elementary expression: he is more simply and entirely occupied with it than any other poet, though there are fine expressions of precisely the same thing in so different a poet as Shelley. There was in his own character a certain contentment, a sort of inborn religious placidity, seldom found united with a sensibility so mobile as his, which was favourable to the quiet, habitual observation of inanimate, or imperfectly animate, existence. . . . This placid life matured a quite unusual sensibility, really innate in him, to the sights and sounds of the natural world—the flower and its shadow on the stone, the cuckoo and its echo. The poem of **"Resolution and Independence"** is a storehouse of such records: for its fulness of imagery it may be compared to Keats's *Saint Agnes' Eve*. To read one of his longer pastoral poems for the first time, is like a day spent in a new country: the memory is crowded for a while with its precise and vivid incidents—

The pliant harebell swinging in the breeze
On some grey rock;—

The single sheep and the one blasted tree
And the bleak music from that old stone wall;—

In the meadows and the lower ground
Was all the sweetness of a common dawn;—

And that green corn all day is rustling in thine ears.

Clear and delicate at once, as he is in the outlining of visible imagery, he is more clear and delicate still, and finely scrupulous, in the noting of sounds; so that he conceives of noble sound as even moulding the human countenance to nobler types, and as something actually "profaned" by colour, by visible form, or image. He has a power likewise of realising, and conveying to the consciousness of the reader, abstract and elementary impressions—silence, darkness, absolute motionlessness: or, again, the whole complex sentiment of a particular place, the abstract expression of desolation in the long white road, of peacefulness in a particular folding of the hills. In the airy building of the brain, a special day or hour even, comes to have for him a sort of personal identity, a spirit or angel given to it, by which, for its exceptional insight, or the happy light upon it, it has a presence in one's history, and acts there, as a separate power or accomplishment; and he has celebrated in many of his poems the "efficacious spirit," which, as he says, resides in these "particular spots" of time. (pp. 45-6)

And so it came about that this sense of a life in natural objects, which in most poetry is but a rhetorical artifice, is with Wordsworth the assertion of what for him is almost literal fact. To him every natural object seemed to possess more or less of a moral or spiritual life, to be capable of a companionship with man, full of expression, of inexplicable affinities and delicacies of intercourse. (pp. 46-7)

[In] Wordsworth, such power of seeing life, such perception of a soul, in inanimate things, came of an exceptional susceptibility to the impressions of eye and ear, and was, in its essence, a kind of sensuousness. At least, it is only in a temperament exceptionally susceptible on the sensuous side, that this sense of the expressiveness of outward things comes to be so large a part of life. That he awakened "a sort of thought in sense," is Shelley's just estimate of this element in Wordsworth's poetry.

And it was through nature, thus ennobled by a semblance of passion and thought, that he approached the spectacle of human life. Human life, indeed, is for him, at first, only an additional, accidental grace on an expressive landscape. When he thought of man, it was of man as in the presence and under the influence of these effective natural objects, and linked to them by many associations. The close connexion of man with natural objects, the habitual association of his thoughts and feelings with a particular spot of earth, has sometimes seemed to degrade those who are subject to its influence, as if it did but reinforce that physical connexion of our nature with the actual lime and clay of the soil, which is always drawing us nearer to our end. But for Wordsworth, these influences tended to the dignity of human nature, because they tended to tranquillise it. By raising nature to the level of human thought he gives it power and expression: he subdues man to the level of nature, and gives him thereby a certain breadth and coolness and solemnity. The leech-gatherer on the moor, the woman "stepping westward," are for him natural objects, almost in the same sense as the aged thorn, or the lichened rock on the heath. In this sense the leader of the "Lake School," in spite of an earnest preoccupation with man, his thoughts, his destiny, is the poet of nature. And of nature, after all, in its modesty. (pp. 48-9)

Wordsworth was able to appreciate passion in the lowly. He chooses to depict people from humble life, because, being nearer to nature than others, they are on the whole more impassioned, certainly more direct in their expression of passion,

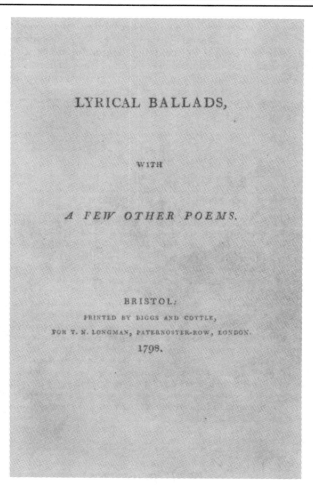

The title page of the first edition of Lyrical Ballads.

than other men: it is for this direct expression of passion, that he values their humble words. In much that he said in exaltation of rural life, he was but pleading indirectly for that sincerity, that perfect fidelity to one's own inward presentations, to the precise features of the picture within, without which any profound poetry is impossible. It was not for their tameness, but for this passionate sincerity, that he chose incidents and situations from common life, "related in a selection of language really used by men." He constantly endeavours to bring his language near to the real language of men: to the real language of men, however, not on the dead level of their ordinary intercourse, but in select moments of vivid sensation, when this language is winnowed and ennobled by excitement. There are poets who have chosen rural life as their subject, for the sake of its passionless repose, and times when Wordsworth himself extols the mere calm and dispassionate survey of things as the highest aim of poetical culture. But it was not for such passionless calm that he preferred the scenes of pastoral life; and the meditative poet, sheltering himself, as it might seem, from the agitations of the outward world, is in reality only clearing the scene for the great exhibitions of emotion, and what he values most is the almost elementary expression of elementary feelings.

And so he has much for those who value highly the concentrated presentment of passion, who appraise men and women by their susceptibility to it, and art and poetry as they afford the spec-

tacle of it. Breaking from time to time into the pensive spectacle of their daily toil, their occupations near to nature, come those great elementary feelings, lifting and solemnising their language and giving it a natural music. . . . A sort of biblical depth and solemnity hangs over this strange, new, passionate, pastoral world, of which he first raised the image, and the reflection of which some of our best modern fiction has caught from him.

He pondered much over the philosophy of his poetry, and reading deeply in the history of his own mind, seems at times to have passed the borders of a world of strange speculations, inconsistent enough, had he cared to note such inconsistencies, with those traditional beliefs, which were otherwise the object of his devout acceptance. Thinking of the high value he set upon customariness, upon all that is habitual, local, rooted in the ground, in matters of religious sentiment, you might sometimes regard him as one tethered down to a world, refined and peaceful indeed, but with no broad outlook, a world protected, but somewhat narrowed, by the influence of received ideas. But he is at times also something very different from this, and something much bolder. A chance expression is overheard and placed in a new connexion, the sudden memory of a thing long past occurs to him, a distant object is relieved for a while by a random gleam of light—accidents turning up for a moment what lies below the surface of our immediate experience—and he passes from the humble graves and lowly arches of "the little rock-like pile" of a Westmoreland church, on bold trains of speculative thought, and comes, from point to point, into strange contact with thoughts which have visited, from time to time, far more venturesome, perhaps errant, spirits. (pp. 51-4)

To him, theories which for other men bring a world of technical diction, brought perfect form and expression, as in those two lofty books of *The Prelude,* which describe the decay and the restoration of Imagination and Taste. Skirting the borders of this world of bewildering heights and depths, he got but the first exciting influence of it, that joyful enthusiasm which great imaginative theories prompt, when the mind first comes to have an understanding of them; and it is not under the influence of these thoughts that his poetry becomes tedious or loses its blitheness. He keeps them, too, always within certain ethical bounds, so that no word of his could offend the simplest of those simple souls which are always the largest portion of mankind. But it is, nevertheless, the contact of these thoughts, the speculative boldness in them, which constitutes, at least for some minds, the secret attraction of much of his best poetry—the sudden passage from lowly thoughts and places to the majestic forms of philosophical imagination, the play of these forms over a world so different, enlarging so strangely the bounds of its humble churchyards, and breaking such a wild light on the graves of christened children.

And these moods always brought with them faultless expression. In regard to expression, as with feeling and thought, the duality of the higher and lower moods was absolute. It belonged to the higher, the imaginative mood, and was the pledge of its reality, to bring the appropriate language with it. In him, when the really poetical motive worked at all, it united, with absolute justice, the word and the idea; each, in the imaginative flame, becoming inseparably one with the other, by that fusion of matter and form, which is the characteristic of the highest poetical expression. His words are themselves thought and feeling; not eloquent, or musical words merely, but that sort of creative language which carries the reality of what it depicts, directly, to the consciousness.

The music of mere metre performs but a limited, yet a very peculiar and subtly ascertained function, in Wordsworth's poetry. With him, metre is but an additional grace, accessory to that deeper music of words and sounds, that moving power, which they exercise in the nobler prose no less than in formal poetry. It is a sedative to that excitement, an excitement sometimes almost painful, under which the language, alike of poetry and prose, attains a rhythmical power, independent of metrical combination, and dependent rather on some subtle adjustment of the elementary sounds of words themselves to the image or feeling they convey. Yet some of his pieces, pieces prompted by a sort of half-playful mysticism, like the **"Daffodil"** and **"The Two April Mornings,"** are distinguished by a certain quaint gaiety of metre, and rival by their perfect execution, in this respect, similar pieces among our own Elizabethan, or contemporary French poetry. (pp. 56-8)

The office of the poet is not that of the moralist, and the first aim of Wordsworth's poetry is to give the reader a peculiar kind of pleasure. But through his poetry, and through this pleasure in it, he does actually convey to the reader an extraordinary wisdom in the things of practice. One lesson, if men must have lessons, he conveys more clearly than all, the supreme importance of contemplation in the conduct of life.

Contemplation—impassioned contemplation—that, is with Wordsworth the end-in-itself, the perfect end. (pp. 59-60)

That the end of life is not action but contemplation—*being* as distinct from *doing*—a certain disposition of the mind: is, in some shape or other, the principle of all the higher morality. In poetry, in art, if you enter into their true spirit at all, you touch this principle, in a measure: these, by their very sterility, are a type of beholding for the mere joy of beholding. To treat life in the spirit of art, is to make life a thing in which means and ends are identified: to encourage such treatment, the true moral significance of art and poetry. Wordsworth, and other poets who have been like him in ancient or more recent times, are the masters, the experts, in this art of impassioned contemplation. Their work is, not to teach lessons, or enforce rules, or even to stimulate us to noble ends; but to withdraw the thoughts for a little while from the mere machinery of life, to fix them, with appropriate emotions, on the spectacle of those great facts in man's existence which no machinery affects, "on the great and universal passions of men, the most general and interesting of their occupations, and the entire world of nature,"—on "the operations of the elements and the appearances of the visible universe, on storm and sunshine, on the revolutions of the seasons, on cold and heat, on loss of friends and kindred, on injuries and resentments, on gratitude and hope, on fear and sorrow." To witness this spectacle with appropriate emotions is the aim of all culture; and of these emotions poetry like Wordsworth's is a great nourisher and stimulant. He sees nature full of sentiment and excitement; he sees men and women as parts of nature, passionate, excited, in strange grouping and connexion with the grandeur and beauty of the natural world:—images, in his own words, "of man suffering, amid awful forms and powers."

Such is the figure of the more powerful and original poet, hidden away, in part, under those weaker elements in Wordsworth's poetry, which for some minds determine their entire character; a poet somewhat bolder and more passionate than might at first sight be supposed, but not too bold for true poetical taste; an unimpassioned writer, you might sometimes fancy, yet thinking the chief aim, in life and art alike, to be a certain deep emotion; seeking most often the great elementary

passions in lowly places; having at least this condition of all impassioned work, that he aims always at an absolute sincerity of feeling and diction, so that he is the true forerunner of the deepest and most passionate poetry of our own day; yet going back also, with something of a protest against the conventional fervour of much of the poetry popular in his own time, to those older English poets, whose unconscious likeness often comes out in him. (pp. 62-4)

Walter Pater, "Wordsworth," in his Appreciations: With an Essay on Style, *Macmillan and Co., Limited, 1889, pp. 39-64.*

JAMES RUSSELL LOWELL   (essay date 1875)

[*Lowell was a celebrated nineteenth-century American poet, critic, essayist, and editor of two leading journals, the* Atlantic Monthly *and the* North American Review. *He is noted today for his satirical and critical writings, including* A Fable for Critics, *a book-length poem featuring witty critical portraits of his contemporaries. Often awkwardly phrased, and occasionally vicious, the* Fable *is distinguished by the enduring value of its literary assessments. Commentators generally agree that Lowell displayed a judicious critical sense, despite the fact that he sometimes relied upon mere impressions rather than critical precepts in his writings. Most literary historians rank him with the major nineteenth-century American critics. Like Pater (1874), Lowell stresses that Wordsworth's poetry ranges from the inspired to the ordinary. He praises Wordsworth's descriptions, especially his "power of particularization," but criticizes his lack of humor and want of unity in longer poems. Lowell observes that Wordsworth's poems often demonstrate surprising originality and have a timeless quality that sometimes makes them "seem rather the productions of nature than of man." Lowell concludes that Wordsworth's most important contributions to poetry are "intuition," "human sympathy," and "purity" of style. This essay was composed in 1875. Other critics who consider Wordsworth's style include Hazlitt (1825), Bradley (1909), Darbishire (1949), Pottle (1950), and Hartman (1964).*]

[In] Wordsworth the very highest powers of the poetic mind were associated with a certain tendency to the diffuse and commonplace. It is in the understanding (always prosaic) that the great golden veins of his imagination are imbedded. He wrote too much to write always well; for it is not a great Xerxes-army of words, but a compact Greek ten thousand, that march safely down to posterity. He set tasks to his divine faculty, which is much the same as trying to make Jove's eagle do the service of a clucking hen. Throughout **The Prelude** and **The Excursion** he seems striving to bind the wizard Imagination with the sand-ropes of dry disquisition, and to have forgotten the potent spellword which would make the particles cohere. There is an arenaceous quality in the style which makes progress wearisome. Yet with what splendors as of mountain-sunsets are we rewarded! what golden rounds of verse do we not see stretching heavenward with angels ascending and descending! what haunting harmonies hover around us deep and eternal like the undying barytone of the sea! and if we are compelled to fare through sands and desert wildernesses, how often do we not hear airy shapes that syllable our names with a startling personal appeal to our highest consciousness and our noblest aspiration, such as we wait for in vain in any other poet! (pp. 399-401)

Take from Wordsworth all which an honest criticism cannot but allow, and what is left will show how truly great he was. He had no humor, no dramatic power, and his temperament was of that dry and juiceless quality, that in all his published correspondence you shall not find a letter, but only essays. If we consider carefully where he was most successful, we shall find that it was not so much in description of natural scenery, or delineation of character, as in vivid expression of the effect produced by external objects and events upon his own mind, and of the shape and hue (perhaps momentary) which they in turn took from his mood or temperament. His finest passages are always monologues. He had a fondness for particulars, and there are parts of his poems which remind us of local histories in the undue relative importance given to trivial matters. He was the historian of Wordsworthshire. This power of particularization (for it is as truly a power as generalization) is what gives such vigor and greatness to single lines and sentiments of Wordsworth, and to poems developing a single thought or sentiment. It was this that made him so fond of the sonnet. That sequestered nook forced upon him the limits which his fecundity (if I may not say his garrulity) was never self-denying enough to impose on itself. . . . Its narrow bounds, but fourteen paces from end to end, turn into a virtue his too common fault of giving undue prominence to every passing emotion. He excels in monologue, and the law of the sonnet tempers monologue with mercy. In *The Excursion* we are driven to the subterfuge of a French verdict of extenuating circumstances. His mind had not that reach and elemental movement of Milton's, which, like the trade-wind, gathered to itself thoughts and images like stately fleets from every quarter; some deep with silks and spicery, some brooding over the silent thunders of their battailous armaments, but all swept forward in their destined track, over the long billows of his verse, every inch of canvas strained by the unifying breath of their common epic impulse. (pp. 401-02)

Wordsworth's absolute want of humor, while it no doubt confirmed his self-confidence by making him insensible both to the comical incongruity into which he was often led by his earlier theory concerning the language of poetry and to the not unnatural ridicule called forth by it, seems to have been indicative of a certain dulness of perception in other directions. We cannot help feeling that the material of his nature was essentially prose, which, in his inspired moments, he had the power of transmuting, but which, whenever the inspiration failed or was factitious, remained obstinately leaden. The normal condition of many poets would seem to approach that temperature to which Wordsworth's mind could be raised only by the white heat of profoundly inward passion. And in proportion to the intensity needful to make his nature thoroughly aglow is the very high quality of his best verses. They seem rather the productions of nature than of man, and have the lastingness of such, delighting our age with the same startle of newness and beauty that pleased our youth. Is it his thought? It has the shifting inward lustre of diamond. Is it his feeling? It is as delicate as the impressions of fossil ferns. He seems to have caught and fixed forever in immutable grace the most evanescent and intangible of our intuitions, the very ripple-marks on the remotest shores of being. But this intensity of mood which insures high quality is by its very nature incapable of prolongation, and Wordsworth, in endeavoring it, falls more below himself, and is, more even than many poets his inferiors in imaginative quality, a poet of passages. Indeed, one cannot help having the feeling sometimes that the poem is there for the sake of these passages, rather than that these are the natural jets and elations of a mind energized by the rapidity of its own motion. In other words, the happy couplet or gracious image seems not to spring from the inspiration of the poem conceived as a whole, but rather to have dropped of itself into the mind of the poet in one of his rambles, who then, in a less rapt

mood, has patiently built up around it a setting of verse too often ungraceful in form and of a material whose cheapness may cast a doubt on the priceless quality of the gem it encumbers. . . . His longer poems (miscalled epical) have no more intimate bond of union than their more or less immediate relation to his own personality. Of character other than his own he had but a faint conception, and all the personages of *The Excursion* that are not Wordsworth are the merest shadows of himself upon mist, for his self-concentrated nature was incapable of projecting itself into the consciousness of other men and seeing the springs of action at their source in the recesses of individual character. The best parts of these longer poems are bursts of impassioned soliloquy, and his fingers were always clumsy at the *callida junctura*. The stream of narration is sluggish, if varied by times with pleasing reflections *(viridesque placido aequore sylvas)*; we are forced to do our own rowing, and only when the current is hemmed in by some narrow gorge of the poet's personal consciousness do we feel ourselves snatched along on the smooth but impetuous rush of unmistakable inspiration. The fact that what is precious in Wordsworth's poetry was (more truly even than with some greater poets than he) a gift rather than an achievement should always be borne in mind in taking the measure of his power. I know not whether to call it height or depth, this peculiarity of his, but it certainly endows those parts of his work which we should distinguish as Wordsworthian with an unexpectedness and impressiveness of originality such as we feel in the presence of Nature herself. . . . Wordsworth's better utterances have the bare sincerity, the absolute abstraction from time and place, the immunity from decay, that belong to the grand simplicities of the Bible. They seem not more his own than ours and every man's, the word of the inalterable Mind. This gift of his was naturally very much a matter of temperament, and accordingly by far the greater part of his finer product belongs to the period of his prime, ere Time had set his lumpish foot on the pedal that deadens the nerves of animal sensibility. He did not grow as those poets do in whom the artistic sense is predominant. . . . Many of Wordsworth's later poems seem like rather unsuccessful efforts to resemble his former self. (pp. 403-09)

Wordsworth has [the] fault of enforcing and restating obvious points till the reader feels as if his own intelligence were somewhat underrated. He is over-conscientious in giving us full measure, and once profoundly absorbed in the sound of his own voice, he knows not when to stop. If he feel himself flagging, he has a droll way of keeping the floor, as it were, by asking himself a series of questions sometimes not needing, and often incapable of answer. There are three stanzas of such near the close of the First Part of *Peter Bell*, where Peter first catches a glimpse of the dead body in the water, all happily incongruous, and ending with one which reaches the height of comicality:—

> Is it a fiend that to a stake
> Of fire his desperate self is tethering?
> Or stubborn spirit doomed to yell,
> In solitary ward or cell,
> Ten thousand miles from all his brethren?

The same want of humor which made him insensible to incongruity may perhaps account also for the singular unconsciousness of disproportion which so often strikes us in his poetry. For example, a little farther on in *Peter Bell* we find:—

> *Now*—like a tempest-shattered bark
> That overwhelmed and prostrate lies,

And in a moment to the verge
Is lifted of a foaming surge—
Full suddenly the Ass doth rise!

And one cannot help thinking that the similes of the huge stone, the sea-beast, and the cloud, noble as they are in themselves, are somewhat too lofty for the service to which they are put.

The movement of Wordsworth's mind was too slow and his mood too meditative for narrative poetry. He values his own thoughts and reflections too much to sacrifice the least of them to the interests of his story. Moreover, it is never action that interests him, but the subtle motives that lead to or hinder it. *The Wagoner* involuntarily suggests a comparison with ''Tam O'Shanter'' infinitely to its own disadvantage. *Peter Bell,* full though it be of profound touches and subtle analysis, is lumbering and disjointed. . . . *The White Doe,* the most Wordsworthian of them all in the best meaning of the epithet, is also only the more truly so for being diffuse and reluctant. What charms in Wordsworth and will charm forever is the

Happy tone
Of meditation slipping in between
The beauty coming and the beauty gone.

A few poets, in the exquisite adaptation of their words to the tune of our own feelings and fancies, in the charm of their manner, indefinable as the sympathetic grace of woman, *are* everything to us without our being able to say that they are much in themselves. They rather narcotize than fortify. Wordsworth must subject our mood to his own before he admits us to his intimacy; but, once admitted, it is for life, and we find ourselves in his debt, not for what he has been to us in our hours of relaxation, but for what he has done for us as a reinforcement of faltering purpose and personal independence of character. (pp. 409-11)

[When] our impartiality has made all those qualifications and deductions against which even the greatest poet may not plead his privilege, what is left to Wordsworth is enough to justify his fame. Even where his genius is wrapped in clouds, the unconquerable lightning of imagination struggles through, flashing out unexpected vistas, and illuminating the humdrum pathway of our daily thought with a radiance of momentary consciousness that seems like a revelation. . . . [He] was a masculine thinker, and in his more characteristic poems there is always a kernel of firm conclusion from far-reaching principles that stimulates thought and challenges meditation. Groping in the dark passages of life, we come upon some axiom of his, as it were a wall that gives us our bearings and enables us to find an outlet. Compared with Goethe we feel that he lacks that serene impartiality of mind which results from breadth of culture; nay, he seems narrow, insular, almost provincial. He reminds us of those saints of Dante who gather brightness by revolving on their own axis. But through this very limitation of range he gains perhaps in intensity and the impressiveness which results from eagerness of personal conviction. If we read Wordsworth through, . . . we find ourselves changing our mind about him at every other page, so uneven is he. If we read our favorite poems or passages only, he will seem uniformly great. And even as regards *The Excursion* we should remember how few long poems will bear consecutive reading. For my part I know of but one,—the Odyssey.

None of our great poets can be called popular in any exact sense of the word, for the highest poetry deals with thoughts and emotions which inhabit, like rarest sea-mosses, the doubtful limits of that shore between our abiding divine and our

fluctuating human nature, rooted in the one, but living in the other, seldom laid bare, and otherwise visible only at exceptional moments of entire calm and clearness. Of no other poet except Shakespeare have so many phrases become household words as of Wordsworth. If Pope has made current more epigrams of worldly wisdom, to Wordsworth belongs the nobler praise of having defined for us, and given us for a daily possession, those faint and vague suggestions of other-worldliness of whose gentle ministry with our baser nature the hurry and bustle of life scarcely ever allowed us to be conscious. He has won for himself a secure immortality by a depth of intuition which makes only the best minds at their best hours worthy, or indeed capable, of his companionship, and by a homely sincerity of human sympathy which reaches the humblest heart. Our language owes him gratitude for the habitual purity and abstinence of his style, and we who speak it, for having emboldened us to take delight in simple things, and to trust ourselves to our own instincts. (pp. 412-15)

James Russell Lowell, ''Wordsworth,'' in his The Writings of James Russell Lowell: Literary Essays, Vol. IV, *revised edition, Houghton Mifflin and Company, 1890, pp. 354-415.*

[LESLIE STEPHEN]   (essay date 1876)

[Stephen is considered one of the most important English literary critics of the late Victorian and early Edwardian era. In his criticism, which was often moralistic, Stephen argues that all literature is nothing more than an imaginative rendering, in concrete terms, of a writer's philosophy or beliefs. It is the role of criticism, he contends, to translate into intellectual terms what the writer has told the reader through character, symbol, and plot. Stephen's analyses often include biographical judgments of the writer as well as the work. As Stephen once observed: ''The whole art of criticism consists in learning to know the human being who is partially revealed to us in his spoken or his written words.'' Stephen maintains that Wordsworth's ideas cohere into ''a scientific system of thought,'' and he identifies and discusses the main elements of that system in the excerpt below. Wordsworth's most characteristic doctrines, Stephen claims, include the belief in pre-existence, love of nature, sustaining the social order, advocating a contemplative life, turning grief into strength, and discerning a ''Divine order.'' Stephen underscores the fact that Wordsworth's poetry and philosophy derive from the same source and that both reflect a profound depth. For an opposing approach to Wordsworth's philosophy, see the excerpt by Arnold (1879). Other critics who write about Wordsworth's philosophical doctrine include Havens (1941), Stallknecht (1958), Perkins (1964), and Langbaum (1977).]

[Wordsworth] in his best moods reaches a greater height than any other modern Englishman. The word ''inspiration'' is less forced when applied to his loftiest poetry than when used of any of his contemporaries. With defects too obvious to be mentioned, he can yet pierce furthest behind the veil; and embody most efficiently the thoughts and emotions which come to us in our most solemn and reflective moods. Other poetry becomes trifling when we are making our inevitable passages through the Valley of the Shadow of Death. Wordsworth's alone retains its power. We love him the more as we grow older and become more deeply impressed with the sadness and seriousness of life; we are apt to grow weary of his rivals when we have finally quitted the regions of youthful enchantment. And I take the explanation to be that he is not merely a melodious writer, or a powerful utterer of deep emotion, but a true philosopher. His poetry wears well because it has solid substance. He is a prophet and a moralist, as well as a mere singer. His ethical system, in particular, is as distinctive and capable of systematic exposition as that of Butler. By endeavouring to state it in plain prose, we shall see how the poetical power implies a sensitiveness to ideas which, when extracted from the symbolical embodiment, fall spontaneously into a scientific system of thought. (pp. 209-10)

The most characteristic of all his doctrines is that which is embodied in the great ode upon the **"Intimations of Immortality."** The doctrine itself—the theory that the instincts of childhood testify to the pre-existence of the soul—sounds fanciful enough; and Wordsworth took rather unnecessary pains to say that he did not hold it as a serious dogma. We certainly need not ask whether it is reasonable or orthodox to believe that "our birth is but a sleep and a forgetting." The fact symbolised by the poetic fancy—the glory and freshness of our childish instincts—is equally noteworthy, whatever its cause. Some modern reasoners would explain its significance by reference to a very different kind of pre-existence. The instincts, they would say, are valuable, because they register the accumulated and inherited experience of past generations. Wordsworth's delight in wild scenery is regarded by them as due to the "combination of states that were organised in the race during barbarous times, when its pleasurable activities were amongst the mountains, woods, and waters." In childhood we are most completely under the dominion of these inherited impulses. The correlation between the organism and its medium is then most perfect, and hence the peculiar theme of childish communion with nature.

Wordsworth would have repudiated the doctrine with disgust. He would have been "on the side of the angels." No memories of the savage and the monkey, but the reminiscences of the once glorious soul, could explain his emotions. Yet there is this much in common between him and the men of science whom he denounced with too little discrimination. The fact of the value of these primitive instincts is admitted, and admitted for the same purpose. Man, it is agreed, is furnished with sentiments which cannot be explained as the result of his individual experience. They may be intelligible, according to the evolutionist, when regarded as embodying the past experience of the race; or, according to Wordsworth, as implying a certain mysterious faculty imprinted upon the soul. The scientific doctrine, whether sound or not, has modified the whole mode of approaching ethical problems; and Wordsworth, though with a very different purpose, gives a new emphasis to the facts, upon a recognition of which, according to some theorists, must be based the reconciliation of the great rival schools—the intuitionists and the utilitarians. The parallel may at first sight seem fanciful; and it would be too daring to claim for Wordsworth the discovery of the most remarkable phenomenon which modern psychology must take into account. There is, however, a real connection between the two doctrines, though in one sense they are almost antithetical. Meanwhile we observe that the same sensibility which gives poetical power is necessary to the scientific observer. The magic of the ode, and of many other passages in Wordsworth's poetry, is due to his recognition of this mysterious efficacy of our childish instincts. He gives emphasis to one of the most striking facts of our spiritual experience, which had passed with little notice from professed psychologists. He feels what they afterwards tried to explain. (pp. 211-12)

The doctrine of the love of nature, regarded as Wordsworth's great lesson to mankind, means, as interpreted by himself and others, a love of the wilder and grander objects of natural scenery; a passion for the "sounding cataract," the rock, the mountain, and the forest; a preference, therefore, of the country to the town, and of the simpler to the more complex forms of social life. But what is the true value of this sentiment? . . . The purpose . . . of the *Excursion,* and of Wordsworth's poetry in general, is to show how the higher faculty reveals a harmony which we overlook when, with the Solitary, we

> Skim along the surfaces of things.

The rightly prepared mind can recognise the divine harmony which underlies all apparent disorder. The universe is to its perceptions like the shell whose murmur in a child's ear seems to express a mysterious union with the sea. But the mind must be rightly prepared. Everything depends upon the point of view. . . . Our philosophy must be finally based, not upon abstract speculation and metaphysical arguments, but on the diffused consciousness of the healthy mind. As Butler sees the universe by the light of conscience, Wordsworth sees it through the wider emotions of awe, reverence, and love, produced in a sound nature.

The pantheistic conception, in short, leads to an unsatisfactory optimism in the general view of nature, and to an equal tolerance of all passions as equally "natural." To escape from this difficulty we must establish some more discriminative mode of interpreting nature. Man is the instrument played upon by all impulses, good or bad. The music which results may be harmonious or discordant. When the instrument is in tune, the music will be perfect; but when is it in tune, and how are we to know that it is in tune? That problem once solved, we can tell which are the authentic utterances and which are the accidental discords. And by solving it, or by saying what is the right constitution of human beings, we shall discover which is the true philosophy of the universe, and what are the dictates of a sound moral sense. Wordsworth implicitly answers the question by explaining, in his favourite phrase, how we are to build up our moral being.

The voice of nature speaks at first in vague emotions, scarcely distinguishable from mere animal bouyancy. The boy, hooting in mimicry of the owls, receives in his heart the voice of mountain torrents and the solemn imagery of rocks, and woods, and stars. The sportive girl is unconsciously moulded into stateliness and grace by the floating clouds, the bending willow, and even by silent sympathy with the motions of the storm. Nobody has ever shown with such exquisite power as Wordsworth how much of the charm of natural objects in later life is due to early associations thus formed in a mind not yet capable of contemplating its own processes. (pp. 215-17)

From this natural law follows another of Wordsworth's favourite precepts. The mountains are not with him a symbol of anti-social feelings. On the contrary, they are in their proper place as the background of the simple domestic affections. He loves his native hills, not in the Byronic fashion, as a savage wilderness, but as the appropriate framework in which a healthy social order can permanently maintain itself. (p. 218)

Wordsworth's favourite teaching . . . [concerns] the advantages of the contemplative life. He is fond of enforcing the doctrine of the familiar lines, that we can feed our minds "in a wise passiveness," and that

> One impulse from the vernal wood
>   Can teach you more of man,
> Of moral evil and of good,
>   Than all the sages can.

And, according to some commentators, this would seem to express the doctrine that the ultimate end of life is the cultivation of tender emotions without reference to action. The doctrine, thus absolutely stated, would be immoral and illogical. To recommend contemplation in preference to action is like preferring sleeping to waking; or saying, as a full expression of the truth, that silence is golden and speech silvern. Like that familiar phrase, Wordsworth's teaching is not to be interpreted literally. The essence of such maxims is to be one-sided. They are paradoxical in order to be emphatic. To have seasons of contemplation, of withdrawal from the world and from books, of calm surrendering of ourselves to the influences of nature, is a practice commended in one form or other by all moral teachers. It is a sanitary rule, resting upon obvious principles. The mind which is always occupied in a multiplicity of small observations, or the regulation of practical details, loses the power of seeing general principles and of associating all objects with the central emotions of "admiration, hope, and love." The philosophic mind is that which habitually sees the general in the particular, and finds food for the deepest thought in the simplest objects. It requires, therefore, periods of repose, in which the fragmentary and complex atoms of distracted feeling which make up the incessant whirl of daily life may have time to crystallise round the central thoughts. But it must feed in order to assimilate; and each process implies the other as its correlative. A constant interest, therefore, in the joys and sorrows of our neighbours is as essential as quiet, self-centred rumination. (p. 219)

The value of silent thought is so to cultivate the primitive emotions that they may flow spontaneously upon every common incident, and that every familiar object becomes symbolic of them. It is a familiar remark that a philosopher or man of science who has devoted himself to meditation upon some principle or law of nature, is always finding new illustrations in the most unexpected quarters. He cannot take up a novel or walk across the street without hitting upon appropriate instances. Wordsworth would apply the principle to the building up of our "moral being." Admiration, hope, and love should be so constantly in our thoughts, that innumerable sights and sounds which are meaningless to the world, should become to us a language incessantly suggestive of the deepest topics of thought.

This explains his dislike to science, as he understood the word, and his denunciations of the "world." The man of science is one who cuts up nature into fragments, and not only neglects their possible significance for our higher feelings, but refrains on principle from taking it into account. The primrose suggests to him some new device in classification, and he would be worried by the suggestion of any spiritual significance as an annoying distraction. . . . Science, in short, requires to be brought into intimate connection with morality and religion. If we are forced for our immediate purpose to pursue truth for itself, regardless of consequences, we must remember all the more carefully that truth is a whole; and that fragmentary bits of knowledge become valuable as they are incorporated into a general system. The tendency of modern times to specialism brings with it a characteristic danger. It requires to be supplemented by a correlative process of integration. We must study details to increase our knowledge; we must accustom ourselves to look at the detail in the light of the general principles in order to make it fruitful.

The influence of that world which "is too much with us late and soon" is of the same kind. The man of science loves barren facts for their own sake. The man of the world becomes devoted to some petty pursuit without reference to ultimate ends. He becomes a slave to money, or power, or praise, without caring for their effect upon his moral character. As social organisation becomes more complete, the social unit becomes a mere fragment instead of being a complete whole in himself. Man becomes

> The senseless member of a vast machine,
> Servin as doth a spindle or a wheel.

The division of labour, celebrated with such enthusiasm by Adam Smith, tends to crush all real life out of its victims. The soul of the political economist may rejoice when he sees a human being devoting his whole faculties to the performance of one subsidiary operation in the manufacture of a pin. The poet and the moralist must notice with anxiety the contrast between the old-fashioned peasant who, if he discharged each particular function clumsily, discharged at least many functions, and found exercise for all the intellectual and moral faculties of his nature, and the modern artisan doomed to the incessant repetition of one petty set of muscular expansions and contractions, and whose soul, if he has one, is therefore rather an encumbrance than otherwise. This is the evil which is constantly before Wordsworth's eyes, as it has certainly not become less prominent since his time. The danger of crushing the individual is a serious one according to his view; not because it implies the neglect of some abstract political rights, but from the impoverishment of character which is implied in the process. Give every man a vote, and abolish all interference with each man's private tastes, and the danger may still be as great as ever. The tendency to "differentiation"—as we call it in modern phraseology—the social pulverisation, the lowering and narrowing of the individual's sphere of action and feeling to the pettiest details, depends upon processes underlying all political changes. It cannot, therefore, be cured by any nostrum of constitution-mongers, or by the negative remedy of removing old barriers. It requires to be met by profounder moral and religious teaching. Men must be taught what is the really valuable part of their natures and what is the purest happiness to be extracted from life, as well as allowed to gratify fully their own tastes; for who can say that men encouraged by all their surroundings and appeals to the most obvious motives to turn themselves into machines, will not deliberately choose to be machines? Many powerful thinkers have illustrated Wordsworth's doctrine more elaborately; but nobody has gone more decisively to the root of the matter.

One other side of Wordsworth's teaching is still more significant and original. Our vague instincts are consolidated into reason by meditation, sympathy with our fellows, communion with nature, and a constant devotion to "high endeavours." If life run smoothly, the transformation may be easy, and our primitive optimism turn imperceptibly into general complacency. The trial comes when we make personal acquaintance with sorrow, and our early buoyancy begins to fail. We are tempted to become querulous or to lap ourselves in indifference. Most poets are content to bewail our lot melodiously, and admit that there is no remedy unless a remedy be found in "the luxury of grief." Prosaic people become selfish, though not sentimental. They laugh at their old illusions, and turn to the solid consolations of comfort. Nothing is more melancholy than to study many biographies and note—not the failure of early promise which may mean merely an aiming above the mark—but the progressive deterioration of character which so often follows grief and disappointment. If it be not true that most men grow worse as they grow old, it is surely true that few men pass through the world without being corrupted as much as purified.

Now Wordsworth's favourite lesson is the possibility of turning grief and disappointment into account. He teaches in many forms the necessity of "transmuting" sorrow into strength. . . . It is owing to the constant presence of this thought, to his sensibility to the refining influence of sorrow, that Wordsworth is the only poet who will bear reading in times of distress. Other poets mock us by an impossible optimism, or merely reflect the feelings which, however we may play with them in times of cheerfulness, have now become an intolerable burden. Wordsworth suggests the single topic which, so far at least as this world is concerned, can really be called consolatory. None of the ordinary commonplaces will serve, or serve at most as indications of human sympathy. But there is some consolation in the thought that even death may bind the survivors closer, and leave as a legacy enduring motives to noble action. It is easy to say this; but Wordsworth has the merit of feeling the truth in all its force, and expressing it by the most forcible images. In one shape or another the sentiment is embodied in most of his really powerful poetry. (pp. 220-23)

We may now see what ethical theory underlies Wordsworth's teaching of the transformation of instinct into reason. We must start from the postulate that there is in fact a divine order in the universe; and that conformity to this order produces beauty as embodied in the external world, and is the condition of virtue as regulating our character. It is by obedience to the "stern lawgiver," Duty, that flowers gain their fragrance, and that "the most ancient heavens" preserve their freshness and strength. But this postulate does not seek for justification in abstract metaphysical reasoning. The **"Intimations of Immortality"** are precisely intimations, not intellectual intuitions. They are vague and emotional, not distinct and logical. They are a feeling of harmony, not a perception of innate ideas. And, on the other hand, our instincts are not a mere chaotic mass of passions, to be gratified without considering their place and function in a certain definite scheme. They have been implanted by the Divine hand, and the harmony which we feel corresponds to a real order. To justify them we must appeal to experience, but to experience interrogated by a certain definite procedure. Acting upon the assumption that the Divine order exists, we shall come to recognise it, though we could not deduce it by an à priori method. (pp. 224-25)

It only remains to be added once more that Wordsworth's poetry derives its power from the same source as his philosophy. It speaks to our strongest feelings because his speculation rests upon our deepest thoughts. His singular capacity for investing all objects with a gloss derived from early associations; his keen sympathy with natural and simple emotions; his sense of the sanctifying influences which can be extracted from sorrow, are of equal value to his power over our intellects and our imaginations. His psychology, stated systematically, is rational; and, when expressed passionately, turns into poetry. To be sensitive to the most important phenomena is the first step equally towards a poetical or a scientific exposition. To see these truly is the condition of making the poetry harmonious and the philosophy logical. And it is often difficult to say which power is most remarkable in Wordsworth. . . .

Finally, we might look at the reverse side of the picture, and endeavour to show how the narrow limits of Wordsworth's power are connected with certain moral aspects; with the want of quick sympathy which shows itself in his dramatic feeble-

ness, and the austerity of character which caused him to lose his special gifts too early and become a rather commonplace defender of conservatism; and that curious diffidence (he assures us that it was "diffidence") which induced him to write many thousand lines of blank verse entirely about himself. But the task would be superfluous as well as ungrateful. It was his aim, he tells us, "to console the afflicted; to add sunshine to daylight by making the happy happier; to teach the young and the gracious of every age to see, to think, and therefore to become more actively and securely virtuous;" and, high as was the aim, he did much towards its accomplishment. (p. 226)

[Leslie Stephen], "Wordsworth's Ethics," in The Cornhill Magazine, Vol. XXXIV, No. 200, August, 1876, pp. 206-26.

MATTHEW ARNOLD   (essay date 1879)

[Arnold is considered one of the most influential authors of the later Victorian period in England. While he is well known today as a poet, in his own time he asserted his greatest influence through his prose writings. Arnold's forceful literary criticism, which is based on his humanistic belief in the value of balance and clarity in literature, significantly shaped modern theory. His appraisal of Wordsworth's poetry, excerpted below, proved influential because of the critic's honesty and objectivity despite the fact that he himself was a Wordsworthian. Arnold contends that Wordsworth, though he is not yet fully recognized as such, is the greatest English poet after Shakespeare and Milton. Acknowledging the uneven quality of his poetry, Arnold considers Wordsworth's shorter pieces his best, describing his ability to deal with life and the extraordinary power of his nature poetry as his strongest qualities. According to Arnold, Wordsworthians have hindered his reputation because they have stressed his philosophic and scientific system and lavished indiscriminate praise on his poetry. His greatness, Arnold writes, lies in those poems in which he balanced truth of subject and truth of execution. Arnold warns that Wordsworth's champions harm their hero by presenting him as the property of a clique. For an opposing approach to Wordsworth's system of thought, see the excerpt by Stephen (1876).]

[Wordsworth] is not fully recognised at home; he is not recognised at all abroad. Yet I firmly believe that the poetical performance of Wordsworth is, after that of Shakspeare and Milton, of which all the world now recognises the worth, undoubtedly the most considerable in our language from the Elizabethan age to the present time. (p. 196)

This is a high claim to make for Wordsworth. But if it is a just claim . . . , Wordsworth will have his due. We shall recognise him in his place, as we recognise Shakspeare and Milton; and not only we ourselves shall recognise him, but he will be recognised by Europe also. Meanwhile, those who recognise him already may do well, perhaps, to ask themselves whether there are not in the case of Wordsworth certain special obstacles which hinder or delay his due recognition by others, and whether these obstacles are not in some measure removable.

The *Excursion* and the *Prelude,* his poems of greatest bulk, are by no means Wordsworth's best work. His best work is in his shorter pieces, and many indeed are there of these which are of first-rate excellence. But in his seven volumes the pieces of high merit are mingled with a mass of pieces very inferior to them; so inferior to them that it seems wonderful how the same poet should have produced both. Shakspeare frequently has lines and passages in a strain quite false, and which are entirely unworthy of him. But one can imagine his smiling if one could meet him in the Elysian Fields and tell him so; smiling and replying that he knew it perfectly well himself, and what did it matter? But with Wordsworth the case is different. Work altogether inferior, work quite uninspired, flat and dull, is produced by him with evident unconsciousness of its defects, and he presents it to us with the same faith and seriousness as his best work. Now a drama or an epic fill the mind, and one does not look beyond them; but in a collection of short pieces the impression made by one piece requires to be continued and sustained by the piece following. In reading Wordsworth, the impression made by one of his fine pieces is constantly dulled and spoiled by a very inferior piece coming after it.

Wordsworth composed verses during a space of some sixty years; and it is not much of an exaggeration to say that within one single decade of those years, between 1798 and 1808, almost all his really first-rate work was produced. A mass of inferior work remains, work done before and after this golden prime, imbedding the first-rate work and clogging it, obstructing our approach to it, chilling the high-wrought mood with which we leave it. To be recognised far and wide as a great poet, to be possible and receivable as a classic, Wordsworth needs to be relieved of a great deal of the poetical baggage which now encumbers him. To administer this relief is indispensable, unless he is to continue to be a poet for the few only, a poet valued far below his real worth by the world. (p. 197)

[Wordsworth] deals with *life,* because he deals with that in which life really consists. This is what Voltaire means to praise in the English poets—this dealing with what is really life. But always it is the mark of the greatest poets that they deal with it; and to say that the English poets are remarkable for dealing with it, is only another way of saying, what is true, that in poetry the English genius has especially shown its power.

Wordsworth deals with it, and his greatness lies in his dealing with it so powerfully. (p. 200)

But we must be on our guard against the Wordsworthians, if we want to secure for Wordsworth his due rank as a poet. The Wordsworthians are apt to praise him for the wrong things, and to lay far too much stress upon what they call his philosophy. His poetry is the reality, his philosophy the illusion. Perhaps we shall one day learn to make this proposition more general, and to say: Poetry is the reality, philosophy the illusion. But in Wordsworth's case, at any rate, we cannot do him justice until we dismiss his philosophy.

The *Excursion* abounds with philosophy, and therefore the *Excursion* is to the Wordsworthian what it never can be to the disinterested lover of poetry—a satisfactory work. . . .

[However] true the doctrine may be, it has . . . none of the characters of *poetic* truth, the kind of truth which we require from a poet, and in which Wordsworth is really strong.

Even the "intimations" of the famous Ode, those corner stones of the supposed philosophic system of Wordsworth—the idea of the high instincts and affections coming out in childhood, testifying of a divine home recently left, and fading away as our life proceeds—this idea, of undeniable beauty as a play of fancy, has itself not the character of poetic truth of the best kind; it has no real solidity. The instinct of delight in Nature and her beauty had no doubt extraordinary strength in Wordsworth himself as a child. But to say that universally this instinct is mighty in childhood, and tends to die away afterwards, is to say what is extremely doubtful. (p. 201)

And let us be on our guard, too, against the exhibitors and extollers of a "scientific system of thought" in Wordsworth's poetry. The poetry will never be seen aright while they thus

J.M.W. Turner's painting of Tintern Abbey.

exhibit it. The cause of its greatness is simple and may be told quite simply. It is great because of the extraordinary power with which Wordsworth feels the joy offered to us in nature, the joy offered to us in the simple elementary affections and duties; and because of the extraordinary power with which, in case after case, he shows us this joy, and renders it so as to make us share it.

The source of joy from which he thus draws is the truest and most unfailing source of joy accessible to man. It is also accessible universally. Wordsworth brings us word, therefore, according to his own strong and characteristic line, he brings us word

Of joy in widest commonalty spread.

Here is an immense advantage for a poet. Wordsworth tells of what all seek, and tells of it at its truest and best source, and yet a source where all may go and draw for it.

Nevertheless we are not to suppose that everything is precious which Wordsworth, standing even at this perennial and beautiful source, may give us. Wordsworthians are apt to talk as if it must be. They will speak with the same reverence of "**The Sailor's Mother,**" for example, as of "**Lucy Gray.**" They do their master harm by such lack of discrimination. "**Lucy Gray**" is a beautiful success; "**The Sailor's Mother**" is a failure. To give aright what he wishes to give, to interpret and render successfully, is not always within Wordsworth's own command. It is within no poet's command; here is the part of the Muse, the inspiration, the God, the "not ourselves." In Wordsworth's case, the accident, for so it may almost be called, of inspiration, is of peculiar importance. No poet, perhaps, is so evidently filled with a new and sacred energy when the inspiration is upon him; no poet, when it fails him, is so left "weak as is a breaking wave." . . . Wordsworth's poetry, when he is at his best, is inevitable, as inevitable as Nature herself. It might seem that Nature not only gave him the matter for his poem but wrote his poem for him. He has no style. He was too conversant with Milton not to catch at times his master's manner, and he has fine Miltonic lines; but he has no assured poetic style of his own, like Milton. When he seeks to have a style he falls into ponderosity and pomposity. (pp. 202-03)

Wordsworth owed much to Burns, and a style of perfect plainness, relying for effect solely on the weight and force of that which with entire fidelity it utters, Burns could show him.

> The poor inhabitant below
> Was quick to learn and wise to know,
> And keenly felt the friendly glow
>   And softer flame;
> But thoughtless follies laid him low
>   And stain'd his name.

Every one will be conscious of a likeness here to Wordsworth; and if Wordsworth did great things with this nobly plain manner, we must remember, what indeed he himself would always have been forward to acknowledge, that Burns used it before him.

Still Wordsworth's use of it has something unique and unmatchable. Nature herself seems, I say, to take the pen out of his hand, and to write for him with her own bare, sheer, penetrating power. This arises from two causes: from the profound sincereness with which Wordsworth feels his subject, and also from the profoundly sincere and natural character of his subject itself. He can and will treat such a subject with nothing but the most plain, first-hand, almost austere naturalness. His expression may often be called bald, as, for instance, in the poem of **"Resolution and Independence"**; but it is bald as the bare mountain tops are bald, with a baldness which is full of grandeur.

Wherever we meet with the successful balance, in Wordsworth, of profound truth of subject with profound truth of execution, he is unique. His best poems are those which most perfectly exhibit this balance. I have a warm admiration for **"Laodameia"** and for the great **"Ode"**; but if I am to tell the very truth, I find **"Laodameia"** not wholly free from something artificial, and the great **"Ode"** not wholly free from something declamatory. If I had to pick out the kind of poems which most perfectly show Wordsworth's unique power, I should rather choose poems such as **"Michael," "The Fountain," "The Highland Reaper."** And poems with the peculiar and unique beauty which distinguishes these he produced in considerable number; besides very many other poems of which the worth, although not so rare as the worth of these, is still exceedingly high.

On the whole, then, . . . not only is Wordsworth eminent because of the goodness of his best work, but he is eminent, also, because of the great body of good work which he has left to us. (pp. 203-04)

I have spoken lightly of Wordsworthians; and if we are to get Wordsworth recognised by the public and by the world, we must recommend him not in the spirit of a clique, but in the spirit of disinterested lovers of poetry. . . . No Wordsworthian has a tenderer affection for this pure and sage master than I, or is less really offended by his defects. But Wordsworth is something more than the pure and sage master of a small band of devoted followers, and we ought not to rest satisfied until he is seen to be what he is. He is one of the very chief glories of English poetry; and by nothing is England so glorious as by her poetry. Let us lay aside every weight which hinders our getting him recognised as this, and let our one study be to bring to pass, as widely as possible and as truly as possible, his own word concerning his poems:—"They will cooperate with the benign tendencies in human nature and society, and will, in their degree, be efficacious in making men wiser, better, and happier." (p. 204)

Matthew Arnold, "Wordsworth," in Macmillan's Magazine, *Vol. XL, No. 237, July, 1879, pp. 193-204.*

JOHN ADDINGTON SYMONDS   (essay date 1879)

[*Symonds was a noted nineteenth-century English critic, poet, historian, and translator. Although primarily remembered for his translations of the Greek poets, Symonds is also known for his aesthetic theory and impressionistic essays. Portraying Wordsworth as primarily a moral poet, Symonds cites his "humanity" and his "grasp upon . . . realities" as those qualities which have made Wordsworth's poetry endure. He does, however, fault Wordsworth's tendency to shift too easily into a didactic or moralistic mode in his poetry. Symonds attributes this in part to Wordsworth's parochialism as an English poet. This essay first appeared on November 1, 1879, in* The Fortnightly Review.]

It is the superior depth, genuineness, sincerity, and truth of Wordsworth's humanity, the solid and abiding vigour of his grasp upon the realities of existence, upon the joys that cannot be taken from us, upon the goods of life which suffer no deduction by chance and change, and are independent of all accidents of fortune, that render Wordsworth's poems indestructible. He is always found upon the side of that which stimulates the stored-up moral forces of mankind. If I remember rightly, he says that he meant his works "to console the afflicted, to add sunshine to daylight, by making the happy happier, to teach the young and the gracious of every age to see, to think, and feel, and therefore to become more actively and securely virtuous." This promise he has kept. When he touches the antique, it is to draw from classic myth or history a lesson weighty with wisdom applicable to our present experience. **"Laodamia"** has no magic to compete with the "Bride of Corinth;" but we rise from its perusal with passions purified by terror and compassion. **"Dion"** closes on this note:

> Him only pleasure leads, and peace attends,
> Him, only him, the shield of Jove defends,
> Whose means are fair and spotless as his ends.

When he writes a poem on a flower, it is to draw forth thoughts of joy, or strength, or consolation. His **"Daffodils"** have not the pathos which belongs to Herrick's, nor has he composed anything in this style to match the sublimity of Leopardi's "Ginestra." But Leopardi crushes the soul of hope out of us by the abyss of dreadful contemplation into which the broom upon the lava of Vesuvius plunges him. Wordsworth never does this. . . . Wordsworth has said nothing so exquisite as Poliziano upon the fragility of rose-leaves, nor has he used the rose, like Ariosto, for similitudes of youthful beauty. But the moralising of these Italian amourists softens and relaxes. Wordsworth's poems on the Celandine brace and invigorate. His enthusiasms are sober and solid. Excepting the **"Ode on Immortality,"** where much that cannot be proved is taken for granted, and excepting an occasional exaggeration of some favourite tenet, as in this famous stanza—

> One impulse from a vernal wood
>   May teach you more of man,
> Of moral evil, and of good,
>   Than all the sages can—

his impulsive utterances are based on a sound foundation, and will bear the test both of experience and analysis. In this respect he differs from Shelley, whose far more fiery and magnetic enthusiasms do not convince us of their absolute sincerity, and are often at variance with probability. In the case of Shelley we must be contented with the noble, the audacious ardour he communicates. The further satisfaction of feeling that his judgments are as right as his aspirations are generous, is too frequently denied. Wordsworth does not soar so high, nor on so powerful a pinion, but he is a safer guide. His own comparison between the nightingale and the stock-dove might be used as an allegory of the two poets. Their several addresses to the skylark give some measure of their different qualities.

The tone of a poet, the mood he communicates, the atmosphere he surrounds us with, is more important even than what he says. This tone is the best or the worst we get from him; it makes it good or bad to be with him. Now it is always good to be with Wordsworth. His personality is like a climate at once sedative and stimulative. I feel inclined to compare it to the influence of the high Alps, austere but kindly, demanding some effort of renunciation, but yielding in return a constant sustenance, and soothing the tired nerves that need a respite from the passions and the fever of the world. The landscape in these regions, far above the plains and cities where men strive, is grave and sober. It has none of the allurements of the south—no waving forests, or dancing waves, or fret-work of sun and shadow cast by olive branches on the flowers. But it has also no deception, and no languor, and no decay. In autumn the bald hillsides assume their robes of orange and of crimson, faintly, delicately spread upon the barren rocks. The air is singularly clear and lucid, suffering no illusion, but satisfying the sense of vision with a marvellous sincerity. And when winter comes, the world for months together is clad in flawless purity of blue and white, with shy, rare, unexpected beauty shed upon the scene from hues of sunrise or sunset. On first acquaintance this Alpine landscape is repellent and severe. We think it too ascetic to be lived in. But familiarity convinces us that it is good and wholesome to abide in it. We learn to love its reserve even more than the prodigality of beauty showered on fortunate islands where the orange and the myrtle flower in never-ending summer. Something of the sort is experienced by those who have yielded themselves to Wordsworth's influence. The luxuriance of Keats, the splendour of Shelley, the oriental glow of Coleridge, the torrid energy of Byron, though good in themselves and infinitely precious, are felt to be less permanent, less uniformly satisfying, less continuously bracing, than the sober simplicity of the poet from whose ruggedness at first we shrank.

It is a pity that Wordsworth could not rest satisfied in leaving this tone to its natural operation on his readers "in a wise passiveness." He passes too readily over from the poet to the moraliser, clenching lessons which need no enforcement by precepts that remind us of the preacher. This leads to a not unnatural movement of revolt in his audience, and often spoils the severe beauty of his art. We do not care to have a somewhat dull but instructive episode from ordinary village life interrupted by a stanza of admonition like the following:

> O Reader! had you in your mind
> Such stores as silent thought can bring,
> O gentle Reader! you would find
> A tale in everything.
> What more I have to say is short,
> And you must kindly take it:
> It is no tale; but, should you *think*,
> Perhaps a tale you'll make it.

After this the real pathos of **"Simon Lee"** cannot fail to fall somewhat flat. And yet it is not seldom that Wordsworth's didactic reflections contain the pith of his sublimest poetry. (pp. 169-74)

The tone I have attempted to describe, as of some clear upland climate, at once soothing and invigorating, austere but gifted with rare charms for those who have submitted to its influence, this tone, unique in poetry, outside the range, perhaps, of Scandinavian literature, will secure for Wordsworth, in England at any rate, an immortality of love and fame. He is, moreover, the poet of man's dependence upon Nature. More deeply, because more calmly, than Shelley, with the passionate enthusiasms of youth subdued to the firm convictions of maturity, he expressed for modern men that creed which, for want of a better word, we designate as Pantheism, but which might be described as the inner soul of Science, the bloom of feeling and enthusiasm destined to ennoble and to poetise our knowledge of the world and of ourselves. In proportion as the sciences make us more intimately acquainted with man's relation to the universe, while the sources of life and thought remain still inscrutable, Wordsworth must take stronger and firmer hold on minds which recognise a mystery in Nature far beyond our ken. What Science is not called on to supply, the fervour and the piety that humanise her truths, and bring them into harmony with permanent emotions of the soul, may be found in all that Wordsworth wrote.

The time might come, indeed may not be distant, when lines like those which . . . [are contained in] the poem composed at Tintern Abbey should be sung in hours of worship by congregations for whom the "cosmic emotion" is a reality and a religion.

Wordsworth, again, is the poet of the simple and the permanent in social life. He has shown that average human nature may be made to yield the motives of the noblest poems, instinct with passion, glowing with beauty, needing only the insight and the touch of the artist to disengage them from the coarse material of commonplace.

> The moving accident is not my trade:
> To freeze the blood I have no ready arts:
> 'Tis my delight, alone in summer shade,
> To pipe a simple song for thinking hearts.

Should the day arrive when society shall be remodelled upon principles of true democracy, when "plain living and high thinking" shall become the rule, when the vulgarity of manners inseparable from decaying feudalism shall have disappeared, when equality shall be rightly apprehended and refinement be the common mark of humble and wealthy homes—should this golden age of a grander civilisation dawn upon the nations, then Wordsworth will be recognised as the prophet and apostle of the world's rejuvenescence. He, too, has something to give, a quiet dignity, a nobleness and loftiness of feeling joined to primitive simplicity, the tranquillity of self-respect, the calm of self-assured uprightness, which it would be very desirable for the advocates of fraternity and equality to assimilate. Of science and democracy Wordsworth in his lifetime was suspicious. It is almost a paradox to proclaim him the poet of democracy and science. Yet there is that in his work which renders it congenial to the mood of men powerfully influenced by scientific ideas, and expecting from democracy the regeneration of society at no incalculably distant future.

After all, Wordsworth is essentially an English poet. He has the limitations no less than the noble qualities of the English character powerfully impressed upon him. Shelley brought into English literature a new ideality, a new element of freedom and expansion. Mazzini greeted Byron with enthusiastic panegyric as the poet of emancipation. Wordsworth moves in a very different region from that of either Byron or Shelley. He remains a stiff, consistent, immitigable Englishman; and it may be questioned whether his stubborn English temperament, his tough insular and local personality, no less than a certain homeliness in his expression, may not prove an obstacle to his acceptance as a cosmopolitan poet. (pp. 175-78)

[In] Wordsworth we find a ponderosity, a personal and patriotic egoism, a pompousness, a self-importance in dwelling upon details that have value chiefly for the poet himself or for the neighbourhood he lives in, which may not unnaturally appear impertinent or irksome to readers of a different nationality. Will the essential greatness of Wordsworth, whereof so much has been already said, his humanity, his wisdom, his healthiness, his bracing tone, his adequacy to the finer inner spirit of a scientific and democratic age—will these solid and imperishable qualities overcome the occasionally defective utterance, the want of humour and lightness, the obstinate insularity of character, the somewhat repellent intensity of local interest, which cannot but be found in him? (p. 180)

> *John Addington Symonds, "Is Poetry at Bottom a Criticism of Life?" in his* Essays, Speculative and Suggestive, Vol. II, *Chapman and Hall, Limited, 1890, pp. 150-80.*

JOHN RUSKIN   (essay date 1880)

[*Ruskin was an English critic, essayist, historian, poet, novella writer, autobiographer, and diarist. Endowed with a passion for reforming what he considered his "blind and wandering fellowmen" and convinced that he had "perfect judgment" in aesthetic matters, Ruskin was the author of over forty books and several hundred essays and lectures that expounded his theories of aesthetics, morality, history, economics, and social reform. Although his views were often controversial and critical reception of his works was frequently hostile, Ruskin became one of the Victorian era's most prominent and influential critics of art and society. Perhaps as well known today for the eloquence of his prose as for the content of his works, Ruskin is considered one of the greatest prose stylists in the English language. In the following brief commentary on Wordsworth, Ruskin, like Lowell (1875), objects to Wordsworth's lack of humor, but grants the beauty of his nature poetry. Still, he does not, in Ruskin's estimate, rank as a great poet. In fact, in formulating his theory of the "Pathetic Fallacy" in his* Modern Painters, *Ruskin included Wordsworth in a group of lesser poets who erroneously ascribe human actions or emotions to inanimate objects.*]

Wordsworth is simply a Westmoreland peasant, with considerably less shrewdness than most border Englishmen or Scotsmen inherit; and no sense of humour: but gifted (in this singularly) with vivid sense of natural beauty, and a pretty turn for reflections, not always acute, but, as far as they reach, medicinal to the fever of the restless and corrupted life around him. Water to parched lips may be better than Samian wine, but do not let us therefore confuse the qualities of wine and water. I much doubt there being many inglorious Miltons in our country churchyards; but I am very sure there are many Wordsworths resting there, who were inferior to the renowned one only in caring less to hear themselves talk.

With an honest and kindly heart, a stimulating egoism, a wholesome contentment in modest circumstances, and such sufficient ease, in that accepted state, as permitted the passing of a good deal of time in wishing that daisies could see the beauty of their own shadows, and other such profitable mental exercises, Wordsworth has left us a series of studies of the graceful and happy shepherd life of our lake country, which to me personally, for one, are entirely sweet and precious; but they are only so as the mirror of an existent reality in many ways more beautiful than its picture. (p. 205)

> *John Ruskin, "Fiction, Fair and Foul," in* The Nineteenth Century, *Vol. VIII, No. XLII, August, 1880, pp. 195-206.**

ALGERNON CHARLES SWINBURNE   (essay date 1884)

[*Swinburne was an English poet, dramatist, and critic. Though renowned during his lifetime for the explicitly sensual themes of his lyric poetry, he is remembered today for his rejection of the mores of the Victorian age. To focus on what is sensational in Swinburne, however, is to miss the assertion, implicit in his poetry and explicit in his critical writings, that in a time when poets were expected to reflect and uphold contemporary morality, Swinburne's only goal was to express beauty. His poetry criticism avoided balanced comparative judgments in favor of ranking poets' achievements; his assessments varied between praise for Shelley, Blake, and Victor Hugo and attacks on Byron, Keats, and, at times, Wordsworth. His critical method is based on his impression and understanding of the work rather than on technical analysis. Yet while some consider this a limitation, others value his judgement; René Wellek considered Swinburne "a genuine critic who succeeded in defining and upholding a specific coherent taste for the imaginative sublime and the moment of poetic magic." In the following excerpt, Swinburne pronounces Wordsworth's attempts to incorporate the "semi-dramatic" form in his poem "Margaret" a failure. However, he admits that no other poet could imbue his subjects with such "sublimity in tenderness" as Wordsworth and praises in particular the emotive power of his "Tribute to the Memory of a Dog."*]

It is through no pleasure in contradiction, but with genuine reluctance to differ from the majority of Wordsworth's ablest and most sympathetic admirers, that I say what I have always thought, when I avow an opinion that as surely as **"Michael"** is a beautiful success, **"Margaret"** is a failure. Its idyllic effect is not heightened but impaired by the semi-dramatic form of narrative—a form so generally alien to Wordsworth's genius that its adoption throughout so great a part of the *Excursion* would of itself suffice at once to establish and to explain the inferiority of that poem to the *Prelude.* . . . Whatever of interest or pathos there may be in the Wanderer's record of Margaret's troubles is fairly swamped in a watery world of words as monotonous and colourless as drizzling mist. The story would be sad enough, if there were any story to tell: and Wordsworth, in his 'wiser mind,' might have turned the subject to some elegiac account: but all the main effect—in spite of certain details and certain passages or phrases impossible to any but a master of pathetic emotion—is washed away by the drowsy and dreary overflow of verses without limit or landmark. The truth is that Wordsworth, of all poets worthy to be named in the same day with him, stood the most in need of artificial confinement and support to prevent his work from sprawling into shapeless efflorescence and running to unprofitable seed; though, if any one were to speak of his blank verse in a tone of sweeping and intemperate irreverence, no doubt the great names of Lorton Vale and Tintern Abbey would rise up before all our memories to shame the speaker into silence: Milton alone could surpass, perhaps Milton alone has equalled, the very finest work of his great disciple in this majestic kind: the music of some few almost incomparable passages seems to widen and deepen the capacity of the sense for reception and enjoyment and understanding of the sublimest harmonies. . . . ["Ode on Intimations of Immortality," that] famous, ambitious, and occasionally magnificent poem—which by the way is no more an ode than it is an epic—reveals the partiality and inequality of Wordsworth's inspiration as unmistakably as its purity and its power. Five stanzas or sections—from the opening of the fifth to the close of the ninth—would be utterly above all praise, if the note they are pitched in were sustained throughout: but after its unspeakably beautiful opening the seventh stanza falls suddenly far down beneath the level of those five first lines, so superb in the majesty of their sweetness, the magnificence of their tenderness, that to have written but the two last of them would have added glory to any poet's crown of fame. The details which follow on the close of this opening cadence do but impair its charm with a sense of incongruous realism and triviality, to which the suddenly halting and disjointed metre bears only too direct and significant a correspondence. No poet, surely, ever 'changed his hand' with such inharmonious awkwardness, or 'checked his pride' with such unseasonable humility, as Wordsworth. He of all others should have been careful to eschew the lawless discord of Cowley's 'immetrical' irregularity: for, to say the least, he had not enough of 'music in himself' to supply in any measure or degree whatever the lack of ordered rhythm and lyric law. . . . The peculiar note of Wordsworth's genius at its very highest is that of sublimity in tenderness. . . . And sometimes, even where no such profound note of emotion is touched as to evoke this peculiar sense of power, the utter sincerity and perfect singleness of heart and spirit by which that highest effect is elsewhere produced may be no less distinctly and no less delightedly recognized. This quality of itself is no doubt insufficient to produce any such effect: and Wordsworth, it may be confessed, was liable to failure as complete as might have been expected, when, having no other merit of subject or of treatment to rely on, he was content to rely on his sincerity and simplicity alone; with a result sometimes merely trivial and unmeritable, sometimes actually repulsive or oppressive. At other times again the success of his method, or rather perhaps the felicity of his instinct, was no less absolute and complete, even when the homeliness or humility of the subject chosen would have seemed incompatible with loftiness of feeling or grandeur of style. All readers who know good work when they see it must appreciate the beauty of his "Tribute to the Memory of a Dog": all must feel the truth and the sweetness of its simplicity: but hardly any, I should suppose, have perceived on a first reading how grand it is—how noble, how lofty, how exalted, is the tone of its emotion. Here is that very sublimity of tenderness which I have ventured to indicate as Wordsworth's distinctive and

crowning quality: a quality with which no other poet could have imbued his verse on such a subject and escaped all risk of apparent incongruity or insincerity. To praise a poem of this class on the score of dignity would seem to imply its deficiency in the proper and necessary qualities of simplicity and tenderness: yet here the loftier quality seems to grow as naturally as a flower out of the homelier and humbler element of feeling and expression. On the other hand, it seems to me undeniable that Wordsworth, who could endow such daily domestic matters, such modest emotion and experience, with a force of contagious and irresistible sympathy which makes their interest universal and eternal, had no such birthright of power, showed no such certitude of hand, when dealing with the proper and natural elements of tragedy. A subject of such naked and untempered horror as he attempted to manage in his semi-dramatic idyl of "The Thorn"—one of the poems elected by himself for especial mention as a representative example of his work, and of its guiding principle,—instead of being harmonized by his genius into tragic and pitiful and terrible beauty, retains in his hands the whole ghastliness and dreadfulness of a merely shocking and hideous reality. (pp. 777-79)

Algernon Charles Swinburne, "Wordsworth and Byron (Concluded)," in The Nineteenth Century, *Vol. XV, No. LXXXVII, May, 1884, pp. 764-90.**

GEORGE SAINTSBURY (essay date 1896)

[*Saintsbury was an English literary historian and critic of the late nineteenth and early twentieth centuries. A prolific writer, he composed several histories of English and European literature as well as numerous critical works on individual authors, styles, and periods. Saintsbury here asserts that Wordsworth's poetical experiment "was and is far more ludicrous than touching." He enumerates the poet's merits as his "felicity of phrase," masterly nature descriptions, and mysticism. Saintsbury concludes that at his best, Wordsworth is one of the finest poets in England, but adds that at his worst, he is very dull indeed. For other views on Wordsworth's critical theory, see the excerpts by Wordsworth (1802), Coleridge (1817), De Quincey (1845), and Abrams (1953).*]

Few except extreme and hopeless Wordsworthians now deny that the result of [Wordsworth's] attempts at simple language was and is far more ludicrous than touching. The wonderful "Affliction of Margaret" does not draw its power from the neglect of poetic diction, but from the intensity of emotion which would carry off almost any diction, simple or affected; while on the other hand such pieces as "We are Seven," as the "Anecdote for Fathers," and as "Alice Fell," not to mention "Betty Foy" and others, which specially infuriated Wordsworth's own contemporaries, certainly gain nothing from their namby-pamby dialect, and sometimes go near to losing the beauty that really is in them by dint of it. Moreover, the Miltonic blank verse and sonnets—at their best of a stately magnificence surpassed by no poet—have a tendency to become heavy and even dull when the poetic fire fails to fuse and shine through them. In fact it may be said of Wordsworth, as of most poets with theories, that his theories helped him very little, and sometimes hindered him a great deal.

His real poetical merits are threefold, and lie first in the inexplicable, the ultimate, felicity of phrase which all great poets must have, and which only great poets have; secondly, in his matchless power of delineating natural objects; and lastly, more properly, and with most special rarity of all, in the half-pantheistic mysticism which always lies behind this observation, and which every now and then breaks through it, puts it, as mere observation, aside, and blazes in unmasked fire of rapture. The summits of Wordsworth's poetry, the **"Lines Written at Tintern Abbey"** and the **"Ode on Intimations of Immortality,"**—poems of such astonishing magnificence that it is only more astonishing that any one should have read them and failed to see what a poet had come before the world,—are the greatest of many of these revelations or inspirations. It is indeed necessary to read Wordsworth straight through—a proceeding which requires that the reader shall be in good literary training, but is then feasible, profitable, and even pleasant enough—to discern the enormous height at which the great **"Ode"** stands above its author's other work. The **"Tintern Abbey"** lines certainly approach it nearest: many smaller things—**"The Affliction of Margaret,"** **"The Daffodils,"** and others—group well under its shadow, and innumerable passages and even single lines, such as that which all good critics have noted as lightening the darkness of the *Prelude*—

Voyaging through strange seas of thought, alone—

must of course be added to the poet's credit. But the **"Ode"** remains not merely the greatest, but the one really, dazzlingly, supremely great thing he ever did. Its theory has been scorned or impugned by some; parts of it have even been called nonsense by critics of weight. But, sound or unsound, sense or nonsense, it is poetry, and magnificent poetry, from the first line to the last—poetry than which there is none better in any language, poetry such as there is not perhaps more than a small volume-full in all languages. The second class of merit, that of vivid observation, abounds wherever the poems are opened. But the examples of the first are chiefly found in the lyrics **"My Heart Leaps up,"** **"The Sparrow's Nest"**; the famous daffodil poem which Jeffrey thought "stuff," which some say Dorothy wrote chiefly, and which is almost perfect of its kind; the splendid opening of the **"Lines to Hartley Coleridge,"** which connect themselves with the **"Immortality Ode"**; the exquisite group of the **"Cuckoo,"** the best patches of the Burns poems, and the three **"Yarrows"**; the **"Peele Castle"** stanzas; and, to cut a tedious catalogue short, the hideously named but in parts perfectly beautiful **"Effusion on the Death of James Hogg,"** the last really masterly thing that the poet did. In some of these we may care little for the poem as a whole, nothing for the moral the poet wishes to draw. But the poetic moments seize us, the poetic flash dazzles our eyes, and the whole divine despair or not more divine rapture which poetry causes comes upon us.

One division of Wordsworth's work is so remarkable that it must have such special and separate mention as it is here possible to give it; and that is his exercises in the sonnet, wherein to some tastes he stands only below Shakespeare and on a level with Milton. (pp. 53-5)

Its thoughtfulness suited his bent, and its limits frustrated his prolixity, though, it must be owned, he somewhat evaded this benign influence by writing in series. And the sonnets on **"The Venetian Republic,"** on the **"Subjugation of Switzerland,"** that beginning "The world is too much with us," that in November 1806, the first **"Personal Talk,"** the magnificent **"Westminster Bridge,"** and the opening at least of that on Scott's departure from Abbotsford, are not merely among the glories of Wordsworth, they are among the glories of English poetry.

Unfortunately these moments of perfection are, in the poet's whole work, and especially in that part of it which was composed in the later half of his long life, by no means very

frequent. Wordsworth was absolutely destitute of humour, from which it necessarily followed that his self-criticism was either non-existent or constantly at fault. His verse was so little facile, it paid so little regard to any of the common allurements of narrative-interest or varied subject, it was so necessary for it to reach the full white heat, the absolute instant of poetic projection, that when it was not very good it was apt to be scarcely tolerable. It is nearly impossible to be duller than Wordsworth at his dullest, and unluckily it is as impossible to find a poet of anything like his powers who has given himself the license to be dull so often and at such length. The famous "Would he had blotted a thousand" applies to him with as much justice as it was unjust in its original application; and it is sometimes for pages together a positive struggle to remember that one is reading one of the greatest of English poets, and a poet whose influence in making other poets has been second hardly to that of Spenser, of Keats, or of [Coleridge]. . . . (pp. 55-6)

> *George Saintsbury, "The New Poetry," in his* A History of Nineteenth Century Literature (1780-1895), *The Macmillan Company, 1896, pp. 49-124.* *

WALTER RALEIGH   (essay date 1903)

[*A renowned lecturer and literary critic, Raleigh was appointed in 1904 the first professor of English literature at Oxford. His critical approach to literature, in both his lectures and in such works as* The English Novel *and* Shakespeare, *was that of a highly perceptive, urbane commentator whose literary exegesis served to facilitate the non-specialist's understanding of English literature through concise textual commentary. In addition, Raleigh often illuminated his subject by examining the personality of the writer under discussion. In the following excerpt from Raleigh's full-length study of Wordsworth, he explores the poet's fascination with nature and theorizes that he "became a psychologist" when he turned inward to interpret nature's signs. He constantly looked for correspondences between humankind and nature, Raleigh adds, and interpreted outward events using emotion as his guide; many of his poems have their origins in a sudden moment of illumination. Maintaining that Wordsworth was "a true visionary," Raleigh attributes his greatness as a poet to his sense of the unity of the universe. For other discussions of Wordsworth's relation to nature, see Whitehead (1925), Beatty (1927), Huxley (1929), and Beach (1936).*]

[To Wordsworth, nature and human life] together make up a book of wonder and power, composed in a strange language, unlike the speech that men use for the business of life, and written in unknown characters. The book has never been read, but glimpses of its meaning are obtainable by those who pore over it lovingly and long, and who do not despise small aids and chance suggestions towards its interpretation. The poet makes it the business of his life to read at least some part of it; and we have seen him at work, trying this way and that, gazing at the pages so fixedly that he stamps them, down to the minutest detail, on his memory, testing likely theories of the cipher, listening with rapt attention to the casual comments of those innocent and idle spirits who, seeking no hidden meaning, find no difficulty in the book, but turn over its pages for pure delight, and notice, from time to time, features of the script that have escaped the eye of more methodical observers. The last resource of the poet still remains to him. The little that he has been able to read comes to him not as the conclusion of a laboured and triumphant series of syllogisms, but in sudden flashes of intelligence, often lost before they can be directed to the dark places. Whence are these lights that spring up in the mind and flicker and die? Does the mind hold the secret after all, and has it bewildered itself chiefly by too servile an attention to outward things? It was to answer these questions that Wordsworth turned his gaze inward and attempted to explore the recesses of his own mind.

This was held by himself to be, and was indeed, the most significant part of his work. He found the mind vast and immeasurable and shadowy; beyond the empyrean it was there, and it stretched under the lowest reaches of the abyss. (pp. 197-98)

Without other apparatus than introspection and the observation of his fellows, Wordsworth became a psychologist. He concerned himself especially, as we have seen, with those moments of suddenly awakened feeling when something comes to the mind in a flash. There is a regular and customary perspective imposed by the mind upon the world of objects perceived. But these objects, whether they be sensations, or perceptions, or emotions, do not invariably submit to the imposition. They assert their independence in movements that defy control. The humblest of them, on no assignable provocation, will put on the demeanour of a tyrant. In social relations it is familiar to everyone how a word or a gesture of no particular import will sometimes recur to the mind with as much insistence and self-importance as if it were the sentence or the nod of a presiding judge. And so with the feelings; they will not accept their ceremonial status; they break loose from their allotted places and subvert the natural order of expectation:—

> I drew my bride, beneath the moon,
> Across my threshold; happy hour!
> But, ah, the walk that afternoon,
> We saw the water-flags in flower!

To Wordsworth these insurgent movements seemed worth the watching, for they give a clue to what is in progress in the depths below. It is this that he intends when he speaks of presenting ordinary things to the mind in an unusual aspect, and of making the incidents and situations of common life interesting by tracing in them "the primary laws of our nature: chiefly, as far as regards the manner in which we associate ideas in a state of excitement." In the unprepared and unforeseen illumination of the dark recesses, which comes and is gone, he found the genesis of poetry.

The inexplicable and almost incredible quickness of movement which is produced in the mind by the presence of a strong emotion seemed favourable to these appearances. (pp. 199-200)

Many of his poems owe their origin to a curious study of these significant moments when the mind, acting spontaneously and without forethought, reads new values into life and experience. It would be tedious to attempt exhaustive illustration. Without these self-directing movements of the mind, which take a man at unawares and leave him in the position of an amazed watcher, the huddled chaos of experience would have no power save to confuse and deaden the receptive faculties. Curiously and intently Wordsworth watched the rise of unexplained impulses and feelings in his own mind and in the minds of others. (p. 202)

Often it is his own mind that he surprises at its work of bringing order into experience, and, under the influence of some obscure emotion, selecting among a thousand objects indifferently presented. These preferences, he holds, are not caprices of the idle fancy; they are portents and reminiscences. In two sonnets he describes himself watching a wide expanse of the sea, sprin-

kled all over with ships. One ship among them engages all his attention:—

> This Ship was nought to me, nor I to her,
> Yet I pursued her with a Lover's look;
> This Ship to all the rest did I prefer:
> When will she turn, and whither?

What land or haven is she bound for as she puts forth thus in fresh and joyous array? And then there crosses his mind a foreboding of

> doubt, and something dark,
> Of the old Sea some reverential fear.

He offers no argument, but is content to record the feeling as simply as it arose in his mind.

These vigils of contemplation were the chief sources of his poetry. (pp. 203-04)

In his exploration of the world of the mind he found [a] strong tendency to interpret events by the light of the emotions. He did not believe that the interpretation was necessarily or usually valid. He believed in the existence of the tendency, and held that its very existence is a fact to be reckoned with. He was far now from the pedantic rationalism of Godwin. All that he had seen in what is called the known world had been revealed to him by his emotions—by admiration, and fear, and hope, and love. In these emotions he found the secret and spring of man's life—that is, of his existence. When, therefore, they arise mysteriously in the mind he was not prepared to call them idle and unmeaning because no rational cause, as the phrase goes, was assignable to them. His wide imagination, which refused to recognise the arbitrary boundary set between Nature and Man, sought for correspondences everywhere. The stars are kept in their places by the law of duty; the humblest fears and hopes of man tenant the same universe as the stars, and move to the same music. He did not transgress the modesty of human science or poorly and fantastically tether symbolic meanings to individual objects. He invented no language of flowers. A flower, in its place, as it grew, was more to him than any symbol; it was a part of the eternal order, and, if it could be understood, a key to the whole. (pp. 206-07)

Running through all Wordsworth's poetry this is the deepest strain. While he limits himself to expressing a sense of the unbroken chain that binds the least things to the greatest in the outward world, he may be called philosophical. When he goes farther, and finds in the instincts and presentiments and impulses of the heart and mind of man movements that obey the same law, low-breathed messages from a hidden source, he is called mystical. Neither does he violate science here; he pins his faith to no particular code, but he refuses to isolate and neglect one whole world of experience only because it cannot be exactly interpreted, and, by certain "busy foes to good," has been used as a refuge and warrant for their baser thoughts and cravings.

It is this deep imaginative sense of unity in things, of real correspondences and connections working throughout the universe of perception and thought, which gives profundity to Wordsworth's treatment of Nature. His imagination is essentially scientific, and quite unlike the fancy that decorates and falsifies fact to gratify an idle mind with a sense of neatness and ingenuity. (p. 208)

The distinction between the Fancy and the Imagination, so often set forth by Coleridge, is admirably exemplified by Wordsworth. He never confuses the two faculties, never passes unwittingly from the one form of energy to the other. The human mind is playful, and will not be denied its sportive indulgences. Yet Fancy claims a comparatively small share in his works; "Natures's secondary grace," as he calls it,—

> The charm more superficial that attends
> Her works, as they present to Fancy's choice
> Apt illustrations of the moral world,
> Caught at a glance, or traced with curious pain,—

is barely touched upon in his greater poems, and never without the clearest indication of its trivial origin and office.

As might be expected, it follows from this that the moral reflections which conclude some of Wordsworth's shorter poems are quite unlike the stale, trite aphorisms of the didactic school of poetry. Wordsworth's morals, so to call them, are discoveries made by a vital sympathy which searches deep into the heart of things. They must be pondered long to be understood. . . .

[They] are the reflections of one who has studied the mind of man as reverently and patiently as the scientific observer studies the works of Nature. They are strange and surprising, as all discoveries are surprising, and are expressed with no homiletic intent, but in a spirit of wonder and awe. It is not from the shallows swept by a thousand nets that these mysterious findings come; they tell of a depth "where fathom-line could never touch the ground," a depth where also there is life.

Whoever, then, desires to read Wordsworth aright must not look for proverbs, or maxims, or any of those condensed and generalised statements whereby mankind seeks to preserve experience in a form suitable for practical application. Nor must

A caricature of Wordsworth and Hartley Coleridge, drawn in 1844.

he look for a second sense. This poet is a true visionary, and deals not in allegories or dreams. . . . It is the mark of the mystic that he never despises sense, never uses it as a means to an end, a stepping-stone to be spurned when he has raised himself higher. He does not look beyond this world, but gazes intently on what is presented to him, and, if his quest fail, looks still nearer and closer. In the earth under his boot-soles, in the garments that cling closest to him, and, if not there, in the beatings of his heart, he tries to find the secret. Heaven is not for him a far place, nor eternity a long time. Here or nowhere, now or never, the soul of all things is to be found. (pp. 210-14)

> *Walter Raleigh, in his* Wordsworth, *Edward Arnold, 1903, 232 p.*

A. C. BRADLEY (essay date 1909)

[*Bradley was a renowned Shakespearean scholar and influential literary critic. In the excerpt below, he focuses on Wordsworth's paradoxical manner. Terming his style "peculiar," Bradley discusses realistic, mystical, and sublime elements in Wordsworth's poetry. Other critics who consider Wordsworth's style include Hazlitt (1825), Pater (1874), Lowell (1875), Darbishire (1949), Pottle (1950), and Hartman (1964).*]

There have been greater poets than Wordsworth, but none more original. He saw new things, or he saw things in a new way. Naturally, this would have availed us little if his new things had been private fancies, or if his new perception had been superficial. But that was not so. If it had been, Wordsworth might have won acceptance more quickly, but he would not have gained his lasting hold on poetic minds. . . . [His way of seeing] is not like Shakespeare's myriad-mindedness; it is, for good or evil or both, peculiar. . . .

If this is so, the road into Wordsworth's mind must be through his strangeness and his paradoxes, and not round them. I do not mean that they are everywhere in his poetry. Much of it, not to speak of occasional platitudes, is beautiful without being peculiar or difficult; and some of this may be as valuable as that which is audacious or strange. But unless we get hold of that, we remain outside Wordsworth's centre; and, if we have not a most unusual affinity to him, we cannot get hold of that unless we realise its strangeness, and refuse to blunt the sharpness of its edge. (pp. 100-01)

However much Wordsworth was the poet of small and humble things, and the poet who saw his ideal realised, not in Utopia, but here and now before his eyes, he was, quite as much, what some would call a mystic. He saw everything in the light of 'the visionary power.' He was, for himself,

> The transitory being that beheld
> This Vision.

He apprehended all things, natural or human, as the expression of something which, while manifested in them, immeasurably transcends them. And nothing can be more intensely Wordsworthian than the poems and passages most marked by this visionary power and most directly issuing from this apprehension. (pp. 126-27)

My main object [is] to insist that the 'mystic,' 'visionary,' 'sublime,' aspect of Wordsworth's poetry must not be slighted. (p. 129)

There is, for instance, in *Prelude,* xii., the description of the crag, from which, on a wild dark day, the boy watched eagerly the two highways below for the ponies that were coming to take him home for the holidays. It is too long to quote, but every reader of it will remember

> the wind and sleety rain,
> And all the business of the elements,
> The single sheep, and the one blasted tree,
> And the bleak music from that old stone wall,
> The noise of wood and water, and the mist
> That on the line of each of those two roads
> Advanced in such indisputable shapes.

Everything here is natural, but everything is apocalyptic. And we happen to know why. Wordsworth is describing the scene in the light of memory. In that eagerly expected holiday his father died; and the scene, as he recalled it, was charged with the sense of contrast between the narrow world of common pleasures and blind and easy hopes, and the vast unseen world which encloses it in beneficent yet dark and inexorable arms. The visionary feeling has here a peculiar tone; but always, openly or covertly, it is the intimation of something illimitable, over-arching or breaking into the customary 'reality.' Its character varies; and so sometimes at its touch the soul, suddenly conscious of its own infinity, melts in rapture into that infinite being; while at other times the 'mortal nature' stands dumb, incapable of thought, or shrinking from some presence

> Not un-informed with Phantasy, and looks
> That threaten the profane.

This feeling is so essential to many of Wordsworth's most characteristic poems that it may almost be called their soul; and failure to understand them frequently arises from obtuseness to it. It appears in a mild and tender form, but quite openly, in the lines **"To a Highland Girl,"** where the child, and the rocks and trees and lake and road by her home, seem to the poet

> Like something fashioned in a dream.

It gives to **"The Solitary Reaper"** its note of remoteness and wonder; and even the slight shock of bewilderment due to it is felt in the opening line of the most famous stanza:

> Will no one tell me what she sings?

Its etherial music accompanies every vision of the White Doe, and sounds faintly to us from far away through all the tale of failure and anguish. Without it such shorter narratives as **"Hartleap Well"** and **"Resolution and Independence"** would lose the imaginative atmosphere which adds mystery and grandeur to the apparently simple 'moral.'

In **"Hartleap Well"** it is conveyed at first by slight touches of contrast. Sir Walter, in his long pursuit of the Hart, has mounted his third horse.

> Joy sparkled in the prancing courser's eyes;
> The horse and horseman are a happy pair;
> But, though Sir Walter like a falcon flies,
> There is a doleful silence in the air.
>
> A rout this morning left Sir Walter's hall,
> That as they galloped made the echoes roar;
> But horse and man are vanished, one and all;
> Such race, I think, was never seen before.

At last even the dogs are left behind, stretched one by one among the mountain fern.

> Where is the throng, the tumult of the race?
> The bugles that so joyfully were blown?

> —This chase it looks not like an earthly chase;
> Sir Walter and the Hart are left alone.

Thus the poem begins. At the end we have the old shepherd's description of the utter desolation of the spot where the waters of the little spring had trembled with the last deep groan of the dying stag, and where the Knight, to commemorate his exploit, had built a basin for the spring, three pillars to mark the last three leaps of his victim, and a pleasure-house, surrounded by trees and trailing plants, for the summer joy of himself and his paramour. But now 'the pleasure-house is dust,' and the trees are grey, 'with neither arms nor head':

> Now, here is neither grass nor pleasant shade;
> The sun on drearier hollow never shone;
> So will it be, as I have often said,
> Till trees, and stones, and fountain all are gone.

It is only this feeling of the presence of mysterious inviolable Powers, behind the momentary powers of hard pleasure and empty pride, that justifies the solemnity of the stanza:

> The Being, that is in the clouds and air,
> That is in the green leaves among the groves,
> Maintains a deep and reverential care
> For the unoffending creatures whom he loves.

"Hartleap Well" is a beautiful poem, but whether it is entirely successful is, perhaps, doubtful. There can be no sort of doubt as to **"Resolution and Independence,"** probably, if we must choose, the most Wordsworthian of Wordsworth's poems, and the best test of ability to understand him. The story, if given in a brief argument, would sound far from promising. We should expect for it, too, a ballad form somewhat like that of **"Simon Lee."** When we read it, we find instead lines of extraordinary grandeur, but, mingled with them, lines more pedestrian than could be found in an impressive poem from any other hand,—for instance,

> And, drawing to his side, to him did say,
> 'This morning gives us promise of a glorious day.'

or,

> 'How is it that you live, and what is it you do?'

We meet also with that perplexed persistence, and that helpless reiteration of a question (in this case one already clearly answered), which in other poems threatens to become ludicrous, and on which a writer with a keener sense of the ludicrous would hardly have ventured. Yet with all this, and by dint of all this, we read with bated breath, almost as if we were in the presence of that 'majestical' Spirit in *Hamlet,* come to 'admonish' from another world, though not this time by terror. And one source of this effect is the confusion, the almost hypnotic obliteration of the habitual reasoning mind, that falls on the poet as he gazes at the leechgatherer, and hears, without understanding, his plain reply to the enquiry about himself and the prosaic 'occupation' he 'pursues':

> The old man still stood talking by my side;
> But now his voice to me was like a stream
> Scarce heard; nor word from word could I divide;
> And the whole body of the man did seem
> Like one whom I had met with in a dream;
> Or like a man from some far region sent,
> To give me human strength, by apt admonishment.

The same question was asked again, and the answer was repeated. But

> While he was talking thus, the lonely place,
> The old man's shape, and speech, all troubled me.

'Trouble' is a word not seldom employed by the poet to denote the confusion caused by some visionary experience. Here are, again, the fallings from us, vanishings, blank misgivings, dim fore-feelings of the soul's infinity. (pp. 133-37)

The solitariness which exerted so potent a spell on Wordsworth had in it nothing 'Byronic.' He preached in the *Excursion* against the solitude of 'self-indulging spleen.' He was even aware that he himself, though free from that weakness, had felt

> perhaps too much
> The self-sufficing power of Solitude.

No poet is more emphatically the poet of community. A great part of his verse—a part as characteristic and as precious as the part on which I have been dwelling—is dedicated to the affections of home and neighbourhood and country, and to that soul of joy and love which links together all Nature's children, and 'steals from earth to man, from man to earth.' And this soul is for him as truly the presence of 'the Being that is in the clouds and air' and in the mind of man as are the power, the darkness, the silence, the strange gleams and mysterious visitations which startle and confuse with intimations of infinity. But solitude and solitariness were to him, in the main, one of these intimations. . . . Thus, in whatever guise it might present itself, solitariness 'carried far into his heart' the haunting sense of an 'invisible world'; of some Life beyond this 'transitory being' and 'unapproachable by death';

> Of Life continuous, Being unimpaired;
> That hath been, is, and where it was and is
> There shall endure,—existence unexposed
> To the blind walk of mortal accident;
> From diminution safe and weakening age;
> While man grows old, and dwindles, and decays;
> And countless generations of mankind
> Depart; and leave no vestige where they trod.

For me, I confess, all this is far from being 'mere poetry'—partly because I do not believe that any such thing as 'mere poetry' exists. But whatever kind or degree of truth we may find in all this, everything in Wordsworth that is sublime or approaches sublimity has, directly or more remotely, to do with it. And without this part of his poetry Wordsworth would be 'shorn of his strength,' and would no longer stand, as he does stand, nearer than any other poet of the Nineteenth Century to Milton. (pp. 143-45)

A. C. Bradley, "Wordsworth," in his Oxford Lectures on Poetry, *1909. Reprint by Indiana University Press, 1961, pp. 99-148.*

ALFRED NORTH WHITEHEAD   (lecture date 1925)

[*Whitehead was a respected English mathematician and philosopher. In this brief excerpt from his study of science in the nineteenth century, Whitehead, like Raleigh (1903), maintains that Wordsworth conceived of nature as "the field of enduring permanences" and was, therefore, hostile to the analytical, fragmenting aspects of science. For other discussions of Wordsworth's relation to nature, see the excerpts by Raleigh (1903), Beatty (1927), Huxley (1929), and Beach (1936).*]

Wordsworth was passionately absorbed in nature. It has been said of Spinoza, that he was drunk with God. It is equally true that Wordsworth was drunk with nature. But he was a thoughtful, well-read man, with philosophical interests, and sane even to the point of prosiness. In addition, he was a genius. He weakens his evidence by his dislike of science. We all remember his scorn of the poor man whom he somewhat hastily accuses of peeping and botanising on his mother's grave. Passage after passage could be quoted from him, expressing this repulsion. In this respect, his characteristic thought can be summed up in his phrase, 'We murder to dissect.'

In this latter passage, he discloses the intellectual basis of his criticism of science. He alleges against science its absorption in abstractions. His consistent theme is that the important facts of nature elude the scientific method. It is important therefore to ask, what Wordsworth found in nature that failed to receive expression in science. I ask this question in the interest of science itself. . . . Now it is emphatically not the case that Wordsworth hands over inorganic matter to the mercy of science, and concentrates on the faith that in the living organism there is some element that science cannot analyse. Of course he recognises, what no one doubts, that in some sense living things are different from lifeless things. But that is not his main point. It is the brooding presence of the hills which haunts him. His theme is nature *in solido*, that is to say, he dwells on that mysterious presence of surrounding things, which imposes itself on any separate element that we set up as an individual for its own sake. He always grasps the whole of nature as involved in the tonality of the particular instance. That is why he laughs with the daffodils, and finds in the primrose thoughts 'too deep for tears.'

Wordsworth's greatest poem is, by far, the first book of *The Prelude*. It is pervaded by this sense of the haunting presences of nature. A series of magnificent passages, too long for quotation, express this idea. Of course, Wordsworth is a poet writing a poem, and is not concerned with dry philosophical statements. But it would hardly be possible to express more clearly a feeling for nature, as exhibiting entwined prehensive unities, each suffused with modal presences of others:

> Ye Presences of Nature in the sky
> And on the earth! Ye Visions of the hills!
> And Souls of lonely places! can I think
> A vulgar hope was yours when ye employed
> Such ministry, when ye through many a year
> Haunting me thus among my boyish sports,
> On caves and trees, upon the woods and hills,
> Impressed upon all forms the characters
> Of danger or desire; and thus did make
> The surface of the universal earth,
> With triumph and delight, with hope and fear,
> Work like a sea? . . .

In thus citing Wordsworth, the point which I wish to make is that we forget how strained and paradoxical is the view of nature which modern science imposes on our thoughts. Wordsworth, to the height of genius, expresses the concrete facts of our apprehension, facts which are distorted in the scientific analysis. Is it not possible that the standardised concepts of science are only valid within narrow limitations, perhaps too narrow for science itself? (pp. 121-23)

The literature of the nineteenth century, especially its English poetic literature, is a witness to the discord between the aesthetic intuitions of mankind and the mechanism of science.

Shelley brings vividly before us the elusiveness of the eternal objects of sense as they haunt the change which infects underlying organisms. Wordsworth is the poet of nature as being the field of enduring permanences carrying within themselves a message of tremendous significance. The eternal objects are also there for him,

> The light that never was, on sea or land.

Both Shelley and Wordsworth emphatically bear witness that nature cannot be divorced from its aesthetic values; and that these values arise from the cumulation, in some sense, of the brooding presence of the whole on to its various parts. Thus we gain from the poets the doctrine that a philosophy of nature must concern itself at least with these six notions: change, value, eternal objects, endurance, organism, interfusion. (p. 127)

> *Alfred North Whitehead, "The Romantic Reaction,"* in his Science and the Modern World: Lowell Lectures, 1925, *The Macmillan Company, 1925, pp. 109-38.*

ARTHUR BEATTY (essay date 1927)

[*Beatty's work is an important study of the historical and philosophic context of Wordsworth's ideas. The following excerpt concerns the poet's view of nature. Emphasizing that nature was to Wordsworth "only one aspect of his doctrine of the development of the individual mind," Beatty traces the influences on Wordsworth's perception of nature to Bacon, Hobbes, Locke, and Rousseau. Though he acknowledges that Wordsworth's nature is a complex amalgam, Beatty concludes that Wordsworth adhered to the rational rather than to the Rousseauistic school of nature. He also probes Wordsworth's model for the three stages of man's development and the relation of each to nature. For other discussions of Wordsworth's relation to nature, see the excerpts by Raleigh (1903), Whitehead (1925), Huxley (1929), and Beach (1936).*]

Wordsworth's doctrine of Nature is of primary importance for the proper understanding of his poetry and criticism, as it forms an essential part of the whole body of his writings, not only of those poems which avowedly deal with matters of doctrine on man and nature, but also of those which seem on the surface to be the simple outpouring of a naive and simple mind, and to be wholly innocent of theory. This is to say that his doctrine of Nature permeates not only *The Excursion, The Prelude,* and the prose **Prefaces** and **Essays,** but also **"Tintern Abbey," "The Cuckoo," "Michael," "Peele Castle," "Resolution and Independence," "Lines Written in Early Spring," "Expostulation and Reply,"** and the **"Ode: Intimations of Immortality."** I mention specimens of diverse classes of his work quite purposely; for I wish to make clear that, so far as the doctrine of Nature is concerned, Wordsworth has not put his doctrines into one set of poems and his poetry into another.

But, while it is true that Nature is of great importance in the poetry and prose of Wordsworth and permeates the whole body of his work, it is equally true that his doctrine of Nature is strictly subordinate to another and much more fundamental, comprehensive, and complex one, of which it is a part, and a necessary part; but only a part. In other words, his doctrine of Nature is only one aspect of his doctrine of the development of the individual mind, according to the scheme of the three ages of man. (p. 129)

[We] have an abundance of evidence that in intention the whole body of Wordsworth's poetry, the short poems as well as the long poems, is philosophic in content; and therefore its interest lies in the problems of psychology and philosophy. This is to say that the problem of Nature is not approached directly as a distinct and separate question, but always in connection with the problem of the development of the mind. The question of Nature is always a part of the question of the development of the individual mind: and the varying attitudes of the mind toward Nature, or the more general reactions towards Nature, as the mark of the mind's development. More explicitly, the poet deals with Nature in terms of his own peculiar theory of the development of the mind. . . . It is absolutely essential to keep this in mind, and to realize that Wordsworth is dealing with the problem of mental development for only then can we see that he describes his relationships to Nature at each period of life, and that what he holds true of one period he does not regard as true of the others. (pp. 131-32)

It must further be noted that Wordsworth does not use the term "nature" in a naive way: but in a highly technical meaning, or series of meanings. He inherited the term from the eighteenth century; and not the term only but the controversy which had raged around it for a century and a half; and hence it was almost inevitable that he should make an important use of it in any discussion of man in his social, ethical, or religious associations, making his choice of the various meanings which best suited his purpose. For the meanings which were given to the term were many; but for our purposes we shall consider only two; which, while they are distinct, merge into each other and into other quite distinct uses. There is the use which may be said to derive from Bacon and Hobbes, continued through Locke and the "sensational school" of philosophy, in which nature is held as the source of truth and reason. "Natural law" is a favorite phrase with those who view nature in this way; and reason and nature are one. The only validity which anything can claim is its "naturalness," and its naturalness is its reasonableness. In Bacon this takes the form of seeking to master nature by understanding her; in Hobbes, of the "natural" laws of society and the ordering of a commonwealth in the light of those immutable and eternal principles on which both natural and moral laws alike are based; in Locke, of endeavoring to arrive at the reality of "those parts of knowledge that men are most concerned to be clear in," and to investigate the nature and conditions of knowledge that conforms to external reality. (pp. 132-33)

[The second attitude to nature] is the attitude which is associated with the phrase "the return to Nature," and most persistently with its chief apostle Rousseau. This attitude is marked by a few leading characteristics which we shall note briefly. The first is the meaning of "nature," and its allied phrases "natural," and "the state of Nature." With this school of thought Nature is opposed to man, in that it is always good, while man as he is in society is evil. Thus the "natural" is the good, and the "state of Nature" is the state of felicity, because man with his contaminating thoughts has not broken in upon the harmony of things as they are in their pristine, natural state. (pp. 133-34)

Now, to which one of these attitudes does Wordsworth adhere? In answering this question, we must . . . be prepared to find extreme complexity in the poet. With this reservation, and having in mind his characteristic and mature attitude, we can unhesitatingly say that he adhered to the rationalistic, intellectual, and anti-sentimental party. (p. 135)

In his description of the three periods of man's life Wordsworth habitually regards the first two as being most closely related to external nature and to each other, as has been noted in the previous chapter. They are both marked by a lack of self-consciousness and by absorption in sensation. They are differentiated, however, in that the child is wholly unconscious and passive, and of the child it is especially and characteristically true that

> The eye it cannot chuse but see,
> We cannot bid the ear be still;
> Our bodies feel, where'er we be,
> Against, or with our will.

All unknown to the infant, the education of the senses proceeds, and through those "blind impulses of deeper birth" and those "dumb yearnings, hidden appetites" which are characteristic of childhood, and which "must have their food" the soul is impelled towards physical and mental connections with the world of sense and experience. But there is no conscious reaction to this world, and the soul is passive to life, so far as the active soul of man can be such. (p. 136)

Youth is closely related to external nature, but in an entirely different way. At this period the soul becomes active in its relationships with the world of sense in a great variety of ways, some of which the poet describes in considerable detail. (p. 137)

[The] power of observation and [the] desire to see had one great defect in the period of youth: the poet's world was one in which all things were in disunity. He was under the domination of the senses, and of those less "pure" forms of mental activity which are related to the immediate sensations, and the only unity of his world was that which is supplied by the "eye":

> the bodily eye
> Amid my strongest workings evermore
> Was searching out the lines of difference
> As they lie hid in all external forms,
> Near or remote, minute or vast; an eye
> Which, from a tree, a stone, a withered leaf,
> To the broad ocean and the azure heavens
> Spangled with kindred multitudes of stars,
> Could find no surface where its powers might sleep;
> Which spake perpetual logic to my soul,
> And by an unrelenting agency
> Did bind my feelings even as in a chain.

But this disconnection in his world was not accepted as a matter of course, for the poet felt the need of unity. This unity he found in one department of his knowledge—in geometry, for he tells us that here he first found relief for a mind "beset with images," that is, with particular experiences. It was his first insight into the ordered world of intelligence and imagination:

> Mighty is the charm
> Of those abstractions to a mind beset
> With images, and haunted by herself,
> And specially delightful unto me
> Was that clear synthesis built up aloft
> So gracefully; even then when it appeared
> Not more than a mere plaything, or a toy
> To sense embodied: not the thing it is
> In verity, an independent world,
> Created out of pure intelligence.

This was the first means of producing unity in his disrupted world; but another more important one existed in the very constitution of his youthful mind. He tells us that when he attained maturity he discovered that he had "two natures," which he had learned "to keep in wholesome separation," the one that feels and the other that observes. This important fact

he did not know in youth; and he mingled objective and subjective, transferring his own feelings to the objects of nature and making his feelings a part of them. (pp. 138-39)

Thus the mind in its activity of youth asserts its independence and active power, rising superior to mere sense-impressions, even though the world which it creates is not a true one. (p. 140)

The transition in the life of man from youth to maturity is signalized in the sub-title of the eighth book of *The Prelude:* "Love of Nature leading to Love of Man"; and the processes by which this is accomplished are detailed in this and the succeeding books of this poem. In childhood, nature was "secondary" to his "own pursuits and animal activities, and all their trivial pleasures." Then, with youth, Nature became prized "for her own sake" and became his joy, to the exclusion of man, "until two-and-twenty summers had been told," "his hour being not yet come." (pp. 142-43)

Youth was the time,

> When the bodily eye, in every stage of life
> The most despotic of the senses, gained
> Such strength in *me* as often held my mind
> In absolute dominion.

But this thraldom was to be changed. By those abstruse operations of life, Liberty and Power were achieved by the mind through the means employed by Nature, to cause the senses each to counteract the other and themselves. Nature no longer was the prime mover of the soul. Imagination and Intellect became the guiding forces, and he now stood in nature's presence, contemplating her, and knowing himself distinct from her and above her, a sensitive being, a creative soul. Now it was that Nature, which had been destined to remain so long foremost in his affections,—that is, up to his twenty-third year,—fell back into the second place, pleased to become a handmaid to a nobler than herself: that is, to Imagination,

> which in truth,
> Is but another name for absolute power
> And clearest insight, amplitude of mind,
> And Reason in her most exalted mood.

To this conclusion he came at maturity, by "the progressive powers" of life, through which the mind is fitted to the World.

It follows logically from this that Wordsworth should hold the opinion that the love of Nature is an intermediate step, and a necessary one, if the individual is to attain the "purer mind" of maturity. Thus in maturity the emotions are intellectualized and rationalized. It follows that in Wordsworth there is not that dwelling upon the sentiments and emotions, such as we find in Rousseau; nor that worship of "The Lady Sorrow." Such false knowledge breaks up the unity of reality, and establishes "puny boundaries" and multiplies "distinctions," not in accordance with observed realities, but out of unreal knowledge which in no way corresponds to external truth. . . . Nor is there in Wordsworth any of that distrust of intellect which we find in the Rousseauists. The passages which have been so interpreted clearly show that he has in mind false knowledge, or reasonings which are based on unreal knowledge, as can be seen in his criticism of the "false secondary power by which we multiply distinctions;" for the poet explains that such false knowledge breaks up the unity of reality, and establishes "puny boundaries" and multiplies "distinctions," not in accordance with observed realities, but out of unreal knowledge which in no way corresponds to external truth. (pp. 143-45)

It follows as a matter of course that the "noble savage" of the Rousseau tradition never appears in Wordsworth. Man, as he is, not "ideal" man, is his theme. This is constantly implied; and it is rather fully developed in the third book of *The Excursion*. (p. 148)

His attitude towards the savage is that of a famous book, certainly known to him, Robertson's *History of America*, which deliberately elaborately combats Rousseau's opinion that the savage is the archetype of man. Instead, the savage is revengeful, remorseless, slothful, with his affections checked, insensible, hard of heart, superstitious, and unintellectual. . . .

Thus the function of Nature is to furnish us with the materials of a true knowledge, and the education of man is to adjust his relations to her so that she becomes the helper, and not the usurper, of a power and place which she should not possess. But she is the necessary aid to the attainment of Imagination and right reason; and the function of Imagination and right reason, when they are attained, is to view her in due proportion to the whole of life and knowledge. (p. 149)

> *Arthur Beatty, in his* William Wordsworth: His Doctrine and Art in Their Historical Relations, *second edition, The University of Wisconsin Studies in Language and Literature, 1927, 310 p.*

ALDOUS HUXLEY   (essay date 1929)

[*Known primarily for his dystopian novel* Brave New World, *Huxley was a British writer who is considered a novelist of ideas. The grandson of noted Darwinist T. H. Huxley and the brother of scientist Julian Huxley, he was interested in many fields of knowledge, and daring conceptions of science, philosophy, and religion are woven throughout his fiction. Huxley's notorious essay on Wordsworth, excerpted below, has prompted reactions by many later critics. His thesis is that Wordsworth's idea of nature as benign stems from the fact that the poet had never witnessed its harsh and inhuman aspects. Such a view, Huxley asserts, is possible only when nature has been tamed or when people are "prepared to falsify their immediate intuitions of Nature." Remarking that Wordsworth simplifies nature by interpreting it through a rationalistic and Anglican perspective, Huxley notes that Wordsworth transformed himself from a natural aesthete into a moralist, preferring to "think his gifts away." For other discussions of Wordsworth's relation to nature, see the excerpts by Raleigh (1903), Whitehead (1925), Beatty (1927), and Beach (1936).*]

In the neighborhood of latitude fifty north and for the last hundred years or thereabouts, it has been an axiom that Nature is divine and morally uplifting. For good Wordsworthians—and most serious-minded people are now Wordsworthians, either by direct inspiration or at second hand—a walk in the country is the equivalent of going to church, a tour through Westmoreland is as good as a pilgrimage to Jerusalem. To commune with the fields and waters, the woodlands and the hills, is to commune, according to our modern and Northern ideas, with the visible manifestations of the "Wisdom and Spirit of the Universe."

The Wordsworthian who exports this pantheistic worship of Nature to the tropics is liable to have his religious convictions somewhat rudely disturbed. Nature under a vertical sun, and nourished by the equatorial rains, is not at all like that chaste, mild deity who presides over the *gemütlichkeit*, the prettiness, the cosy sublimities of the Lake District. The worst that Wordsworth's goddess ever did to him was to make him hear

> Low breathings coming after me and sounds
> Of undistinguishable motion, steps
> Almost as silent as the turf they trod;

was to make him realize, in the shape of "a huge peak, black and huge," the existence of "unknown modes of being." He seems to have imagined that this was the worst nature *could* do. A few weeks in Malaya or Borneo would have undeceived him. Wandering in the hothouse darkness of the jungle, Wordsworth would not have felt so serenely certain of those "Presences of Nature," those "Souls of Lonely Places," which he was in the habit of worshipping on the shores of Windermere and Rydal. The sparse inhabitants of the equatorial forest are all believers in devils. When one has visited, in even the most superficial manner, the places where they live, it is difficult not to share their faith. The jungle is marvellous, fantastic, beautiful; but it is also terrifying, it is also profoundly sinister. (pp. 672-73)

The Wordsworthian adoration of nature has two principal defects. The first, as we have seen, is that it is only possible in a country where Nature has been nearly or quite enslaved to man. The second is that it is only possible for those who are prepared to falsify their immediate intuitions of Nature. For Nature, even in the temperate zone, is always alien and inhuman, and occasionally diabolic. . . . Wordsworth asks us to make [a] falsification of immediate experience. It is only very occasionally that he admits the existence in the world around him of those "unknown modes of being" of which our immediate intuitions of things make us so disquietingly aware. Normally what he does is to pump the dangerous Unknown out of Nature and re-fill the emptied forms of hills and woods, flowers and waters, with something more reassuringly familiar—with humanity, with Anglicanism. He will not admit that a yellow primrose is simply a yellow primrose—beautiful, but essentially strange, having its own alien life apart. He wants it to possess some sort of soul, to exist humanly, not simply flowerly. He wants the earth to be more than earthy, to be a divine person.

But the life of vegetation is radically unlike the life of man; the earth has a mode of being that is certainly not the mode of being of a person. "Let Nature be your teacher," says Wordsworth. The advice is excellent. But how strangely he himself puts it into practice! Instead of listening humbly to what the teacher says, he shuts his ears and himself dictates the lesson he desires to hear. The pupil knows better than his master; the worshipper substitutes his own oracles for those of the god. Instead of accepting the lesson as it is given to his immediate intuitions, he distorts it rationalistically into the likeness of a parson's sermon or a professorial lecture. Our direct intuitions of Nature tell us that the world is bottomlessly strange; alien, even when it is kind and beautiful; having innumerable modes of being that are not our modes; always mysteriously not personal, not conscious, not moral; often hostile and sinister; sometimes even unimaginably, because inhumanly, evil. In his youth, it would seem, Wordsworth left his direct intuitions of the world unwarped.

> . . . The sounding cataract
> Haunted me like a passion; the tall rock,
> The mountain, and the deep and gloomy wood,
> Their colours and their forms, were then to me

An appetite; a feeling and a love,
That had no need of a remoter charm,
By thought supplied, nor any interest
Unborrowed from the eye.

As the years passed, however, he began to interpret them in terms of a preconceived philosophy. Procrustes-like, he tortured his feelings and perceptions until they fitted his system. By the time he was thirty,

   . . . The immeasurable height
Of woods decaying, never to be decayed,
The stationary blasts of waterfalls . . . ,
The torrents shooting from the clear blue sky,
The rocks that muttered close upon our ears,
Black drizzling crags that spake by the wayside
As if a voice were in them, the sick sight
And giddy prospect of the raving stream,
The unfettered clouds and region of the heavens,
Tumult and peace, the darkness and the light—
Were all like workings of one mind, the features
Of the same face, blossoms upon one tree,
Characters of the great Apocalypse,
The types and symbols of eternity,
Of first, and last, and midst, and without end.

"Something far more deeply interfused" had made its appearance on the Wordsworthian scene. The god of Anglicanism had crept under the skin of things, and all the stimulatingly inhuman strangeness of Nature had become as flatly familiar as a page from a text-book of metaphysics or theology. As familiar and as safely simple. Pantheistically interpreted, our intuitions of Nature's endless varieties of impersonal mysteriousness lose all their exciting and disturbing quality. It makes the world seem delightfully cosy, if you can pretend that all the many alien things about you are really only manifestations of one person. It is fear of the labyrinthine flux and complexity of phenomena that has driven men to philosophy, to science, to theology—fear of the complex reality driving them to invent a simpler, more manageable and, therefore, consoling fiction. For simple, in comparison with the external reality of which we have direct intuitions, childishly simple is even the most elaborate and subtle system devised by the human mind. (pp. 674-77)

The change in Wordsworth's attitude towards Nature is symptomatic of his general apostasy. Beginning as what I may call a natural aesthete, he transformed himself, in the course of years, into a moralist, a thinker. He used his intellect to distort his exquisitely acute and subtle intuitions of the world, to explain away their often disquieting strangeness, to simplify them into a comfortable metaphysical unreality. Nature had endowed him with the poet's gift of seeing more than ordinarily far into the brick walls of external reality, of intuitively comprehending the character of the bricks, of feeling the quality of their being and establishing the appropriate relationship with them. But he preferred to think his gifts away. He preferred, in the interests of a preconceived religious theory, to ignore the disquieting strangeness of things, to interpret the impersonal diversity of Nature in terms of a divine, Anglican unity. He chose, in a word, to be a philosopher, comfortably at home with a man-made and, therefore, thoroughly comprehensible system, rather than a poet adventuring for adventure's sake through the mysterious world revealed by his direct and undistorted intuitions.

It is a pity that he never travelled beyond the boundaries of Europe. A voyage through the tropics would have cured him of his too easy and comfortable pantheism. A few months in the jungle would have convinced him that the diversity and utter strangeness of Nature are at least as real and significant as its intellectually discovered unity. Nor would he have felt so certain, in the damp and stifling darkness, among the leeches and the malevolently tangled rattans, of the divinely Anglican character of that fundamental unity. He would have learned once more to treat Nature naturally, as he treated it in his youth; to react to it spontaneously, loving where love was the appropriate emotion, fearing, hating, fighting, whenever Nature presented itself to his intuition as being, not merely strange, but hostile, inhumanly evil. A voyage would have taught him this. But Wordsworth never left his native continent. Europe is so well gardened that it resembles a work of art, a scientific theory, a neat metaphysical system. Man has re-created Europe in his own image. Its tamed and temperate Nature confirmed Wordsworth in his philosophizings. The poet, the devil's partisan were doomed; the angels triumphed. Alas! (pp. 682-83)

> *Aldous Huxley, "Wordsworth in the Tropics," in*
> The Yale Review, *Vol. XVIII, No. 4, June, 1929,*
> *pp. 672-83.*

T. S. ELIOT (lecture date 1932)

[*Eliot, an American-born English poet, essayist, and critic, is regarded as one of the most influential literary figures of the first half of the twentieth century. As a poet, he is closely identified with many of the qualities denoted by the term Modernism, including experimentation, formal complexity, artistic and intellectual eclecticism, and a classicist view of the artist working at an emotional distance from his or her creation. As a critic, he introduced a number of terms and concepts that strongly affected critical thought in his lifetime, such as his concept of the "objective correlative," which he defined in his* Selected Essays *as "a set of objects, a situation, a chain of events which shall be the formula of (a) particular emotion in the reader." His overall emphasis on imagery, symbolism, and meaning and his shunning of extratextual elements as aids in literary criticism helped to establish the theories of New Criticism. Eliot, who converted to the Anglican Church in 1928, stressed the importance of tradition, religion, and morality in literature. Eliot here briefly compares Wordsworth and Coleridge; his remarks, delivered on December 9, 1932, were part of the Charles Eliot Norton Lectures for 1932-33.*]

[Wordsworth] was of an opposite poetic type to Coleridge. Whether the bulk of his genuine poetic achievement is so much greater than Coleridge's as it appears, is uncertain. Whether his power and inspiration remained with him to the end is, alas, not even doubtful. But Wordsworth had no ghastly shadows at his back, no Eumenides to pursue him; or if he did, he gave no sign and took no notice; and he went droning on the still sad music of infirmity to the verge of the grave. His inspiration never having been of that sudden, fitful and terrifying kind that visited Coleridge, he was never, apparently, troubled by the consciousness of having lost it. (p. 60)

> *T. S. Eliot, "Wordsworth and Coleridge," in his*
> The Use of Poetry and the Use of Criticism: Studies
> in the Relation of Criticism to Poetry in England,
> *Cambridge, Mass.: Harvard University Press, 1933,*
> *pp. 58-77.**

JOSEPH WARREN BEACH (essay date 1936)

[*Beach was an American critic and educator who specialized in American literature and English literature of the Romantic and Victorian eras. Of his work, Beach noted: "I do not aim so much*

Dove Cottage, Grasmere, where the Wordsworths lived from 1799 to 1808.

to render final judgments and deliver certificates of greatness, which is something manifestly impossible and a trifle ridiculous, as to analyze and interpret stories and poems as expressions of our humanity and as effective works of art." Here, Beach provides a summary and analysis of Wordsworth's concept of nature. He argues that although Wordsworth conceived of nature as a system which was "the result of providential design," in his early poetry he thought of nature as an active entity independent of any theology. Beach traces the beginnings of Wordsworth's more conservative and religious attitude toward nature to his change of opinion about the French Revolution, which he had initially supported, and to the influence of Hartley. Despite Wordsworth's apparent lack of awareness that his philosophy was changing, "intuitionism" and its reference to the soul replaced "naturalism" in his later poetry, as Beach demonstrates. For other discussions of Wordsworth's relation to nature, see the excerpts by Raleigh (1903), Whitehead (1925), Beatty (1927), and Huxley (1929).]

In the poetry of Wordsworth, the pleasure taken in the forms of the natural world, especially in rural scenes, is almost invariably associated, more or less consciously, with the thought of universal nature conceived as an orderly system. The esthetic synthesis of Shaftesbury and of many eighteenth-century poets is in him continued and given greater volume, depth and variety of content. The mere imaginative pleasure taken in natural objects is reinforced by the conviction, shared by scientists and theologians alike, that nature, in the whole and in every detail,

is the result of providential design. The order of nature may be taken by men as a norm of conduct. The well-being of men is provided for within the frame of nature. With men, as with the lower animals and vegetable organisms, natural impulses tend towards the well-being of the individual, and we are guided by the admonitions of pain and pleasure, especially the latter. Virtue is more natural to us than vice, providing us with greater and more lasting gratifications. Whatever defects are found in life in a narrow view are seen to be, or may be assumed to be, contributory to the general scheme of things and therefore good in the large view. Communion with nature in the country, where her forms have not been obscured by man's artificial inventions, is therefore beneficial to man, leading him as it does to reflection on her benevolent dispositions and harmonies. Wordsworth's preference of country to town, like that of many eighteenth-century poets, is probably somewhat colored by the romantic legend of a Golden Age, in which man's heart and manners were still natural, uncorrupted by institutions and ideas which had swerved from the simplicity of nature. Wordsworth's view of the child and the peasant as beings particularly close to nature and sharing in her wisdom is analogous to the romantic view of the savage, or primitive man, though Wordsworth does not seem to have taken much stock himself in this conception of the "noble savage."

In order to represent the operations of nature as a whole, to account for her (as-it-were) purposive and rational procedure, and to keep clear of the odium and the logical difficulties inherent in pure materialism, or mechanism, Wordsworth, following the lead of many philosophers, theologians and poets, conceives of nature as a spirit, a soul of things, an active principle. This view is given countenance by the speculations of Newton and of many theological expositors of his system. (pp. 202-03)

[Perhaps] it is significant that, in the period of **"Tintern Abbey,"** in his reference to the active principle of the universe, he does not have recourse to the deity in order to explain the goodness and purposiveness of nature. And what makes it significant is the prevalent fashion, in eighteenth-century poems of this character, of referring to nature in terms strongly marked with a kind of platonic deism. It seems possible that Wordsworth was still measurably under the influence of writers like d'Holbach and Godwin, and was desirous of avoiding any suggestion of supernaturalism. He wished perhaps to attribute to nature the self-active power of a non-materialistic philosophy without referring this power to any theological source. Nature seems to have with him at this period a more autonomous character than it has with Cudworth, Shaftesbury, Thomson, or even with Newton. If Wordsworth were more of a systematic philosopher, one might almost suspect that he had for the moment espoused the doctrine of hylozoism,—a doctrine repudiated by Cudworth with such gentle disparagement and by Coleridge with the greater vehemence befitting a time in which there was more danger of its prevailing. So that Wordsworth does perhaps bear out in **"Tintern Abbey"** the popular view deprecated by Bayle that "whatever one gives to nature is so much taken from the claims of God." His nature-philosophy derived much of its force and many of its characteristic features from theology and theological metaphysics. But it was trying hard to stand by itself as an independent system. It is at any rate true that the main period of Wordsworth's nature-poetry was that in which he was least dominated by the theological doctrines of Christianity. Nature may be regarded as then in very large measure a kind of substitute religion, which we may call the religion of naturalism.

A central problem of naturalism is the place of man and man's spirit in the system of nature. It was Wordsworth's earnest desire to establish man's close kinship with the nature which he revered.

> To her fair works did Nature link
> The human soul that through me ran. . . .

In this he was greatly helped by the associationist psychology, which enabled him to realize how man's spiritual life is built up out of the materials furnished by nature—sensations, as Hartley designates them; the fair forms of nature, as they show themselves to the poet. But even Hartley must start with the soul, in which this building-up process is carried on. Whence comes the soul, and what part does *it* play in the building-up process, are problems not faced by Hartley; the soul is conceived of as a passive recipient of sensations, or as a substance to be shaped by sensations and their derivative ideas. This appears to have been pretty much the situation with Wordsworth at first. But gradually the active part played by a man's own soul, or his creative faculty, the imagination, in shaping the materials offered by the senses, came to be more and more stressed by him.

Many factors doubtless contributed to bring about this radical change of emphasis in Wordsworth's thinking. . . . The mere influence of Coleridge must be given a major place in the picture. The gradual reaction of Wordsworth against the ideals of the French Revolution, and against all things French, including the religion of reason, would be a factor of great and incalculable importance. This threw him back, in politics, religion and social philosophy, upon views less congenial with the naturalism which he had once espoused. His passion for English scenery lent a glamour to the time-hallowed institutions there enshrined. The very deepening of his patriotism tended to endear to him the national church and restore him more and more to religious orthodoxy. The influence of rationalists and anti-clericals like Godwin gave way to that of theological writers of a traditional stamp. The entire complex of his opinions and emotional reactions came to work against the assumptions of naturalism, just as with Swinburne and Meredith they worked in favor of them. . . . He naturally came to distrust the inspirations of "nature," and to rely more and more on the prescriptive admonitions of Duty as voiced by religion. "Me this unchartered freedom tires." During the long period of disenchantment, when he had "given up moral questions in despair," he was compelled to a very vigorous effort of "compensation," sublimation and reconstruction of faith. He was led to have more reliance on various "transcendental" faculties,—on the heart, the intuition, the "higher reason," or on religious faith. It has been variously suggested that, under these circumstances, he was influenced by the philosophy of Rousseau, of Spinoza, of Kant; and it is obvious that he was strongly influenced by the element of "mysticism" which was never absent from Christian theology, even in the eighteenth century.

One result of this change of attitude was the increasing emphasis laid on the creative activity of the poetic imagination. And this brought to the fore a problem which he had scantily provided for in his earlier thinking—the origin of the human soul, of which the imagination is a constituent faculty. However much he might credit nature with a major part in the *education* of the spirit, he had not ruled out the important circumstance that the child comes into existence already possessed of a spirit susceptible of being educated. The soul may be the nursling of nature, its ward and pupil; but it is not nature's child, but the child of God, "who is our home."

Thus Wordsworth, like so many reflective minds, like some of the greatest of professional philosophers, is a Janus-thinker, facing in two opposite directions. In his naturalist phase, he looks towards the scientific rationalism associated with the names of Newton and Locke. In his "transcendental" phase he looks towards religious intuitionism. His intuitionism serves as a check on his naturalism, and in the end largely replaces it. At his peak of poetic inspiration, represented by **"Tintern Abbey,"** the two tendencies were maintained in equilibrium, and together gave its force to the romantic concept of nature. Ambiguous as this concept may have been—nay, by virtue of its very ambiguity—it was for Wordsworth a fairy wand by which he transformed "the common countenance of earth and sky" into a spiritual paradise, and the children of earth to spirits "trailing clouds of glory." (pp. 204-07)

Wordsworth is, of all English poets, the one who gave the most impressive and the most emotionally satisfying account of man's relation to universal nature. This is partly due to his peculiar imaginative endowments; and partly to the fact that his poetry held in solution more of the philosophic ideas implied in the "worship of nature" than that of any other English poet, or held them more perfectly in solution.

It is probable that Wordsworth was not fully conscious how many ideas derived from religion and science, as well as from romantic tradition, underlay and gave color to his concept of nature. He was probably not aware of all the metaphysical considerations involved in his view of nature as a spirit or active principle; of the range of considerations involved in his "naturalism," or the precise reasons for his drift away from naturalism. Indeed, it is obvious both in *The Prelude* and *The Excursion* that he was scarcely aware of the radical change of thought involved in the marked, if gradual, change of emphasis in his poetry, by which nature yielded more and more to the constructions of orthodox religion. In the period of his writing when it is most stimulating and inspiring, this is doubtless partly due to the very fact that the intellectual ideas involved are implicit rather than explicit. They are not something that must be labored for and defended by an arduous exercise of the mind. They are something inherited, taken for granted, an element which he took in with the very air he breathed. So that, while his poetry belongs so largely to the category of the reflective, it has, at its best, the sureness, grace and buoyancy of movements and expressions that are instinctive rather than reasoned. (p. 208)

> *Joseph Warren Beach, "Nature in Wordsworth: Summary," in his* The Concept of Nature in Nineteenth-Century English Poetry, *1936. Reprint by Russell & Russell, 1966, pp. 202-08.*

F. R. LEAVIS (essay date 1936)

[*An influential English critic and teacher, Leavis articulated his views in his lectures, in his many critical works, and in* Scrutiny, *a quarterly which he co-founded and edited from 1932 to 1953. His methodology combines close textual analysis, predominantly moral and social concerns, and emphasis on the development of "the individual sensibility." Leavis believed that the artist should strive to eliminate "ego-centered distortion and all impure motives" in order to be able to explore the proper place of persons in society. Although his advocacy of a cultural elite and the occasional vagueness of his moral assumptions were sometimes criticized, his writings remain an important, if controversial, force in literary criticism. Leavis here stresses that the complexity of Wordsworth's philosophy cannot be easily reduced to a simple paraphrase. His poetry and thought were inextricable and they were able "to command a certain kind of attention . . . and permit no other." Leavis also discusses the issues of Wordsworth's naturalism and his "essential sanity and normality." The critic contends that Wordsworth withdrew from what was painful and difficult in life and assumed a stance of "equipoise." Leavis points out that, "in the pursuit of formal orthodoxy he freely falsified and blunted the record of experience."*]

Wordsworth's greatness and its nature seem to be, in a general way, pretty justly recognized in current acceptance, the established habit of many years. Clear critical recognition, however, explicit in critical statement, is another matter, and those who really read him to-day—who read him as they read contemporary literature—will agree that, in spite of the number of distinguished critics who have written on him, satisfactory statement is still something to be attempted. And to attempt it with any measure of success would be to revalue Wordsworth, to achieve a clearer insight and a fresh realization.

There is—a time-honoured critical blur or indecision—the question of Wordsworth's 'thought.' (p. 154)

Wordsworth's 'philosophy' certainly appears, as such, to invite discussion, and there is a general belief that we all know, or could know by re-reading *The Prelude,* what his doctrines concerning the growth of the mind and relation of Man to nature are. His philosophic verse has a convincingly expository tone

and manner, and it is difficult not to believe, after reading, say, Book II of *The Prelude,* that one has been reading a paraphrasable argument—difficult not to believe, though the paraphrase, if resolutely attempted, would turn out to be impossible. Few readers, it would seem, have ever made the attempt, and, in fact, to make it resolutely is the real difficulty—if 'difficulty' can describe the effect of a subtle, pervasive and almost irresistible dissuasion from effort.

This, at any rate, describes fairly the working of Wordsworth's philosophic verse. His triumph is to command the kind of attention he requires and to permit no other. (pp. 155-56)

[Wordsworth's essential habit is to produce] the mood, feeling or experience and at the same time [to appear] to be giving an explanation of it. The expository effect sorts well with—blends into—the characteristic meditative gravity of the emotional presentment ('emotion recollected in tranquillity'), and in the key passages, where significance seems specially to reside, the convincing success of the poetry covers the argument: it is only by the most resolute and sustained effort (once it occurs to one that effort is needed) that one can pay to the argument, as such, the attention it appears to have invited and satisfied. (p. 159)

Even if there were not so much poetry to hold the mind in a subtly incompatible mode of attention, it would still be difficult to continue attending to the philosophic argument, because of the way in which the verse, evenly meditative in tone and movement, goes on and on, without dialectical suspense and crisis or rise and fall. By an innocently insidious trick Wordsworth, in this calm ruminative progression, will appear to be preoccupied with a scrupulous nicety of statement, with a judicial weighing of alternative possibilities, while actually making it more difficult to check the argument from which he will emerge, as it were inevitably, with a far from inevitable conclusion. (p. 162)

He had, if not a philosophy, a wisdom to communicate . . . . It may be said, fairly, that Wordsworth went on tinkering with *The Prelude* through his life instead of completing the great 'philosophic poem' [*The Recluse*] because, as he had in the end tacitly to recognize, his resources weren't adequate to the ambition—he very obviously hadn't enough material. But it must also be said that in letting the ambition lapse he was equally recognizing its superfluity: his real business was achieved. His wisdom is sufficiently presented in the body of his living work.

What he had for presentment was a type and a standard of human normality, a way of life; his preoccupation with sanity and spontaneity working at a level and in a spirit that it seems appropriate to call religious. His philosophizing (in the sense of the Hartleian studies and applications) had not the value he meant it to have; but it is an expression of his intense moral seriousness and a mode of the essential discipline of contemplation that gave consistency and stability to his experience. Wordsworth, we know, is the 'poet of Nature,' and the associations of the term 'Nature' here are unfortunate, suggesting as it does a vaguely pantheistic religion-substitute. . . . But Wordsworth himself, in the famous passage that, 'taken from the conclusion of the first book of *The Recluse,*' he offers 'as a kind of **"Prospectus"** of the design and scope of the whole Poem,' proposes something decidedly different when he stresses 'the Mind of Man' as

> My haunt, and the main region of my song.

And Wordsworth here, as a matter of fact, is critically justified.

Creative power in him, as in most great poets, was accompanied by a high degree of critical consciousness in the use of it. His critical writings give a good view of his creative preoccupations. . . . (pp. 163-65)

Wordsworth's preoccupation was with a distinctively human naturalness, with sanity and spiritual health, and his interest in mountains was subsidiary. His mode of preoccupation, it is true, was that of a mind intent always upon ultimate sanctions, and upon the living connexions between man and the extra-human universe. . . . (p. 165)

[One] of the most remarkable facts about Wordsworth's poetry is the virtual absence from it of . . . [erotic] associations and suggestions, and it is this absence that Shelley, when he calls Wordsworth 'cold,' is remarking upon. . . . (p. 168)

The absence no doubt constitutes a limitation, a restriction of interest; but it constitutes at the same time an aspect of Wordsworth's importance. (p. 169)

Spontaneity, . . . as Wordsworth seeks it, involves no cult of the instinctive and primitive at the expense of the rationalized and civilized; it is the spontaneity supervening upon complex development, a spontaneity engaging an advanced and delicate organization. He stands for a distinctly human naturalness; one, that is, consummating a discipline, moral and other. A poet who can bring home to us the possibility of such a naturalness should to-day be found important. In Wordsworth's poetry the possibility is offered us realized—realized in a mode central and compelling enough to enforce the bearing of poetry upon life, the significance of this poetry for actual living. The absence both of the specifically sexual in any recognizable form and of any sign of repression serves to emphasize this significance, the significance of this achieved naturalness, spontaneous, and yet the expression of an order and the product of an emotional and moral training.

No one should, after what has been said, find it necessary to impute to the critic at this point, or to suppose him to be applauding in Wordsworth, a puritanic warp. Wordsworth was, on the showing of his poetry and everything else, normally and robustly human. The selectiveness and the habit of decorum involved in 'recollection in tranquillity' were normal and, in a wholly laudatory sense of the word, conventional; that is, so endorsed by common usage as to be natural. The poetic process engaged an organization that had, by his own account, been determined by an upbringing in a congenial social environment, with its wholesome simple pieties and the traditional sanity of its moral culture, which to him were nature. He may have been a 'Romantic,' but it would be misleading to think of him as an individualist. (pp. 170-71)

Wordsworth is often spoken of as a 'mystic,' and the current valuation would appear to rest his greatness largely upon the 'visionary moments' and 'spots of time.' Wordsworth himself undoubtedly valued the 'visionary' element in his experience very highly, and it is important to determine what significance he attributes to it. (p. 173)

If these 'moments' have any significance for the critic (whose business it is to define the significance of Wordsworth's poetry), it will be established, not by dwelling upon or in them, in the hope of exploring something that lies hidden in or behind their vagueness, but by holding firmly on to that sober verse in which they are presented. (p. 174)

Wordsworth's roots were deep in the eighteenth century. To say this is to lay the stress again—where it ought to rest—on his essential sanity and normality.

But though he is so surely and centrally poised, the sureness had nothing of complacency about it. It rests consciously over unsounded depths and among mysteries, itself a mystery. This recognition has its value in the greater validity of the poise—in a kind of sanction resulting. So, too, Wordsworth's firm hold upon the world of common perception is the more notable in one who knows of 'fallings from us, vanishings, blank misgivings' ('when the light of sense goes out'), and is capable of recording such moments as when

> I forgot,
> That I had bodily eyes, and what I saw
> Appear'd like something in myself, a dream,
> A prospect in my mind.
>
> (pp. 174-75)

[It] is now time to qualify the present account of [Wordsworth], as it stands now, by taking note of . . . [opposing criticism]. Does not, for instance, the formula, 'recollection in tranquillity,' apply to Wordsworth's poetry with a limiting effect that has as yet not been recognized? Is the tranquillity of this wisdom really at all close to any 'spontaneous overflow of powerful feelings'? Are the feelings, as recollected, so very powerful?

It has to be admitted that the present of this poetry is, for the most part, decidedly tranquil and that the emotion—anything in the nature of strong excitement or disturbance—seems to belong decidedly to the past. If, as might be said, the strength of the poetry is that it brings maturity and youth into relation, the weakness is that the experience from which it draws life is confined mainly to youth, and lies at a distance. What, an intelligent contemporary reader might have asked at the creative period, will happen as youth recedes? What did happen we know, in any case, and the fact of the decline may reasonably be held to have a bearing on the due estimate of Wordsworth's wisdom. (p. 176)

[The description of the Wanderer in *The Excursion*] is, fairly obviously, very much in the nature of an idealized self-portrait. If Wordsworth, even when well embarked on *The Excursion,* was not quite this, this clearly is what he would have liked to be. That he should have wished to be this is significant. That he should have needed to wish it is the great difference between himself and the Wanderer. For Wordsworth's course had not been steady; he sought the Wanderer's 'equipoise' just because of the 'piteous revolutions' and the 'wild varieties of joy and grief' that he had so disturbingly known. The Wanderer could not have written Wordsworth's poetry; it emerges out of Wordsworth's urgent personal problem; it is the answer to the question: 'How, in a world that has shown itself to be like this, is it possible to go on living?'

Behind, then, the impersonality of Wordsworth's wisdom there is an immediately personal urgency. Impelling him back to childhood and youth—to their recovery in a present of tranquil seclusion—there are the emotional storms and disasters of the intervening period, and these are also implicitly remembered, if not 'recollected,' in the tranquillity of his best poetry. In so far as his eyes may fairly be said to 'avert their ken from half of human fate,' extremely painful awareness of this half is his excuse. For if his problem was personal, it was not selfishly so, not merely self-regarding; and it is also a general one: if (and how shall they not?) the sensitive and imaginative freely let their 'hearts lie open' to the suffering of the world, how are they to retain any health or faith for living? Conflicting duties seem to be imposed (for it is no mere blind instinct of self-preservation that is in question). Wordsworth is not one of the few great tragic artists, but probably not many readers will care to censure him for weakness or cowardice. His heart was far from 'unoccupied by sorrow of its own,' and his sense of responsibility for human distress and his generously active sympathies had involved him in emotional disasters that threatened his hold on life. A disciplined limiting of contemplation to the endurable, and, consequently, a withdrawal to a reassuring environment, became terrible necessities for him.

It is significant that (whatever reason Wordsworth may have had for putting it there) the story of Margaret should also, following, as it does, close upon the description of the Wanderer, appear in Book I of **The Excursion**. It seems to me the finest thing that Wordsworth wrote, and it is certainly the most disturbingly poignant. The poignancy assures us with great force that the Wanderer, for all his familiarity with the Preface to the **Lyrical Ballads,** is not Wordsworth—not, at any rate, the poet. . . . (pp. 178-79)

The difficulty does not merely appear in the poignancy of the poetry, which contrasts so with the surrounding verse; it gets its implicit comment in the byplay between Wordsworth and the Wanderer. At a painful point in the story 'the Wanderer paused' . . . :

> 'Why should we thus, with an untoward mind,
> And in the weakness of humanity,
> From natural wisdom turn our hearts away;
> To natural comfort shut our eyes and ears;
> And, feeding on disquiet, thus disturb
> The calm of nature with our restless thoughts?'

Wordsworth gladly acquiesced:

> That simple tale
> Passed from my mind like a forgotten sound.

But it refused to be dismissed; it rose insistently up through the distracting idle talk:

> In my own despite
> I thought of that poor Woman as of one
> Whom I had known and loved.

No doubt the particular memory of Annette asserts itself here, but that recognition (or guess) makes it all the more important to give due weight to the corrective hint thrown out by the Wanderer a little later:

> ''Tis a common tale,
> An ordinary sorrow of man's life . . .'

—Wordsworth at this date cannot easily afford to suffer with those whom he sees suffer.

That is very apparent in the way 'that Woman's sufferings' (which had 'seemed present') are, at the end of the story, distanced. (pp. 179-80)

[In "**Michael**" Wordsworth] has no need to withdraw his mind from the theme to a present 'image of tranquillity.' The things of which he speaks never 'seem present' in this story; they are seen always as belonging, in their moving dignity, to the past. 'Recollection' holds them at such a distance that serenity, for all the pathos, never falters; and an idealizing process, making subtle use of the mountain background, gives to 'human suffering' a reconciling grandeur. "**Michael**," of course, is only

one poem (and an exceptionally fine one), but the implied representative significance of this comparison with "**Margaret**" is justly implied. When in the characteristic good poetry of Wordsworth painful things are dealt with, we find them presented in modes, more and less subtle, that are fairly intimated by his own phrase (the context of which is very relevant):

> Remov'd and to a distance that was fit.

In "**Michael**" Wordsworth is very much more like the Wanderer. What, the contemporary reader already invoked may be imagined as asking, will be the next phase in the development? What will happen as youth, where lie the emotional sources of his poetry—'the hiding-places of my power'—and young manhood, which, in the way suggested, provides the creative pressure and incitement, recede further and further into the past, and the 'equipoise' becomes a settled habit? (pp. 181-82)

The Wordsworth who in the "**Ode to Duty**" spoke of the 'genial sense of youth' as something he happily surrendered had seen the hiding-places of his power close. The 'equipoise' had lost its vitality; the exquisitely fine and sensitive organization of the poet no longer informed and controlled his pen. The energy of the new patriotic moral interests, far from bringing the poet new life, took the place of creative sensibility, and confirmed and ensured its loss.

In fact, the new power belongs, it might be said, not to the 'hiding-places'—it has no connexion with them—but to the public platform (a metaphor applying obviously to the patriotic development, with which, it should be noted, the religious is not accidentally associated): the public voice is a substitute for the inner voice, and engenders an insensitiveness to this—to its remembered (or, at least, to its recorded) burden and tone. For the sentiments and attitudes of the patriotic and Anglican Wordsworth do not come as the intimately and particularly realized experience of an unusually and finely conscious individual; they are external, general and conventional; their quality is that of the medium they are proffered in, which is insensitively Miltonic, a medium not felt into from within as something at the nerve-tips, but handled from outside. This is to question, not their sincerity, but their value and interest; their representativeness is not of the important kind. Their relation to poetry may be gathered from the process to which, at their dictation, Wordsworth subjected **The Prelude:** in the pursuit of formal orthodoxy he freely falsified and blunted the record of experience. (pp. 183-84)

F. R. Leavis, "Wordsworth," in his Revaluation:
Tradition & Development in English Poetry, *Chatto
& Windus, 1936, pp. 154-202.*

RAYMOND DEXTER HAVENS (essay date 1941)

[In this excerpt from his full-length study of Wordsworth's philosophy, Havens discusses his style with particular attention to what he terms his "prolixity and matter-of-factness." Though he determines that a tendency to extraneous detail was natural for Wordsworth, Havens suggests that the habit of recollection in tranquility helped him to control it. Havens adds that opposed to Wordsworth's tendency toward prolixity were his "love of romance" and rootedness in the real world, which were equally important elements of his style. Though Wordsworth valued the imagination, according to the critic, he treated it as "a servant of truth and reason." To Havens, the combination of such disparate elements in Wordsworth's poetry was "like the two wings of a great kite which requires a heavy tail to keep it steady, head up, and free from the danger of plunging suddenly to earth." Other critics who write about Wordsworth's philosophical doc-

trine include Stephen (1876), Stallknecht (1958), Perkins (1964), and Langbaum (1977).]

Hazlitt records that on a memorable evening walk to Nether Stowey "as we passed through echoing grove, by fairy stream or waterfall, gleaming in the summer moonlight" Coleridge "lamented that Wordsworth was not prone enough to believe in the traditional superstitions of the place, and that there was a something corporeal, a *matter-of-fact-ness*, a clinging to the palpable, or often to the petty, in his poetry, in consequence." We have Coleridge's own words to a similar effect in a letter to Southey of July 29, 1802, which speaks of "a daring humbleness of language and versification [in Wordsworth's poems], and a strict adherence to matter of fact, even to prolixity, that startled me." Coleridge presumably had in mind not only the passage from *The Excursion* which he cited but **"Goody Blake," "Simon Lee," "The Idiot Boy," "Strange fits of passion,"** the Prologue and some lines about the ass in *Peter Bell*, and such verses as

> I've measured it from side to side:
> 'Tis three feet long, and two feet wide

in **"The Thorn."** This prolix, anxious adherence to reality, this dwelling upon unessential details, is ludicrously apparent in the titles of some of the short pieces: **"Lines Left upon a Seat in a Yew-tree, which stands near the lake of Esthwaite, on a desolate part of the shore, commanding a beautiful prospect," "Inscription, Written at the Request of Sir George Beaumont, Bart., and in his Name, for an Urn, Placed by him at the Termination of a Newly-planted Avenue, in the same Grounds."** Nor is it limited to Wordsworth's early work; it is found in *The Recluse*, I. i, *The Excursion, The Prelude,* the Fenwick notes,—indeed everywhere.

The early manuscripts of *The Prelude* suggest that if we had more first drafts we should find much more of this sort of thing. In the A text [1805], for example, the great passage about Newton's statue contains the distressing line, "Could see, right opposite, a few yards off" . . . ; the memorable picture of the sunrise which left Wordsworth "a dedicated Spirit" was at first introduced with the explanation,

> Two miles I had to walk along the fields
> Before I reached my home; . . .

and the account of the "borrowed" boat originally began with these irrelevancies:

> I went alone into a Shepherd's Boat,
> A Skiff that to a Willow tree was tied
> Within a rocky Cave, its usual home.
> 'Twas by the shores of Patterdale, a Vale
> Wherein I was a Stranger, thither come
> A School-boy Traveller, at the Holidays.
> Forth rambled from the Village Inn alone
> No sooner had I sight of this small Skiff,
> Discover'd thus by unexpected chance,
> Than I unloos'd her tether and embark'd. . . .

The superb description of the Simplon Pass is followed, in the earliest version, by

> That night our lodging was an Alpine House,
> An Inn, or Hospital, as they are nam'd,
> Standing in that same valley by itself.

Ultimately this was reduced to

> That night our lodging was a house that stood
> Alone within the valley. . . .

The blue chasm seen in the "vision" from Snowdon was at first located as "not distant more perchance than half a mile"; later this became "at distance not the third part of a mile"; then "not twice the measure of an arrow's flight"; and finally "not distant". . . . It took the poet nearly fifty years to realize that the facts mentioned in the title, **"Lines written at a small distance from my house, and sent by my little boy to the person to whom they are addressed,"** meant nothing to the reader; that there was no loss and much gain in calling the poem simply **"To my Sister."** Likewise he did not at first see that if the purpose of a poem is to commemorate the devotion of a dog to her dead master, it need not include a description of the deceased, of how he met his death, and all the ghastly particulars as to the condition in which the body was found. As first written, **"Resolution and Independence"** contained the following pedestrian stanza:

> He wore a Cloak the same as women wear
> As one whose blood did needful comfort lack;
> His face look'd pale as if it had grown fair;
> And, furthermore he had upon his back,
> Beneath his cloak, a round and bulky Pack;
> A load of wool or raiment as might seem,
> That on his shoulders lay as if it clave to him.

These needless and ineffectual details are due, as is clear from Dorothy's Journal of October 3, 1800, to the attempt to describe the leech-gatherer just as he appeared; that is, they furnish one more illustration of how hard it was for Wordsworth to free himself from the actual.

To some extent, then, the prolixity and matter-of-factness of Wordsworth's poetry is due to the difficulty its author found in distinguishing the essential from the accidental. So strong and definite were his sense impressions that in his youth "nor day nor night, evening or morn, was free From . . . [their] oppression," and his memory of such impressions was equally remarkable, not alone in its vividness but in its tenacity of details. Of *An Evening Walk,* composed in his eighteenth and nineteenth years, he remarked: "There is not an image in it which I have not observed; and, now in my seventy-third year, I recollect the time and place where most of them were noticed." Accordingly the artist in him had to be on guard against the tyranny of memory. Furthermore the material he dealt with was so simple and quiet—incidents that seem commonplace and "souls that appear to have no depth at all To careless eyes"—that he found it hard to say which particulars helped to make his account authentic and vital and which weighed it down, which clarified his meaning and which obscured it. The distinction was the more difficult because Wordsworth was an innovator, because *all* of his work seemed to most of his contemporaries tedious and meaningless. Hence, although much of the labor he expended in composing and revising his poems went to the elimination of the irrelevant, the unduly factual, and the needlessly explanatory, it is not strange that his surgery was by no means so drastic as it should have been. (pp. 11-15)

The truth is that matter-of-factness, practical sense, thrift, prolix explanation, and attention to prosaic detail were as truly Wordsworth as the vision of childhood trailing clouds of glory or responsiveness to the dancing of the daffodils and the song of the Solitary Reaper. It was in the man as well as in the poetry that Coleridge lamented a deficiency. (p. 16)

[Irrelevant] and pedestrian details often remain through all revisions. A distressing instance is "that rural castle, name now slipped From my remembrance"; the name did not matter but, as Wordsworth had tried to recall it and had failed, he felt bound to record the fact however awkwardly he expressed it. So it is with the lines in which the machinery of the poem creaks:

> The song would speak, . . .

> We need not linger o'er the ensuing time,
> But let me add at once that, . . .

> The circumstances here I will relate
> Even as they were, . . .

> 'Twould be a waste of labour to detail
> The rambling studies of a truant Youth,
> Which further may be easily divin'd,
> What, and what kind they were. My inner knowledge,
> (This barely will I note) was . . . . . .

Wordsworth's first volume was marked by unusually exact observation, and at the beginning of his great period the influence of Dorothy combined with his reaction from the abstract theorizing into which Paine, Godwin, and the French radical philosophers had led him resulted in an absorption in the concrete, the immediate, and the contemporary—the phenomena of nature and the daily life of his humble neighbors—which found expression in **"The Idiot Boy," "Anecdote for Fathers," "Simon Lee," "A Night-Piece," "A whirl-blast from behind the hill,"** and the like. Although some of these are excellent, some approach if they do not reach the trivial, and in not a few the interest is psychological or sociological rather than poetic. Here at least lay a danger, a danger that was more acute in *The Prelude,* where the personal might easily obscure the universal and where the episodes, if care were not taken, might become merely events in the life of an individual rather than illustrations of the development of The Poet. Besides, the incidents recorded in *The Prelude* are commonly little things, undramatic and outwardly unimportant, which must be told vividly—that is in detail—if they are to be felt but from which explanations, unessential or merely personal facts—whatever does not contribute to a vivid presentation of the universally significant—must be rigorously excluded. That Wordsworth always made such exclusion cannot be maintained. Often he forgot his ultimate purpose and told a story for its own sake, or one thing led on to another until he was astray, or he mistook the personal for the essential, or, most often, his matter-of-factness, his inability to escape the minutiae of actuality hampered him.

From this danger his poetry would have suffered more severely had it not been derived chiefly from "emotion recollected in tranquillity." The stream of time acted as other streams do, sifting out small things and allowing them to drop from sight. (pp. 17-18)

But all this is only half the story. In Wordsworth's personality, in his literary tastes, and in his poetry, there were forces strongly opposed to matter-of-factness. For there was in him and there appears in his work a deep love of romance,—not the superficial pseudo-romanticism of grave-yard poets and Gothic novelists, but a fondness for "daring feat" and "enterprize forlorn," for travellers' tales of distant lands with strange fauna and flora, for "old, unhappy, far-off things, And battles long ago." He exclaimed:

> Avaunt this oeconomic rage!
> What would it bring?—an iron age,
> When Fact with heartless search explored
> Shall be Imagination's Lord,

> And sway with absolute controul
> The god-like Functions of the Soul.
>   **("To the Utilitarians,")** . . .

He referred to the

> wish for something loftier, more adorned,
> Than is the common aspect, daily garb,
> Of human life

as "that most noble attribute of man"; he was pleased with the greeting, "What, you are stepping westward?" as "a sound Of something without place or bound"; he was glad that the Yarrow of his imagination was not to be supplanted by sight of the actual stream; and he emphasized the blind highland boy's delight in his perilous voyage and his disappointment at being rescued:

> So all his dreams—that inward light
> With which his soul had shone so bright—
> All vanished;—'twas a heartfelt cross
> To him, a heavy, bitter loss,
>   As he had ever known.

Well might Wordsworth write:

> Beauty . . . waits upon my steps;
> Pitches her tents before me as I move,
> An hourly neighbour,
>   (*Recluse,* "Prospectus," . . .)

for he saw beauty, nobility, romance at every hand: in the old and poor as in the young and gay, in beggars and city streets as in stars and mountains. (pp. 18-20)

True, he renounced "the dragon's wing, the magic ring," and asserted that "the common growth of mother-earth" sufficed him, but it was only at times that he felt thus. There is abundant and varied evidence that he craved more, that only the literature which gives more, such as the poetry of Spenser and Milton, satisfied him. . . . [In] speaking of **"Lucy Gray"** he said:

> The way in which the incident was treated, and
> the spiritualising of the character, might furnish
> hints for contrasting the imaginative influences,
> which I have endeavoured to throw over common life, with Crabbe's matter-of-fact style of
> handling subjects of the same kind.

These are not the words of a realist but of one who asserted his "unwillingness to submit the poetic spirit to the chains of fact and real circumstance," who affirmed the true antithesis of poetry to be, not prose but "Matter of Fact, or Science," who held that in verse "forms and substances"

> Present themselves as objects recognised,
> In flashes, and with glory not their own. . . .

Indeed, few poets have felt more strongly than Wordsworth did that their art required the transformation of reality by the creative imagination, few have differentiated it more clearly from photography or the making of phonograph discs.

Yet there can be no question as to Wordsworth's love of the real. "All the little incidents of the neighbourhood were to him important." The "Beauty" which, he declared, "waits upon my steps. . . . An hourly neighbour" was "a living Presence of the earth, Surpassing the most fair ideal Forms." The Cumberland dalesman, "intent on little but substantial needs," he found

> Far more of an imaginative form
> Then the gay Corin of the groves, who lives
> For his own fancies, . . .

and undoubtedly he expressed his own feelings in the words of the Solitary:

> How rich in animation and delight,
> How bountiful these elements—compared
> With aught, as more desirable and fair,
> Devised by fancy for the golden age;
> Or the perpetual warbling that prevails
> In Arcady, beneath unaltered skies.
>
> (*Excursion* . . .)
> (pp. 20-21)

So exigent a veracity, such an insistence on accuracy of detail, on flesh and blood, such a preference for "even coarse nature" over what is "too ideal" is almost the antipodes of the usual conception of the poetic. Realism is often thought the negation of imagination, and imagination an escape from realism. "Natural objects," wrote Blake, "always did & now do weaken, deaden & obliterate Imagination in me." Not so Wordsworth; for him natural objects were the ladder on which he ascended into the heavens, into the heaven of heavens. Even in those "visitings Of awful promise," the supreme moments of the mystic experience, although the light of sense goes out it does so "in flashes that have shewn to us The invisible world." . . . A great part of his poetry springs from actual occurrences, and in many cases he is able to tell how and where he first observed the phenomena that gave rise to certain images, the incidents (and the circumstances leading up to them) which suggested certain poems. Imaginative transformation is all-important but, as the imagination is not a playful will o' the wisp but the servant of truth and reason, the materials with which it works must be true, that is, they must rest upon careful observation and sound reflection. Such materials, we should remember, are not limited to the phenomena of external nature but include "the Mind of Man—. . . the main region of my song." Wordsworth's early work reveals a marked interest in human psychology and much of that produced in his great decade turns on the mystery of man and the hiding places of his power; yet whether he treats of man or of nature he has his eye on the object. The leech-gatherer and the small celandine, though not presented as a camera would show them, have been clearly seen and attentively considered. The "plastic power" which abode with the poet was, he explains, "subservient strictly to external things With which it communed." Such lines as the following reveal not merely a strong imagination but a love of reality that has inspired close observation:

> And, afterwards, the wind and sleety rain,
> And all the business of the elements,
> The single sheep, and the one blasted tree,
> And the bleak music from that old stone wall,
> The noise of wood and water, and the mist
> That on the line of each of those two roads
> Advanced in such indisputable shapes;
> All these were kindred spectacles and sounds
> To which I oft repaired. . . .

If, then, Wordsworth's eye was often too closely fixed on its object and his feet were frequently too securely fastened to the ground, these were but the defects of the excellences to which his poetry owed its freedom from the conventional and the

vague, its truth, and much of its substance. His unusual sensitiveness to natural beauty and his powerful imagination were like the two wings of a great kite which requires a heavy tail to keep it steady, head up, and free from the danger of plunging suddenly to earth. (pp. 22-3)

The imaginative transmutation of reality rests upon observation and does not consist in throwing a cloud of idealism around objects vaguely seen and imperfectly understood. The poetry of Shelley, great as it is, suffers from the failure to observe either man or nature closely. On the other hand, much of Wordsworth's best work—**"Michael," "Resolution and Independence," "Peele Castle," "The Cock is crowing,"** many of the sonnets, the first book of *The Excursion,* and a great part of *The Prelude*—not only rests upon careful observation but is the flowering of that matter-of-factness, that pre-occupation with reality, which, when unfertilized by the imagination and unpruned by the critical faculty, reduces poetry to the commonplace, the pedestrian, or even the absurd. (p. 25)

> *Raymond Dexter Havens, in his* The Mind of a Poet: A Study of Wordsworth's Thought with Particular Reference to "The Prelude," *The Johns Hopkins University Press, 1941, 670 p.*

G. WILSON KNIGHT   (essay date 1941)

[*A Canadian literary critic, Knight is one of the most influential Shakespearean scholars of the twentieth century. In helping to shape a new interpretive approach to Shakespeare's work, Knight promoted a greater appreciation of many of the plays. His criticism most often focuses on interpreting patterns of imagery and symbolism in literary works. In this excerpt from his discussion of Wordsworth's "Intimations" ode, Knight concentrates on his*

A portrait of Wordsworth in 1806.

The **"Ode on Intimations of Immortality"** is probably Wordsworth's most finally satisfying human work. Here he houses many favourite intuitions in majestic light; marries his dearest inward feelings to a highly charged impressionism, pastoral and royalistic; and faces the intoxication of a sunlight creation. It is his only poem at once human, happy, and powerful. The **"Ode"** stands the test of his description of great poetry in *The Prelude;* in it that 'host of *shadowy* things' ('shadow' is an important word in Coleridge too) finds its proper home; all mysterious substances are suffused with 'light divine', the 'turnings intricate of verse', a phrase peculiarly apt to this poem, aiding poetic mastery. Though the subject still be childhood, the poem is more technically erotic than most, a symbolic union with the child-symbol performing a central and most important resolution of dynamic immediacy: poetic excitement locked imperishably to live as a tranquil yet pulsing memorial of creative joy. Technical and formal elaboration, whether in symbolism or rhyme-scheme, forces the poet into an especially condensed precision. Art is born from a jerking of consciousness outside and above itself, throwing responsibility on to a higher centre, and technical strictures are the medium through which this other domination is conjured into existence. That sense of young joy so often mentioned in *The Prelude* now very subtly possesses the reader too; we are inside Wordsworth's own ecstasy. In *The Prelude* a very personal feeling tends, except in the great numinous passages, to suffuse bare narration of objective fact. Though the central experience of *The Prelude* is directly included, its method is here diametrically reversed: a subjective experience is, through a clear technique, perfectly objectified.

The poem is far from easy. The term 'immortality' means 'death negated': it is a dramatic word and may be equated with life itself provided some recognition of death is incorporated. Such recognition our ode gives, celebrating life victorious over death. In poetic study we must never limit too closely a vast unknowable which the poem itself is created to define. So, though Wordsworth's **"Ode,"** like Shakespeare's *Pericles* or Shelley's *Prometheus,* is a vision of immortality or life victorious, it need have nothing to say about life-after-death. It is rather a vision of essential, all-conquering, life. The symbols which carry this over to us are flowers, springtime joy, bird music, all young life, and, pre-eminently, the child.

The 'spring' references need not be emphasized: they are clear and obvious. But the 'child' is so important that I note first its continual presence in the poem. 'Early childhood' occurs in the title, and at the head of the poem are the lines commencing, 'The Child is father of the Man'. 'Child' and 'birth' images are frequent. The sunshine is 'a glorious birth', the 'young lambs' bound as to the tabor. (pp. 37-8)

We have the poet's references to his own childhood's faded magic, to the time when all nature

> To me did seem
> Apparelled in celestial light,
> The glory and the freshness of a dream.

The radiance is gone:

> But yet I know, where'ere I go,
> That there hath passed away a glory from the earth.

Next, he expresses sorrow that he alone should have shown grief amid universal joyousness. A second wave of poetic rapture floods on in this and the next stanza; then, again, the bitter remembrance alternating. A tree, a field, both speak of 'something that is gone':

> Whither is fled the visionary gleam?
> Where is it now, the glory and the dream?

Then he expands this personal recollection into the general pilgrimage of mortality from birth, the fount of life, to life, the beginning of death. (pp. 39-40)

Yet the poet confuses us with two uses of 'nature'. One is the nature transfigured, indistinguishable from the antenatal glory, indeed itself the essential life of which that glory is an intellectual aspect. But we also have quite another 'nature'. Earth is a kindly foster-mother to the divine life born to her arms: 'yearnings she hath in her own natural kind.' So

> The homely nurse doth all she can
> To make her Foster-child, her Inmate Man,
> Forget the glories he hath known
> And that imperial palace whence he came.

In these passages 'natural' and 'earth' are to be contrasted with the divine. This, then, is rather the 'nature' of clouded vision: the nature of Wordsworth's manhood. Now, after the great central invocation, which I inspect later, the poem again returns to this secondary nature, joying

> That nature yet remembers
> What was so fugitive!

His manhood is leavened and purified by fitful recollections, and such memories bring him 'perpetual benediction'. They take the form of

> obstinate questionings
> Of sense and outward things,
> Fallings from us, vanishings,
> Blank misgivings of a Creature
> Moving about in worlds not realized,
> High instincts before which our mortal Nature
> Did tremble like a guilty thing surprised. . . .

Observe how here 'sense and outward things' are 'questioned'. This is an intellectual falsification. In the moment of child vision, nature was itself the divine glory, and the youth therefore 'nature's priest'. Remembering the quality of that vision, without being able to re-experience it in direct contact with the actual, the mind is forced into an idealism which regards the other, lesser nature, as 'questionable'. The poet thus moves in formless worlds, traversing the wide spaceless vacancies of abstract and inhuman recollection, without the creative power to fuse such vision-longing with immediate experience: the process at times evident in *The Prelude,* which is, we may remember, merely a recollection of child-moments in maturity, and not necessarily an authentic autobiographical record. This 'mortal nature', once the vision is gone, is truly a thing of meanness; and indeed a whole universe separates the one nature from the other. So these recollected life-glimmerings, vague and fitful though they be, have yet tremendous authority, and are, indeed, in this poem given a fine and concrete expression:

> But for those first affections,
> Those shadowy recollections,
> Which, be they what they may,
> Are yet a fountain-light of all our day,

Are yet a master-light of all our seeing;
  Uphold us, cherish, and have power to make
Our noisy years seem moments in the being
Of the eternal silence: truths that wake
    To perish never. . . .

The lights of that death-in-life which we live. They 'perish never'; not subject to mortality, because, though 'recollections', they are yet 'shadows' of some transcendent victory, existing with immortal power; and so time itself, 'our noisy years', becomes but a passing moment in the one vast immediacy of the eternal.

Our poem thus imagines the immortality in terms of (i) the child, imaged objectively as a thing enjoying its existence perfectly; and (ii) moments of vision, themselves to be related to the experiences of childhood. The two alternate. Neither by itself is wholly satisfying to us or to the poet suffering his loss of delight. He can see the shepherd-boy in youthful happiness, but he himself is sad; he can remember his own one-time visions, yet they return but fitfully, and then in terms of themselves and vague, 'shadowy' abstractions, rather than nature, thus lacking a certain reality. The immortality will be perfectly incarnated when these two approaches are married; when the poet's own desire is fused with an object, that object or image alight with the poet's immediate vision. Now our two aspects of immortality have been aspects of childhood: and the heart of our poem is a passionate invocation of the child. Here the poet falls into visionary love with his own symbol, and *majestically recreates before our eyes the thing he has lost*. The fusion is not 'recollected': it is in the poetic act. Two styles are, moreover, blended: that of *The Prelude* with that of the more technically objective sonnets. The fusion Wordsworth elsewhere describes is here immediately at work. The poet marries his own birth-visions to the child-symbol. The elements are things of life, and the technical process a creative act, so that we have a miraculous birth, a vivid poetic life shooting its life-ray into the heart of life. The climax of the ode rings out a prophetic and human splendour unique in Wordsworth. Nor has it been properly understood.

This, the vital centre, is preceded by the stanza carefully describing the child at play. The poet first studiously actualizes the symbol with which his passion is to be fused; and indeed closes his grand invocation by again imaging the child in its expressly human actuality. In the invocation we have our vision of the child as immortality. The immortal fire blazes out from this moment of created vision, and the lost immediacy, now incarnated in poetry, is recaptured in its full richness and splendour. The rest of the ode, with all its vivid imagery, is really the structure for this the central towering height, or heart. (pp. 40-3)

The child is the new-minted coin of life, its freshest currency, stamped with the impressure of the latest signature of paradise. It is thus an 'eye among the blind' possessing sight; deaf, silent, passive, its very *being* is a light and a vision. The child is a new eye of life. In later years we most often sleep. But in poetry, religion, music, love, in all ecstatic experience, we may wake to essential life, which is immortality. In that his very existence is an awakening to life, the child is indeed 'a mighty prophet' or blest 'seer'. Nor is he on a lower plane: wherever there is birth and newness, there is sublimity. That is why *height-born mountain-torrents* regularly symbolize birth. Full possession of this miracle is the aim of all poetry and prophecy. The child is therefore one

on whom those truths do rest
Which we are toiling all our lives to find,
In darkness lost, the darkness of the grave.

The child is life, the man, death. Because the child is a symbol of so vast a conception, greater than itself, itself emblematic of sovereign life, its 'immortality' is said to 'brood' over it like 'the day', a *domed* empyrean of light, overarching, expansive, illimitable, and of this the child is a 'slave' or symbol, a momentary expression. Momentary, in terms of time, or logic; yet when fused with contemplating passion, as here, the passion-child is immortality itself, the child being a symbol only when isolated, but actually blending with the poet's emotion and clustering imagery to create the mystery of which it is a reflection. Or, in terms of one of Coleridge's objections, that the child is in no valuable sense conscious of divinity any more than a tree or a ship, we may say indeed that the child alone has life, but not life fully conscious of life, but that that very consciousness the poet himself provides, so that his creation is both child in purity and man in experience. In such marriage of the symbol with poetic passion is created the greatest poetry, and by such welding of a childlike faith with profound experience have been forged the greatest lives on earth. (pp. 45-6)

And so the **"Ode"** dims to a noble conclusion, where the poet assuages his banishment from life eternal by vague intuition that in some sense the pilgrimage into mortality is necessary and just. With him, we must believe it so, or name the universe a medley and human existence a farce. But these thoughts are not our essentials here; or, rather, only important as circling routes to the summit, which is the centre. We must see the **"Ode"** spatially, not merely temporally: that is, must view its pattern simultaneously outrolled, the beginning and end as framework, the outer rose-petals, the centre its fiery heart, wherein we have our vision of the child, transfigured by poetry. (p. 48)

G. Wilson Knight, "The Wordsworthian Profundity," in his The Starlit Dome: Studies in the Poetry of Vision, *1941. Reprint by Methuen & Co. Ltd., 1959, pp. 1-82.*

HELEN DARBISHIRE (lecture date 1949)

[*Darbishire focuses on Wordsworth's style. She praises the naturalness of his descriptions, the simplicity and aptness of his verbal figures, the "inevitablity" of his realism, and the experimental manner of many of his works. Darbishire's remarks were originally delivered as part of the Clark Lectures in 1949. Other critics who consider Wordsworth's style include Hazlitt (1825), Pater (1874), Lowell (1875), Bradley (1909), Pottle (1950), and Hartman (1964).*]

All poetry draws its life from images of the senses: Wordsworth's poetry is steeped in these images, and his words carry them so naturally that we hardly notice them. The word cleaves to the thing like flesh to bone. When he wrote of

the giddy bliss
That like a tempest works along the blood,

he used a strangely living expression. The emotion sweeps through his body as a sudden storm sweeps along a lake—more than sweeps—works along it. . . .

In **"Tintern Abbey"** he speaks of

those sensations sweet
Felt in the blood and felt *along the heart*.

And again, of the sound of the Derwent that entered his infant slumbers,

> The fairest of all rivers sent a voice
> That flowed *along my dreams*.

Something comes into him, flows through him, flows along his blood, along his heart, along his dreams. In **"Lines Written in Early Spring"** he says:

> To her fair works did Nature link
> The human soul that *through me ran*

—another strange expression. Sometimes it seems that the mind *drinks in* what Nature gives. From strange sounds in the night,

> Thence did I drink the visionary power;

and in the early morning he held unconscious intercourse with beauty old as creation,

> drinking in a pure
> Organic pleasure from the silver wreaths
> Of curling mist.

On another unforgettable spring morning he calls his sister out into the woods and tells her,

> Our souls shall drink at every pore
> The Spirit of the Season.

All these phrases tell of spiritual life as if what happened to the spirit was a physical process, a flowing along, a running through, a drinking in at the pores.

This way of using images belongs to all language: our own speech is full of dormant, or dead, or half-alive metaphors. With the poet they are intensely alive, and it is no good reading poetry unless we take pains to be aware of that life.

We are more likely to be aware of the fuller use of imagery that the poet makes, in what the rhetoricians classify as figures—such as the simile. In the *Lyrical Ballads* the similes are of the Ballad kind, swift and short. Harry Gill's cheek is 'ruddy as clover'. Wordsworth was always addicted to such similes. In *The Excursion* the wanderer reflects:

> The good die first,
> And those whose hearts are dry as summer dust
> Burn to the socket.

Is this the kind of thing Hazlitt had in mind when he said, 'His style is vernacular: he delivers household truths'? [see excerpt dated 1825] The pedlar has the memory of dusty roads that he knows only too well in his summer tramps, and of the humble household candle that is offered him in his cottage lodging at the end of the day. Wordsworth's short similes, simple though they be, are singularly apt—right for the speaker that uses them, right for the character or scene they are applied to. The effect of the intense piercing cry that falls on Peter Bell's ear from the wood, is described thus:

> The Ass is startled—and stops short
> Right in the middle of the thicket,
> And Peter, wont to whistle loud,
> Whether alone or in a crowd,
> Is silent as a cricket.

How absolutely right! We all know the uncanny effect of silence when a cricket suddenly ceases his interminable chirp. Peter Bell deserves a sharp, true simile, but a homely one.

When the white doe appears in the churchyard she

> Comes gliding in serene and slow,
> Soft and silent as a dream.

That tells us all we need to know of her natural-supernatural life and being. And how true it is to the noiseless tread of the deer! Another kind of silence is that of Old Matthew in his final rest:

> Poor Matthew, all his frolics o'er,
> Is silent as a standing pool.

In that silence the sound is in our ears of the stream which stirred Matthew's thoughts in the poem of **"The Fountain."** He has the simile he deserves.

'Silent as a cricket', 'silent as a dream', 'silent as a standing pool'—all the phrases seem natural and inevitable in their context, but the imagination that supplies them is no ordinary imagination.

Memorable and haunting images that are crystallized in forms more elaborate than the one-word ballad simile are equally Wordsworthian, because equally true and revealing. He had a fondness for flowers and plants which has enraged some of his critics, from Clough onwards. . . . Rarer with Wordsworth is the long-tailed simile which Spenser inherited from Homer and Virgil through the Italian poets. Now the classical simile starts from a simple point of comparison, and then the new image brought in for illustration is elaborated for its own sake. In *The Faerie Queen,* Una's joy at recovering her knight suggests to Spenser a sea-captain returned to port after storm; his simile launches out into a description of the past voyage and of what happens on board when harbour is sighted: the mariners drink together, the mates pledge the captain. We are far enough by this time from the modest Una and her maidenly joy.

In **"Resolution and Independence,"** where Wordsworth adopts a form of the Spenserian stanza, he introduces a simile which is a fine example of the modern handling of this classical type.

On the desolate moor he is suddenly aware of a solitary figure:

> Beside a pool, bare to the eye of heaven,
> I saw a man before me unawares,
> The oldest man he seemed who ever wore grey hairs.

Now follows the simile:

> As a huge stone is sometimes seen to lie
> Couched on the bald top of an eminence;
> Wonder to all who do the same espy,
> By what means it could thither come, and whence,
> So that it seems a thing endued with sense:
> Like a sea-beast crawled forth, that on a shelf
> Of rock or sand reposeth, there to sun itself;
> Such seemed this Man, not all alive nor dead,
> Nor all asleep—in his extreme old age:

The images of the stone and sea-beast, not beautiful nor arresting in themselves, are not developed independently. They act and react vitally upon each other, and upon the original conception of the still, solitary figure of the old man in the midst of bare nature. As the stanza moves on we are more and more conscious of that strange stillness of his which seems to suggest both death and life. Moreover the simile contributes— no analysis can quite show how—to the inwardness and deep spiritual meaning of the whole poem. The poet is left at the end with a sense of the indomitable, the wellnigh insuperable power of the human spirit revealed to him through his encounter with a derelict old leech-gatherer. 'Motionless as a cloud the old Man stood.' The lonely moor and endless sky surround him. Once again, as in so many of his poems, the mysterious depth of Nature's life enhances and reveals without any exposition the spiritual quality of the human character.

Wordsworth's sense of the infinite and the life of the human mind in its relation with infinity, finds a natural expression in his poetic style in certain obvious ways, and in others not so obvious. A fragment of blank verse which he calls "**A Night Piece**" tells of a vision of the sky when the moon suddenly breaks through a screen of clouds:

> There, in a black-blue vault she sails along,
> Followed by multitudes of stars, that, small
> And sharp, and bright, along the dark abyss
> Drive as she drives: how fast they wheel away,
> Yet vanish not!—the wind is in the tree,
> But they are silent: still they roll along
> Immeasurably distant; and the vault,
> Built round by those white clouds, enormous clouds,
> Still deepens its unfathomable depth.
> At length the Vision closes; and the mind
> Not undisturbed by the deep joy it feels,
> Which slowly settles into peaceful calm,
> Is left to muse upon the solemn scene.

The images physically seen are described with Wordsworth's customary grave verracity. The sense of infinity which they invoke is given partly by words such as Milton taught him to use to contradict earthly limitation: 'immeasurably distant', 'unfathomable depth'. (Wordsworth's phrases in this kind are unforgettable: 'man's unconquerable mind', the 'incommunicable sleep' of death, the 'unimaginable touch of time'.) But there is something else in the lines of "**A Night Piece**" which contributes to the intangible effect: the simplest possible statement of what *is*.

> The wind is in the tree,
> But they are silent.

We remember, from another poem of his,

> The silence that is in the starry sky.

This potency of the verb 'to be' lies latent in many of his most memorable lines: 'The light that never *was* on sea or land'—that is to say, *is*, by *not being* in the physical sense.

> Nor know we anything more fair
> Than is the smile upon thy face; . . .

Sure beyond all physical security is for Wordsworth the smile on duty's face. But there is no need to elaborate.

> Let good men feel the soul of nature,
> And see things *as they are;*

—that is the core of what he has to tell us.

In all the supreme passages of Wordsworth's poetry there is a sense of inevitability, of something that is there because in the resistless movement of life it came there, it was there.

> There is a comfort in the strength of love;
> 'Twill make a thing endurable, which else
> Would overset the brain, or break the heart.

Those lines from "**Michael**" crystallize the quiet certainty of thought and feeling that are found in all his studies of simple men and women who are moved by the great emotions—who

suffer through love, 'that is not pain to hear of', Wordsworth thinks,

> for the glory that redounds
> Therefrom to humankind, and what we are. . . .

Wordsworth's vision of life took a wide sweep: it embraced the mind of man, the inner life of Nature where the mind of man meets it, the sphere of the elementary passions revealed in humble life, the world of high actions in the national and international arena, and that personal world of passing things and lasting truths which his own mind lived in from day to day.

To express all this in a poetic medium he needed an elastic style, and he acquired it by assiduous labour in his art. Coleridge praises the *curiosa felicitas* of his diction, and his austere accuracy in the use of words. In the maturity of his powers he could at one stroke master a style new to him, when occasion called. (pp. 164-73)

As poetic artist Wordsworth was a bold experimenter, and he had his resounding failures as well as his supreme successes; but his skill and range are great, and have not been fully recognized. In diction he moves from the low familiar style of "**The Idiot Boy**," where the owls hob-nob, and Betty Foy fiddle-faddles, to the majestic Miltonic heights of *The Recluse,*

> above the fierce confederate storm
> Of sorrow, barricadoed evermore
> Between the walls of cities.

Though he reaches supreme expression in the simplest of metres—

> A slumber did my spirit seal;
> I had no human fears:
> She seemed a thing that could not feel
> The touch of earthly years—

he had an instinctive liking for elaborate metrical forms; he excelled in the sonnet, and it has been noticed that, out of the 523 that he published, only one is in the easy Shakespearian form: all the rest are in one variety or another of the difficult Petrarcan—the best possible metre for the braced heroic strength of his political utterances. He wrote good Popian couplets as a schoolboy, and though he reverted to ballad forms at the beginning of his great creative period, he proceeded after that to experiment with a variety of metres learnt principally from the Elizabethans and Jacobeans. To my mind he is only unsuccessful in the trisyllabic measures, familiar to him in the Chapbooks (I am speaking of the poetry of his great period).

> An Orpheus! an Orpheus! yes, Faith may grow bold
> And take to herself all the wonders of old;—
> Near the stately Pantheon you'll meet with the same
> In the street that from Oxford hath borrowed its name.

Wordsworth's thought does not move easily in this jigging measure. When he has something gay to express he fares better with the four-beat couplet:

> There liveth in the prime of glee
> A woman whose years are seventy-three.

And, as *The Waggoner* shows, he could sustain this measure with pleasant variation through a long poem.

Like all good artists he knew the meaning and necessity of decorum, 'the grand masterpiece to observe', as Milton said. His choice of metres for the "**Ode to Duty**" and the "**Ode.**

Intimations of Immortality,'' betray it. In his great experiments in short blank-verse poems, where the metre tempts an inexperienced writer to go on and on, Wordsworth knows where to stop; he has a true sense of scale and proportion. Witness **"The Yew Trees"** or any of the **"Poems on the Naming of Places."**

It is hard to find a last word to say on the achievement of Wordsworth as a poet.

He said himself of his cherished theme,

> the might of souls
> And what they do within themselves,

that in the main 'It lies far hidden from the reach of words'. If that is so for the poet, how can a humble critic hope to do justice to him in the unwinged words of prose? I fall back on the naïve but penetrating question with which the engaging Audrey rounded upon Touchstone: 'I do not know what poetical is. Is it honest in deed and word? Is it a true thing?'

For Wordsworth we may answer: Yes, it is a true thing. What he has to express, the inner heart of man, the deepest secrets of the human mind, the mysterious responses of heart and mind to Nature, is perhaps the most difficult thing that any poet has tried to express. But Wordsworth set about it with the conviction that poetry can be a true thing. His method, as he said, was to keep his eye upon his object, to 'look steadily at his subject': he watched intently the surfaces of things so as to read their inner meaning, listened to the words of simple people, beggars, children, rustics, even idiots, to draw from them hints and signs of the ultimate truths that he was after. He developed the power to register the most evanescent movements, the most delicate outward manifestations of the inner life. Louisa is not a propitious name for a spirited girl, who 'winds along the brook' and 'hunts the waterfalls', but Wordsworth gives us something of the magic charm of this young haunter of the mountain streams, in lines unsurpassed, I think, for sensitive portrayal of the human spirit through the bodily form:

> And she has smiles to earth unknown,
> Smiles that with motions of their own
> Do spread, and sink, and rise:
> That come and go with endless play
> And ever as they pass away
> Are hidden in her eyes.

That poem begins simply,

> I met Louisa in the shade.

Wordsworth's simplicity has been mocked at, overemphasized, and misunderstood. But it lies at the very core of his art. He sought the truth and tried to express it with the least possible deviation. In all his artistic experiments his salvation lay in the integrity of his imagination and in his single-minded devotion to what he knew within. Under this severe discipline words answered his need.

> Love had he known in huts where poor men lie;
> His daily teachers had been woods and rills,
> The silence that is in the starry sky,
> The sleep that is among the lonely hills.

Another poet might have written: 'The peace that lies among the lonely hills'—and it would have been a good line. But Wordsworth, out of his deep long knowledge of the mountains, writes,

> The sleep that is among the lonely hills.
>
> (pp. 174-78)

At his greatest moments Wordsworth speaks so quietly that an ear not intent on his meaning catches little.

'The voice which is the voice of my poetry', he once said, 'without imagination cannot be heard.' (p. 179)

> *Helen Darbishire, in her* The Poet Wordsworth, *Oxford at the Clarendon Press, Oxford, 1950, 182 p.*

LIONEL TRILLING   (essay date 1950)

[A respected American critic and literary historian, Trilling was also an essayist, editor, novelist, and short story writer. His exploration of liberal arts theory and its implications for the conduct of life led Trilling to function not only as a literary critic, but as a social commentator as well. A liberal and a humanist, Trilling judged the value of a text by its contribution to culture and, in turn, regarded culture as indispensible for human survival. Trilling focused in particular on the conflict between the individual and culture, maintaining that art had the power to "liberate the individual from the tyranny of his culture in the environmental sense and to permit him to stand beyond it in an autonomy of perception and judgment." Trilling's essay on the "Intimations" ode, excerpted below, is acknowledged as historically important because he refutes the popular critical assessment, first expressed by Dean Sperry, that the poem is "Wordsworth's conscious farewell to his art." Such an interpretation, Trilling argues, is based on two incorrect assumptions: that poetic ability can be classified, and that there is always tension between a poet's philosophic and poetic powers. Preferring to view the ode as Wordsworth's "dedication to new powers," Trilling emphasizes that in the poem Wordsworth is concerned with incorporating a new, more mature vision into his art. This essay was originally delivered as a lecture in a slightly different form in 1941; it was first published in this revised form in 1950 in The Liberal Imagination.]

In speaking about Wordsworth's **"Ode: Intimations of Immortality from Recollections of Early Childhood,"** I should like to begin by considering an interpretation of the poem which is commonly made. According to this interpretation—I choose for its brevity Dean Sperry's statement of a view which is held by many other admirable critics—the Ode is "Wordsworth's conscious farewell to his art, a dirge sung over his departing powers."

How did this interpretation—erroneous, as I believe—come into being? The Ode may indeed be quoted to substantiate it, but I do not think it has been drawn directly from the poem itself. To be sure, the Ode is not wholly perspicuous. Wordsworth himself seems to have thought it difficult, for . . . he speaks of the need for competence and attention in the reader. The difficulty does not lie in the diction, which is simple, or even in the syntax, which is sometimes obscure, but rather in certain contradictory statements which the poem makes, and in the ambiguity of some of its crucial words. Yet the erroneous interpretation I am dealing with does not arise from any intrinsic difficulty of the poem itself but rather from certain extraneous and unexpressed assumptions which some of its readers make about the nature of the mind.

Nowadays it is not difficult for us to understand that such tacit assumptions about the mental processes are likely to lie hidden beneath what we say about poetry. Usually, despite our general awareness of their existence, it requires great effort to bring these assumptions explicitly into consciousness. But in speaking of Wordsworth one of the commonest of our unexpressed ideas comes so close to the surface of our thought that it needs only to be grasped and named. I refer to the belief that poetry is made by means of a particular poetic faculty, a faculty which may be isolated and defined.

It is this belief, based wholly upon assumption, which underlies all the speculations of the critics who attempt to provide us with explanations of Wordsworth's poetic decline by attributing it to one or another of the events of his life. In effect any such explanation is a way of *defining* Wordsworth's poetic faculty: what the biographical critics are telling us is that Wordsworth wrote great poetry by means of a faculty which depended upon his relations with Annette Vallon, or by means of a faculty which operated only so long as he admired the French Revolution, or by means of a faculty which flourished by virtue of a particular pitch of youthful sense-perception or by virtue of a certain attitude toward Jeffrey's criticism or by virtue of a certain relation with Coleridge.

Now no one can reasonably object to the idea of mental determination in general, and I certainly do not intend to make out that poetry is an unconditioned activity. Still, this particular notion of mental determination which implies that Wordsworth's genius failed when it was deprived of some single emotional circumstance is so much too simple and so much too mechanical that I think we must inevitably reject it. Certainly what we know of poetry does not allow us to refer the making of it to any single faculty. Nothing less than the whole mind, the whole man, will suffice for its origin. And such was Wordsworth's own view of the matter.

There is another unsubstantiated assumption at work in the common biographical interpretation of the Ode. This is the belief that a natural and inevitable warfare exists between the poetic faculty and the faculty by which we conceive or comprehend general ideas.... Observing in the Ode a contrast drawn between something called "the visionary gleam" and something called "the philosophic mind," they leap to the conclusion that the Ode is Wordsworth's conscious farewell to his art, a dirge sung over departing powers.

I am so far from agreeing with this conclusion that I believe the Ode is not only not a dirge sung over departing powers but actually a dedication to new powers. Wordsworth did not, to be sure, realize his hopes for these new powers, but that is quite another matter.... (pp. 123-25)

Both formally and in the history of its composition the poem is divided into two main parts. The first part, consisting of four stanzas, states an optical phenomenon and asks a question about it. The second part, consisting of seven stanzas, answers that question and is itself divided into two parts, of which the first is despairing, the second hopeful....

The question which the first part asks is this:

> Whither is fled the visionary gleam?
> Where is it now, the glory and the dream?

All the first part leads to this question, but although it moves in only one direction it takes its way through more than one mood.... (p. 126)

Now, the interpretation which makes the Ode a dirge over departing powers and a conscious farewell to art takes it for granted that the visionary gleam, the glory, and the dream, are Wordsworth's names for the power by which he made poetry. This interpretation gives to the Ode a place in Wordsworth's life exactly analogous to the place that "Dejection: An Ode" has in Coleridge's life. It is well known how intimately the

two poems are connected; the circumstances of their composition makes them symbiotic. Coleridge in his poem most certainly does say that his poetic powers are gone or going; he is very explicit, and the language he uses is very close to Wordsworth's own. He tells us that upon "the inanimate cold world" there must issue from the soul "a light, a glory, a fair luminous cloud," and that this glory *is* Joy, which he himself no longer possesses.... (pp. 128-29)

Wordsworth tells us something quite different about himself. He tells us that he has strength, that he has Joy, but still he has not the glory. In short, we have no reason to assume that, when he asks the question at the end of the fourth stanza, he means, "Where has my creative power gone?" Wordsworth tells us how he made poetry; he says he made it out of the experience of his senses as worked upon by his contemplative intellect, but he nowhere tells us that he made poetry out of visionary gleams, out of glories, or out of dreams.

To be sure, he writes very often about gleams.... His great poems are about moments of enlightenment, in which the metaphoric and the literal meaning of the word are at one—he uses "glory" in the abstract modern sense, but always with an awareness of the old concrete iconographic sense of a visible nimbus. But this momentary and special light is the subject matter of his poetry, not the power of making it. The moments are moments of understanding, but Wordsworth does not say that they make writing poetry any easier. Indeed, in lines 59-131 of the first book of *The Prelude* he expressly says that the moments of clarity are by no means always matched by poetic creativity.... (pp. 129-30)

This great poem is not to be given a crucial meaning in Wordsworth's life. It makes use of a mood to which everyone, certainly every creative person, is now and again a victim.... But although Wordsworth urges himself on to think of all the bad things that can possibly happen to a poet, and mentions solitude, pain of heart, distress and poverty, cold, pain and labor, all fleshly ills, and then even madness, he never says that a poet stands in danger of losing his talent.... (pp. 133-34)

Must we not, then, look with considerable skepticism at such interpretations of the Ode as suppose without question that the "gleam," the "glory," and the "dream" constitute the power of making poetry?—especially when we remember that at a time still three years distant Wordsworth in *The Prelude* will speak of himself as becoming a "*creative* soul" ... despite the fact that, as he says ..., he "sees by glimpses now."

The second half of the Ode is divided into two large movements, each of which gives an answer to the question with which the first part ends. The two answers seem to contradict each other. The first issues in despair, the second in hope; the first uses a language strikingly supernatural, the second is entirely naturalistic. The two parts even differ in the statement of fact, for the first says that the gleam is gone, whereas the second says that it is not gone, but only transmuted. It is necessary to understand this contradiction, but it is not necessary to resolve it, for from the circuit between its two poles comes much of the power of the poem.

The first of the two answers (stanzas V-VIII) tells us where the visionary gleam has gone by telling us where it came from. It is a remnant of a pre-existence in which we enjoyed a way of seeing and knowing now almost wholly gone from us. We come into the world, not with minds that are merely *tabulae rasae*, but with a kind of attendant light, the vestige of an existence otherwise obliterated from our memories. In infancy and childhood the recollection is relatively strong, but it fades as we move forward into earthly life. Maturity, with its habits and its cares and its increase of distance from our celestial origin, wears away the light of recollection. Nothing could be more poignantly sad than the conclusion of this part with the heavy sonority of its last line as Wordsworth addresses the child in whom the glory still lives:

> Full soon thy Soul shall have her earthly freight,
> And custom lie upon thee with a weight,
> Heavy as frost, and deep almost as life!

Between this movement of despair and the following movement of hope there is no clear connection save that of contradiction. But between the question itself and the movement of hope there is an explicit verbal link, for the question is: "Whither has *fled* the visionary gleam?" and the movement of hope answers that "nature yet remembers / What was so *fugitive*."

The second movement of the second part of the Ode tells us again what has happened to the visionary gleam: it has not wholly fled, for it is remembered. This possession of childhood has been passed on as a legacy to the child's heir, the adult man; for the mind, as the rainbow epigraph also says, is one and continuous, and what was so intense a light in childhood becomes "the fountain-light of all our day" and a "master-light of all our seeing," that is, of our adult day and our mature seeing. The child's recollection of his heavenly home exists in the recollection of the adult.

But what exactly is this fountain-light, this master-light? I am sure that when we understand what it is we shall see that the glory that Wordsworth means is very different from Coleridge's glory, which is Joy. Wordsworth says that what he holds in memory as the guiding heritage of childhood is exactly not the Joy of childhood. It is not "delight," not "liberty," not even "hope"—not for these, he says, "I raise / The song of thanks and praise." For what then does he raise the song? For this particular experience of childhood:

> ... those obstinate questionings
> Of sense and outward things,
> Fallings from us, vanishings;
> Blank misgivings of a Creature
> Moving about in worlds not realised.

He mentions other reasons for gratitude, but here for the moment I should like to halt the enumeration.

We are told, then, that light and glory consist, at least in part, of "questionings," "fallings from us," "vanishings," and "blank misgivings" in a world not yet *made real,* for surely Wordsworth uses the word "realised" in its most literal sense. . . . (pp. 134-36)

Wordsworth is talking about something common to us all, the development of the sense of reality. To have once had the visionary gleam of the perfect union of the self and the universe is essential to and definitive of our human nature, and it is in that sense connected with the making of poetry. But the visionary gleam is not in itself the poetry-making power, and its diminution is right and inevitable.

That there should be ambivalence in Wordsworth's response to this diminution is quite natural, and the two answers, that of stanzas V-VIII and that of stanzas IX-XI, comprise both the resistance to and the acceptance of growth. Inevitably we resist change and turn back with passionate nostalgia to the stage we are leaving. Still, we fulfill ourselves by choosing what is

painful and difficult and necessary, and we develop by moving toward death. In short, organic development is a hard paradox which Wordsworth is stating in the discrepant answers of the second part of the Ode. . . . (pp. 140-41)

To speak naturalistically of the quasi-mystical experiences of his childhood does not in the least bring into question the value which Wordsworth attached to them, for, despite its dominating theistical metaphor, the Ode is largely naturalistic in its intention. . . . (p. 141)

[We] must credit Wordsworth with the double vision. Man must be conceived of as "imperial," but he must also be seen as he actually is in the field of life. The earth is not an environment in which the celestial or imperial qualities can easily exist. Wordsworth, who spoke of the notion of imperial pre-existence as being adumbrated by Adam's fall, uses the words "earth" and "earthly" in the common quasi-religious sense to refer to the things of this world. He does not make Earth synonymous with Nature, for although Man may be the true child of Nature, he is the "Foster-child" of Earth. . . . (pp. 142-43)

Wordsworth, in short, is looking at man in a double way, seeing man both in his ideal nature and in his earthly activity. The two views do not so much contradict as supplement each other. If in stanzas V-VIII Wordsworth tells us that we live by decrease, in stanzas IX-XI he tells us of the everlasting connection of the diminished person with his own ideal personality. The child hands on to the hampered adult the imperial nature, the "primal sympathy / Which having been must ever be," the mind fitted to the universe, the universe to the mind. The sympathy is not so pure and intense in maturity as in childhood, but only because another relation grows up beside the relation of man to Nature—the relation of man to his fellows in the moral world of difficulty and pain. Given Wordsworth's epistemology the new relation is bound to change the very aspect of Nature itself: the clouds will take a sober coloring from an eye that hath kept watch o'er man's mortality, but a sober color is a color still.

There is sorrow in the Ode, the inevitable sorrow of giving up an old habit of vision for a new one. In shifting the center of his interest from Nature to man in the field of morality Wordsworth is fulfilling his own conception of the three ages of man. . . . The shift in interest he called the coming of "the philosophic mind," but the word "philosophic" does not have here either of two of its meanings in common usage—it does not mean abstract and it does not mean apathetic. Wordsworth is not saying, and it is sentimental and unimaginative of us to say, that he has become less a feeling man and less a poet. He is only saying that he has become less a youth. Indeed, the Ode is so little a farewell to art, so little a dirge sung over departing powers, that it is actually the very opposite—it is a welcome of new powers and a dedication to a new poetic subject. . . . (pp. 143-44)

Still, was there not, after the composition of the Ode, a great falling off in his genius which we are drawn to connect with the crucial changes the Ode records? That there was a falling off is certain, although we must observe that it was not so sharp as is commonly held and also that it did not occur immediately or even soon after the composition of the first four stanzas with their statement that the visionary gleam had gone; on the contrary, some of the most striking of Wordsworth's verse was written at this time. It must be remembered too that another statement of the loss of the visionary gleam, that made in "**Tintern Abbey**," had been followed by all the superb production of the "great decade"—an objection which is sometimes dealt with by saying that Wordsworth wrote his best work from his near memories of the gleam, and that, as he grew older and moved farther from it, his recollection dimmed and thus he lost his power: it is an explanation which suggests that mechanical and simple notions of the mind and of the poetic process are all too tempting to those who speculate on Wordsworth's decline. Given the fact of the great power, the desire to explain its relative deterioration will no doubt always be irresistible. But we must be aware, in any attempt to make this explanation, that an account of why Wordsworth ceased to write great poetry must at the same time be an account of how he once did write great poetry. And this latter account, in our present state of knowledge, we cannot begin to furnish. (pp. 145-46)

> Lionel Trilling, "The Immortality Ode," in his The Liberal Imagination: Essays on Literature and Society, *Harcourt Brace Jovanovich, 1979, pp. 123-51.*

FREDERICK A. POTTLE   (lecture date 1950)

[*Pottle analyzes Wordsworth's poetic method by considering two of his statements from the Preface to the* Lyrical Ballads *(see excerpt dated 1802): "Poetry takes its origin from emotion recollected in tranquility," and "I have at all times endeavoured to look steadily at my subject." Pottle demonstrates that the statements taken together encapsulate Wordsworth's technique of transfiguring real images into symbolic ones. This essay was originally delivered as a lecture at the Wordsworth Centenary Celebrations held at Cornell and Princeton Universities in 1950. For other studies of Wordsworth's style, see the excerpts by Hazlitt (1825), Pater (1874), Lowell (1875), Bradley (1909), Darbishire (1949), and Hartman (1964).*]

A centenary year invites the publication of a great many essays with some such title as "Wordsworth Today." The purpose

Rydal Mount, where Wordsworth resided from 1813 until his death.

of these essays would be to judge Wordsworth as though he were a contemporary poet, to decide what portion of his works is really available to present-day sensibility. My purpose in the remarks that follow is descriptive rather than judicial: I shall try to isolate qualities of Wordsworth's poetry that look as though they were going to be apparent to all historical varieties of sensibility, though the values assigned to them by different sensibilities may differ. And I think I can best get to what I want to say by the method of texts: by inviting you to consider two prose statements made by Wordsworth himself about poetry in general and about his own poetry in particular. They are both from the famous Preface: "Poetry takes its origin from emotion recollected in tranquility" and "I have at all times endeavoured to look steadily at my subject." It is my notion that the latter of these texts usually gets, if not a false, at least an impoverished, interpretation; and that the two, taken together and rightly understood, go a long way toward placing Wordsworth in literary history.

At first sight it looks as though they were what Bacon calls "cross clauses": that is, they appear to be hopelessly contradictory. The natural image that rises in one's mind as one reads the statement "I have at all times endeavoured to look steadily at my subject" is that of an artist painting from a model or an actual landscape; and since Wordsworth's poetry contains a good deal of landscape, the obvious meaning of his words would appear to be that he composed poetry while looking earnestly and steadily at the natural objects that he introduces into his poems. But if poetry takes its rise from "emotion recollected in tranquility," it is hard to see how this can happen. In fact, the only way in which we can leave any place for the actual model, in poetry that starts from recollection, is to suppose that after poetry *has* taken its rise, the poet goes back to natural objects and pores over them as he composes. And we know that Wordsworth did not do that. His normal practice, like that of other poets, was to paint without the model. He very seldom made a present joy the matter of his song, but rather turned habitually for the matter of poems to joys that sprang from hiding-places ten years deep.

More than that, a good many of his poems, including several of his finest, either have no basis in personal experience at all, or show autobiography so manipulated that the "subject" corresponds to nothing Wordsworth ever saw with the bodily eye. His extensive critical writings deride the matter-of-fact and speak over and over again of the power of the imagination to modify and create. Yet there is a widespread belief that Wordsworth was Nature's Boswell, in the old erroneous sense which defined Boswell as a man who followed Johnson about with a notebook, taking down his utterances on the spot. Actually, like Boswell, Wordsworth relied on memory, and says so quite explicitly. But then he says other things in which he appears to be vindicating the rightness of his poetry, not on the ground that it is well-imagined, but on the ground that the things described in the poem really did happen in that fashion and in no other. (pp. 23-4)

[In] real life Wordsworth met the old man [who served as the model for the leech gatherer in "**Resolution and Independence**"] not on the lonely moor, but in the highway; the old man in real life was not demonstrating resolution and independence by gathering leeches under great difficulties, but was begging. In short, . . . the narrative is from first to last an imaginative construction—the account of an imagined meeting between Wordsworth and the beggar as Wordsworth imagined him to have been before he was finally reduced to beggary.

What, then, are we to make of Wordsworth's boast that he endeavored at all times to look steadily at his subject? (p. 25)

The function of the imagination, as Wordsworth and Coleridge insisted, is, at the first level, to make sense out of the undifferentiated manifold of sensation by organizing it into individual objects or things; at the second, and specifically poetic, level, to reshape this world of common perception in the direction of a unity that shall be even more satisfactory and meaningful. (pp. 27-8)

Wordsworth recollected the scene [that he depicts in **"I Wandered Lonely as a Cloud"** (see excerpt dated 1804)] in tranquillity and wrote his poem a full two years afterwards. . . . The literal, positivistic, "scientific" fact was that Wordsworth and his sister saw a large bed of wild daffodils beside a lake, agitated by a strong, cold spring wind. The rest is all the work of the imagination.

The mark of the poetic imagination is to simplify: to make the manifold of sensation more meaningful by reducing it to a number of objects that can actually be contemplated. (pp. 28-9)

We can now see what Wordsworth meant by looking steadily at his subject. So far as his subject is expressed in imagery drawn from nature (and that means in all his best poetry), there is implied a lifelong habit of close, detailed, and accurate observation of the objects composing the external universe. By "accurate" I mean something the same thing as "naturalistic," but not entirely so. Wordsworth scorned the merely analytic vision of the naturalist ("One that would peep and botanize Upon his mother's grave") because in his opinion that kind of apprehension empties the object of life and meaning by detaching it from its ground. "His theme is nature *in solido,* that is to say, he dwells on that mysterious presence of surrounding things, which imposes itself on any separate element that we set up as an individual for its own sake. He always grasps the whole of nature as involved in the tonality of the particular instance." But, except for those portions of the scientist's vision which require (let us say) dissection and magnification, there is little in the scientist's vision that Wordsworth misses. A *merely* matter-of-fact, an *exclusively* positivistic view of nature fills him with anger, but his own apprehension includes the matter-of-fact view without denying any of it. Dr. Leavis has perhaps put this more intelligibly when he remarks, as the chief virtue of Wordsworth's poetry, a "firm hold upon the world of common perception" [see excerpt dated 1936], though I myself should like to phrase it, "in the mode of perception which has been common in Western civilization since some time in the late eighteenth century." In a literal, physiological sense, Wordsworth did look steadily at the natural objects that appear in his poetry.

But the subject he is talking about in the sentence in the Preface is not an object in external nature; and the eye that looks steadily is not the physical eye. The subject is a mental image, and the eye is that inward eye which is the bliss of solitude. The mental image accompanies or is the source of the emotion recollected in tranquillity; it recurs in memory, not once but many times; and on each occasion he looks at it steadily to see what it *means*. Wordsworth in his best poetry does not start with an abstraction or a generalization, a divine commonplace which he wishes to illustrate. He starts with the mental image of a concrete natural object. He feels this object to be very urgent, but at first he does not know why. As he looks steadily at it, he simplifies it, and as he simplifies it, he sees what it means. He usually continues to simplify and interpret until the object

becomes the correlative of a single emotion. It is a great mistake to consider Wordsworth a descriptive poet. When he is writing in the mode of the imagination, he never gives catalogues, in fact never provides a profusion of imagery. He employs few images. His images are firm and precise ("literal"), but . . . they are very spare. Of the daffodils we are given nothing but their habit of growing in clumps, their color, and their characteristic movement when stirred by the wind. Wordsworth's method (I am trying to be just as hard-headed and precise as I know how) is not the method of beautification (Tennyson), nor the method of distortion (Carlyle); it is the method of transfiguration. The primrose by the river's brim remains a simple primrose but it is also something more: it is a symbol (to use Hartley's quaint terminology) of sympathy, theopathy, or the moral sense. (pp. 31-3)

It is not difficult by Wordsworth's own standards to establish the right of [**"I Wandered Lonely as a Cloud"**] to be considered an imaginative poem. The impression that the daffodils are joyous is not for him what Ruskin called pathetic fallacy. Under steady, prolonged, and serious contemplation daffodils can remain for him a symbol of joy because it is his faith (literally—no figure of speech) that every flower enjoys the air it breathes. Again, [the poem] is imaginative because the impression of joy deepens into *social* joy: since the daffodils stand for men in society, the poem attains to sympathy on Hartley's ladder. But Wordsworth was not willing to rank the poem as an example of the higher exercise of the imagination, because it lacks the fade-out. In it things only just begin to be lost in each other, and limits to vanish, and aspirations to be raised. He was quite aware of the fact that [**"I Wandered Lonely as a Cloud"**] is a very simple poem.

"The Solitary Reaper" has the degree of complexity necessary for full illustration of Wordsworth's theory. The Highland Lass is *single,* is *solitary,* is *alone,* and her song is *melancholy.* I said that the situation of [**"I Wandered Lonely as a Cloud"**] was promising, but here is what is for Wordsworth the optimum situation: solitude, in the single human figure against the landscape with more than a hint of visionary dreariness in it; society, its affections and passions presented not directly but felt in the distanced, muted, managed form of song. Actual men in crowds are to him an unmanageable sight; a crowd of daffodils can stand for humanity if no more is called for than a gush of social joy; but this symbol of the singing reaper will express the whole solemn mystery of human existence. The limits begin to vanish in the first stanza with the figure of the sound overflowing the rim of the vale.

The mystery of human existence: that is the first meaning of the bird metaphors of the second stanza. The song can stand for mystery because it is itself mysterious. Like the song of the nightingale and the song of the cuckoo, it is in a foreign tongue. It is one of those Gaelic occupational chants that go on and on like the drone of a bagpipe ("the Maiden sang As if her song could have no ending"): the poet feels it to be melancholy from its tone and rhythm, though he cannot understand the words. But he is also at work in other ways to make limits vanish: he pushes his boundaries out in space from Arabia to St. Kilda. And the third stanza, besides reinforcing "melancholy" by the more explicit "old, unhappy, far-off things, And battles long ago," extends the boundaries in time: from "long ago" to "to-day," a plane of extension cutting across the plane of space. Again, we have the extension in human experience: from the unnatural sorrows of battles to the natural pain of everyday life. It is by devices such as these that Wordsworth transfigures the matter of common perception.

It would be perverse to attempt to identify the basic ideas of Wordsworth and Blake on the imagination. Blake by his "double vision" no doubt meant much the same thing as Wordsworth with his two ways of looking steadily at objects. Wordsworth might well have joined Blake's prayer to be kept from single vision and Newton's sleep. But Wordsworth believed that poetry must hold firm to the vision of the outward eye, and Blake, I think, wanted to relinquish the control of common perception altogether. "I assert for My Self that I do not behold the outward Creation & that to me it is hindrance & not Action; it is as the dirt upon my feet, No part of Me. . . . I question not my Corporeal or Vegetative Eye any more than I would Question a Window concerning a Sight. I look thro' it & not with it." Still, detached from Blake's private interpretations, his lines state very well what Wordsworth proposed:

To see a World in a Grain of Sand
And a Heaven in a Wild Flower,
Hold Infinity in the palm of your hand
And Eternity in an hour.

(pp. 39-42)

Frederick A. Pottle, "The Eye and the Object in the Poetry of Wordsworth," in Wordsworth: Centenary Studies Presented at Cornell and Princeton Universities *by Douglas Bush & others, edited by Gilbert T. Dunklin, Princeton University Press, 1951, pp. 23-42.*

M. H. ABRAMS (essay date 1953)

[*Abrams is an American critic best known for his writings on English Romanticism. In* The Mirror and the Lamp: Romantic Theory and the Critical Tradition, *from which the following excerpt is drawn, he interprets "the mirror" as a metaphor for the classical conception that art must imitate reality, and "the lamp" as a representation of the Romantic belief that artists should express personal perceptions through their creations. Using these symbols, Abrams traces the development of Romantic critical theory. Though he acknowledges Wordsworth's transitional place in the history of English literary theory, Abrams focuses on the traits that the poet inherited from eighteenth-century thinkers. Wordsworth's "cultural primitivism," Abrams contends, led him to employ nature as a "standard of poetic value" and to base his criticism on his recognition of the importance of the oral tradition. For other views on Wordsworth's critical theory, see the excerpts by Wordsworth (1802), Coleridge (1817), De Quincey (1845), and Saintsbury (1896).*]

[Wordsworth,] the first great romantic poet, may also be accounted the critic whose highly influential writings, by making the feelings of the poet the center of critical reference, mark a turning-point in English literary theory. It is nevertheless remarkable that Wordsworth was more thoroughly immersed in certain currents of eighteenth-century thinking than any of his important contemporaries. There is, for example, almost none of the terminology of post-Kantian aesthetic philosophy in Wordsworth. Only in his poetry, not in his criticism, does Wordsworth make the transition from the eighteenth-century view of man and nature to the concept that the mind is creative in perception, and an integral part of an organically inter-related universe. (pp. 103-04)

[The] critical theory he held during those early years of the nineteenth century, when he formulated his most important literary pronouncements, may in all fairness be classified as a form—though a highly refined and developed form—of cultural primitivism. Wordsworth's cardinal standard of poetic value is 'nature,' and nature, in his usage, is given a triple and primitivistic connotation: Nature is the common denominator of human nature; it is most reliably exhibited among men living 'according to nature' (that is to say, in a culturally simple, and especially a rural environment); and it consists primarily in an elemental simplicity of thought and feeling and a spontaneous and 'unartificial' mode of expressing feeling in words. (p. 105)

By showing that Wordsworth's theory had its roots in earlier primitivistic doctrine, I should by no means be taken to condemn, or even to derogate, Wordsworth's achievement. The attempt to correct earlier tendencies to formalize and freeze the 'art' of poetry by emphasizing the opposing element of 'nature' was historically justifiable, and validated at least in the pragmatic sense that the theory was the working hypothesis, and so helped shape the procedure, of one of the great and original poets of the language. Wordsworth's criticism rests on the solid basis of his recognition of the greatness, and the potentialities as literary models, of the ballads, songs, and stories of oral tradition. It rests also on his perception of the possibilities as literary subject matter of the ways and speech of men living close to the soil, comparatively insulated from the rapid changes of life and manners in the urban world. And if neither the literature nor manners of the folk are 'artless' in the way Wordsworth asserted, and if his attempt to generalize from their attributes to all of poetry is open to serious objection, still Wordsworth, by doctrine and example, brought into the literary province the store of materials which has since been richly exploited by writers from Thomas Hardy to William Faulkner.

In addition, Wordsworth succeeded in elaborating and qualifying the doctrines of earlier enthusiasts for the primitive so as to convert them into a reputable and rewarding, if not in itself a wholly adequate, contribution to our critical tradition. Certainly Wordsworth did not conceive of the great poet as a thoughtless and instinctive child of nature. Just as he required the poet to keep his eye on the subject, and reminded him that he writes not for himself, but for men, so he affirmed that good poems are produced only by a man who has 'thought long and deeply. For our continued influxes of feeling are modified and directed by our thoughts, which are indeed the representatives of all our past feelings . . .' In this way, he refined the key assumption of aesthetic primitivism into the conception of a spontaneity which is the reward of intelligent application and hard-won skills—a spontaneity, as F. R. Leavis has said, 'supervening upon complex development,' and a naturalness 'consummating a discipline, moral and other.' Wordsworth's own practice, as this is described in Dorothy Wordsworth's *Journals,* also gives ample evidence that once they have been composed, poems may be subjected to long and arduous revision. It is the strength of Wordsworth's expressive theory, therefore, that he brings into its purview elements of the older conception that poetry is a deliberate art; it is its peculiarity that these elements are carefully relegated to a temporal position before or after the actual coming-into-being of the poem. For in the immediate act of composition, the best warrant of 'naturalness,' Wordsworth insists, is that the overflow of feeling be spontaneous, and free both from the deliberate adaptation of conventional language to feeling and from the deliberate bending of linguistic means to the achievement of poetic effects.

It is worth emphasizing, finally, that although Wordsworth repudiates the opinion that nature in poetry must be 'to advantage dressed,' he consents to the opinion that it may be

457

'what oft was thought.' In one instance, Wordsworth overtops Dr. Johnson in his demand for uniformity, instead of originality, in the materials of poetry. Johnson, like Wordsworth, was interested in mortuary verse, and had anticipated him in writing essays on epitaphs. Johnson had selected a composition of Pope's for special praise because in it 'there is scarce one line taken from common places.' For this Wordsworth reprimands him:

> It is not only to fault but a primary requisite in an epitaph that it shall contain thoughts and feelings which are in their substance commonplace, and even trite. It is grounded upon the universal intellectual property of man,—sensations which all men have felt and feel in some degree daily and hourly;—truths whose very interest and importance have caused them to be unattended to, as things which should take care of themselves.

The next sentence, however, marks the point at which the two theorists part company: 'But it is required,' says Wordsworth, 'that these truths should be *instinctively* ejaculated or should rise irresistibly from circumstances . . .'

That the great romantic poet should exceed the great neo-classic critic in his quest for uniformity will not seem anomalous if we remember that Johnson, on his part, had balanced his demand for common truths by requiring what 'is at once natural and *new*,' and if we remember also that none of the English romantic poets was of Novalis' opinion that 'the more personal, local, temporal, and peculiar [*eigentümlicher*] a poem is, the nearer it is to the center of poetry.' In England the high-water mark of the worship of uniqueness and originality had come and passed with Young's *Conjectures*. In his demand that the content of poetry be what is central to all mankind, Wordsworth was at one with Boileau, Pope, and Johnson; the substitution of poetry as the overflow of feeling, however, for poetry as a pleasure-giving imitation enforced a change in the application of this criterion. Since a poet is 'a man speaking to men,' to express his spontaneous feelings is the best way to insure a universal content and to appeal to what is universal in mankind. (pp. 112-14)

> *M. H. Abrams, "Varieties of Romantic Theory: Wordsworth and Coleridge," in his* The Mirror and the Lamp: Romantic Theory and the Critical Tradition, *Oxford University Press, 1953, pp. 100-24.*

NEWTON P. STALLKNECHT   (essay date 1958)

[*Stallknecht stresses the importance of political ideas, especially the conception of liberty, in Wordsworth's poems. Focusing on* The Prelude, *Stallknecht discusses the ways in which Wordsworth's later writings repudiate the philosophical doctrine of "enlightened self-assertion" which he incorporated into that poem. The critic theorizes that Wordsworth's early work reveals a philosophy flawed by the "democratic fallacy," the belief that "the gifted man hesitates to make full use of his gifts, is even suspicious of them, because they are not universal." Proposing some possible reasons for Wordsworth's shifting stance, Stallknecht surveys the influences of Godwinism and the ideal of "the ethical imagination" on Wordsworth's thinking, concluding that his tragic flaw lay in his inability to reconcile "the ideal of self-realization and the ideal of self-transcending duty." Other critics who write about Wordsworth's philosophical doctrine include Stephen (1876), Havens (1941), Perkins (1964), and Langbaum (1977).*]

Much of the noble enthusiasm which inspires *The Prelude* is of a social and political origin, and no one can say that Wordsworth's earlier writings are not to a large degree strengthened by his political interests. The ideal of liberty is taken up and absorbed into the development of Wordsworth's early philosophy, becoming inseparably united with the bold romantic individualism of *The Prelude.*

The mind of man, the locus of liberty, is the glory of the world, an awe-inspiring subject for contemplation. Man is worthy of himself only when he realizes the dignity and power of which his mind is capable, owing to his essentially human endowment. This power, the proper energy of mind, is manifest in the creations of the imagination and the syntheses of the inquiring intelligence. It is, indeed, what Coleridge called the *esemplastic* power. Unlike the association of ideas or the unconscious forming of habits, this power is not borne in upon the mind by mechanical repetition: it is the fundamental assertion of the mind itself, genuine liberty, the full exercise of which is at once moral freedom and happiness. The philosophy of *The Prelude* centers upon this concept. The theories of education, of art, and of democratic politics are founded upon it. (p. 223)

[The] human "frame is good and graciously composed"; human beings are worthy of self-government and, once truly awakened, quite capable of it. Such is the noble humanism of *The Prelude,* a philosophy of self-confidence and of enlightened self-assertion, which distinguishes its doctrine from the somewhat too conventional admonitions of *The Excursion* and later poems. But despite the energy with which the teaching of *The Prelude* was presented, its doctrine could not have had so profound a seat in Wordsworth's mind as we often suppose. As we all know, the ink was hardly dry upon the first draft of *The Prelude* when Wordsworth in no equivocal fashion repudiated its philosophy, for "Elegiac Stanzas" and parts of the "Ode to Duty" amount to a recantation. Furthermore, a careful survey of the last books of *The Prelude* itself indicates at least two or three passages where traces of a latent skepticism and dissatisfaction may be found. In Book XII, good men are recognized as the genuine "wealth of nations," but Wordsworth mentions his anxious meditations upon equalitarianism:

> . . . I could not but inquire,
> Not with less interest than heretofore,
> But greater, though in spirit more subdued,
> Why is this glorious Creature to be found
> One only in ten thousand? . . .

Again we must remember that the virtues of the full imaginative life are in the last book of *The Prelude* attributed only to "higher minds," although no mention is here made of any possible conflict between this doctrine and the democratic tenets of earlier passages. In "Elegiac Stanzas," however, there is no difficulty of interpretation. A wholly new attitude appears:

> Farewell, farewell the heart that lives alone,
> Housed in a dream, at distance from the Kind!
> Such happiness, wherever it be known,
> Is to be pitied; for 'tis surely blind.

Here Wordsworth is repudiating the philosophy of *The Prelude*, which has come to appear as selfish and socially unobservant. Again in the "Ode to Duty" occurs a similar repudiation:

> I, loving freedom, and untried;
> No sport of every random gust,

Yet being to myself a guide,
Too blindly have reposed my trust:
And oft, when in my heart was heard
Thy timely mandate, I deferred
The task, in smoother walks to stray;
But thee I now would serve more strictly, if I may.

The doctrine of *The Prelude* is spoken of with tolerance but is nonetheless found to be wanting. It seems to the Wordsworth of 1805-1806 to be pitifully subject to self-deceit and the weakness of rationalization. Man requires a standard of morality so firmly defined and rigorously stated that he can in no way alter its *dicta* or tamper with its integrity by a rationalizing interpretation. We shall presently question the validity of this criticism which Wordsworth directs against his own thought.

But now let us consider Wordsworth's first bit of self-criticism, the notion that in *The Prelude* he had entertained a philosophy "housed in a dream, at distance from the Kind." Certainly a perusal of the magnificent conclusion of *The Prelude* suggests to the reader no strain of selfishness, and, if we understand its doctrine, we can hardly feel that it is based upon a sheltered ignorance of human life. Surely Wordsworth does not deny the existence of evil or of suffering. He insists only that we enrich our understanding of life through concrete insight and so widen our sympathies before judging our fellow men or attempting to influence their lives. Where then lies the flaw in his thinking? I, for one, believe that there is in the conclusion of *The Prelude* no serious or fundamental flaw. The weakness of Wordsworth's philosophy is most clearly manifest not here but in the great ethical poems which follow, in "**Elegiac Stanzas**," "**Ode to Duty**," *The Excursion,* and "**Laodamía**."

There are, most broadly speaking, two attitudes of the intellectual towards democracy: one in which he would raise all men, who, he recognizes, are equal in fundamental capacity, toward a life of responsible self-government; the other in which he recognizes in many if not all of the humble and untutored a strength and wisdom which he may not himself possess, an ability to face the real world, born of stress and its complementary fortitude.

The first of these appears clearly in *The Recluse* and the second occasionally in *The Prelude* and in such poems as "**Resolution and Independence**" and "**Elegiac Stanzas**." These two points of view are not necessarily contradictory. They can exist side by side as they do in Wordsworth's earlier thought. After all, men of intellectual and of moral virtue have much to learn of one another. But there is possible a confusion of these elements, and this we may call the *democratic fallacy,* a sadly perverted form of equalitarian doctrine, which, although frequently arising in democratic communities, is by no means essential to democracy or indeed a necessary outcome of it. This fallacy appears when the gifted man hesitates to make full use of his gifts, is even suspicious of them, because they are not universal. This line of thought becomes even more dangerous if the man of genius has at one time overestimated the power of his less endowed fellows. He may finally come to suspect even his own strength. This I believe to have been the case with Wordsworth.

As we have seen, Wordsworth had drawn from Godwin, if only for a brief period, a certainty that man must free himself from convention and sentiment and solve his problems, individual and social, solely by the aid of analytic intelligence. This philosophy he shortly repudiated, having recognized, not without bitter disappointment, that reason by itself, working

as it does with abstract terms, offers but meager motivation for man's emotions and engenders but little strength of will. He then supplemented his Godwinism with his own doctrine of the ethical imagination above described. In this doctrine Wordsworth retained something, however little, of Godwinism. The individual remains his own arbiter of right and wrong, and man's mind, albeit his imagination rather than his reason, remains its own court of highest appeal. What I really want to do when I have envisaged my situation and the people involved in the full clarity of concrete imagery—that is the right thing to do. There is no other way, rational or traditional of determining right or wrong. I must face the world, "being to myself a guide." And so must all men who are capable of moral life.

While working upon *The Prelude,* Wordsworth had, as we have seen, pondered the problem: How many men are capable of such responsiblity? All, of course, possess the capacity, for all men possess the nucleus of imagination or they would be incapable of the simplest acts of knowing, of the most rudimentary awareness of unity in variety. This fact was at one time enough for Wordsworth. In time, under democratic ideals and wholesome education guided by sound romantic teaching, genuine moral liberty would be the possession of all. Furthermore, men would learn to appreciate the natural religion which must accompany the dominion of imagination. We have already seen that Wordsworth believed all human beings to be at least *capable* of some mystical insight. This hope for the future was enough, and until this happy consummation, the "higher minds," the few romantic intellectuals and the rarely gifted children of Nature, untutored but happily inspired, must preserve this substantial wisdom.

The unenlightened must be brought slowly to the position of the elect, such is the faith of 1800. This belief is tempered somewhat by doubts and qualifications expressed in *The Prelude*. Some men are perhaps almost incapable of enlightenment, and some fortunate souls need very little enlightening. But the faith remains throughout unretracted: Virtue is the child of imagination and the only path to virtue and wisdom lies through expansion of the individual's imaginative powers. The poet, the true romantic poet, the imaginative man par excellence, is the proper teacher of the human race. Thus Wordsworth writes of himself in the last lines of *The Recluse* fragment:

> . . . may my life
> Express the image of a better time. . . .

Suddenly, at least in appearance, this faith is retracted: the poets must discipline their wayward genius and assume the patient fortitude and sturdy endurance of the humble. They have withdrawn themselves and housed their ideals in a dream, and their ideals are selfish and futile. They must go to school to the very people that they had once considered their rightful pupils. They must assume the "unfeeling armor of old time," so admired in the "**Elegiac Stanzas**." (pp. 225-29)

To account for this *volte-face,* we find available three or four possible explanations which have been offered at one time or another by Wordsworth's biographers. (1) In the first place, we may attribute it to the temporary failure of French democracy, and its passage under Napoleon into imperial dictatorship. The philosophers seemed to have betrayed the people or, at least, advised them so badly that the people became willy-nilly the victims of an archadventurer. Certainly at this time the human virtues might easily appear to advantage in contrast with the ideals of revolutionary individualism which seemed to have been treacherously perverted to such foul ends.

(2) Again it may be true that, brooding over his unhappy relations with Annette Vallon and considering the suffering and unhappiness which impulse had produced, Wordsworth may have come to believe that human nature is fundamentally incapable of "being to itself a guide." This unfortunate affair, however, lay well in the past, dating from a time when even the philosophy of *The Prelude* was unformulated. Hence had remorse for the desertion of Annette exercised any effect upon his philosophy, it would have checked the first development of such thinking rather than have caused its decline. Furthermore, impulsive weakness may easily enough be explained according to the psychology of *The Prelude*. We often act impulsively when our impulses are unenlightened by full comprehension, expressed in concrete imagery, of their present significance and possible consequences.

(3) Perhaps most important of all the reasons advanced is that expressed in "Elegiac Stanzas": "A deep distress hath humanized my soul." Under the emotional strain of a cruel bereavement, the loss of his brother John, Wordsworth came to value more highly the virtues of endurance and resignation. This, to be sure, is a natural and quite comprehensible development of his personality. It is only when such insight leads to repudiation of the efficacy of a philosophy of self-enlightenment that we must put it down as a counsel of despair. After all, Wordsworth's bereavement really widened his imaginative sympathies, as the "Elegiac Stanzas" eloquently tell, and included within the sphere of his understanding attitudes never before so clearly envisaged.

(4) It is important to remember in the above connection that at this time, as the "Intimations Ode" suggests, Wordsworth recognized a certain decline in his own gifts of intense esthetic sensibility and of mystical exaltation. The resultant loss of self-confidence might well be reflected in his emphasis upon the humble virtues and the philosophy of duty. Duty may then appear as the one sure foundation of human dignity, without which man is a poor creature, weak and insignificant:

> Possessions vanish, and opinions change,
> And passions hold a fluctuating seat:
> But, by the storms of circumstance unshaken,
> And subject neither to eclipse nor wane,
> Duty exists. . . .

We might call this a philosophy of self-defense as opposed to the philosophy of self-confidence, so clearly expressed in *The Prelude*.

These reasons, offered frequently as explanations of Wordsworth's change of heart, are most assuredly not to be dismissed. Certainly the first, third, and fourth seem to bear out our problem. But it seems clear that no one of these influences could have determined Wordsworth's thinking profoundly had it not been for his unhappy readiness to entertain what we have called the democratic fallacy. Had these circumstances arisen before a thinker quite free of any merely sentimental interest in praising his fellow men or of any desire to be as like them as possible, the outcome must have been very different. And, be it said in defense of *The Prelude*, the benevolence which it teaches does not necessarily involve such a sentimentalism. (pp. 230-32)

The triumph of the democratic fallacy, with its pernicious leveling of great minds and small, leads to an inevitable and ironic conclusion. It finally destroys faith in democracy. If we are to identify ourselves with "the Kind" and accept the virtues of endurance, we will come to accept the traditional supports of the humble and gather stoically beneath the orthodox and conservative strongholds of church and state. With these great fortresses of security we shall not care to tamper. In fact, there seems something indecent in any attempt to recast the scheme of things. Of such development in Wordsworth's thinking we are all only too well aware. The extreme illiberalism which resulted in his political thought is too well known to require much comment. His opposition to reform, expressed with timid and suspicious querulousness, is almost identical with the attitude of an aristocratic arch-conservative, although the fear of change which is its usual aspect has an ultimate origin quite distinct from any aristocratic sentiment. This fear of change led Wordsworth to oppose universal education and the freedom of the press, and this latter as early as 1814, within ten years of the completion of the first draft of *The Prelude*. But Wordsworth's intellectual progress from "Elegiac Stanzas" was inevitable one. Once doubt the value of the intellectual and spiritual independence of the individual, and the rest follows.

We have described the vacillations of Wordsworth's thought while he passes from *The Prelude* to *The Excursion* as a wavering between the philosophies of "I *want*" and of "I *must*," between the ideal of self-realization and the ideal of self-transcending duty. In this his thought is clearly less balanced than that of Dante or even of Goethe, if we consider the latter's thought as expressed in such a poem as his "Vermächtniss." It is this vacillation that reveals the tragic flaw in Wordsworth's philosophy. The moral insight so brilliantly presented in *The Prelude* is very shortly marred and finally, in the later poems, wholly obscured by Wordsworth's failure to perceive that these two approaches to morality can be rendered mutually consistent. Wordsworth faces a fatal disjunction: either we are to develop ourselves, our insights and our sympathies and proceed according to a romantic version of Augustine's formula, *Ama et fac quod vis,* or we are to submit ourselves wholly to the discipline of an established principle of duty. There can be no alternative or middle course. (pp. 234-35)

[Had Wordsworth expanded his ideas in the "Ode to Duty"], the philosophy of *The Prelude* might well have been richly supplemented. But here Wordsworth failed. Imagination and spontaneous enjoyment are discounted in favor of stoic endurance such as appears in the *White Doe*. And I very much fear that this evaluation is founded largely upon the feeling that in accepting dutiful endurance as the prime virtue, we are identifying ourselves with "the Kind." Thus the democratic fallacy seems to triumph.

Wordsworth's failure to integrate the philosophy of *The Prelude* with a theory of duty constitutes a real loss to our modern culture. It is one of our fundamental weaknesses that we habitually see life as divided between play and real enjoyment on the one hand and important work and duty on the other. What we want to do and what we ought to do stand apart in theory. This is perhaps inevitable in an irreligious and commercial civilization. But against this error Wordsworth's teaching might well have proven to be a great force had he overcome his own confusion, for he at least faced our problem and in his happier periods held a key to its solution.

But let us here in fairness to Wordsworth admit that the democratic fallacy, as we have described it, confused and perverse as it is, rests upon one sentiment among others, which is clearly an honorable one. This is an intense dislike of making an exception of oneself. It is from this underlying motive, which in the minds of rationalist philosophers may be interpreted as a respect for strict logical consistency in practical life, that the real power of Kant's categorical imperative derives. Consider Walt Whitman's famous resolve to accept nothing that all men might not enjoy on the same terms. This may be a sound foundation for equalitarian ethical doctrine, but of course it should be read as requiring equal opportunity rather than any limitation of achievement to the common level. (pp. 235-36)

> *Newton P. Stallknecht, in his* Strange Seas of Thought: Studies in William Wordsworth's Philosophy of Man and Nature, *second edition, Indiana University Press, 1958, 290 p.*

DAVID PERKINS (essay date 1964)

[*Describing Wordsworth as "a man dominated by a moral ideal," Perkins focuses in this excerpt on Wordsworth's belief in the importance of sincerity as a personal and artistic ideal. After analyzing the poet's truthfulness, "high-mindedness," and independence, Perkins compares Wordsworth with Leo Tolstoy, observing that both writers imposed moral lessons upon their art. Other critics who write about Wordsworth's philosophical doctrine include Stephen (1876), Havens (1941), Stallknecht (1958), and Langbaum (1977).*]

Wordsworth is the central figure of English romanticism, and, with the exception of Goethe, he is probably the greatest writer of the romantic age. He is also a moving example of a man dominated by a moral ideal. In the transformation of poetry throughout the eighteenth century, nothing is more remarkable than the emergence of sincerity as a major poetic value, and, indeed, as something required of all artists. One can hardly overstress the novelty of this demand. Neither Pope nor his predecessors would have dreamed of asking themselves the dreadful question: is my poetry sincere? (p. 1)

There is, it seems to me, only one sense in which it is even possibly appropriate to say that a poem must be sincere. It may be that in order to write well a poet must deeply feel the emotion he expresses as he creates the poem, though he need not feel it ever before or after. This is what Wordsworth meant by sincerity, but not all that he meant; and if sincerity suggested nothing more, it would have little influence on poetry or criticism. For in this sense sincerity would be merely a sufficient power of sympathetic imagination. It would have nothing to do with personal honesty, and the whole sting and effect of the poetic ideal of sincerity proceed from the fact that it refers to moral qualities—veracity, earnestness, integrity. To expect that a poet will write with a personal truthfulness is obviously naïve, as virtually all poets have recognized. But their more sophisticated views have not prevented them from making the effort. In describing the particular response of Wordsworth to the challenge of sincerity, one also suggests how the ideal of sincerity has influenced poetry throughout the last century and a half; for at the opening phase of this new development, Wordsworth already confronted most of the large dilemmas it engenders, and he felt his way to stylistic expedients that later poets would continue and refine. Moreover, if we stand at a distance, a personal drama of the widest relevance unfolds itself in Wordsworth. He reveals at least one way in which the ideal of sincerity may work itself out in the life of a man—the achievement it may inspire, and the limitations to which it may finally contribute. The achievement is obvious in Wordsworth. Apart from his constant effort to be honest, there would have been neither the power of phrase nor the liberating originality of thought. An ideal that might crush other poets made Wordsworth a great one. (pp. 3-4)

When we read Wordsworth today, it is not likely to be for the beliefs or dogma to which he subscribed at any stage of his life, and least of all for the religion of Nature that pervades his greatest poetry. This poetry took the lead in a major theme of sensibility in the nineteenth century. It encouraged readers to imagine that they felt a sympathy and communion with the natural world, and, in such communion, a quasi-religious experience. For if the natural world was not itself divine, it was haunted by a divine presence. But this particular religious movement has run its course and the sect is disbanded. We now have to read Wordsworth in the same way, and for the same reasons, that we read other poets whose theology we may not share. Partly, of course, we read him for his phrasing— the unforgettable lines and stanzas. We still turn to the Wordsworth finely presented by Arnold and Mill [see excerpts dated 1879 and 1853-54], the poetry that awakens us to sources of happiness in the common things of life. There is the brooding weight and sanity of his wide moral concern, and the manly pathos of poems that are, in Hazlitt's phrase, "mournful *requiems*" over the grave of human hopes." We can also go to Wordsworth for a poetry of visionary symbolism, a few passages mostly in the **Prelude**. Then, too, no poet gives a more vivid picture of the mind encountering and building up its world, and reading Wordsworth we see more clearly the modes and processes of our own consciousness. There is also the Wordsworth who senses the aura of strangeness around any act or object, the sheer inexplicability of it, the mystery and unfathomable depth.

Behind all of these partial descriptions there is the writer who, whenever he is taken seriously, troubles the conscience of poetry. He seems to suggest that even in writing poetry some commitments must be put before art. (pp. 24-5)

He was, at least after his youth, incapable of romantic illusions. His pamphlet on the **Convention of Cintra,** it was agreed in his

A portrait of Wordsworth in 1817.

circle, combined the philosophical and psychological depth of Burke with the moral passion of Milton. Thundering from a summit of idealism, Wordsworth was to recall the English people to strenuous principle in the conduct of foreign affairs. But while the pamphlet was at the printer's, he began to fear that portions of it might expose him to prosecution for sedition or libel. The heroic mood evaporates like a morning mist. The publisher is begged to read it over. "If any such passages occur, let the leaf be cancelled—as to the expense, that I disregard in a case like this." (The last clause is a tremendous proof of Wordsworth's alarm.) Wordsworth reflects that the pamphlet has been long delayed. It will probably have little effect. There is no reason why he should endanger himself. Except that there was little risk, the reaction is quite sensible. It is not the reaction of a Shelley, however. The constrast with Shelley holds in another sphere as well. No man was more "tenderly attached" to family and friends than Wordsworth, but, according to Coleridge, he could not fall in love in a romantic way. (pp. 26-7)

But Coleridge knew that "In all human beings good and bad Qualities are not only found together . . . but they actually tend to produce each other." The same obstinate veracity, the habit of admitting to himself and saying to others what he held to be true, was one of the things that attracted Coleridge in the first place and still attracts readers to Wordsworth's poetry. He was a person one could trust. (p. 28)

In any kind of work, the union of hard common sense with tenacity would have made Wordsworth effective. The addition of an immense high-mindedness plus, of course, some unexplainable gift, made him a poet. He was intensely competitive and ambitious, as much as any captain of industry, with the difference that he would commit himself only to what he held to be best. (p. 29)

[He] was a sort of Cincinnatus of poetry, who could interrupt the writing of the great ode on **"Intimations of Immortality"** to spread manure on the garden. The independence was a way of life as well as of thinking, and it was independence for the sake of achievement. For by the time he was twenty-one, Wordsworth knew as a matter of common sense that "small certainties are the bane of great talents," and upon that principle he acted. As Coleridge put it, Wordsworth "knows the intrinsic value of the Different objects of human Pursuit, and regulates his Wishes in Subordination to that Knowledge . . . he feels, and with a *practical* Faith, the Truth . . . that we can do but one thing well, & that therefore we must make a choice—he has made that choice from his early youth, has pursued & is pursuing it."

The choice, of course, was poetry, but poetry not as offering a momentary release from the actual concerns of life. To Wordsworth, our daily preoccupations—our "business, love, or strife"—are the distraction and escape, the dream, the illusion in which we protect ourselves, until we float out of existence, having cheated ourselves of life. Great art, he thinks, can call us back to reality. It is a record and instrument of man's questing mind seeking to grapple with truth.

Perhaps the best short description of Wordsworth is that he was an English, middle-class, limited version of Tolstoy. There was the same sensuous grip. Though Wordsworth was much more inhibited, there was the same violence of passion, and fundamental sympathy with the energies of life even when they might be lawless. Both men show a clutch for essentials and contempt of trivia. Moreover, it is a drastic understatement to say that they took things hard. Whatever they went through,

there was a passionate concern that dwarfs most writers. Neither did they dwindle as they grew older. If their art gradually withered, the reason lies not so much in any increasing numbness as in their power to care so much about other things. To take some trivial examples: Wordsworth's interminable tirades in his later years against political reform, or his vehement opposition to his daughter's marriage, are not edifying passages in his life, but they show that the fire was not spent. Aubrey de Vere wondered that the aging poet should "speak with passionate grief of the death of a child, as if a bereavement forty years past had befallen him the day before, detailing the minutest circumstances of the illness." In his youth, after the French Revolution, Wordsworth went through a spiritual and intellectual crisis that reminds one of Tolstoy. Both men could commit titanic energies in the struggle for some final certitude, with a questioning that leaves nothing unchallenged, and then, if they thought they had an answer, they would impose it upon their art. (pp. 30-2)

David Perkins, in his Wordsworth and the Poetry of Sincerity, *Cambridge, Mass.: Belknap Press, 1964, 285 p.*

GEOFFREY H. HARTMAN   (essay date 1964)

[An American critic, poet, and editor, Hartman champions the creative imagination in his critical writings, guarding it against formalism and reduction. Though he acknowledges that the mind continually seeks a sense of order, Hartman maintains that the role of imaginative literature is to confront and convey experience without classifying it or turning it into an abstraction. Regarding the writing of criticism, Hartman has written that it "should not be fobbed off as a secondary activity, as a handmaiden to more 'creative' thinking," but instead should be viewed as an imaginative as well as an analytical endeavor. Here Hartman theorizes that in Wordsworth's poetry, "consciousness of self (is) raised to apocalyptic pitch," and he discusses this idea as it relates to the Romantic lyric in general. Through a detailed analysis of "The Solitary Reaper," Hartman develops his argument that Wordsworth's poetry typically starts with the poet's awareness of an arresting image and then proceeds through "surmise." According to Hartman, the process of "surmise" involves self-consciousness, reaction, and expression on the part of the poet, with the final result being the writing of the poem itself. Other critics who consider Wordsworth's style include Hazlitt (1825), Pater (1874), Lowell (1875), Bradley (1909), Darbishire (1949), and Pottle (1950).]

[Wordsworth's egotism] would have been beneath notice had it not contained something precariously "spiritual" which was not exhausted by his overt choice of scenes from low or rural life. Those who objected to Wordsworth often commended Burns, Crabbe, and even Robert Bloomfield, and the magazine poetry of the 1790's is full of compassionate subjects, rural themes, and personal reflections. Modest Christian sentiment was welcome, and to "suck Divinity" (or even metaphysics) from daffodils was too common a poetic indulgence to have roused the contemptuous disgust of a literary lady. What is so precariously spiritual about Wordsworth, and so difficult to separate from egotism, is the minute attention he gives to his own most casual responses, a finer attention than is given to the nature he responds to. He rarely counts the streaks of the tulip, but he constantly details the state of his mind. When Wordsworth depicts an object he is also depicting himself or, rather, a truth about himself, a self-acquired revelation. There is very little "energetic" picture-making in him.

I call this aspect of Wordsworth's poetry spiritual because its only real justification (which few of his contemporaries were willing to entertain) was that it carried the Puritan quest for evidences of election into the most ordinary emotional contexts. Wordsworth did not himself talk of election or salvation but . . . of renovation (regeneration), and he did not seem to be directly aware of his Puritan heritage, although the *Poems* of 1807, which includes both **"I wandered lonely as a cloud"** and **"The Solitary Reaper,"** shows a heightened intimacy with seventeenth-century traditions. Failure or access of emotion (inspiration) vis-à-vis nature was the basis of his spiritual life: his soul either kindled in contact with nature or it died. There was no such thing as a casual joy or disappointment. Such 'justification by nature' was not, however, a simple matter, to be determined by one experience—Wordsworth's response is often delayed for a considerable time. His spirit may be "shy," or stirrings may rise from almost forgotten depths. (pp. 4-5)

It is a dangerous half-truth, however, to connect Wordsworth's spirituality with habits of introspection spread abroad by such different movements as Protestantism, Rationalism, and Rousseauism. . . . **"The Solitary Reaper"** is not a brooding analytic inquiry into the source of an emotion. The poet does not explain why he responded so strongly to the Highland girl but takes advantage of the strength of his response. After expressing the fact that he is moved, he allows the emotion its own life and delights in new accesses of thought and feeling. A poet, we read in the preface to *Lyrical Ballads,* "rejoices more than other men in the spirit of life that is in him."

Neither is this the whole truth, for the poet's spirit, tinged by melancholy, is not completely free-moving. Some burden of mystery is present, linked to his initial mood. To take this mood as expressing nothing more than surprise is to dispell the mystery too quickly. Though the poem begins in surprise— an ordinary sight is modified by an unusual circumstance: the harvester is alone and her song heightens the solitude where communal and joyful activity was expected—surprise turns into something pensive, even elegiac. There is an inward sinking, as if the mind, having been moved by the Highland girl, is now moved by itself. The mystery lies in that sudden deepening, or doubled shock.

I put this in the form of an impression but the text supports it. If the first imperative, "Behold her, single in the field," is addressed to the reader, the second, "Stop here, or gently pass," is certainly said also by the poet to himself. The inward sinking or turning—the reflexive consciousness—is quite clear. The poet himself is made to stop, reflect, and listen, like a traveler who has come on the scene by chance. An image has "singled" him out.

At the end of the first stanza, moreover, we are still in the shadow of the mystery and uncertain why the poet is moved. His third imperative, "O listen!," again addressed either to an auditor or to himself, is followed by an explanation ("for the Vale profound / Is overflowing with the sound") which explains nothing. It would be inane if "listen" did not suggest an activity more intense than hearing, and if "overflowing" did not heighten the idea of strong emotional participation. Even the vale seems to be moved: and should not a passerby, therefore, stop and respond? It would be ungenerous not to enter into communion.

The question why the poet is moved is subordinated to the fact *that* he is moved, that his mind overflows under the influence of song. While the poem begins with a girl who is alone in her work and in her song, which is not expressly for others but which she sings to herself, she and her song reach across the valley to halt the traveler, who then resumes his journey with music in his heart. The last lines of the poem,

> The music in my heart I bore,
> Long after it was heard no more,

have a literal and an extended meaning, which collaborate to express response, repercussion, overflow. The poet heard the girl inwardly after he had passed out of actual range of hearing (the literal import), yet the "long after" may be taken to reach to the moment of composition two years later. **"The Solitary Reaper"** is evidence that the song has survived in his heart.

The overflow of the poet's feelings, and the pleasure he takes in each new mood or thought, can be traced stage by stage. In the second stanza he has already traveled, as through a magic casement, beyond the immediate scene, and though he returns to the present in stanza three, it is only to begin a new 'dallying with surmise.' Even the question on which he returns is significant. "Will no one tell me what she sings?" is a sociable gesture revealing how the song has spread beyond itself to cause this appeal he whimsically makes. His new address to the reader blends outward-directed feeling and inward-going thought.

The third stanza, composed of two surmises, continues to advance *through* the solitary to the social. Does the song, it is asked, "flow" for sufferings associated with a historical or mythical past, or does it treat of familiar things, past, present, and future? This return to the familiar, and from the fixed past to the more open "has been, and may be again," is characteristically Wordsworthian and anticipates the "something evermore about to be" toward which the poem tends. For in the final stanza, though Wordsworth gives up surmise and reverts to the indicative, his variations of the central word (sang, song, singing), his circling back to the figure of the girl at work (is she in a laboring or a thoughtful attitude?), and his first use of feminine rhyme ("ending"/"bending") modify the matter-of-factness of the event. As the poet returns in thought from one solitary, the girl, to another, himself, and therefore uses the "I" more overtly than before, the power for communion in so random an image, and its indefinite echo, are acknowledged. A finitude is removed from the verbs as from the action.

Thus Wordsworth, under the impress of a powerful feeling, turns round both it and its apparent cause, respecting both and never reducing the one to the other. By surmise he multiplies his moods, if not the phenomenon. His surmises have a pattern, which is to proceed through the solitary to the social and from stasis to motion, or to make these interchangeable. Yet everything stays in the realm of surmise, which approves, in any case, of such fluidity. Surmise is fluid in nature; it likes "whether . . . or" formulations, alternatives rather than exclusions, echoing conjecture (Keats' "Do I wake or sleep?") rather than blunt determinateness. The actual is in some way the potential, and in **"The Solitary Reaper"** surmise has unobtrusively influenced even the rhythm and certain verbal figures. Such a line as "Stop here, *or* gently pass" (my italics) is directed in theme and format against the purely determinate. The line contains, in fact, one of the many 'fluidifying' doublings of this poem ("Reaping and singing," "cuts and binds," "Things, and battles," "Perhaps . . . or"). Because the second phrase of each doubling is expanded thematically or in the number of syllables or by an equally subtle increment, the effect is that of expansion: "cuts and binds" flows into "and sings," and a parallel lengthening occurs in each stanza, whose symmetry is beautifully disturbed by the fourth line of six syllables, which expands into regular tetrameter at the end.

An exhaustive analysis of verbal effects is not necessary and may even distract us. The essential fact is that Wordsworth allows the sudden emotion (or, in the daffodil poem, sudden optical impression) to invade and renew his mind instead of reducing the emotion by an act of mind. Knowing that his relation to nature is as unpredictable as a relation of Grace—that whether or not he originally responded, and whether or not he responded fully, the encounter has a secret life that may later flash out and renew his feelings—Wordsworth adopts the stance of surmise which points to liberty and expansiveness of spirit. In **"The Solitary Reaper"** it is impossible to distinguish what originally happened from what happened to the mental traveler. . . . But however we construe the situation, Wordsworth's response reflects the importance of surmise both in his own and in Romantic lyricism. (pp. 6-9)

All is surmise in **"The Solitary Reaper"** except the startled opening: the poet's mind swings far from the present to which it keeps returning until raised to the virtue of the song it hears, apposing to the song the mind's own flowingness. In Keats' odes, however, there is from the outset a strong attempt to transcend surmise, to turn it into real vision, and his poems are this flight and faltering. Wordsworth's more leisurely procedure can lead to a dangerous prolixity rarely felt in Keats; through Keats' sharper vacillations, moreover, we once again feel "the surmise" as a separate movement, although this separateness is not intellectual, as in Milton, but based on levels of imaginative intensity. Surmise, for Keats, is the middle-ground of imaginative activity, not reaching to vision, not falling into blankness. Stanza five of "Ode to a Nightingale," which owes a specific debt to Milton's flower passage in "Lycidas," and which by its profuse tenderness, and this reminiscence, anticipates an easeful death, is a perfect expression of the mood of surmise as such:

> I cannot see what flowers are at my feet,
> Nor what soft incense hangs upon the boughs,
> But, in embalmed darkness, guess each sweet
> Wherewith the seasonable month endows
> The grass, the thicket, and the fruit-tree wild. . . .

It might be useful to consider the Romantic lyric as a development of the surmise. We have no proper definition, formal or historical, of this kind of lyric, which disconcertingly turns all terms descriptive of mode into terms descriptive of mood. When we say, for example, that **"The Solitary Reaper"** is a blend of idyll and elegy we refer more to states of mind expressed by it than to formal genres. Though the surmise is not a genre originally, it is a specific rhetorical form whose rise and modifications one can trace and which significantly becomes a genre in the Romantic period.

Yet the designation "a lyric of surmise" would be too simple and artificial. In **"The Solitary Reaper,"** as in Keats' ode ("Darkling I listen . . ."), surmise is tinged by a *penseroso* element that sinks toward melancholoy. Romantic lyricism, pensiveness, and melancholy are interrelated, even if the exact nature of the relation has remaind obscure. We know that surmise expresses the freedom of a mind aware of itself, aware and not afraid of its moods or potentialities—what darker burden, then, is expressed by this "dewy" melancholoy?

These questions of mood, and the relation of mood to mode, are clarified by a strange line in Wordsworth's poem. "Stop here, or gently pass" is a variant of apostrophes to the passing traveler found on gravestones or commemorative statues. "Look well upon this statue, stranger," is the opening of one of Theocritus' *Inscriptions*. Again: "Stand and look at Archilochus, the old maker of iambic verse." This is sometimes coupled with the wish that soil or tomb lie lightly on the dead man: "Blessed be this tomb for lying so light above the sacred head of Eurymedon." Wordsworth's poem is linked to the epitaph, though we do not know immediately what valor or virtue it mourns, and though it is strange that a harvest scene should suggest this memento mori to the poet. The traveler—man, the secular pilgrim—is halted by an affecting image. And something peculiar in the image, or the suspension itself of habitual motion, or an ensuing, meditative consciousness, brings him into the shadow of death. That shadow is lightened or subsumed as the poem proceeds, and the unusual image pointing like an epitaph to the passerby is transformed into a more internal inscription testifying of continuance rather than death: "The music in my heart I bore, / Long after it was heard no more."

The reflective stopping of the poet, which is like the shock of self-consciousness and may express it in a mild and already distanced form, is a general feature of Romantic lyricism and related to its penseroso or "white" melancholy. The halted traveler, of course, does not always appear so clearly and dramatically. But a meditative slowing of time—a real deepening of mind-time or self-consciousness—is always present and often sharply announced, as in the first strong beats of "My heart aches" (Keats) or the absoluteness of "A sudden blow . . ." (Yeats). In Wordsworth's poetry local traditions of genre are still felt, and many of his poems are recognizably cognate with the Epitaph, or at least the Inscription: the latter is the most contemporary way of being Classical about Spirit of Place. One of Wordsworth's first genuinely lyrical poems is such an epitaph-inscription, namely the **"Lines left upon a Seat in a Yew-tree which stands near the Lake of Esthwaite"**; and even the **"Lines composed a few miles above Tintern Abbey,"** with their specific registry of place and date and a distinctly elegiac and memorializing strain, carry some marks of the genre they transcend.

Is there a more archetypal situation for the self-conscious mind than this figure of the halted traveler confronting an inscription, confronting the knowledge of death and startled by it into feeling "the burden of the mystery"? (pp. 11-13)

The startled, yet subdued, opening of **"The Solitary Reaper"** is . . . not fortuitous. In fact, the more typical a Wordsworth poem the more it arises . . . [from a shock]. This shock, though consonant with the ordinary mechanism of heightened awareness, may also be, as some poems indicate explicitly, a "conversion" or "turning" of the mind. "My mind turned round," Wordsworth can say, "As with the might of waters." In the Lucy poem, **"Strange fits of passion,"** the moon dropping suddenly behind the cottage roof engenders as suddenly a thought of death, and if the poet mutes its implication (it is called "fond and wayward") the thought has some truth, as the ensuing poems telling of Lucy's death suggest. Is Wordsworth aggrandizing the prophetic character of ordinary perception or subduing an extraordinary perception? In **"The Solitary Reaper,"** likewise, ordinary attention blends with a stronger awareness (call it imagination or revelation) as if the poet were afraid of distinguishing them too precisely.

We can understand the blending best if we suppose that the "Behold" by which Wordsworth's attention is engaged or redirected signals the influx of an unusual state of consciousness which is quickly normalized. A Wordsworth poem is then seen to be a *reaction* to this consciousness as well as its *expression*. **"The Solitary Reaper"** may be viewed as the product of two kinds of consciousness, old and new, ordinary and supervening, which gather in tension around the precipitating image. This view introduces a dialectical factor and considers the poem as the synthesis of a mind in conflict with itself.

There is an episode, perhaps the most significant in *The Prelude*, which shows the poet in the actual grip of the special consciousness we are positing. There, too, a halted traveler appears. In 1804, describing how he and a friend crossed the Alps some fourteen years earlier, Wordsworth is usurped by something in his mind which is both a new interpretation of the episode and a new state of consciousness, and he records the fact in place:

> Imagination—here the Power so called
> Through sad incompetence of human speech,
> That awful Power rose from the mind's abyss
> Like an unfathered vapour that enwraps,
> At once, some lonely traveller. I was lost;
> Halted without an effort to break through.
>
> (pp. 15-16)

An ecstatic passage follows . . . in which Wordsworth does break through to resolve partially the stasis, for the usurping consciousness produces its own rush of verses, becomes its own subject as it were, and so retains momentarily a separate existence. Wordsworth calls this separate consciousness "Imagination."

It is a strange name to give it. Imagination, we are usually told, vitalizes and animates. Especially the Romantic Imagination. Yet here it stands closer to death than life, at least in its immediate effect. The poet is isolated and immobilized by it; it obscures rather than reveals nature; the light of the senses goes out. Only in its secondary action does it vitalize and animate, and even then not nature but a soul that realizes its individual greatness, a greatness independent of sense and circumstance. A tertiary effect does finally reach nature, when the soul assured of inner or independent sources of strength goes out from and of itself.

However removed this episode is from **"The Solitary Reaper,"** the halting of the traveler in that poem is also more than part of the random context. It expresses a sudden consciousness and is quietly linked to a memento mori. The great difference, indeed, is that this consciousness blends at once and imperceptibly with a new state or rather motion of mind, stasis being replaced by an evolving sense of continuity, till the traveler proceeds on his journey. The supervening consciousness does not have an abrupt and strongly separate existence as in *Prelude* VI. There is a pause, the mind sinks toward an intimation of death, but the vital rhythm is restored almost at once, and only an echo of that pause remains, as in the desert image and Hebrides-silence of stanza two. The initial halting, so quickly countervailed, is at the source of many Wordsworth poems, and it is time to identify its character precisely. Together with the poem that is at once its overflow and masking, it will tell us something significant about the relation of poetry to the mind.

A definition can now be offered. The supervening consciousness, which Wordsworth names Imagination in *Prelude* VI, and which also halts the mental traveler in the Highlands, is *consciousness of self raised to apocalyptic pitch.* The effects of "Imagination" are always the same: a moment of arrest, the ordinary vital continuum being interrupted; a separation of the traveler-poet from familiar nature; a thought of death or judgment or of the reversal of what is taken to be the order of nature; a feeling of solitude or loss or separation. Not all of these need be present at the same time, and some are obliquely present. But the most important consequence is the poem itself, whose developing structure is an expressive reaction to this consciousness. The poem transforms static into continuous by a gradual crescendo which is the obverse of the fixating initial shock. The Highland girl, a single, lonely figure, startles Wordsworth into an exceptionally strong self-consciousness, yet no stark feelings enter a poem which mellows them from the beginning. The poem here is on the side of "nature" and against the "imagination" which fathered it; it hides the intense and even apocalyptic self-consciousness from which it took its rise; it is generically a veiling of its source. (pp. 16-18)

> *Geoffrey H. Hartman, in his* Wordsworth's Poetry:
> 1787-1814, *1964. Reprint by Yale University Press,*
> *1971, 418 p.*

CARL WOODRING (essay date 1965)

[In his summary of Wordsworth's importance as a poet, Woodring observes that "outside of literature, no English artist . . . has been more influential." He portrays Wordsworth as one who extended the boundaries of poetry by "proclaiming the value of his own independent practice." According to Woodring, Wordsworth's greatness lies in his simplicity, iconoclasm, and wide knowledge of meter and form.]

[Wordsworth] grew into the greatest English poet since Milton. Between 1789 and 1847, he had eight formative years, ten stupendous years, nine or ten important years, and thirty years of decent productivity and consolidation. His historical influence on language, ideas, and manners has been immense. Outside of literature, no English artist, whether painter, sculptor, musician, choreographer, or architect, has been more influential. Although he has been translated to little effect—little, that is, relative to a Dante, a Shakespeare, a Bunyan, or a Dostoevsky—his influence on the people who speak or read English has been sufficient to sway art and affairs universally. His indirect effect on Proust, for example, is similar to Rousseau's indirect effect on *him*, and a line of some rectitude could be drawn from Wordsworth through Thoreau to Gandhi.

What Coleridge admired as much as anything else in Wordsworth, and what we shall not do wrong to admire, was the application of a powerful intellect, combined with powerful emotions, toward the solution of the general but immediate problems of man. This application of power is notable even in the **"Memorials of a Tour in Italy, 1837,"** where strength of imagination has flagged. His was no metaphysical intellect, like Coleridge's; it was practical, like Swift's.

Most of all, Wordsworth turned the course of English poetry. As both the Preface and the "lyrical ballads" indicate, he sensed very early the importance of his leadership. Of more than one poem in the volume of 1798 it could be said that he did not invent the form but he invented the idea that it was art. This extension of boundaries has had limitless implications for the nineteenth and twentieth centuries. Alexander Calder was not the first to make a mobile, but he first conceived, for our time, the idea that a continuously changing work could extend the plastic arts. Historical relativism in the judgment of works of art had been introduced in the eighteenth century, but no English artist before Wordsworth, in any medium, had anything like his effect in overthrowing the canons of taste by proclaiming the value of his own independent practice. For English-speaking peoples, only Beethoven had an equivalent effect, and there was no English musician worthy of the lesson. Giving to the word *experiment,* as applied to poetry, a meaning of something more permanent than an impromptu, *esquisse,* improvisation, or *commedia dell'arte all'improvviso,* Wordsworth pioneered in the movement of modern arts that has in fact given stature to improvisation as "something far more deeply interfused" than imitation of the masters.

Coleridge's ultimate commendation of Wordsworth may be put in the terms that a later poet and critic devised for a different purpose: In altering the whole existing order of the poetic past, Wordsworth restored poetry to the wholeness of its tradition after the dissociation of sensibility in Dryden and Pope and the Chinese wall of unfeeling language erected by Pope's followers. In Coleridge's view, Wordsworth brought thought and feeling together in the Elizabethan way after several generations had "thought and felt by fits, unbalanced." That he and Wordsworth disparaged Dryden and Pope unduly goes without saying.

When Coleridge makes a memorandum to write to the author of *The Recluse* "that he may insert something concerning *Ego,* its metaphysical Sublimity and intimte Synthesis with the principle of Co-adunation," we know that Colerdge recognizes Wordsworth's intellectual acumen, but we know also that Wordsworth would blur the edges of the idea and change the language drastically. Wordsworth's poetry is not ultimately simple, but its great historical influence has come from its relative simplicity of surface. In "Lines Written in Early Spring," he presents a characteristic observation that the birds and flowers seem to enjoy the air they breathe:

> And I must think, do all I can,
> That there was pleasure there.

What other poet would have expressed the qualification in terms even as simple as, say, "try as hard as I may"? The phrase "do all I can" has the daring of a child, a Beethoven, or a Wordsworth.

With simplification as his guide, he made everything he assimilated into his own. Like T. S. Eliot, he put borrowed words to many uses, but he created enough memorable phrases of his own to prove his right even to "human form divine," which Blake also thought too universal for Milton to keep to himself.

Egotism aside, Wordsworth's virtues are those of a prophet rather than of a polymath or a universal man. He is no Michelangelo, and no Goethe. Despite his kinship with Roman moralists, he is a poet of English solitude. Despite his wide knowledge of Italian poetry, he is less like Tasso or Ariosto than he is like Thomson and Beattie—except in the essential of genius. Despite his experiences near the heart of the French Revolution, he turns for guidance to Milton. He toured the Continent in search of images, but his skylarks are as English as his daisies. His view is not even as ample as the British Isles. He tried harder than the average Englishman, in the *Ecclesiastical Sonnets* and similar pieces, to remember the significance of Scotland, Wales, and Ireland for British institutions; but the confluence he honors is that of English throne, English Parliament, English Church, and English tongue.

Thomas Love Peacock was one of the first, but certainly not the last, to notice the absence from Wordsworth's poems of sexual passion. What is omitted from *The Prelude* is all that a diarist like Boswell would put into it. Love, and especially love for his wife, runs through the crevices of the later poetry, but the sexual images usually resemble the virginal dedication to poetry described in *The Prelude:*

> Gently did my soul
> Put off her veil, and, self-transmuted, stood
> Naked as in the presence of her God. . . .

Arnold's arithmetic was bad. Wordsworth averted his ken from no more than a third of human fate; but his "internal brightness" told him never to linger over sex, squalor, or spasms of despair merely because the artist can claim a franchise to linger over what exists. Agreeing that an artist should express "all he sees," Wordsworth took the phrase qualitatively rather than quantitatively.

No feminist ever used as handbook *The White Doe of Rylstone.* Although Wordsworth spoke for nationalism, for the sanctity of childhood, and—before the Oxford Movement—for the doctrine of Incarnation above the doctrine of Atonement, it is hard, on our side of Baudelaire, Marx, and Nietzsche, to think of him as iconoclastic. Yet he was iconoclastic, as well as independent and stubborn. He opposed the whole modern megalomania of analysis and measurement. The discoveries of Freud and Einstein would not have shocked him. What he deplored in advance is not the discoveries but the amoral application of them. About amorality he was as stubborn as God.

His poetry has a remarkable range in matter, forms, and artistry. Precision and delicacy do not belong to the Wordsworth of conventional literary history. . . .

Yet William Wordsworth is also that master of brevity and condensation who wrote the Lucy poems, "The Solitary Reaper," and a golden collection of such sonnets as those beginning "The world is too much with us," "Earth has not anything to show more fair," "Surprised by joy," and "I thought of thee, my partner and my guide." In my opinion, he earned the very highest rank among the precise artists who have—in Dr. Johnson's contemptuous phrase—carved heads on cherry stones.

Above all, it needs to be said that the many studies to date have left the mysteries of Wordsworth's performance far from exhausted.

All historical judgments are relative. But the absolute accomplishment endures, from his simple songs for thinking hearts to his explorations along the chasms and abysms of normal experience. Day in and day out, he proclaims in hammered verse the thrill of the ordinary. That, in our time, is a rarity indeed. (pp. 211-14)

> *Carl Woodring, in his* Wordsworth, *Houghton Mifflin Company, 1965, 227 p.*

PAUL M. ZALL (essay date 1966)

[*Zall maintains that Wordsworth was "primarily a practicing critic" who believed that poetry could bring about positive change in society. According to Zall, the poet hoped to enhance man's spirituality; therefore, Wordsworth concentrated on teaching his readers that the imagination is synonymous with "right reason" and that poetry is capable of uniting the inner and the outer worlds.*]

Wordsworth was primarily a practicing critic. His critical essays synthesize a number of principles current in the eighteenth century and redirect the focus of criticism to the operations of the mind in creating and appreciating poetry. But he was less concerned with setting up a consistent aesthetic system than with explaining the practical powers of poetry to a practical-minded public. He believed that poetry had the power to medicine men's minds by providing the inner man release from the pressures of the outer world. In an age when social, political, and economic pressures mounted "almost hourly," men's need for poetry increased proportionally. Poetry could provide healing sensations that would exercise the imagination in creative activity and stimulate awareness of man's brotherhood in a universe bonded by love. Wordsworth believed, in short, that the ultimate aim of poetry was no less than the regeneration of society.

As a practicing poet, Wordsworth wrote about poetry in terms of his own work, explaining or defending his practice, especially when it conflicted with conventional ideas of what poetry ought to be. To Wordsworth, contemporary ideas about poetry were based on the practice of Alexander Pope, but Wordsworth found Pope overly concerned with "manners," his language incongruous with the feelings of men, his descriptions of nature inaccurate. Moreover, he thought Pope's antithetical mode of expression in the heroic couplet placed equal emphasis on agreeable and disagreeable passions. If poetry were to achieve its highest aim, Wordsworth insisted, it must emphasize agreeable passions only. Dissatisfied with Pope, then, he turned for his models to earlier poets—Chaucer, Spenser, Shakespeare, Milton. Their concerns were with morals rather than manners; their language was accurately expressive of recognizable passions; their descriptions had the fidelity of eye-witness reports; and their subjects were healthy, elemental passions. They were to provide the pattern for the resurrection of poetry. (p. ix)

Wordsworth's chief concern is with the capability of poetry to restore man's spiritual powers by bridging the gap between the world about him and the world within. Since John Locke's time, it had been generally accepted that the world and its perceiver were separate entities; that the "secondary qualities" of abstraction and the "primary qualities" of sensation were distinctly discrete; and that sensation was the only mode of perceiving the world, while subsequent reflection led to developing abstract ideas about it. The problem for Wordsworth is that man is now lost to the tranquillizing, uplifing sensations abounding in natural surroundings. Further, selfish pursuits have separated him from other men; neglect of reflection has blinded him to the connection between the natural and the moral worlds. Wordsworth's solution is poetry that will stimulate beneficent sensations, reawaken sympathy, and revivify the reflective powers of the mind. He tries to link the external and the internal worlds by recreating precise forms of nature with all the breath and spirit of associations inherent in them. As the forms of nature are symbols of some higher order, so Wordsworth displays them "not as they exist in themselves, but as they *seem* to exist to the *senses* and to the *passions.*" In this aspect, nothing in nature exists in absolute singleness, but in the context of all past experience and in relation to the present state of the mind perceiving it (as dramatically projected in **"Tintern Abbey"**).

The real concerns of poetry, like those of religion, are with abstractions "too weighty for the mind to support them without relieving itself by resting a great part of the burthen upon words and symbols." Thus Wordsworth employs language as a symbolic reflection of the mind in motion, reacting with its environment, which takes on the coloration of both primary qualities inherent in natural forms and secondary qualities developed

and developing in the mind. In this way his poetry conveys the spirit as well as the letter of what it is talking about, bridging the two worlds of man, internal and external, spiritual and material, subjective and objective.

This kind of poetry requires a high order of poetic skill. Wordsworth insists upon poetic language that is more than Pope's "dress of thought," but that is also an incarnation of the process that created it with impurities pruned by the poet's judgment. The poet had first to identify the experience he would describe, then analyze and reflect upon it, working it over in the crucible of his imagination. Then he would decide upon the fittest vehicle for its expression, and rigorously select his words for accuracy of connotation as well as denotation. Properly expressive language would be at once rhythmical and figuratively exact because it is associated with elemental feelings. Meter would provide added pleasure through recognizable regularity in constant change, similitude in dissimilitude. Prose might serve to convey the expression, but it would be less pleasurable; and pleasure was essential to the operations of the mind Wordsworth aimed to simulate and stimulate.

Obviously skill alone is not enough. The true poet is blessed, in addition, with a highly sensitized mind that rediscovers truths so common as to have been ignored and forgotten, yet laden with beneficent associations. To foster this sensitivity in the minds of less fortunate men, Wordsworth proposed to provide his imagination as surrogate for theirs, and thus concentrates on analyzing and demonstrating its operations. (pp. xiii-xiv)

Wordsworth often uses "imagination" in a sense synonymous with earlier notions of "right reason." In this aspect, the faculty plays the crucial role in the creative process, actively striving to achieve mastery of both the internal and the external worlds, not satisfied with knowledge of either world alone. The poet may receive intense delight from his sensations, and an equal pleasure from realizing the imagination's dominance over his sense impressions, but it is this higher faculty that combines both kinds of pleasure for a higher pleasure still, such as is experienced when the "intimations" celebrated in the **"Intimations Ode"** are refined into "assurances." Even discursive reason plays a role in the poetic process, as the "recollecting" or organizing faculty that channels overflow of feeling and prunes expression of disagreeable elements. Applied in criticism, discursive reason, along with imagination in all its operations, engages the letter and the spirit of the text in a search for common sense and psychological accuracy, summed up as "truth to nature." Lacking this truth, a work cannot find a place in a healthy mind and fails in its fundamental aim.

The practical problem Wordsworth faced was to create the taste that would enable his poetry to achieve its aim, when it was much easier for people to appreciate the titillating sensations and facile abstractions of the followers of Pope. Yet he insisted upon doing it his way: "I have not written down to the level of superficial observers and unthinking minds. Every great Poet is a Teacher; I wish either to be considered as a Teacher, or as nothing." He insisted on truth in the letter as well as the spirit. When a critic alluded to the poem "on Daffodils reflected in the water," Wordsworth exclaimed: "How is it possible for flowers to be *reflected* in water where there are *waves*?" This passion for accuracy carried over into his criticism also, and he read the texts of others as carefully as he composed his own. He had selected his language with care and expected readers to read it accordingly. But this, of course, put too much of a burden on readers who looked upon poetry as mere entertainment or memorable restatements of "what oft was thought." Wordsworth shifted the focus of poetry to "what oft was felt" and was forced to wait until people realigned their reading habits.

Rightly confident that he would eventually be appreciated, Wordsworth received fame, honors, and financial satisfaction in his later years. Yet his greatest personal satisfaction is found reflected in the Postscript to the 1835 edition of his *Poems.* It is concerned almost entirely with discussion of public morality and civic affairs, but he concluded with fifty-four lines from Book XII of the (then unpublished) *Prelude,* recapitulating his service to the people in medicining their minds. There was no longer need for explanation or defense of his poetic principles or his practice, for his way had been justified. (pp. xv-xvi)

> *Paul M. Zall, in an introduction to* Literary Criticism of William Wordsworth, *edited by Paul M. Zall, University of Nebraska Press, 1966, pp. ix-xvii.*

HAROLD BLOOM (essay date 1971)

[*Bloom, an American critic and editor, is best known as the formulator of "revisionism," a controversial theory of literary creation based on the concept that all poets are subject to the influence of earlier poets, and that, to develop their own voice, they attempt to overcome this influence through a deliberate process of "creative correction," which Bloom calls "misreading." Bloom also extended this theory, introduced in 1973 in his* The Anxiety of Influence, *to include the critic or reader as another willful misreader of literary texts. His theories are largely based on his readings of English poetry from the Romantic period to the present. Discussing "Tintern Abbey" in the context of the Romantic mind-nature dialectic, Bloom comments that the poem is "a history in little of Wordsworth's imagination." He traces Wordsworth's exploration of his relation to nature, especially his rejection of simple reciprocity between his imagination and the outside world. In "Tintern Abbey," according to Bloom, the poet succeeds in uniting the two only through sustained meditation and the creative power of memory. Bloom concludes that Wordsworth's coming to terms with mortality in the poem is a "sublime act of honesty."*]

"Tintern Abbey" is a minature of the long poem Wordsworth never quite wrote, the philosophical and autobiographical epic of which *The Prelude,* the *Recluse* fragment, and *The Excursion* would have been only parts. As such, "Tintern Abbey" is a history in little of Wordsworth's imagination. The procedure and kind of the poem are both determined by Coleridge's influence, for *The Eolian Harp* . . . and *Frost at Midnight* . . . are its immediate ancestors, with the eighteenth-century sublime ode in the farther background. Yet we speak justly of the form of "Tintern Abbey" as being Wordsworth's, for he turns this kind of poem to its destined theme, the nature of a poet's imagination and that imagination's relation to external Nature. Coleridge begins the theme in his "conversation poems," but allows himself to be distracted from it by theological misgivings and self-abnegation. "Tintern Abbey," and not *The Eolian Harp,* is the father of Shelley's *Mont Blanc* and Keats's *Sleep and Poetry.*

In the renewed presence of a remembered scene, Wordsworth comes to a full understanding of his poetic self. This revelation, though it touches on infinity, is extraordinarily simple. All that Wordsworth learns by it is a principle of reciprocity between the external world and his own mind, but the story of that reciprocity becomes the central story of Wordsworth's best poetry. The poet loves Nature for its own sake alone, and the

Benjamin Robert Haydon's portrait of Wordsworth in 1818.

presences of Nature give beauty to the poet's mind, again only for that mind's sake. Even the initiative is mutual; neither Nature nor poet gives in hope of recompense, but out of this mutual generosity an identity is established between one giver's love and the other's beauty. The process of reciprocity is like a conversation that never stops, and cannot therefore be summed up discursively or analyzed into static elements. The most immediate consequence of this process is a certain "wide quietness," as Keats was to call it in his *Ode to Psyche.* As the dialogue of love and beauty ensues, love does not try to find an object, nor beauty an expression in direct emotion, but a likeness between man and Nature is suggested. The suggestion is made through an intensification of the dominant aspect of the given landscape, its seclusion, which implies also a deepening of the mood of seclusion in the poet's mind:

> —Once again
> Do I behold these steep and lofty cliffs,
> That on a wild secluded scene impress
> Thoughts of more deep seclusion; and connect
> The landscape with the quiet of the sky.

The further connection is with the quiet of Wordsworth's mind, for the thoughts of more deep seclusion are impressed simultaneously on the landscape and on its human perceiver.

We murder to dissect, Wordsworth wrote in another context, and to dissect the renewed relationship between the poet and this particular landscape ought not to be our concern. Wordsworth wants to understand the interplay between Mind and Nature without asking *how* such dialogue can be, and this deliberate refusal to seek explanation is itself part of the meaning of "Tintern Abbey". (pp. 131-32)

Until **"Peele Castle,"** natural seeming and reality are one for Wordsworth, and so this theory of poetry is a theory of description also. The language of description is employed by him both for the external world and for himself; if he will not analyze Nature, still less will he care to analyze man. The peculiar *nakedness* of Wordsworth's poetry, its strong sense of being alone with the visible universe, with no myth or figure to mediate between ego and phenomena, is to a surprisingly large extent not so much a result of history as it is of Wordsworth's personal faith in the reality of the body of Nature.

Away from the landscape he now rejoins, the poet had not forgotten it, but indeed had owed to memories of its sensations sweet, felt in hours of urban weariness, and therapeutic of the lonely ills he has experienced. Such tranquil restoration is only one gift of memory. Another is of more sublime aspect:

> that blessed mood,
> In which the burthen of the mystery,
> In which the heavy and the weary weight
> Of all this unintelligible world,
> Is lightened:—that serene and blessed mood,
> In which the affections gently lead us on,—
> Until, the breath of this corporeal frame
> And even the motion of our human blood
> Almost suspended, we are laid asleep
> In body, and become a living soul:
> While with an eye made quiet by the power
> Of harmony, and the deep power of joy,
> We see into the life of things.

This is not mysticism but, rather, a state of aesthetic contemplation. All contemplation of objects except the aesthetic is essentially practical, and so directed toward personal ends. The poet's genius frees contemplation from the drive of the will, and consequently the poet is able to see with a quiet eye. To see into the life of things is to see things for themselves and not their potential use. The poet attains to this state through memories of Nature's presence, which give a quietness that is a blessed mood, one in which the object world becomes near and familiar, and ceases to be a burden. The best analogue is the difference we feel in the presence of a stranger or a good friend. From this serenity the affections lead us on to the highest kind of naturalistic contemplation, when we cease to *have* our bodies, but *are* our bodies, and so are "laid asleep / In body, and become a living soul."

Having made this declaration, Wordsworth gives his first intimation of doubt as to the efficacy of Nature's presences:

> And now, with gleams of half-extinguished thought,
> With many recognitions dim and faint,
> And somewhat of a sad perplexity,
> The picture of the mind revives again.

The "sad perplexity" concerns the future and the enigma of the imagination when transposed from past to future time. In this moment of renewed covenant with a remembered and beloved landscape, is there indeed life and food and for future years?

> And so I dare to hope,
> Though changed, no doubt, from what I was then first
> I came among these hills.

The process of change is what troubles Wordsworth. He speaks of three stages of development already accomplished, and fears the onset of a fourth. The "glad animal movements" of his boyish days preceded any awareness of nature. Then came the time when his perception of natural objects brought an immediate joy, so that he speaks of the simultaneity of vision and emotion as

> An appetite; a feeling and a love,
> That had no need of a remoter charm,
> By thought supplied, nor any interest
> Unborrowed from the eye.

That time is past, and Wordsworth has lost its "aching joys" and "dizzy raptures." He has entered into a third time, and other gifts have recompensed him for such loss. In this mature stage he *looks* on Nature, and *hears* in it

> The still, sad music of humanity,
> Nor harsh nor grating, though of ample power
> To chasten and subdue.

The dialectic of the senses here is vital in Wordsworth. The young child has an organic sense that combines seeing and hearing. The older child, awakening to the phenomenal world, sees a gleam in it that the mature man cannot see again. But the man gains an intimation of immortality, of his renewed continuity with the young child, by hearing a still, sad music *as* he sees a soberer coloring in Nature. Here in **"Tintern Abbey,"** eight years before the completion of the Great Ode, Wordsworth anticipates the totality of its myth. As he listens to the sad music ("still" because it pipes to the spirit, not to the sensual ear of man) he hears evidence not only of man's mortality but of man's inseparable bond with Nature. But perception and response are no longer simultaneous, and it is an act of mediation that must bring the riven halves together. This mediation does not start in the mind, but is first felt as a presence that disturbs the mind with the joy of elevated thoughts:

> a sense sublime
> Of something far more deeply interfused,
> Whose dwelling is the light of setting suns,
> And the round ocean and the living air,
> And the blue sky, and in the mind of man:
> A motion and a spirit, that impels
> All thinking things, all objects of all thought
> And rolls through all things.

As a consecration or sacramental vision this becomes the main burden of Wordsworth's song, until in **"Peele Castle"** it is exposed as only a dream, and the great light pervading it is deprecated as "the light that never was, on sea or land." When Wordsworth still believed in that light, as in this crucial passage from **"Tintern Abbey,"** he was able to see and hear a primal unity manifested simultaneously in all subjects and all objects. Again, it is a laziness of our imaginations that tempts us to call this vision mystical, for the mystical is finally incommunicable and Wordsworth desires to be a man talking to men about matters of common experience. The emphasis in **"Tintern Abbey"** is on things seen and things remembered, on the light of sense, not on the invisible world. The presence of outer Nature disturbs the mind, sets it into motion, until it realizes that Nature and itself are not utterly distinct, that they are mixed together, interfused. They are more interfused than the reciprocal relation between the outer presence and the mind's inner elevation in response would seem to indicate, for in speaking of that relation the poet still uses the vocabulary of definiteness and fixity. But the imagination dissolves such separateness. Within both nature and Wordsworth is something that moves and breathes, and that blends subject and object as it animates them. *Therefore* the poet, though he has lost the aching joy that is Nature's direct gift, still loves Nature as he can apprehend it by eye and ear:

> —both what they half create,
> And what perceive; well pleased to recognise
> In nature and the language of the sense
> The anchor of my purest thoughts, the nurse,
> The guide, the guardian of my heart, and soul
> Of all my moral being.

But why "half create"? Though the boundaries between man and Nature have wavered, Wordsworth wishes to avoid the suggestion of a total absorption of Nature into man. Man is almost totally absorbed in Nature in his childhood, and again in extreme old age, as in **"The Old Cumberland Beggar"** and the Leech Gatherer of **"Resolution and Independence."** But for the mature man, outward Nature must be recognized as external. That is his freedom and his grief. His consolation is that he half creates as well as perceives "outward" Nature, for what is outward comes to him only through the gates of his own perception, and whatever cannot come to him is not relevant to his condition. Eyes and ears, the gates of perception, are not passive but selective. He cannot create the phenomena that present themselves to him; they are given. But his choice among them is a kind of creation, and his choice is guided by memory. Memory is the mother of poetry for Wordsworth because the poem's half of the act of creation cannot proceed without the catalyst of recollecting the poet's response to an earlier version of the outward presence of Nature. Nature's half of the act is mysterious, except that Wordsworth inists that it cannot proceed without the initiating expression of man's love for what is outside himself.

This mature love for Nature leads to love for other men, to hearing the still, sad music of *humanity*. The soul of a man's moral being, its inwardness, *is* Nature once the earlier relation between man and Nature, where no meditation was necessary between perception of natural beauty and the deep joy of the perceiver's response, is in the past. The meditation of the later stage, the time of mature imagination, brings vision and joy together again by linking both with the heart's generosity toward our fellow men.

This is the teaching that preserves Wordsworth's "genial spirits" from decay, but the teacher himself is uncertain of the efficacy of his doctrine in the fourth stage that is to come, when natural decay may dull his responsiveness to the presences of beauty. (pp. 133-37)

The misgivings and the ultimate fear of mortality are part of the poem because of Wordsworth's insistence upon autobiographical honesty. They help to make **"Tintern Abbey"** the major testament it is, for through them the poem convinces us it has earned the heights upon which it moves.... [Wordsworth's "nakedness"] is a sublime act of honesty, and prepares us for the Wordsworth who is the first poet ever to present our human condition in its naturalistic truth, vulnerable and dignified, and irreducible, not to be explained away in any terms, theological or analytical, but to be accepted as what it is. The mind, knowing only itself and Nature, but remembering a time when Nature gave it direct joy, and having remoter memories of an earlier time when it knew itself only in union with Nature, is able to turn back through memory for a faith that at last gives courage and a love for others. Blake did not believe in the goodness of the natural heart, and Coleridge could neither believe in nor deny it, but Wordsworth brings its possibility as truth alive into our hearts, as he did into the heart of Keats.

There are greater Romantic poems than **"Tintern Abbey,"** but they surpass it as vision or rhetoric, not as consolation. No poem, unless it be **"The Old Cumberland Beggar,"** humanizes us more. (p. 140)

> *Harold Bloom, "William Wordsworth," in his* The Visionary Company: A Reading of English Romantic Poetry, *revised edition, Cornell University Press, 1971, pp. 124-99.*

ROBERT LANGBAUM (essay date 1977)

[*Langbaum's main critical concern has been to reestablish a vital connection between the literature of the nineteenth and twentieth centuries, to "connect romanticism with the so-called reactions against it." In his best-known work,* The Poetry of Experience, *Langbaum makes a distinction between an older, ordered "poetry of meaning" and a more modern "poetry of experience" in which the imagination and the writing process itself help to shape the meaning of the poem. In the following excerpt from his* Mysteries of Identity, *Langbaum discusses Wordsworth's contributions to the Romantic concept of identity as they are illustrated in some key passages in* The Prelude. *Tracing the influence of Lockean and Platonic ideas on Wordsworth's thinking, Langbaum demonstrates how Wordsworth modified the Lockean model for the mind by emphasizing the roles of process, memory, and man's close connection with nature. For other studies of Wordsworth's philosophical doctrine, see the excerpts by Stephen (1876), Havens (1941), Stallknecht (1958), and Perkins (1964).*]

More completely than the other English romanticists, Wordsworth works out in his poetry the new romantic concept of self. When Keats in a letter calls this world "The vale of Soul-making," he comes close to Wordsworth's thinking and helps us understand how Wordsworth, by answering the empiricist attack on the Christian concept of soul, is able to use the word *soul* in a new way. For Keats says that we come into the world as pure potentiality or "Intelligence" and that we acquire a "Soul" or "sense of Idenity" through "Circumstances." And it is the main purport of Wordsworth's poetry to show the spiritual significance of this world, to show that we evolve a soul or identity through experience and that the very process of evolution is what we mean by *soul*.

To understand the implications of Wordsworth's view and why it is distinctively modern, we have to go back to the psychological assertions of Locke and Locke's disciple Hartley that Wordsworth was both absorbing and answering. The best analogy to the challenge raised by Locke is the challenge raised in our time by computers. For Lockean man is like a computer in that everything inside him comes from outside, through sensation; so that Lockean man gives back only what has been "programmed" into him. Even his choices are no evidence of free will; for once the idea of choice has entered his head, he must choose—and he must choose between predetermined alternatives. "A man that is walking," says Locke, "to whom it is proposed to give off walking, is not at liberty, whether he will determine himself to walk, or give off walking or not: he must necessarily prefer one or the other of them; walking or not walking." One would use the same line of reasoning to show that a computer, for all its ability to make choices, is not free; for its choices are limited. (pp. 29-30)

As computers become increasingly complex, as they become capable of making choices, learning, and giving orders, we inevitably wonder at what point of complexity they can be considered human, as having a soul. Now in *The Prelude* Wordsworth was trying to answer some such question as this regarding Lockean man. If we consider that the human psyche is built up of sensations, then at what point do sensations add up to soul, or how do we jump from sensations to soul? We can understand Wordsworth's answer to Locke if we imagine him answering the question in regard to computers. His answer would be that computers will never be human—will never have continuity or identity—until they are born and grow up and can therefore have the changing memory of change that constitutes awareness of one's own identity.

If sensations turn into soul—into an ineffable quality that can never be accounted for by the sensations themselves—it is because the sensations reach an ever-changing mind that transforms them, as a merely passive receiver, the sort of mind Locke likens to blank paper, could not. No two succeeding sensations from the same object can be the same, because the later sensation reaches a mind already modified by the earlier sensation. Locke recognizes all this, but it remains for Wordsworth to draw the necessary conclusions in his poetry and for Coleridge to formulate them in his theory of imagination. The necessary conclusions are summed up in the idea of interchange between man and nature—the idea that the mind modifies sensation as much as sensation modifies the mind.

It may be argued that computers, too, as they learn, offer a changing receiver to external data. This brings us to the second important point in Wordsworth's answer to Locke. Wordsworth portrays the mind as itself part of the nature it perceives; and it is this connection, sensed through what Wordsworth calls *joy*—an intensification of Hume's "vivacity"—that gives us confidence in the reality of ourselves and the external world. Dare one predict that no computer is likely to have this organic connection or to sense it through *joy*?

In *The Prelude,* Wordsworth tells us that his life began to the sound of the Derwent Riever that "loved / To blend his murmurs with my nurse's song" and "sent a voice / That flowed along my dreams," making

> ceaseless music that composed my thoughts
> To more than infant softness, giving me
> Amid the fretful dwellings of mankind
> A foretaste, a dim earnest, of the calm
> That Nature breathes among the hills and groves. . . .

There, in the best Lockean fashion, Wordsworth traces all his mature thoughts back to the sound of the river. But unlike Locke, Wordsworth presents the perceiving mind as active. The fact that the nurse's song blends with the river suggests a correspondence between mind and river; that is why the river's voice flows along the dreams of the growing Wordsworth. When we read that the river "loved / To blend," we understand that the baby did not merely receive but loved the river's sound, reached out to it as a flower reaches out to the sun and air and rain it has the potentiality to receive. The blending and interchange turn sensation into experience, an experience of joy that will in future years spread around the mature man's thoughts an affective tone—a tone objectified in "the calm / That Nature breathes." This tone, this atmosphere of the mind, sensed as at once inside and outside the mind, is what the mature man will call *soul*.

The river received on its "smooth breast the shadow of those towers" of Cockermouth Castle. . . . The reflection of the towers was perceived, we gather, at a somewhat later age than the sound of the river. Visual sensations are in Wordsworth more intellectual than sensations of sound. The composite experience of river and towers—which might be understood as an expe-

rience of female and male principles—stands behind the experience of beauty and fear described in the rest of Book I, which are composite experiences of natural and moral power.

In Book II, the mature man's capacity for love is traced back to the contentment of the infant.

> who sinks to sleep
> Rocked on his Mother's breast; who with his soul
> Drinks in the feelings of his Mother's eye!

Through his connection with his mother, he gains a sense of connection with nature, a connection portrayed through the imagery of flow and blending:

> No outcast he, bewildered and depressed:
> Along his infant veins are interfused
> The gravitation and the filial bond
> Of nature that connect him with the world.

The infant is from the start an active agent of perception who "drinks in" feelings. Because he inhabits the loving universe circumscribed for him by his mother's "Presence," he loves or reaches out to all that he beholds. That sense of "Presence," the baby's first apprehension of Deity, is produced by the sympathetic relation of mind to universe which is, says Wordsworth, the "Poetic spirit of our human life." The mind is portrayed as a relation and a process—a process *growing* from feeling through power, sense, thought, into the one great Mind and between subject and object, in such a way that the parts flow one into the other and can hardly be discriminated.

> For feeling has to him imparted power
> That through the growing faculties of sense
> Doth like an agent of the one great Mind
> Create, creator and receiver both,
> Working but in alliance with the works
> Which it beholds.

This poetic spirit, says Wordsworth, is in most people "abated or suppressed" in later years. But in some few it remains "Preeminent till death," and those few are, we gather, poets. . . .

We have here a psychological accounting for affect, for the value or "glory" we find in the world, which seems to contradict the Platonic accounting in the **"Immortality Ode."** The accounting in *The Prelude* is the authentically Wordsworthian one, because it is naturalistic, psychological and sensationalist. The Platonic idea of pre-existence is advanced in the **"Ode,"** Wordsworth tells us in the Fenwick note to that poem, merely as a figure of speech, as a fanciful and traditional way of generalizing the psychological phenomenon revealed to him by his own life—that "the Child is Father of the Man," that spirit is to be found in the primitive. "I took hold of the notion of pre-existence," says Wordsworth, "as having sufficient foundation in humanity for authorizing me to make for my purpose the best use of it I could as a Poet." The Platonic idea is used with fine artistry in the **"Ode,"** as a counterpoint to the primitivist idea. It is the primitivist idea that takes over when in stanza IX Wordsworth gets down to the serious business of answering the question of the poem, the question posed by the adult's sense of loss. His answer is that nothing is lost. Even if we no longer experience the "glory" we experienced in childhood, "nature yet remembers." Our souls, he concludes in a strikingly primitivist image, can in a moment travel backward

> And see the Children sport upon the shore,
> And hear the mighty waters rolling evermore.

(pp. 30-4)

Much ink has been spilled over the question whether Words-worth believed that his apprehension of spirit came from out-side or inside, whether he was a Lockean empiricist or a Pla-tonic believer in innate ideas. The answer is that Wordsworth, when he is writing his best poetry, uses both doctrines as possibilities, blending them in such a way as to evoke the mystery he is talking about—the mystery of life, vitality, or-ganic connection. The case should teach us something about the proper relation of ideas to poetry. And, indeed, Wordsworth himself pronounces on the subject in his first **"Essay Upon Epitaphs,"** where he speaks of the antithetical ideas of two Greek philosophers about the value of body in relation to soul. In spite of their opposite ideas, says Wordsworth, modulating from talk of thought to talk of feelings,

> Each of these Sages was in sympathy with the best feelings of our nature; feelings which, though they seem opposite to each other, have another and a finer connection than that of con-trast. It is a connection formed through the sub-tle progress by which, both in the natural and the moral world, qualities pass insensibly into their contraries, and things revolve upon each other.

Wordsworth praises the insensible passing between contraries that Hume calls error; for Wordsworth employs dialectical thinking. (pp. 36-7)

For Locke, we apprehend infinity as an idea of quantity—the result of our understanding that we can count indefinitely and can indefinitely add line segments to a given line segment. The idea is inapplicable, in the same way, to quality: "nobody ever thinks of infinite sweetness, or infinite whiteness." For Words-worth, instead, we apprehend infinity as a feeling having to do with quality and organic wholeness—we cannot add to an organism as to a line segment. For Locke, the idea of infinity follows from our experience. For Wordsworth, we not only bring the feeling of infinity to later experiences through as-sociated memory of earlier experiences, but the feeling some-how both rises out of and is anterior to even our primal ex-periences. This original feeling of infinity envelops all subsequent experiences, giving the sense that they all fold into the same self.

The ambiguity is suggested through the use of both memory and the fading-out of memory. Because the soul remembers not what but how she felt, we carry with us a feeling larger than anything we can remember of our primal experiences; and the soul grows, in this vale of soul-making, toward a feeling of wholeness that seems recollected though we cannot say from where. Locke refutes the theory of pre-existence by saying that if a man has no memory at all of his previous existence, if he has "a consciousness that *cannot* reach beyond this new state," then he is not the same person who led the previous existence since "personal idenity"—here Locke is at one with Descartes and Hume—reaches "no further than consciousness reaches." Wordsworth's answer is to blur the line between remembering and forgetting, to introduce a notion of unconscious memory. By combining memory and association, Wordsworth sets the Lockean system in motion, infusing it with vitality, surround-ing it with mystery, and carrying the mind back beyond con-scious memory to the "dawn of being" where it is undistin-guishable from its first sensation. (pp. 40-1)

In one of the earliest written passages of *The Prelude,* one of those passages that must have helped Wordsworth find his theme, the poet thanks nature, in a tone of religious solemnity, for having from his "first dawn / Of childhood" intertwined for him "The passions that build up our human soul". . . . The whole poem traces this building-up process, but the words *soul* and *imagination* are used interchangeably and Wordsworth speaks more often of the building up of imagination. That is because the poet or man of imagination is being used to epitomize a psychological process.

The poet, we are being told, is more spiritual than the rest of us because he *remembers* more than we do—though his re-membering is often spoken of as a kind of forgetting: "By such forgetfulness the Soul becomes / Words cannot say how beautiful". . . . The poet filters a present experience back through memory and the unconscious river in his veins—Wordsworth habitually speaks of thought as flowing in and out of the veins—to the external river that was his first sensation. That is why the poet can respond to the world and see it symbolically. That is why seeing is better than faith—it is revelation. "Nor did he believe,—he *saw*," says Wordsworth of the poetical Pedlar in *The Excursion.* . . . (p. 42)

In *The Prelude*'s climactic "spot of time," the epiphany on Mt. Snowdon in Book XIV, the whole world seems under moonlight to be returned to water. The mist below is a silent sea, the hills around static billows; and this illusory sea stretches out into the real Atlantic. The optical illusion is substantiated when, through a rift in the mist, Wordsworth hears the roar of inland waters. The movement from sight to sound is always in Wordsworth a movement backward to the beginning of things, to sensation and the sentiment of Being; later in Book XIV, Wordsworth says that he has in *The Prelude* traced the stream of imagination back from "light / And open day" to "the blind cavern whence is faintly heard / Its natal murmur". . . . Words-worth understands, therefore, that he has had on Mt. Snowdon an epiphany of pure imagination or pure potentiality. He has beheld, in the moon over the waters, "the emblem of a mind" brooding over the abyss—waiting, like God in the opening passage of *Paradise Lost,* to bring forth the world. We have here an image of externalized self repeating God's act of cre-ation. We have only to compare this image with the image Beckett draws from Descartes of a mind surrounded by void to realize that for Beckett the self reverses God's act of creation by withdrawing through an act of thought from nature, leaving it dead and mechanical. The self is thus imprisoned, cannot go forth to create the world because "of the impenetrability (isolation)," as Beckett puts it, "of all that is not 'cosa mental.'"

The Wordsworthian self goes forth, achieves transcendence, because it connects with the external world through sensation. On Mt. Snowdon, Wordsworth transcends even the beginning of things by moving back from sight to sound and then to an inextricable blending of sight and sound:

> the emblem of a mind
> That feeds upon infinity, that broods
> Over the dark abyss, intent to hear
> Its voices issuing forth to silent light
> In one continuous stream. . . .

"This," says Wordsworth, "is the very spirit" with which "higher" or imaginative "minds" deal "With the whole com-pass of the universe." . . . Confronted with sensory experience, the poetical man travels back *that far* in order to perceive it imaginatively. He re-creates the world in his imagination; so that he can return to the scene before him, imposing upon it the picture in his mind and thus finding there the surrounding aura of calm that is his soul.

Thus Wordsworth establishes, on naturalistic, psychological grounds, a self as transcendent as the old Christian self created and sustained by God. He establishes a new certainty about self and the self's perceptions, after the dissolution of the old Christian certainty had been articulated by Locke and the other empiricists. Wordsworth's answer to Locke (which serves also as an answer to the rationalist Descartes) is that the mind belongs to, and therefore *actively* connects with, the nature it perceives. It is this connection, sensed through what Wordsworth calls *joy,* that gives us confidence in the reality of ourselves and the external world. For Wordsworth the self is memory and process—the memory of all its phases and the process of interchange with the external world. The movement of thought into sensation and back again corresponds to the circular movement of self into nature and back again and to the circular movement from the subjectively individual to the objectively archetypal phases of identity and back again. Each such circular movement, which could be conceived as starting from outside as well as inside, is a new creation, a new confirmation, of self—and is impelled by joy. (pp. 45-6)

> Robert Langbaum, "Wordsworth: The Self as Process," in his The Mysteries of Identity: A Theme in Modern Literature, 1977. Reprint by The University of Chicago Press, 1982, pp. 25-47.

ROBERT REHDER (essay date 1981)

[*Rehder's approach to Wordsworth's understanding of the mind and its role in composition centers on a study of the Mount Snowdon episode which concludes* The Prelude. *Hypothesizing that the mind represented an abyss to Wordsworth and that he thought of himself as traveling between the inner and the outer world, Rehder suggests that Wordsworth both feared and nourished the creative process. Since he associated the mind with chaos, Wordsworth looked to poetry for a sense of order and completion.*]

Wordsworth was a man who continually struggled not to be overwhelmed by his feelings. The difficulty of the struggle in his early years determined in part the deliberate order, self-isolation and conservatism of his later years. Evidence of the intensity and turbulence of Wordsworth's inner life can be found throughout his work, but there is no better example than the remarks that he made to Isabella Fenwick in 1843 on the subject of his great **"Ode: Intimations of Immortality from Recollections of Early Childhood."** He tells her:

> . . . I was often unable to think of external things as having external existence, and I communed with all that I saw as something not apart from, but inherent in, my own immaterial nature. Many times while going to school I have grasped at a wall or tree to recall myself from this abyss of idealism to the reality. At that time I was afraid of such processes.

This is an extraordinary confession: that often the world existed for him only when he made an effort and that without this effort he could not escape from his phantasies. . . . Wordsworth reaches out to the wall and the tree like a drowning man, in a gesture of desperate need. He was, he says, afraid. The fear of being engulfed and the fear of falling seem to be united in this experience, and as Wordsworth relates it we have the illusion that he is still walking to the school: 'Many times while going to school have I grasped at a wall or tree . . .' He says 'this abyss' as if it is yawning in front of him. (p. 146)

For Wordsworth writing poetry was like reaching out a hand to steady himself. His poems were a way of pushing against these primitive moods that sometimes threatened to overpower him and that he thought of as forming 'the starting-place of being.' Because the imagination has its source in this abyss of the mind, and because composing meant facing up to the totality of the inner situation (including the imagination), Wordsworth cultivated as well as feared these moods. Self-absorption was a means of holding on to the self, a defence against vanishing into thought—and a way of wooing the muse.

These accounts reveal how great was Wordsworth's sense of the separateness of the inner and outer worlds, and how conscious he was of moving back and forth between two realms, the one dream-like and cloudy, the other substantial and definite. His realisation of the degree to which perception is creation might have been impossible without the memory of the world intermittently emerging from the mists of phantasy. This is a recurring image in his poetry and one that he constantly uses to describe the mind. Nowhere is this clearer than in his description of climbing to the top of Snowdon to watch the sunrise. This passage is the great conclusion to his greatest poem [*The Prelude*], and, as soon as he had drafted it, he recognised its value. (p. 147)

Wordsworth starts by carefully locating the episode in his own life. The narration is elaborately circumstantial and full of the almost euphemistic expressions that are so characteristic of him. They abound at the beginning: 'youthful Friend,' 'couching-time,' 'Rouz'd up the Shepherd,' 'by ancient right / Of office' 'the Stranger's usual Guide,' 'short refreshment,' 'sallied forth,' and show us Wordsworth's need to transform his experience. The opening is like a diary entry, but in the grand style. The place name, 'Bethkelet,' that the shepherd living at the foot of the mountain had the right by custom to be the guide, the encounter of the dog and the hedgehog, none of these things seems crucial to the description of the 'sea of mist,' but they are necessary to establish the reality of the experience. They balance it as our waking life balances our dreams. This is Wordsworth grasping at a tree or pushing against a five-bar gate. These particulars emphasise the uniqueness of the experience. They make it a moment distinguishable from all other moments and ward off the chaos of undifferentiated sensation.

The progress up the mountain is a movement from the outer to the inner world. The climbers are soon isolated, 'Hemm'd round on every side with fog and damp.' After some polite conversation, each of the three men sinks 'into commerce with his private thoughts.' The poet becomes completely self-absorbed:

>   and by myself
> Was nothing either seen or heard the while
> Which took me from my musings . . .

These are interrupted only by the dog barking at the hedgehog. The smallness of this incident serves as a measurement of the larger silence. The mountain is 'lonely.' The moon and clouds seem to emerge from the poet's thoughts just as the 'sea of mist' merges with 'the real sea.' Here the inner world is made continuous with the outer world and the whole scene becomes 'The perfect image of a mighty Mind.' This is the end to which this poem on the growth of the poet's mind builds.

The progress up the mountain is also a movement from darkness to enlightenment. At the foot of Snowdon they were under the mist, 'Low-hung and thick that cover'd all the sky,' and were soon engulfed by it. 'Little could we see,' the poet says. The time is 'the dead of night.' Then a sudden flash of light intrudes upon his day-dreams like an idea and he, who has been looking down at nothing, looks about. The moon reveals a vast panorama of earth and sky of which it is a part. The poet gazes 'as far as sight could reach.' The darkness is illuminated by the moon, instead of fog there is a landscape, the fog forms tongues, the roar of waters becomes a voice, then the scene passes and is replaced by understanding. The description is followed by a long interpretation of the event.

Knowledge has to be paid for. The idea is as old as the myth of Eden that tells us that its price is innocence and shows us that in the world of experience what we are is always at risk. . . . The 'shadowy ground' resembles the 'huge sea of mist.' The poet must 'sink / Deep' (as into the 'blue chasm') and ascend 'aloft' (as to the mountain top) to breathe in the new worlds. This means confronting: 'All strength, all terror . . . / That ever was put forth in personal form.' Although Wordsworth declares himself 'unalarmed' by Jehovah's thunder and the angels' shouting, there is nothing that he finds more fearful or awful than looking into the human mind:

> Not Chaos, not
> The darkest pit of lowest Erebus,
> Nor aught of blinder vacancy scooped out
> By help of dreams can breed such fear and awe
> As fall upon us often when we look
> Into our Minds, into the Mind of Man,
> My haunt and the main region of my Song. . . .

Haunt summons up an underworld of ghosts, '*My* haunt' shows us that Wordsworth felt himself irresistibly drawn to the twilight of his subject. The 'blue chasm' is 'deep and gloomy,' and a 'dark deep thoroughfare,'—a road into the night of the mind. *Homeless* to describe the 'voice of waters' is like *haunt* in that it conjures up rootless, restless, ever-changing spirits, who press to speak to us in an uncanny language.

That poets are explorers and likewise exposed to dangers is implied by the passage of over a hundred lines that Wordsworth later thought of including in his analysis of what he saw from the peak of Snowdon. He relates two mundane experiences of his own of how nature imposes herself on man, and then episodes from the lives of Columbus, Gilbert, Park and Dampier, all stories of great fear or suffering. Wordsworth's feelings when watching a storm blow over Coniston and when seeing a horse standing motionless against 'a clear silver moonlight sky' near Grasmere are set equal to Mungo Park's despair in the jungle of the Niger and to James Dampier's narrow escape from death in a canoe off Nicobas in the worst storm that he had ever known.

The mind for Wordsworth is an abyss. He associates it with chaos (when 'the earth was without form, and void; and darkness *was* upon the face of the deep'), the bottom of the underworld and threatening dreams,—with something blind, vacant and 'scooped out' that we can 'look into.' That 'fear and awe' then *fall* upon us suggests the vertigo of looking over the edge of a precipice. He refers in his great *Ode* to the child's ability to read:

> the eternal deep,
> Haunted for ever by the eternal mind . . .

This is the 'mighty mind' 'exalted by an underpresence'. . . . The sources of the poet's power are conceived of as coming from below, and this is perhaps why Wordsworth's two greatest descriptions of the imagination are set high in the mountains: near the top of the Simplon Pass and on the summit of Snowdon. Thus, the whole world is revealed as subject to the imagination and made a metaphor for the mind itself. . . . Wordsworth's poetry about nature is not any more specific than it is, because he is constantly trying to look through nature to his own mind and being. (pp. 147-53)

Repeatedly Wordsworth calls attention to the tremendous energies at play in the mind. His language suggests that consciousness is a war between sensation and the will. 'Nature' *exerts* a *domination, makes* one object *impress* itself upon another and *thrusts forth upon the senses.* The grossest minds *cannot chuse but feel.* As for the higher minds, *they are Powers.* The syllogistic form of the meditation . . . represents part of Wordsworth's attempt to encompass the totality of these energies. He includes 'all the objects in the universe,' and, refers to 'every image' and 'every thought, / And all impressions,' that pass through a 'higher' mind. The many superlatives and commodious abstractions are part of the struggle to comprehend the whole by connecting everything to something else. (pp. 156-57)

The poet's mind . . . is a vast structure of connections, an 'interminable building,' and Wordsworth's religion may be described as an attempt to find a mirror image of this structure in the world. He obtained from religion the same satisfactions that he obtained from geometry:

> Mighty is the charm
> Of those abstractions to a mind beset
> With images, and haunted by itself;
> And specially delightful unto me
> Was that clear Synthesis built up aloft
> So gracefully, even then when it appear'd
> No more than as a plaything, or a toy
> Embodied to the sense, not what it is
> In verity, an independent world
> Created out of pure Intelligence.
>
> (p. 158)

When in the Snowdon meditation Wordsworth actually describes how 'higher minds' work, his language becomes sharper and more confident, and he has no need of religious language:

> This is the very spirit in which they deal
> With all the objects of the universe;
> They from their native selves can send abroad
> Like transformations, for themselves create
> A like existence, and, whene'er it is
> Created for them, catch it by an instinct;
> Them the enduring and the transient both
> Serve to exalt; they build up greatest things
> From least suggestions, ever on the watch,
> Willing to work and to be wrought upon,
> They need not extraordinary calls
> To rouze them, in a world of life they live,
> By sensible impressions not enthrall'd,
> But quicken'd, rouz'd, and made thereby more fit
> To hold communion with the invisible world. . . .

Although he uses the third person plural and makes no mention of poetry, this is introspection. What the poet sends abroad—the world here is a foreign country—is a transformation of his native self, and *native* seems to be an attempt in this context to distinguish a primitive version of the self, the self of infancy as opposed to the self of maturity. The passage is completely abstract, an abstractness that is a measurement of Wordsworth's self-consciousness. Wordsworth stands outside the mental processes and observes them; he is concerned to define the mind in terms of its operations. . . . (pp. 159-60)

Wordsworth's poetry contains many passages like this one where he first describes his feelings and then derives theoretical conclusions from them, developing what might be called an *ad hoc* theory of the mind. This, such as it is, is never fully articulated, but is present as a set of unspoken (or half-spoken) assumptions, that he has not worked out systematically, and that find their way into his poetry when he needs to follow his feelings to something that he can believe in as a conclusion. Often these conclusions are rather perfunctory religious statements or, as in this case, shade off into such statements. His religious beliefs mark the limits of his knowledge of the mind. The very abstract passages are never far away from the description of a definite moment or a particular feeling; they are the result of Wordsworth's capacity to enter into reality in very specific terms. Although many of his successors have been freer, few, perhaps only Valéry and Stevens, have been as successful in making great poetry about the data of consciousness.

Why did Wordsworth in his theory-making stop where he did and why is he less thoroughgoing than Valéry or Stevens? The answer is hidden in the details of his life (which perhaps we could not interpret even if we could recover them) and leads to the question of why he wrote poetry. Some suggestions can be made instead of answers. R. D. Laing says that:

> Orphans and adopted children sometimes develop a tremendously strong desire to find out 'who they are' by tracing the father and mother who conceived them. They feel incomplete for want of a father or mother, whose absence leaves their concept of self incomplete.

This desire may be satisfied by seeing something tangible, such as a tombstone which 'seems to allow "closure".' The poem is to the poet as the tombstone is to the child and provides him with an analogous sense of completion. Poem and tombstone both are objects, concrete, palpable, that supply unchanging form to the dimmest feelings. Wordsworth wrote to reaffirm his sentiment of being. His invention of the autobiographical poem was the invention of a self. This involved not only making an order of his feelings and coping with his guilt, but also coming to terms with his genius, as so many of his most theoretical and greatest passages are on the subject of the creative power of the mind. Autobiography to Wordsworth meant an examination of the sources of poetry, and more theory would have taken him too far away from his subject: himself. (pp. 160-61)

> Robert Rehder, "The Poetry of Consciousness," in his Wordsworth and the Beginnings of Modern Poetry, *Barnes & Noble Books, 1981, pp. 146-77.**

ADDITIONAL BIBLIOGRAPHY

Abercrombie, Lascelles. *The Art of Wordsworth*. 1952. Reprint. Hamden, Conn.: Archon Books, 1965, 157 p.

Haydon's portrait of Wordsworth on Mount Helvellyn, painted in 1842.

A study of the art of Wordsworth's poetry, focusing on the early writings. Abercrombie believes that Wordsworth's inspiration waned and that his poetry markedly declined after 1816.

Abrams, M. H. "Wordsworth's *Prelude* and the Crisis-Autobiography." In his *Natural Supernaturalism: Tradition and Revolution in Romantic Literature*, pp. 71-140. New York: W. W. Norton & Co., 1973.
Studies Wordsworth's intent and use of form in *The Prelude*. Abrams also traces the influences, literary forerunners, and religious implications of the poem.

————,ed. *Wordsworth: A Collection of Critical Essays*. Englewood Cliffs, N.J.: Prentice-Hall, 1972, 214 p.
A collection of essays on Wordsworth's style, the early poems, *The Prelude*, and the later poems. Represented are such critics as David Ferry, Stephen Maxfield Parrish, Paul de Man, and John Jones.

Babbitt, Irving. "The Primitivism of Wordsworth." In his *On Being Creative and Other Essays*, pp. 34-79. Boston: Houghton Mifflin Co., The Riverside Press, 1932.
A New Critical analysis of Wordsworth's philosophy. Babbitt discusses the primitivism and pantheism in Wordsworth's poetry and how he employed them in reaction to the neoclassical ideals of analytical thinking and decorum.

Bateson, F. W. *Wordsworth: A Re-Interpretation*. London: Longmans, 1954, 227 p.
A critical biography of Wordsworth. Bateson makes the controversial claim that Wordsworth acted out his incestuous feelings

for Dorothy in writing the Lucy poems, and that Lucy is, in fact, Dorothy.

Batho, Edith C. *The Later Wordsworth*. New York: Russell & Russell, 1963, 417 p.

A critical biography that focuses on Wordsworth's later years. Attempting to correct the bias of earlier biographers, Batho treats her subject in a detailed and sympathetic manner.

Bauer, N. S. *William Wordsworth: A Reference Guide to British Criticism, 1793-1899*. Boston: G. K. Hall & Co., 1978, 467 p.

An annotated bibliography, chronologically arranged, of English writings about Wordsworth in the eighteenth and nineteenth centuries.

Brooks, Cleanth. "The Intimations of the Ode." *The Kenyon Review* VIII, No. 1 (Winter 1946): 81-102.

A detailed analysis of Wordsworth's use of imagery, paradox, symbol, irony, and theme in the "Intimations" ode. Brooks reads the poem "as independent poetic structure" rather than as a biographical document. He concludes that the ode is flawed because its conclusion "is asserted rather than dramatized."

Bush, Douglas. "Coleridge, Wordsworth, Byron." In his *Mythology and the Romantic Tradition in English Poetry*, pp. 51-80. New York: W. W. Norton & Co., 1963.*

Examines Wordsworth's use of classical mythology in his poems. Bush asserts that Wordsworth "re-established the classical genre" in *Laodamia* and used mythology more frequently in his later poetry.

Clarke, C. C. *Romantic Paradox: An Essay on the Poetry of Wordsworth*. London: Routledge & Kegan Paul, 1962, 101 p.

Discusses Wordsworth's "largely unconscious" use of paradox in his poetry. Contending that some of Wordsworth's best poems are contingent on his successful treatment of paradox, Clarke probes the idea that "the place of the mind in the natural world is equivocal."

Cooper, Lane, ed. *A Concordance to the Poems of William Wordsworth*. New York: E. P. Dutton & Co., 1911, 1136 p.

A listing of individual words used by Wordsworth in his poems, their frequency of occurrence, and their location in the text.

Cowell, Raymond, ed. *Critics on Wordsworth*. Readings in Literary Criticism, no. 12. London: George Allen and Unwin, 1973, 114 p.

A selection of Wordsworth criticism from the nineteenth and twentieth centuries. Included are pieces by such commentators as Henry Crabb Robinson, Thomas Love Peacock, William Minto, Salvador de Madariaga, and Albert S. Gérard.

Curtis, Jared R. *Wordsworth's Experiments with Tradition: The Lyric Poems of 1802*. Ithaca: Cornell University Press, 1971, 227 p.

Explores the biographical, theoretical, and artistic context of Wordsworth's poetical experiments of 1802. Curtis devotes special attention to "Resolution and Independence" and the "Immortality" ode.

Danby, John F. *The Simple Wordsworth: Studies in the Poems, 1797-1807*. London: Routledge & Kegan Paul, 1960, 144 p.

A study of the themes, imagery, and structure of Wordsworth's early poetry. Danby especially emphasizes the poet's development and his "interesting spiritual journey from 'The Reverie of Poor Susan' to 'The White Doe of Rylstone'."

Davis, Jack, ed. *Discussions of William Wordsworth*. Discussions of Literature. Boston: D. C. Heath and Co., 1964, 178 p.

A collection of important essays on Wordsworth by such critics as Coleridge, Abrams, Leavis, Jones, and Paul Goodman.

De Selincourt, E. *The Early Wordsworth*. Oxford: Oxford University Press, 1936, 28 p.

A sketch of Wordsworth's early life, political concerns, artistic development, and poetic achievement. According to De Selincourt, Wordsworth's two main intellectual crises during this period revolved around the war between England and France and his disillusionment with the French Revolution.

Devlin, D. D. *Wordsworth and the Poetry of Epitaphs*. Totowa, N.J.: Barnes & Noble Books, 1981, 143 p.

An analysis of Wordsworth's *Essays upon Epitaphs*. Devlin argues that in the essays, which he considers unusually free of defensiveness and self-justification, "a description emerges of his own finest and most typical work and his characteristic mode of 'reconcilement of opposites'."

Dicey, A. V. *The Statesmanship of Wordsworth: An Essay*. Oxford: Clarendon Press, 1917, 134 p.

Surveys Wordsworth's political thought from his statements on the French Revolution through the full articulation of his political convictions concerning both France and England. In the later chapters, Dicey specifically addresses the questions of Wordsworth's nationalism and statesmanship.

Dunklin, Gilbert T., ed. *Wordsworth Centenary Studies Presented at Cornell and Princeton Universities*. Princeton: Princeton University Press, 1951, 169 p.

A collection of centenary essays by Bush, Pottle, Trilling, Earl Leslie Griggs, John Crowe Ransom, B. Ifor Evans, and Willard L. Sperry that evaluate various aspects of Wordsworth's art.

Empson, William. "Chapter IV." In his *Seven Types of Ambiguity*, pp. 133-54. Rev. ed. London: Chatto and Windus, 1947.*

Discusses Wordsworth's ambiguous attitude toward religion in "Tintern Abbey." Empson regards the poem's shifting tone as necessary to Wordsworth's goal of being "uplifting yet nondenominational."

Ferguson, Frances. *Wordsworth: Language as Counter-Spirit*. New Haven: Yale University Press, 1977, 263 p.

Studies the relationship between language and consciousness in Wordsworth's poetry. Ferguson theorizes that for Wordsworth, neither the self nor language were fixed or continuous, and that his emphasis on memory in the poetry testifies to his belief in "the impossibility of constructing one individual self which would be 'there' for language to imitate."

Ferry, David. *The Limits of Mortality: An Essay on Wordsworth's Major Poems*. Middletown, Conn.: Wesleyan University Press, 1959, 181 p.

A study of style and theme in Wordsworth's poetry. Ferry includes detailed readings of some of the major poems.

Garber, Frederick. *Wordsworth and the Poetry of Encounter*. Urbana: University of Illinois Press, 1971, 195 p.

Explores Wordsworth's epistemology. Garber delves into the poet's interaction with the world around him—his "object-consciousness"—as well as into Wordsworth's treatment of "the speaker as witness of himself."

Garrod, H. W. *Wordsworth: Lectures and Essays*. Oxford: Clarendon Press, 1927, 231 p.

A detailed analysis of Wordsworth's poetry to 1805.

Greenbie, Marjorie L. Barstow. *Wordsworth's Theory of Poetic Diction: A Study of the Historical and Personal Background of the "Lyrical Ballads."* Yale Studies in English, edited by Albert S. Cook, no. LVII. New Haven: Yale University Press, 1917, 191 p.

Outlines the biographical, historical, and literary influences on Wordsworth's thought in the *Lyrical Ballads*.

Grob, Alan. *The Philosophic Mind: A Study of Wordsworth's Poetry and Thought, 1797-1805*. Columbus: Ohio University Press, 1973, 279 p.

Discusses Wordsworth's philosophy from the time he wrote "Tintern Abbey" to the "Immortality" ode. Grob concentrates on the poet's theories of the mind, nature, morality, and anthropocentrism.

Harper, George McLean. *William Wordsworth: His Life, Works, and Influence*. 2 vols. London: John Murray, 1923.

Considered an important study of Wordsworth's life, although superseded in some respects by Moorman's biography.

Hartman, Geoffrey H. "Wordsworth." In his *The Unmediated Vision: An Interpretation of Wordsworth, Hopkins, Rilke, and Valéry*, pp. 1-46. New Haven: Yale University Press, 1954.

An analysis of Wordsworth's poetry, especially his technique of juxtaposing the subject and the object, in relation to the development of modern poetry.

————, ed. *New Perspectives on Coleridge and Wordsworth: Selected Papers from the English Institute*. New York: Columbia University Press, 1972, 284 p.*

Includes two essays on Wordsworth. Kenneth R. Johnston's piece treats visual imagery in Wordsworth's poetry; John Hollander's study describes Wordsworth's use of acoustics.

Hayden, John O., ed. "Wordsworth." In his *Romantic Bards and British Reviewers: A Selected Edition of the Contemporary Reviews of the Works of Wordsworth, Coleridge, Byron, Keats, and Shelley*, pp. 3-118. Lincoln: University of Nebraska Press, 1971.

A selection of early reviews of Wordsworth's works.

Hearn, Ronald B., and others. *Wordsworth Criticism since 1952: A Bibliography*. Salzburg Studies in English Literature: Romantic Reassessment, edited by James Hogg, vol. 83. Salzburg: Universität Salzburg, 1978, 93 p.

A bibliography of articles, books, dissertations, and theses on Wordsworth from 1952 to 1977.

Henley, Elton F., and Stam, David H. *Wordsworthian Criticism 1945-1964: An Annotated Bibliography*. Rev. ed. New York: New York Public Library, 1965, 107 p.

An annotated bibliography of editions, bibliographies, and criticism of Wordsworth from 1945 to 1964.

Jacobus, Mary. *Tradition and Experiment in Wordsworth's "Lyrical Ballads" (1798)*. Oxford: Clarendon Press, 1976, 301 p.

An in-depth assessment of Wordsworth's employment of and departures from poetic tradition in the *Lyrical Ballads*. Jacobus touches on such topics as Godwinian philosophy, eighteenth-century ideas about nature, and the revival of the ballad form, and she examines their influence on Wordsworth's poetic experiments.

Johnston, Kenneth R. *Wordsworth and "The Recluse."* New Haven: Yale University Press, 1984, 397 p.

An interpretive reconstruction of *The Recluse*. Johnston discusses Wordsworth's original plan for the structure of the poem, its theoretical framework, and the development and interrelationship of its parts.

Jones, Alun R., and Tydeman, William, eds. *Wordsworth: "Lyrical Ballads," a Casebook*. Casebook Series, edited by A. E. Dyson. London: Macmillan, 1972, 253 p.

A collection of key nineteenth- and twentieth-century essays on the *Lyrical Ballads*. The editors also include tables of contents for the 1798 and 1800 editions of the work and a critical bibliography.

Jones, John. *The Egotistical Sublime: A History of Wordsworth's Imagination*. London: Chatto & Windus, 1954, 212 p.

Traces the progression of Wordsworth's poetry through three distinct creative stages. Jones theorizes that in his search for synthesis Wordsworth first moved toward solitude, but eventually abandoned it as an ideal.

Jordan, John E. "Wordsworth's Humor." *PMLA* LXXIII, No. 1 (March 1958): 81-93.

Argues that in Wordsworth's works "there is much more humor than has been generally recognized." Citing evidence from Wordsworth's poems and biographical accounts, Jordan concludes that there was a comic strain in the poet's early works, but that it was almost extinguished by his later seriousness and didacticism.

————. *Why the "Lyrical Ballads"?: The Background, Writing, and Character of Wordsworth's 1798 "Lyrical Ballads."* Berkeley: University of California Press, 1976, 212 p.

Explores the evolution, form, and literary context of the *Lyrical Ballads*. Jordan also evaluates Wordsworth's poetic innovations and addresses the style and critical reception of the volume.

Krieger, Murray. "William Wordsworth and the *Felix Culpa*." In his *The Classic Vision: The Retreat from Extremity in Modern Literature*, pp. 149-96. Baltimore: Johns Hopkins Press, 1971.

A discussion of classical elements in Wordsworth's poetry. Krieger argues that Wordsworth's mature poetry is free from the excessive self-consciousness of some of his earlier works and embodies "an awareness of our historic dimension which helps lose us in the human whole."

Kroeber, Karl. *Romantic Landscape Vision: Constable and Wordsworth*. Madison: University of Wisconsin Press, 1975, 142 p.

A study of Wordsworth and the English painter John Constable in relation to nineteenth-century picturesque aesthetics. Pairing poems and paintings in each chapter, Kroeber explores their analogies and differences.

Legouis, Émile. *William Wordsworth and Annette Vallon*. Rev. ed. Hamden, Conn.: Archon Books, 1967, 176 p.

A landmark work that documents Wordsworth's relationship with Vallon. Legouis includes, among other information, a genealogy of the Vallon family and Annette Vallon's letters to William and Dorothy Wordsworth.

Lindenberger, Herbert. *On Wordsworth's "Prelude."* Princeton: Princeton University Press, 1963, 316 p.

An in-depth analysis of various aspects of *The Prelude*. Lindenberger examines such topics as rhetoric, form, imagery, and the historical significance of the poem.

Logan, James V. *Wordsworthian Criticism: A Guide and Bibliography*. Columbus: Ohio State University Press, 1961, 304 p.

A guide to Wordsworthian criticism, arranged by date and topic. Each chapter discusses a segment of Wordsworthian criticism, ranging from early periodical reviews to 1944.

Marchant, Robert. *Principles of Wordsworth's Poetry*. Swansea, Wales: Brynmill Publishing Co., 1974, 112 p.

Focuses on lyric, discursive, and narrative elements in Wordsworth's poetry. Emphasizing Wordsworth's poetic stance as an observer and judge, Marchant concludes that this "act of commitment" contributes to the realism of his poetry.

Marsh, Florence. *Wordsworth's Imagery: A Study in Poetic Vision*. Yale Studies in English, edited by Benjamin Christie Nangle, vol. 121. New Haven: Yale University Press, 1952, 146 p.

Explores landscape, color, human, and sound imagery in Wordsworth's poetry and discusses his general theories of symbolism and imagery.

Martin, A. D. *The Religion of Wordsworth*. London: George Allen & Unwin, 1936, 100 p.

A study of religious themes, images, and references in Wordsworth's poetry. Martin also includes an index of his use of biblical references.

Mead, Marian. *Four Studies in Wordsworth*. New York: Haskell House, 1964, 274 p.

Analyzes light and color imagery in Wordsworth's poems and includes an appendix of references to such images.

Meyer, George Wilbur. *Wordsworth's Formative Years*. University of Michigan Publications: Language and Literature, vol. XX. Ann Arbor: The University of Michigan Press, 1943, 265 p.

A study of Wordsworth's artistic development from 1787 to 1798. Focusing on both the poet and his letters, Meyer traces Wordsworth's growth from his first poems to *The Borderers* and the naturalistic poems of 1798.

Miles, Josephine. *Wordsworth and the Vocabulary of Emotion*. 1942. Reprint. New York: Octagon Books, 1965, 181 p.

Examines Wordsworth's use of emotionally charged language in the context of eighteenth- and nineteenth-century critical theory.

Miles also relates Wordsworth's critical acceptance to changing attitudes about the role of feeling in poetry.

Moorman, Mary. *William Wordsworth, A Biography: The Early Years, 1770-1803.* Rev. ed. Oxford: Clarendon Press, 1965, 632 p.

————. *William Wordsworth, A Biography: The Later Years, 1803-1850.* Rev. ed. Oxford: Clarendon Press, 1966, 632 p.

A two-part study that is considered the standard modern biography of Wordsworth.

Murray, Roger N. *Wordsworth's Style: Figures and Themes in the "Lyrical Ballads" of 1800.* Lincoln: University of Nebraska Press, 1967, 166 p.

An analysis of Wordsworth's diction in the 1800 edition of *Lyrical Ballads.* Murray focuses on Wordsworth's treatment of paradox, synecdoche, simile, personification, and metaphor.

Owen, W.J.B. *Wordsworth as Critic.* Toronto: University of Toronto Press, 1969, 239 p.

Charts the growth of Wordsworth's critical thinking, drawing on his poetry, prefaces, and letters. This work is considered the fullest account of Wordsworth's critical theories.

Parrish, Stephen Maxfield. *The Art of the "Lyrical Ballads."* Cambridge: Harvard University Press, 1973, 250 p.

A detailed account of the conception and writing of the *Lyrical Ballads.* Parrish analyzes Wordsworth's collaboration with Coleridge and emphasizes the theoretical framework and artistry of their poetry.

Perkins, David. "Wordsworth: The Isolation of the Human Mind," "Wordsworth: The Linking of Man and Nature," and "The Wordsworthian Withdrawal." In his *The Quest for Permanence: The Symbolism of Wordsworth, Shelley, and Keats,* pp. 1-100. Cambridge: Harvard University Press, 1965.

Traces Wordsworth's creation and use of symbols and their influence on style and form in his poetry. Perkins suggests that while Wordsworth's subjectivism "mirrors . . . one of the central problems of the contemporary poet," it was also his main limitation as an artist.

Potts, Abbie Findlay. *Wordsworth's "Prelude": A Study of Its Literary Form.* Ithaca: Cornell University Press, 1953, 392 p.

A detailed study of various influences on Wordsworth and on his writing of *The Prelude.* Potts probes Wordsworth's reading of such authors as Alexander Pope, James Beattie, Thomas Gray, James Thomson, Oliver Goldsmith, William Shakespeare, and John Bunyan.

Purkis, John. *A Preface to Wordsworth.* Preface Books, edited by Maurice Hussey. New York: Charles Scribner's Sons, 1970, 208 p.

Presents concise background information on Wordsworth and his era. Besides providing a section on the poet's life, Purkis also surveys the economic history, philosophy, religion, and audience of Wordsworth's time. Purkis also includes an overview of critical response to Wordsworth's poetry.

Rader, Melvin. *Wordsworth: A Philosophical Approach.* Oxford: Clarendon Press, 1967, 217 p.

Concentrates on philosophical influences on Wordsworth's thinking and on the development of his personal philosophy. Rader stresses the idealism inherent in Wordsworth's views of nature, animism, and God.

Read, Herbert. *Wordsworth: The Clark Lectures, 1929-1930.* New York: Jonathan Cape and Harrison Smith, 1931, 271 p.

Traces Wordsworth's emotional development and its effect on his literary efforts. Read then extends his discussion to hypothesize about Wordsworth as a type of the poetic mind.

————. "A Complex Delight: Wordsworth" and "Wordsworth's Philosophical Faith." In his *The True Voice of Feeling: Studies in English Romantic Poetry,* pp. 38-54, 189-211. New York: Pantheon Books, 1953.

Discusses Wordsworth's treatment of organic form and its implications for his philosophical faith.

Rountree, Thomas J. *This Mighty Sum of Things: Wordsworth's Theme of Benevolent Necessity.* Tuscaloosa: University of Alabama Press, 1965, 142 p.

Explores Wordsworth's philosophy of benevolent necessity—"an optimistic concept of the world as directed inevitably toward perfectibility by a cosmic force that pays special attention to the educative effect of nature in the mental and moral progress of man."

Salvesen, Christopher. *The Landscape of Memory: A Study of Wordsworth's Poetry.* London: Edward Arnold (Publishers), 1965, 207 p.

Emphasizes the role of memory in Wordsworth's poetry. Salvesen asserts that much of Wordsworth's originality, poetic development, and historical importance are dependent on his treatment of his past.

Scoggins, James. *Imagination and Fancy: Complementary Modes in the Poetry of Wordsworth.* Lincoln: University of Nebraska Press, 1966, 264 p.

Chronicles the evolution of Wordsworth's perception of imagination and fancy and its effect on his classification of his poetry.

Sheats, Paul D. *The Making of Wordsworth's Poetry, 1785-1798.* Cambridge: Harvard University Press, 1973, 301 p.

Argues that the development of Wordsworth's poetry is directly related to the history of his era and to his personal growth. Though he remarks that in his later poetry Wordsworth idealizes nature and shrinks from the painful experiences of this world, Sheats stresses that in his greatest poetry Wordsworth accepts the full spectrum of life.

Shelley, Percy Bysshe. "Peter Bell the Third." In his *The Works of Percy Bysshe Shelley,* Vol. III edited by Roger Ingpen and Walter E. Peck, pp. 255-86. New York: Gordian Press, 1965.

A notorious parody, written in 1819, of Wordsworth's *Peter Bell.*

Smith, J. C. *A Study of Wordsworth.* 1944. Reprint. Edinburgh: Oliver & Boyd, 1958, 103 p.

Discusses the role of organic sensibility, memory, pleasure, vision, politics, and religion in Wordsworth's poetry. Smith also includes a chapter on Wordsworth's theory of poetry.

Spark, Muriel, and Stanford, Derek. *Tribute to Wordsworth: A Miscellany of Opinion for the Centenary of the Poet's Death.* London: Brun, 1950, 232 p.

A collection of nineteenth- and twentieth-century assessments of Wordsworth's poetry, occasioned by the centenary of his birth, with an introductory critical essay by Stanford and Spark.

Sperry, Willard L. *Wordsworth's Anti-Climax.* Harvard Studies in English. 1935. Reprint. New York: Russell & Russell, 1966, 228 p.

Gathers evidence from Wordsworth's life and his doctrines of nature, religion, and ethics to document the theory that Wordsworth's artistic power measurably declined after 1808.

Todd, F. M. *Politics and the Poet: A Study of Wordsworth.* London: Methuen & Co., 1957, 238 p.

An important study of Wordsworth's political ideas from his early sympathy with the French Revolution to his later years as a supporter of conservative politics in England.

Weaver, Bennett. *Wordsworth: Poet of the Unconquerable Mind.* Edited by Charles L. Proudfit. Ann Arbor, Mich.: George Wahr Publishing Co., 1965, 109 p.

A collection of influential essays written between 1934 and 1940. Three of the pieces focus on *The Prelude,* while the remaining four treat Wordsworth's style, imagery, and general critical reputation.

Wellek, René. "Wordsworth." In his *A History of Modern Criticism, 1750-1950: The Romantic Age,* Vol. 2, pp. 130-50. New Haven: Yale University Press, 1955.

Emphasizes Wordsworth's transitional position in literary history and discusses his relationship to eighteenth-century poetic traditions. Wellek's commentary centers on Wordsworth's ideas concerning language, primitivism, emotionalism, didacticism, and imagination.

Welsford, Enid. *Salisbury Plain: A Study in the Development of Wordsworth's Mind and Art.* Oxford: Basil Blackwell, 1966, 171 p.
> Traces Wordsworth's personal and artistic growth from 1793 to 1814 as reflected in a group of poems inspired by his travels near Stonehenge. The poems, Welsford asserts, "throw light, not only on the poet's thought, but on his artistry, and particularly on the care he expended on architectonics."

Willey, Basil. "Postscript: On Wordsworth and the Locke Tradition." In his *The Seventeenth Century Background: Studies in the Thought of the Age in Relation to Poetry and Religion,* pp. 296-309. 1934. Reprint. London: Chatto and Windus, 1962.
> A seminal essay on Wordsworth's relation to the scientific tradition. Willey theorizes that although Wordsworth was violently opposed to scientific knowledge, his "root-assumption that truth could only be achieved by 'making verse deal boldly with substantial things'" owes a debt to the scientific method.

Wlecke, Albert O. *Wordsworth and the Sublime.* Perspectives in Criticism, no. 23. Berkeley: University of California Press, 1973, 163 p.
> Examines the visionary dimensions of Wordsworth's imagination. Wlecke first presents his hypothesis about "the structure of consciousness" in Wordsworth's "Tintern Abbey," then develops and generalizes this theory to encompass all of Wordsworth's work.

The Wordsworth Circle. Washington, D.C.: Heldref Publications, 1970-
> A quarterly journal devoted to criticism about Wordsworth and such contemporaries as Coleridge, Hazlitt, Lamb, and Austen.

Appendix

The following is a listing of all sources used in Volume 12 of *Nineteenth-Century Literature Criticism*. Included in this list are all copyright and reprint rights and acknowledgments for those essays for which permission was obtained. Every effort has been made to trace copyright, but if omissions have been made, please let us know.

THE EXCERPTS IN NCLC, VOLUME 12, WERE REPRINTED FROM THE FOLLOWING PERIODICALS:

Accent, v. 5, Autumn, 1944.

American Heritage, v. XII, December, 1960. © 1960 by American Heritage Publishing Co., Inc. All rights reserved. Reprinted by permission from *American Heritage,* 1960.

The American Review, and Literary Journal, v. II, January-March, 1802.

The Analytical Review, v. XXIV, August, 1796.

The Antijacobin Review, v. XLVI, April, 1814.

The Athenaeum, n. 1257, November 29, 1851.

The Atlantic Monthly, v. XXXIV, November, 1874; v. 99, April, 1907.

The Australasian, v. VI, January 16, 1869.

Australian Literary Studies, v. 4, May, 1969 for "The Radiant Dream: Notes on Henry Kendall" by A.C.W. Mitchell. Reprinted by permission of the publisher and the author.

Australian Writers, v. I, 1928.

Blackwood's Edinburgh Magazine, v. III, July, 1818; v. V, August, 1819; v. VI, November, 1819.

Bookfellow, December 15, 1919.

The British Review, v. XIV, August, 1819.

Broom, v. 3, August, 1922.

The Canadian Bookman, v. IX, May, 1927.

Canadian Children's Literature: A Journal of Criticism and Review, n. 22, 1981. Box 335, Guelph, Ontario, Canada N1H 6K5. Reprinted by permission.

Canadian Literature, n. 34, Autumn, 1967 for "Isabella Valancy Crawford: 'The Canoe'" by John B. Ower; n. 55, Winter, 1973 for "The Hunter's Twain" by Dorothy Livesay; n. 78, Autumn, 1978 for "Crawford's Fairies" by Frances Frazer. All reprinted by permission of the respective authors.

The Canadian Magazine of Politics, Science, Art and Literature, v. I, May, 1893; v. V, October, 1895.

The Century, v. XLV, November, 1892.

Contemporary Review, v. XLII, December, 1882.

The Cornhill Magazine, v. XXXIV, August, 1876.

The Criterion, v. XVIII, January, 1939.

The Critic, New York, v. XIX, April 15, 1893.

The Critical Review, v. XLVI, September, 1778; n.s. v. XXIV, October, 1798.

The Edinburgh Annual Register, v. I, 1808.

The Edinburgh Review, v. I, October, 1802; v. XI, October, 1807; v. XXIV, November, 1814; v. XXIV, February, 1815; v. XXV, October, 1815; v. XXXVI, February, 1822; v. XXXVII, November, 1822; v. LXXVI, January, 1843.

ELH, Vol. II, March, 1944.

L'Esprit Créateur, v. XVII, Fall, 1977. Copyright © 1977 by *L'Esprit Créateur.* Reprinted by permission.

The European Magazine, and London Review, v. XXVII, April, 1795.

The Examiner, n. 618, October 31, 1819; n. 1589, July 15, 1838.

The Fortnightly Review, n.s. v. XXVI, November 1, 1879.

Fraser's Magazine, v. VI, October, 1832.

The Freeman, v. V, August 23 & August 30, 1922.

Illinois Quarterly, v. 37, Spring, 1975 for "A Wreath for Fanny Burney's Last Novel" by Rose Marie Cutting. Copyright, Illinois State University, 1975. Reprinted by permission of the publisher and the author.

The Illustrated London News, v. LXXXVIII, April 3, 1886.

The Independent Review II, February, 1904.

John Bull, October 25, 1851.

The Liberal, v. 1, October, 1822.

The Literary Gazette, London, n. 1820, December 6, 1851.

The Literary Review, November 5, 1921.

The Literary World, v. IV, March 31, 1849; v. IX, November 15 and November 22, 1851.

The London Literary Gazette, n. 271, March 30, 1822.

Macmillan's Magazine, v. XL, July, 1879.

The Melbourne Review, v. I, April, 1876.

The Mississippi Valley Historical Review, v. X, March, 1924.

Modern Fiction Studies, v. VIII, Autumn, 1962. Copyright 1962 by Purdue Research Foundation, West Lafayette, IN 47907. Reprinted with permission.

Modern Language Notes, v. LXV, June, 1950.

Monthly Literary Recreations, July, 1807.

The Monthly Magazine, London, v. LII, August 1, 1821.

The Monthly Review, London, v. LVIII, April, 1778; v. LXVII, December, 1782; v. XII, October, 1793; v. XII, October, 1793; v. XXI, October, 1796; v. XXIX, June, 1799; v. LXXVIII, November, 1815; n.s. v. LXXXIX, August, 1819.

Morning Chronicle, London, September 25, 1846.

The Nation, v. IV, June 6, 1867; v. CXVII, October 10, 1923.

The National Review, London, n.s. v. 19, November, 1864.

The New England Quarterly, v. XXIV, December, 1951.

The New Monthly Magazine, n.s. v. XCVIII, July, 1853.

The New Statesman & Nation, v. XXXVIII, August 20, 1949.

The New York Review of Books, v. XXX, October 13, 1983. Copyright © 1983 Nyrev, Inc. Reprinted with permission from *The New York Review of Books.*

The New Yorker, v. XL, November 14, 1964 for "O Canada: An American's Notes on Canadian Culture—I" by Edmund Wilson. © 1964 by The New Yorker Magazine, Inc. Reprinted by permission of Farrar, Straus and Giroux, Inc.

The Nineteenth Century, v. VIII, August, 1880; v. XV, May, 1884.

The North American Review, v. LXIX, July, 1849; v. LXXIII, October, 1851; v. CXX, January, 1875./ v. CXCIX, January, 1914 for "Madame D'Arblay" by Gamaliel Bradford. Copyright 1914 by North American Review Publishing Company. Renewed 1941 by Helen F. Bradford. Reprinted by permission of the University of Northern Iowa.

Novel: A Forum on Fiction, v. 12, Spring, 1979. Copyright © Novel Corp., 1979. Reprinted by permission.

Partisan Review, v. XXI, September-October, 1954. Copyright 1954 by *Partisan Review.* Reprinted by permission of *Partisan Review.*

Poet Lore, v. XIII, Winter, 1901.

Proceedings of the American Academy of Arts and Sciences, v. XXIX, May, 1893-May, 1894.

Proceedings of the Massachusetts Historical Society, n.s. v. VIII, 1892-1894.

The Quarterly Review, v. XI, April, 1814; v. XII, October, 1814; v. XXVII, July, 1822; v. XLIX, April, 1833; v. LXX, June, 1842.

Queen's Quarterly, v. VII, October, 1899./ v. LXXVII, Autumn, 1970 for "The Ambivalence of Love in the Poetry of Isabella Valancy Crawford" by Frank Bessai. Copyright © 1970 by the author. Reprinted by permission of the Literary Estate of Frank Bessai.

The Review of English Studies, n.s. v. X, August, 1959. Reprinted by permission of Oxford University Press.

Romance Notes, v. XXI, Fall, 1980. Reprinted by permission.

The Romanic Review, v. XXII, (October-December, 1931).

The Saturday Review, London, v. 59, May 23, 1885.

The Scots Magazine, v. 58, October, 1796.

The Sewanee Review, v. X, July, 1902.

The Spectator, v. 24, October 25, 1851; v. 57, October 18, 1884; v. 59, February 6, 1886./ v. 236, February 21, 1976. © 1976 by *The Spectator.* Reprinted by permission of *The Spectator.*

Spirit of the Times, December 6, 1851.

Tait's Edinburgh Magazine, v. XII, September, 1845; v. XVII, September, 1850.

The Westminster Review, v. CXLIV, November, 1895.

The William and Mary Quarterly, third series, v. XVIII, April, 1961 for ''The History of New France According to Francis Parkman'' by W. J. Eccles. Copyright, 1961, by the Institute of Early American History and Culture. Reprinted by permission of the Institute and the author.

The Yale Review, v. XIII, April, 1924./ v. XVIII, June, 1929 for ''Wordsworth in the Tropics'' by Aldous Huxley. Copyright 1929, by Yale University. Renewed 1956 by Aldous Huxley. Reprinted by permission of the author and the author's agents, Scott Meredith Literary Agency, Inc., 845 Third Avenue, New York, NY 10022./ v. XL, Autumn, 1950. Copyright 1950, renewed 1978, by Yale University. Reprinted by permission of the editors.

Abrams, M. H. From *The Mirror and the Lamp: Romantic Theory and the Critical Tradition.* Oxford University Press, 1953. Copyright 1953 by Oxford University Press, Inc. Renewed 1981 by Meyer Howard Abrams. Reprinted by permission of the publisher.

Adams, Henry. From a letter to Francis Parkman on December 21, 1884, in *Francis Parkman.* By Henry Dwight Sedgwick. Houghton, Mifflin and Company, 1904.

Arvin, Newton. From *Herman Melville.* Sloane Associates, 1950. Copyright, 1950, by William Sloane Associates, Inc. Renewed 1978 by John A. Zeigler and Jean E. Fischer. Abridged by permission of William Morrow & Company, Inc.

Auden, W. H. From *The Enchafèd Flood; or, The Romantic Iconography of the Sea.* Random House, 1950. Copyright, 1950, by the Rector and Visitors of the University of Virginia. Renewed 1977 by Monroe K. Spears and William Meredith. All rights reserved. Reprinted by permission of Random House, Inc.

Austen, Jane. From *Northanger Abbey and Persuasion.* John Murray, 1818.

Bachelard, Gaston. From *On Poetic Imagination and Reverie: Selections from the Works of Gaston Bachelard.* Translated by Colette Gaudin. Revised edition. To be published by Spring Publications, Dallas, 1987. Reprinted by permission of Colette Gaudin.

Baker, Ernest A. From *The History of the English Novel: The Novel of Sentiment and the Gothic Romance, Vol. 5.* H. F. & G. Witherby, 1934.

Balakian, Anna. From *Surrealism: The Road to the Absolute.* Revised edition. Dutton, 1970. Copyright © 1959, 1970 by Anna Balakian. Reprinted by permission of the author.

Bancroft, George. From a letter to Francis Parkman on November 28, 1884, in *Francis Parkman.* By Henry Dwight Sedgwick. Houghton, Mifflin and Company, 1904.

Barton, G. B. From "Henry Kendall," in *The Poets and Prose Writers of New South Wales.* Edited by G. B. Barton. Gibbs, Shallard, & Co., 1866.

Beach, Joseph Warren. From *The Concept of Nature in Nineteenth-Century English Poetry.* The Macmillan Company, 1936.

Beatty, Arthur. From *William Wordsworth: His Doctrine and Art in Their Historical Relations.* Second edition. The University of Wisconsin Studies in Language and Literature, 1927.

Beaty, Frederick L. From *Byron the Satirist.* Northern Illinois University Press, 1985. Copyright © 1985 by Northern Illinois University Press. All rights reserved. Reprinted with permission of Northern Illinois University Press, DeKalb, IL.

Benkovitz, Miriam J. From an introduction to *Edwy and Elgiva.* By Madame d'Arblay, edited by Miriam J. Benkovitz. Shoe String Press, 1957. Copyright, 1957 by Miriam J. Benkovitz. Reprinted by permission of Miriam J. Benkovitz.

Bersani, Leo. From *A Future for Astyanax: Character and Desire in Literature.* Little, Brown, 1976. Copyright © 1969, 1974, 1975, 1976 by Leo Bersani. All rights reserved. Reprinted by permission of Little, Brown and Company.

Berthoff, Warner. From *The Example of Melville.* Princeton University Press, 1962. Copyright © 1962 by Princeton University Press. All rights reserved. Excerpts reprinted with permission of Princeton University Press.

Bewley, Marius. From *The Eccentric Design: Form in the Classic American Novel.* Columbia University Press, 1959. © 1959, Columbia University Press. Reprinted by permission of the publisher.

Blake, William. From *The Complete Writings of William Blake.* Edited by Geoffrey Keynes. Nonesuch Press, 1957.

Bloom, Harold. From *The Visionary Company: A Reading of English Romantic Poetry.* Revised edition. Cornell University Press, 1971. Copyright © 1961 by Harold Bloom. Copyright © 1971 by Cornell University. All rights reserved. Used by permission of the publisher, Cornell University Press.

Bowra, C. M. From *The Romantic Imagination.* Cambridge, Mass.: Harvard University Press, 1949. Copyright 1949 by the President and Fellows of Harvard College. Renewed © 1977 by the Literary Estate of Cecil Maurice Bowra. Excerpted by permission.

Boyd, Elizabeth French. From *Byron's "Don Juan": A Critical Study.* Rutgers University Press, 1945.

Bradley, A. C. From *Oxford Lectures on Poetry*. Macmillan and Co., Limited, 1909.

Brandes, George. From *Main Currents in Nineteenth Century Literature: Naturalism in England, Vol. IV*. Translated by Mary Morison. William Heinemann, 1905.

Breton, André. From " 'Anthology of Black Humour': Isidore Ducasse, Comte de Lautréamont," translated by Stephen Schwartz, in *What is Surrealism? Selected Writings*. By André Breton, edited by Franklin Rosemont. Pluto Press, 1978. This selection copyright © 1978 by Franklin Rosemont. Reprinted by permission.

Brophy, Brigid, Michael Levey, and Charles Osborne. From *Fifty Works of English and American Literature We Could Do Without*. Stein and Day, 1968. Copyright © 1967 by Brigid Brophy, Michael Levey, Charles Osborne. All rights reserved. Reprinted with permission of Stein and Day Publishers.

Brown, E. K. From *On Canadian Poetry*. Revised edition. Ryerson Press, 1944.

Burke, Edmund. From a letter to F. Burney on July 29, 1782, in *Cecilia; or, Memoirs of an Heiress, Vol. 1*. By Frances Burney, edited by Annie Raine Ellis. G. Bell and Sons, Ltd., 1914.

Burney, Fanny. From a preface to *Evelina; or, A Young Lady's Entrance into the World*. By Fanny Burney. N.p., 1778.

Byron, Lord. From *Don Juan: Cantos I and II*. Thomas Davison, 1819.

Byron, Lord. From *Don Juan: Cantos III, IV, and V*. Thomas Davison, 1821.

Byron, Lord. From *Don Juan: Cantos VI, VII, and VIII*. John Hunt, 1823.

Byron, Lord. From a conversation with Thomas Medwin in 1822, in *Journal of the Conversations of Lord Byron*. By Thomas Medwin. Henry Colburn, 1824.

Byron, Lord. From letters to Thomas Moore on August 8, 1822 and September 19, 1818, in *Letters and Journals of Lord Byron, Vol. II*. By Lord Byron, edited by Thomas Moore. John Murray, 1830.

Byron, Lord. From *The Works of Lord Byron, Vol. XV*. By Thomas Moore, edited by John Wright. John Murray, 1833.

Byron, Lord. From a letter to Bryan Waller Procter on March 5, 1823, in *An Autobiographical Fragment and Biographical Notes*. By Bryan Waller Procter, edited by Coventry Patmore. G. Bell and Sons, 1877.

Byron, Lord. From *The Works of Lord Byron: Letters and Journals, Vol. VI*. Edited by Rowland E. Prothero. John Murray, 1901.

Byron, Lord. From letters to John Cam Hobhouse on November 11, 1818; John Cam Hobhouse and Douglas Kinnaird on January 19, 1819; John Murray on January 25, 1819, February 1, 1819, April 6, 1819, August 12, 1819, December 10, 1819; Douglas Kinnaird on October 26, 1819 and Richard Belgrave Hoppner on October 29, 1819 in *"The Flesh Is Frail:" Byron's Letters and Journals, 1818-1819, Vol. 6*. By Lord Byron, edited by Leslie A. Marchand. Cambridge, Mass.: Belknap Press, 1976, J. Murray, 1976. © Byron copyright material, John Murray 1976. All rights reserved. Reprinted by permission of the President and Fellows of Harvard College. In Canada by John Murray (Publishers) Ltd.

Byron, Lord. From letters to John Murray on February 6, 1821, June 29, 1821, August 23, 1821 and August 31, 1821, in *"Born for Opposition;" Byron's Letters and Journals, 1821, Vol. 8*. By Lord Byron, edited by Leslie A. Marchand. Cambridge, Mass.: Belknap Press, 1978, John Murray, 1978. © Byron copyright material, John Murray, 1978. All rights reserved. Excerpted by permission of the President and Fellows of Harvard College. In Canada by John Murray (Publishers) Ltd.

Byron, Lord. From a letter to John Murray on December 25, 1822, in *"A Heart for Every Fate": Byron's Letters and Journals, 1822-1823, Vol. 10*. By Lord Byron, edited by Leslie A. Marchand. Cambridge, Mass.: Belknap Press, 1980, J. Murray, 1980. © Byron copyright material, John Murray 1980. All rights reserved. Excerpted by permission of the President and Fellows of Harvard College. In Canada by John Murray (Publishers) Ltd.

Calvert, William J. From *Byron: Romantic Paradox*. The University of North Carolina Press, 1935.

Camus, Albert. From *The Rebel: An Essay on Man in Revolt*. Translated by Anthony Bower. Revised edition. Vintage Books, 1956. Copyright © 1956, renewed 1984, by Alfred A. Knopf, Inc. All rights reserved. Reprinted by permission of the publisher.

Carlyle, Thomas. From *Reminiscences*. Edited by James Anthony Froude. Harper & Brothers, 1881.

Cecil, David. From *Poets and Story-Tellers: A Book of Critical Essays*. Constable & Company, Ltd., 1949.

From "The 'Athenaeum' Review of Kendall's Manuscript Poems," in *A Century of Australian Song*. Edited by Douglas B.W. Sladen. W. Scott, 1888.

Chase, Richard. From *Herman Melville: A Critical Study*. Macmillan, 1949. Copyright 1949 by Richard Chase. Renewed 1976 by Frances W. Chase. Reprinted with permission of Macmillan Publishing Company.

Coleridge, Ernest Hartley. From "Introduction to 'Don Juan'," in *The Works of Lord Byron: Poetry, Vol. VI*. By Lord Byron, edited by Ernest Hartley Coleridge. Revised edition. Charles Scribner's Sons, 1903.

Coleridge, Samuel Taylor. From *Biographia Literaria; or, Biographical Sketches of My Literary Life and Opinions*. Kirk and Mercein, 1817.

Commager, Henry Steele. From an introduction to *The Oregon Trail: Sketches of Prairie and Rocky-Mountain Life*. By Francis Parkman. The Modern Library, 1949. Copyright, 1949, by Random House, Inc. Renewed 1976 by Henry Steele Commager. Reprinted by permission of Random House, Inc.

Conrad, Joseph. From a letter to Humphrey Milford on January 15, 1907, in *Moby-Dick as Doubloon: Essays and Extracts (1851-1970)*. Edited by Hershel Parker and Harrison Hayford. W. W. Norton & Company, Inc., 1970. Reprinted by permission of the Literary Estate of Joseph Conrad.

Coombs, Archie James. From *Some Australian Poets*. Angus & Robertson Limited, 1938.

Crane, Hart. From a letter to Solomon Grunberg on March 20, 1932, in *The Letters of Hart Crane: 1916-1932*. By Hart Crane, edited by Brom Weber. University of California Press, 1965. Copyright © 1965 by Brom Weber. All rights reserved. Reprinted by permission of the University of California Press.

d'Arblay, Frances. From an introduction to *Diary & Letters of Madame d'Arblay: 1778-1840, Vol. I*. By Frances d'Arblay, edited by Charlotte Barrett. The Macmillan Company, 1904.

Daniells, Roy. From "Crawford, Carman, and D. C. Scott," in *Literary History of Canada: Canadian Literature in English, Vol. I*. Edited by Carl F. Klinck. Second edition. University of Toronto Press, 1976. © University of Toronto Press 1976. Reprinted by permission of the Literary Estate of Roy Daniells.

Darbishire, Helen. From *The Poet Wordsworth*. Oxford at the Clarendon Press, Oxford, 1950.

de Jonge, Alex. From *Nightmare Culture: Lautréamont and "Les Chants de Maldoror"* Secker & Warburg, 1973. Copyright © Alex de Jonge 1973. All rights reserved. Reprinted by permission.

DeVoto, Bernard. From *The Year of Decision: 1846*. Little, Brown and Company, 1943.

Drinkwater, John. From *The Pilgrim of Eternity: Byron—A Conflict*. Hodder and Stoughton Limited, 1925. Copyright 1925 by John Drinkwater. Renewed 1952 by Daisy Drinkwater. Reprinted by permission of the Literary Estate of John Drinkwater.

Edgeworth, Maria. From a letter to Rachel Mordecai Lazarus on June 27, 1833, in *The Education of the Heart: The Correspondence of Rachel Mordecai Lazarus and Maria Edgeworth*. Edited by Edgar E. MacDonald. University of North Carolina Press, 1977. Copyright © 1977 by The University of North Carolina Press. All rights reserved. Reprinted by permission.

Eliot, T. S. From *The Use of Poetry and the Use of Criticism: Studies in the Relation of Criticism to Poetry in England*. Cambridge, Mass.: Harvard University Press, 1933, Faber and Faber, 1933. Copyright 1933 by the President and Fellows of Harvard College. Renewed © 1961 by T. S. Eliot. All rights reserved. Excerpted by permission of Harvard University Press. In Canada by Faber and Faber Ltd.

Éluard, Paul. From "Poetic Evidence," in *Surrealism*. Edited by Herbert Read. Faber and Faber Limited, 1936.

England, A. B. From "The Style of 'Don Juan' and Augustan Poetry," in *Byron: A Symposium*. Edited by John D. Jump. Macmillan, 1975. All rights reserved. Reprinted by permission of Macmillan, London and Basingstoke.

Farmiloe, Dorothy. From *Isabella Valancy Crawford: The Life and the Legends*. Tecumseh Press, 1983. Copyright © by The Tecumseh Press Limited, 1983. All rights reserved. Reprinted by permission of The Tecumseh Press.

Fiedler, Leslie A. From *Love and Death in the American Novel*. Revised edition. Stein and Day, 1966. Copyright © 1960, 1966 by Leslie A. Fiedler. Reprinted with permission of Stein and Day Publishers.

Fiske, John. From an introduction to *The Works of Francis Parkman, Vol. I*. By Francis Parkman. Little, Brown & Co., 1897.

Fowlie, Wallace. From *Age of Surrealism*. The Swallow Press, 1950.

Fowlie, Wallace. From *Climate of Violence: The French Literary Tradition from Baudelaire to the Present*. Macmillan, 1967. Copyright © 1967 by Wallace Fowlie. All rights reserved. Reprinted with permission of Macmillan Publishing Company.

Fuess, Claude M. From *Lord Byron as a Satirist in Verse*. Columbia University Press, 1912.

Gleckner, Robert F. From *Byron and the Ruins of Paradise*. The Johns Hopkins University Press, 1967. Copyright © 1967 by The Johns Hopkins Press. All rights reserved. Reprinted by permission.

Goethe, Johann Wolfgang von. From *Goethe's Literary Essays*. Edited by J. E. Spingarn. Harcourt Brace Jovanovich, 1921.

Gourmont, Remy de. From *The Book of Masks*. Translated by Jack Lewis. J. W. Luce and Company, 1921.

Hale, Katherine. From *Isabella Valancy Crawford*. The Ryerson Press, 1923.

Hartman, Geoffrey H. From *Wordsworth's Poetry: 1787-1814*. Yale University Press, 1964. Copyright © 1964 and 1971 by Yale University. All rights reserved. Reprinted by permission.

Havens, Raymond Dexter. From *The Mind of a Poet: A Study of Wordsworth's Thought with Particular Reference to "The Prelude."* The Johns Hopkins University Press, 1941. Copyright 1941, The Johns Hopkins Press. Renewed 1969 by Raymond Dexter Havens. Reprinted by permission.

Hazlitt, William. From *The Spirit of the Age; or, Contemporary Portraits*. H. Colburn, 1825.

Hemingway, Ernest. From *Green Hills of Africa*. Charles Scribner's Sons, 1935. Copyright, 1935, by Charles Scribner's Sons. Renewed © 1963 by Mary Hemingway. All rights reserved. Reprinted with the permission of Charles Scribner's Sons.

Hillway, Tyrus. From *Herman Melville*. Revised edition. Twayne, 1979. Copyright 1979 by Twayne Publishers. All rights reserved. Reprinted with the permission of Twayne Publishers, a division of G. K. Hall & Co., Boston.

Hope, A. D. From an introduction to *Henry Kendall*. By Henry Kendall, edited by Leonie Kramer and A. D. Hope. Sun Books, 1973. Copyright © Leonie Kramer and A. D. Hope, 1973. Reprinted by permission of A. D. Hope.

Howells, W. D. From *Heroines of Fiction, Vol. I*. Harper & Brothers Publishers, 1901.

Hugnet, Georges. from "1870 to 1936," in *Surrealism*. Edited by Herbert Read. Faber and Faber Limited, 1936.

James, Henry. From a letter to Francis Parkman on August 24, 1885, in *Francis Parkman*. By Henry Dwight Sedgwick. Houghton, Mifflin and Company, 1904.

Johnson, Reginald Brimley. From *The Women Novelists*. William Collins Sons & Co., Ltd., 1918.

Johnson, Samuel. From "On Miss Burney's 'Evelina'," in *Library of Literary Criticism of English and American Authors through the Beginning of the Twentieth Century: 1730-1784, Vol. III*. Edited by Charles Wells Moulton. The Moulton Publishing Company, 1904?

Joseph, M. K. From *Byron the Poet*. Victor Gollancz Ltd., 1964. © M. K. Joseph 1964. Reprinted by permission.

Keats, John, as reported by Joseph Severn. From comments of October, 1820, in *The Keats Circle: Letters and Papers, 1816-1878, Vol. 2*. Edited by Hyder Edward Rollins. Cambridge, Mass.: Harvard University Press, 1948. Copyright 1948 by the President and Fellows of Harvard College. Renewed © 1975 by the Literary Estate of Hyder Edward Rollins. All rights reserved. Excerpted by permission.

Keats, John. From a letter to John Hamilton Reynolds on May 3, 1818, in *The Letters of John Keats, Vol. I*. By John Keats, edited by Maurice Buxton Forman. Oxford University Press, London, 1931.

Kendall, Henry. From a letter to the editor of "The Athenaeum" on July 19, 1862, in *A Century of Australian Song*. Edited by Douglas B. W. Sladen. W. Scott, 1888.

Kennedy, James, and Lord Byron. From a conversation in 1823, in *Conversations on Religion, with Lord Byron and Others*. By James Kennedy. John Murray, 1830.

Kernan, Alvin B. From *The Plot of Satire*. Yale University Press, 1965. Copyright © 1965 by Yale University. All rights reserved. Reprinted by permission.

Knight, G. William. From *The Starlit Dome: Studies in the Poetry of Vision*. Oxford University Press, 1941.

Knight, Paul. From "Introduction to 'Poems'," in *Maldoror and Poems*. By Comte de Lautréamont, translated by Paul Knight. Penguin Books, 1978. Copyright © Paul Knight, 1978. All rights reserved. Reprinted by permission of Penguin Books Ltd.

Kulkarni, H. B. From *"Moby-Dick," a Hindu Avatar: A Study of Hindu Myth and Thought in "Moby-Dick."* Utah State University Press, 1970. Copyrighted, 1970, Utah State University. Reprinted by permission.

Langbaum, Robert. From *The Mysteries of Identity: A Theme in Modern Literature*. The University of Chicago Press, 1982. Copyright © 1977, 1982 by Robert Langbaum. Reprinted by permission of the author.

Lautréamont, Comte de. From *Maldoror and Poems*. Translated by Paul Knight. Penguin Books, 1978. Copyright © Paul Knight, 1978. All rights reserved. Reprinted by permission of Penguin Books Ltd.

Lautréamont, Comte de. From three letters: to Monsieur Verboeckhoven on October 23, 1869 and February 21, 1870 and Monsieur Darasse on March 12, 1870, in *Poésies and Complete Miscellanea*. By Isidore Ducasse, edited and translated by Alexis Lykiard. Allison & Busby, 1978. Translation, preface, notes, bibliography and additional material copyright © 1978 Alexis Lykiard. Reprinted by permission.

Lawrence, D. H. From *Studies in Classic American Literature*. The Viking Press, 1964. Copyright 1923 by Thomas Seltzer, Inc., renewed 1950 by Frieda Lawrence. Copyright © 1961 by The Estate of the late Mrs. Frieda Lawrence. Reprinted by permission of Viking Penguin Inc.

Leavis, F. R. From *Revaluation: Tradition & Development in English Poetry*. Chatto & Windus, 1936.

Lamaître, Georges. From *From Cubism to Surrealism in French Literature*. Revised edition. Cambridge, Mass.: Harvard University Press, 1947. Copyright, 1941 and 1947 by the President and Fellows of Harvard College. Renewed © 1974 by Wynifred E. Lemaître. Excerpted by permission.

Levin, David. From *History as Romantic Art: Bancroft, Prescott, Motley, and Parkman*. Stanford University Press, 1959. © 1959 by the Board of Trustees of the Leland Stanford Junior University. All rights reserved. Excerpted with the permission of the publishers, Stanford University Press.

Lockhart, John Gibson. From *Letter to the Right Hon. Lord Byron*. By John Bull. William Wright, 1821.

Lovell, Ernest J., Jr. From "Irony and Image in Byron's 'Don Juan'," in *The Major English Romantic Poets: A Symposium in Reappraisal*. Clarence D. Thorpe, Carlos Baker, Bennett Weaver, eds. Southern Illinois University Press, 1957. Copyright © 1957 by Southern Illinois University Press. Reprinted by permission of the publisher.

Lowell, James Russell. From *The Writings of James Russell Lowell: Literary Essays, Vol. IV*. Revised edition. Houghton Mifflin and Company, 1890.

McGann, Jerome J. From *"Don Juan" in Context*. University of Chicago Press, 1976. © 1976 by The University of Chicago. All rights reserved. Reprinted by permission of The University of Chicago Press and the author.

Melville, Herman. From a letter to Nathaniel Hawthorne in June, 1851, in *Herman Melville: Representative Selections*. By Herman Melville, edited by Willard Thorp. American Book, 1938. Copyright, 1938, by American Book Company. Renewed 1966 by Willard Thorp. All rights reserved. Reprinted by permission of D. C. Heath & Company.

Melville, Herman. From a letter to Nathaniel Hawthorne in November, 1851, in *Herman Melville: Representative Selections*. By Herman Melville, edited by Willard Thorpe. American Book, 1938. Copyright, 1938, by American Book Company. Renewed 1966 by Willard Thorp. All rights reserved. Reprinted by permission of D. C. Heath & Company.

Mill, John Stuart. From *Autobiography of John Stuart Mill*. Columbia University Press, 1924.

Moore, T. Inglis. From an introduction to *Selected Poems of Henry Kendall*. By Henry Kendall. Angus & Robertson, 1957. Reprinted with the permission of Angus & Robertson (UK) Ltd. Publishers.

Moore, Thomas. From an extract from *Letters and Journals of Lord Byron*. By Lord Byron, edited by Thomas Moore. J. Murray, 1830.

More, Paul Elmer. From *Shelburne Essays, fourth series*. G. P. Putnam's Sons, 1906.

Morison, Samuel Eliot. From an introduction to *The Parkman Reader*. By Francis Parkman, edited by Samuel Eliot Morison. Little, Brown, 1955. Copyright 1955, by Samuel Eliot Morison. Renewed 1983 by Emily Morison Beck. All rights reserved. Reprinted by permission of Little, Brown and Company.

Mumford, Lewis. From *Herman Melville*. Harcourt Brace Jovanovich, 1929. Copyright 1929, renewed 1956, by Lewis Mumford. Reprinted by permission of Russell & Volkening, Inc. as agents for the author.

Mushabac, Jane. From *Melville's Humor: A Critical Study*. Archon Books, Hamden, CT. 1981. © 1981 Jane Mushabac. All rights reserved. Reprinted by permission of Archon Books, an imprint of The Shoe String Press, Inc.

Nechas, James William. From *Synonomy, Repetition, and Restatement in the Vocabulary of Herman Melville's "Moby-Dick."* Norwood Editions, 1978. © 1978 by James William Nechas. Reprinted by permission of the author.

Nevins, Allan. From "The Achievement of Francis Parkman," in *France and England in North America: Pioneers of France in the New World, Vol. I*. By Francis Parkman. Ungar, 1965. Copyright © 1965 by Frederick Ungar Publishing Co., Inc. Reprinted by permission.

O'Leary, Patrick Ignatius. From *Bard in Bondage*. Edited by Joseph O'Dwyer. The Hawthorn Press, 1954.

Olson, Charles. From *Call Me Ishmael*. Reynal & Hitchcock, 1947.

Pacey, Desmond. From *Creative Writing in Canada: A Short History of English-Canadian Literature*. Ryerson Press, 1952.

Parker, Theodore. From a letter to Francis Parkman on December 22, 1851, in *A Life of Francis Parkman*. By Charles Haight Farnham. Little, Brown and Company, 1900.

Parkman, Francis. From a preface to *History of the Conspiracy of Pontiac, and the War of the North American Tribes against the English Colonies after the Conquest of Canada*. By Francis Parkman. C. C. Little and J. Brown, 1851.

Parkman, Francis. From an introduction to *Pioneers of France in the New World: France and England in North America, Part First*. By Francis Parkman. Little, Brown and Company, 1865.

Parkman, Francis. Jr. From a preface to *The California and Oregon Trail: Being Sketches of Prairie and Rocky Mountain Life*. By Francis Parkman, Jr. George P. Putnam, 1849.

Pater, Walter. From *Appreciations: With an Essay on Style*. Macmillan and Co., Limited, 1889.

Pease, Otis A. From *Parkman's History: The Historian as Literary Artist*. Yale University Press, 1953. Copyright, 1953, by Yale University Press. Renewed 1981 by Otis A. Pease. All rights reserved. Reprinted by permission.

Perkins, David. From *Wordsworth and the Poetry of Sincerity*. Cambridge, Mass.: Belknap Press, 1964. Copyright © 1964 by the President and Fellows of Harvard College. All rights reserved. Excerpted by permission.

Petrone, Penny. From an introduction to *Selected Stories of Isabella Valancy Crawford*. By Isabella Valancy Crawford, edited by Penny Petrone. University of Ottawa Press, 1975. All rights reserved. Reprinted by permission.

"Contemporary Reactions to Lautréamont: Extract from 'Bulletin du bibliophile et du bibliothécaire', Issue of May, 1870," in *Poésies and Complete Miscellanea*. By Isidore Ducasse, edited and translated by Alexis Lykiard. Allison & Busby, 1978. Translation, preface, notes, bibliography and additional material copyright © 1978 Alexis Lykiard. Reprinted by permission.

Raleigh, Walter. From *Wordsworth*. Edward Arnold, 1903.

Rashley, R. E. From *Poetry in Canada: The First Three Steps*. The Ryerson Press, 1958. Copyright © McGraw-Hill Ryerson Limited, 1958. All rights reserved. Reprinted by permission of the Literary Estate of R. E. Rashley.

Reaney, James. From "Isabella Valancy Crawford," in *Our Living Tradition, second and third series*. Edited by Robert L. McDougall. University of Toronto Press, 1959. Copyright © 1959, by University of Toronto Press. Reprinted by permission of James Reaney.

Reed, Thomas Thornton. From *Henry Kendall: A Critical Appreciation*. Rigby Limited, 1960. © Dr. T. T. Reed, 1960. Reprinted by permission.

Rehder, Robert. From *Wordsworth and the Beginnings of Modern Poetry*. Barnes & Noble, 1981. © 1981 Robert Rehder. By permission of Barnes & Noble Books, a Division of Littlefield, Adams & Co., Inc.

Rexroth, Kenneth. From *Assays*. New Directions, 1961. Copyright © 1961 by Kenneth Rexroth. Used by permission of Bradford Morrow for The Kenneth Rexroth Trust.

Rhodenizer, V. B. From *A Handbook of Canadian Literature*. Graphic Publishers Limited, 1930.

Ridenour, George M. From *The Style of "Don Juan."* Yale University Press, 1960. © copyright, 1960, by Yale University Press. Reprinted by permission.

Roosevelt, Theodore. From a letter to Francis Parkman on April 23, 1888, in *Francis Parkman*. By Henry Dwight Sedgwick. Houghton, Mifflin and Company, 1904.

Saintsbury, George. From *Essays in English Literature: 1780-1860, second series*. J. M. Dent & Co., 1895.

Saintsbury, George. From *A History of Nineteenth Century Literature (1780-1895)*. The Macmillan Company, 1896.

Schramm, Wilbur L. From an introduction to *Francis Parkman: Representative Selections*. By Francis Parkman, edited by Wilbur L. Schramm. American Book Company, 1938.

Scott, Sir Walter. From a journal entry of January 1, 1827, in *The Journal of Sir Walter Scott*. By Sir Walter Scott, edited by David Douglas. Harper & Brothers, 1890.

Sedgwick, William Ellery. From *Herman Melville: The Tragedy of Mind*. Cambridge, Mass.: Harvard University Press, 1944. Copyright 1944, renewed © 1972, by the President and Fellows of Harvard College. Excerpted by permission.

Shelley, Percy Bysshe. From *Alastor; or, The Spirit of Solitude and Other Poems*. S. Hamilton, 1816.

Shelley, P. B. From a letter to Lord Byron on May 26, 1820, in *Lord Byron's Correspondence, Vol. II*. By Lord Byron, edited by John Murray. John Murray, 1922.

Shelley, P. B. From a letter to Lord Byron on October 21, 1821, in *The Works of Lord Byron: Letters and Journals, Vol. V*. By Lord Byron, edited by Rowland E. Prothero. John Murray, 1901.

Sircos, Alfred. From "Contemporary Reactions to Lautréamont: The First Review," in *Poésies and Complete Miscellanea*. By Isidore Ducasse, edited and translated by Alexis Lykiard. Allison & Busby, 1978. Translation, preface, notes, bibliography and additional material copyright © 1978 Alexis Lykiard. Reprinted by permission.

Sladen, Douglas B. W. From an introduction to *A Century of Australian Song*. Edited by Douglas B. W. Sladen. White and Allen, 1887.

Slessor, Kenneth. From *Bread and Wine: Selected Prose*. Angus and Robertson, 1970. Copyright © Kenneth Slessor 1970. Reprinted with the permission of Angus & Robertson (UK) Ltd. Publishers.

Southey, Robert. From a letter to Walter Savage Landor on February 20, 1820, in *The Life and Correspondence of Robert Southey, Vol. V*. By Robert Southey, edited by Rev. Charles Cuthbert Southey. Longman, Brown, Green and Longmans, 1850.

Spacks, Patricia Meyer. From *Imagining a Self: Autobiography and Novel in Eighteenth-Century England*. Cambridge, Mass.: Harvard University Press, 1976. Copyright © 1976 by the President and Fellows of Harvard College. All rights reserved. Excerpted by permission.

Stallknecht, Newton P. From *Strange Seas of Thought: Studies in William Wordsworth's Philosophy of Man and Nature*. Second edition. Indiana University Press, 1958. Copyright © 1958 by Indiana University Press. Reprinted by permission.

Steeves, Harrison R. From *Before Jane Austen: The Shaping of the English Novel in the Eighteenth Century*. Holt, Rinehart and Winston, 1965. Copyright © 1965 by Harrison R. Steeves. All rights reserved. Reprinted by permission of McIntosh and Otis, Inc.

Taine, H. A. From *History of English Literature, Vol. II*. Translated by H. van Laun. Holt & Williams, 1871.

Thibaudet, Albert. From *French Literature from 1795 to Our Era*. Translated by Charles Lam Markmann. Funk & Wagnalls, 1968. Copyright 1938 by Librairie Stock, Paris. Translation copyright © 1967 by Harper & Row, Publishers, Inc. All rights reserved. Reprinted by permission of Harper & Row, Publishers, Inc.

Thompson, Lawrence. From *Melville's Quarrel with God*. Princeton University Press, 1952. Copyright 1952, renewed © 1980, by Princeton University Press. Excerpts reprinted with permission of Princeton University Press.

Thorp, Willard. From an introduction to *Hermann Melville: Representative Selections*. By Herman Melville, edited by Willard Thorp. American Book, 1938. Copyright, 1938, by American Book Company. Renewed 1966 by Willard Thorp. All rights reserved. Reprinted by permission of D. C. Heath & Company.

Thrale, Hester Lynch. From a diary entry of May 19, 1782, in *Thraliana, The Diary of Mrs. Hester Lynch Thrale, 1776-1809: 1776-1784, Vol. 1*, Edited by Katharine C. Balderston. Oxford at the Clarendon Press, 1942.

Todd, Janet. From *Women's Friendship in Literature*. Columbia University Press, 1980. © 1980, Columbia University Press. All rights reserved. Reprinted by permission of the publisher.

Trilling, Lionel. From *The Liberal Imagination: Essays on Literature and Society*. Charles Scribner's Sons, 1976. Copyright 1950 Lionel Trilling. Copyright renewed © 1978 Diana Trilling and James Trilling. Reprinted with the permission of Charles Scribner's Sons.

Tzara, Tristan. From *Seven Dada Manifestos and Lampisteries*. Translated by Barbara Wright. John Calder, 1977. © this translation John Calder (Publishers) Ltd. 1977. All rights reserved. Reprinted by permission.

Vitzthum, Richard C. From *The American Compromise: Theme and Method in the Histories of Bancroft, Parkman, and Adams*. University of Oklahoma Press, 1974. Copyright 1974 by the University of Oklahoma Press, Publishing Division of the University. Reprinted by permission.

Wade, Mason. From *Francis Parkman: Heroic Historian*. The Viking Press, 1942. Copyright 1942, renewed © 1969 by Hugh Mason Wade. Reprinted by permission of Viking Penguin Inc.

Walpole, Horace. From a letter to Hannah More on August 29, 1796, in *The Letters of Horace Walpole, Earl of Orford, Vol. VIII*. By Horace Walpole, edited by Peter Cunningham. Henry G. Bohn, 1866.

Wetherald, Ethelwyn. From an introduction to *The Collected Poems of Isabella Valancy Crawford*. By Isabella Valancy Crawford, edited by J. W. Garvin. William Briggs, 1905.

Whitehead, Alfred North. From *Science and the Modern World: Lowell Lectures, 1925*. Macmillan, 1925. Copyright, 1925, by Macmillan Publishing Company. Renewed 1953 by Evelyn Whitehead. All rights reserved. Reprinted with permission of Macmillan Publishing Company.

Wilder, Thornton. From *American Characteristics and Other Essays*. Edited by Donald Gallup. Harper & Row, 1979. Copyright 1952 by Thornton Wilder. Compilation copyright © 1979 by Union Trust Company, Executor of the will of the Estate of Thornton Wilder. Reprinted by special permission of Harper & Row, Publishers, Inc. and the Estate of Thornton Wilder.

Wilkie, Brian. From *Romantic Poets and Epic Tradition*. The University of Wisconsin Press, 1965. Copyright © 1965 by the Regents of the University of Wisconsin. Reprinted by permission.

Wilson, Edmund. From *Axel's Castle: A Study in the Imaginative Literature of 1870-1930*. Charles Scribner's Sons, 1931. Copyright 1931 by Charles Scribner's Sons. Renewal copyright © 1959 by Edmund Wilson. Reprinted with the permission of Charles Scribner's Sons.

Winters, Yvor. From *In Defense of Reason*. The Swallow Press Inc., 1947. Copyright 1937 by Yvor Winters. Copyright 1938, 1943 by New Directions. Copyright renewed © 1965 by Yvor Winters. Reprinted by permission of Ohio University Press/Swallow Press.

Woodring, Carl. From *Wordsworth*. Houghton Mifflin, 1965. Copyright © 1965 by Carl Woodring. All rights reserved. Reprinted by permission of Houghton Mifflin Company.

Woolf, Virginia. From a diary entry of August 8, 1918, in *The Diary of Virginia Woolf: 1915-1919, Vol. I*. By Virginia Woolf, edited by Anne Olivier Bell. Harcourt Brace Jovanovich, 1977, Hogarth Press, 1977. Diary © Quentin Bell and Angelica Garnett 1977. Reprinted by permission of Harcourt Brace Jovanovich, Inc. In Canada by the Literary Estate of Virginia Woolf and The Hogarth Press.

Wordsworth, Dorothy. From a journal entry of April 14, 1802 in *Journals of Dorothy Wordsworth*. By Dorothy Wordsworth, edited by William Knight. Macmillan and Co., Ltd., 1897.

Wordsworth, William. From an extract of a letter to Henry Crabb Robinson in January, 1820? in *The Correspondence of Henry Crabb Robinson with the Wordsworth Circle (1808-1866): 1844-1866, Vol. II*. Edited by Edith J. Morley. Oxford at the Clarendon Press, Oxford, 1927.

Wordsworth, William. From a preface to *Lyrical Ballads, with Other Poems*. By William Wordsworth. James Humphreys, 1802.

Wordsworth, William. From *Poems*. Longman, 1807.

Zall, Paul M. From an introduction to *Literary Criticism of William Wordsworth*. Edited by Paul M. Zall. University of Nebraska Press, 1966. © 1966 by the University of Nebraska Press. All rights reserved. Reprinted by permission of University of Nebraska Press.

Zoellner, Robert. From *The Salt-Sea Mastodon: A Reading of Moby-Dick*. University of California Press, 1973. Copyright © 1973 by The Regents of the University of California. Reprinted by permission of the University of California Press.

Zweig, Paul. From *Lautréamont: The Violent Narcissus*. Kennikat Press, 1972. Copyright © 1972 by Paul Zweig. All rights reserved. Reprinted by permission of Associate Faculty Press, Inc., Port Washington, NY.

ISBN 0-8103-5812-3

90000

9 780810 358126